A NEW
TESTAMENT
BIBLICAL
THEOLOGY

A NEW TESTAMENT BIBLICAL THEOLOGY

THE UNFOLDING OF THE
OLD TESTAMENT IN THE NEW

G. K. BEALE

Baker Academic

a division of Baker Publishing Group
Grand Rapids, Michigan

Published by Baker Academic
a division of Baker Publishing Group
P.O. Box 6287, Grand Rapids, MI 49516-6287
www.bakeracademic.com

Printed in the United States of America

Library of Congress Cataloging-in-Publication Data
Beale, G. K. (Gregory K.), 1949–
    A New Testament biblical theology : the unfolding of the Old Testament in the New /
G. K. Beale.
        p.   cm.
    Includes bibliographical references (p.   ) and indexes.
    ISBN 978-0-8010-2697-3 (cloth : alk. paper.)
    1. Bible. N.T.—Theology. 2. Bible. N.T.—Relation to the Old Testament. I. Title.
BS2397.B39 2011
230′.0415—dc23   2011027290

11   12   13   14   15   16   17   7   6   5   4   3   2   1

To Meredith G. Kline and Gordon P. Hugenberger,
who have helped me to understand better the riches
of Old Testament biblical theology,
and to David F. Wells,
who helped me to understand Christology better
within an "already and not yet" framework.

Contents

Preface

This book had its birth in a class on New Testament theology at Gordon-Conwell Theological Seminary that I began teaching in 1989. In the summer of 2007, I gave a plenary paper titled "The Eschatological Conception of New Testament Theology" at the third Triennial Plenary Conference of the Tyndale Fellowship at Swanwick, Derbyshire. This paper was a summary of the course that I had begun teaching in 1989, and it was subsequently published as "The Eschatological Conception of New Testament Theology" in *The Reader Must Understand: Eschatology in Bible and Theology* (Leicester: Apollos, 1997) and *Eschatology in Bible and Theology: Evangelical Essays at the Dawn of a New Millennium* (Downers Grove, IL: InterVarsity, 1997), both edited by Kent Brower and Mark Elliott. I am grateful to the conveners of the Tyndale Fellowship Conference for giving me the opportunity to deliver this paper and for including it in the published volume of papers from the conference.

The same paper was delivered at the Wheaton Conference of 2000 in Wheaton, Illinois, and an abbreviated and revised version of that paper and earlier article was published in *Biblical Theology: Retrospect and Prospect* (Downers Grove, IL: InterVarsity, 2002), edited by Scott Hafemann.

From there on, I published various articles that would be revised and integrated into parts of the present book. I continued to develop my thinking in this area as I continued to teach the New Testament theology course at Wheaton College Graduate School, beginning in 2002. Then in 2005, I began to work only on this project. Afterward, however, other projects crowded in and prevented me from bringing this book to its final form, though I continued to work on it here and there. Then, in the summer of 2008, I began working only on this project, and finally I submitted the manuscript to Baker at the end of the summer of 2010.

This New Testament biblical theology, therefore, is an expansion of the aforementioned article and the course on New Testament theology that I taught. I have discovered along the way that some of the book's chapters themselves deserve full-length book treatments and need even further elaboration, but one has to stop somewhere. (I leave it to others to develop further some of the ideas proposed in the book.) I have come to recognize the impossibility of writing a New Testament biblical theology that covers everything one would want to cover. As it is, this book is already long. In chapter 27, I not only give a summary of the book but also discuss topics not directly developed in the book in order to give some indication of the direction in which I would take them. But even there, I am sure that some topics have been left out. If readers want a more in-depth overview of this book after perusing the table of contents, I would suggest they read the introduction and the two concluding chapters (27–28). This book may also be used as a reference or encyclopedic source, since I have written each chapter on one general theme that can be sufficiently understood independently from the rest of the book. Of course, a reading of the whole book will enhance the understanding of each chapter.

Working on this book has opened my eyes to themes that I had seen only dimly before. In particular, I have seen more clearly than ever that the already–not yet end-time new creation and kingdom is a lens that sheds much light on the Scriptures and enables one to see better the deeper riches of the major theological ideas of the New Testament. In addition, this approach to the New Testament has helped me to appreciate better the role of believers and the mission of the church within the redemptive-historical storyline of Scripture. It is my hope that the biblical-theological perspective of this book will provide greater fuel to fire the church's motivation to understand itself in the light of this stage of redemptive history and to fulfill its mission to the world.

I am indebted beyond words to my wife, Dorinda, who has discussed the theology of this book with me during the past years, and who remains as excited as I am about the subject. She has been one of the main instruments through which I have been able to understand this topic in more depth.

I am thankful for the careful editorial work done by the staff at Baker 'Academic, especially Brian Bolger. I thank Jim Weaver for initially accepting this book for publication and Jim Kinney for his flexibility and ongoing work with me as the project developed and grew.

I am grateful to a number of churches that over the years have asked me to speak at conferences on the themes of this book. Likewise, I am grateful to many students from Gordon-Conwell Theological Seminary and Wheaton College Graduate School who have asked insightful questions about the topic that have caused me to reflect more deeply and to clarify my perspectives. I am also grateful to the Greek Bible School of Athens, Greece, and the Evangelical Theological College in Addis Ababa, Ethiopia, for inviting me to teach the course on New Testament theology and helping me to better situate my views in different cultural contexts.

I also express my appreciation to the following students who either helped with research or checked and edited the manuscript of this book: Stefanos Mihalios, Mike Daling, Ben Gladd, Mitch Kim, Matt Newkirk, Matt Dudreck, and especially Dan Brendsel, who labored beyond the call of duty (and among many other things compiled excursus 1 in chap. 20). A number of Wheaton College graduate students from my New Testament theology course and canonical biblical interpretation course in the spring of 2010 also helped with various aspects of editing and checking of primary source references.

Above all, I am grateful to God for enabling me to conceive the idea for this book, building on the shoulders of others before me, and for giving me the energy and discipline to write it. It is my prayer that through this book God's glory in some way will be more greatly manifested.

I am also indebted to Daniel Bailey, who sent to me the vast majority of his English translation of Peter Stuhlmacher's *Biblische Theologie des Neuen Testaments*, 2 vols., Göttingen: Vandenhoeck & Ruprecht, 1992–99, which will soon be published by Eerdmans. I believe this to be an important book, especially with respect to the influence of the OT and Jewish background upon NT biblical theology. I have made several references to Stuhlmacher's work throughout my book, though these references are to the German edition, since the English translation has not yet been published.

A few comments about some stylistic aspects of the book are in order. Unless otherwise indicated, English translations follow the New American Standard Bible (sometimes using the marginal readings, and with some variation in the use of capitalization, italics, and quotation marks) or, when different, are my own. With respect to ancient works, when the translation differs from the standard editions usually referred to, it is mine or someone else's (in the latter case I indicate whose).

At various points in Scripture quotations italics or underlining of words or phrases is used. The default translation that I am using (the NASB) italicizes words that the translators supply but are not found in the Hebrew or Greek. Underlining is used to indicate key words or phrases that are in parallel, usually when two or more passages are compared with each other. Most of the time these lexical or cognate parallels indicate that the later text is alluding to the earlier text (e.g., OT in the NT) or has some kind of organically parallel relationship with it. Sometimes broken underlining is used to indicate conceptual parallels that likely indicate an allusion.

References to the Greek New Testament are from the *Novum Testamentum Graece* (27th ed.). References to the Hebrew Old Testament are from the *Biblia Hebraica Stuttgartensia*. For the Septuagint, I refer to the Greek text of *The Septuagint Version of the Old Testament and Apocrypha with an English Translation* (Grand Rapids: Zondervan, 1972), which is dependent on Codex B, published by special arrangement with Samuel Bagster and Sons,

London. This will enable those not knowing Greek to follow the Septuagint in a readily available English edition.

My references to the Dead Sea Scrolls come primarily from the edition by Florentino García Martínez, *The Dead Sea Scrolls Translated* (Leiden: Brill, 1994); sometimes reference is made to the two-volume *Dead Sea Scrolls Study Edition*, edited by Florentino García Martínez and Eibert J. C. Tigchelaar (Leiden: Brill, 2000). In addition, other translations of Dead Sea Scrolls were consulted and sometimes are preferred in quotations (A. Dupont-Sommer, *The Essene Writings from Qumran*, translated by G. Vermes [Oxford: Basil Blackwell, 1961]). At times, variations in the translation from the primary text of García Martinez are due to my own translation.

The primary sources for references to and quotations from various Jewish works are the following English editions: *The Babylonian Talmud*, edited by I. Epstein (London: Soncino, 1948); *The Talmud of the Land of Israel: A Preliminary Translation and Explanation* (the Jerusalem Talmud), edited by Jacob Neusner (Chicago: University of Chicago Press, 1982–); *Mekilta de-Rabbi Ishmael*, translated and edited by Jacob Lauterbach (Philadelphia: Jewish Publication Society of America, 1976); *The Midrash on Proverbs*, translated by Burton Visotzky (New Haven: Yale University Press, 1992); *The Midrash on Psalms*, translated and edited by William Braude (New Haven: Yale University Press, 1976); *Midrash Rabbah*, edited by H. Freedman and Maurice Simon (London: Soncino, 1961); *Midrash Sifre on Numbers*, translated and edited by Paul Levertoff (London: SPCK, 1926); *Midrash Tanhuma*, translated and edited by John Townsend (Hoboken, NJ: KTAV, 1989); *Midrash Tanhuma-Yelammedenu: An English Translation of Genesis and Exodus from the Printed Version of Tanhuma-Yehammedenu with Introduction, Notes, and Indexes*, translated by Samuel Berman (Hoboken, NJ: KTAV, 1996); *The Minor Tractates of the Talmud*, edited by A. Cohen (London: Soncino, 1965); *The Mishnah*, translated and edited by Herbert Danby (Oxford: Oxford University Press, 1980); *The Old Testament Pseudepigrapha*, edited by James Charlesworth (Garden City, NY: Doubleday, 1983) (though sometimes reference is made to volume 2 of *The Apocrypha and Pseudepigrapha of the Old Testament*, edited by R. H. Charles [Oxford: Clarendon, 1977]); *The Pesikta de-Rab Kahana*, translated and edited by William Braude and Israel Kapstein (Philadelphia: Jewish Publication Society of America, 1975); *Pesikta Rabbati*, translated and edited by William Braude (New Haven: Yale University Press, 1968); *Pirke de Rabbi Eliezer*, translated and edited by Gerald Friedlander (New York: Hermon Press, 1916); *Sifre: A Tannaitic Commentary on the Book of Deuteronomy*, translated and edited by Reuven Hammer (New Haven: Yale University Press, 1986); *Tanna debe Eliyyahu*, translated and edited by William Braude and Israel Kapstein (Philadelphia: Jewish Publication Society of America, 1981); *The Targums of Onkelos and Jonathan Ben Uzziel on the Pentateuch, with the Fragments of the Jerusalem Targum, on Genesis and Exodus*, translated and edited by J. W. Etheridge (New York: KTAV, 1968); the available volumes published in *The Aramaic Bible: The Targums*, edited by Martin McNamara et al. (Collegeville, MN: Liturgical Press, 1987).

References to ancient Greek works, especially those of Philo and Josephus (including English translations), are from the Loeb Classical Library. References and some English translations of the Apostolic Fathers come from the second edition of *The Apostolic Fathers: Greek Texts and English Translations of Their Writings*, translated by J. B. Lightfoot and J. R. Harmer, edited and revised by Michael Holmes (Grand Rapids: Baker Academic, 1992).

G. K. B.

Abbreviations

General

Aram.	Aramaic	idem	by the same author
chap(s).	chapter(s)	lit.	literally
col(s).	column(s)	p(p).	page(s)
esp.	especially		
frg(s).	fragment(s)	repr.	reprint
Gk.	Greek	rev.	revised
Heb.	Hebrew	sect(s).	section(s)
ibid.	in the same source	v(v).	verse(s)

Divisions of the Canon

NT	New Testament	OT	Old Testament

Ancient Texts, Text Types, and Versions

Aq	Aquila	OG	Old Greek
DSS	Dead Sea Scrolls	Sym	Symmachus
LXX	Septuagint	Tg.	Targum
MT	Masoretic Text	TH	Theodotion (Θ)

Modern Editions

NA²⁷   *Novum Testamentum Graece.* Edited by [E. and E. Nestle], B. Aland, K. Aland, J. Karavidopoulos, C. M. Martini, and B. M. Metzger. 27th rev. ed. Stuttgart: Deutsche Bibelgesellschaft, 1993

Modern Versions

ESV	English Standard Version
GNB	Good News Bible
HCSB	Holman Christian Standard Bible
JB	Jerusalem Bible
KJV	King James Version

Moffatt	*The New Testament: A New Translation*, James Moffatt		
NAB	New American Bible		
NASB	New American Standard Bible		
NEB	New English Bible		
NET	New English Translation (The NET Bible)		
NIV	New International Version		
NJB	New Jerusalem Bible		
NJPS	*Tanakh: The Holy Scriptures: The New JPS Translation according to the Traditional Hebrew Text*		
NLT	New Living Translation		
NRSV	New Revised Standard Version		
REB	Revised English Bible		
RSV	Revised Standard Version		
RSVA	Revised Standard Version Apocrypha		
TNIV	Today's New International Version		

Hebrew Bible/Old Testament

Gen.	Genesis	Song	Song of Songs
Exod.	Exodus	Isa.	Isaiah
Lev.	Leviticus	Jer.	Jeremiah
Num.	Numbers	Lam.	Lamentations
Deut.	Deuteronomy	Ezek.	Ezekiel
Josh.	Joshua	Dan.	Daniel
Judg.	Judges	Hos.	Hosea
Ruth	Ruth	Joel	Joel
1–2 Sam.	1–2 Samuel	Amos	Amos
1–2 Kings	1–2 Kings	Obad.	Obadiah
1–2 Chron.	1–2 Chronicles	Jon.	Jonah
Ezra	Ezra	Mic.	Micah
Neh.	Nehemiah	Nah.	Nahum
Esther	Esther	Hab.	Habakkuk
Job	Job	Zeph.	Zephaniah
Ps./Pss.	Psalms	Hag.	Haggai
Prov.	Proverbs	Zech.	Zechariah
Eccles.	Ecclesiastes	Mal.	Malachi

New Testament

Matt.	Matthew	1–2 Thess.	1–2 Thessalonians
Mark	Mark	1–2 Tim.	1–2 Timothy
Luke	Luke	Titus	Titus
John	John	Philem.	Philemon
Acts	Acts	Heb.	Hebrews
Rom.	Romans	James	James
1–2 Cor.	1–2 Corinthians	1–2 Pet.	1–2 Peter
Gal.	Galatians	1–3 John	1–3 John
Eph.	Ephesians	Jude	Jude
Phil.	Philippians	Rev.	Revelation
Col.	Colossians		

Apocrypha and Septuagint

Add. Esth.	Additions to Esther		1–4 Macc.	1–4 Maccabees
Bar.	Baruch		Sir.	Sirach
1–2 Esd.	1–2 Esdras		Tob.	Tobit
Jdt.	Judith		Wis.	Wisdom of Solomon

Old Testament Pseudepigrapha

Apoc. Ab.	Apocalypse of Abraham
Apoc. El.	Apocalypse of Elijah
Apoc. Ezek.	Apocalypse of Ezekiel
Apoc. Mos.	Apocalypse of Moses
Apoc. Zeph.	Apocalypse of Zephaniah
As. Mos.	Assumption of Moses
2 Bar.	2 Baruch (Syriac Apocalypse)
1 En.	1 Enoch (Ethiopic Apocalypse)
2 En.	2 Enoch (Slavonic Apocalypse)
3 En.	3 Enoch (Hebrew Apocalypse)
4 Ezra	4 Ezra
Gk. Apoc. Ezra	Greek Apocalypse of Ezra
Hel. Syn. Pr.	Hellenistic Synagogal Prayers
Hist. Rech.	History of the Rechabites
Jos. Asen.	Joseph and Aseneth
Jub.	Jubilees
L.A.B.	Liber antiquitatum biblicarum (Pseudo-Philo)
L.A.E.	Life of Adam and Eve
Lad. Jac.	Ladder of Jacob
Let. Aris.	Letter of Aristeas
Liv. Pro.	Lives of the Prophets
Mart. Ascen. Isa.	Martyrdom and Ascension of Isaiah
Odes Sol.	Odes of Solomon
Ps.-Phoc.	Pseudo-Phocylides
Pss. Sol.	Psalms of Solomon
Sib. Or.	Sibylline Oracles
T. Ab.	Testament of Abraham
T. Adam	Testament of Adam
T. Benj.	Testament of Benjamin
T. Dan	Testament of Dan
T. Gad	Testament of Gad
T. Iss.	Testament of Issachar
T. Job	Testament of Job
T. Jos.	Testament of Joseph
T. Jud.	Testament of Judah
T. Levi	Testament of Levi
T. Mos.	Testament of Moses
T. Naph.	Testament of Naphtali
T. Reub.	Testament of Reuben
T. Sim.	Testament of Simeon
T. Zeb.	Testament of Zebulon

Dead Sea Scrolls

CD-A	*Damascus Document*[a]
CD-B	*Damascus Document*[b]
1QH[a]	*1QHodayot*[a]
1QIsa[a]	*1QIsaiah*[a]
1QIsa[b]	*1QIsaiah*[b]
1QM	*1QWar Scroll*
1QpHab	*1QPesher to Habakkuk*
1QS	*1QRule of the Community*
1Q28a (1QSa)	*1QRule of the Congregation*
1Q29	*1QLiturgy of the Three Tongues of Fire*
4Q58	*4QIsaiah*[d]
4Q162 (4QpIsa[b])	*4QIsaiah Pesher*[b]
4Q163 (4Qpap pIsa[c])	*4QIsaiah Pesher*[c]
4Q169 (4QpNah)	*4QNahum Pesher*
4Q174 (4QFlor)	*4QFlorilegium*
4Q177	*4QCatena A*
4Q213b (4QLevi[c] ar)	*4QAramaic Levi*[c]
4Q246	*4QAramaic Apocalypse*
4Q252 (4QcommGen A)	*4QCommentary on Genesis A*
4Q266 (4QD[a])	*4QDamascus Document*[a]
4Q376 (4QapocrMoses[b]?)	*4QApocryphon of Moses*[b]?
4Q418	*4QInstruction*[d]
4Q423	*4QInstruction*[g]
4Q444	*4QIncantation*
4Q475	*4QRenewed Earth*
4Q504 (4QDibHam[a])	*4QWords of the Luminaries*[a]
4Q511 (4QShir[b])	*4QSongs of the Sage*[b]
4Q521	*4QMessianic Apocalypse*
11Q13 (11QMelch)	*11QMelchizedek*

Targumic Texts

Tg. Isa.	*Targum Isaiah*		*Tg. Onq.*	*Targum Onqelos*
Tg. Mic.	*Targum Micah*		*Tg. Ps.-J.*	*Targum Pseudo-Jonathan*
Tg. Neof.	*Targum Neofiti*			

Mishnah and Talmud

b.	Babylonian Talmud		*Qidd.*	*Qiddušin*
m.	Mishnah		*Roš Haš.*	*Roš Haššanah*
y.	Jerusalem Talmud		*Šabb.*	*Šabbat*
			Sanh.	*Sanhedrin*
'Abod. Zar.	*'Abodah Zarah*		*Šeqal.*	*Šeqalim*
'Arak.	*'Arakin*		*Soṭah*	*Soṭah*
B. Bat.	*Baba Batra*		*Sukkah*	*Sukkah*
Ber.	*Berakot*		*Taʿan.*	*Taʿanit*
Ḥag.	*Ḥagigah*		*Tamid*	*Tamid*
Mek.	*Mekilta*		*Yebam.*	*Yebamot*
Ned.	*Nedarim*		*Yoma*	*Yoma* (= *Kippurim*)
Pesaḥ.	*Pesaḥim*			

Other Rabbinic Works

'Abot R. Nat.	*'Abot de Rabbi Nathan*	*Pesiq. Rab Kah.*	*Pesiqta de Rab Kahana*
Mek.	*Mekilta*	*Pirqe R. El.*	*Pirqe Rabbi Eliezer*
Midr.	*Midrash*	*Rab.*	(biblical book +) *Rabbah*
Midr. Rab.	*Midrash Rabbah*	*S. Eli. Rab.*	*Seder Eliyahu Rabbah*
Pesiq. Rab.	*Pesiqta Rabbati*	*Tanḥ.*	*Tanḥuma*

Apostolic Fathers

Barn.	*Barnabas*	Ign. *Eph.*	Ignatius, *To the Ephesians*
1–2 Clem.	*1–2 Clement*	Ign. *Magn.*	Ignatius, *To the Magnesians*
Did.	*Didache*	Ign. *Phld.*	Ignatius, *To the Philadelphians*
Diogn.	*Diognetus*	Ign. *Trall.*	Ignatius, *To the Trallians*
Frag. Papias	*Fragments of Papias*	*Mart. Pol.*	*Martyrdom of Polycarp*
Herm.	*Shepherd of Hermas*	*Pol. Phil.*	Polycarp, *To the Philippians*

Nag Hammadi

Gos. Truth	*Gospel of Truth*

New Testament Apocrypha and Pseudepigrapha

Apos. Con.	*Apostolic Constitutions and Canons*
Gos. Thom.	*Gospel of Thomas*
Mart. Pet. Paul	*Martyrdom of Peter and Paul*

Greek and Latin Works

Augustine

Conf.	*Confessionum libri XIII (Confessions)*
Quaest. Hept.	*Quaestiones in Heptateuchum*

Clement of Alexandria

Strom.	*Stromata (Miscellanies)*

Epiphanius

Pan.	*Panarion (Refutation of All Heresies)*

Hippolytus

Comm. Dan.	*Commentarium in Danielem*

Irenaeus

Haer.	*Adversus haereses (Against Heresies)*

Josephus

Ag. Ap.	*Against Apion*
Ant.	*Jewish Antiquities*
J.W.	*Jewish War*

Justin

1 Apol.	*Apologia i (First Apology)*
Dial.	*Dialogus cum Tryphone (Dialogue with Trypho)*

Philo

Aet.	*De aeternitate (On the Eternity of the World)*
Agr.	*De agricultura (On Agriculture)*
Cher.	*De cherubim (On the Cherubim)*
Conf.	*De confusione linguarum (On the Confusion of Tongues)*
Decal.	*De decalogo (On the Decalogue)*
Det.	*Quod deterius potiori insidari soleat (That the Worse Attacks the Better)*
Fug.	*De fuga et inventione (On Flight and Finding)*
Gig.	*De gigantibus (On Giants)*
Her.	*Quis rerum divinarum heres sit (Who Is the Heir?)*
Leg.	*Legum allegoriae (Allegorical Interpretation)*
Legat.	*Legatio ad Gaium (On the Embassy to Gaius)*
Migr.	*De migratione Abrahami (On the Migration of Abraham)*
Mos.	*De vita Mosis (On the Life of Moses)*
Mut.	*De mutatione nominum (On the Change of Names)*
Opif.	*De opificio mundi (On the Creation of the World)*
Plant.	*De plantatione (On Planting)*
Post.	*De posteritate Caini (On the Posterity of Cain)*
QE	*Quaestiones et solutiones in Exodum (Questions and Answers on Exodus)*
Somn.	*De somniis (On Dreams)*
Spec.	*De specialibus legibus (On the Special Laws)*

Plutarch

Mor.	*Moralia*
Superst.	*De superstitione*

Secondary Sources

AB	Anchor Bible
ABD	*Anchor Bible Dictionary*. Edited by D. N. Freedman. 6 vols. New York, 1992
ABR	*Australian Biblical Review*
AnBib	Analecta biblica
ANTC	Abingdon New Testament Commentaries
ANTJ	Arbeiten zum Neuen Testament und Judentum
AOTC	Apollos Old Testament Commentary
ArBib	The Aramaic Bible
AUMSR	Andrews University Monographs: Studies in Religion
AUSDDS	Andrews University Seminary Doctoral Dissertation Series
AYBRL	Anchor Yale Bible Reference Library
BAGD	Bauer, W., W. F. Arndt, F. W. Gingrich, and F. W. Danker. *Greek-English Lexicon of the New Testament and Other Early Christian Literature*. 2nd. ed. Chicago, 1979
BBR	*Bulletin for Biblical Research*
BCOTWP	Baker Commentary on the Old Testament Wisdom and Psalms
BDAG	Bauer, W., F. W. Danker, W. F. Arndt, and F. W. Gingrich. *Greek-English Lexicon of the New Testament and Other Early Christian Literature*. 3rd ed. Chicago, 1999
BDB	Brown, F., S. R. Driver, and C. A. Briggs. *A Hebrew and English Lexicon of the Old Testament*. Oxford, 1907

BDF	Blass, F., A. Debrunner, and R. W. Funk. *A Greek Grammar of the New Testament and Other Early Christian Literature.* Chicago, 1961
BECNT	Baker Exegetical Commentary on the New Testament
Bib	*Biblica*
BIS	Biblical Interpretation Series
BJS	Biblical and Judaic Studies
BLS	Bible and Literature Series
BNTC	Black's New Testament Commentaries
BSac	*Bibliotheca sacra*
BTB	*Biblical Theology Bulletin*
BTCB	Brazos Theological Commentary on the Bible
BZ	*Biblische Zeitschrift*
BZNW	Beihefte zur Zeitschrift für die neutestamentliche Wissenschaft
CBET	Contributions to Biblical Exegesis and Theology
CBQ	*Catholic Biblical Quarterly*
CBQMS	Catholic Biblical Quarterly Monograph Series
CC	Continental Commentaries
CCL	Classic Commentary Library
CEB	Commentaire évangélique de la Bible
CGTC	Cambridge Greek Testament Commentary
ConBNT	Coniectanea biblica: New Testament Series
CTJ	*Calvin Theological Journal*
CTM	*Concordia Theological Monthly*
DJG	*Dictionary of Jesus and the Gospels.* Edited by J. B. Green and S. Mc-Knight. Downers Grove, 1992
DLNTD	*Dictionary of the Later New Testament and Its Developments.* Edited by R. P. Martin and Peter H. Davids. Downers Grove, 1997
DPL	*Dictionary of Paul and His Letters.* Edited by G. F. Hawthorne and R. P. Martin. Downers Grove, 1993
EBC	Expositor's Bible Commentary
EBib	Etudes bibliques
ECC	Eerdmans Critical Commentary
EncJud	*Encyclopedia Judaica.* 16 vols. Jerusalem, 1972
EvQ	*Evangelical Quarterly*
EvT	*Evangelische Theologie*
ExpTim	*Expository Times*
FB	Forschung zur Bibel
GKC	*Gesenius' Hebrew Grammar.* Edited by E. Kautzsch. Translated by A. E. Cowley. 2nd ed. Oxford, 1910
GNC	Good News Commentary
GTJ	*Grace Theological Journal*
HBM	Hebrew Bible Monographs
HBS	Herders biblische Studien
HCOT	Historical Commentary on the Old Testament
HNT	Handbuch zum Neuen Testament
HSM	Harvard Semitic Monographs
HSS	Harvard Semitic Studies
HTKAT	Herders theologischer Kommentar zum Alten Testament
HTKNT	Herders theologischer Kommentar zum Neuen Testament
IBC	Interpretation: A Bible Commentary for Teaching and Preaching
IBS	*Irish Biblical Studies*

ICC	International Critical Commentary
Int	*Interpretation*
IVPNTC	IVP New Testament Commentary
JAAR	*Journal of the American Academy of Religion*
JBL	*Journal of Biblical Literature*
JETS	*Journal of the Evangelical Theological Society*
JNES	*Journal of Near Eastern Studies*
JPSTC	Jewish Publication Society Torah Commentary
JPTSup	Journal of Pentecostal Theology: Supplement Series
JSNT	*Journal for the Study of the New Testament*
JSNTSup	Journal for the Study of the New Testament: Supplement Series
JSOT	*Journal for the Study of the Old Testament*
JSOTSup	Journal for the Study of the Old Testament: Supplement Series
JTI	*Journal of Theological Interpretation*
JTS	*Journal of Theological Studies*
K&D	Keil, C. F., and F. Delitzsch, *Biblical Commentary on the Old Testament*. Translated by J. Martin et al. 10 vols. Repr., Grand Rapids, 1949–71
KEK	Kritisch-exegetischer Kommentar über das Neue Testament (Meyer-Kommentar)
LCL	Loeb Classical Library
LNTS	Library of New Testament Studies
LSJ	Liddell, H. G., R. Scott, and H. S. Jones. *A Greek-English Lexicon*. 9th ed. with rev. supplement. Oxford, 1996
LW	Luther's Works
MM	Moulton, J. H., and G. Milligan. *The Vocabulary of the Greek New Testament: Illustrated from the Papyri and Other Non-literary Sources*. Grand Rapids, 1972
MNTC	Moffatt New Testament Commentary
NAC	New American Commentary
NCB	New Century Bible
NClarB	New Clarendon Bible
NDBT	*New Dictionary of Biblical Theology*. Edited by T. D. Alexander and B. S. Rosner. Downers Grove, 2000
NIB	*The New Interpreter' Bible*. Edited by Leander E. Keck. 12 vols. Nashville, 1994–2004
NIBC	New International Bible Commentary
NICNT	New International Commentary on the New Testament
NICOT	New International Commentary on the Old Testament
NIDNTT	*New International Dictionary of New Testament Theology*. Edited by Colin Brown. 4 vols. Grand Rapids, 1975–85
NIGTC	New International Greek Testament Commentary
NIVAC	NIV Application Commentary
NovT	*Novum Testamentum*
NovTSup	Novum Testamentum Supplements
NSBT	New Studies in Biblical Theology
NSKAT	Neuer Stuttgarter Kommentar: Altes Testament
NTG	New Testament Guides
NTL	New Testament Library
NTS	*New Testament Studies*
ÖTK	Ökumenischer Taschenbuch-Kommentar
OTL	Old Testament Library

OtSt	Oudtestamentische Studiën
PFES	Publications of the Finnish Exegetical Society
PNTC	Pillar New Testament Commentary
PS	Pauline Studies
PTMS	Princeton Theological Monograph Series
ResQ	*Restoration Quarterly*
RevQ	*Revue de Qumran*
RIMA	The Royal Inscriptions of Mesopotamia, Assyrian Periods
RTR	*Reformed Theological Review*
SBL	Studies in Biblical Literature
SBLDS	Society of Biblical Literature Dissertation Series
SBLMS	Society of Biblical Literature Monograph Series
SBLSP	*Society of Biblical Literature Seminar Papers*
SBS	Stuttgarter Bibelstudien
SBT	Studies in Biblical Theology
SHBC	Smith & Helwys Bible Commentary
SJT	*Scottish Journal of Theology*
SJTOP	Scottish Journal of Theology Occasional Papers
SM	*Studia Missionalia*
SNTSMS	Society for New Testament Studies Monograph Series
SNTW	Studies of the New Testament and Its World
SP	Sacra pagina
ST	*Studia theologica*
StPB	Studia post-biblica
StudBT	*Studia Biblica et Theologica*
SubBi	Subsidia biblica
TANZ	Texte und Arbeiten zum neutestamentlichen Zeitalter
TDNT	*Theological Dictionary of the New Testament.* Edited by G. Kittel and G. Friedrich. Translated by G. W. Bromiley. 10 vols. Grand Rapids, 1964–76
TDOT	*Theological Dictionary of the Old Testament.* Edited by G. J. Botterweck and H. Ringgren. Translated by J. T. Willis, G. W. Bromiley, D. E. Green, and Douglas W. Stott. 8 vols. Grand Rapids, 1974–
TJ	*Trinity Journal*
TNTC	Tyndale New Testament Commentaries
TOTC	Tyndale Old Testament Commentaries
TQ	*Theologische Quartalschrift*
TSAJ	Texte und Studien zum antiken Judentum
TTE	*The Theological Educator*
TUGAL	Texte und Untersuchungen zur Geschichte der altchristlichen Literatur
TynBul	*Tyndale Bulletin*
VT	*Vetus Testamentum*
VTSup	Vetus Testamentum Supplements
WBC	Word Biblical Commentary
WEC	Wycliffe Exegetical Commentary
WestBC	Westminster Bible Companion
WMANT	Wissenschaftliche Monographien zum Alten und Neuen Testament
WTJ	*Westminster Theological Journal*
WUNT	Wissenschaftliche Untersuchungen zum Neuen Testament
ZNW	*Zeitschrift für die neutestamentliche Wissenschaft und die Kunde der älteren Kirche*
ZTK	*Zeitschrift für Theologie und Kirche*

1

Introduction

Of the writing of NT theologies there seems to be no end. When I teach a class on NT theology, I distribute a three-page bibliography of only NT theologies, the majority of which were written in the twentieth century. My attempt in this book is not to write a NT theology but rather a NT *biblical* theology. To some ears this may not sound like much of a distinction. Nevertheless, this introductory chapter and the following body of this book will indicate how different my project is from that of the typical NT theology genre.

The Principles and Definition of a Biblical Theology of the New Testament

The first task is to describe the particular discipline of NT biblical theology to be adopted in this book, which overlaps to some degree not only with whole-Bible biblical theologies but also with OT biblical theologies. The increasing focus will be on the unique aspects of doing NT biblical theology. Some parts of this description will overlap with the task of the NT theology genre, but the differences will increasingly become apparent.

First, many NT theologies spend much time discussing the question of the historical Jesus and whether a theology of the NT can begin with the life and teachings of Jesus. Some scholars conclude negatively about this (e.g., Rudolf Bultmann), whereas more conservative writers base the beginning of their theologies on Jesus as he was portrayed in the Gospels. I will not spend time analyzing this issue, but I will assume the conclusion of conservative scholars, including conservative NT theologians, who decide that the Gospels portray a historically reliable picture of Jesus's ministry and thus start their study of the NT on that basis.[1]

Second, more recent NT theologies directly address the issue of postmodern hermeneutics, especially with respect to whether it is possible to interpret scriptural texts without one's theological biases detrimentally affecting the interpretations.[2] This book will not address this issue, but a few comments are appropriate here. In the twentieth century, both liberal historical critics and many conservative scholars believed that readers could interpret texts "objectively," without their own presuppositions influencing their interpretations. Few, whether conservative or liberal, hold this view today, though some still do. The question now is whether one's presuppositions result in distorting the original meaning of a text and whether interpreters come away only with interpretive conclusions that reflect their own theological predispositions. Entire books can be, and have been, written on this issue.[3] My assumption in this book is that all interpreters have presuppositions, and that some presuppositions are bad and distort the originally intended meanings of ancient texts, while other presuppositions are good and actually guide one into the truth of texts. The presuppositions of the biblical writers themselves as expressed in Scripture have the power through the Spirit to regrind the presuppositional lenses of its readers.

One such presupposition, for example, is that the Protestant canon of the OT and the NT composes the divinely inspired, authoritative material for doing biblical theology. This differs from some who do not want to limit NT theology to this database and want to include the Apocrypha, the Pseudepigrapha, and other early Jewish works as part of the authoritative framework.[4] Although

1. See, e.g., I. Howard Marshall, *New Testament Theology: Many Witnesses, One Gospel* (Downers Grove, IL: InterVarsity, 2004); Frank Thielman, *Theology of the New Testament: A Canonical and Synthetic Approach* (Grand Rapids: Zondervan, 2005). See the very important discussion of Peter Stuhlmacher, *Biblische Theologie des Neuen Testaments*, vol. 1 (Göttingen: Vandenhoeck & Ruprecht, 1992), chaps. 2–13 (and at several other points throughout vol. 1), who well demonstrates in a balanced manner the historical reliability of the Gospels from a biblical-theological perspective, particularly in light of the OT and Jewish backgrounds. This section of Stuhlmacher's book is especially a response to his own recognition of the critical problems involved in basing a biblical theology of Jesus on the portrayal of the earthly Jesus in the Gospels (in chap. 2 of his book).
2. See Thomas R. Schreiner, *New Testament Theology: Magnifying God in Christ* (Grand Rapids: Baker Academic, 2008), 882–88; Thielman, *Theology of the New Testament*, 30–33.
3. See, e.g., E. D. Hirsch, *Validity in Interpretation* (New Haven: Yale University Press, 1967); Kevin Vanhoozer, *Is There a Meaning in This Text? The Bible, the Reader, and the Morality of Literary Knowledge* (Grand Rapids: Zondervan, 1998). These two scholars are optimistic about readers being able to discern sufficiently, though not exhaustively, authorial intentions of writers. For interaction with those who are skeptical, see Vanhoozer.
4. This was a typical approach of the Tübingen school in the second half of the twentieth century, especially characterized by Hartmut Gese and Peter Stuhlmacher (in this respect, see

these extracanonical sources do need to be considered in the interpretation of NT texts, I will assume that they are not on the same authoritative level as those texts. I will make the same assumption about the LXX in relation to the OT Hebrew text, the latter of which I take to be authoritative.[5] Of course, there could be much discussion of the thorny issue of canon, but since the scope of this work does not allow for such elaboration, I must simply take the Protestant canon as my presuppositional starting point.

Another such presupposition is a particular definition of "intertextuality." I will assume that later biblical quotations of and allusions to earlier Scripture unpack the meaning of that earlier Scripture, and yet the earlier passage also sheds light on the later passage.[6] This is my view of the famous dictum "Scripture interprets Scripture." Or, as Augustine put it, "The New Testament lies concealed in the Old, the Old lies revealed in the New" (*Quaest. Hept.* 2.73). I do not follow some postmodern understandings of intertextuality, which, for example, contend that later references to earlier texts interact in such a way that new meanings are produced that are completely unlinked and dislodged from the originally intended meaning of the earlier text.[7] In this respect, I will study quotations of earlier Scripture by later Scripture as well as allusions. There has been much discussion about the criteria for validating whether a reference is actually a probable allusion. I have discussed these criteria at numerous points in my writings over the past years.[8] The most important criterion is the recognition of sufficient verbal and thematic parallels, though interpreters will still debate whether such parallels exist in particular cases.

Thus, readers will make different judgments on the basis of the same evidence, some categorizing a reference as "probable," others viewing the same reference as only "possible" or even so faint as not to merit analysis. I have

---

further discussion below of Gese and Stuhlmacher). However, I do agree with Stuhlmacher's assessment that because the NT is Scripture inspired by the Spirit, anyone who does biblical theology of the NT documents should read and interpret them "in the way in which they want to be interpreted, namely, as inspired witnesses of the path which God in and through Christ took to humanity to lead them to himself and thereby to salvation" (*How to Do Biblical Theology,* PTMS 38 [Allison Park, PA: Pickwick, 1995], 88).

5. Though, of course, it is true that NT writers quote from the LXX and cite it as Scripture (e.g., the author of Hebrews). However, this is similar to a preacher today quoting an OT passage from the NLT of the Bible and calling it Scripture, even though that preacher would make a distinction between the originally inspired Hebrew OT and the NLT.

6. Another presupposition, in this respect, is that I will assume a typically conservative view for the dating and authorship of the OT and NT books. However, when critical views on dating differ from my approach, it merely means that the intertextual relationship will be reversed, but hermeneutically in such cases one can still hold to a mutually interpretative relationship.

7. For further reference to this hermeneutical debate, see G. K. Beale, *We Become What We Worship: A Biblical Theology of Idolatry* (Downers Grove, IL: IVP Academic, 2008), 23n23.

8. In connection to issues concerning intertextuality, see ibid., 22–34.

tried to include for study in this book those OT allusions whose validity are attested by sufficient evidence and that I consider to be probable (this includes not only references made by NT writers but also those made by later OT writers of earlier OT texts). I am sure, however, that some interpreters will still debate the validity of some of the references that I discuss.

Along these lines, Richard Hays touches on the problematic issue of how much a NT author (and I would include OT authors) can develop an earlier OT text and whether such creative developments still remain within the original conceptual contours of the OT context. He speaks about "the power of texts to engender unforeseen interpretations that may transcend the original authorial intention and historical setting."[9] This is to be seen not as an argument for a radical reader-response approach (where there is lack of concern for original authorial intention) but rather as a reading whereby one continues to see how an OT text keeps imposing its original sense on the later text's author (albeit sometimes subliminally), even as that author is creatively developing that original sense beyond what may appear to be the "surface meaning" of the OT text.[10] The notion of whether NT writers refer to OT texts with their broader context in mind is debated in the academic guild. My own assessment is in line with Hays's approach and the earlier approach of C. H. Dodd.[11]

Thus, Paul or later OT writers build on earlier OT texts that they interpret and develop creatively. This creativity is to be seen in understanding such earlier texts in the light of the further developments of the redemptive-historical epoch in which the writer lives. For example, NT writers interpret the OT in the light of the later events of Christ's coming and work. In this respect, part of the creative interpretative development lies merely in the fact that fulfillment always fleshes out prior prophecy in a way that, to some degree, was unforeseen by earlier OT prophets. Another way to say this is that progressive revelation always reveals things not seen as clearly earlier. Geerhardus Vos's metaphor for this creative development between the two Testaments is that earlier OT prophecies and texts are like seeds, and later OT texts develop the seeds into roots from which stems and leaves imperceptibly grow, and then in the NT the bud emerges and begins to flower; from one angle the blooming plant may not look like the seed or the root (as in botanical comparisons),

9. Richard B. Hays, *The Conversion of the Imagination: Paul as Interpreter of Israel's Scripture* (Grand Rapids: Eerdmans, 2005), 169.

10. Ibid., 173–76.

11. C. H. Dodd, *According to the Scriptures: The Sub-Structure of New Testament Theology* (London: Nisbet, 1952). For an example of the debate between scholars on both sides of this issue, see G. K. Beale, ed., *The Right Doctrine from the Wrong Texts? Essays on the Use of the Old Testament in the New* (Grand Rapids: Baker Academic, 1984). For a programmatic essay in which I argue for the contextual use of the OT in the NT, see G. K. Beale, "Did Jesus and His Followers Preach the Right Doctrine from the Wrong Texts? An Examination of the Presuppositions of the Apostles' Exegetical Method," *Themelios* 14 (1989): 89–96.

but careful exegesis of both OT and NT contexts can show at least some of the organic connections.[12]

Another important presupposition of this book is that the divine authorial intentions communicated through human authors are accessible to contemporary readers. Although no one can exhaustively comprehend these intentions, they can be sufficiently understood, especially for the purposes of salvation, sanctification, and glorification of God.

These three preceding presuppositions about canon, intertextuality, and authorial intention being accessible to modern readers overlap to varying degrees with the approach of more recent classic conservative NT theologies.[13]

In addition, a proper understanding and development of OT and NT theology reveals that theology is not only descriptive but also prescriptive. That is, the mere development of a theology of either Testament is a descriptive task, but the content of that theology manifests an imperative for God's people to follow and obey. For example, we will see that one of the important biblical-theological ideas formulated in this book entails that believers ought to take part in expanding God's new-creational kingdom and that they glorify God. This kind of prescriptive element, however, is found to varying degrees in other NT theologies.

The preceding discussion has shown some slight differences but also primarily commonalities between this project and other NT theologies that have been written. However, the following shows the unique traits of my approach to a NT biblical theology in distinction from the usual NT theologies.

(1) The approach of this book overlaps with that of a whole-Bible biblical theology in that it addresses more directly the theological storyline of the OT. I will discuss early in the book precisely what I mean by a "storyline."[14] In this respect, my work begins formally in the next chapter with a focus only on a thumbnail sketch of the development of the OT storyline beginning in Genesis and developing throughout the OT. This storyline consists of a synthetic formulation about God's purposes in creation, fall, redemption, and consummation. In contrast, classic NT theologies stay formally only within the bounds of the NT canon. Of course, a long book could be written on the tracing of such an OT storyline, so that I will have to rest content with attempting to discern the main thrusts of such a storyline in two substantive introductory chapters (see chaps. 2–3). Thus, the OT storyline formulated in this book is based on a

<hr/>

12. On which, see Geerhardus Vos, "The Idea of Biblical Theology as a Science and a Theological Discipline," in *Redemptive History and Biblical Interpretation: The Shorter Writings of Geerhardus Vos*, ed. Richard B. Gaffin Jr. (Phillipsburg, NJ: P&R, 1980), 11–15.

13. Marshall, *New Testament Theology*; Thielman, *Theology of the New Testament*; Schreiner, *New Testament Theology*.

14. For a fuller discussion of what I mean by "storyline," see chap. 2 under the heading "The Repeated Cosmic Judgment and New Creation Episodes of the Old Testament," and esp. chap. 6.

study of OT theology and especially how the theological threads of Gen. 1–3 are developed throughout the rest of the OT. Many would be skeptical that a unifying storyline of the OT is possible,[15] and others would say that this is difficult to do in one or two chapters (see chaps. 2–3). Nevertheless, the hope here is that the main outline of this kind of study is sufficiently headed in the right direction such that it holds potential to be fleshed out and validated by subsequent substantive research by others.

(2) The main facets of the OT narrative story are then traced into and throughout the NT. The main elements of the OT plotline become the basis for the formulation of the NT storyline. Of course, insofar as the OT plotline is somewhat provisional, so will be its basis for the NT storyline. But this is a problem inherent to any project that focuses on the NT, even a NT biblical theology. A volume longer than the present one would need to be written to validate further both the OT and the NT storylines proposed here.

Thus, the NT storyline will be a transformation of the OT one in the light of how the NT is seen to be an unfolding of the OT, especially through fulfillment of the OT. The main theological categories for the tracing of OT and NT theology therefore arise not first from considering the categories of systematic theology but from attempting to trace the respective canonical storylines in the two Testaments. I will try to determine how the NT develops the OT plotline and then let the major parts of the transformed storyline of the NT form the major subjects to be considered in the biblical theology of the NT.[16]

Consequently, it is the main categories of the NT storyline that then become the main conceptual categories for the organization or outline of the biblical theology of the NT (which this book develops in chaps. 5–28).

(3) The bulk of discussion in this biblical theology of the NT consists of attempts to elaborate on the main plotline categories of thought through surveying the places in the NT where that thought is expressed. Such a survey occurs through studying the use of key words and concepts relevant to the major category of focus. Also, discussion of each category will occur

15. See, e.g., James Barr, *The Concept of Biblical Theology: An Old Testament Perspective* (Minneapolis: Fortress, 1999), 375–76.

16. Some topics of chapters that I have chosen do overlap with systematic categories—e.g., chap. 15 on justification and chap. 16 on reconciliation. There is truth to the overlap, though I contend that these are also biblical-theological notions, and they will be developed as such. Likewise, chaps. 23–24 on "The Church's New Creational Transformation of Israel's Distinguishing Marks" discuss topics such as the Sabbath, baptism, the Lord's Supper, the office of elders, and the NT canon. In addition, chaps. 13 and 14 deal directly with the image of God, but the focus on this is through the biblical-theological lens of Gen. 1–3 and how Christ relates to restoring the divine image that became distorted in the first Adam. All these topics are addressed in systematic theologies, but I will attempt to discuss them as biblical-theological concepts. These systematic topics thus also fit naturally into various components of the biblical-theological storyline proposed in this book.

through exegetical analysis of crucial passages and of OT quotations, allusions, and sometimes of discernible themes. Such concentrated studies, especially of the NT's use of the OT, are not characteristic features of most NT theologies. Although many are doubtful that it is possible to find a theological unity among the NT writings,[17] I am more optimistic and hope that my proposed storyline proves fruitful to others in perceiving more of a unity to the NT.

In contrast, some NT theologies try to place the documents in chronological order and focus on an attempt to trace the historical genealogical development of concepts. This often involves also studying what lies behind these documents, so that the full purported process of historical development can be more precisely reconstructed. This then entails that one also speculate about the theology of the sources behind the written document (e.g., in the Gospels), which of course are no longer extant in any literary form. The weakness of the approach is that it has to speculate about hypothetical sources and becomes too much a study of the theology of such sources instead of focusing on the study of the theology of the NT documents themselves.[18] Furthermore, apart from the problem of hypothetical sources is, among other problems, the difficulty of dating the NT documents with enough certainty that a development among them can be traced chronologically.[19]

NT theologies are organized in a variety of ways,[20] but the habit of a number of classic NT theologies is to conduct a consecutive theological analysis of each NT book,[21] usually in the canonical order of each corpus,[22] and then to draw up a final comparison of each of the theological emphases of each of the books.[23] Such projects sometimes conclude with an attempt to find a major theological thrust in the NT.[24] Others who do NT theologies set up certain major themes for the whole NT and then trace those themes consecutively

17. See, e.g., G. B. Caird and L. D. Hurst, *New Testament Theology* (Oxford: Clarendon, 1994), 15–17.

18. Here I am following Marshall, *New Testament Theology*, 25–27.

19. On which, see further the critique by Caird and Hurst, *New Testament Theology*, 8–15, which lays out several problems with the developmental approach.

20. On which, see D. A. Carson, "New Testament Theology," *DLNTD* 799–804.

21. Often the books in each corpus are arranged by date.

22. E.g., see Frank J. Matera, *New Testament Theology: Exploring Diversity and Unity* (Louisville: Westminster John Knox, 2007), who, however, groups John's Gospel with the Johannine Epistles and places them after discussion of the Synoptics and Paul's epistles (which he studies in order of date), and he places Acts together with Luke. Within the evangelical sector, e.g., see Roy Zuck and Darrell Bock, eds., *A Biblical Theology of the New Testament* (Chicago: Moody, 1994), which is like Matera's order except for the primary difference that it groups John's Gospel, the Johannine Epistles, and Revelation together directly after the Synoptic Gospels. The book is a broad survey of various themes in each book and corpus of the NT.

23. E.g., Marshall, *New Testament Theology*; Thielman, *Theology of the New Testament*.

24. E.g., Marshall (*New Testament Theology*) determines that the major thrust of NT theology is mission, which I find helpful but not sufficiently comprehensive.

through its books, usually in the order of the canon.[25] The challenge for these thematic approaches is validating the probability of whether the major themes chosen are in fact the major themes of the NT. The themes chosen according to this approach sometimes are derived from systematic theology.[26] On the one hand, the whole-Bible biblical theology of Charles H. H. Scobie's work is closest in this respect to my approach, since he is much more synthetic and does not trace themes in the OT or the NT consecutively book by book or corpus by corpus. On the other hand, his work is different in that it is structured by themes and not by the elements of a formally postulated storyline, though I think that he would say that ultimately he has derived these themes from a biblical storyline.[27]

(4) Another unique feature of this biblical theology of the NT in contrast with most other NT theologies is that it is concerned with how important components of the OT storyline are understood and developed in Judaism.[28] This is significant because it is important to see how the major biblical-theological notions in the NT develop these same OT components and whether they do so in dependence on Judaism or in line with Judaism or in contrast to it. The results from such a comparison and contrast should shed interpretative light on the development of the NT. Accordingly, most chapters in this book have discrete sections on how Judaism developed the

25. E.g., George Eldon Ladd, *A Theology of the New Testament* (Grand Rapids: Eerdmans, 1974), though he sets up relatively different themes for each major NT corpus, including Acts and Revelation, and conducts only a general survey of the Johannine Epistles without setting up themes; Schreiner, *New Testament Theology*. This is also the procedure of the whole-Bible biblical theologies of Brevard S. Childs, *Biblical Theology of the Old and New Testaments: Theological Reflection on the Christian Bible* (Minneapolis: Fortress, 1993), and Charles H. H. Scobie, *The Ways of Our God: An Approach to Biblical Theology* (Grand Rapids: Eerdmans, 2003), though he does not proceed book by book or corpus by corpus.

26. E.g., Donald Guthrie, *New Testament Theology* (Downers Grove, IL: InterVarsity, 1981), though he does integrate biblical-theological topics into his broad systematic scheme and provides brief introductory sections on OT and Jewish background for a number of the major themes that he studies, which give his book a biblical-theological flavor; so also, to some degree, Leon Morris, *New Testament Theology* (Grand Rapids: Zondervan, 1986), which, while structured corpus by corpus (with Paul first), tends to organize the themes within each corpus by systematic topics, though it also integrates biblical-theological themes into the organization.

27. See Scobie, *Ways of Our God*, 91–99, where he proposes the broad fourfold framework of proclamation, promise, fulfillment, and consummation, though the specific themes that he traces through each of these four categories he derives from "an extensive study of the numerous proposals that have been made by biblical scholars, especially for a so-called center or focal point of BT" (p. 93). See also the whole-Bible biblical theology of Keith A. Mathison, *From Age to Age: The Unfolding of Biblical Eschatology* (Phillipsburg, NJ: P&R, 2009), who looks at each book and corpus consecutively in general canonical order (with a few exceptions) in the OT and then in the NT and attempts conceptually to trace the developing theme of eschatology throughout Scripture.

28. Though, as we will see in this chapter, the NT theologies of Hans Hübner and Peter Stuhlmacher make significant references throughout to Judaism.

OT notion under study.[29] Such analysis will also show the historical rooted-ness of the theology of the NT.

(5) This approach to NT biblical theology will focus more on the unity of the NT than on its diversity. The reason for this is that such a theology attempts to trace how the overall storyline of the NT develops from the OT and develops throughout the NT material. In this respect, more classic NT theologies have opportunity to show more of this diversity and historical particularity than the biblical theology being done in this book. This is a limitation of the present project. Such diversity could, however, be discussed sufficiently if twice the space were allotted to the present book. Nevertheless, discontinuities will be shown between the major themes of the OT and those of the NT, especially in terms of how the NT transforms these notions.[30]

(6) On the one hand, it is not usual to find a concise definition of what is a classic NT theology. On the other hand, my working definition of NT biblical theology is the following, in dependence on Geerhardus Vos's definition of a whole-Bible biblical theology: "Biblical theology, rightly defined, is nothing else than *the exhibition of the organic progress of supernatural revelation in its historic continuity and multiformity.*"[31] In this light, a biblical-theological approach to a particular text seeks to give its interpretation first with regard to its own literary context and primarily in relation to its own redemptive-historical epoch, and then to the epoch or epochs preceding and following it. This definition, while true of a whole-Bible biblical theology, is equally applicable to the doing of a NT biblical theology and differs from the usual approach of standard NT theologies. In particular, the present project places the interpretation of NT texts in relation to the preceding epochs found in the OT, which often occurs through analyzing the use of particular OT passages in the NT. I will also try to be sensitive to how parts of the NT relate to one another in the development of the storyline, and how the NT era of inaugurated fulfillment of the OT relates to the consummative era.[32] In fact, chapter 27

29. While the majority of chapters on the NT (chaps. 3–26) have such sections, a few do not, since it was deemed less important in these chapters (i.e., chaps. 20–21 on the church as eschatological Israel and chap. 25 on Christian living). However, there are a few chapters where such sections on Jewish interpretation would have been helpful, but, among other factors, lack of space hindered such an inclusion (see chap. 15 on justification, chap. 16 on reconciliation, chap. 22 on the land promises, chap. 23 on the Sabbath in relation to the church, the sections in chap. 24 on baptism and the Lord's Supper, and chap. 26 on the law and marriage).

30. See, e.g., chap. 27.

31. Vos, "Idea of Biblical Theology," 15. Carson ("New Testament Theology," 807–8) agrees with Vos's definition and elaborates well upon it.

32. The definition of biblical theology offered so far in this paragraph is in line with pro-grammatic essays by D. A. Carson, "Current Issues in Biblical Theology: A New Testament Perspective," *BBR* 5 (1995): 17–41; idem, "New Testament Theology," 798–814. The latter especially should also be consulted for the history of the problematic issues involved in biblical theology (esp. NT theology), for the massive relevant literature on the subject of NT theology, and various perspectives on the topic, especially from the early part of the twentieth century

tries to summarize the main thematic storyline components discussed in the book by showing how the NT theme relates to the OT through observing its various inaugurated fulfillments of the OT and then how these inaugurated fulfillments relate to the time of the consummation of these fulfillments.

(7) The scheme of this book is generally closer to a couple of works that also style themselves as NT biblical theologies: both Hans Hübner[33] and Peter Stuhlmacher[34] have written such books with the identical title *Biblische Theologie des Neuen Testaments* (*Biblical Theology of the New Testament*). Hübner sees that the key beginning point of his work is that of determining how the NT writers interpret particular OT quotations and allusions. This is a promising approach. He has numerous references to the OT in the NT and interesting discussions of them. Hübner's focus, however, is on how the OT is "received" in the NT rather than on how the OT itself relates to and informs the NT. While showing some continuity between the two Testaments, he highlights more discontinuity.[35] He sees that there is more of a separation or gap than a conceptual bridge between the original meaning of OT passages and the meaning that NT writers gave such passages. In this respect, his program can be described as the "New Testament takeover (*in novo receptum*) of the Old."[36] The NT writers' perspective "in Christ" overrides the original contextual meanings of the OT texts that are referred to.[37]

Following Brevard S. Childs, Stuhlmacher criticizes Hübner's project. Stuhlmacher asserts that using only OT citations and allusions as the starting point for a NT theology does not result in a deep and comprehensive enough understanding on how the two Testaments are related. Each Testament deserves to have its own witness heard separately on its own terms, after which and in light of which the two can then be related to each other.[38] I would also add

---

up until the early 1990s. Also helpful is Brian S. Rosner, "Biblical Theology," *NDBT* 3–11; Stuhlmacher, *Biblische Theologie*, 1:13–28.

33. Hans Hübner, *Biblische Theologie des Neuen Testaments*, 3 vols. (Göttingen: Vandenhoeck & Ruprecht, 1990–95).

34. Stuhlmacher, *Biblische Theologie*.

35. On which, see the criticism by Carson, "New Testament Theology," 802. However, Hübner (*Biblische Theologie*, 1:258–59) rightly says that Jewish exegetical methodology should not be seen as the key to understanding Paul's interpretation of the OT, but rather Paul's approach must be based primarily on an examination of his letters themselves.

36. Carson, "New Testament Theology," 802.

37. For a succinct summary of Hübner's programmatic discussion of his view on "Vetus Testamentum in novo receptum," see *Biblische Theologie*, 1:64–70, 2:344.

38. Stuhlmacher, *How to Do Biblical Theology*, 77, following Childs, *Biblical Theology*, 77–78, 225–27. In this introductory section, I will focus on the English translation of this work by Stuhlmacher because it summarizes his general approach in his German NT biblical theology and thus is more accessible to English readers. I have also read a prepublication copy of the English translation of Stuhlmacher's two-volume *Biblische Theologie des Neuen Testaments* (trans. Daniel Bailey and forthcoming by Eerdmans); however, after this introductory section, I will refer to the published German edition.

specifically that the NT use of OT passages is significantly influenced by the context of those OT texts, even though there is development of the meaning in the NT. Stuhlmacher's approach is the beginning of a recent trend among NT theologies that attempt, to varying degrees, to understand the significance of Christ and his redemptive work in light of the conceptual categories of the OT.[39]

Therefore, in distinction to Hübner's procedure, Stuhlmacher wants to focus not only on the particular use of OT texts in the NT but also on the wider theological framework of the OT.[40] He sees that the OT truly sheds light on the NT and vice versa.[41] Accordingly, the OT is not, as entailed in Hübner's position, "a preliminary stage to the New, the significance and worth of which will only be decided on the basis of the New Testament revelation."[42] In this respect, in the view of Stuhlmacher, Hübner's hermeneutical strategy faces a very difficult main question of whether the God of Israel is the same God as the Father of Jesus and the Lord of humanity.[43]

In the English-speaking world, C. H. Dodd's small yet profound book *According to the Scriptures* made two major points in line with Stuhlmacher's general approach, but preceding him. Dodd argued that OT quotations and allusions in the NT have in mind the broader context of the OT passage from where they come. Furthermore, he contended that the OT formed the "substructure" of NT theology, providing the NT writers with major theological categories and their framework of thought, which was finally interpreted by the saving event of Jesus's coming.[44]

The approach of this book is most in line with Stuhlmacher's and Dodd's theory of NT biblical theology (though in the case of Stuhlmacher there is a different understanding of the canon).[45] Nevertheless, this book sets out in a

---

39. See Marshall, *New Testament Theology*; Thielman, *Theology of the New Testament*; Schreiner, *New Testament Theology*, on which see the further survey in D. A. Carson, "Locating Udo Schnelle's *Theology of the New Testament* in the Contemporary Discussion," *JETS* 53 (2010): 133–34, which also summarizes some German NT theologies that are a part of this recent trend. See, e.g., Ulrich Wilckens, *Theologie des Neuen Testaments*, 5 vols. (Neukirchen-Vluyn: Neukirchener Verlag, 2002–5), which especially in the first volume has significant discussions of the OT and Judaism as significant background for the following study of NT theology. Already in the mid-1970s, Leonhard Goppelt, in introducing his theology of Paul, affirmed that the OT provided a framework of "promise and typology" within which Paul interpreted the OT and applied it to Christ and the church (*Theology of the New Testament*, trans. John E. Alsup, ed. Jürgen Roloff, 2 vols. [Grand Rapids: Eerdmans, 1981–82], 2:52–62).

40. See, e.g, Stuhlmacher, *How to Do Biblical Theology*, 79.

41. Ibid., 2–12.

42. Ibid., 79.

43. Ibid. See Stuhlmacher, *Biblische Theologie* 1:37–38, for similar and further critique of Hübner's position.

44. I agree with Marshall, *New Testament Theology*, 39–40, on this significance of Dodd's work.

45. Stuhlmacher says that "*one must speak of one canonical process from which the Hebrew Bible, the Septuagint* [including the apocryphal books] *and the New Testament all proceed and*

different direction in the way it executes how the two Testaments are related. The first major section of this book attempts to summarize the main storyline of the OT (chaps. 2–3), whereas Dodd and Stuhlmacher, among others, make no substantive attempt to do so. Stuhlmacher's first segment begins with Jesus. Furthermore, neither Dodd nor Stuhlmacher attempts in a significant manner to see how the broad OT storyline relates to that of the NT. In general—and this is the major difference between their work and the present project—they do not attempt an in-depth examination of how the OT influences each of the major theological concepts of the NT. Dodd's book is especially thin on this score (and we should note that it was not his aim to do such a thorough study). Stuhlmacher chooses God's righteousness and justification as the central concern of the OT and especially of the NT.[46] To be fair, however, Stuhlmacher would see his "center" of God's righteousness and justification to be the essence of the biblical story.[47]

Howard Marshall has said that Hübner and Stuhlmacher have "so thoroughly demonstrated" the OT background for a biblical theology of the NT that "no further demonstration here" is required, and he "is content to assume this approach rather than to justify it."[48] I think that Marshall's assessment needs some modification. Indeed, as late as 1999 James Barr could say that classic NT theologies have had "even less eagerness to establish connections with the Old Testament" than have OT theologies tried to make links with the NT.[49] Barr may be overstating the situation somewhat, since Hübner and

---

which, although multi-layered, represents a continuum" (How to Do Biblical Theology, 78). This canonical "process ends with the formation of the two-part Christian canon in the fourth century CE" (ibid., 81). Hartmut Gese held that the NT writers accepted the Apocrypha, Qumran writings, and other early Jewish writings as Scripture, and that the NT was responsible for closing the OT canon (see Gese, "Tradition and Biblical Theology," in Tradition and Theology in the Old Testament, ed. Douglas A. Knight [Philadelphia: Fortress, 1977], 317–26; for a summary and critical evaluation of Gese's position, see Barr, Concept of Biblical Theology, 362–77). My view is that there was a distinct canonization of the Hebrew OT and later of the NT, though it is better to speak of a recognition of the divine canonical authority of books, not a process of the church creating a canon, as some scholars hold. In this respect, as alluded to earlier, I do not see the LXX to have been originally divinely inspired like the Hebrew text, but to be a noninspired translation.

46. Stuhlmacher, How to Do Biblical Theology, 26–27, 33, 36–38, 63 (where apparently he uses "salvation" synonymously with the concept of justification; so also 81). See Scott J. Hafemann, "'The Righteousness of God': An Introduction to the Theological and Historical Foundation of Peter Stuhlmacher's Biblical Theology of the New Testament," in Stuhlmacher, How to Do Biblical Theology, xv–xli. Hafemann shows that Stuhlmacher saw that the central notion of the OT and especially of the NT is the righteousness of God and justification, and that the NT develops this idea from the OT. Hübner's work also emphasizes justification in the NT (on which, see Stuhlmacher, How to Do Biblical Theology, 79).

47. See Stuhlmacher, How to Do Biblical Theology, 63, where he gives a brief formulation of a storyline, though with emphasis on the NT role in that storyline; see likewise p. 81.

48. Marshall, New Testament Theology, 708–9.

49. Barr, Concept of Biblical Theology, 183.

especially Stuhlmacher and Dodd have made significant strides in showing the connection between OT and NT theology. Indeed, Stuhlmacher's project should be seen as the best attempt to show most consistently the continuity between the OT and the NT in the area of NT theology. Nevertheless, Barr's critique still had some force up until the beginning of the twenty-first century. A more thoroughgoing demonstration of the relation of the OT to NT theology still had not been written.

The need to demonstrate the OT background to NT theology has begun to be met in the recently published *Commentary on the New Testament Use of the Old Testament*,[50] where nineteen NT scholars have analyzed every major OT quotation and significant allusion in the NT. This is the first time in the history of biblical scholarship that this kind of material has been brought together in one volume. This is a major step forward in understanding the biblical theology of the NT, since all the contributors affirm in one way or another that the two Testaments hang together theologically, and that the NT writers to varying degrees have referred to OT passages with their broader OT context in mind. However, this project did not attempt to synthesize the results of each contributor's interpretative work on the use of the OT in the NT. Consequently, the unifying threads of the NT arising out of the use of the OT are not analyzed and discussed. Furthermore, as Stuhlmacher mentioned earlier, focusing only on OT quotations and allusions does not give a deep and comprehensive enough understanding of how the two Testaments relate and how this bears on NT biblical theology. Each Testament needs to be heard on its own, and then how they relate can be focused upon. In particular, the storylines of both Testaments need to be reflected upon, and then one can try to determine how these storylines relate to each other.

Therefore, I believe that more work needs to be done to validate further the program of Stuhlmacher, as well as that of Dodd and others who have shown agreement with them. Consequently, one of the main goals of this book is to demonstrate further the OT background for the theology of the NT. The hope is that others will also contribute to this goal from other various angles.[51] Of course, in a NT biblical theology project like this one, the coverage of the OT must be abbreviated in comparison with that of the NT, which is a limitation. But this will always be a limitation of theologies of the NT, even of the NT biblical theology genre.

50. G. K. Beale and D. A. Carson, eds., *Commentary on the New Testament Use of the Old Testament* (Grand Rapids: Baker Academic, 2007).

51. Even though the earlier-mentioned book edited by Zuck and Bock is titled *A Biblical Theology of the New Testament*, it does not have significant discussion either of how the storyline (or broad themes) of the OT relates to the NT, or of how particular OT texts are used in the New (though there are a few exceptions with respect to the latter). It might better have been titled merely *A New Testament Theology*, since it deals only broadly with themes of the respective NT books.

Before leaving this topic, I should also again acknowledge the whole-Bible biblical theology of Charles H. H. Scobie, whose work has more consistently and on a larger scale attempted to relate the OT thematic background to major NT themes than any other that I know of.[52] My project tries to do this in more depth, even though some scholars believe that it is impossible on an exegetical or biblical-theological level to demonstrate the unity and coherence of the two Testaments.[53]

(8) As alluded to briefly above, another distinction between several NT theologies in comparison with the scheme of the present project is that they conduct their discussions generally corpus by corpus.[54] This is the case, for example, with the theologies of Marshall, Thielman, and Schreiner, as well as that of Hübner and Stuhlmacher.[55] Also in contrast, as noted earlier, my approach is organized by the major components of my formulation of the NT storyline.[56] In this respect, this project attempts to begin to meet the need, recognized by others, for NT theologies to pay attention to the narrative plotline of the biblical witness.[57] In further contrast to many of these NT theologies, I will not as consistently survey every NT book and sometimes corpus in examining each of the themes. Indeed, such a partial corpus-by-corpus or book-by-book outline in the NT section will not be followed at all in some chapters of this study.[58]

Thus, this project is not an attempt to focus directly and discretely on how each book of the NT[59] contributes to the theology of the NT but rather concentrates on those parts of the NT that most develop the storyline that I have formulated, which I believe is the essential thread of the NT. Furthermore, my studies of the major themes tend to be deeper exegetically,

52. Scobie, *Ways of Our God*.
53. See, e.g., Barr, *Concept of Biblical Theology*, 375–76.
54. And within each corpus each book is surveyed.
55. Here should also be mentioned Wilckens, *Theologie des Neuen Testaments*, which, after an extended discussion of introductory matters, deals corpus by corpus, though the last volume again covers the Gospels, then Acts, the Johannine Epistles, Revelation, and finally issues of canon.
56. This is not to say that some NT theologies lack reference to the importance of a storyline, but they do not formulate it very clearly, nor does it play a role in organizing their project but instead emerges as a result at the end of their inductive studies. E.g., Thielman (*Theology of the New Testament*, 681–725) sees the following five elements as a summary of the key themes of the NT, which do form a general storyline with Jesus as the center of it: (1) Jesus and sin; (2) response of faith; (3) the Spirit as God's presence; (4) the church as the people of God; (5) the consummation. Likewise Marshall, *New Testament Theology*, 709–31, who mentions virtually the same five elements, though stressing that the best framework for understanding them is that of "mission," which enhances the storyline nature of these elements together.
57. See Richard B. Hays, "Can Narrative Criticism Recover the Theological Unity of Scripture?" *JTI* 2 (2008): 205; see the entire article for his attempt at a thumbnail sketch of how viewing Scripture as a unified and coherent dramatic narrative can contribute to the doing of NT theology.
58. E.g., in chaps. 12, 15–16, 18–20, 22–24, 26.
59. Especially in mind here are the smaller epistles, such as Jude and 2–3 John.

though this means that I cannot cover as many subtopics as typical NT theologies cover.

(9) In light of what I have discussed thus far, I categorize my biblical-theological approach to be canonical, genetic-progressive (or organically developmental, as a flower develops from a seed and bud), exegetical, and intertextual. This approach could be summarized as a "biblical-theological-oriented exegesis."[60] My methodology indicates no weakness on the part of NT theologies such as those of Stuhlmacher, Ladd, Guthrie, Marshall, Thielman, and Schreiner, but only the different nature of my project.[61]

The Specific Content of This Biblical Theology of the New Testament

As discussed briefly above, this biblical theology of the NT first attempts to trace the canonical storyline of the OT and tries to distill the major biblical-theological themes from that storyline (chap. 2). Since, as we will see, "movement toward an eschatological goal" is one of the major themes of the OT storyline, the third, fourth, and fifth chapters look respectively at the eschatology of the OT, then of Judaism, and finally of the NT. The themes composing the OT storyline found in chapters 2–3 become the basis for the NT storyline, which is stated in chapter 6. The NT plotline is a transformation of the OT storyline through developing it and fulfilling its prophetic features.

Chapter 6 then discusses methodological problems in the search for "centers" in the OT and the NT and how this is similar yet different from the search for a storyline, the latter of which the present project prefers. What is meant by the word "storyline" is explained further in chapter 2 (under the heading "The Repeated Cosmic Judgment and New Creation Episodes of the Old Testament") and especially in chapter 6. It is argued that a storyline reflects a unified story yet contains multiple themes that are incased in a narratival canonical plotline.[62]

Then the components of the NT storyline, as noted earlier, serve as the organizing outline of the remainder of the book (chaps. 7–28). Each chapter discusses and traces throughout the NT a thematic component of the storyline (along with subthemes to be traced that are subordinate to each major

60. See Carson, "New Testament Theology," 807.
61. E.g., Marshall says that his work has "attempted the more limited objective of establishing that there is a common, basic theology that can be traced in all of our witnesses, but without developing this theology in detail" (*New Testament Theology*, 726). My work attempts to do the latter by laying out the core storyline at the beginning in the light of the OT storyline and then developing more deeply the theological-thematic components of that story. In this respect, my plotline statement finds general support not only in the OT narrative line but also in the conclusions of theologies such as those of Marshall and Thielman, whose conclusions about the core elements of the NT are consistent with the main elements of my proposed NT plotline.
62. Also in chap. 6 is discussion about how the concept of a storyline relates to history and to theology.

15

thematic component). This NT section is the bulk of the book. Each theme discussed in the NT section is seen from the perspective of its roots in the OT, its development in Judaism, and through the lens of the "already and not yet end-time fulfillment" in the NT. Accordingly, chapters typically are structured, to one degree or another, by discussion of relevant OT background, then Jewish developments, followed by analysis of the NT material (sometimes but not always in the order of Gospels, Acts, Paul, General Epistles, and Revelation). In some cases, when the relevant material is concentrated in only certain parts of the NT, there is more focus on those parts than others, as alluded to earlier.

The OT storyline that I posit as the basis for the NT storyline is this: *The Old Testament is the story of God, who progressively reestablishes his new-creational kingdom out of chaos over a sinful people by his word and Spirit through promise, covenant, and redemption, resulting in worldwide commission to the faithful to advance this kingdom and judgment (defeat or exile) for the unfaithful, unto his glory.* The inductive basis for the formulation of this statement is found in chapters 2–3.

The NT transformation of the storyline of the OT that I propose is this: *Jesus's life, trials, death for sinners, and especially resurrection by the Spirit have launched the fulfillment of the eschatological already–not yet new-creational reign, bestowed by grace through faith and resulting in worldwide commission to the faithful to advance this new-creational reign and resulting in judgment for the unbelieving, unto the triune God's glory.* At first glance, some of the conceptual categories that compose various chapters may not seem to grow out of the foregoing storyline components, but I will argue that they indeed do.[63]

I contend that the goal of the NT storyline is God's glory, and that the main stepping-stone to that goal is Christ's establishment of an eschatological new-creational kingdom and its expansion. The main focus of this book is on the development of this new-creational kingdom and its spread as the penultimate means to divine glory. Others have argued well that the glory of God is the final goal of Scripture,[64] so I concentrate my efforts here on the major instrumentation that accomplishes that goal.

A key element of the aforementioned storyline is the "eschatological already–not yet" fulfillment in the NT. Others have also emphasized in various ways the eschatological focus of NT theology. My primary thesis, in general, is that in order to understand the NT in its full richness, we must have a keen acquaintance with how the biblical authors viewed the "end times," especially as it forms an essential part of the NT story. This may sound like an extreme

---

63. E.g., chaps. 15 and 16, respectively on justification and reconciliation, may not appear formally linked to the words of this storyline, but they are conceptual explanations of it; i.e., they unpack that part of the storyline dealing with Jesus's death for sinners and his resurrection. Likewise, chaps. 20–24, pertaining to the church, are conceptual developments of various aspects of the faithful who advance the new-creational reign.

64. I will refer to such commentators as the book develops, esp. in chap. 28.

proposition to Christians outside scholarly circles, since many in the church often think of the end times as a period that will happen only at the very climax of history. After all, can we not have an excellent understanding of the NT without knowing about exactly how the world is going to end?

The popular understanding that the latter days refer only to the future end of the world needs radical adjustment. On a scholarly level, NT research over past decades has made great strides in increasing our understanding that the beginning of Christian history was perceived by the first Christians as the beginning of the end times but not their consummation.[65] There is, however, still much study to be done in synthesizing this work, developing a NT theology in the light of such work, and refining the focus of eschatology in its relation to NT theology. NT scholarship has still been atomistic enough to prevent serious broad theological reflection on the already–not yet eschatological perspective of the entire NT corpus (though there are significant exceptions, such as N. T. Wright's work). Along these lines, as late as the mid-1980s Dale Allison could complain that the history of NT theology was responsible for influencing scholars to focus specifically on the atoning nature of Christ's death and pay insufficient attention to its eschatological ramifications. He continues by saying,

> Christian theology has rarely grappled seriously with the eschatological presuppositions that permeate the New Testament, and although the twentieth century is the century of Albert Schweitzer, contemporary students of the New Testament have yet to explore *fully* the importance of eschatological language for the early followers of Jesus.[66]

The NT writers assert that Christians experience only a part of what will be completely experienced in the final form of the new heavens and earth. There is what has become famously called an "already and not yet" dimension of the end times. In this respect, Oscar Cullmann has metaphorically described Jesus's first coming as "D-day" because this is when Satan was decisively defeated. "V-day" is the second coming, when Jesus's enemies will totally surrender and bow down to him. Cullman says it this way: "The hope of the final victory is so much the more vivid because of the unshakably firm conviction that the battle that decides the victory has already taken place."[67]

65. For articles and relevant bibliography on the eschatology of the Gospels, Paul, and the remainder of the NT, see respectively Dale C. Allison Jr., "Eschatology," *DJG* 206–9; Larry J. Kreitzer, "Eschatology," *DPL* 253–69; G. K. Beale, "Eschatology," *DLNTD* 330–45. See also David E. Aune, "Early Christian Eschatology," *ABD* 2:594–609.

66. Dale C. Allison Jr., *The End of the Ages Has Come: An Early Interpretation of the Passion and Resurrection of Jesus* (Philadelphia: Fortress, 1985), 169 (my italics).

67. Oscar Cullmann, *Christ and Time: The Primitive Christian Conception of Time and History*, trans. Floyd V. Filson (Philadelphia: Westminster, 1950), 87.

But the point of the present discussion is that the great end-time predictions have already begun the process of fulfillment. William Manson has well said,

> When we turn to the New Testament, we pass from the climate of prediction to that of fulfillment. The things which God had foreshadowed by the lips of His holy prophets He has now, in part at least, brought to accomplishment. . . . The supreme sign of the Eschaton is the Resurrection of Jesus and the descent of the Holy Spirit on the Church. The Resurrection of Jesus is not simply a sign which God has granted in favour of His son, but is the inauguration, the entrance into history, *of the times of the End.*
>
> Christians, therefore, have entered through the Christ into the new age. . . . What had been predicted in Holy Scripture as to happen to Israel or to man in the Eschaton, has happened to and in Jesus. *The foundation-stone of the New Creation has come into position.*[68]

Therefore, the apostles understood eschatology not merely as futurology but as a mind-set for understanding the present within the climaxing context of redemptive history. That is, the apostles understood that they were already living in the end times, and that they were to understand their present salvation in Christ to be already an end-time reality. *Every aspect of their salvation was to be conceived of as eschatological in nature.* To put this another way, the major doctrines of the Christian faith are charged with eschatological electricity. Just as when you put on green sunglasses, everything you see is green, so Christ through the Spirit had placed eschatological sunglasses on his disciples so that everything they looked at in the Christian faith had an end-time tint. This means that the doctrine of eschatology in NT theology textbooks should not merely be one among many doctrines that are addressed but should be the lens through which all the doctrines are best understood. Furthermore, eschatology should not be placed at the end of NT theology textbooks or at the end of chapters dealing with the different NT corpuses because it purportedly describes only the very end of the world as we know it. Rather, the doctrine of eschatology could be part of the title of such a textbook because every major theological concept breathes the air of a latter-day atmosphere. For the same reason, systematic theology textbooks should integrate the inaugurated aspect of eschatology more into the discussion of other NT doctrines, even if they still put a section of consummative eschatology as the last chapter.

It is important to say that our understanding of most of the traditional doctrines is not so much changed as radically enriched by seeing them through end-time lenses. But how are some of the crucial doctrines of our faith so

68. William Manson, "Eschatology in the New Testament," in *Eschatology: Four Papers Read to the Society for the Study of Theology,* SJTOP 2 (Edinburgh: Oliver & Boyd, 1953), 6 (my italics). Although this sounds like "overrealized eschatology," Manson qualifies it by saying, "The End has come! The End has not come!" (ibid., 7).

enriched when seen as eschatological doctrines? To put it another way: how can our hermeneutical lenses be reground in order to see better the end-time reality of the NT? I believe that the concluding part of William Manson's quotation above is a good place to start answering this question. He said that the *resurrected* Christ is "the foundation-stone of the New Creation [that] has come into position."[69]

We should think of Christ's life, trials, and especially his death and resurrection as the central events that launched the latter days. These pivotal events of Christ's life, trials, death, and resurrection are eschatological in particular because they launched the beginning of the new creation and kingdom. The end-time new-creational kingdom has not been recognized sufficiently heretofore as of vital importance to a biblical theology of the NT, and it is this concept that I believe has the potential to refine significantly the general scholarly view of the eschatological already–not yet.

It is at this precise point that I hope to build on the foundational work of theologians such as Geerhardus Vos,[70] Oscar Cullmann,[71] Herman Ridderbos,[72] and George Eldon Ladd,[73] among others.[74] Though more recent theologians have increasingly seen some important aspects of NT theology to be colored with an eschatological tint,[75] these earlier scholars saw more consistently that

69. Ibid., 6.

70. Geerhardus Vos, *The Pauline Eschatology* (1930; repr., Grand Rapids: Baker Academic, 1979); see also idem, *Redemptive History and Biblical Interpretation*, passim; idem, *Biblical Theology: Old and New Testaments* (Grand Rapids: Eerdmans, 1948).

71. Cullmann, *Christ and Time*.

72. Herman Ridderbos, *The Coming of the Kingdom*, trans. H. de Jongste, ed. Raymond O. Zorn (Philadelphia: P&R, 1962); idem, *Paul: An Outline of His Theology* (Grand Rapids: Eerdmans, 1975).

73. George Eldon Ladd, *The Presence of the Future: The Eschatology of Biblical Realism* (Grand Rapids: Eerdmans, 1974).

74. See, e.g., Rudolf Bultmann, *Theology of the New Testament*, trans. Kendrick Grobel, 2 vols. (London: SCM, 1952–55). In the first volume Bultmann integrates already–not yet eschatology into topics such as Christ's message, justification, reconciliation, the Spirit, and the church's existence; however, he does not conduct penetrating studies on the eschatological nature of these ideas (though, of course, he demythologizes the supernatural aspects of these notions). Note also Werner Georg Kümmel's observation that "God has caused his salvation promised for the end of the world to begin in Jesus Christ" (*The Theology of the New Testament according to Its Major Witnesses*, trans. John E. Steely [Nashville: Abingdon, 1973], 332).

75. See, e.g., Thielman, *Theology of the New Testament*, 692–94, 698–714; Schreiner, *New Testament Theology*. Schreiner dedicates the first section of his book to "already and not yet eschatology" (pp. 41–116), and while referring to this theme throughout the topics of the rest of his work, it was apparently not his purpose to work it through trenchantly. See also the whole-Bible biblical theology by Scobie, *Ways of Our God*. Scobie, as already noted, sets out the following fourfold scheme for each of his major themes that structure his work: OT proclamation, OT promise, NT fulfillment, and consummation. However, in his NT discussions he generally emphasizes fulfillment more than the notion that the nature of this fulfillment is eschatological, though he does briefly discuss the inaugurated eschatological element of fulfillment

Christ's redemptive work inaugurated the latter days, and that the eschatological period would be consummated at some point in the future.[76] These scholars understood that eschatology was a crucial influence upon the thinking of the NT writers.

Geerhardus Vos taught at Princeton Theological Seminary from 1892 to 1932, and he anticipated later twentieth-century biblical theology and NT scholarship that emphasized inaugurated eschatology and a redemptive-historical approach. He stressed more than the others just noted that the notion of new creation was the main thrust of NT theology.[77] In particular, Vos saw Christ's resurrection as the beginning of new creation and viewed it as the central focus of the NT.[78] The reason for this was that it represented the further redemptive-historical progression from Christ's death and because it was from his resurrected position that he dispensed the Spirit, who brings believers into union with him and causes them to participate in the eschatological benefits of the new-creational age to come. The present volume is my attempt to develop further Vos's program, since he never wrote a full biblical theology of the NT.[79]

---

at several significant points throughout the book (e.g., see his programmatic statement in this latter respect on p. 93).

76. Though there were a few others who held this view. These scholars brought together the polar positions of Albert Schweitzer and C. H. Dodd, who believed respectively that the end times were imminent but not yet fulfilled and that the latter days had fully arrived in the coming of Jesus (for a brief overview of the two positions, see Aune, "Early Christian Eschatology," 599–600, where he also cites Joachim Jeremias and Werner Kummel as holding a synthesis of the two perspectives). Interestingly, Vos appears to be the first European or American scholar to espouse an already–not yet eschatology as a major theological approach to Paul! See Henry M. Shires, *The Eschatology of Paul in the Light of Modern Scholarship* (Philadelphia: Westminster Press, 1966), which is helpful, though having some affinities with Bultmann's approach and apparently unaware of Vos's work. Recently, C. Marvin Pate has developed Vos's view of eschatology as the framework within which to understand best Pauline theology in a more thoroughgoing manner than before, though, interestingly, he does not interact with Vos (*The End of the Age Has Come: The Theology of Paul* [Grand Rapids: Zondervan, 1995]). See also the New Testament section of the whole-Bible biblical theology by Mathison, *From Age to Age*, 337–698, who also follows Vos, Ridderbos, and Dumbrell in seeing and attempting to trace an already and not yet eschatological perspective throughout the NT. While helpful, Mathison's work operates at a broad general level through a brushstroke survey of eschatology in each NT book and typically does not reflect exegetical depth (esp. with respect to the use of the OT in the NT and associated Jewish interpretations of these OT uses), though this does not appear to have been part of his purpose.

77. Here also should be included Graeme Goldsworthy, *According to Plan: The Unfolding Revelation of God in the Bible* (Leicester: Inter-Varsity, 1991), which also sees the new creation and kingdom as the thrust of the Bible's redemptive-historical and eschatological development and is written explicitly at a popular level for people in the church.

78. On which, see Bradley J. Bitner, "The Biblical Theology of Geerhardus Vos" (MA thesis, Gordon-Conwell Theological Seminary, 2000). Accordingly, see esp., e.g., Vos, "Idea of Biblical Theology," 11–12.

79. Note that Vos's *Biblical Theology* included only a section on the Gospels in the NT segment (in about one hundred pages), though he did develop some significant biblical-theological

Richard Gaffin, in *The Centrality of the Resurrection*,[80] following in the wake of Vos, affirms that the resurrection as an end-time event is the all-encompassing thought for Paul. Seyoon Kim, in *The Origin of Paul's Gospel*,[81] explains why the resurrection dominated Paul's thinking: the risen Christ's confrontation with Paul on the Damascus Road left such a lasting impact and indelible mark on Paul that it continued to dominate his thinking as he wrote his letters.

But these scholars, as suggestive and helpful as they were, did not aim to explain in programmatic fashion how inaugurated eschatology relates to and sheds light on the major theological doctrines of the NT, though Vos and Pate come closer than others in having done this.[82] Nor, significantly, did they see that the controlling conception of eschatology was the new-creational kingdom. William Dumbrell is the only consistent exception to this, since he sees creation as the central theme of both Testaments: all of the OT works toward the goal of new creation, and the NT begins to fulfill that primary goal.[83]

Dumbrell identifies five related themes that are interrelated through their overlapping relation to Scripture's wider concept of government and God's kingdom.[84] Interestingly, Scobie surveys past proposals of "centres" for the OT, the NT, and the entire canon,[85] and he criticizes all of them except Dumbrell's, though he does say that Dumbrell's is "not a full-fledged Biblical Theology."[86] Scobie himself offers a biblical-theological scheme of the entire canon not far different from Dumbrell's. What he does is combine the numerous suggestions for a "single centre" and organize them broadly into four groups that become the basis for his multithematic approach: (1) God's creative order; (2) God's servant (Christ); (3) God's people; (4) God's way (ethics).[87]

---

material on Paul in his *Pauline Eschatology* and in other articles found in *Redemptive History and Biblical Interpretation* (e.g., chap. 4, "The Eschatological Aspect of the Pauline Conception of the Spirit").

80. Richard B. Gaffin Jr., *The Centrality of the Resurrection: A Study in Paul's Soteriology* (Grand Rapids: Baker Academic, 1978).

81. Seyoon Kim, *The Origin of Paul's Gospel* (Grand Rapids: Eerdmans, 1982).

82. See Pate, *End of the Age*. He, along with Vos, has made a better attempt at this in regard to Paul than have others.

83. See William J. Dumbrell, *The Search for Order: Biblical Eschatology in Focus* (Grand Rapids: Baker Academic, 1994); idem, *The End of the Beginning: Revelation 21–22 and the Old Testament* (Homebush West, NSW: Lancer, 1985); see also his OT theology, *Covenant and Creation: A Theology of the Old Testament Covenants* (Nashville: Thomas Nelson, 1984).

84. Dumbrell, *End of the Beginning*, "Introduction."

85. Charles H. H. Scobie, "The Structure of Biblical Theology," *TynBul* 42, no. 2 (1991): 173–79. He surveys significant "centres" for a canonical biblical theology such as "covenant," "kingdom," and "life," and for the NT he discusses "centres" such as "the Christ event," "christology," "justification," and "reconciliation."

86. Ibid., 180–81.

87. Ibid., 187–94. See Scobie, *Ways of Our God*, where he works this structure out in far more detail than in his *Tyndale Bulletin* article.

Scobie apparently is attracted to Dumbrell's view because it seems also to be multiperspectival; Dumbrell traces five major themes throughout both Testaments: (1) new creation; (2) new covenant; (3) new temple; (4) new Israel; (5) new Jerusalem.[88] Each theme is not to be viewed as of equal importance, but they are the most important ones in the Bible for him. The new Jerusalem is the symbol of government (= the kingdom) and those governed; the new temple is the seat of government; the new covenant is the instrument of government; the new Israel reveals those governed and their role; and the new creation is a final comprehensive presentation of both the governed and the governor.

Dumbrell rightly, in my view, opts for new creation as the comprehensive presentation of government (= kingdom) and thus as the most comprehensive notion of the Bible, being a summary of the four other ideas (a point apparently overlooked by Scobie, who views Dumbrell as a thoroughgoing biblical-theological multiperspectivalist). But note that *new creation and kingdom* appear to be virtually overlapping, so that Dumbrell's core idea is really that of a new-creational kingdom and not merely a new creation. The entire scheme of the Bible is structured around the movement "from creation to new creation by means of divine redemptive interventions," climaxing in Christ's death, resurrection, enthronement, and second coming, which concludes all things.[89] Dumbrell asserts that redemption is always subordinate to creation in that it is the means of reintroducing the conditions of the new creation.[90] All events since the fall of humankind are to be seen as a process leading to the reintroduction of the original creation. I believe that Dumbrell is correct in understanding that the new-creational kingdom is of vital importance to biblical theology because new creation is the main instrumentation of God's redemptive-historical plan in achieving the final goal of God's glory. As proposed earlier, the new-creational reign is the penultimate logical main point (leading to divine glory) of the scriptural storyline, which points further to the kingdom of the new creation as the main lens of a canonical biblical theology, which I will attempt to demonstrate in the remaining chapters of this book.

There are, nevertheless, shortcomings in Dumbrell's approach, but to be fair, his design was not to address these areas. His work is too much a sweeping brushstroke that surveys broad themes (with brief summaries of important passages), does not work trenchantly at the exegetical level,[91] does not try organically to relate the major NT doctrines specifically to Christ's life, death, and resurrection, nor does it attempt to explain specifically how the notions

---

88. For an expansion of the following summary of Dumbrell, see G. K. Beale, review of *The End of the Beginning*, by William J. Dumbrell, *Themelios* 15 (1990): 69–70.

89. Dumbrell, *End of the Beginning*, 166, 196.

90. Ibid., 184–85, 191, 194.

91. E.g., there needed to be serious discussion of texts in the NT that actually associate Christ with the language of new creation (esp. 2 Cor. 5:14–17; Gal. 6:14–18; Eph. 2:13–22 [cf. 1:20–23; 2:10]; Col. 1:15–18; Rev. 3:14 [cf. with 1:5]).

of new creation and kingdom relate organically to the major NT ideas and doctrines. Nowhere is there a sufficiently precise explanation of how Christ's life, death, and resurrection relate to or inaugurate the new creation. Also, Dumbrell does not work enough at a scholarly exegetical level, nor does he interact much with contemporary scholarship (though again, these were not his aims). Consequently, his work has not received the recognition that it deserves in scholarly works on biblical theology, including NT theology.

Despite these weaknesses, Dumbrell's is among the better canonical biblical theologies that I have read, and his work is highly relevant to and informative for NT theology. Although Dumbrell does not provide a specific answer, his thesis demands that the question of how Christ's death and resurrection relate to the kingdom of the new creation be answered in a clear and thorough manner. Therefore, even though Dumbrell was writing not a NT theology but rather a broader biblical theology, his work is a broad thematic sketch supporting my proposal that the movement toward new creation and kingdom is the main thrust of the NT storyline. What Dumbrell lacks in exegetical depth, Vos supplies, even if he is not as consistent in tracing the theme of the new-creational kingdom throughout the Scriptures.

My own view, then, is broadly similar to those of Dumbrell, Vos, and Gaffin, but I am trying to establish the crucial role of the kingdom of the new creation in a much more consistently exegetical and theologically trenchant manner. My thesis is that the major theological ideas of the NT flow out of the following NT storyline (which I repeat from above), of which the new-creational kingdom and its expansion are the central element (underlined in the following idea) leading to God's glory: *Jesus's life, trials, <u>death for sinners, and especially resurrection by the Spirit have launched the fulfillment of the eschatological already–not yet new-creational reign</u>, bestowed by grace through faith and <u>resulting in worldwide commission to the faithful to advance this new-creational reign</u> and resulting in judgment for the unbelieving, unto the triune God's glory.*

In fact, it is my contention that the definition of *eschatology* should be refined as the movement toward the new-creational reign, with other associated eschatological concepts being understood as subcategories of this. This eschatological new creation reign is a movement toward a regaining of what was in Eden before sin. Accordingly, the topical subcategories of this book given from chapters 3–28 are not chosen in a completely subjective manner but are controlled to a significant degree by perceiving that these are topics that are prominent facets of Gen. 1–3 and are prominent in the final vision of the consummated regaining of Eden and the eschatological new-creational kingdom in Rev. 21–22. At the very end of chapter 6, I will address in more detail the rationale of why I have chosen some chapter topics and not included others.

Therefore, the major theological ideas in the NT gain their fullest meaning within the framework of this overriding plotline thrust of the new creation and kingdom and are but facets of it. In this regard, what Vos says about the dominating notion of eschatology in Paul's thought is, I will argue, true of the NT as a whole:[92]

> The eschatology [of Paul] . . . no longer forms one item in the sum-total of revealed teaching, but draws within its circle as correlated and eschatologically-complexioned parts practically all of the fundamental tenets of Pauline Christianity . . . [and] to unfold the Apostle's eschatology means to set forth his theology as a whole.[93]

Although it is true that ideas others may think are significant in NT theology may not be included in this book, I will try to focus on those I believe to be the most important. Other NT theologies may also include more themes. The present project, however, while containing fewer thematic studies than others, provides more in-depth analysis of each theological topic to be studied.

Thus, we can think of Christ's life, particularly his death and resurrected kingship, as a diamond that represents the new-creational reign. The various theological ideas are the facets of the diamond, which are inseparable from the diamond itself. This book is an attempt to give some of the most significant examples of how this is so and how the eschatological enhancement of the various doctrines also gives insight into the practical application of these doctrines to the lives of Christians. I am sure that many readers will not agree with my proposal of the new-creational kingdom and its expansion being the major stepping-stone to God's glory and the major thrust of the NT storyline. Nevertheless, I am hopeful at least that the eschatological lens that I am offering will yield insights that can still be appreciated. This book represents the biblical-theological thought that I have been developing for about thirty years in various articles and books, and that took its first "seed" form in a class on NT theology that I have taught since the late 1980s.

Conclusion

Each topic addressed in this introduction could legitimately receive book-length treatment. The purpose of this introduction is not to elaborate fully on

92. Recalling that Vos saw the central aspect of Pauline eschatology to lie in the resurrected and ascended Christ (on which, see further, e.g., Vos, *Pauline Eschatology*, 151).

93. Vos, *Pauline Eschatology*, 11. See likewise Herman Ridderbos, *Paul: An Outline of His Theology*, 44, who, possibly inspired by the earlier Vosian Dutch tradition, says, "The whole content of this preaching [by Paul] can be summarized as the proclamation and explication of the eschatological time of salvation inaugurated with Christ's advent, death and resurrection. It is from this principal point of view and under this denominator that all the separate themes of Paul's preaching can be understood and penetrated in their unity and relation to each other." So similarly ibid., 57, where he says the focus of Paul's eschatology is on Christ's death and especially resurrection.

such matters but rather to lay out the presuppositions and the uniqueness of this biblical theology of the NT, as well as the direction this book will take. Other works on NT theology have summarized in much more depth than this one things such as the history of the discipline, issues of prolegomena, critical problems concerning history in relation to revelation and theology, and a survey of the various significant works, especially the flourishing of the discipline in the twentieth century.[94] To such works I refer the reader. The aim and hope are that the substance of the book itself will demonstrate the viability of this project. The goal is that "the proof will be in the pudding." The greatest goal, however, is that the book will call forth worship and glorification of the triune God, which, we will see, is the final descriptive and prescriptive goal of the NT storyline.

A final word about the intended audience of this book is important. This book, like my books on the temple[95] and idolatry,[96] is primarily aimed at serious Christian readers, whether they be people in the church who are not scholars or college or graduate theology students. I hope, however, that the book will also contribute to biblical scholarship, especially in the area of NT *biblical* theology. Attempting to communicate to serious lay audiences as well as to theological students and scholars is a bit of a tightrope act: insufficient academic argumentation in a number of areas may cause dissatisfaction among scholars, but tailoring material to scholars may cause interested lay readers to become overwhelmed. So I will try to walk that tightrope as best I can, though I will tilt my book toward readers who want to delve more deeply into the Scriptures and theology. I suggest that readers of a more popular bent ignore the footnotes (or read them after reading through the body of each chapter). I must emphasize that this book focuses on biblical interpretation and biblical theology and much less on practical application of these truths in the modern world (though this last topic will be addressed at points throughout and at the very end of the book, the last part of chap. 28). Nevertheless, I hope that readers can glean theological principles with a view to living as faithful Christians who have one foot in the old world and the other in the emerging new world.

94. See again Carson, "New Testament Theology," as well as the earlier evaluative survey by Gerhard F. Hasel, *New Testament Theology: Basic Issues in the Current Debate* (Grand Rapids: Eerdmans, 1978). See also the brief but helpful sketch of the history of the major problems facing NT biblical theology in Thielman, *Theology of the New Testament*, 19–42, and Schreiner, *New Testament Theology*, 867–88, especially with respect to the problems revolving around issues concerning the canon, diversity, and presuppositions of interpretation. For the NT theologies in Germany that Stuhlmacher considers most significant, among which he includes the American works of Ladd and Childs, see *How to Do Biblical Theology*, 74–75. See also Matera, *New Testament Theology*, xix–xxviii, for a brief but helpful discussion of the major New Testament theologies of the twentieth and twenty-first centuries.

95. G. K. Beale, *The Temple and the Church's Mission: A Biblical Theology of the Dwelling Place of God*, NSBT 17 (Downers Grove, IL: InterVarsity, 2004).

96. Beale, *We Become What We Worship*.

PART 1

THE BIBLICAL-THEOLOGICAL STORYLINE OF SCRIPTURE

2

The Redemptive-Historical Storyline
of the Old Testament

The presupposition of this book is that the NT is the continuation of the storyline of the OT, although I will attempt to demonstrate this inductively throughout. Therefore, it is fitting to summarize in this chapter the development of the storyline in the OT before elaborating on how the various aspects of NT theology relate to this storyline. Obviously, this initial task deserves the writing of a full biblical theology of the OT, but that is a luxury that the scope of the present project cannot afford. Hopefully, what is laid out here will be seen to have potential as providing an outline for an OT biblical theology that could viably be fleshed out in more detail. The analysis here will be from a canonical perspective, since I believe that would have been the perspective of the NT writers, though it is also an increasingly popular perspective among some sectors of modern biblical scholarship.[1]

My thesis in this respect is that Gen. 1–3 lays out the basic themes for the rest of the OT, which, as we will see, are essentially eschatological themes.

1. My own method and perspective come closest to that of Stephen G. Dempster, *Dominion and Dynasty: A Theology of the Hebrew Bible*, NSBT 15 (Downers Grove, IL: InterVarsity, 2003), as well as Geerhardus Vos, *Biblical Theology: Old and New Testaments* (Grand Rapids: Eerdmans, 1948), and various works by William J. Dumbrell, especially *The End of the Beginning: Revelation 21–22 and the Old Testament* (Homebush West, NSW: Lancer, 1985); idem, *The Search for Order: Biblical Eschatology in Focus* (Grand Rapids: Baker Academic, 1994); idem, *The Faith of Israel: A Theological Survey of the Old Testament*, 2nd ed. (Grand Rapids: Baker Academic, 2002).

These themes are then developed in the NT. The works that have attempted to affirm this have merely demonstrated general thematic connections between the first three chapters of the Bible and the rest of Genesis and of the OT.[2] None that I am aware of have tried to do this also by actually focusing on specific literary allusions to Gen. 1–3 elsewhere in subsequent Scripture (though Stephen Dempster comes closest).[3] Thus, this chapter falls into four sections:

1. a sketch of the thought in Gen. 1–3;
2. allusions to Gen. 1–3 elsewhere in the OT and how they develop that initial narrative;
3. observation of the themes from Gen. 1–3 elsewhere in the OT and how they develop that initial narrative;
4. the relation of the Adamic storyline derived from the above analysis to past proposals of the "center" of the OT.

Adam's Commission in the First Creation and the Passing On of the Commission to Other Adam-Like Figures

The commission of Gen. 1:26–28 involves the following elements, especially as summarized in 1:28: (1) "God blessed them"; (2) "be fruitful and multiply"; (3) "fill the earth"; (4) "subdue" the "earth"; (5) "rule over . . . all the earth."

It also appears that God's making of Adam in his "image and likeness" is what enables Adam to carry out the particular parts of the commission. God's creation of Adam in his image as the crown of creation is probably to be seen as the content of the "blessing" at the beginning of verse 28. The "ruling" and "subduing" "over all the earth" expresses Adam's kingship[4] and is plausibly part of a functional definition of the divine image in which Adam was made. This functional aspect is likely the focus of what it means that Adam and Eve were created in God's image. Such a functional view of the image is suggested by images of gods in the ancient Near East, which neither represented the actual form of the god nor indicated primarily the attributes of the god (though this sometimes was included) but rather were the place through which the god manifested his presence and conveyed his blessings. When ancient Near Eastern kings were conceived to be images of a god, the idea of the god's subduing and ruling through him are in mind, and this appears to be the best background against which to understand Adam as a king and in the image of God in Gen.

2. See, e.g., Dumbrell, *Search for Order*, 9–12. He is the only other commentator apparently underscoring that the major ideas in Gen. 1–3 are also eschatological in nature.
3. Dempster, *Dominion and Dynasty*.
4. Note the use of *rādâ* ("rule") and its uses elsewhere in the OT, at least half of which refer to a king's rule (following Dumbrell).

1:26–28.[5] For example, note King Adad-nirari II of Assyria (911–891 BC), who says that the gods "intervened to alter my appearance to lordly appearance, [and] fixed/established and perfected my features," which resulted in the king "being fit to rule."[6] Likewise, King Assurbanipal affirms that the gods "gave me a splendid figure and made my strength great."[7] And to be in the image of a god meant that the king reflected the god's glory.[8] Thus, ancient Near Eastern kings being said to be in the image of their gods was part of *"the institution of kingship itself,* giving concrete form to underlying concepts of divinely sanctioned rule and ideal qualities of the ruler."[9] Therefore, the king as the image of God was understood as a royal figure who *"represents* the god by virtue of his royal office and is portrayed as *acting like* the god in specific behavioral ways."[10]

J. Richard Middleton concludes,

> The description of ancient Near Eastern kings as the image of a god, when understood as an integral component of Egyptian and/or Mesopotamian royal ideology, provides the most plausible set of parallels for interpreting the *imago Dei* in Genesis 1. If such texts . . . influenced the biblical *imago Dei*, this suggests that humanity is dignified with a status and role vis-à-vis the nonhuman creation that is analogous to the status and role of kings in the ancient Near East vis-à-vis their subjects. Genesis 1 . . . thus constitutes a genuine democratization of ancient Near Eastern royal ideology. As *imago Dei*, then, humanity in Genesis 1 is called to be the representative and intermediary of God's power and blessing on earth.[11]

Likewise, when ancient Near Eastern kings set up images of themselves in various parts of their territories, their image generally represented their sovereign presence and rule over that particular area. This probably provides

5. Edward M. Curtis, "Image of God (OT)," *ABD* 3:390–91.
6. Irene J. Winter, "Art *in* Empire: The Royal Image and the Visual Dimensions of Assyrian Ideology," in *Assyria 1995: Proceedings of the 10th Anniversary Symposium of the Neo-Assyrian Text Corpus Project, Helsinki, September 7–11, 1995,* ed. S. Parpola and R. M. Whiting (Helsinki: The Neo-Assyrian Text Corpus Project, 1997), 372, on which see A. Kirk Grayson, *Assyrian Rulers of the Third and Second Millennia BC (1114–859 BC),* RIMA 2 (Toronto: University of Toronto Press, 1991), 147.
7. Winter, "Art *in* Empire," 372. For other references to Assyrian kings being "in the very image of" or "in the perfect likeness of" various gods, see ibid., 374–75.
8. For examples, see ibid., 380n52. So also along the same lines, see J. Richard Middleton, *The Liberating Image: The Imago Dei in Genesis 1* (Grand Rapids: Brazos, 2005), 108–11. Middleton shows numerous examples of pharaohs said to be in the image of a god, so that the god's presence was manifested through the king's human image. This could be taken to support a functional or ontological view.
9. Winter, "Art *in* Empire," 377.
10. Middleton, *Liberating Image,* 121.
11. Ibid. Middleton also concludes that the Mesopotamian background is more probable than the Egyptian, though allowing for the possible influence of the latter (see also ibid., 122–45).

insight into God setting up Adam as his image on the territory of the earth: Adam represents God's sovereign presence and rule on earth.[12]

Nevertheless, there is likely an additional ontological aspect of the "image" by which humanity was enabled to reflect the functional image.[13] For example, Adam was made in the volitional, rational, and moral image of God, so that, with regard to the latter, he was to reflect moral attributes such as righteousness, knowledge, holiness, justice, love, faithfulness, and integrity (for the first three attributes as part of the divine image, see Eph. 4:24; Col. 3:10), and above all he was to reflect God's glory.

Some commentators have noticed that Adam's role in Eden is part of the initial carrying out of the mandate given to him in Gen. 1:26–28. Just as God, after his initial work of creation, subdued the chaos, ruled over it, and further created and filled the earth with all kinds of animate life, so Adam and Eve, in their garden abode, were to reflect God's activities in Gen. 1 by fulfilling the commission to "subdue" and "rule over all the earth" and to "be fruitful and multiply" (Gen. 1:26, 28).[14] Thus, the focus of the divine image in Adam in Gen. 1–2 is on how Adam's activities copy God's, though there is the underlying assumption that Adam was created with attributes that were reflective of God's attributes. Adam's commission to "cultivate" (with connotations of "serving") and "guard" in Gen. 2:15 as a priest-king is probably part of the commission given in 1:26–28.[15] Hence, Gen. 2:15 continues the theme of subduing and filling the earth by humanity created in the divine image, which has been placed in the first temple.[16]

Adam was to be God's obedient servant in maintaining both the physical and the spiritual welfare of the garden abode, which included dutifully keeping evil influences from invading the arboreal sanctuary. In fact, the physical and spiritual dimensions of Adam's responsibilities in relation to the Gen. 1 commission are

12. On which, see ibid., 104–8, where Middleton sufficiently establishes this point.

13. For evidence that God's "image" in Gen. 1:26a, 27 has both ontological and functional aspects, see Jeremy Cohen, *"Be Fertile and Increase, Fill the Earth and Master It": The Ancient and Medieval Career of a Biblical Text* (Ithaca, NY: Cornell University Press, 1989), 22–23. It is likely, however, that the latter is the emphasis in Gen. 1, which is also the emphasis of John H. Walton, *Genesis*, NIVAC (Grand Rapids: Zondervan), 130–31. See also the helpful summary, discussion, and reasonably broad definition with biblical rationale offered by John Piper, "The Image of God: An Approach from Biblical and Systematic Theology," *StudBT* 1 (1971): 15–32. Piper discusses the strengths and weaknesses of the functional and ontological perspectives, preferring the latter.

14. Following Warren Austin Gage, *The Gospel of Genesis: Studies in Protology and Eschatology* (Winona Lake, IN: Carpenter Books, 1984), 27–36. There is debate about whether Gen. 1 depicts God first creating the chaos from nothing or portrays the chaos already present before God's work of creation. The former, traditional view is assumed here, for which limits of space do not allow argumentation.

15. I have found support for this link in Cohen, *"Be Fertile and Increase,"* 18, which also cites James Barr and Claus Westermann in support.

16. So also Dumbrell, *Search for Order*, 24–26.

apparent from the recognition that Adam was like a primordial priest serving in a primeval temple. Adam was to be like Israel's later priests, who both physically protected the temple and spiritually were to be experts in the recollection, interpretation, and application of God's word in the Torah.[17] Accordingly, essential to Adam and Eve's raising of their children was spiritual instruction in God's word that the parents themselves were to remember and pass on.

In this respect, it is apparent that knowing and being obedient to God's word was crucial to carrying out the task of Gen. 1:26, 28 (and disobedience to it led to failure [cf. Gen. 2:16–17 with 3:1–7]). Thus, knowing God's will as expressed in his word of command (Gen. 2:16–17) is part of the functional manner in which humanity was to reflect the divine image (Gen. 1:26, 28), which assumes that Adam was created with the rational and moral capacities to comprehend and carry out such a command. The first two humans were to think God's thoughts after him. Thus, Adam and his wife's "knowledge" of God also included remembering God's word addressed to Adam in Gen. 2:16–17, which Adam's wife failed to recall in Gen. 3:2–3. After God puts Adam into the garden in Gen. 2:15 to serve him, he gives Adam a positive command, a negative command, and a warning to remember: "From any tree of the garden you may eat freely; but from the tree of the knowledge [LXX: infinitive of *ginōskō*] of good and evil you shall not eat, for in the day that you eat from it you will surely die" (Gen. 2:16–17).

When confronted by the satanic serpent, Adam's wife responds by quoting Gen. 2:16–17 but changes the wording in at least three major places (Gen. 3:2–3). It is possible that the changes are incidental and are a mere paraphrase still retaining the same meaning as in 2:16–17. It is more likely, however, that she either failed to remember God's word accurately or intentionally changed it for her own purposes.[18] The telltale sign of this is that each change appears to have theological significance. First, she minimizes their privileges by saying merely, "We may eat," whereas God had said, "You may eat freely"; second, she minimizes the judgment by saying, "You will die," whereas God said, "You will surely die"; third, she maximizes the prohibition by affirming, "You shall not . . . touch," whereas God originally said only, "You shall not eat."

The Design of Escalated Blessings of Adam in His Prefall State

There are indications in Gen. 1–3 that if Adam had been faithful and obedient, he would have experienced even greater blessings than he had before his

---

17. For the argument that Adam was a priest-king serving in the Edenic temple, see G. K. Beale, *The Temple and the Church's Mission: A Biblical Theology of the Dwelling Place of God*, NSBT 17 (Downers Grove, IL: InterVarsity, 2004), 66–70, and secondary sources cited therein.

18. See further Allen P. Ross, *Creation and Blessing: A Guide to the Study and Exposition of the Book of Genesis* (Grand Rapids: Baker Academic, 1988), 134–35. Ross observes three changes in the original wording of Gen. 2:16–17 as it is cited in Gen. 3:2–3.

sin. In particular, for example, Gen. 1:28 is best taken as a command, possibly with an implied promise that God will provide the ability to humanity to carry it out.[19] It seems that Adam was promised some kind of greater blessing if he remained faithful. He was set up in the first pristine creation, and he was commanded to be obedient, with the reward of receiving heightened blessings. The following points to this conclusion of escalated blessings coming in response to Adam's faithful obedience.

(1) First, included in carrying out the mandate of Gen. 1:28 likely was defeating and ruling over the evil serpent partly by remembering and trusting in God's word of command in 2:16–17 (note the emphasis on God "said" or "saying" with reference to 2:16–17 in 2:15; 3:1a, 1b, 3). Adam as the priest-king, who prevented unclean things from entering the temple, should have discerned Eve's misquotation of God's word and the serpent's capitalizing on it. Here it is important to recall that later priests in Israel's temple were to be guardians who were to slay any unclean animal or person entering the temple precincts. Adam was to do the same.[20] Furthermore, Adam should have slain and thus judged the serpent in carrying out the mandate of Gen. 1:28 to "rule and subdue." Thus, he was to rule over and subdue the serpent, which was to be reflective of God's own activity in Gen. 1 of subduing the chaotic darkness of creation and ruling over it by his word.

19. Here I cannot enter into the problem of whether Gen. 1:28 is merely a "blessing . . . delineating a privilege" (Walton, *Genesis*, 134) or is a blessing that includes a mandate or command. Traditionally, it has been called a "creation mandate," and with this I essentially agree. Paul Joüon concludes that in Gen. 1:28 all "five imperatives are direct imperatives," with the explicit sense of a direct command (*A Grammar of Biblical Hebrew*, trans. and rev. T. Muraoka, 2 vols., SubBi 14 [Rome: Editrice Pontificio Istituto Biblio, 1991–93], 2:373). Gesenius construes Gen. 1:28 as a command, "the fulfillment of which is altogether out of the power of the one addressed," which has the force of an "assurance" or "promise" (GKC 324). Gordon Wenham combines the two preceding views: "This command . . . carries with it an implicit promise that God will enable man to fulfill it" (*Genesis 1–15*, WBC 1 [Waco: Word, 1987], 33). Wenham's conclusion is pointed to by observing that imperatives are used as commands in the restatement of Gen. 1:28 to Abraham (Gen. 12:1–2: "Go forth from your country . . . and so you shall be a blessing") and to Jacob (Gen. 35:11: "Be fruitful and multiply"). Some see the verb "bless" in Gen. 12:2 to be a basic imperative (so M. Daniel Carroll R., "Blessing the Nations: Toward a Biblical Theology of Mission from Genesis," *BBR* 10 [2000]: 22, which cites others in support). Some grammarians see Gen. 12:2 as part of a promise (see, e.g., GKC 325), while others view it as an "indirect imperative" expressing purpose or result (Joüon, *Grammar of Biblical Hebrew*, 385; cf. Carroll R., "Blessing the Nations," 22, citing others who view the construction to be conveying consequence or purpose). But the context of such "indirect" uses of the imperative may indicate that they retain a notion of "command" (e.g., Exod. 3:10, an example adduced in GKC 325: "Therefore, come now, and I will send you to Pharaoh, *so that you may bring my people out*"; cf. in light of Exod. 3:11; 4:21–23; 6:10–13). Apparently, on this basis, Ross (*Creation and Blessing*, 263) sees that the last imperative of Gen. 12:2 emphasizes the purpose of the divine blessing yet still "retains an imperatival force" (Carroll R.'s discussion approaches the same conclusion).

20. On the idea of Eden as a temple and that Adam's task as a priest-king was to expand it until it covered all creation, see Beale, *Temple*.

In this light, the tree in Eden seems to have been the symbolic place where judgment was to be carried out (much as courthouses and courtrooms are adorned with the symbol of Lady Justice). The name of the tree—"the tree of the knowledge of good and evil"—of which Adam was not to eat, was suggestive of his magisterial duty. "Discerning between good and evil" is a Hebrew expression that refers to kings or authoritative figures being able to make judgments in carrying out justice. Elsewhere the phrase usually refers to figures in a position of judging or ruling over others (2 Sam. 14:17; 19:35; 1 Kings 3:9; Isa. 7:15–16).[21] In this connection, that Solomon prays to have "an understanding heart to judge . . . to discern between good and evil" (1 Kings 3:9 [cf. 3:28]) not only reflects his great wisdom but also appears to echo "the tree of the knowledge [or discerning] of good and evil" (Gen. 2:9), from which Adam and Eve were prohibited to eat (Gen. 2:17; 3:5, 22). Commentators differ over the meaning of this tree in Eden, but the most promising approach explains the tree by determining the use of "know/discern good and evil" elsewhere in the OT. In this respect, the tree in Eden seems to have functioned as a judgment tree, the place where Adam should have gone to "discern between good and evil" and, thus, where he should have judged the serpent as evil and pronounced judgment on it, as it entered the garden.[22] Trees also were places where judgments were pronounced elsewhere in the OT (Judg. 4:5; 1 Sam. 22:6–19; cf. 1 Sam. 14:2) and thus were symbolic of judgment, usually pronounced by a prophet. So Adam should have discerned that the serpent was evil and should have judged the serpent in the name of God at the place of the judgment tree.[23]

Nevertheless, the serpent ended up ruling over Adam and Eve by persuading them with deceptive words.

With regard to Adam's royal position, Gen. 1:26 specifies that Adam was to "rule" not just over the animals in Eden but "over all the earth," and 1:28

21. The last reference to Isaiah is best taken to refer not to an age of accountability but rather to the beginning exercise of rule, if, as a number of commentators think, Isa. 9:6–7 is part of the fulfillment of Isa. 7:14–15, the former focusing on governmental rule and judging. Similarly, Deut. 1:39 refers to young people having "no knowledge of good or evil" but who will enter into the promised land and "shall possess it." This may well refer to those who are not yet qualified to evaluate the good from the evil and, accordingly, to reward and punish, which they must be able to do in conquering the land with enemies in it. Also, note the use of "good" and "evil" where it refers to those in positions of rendering legal judgment but who misuse their position (Isa. 5:20–23; Mic. 3:1–2; Mal. 2:17).

22. See Meredith G. Kline, *Kingdom Prologue: Genesis Foundations for a Covenantal Worldview* (Overland Park, KS: Two Age Press, 2000), 103–7.

23. This paragraph is adapted from G. K. Beale, *We Become What We Worship: A Biblical Theology of Idolatry* (Downers Grove, IL: IVP Academic, 2008), 128–29. My conclusion about the symbolic identification of the tree is not exclusive of, but is in line with, the traditional view that God is the only autonomous arbiter of what is good and evil, to which Adam was to submit and recognize (see, e.g., Henri Blocher, *In the Beginning: The Opening Chapters of Genesis*, trans. David G. Preston [Downers Grove, IL: InterVarsity, 1984], 126–34).

asserts that he is to "subdue" the entire "earth," a goal that could not have been completed by staying in the confines of the garden. He would begin to rule in the arboreal sacred space partly by subduing the serpent, and then he would continue to fulfill the goal, moving outward and reigning until his rule was extended over the entire earth. This means that there would be a heightened phase of his ruling and a climactic point at which he would fulfill the goal of worldwide dominion.

There are references to an eschatological Adam figure who will rule over opposition (Pss. 72:4, 8–14; 89:19–27) forever (Ps. 72:5–7, 17 in comparison to 72:19 [on which, see discussion below in this chapter]) and whose throne lasts forever (Ps. 89:27–29, 33–37 [on which, see discussion below, including links to 2 Sam. 7:12–19, where also David's throne is repeatedly said to last "forever"]). This rule entails overcoming opposition. Similarly, Dan. 7 prophesies about a "Son of Man" who will replace the rule of ungodly world kingdoms and will rule eternally in an incorruptible kingdom (vv. 13–14), the clear implication being that he and his people will sit in judgment over the evil kingdoms (vv. 16–27). These prophecies foretell an end-time kingdom that will never cease and the victorious and blessed conditions of which will never be reversed.

Are such blessed conditions a unique response only to postfall sinful opposition, or can one perceive that the goals of these two psalms and of Dan. 7 reflect the original design inherent in Gen. 1–3? The latter appears to be the case. Adam's inaugurated but losable kingship in the garden also was designed originally to reach a climactic point of irreversibility, so that his reign would never have been lost. If so, then Adam's own *potentially* corrupt kingly existence would have reached a point of transformation into an irreversible, incorruptible kingly existence. If Adam had faithfully executed his kingly and priestly task of defeating the serpent, then evil in the midst of the good creation would have been decisively judged, and from that point forward Adam and his progeny would have enjoyed endless security from the lethal threat of evil. This security would entail Adam's endless and irreversible kingly existence. Such a defeat and consequent security appear to be a discernible design of greater blessing within the Gen. 1–3 narrative itself.

(2) Another intensified stage of blessing in response to Adam's obedience appears to be inextricably linked to Adam as an image-bearer who was to reflect the character of God, which included mirroring the divine glory. Just as Adam's son was in Adam's "likeness" and "image" (Gen. 5:1–3) and was to resemble his human father in appearance and character, so Adam was a son of God who was to reflect his Father, since he was in the "image" and "likeness" of God (Gen. 1:26). This means that the command for Adam to "subdue, rule, and fill the earth" includes uppermost that of him as a king functionally filling the earth, not merely with progeny, but with image-bearing progeny who will reflect God's glory and special revelatory presence. Ancient Near Eastern kings were considered to be "sons" of their god and to represent

the image of their god in their rule, especially reflecting the god's glory[24] and, accordingly, the manifestation of its presence. In fact, the images of gods in Mesopotamia and Egypt were intended to represent the god and manifest its presence.[25] Although the word "glory" is not found in Gen. 1–3, it is likely conceptually included in the notion of Adam and Eve as image-bearers of God's attributes, which is further pointed to by the directly following comments.

The inclusion of subduing in conjunction with "filling the earth" with glory is expressed well in Ps. 8, which alludes to Gen. 1:26–28 and concerns the ideal eschatological Adam. The psalmist, commenting on the purpose of Adam and humanity, also indicates that the ultimate, ideal goal of humanity, even before the fall, was to fill the whole earth with God's glory. Psalm 8 begins in verse 1 and concludes in verse 9 with the same stated goal: "O Lord, our Lord, how majestic is Your name in all the earth." This "majesty" is God's glorious "splendor" (cf. v. 1). The goal of divine splendor is to be achieved "in all the earth" by humanity, whom God has crowned "with glory and majesty" by making him in his image (v. 5). In particular, Ps. 8 says that God's glory is to be spread throughout the earth by humanity "ruling" over all "the works of Your hands" (vv. 6–8). Included in this rule is making "the enemy and the revengeful cease" (v. 2), which the Aramaic translation of the psalm identifies with "the enemy and the violent man," which could include satanic powers.

Being "fruitful and multiplying" in Gen. 1:28 refers to the increase of Adam and Eve's progeny, who were also to reflect God's glorious image and be part of the vanguard movement, spreading out over the earth with the goal of filling it with divine glory. Thus, Adam and Eve and their progeny were to be vice-regents who were to act as God's obedient children, reflecting God's ultimate glorious kingship over the earth. The task itself of creating progeny with the goal of "filling the earth" mirrored God's own creative work in Gen. 1, which also was to climax with the goal of filling the earth with his creation.

Interestingly, Isa. 45:18 says about even the prefall design of creation that God "formed the earth and made it . . . and did not create it a waste place [allusion to Gen. 1:2], but formed it to be inhabited." This verse is given as the basis for the preceding verse, which prophesies God's future "everlasting salvation" of his people and the fact that they "will not be put to shame or humiliated to all eternity." This also shows that God's original intention for his creation from the beginning was that humanity, as image-bearers of divine glory, would "fill the earth" (Gen. 1:28) and inhabit it forever, so that the entire earth would be filled with God's glorious image-bearers (and thus God's own glorious presence) forever. The eschatological Ps. 72 ends with the

24. For elaboration on Adam's kingship, especially against the ancient Near Eastern background, see Beale, *Temple*, 81–93.
25. Curtis, "Image of God," 390.

same goal of the end-time king's reign: "And may the whole earth be filled with His glory" (v. 19b).

Adam failed to be faithful, so that this irreversible condition of humanity filling and inhabiting the entire earth and consummately reflecting the divine glory was not realized with him. Another had to come to carry out God's design. The achievement of such a goal would have represented a greater blessing for humanity starting out in the same garden-temple. In fact, the aim of spreading God's glory worldwide through glorious image-bearers is to be understood more specifically as extending the boundaries of the Eden temple (which contained the divine glory) around the entire earth.[26]

(3) The implication of Gen. 3:22–23a points to another heightened goal of blessing in response to Adam's faithfulness: "Then the LORD God said, 'Behold, the man has become like one of Us, knowing good and evil; and now, lest he stretch out his hand, and take also from the tree of life, and eat, and live forever'—therefore the LORD God sent him out from the garden of Eden." Some believe that this means that Adam and his wife had been prohibited from eating from the tree of life, and that if he were faithful for a period of time, he would be rewarded by eating of this tree and experiencing eternal life. Others believe that Adam and Eve had been eating from this tree all along because Gen. 2:16–17 says, "From any tree of the garden you may eat freely" except from the "tree of the knowledge of good and evil." This seems to mean that the tree of life was included among those trees from which the first couple could eat.[27]

Whether or not Adam was able to eat of the tree of life before his sin, it is likely that there is reference in Gen. 3:22 to what might be termed a "consummative eating." The word "also" is the first indication that this was a decisive "onetime" act of eating: "And now, lest he stretch out his hand and take also [gam] from the tree of life, and eat. . . ." This word "also" appears to put on a par the eating from "the tree of life" with the directly prior decisive eating from the "tree of the knowledge of good and evil," which has just tragically occurred (Gen. 3:6). Thus, even if Adam had been eating previously of the tree of life, this was to be a more decisive act of eating of that tree than had ever occurred. The eating from the tree of life also appears to be a decisive partaking, since 3:22 says that from that point on Adam would "live forever." It is not that he would have kept on living the kind of life he had previously, but rather that he would have possessed a longevity of life, of which he was not guaranteed before and which many translations render as an "eternal" (lit., "forever") life.[28] The reference is to a guarantee of "living forever" if he

---

26. Again, for the idea of Eden as a temple and that Adam's task as a priest-king was to expand it until it covered all creation, see Beale, *Temple* (this is summarized in chap. 19 below).

27. So, e.g., Blocher, *In the Beginning*, 122–23.

28. The Hebrew word for "forever" is *ʿōlām*, which all the numerous translations that I checked render as "forever," indicating an unending period, not a long period with an end (which in some contexts this Hebrew word [with various prepositions] can connote). The remaining

eats decisively of this tree. This would result in an irreversible possession of life. Such an assurance was not given prior to this. But even if this were not to be understood to connote an everlasting state, it certainly connotes a very long period of time. Although the notion of an unending life is likely, either meaning points strongly to an escalation of the security of Adam's life. Adam's exclusion from the garden and from partaking of the tree indicates that he would be prohibited from decisively eating of the tree of life and enjoying the consequent escalated blessing of eternal life.[29]

Other Possible Escalated Blessings of Adam in His Prefall State

Thus far, I have attempted to isolate from within Gen. 1–3 three discernible goals that Adam was designed to obtain, which are also reflected in some subsequent parts of the OT (Ps. 8; Isa. 45). There may be other heightened conditions that he would have experienced, though these are not as clearly discernible in Gen. 1–3.

(1) First, it is plausible that Adam's decisive defeat of the evil force on the perimeter of the garden would have resulted in him experiencing unending eschatological "rest."[30] Of course, explicit reference to an ordinance of a Sabbath rest for humans is nowhere stated in Gen. 1–3, but it may be suggested from the following considerations. Clearly, God experienced "rest" (*šbt*) on the seventh day, after he overcame chaos and established creational order (Gen. 2:2). And Adam himself is said to be "caused to rest" (*yanniḥēhû*) in Eden (Gen. 2:15). Both the creation made by God and the garden in which Adam was placed are to be considered temples, though not finally perfected for eternity, as suggested by the preceding three points about escalated creational conditions that had not yet occurred. If this is so,[31] then Adam's rest was of an inaugurated and not consummated nature. The likely intention of Gen. 2:3 is that Adam was to observe a Sabbath rest every seventh day as a token of the eternal, eschatological life and rest to come.[32]

---

twelve uses of this word in Genesis almost always have the sense of open-ended everlastingness, though one text is figurative for an "ancient time" (6:4).

29. Judaism sometimes reflected the same view of potentially escalated blessings of immortality for Adam. For example, see *Hel. Syn. Pr.* 12:43–45, where it is said that God had "given to him [Adam] an implanted law to do. . . . But of only one thing did you [God] refuse him the taste; in hope of greater things, in order that, if he should keep the commandment, he might receive immortality as a reward for this." Other escalated blessings for Adam are mentioned in *L.A.B.* 13:8; *Tg. Neof.* Gen. 3:23.

30. For this notion, see Dumbrell, *Search for Order*, 48–49, 68–72, 323–24.

31. I cannot present the full argument here. See Beale, *Temple*, 31–50, 66–80, and chap. 19 below on the sanctuary of Eden, Israel's temple, and the church as a temple, where also other supporting secondary sources may be found.

32. Again, the full argument for the Sabbath as a creational ordinance for humanity with eschatological implications cannot be given here, though it is addressed in much more detail in chap. 23 below.

The validity of the Sabbath as a creational ordinance for humanity is suggested by recalling that Gen. 2:2–3 is given as the basis of why Israelites later should cease to do labor on the Sabbath (Exod. 20:8–11). If Adam is in God's image, then he should rest from his work, since God also had already rested from his.[33] Just as God had achieved heavenly rest after overcoming creational chaos and constructing the beginning of his creational temple, so Adam presumably would achieve unending rest after overcoming the opposition of the serpent and the opposing temptation to sin and extending the boundaries of the glorious Eden temple around the entire earth.[34] This also finds an important analogy later with David, who cannot build the temple because although he had achieved rest by overcoming outside enemies, there were still internal forces of opposition that were suppressed only after his death. Thus, Solomon built the temple because all enemies, both outside and within Israel, had been conquered for a period. At this time, God is said to have found rest in the holy of holies of the temple because all his earthly enemies, who also were Israel's enemies, had been defeated.[35] The ancient Near East also reflects the same pattern of overcoming opposition resulting in "rest," which is indicated by the building of a temple.[36]

Is it possible that this rest involved ultimate security not only from external evil but also from potential internal evil? While Adam had the potential to sin, would there come a time in which there would no longer be such potential? If Adam was continually able to sin at any point, how could he have "fully rested"? If he at any moment could sin and thrust himself and humanity into a corruptible state, how could he have been at true rest? It is possible to answer these questions by saying that though Adam had this potential to disobey, he was unaware of such a potential and thus would be able to maintain psychological rest. But this seems unsatisfactory because the very command that threatens potential death would in some way have impressed him with awareness of this fateful potential. It is unlikely that he could fully rest if faced with the potential of dying in judgment at any time. Adam's spirit or soul would have become morally incorruptible (i.e., unable ever to sin again), and this would have resulted in true rest for him.

(2) The same thing appears to be the case with his body: if he could sin and incur judgment, it would be not only a spiritual but also a physical judgment

33. So Wenham, who says, "If the other parts of creation were designed for man's benefit, so too was the Sabbath" (*Genesis 1–15*, 38).
34. For the relationship of God's rest after his creating work and the similar rest that Adam was designed to achieve, see Beale, *Temple*, 60–66, and chap. 23 below. For the nature of God's "rest" as being in a position to exercise kingship, after overcoming forces of chaos, see John H. Walton, *The Lost World of Genesis One: Ancient Cosmology and the Origins Debate* (Downers Grove, IL: IVP Academic, 2009), 72–79.
35. For the various references supporting these ideas in Samuel, Kings, Chronicles, and elsewhere, see Beale, *Temple*, 61–63; Dumbrell, *Search for Order*, 68–72.
36. Beale, *Temple*, 63–64.

of death. In the same way that there could be no moral or spiritual rest with the threat of spiritual death, so entailed with this is that there would be no physical rest without the removal of the danger of physical death. The converse is that there appears to be a goal that Adam's body would have been permanently protected from corruption (i.e., perhaps by being transformed into an incorruptible, glorified body). I comment below on the NT evidence for this (see below in this chapter, "Excursus on the Possible Goal of the Prefall Adam Experiencing Full Security from Death").

(3) An even further corollary of the apparent purpose of Adam obtaining decisive protection from death and corruption is the notion that the earth itself likewise would have been secured forever (on which, see 2 Bar. 44:12; 74:2–4; 2 En. [J] 65:6–11; Rev. 21:1–22:5). Again, we might ask, how could Adam experience complete rest with the knowledge that the place in which he lived could be destroyed at any time?

(4) The marriage relationship of Adam and Eve and of all their progeny appears to have been established as a kind of shadow to point to the consummated end-time relationship of God and his bridal people (cf. Isa. 54:1–6; 62:2–5; Eph. 5:29–32).[37] That is, human marriage originally was designed even before the fall to be transcended by God's relationship with his people (this seems to suggest that human marriage will no longer have the purpose of procreation, nor, presumably, will it include a sexual relationship, which appears to be the implication of Matt. 22:30).

(5) It seems likely also that Adam and Eve's nakedness at the end of Gen. 2 is meant to point to the need for clothing, the bestowal of which would have been part of their later escalated blessing. They grasp for their reward in the wrong way and at the wrong time. They ineptly try to provide clothing for themselves (Gen. 3:7), but God subsequently clothes them to signify their inaugurated restoration to him (Gen. 3:21). This second set of clothing was not the full clothing originally designed for them; it symbolically represented their future consummate inheritance as kings of the earth. This second set of clothing thus symbolized a permanent inheritance that they would receive at some consummative point in the future, which would entail a greater, glorious royal investiture of clothing when they would completely fulfill the mandate to rule as kings over the earth.[38]

37. For analysis of this idea in Eph. 5:29–32, see chap. 26 under the heading "Marriage as a Transformed New-Creational Institution in Ephesians 5."

38. For a fuller argument than can be provided here, see William N. Wilder, "Illumination and Investiture: The Royal Significance of the Tree of Wisdom," WTJ 68 (2006): 56–69, which indicates the significance of investiture with clothing and clothing as symbolizing inheritance with respect to Adam and Eve, and which I find compatible with my discussion (chap. 14 under the subheading "The Image of the Last Adam in Colossians 1:15–18; 3:9–10") of the significance of clothing in Col. 3 and Gen. 3 (Wilder provides numerous secondary sources on which he partly depends for his discussion). For other possible escalations of blessing that may be reflected in

In light of these observations, we can speak of the prefall conditions as a "beginning first creation" and the yet-to-come escalated creation conditions to be a consummate "eschatologically" enhanced stage of final blessedness. The period leading up to the reception of these escalated conditions is the time when it would be decided whether Adam would obey or disobey. These escalated conditions indicate that Adam was in a covenant relationship with God. Although the word "covenant" is not used to describe the relationship between God and Adam, the concept of covenant is there. God chooses to initiate a relationship with Adam by imposing an obligation on him (Gen. 2:16–17). This obligation was part of the larger task with which Adam had been commissioned in Gen. 1:28: to "rule" and "subdue" creation and in the process to "be fruitful and multiply and fill the earth." Adam's "ruling and subduing" commission included guarding the garden from any threat to its peaceful maintenance. In light of Gen. 2:16–17 and 3:22, Adam would receive irreversible blessings of eternal life on the condition of perfect faith and obedience, and he would receive the decisive curse of death if he was unfaithful and disobedient.[39] Thus, the discernment of irreversible escalated creation conditions discussed above is the best argument for such a covenant notion.

Consequently, the argument that the word "covenant" is not used in Gen. 2–3 does not provide proof that there is no covenant relationship,[40] just as Adam and Eve's marriage relationship is not termed a "covenant" in Gen. 2:21–24 but expresses covenantal concepts[41] and, in fact, is identified as a covenant elsewhere.[42] Likewise, it is probable that God's covenant with Adam[43] is re-

---

Gen. 1–3, including references to early church commentators as well as later ones who hold that Adam was designed to receive greater blessings than he had been created with, see ibid., 51–56.

39. In this respect, see the Westminster Confession of Faith, VII.2. A biblical covenant may best be defined as "an elected relationship of obligation established under divine sanction and indicated by an oath—commitment" (often with cursings for disobedience and blessings for obedience). For this definition, see Gordon P. Hugenberger, *Marriage as a Covenant: Biblical Law and Ethics as Developed from Malachi*, VTSup 52 (Leiden: Brill, 1994), 168–215; see likewise Scott W. Hahn, *Kinship by Covenant: A Canonical Approach to the Fulfillment of God's Saving Promises*, AYBRL (New Haven: Yale University Press, 2009), 1–216; Kline, *Kingdom Prologue*, 1–7.

40. Hugenberger notes the emergence of "a scholarly consensus that warns against the frequent error of denying the presence of a בְּרִית merely because of the absence of the term" (*Marriage as a Covenant*, 157n133). On which, see E. P. Sanders, *Paul and Palestinian Judaism* (Philadelphia: Fortress, 1977), 420–21.

41. So Hugenberger, *Marriage as a Covenant*, 156–67. Hugenberger observes that the following notions in Gen. 2:23–24 parallel covenantal ideas: (1) to establish a unified relationship between unrelated people; (2) "leave" and "cleave" are words often associated with other covenantal contexts; (3) the phrase "bone of my bones and flesh of my flesh" closely parallels a "covenant-ratifying formula" in other texts (2 Sam. 5:1; 1 Chron. 11:1). Consequently, he concludes that marriage is a covenant in Gen. 2:23–24.

42. See Mal. 2:14 (on which, see Hugenberger, *Marriage as a Covenant*, esp. 124–67).

43. Sometimes referred to as a "covenant of works" or a "covenant of creation."

ferred to as a covenant elsewhere in the OT.[44] The essential elements of a covenant are found in the Gen. 1–3 narrative: (1) two parties are named; (2) a condition of obedience is set forth; (3) a curse for transgression is threatened; (4) a clear implication of a blessing is promised for obedience.[45] It could be objected that there is no reference to either party reaching a clear agreement or, especially, to Adam accepting the terms set forth in this so-called covenant. However, neither is this the case with Noah and Abraham, with whom God made explicit covenants.[46]

Excursus On the Possible Goal of the Prefall Adam Experiencing Full Security from Death

With respect to Adam receiving absolute security from death, there is no explicit reference within Gen. 1–3 or, indeed, anywhere in the OT that Adam's faithfulness would have eventually been rewarded with such a thing. However, 1 Cor.

---

44. Note Hos. 6:7: "But like Adam they have transgressed the covenant; there they have dealt treacherously against me." Some commentators do not believe that this alludes to the covenant that God made with Adam, while others do. See Byron G. Curtis, "Hosea 6:7 and the Covenant-Breaking like/at Adam," in *The Law Is Not of Faith: Essays on Works and Grace in the Mosaic Covenant*, ed. Bryan D. Estelle, J. V. Fesko, and David VanDrunen (Phillipsburg, NJ: P&R, 2009), 170–209. Curtis argues in favor of an allusion to the covenant with Adam and provides an interpretative overview of the debate revolving around this passage. In addition to those in support of an Adamic allusion, see also Duane Garrett, *Hosea, Joel*, NAC 19A (Nashville: Broadman & Holman, 1997), 163–64; Derek Drummond Bass, "Hosea's Use of Scripture: An Analysis of His Hermeneutics" (PhD diss., Southern Baptist Theological Seminary, 2008), 186–87. See also *Selected Shorter Writings of Benjamin B. Warfield*, ed. John E. Meeter (Nutley, NJ: P&R, 1970–73), 1:116–29, where Warfield gives a review of the earliest interpretations up through to the end of the nineteenth century and argues in support of an allusion to Adam in Gen. 3. The two main objections to an allusion to Adam in Hos. 6:7 are (1) "Adam" is better translated generically as "men" or "mankind" (referring to past generations of Israel or to humanity in general), or (2) it refers to a place name where a grievous sin was committed (the latter especially because of the initial "there" in v. 7b, which would fit better with a geographical reference in v. 7a). The problem with the first view is that it does not fit with the geographical reference of "there" in v. 7b, while the second view is forced to emend the Hebrew text of v. 7a without any extant manuscript evidence, changing the preposition from *k*, reading "like Adam," to *b* to read "at Adam," as a place name. Thus, the extant form of the Hebrew "like Adam" most favors an allusion to Adam in Gen. 3, though limits of space here do not allow further elaboration on this debate. For how a reference to the singular "Adam" could fit with the geographical reference in v. 7b, see the aforementioned discussions by Curtis, Garrett, and Warfield.

45. Following Louis Berkhof, *Systematic Theology* (Grand Rapids: Eerdmans, 1976), 213.

46. Ibid. Judaism sometimes held to the notion of a covenantal agreement in Eden: *2 En.* [J] 31:1 says that God "created a garden in Eden, in the east, so that he [Adam] might keep the agreement and preserve the commandment." So too other Jewish texts mention an actual "covenant" with Adam: *L.A.E.* [*Apocalypse*] 8:1–2; Sir. 17:11–12; 1QS IV:22–23; cf. Philo, *Leg.* 3.246: Adam "made a covenant with wickedness" (see *The Works of Philo: Complete and Unabridged*, trans. C. D. Yonge [Peabody, MA: Hendrickson, 1993], and the Greek text of Philo).

15:45 is perhaps the preeminent biblical text attesting to such an eschatologically escalated existence as the final goal for the prefall Adam: "So also it is written, 'The first man, Adam, became a living soul.' The last Adam became a life-giving spirit." Here the first Adam in his prefall and sinless condition is contrasted with the last Adam in his glorious resurrected state. Remarkably, Paul draws the contrast not with the first Adam's sinful, corruptible condition but rather with his prefall sinless condition as recorded in Gen. 2:7 ("Adam became a living soul"), and he concludes that even this prefall condition was insufficient for qualification to "inherit the kingdom of God" (1 Cor. 15:50). Verse 45 is a contrast of lesser and greater glorious states. In fact, Paul's argument throughout 1 Cor. 15:39–53 appears to involve contrasts of lesser and greater glories, in addition to contrasts of sinful realities and nonsinful realities or of sinful life and death versus resurrection life. Paul employs illustrative contrasts of different kinds of seeds, animals, and heavenly light sources (sun, moon, and stars), each with differing degrees of glory. These are illustrations also drawn from the prefall description of Gen. 1[47] to demonstrate the contrast between the "earthly" perishable and corruptible bodies of believers, which have a degree of glory, and their destined "heavenly" imperishable and incorruptible bodies, which have greater glory (15:38–41).

Paul then says that "in the same manner" (houtōs)[48] that there are lesser and greater glories observable in the earth and heavens, so also is the resurrection of the dead. "It is sown a perishable [corruptible] body, it is raised an imperishable body; it is sown in dishonor [corruptibility],[49] it is raised in glory; it is sown in weakness, it is raised in power; it is sown a natural body, it is raised a spiritual body. If there is a natural[50] body, there is also a spiritual body" (15:42–44). Since the contrast of relative glories does not involve black-and-white contrasts, "in the same manner also" it is the case with the preconsummate human body and the consummated, resurrected body. Verse 45 says that "in the same manner" Adam's prefall body had a degree of glory (indeed, it was included with all the creation, which God had declared "very good" [Gen. 1:31]).

To explain the contrast between the first Adam and the last Adam, Paul refers to the "natural" or "physical" (not sinful) versus the "spiritual" (v. 46), "the first man from the earth, earthy" or "made of dust [choïkos]" versus "the second man . . . from heaven" (vv. 47–48a). Indeed, verses 46–48 continue the contrast in verse 45 of the prefall, sinless Adam with the resurrected last Adam. Verse 47 continues the allusion to Gen. 2:7, this time by alluding to the first

47. See margin of NA[27], which lists allusions to Gen. 1:11–12, 20, 24; 8:17 for 1 Cor. 15:38–39.
48. The NASB renders this as "so."
49. The Greek word atimia can mean "dishonor" (Rom. 1:26; 1 Cor. 11:14; 2 Cor. 6:8), though it can also have the notion of clay vessels for "common" use and vessels of precious metal for a more refined use (Rom. 9:21; 2 Tim. 2:20; though the metaphorical application to people in context has to do with "honor" and "dishonor"). The idea in 15:43 may be expressed in 12:23: "And those members of the body which we deem less honorable, on these we bestow more abundant honor, and our less presentable members become much more presentable." Thus, "dishonor" versus "glory" in 15:42–43 may continue the notion of degrees of honor of the luminaries from 15:40–41.
50. For this meaning of psychikos, see BDAG 1100a.

part of that verse: "The first man is from the earth, made of dust" (Gen. 2:7: "God formed man of dust from the ground"). Paul concludes by saying that there are also people "made of dust" and bearing "the image of the one made of dust" and people who will become "heavenly" and those also who will "bear the image of the heavenly" (vv. 48b–49).[51] Paul makes the conclusion that "flesh and blood," "the perishable," and "the mortal" cannot "inherit the kingdom of God," but only the "imperishable" and "immortal" will inherit that kingdom (vv. 50–53). Resuming the idea of actual death from verse 36, it appears that in verses 54–57 there comes into Paul's view again the notion that not only is the present body mortal like Adam's prefall body (since neither was qualified to enter the eternal kingdom), but also it will die because of sin; nevertheless, Christ will give his people victory over death.

But even if verses 39–44 and verses 49–53 have in view contrasts of postfall sinful, earthly human reality versus sinless resurrected reality, it appears probable, at least, that verses 45–48 go back beyond even Adam's fall to his prefall state and contrast that with resurrected human reality. Paul's understanding, therefore, is that even if Adam had never sinned, his prefall existence still needed to be transformed at some climactic point into an irreversible glorious existence, which Paul identifies as resurrection existence. Accordingly, Paul understood that Adam would have been rewarded with a transformed, incorruptible body if he had remained faithful. Of course, such a transformation would necessitate that Adam's spirit or soul become morally incorruptible (i.e., he would be unable ever to sin again).

Summary of the Escalated Blessings of Adam in His Prefall State

The foregoing discussion, I believe, provides cumulative evidence from various angles that Adam would have experienced heightened conditions of a permanent and irreversible nature if he had been faithful to the covenant obligations imposed on him by God.

Adam's failure in the task with which he was commissioned includes his permitting entrance into the garden to an antagonistic and unclean being. Although Gen. 2–3 does not explicitly say that Adam's "ruling and subduing" task was to guard the garden from the satanic snake, this is likely conceptually in mind in light of the following two considerations: (1) the commission in Gen. 1:26, 28 to subdue and rule over every creature that "creeps on the earth";[52] (2) Eden was a temple in which Adam was placed as a living image of God and as God's priest who was to guard the sanctuary from unclean creatures. Thus, Adam did not rule well because he did not guard the garden, allowing entrance to a foul snake that brought sin, chaos, and disorder into the sanctuary and into Adam

51. Some commentators and the margins of some translations (e.g., NASB), as well as the margin of NA[27], posit an allusion to Gen. 5:3 in 1 Cor. 15:49, though the only word in common between the two texts is "image," a word also found twice in Gen. 1:26–27, so that the allusion may just as likely be to Gen. 1:26–27, a prefall text.
52. On which, see further Kline, *Kingdom Prologue*, 54–55, 65–67; Beale, *Temple*, 66–87.

and Eve's lives. He allowed the serpent to "rule over" him rather than "ruling over" it and, as an obedient priest, casting it out of the garden.

Rather than extending the glorious divine presence of the garden sanctuary, Adam and Eve were expelled from it and excluded from the eternal life for which they were designed. Consequently, Adam and Eve disobeyed God's mandate in Gen. 1:28, and they did not inherit the more intensified stage of blessings that full faithfulness would have entailed.[53]

As we will see below, after Adam's failure to fulfill God's mandate, God raised up other Adam-like figures to whom his kingly and priestly commission was passed on. We will find that some changes in the commission occurred as a result of sin entering into the world. Adam's descendants, like him, however, fail. Failure would continue until there arose a "last Adam" who finally fulfilled the commission on behalf of humanity.

The Passing On of Adam's Commission to His Descendants[54]

Some commentators have noticed that Adam's commission was passed on to Noah, to Abraham, and on to his descendants. The directly following observations of the repeated application of the mandate are made on the basis of discerning actual allusions back to Gen. 1:28 or one of its subsequent reformulations:

Gen. 1:28 <u>God blessed them</u>; and God said to them, "<u>Be fruitful and multiply, and fill the earth</u>, and <u>subdue it; and rule</u> over the fish of the sea and over the birds of the sky, and over every living thing that moves on the earth."

Gen. 9:1, 7 And <u>God blessed Noah and his sons</u> and said to them, "<u>Be fruitful and multiply, and fill the earth</u>. . . . <u>Be fruitful and multiply; populate the earth abundantly and multiply in it</u>."

Gen. 12:2–3 "And I will make you a great nation, and <u>I will bless you</u>, and make your name great; and so be a blessing; and <u>I will bless those who bless you</u>, and the one who curses you I will curse. And in you <u>all the families of the earth</u> will be blessed."

Gen. 17:2, 6, 8 "I will establish My covenant between Me and you, and <u>I will multiply you exceedingly</u>. . . . <u>I will make you exceedingly fruitful</u>. . . .

---

53. In fact, they began to experience eschatological death through the death of their bodies in fulfillment of Gen. 2:17, though the consummation of that death would also be spiritual; however, God intervened (Gen. 3:20–21) and brought Adam and Even out from a state of spiritual death that was not yet consummated into an inaugurated living spiritual relationship with him that remained to be consummated in physical resurrection life, which would reverse their inevitable physical death.

54. The following sections "The Passing On of Adam's Commission to His Descendants," "The Differences between the Commission to Adam and What Was Passed On to His Descendants," and "Conclusion" are an abbreviated revision of my longer discussion in *Temple*, 93–121.

I will give to you and to your descendants after you, the land of your sojournings, all the land of Canaan."

Gen. 22:17–18 "Indeed <u>I will greatly bless you, and I will greatly multiply your seed</u> as the stars of the heavens and as the sand which is on the seashore; and your seed shall possess the gate of his [singular pronoun] enemies. In your seed <u>all the nations of the earth</u> shall be blessed, because you have obeyed My voice."

Gen. 26:3 "Sojourn in this land and I will be with you and <u>bless you</u>, for to you and to your descendants I will give all these lands, and I will establish the oath which I swore to your father Abraham."

Gen. 26:4 "<u>I will multiply your descendants</u> as the stars of heaven, and will give your descendants all these lands; and by your descendants <u>all the nations of the earth shall be blessed</u>."

Gen. 26:24 The LORD appeared to him the same night and said, "I am the God of your father Abraham; do not fear, for I am with you. <u>I will bless you, and multiply your descendants</u>, for the sake of my servant Abraham."

Gen. 28:3–4 "May <u>God Almighty bless you and make you fruitful and multiply you</u>, that you may become a company of peoples. May he also give you <u>the blessing</u> of Abraham, to you and to your descendants with you, that you may possess the land of your sojournings, which God gave to Abraham."

Gen. 28:13–14 "I will give it [the land] to you and to your seed. <u>Your seed will also be like the dust of the earth</u>, and you will spread out to the west and to the east . . . ; and in you and in your seed shall <u>all the families of the earth be blessed</u>."

Gen. 35:11–12 God also said to him, "I am God Almighty; <u>be fruitful and multiply</u>; a nation and a company of nations shall come from you, and <u>kings shall come forth from you</u>. The land which I gave to Abraham and Isaac, I will give it to you, and I will give the land to your descendants after you."

The same commission repeatedly given to the patriarchs is restated numerous times in subsequent OT books to Israel and eschatological Israel. Like Adam, Noah and his children failed to perform this commission. God then gave the essence of the commission of Gen. 1:28 to Abraham (Gen. 12:2; 17:2, 6, 8, 16; 22:18), Isaac (Gen. 26:3–4, 24), Jacob (Gen. 28:3–4, 14; 35:11–12; 48:3, 15–16), and Israel (see Deut. 7:13 and Gen. 47:27; Exod. 1:7; Ps. 107:38; Isa. 51:2, the latter four of which state the beginning fulfillment of the promise to Abraham in Israel).[55] Recall that the commission of Gen. 1:26–28 involves the

55. This was first brought to my attention by N. T. Wright, *The Climax of the Covenant: Christ and the Law in Pauline Theology* (Minneapolis: Fortress, 1992), 21–26, on which the above

following elements, especially as summarized in 1:28: (1) "God blessed them"; (2) "be fruitful and multiply"; (3) "fill the earth"; (4) "subdue" the "earth"; (5) "rule over . . . all the earth."

The commission is repeated to, for example, Abraham: "I will greatly *bless you*, and I will greatly *multiply your seed* . . . ; and *your seed shall possess the gate of their enemies* [= 'subdue and rule']. In your seed all the nations of *the earth* shall be *blessed*" (Gen. 22:17–18).[56] God placed Adam in a garden, and he promised Abraham a fertile land. God expresses the universal scope of the commission by underscoring that the goal is to "bless" "all the nations of the earth."[57] It is natural, therefore, that in the initial statement of the commission in Gen. 12:1–3 that God says to Abraham, "Go forth from your country. . . . And so be a blessing. . . . And in you all the families of the earth will be blessed." Gordon Wenham observes in this respect that "the promises to Abraham renew the vision for humanity set out in Gen. 1–2," so that "he, like Noah before him, is a second Adam figure"[58] or a "new Adam."[59]

After the majority of the book of Genesis reiterates the promissory application of the Gen. 1:28 commission to the patriarchs, it is portrayed as beginning to be fulfilled in the nation of Israel in Egypt:

Gen. 47:27 Now Israel lived in the land of Egypt, in Goshen, and they acquired property in it and <u>were fruitful and became very numerous.</u>

Gen. 48:3–4 "God . . . <u>blessed me</u>, and He said to me, 'Behold, <u>I will make you fruitful and numerous</u>, and I will make you a company of peoples,

list of references in Genesis is based. Wright sees that the command to Adam in Gen. 1:26–28 has been applied to the patriarchs and Israel; he also cites other texts where he sees Gen. 1:28 applied to Israel (Exod. 32:13; Lev. 26:9; Deut. 1:10–11; 7:13–14; 8:1; 28:63; 30:5, 16). I have subsequently likewise discovered that Cohen ("*Be Fertile and Increase*," 28–31, 39) makes the same observation in dependence on Gary Smith, "Structure and Purpose in Genesis 1–11," *JETS* 20 (1977): 307–19, both of whom include Noah. For the notion that the blessings conditionally promised to Adam are given to Israel, see also Dumbrell, *Search for Order*, 29–30, 37, 72–73, 143. Likewise, Gage affirms only generally that the "divine command (or creative mandate) originally pronounced to Adam . . . (Gen. 1:28), is formalized covenantally through three administrations (i.e., three mediators: Noah, Abraham and David)" (*Gospel of Genesis*, 29). See also Carroll R., "Blessing the Nations," 27, saying only briefly that the divine intention to bless humankind is reaffirmed in Gen. 12:1–3. See similarly Michael Fishbane, *Text and Texture: Close Readings of Selected Biblical Texts* (New York: Schocken, 1979), 112–13. Jewish tradition applies the Gen. 1:28 commission to Noah and Abraham (*Midr. Tanḥ. Gen.* 3.5; likewise *Midr. Tanḥ. Yelammedenu Gen.* 2.12).

56. Notice that the ruling aspect of the commission is expressed to Abraham elsewhere as a role of "kingship" (Gen. 17:6, 16), and likewise with respect to Jacob (Gen. 35:11).

57. See Gordon J. Wenham, *Story as Torah: Reading the Old Testament Ethically* (Edinburgh: T&T Clark, 2000), 37.

58. Ibid.; so also Dumbrell, *Search for Order*, 29–30.

59. Fishbane, *Text and Texture*, 112.

and will give this land to your descendants after you for an everlasting possession'" [in partial application to Joseph's sons].

Exod. 1:7 But the sons of Israel were <u>fruitful and increased greatly</u>, and <u>multiplied</u>, and became exceedingly mighty, so that <u>the land was filled</u> with them.

Exod. 1:12 The more they <u>multiplied</u> and the more they <u>spread out</u>.

Exod. 1:20 The people <u>multiplied</u>, and became very mighty.

Num. 23:10–11 "Who <u>can count the dust</u> of Jacob, or <u>number</u> the fourth part of Israel?" . . . Then Balak said to Balaam, ". . . Behold, you have actually <u>blessed them</u>!"

But, after the events of Israel's rebellious attitude in Egypt and at the event of the golden calf, it becomes clear that the promise is not consummated in the first generation of Israel, since it does not fully obey the commission. Moses prayed that, nevertheless, God would fulfill the promise (Exod. 32:13). And so the promise that the nation would fulfill the commission at some point in the future is reiterated, as it was to the patriarchs in Genesis:

Lev. 26:9 "I will turn toward you and <u>make you fruitful and multiply you</u>, and I will confirm My covenant with you."

Deut. 7:13 "He will love you and <u>bless you and multiply you</u>; He will also <u>bless the fruit of your womb</u> . . . in the land which He swore to your forefathers to give you." [Cf. Deut. 6:3; 8:1.]

Deut. 15:4, 6 "<u>The LORD will surely bless you</u> in the land which the LORD your God is giving you as an inheritance <u>to possess</u>. . . . <u>For the LORD your God will bless you</u> as He has promised you . . . ; and <u>you will rule over</u> many nations."

Deut. 28:11–12 (LXX) "And the Lord your <u>God will multiply you</u> with respect to good things concerning <u>the offspring</u> of your womb . . . <u>to bless</u> all the works of your hands. . . . And <u>you will rule over</u> many nations."

Deut. 30:16 "I command you today to love the LORD your God, to walk in His ways and to keep His commandments and His statutes and His judgments, that you may live and <u>multiply</u>, and that <u>the LORD your God may bless you</u> in the land where you are entering to possess it." [Cf. Deut. 30:5.]

2 Sam. 7:29 (LXX) "And now <u>rule and bless</u> the house of your servant . . . ; and now from your <u>blessing</u> the house of your servant <u>will be blessed forever</u>."

Despite the promise of future blessing, at various points throughout the succeeding history of Israel the language of the Gen. 1:28 commission is reapplied to individual Israelites or the nation to indicate some degree of beginning fulfillment:

> **1 Chron. 4:10** Now Jabez called on the God of Israel, saying, "Oh that You would <u>bless me indeed and enlarge</u> my border, and that Your hand might be with me, and that You would keep me from harm that it may not pain me!" And God granted him what he requested.

> **1 Chron. 17:9–11, 27** [God speaks through Nathan.] "I . . . will plant them [Israel]. . . . And <u>I will subdue</u> all your enemies [LXX adds '<u>I will cause you to increase</u>']. . . . And I will establish his kingdom." [David affirms initial realization.] "And now it has pleased You to bless the house of Your servant, that it may continue forever before You; for You, O LORD, have <u>blessed, and it is blessed forever</u>."

> **Ps. 8:5–8** Yet You have made him a little lower than God, and <u>You crown him with glory and majesty! You make him to rule over the works of Your hands; You have put all things under his feet</u>, all sheep and oxen, and also the beasts of the field, the birds of the heavens and the fish of the sea, whatever passes through the paths of the sea. [Although some commentators would place Ps. 8 in this category, which is possible, it better fits into an overt eschatological category directly below.]

> **Ps. 107:37–38** And sow fields and plant vineyards, and gather a fruitful harvest. Also <u>He blesses them and they multiply greatly</u>, and He does not let their cattle decrease.

> **Isa. 51:2–3** "Then <u>I blessed him</u> [Abraham] and <u>multiplied him</u>." . . . And her [Israel's] wilderness He will make like Eden, and her desert like the garden of the LORD. [Note that the concluding wording is a promise for the future, which is repeated below.]

However, sinful events occur that make it clear that the king and nation only partly accomplish the commission. Ultimately, they also fail in attempting to do what Adam and their ancestors had failed to do. Therefore, there is reiteration of the promise that eschatological Israel and their end-time king will finally succeed in fully accomplishing the Adamic commission:

> **Ps. 8:5–8** Yet You have made him a little lower than God, and <u>You crown him with glory and majesty! You make him to rule over the works of your hands; You have put all things under his feet</u>, all sheep and oxen, and also the beasts of the field, the birds of the heavens and the fish of the sea, whatever passes through the paths of the sea.

> **Ps. 72:8, 17, 19** May he [the end-time king] also <u>rule</u> from sea to sea and from the River to the ends of the earth. . . . And let men bless themselves by him; <u>let all nations call him blessed</u> [allusion possibly to Gen. 12:2–3;

28:14, and above all to Gen. 22:18]. . . . And <u>may all the earth be filled</u> with His glory.

Isa. 51:2–3 "Then <u>I blessed him</u> [Abraham] <u>and multiplied him</u>." . . . Her [Israel's] wilderness He will make like Eden, and her desert like the garden of the LORD.

Isa. 54:1–3 "The sons of the desolate one <u>will be more numerous</u>. . . . Enlarge the place of your tent; stretch out the curtains of your dwellings. . . . Lengthen your cords and strengthen your pegs. For you <u>will spread abroad to the right and to the left. And your seed will possess the nations</u>" (the last two sentences are an allusion to Gen. 28:4, 13–14, which is part of the intertextual network of allusions to Gen. 1:28 and 12:23).

Jer. 3:16, 18 "It shall be in those days when you <u>are multiplied and increased</u> in the land . . . the land that I gave your forefathers as an inheritance."

Jer. 23:3 "Then I Myself will gather the remnant of My flock out of all the countries where I have driven them and bring them back to their pasture, and <u>they will be fruitful and multiply</u>." [Cf. Jer. 29:6; 30:19; 33:22.]

Ezek. 36:9–12 "You [the promised land] will be cultivated and sown. <u>I will multiply men</u> on you [the land]. . . . <u>I will multiply on you</u> [the land] <u>man</u> [Israel] and beast; and <u>they will increase and be fruitful</u> . . . <u>and possess you</u>." [Cf. Ezek. 36:27.]

Dan. 7:13–14 "With the clouds of heaven one like a Son of Man was coming. . . . And to Him was given dominion . . . that <u>all the</u> peoples, <u>nations</u> and men of every language[60] . . . [will] serve him." [His rule will replace that of the "beasts."]

Hos. 1:10 Yet the <u>number of the sons of Israel will be like the sand of the sea, which cannot be measured or numbered</u>. . . . "You are the sons of the living God."

---

60. This appears to confirm Dan. 7:13–14 as an allusion to Gen. 22:18, especially since the latter is the only reiterated promise that also contains "possessing the gate of your enemy," a major theme in Dan. 7 concerning the "Son of Man" and the Israelite saints. Also the Son of Man's rule of sea beasts (portraying the enemy) reflects Adam's original commission to do the same. The allusion to the Adamic commissions, esp. Gen. 22:18, in Dan. 7 is further confirmed from observing that the precise phrase (in the OG) "all the nations of the earth" (*panta ta ethnē tēs gēs*) occurs only five other times in the OT, two of which are Gen. 22:18; 26:4, which are among the repetitions of Adam's commission; two more occur in Deut. 28:10; Josh. 4:24, likely also a part of allusions to the earlier phrases in Genesis (though Zech. 12:3 appears not to be an allusion). Other case forms of the phrase also occur in Deut. 28:1, which together with the same expression in Deut. 28:10, directly following mention of repeated blessings, and the phrase "the LORD will multiply you for good in your offspring" in Deut. 28:11 would enhance the two Deut. 28 phrases as allusions to the earlier Genesis texts. The phrase occurs also in Jer. 33:6; 51:8, which do not appear to be allusions to Genesis.

Interestingly, the Qumran community also believed that they were the beginning end-time fulfillment of these promises. In 4Q418 frg. 81 (= 4Q423 8 + 24?), God is said to be "your portion and your inheritance among the sons of Adam, [and over] his [in]heritance he has given them authority" (line 3). Thus, the members of the Qumran community are those who are the true "sons of Adam" to whom God has given authority over an "inheritance." Those who "inherit the earth" will "walk" in an "eter[nal] plantation" (lines 13–14), likely referring to the whole earth as a large Eden.[61] They "shall fill [apparently the earth] and . . . be satiated with the abundance of good" (line 19). So far, the description of the community echoes the commission of Gen. 1:26, 28, which they have begun to fulfill. They are also commanded to "honor" God "by consecrating yourself to him, in accordance to the fact that he has placed you as a holy of holies [over all][62] the earth" (line 4 [see also 1QH^a XIV:12–19; XVI:20–22]). Sprinkled throughout the passage are other imperatives: "in faithfulness to him walk continuously" (line 6) and "love him" (line 8).

Similarly *Sib. Or.* 5:414–416 affirms the same thing: "For there has come from the plains of heaven a blessed man with the sceptre in his hand which God has committed to his clasp: and he has won fair dominion over all." Similarly, Isaac gives Jacob the following blessings in *Jub.* 22:13: "May the Most High God give thee all the blessings wherewith he has blessed me and wherewith he blessed Noah and Adam; may they rest on the sacred head of thy seed from generation to generation for ever" (likewise *Jub.* 19:27).[63]

It became clear after the AD 70 ransacking of Jerusalem, as well as the desolation of the Qumran community around that time, that neither Qumran nor any other part of Israel was the fulfillment of the eschatological promise about the Adamic commission.

The Differences between the Commission to Adam and What Was Passed On to His Descendants

Despite the many similarities between the original commission in Gen. 1 (and that repeated to Noah) and that given to Abraham and his Israelite seed, some differences exist. Before Adam's disobedience, he would have fulfilled the

---

61. A closely related passage in 4Q475 is apparently the most explicit Qumran text affirming that the earth will become Eden: after all sin has been extinguished from the earth, "all the world will be like Eden, and all . . . the earth will be at peace for ever, and . . . a beloved son . . . will . . . inherit it all" (lines 5–6).

62. The Martínez and Tigchelaar Hebrew-English edition rightly fills the lacuna with "over all" because of the following parallelism with "over all the angels" (lit. "gods"), though in Martínez's earlier English edition he did not do so and gave an otherwise quite different translation, which does not reflect the Hebrew as well as the later translation.

63. Note likewise *Pesiq. Rab Kah.* Piska 15.1: "As with Adam, said God, so with his children: I brought them into the Land of Israel, I gave them commands, but they transgressed my commands."

"subduing and ruling" part of the commission by demonstrating sovereignty through cultivating the earth and having mastery over all the creatures of the earth, including the satanic "serpent," which existed outside the garden and subsequently would enter into it. After Adam's sin, the commission would be expanded to include renewed humanity's reign over unregenerate human forces arrayed against it. Hence, the language of "possessing the gate of their enemies" is included, which elsewhere is stated as "subduing the land" (note here Num. 32:22: "and the land is subdued before the Lord," where the same word (*kbs̆*) is used for "subdue" as in Gen. 1:28).[64]

Thus, in the repetition of the commission to the patriarchs noted above, the mention of "all the nations of the earth" being "blessed" by Abraham's "seed" alludes to a renewed human community bearing God's image and "filling the earth" with regenerated progeny who also reflect God's image and shine out its luminosity to others in the "city of man" who do not rebel and also come to reflect God. Thus, these new converts are "blessed" with the favor of God's glorious presence and become a part of God's ever-increasing kingdom and rule, which the first Adam had forfeited. Hence, the "ruling and subduing" of Gen. 1:28 now includes *spiritually* overcoming the influence of evil in the hearts of unregenerate humanity that has multiplied upon the earth. The implication is that the notion of physical newborn children "increasing and multiplying" in the original Gen. 1:28 commission now includes people who have left their old way of life and have become spiritually newborn and have come to reflect the image of God's glorious presence and participate in the expanding nature of the Gen. 1:26–28 commission.

Abraham's descendants were to be a renewed humanity. They were to bear God's image and "fill the earth" with children who also bore that image, being beacons of light to others living in spiritual darkness. They were to be God's instruments through whom God caused the light of his presence to shine in the dark hearts of people in order that they too might become part of the increasing expansion of God's glorious presence and of the kingdom. This is none other than performing the role of "witness" to God throughout the earth.

Presumably, part of the point of the repeated reference to the "tabernacle of testimony" and the "ark of testimony" is that Israel itself was to accept God's "testimony" of his presence and then bear witness to God's saving presence in the past and present by declaring God's own "testimony" to his law and to the various redemptive acts performed on Israel's behalf. In addition, the nation was to be a "testimony" by obeying the law. All of this would bear witness to the truth of God's presence.

God commanded the people of Israel that, directly after their restoration, they were to be "witnesses"[65] to their "knowledge" and "belief" that he is the

64. So Wright, *Climax of the Covenant*, 23.
65. Cf. the use here of the cognate *ēd*, and the LXX's *martys*.

only true God. At this time, they were also to testify that God had expressed his divine omnipotence again by delivering Israel out of a second bondage and performing a second exodus to the promised land (Isa. 43:10–12; 44:6–8). That Israel was to be a witness to the nations is implied at various points (cf. Isa. 43:9) but made explicit in Isa. 55:4, where God says that he had made David "a witness to the peoples," a commission that Israel should share. Israel's kings were to be leaders in bearing this "testimony."[66] This commission was Israel's task to "call" the nations to God (Isa. 55:5). To accomplish this mission, Israel was first to "seek the LORD while He may be found" and "call upon Him while He is near" (Isa. 55:6).

Another difference in the repetition of the Gen. 1 commission is that whereas Gen. 1:28 and Gen. 9:1, 6–7 are expressed only as commands, the restatements beginning with the patriarchs are now stated formally as a promise.[67] Even in these reiterations, however, parts of the commission usually are retained and are explicitly reiterated in an inextricable way to the restated promise. That the aspect of the commission is retained is apparent from the imperatives introducing the commission in Gen. 12:1–3: "Go forth from your country. . . . You shall be a blessing." Likewise, the Gen. 35:11–12 promise includes the statement with imperatives: "I am God Almighty; be fruitful and multiply." The implication is that humanity cannot carry out this commission on its own, but God will enable humanity in some way to perform it, which he promises to do.

Most of the promissory reapplications of the commission given to Adam and Noah are shot through with commands as well, not only to a patriarch[68] but also to the promised eschatological seed of the patriarch. For example, note the following in Gen. 17: "Walk before Me and be blameless. And I will establish My covenant between Me and you, and I will multiply you exceedingly" (vv. 1–2); "I will make you exceedingly fruitful," and "I will establish My covenant between Me and you and your seed," and "I will give to . . . your seed . . . the land . . . for an everlasting possession," and "you shall keep My covenant, you and your seed after you [i.e., the promised seed] throughout their generations. This is My covenant, which you shall keep, between Me and you and your seed after you [i.e., including the promised seed]" (vv. 6–10).

66. E.g., 2 Chron. 23:11 says that when Joash was crowned king, they placed the "testimony" in his hands, indicating that he was to uphold the law and all it stood for; see also 2 Chron. 34:29–33.

67. Wright (*Climax of the Covenant*, 22) sees only the aspect of "becoming fruitful" being transformed into a promise.

68. Note, e.g., the following, which directly precedes or follows most of the reapplications of the Adamic promises listed earlier: "For I have chosen him [Abraham], so that he may command his children . . . to keep the way of the LORD by doing righteousness and justice, so that the LORD may bring upon Abraham what He has spoken about him" (Gen. 18:19). In Gen. 22:16–18 Abraham's obedience in sacrificing Isaac is viewed as the basis for God promising that he will cause the reiterated Adamic commission to be fulfilled in the future. So also Gen. 26:3–5; 26:24 (note the imperative "do not fear"); 28:1–4 (note the imperative in vv. 1–2 to marry in a way that is faithful to God).

Likewise, observe the promise mixed with commands addressed to latter-day Israel in Isa. 54:1–3: "The sons of the desolate one will be more numerous. . . . Enlarge the place of your tent; stretch out the curtains of your dwellings. . . . Lengthen your cords and strengthen your pegs. For you will spread abroad to the right and to the left. And your seed will possess the nations" (note here allusion to the earlier Abrahamic promise in Gen. 28:4, 13–14). Other examples of the same phenomenon may also be found with respect to reiterations of the promise to end-time Israel.[69]

Other commands in conjunction with these promises are given to the patriarchs and later to Israel, which is further evidence suggesting that the expectations of the original Adamic commission were still in force, though together now with God's promise that he will enable the Abrahamic seed to carry out the commission.

God's assurance that "I am with you" was not addressed to Adam or Noah and is not formulated until the promise is repeated to Isaac. This assurance is the basis for God's promise and commission to spread out in order that his presence would spread (see with respect to Isaac [Gen. 26:24], Jacob [Gen. 28:15], and Moses [Exod. 3:12]). It was this very presence that provided enablement of the task and assured the fulfillment of the promise.[70] In response to God's presence, Israel was "to walk in His ways and to keep His commandments" in order to fulfill the original Adamic commission: to "live and multiply, and that the LORD your God may bless you in the land where you are entering to possess it" (Deut. 30:16). Ultimately, only if God "circumcised their heart" would they be able to love and obey him, continue in his presence, and inherit the promise and truly "live" (Deut. 30:5–6, 16).

Essentially the same formula is repeated to Solomon. David says to his son, "The LORD be with you that you may be successful, and build the house of the LORD your God just as He has spoken concerning you. Only the LORD give you . . . understanding . . . so that you may keep the law of the LORD your God" (1 Chron. 22:11–12).

God pronounces the same accompaniment formula in the book of Jeremiah when he commissions Jeremiah and enables him to be a "prophet to the nations" (1:5) and "to destroy and to overthrow, to build and to plant" (1:10 [for the formula, see 1:8, 19]). God speaks the same formula to the people of

---

69. See also Lev. 26:9–16 (eschatological Israel will receive the promise if they also obey); cf. Isa. 51:1–2a (end-time Israel is commanded to "look to the rock from which you were hewn, and to the quarry from which you were dug. Look to Abraham your father, and to Sarah who gave birth to you in pain," which is then followed by a restatement of the Abrahamic promise in vv. 2b–3); Jer. 3:16, 18 is directly preceded by this command to end-time Israel: "Return, O faithless sons, . . . for I am a master to you" (v. 14).

70. The same promise could be made to individual Israelites other than the patriarchs; note, e.g., 1 Chron. 4:10: "Now Jabez called on the God of Israel, saying, 'Oh that You would bless me indeed and enlarge my border, and that Your hand might be with me, and that You would keep me from harm that it may not pain me!' And God granted him what he requested."

Israel when he tells them that his purpose in regathering them from exile is to renew their commission to be a "witness" to the nations about his purpose in creating "new things" (Isa. 43:5–21). These "divine accompaniment formulas" addressed to Solomon, Jeremiah, and Israel may be rooted in the promissory reapplication of Gen. 1:28 to the patriarchs, where the formula first occurs.

Certainly Adam's obedience within the garden sanctuary was key to carrying out his mandate by means of God's presence with him (recall the divine presence in the garden: "God walking in the garden" [Gen. 3:8]). But there is no scriptural record that God promised to Adam that his presence would always be with him in carrying out his mandate. Indeed, God withdrew his presence from Adam. As a result of sin, Adam was cast out of the sanctuary of God's glorious presence and was not able to fulfill the divine commission.

Just as in the case of Adam, Israel's obedience within its "garden of Eden" to the laws regulating the temple was a part of carrying out its renewed commission as a corporate Adam. Israel's temple[71] and land are explicitly compared to the garden of Eden (for the latter, see Isa. 51:3; Ezek. 36:35; Joel 2:3; cf. Gen. 13:10; Ezek. 47:12) and are portrayed as very fruitful in order to heighten the correspondence to Eden (cf. Deut. 8:7–10; 11:8–17; Ezek. 47:1–12).[72] The promised land itself is called God's "holy land" (Ps. 78:54; Zech. 2:12) because it was to be a garden of Eden on a grander scale.[73] The commission to have cosmic dominion (Gen. 1:26–28), first expressed through Adam's role in Eden, is now addressed to Israel, which apparently is conceived of as a corporate Adam.[74]

This commission is expressed well in Exod. 19:6, where God says of the whole nation, "You shall be to Me a kingdom of priests and a holy nation." They were to be mediators in spreading the light of God's tabernacling presence to the rest of the dark world. Such a connection of Gen. 1:28 to Eden and the temple may have sparked off the following thought in the *Hymn Scroll* of Qumran: "My dominion shall be over the sons [of the ear]th. . . . I will shine

71. On which, see Beale, *Temple*, 66–80.

72. For the latter point, see William J. Dumbrell, "Genesis 2:1–17: A Foreshadowing of the New Creation," in *Biblical Theology: Retrospect and Prospect*, ed. Scott J. Hafemann (Downers Grove, IL: InterVarsity, 2002), 58–59.

73. Ibid., 58–61.

74. Israel's temple is also related to the nation's carrying out the Gen. 1:28 commission. So R. E. Clements, *God and Temple* (Philadelphia: Fortress, 1965), 67–73. Later midrashic exegesis on the temple may have been partly inspired by Gen. 1:26–28 in its understanding that the temple brought the blessing of fertility, even of children (*Midrash Tanḥuma Numbers* [ed. Buber, p. 33]; *y. Yebam.* 6b, cited in Raphael Patai, *Man and Temple in Ancient Jewish Myth and Ritual*, 2nd ed. [New York: KTAV, 1967], 90; cf. *b. Ber.* 63b–64a; *Num. Rab.* 4.20; 11.3; *Song Rab.* 2.5; *b. Yoma* 39b, to which I was alerted by Patai). Likewise, the existence of the temple and the rites performed therein procured blessing and fruitfulness for Israel (and implicitly the earth in general) (so Patai, *Man and Temple*, 122–28, who cites, e.g., *The Fathers according to Rabbi Nathan* 4).

with a sevenfold li[ght] in the E[den which]⁷⁵ Thou hast [m]ade for Thy glory"
(1QHᵃ XV:23–24, where the temple lampstand with seven lamps is probably
behind the image of the "sevenfold light").

Israel sinned and was cast away from God's presence and out of the land.
At the same time, God withdrew his presence from their temple (Ezek. 9:3;
10:4, 18–19; 11:22–23). The same thing happened to restored Israel in AD 70,
when the Romans destroyed Jerusalem and the temple, though God's presence
had long since left that temple.⁷⁶ Thus, the promise of divine accompaniment
to enable fulfillment of the Gen. 1 mandate was not ultimately fulfilled in
Abraham or any of the physical descendants, nor in Israel or the temple, but
remained yet to be realized.

Just as Adam "hid . . . from the presence of the LORD" (Gen. 3:8), thus en-
suring failure to accomplish his mission, Noah and Israel, as representative of
God's true humanity, likewise separated themselves from the divine presence
and failed to carry out the commission. Thus, it is not an overstatement to say
that Noah was commissioned in a new creation to be another individual Adam
figure, and Israel to be a "corporate Adam." The nation's task was to do what
Adam had first been commissioned to do. Noah and his seed and Israel and
its seed failed even as had Adam. And like Adam, Noah's seed and Israel were
exiled, the latter also banished from its "garden land." The pattern occurs twice
in Israel's history, the first commencing in Egypt and the second in Babylon.
Although a remnant of Israel returned from Babylonian exile, its failure to
carry out the Adamic task continued until the beginning of the first century AD.

Conclusion

We can speak of Gen. 1:28 as the first "Great Commission," which was
repeatedly applied to humanity. The commission was to bless the earth, and
part of the essence of this blessing was God's salvific presence. Before the fall,
Adam and Eve were to produce progeny who would fill the earth with God's
glory being reflected from each of them in the image of God. After the fall,
a remnant, created by God in his restored image, was to go out and spread
God's glorious presence among the rest of darkened humanity. This witness
was to continue until the entire world would be filled with divine glory. Thus,
Israel's witness was reflective of its role as a corporate Adam, which highlights
the notion of missions in the OT.⁷⁷

75. This follows the translation by A. Dupont-Sommer, *The Essene Writings from Qumran*,
trans. G. Vermes (Oxford: Blackwell, 1961), though his is the only translation that fills the
lacunae with "Eden." For elaboration on this debated translation, see Beale, *Temple*, 79n125.
76. God's presence had left the temple at least by the time of Christ's coming, since he himself
became the place of the special divine presence in the midst of the nation instead of the temple
in ultimate fulfillment of Hag. 2:5. It is quite possible that the divine presence never returned
to the postexilic temple.
77. For elaboration of this, see Beale, *Temple*.

Without exception, the reapplications of the Adamic commission are stated positively in terms of what Noah, the patriarchs, Israel, and eschatological Israel or its king should do or were promised to do. Always the expression is that of actual conquering of the land, increasing and multiplying population, and filling the promised land and the earth with people who will reflect God's glory. Never is there a hint that this commission is to be carried out by what we might call a negative act—that is, by death. Of course, Isa. 53, Dan. 9, and Zech. 12 (and a handful of typological Davidic texts such as Ps. 22) prophesy the Messiah's death as crucial to achieving Israel's restoration, but these texts are the minority, and they are never directly associated with the repetitions of the Adamic commission. Therefore, the Adamic expectations and promises of obedience for Israel's patriarchs, the nation, and its king are always stated in positive terms of what they were to do or were promised to do.

One important observation from the analysis so far in this chapter can be made: Gen. 1:28 has more intertextual connections with the rest of Genesis and the remaining OT books than any other text in Gen. 1–11, and this is an initial pointer to it being the most formal thread from that initial section of Genesis being developed elsewhere in the OT.

The Repeated Cosmic Judgment and New Creation Episodes of the Old Testament

Essential to the storyline so far formulated is the kingdom of a new creation. The pattern of judgment in the form of (1) cosmic chaos followed by (2) new creation, (3) commission of kingship for divine glory, (4) sinful fall, and (5) exile is one that composes the major events of redemptive history. The following tables (2.1, 2.2, and 2.3) are an attempt to show how these patterns repeat themselves, though any table like this will be too simplistic, since further explanation is needed to flesh it out (which I try to do to some degree in the remainder of the chapter). Patterns in the NT are included in order to provide a full canonical overview, although thorough discussion of the NT part will have to wait until later chapters.

The beginning of history in Gen. 1–3 and the ending of history in Rev. 21 are like bookends to canonical world history. Richard Hooker (*Of the Laws of Ecclesiastical Politie* [1593]) said, "Is there any thing which can either be thoroughly understood, or soundly judged of, till the very first cause and principles from which originally it springeth be made manifest?"[78] Thus, the various books of the OT and its postdiluvian history are best understood as flowing out of Gen. 1–3 and, hence, in one way or another, related ultimately to the first three chapters of the Bible.

78. Cited in Norman Cohn, *Cosmos, Chaos, and the World to Come: The Ancient Roots of Apocalyptic Faith* (New Haven: Yale University Press, 1993), v.

Table 2.1
Beginning of History
as the Inaugurated First-Creational Kingship
in Genesis 1–3

first chaos of earth and waters[a]
first creation
first commission of first Adam as king for divine glory
first Adam's sin
first Adam's judgment[b] and exile

[a]There is debate about whether the earth being "formless and void" conveys a notion of some kind of primordial judgment, for which the limits of this discussion do not allow elaboration.
[b]See Jeffrey J. Niehaus, "In the Wind of the Storm: Another Look at Genesis III 8," *VT* 46 (1994): 263–67. Niehaus renders the Hebrew *rûaḥ hayyôm* as "the wind of the storm" instead of the traditional rendering of "the cool of the day"; accordingly, he translates the entire verse as follows: "Then the man and his wife heard the thunder (*qwl*) of Yahweh God as he was going back and forth (*mthlk*) in the garden in the wind of the storm (*lrwḥ hywm*), and they hid from Yahweh God among the trees of the garden." If Niehaus is correct, then this is the first judgmental theophany of God, foreshadowing the eschatological theophany in judgment (e.g., Rev. 6:15–17).

But more needs to be said. On the basis of the presupposition that the entire canon is the inspired database of God's revelation, the two bookends of Gen. 1–3 and Rev. 21 interpret everything between them. This means that the biblical material between these two poles is to be read not only in light of its origins in Gen. 1–3 but also in view of its goal in Revelation. Consequently, the foregoing evidence broadly supports the notion that everything in the biblical canon should be seen to have its roots in Gen. 1–3 and to move toward its final goal in Rev. 21. Furthermore, the material and events of each cycle within the canonical bookends of Gen. 1–3 and Rev. 21 should also be viewed in light of the preceding and succeeding cycle. This interpretative angle is justified on the basis that Scripture has one ultimate divine author, who has intentionally caused these cycles to be modeled on the basic "chaos followed by new creation" pattern of Gen. 1 and to be placed one after another in a mutually interpretative relationship.[79] The following analysis of the OT depends to a significant extent on this conclusion as a presupposition.

79. The table above probably could have included more such cycles, but those depicted are the major and most complete ones. Perhaps the episode of the tower of Babel followed by Abraham's departure from idolatrous captivity in Ur and subsequent Adamic recommission (e.g., in Gen. 12:1–2) is one such example of the pattern. Later Judaism accordingly understood that Abraham's commission in Gen. 12:1–2 represented God making the patriarch a new creation like that which began in Gen. 1 (e.g., see *Midr. Tanḥ. Gen.* 3.5; 5.5; likely also *Gen. Rab.* 39.11; cf. *Midr. Tanḥ. Gen.* 5.1). The reasons for this involve Gen. 12:1–3 being the reapplication of the Gen. 1:28 commission to Abraham.

Table 2.2
Cycles of Inaugurated Eschatology within Biblical History

chaos of earth and waters at flood	chaos of oppression and Egyptian plagues[a]	chaos of exile in wilderness for second generation	chaos of oppression and destruction in Israel's land and exile[b]	chaos of oppression and destruction in Israel's land as continuing exile[c]
new creation	exodus and new creation through Red Sea[d]	exodus and new creation through small Red Sea (Jordan)	exodus and new creation through return from Babylonian exile	escalated new creation in Christ's life (and later at his death, and resurrection)
commission of Noah as new Adam for divine glory[e]	commission of Israel as a corporate Adam for divine glory	commission of Israel as corporate Adam for glory (repeated)	promised commission of Israel as an eschatological corporate Adam for divine glory	commission of Christ as eschatological Israel/Son of Man ("Adam") for God's glory
new Adam's sin	sin of Israel (corporate Adam) at the "golden calf" episode and in wilderness	repeated sin of Israel from Judges up to destruction in land[f] and exile in Babylon	Israel's sin in the land and forfeiture of the eschatological role	Christ as eschatological Israel and last Adam resists sin
judgment and exile throughout the earth at Babel	judgment and exile in wilderness for first generation	judgment in land and exile in Babylon	judgment of continuing exile even though Israel had returned to the land	continuing physical exile for God's people in the world even though they had begun to be restored spiritually

[a]See in this respect Archie Lee, "Gen. 1 and the Plagues Tradition in Ps. 105," *VT* 40 (1990): 257–63. Lee contends that the exodus plagues rehearsed in Ps. 105 represent a de-creation or reversal of the elements of creation in Gen. 1.
[b]So Jer. 4:23–28, where Israel's land is spoken of as "the earth . . . formless and void; and . . . the heavens . . . had no light," a place where no creatures dwelled, "a wilderness," a "desolation," and "the heavens . . . dark." So also Isa. 45:18–19 either describes Israel's land or its exile in Babylon in the same manner.
[c]Note that the "chaos of Israel's exile" is repeated as both the last stage of each cycle pertaining to Israel and the first stage of the following cycle about Israel, since on the one hand it is judgment, and on the other hand it is the context from which new creation arises, in imitation of the Gen. 1 pattern.
[d]On the new-creational motifs of the first exodus (e.g., in Exod. 15), see Dumbrell, *End of the Beginning*, 167–71; see Wis. 19:6; note also *Pesiq. Rab Kah.* Piska 12.19, which depicts God saying to Israel at Sinai, "As I make you new again, I show you a kind of earnest of the world-to-come."
[e]For the parallels between chaos waters, new creation, and Noah as a new Adam in the Noahic flood narrative in Gen. 6–9 and Gen. 1–3, see, e.g., Gage, *Gospel of Genesis*, 7–16. Early Judaism also understood the new world resulting from the flood to be a new creation (*1 En.* 106:13; Philo, *Mos.* 2.64–65; cf. *Jub.* 5:12).
[f]Here is included significantly the sin of Jeroboam setting up the golden calves in typological reproduction of the first worship of the golden calf at Sinai, both of which were corporate sinful acts affecting subsequent generations of Israel. This ultimately climaxes in northern Israel's judgment in exile. Southern Israel subsequently followed northern Israel's idolatry, likewise resulting in judgment and exile.

These cyclic patterns show that there were apparent inaugurated new-creational movements of God's kingdom following crisis points of chaos at various stages in the OT that, from the human perspective, could have developed into consummative eschatological conditions. Such final and irreversible conditions, however, did not eventuate due to sin. In addition, when it is recalled that the chaos of the first creation was resolved by God bringing

Table 2.3
Ending of History
as Consummative Eschatology
in Revelation 21

chaos of last destruction of heavens and earth
last new creation
last commission of saints as a corporate Adam
last resistance to sin by saints
last deliverance of saints from exile

about an ordered creation, the subsequent judgments of the flood, the Egyptian plagues, and Israel's desolated land can be understood as recapitulations of the primordial chaos that precedes new creation.[80] This order is not merely the proper arrangement of created cosmic realities but also the personal and social order of human beings.[81] The failure of God's people to carry out the Adamic mandate in these apparent new-creational start-ups then came to be typological in the scriptural record of a new creation yet to come, when an eschatological Adam would come and finally do what the first Adam should have done.

Thus I am not positing a center or single topic as the key to OT theology but rather a storyline around which the major thematic strands of the OT narratives and writings revolve. Although story as a hermeneutical approach to biblical literature has become popular in recent biblical scholarship[82] and accordingly has even been applied to the doing of whole biblical theologies,[83] the older Dutch Reformed scholars sometimes employed the notion of tracing the "redemptive-historical story" of "creation-fall-restoration."[84] It is also

80. On which, see Patrick D. Miller, "Creation and Covenant," in *Biblical Theology: Problems and Perspectives*, ed. Steven J. Kraftchick, Charles D. Myers Jr., and Ben C. Ollenburger (Nashville: Abingdon, 1995), 155–68; Robert R. Wilson, "Creation and New Creation: The Role of Creation Imagery in the Book of Daniel," in *God Who Creates: Essays in Honor of W. Sibley Towner*, ed. William P. Brown and S. Dean McBride Jr. (Grand Rapids: Eerdmans, 2000), 190 203. Note also the depictions of Babylon in Isa. 13:1–13 and of Edom in Isa. 34:1–15 as examples of judgment as "de-creation," which can be found elsewhere of the judgment of other nations, including Israel.

81. Dumbrell, *Search for Order*, 11.

82. See the sources cited in Craig G. Bartholomew and Micahel W. Goheen, eds., *The Drama of Scripture: Finding Our Place in the Biblical Story* (Grand Rapids: Baker Academic, 2004), 215–16. This is an approached favored by, e.g., N. T. Wright.

83. Bartholomew and Goheen, *Drama of Scripture*; C. Marvin Pate et al., *The Story of Israel: A Biblical Theology* (Downers Grove, IL: InterVarsity, 2004).

84. See, e.g., Geerhardus Vos, *Biblical Theology: Old and New Testaments* (Grand Rapids: Eerdmans, 1948). Although "story" is not a favorite term of his, the notion of "progressive organic development of God's revelation" is crucial, which comes quite close to the idea of an unfolding story or drama. See likewise Vos, "The Idea of Biblical Theology as a Science and a Theological Discipline," in *Redemptive History and Biblical Interpretation: The Shorter Writings*

significant to recall that all the ancient creeds and confessions had a basic skeletal plotline of creation, fall, redemption, and consummation. The threefold pattern of "sin-exile-restoration" of Israel has been proposed recently as the framework of a biblical theology,[85] as has a six-act structure of the Bible as a drama with kingdom as the overarching motif: (1) kingdom establishment; (2) rebellion; (3) the king chooses Israel—interlude: the kingdom story awaits ending during the intertestamental period—(4) coming of the king; (5) mission of the king's message; (6) return of the king.[86] As evident from the preceding, both the threefold and the sixfold pattern are included here but compose only some of the elements of a larger overall cyclic pattern of sacred history.

In the light of the above, my formulation of the storyline of the OT is as follows: *The Old Testament is the story of God, who progressively reestablishes his new-creational kingdom out of chaos over a sinful people by his word and Spirit through promise, covenant, and redemption, resulting in worldwide commission to the faithful to advance this kingdom and judgment (defeat or exile) for the unfaithful, unto his glory.* Rather than referring to this as the "center" of the OT, I prefer to see it as the primary strand of the biblical storyline thread, composed of other minor strands that are held together by the primary one.

The kingdom of the new creation and its missional expansion likely form the major stepping-stone for the accomplishment of divine glory.[87] Accordingly, in the classic fourfold division of the scriptural story as creation, fall, redemption, and consummation, the last two elements are better revised as redemption through new creation and consummation of that new creation. Thus, the story of the Bible in this formulation begins with creation and ends with the restoration of creation. The last phrase of the storyline, "unto his glory," is the goal and needs a little more elaboration. Above, we saw that the first Adam's role as king in God's image was for the purpose of reflecting God's glorious image throughout all the earth—that is, his glory. Noah's

---

of *Geerhardus Vos*, ed. Richard B. Gaffin Jr. (Phillipsburg, NJ: P&R, 1980), 23, where he speaks of Scripture as "a book of history, the parallel to which in dramatic interest and simple eloquence is nowhere to be found." Similarly, note Vos, *The Pauline Eschatology* (1930; repr., Grand Rapids: Baker Academic, 1979), 26, where he refers to the eschatological perspective of Paul's writings as a "drama." On Vos's view in this respect, see Michael S. Horton, *Covenant and Eschatology: The Divine Drama* (Louisville: Westminster John Knox, 2002), 237–38, 241–42. For a more practical application of this in the Dutch Reformed tradition, see S. G. de Graaf, *Promise and Deliverance*, trans. H. Evan Runner and Elisabeth Wichers Runner, 4 vols. (St. Catherines, ON: Paideia, 1977–81), vols. 1–2.

85. Pate et al., *Story of Israel*. This threefold pattern is focused on also by the sources cited in J. Ross Wagner, *Heralds of the Good News: Isaiah and Paul in Concert in the Letter to the Romans*, NovTSup 101 (Leiden: Brill, 2001), 355n39.

86. Bartholomew and Goheen, *Drama of Scripture*.

87. On which, see further discussion below in chap. 6, where more elaboration on the nature of a "storyline" is found.

commission likewise as a second Adam in God's image (Gen. 9:6–7) probably should be construed as being for the same glorious purpose. Other major redemptive-historical events also have as their goal God's glory.

1. Israel's deliverance out of Egypt was to result in God's glorious presence residing among them in the tabernacle (Exod. 40:34–38).
2. The beginnings of Israel's sinful monarchy would still exalt God's "great name" (1 Sam. 12:22).
3. The final conquest of Canaan (2 Sam. 7:1–11), the confirmation of Israel's kingdom (2 Sam. 7:12–16), and the building of the temple (2 Sam. 7:13, 27) were for the purpose that God's "name may be magnified forever" (2 Sam. 7:26; with specific reference only to the temple, see 1 Kings 8:10–13, 41–45).
4. Israel's exile and promised restoration were for God's "name" and "glory" (cf. Isa. 48:11 in the context of 48:5–19).
5. The rebuilding of Jerusalem and the temple was to be for God's glory (Hag. 1:8; 2:7–9; Zech. 2:5, 8–11).[88]

Consequently, the final goal of various significant redemptive-historical episodes throughout scriptural history was God's glory. All these events with glorious goals point to the glorious goal of the final events of history, in which God will definitively execute judgment, accomplish redemption, and establish the eternal new creation. At this time, God's glorious presence will permeate every part of the new heavens and earth and all will exalt and glorify him for his glorious attributes, which have been manifested through his culminating acts at the eschaton.

The Repeated New-Creational Expectation of an Adamic King throughout the Old Testament

My attempt here is to provide a thumbnail sketch of the way I see the Gen. 1:26–28 notion of the Adamic king of the new creation forming the central storyline that is threaded throughout all the various books of the OT to one significant degree or another. At various stages in the OT the engine of the new creation gets started again, and its missional expansion seems to begin but stalls and ultimately breaks down because of sin. The following is merely the direction where I see the evidence of the various OT books pointing. The primary purpose of this section is to set out my understanding of the way the OT develops the cyclic yet progressing storyline that I formulated above in order to see how that relates to the NT and its development of the same storyline.

88. This survey of divine glory is based on John Piper, *Desiring God: Meditations of a Christian Hedonist* (Portland: Multnomah, 1986), 227–35.

Pentateuch

The most reused verse in Genesis, as we have seen, is the repeated application of the Adamic commission from Gen. 1:28. The passing on of this expectation is the main thread throughout the book. Despite opposition to and disobedience by the faithful seed, the hope remains alive that a future seed of Adam and the patriarchs will finally succeed in performing the mandate of Gen. 1:28.

The remaining books of the Pentateuch show that the first generation of Israel was not faithful enough to fulfill the commission. Exodus narrates God bringing Israel out of Egypt in order that it would be "a kingdom of priests" (Exod. 19:6), and at Sinai Israel was given a charter that delineated further the conditions of the Adamic commission, which Israel immediately broke by committing idolatry. The goal of the book of Exodus was that God's glorious presence would dwell in the midst of the nation in the tabernacle. This goal is imperfectly achieved, since Moses must wear a veil over his face so that the divine glory radiating from his face would not strike the hardened hearts of the majority of the nation.[89] Despite the realization of the goal in Exodus, Leviticus explains the laws that Israel must keep in order to be clean and qualified to approach the tabernacle to be near to God's presence and thus qualified to be "a kingdom of priests." Numbers describes the various obstacles that Israel had to overcome in order to reach the promised land, where Israel was to function as a corporate Adam in a new garden of Eden. Deuteronomy addresses the second generation with the same obligations of the first, and it is they who enter into the land of promise, the new Eden, flowing with milk and honey. As we saw earlier, several OT texts refer to the promised land as "Eden" or the "garden" because Israel was conceived to have been a corporate Adam who was given the commission of Adam to carry out.

Joshua, Judges, and Ruth

Joshua recounts how the second generation entered and possessed the land. Possession of the land or judgment through oppression while still in the land due respectively to obedience or disobedience becomes the overriding theme, not only in Joshua but also in the rest of the OT (where judgment is expressed as exile from the land). In this respect, the promise to the patriarchs is often referred to, but it should be remembered that this is part of the development of the Gen. 1:28 commission of subduing and ruling over the earth.

The book of Joshua depicts Israel experiencing a small-scale exodus (Josh. 3) and then progressively dispossessing the antagonistic peoples living in the land. The book concludes on a very positive note by repeatedly affirming that "the LORD gave them rest [from their enemies] on every side" (21:44; 3:1), and that

---

89. See Scott J. Hafemann, *Paul, Moses, and the History of Israel: The Letter/Spirit Contrast and the Argument from Scripture in 2 Corinthians 3*, WUNT 81 (Tübingen: Mohr Siebeck, 1995).

"not one of the good promises which the LORD had made to the house of Israel failed; all came to pass" (21:45 [cf. 23:14–15]). However, it is clear that these statements are to be understood as indicating not the consummate fulfillment of the promises but only that all the promises had begun fulfillment. This is apparent from observing that enemy nations still reside in the promised land and pose a threat to Israel's complete possession of it (23:12–16). Accordingly, Joshua warns that if Israel is not faithful, they "will perish quickly from off the good land which He has given you" (23:16).

In Exodus, Leviticus, Numbers, Deuteronomy, and Joshua there is clear reference to the beginning fulfillment of the end-time promises to the patriarchs, especially with reference to possession of the land, but the fulfillment never reaches its eschatological consummate form because of the nation's disobedience, expressed already and incipiently by the sin of Achan and in Israel's failure to expel all the enemy nations. This lack of fulfillment mirrors the same pattern in Gen. 1–3, where Adam was set up in the first creation, was commanded to be faithful but was disobedient, and did not inherit the conditions of full eschatological blessing in a "completely glorified" new cosmos.

The book of Judges shows the incipient sin briefly noted in Joshua running rampant. The book narrates a repeated cyclical pattern of Israel (1) sinning, (2) being judged by coming under bondage to a surrounding enemy power, and then (3) being delivered by a judge raised up by God. The book of Ruth gives a personal snapshot of life in Israel during this time: occasional famine, exile, and blessing, in the midst of which the line leading to Davidic kingship is preserved.

The book of Ruth reveals that during the final phase of the period of the judges God was superintending events so that his plan of Davidic kingship would come to fruition (see Ruth 4). Its placement in the Hebrew canon among the "writings" after the return from exile may show that the story of Ruth was taken as an anticipation of God's sending Israel into exile and then delivering it and restoring it to the land and similarly preserving David's line in order to establish a new Davidic king over Israel after the return from exile.

Establishment of Kingship in Israel in Relation to Genesis 1–3 (1 and 2 Samuel and 1 Kings)

The book of 1 Samuel tells the story of the transition from the rule of the judges, concluding with Samuel and his sons, to that of kingship in Israel. Kingship itself was not evil (according to Deut. 17:14–20), especially since, as we have noted, God had installed Adam as a king over creation. Thus, keeping in mind the first chapters of Genesis, we could see kingship as a step back in the direction of achieving the commission of Gen. 1:28. The first king, Saul, was disobedient like the first human king, Adam. His kingship was taken away and given to David, whom he had persecuted. David initially displayed the marks of a faithful king by waiting for God to install him at the right time, though he had repeated opportunity to kill Saul.

After Saul's demise as king, David's promising start toward successful king-ship did not come to fruition, as 2 Samuel (and 1 Chronicles) sadly recounts. His adultery with Bathsheba and murder of Uriah signal the beginning of his demise, inaugurated by the rebellion of his own son, Absalom. Although David regained his kingdom, 1 Kings 1–2 relates how his chosen heir, Solomon, inaugurated his reign only after an attempted coup to replace him. Then the kingdom of Israel reached its zenith under Solomon, who successfully built the prophesied temple and established his kingdom more widely than had the two previous kings (1 Kings 3–10 // 2 Chron. 1–9). The description of the height of Solomon's kingship has more literary resonances with Gen. 1:26–28 and its immediate context than any other narrative about Israelite kings. The affinities between Solomon's reign and Gen. 1–3 probably are drawn because Solomon represents the height of Israelite kingship in the OT, thus also representing the epitome of Israel fulfilling the promises and hopes of the repeated Gen. 1:28 promissory commission. While only a few parallels would be insufficient to establish a connection with Gen. 1:26–28, it is the cumulative effect of the following points of correspondence that point to a relationship.

(1) Solomon's "wisdom surpassed the wisdom of all," even "all the kings of the earth" (1 Kings 4:30, 34), and is repeatedly referred to (14x in 1 Kings 2–11), being applied to him more than to any other Israelite king. He thus is viewed as an Adamic kind of king, since Adam was one who was to be perfectly wise. Although this is not explicit in Gen. 1–2, Job 15:7–8 is clearer about Adam possessing wisdom: "Were you [Job] the first man to be born, or were you brought forth before the hills? Do you hear the secret counsel of God [as did Adam], and limit wisdom to yourself [which was limited to Adam in the first garden enclosure]?"[90] Similarly, Ezek. 28:12–13 says that Eden was the place where wisdom was first found ("You had the seal of perfection, full of wisdom and perfect in beauty. You were in Eden, the garden of God"), but that this wisdom became corrupted (Ezek. 28:17).[91] Interestingly, the clos-est parallel to Ezek. 28:12 ("full of wisdom") is not coincidentally 1 Kings

90. For discussion of this text in context, see Dexter E. Callender Jr., *Adam in Myth and History: Ancient Israelite Perspectives on the Primal Human*, HSS 48 (Winona Lake, IN: Eisenbrauns, 2000), 137–76.

91. It is highly probable that the LXX version of Ezek. 28:14, 16 views the glorious being who had "fallen" to be Adam: "From the day that you were created you were with the cherub" (v. 14 [likewise Syriac Peshitta]); "you sinned; therefore, you have been cast down wounded from the mount of God [where Eden was]" (v. 16). For the notion that the Hebrew text of Ezek. 28:14 refers to Adam (i.e., "you were with the anointed cherub who covers"), see Callender, *Adam in Myth and History*, 87–135, and see further chaps. 12 (under the heading "Genesis 1–3 and Idolatry") and 19 below (under the heading "Adam's Commission as a Priest-King to Rule and Expand the Temple Is Passed On to the Patriarchs"). Note also directly below 2 *En.* [J] 30:11–12, which also refers to Adam as an "angel."

7:14, where Hiram was employed by wise Solomon to help build the temple (Hiram was "filled with wisdom," though note the next closest parallels, most of which are in conjunction with building the tabernacle: Exod. 28:3; 31:3; 35:31, 35; Deut. 34:9).

Second Enoch [J] 30:11–12 paraphrases Gen. 1:26, 28 in the following striking manner, applying the attribute of wisdom to Adam: "And on the earth I [God] assigned him [Adam] to be a second angel, honored and great and glorious. And I assigned him to be a king, to reign [on] the earth, [and] to have my wisdom" (likewise 4Q504 frg. 8, I:4–6). Early Judaism directly applies wisdom to Adam in comparison to kingship or to Solomon's reign. Philo says that Adam's assigning of names to all the creatures was evidence of "wisdom and royalty," since "the first man was wise with . . . wisdom," and "he was, moreover, a king" (*Opif.* 148). In the book of Wisdom's commentary on 1 Kings 3, Solomon is depicted as being given wisdom by God (7:7), which is "an image of his goodness" (7:26). This wisdom had been given to the king as an answer to his prayer that he be given the wisdom by which God had "formed man to have dominion over the creatures you have made" (9:2–4) and by which he could be "guided" to "judge . . . and . . . be worthy of the throne" of his father (9:10–12). Although "the first man did not know her [wisdom] perfectly" (Sir. 24:28), it was this very wisdom that "protected the first-formed father of the world, when he alone had been created; she delivered him from his transgression, and gave him strength to rule all things" (Wis. 10:1–2). Then, according to Wisdom, this same wisdom is said to have guided Noah (10:4), Abraham (10:6), Jacob (10:10–12 [in connection to God's "kingdom" and the patriarch's "victory"]), Joseph (10:13–14 [wisdom "brought him the scepter of a kingdom and authority"]), and Israel in its exodus from Egypt and sojourn in the wilderness (10:15–11:14).

These early Jewish notions presumably formed part of the matrix for understanding Adam in earliest Christianity and appear to be viable interpretations of Gen. 1–3 itself. "The tree of the knowledge [or 'discerning'] of good and evil" (Gen. 2:17) appears to be associated with wisdom, which is confirmed explicitly from Gen. 3:6 ("the tree was desirable to make one wise" [see also 3:5, 22]). Thus, wisdom is directly linked to Adam and Eve in the garden. The wisdom that Solomon was said to have had sounds similar to that which Adam must have had, since it had to do with a knowledge of how creation operates: "how the world was made, and the operation of the elements . . . the alterations of the turning of the sun, and change of seasons . . . positions of stars; the natures of living creatures . . . the violence of winds . . . the diversities of plants, and the virtues of roots; and all such things as are either secret or manifest" (Wis. 7:17–21).

(2) The wisdom in 1 Kings is directly related to Solomon's knowledge about "trees, from the cedar . . . even to the hyssop" (4:33). Could this be reminiscent of the garden atmosphere of Eden, of which Adam would have

had expert knowledge? This is pointed to by noticing that only two chapters later Solomon is said repeatedly to have built the entire temple (6:2, 9, 12, 14), and is repeatedly said to have built the particular constituent parts of it like a garden, including "carved . . . gourds and open flowers" in the "cedar" walls of the holy place (6:18).[92] Likewise, he is said to have "carved all the walls of the house round about with carved engravings of cherubim, palm trees, and open flowers" (6:29), and he made "two doors of olive wood" and "two doors of cypress wood" with the very same carved figures (6:31–35).

It is probable that these arboreal and floral images were intended to be reminiscent of the same images in the garden of Eden, thus connecting the mention of Solomon's vast knowledge of trees to Adam's knowledge and association with the trees of Eden (as well as with the cherubim stationed at the doors of Eden [Gen. 3:24]). In fact, many more features of Solomon's temple reflected features of Eden (which cannot be discussed in detail here due to space limitations). For example, note in 1 Kings 7 the garden imagery of the lily and pomegranate designs on the top of the temple pillars (vv. 18–19, 22), the lily blossoms on the brim of the molten sea and the gourds under the brim (vv. 24–26), engravings of "cherubim, lions and palm trees" on the ten washstands (v. 36), and the ten flowering lampstands (v. 49 [patterned after almond trees, according to Exod. 25:31–40]); see also 1 Kings 10:12 and 2 Chron. 9:11 with respect to algum trees used as foundations for the temple.[93]

Solomon's arboreal knowledge and wisdom to apply that knowledge extended beyond the temple. He was also a master gardener: he "made cedars as plentiful as sycamore trees" (1 Kings 10:27). He "planted vineyards . . . made gardens and parks . . . and . . . planted in them all kinds of fruit trees" and made "ponds of water . . . to irrigate a forest of growing trees" (Eccles. 2:4–6).[94] That during Solomon's rule all Israel "lived in safety, every man under his vine and his fig tree" (1 Kings 4:25) may recall the safety of the garden haven of Eden. The first occurrence of "fig" occurs in Gen. 3:17, and the healthy growth of the "vine and fig tree" indicates blessing (2 Kings 18:31; Joel 2:22), especially of an eschatological nature when expressed in the wording of "sit under his vine and under his fig tree" (Mic. 4:4; Zech. 3:10).

Could even the mention of gold and precious stones in association with the height and majesty of Solomon's reign echo the "gold . . . bdellium and the onyx" in Eden (Gen. 2:11–12)? The repetition of the mention of gold with respect to Solomon's kingdom (over 30x) is greater than with respect to any

---

92. Of course, it is actually Hiram from Tyre, "filled with wisdom," who carried out the actual work in "bronze" (1 Kings 7:13–14), and, presumably, either he or others also did the carved work in other materials (in light of 2 Chron. 2:13–14 and on analogy with Exod. 28:3; 31:3; 35:31). Nevertheless, the point in attributing the overall work to Solomon is to show that he was the ultimate manager in wisely guiding the building of the entire temple complex.

93. On which, see further Beale, *Temple*, 66–80.

94. On the assumption that Solomon is the narrator.

other narrative in the OT except Exodus. This is understandable, since both Exod. 25–40 (likewise Num. 7–8) and 1 Kings 6–10 (// 2 Chron. 2–9)[95] record respectively the building of the tabernacle and the building of the temple, both of which some see to be allusive developments of the Genesis conception of Eden as the first sacred sanctuary,[96] where also the gold and precious stones were found nearby. That Solomon covered with gold the wooden door carvings of "cherubim, palm trees, and open flowers" more directly associates the gold with overt Edenic features (1 Kings 6:32; so also 6:35). Similarly, the ten almond-tree-patterned lampstands were covered in gold (1 Kings 7:49) together with its flowers (2 Chron. 4:20–21), which some scholars also believe is reminiscent of the tree of life in Eden.[97] The repeated mention of gold goes beyond description of the temple and is applied to other features of Solomon's kingdom. Silver was in such abundance during his time that "it was not considered valuable" (1 Kings 10:21 // 2 Chron. 9:20 [cf. 1 Chron. 22:14]); indeed, Solomon "made silver and gold as plentiful . . . as stones" (2 Chron. 1:15).

(3) That Solomon prays to have "an understanding heart to judge . . . to discern between good and evil" (1 Kings 3:9 [cf. 3:28]) not only reflects his great wisdom but appears to echo "the tree of the knowledge [or discerning] of good and evil" (Gen. 2:9), from which Adam and Eve were prohibited to eat (Gen. 2:17; 3:5, 22). Commentators differ over the meaning of this tree, but the most promising approach explains the tree by determining the use of "know/discern good and evil" elsewhere in the OT. Elsewhere the phrase usually refers to figures in a position of judging or ruling over others (2 Sam. 14:17; 19:35; 1 Kings 3:9; Isa. 7:15–16).[98] In this light, the tree in Eden seems to have functioned as a judgment tree, the place where Adam should have gone to discern between good and evil and, thus, where he should have judged the serpent as evil and pronounced judgment on it, as it entered the garden.[99] Trees were also places where judgments were pronounced elsewhere in the OT (Judg. 4:5; 1 Sam. 22:6–19; cf. 1 Sam. 14:2). Accordingly, 1 Kings 3:9 is likely one more way to depict Solomon as an Adam figure.

(4) Adam was skillful in determining names to describe animals: "Whatever the man called a living creature, that was its name. And the man gave names to all the cattle, and to the birds of the sky, and to every beast of the field" (Gen. 2:19–20). So also Solomon was a wise master at proverbial description of "animals and birds and creeping things and fish" (1 Kings 4:33). This fourfold

95. See also 1 Chron. 28–29, where there is also repetition of "gold," where David is preparing the materials for the temple that Solomon built.
96. On which, see further Beale, *Temple*, 66–80.
97. On which, see ibid., 70.
98. See discussion of these uses in my analysis of Gen. 1–3 at the beginning of this chapter (under the subheading "The Design of Escalated Blessings of Adam in His Prefall State").
99. See esp. Kline, *Kingdom Prologue*, 103–7, and my earlier discussion under the subheading "The Design of Escalated Blessings of Adam in His Prefall State."

phrase describing earth's animate life is uniquely found in the OT only in Gen. 1:26; Deut. 4:17–18; 1 Kings 4:33.[100] Indeed, 1 Kings 4:33 is likely alluding to Gen. 1:26 (perhaps together with Gen. 2:19–20), since the Deuteronomy text concerns parts of the creation becoming objects of idolatry, and Gen. 1:26 is much more comparable to 1 Kings, being about Adam as a king ruling over the creation. (Though the Deuteronomy text itself likely alludes to Gen. 1:26: humans were created to reflect God's image and worship him, but they sinned by creating gods in the image of created things.) The notation that "apes and peacocks" (1 Kings 10:22; 2 Chron. 9:21) were increasingly common commodities shipped into Israel may also enhance the zoological connection with Eden, as does the mention also of an abundance of "horses and mules" (1 Kings 10:25; 2 Chron. 9:24). This is enhanced by the mention of numerous "fat oxen . . . sheep besides deer, gazelles, roebucks, and fattened fowl," which were part of the daily food for Solomon's royal table (1 Kings 4:23), thus showing that such animals were plentiful in Israel at the time.

(5) These Adam-like traits are compared to Solomon more than any other Israelite king probably because, for a time, he had achieved the position of being the greatest king in Israel (1 Kings 4:21, 24; cf. 1:47) and greater than the kings of the earth (1 Kings 4:34; 10:23). An echo of Gen. 1:26 ("let them rule . . . over all the earth") may also be heard in the description of Solomon's wisdom and rule: "Solomon became greater than all the kings of the earth. . . . All the earth was seeking the presence of Solomon" (1 Kings 10:23–24).[101] Although geographically qualified, it is also said that "Solomon ruled over all the kingdoms" and "had dominion [rdh, as in Gen. 1:26, 28] over everything" (1 Kings 4:21, 24). In correlation with the large-scale rule of Solomon, in the same immediate context, is noted the large-scale size of Israel: "Judah and Israel were as numerous as the sand that is on the seashore" (1 Kings 4:20), an allusion to the Abrahamic promise, which itself, as we have seen, develops the Gen. 1:28 commission.[102] In the same way, 1 Kings 3:8 (alluding to Gen. 15:5; 22:17) refers to Israel as "a great people who cannot be numbered or counted for multitude." In conjunction with the worldwide association of his kingdom, Solomon is "blessed" (1 Kings 2:45; 8:66; implicitly in 10:9), likewise a key linguistic feature in Gen. 1:26–28.

There are also links in the Davidic narrative of Chronicles and parallels in 2 Sam. with Gen. 1:28, though not as explicitly. In direct connection with his preparations for the building of the temple by Solomon in 1 Chron. 29:10–12, David praises God:

100. See also Gen. 1:28 in the LXX. Note comparably Gen. 9:2; Ezek. 38:20, though "living thing" (ḥayyâ) replaces "beast" (bēhēmâ), as well as Gen. 7:14, 21.

101. The first phrase in 10:23 repeats that of 4:34, which we saw above is directly linked to the Gen. 1:26 allusion concerning the four kinds of created beings in 4:33.

102. Genesis 22:17–18; 32:12; Jer. 33:22, the last of which connects the patriarchal promise to David's reign (likewise 2 Chron. 1:9); cf. 2 Sam. 17:11; Isa. 10:22, which are shorter descriptions, though probably echoing Gen. 22:17.

Blessed are you, O LORD. . . . Yours . . . is the greatness and the power and the glory and the victory and the majesty, indeed everything that is in the heavens and the earth; Yours is the dominion. . . . You exalt Yourself as head over all. . . . You rule over all, . . . and it lies in Your hand to make great and to strengthen everyone.

David uses language synonymous with that of Gen. 1:28 to praise God because he is the one who "makes great and strengthens" his human vice-regents to rule under his hand. Then Solomon is designated in the following verses as the example par excellence of such a vice-regent: "Then Solomon sat on the throne of the LORD as king. . . . The LORD highly exalted Solomon . . . and bestowed on him royal majesty which had not been on any king before him in Israel" (1 Chron. 29:23–25). It is probably not accidental that a few verses earlier David refers explicitly to the nation's identification with the patriarchs: he petitions "the God of Abraham, Isaac and Israel, our fathers" to preserve the peoples' godly desires and "to give to my son Solomon a perfect heart to keep Your commandments . . . and to build the temple, for which I have made provision" (1 Chron. 29:18–19).

Solomon completed the foundation-laying activities of his father: "Then Solomon began to build the house of the LORD in Jerusalem on Mount Moriah" (2 Chron. 3:1). In 2 Sam. 7 (// 1 Chron. 17) the need to build a temple (vv. 2–13) is closely linked with the following aspects of Gen. 1:28: (1) ruling and subduing (vv. 9–16), and (2) a blessing on God's kingly vice-regent (v. 29). It may also not be unexpected, therefore, that 2 Sam. 7:9, "I will make you a great name," would allude to Gen. 12:2, "I will . . . make your name great," which itself is part of the development of Gen. 1:28. Accordingly, it is natural that the overall purpose is linked to God giving "rest" to Israel's king from his enemies (2 Sam. 7:1, 11). Even more explicitly with reference to Gen. 1:28 is 1 Chron. 17:9–11: "I . . . will plant them [Israel]. . . . And I will subdue all your enemies [LXX adds 'I will cause you to increase']. . . . And I will establish his kingdom," followed by the repeated blessing, "And now it has pleased You to bless the house of Your servant, that it may continue forever before You; for You . . . have blessed, and it is blessed forever" (1 Chron. 17:27).

(6) Last, Solomon is depicted more than any other king, except perhaps David, to be functioning like a priest, which reflects Adam's portrayal as a priest-king.[103] He commands the priests to bring the ark into the new temple (1 Kings 8:1–6), blesses all Israel from the court of the temple (1 Kings 8:14, 55), and prays "before the altar" (1 Kings 8:22–54) for all Israel as a representative mediator (2 Chron. 6:13, 21–42). The ultimate purpose of his dedicatory

---

103. For argument that Adam was a priest-king, including additional ancient Near Eastern evidence for the notion, see Beale, *Temple*, 66–93. I have subsequently found that John A. Davies, "Solomon as a New Adam in 1 Kings," *WTJ* 73 (2011), 39–57, has argued in a very similar manner as I have here and above that Solomon was depicted in 1 Kings as an Adam figure.

prayer for the temple is that he as king and Israel as a nation would be priestlike mediators (cf. Exod. 19:6), "so that all the peoples of the earth may know that the LORD is God; there is no one else" (1 Kings 8:60). His numerous sacrificial offerings are singled out among all others (1 Kings 8:62–64; 9:25), perhaps also adding to his priestly aura. That he also "appointed the divisions of the priests for their service" and "the Levites for . . . ministering" in the temple further enhances his association with the priesthood (2 Chron. 8:14–15).

Solomon was following in the tradition of David, who functioned essentially as a priest, though he was never identified as such. When David brought the ark to Jerusalem, he was "wearing a linen ephod" (2 Sam. 6:14), a piece of ceremonial clothing unique to priests (1 Sam. 2:18, 28; 14:3; 22:18; 1 Chron. 15:27).[104] He also offered sacrifices (2 Sam. 6:13, 17; 24:25). In addition, in his rise to the zenith of his kingship, the highest officers in his kingdom are noted, among whom are Zadok and Ahimelech, who were "priests" (kōhănîm), and David's sons, who were "chief ministers" (kōhănîm) (2 Sam. 8:15–18).[105] Although Solomon was not yet born, it appears that some significant aspect of priestly function was part of the Davidic and Solomonic kingship. This was common in the ancient Near East, where Egyptian and Assyrian kings were also considered to be priests of their gods.[106]

As in the case of Israel's possession of the land in Joshua, so toward the end of narrating the zenith of Israelite kingship in Solomon, 1 Kings 8:56 says that Solomon's reign and building of the temple happened "according to all that He promised; not one word . . . failed of all His good promise, which He promised through Moses His servant."[107] This is not mere fulfillment of prophecies about a kingdom and a temple; in the light of the links to Gen. 1–2, this is also the realization of a kingdom and a temple in what appeared to be an emerging new creation. And, as with Joshua, although there was an escalated fulfillment of prophecies of the Israelite kingship and of the temple (and even more so with Solomon), these fulfillments were

104. The phrase "linen ephod" appears twenty-nine times in the OT outside of 2 Sam. 6:14 and is always associated with priestly apparel.

105. Although some translations refer to David's sons as "chief ministers" apparently in a governmental sense, the Hebrew word describing them is kōhēn, which occurs about 770 times in the OT and without exception refers to actual priests. The same is most likely the case here (thanks to my student D. Lincicum for research on this point and on the ephod above).

106. See Henri Cazelles, "Sacral Kingship," ABD 5:863–64; Jeremy Black, "Ashur (god)," in Dictionary of the Ancient Near East, ed. Piotr Bienkowski and Alan Millard (Philadelphia: University of Pennsylvania Press, 2000), 36. I am grateful to Christopher A. Beetham for pointing out these sources, as well as the observations about David's and his sons' priestly functions (on which, see his Echoes of Scripture in the Letter of Paul to the Colossians, BIS 96 [Leiden: Brill, 2008], 223).

107. So likewise 1 Kings 8:20, 24, 56. The promises in mind include the promise of possessing the land, being secure in it, and worshiping at the temple (Deut. 12:9–11), which was also prophesied to be built (Exod. 15:17–18).

not consummated. Subsequent history reveals this lack of consummation in that sin by both Solomon and Israel occurred, resulting not in elevation of conditions into a new creation where perfect righteousness dwells but rather in the deleterious consequences of the splintering of Israelite kingship and kingdom, destruction of the temple, and dismantling of the nation itself in exile. Also, both Moses's prophecy in Exod. 15:17–18 and God's promise in 2 Sam. 7:10–16 (an allusive development itself of the Exod. 15 passage) affirm that the kingdom and the temple will be established "forever,"[108] which did not happen with Solomon. Lack of complete fulfillment is indicated also by the conditional way that the fulfillment is expressed (1 Kings 2:4; 8:25; 9:1–9), as well as by the observation, as in Joshua, that left in Israel were some of the people remaining from the enemy nations, "whom the sons of Israel were unable to destroy utterly" (1 Kings 9:21). Thus, the purpose of emphasizing that God had fulfilled all the promises is to highlight that the beginning fulfillment of the promises had begun but not their consummation. This lack of consummation with Solomon means that he becomes a prototype of the true eschatological king who would come, who would achieve the greater escalated and consummated blessings of which Solomon fell short (cf. Matt. 12:42).

Demise and Corruption of Kingship in Israel (1 and 2 Kings)

First Kings 11 through 2 Kings (// roughly 2 Chron. 10–36) narrates the immediate demise of kingship in Israel. Solomon's sinful demise commences the narration in 1 Kings 11, though it probably begins in chapter 10 with the mention of proliferating silver and gold and of horses, which was contrary to the depiction of the ideal Israelite king in Deut. 17. Further deterioration directly occurs with the division of the monarchy of southern and northern Israel and the subsequent predominantly sinful behavior of the kings and often their consequent judgment. The righteous rule of kings during this period was the exception that proved the rule.[109]

Israel's Wisdom Literature in Relation to Kingship and New Creation

The so-called wisdom literature of the OT appears best to fit to varying degrees into the paradigm of Solomon as a kind of ideal wise and kingly

---

108. Sometimes the Hebrew word *'ôlām* connotes a long time or an "eternal" period. Although there is debate, the word in 2 Sam. 7:13, 16 best refers to an eternal epoch because of its links with the eschatological purposes of Eden that are developed with the patriarchs and because of the links with the eternal eschatological temple and kingdom later in the OT and the NT (see, e.g., Heb. 1:5; similarly Acts 2:30; 13:23), on which, see further Beale, *Temple*, 66–121.

109. E.g., Asa (1 Kings 15:11–15), Jehoshaphat (1 Kings 22:41–44), Hezekiah (2 Kings 18–20), and Josiah (2 Kings 22–23), who, in terms of righteousness, was greater even than Solomon.

Adam figure.[110] The majority of Proverbs is attributed to Solomon, enhancing his stature as the epitome of the wise human in the tradition of Adam. Others also wrote parts of Proverbs, and they express the notion that Israel itself should have functioned as a corporate wise Adam.

Song of Songs, also attributed to or for Solomon (Song 1:1; 3:7–11), fits nicely within a notion that the book pictures the ideal marriage relationship and unity that Adam and Eve should have had in their first garden as king and queen of the earth. Both the repeated hyperbolic garden imagery and specific allusions to Gen. 1–3 make this an attractive way to view the book. Examples of the latter in Song of Songs are "his [the husband's] desire is for me" in 7:10, which alludes to part of the curse in Gen. 3:16, where the wife's "desire shall be for your husband" (so also Gen. 4:7) and may be pictured as being reversed here; "the cool of the day" in 2:17; 4:6 (= Gen. 3:8); streams of water flowing from a garden on a hill or mountain in 4:15 (= Gen. 2:10 // Ezek. 28:13–14; 40:2; 47:1–12); the king's body portrayed as covered with precious stones, such as gold, beryl, and lapis lazuli in 5:14–15, which finds unique correspondence to the description of one other king in the OT, who is pictured as being in the garden of Eden (Ezek. 28:13), and who appears to be Adam, as Ezek. 28:14 in the LXX explicitly identifies the figure.[111] While the garden imagery for both the setting of the book and for the lovers themselves may merely be attributed to associating love with the fertility of springtime, as in other love genres of the ancient Near East, this imagery may also reflect the author's intention to draw connections with the love of the first primal married couple in the first garden.[112]

The book of Ecclesiastes reflects on the fragmented nature of an earthly reality, which sometimes thwarts the efforts of righteous people to fulfill their Adamic calling and rewards the sinful work of the ungodly, so that they prosper. This situation the book calls "vanity," which is a result of the fall (cf. 3:20; 12:7

110. See Christopher B. Ansberry, "Be Wise, My Son, and Make My Heart Glad: An Exploration of the Courtly Nature of Proverbs" (PhD diss., Wheaton College Graduate School, 2009). Ansberry argues that Proverbs is fundamentally a "courtly" document that addresses the Israelite king and the members of his royal court, especially highlighting that the king and other courtly leaders were to be the models of Torah life and the ideal representatives of Yahweh to the people. This fits well with my contention about Solomon being portrayed in Proverbs as an ideal wise and kingly figure.

111. On which, see the earlier note about Ezek. 28 under the subheading "Establishment of Kingship in Israel in Relation to Genesis 1–3 (1 and 2 Samuel and 1 Kings)." Although, Exod. 28:17–20; 39:10–13 mention precious stones on the high priest's breastpiece, which may suggest that the figure in Ezek. 28 is also a priestly figure.

112. On which, see further Dumbrell, *Faith of Israel*, 282–83; similarly, Albert H. Baylis, *From Creation to the Cross: Understanding the First Half of the Bible* (Grand Rapids: Zondervan, 1996), 265; Francis Landy, "The Song of Songs," in *The Literary Guide to the Bible*, ed. Robert Alter and Frank Kermode (London: Collins, 1987), 318; idem, *Paradoxes of Paradise: Identity and Difference in the Song of Songs*, BLS 7 (Sheffield: Almond, 1983), though many of the arguments for parallels are suggestive rather than fully convincing.

with Gen. 3:19). Although God had made humans "upright," because of their sinful devices vanity has been introduced into the world (cf. 7:29 with Gen. 1:27). Solomon is portrayed as the wisest man of his time and the greatest king, yet he concludes that even such kingly wisdom is ultimately vanity (1:16–18; 2:9–11). Thus, the fall has continued to thwart the efforts of human kings to fulfill the mandate to the first man in Eden. Nevertheless, the book affirms that work, food, and marriage are good gifts of God that can be enjoyed in the midst of life's futility (2:24–25; 5:18–20; 8:15–9:1; 9:9). Furthermore, there is the affirmation that God is sovereign over every event (whether good or bad from the human perspective), and the ultimate hope is expressed of reward for those fearing God and judgment for those who do not (3:1–18; 12:11–14).

Both Job and Ecclesiastes conduct a polemic against conventional wisdom about how the cosmos operates: contrary to the notion that suffering is always an indication of punishment for sin, God's sovereign plan can bring suffering for other reasons, such as to test the faithful and to vindicate God's own character by showing that the true saint will continue to trust God even when not receiving earthly blessings.[113] Both books also focus on wisdom as the knowledge of how the cosmos operates under God's providential guidance. In relation to this, Job is repeatedly asked whether he knows the inner workings of the cosmos in the way that God knows these matters, which highlights the inadequacy of human wisdom in contrast to God's (Job 36:24–42:6).

Generally, there is an absence of redemptive-historical themes in the wisdom literature (excluding Psalms), since it reflects on the harmonization of orders in the created structures, both inanimate and animate, that should be exhibited. To the best of their God-given ability, humans need to gain sufficient wisdom about these structures in order to live as harmoniously as possible within them.[114]

While the psalms are usually categorized as part of the wisdom literature, they are different because they speak repeatedly and often about God's specific salvation-historical deliverances and judgments in the history of Israel, as well as the future eschatological deliverance and judgment. The book of Psalms is divided into five smaller books (Pss. 1–41; 42–72; 73–89; 90–106; 107–150).[115] The main thematic emphases of the ending and the beginning of each book provides the primary clue to the main theme of each and, when seen together, of the entire Psalter.

The first observation is that most of these beginning and ending psalms deal with God's rule through Israel's kings. Psalms 1–2 are probably best

---

113. Dumbrell, *Faith of Israel*, 284–94.

114. Ibid., 253.

115. This fivefold division is not designated in the OT, but it is noted in the Jewish literature and by modern translations. At the least, the formal divisions are an interpretation seeking to illuminate the original literary divisions of Psalms. See C. Hassell Bullock, *Encountering the Book of Psalms: A Literary and Theological Introduction* (Grand Rapids: Baker Academic, 2001), 57–71, on which subsequent comments here on structure are based.

viewed as the introduction not only to the first few books but also to the entire Psalter. They focus on different topics, but there are parallels between them that reveal a discernible unity (the lack of a superscription before Ps. 2 may enhance this). While Ps. 1 speaks of the individual's relationship with God and Ps. 2 of God's redemptive-historical plan to install his "son" as king over the earth, both conclude by highlighting judgment of the individual (1:6b; 2:12). Table 2.4 shows linguistic parallels that are conceptual as well.

Table 2.4

Psalm 1	Psalm 2
1:1–2: "How blessed is the man [whose] . . . delight is in the law of the LORD."	2:12c: "How blessed are all who take refuge in Him."

Psalm 2 ends as Ps. 1 began, thus forming a nice literary inclusio as an overall introduction to the Psalter, focusing on the blessing of the godly. This inclusio is strengthened by another parallel: those who "stand in the path of sinners" (1:1b) will "perish" in this "way" (1:6b); this is reiterated in 2:12b: those angering the "son" will "perish in the way." Thus, both Ps. 1 and Ps. 2 also end the same way. Those who "walk in the counsel of the wicked" and "stand in the path of sinners" (1:1) will be identified with "the kings of the earth" who "take their stand, and . . . take counsel together against the LORD and against his Messiah" (2:2 [though different Hebrew words occur]). In contrast to the godly who meditate on God's law (1:2b), the ungodly meditate on a vain thing (2:1b). Whereas the righteous delight in being subject to God's law (1:2a), the impious rebel against the law, as if it were a shackle around their neck (2:3). The judged condition of the wicked is strikingly comparable: chaff (1:4) and shattered pottery (2:9b).

Not only does the climax of eschatological judgment bring Ps. 1 closer to Ps. 2, but also there are some intertextual references in Ps. 1 indicating that it appears to be tying the description of the individual Israelite saint to the redemptive-historical realities of the past and the future. Psalm 1:2–3 alludes to Josh. 1:8, where "meditating on" the law "day and night" will lead to being "prosperous," which is defined as gaining "possession of the land" that God "swore to their fathers to give them" (Josh. 1:6; see also 1:2, 11). According to the psalm, the same thing holds true for later generations of Israel. Also, the psalm's description of the meditative person being compared to a tree whose "leaf does not wither" is found elsewhere only in Ezek. 47:12. There, the nonwithering leaf is on trees in an expanded garden of Eden in a renewed creation, which are made fruitful by water flowing from the eschatological temple, a development of Ezek. 36:35 (see Ezek. 47:1–11, which itself is alluded to in Rev. 22:1–2). Perhaps not coincidentally, the description of Ezek. 47:12 is followed up directly by a description of Israel's "inheritance" in the land that God "swore to give . . . to your forefathers" (Ezek. 47:13–14 [see also 47:14–23]), virtually identical to the Josh. 1:6 phrase (that Ps. 2:8 also highlights the eschatological king's inheritance of the earth is, presumably, linked to these ideas). Finally, Jer. 17:7–8 alludes to Ps. 1:1–3 to describe the faithful person in contrast to sinners who will cause the nation to go into exile. These three intertextual connections[116] show that Ps. 1 is associated with Israel's possession of the land and new creation, both ideas stemming from Gen. 1:28 and its repetitions elsewhere in Genesis.

These literary links point further to Ps. 1's affinity with Ps. 2's focus on major redemptive-historical realities, especially the reign of Israel's eschatological king throughout the creation ("the ends of the earth") and judgment of the latter-day enemy. The introductory function of Pss. 1–2 indicates that this theme of eschatological kingship throughout all creation and judgment is going to be the heartbeat of the whole Psalter, and that the individual's behavior is inextricably linked to this cosmic theme. The fact that most of the psalms were written by King David (at least about eighty-four of them)[117] also underscores the kingship theme running throughout. Psalm 41 appropriately closes Book 1, since it is written by King David and is a prayer that he will triumph over his enemies (note the use of Ps. 41:9 in John 13:18 in application to Judas's betrayal of Jesus).

Psalm 42 begins Book 2 of the Psalter and continues the theme of Ps. 41, though it focuses more on the element of distress (again, likely experienced by David) due to oppression by the enemy. The conclusion of Book 2, Ps. 72, is attributed to King Solomon, one of the two psalms said to be written by (or for) him. The first part of the psalm appears to be a majestic description of Solomon's kingship, but some of the depictions go beyond anything that happened during his reign.[118] The allusions to Isa. 11:2–5 in verses 2, 4 also enhance the ideal or messianic nature of the royal figure in the psalm. Psalm 72 (vv. 8, 17, 19) also is one of the key OT passages observed above containing reiteration of the promise that eschatological Israel and its end-time king will finally succeed in fully accomplishing the Adamic commission first set out in Gen. 1:28:

> May he [the end-time king] also <u>rule</u> from sea to sea, and from the River to the ends of the earth. . . . <u>Let all nations be blessed in him; let all nations call him blessed</u> [allusion possibly to Gen. 12:2–3; 28:14; and esp. 22:18]. . . . And <u>may all the earth be filled</u> with His glory.

116. Both Ezek. 47:12 and Jer. 17 probably allude to Ps. 1:3, though it is possible that it is the psalm that alludes to them.

117. Bullock, *Book of Psalms*, 72.

118. E.g., note the worldwide extent of the rule (vv. 8–11) and its eternal duration (vv. 7, 17, 19), the latter a feature observed earlier with respect to why Solomon was not seen to have been the complete fulfillment of the prophecy of an eternal kingdom in 2 Sam. 7.

Striking also in Ps. 72 are the references to superabundant fertility (v. 16a), as well as portrayals of the righteous with metaphors of water causing flourishing vegetation (vv. 6, 16b), much like that in Ps. 1:3. Even reference to the eternal duration of the sun and moon (v. 5) may add to the notion of a renovated creation that cannot wear out. Thus, again, we have the themes of universal Adamic rule together with new-creational imagery. Important also to note is that the conclusion and goal of the psalm is that "all the earth be filled with His glory," a main goal also of Ps. 8, the clearest and most elaborate interpretative reflection on Gen. 1:26–28 in the entire OT. It recalls the implicit notion itself in Gen. 1:26–28 that the king and his seed were to be images of God, bearing his glorious image throughout creation. That this psalm concludes Book 2 again underscores for the Psalter the themes of kingship in a new creation.

Psalm 73, which begins Book 3 of the Psalter, has been difficult to place among the typical types of psalms. Perhaps it is best seen as an individual wisdom psalm (with concerns similar to those of Job and Ecclesiastes), since it addresses problems of justice in a world where the wicked appear to prosper and the righteous can suffer (vv. 2–16).[119] Yet, as in Job and Ecclesiastes, assurance is expressed that God will reward the faithful and judge the wicked (vv. 1, 17–28). This notion of ultimate justice may continue Ps. 72's theme of the justice that will be executed by the end-time ideal king of Israel (see 72:1–4, 7, 12–14). The individual perspective of Ps. 73 is like that of Ps. 1 and, again, reflects that the individual believers and their behavior are a part of larger patterns of redemptive-historical movements, such as final judgment and reward (vv. 24–27).

The observation that Ps. 89 concludes Book 3 further enhances the motif of kingship, not only in its parallelism with Ps. 72 (e.g., cf. 72:8 with 89:25; and 72:5, 7 with 89:36–37) forming an inclusio for Book 3,[120] but also in its forming a larger inclusio for Books 1–3 because of its parallelism with Ps. 2. Psalm 89 elaborates further on Ps. 2 and Ps. 72 in expressing hope in God's fulfillment of his promise to David that a descendant would rule on his throne forever (vv. 1–4, 19–37).[121] And, as in Ps. 72:5, the eternal duration of the king's monarchy is paralleled by the eternal duration of the creation within which that monarchy will exist (in 89:36–37 the sun's and the moon's existence is implied to be forever, since they are compared to the eternal establishment of the king's throne). The reference to the ideal king as "firstborn" (89:27) suggests

119. Bullock, *Book of Psalms*, 64.
120. It may be a problem that this inclusio technically is formed not by the first and last psalms of Book 3 but rather by the last psalm of Book 2 and the last psalm of Book 3, unless Ps. 73 is seen as a continuation of the themes of Ps. 72.
121. Note even the allusions to 2 Sam. 7 in Ps. 89:4, 22–24, 29–33 respectively to the eternal victorious aspects of rule and to the possibility that successive descendants will nevertheless be disobedient.

that he will be an Adam figure who represents Israel.[122] Psalm 89 concludes by expressing anxiety over lack of fulfillment of this promise and present defeat by enemies (vv. 38–48), yet still affirming trust that God will fulfill his promises (vv. 49–52). Once more, this psalm expresses that the hope for kingship is placed within the context of a renewed creation. This intimation is clarified by the NT, which later understands this reference to have its ultimate fulfillment in Christ as the resurrected, newborn Adamic king of the new creation; so Col. 1:15–18[123] and Rev. 1:5 with 3:14.[124]

Psalm 90, the beginning of Book 4, speaks of God's people corporately living apart from God's blessing (vv. 3–6) and under judgment (vv. 7–11), and it concludes with a hope that God will "return" to bless them (vv. 13–17). The conditions of the psalm reflect the cursed conditions of the first-generation Israelites, who did not reach the promised land (cf. Ps. 95:8–11), which likely was seen as applicable to the later generation of Israelites who went into exile, and even to the remnant who returned but without experiencing the blessings promised to occur with that return.

The conclusion to Book 4 in Ps. 106 continues the theme of Ps. 90: a later Israelite generation bewails that it is as sinful as the first generation (v. 6) and has suffered judgment like that initial generation. The description of the sin of the first generation and its judgment is expanded in more concreteness (vv. 7–33), as is that of the sin and judgment of the successive generations (vv. 34–43). Yet despite their sin, God would save them from oppression (vv. 10, 44–45), only to see Israel sin once more. Nevertheless, the present generation of the psalmist, which also experiences conditions of judgment, expresses hope that God will deliver it, presumably out of exile or from the oppressors of the remnant after return from exile (vv. 1–5, 47–48).

Psalm 107, the beginning of Book 5, is the answer to the cry and hope for deliverance from the judgment of exile expressed in Pss. 90 and 106. Psalm 107 presumably celebrates God's deliverance of the people of Israel from Babylonian exile (e.g., vv. 2–3, 6–7, 36). This deliverance has led them to "gather a fruitful harvest" (v. 37), and God "blesses" them and makes them "multiply greatly" (v. 38), an allusion to Gen. 1:28 and its repetitions.[125] This deliverance in connection to these Gen. 1 themes found later in Ps. 107 may be anticipated

---

122. Israel was sometimes called "firstborn" (see Exod. 4:22; Jer. 31:9), which later Judaism projected back onto Adam, who was the firstborn king of all creation. See further G. K. Beale, "Colossians," in *Commentary on the New Testament Use of the Old Testament*, ed. G. K. Beale and D. A. Carson (Grand Rapids: Baker Academic, 2007), 853–55.

123. For further elaboration, see ibid.

124. For further elaboration, see G. K. Beale, *The Book of Revelation: A Commentary on the Greek Text*, NIGTC (Grand Rapids: Eerdmans, 1999), 190–92, 297–301.

125. See Gen. 1:28 and the list of reiterated Gen. 1:28 references above, esp. Gen. 9:1, 6–7; 28:3–4; 48:3–4, all of which refer to "blessing," "multiplying," and producing "fruit"; cf. also Ps. 107:41b, where God "makes his [Israel's] families like a flock," with Jer. 23:2, one of the Gen. 1:28 reiterations.

in verse 3 of the psalm: the Israelites have been "gathered from the lands, from the east and from the west, from the north and from the south," which also alludes to Gen. 28:14–15: "You will spread out to the west and to the east and to the north and to the south. . . . I . . . will bring you [Jacob] back to this land." Thus, the deliverance from exile is viewed as an event placing Israel again in position to carry out the mandate to Adam to rule, multiply, and fill the earth, which he, Noah, the patriarchs, and subsequent Israelite generations had not fulfilled. Also leading up to the Gen. 1:28 allusion are new-creational conditions, in keeping with the renewal of the original mandate, which was to be carried out in a new creation: "He changes a wilderness into a pool of water, and a dry land into springs of water. . . . And [they] sow fields and plant vineyards, and gather a fruitful harvest" (Ps. 107:35, 37).[126] The link with new creation and abundant fertility together with the allusion to Gen. 1:28 and its later developments in Genesis fits with themes discerned in the inclusio markers of the earlier books of the Psalms, thus confirming that kingship, new creation, eschatological victory, and judgment in relation to fulfilling Gen. 1:28 is the major thematic tone of the Psalter.

The thematic transition between Ps. 89 and Pss. 90, 106, and 107 may seem abrupt. The focus on national, corporate sin in Pss. 90 and 106 and corporate restoration in Ps. 107 is not unrelated to the strands of individual kingship and new creation discussed in the previous psalms. The themes of kingship, new creation, final vindication, and judgment are various strands that are loosely related in that all of them can be tied back to Gen. 1:28 but are not necessarily always bound together or found to develop one from another. Nonetheless, it is strange that certain elements of this thematic web (e.g., kingship) seem to drop out of these later books of the Psalms.

The concluding psalm of Book 5 and of the whole Psalter, Ps. 150, is a repeated thirteenfold praise of God, concluding with an exhortation for all animate creation to praise God. It is the crescendo of four prior "praise" psalms, which call for every part of the creation to extol God (148:1–14) for (1) being the Creator (146:6) and (2) sustainer of creation (147:4, 8–9, 14–18), (3) who will reign forever (146:10) and (4) who executes justice (146:7, 9), (5) delivers his people from exile (146:8; 147:2–6), (6) restores them (147:12–14), and (7) gives them salvation, victory over their enemies, and the right to execute judgment upon them (149:1–9). Images of God as creator and providential sustainer of his creation are repeatedly interspersed with acclamations of his sovereign sustaining of his people through deliverance from exile and restoration and victory over the enemy (cf. Ps. 146:5–7; Pss. 147–148). The purpose of this interspersion is to indicate that if God is committed to preserve his creation, he certainly is committed to preserve the crown of his creation, his people

---

126. The language is very close to the new creation and new exodus expected by Isaiah (e.g., Isa. 35:6–7; 41:18; 65:21).

Israel, the corporate Adam. The fact that the establishment of creation is said to be "forever and ever" (Ps. 148:6), and that God's reign is to be "forever," suggests that he will rule in a renewed creation over his restored people.

All the themes of the earlier psalms are picked up in these concluding psalms, though there is no mention of an Israelite king figure. The observation that Ps. 145 is the last psalm "of David" may help us to understand this lack of mention of an individual king. In Ps. 145 David also "praises" God at both its beginning and ending (vv. 2, 21: "praise" God's "name forever and ever"), which actually appears to function as the transition to the final four psalms, which have a formal "praise" inclusio ("praise the LORD") at their first and last verses. David focuses not explicitly on what God has done through him as king but only on what God has done in general. He expresses this in general trans-temporal terms, especially with respect to God's goodness toward his creation (vv. 9–10, 15–16) and his wonderful acts in history on behalf of his people (vv. 1–8, 11–12a), particularly in delivering them (vv. 14, 18–20a) and judging their enemies (v. 20b), which will lead to God's eternal kingship (vv. 12b–13). Hence, particular identifiable historical acts have been generalized in order to take the focus off individual human deliverers and place it on God as the ultimate deliverer and preserver of his creation, the only one to whom praise is due.

Israel's Major Prophets in Relation to Kingship and New Creation

The major prophets (Isaiah, Jeremiah, and Ezekiel) focus on Israel's sin (especially idolatry), for which the nation is prophesied to go into captivity. The book of Lamentations laments the desolated condition of Jerusalem, which led to the exile of the majority of the land's inhabitants; this sorrow is mixed with prayers for God's mercy. Both Isa. 40–66 and Ezek. 36–48 predict Israel's deliverance from exile and restoration into a new creation, though these themes also occur earlier in these books.[127]

The most explicit hopes for new creation are expressed in these major prophets, especially the book of Isaiah. The return from exile is prophesied as an eschatological period when new-creational conditions will exist on the earth. The idea of end-time new creation is not anomalous within the book but rather is a natural part of a broader theme of new creation woven throughout chapters 40–66, the most explicit texts being 43:18–19; 65:17; 66:22. The text of 43:18–20 is but part of a series of pericopae in the so-called Book of Consolation (chaps. 40–55) that explain the restoration of exiled Israel as a new creation or at least integrally associates the two concepts of restoration and creation.[128]

127. E.g., Isa. 2; 4; 9; 11–12; 14; 24–27; 32:15–20; 35; Ezek. 11:16–19; 20:33–44; 28:25–26; 34:23–31; see also Jer. 29:10–14; 30:9–11, 18–24; 31:1–15, 21–40; 32:37–44; 33:6–26.
128. Isaiah 40:28–31; 41:17–20; 42:5–9; 44:21–23, 24–28; 45:1–8, 9–13, 18–20; 49:8–13; 51:1–3, 9–10, 11–12; 54:1–10 (cf. v. 5); 55:6–13; on which, see Carroll Stuhlmueller, *Creative Redemption*

This same thematic emphasis is continued in 57:15–19;[129] 60:15–22; 65:17–25; 66:19–24. The latter-day work of the Spirit is part of an introduction to two of these pericopae (42:1; 44:3), which continues an earlier theme of new creation by the Spirit in 32:15–18 (and possibly 30:23–28).[130] God's act of new creation as restoration is also described outside of chapter 43 as his "redemption" of Israel (e.g., 44:1–8; 44:24–45:7; 54:1–10)[131] and as a new exodus (see 40:3–11; 41:17–20; 44:24–28; 51:1–13; 52:7–10; also 43:16–21).[132] Some of the specific links between the "Spirit" and "fruit" in Isaiah, which are part of the theme of new creation, likely reflect the same original link at the first creation, where the "Spirit" (*pneuma* [Gen. 1:2 LXX]) was the agent of the creation, including the creation of fruit-bearing trees (*karpos* [Gen. 1:11–12, 29 LXX]).

Accordingly, Isa. 51:3 contains the promise that God will make Israel's land like "Eden . . . the garden of the LORD" (cf. Ezek. 36:35; 47:1–12; it is in this light that restored Israel's depiction of being "like a watered garden" is to be seen [Isa. 58:11; Jer. 31:12]). We saw earlier that Isaiah also closely links the restoration to development of Gen. 1:28 (Isa. 51:2–3; 54:2–3; so also Jer. 3:16; 23:3; Ezek. 36:10–12), sometimes in association specifically with promises of the restoration of Eden (Isa. 51:2–3; cf. Ezek. 36:10 with 36:8–9, 34–35). The main theme of Isa. 1–39 anticipates the last part of the book: holy Yahweh judges unholy humanity (including Israel) for the purpose of executing justice, purging a remnant (to go into exile and return), and reestablishing a Davidic kingdom.

Much more could be said about kingship and new creation, especially in Jeremiah and Ezekiel, but the limitations of the present project prevent further analysis.

Minor Prophets, Daniel, and Ezra–Nehemiah in Relation to Kingship and New Creation

Other preexilic prophets express overlapping themes of those found in Isaiah, Jeremiah, and Ezekiel. Hosea recounts Israel's sin and disloyalty to God, while affirming that God ultimately will remain faithful to the patriarchal

---

in Deutero-Isaiah, AnBib 43 (Rome: Biblical Institute Press, 1970), 66–98, 109–61, 193–208; Dumbrell, *End of the Beginning*, 97–100.

129. For elaboration of the concept of new creation inherent in this text, see G. K. Beale, "The Old Testament Background of Paul's Reference to the 'Fruit of the Spirit' in Gal. 5:22," *BBR* 15 (2005): 1–38.

130. Isaiah 30:27–28 LXX interprets the MT's apparent reference to God's "breath" (*rûaḥ*) to be God's Spirit, since it also interprets the MT's reference to "lips" and "tongue" as God's "word": "And his Spirit, as rushing water in a valley, will come [*hēxei*] as far as the neck, and be divided, to confound the nations for vain error." The MT of Isa. 30:27 also says that God "comes from a remote place" (i.e., high heavens). See also Isa. 26:18–19, though only resurrection and new creation are in mind.

131. Stuhlmueller, *Creative Redemption*, 112–34, 196–208.

132. Dumbrell, *End of the Beginning*, 15–18, 97; Stuhlmueller, *Creative Redemption*, 66–73, 82–94.

promises (e.g., 1:10), so that both northern and southern Israel will be restored in the future, which is pictured in new-creational language (2:14–23; 6:1–3; 14:4–8). Amos recounts the judgment of Israel's enemies and then predicts judgment on Israel too because it is no better. Only the last verses of the book give a ray of hope for Israel: its enemies will be conquered, the Davidic kingdom will be restored, and the nation itself will be restored to the land, which will be renewed as an idyllic garden (9:11–15). Micah sounds the same note as Amos, though with a bit less mention of the nations being judged and with added mention of them being redeemed (4:1–8; 5; 7). Zephaniah also intersperses judgment of Judah and the nations with restoration of Judah and the nations. Joel focuses on imminent judgment on Israel (1:1–2:17) and God's promise of subsequent blessing, as well as judgment of the nations (2:18–3:21). As also highlighted in the conclusion to Amos, Joel underscores that Israel's eschatological blessing will include a return to Edenic conditions (cf. 2:3 with 3:18–20). Obadiah stresses judgment on Edom and deliverance for Israel, and Nahum does the same thing respectively with Nineveh and Israel. Habakkuk prophesies only the imminent coming judgment on Judah by the Babylonians and urges trust in God in the face of such judgment. Although Jonah is hard to date, the book appears to have been written before the exile of northern or southern Israel. Jonah's main point is to assert that Israel had a prophetic mission to the nations to witness to God, and that at times, even when they disobeyed this commission, God caused Israel to carry this mission out anyway because of his compassion.

The exilic prophet Daniel draws attention to events of ancient world history more than any other OT book. While most of the first half of the book narrates episodes of Daniel and his friends persevering through the persecution of exile and finally prospering as loyal Israelites in a pagan society,[133] chapter 2 and the second half of the book (chaps. 7–12) predict the rise and demise of antagonistic world empires and Israel's restoration to the land and its final rule over the earth at the end of history. The two most famous prophecies of Israel's eschatological judgment of evil kingdoms and its world rule are Dan. 2 and 7, both of which make rich use of Gen. 1–2 allusions. The portrayal of Babylon in Dan. 2 makes allusion to Gen. 1:26–28[134] in order to set it up as the pseudocounterpart to Israel's end-time kingdom headed up by the Son of Man, who is portrayed as a latter-day Adam figure ("the son of Adam"), who is king over all the beasts and people of the earth (the figure is likely individual and corporate, an example of the "one and the many" notion in the OT). The image is an eschatological king who represents Israel. We saw earlier that Dan. 7:13–14 is one of the OT texts that develop Gen. 1:28, especially through allusion to

133. The book of Esther narrates virtually the same thing, though the persecution threatened is on a more explicit national scale.
134. On the Gen. 1 allusion in Dan. 2, see Beale, *Temple*, 144–45.

Gen. 22:18 (on which, see n. 134).[135] The Gen. 1 background is enhanced by observing that Dan. 7:2 ("the four winds of heaven were stirring up the great sea") echoes Gen. 1:2 ("the earth was formless and void, and . . . the Spirit [wind] of God was hovering over the surface of the waters"), thus expressing God's sovereignty over the rise and fall of world kingdoms narrated in the verses directly following.[136] The chaotic sea and the hybrid mutant animals arising from it convey a notion of "de-creation," which implies a move to an ordered new creation in the rule of the Son of Man (Dan. 7:13–14) and the saints (Dan. 7:18, 22, 27).[137] Psalm 8, another development of Gen. 1:26–28, may also lie in the background of Dan. 7 in the light of the following common themes: (1) the defeat or judgment of God's enemies; (2) the rule of the Son of Man; (3) the rule over sea creatures (the Targum of Ps. 8 identifies the sea creature as Leviathan); (4) the glory of the Son of Man; (5) allusion to Gen. 1:28 in Ps. 8 and Dan. 7:13–14.

Ezra narrates the initial stage of the rebuilding of the temple, and Nehemiah the beginning of the reconstruction of Jerusalem. The postexilic prophets speak to conditions after the exile and expectations for the future. Soon after the beginning efforts of temple rebuilding narrated in Ezra, Haggai exhorts the returnees to continue their efforts in the initial stages of rebuilding the temple and promises that God will be with them in the reconstruction. In addition, God promises to defeat all antagonistic nations of the earth. Therefore, it is clear that although Israel had returned from exile, all the promises about that return (e.g., a grander temple and complete defeat of Israel's enemies) had not yet been fulfilled. Zechariah 1–6, also written around the time of Haggai, likewise encourages the leadership to continue with the temple project and is a prophecy that God will build the temple through the leaders at some future point and that his tabernacling presence will emanate from the temple and cover Jerusalem and apparently even the whole land (on the latter point, see Zech. 14:20–21). Nevertheless, the disobedience of the returned exiles will prevent the promises of the temple from being realized in their time (Zech. 6:15–7:14). In addition to the likely expectation that the successful eschatological rebuilding of the temple will not occur in the present generation, Zechariah predicts that a time will still come when that rebuilding will definitively happen, along with a greater return of Israel from exile, Israel's repentance and salvation, the coming of a messianic leader (partly by allusion to Ps. 72:8 in Zech. 9:10), and the conversion of some among the nations, as well as the defeat of the enemy nations (Zech. 8; 9–14). At points throughout the book, the conditions of restoration are portrayed in terms of great fertility (Zech. 3:10; 8:12; 9:17; 14:4–11).

135. See also John E. Goldingay, *Daniel*, WBC 30 (Dallas: Word, 1989), 150, 190. Goldingay sees a link to Gen. 1–2.
136. See ibid., 160, 185.
137. On which, see Wilson, "Creation and New Creation," 200–203.

Malachi shows that despite God's mercy in choosing Israel over Edom (1:1–5), Israel's response to exhortations to faithfulness has been negative. The priests are presenting unclean sacrifices (1:6–14) and have broken their covenant as Levitical priests (2:1–13), just as many Israelite men (especially priests, apparently) had broken covenant with their wives (2:14–17). In response, God promises to "come to his temple" and purify it and the priests who serve in it (3:1–4). If Israel will repent of its many sins, God will bless the people again in the future (3:5–18). Judgment is coming, but the faithful will be spared (4:1–6).

Conclusion

The main strands of the biblical story traced above in the OT books are those of Israel (and its king) being commissioned to fulfill the Adamic commission to reign over a renewed earth but repeatedly failing to do so.[138] As a result of this failure, Israel suffers judgment and exile, and these patterns of renewal and failure become typological patterns of the true, final eschatological rule in a new creation that will inevitably come. Thus, promises of future restoration in a new creation continue to be reiterated in the OT narratives.

One significant aspect of the biblical narrative beginning also in Gen. 1–3 but not tracked as much in the preceding summary is that of God's glorious tabernacling presence with his priestly people in a sanctuary as the goal of God's redemptive work. We saw in the discussion of Gen. 1–3 that Adam was not only a king but also a priest in Eden, which was a primordial sanctuary. Functioning as a priest in the Eden temple was essential to carrying out the commission of Gen. 1:26–28. The Adamic commission often is combined with the notion of priestly service in a temple when it is repeated to Noah, the patriarchs, Israel, and in the promises to end-time Israel. This will be elaborated on in a following chapter on the role of the temple in biblical theology.

The Relation of the New-Creational Adamic Storyline to Past Proposals of the "Center" of the Old Testament

The foregoing proposal of the main storyline of the OT is that Israel (and its king) was commissioned to fulfill the Adamic commission to reign over a renewed earth but repeatedly failed to do so, consequently suffering judgment and exile. Nevertheless, a promise of future restoration in a renewed creation continued to be reiterated. How does this proposal relate to the work of past

---

138. For a broad thumbnail sketch of this theme but from somewhat different angles than traced in this chapter, see T. Desmond Alexander, *From Eden to the New Jerusalem: An Introduction to Biblical Theology* (Grand Rapids: Kregel, 2008), 74–89.

OT scholars who have proposed what they believe are different central themes of the OT?

A summary of the various "centers" has been given by others, so here the purpose is merely to summarize briefly the various past proposals and then relate them to the proposal of this book. The following are some of the prominent central ideas of the OT that have been offered: (1) God or God's presence; (2) Israel; (3) the relationship between God and Israel; (4) the law; (5) election; (6) promise; (7) covenant; (8) the kingdom or rule of God; (9) God's demand for exclusive worship; (10) the revelation of God's redemptive activity by his word, leading salvation history to its goal; (11) Israel's experience of God in history.[139]

One qualification needs to be made immediately. It is perhaps best not to speak of "centers" because, as we will see, such proposals tend to be reductionistic. This kind of suggested scheme for the OT has the same problems as similar proposals for the NT. A focus on a single theme can lead to overlooking other important notions, which sometimes can happen when systematic theological categories are appealed to. Some who are discontented with referring to centers nevertheless eventually end up positing their own center or essential principle. Instead, it is more fitting and suitable to the Bible as narrative and literature to talk of a "storyline" that is woven throughout the various genres of the OT (historical narrative, prophetic, poetic, wisdom, etc.), from which most other significant ideas are derived and are to be seen as subordinate and explanatory of parts of the storyline.[140]

Charles Scobie plausibly sees that many of these proposed centers can be summarized and combined into a multiperspectival approach to the OT in which the major themes of God's order, God's servant (leaders), God's people, and God's way (ethics) can be discussed, with each one having several subthemes, all of which is to be understood within the categories of proclamation (about what God has done in each of these four areas) and promise (about what God will do in each of these four areas).[141] Scobie thinks that to speak of a "storyline" is less encompassing than his above proposal, since he believes as traditionally stated such "salvation-historical storylines are concerned only about God and his people and not all peoples or the entire cosmos."[142] However, such things are indeed included in the storyline as I have tried to formulate it,

---

139. For a good though dated survey, see Gerhard F. Hasel, *Old Testament Theology: Basic Issues in the Current Debate* (Grand Rapids: Eerdmans, 1972), 49–63. For a more recent survey, see Charles H. H. Scobie, *The Ways of Our God: An Approach to Biblical Theology* (Grand Rapids: Eerdmans, 2003), 93–102, though some of these included "whole-Bible" proposals.

140. In this paragraph I have benefited from the discussion by Frank Thielman, *Theology of the New Testament: A Canonical and Synthetic Approach* (Grand Rapids: Zondervan, 2005), 230–33, with regard to the problem of proposed centers for Pauline theology.

141. Scobie, *Ways of Our God*, 90. Hasel (*Old Testament Theology*, 91) also takes a multiplex approach, though he does affirm that "God is the center of the Old Testament as its central subject."

142. Scobie, *Ways of Our God*, 90.

and Scobie's own view naturally can be expressed and incorporated into the form of the storyline that I proposed earlier: *The Old Testament is the story of God, who progressively reestablishes his new-creational kingdom out of chaos over a sinful people by his word and Spirit through promise, covenant, and redemption, resulting in worldwide commission to the faithful to advance this kingdom and judgment (defeat or exile) for the unfaithful, unto his glory.* Although there are numerous subplots, this dominating storyline appears to be the main one that is told throughout the OT; some of the themes suggested above serve as major OT ideas around which this basic plot and message can be organized.[143] Some might contend that this storyline is a canonically narratival center, but I think that it differs from the centers formerly suggested. It is best, then, to refer to this as an OT canonical "storyline" or "plotline."

One validation of the probability of this storyline over other proposed storylines or even suggested centers is its heuristic force: does it shed light on more of the data and difficulties of the OT than other suggested ones? Of course, the heuristic power of various proposals can be debated. I believe that the one just stated has more heuristic power than any other. It would take massive work to make a detailed comparison of my proposal with others (including other proposed centers) with regard to their heuristic effect. This suggested storyline, I contend, is neither too broad to be useful nor too narrow to be exclusive of other important but subordinate ideas, though, of course, readers will judge this for themselves.[144] I will be content if readers merely see the viability of my proposed storyline and find it useful as a lens for better understanding the OT. At the end of the day, it is best to see my proposed storyline not as a center of the OT but rather as the primary strand of the biblical storyline thread, around which other minor or thinner narratival and conceptual strands are woven and are held together. Thus, the other storyline threads (which some might call "centers") are not competing but complementary, and some may perhaps be almost as thick as the primary strand for which I am contending.

But it is difficult to talk about a "center" or "centers" of the OT or, my preference, a "storyline" without including consideration of that of the NT. For, on the assumption of the validity of a Protestant canonical database for doing biblical theology, the consideration of the OT must include its completion in the NT.[145] And to this we turn in the next few chapters on the significance of the conceptual role of "latter-day" language in Scripture. There, I will also attempt to address in more detail the validity of searching for a storyline in Scripture and whether this is all that different from searching for a center of the Bible.

143. For this formulation of storyline, I have found helpful the methodological discussion by Brian S. Rosner, "Biblical Theology," *NDBT* 9.
144. On this way of describing one of the criteria for validity, see Thielman, *Theology of the New Testament*, 232.
145. In line with Hasel, *Old Testament Theology*, 62–63.

3

The Eschatological Storyline of the Old Testament

The Old Testament Focus on the Latter Days

The preceding chapter attempted to trace the major themes of Gen. 1–3 throughout the OT, especially kingship in an inaugurated renewed creation that pointed to a consummated creation. The themes explored were essentially of an eschatological nature. That is, Adam was established as a priest-king in a pristine creation, but his kingship and the creation itself did not reach their destined goal of victory over evil and ultimate security against sin, against corruption of the body, and against corruption of the creation itself. This goal was eschatological in nature, since it is apparent that the eternal state would have commenced for Adam and creation once this objective was reached, and final judgment would have been pronounced and executed upon the primordial antagonist. Thus, in Eden there was the commencement of the first sinless world order that was yet incomplete and still needed consummation. In the preceding chapter I referred a few times to the notion that Adam's goal as a priest-king was to rule in a consummated eschatological creation in which the blessings of Eden would reach a final escalation. So here I want to reflect a bit more on the meaning of eschatology as it relates to Adam's goal.

In that Adam's establishment in the Eden temple as a priest-king reflecting God's glory was the beginning of the first created order, may we not say that it was also the very beginning of a process that was never eschatologically completed? Genesis 1–2 represented a condition of creation that was subeschatological or even contained within it the seed that would sprout eschatologically. Thus, in Eden there was a beginning establishment of a priest-king in a sinless world order who was to be faithful and obedient to God *until that first creation was consummated.* On the one hand, the beginning of the first creation untainted by sin would be the inception of a process to be eschatologically completed through final glorification in incorruptibility. On the other hand, eschatology after Eden and the sin of humanity was to be redemptive eschatology consisting of both restoration from sin and consummation.[1] In this respect, the beginning of restoration from sin often is portrayed later as a restoration of Eden and a beginning new creation, which becomes an eschatological notion, as in, for example, Isa. 65:17; 66:22, as well as in Rev. 21:1–22:5. This restoration of Eden is not merely a return of the conditions of the prefall state but rather is the inauguration of the escalated and eternally consummated conditions of incorruptibility. The same phenomenon can be observed in Jewish apocalyptic literature and in the NT.[2] Looking at Gen. 1–2 in light of this later biblical notion of beginning new creation and its consummation allows one to perceive in the first two chapters of Genesis that consummative eschatology was a goal to be achieved by Adam. In this respect, we may say that eschatology originally preceded soteriology, but with the fall, eschatology is now restoration from sin followed by a consummation of an eternal new creation.

While it is not preferable to refer to prefall Eden as "semieschatological" or as an "inaugurated eschatological" condition, it is a condition that is to be brought to eschatological completion by God escalating the conditions and blessings of the prefall state into a permanent, indestructible creation. Thus, the original beatitude of Adam and Eve in Eden before sin contained "eschatological potential"[3] or an "increased earnest of [eschatological] fullness"[4] that was designed to be realized by permanently confirming them in their condition of blessedness.[5] In particular, the image of God in which Adam and Eve were created contained an eschatological latency that was to be actualized.[6] Their beginning life, while sinless though still capable of sin, was to be confirmed in eternal life.[7] Adam's initial, original kingship and beginning reflection of God's glory were to experience an "eschatological advance in kingdom glory."[8] The same may be said of the environment of

---

1. Here I follow Geerhardus Vos, *The Eschatology of the Old Testament* (Phillipsburg, NJ: P&R, 2001), 74–75.

2. On which, see the section on Revelation 21 in chap. 19.

3. So Meredith G. Kline, *Kingdom Prologue: Genesis Foundations for a Covenantal Worldview* (Overland Park, KS: Two Age Press, 2000), 113.

4. Ibid., 111 (the bracketed wording is mine).

5. Ibid., 104.

6. Ibid., 101; see also 96, 98, 111.

7. Ibid., 114.

8. Ibid., 104.

Eden and the earth before the onset of disobedience. The goal of the original Eden and Adam and Eve's covenantal order therein was that its beatitude was to be eschatologically perfected in greater blessedness.[9] The various features of this eschatologial consummation have already been delineated in the first part of the preceding chapter.

This is to say that protology presupposes an eschatology, that a beginning implies an end.[10] Because of their unfaithfulness, Adam and Eve never reached the end. In subsequent Scripture we will see that the return and beginning escalation of the prefall Eden indeed can legitimately be called "inaugurated eschatology," and the final completion of that condition is consummated eschatology, when the old creation is destroyed and the new eternally established. From this retrospective vantage point, the original state of Adam and Eden becomes a prototype of the escalated conditions of new creation that appear to be introduced at repeated points in certain subsequent historical accounts in the OT era.[11] These apparent inaugurated eschatological episodes do not materialize in a consummated end-time state, and they themselves then come to be seen as eschatological prototypes by later OT writers. As I will argue later, at Christ's first coming there is an inaugurated end-time state that will effectually be culminated at his final advent into a permanently glorious new-creational kingdom. Accordingly, Adam's failure in Eden and the other OT patterns of new-creational start-ups and failures become typological foreshadowings of what finally is successfully accomplished in Christ (see, e.g., Rom. 5:14; 1 Cor. 15:45).

The question about the viability of the foregoing description of Eden is whether there can be discerned in Gen. 1–3 a process leading to an eschatological culmination or escalation of conditions, or whether Adam and Eve would have merely continued to live in the very same conditions eternally if they had remained faithful. I have argued that the former is most probable.[12]

Some define eschatology narrowly as "the end of this world's time . . . a consummation of the historical process in events which lie beyond the scope of the world's history."[13] As we will see, most definitions of OT eschatology focus on conditions that have significant and decisively irreversible discontinuities with the prior sinful course of history, where there will be radically transformed people (forgiven and newly created), society (restored Israel and

9. Ibid., 101.
10. See Walther Eichrodt, *Theology of the Old Testament*, trans. J. A. Baker, 2 vols., OTL (Philadelphia: Westminster, 1961–67), 2:110. Eichrodt says that the commission "be fruitful and multiply" in Gen. 1:28 "subordinates Man to the mighty teleological world movement," and that possibly even "$b^e r\bar{e}'\check{s}\bar{\imath}t$, in the beginning" already conveys the notion of "distant goal of the world process, the '$ah^a r\hat{\imath}t$ $hayy\bar{a}m\bar{\imath}m$, the end of days."
11. On these repeated episodes, see table 2.2 in chap. 2.
12. On which, see the initial section of chap. 2 on Gen. 1–3.
13. Gerhard von Rad, *Old Testament Theology*, trans. D. M. G. Stalker, 2 vols., OTL (New York: Harper, 1962–65), 2:114. Von Rad cites some who hold this position.

nations led by a messianic figure and centered in Zion), and nature (renewed creation).[14] This is a helpful definition, but it means that eschatology is only about future conditions, whereas I have suggested the possibility that there may be in the OT itself a temporary sense of inaugurated eschatology or semieschatological conditions that can exist prior to their consummated, future form. While I think this is the case, such apparent eschatological conditions never eventuate into true, decisively irreversible conditions until the first coming of Christ.

Accordingly, I made an effort in the preceding chapter to show how this apparent "already and not yet" end-time idea was developed at points throughout the OT. For example, the major episodes of OT history were seen to be reiterations, to varying significant degrees, of the pattern of beginning kingship in a beginning new creation. Thus, these subsequent episodes in the OT represent events that have the appearance of commencing an end-time process that is never completed. In the postfall sinful cosmos, in contrast to prefall Eden, it seems more understandable that the beginning process of restoration from sin would be charged with notions of a commencement toward an eschatological consummation. This is the case, as we saw in the preceding chapter, with Isaiah's prophecy of new creation, which is portrayed as a part of Israel's return from exile (though Isaiah portrays it as an apparently single event and not an extended new-creational process).[15] We will see below that prophecies of Israel's restoration from exile are said explicitly to take place "in the latter days" (Deut. 4:30; 31:29; Hos. 3:5; and possibly Jer. 23:20; 30:24, the latter especially in light of 31:1–40).

Nevertheless, the definition of eschatology as that of a later period with significant irreversible discontinuities with an earlier period would fit my definition of primeval eschatology in Eden. Even though the preconsummate stage in Eden was without the contamination of sin, it was to reach a completed and irreversible stage that was significantly different because of the following escalated conditions, which were elaborated in the first part of the preceding chapter:

1. victory over evil;
2. ultimate security against committing sin;
3. protection from corruption of the body;
4. protection from corruption of the creation;
5. as I will argue later, even marriage itself was to be transcended, since it likely was a foreshadowing of the unity humanity was to have with God in the eternal state.[16]

14. See, e.g., Donald E. Gowan, *Eschatology in the Old Testament* (Philadelphia: Fortress, 1986).
15. On which, see chap. 16 below on new creation and reconciliation.
16. On which, see chap. 26 below on new creation and marriage.

Other OT episodes subsequent to Eden also appear to be reinstating the conditions of Eden and marching toward a final consummation, but they never reach it. Such potential but failed eschatological-like narratives come to be seen by subsequent OT narrators and the NT as patterns foreshadowing the eschaton that will indeed finally come to pass at some future point.

This chapter also looks at key aspects of eschatology in the OT, though the focus is on end-time expectations of the future, especially as these are expressed through the phrase "latter days" and its various synonyms. As in the prior chapter, there is no intent to be exhaustive; rather, I examine only those expressions that are overtly eschatological. This means that OT passages containing end-time *concepts* but without the precise language are not surveyed here.[17] The purpose in this and the following two chapters is to look at the explicit "latter-day" language in order to see how that language is alluded to and developed in Judaism and in the NT. We will see that there are intertextual relationships between the wording of these expressions within the OT itself. Although the survey in this chapter is selective and limited, we will see that analysis of texts with the explicit language of the eschaton addresses virtually all the future promises of the OT that are expressed conceptually elsewhere but without the technical eschatological terminology.

The relevant passages are surveyed in the order that they would have been perceived to have been written from the standpoint of the NT writers, since that is the ultimate perspective of concern in this book.

The Latter Days in the Old Testament

Genesis 49:1

The first place an explicit expression of "latter days" occurs is in Gen. 49:1, where Jacob's prophecy about the destiny of his twelve sons and their descendants is introduced by him saying, "Assemble yourselves that I may tell you what will befall you in the latter days [*bĕ'aḥărît hayyāmîm*]." Much of what he predicts does not appear to be explicitly eschatological but merely descriptive of the future of the tribes of Israel. The prophetic pronouncements may be fulfilled at various stages of the history of the twelve tribes within the OT epoch itself. Because of this observation, translations render the last phrase as "in the days to come," and, accordingly, some scholars conclude that it indicates only the indefinite future and has nothing to do with any explicit notion of eschatology.[18]

---

17. E.g., we could survey the many eschatological references to "day" in the prophets (usually referring to a time of judgment), but the present survey of more explicit eschatological language will be sufficient to cover the basic range of eschatological concepts found in the OT, though various subcategories within this range will not be elaborated.

18. Along these lines, see G. W. Buchanan, "Eschatology and the 'End of Days,'" *JNES* 20 (1961): 188–93, esp. 189; J. P. M. Van Der Ploeg, "Eschatology in the Old Testament," in *The*

I have argued that Gen. 1–3 already contains an expectation of consummate eschatological notions, even though technical eschatological expressions do not occur there. The same may be the case in Gen. 49, though there an explicit eschatological expression does occur.

But the storyline of Genesis and Exodus needs to be remembered at this point in order to have a full contextual sense of what "latter days" means: (1) Adam and Eve before their sin were part of an original sinless creation in Eden that was designed to "end" in a consummated eternal and glorified state of new creation; (2) Noah was a second Adam, emerging out of the chaotic flood, who was given the same commission as the first Adam in a beginning renewed creation that was designed to "end" in a consummated eternal and glorified condition of new creation; (3) Israel was designed to be a corporate Adam, emerging out of the plague chaos of Egypt and in a beginning new creation of the exodus, taking residence again in another garden of Eden (the promised land) and obeying the mandate that the first Adam should have obeyed and finally achieving complete eternal rest in a glorified new creation.[19] Thus, Genesis and Exodus portray history as a repeated cycle of new-creational commencements that never reach their designed eschatological goal of irreversibly completed and incorruptible new-creational conditions. Hence, the first creation is a process that is designed to "end" with the successful obedience of that figure, who receives the reward of living in a glorified and incorruptible state of new creation.

Genesis 49 is to be viewed within the framework of these cyclical eschatological-like movements, in particular as the first extended prophecy of the third cycle (after the Adamic and Noahic cycles) involving the nation Israel. Although parts of Jacob's discourse are opaque and, at the same time, positive (e.g., vv. 13, 19–21, 27), it is apparent that he prophetically narrates how some of his sons and their seed would fail in carrying out this mandate. An inference from the wider narrative context is that all the tribes of Israel, except for Judah, that fail in doing their corporate part in following the original mandate likely fail to some degree in the way that Adam did. This suggests that up to the point of their failure they were involved in an apparent process of restorative new

---

Witness of Tradition: Papers Read at the Joint British-Dutch Old Testament Conference Held at Woudschoten, 1970, ed. A. S. Van Der Woude, OtSt 17 (Leiden: Brill, 1972), 89–99; A. D. H. Mayes, *Deuteronomy*, NCB (Grand Rapids: Eerdmans, 1979), 156–57. S. R. Driver similarly but more generally describes the use of the expression to denote "the final period of the future so far as it falls within the range of the speaker's perspective," so that context defines the use in each case (*A Critical and Exegetical Commentary on Deuteronomy*, ICC [1895; repr., Edinburgh: T&T Clark, 1996], 74).

19. Both directly preceding Noah's exit from the ark and Israel's exit from Egypt there are "chaos" conditions intentionally comparable to the initial chaos of Gen. 1:2. For example, each plague of Egypt is a corresponding antithesis of something that was created in Gen. 1, so that the chaos is a condition of de-creation (on which, see chap. 2 under the heading "The Repeated Cosmic Judgment and New Creation Episodes of the Old Testament").

creation and rule that was designed to culminate in a successful eschatological climax.[20] However, this process of restoration then ceases when corporate sin and judgment occur, though even the stage of judgment[21] anticipates a final climactic judgment at the very end of history.[22]

One of Jacob's descendants, however, clearly will carry out this mandate to extend the divine kingdom over the earth. In Gen. 49 Judah is prophesied to be victor over all his enemies (vv. 8a, 11–12)[23] and to be the leading tribe in Israel (v. 8b). He will be mighty as a lion (v. 9) and will rule *until all the nations become obedient* to him (v. 10). This is not some mere victory in a few local battles in Canaan but rather decisive and ultimate victory over all possible enemies of Israel. That this is not merely about subduing all the nations living in Canaan but probably is an ultimately universal reference is apparent when we recall that Israel was to be a corporate Adam fulfilling the universal earthly mandate in Gen. 1:28.

Therefore, this indicates a climactic and irreversible point in history and thus represents an eschatological zenith of Jacob's prophecy.[24] According to Gen. 49, this prophesied king from Judah will lead the entire nation in finally doing what Adam should have done (vv. 9–10), especially in defeating the satanic eschatological enemy,[25] and being rewarded with living in climactic conditions of a renewed creation (vv. 11–12). This is the "final" point of history toward which Jacob's prophecy focuses. Descriptions of the destiny of the other tribes may have appeared telescoped or condensed from Jacob's perspective, so that they could have been seen as events happening directly before and leading up

20. E.g., see this with respect to the prophecies especially about Zebulon, Gad, Asher, and Joseph, though these prophecies are still ambiguous.

21. The vague reference to the judgment of Simeon and Levi could be "thick" enough to include the final end-time judgment of Israel as a nation, which Matt. 23:29–39 narrates as occurring in the generation that was accountable for putting Jesus to death.

22. In this respect, Adam's judgment, the Genesis flood, and Israel's judgment are applied analogically, and probably typologically, by the NT to prophecies of the final judgment. See, e.g., for Adam's judgment, the "hiding" of Rev. 6:16b as an allusion to Gen. 3:8; for the Genesis flood, Matt. 24:35–39; 2 Pet. 3:5–7; see also Rev. 17:16 as an allusion to Israel's judgment by way of allusion to Ezek. 16:39; 23:29.

23. Genesis 49:11–12 appears also to express the fruitfulness in the sphere of a peaceful renewed creation ruled over by Judah's end-time king (see similar imagery in 49:22, 25–26). Isaiah 63:1–3 alludes to Gen. 49:11c–d and views it as imagery of God as a warrior defeating the enemy nations (on which, see further G. K. Beale, *The Book of Revelation: A Commentary on the Greek Text*, NIGTC [Grand Rapids: Eerdmans, 1999], 958–60).

24. John Walton notes that the phrase usually translated "until" in the third line of Gen. 49:10 is not the usual expression for "until" (which is *ʿad*) but rather is wording (*ʿad kî*) that connotes a climax and could be rendered "at last Shiloh will come" (*Genesis*, NIVAC [Grand Rapids: Zondervan], 714–15); so likewise Vos, *Eschatology of the Old Testament*, 92, 103.

25. The phrase in Gen. 4:7, contextually applied to Cain in his defeat by evil, ". . . be lifted up . . . Sin is crouching [*rābaṣ*] at the door, and its desire is for you, but you must rule over it," appears to be reapplied in 49:9 to Judah's king (". . . you have gone up. He couches, he lies down [*rābaṣ*] as a lion, and as a lion who dares rouse him up?"), who conquers all opposition in 49:8–12.

to and, therefore, linked with that of the climactic end-time rule of Judah. In this respect, the other tribes find their ultimate eschatological destiny in Judah: "Judah, your brothers shall praise you. . . . Your father's sons shall bow down to you" (v. 8). This may be illustrated by the apparently negative prophecy about Dan's future sin ("Dan shall be a serpent in the way . . . that bites"), which concludes with "For your salvation I wait, O LORD" (vv. 17–18). The end-time "waiting" appears to refer to the expectation about the tribe of Judah's ultimate victory (vv. 9–12). Thus, at least, in that the other eleven tribes will find their final end-time success bound up with that of Judah, the initial reference to "the latter days" refers to all the tribes.

This climax of history fits the definition of eschatology proposed above in that conditions are reached that have significant discontinuity with the preceding era, and such conditions appear to be irreversible: whereas Israel was beset by opposition from enemy nations during most of its history, Gen. 49:8–12 pictures a period in which Judah will defeat all enemies and bring about their "obedience." In this sense, all the prophesied events of Gen. 49 would roughly fit the pattern of the Gen. 1–3 perspective, where a process occurs with both a beginning and an intended eschatological culmination. Although many cite Brown, Driver, and Briggs's definition of "in the end of days" in support of a reference to a mere "indefinite non-eschatological future" in Gen. 49:1, this definition could fit well within the contours of the approach here: "a prophetic phrase denoting the final period of the history so far as the speaker's perspective reaches; the sense thus varies with the context, but it often = the ideal or Messianic future."[26] Similarly, Driver adds elsewhere that the phrase denotes "the final period of the future so far as it falls within the range of the speaker's perspective," so that context defines the use in each case.[27] These two definitions admirably fit within the present perspective because they can easily be viewed to describe well ancient prophecies of various aspects of the eschaton at an early stage of redemptive history and progressive revelation, though Brown, Driver, and Briggs unlikely perceived their comments within such a more explicit biblical-theological framework.

Accordingly, Jacob's prophecy is similar, in a sense, to inhabitants of another planet in a spaceship some distance from the earth. They can see with the naked eye the earth and its various shades of white, blue, green, and brown (representing clouds, bodies of water, and land masses). They radio back to their home planet and describe what they see from this distance. It does not appear to the naked eye that there is much distance between the spacecraft and the final destination of earth, only empty space and a few other planets and stars stand between them. When their spaceship approaches closer to the earth, however, the stars and planets are better recognized as actually far

26. BDB 31a.
27. Driver, *Deuteronomy*, 74, for virtually the same definition.

from earth after all. Then when their spacecraft reaches earth and begins to descend into the atmosphere over, say, New York City, they are able to make out the rivers, forests, valleys, and particularly the city, buildings, houses, streets, cars, and people. Both the distant and the close-up views are "literal." The close-up picture reveals details that someone with only a distant view could not have seen. The close-up view even offers what looks like a different reality from the one seen from the distant vantage point. Nevertheless, both are literal depictions of what is actually there. Jacob's focus on the distant, prophetic climactic destination of Judah's reign is compacted together with other events involving other tribes that appear to him perhaps close to and leading directly up to the historical end-time climax, but as redemptive-historical revelation develops, these other events take place long before the zenith point in Judah is reached (just as the planets and stars are finally seen to be farther from earth than formerly perceived).

The picture of Jacob's prophecy depicts events that are moving toward a final, historical consummation, and this may be one reason that even they can be included, together with the Judah prophecy, under the rubric of what will happen "in the latter days." Jacob's prophetic portrait is magnified by the various intertextual developments of it by subsequent OT writers in later times (which we will see presently below), which enlarges the details of the initial "thick" prophetic portrait of what "will befall" the tribes of Israel "in the latter days" (Gen. 49:1). Jacob's vantage point becomes sharpened and the details clarified, indeed, magnified. As we will soon see, NT revelation further clarifies and magnifies the OT portrait of the Judah prophecy and how it was specifically fulfilled in Christ[28] (which is comparable to the space travelers seeing the full clarity of New York City). It is for this reason that Jacob can refer to the entire vision as pertaining to events to take place "in the latter days." In fact, not only do parts of Jacob's prophecy begin end-time fulfillment in the "lion of Judah" in the NT, but also already in the OT the destinies of some of Israel's tribes are referred to as occurring "in the latter days," as we will soon see in this very chapter. Thus, the actual plural form of "latter days" may refer to some degree to an extended eschatological period composed of several events, whereas the singular "end" or "last" refers more to the definitive end (e.g., see Job 19:25; Isa. 46:10), a distinction that we will find also in the NT use of the two phrases (though there are exceptions to the pattern in both Testaments).[29]

Another end-time aspect of Jacob's prophecy concerns Joseph, though it is more vague than the prediction about Judah. With new-creational imagery

28. Bruce K. Waltke sees the expression "the latter days" of Gen. 49:1 as having a "thickness" of expression that "embraces the entire history of Israel from the conquest and distribution of the land to the consummate reign of Jesus Christ" (*Genesis* [Grand Rapids: Zondervan, 2001], 605). See similarly, Allen P. Ross, *Creation and Blessing: A Guide to the Study and Exposition of the Book of Genesis* (Grand Rapids: Baker Academic, 1988), 700.
29. See, e.g., Dan. 12:13.

that likely derives from reflections on Gen. 1:28 and the garden of Eden in Gen. 2, the career of Joseph and the destiny of his descendants are described in Gen. 49:22, 25–26:

> Joseph is a fruitful bough,
> A fruitful bough by a spring;
> Its branches run over a wall. . . .
> From the God of your father who helps you,
> And by the Almighty who blesses you
> With blessings of heaven above,
> Blessings of the deep that lies beneath,
> Blessings of the breasts and of the womb.
> The blessings of your father
> Have surpassed the blessings of my ancestors
> Up to the utmost bound of the everlasting hills;
> May they be on the head of Joseph,
> And on the crown of the head of the one distinguished among his
> brothers.

Joseph's portrayal as a "fruitful bough by a spring" echoes the trees bearing fruit in Eden that were watered by the source in the midst of the garden. The fecundity of the first garden is applied to the fruitfulness and prosperity of Joseph and his children (a precursor of Ps. 1:3). The sixfold blessing pronounced on Joseph in verses 25–26 affirms that both literal fecundity of the womb and general prosperity are in mind, which also seems to be a development of the initial blessing of Gen. 1:28:[30]

> God blessed them; and God said to them, "Be fruitful and multiply, and fill the earth, and subdue it; and rule over the fish of the sea and over the birds of the sky and over every living thing that moves on the earth."

The double use of the participial form of "bear fruit" (pārâ) in verse 22[31] followed by the repeated mention of "blessing" in verses 25–26 also reflects the close placement of "bless" and "bear fruit" in Gen. 1:28. There is even evocation of "filling the earth" prosperously in the mention that "the blessings of your father [Jacob's blessing on Joseph] have surpassed the blessings of my [Jacob's] ancestors [beginning with Adam] up to the utmost bound of the everlasting hills." Although Adam had failed to possess full end-time blessings, Joseph received them at some point in the future. Although an end-time

---

30. So also Waltke, *Genesis*, 614.

31. Though see Victor P. Hamilton, *The Book of Genesis: Chapters 18–50*, NICOT (Grand Rapids: Eerdmans, 1995), 678–79, 683. Hamilton understands the Hebrew word that many see behind "fruit" to be *pere'*, "wild donkey." His full discussion is, I think, plausible though unpersuasive.

climax is not as clear here as in the Judah prophecy, the Joseph prophecy may overlap with its fulfillment in conjunction with the Judah prophecy because it is so saturated with new-creational motifs related also to Joseph's descendants that a culminating eschatological notion of a renewed creation is likely elicited. Furthermore, the reference to "surpassing the blessings . . . up to the utmost bound of the everlasting hills" may suggest not some figuratively vague future condition but rather a zenith point of blessings beyond which no more blessing can be given and that will not be reversible.

Consequently, the expression *bě'aḥărît hayyāmîm* in Gen. 49:1 is to be rendered "in the latter days," referring to Israel's movement in eventually fulfilling what Adam was commanded to do[32] in a renewed and eschatologically consummated Eden (*Tg. Neof.* Gen. 49:1 adds that the latter days about which Jacob was prophesying included "what the happiness of Eden is"; so also *Tg. Ps.-J.* Gen. 49:1). This history will be marked with some of the tribes participating in unsuccessful small-scale attempts to fulfill the Adamic commission, which do not reach eschatological completion until the ruler "comes to whom it [the kingdom] belongs,[33] and to him will be the obedience of the peoples" (Gen. 49:10c–d [my translation]).[34] In this respect, the destiny of the other Israelite tribes that fail in fulfilling their Adamic mandate continues to leave open the necessity for fulfilling it and thus comes to point forward typologically to that eschatological time when it will finally be carried out. Thus, "the latter days" refers not to the future in general but rather to the final outcome of future events, involving all of Israel's tribes, which dovetails in Judah.[35]

32. See C. F. Keil and F. Delitzsch, *The Pentateuch*, vol. 1 of *Biblical Commentary on the Old Testament* (repr., Grand Rapids: Eerdmans, 1971), 387. They take a similar approach and view the concept of eschatology in Gen. 49:1–27 as referring to the "future as bringing the work of God to its ultimate completion, though modified by the particular age to which the work of God had advanced in any particular age." See similarly Waltke, *Genesis*, 605; likewise H. C. Leupold, *Exposition of Genesis*, 2 vols. (Grand Rapids: Baker Academic, 1942), 2:1167.

33. This is in line with the paraphrastic rendering of Qumran (4Q252 V:1–5) and with the way the LXX reads the Hebrew ("until there come the things stored up for him").

34. Genesis 49:10c, one of the longest-debated Hebrew phrases in Genesis, may also be translated "until tribute comes to him" or "until Shiloh comes" or, less probably, "until he comes to Shiloh" (for discussion of the options, see Hamilton, *Genesis*, 658–61; Walton, *Genesis*, 714–16). For a discussion of the various interpretations, see Vos, *Eschatology of the Old Testament*, 89–104. Vos takes it as an eschatological messianic prophecy, in line with my conclusion, as does also, e.g., Waltke (*Genesis*, 609) and Ross (*Creation and Blessing*, 703–4). All three commentators also favor the translation "he comes to whom it belongs," though, as seen just above, there are other translation options that would not exclude an ultimate eschatological messianic interpretation. Any of these translations, in this context, would express the coming of a kingly figure to rule. The LXX viewed Gen. 49:10d to be messianic: "he is the expectation of the nations." As we saw above, *Tg. Onq.* Gen. 49:9–11 applies the text to the end-time Messiah and his universal rule.

35. So also Geerhardus Vos, *The Pauline Eschatology* (1930; repr., Grand Rapids: Baker Academic, 1979), 2–3. See H. Seebass, "אַחֲרִית," *TDOT* 1:211; his same conclusion about the phrase in Dan. 2:28 has influenced the conclusion here.

We will see below that the earliest interpretation of Gen. 49:10, Num. 24:14–19, understands it to be an eschatological event in which an Israelite king gains victory over foes. The eschatological meaning of Gen. 49:1 is attested not only by Judaism but also by the NT, since the NT understands parts of Jacob's following prophecy in Gen. 49 to be eschatological and the beginning fulfillment in Christ's first coming. Romans 1:4–5; 16:25–26 allude to Gen. 49:10 (see table 3.1).[36]

Table 3.1

Genesis 49:10	Romans 1:4–5 (cf. almost identically 16:25–26)
"Unto him [the coming Israelite conqueror] will be the obedience of the nations."	"Jesus Christ . . . through whom we received grace and apostleship unto the obedience of faith among all the nations."

Likewise Rev. 5:5 ("the Lion that is from the tribe of Judah . . . has overcome") applies Gen. 49:9 to Jesus's resurrection, which inaugurated the end-time prophecy of the final resurrection.

Numbers 24:14

The second appearance of the expression "in the latter days" is in Num. 24:14: "And now, behold, I [Balaam] am going to my people; come, and I will advise you what this people will do to your people in the latter days to come [*bĕ'aḥărît hayyāmîm*]." As in Gen. 49:1, the phrase here is not merely a vague reference to the future but rather is an eschatological reference, which is indicated by its connection to Gen. 49, the context of the phrase in Num. 24, and its use in later biblical and extrabiblical literature. As mentioned earlier, this passage and its immediate context allude to Gen. 49:1, which is evident from the following:

1. Virtually the same wording in Gen. 49:9 occurs in Num. 24:9: "He couches, he lies down as a lion, and as a lion, who dares rouse him?"
2. The term "scepter" is used in Gen. 49:10 and Num. 24:17.
3. Both the Genesis and Numbers texts identify their respective prophecies to be about "the latter days" (cf. Num. 24:14).
4. Numbers 24:8, like Gen. 49, explicitly refers to the "nations" as Israel's enemies who are to be defeated.
5. Just as the prophecy of Israel's future conqueror in Gen. 49 is directly linked to new-creational imagery (vv. 11–12, as well as vv. 22, 25–26),

36. For discussion of the validity and use of this allusion, see G. K. Beale, *John's Use of the Old Testament in Revelation*, JSNTSup 166 (Sheffield: Sheffield Academic Press, 1998), 238–42.

so is the case in Num. 24 (cf. vv. 7b–9 with vv. 5–7a). Numbers 24:5–7a says,

> How fair are your tents, O Jacob,[37]
> Your dwellings, O Israel![38]
> Like palm trees that stretch out,
> Like gardens beside the river,
> Like aloes planted by the Lord,[39]
> Like cedars beside the waters.
> Water will flow from his buckets,
> And his seed will be by many waters.

The depiction of Num. 24:5–8 is also associated with the Abrahamic promise (cf. an increase of "seed" in v. 7; the "blessing and cursing" in v. 9 repeats Gen. 12:3b). There may also be an echo of the original Adamic commission (note "king" and "kingdom" in v. 7 and "dominion" in v. 19) and of the manner in which the promised seed in Gen. 3:15 ("he shall bruise you on the head") is to defeat the divine enemy (cf. "a scepter . . . shall crush through the forehead of Moab" in Num. 24:17).

The climactic point of Balaam's discourse to Balak comes in Num. 24:17–19, where a messianic-like king from Israel will defeat its enemies:

> I see him, but not now;
> I behold him, but not near;
> A star shall come forth from Jacob,
> A scepter shall rise from Israel,
> And shall crush through the forehead of Moab,
> And tear down all the sons of Sheth.
> Edom shall be a possession,
> Seir, its enemies, also will be a possession,
> While Israel performs valiantly.
> One from Jacob shall have dominion,
> And will destroy the remnant from the city.

37. *Targum Neofiti* and *Targum Pseudo-Jonathan* render the Hebrew of this line partly as "How beautiful is *the tent of meeting*," thus clearly identifying the "tents" as Israel's tabernacle.

38. On analogy with later OT texts referring to the temple in the plural, the same may well be the case in Num. 24:5. Furthermore, when these two Hebrew words for "tent" and "dwelling" occur together everywhere else in the Pentateuch (so 25x up to Num. 24), only once (Num. 16:27, in the plural) do they refer generally to Israel's dwellings around the tabernacle, and twenty-four times they refer to the tabernacle. If "tents" and "dwellings" in Num. 24:5 are plural references to the tabernacle, then this is a passage explaining Israel's task by linking a portrayal of Israel as a tabernacle with the picture of vegetation and waters spreading out over the earth, which is likely rooted in the Gen. 2 portrayal of Eden as a garden sanctuary. On this, see further G. K. Beale, *The Temple and the Church's Mission: A Biblical Theology of the Dwelling Place of God*, NSBT 17 (Downers Grove, IL: InterVarsity, 2004), 66–126.

39. The LXX here reads "as tabernacles [or 'tents'] pitched by the Lord," on which see further below.

Part of this prophecy ("Edom shall be a possession") is alluded to in Amos 9:12a ("that they [Israel] possess the remnant of Edom"), which is a prophecy of Israel's end-time defeat of the nations at the time of Israel's restoration (Amos 9:11) to the land, which is described in paradisical language, much like that in Gen. 49:11–12 and Num. 24:6–7.[40] Amos 9:11–12 is quoted in Acts 15:16–18 to explain the gospel's relationship to the gentiles and how Amos 9 has begun fulfillment.

Both Judaism and the NT identify this figure with the Messiah and his eschatological defeat of God's enemy.[41] Revelation 2:28 ("and I will give him [the overcomer] the morning star") and 22:16 ("I am . . . the bright morning star") allude to Num. 24:17 and apply it to Christ (as does possibly 2 Pet. 1:19).[42] This shows that the early Christian community understood "the latter days" of the Num. 24 prophecy commencing fulfillment with the first coming of Christ.[43]

Deuteronomy 4:30; 31:29

The next occurrences of the phrase "the latter days" are in Deuteronomy. After Israel commits idolatry, God will expel them from their land and scatter them throughout the nations, from where they will seek God (4:25–29). At this time, "When you are in distress and all these things have come upon you, in the latter days [bĕ'aḥărît hayyāmîm] you will return to the LORD your God and listen to His voice" (4:30). Here "the latter days" includes both the distress that is to come upon Israel and its returning to God as a result of that distress. The basis for Israel's return to God lies in that he will not "forget the covenant with your fathers which he swore to them" (4:31). This covenant, of course, is the covenant made with the patriarchs, the core of which, as I have argued earlier, is a repetition of Gen. 1:28. Thus, this covenant involves a mandate to the patriarchs and Israel to do what Adam should have done and a promise that their seed will ultimately carry this out to bless the world and spread God's glory throughout the earth. And, as I have also contended, the concluding fulfillment of this mandate in Gen. 1:28 is eschatological in nature, which is in mind in 4:30, as it refers to Israel "returning" in faith to fulfill this covenant.

40. Cf. Amos 9:13–15: "The mountains will drip sweet wine. . . . They [Israel] will also plant vineyards and drink their wine, and make gardens and eat their fruit. . . . They will not again be rooted out from their land."

41. See, e.g., 4Q266 frg. 3, III:18–21; *Tg. Onq.* Num. 24:17; *Tg. Ps.-J.* Num. 24:14; Num. 24:17 in particular was interpreted messianically in early Jewish writings: *T. Levi* 18:3; *T. Jud.* 24:1; CD-A VII:18–21; 1QM XI:6–7; in later Judaism, see *y. Taʿan.* 4.5. It is well known that "Bar Kokhba" ("Son of the Star") was the name of a messianic figure in the final Jewish uprising against Rome early in the second century AD, but his movement was defeated.

42. On which, see further Beale, *Revelation*, 268–69.

43. So also Num. 24:17 is understood the same way by Justin Martyr (*Dial.* 106) and Irenaeus (*Haer.* 3.9.2).

Commentators sometimes do not see Deut. 4:30 as "eschatological."[44] However, if I am correct in linking this verse with the pattern that begins in the early chapters of Genesis and is repeated, and if this pattern is eschatological, then Deut. 4:30 can be considered so. Other commentators consider Israel's restoration to the land in repentance[45] to be eschatological because conditions inextricably linked with that restoration are a radical break with prior conditions.[46]

Consequently, Deut. 4:30 understands that Israel's judgment and exile for not fulfilling its part of the covenant and its return to begin to fulfill its covenantal obligations again are eschatological. This is why the repeated reference later in Deut. 31:29 is to be understood as part of an end-time process: "For I know that after my [Moses's] death you will act corruptly and turn from the way which I have commanded you; and evil will befall you in the latter days [bĕ'aḥărît hayyāmîm], for you will do that which is evil in the sight of the LORD, provoking Him to anger with the work of your hands." Although, more precisely, exile has been construed to be part of a de-creation pattern, it may be viewed also either as an eschatological-like judgment against violation of the Adamic mandate or a judgment anticipating the final judgment of exile from God's presence and the consummated form of the cosmos. This is the idea in Deut. 31:29, though likely an intense time of tribulation toward the end of exile may be the focus, so that the "latter days" there presumably overlap with the conclusion of the exilic period, when the "return" of Deut. 4:30 begins (cf. Ps. 107:6, 13).[47] However, since Israel's restoration from Babylon after seventy years of exile did not eventuate in truly decisive and irreversible eschatological conditions of new creation, the end-time prophecy of Deut. 4 and Deut. 31 still awaited a future time when Israel would again do eschatological evil and then repent and turn to God. Accordingly, Israel's sin, exile, and restoration would become a historical pattern pointing to the true eschaton, a perspective that, as we will see, is taken up by NT writers.

44. So, e.g., Peter C. Craigie, *Deuteronomy*, NICOT (Grand Rapids: Eerdmans, 1976), 140; J. G. McConville, *Deuteronomy*, AOTC 5 (Leicester: Apollos, 2002), 111.

45. The use of "return" (*šûb*) in Deut. 4:30 in this context likely carries the pregnant notion of both return to the land physically and return to God spiritually, as it does in similar contexts, especially in the prophets. If repentance is mainly in mind, then physical return is implicit, since the land represented blessings for Israel; if physical return is primarily the focus, then repentance is implied, since Israel could truly return to the land only by repentance.

46. See, e.g., Gowan, *Eschatology*, 21–27. Note that *Tg. Neof.* Deut. 4:30 specifies that the "*very* end of the days" is what is in mind.

47. Joshua 24:27 reads, "And Joshua said to all the people, 'Behold, this stone shall be for a witness against us, for it has heard all the words of the LORD which He spoke to us; thus it shall be for a witness against you, so that you do not deny your God." The Greek version paraphrases this conclusion as "And this [stone] shall be among you for a witness in the latter days [ep' eschatōn tōn hēmerōn], at the time when you deal falsely with the Lord my God," apparently interpreting in line with Deut. 31:29 and applying "latter days" to a time of Israel's eschatological apostasy.

Hosea 3:5

Hosea 3:4 depicts a time when the people of Israel will endure a period of captivity when no Israelite king will rule over them (they will be "without king or prince"), they will not have the benefits of their temple (they will be "without sacrifice"), and they will not have the benefits of the functions of a priest (they will be "without ephod"), presumably because of the temple's destruction. Consequently, they will not even have opportunity to defile their temple worship as they previously had done (they will be without "sacred pillar," likely an idolatrous object, and "household idols"). The next verse, however, says that "afterward the sons of Israel will return and seek the LORD their God and David their king; and they will come trembling to the LORD and to His goodness in the latter days [bĕ'aḥărît hayyāmîm]" (Hos. 3:5). An eschatological time will come when God will restore Israel from captivity and reinstall Davidic kingship, and the nation will trust in God (so also Hos. 1:10–11; 2:21–23).[48] The implication from 3:4 is that God will also reestablish the temple for worship (note that the introductory "afterward" ['aḥar] in 3:5 is a parallel expression with "in the latter days" [bĕ'aḥărît hayyāmîm], which suggests that "afterward" and other synonymous expressions elsewhere in the prophets are eschatologically charged; cf., e.g., 'aḥărê-kēn in Joel 2:28 [3:1 MT]).[49]

Hosea elsewhere has close connections with the covenant cursings and blessings of Deuteronomy, and the reference to "in the latter days" in Hos. 3:5 appears to pick up and develop the earlier identical reference in Deut. 4:30 (cf. 30:29), which predicts the blessings for Israel in the end time.[50] In fact, the validity of Hosea's allusion to Deut. 4:30 is apparent from the observation that the combined Hebrew wording of "return to the LORD their [or your] God" + "in the latter days" occurs nowhere else in the OT except these two passages.

Isaiah

Isaiah 2:2 contains the identical phrase "in the latter days" as in the preceding OT verses. In line with Hosea, and possibly under its influence, Isaiah focuses on God's kingship and temple that will be established "in the latter days." Whereas it is not clear whether the Deuteronomy texts are alluding to the earlier Genesis or Numbers or Hosea texts, Isa. 2:2 appears to be developing Gen. 49:1, 10, where at the eschatological zenith of the "latter

48. For a similar conclusion, see Duane Garrett, *Hosea, Joel*, NAC 19A (Nashville: Broadman & Holman, 1997), 104.

49. Here I also have in mind eschatologically charged expressions such as Isa. 1:26; Jer. 49:6 (cf. with Jer. 48:47); similarly Jer. 31:33; Dan. 2:28–29.

50. So Douglas Stuart, *Hosea–Jonah*, WBC 31 (Waco: Word, 1987), 68. Stuart also sees Hos. 3:5 as a classic end-time prophecy of the Messiah that began fulfillment in Christ.

days" "the obedience of the peoples ['ammîm]" will be given to the king of Israel. Isaiah 2:2–3 likewise views "the peoples ['ammîm]" coming to Jerusalem in subservience to God and his law. The only places in the OT where the subservience of the "peoples" ('ammîm) appears together with "in the latter days" (bĕ'aḥărît hayyāmîm) are Gen. 49:1, 10; Isa. 2:2–3; Mic. 4:1 (on which, see directly below). Isaiah also portrays "the mountain of the house of the LORD" being "established as the chief of the mountains," which is part of an eschatological hope that Israel's temple would begin to be expanded in the eschaton.[51] Another explicit eschatological feature is that there will no longer be war on the earth (Isa. 2:4). In light of this passage, which predicts the permanent end of strife among nations in history, it is difficult to understand why some commentators see a reference to an indeterminate future without any eschatological sense.[52] This latter-day prophecy appeared to begin fulfillment with Israel's restoration from Babylonian captivity but did not find fulfillment in all the other associated promises (eschatological temple, pilgrimage of gentiles to Jerusalem, etc.). Therefore, this prophecy still awaited true inaugurated and irreversible fulfillment with the events of Christ's coming.[53]

Acts 2:17 alludes to the "latter days" of Isa. 2:2 (both read *estai en tais eschatais hēmerais*, an expression occurring nowhere else in the LXX or the NT). Acts interprets Joel 2:28–32, its main focus text, by Isa. 2:2.[54] Apparently, Joel's promise of the Spirit for Israel is being anticipated as a promise to be fulfilled among gentiles, which the remainder of Acts will narrate (e.g., Acts 10:44–47). Furthermore, the promise of an expanding temple in Isaiah is viewed as beginning fulfillment with the outpouring and expansion of the divine Spirit.[55] Revelation 15:4 pictures the final fulfillment of the Isa. 2:2 prophecy about the nations coming to the Lord in connection also with the revelation of the eschatological temple (Rev. 15:5: "And after these

---

51. On which, see Beale, *Temple*, 81–167.

52. As does, e.g., Otto Kaiser, *Isaiah 1–12*, trans. John Bowden, 2nd ed., OTL (Philadelphia: Westminster, 1983), 53.

53. Bruce K. Waltke argues this for the Mic. 4:1 prophecy, which is parallel to Isa. 2:2 ("Micah," in vol. 2 of *The Minor Prophets: An Exegetical and Expository Commentary*, ed. Thomas Edward McComiskey [Grand Rapids: Baker Academic, 1993], 679).

54. Some Greek manuscripts of Joel 2:28 also read *en tais eschatais hēmerais*, probably under the influence of Isa. 2:2 (Theodoret Ii. 183 et al. [according to the Holmes and Parsons LXX apparatus]), which shows that the interpretative move in Acts 2:17 had already been made by some scribes when copying the Greek of Joel (though the variant could have arisen by Christian scribes copying Joel under the influence of Acts 2:17).

55. On which, see further G. K. Beale, "The Descent of the Eschatological Temple in the Form of the Spirit at Pentecost: Part I," *TynBul* 56, no. 1 (2005): 73–102; idem, "The Descent of the Eschatological Temple in the Form of the Spirit at Pentecost: Part II," *TynBul* 56, no. 2 (2005): 63–90.

things I looked, and the temple of the tabernacle of testimony in heaven was opened").[56]

There are other explicit eschatological texts in Isaiah. Among these is Isa. 41:22–23, which speaks of the idols as unable to announce the "end" (MT: *'ahărîtān*; LXX: *ta eschata*),[57] in contrast to Israel's God, who is the only one "declaring the end [MT: *'ahărît*; LXX: *ta eschata*, 'latter events'] from the beginning" (Isa. 46:10). The "end" in these contexts refers to the promised restoration of Israel to the land in a new creation,[58] especially in light of the directly preceding context set by Isa. 41:18–20:

> I will open rivers on the bare heights
> And springs in the midst of the valleys;
> I will make the wilderness a pool of water
> And the dry land fountains of water.
> I will put the cedar in the wilderness,
> The acacia and the myrtle and the olive tree;
> I will place the juniper in the desert
> Together with the box tree and the cypress,
> That they may see and recognize,
> And consider and gain insight as well,
> That the hand of the LORD has done this,
> And the Holy One of Israel has created it.

Micah

Micah 4:1–4 is identical to Isa. 2:1b–4 (see above), but it adds new creation imagery (4:4: "Each of them will sit under his vine and under his fig tree, with no one to make them afraid") and underscores that God will be the ruler in Zion. The paradisical garden imagery of 4:4 is not unexpected in a passage that has just pictured a latter-day temple-mountain, especially since Eden was a garden on a mountain (see Ezek. 28:14, 16, 18, to be compared with Mic. 4:4). Thus, primal history is repeated in eschatological history (*Barn.* 6:13 says, "Behold, I make the last things as the first"). Neither is Isaiah unfamiliar with an eschatological arboreal temple atmosphere: "The glory of Lebanon will come to you, the juniper, the box tree, and the cypress together, to beautify the place of My sanctuary, and I shall make the place of My feet [the ark of the covenant] glorious" (Isa. 60:13).

56. On which, see also Beale, *Revelation*, 797, where Isa. 2:2 is seen to be woven into the broader allusion to Ps. 86:9–10.
57. Likewise Isa. 41:23 has "afterward" (*lĕ'āḥôr*), which the LXX renders as "at the end" (*ep' eschatou*).
58. For an elaboration of this context of restoraton and new creation as the content of these eschatological statements in Isa. 40–66, see chap. 16 under the heading "Paul's View of Reconciliation as New Creation and Restoration from Exile."

Jeremiah

The phrase "in the latter days" appears four times in Jeremiah. Jeremiah 23:20 says, "The anger of the LORD will not turn back until He has performed and carried out the purposes of his heart; in the latter days [bĕ'aḥărît hayyāmîm] you will clearly understand it." The phrase "in the latter days" is identical in Hebrew to all the passages surveyed above, but it appears to be a reference to Deut. 31:27–29, where Israel's "stubbornness" is mentioned together with the "anger" of the "LORD" (so also Jer. 23:17–20). Thus, in the light of the earlier parallel in Deut. 4:30, this may refer to the latter-day tribulation to come upon the people of Israel because of their sin, at the end of which God will cause them to return to him and bring them out of distress. However much the Deuteronomy text may be in mind, the emphasis here is the same as Deut. 4:30, where restoration in the latter days from distress is the focus. Especially, Jer. 23:20 underscores that "in the latter days," when restoration has occurred, the false prophecy of the false prophets will not blind God's people, and they will have a fuller redemptive-historical "understanding" of why he expressed his anger against Israel.

An eschatological view of Jer. 23:20 is further indicated by Jer. 30:24 (37:24 LXX), which reiterates the statement of the former and places it more clearly into a context of eschatological restoration, as the preceding context of both 30:17–22 and 31:1–40 make clear.[59] The "latter days" of 30:24 are equivalent to "at that time" (31:1), "the days are coming" (31:27, 31, 38), "in those days" (31:29), and "after those days" (31:33), all of which designate the end-time of restoration. This is a time when Israel will begin to fulfill the mandate and later reiterated promise of Gen. 1:28 ("And I will cause them to be multiplied, and they will not be diminished; and I will cause them to be glorified, and they will not be insignificant" [Jer. 30:19]). The following context shows that this will happen in a renewed creation (31:12–14). Above all, however, the following context expands on the eschatological "understanding" of 30:24 by explaining that at the end-time restoration God will make a "new covenant" with Israel in which he will forgive its sin and in which it will have a greater understanding of God's law and of God himself than previous generations had (31:31–34).[60] Presumably, this latter-day "understanding" will enable Israel to perceive that its suffering was part of God's just judgment on

---

59. See, e.g., F. B. Huey Jr., *Jeremiah, Lamentations*, NAC 16 (Nashville: Broadman, 1993), 216; Charles L. Feinberg, "Jeremiah," in vol. 6 of *The Expositor's Bible Commentary*, ed. Frank E. Gaebelein (Grand Rapids: Zondervan, 1986), 523. Neither commentator thinks that Jer. 23:20 is eschatological, though Feinberg (pp. 663, 671) sees the very same phrase in Jer. 48:47; 49:39 to refer to the eschatological messianic times. Commentators also generally view Jer. 30:24 to be noneschatological.

60. That Jer. 31:31–34 develops 30:24 is clear not only from the synonymous expressions for "latter days" there (see above) and the focus on end-time understanding, but also from the repetition of the phrase "I will be their God, and they shall be My people" in 31:33 (on which,

it, that God had ordained that a faithful remnant be produced and refined by the fire of judgment, and that his deliverance of the faithful from such suffering was an expression of his grace and that he would "forgive their iniquity" (on which, see also Jer. 32:37–43).

"In the latter days" occurs twice more in Jeremiah: 48:47; 49:39 (25:19 LXX). Strikingly, it refers to gentile nations (respectively Moab and Elam) being restored to God in the end time. Like Israel, these nations will suffer punishment under God's judicial hand and even go into exile (see 48:46), but "in the latter days" God "will restore the captivity" of these peoples (so likewise with respect to Ammon, on which, see 49:6). The restoration of the faithful among these nations appears to coincide with the restoration of the remnant of Israel, as is the case also in Isa. 40–66. This use of "in the latter days" together with nations (though 'ammîm is not present as in Isaiah and Micah) being positively related to God probably develops Gen. 49:1, 10 and Isa. 2:2–4, where the same eschatological idea is expressed.

Ezekiel

Ezekiel 38:14–16 refers to God bringing an enemy (called "Gog") against Israel to oppress it "in the latter days," so that again we have reference to Israel's end-time tribulation, which we have seen in Deut. 31:29, as well as possibly in Deut. 4:30. After this oppression, God promises to pour out his Spirit on the people of Israel (Ezek. 39:28–29) and establish his eschatological temple among them (Ezek. 40–47).

Daniel

THE LATTER-DAY STONE-MOUNTAIN OF DANIEL 2

The book of Daniel contains several references to "the latter days." The first appears in Dan. 2:28–29, 45:

However, there is a God in heaven who reveals mysteries, and He has made known to King Nebuchadnezzar what will take place in the latter days [bĕ'ahărît yômayyā'].This was your dream and the visions in your mind while on your bed. As for you, O king, while on your bed your thoughts turned to what would take place after this ['ahărê]; and he who reveals mysteries has made known to you what will take place. . . .

Inasmuch as you saw that a stone was cut out of the mountain without hands and that it crushed the iron, the bronze, the clay, the silver and the gold, the great God has made known to the king what will take place after this ['ahărê]; so the dream is true and its interpretation is trustworthy.

---

see 30:22; 31:1; for discussion of this eschatological fellowship formula, see Beale, *Revelation*, 1046–48).

The OG of Daniel renders "after this" in verses 29, 45 as "in the latter days," most likely because they are in parallelism with "in the latter days" of verse 28. The vision was of a huge statue composed of four sections, each of which represented a world empire. The climax of the vision portrays a stone coming from nowhere that smashes the statue and grows and fills the entire world. Daniel explains that the stone's smashing of the statue represents the kingdom of God's defeat of evil empires at the end of time and the eternal establishment of God's kingdom on earth (vv. 44–45). Daniel 2:28 and the verses that follow have so many unique correspondences to Isa. 2:2 (// Mic. 4:1) that it probably has been influenced by the Isaiah passage.

There are indications that Daniel's eschatological stone-mountain may indeed be closely associated with the gigantic end-time temple in Isa. 2, further confirming its eschatological nature. First, not only does Isa. 2:2–3 utilize a mountain to symbolize Israel, but also the image is integrally connected to the temple, "the mountain of the house of the LORD." Such a close link between mountain and temple is made throughout the OT, so that Mount Zion is sometimes merely referred to as "mountain," "hill," or a similar image. These ways of speaking about Mount Zion either closely associate it or virtually equate it with the temple as a synecdoche of the whole for the part (the entire mountain is substituted for the top part, where the temple is located).[61] For example, repeatedly occurring are phrases such as "mountain of the house" (Jer. 26:18; Mic. 4:1), "holy mountain" (about 20x in the OT), "holy hill" (Pss. 15:1; 43:3; 99:9; Jer. 31:23), and "temple hill" (1 Macc. 13:52; 16:20). Sometimes these references are equated with the temple, for example, in the following contexts: in Isa. 66:20 "holy mountain" = "house of the LORD"; in Ps. 15:1 "holy hill" = "your tent"; in Ps. 24:3 "hill of the LORD" = "his holy place" (cf. Ps. 43:3).

Thus, "mountain," when referring to Zion, often includes reference to the temple.[62] Among the best illustrations of this are Isa. 2:2–3 and Mic. 4:1–2, which equate "the mountain of the house of the LORD" with "the mountain of the LORD . . . the house of the God of Jacob." The description of the mountain in Dan. 2 rings with the same intonations of these descriptions in Isaiah and Micah.

Second, what is further attractive about linking Dan. 2 and Isa. 2:2–3 (// Mic. 4:1–2) as "eschatological temple" texts is that both are introduced as containing events that are to occur "in the latter days" (Dan. 2:28 [so also Dan. 2:29 LXX]; Isa. 2:2; Mic. 4:1). Micah even equates "the mountain of the house of the LORD" (Mic. 4:1) with God's eternal kingdom, the latter an explicit element of the mountain in Dan. 2: "The LORD will reign over them in Mount

61. A synecdoche is a figure of speech wherein the whole represents the part or the part represents the whole.
62. In *4 Ezra* 13:6–7, 35–36 the Dan. 2 mountain is equated with "Mount Zion" and "Zion."

Zion . . . forever" (Mic. 4:7). Exodus 15:17–18 also equates "the mountain of Your inheritance" with "the place, O LORD, which You have made for Your dwelling, the sanctuary," from where "the LORD shall reign forever and ever." Additionally, it is clear that the eschatological temple was to be situated on a mountain (Ezek. 40:2; Rev. 21:10).

Third, both Isa. 2:2–3 and Mic. 4:1–2 portray the mountain on which the temple sits as growing: it "will be raised above the hills." Although this is not as explicit as Daniel's rock that becomes a mountain and fills the earth, it is not far from that picture. Both portray a growing mountain temple. Both the Daniel and Isaiah/Micah passages, being eschatologically oriented, reverberate with echoes of new creation. The image of an emerging new creation may be perceived in the depiction of a growing holy mountain because the emergence of mountains certainly was a feature of the original creation.

Fourth, both Isa. 2 and Dan. 2 have in common the background of the ancient Near Eastern picture of temples growing like a mountain from a stone, which was linked with the dominion of the kingdom in which the temple started its growth. This is well illustrated by the Sumerian Cylinders of Gudea, which commemorate King Gudea's building and dedication of a temple for the god Ningirsu in Lagash.[63] The narrative about King Gudea even says that "all the foreign lands assemble from the horizon" to this gigantic temple (Cylinder A ix.15), and that from the temple the king will issue "laws" during "a day of majestic justice" (Cylinder B xvii.15).[64]

These four observations point to the probability that Dan. 2:28 and its context about the growing stone are developing the eschatological picture in Isa. 2:2 (// Mic. 4:1).[65]

C. F. Keil affirms that the events "which must occur afterwards" in Dan. 2:29 include the immediate future of the then-reigning king, Nebuchadnezzar, as well, and, therefore, of the writer himself.[66] But even in contrast to Keil, strictly speaking, the "latter days" of Dan. 2:28 (= "after this" [Dan. 2:29, 45]), to which the entire dream and interpretation are said to refer, include not only the immediate and distant future but also the immediate past and present. This is evident from observing that the head of gold in Dan. 2:37–38 is identified as Nebuchadnezzar in his present reign ("You *are* the head of gold"). Yet, the

---

63. For elaboration, see Beale, *Temple*, 148–52.

64. See Hans Wildberger, *Isaiah 1–12*, trans. Thomas H. Trapp, CC (Minneapolis: Fortress, 1991), 89–90. Wildberger notes these two additional parallels with Isa. 2. For the full text of the Sumerian Cylinders of Gudea, see Richard E. Averbeck, "The Cylinders of Gudea (2.155)," in *Monumental Inscriptions from the Biblical World*, vol. 2 of *The Context of Scripture: Archival Documents from the Biblical World*, ed. William. W. Hallo and K. Lawson Younger Jr. (Leiden: Brill, 2000), 418–33.

65. The discussion of Dan. 2 up to this point has been an abbreviated revision of Beale, *Temple*, 145–52.

66. C. F. Keil, *Biblical Commentary on the Book of Daniel*, trans. M. G. Easton, K&D (repr., Grand Rapids: Eerdmans, 1971), 111–12.

description of his reign in verses 37–38 is holistic, so that not only the immediate future is included in the identification but also the recent past.

As in Gen. 49:1, so also here commentators take this to mean that an idea of "eschatology" is not in mind, but only the indefinite future. Alternatively, this could further support my conclusion above that "latter days" in Gen. 49:1 (in relation to 49:2–27) refers to events that are designed to move toward, and therefore are inextricably linked to, a final, historical end-time climax, and this may be one reason that even they can be vaguely included, together with the Judah prophecy, under the rubric of what will happen "in the latter days." In particular, in Gen. 49 the failure of Israel's other tribes to achieve end-time success points to Judah's final triumph, and the tribes find their ultimate successful destiny in that of Judah.

Likewise, the focus of Daniel's "latter days" is on the establishment of God's kingdom in the future, which, I will argue, various NT writers view to have been inaugurated in their own time. Interestingly, Daniel's portrayal of God's defeat of the end-time evil kingdom pictures the defeat not merely of the final kingdom but also of the three preceding kingdoms leading up to the last kingdom as being destroyed "like one" kingdom with it (Dan. 2:35; cf. 2:45). This may be another way to indicate that although the focus of "the latter days" is on the final defeat of the enemy kingdom at the end of history, preceding events are part of a sovereignly designed historical movement and are part of an eschatological process inextricably linked to the "end" of that process and culminate in final judgment.[67] Perhaps another way to state this is that the first three kingdoms are part of eschatological patterns, especially in their judgmental demise, so that they are prototypical harbingers that foreshadow the final demise at the very end of history pictured in Dan. 2:34–35, 44–45. That the first three kingdoms are part of an eschatological portrayal is apparent from recalling that they all undergo end-time judgment *together* with the fourth and last kingdom (Dan. 2:34–35, 44–45). The theological reason for the identification of the first three kingdoms' judgment with the fourth kingdom's judgment is that they were corporately represented by that last kingdom. Thus, their very historical sinful existence lays the basis for their future inevitable judgment. Just as in a similar manner Judaism and the NT saw sinful humanity as corporately represented by Adam's sin at the beginning of history, so Dan. 2 sees the sinful kingdoms leading up to the last kingdom to be corporately represented by that kingdom's final end-time judgment. Consequently, Dan. 2's expression "in the latter days" refers to "the outcome of the future and not the future in general."[68]

67. For similar assessment, see Norman W. Porteous, *Daniel*, OTL (Philadelphia: Westminster, 1965), 44. The same kind of phenomenon is observable in Dan. 11:1–12:13 as an elaboration of the content of "the latter days" in Dan. 10:14.

68. H. Seebass, "אַחֲרִית," *TDOT* 1:211.

In support of this extended notion of the first three kingdoms being part of a prototypical eschatology is the portrayal of one of the kings of the first kingdom (Babylon) as an Adam-like figure. An allusion to Gen. 1:28 is apparent in Dan. 2:38 LXX, where Daniel says that God has given the Babylonian king rule over "the birds of the sky and the fish of the sea," almost verbatim with the LXX of Gen. 1:28[69] (the same observation may be made of the warped universal kingdoms of Assyria and Egypt portrayed by Ezek. 31 with language from Gen. 1–2).[70] This may indicate that other human kingdoms besides those of Israel were also involved in the process of what appear to be eschatological "start-ups" wherein a king is commissioned by God to do what Adam should have done, but, like Adam, he also fails, and the eschatological motor stalls and ultimately breaks down. Further evidence of an allusion to Gen. 1:28 in Daniel is that the former sees that God's kingdom will permeate the entire earth: the "stone" that became a "great mountain . . . filled the whole earth." The notion of God's kingdom "filling the whole earth" echoes Gen. 1:26, 28, where God commissions Adam to "fill the earth" and to "rule . . . over all the earth." What Adam, as well as Babylonian and Assyrian kings, tried to fulfill[71] will be fulfilled only by God's agent in the end time (Dan. 7:13–14 identifies this divine agent to be the "Son of Man").

Other References to Latter Days in Daniel

The next reference to the actual phrase "in the latter days" is in Dan. 10:14, where a heavenly being comes to Daniel to give him "an understanding of what will happen to your people in the latter days [bě'aḥărît hayyāmîm]." The content of this eschatological revelation is given in chapters 11–12, which focuses on the historical climax of a final tribulation for Israel and a subsequent resurrection of the righteous and unrighteous (11:28–12:13). The final tribulation has already been alluded to in 7:21, 23, 25; 8:17–26, the latter of which calls this period of distress and deception by the end-time opponent one that pertains "to the time of the end" (lě'et-qēṣ [8:17]) and "to the appointed time of the end" (lěmô'ēd qēṣ [8:19]). Likewise, chapters 11–12 use various kinds of "latter-day" expressions[72] to indicate facets of Israel's final distress of deception and persecution instigated by the eschatological opponent. At

---

69. Following André Lacocque, *The Book of Daniel*, trans. David Pellauer (London: SPCK, 1979), 50. Lacocque notes also the same parallel with Ps. 8:8. Similarly in line with the LXX of Gen. 1:28 is mention that the second kingdom "will have dominion over all the earth" (Dan. 2:39).

70. On which, see Beale, *Temple*, 126–29.

71. Of course, the pagan kings were not consciously trying to fulfill an Adamic mandate, but they were trying to dominate the earth, so that one might say that in the common grace realm their drive to rule is a reflection of that original mandate. However, in the case of Nebuchadnezzar, this Adamic mandate was revealed by God to the king through Daniel (Dan. 2:37–38).

72. Each of which have "end" (qēṣ) as part of the expression, like those in Dan. 8. For the interpretative renderings in TH and the OG of the "latter-day" Hebrew clauses in Dan. 8; 10; 11–12, see chap. 5 under the heading "Eschatological References in the General Epistles."

the "end," the antitheocratic antagonist will intend to "do evil" (11:27), will persecute the saints and try to deceive them (11:32–35, 40–41), but they will not compromise because of their wisdom (here also see 12:3–4, 9–10). Interestingly, the activities of this final enemy are enigmatically associated with "ships of Kittim" (11:30), which come against him. Likewise, Num. 24:24 portrays "ships of Kittim" that are to come against Israel's enemy "in the latter days" (Num. 24:14), which is the only other place in biblical literature that the phrase "ships of Kittim" occurs. This indicates that Dan. 11 is developing in some way the latter-day portrayal of Num. 24 as it relates to Israel's opponents. After the time of tribulation and deception (Dan. 12:1, 10), the saints will be raised from the dead (12:2, 13). Daniel again says that these events will happen at "the end time" (*'ēt qēṣ* [12:4]) and "at the end of the days" (*lĕqēṣ hayyāmîn* [12:13]).

Conclusion

G. B. Caird has written a helpful chapter on "The Language of Eschatology,"[73] where he summarizes the major definitions given to the term "eschatology":

1. the last things of death, judgment, heaven, and hell;
2. the final destiny of Israel as a nation (with only secondary thought of the individual) and the universal victory of Israel's God;
3. the end of the cosmos, which is expected to be imminent;
4. "inaugurated" or "already and not yet" coming of the end of the world;
5. the end reaching out from the past and impeling one to an existential decision and, hence, encounter with God;
6. some significant OT definitions see the essence of eschatology to be not "finality" but "newness" or
7. "purpose," the latter understood in terms of God working out a purpose in history to reach a goal.

These definitions are not mutually exclusive unless they are taken too narrowly, as too often has been the case. This can easily be seen with the first two. The third and the fourth are compatible as long as the imminent end of the former is viewed to be something that can happen at any time and no date-setting is proposed. Accordingly, the second two are not inconsistent with the first two. The sixth and the seventh would be mutually exclusive of the prior five if the notion of "nonfinality" is retained, but when that notion is jettisoned, both can easily fit into a traditionally understood eschatological concept, especially as this is viewed as a historical process worked out over time that eventuates in a definitive historical climax beyond which there will

73. G. B. Caird, *The Language and Imagery of the Bible* (Philadelphia: Westminster, 1980), 243–71.

be no reversal. Truly incompatible is the fifth definition (Rudolf Bultmann's), which understands Jesus's teaching of the end reaching out from the past into the present and resulting in an existential decision. However, this does not refer to true eschatological realities that are a part of true history, since through "demythologization" eschatology is purely metaphorical. Since Bultmann held that Jesus was wrong about when the "end" would come, Jesus's teachings about eschatology must be demythologized and made completely metaphorical. But if this definition is restated as "the literal end reaching back from the literal future into the present to result in an existential decision," then this is quite consistent with inaugurated eschatology that takes place in space-time history.

Thus, most of the definitions are compatible, and the others form important complements also when they are altered as above. Accordingly, these definitions are not inconsistent with the various aspects of OT eschatology observed in the main body of this chapter (nor are they inconsistent, I might add, with NT eschatology to be observed below).

After elaborating on these definitions, Caird gives his own threefold definition of eschatology:

1. The biblical writers believed literally that the world had had a beginning in the past and would have an end in the future.
2. They regularly use "end of the world" language metaphorically to refer to that which they well knew was not the end of the world.
3. As with all other uses of metaphor, we have to allow for the likelihood of some literalist misinterpretation on the part of the hearer, and for the possibility of some blurring of the edges between vehicle and tenor on the part of the speaker.[74]

Caird's third category acknowledges that sometimes metaphorical uses of eschatological language can blur the literal reference with the picture to include some degree of literal reference to the eschaton. Furthermore, although at times Caird says that references in the second category are pure metaphor (in the same way that the psalmist in Ps. 23 depicted himself as a sheep), at other times he refers to such uses "as an anticipation and embodiment of the universal judgment to come."[75] He gives an illustration that fits well with this: the prophets had "bifocal vision" whereby with the near-sight lens they saw imminent historical events, and with the long-sight lens they saw the final historical end.[76] This is quite close to the definition of typology given by many in which an OT historical person, institution, or event has analogous corre-

74. Ibid., 256.
75. Ibid., 260.
76. Ibid., 258.

spondence to and is a foreshadowing of a later event in the NT age. Although it certainly is possible, even likely, that there are purely metaphorical uses of eschatological language, the OT uses of eschatological phraseology that we have surveyed (e.g., "latter days") most likely fall into any of Caird's three categories, the latter two understood as "anticipations and embodiments" of the very end. Indeed, Caird quotes the definition of the phrase "in the latter days" (bĕʾaḥărît hayyāmîm) by Brown, Driver, and Briggs, which, we have seen, fits well within the contours of the approach in this chapter: "a prophetic phrase denoting the final period of the history so far as the speaker's perspective reaches." Caird summarizes this as "the equivalent of the English expression 'in the end' or 'ultimately' when we use them to mean 'sooner or later' or 'in the future'; and it has precisely that vagueness which makes for the blurring of the edges mentioned in Proposition 3."[77] This comports excellently with a view of progressive revelation throughout the development of the writing of the biblical books of the canon, as we also observed earlier.

We have seen that the phrase "latter days" occurs at points throughout the OT to refer not to the mere indefinite future[78] but rather to the culmination of history from the various writers' perspectives. Although earlier OT authors have more vague or "thicker" prophetic portraits of "the latter days," some of which we have observed in this chapter, all include in a variety of ways reference to a future period that represents *an irreversible radical break with a former period*. I define these uses of "latter days" to be overtly eschatological because all refer to a permanent and radical break with the preceding historical epoch. A filling out of the notion of "the latter days" occurs as the OT writings develop and revelation progresses. It is like a seed germinating, sprouting, and then growing into a small plant and then developing into a full plant. A developing organic eschatological perspective is pointed to by my earlier observation in this chapter that the phrase "in the latter days" is used across the OT almost always in intertextual development of earlier uses of the same phrase.[79]

---

77. Ibid., 257–58.

78. See John T. Willis, "The Expression *beʾacharith hayyamim* in the Old Testament," *ResQ* 22 (1979): 54–71. Willis affirms, unpersuasively in my view, that every use of "latter days" in the OT, DSS, and NT refers to mere indefinite future. This position is held by no one else whose work I have surveyed.

79. Some may want to argue that merely because a later OT writer understands earlier passages to be eschatological does not mean that these earlier passages are eschatological. Some may say this because the later author may merely use earlier wording analogically or in some way that does not pay attention to the earlier contextual meaning. The presupposition of this book is that later biblical authors refer to earlier texts in ways that reflect varying degrees of significant commensurate contextual awareness of the earlier texts, so that there is some kind of noteworthy organic conceptual connection between the two texts. One of the validations of this approach is that there is always enriched interpretive light shed on the earlier text and the later alluding text.

The following eschatological conditions represent various aspects of the eschatological discontinuity:

1. a final, unsurpassed and incomparable period of tribulation for God's people by an end-time opponent who deceives and persecutes, in the face of which they will need wisdom not to compromise; afterward they are
2. delivered,
3. resurrected, and their kingdom reestablished;
4. at this future time, God will rule on earth
5. through a coming Davidic king who will defeat all opposition and reign in peace in a new creation over both
6. the nations and
7. restored Israel,
8. with whom God will make a new covenant, and
9. upon whom God will bestow the Spirit, and
10. among whom the temple will be rebuilt.

These ten ideas compose in various OT contexts the content of the expression "the latter days" (and its near equivalents in Daniel). The notions of kingdom, king, and rule over nations are sometimes developed in connection with the fulfillment of the Adamic-patriarchal promises of blessing. In this connection, the protological beginning chapters of Gen. 1–3 reveal the expectation that Adam should have reigned as a consummate priest-king in God's perfect image. His failure to accomplish this left open the necessity for another Adam figure to accomplish the first Adam's commission. The subsequent chapters of Genesis and, indeed, of the OT show repeated allusion to Gen. 1:28 and hope for such a figure, but no significant fulfillment occurs. It had to await another who would come after the formal close of the OT period of expectation.

Although it is true that there are numerous other OT passages about eschatology where the technical language of "latter days" and its synonyms do not appear, the texts surveyed above cover all the major topics of eschatology found elsewhere in the OT (though there are subcategories of these major topics). We have seen that some scholars view the expression "in the latter days" to refer to the indefinite future, while others, though acknowledging this meaning in some cases, also see an overt eschatological nuance in other uses.[80] The focus of the expression "in the latter days" refers to a period at the end of history, but it also includes secondarily what we may call "protoeschatological"

---

80. E.g., BDB 31; H. Seebass, "אַחֲרִית," *TDOT* 1:207–12; Jack R. Lundbom, *Jeremiah 21–36*, AB 21B (New York: Doubleday, 2004), 197. Lundbom understands this to be the consensus among commentators.

or apparent "semieschatological" events (e.g., tribulation, return from exile) that occur at points in the OT epoch before the climactic world-ending happenings and are inextricably linked to and lead up to such final happenings.

The main storyline of the OT was formulated at the end of the preceding chapter. This chapter has revealed that eschatology is an essential part of this storyline, which we have seen was already implied in the Gen. 1–3 narrative itself. Thus, the formulation of the OT storyline at the end of chapter 2 may be slightly revised in the following manner: *The Old Testament is the story of God, who progressively reestablishes his <u>eschatological</u> new-creational kingdom out of chaos over a sinful people by his word and Spirit through promise, covenant, and redemption, resulting in worldwide commission to the faithful to advance this kingdom and judgment (defeat or exile) for the unfaithful, unto his glory.*

4

The Eschatological Storyline
of the Old Testament in Relation to Judaism

The Jewish Focus on the Latter Days

Since eschatology is a major thematic part of the storyline of the OT, it should not be surprising to find it also in early Jewish writings.

Allusions in Judaism to Old Testament Texts
containing Eschatological Language

First, it is helpful to study how Judaism understood the OT passages containing the phrase "latter days," discussed in the preceding chapter. The Greek OT renders the Hebrew phrase *bĕ'aḥărît hayyāmîm* in all the aforementioned OT passages as *ep' eschatōn tōn hēmerōn*, "in the latter days" (though the initial Greek prepositions and case form differs).

Philo (*Her.* 261) cites Gen. 49:1 according to its virtually identical LXX form (*ep' eschatō tōn hēmerōn*, "in the latter days"). Some of the later Jewish midrashic writings (*Midr. Ps.* 31.7; *Gen. Rab.* 96; 99.5; *b. Pesaḥ.* 56a) apply Gen. 49:1 to Jacob's intent to reveal end-time redemption, though these texts go on to say that God hid from Jacob the actual eschatological events that were to happen in the future (*Midr. Tanḥ. Gen.* 12.9 likewise applies this to Jacob's intent to reveal the "end" of history). One of the Aramaic translations of Gen. 49:1 (*Targum Onqelos*) refers to "the end of days," and Gen. 49:9

develops this with the interpretation that "a king shall be raised *in the end*" (4Q252 V:1–7 interprets Gen. 49:10 to refer to the coming of "the messiah of righteousness"). Another Aramaic translation (*Targum Pseudo-Jonathan*) interpretatively paraphrases Gen. 49:1 to refer to the time of "the giving of the reward to the righteous" and "the time in which the King Messiah was destined to come" (so also 4Q252 V:1–7).

Testaments of the Twelve Patriarchs, an interpretive expansion of Jacob's prophecy about Israel in Gen. 49, portrays the eschatological aspect of Jacob's prophecy to extend to almost every one of the tribes (see the general statement to this effect in *T. Naph.* 8:1). From Levi will come "an eternal king" (*T. Reub.* 6:8–12); "in the end of the ages [*epi ta telei tōn aiōnōn*][1] you will act impiously against the Lord, setting your hands to do every evil deed," which will result in Israel's exile (*T. Levi* 14:1; see 14:1–8; likewise *T. Dan* 5:4; *T. Gad* 8:2, the latter of which refers only to Israel's sin); Judah will do "evil things . . . in the last days [*en eschatais hēmerais*]" (*T. Jud.* 18:1–3), which will result in its exile and captivity (*T. Jud.* 23). Both references associate Judah's sin and exile with classic eschatological notions, since they allude to such notions in *1 Enoch*.[2] *Testament of Judah* says that directly after Israel's exile the Messiah's reign will be established ("There shall arise for you a star from Jacob" [24:1]), a reference to the end-time prediction of Num. 24:17. Similarly, *T. Iss.* 6:1–4 says that Israel will sin greatly "in the last times" (*en eschatois kairois*), resulting in exile and followed directly by end-time restoration.[3] *Testament of Zebulon* 9:5–9 says virtually the same thing (see "in the last days" in 9:5) but adds that Israel will be wicked and rejected by God "until the time of the end" (9:9), even during the time of final restoration. *Testament of Joseph* 19:1–12 likely refers to the end-time kingship prophecy of Gen. 49:8–10 and directly connects it to what will occur

1. So manuscripts *c h i j*, whereas all others have only "in the end."
2. *Testament of Levi* 14:1 is likely a partial allusion to *1 Enoch* (since some manuscripts preface the eschatological expression there with "I have learned from the writing of Enoch"), particularly *1 En.* 91:6 and especially 93:9, since they come closest in all of *1 Enoch* to *T. Levi* 14:1 (on which, see R. H. Charles, *The Apocrypha and Pseudepigrapha of the Old Testament*, 2 vols. [Oxford: Clarendon, 1913], 2:312). Quite similar to *T. Lev.* 14:1, so also here part of the manuscript tradition prefaces the eschatological expression with "for in the books of Enoch the Righteous I have read," which probably alludes to the same eschatological passages to which *Testament of Levi* alludes. The significance of this is that the *1 Enoch* phrases are contextually part of overt eschatological predictions, making the *Testament of Levi* and *Testament of Judah* statements eschatologically charged. Deuteronomy 4:30 and 31:29 may have exercised some influence on these two texts, since they also have the expression "in the latter days" together with a prediction that Israel would sin in that time.
3. This appears to allude specifically to Deut. 4:30, where Israel's sin, distress, and restoration are linked to "the latter days." Likewise, 4Q163 frgs. 4–6, II:8–13 interprets Isa. 10:22 ("For though your people, O Israel, may be like the sand of the sea, only a remnant within them will return") to refer to "the final [days . . .]" in which "they will go into cap[tivity]," with the implication that a restoration for Israel will follow.

"in the latter days" (*T. Jos.* 19:10).[4] *Testament of Benjamin* refers also to the same Judah prophecy and says that it will occur "in later times" (11:2) and at "the consummation of the ages" (11:3).

Pseudo-Philo alludes to Jer. 30:24 ("The fierce anger of the LORD will not turn back . . . ; in the latter days you will understand this"): "For they will know in the last days that on account of their own sins their seed has been abandoned" (*L.A.B.* 13:10) (note also the common reference to the Abrahamic promise in the Pseudo-Philo passage and in Jer. 30:19). The reference to "the last days," as in Jer. 30, refers to the eschatological restoration, when God's people will be able fully to understand the redemptive-historical purpose of the sufferings that they have endured. *Second Baruch* 78:5–7 appears to be an interpretative expansion of Jer. 23:20 ("The anger of the LORD will not turn back . . . ; in the latter days you will clearly understand this"), which is virtually identical to Jer. 30:24. The point of the *2 Baruch* passage is to explain that the people of Israel should understand that the sufferings of their exile are ultimately designed "for your good" by God to cause them to "be found worthy of your fathers in the last times" (note also the parallel notion of the regathering of the remnant of dispersed Israel in Jer. 23:3 and *2 Bar.* 78:7b).

General Use of Eschatological Language in Judaism

In addition to allusion to OT texts containing eschatological language, early Judaism associates "the latter days" with most of the same topics as does the OT. As in the preceding survey of the OT, the present one also focuses on actual eschatological language and not on concepts; analysis of the latter certainly would fill out the picture, but the limits of this study do not allow the luxury of such a massive survey. All the major concepts found linked with formal end-time wording can also be found elsewhere without such wording. This is a legitimate and abbreviated way to cover the eschatology of early Judaism, since the various places where precise eschatological wording occurs pertain to almost all the relevant major eschatological topics found elsewhere without such exact wording.

There are several references to the end-time that, in their immediate contexts, make no mention of specific events that will characterize the period, and there are other, full-orbed references with specific mention of many kinds of events that will occur. Both kinds of references are very general.

For a sampling of general references, without mention of specific events, see the following: *4 Ezra* 8:63 ("You have now shown me a multitude of the signs

---

4. For the classic eschatological nature of *T. Jos.* 19 (e.g., its heavy indebtedness to Dan. 7–8), see G. K. Beale, *The Use of Daniel in Jewish Apocalyptic Literature and in the Revelation of St. John* (Lanham, MD: University Press of America, 1984), 90–96.

which you will do in the last times"); 10:59 ("The Most High will show you
. . . what the Most High will do to those who dwell on earth in the last days").[5]

There are also numerous passages that focus on a very specific description
of what will happen in the eschatological period.

Eschatological Judgment

Early Jewish apocalyptic writings affirm that the final judgment will happen at the very end of time, which is usually spoken of in the singular: "the
day of the great conclusion . . . until the great age is consummated" (*1 En.*
16:1); there will be a "judgment in the last days" (*1 En.* 27:2 [see also *2 En.*
65:6–7]); "the time of threshing" (*4 Ezra* 4:30); "torment laid up for themselves
in the last days" (*4 Ezra* 7:84); "they are to be judged in the last times" (*4 Ezra*
7:87); "the day of judgment will be the end of this age" (*4 Ezra* 7:113); "the
end" will manifest itself in "requital" (*4 Ezra* 9:6); "at the end of the world,
a retribution will be demanded with regard to those who have done wickedly
in accordance with their wickedness" (*2 Bar.* 54:21).[6] The Qumran writings
testify to the same thing: the wicked in Israel will be judged "in the last time"
(*lqṣ h'ḥrwn*) (4Q169 frgs. 3–4, IV:3); judgment of those who do not seek the
truth take place at "the last time" (*qṣ 'ḥrwn*), and there is "the time appointed
for the judgment" (1QS IV:15–20 [see also IV:25]).

Quite similar to the notion of judgment is the belief that in the final age
the enemy of God's people will be decisively defeated. The DSS affirm that the
"sons of light" will defeat the "sons of darkness" at "the end of all the periods
of darkness" (1QM I:8–16). The Aramaic OT asserts that the "sons" of the
woman in Gen. 3:15 will defeat the serpent "in the end" (*Tg. Neof.* Gen. 3:15).

---

5. So see further *4 Ezra* 12:9 (Ezra was "shown the end of the times"); 14:5, 9–10 (Ezra was
shown what will happen at "the end of the times); *Apoc. Ab.* 23:2 ("in the last days"); 24:2 ("in
the last days"); 32:5 ("in the last days"); *Mart. Ascen. Isa.* 11:37–38 ("the end of this world and
all this vision" includes Christ's first coming up to his second coming [though this is a compos-
ite work]); *2 Bar.* 10:2–3 ("I will show you . . . what will happen at the end of days"); 59:1–12
(59:4: "the end of time"; 59:8: "the end of the periods"); 83:5 ("that which has been promised
to us regarding the end").

6. Additional references affirming that judgment will occur at the end of time are the following: *2 Bar.* 78:6 ("so that you may not be condemned at the end"); 82:2–4 (judgment of the
nations at "the end"); 83:7 (at "the end of the world . . . everything will come to judgment");
Sib. Or. 3:741–744 ("this fated day also reaches its consummation"); *Apoc. El.* 4:25–26 (an early
Christian source); *L.A.B.* 3:10 ("when the years appointed for the world have been fulfilled");
4 Ezra 11:44 ("his [the Most High's] times . . . they are ended . . . his ages are completed");
Apoc. Ab. 22:4 ("at the end of the age"); *2 Bar.* 13:2–6 ("the end times"); 30:3–5 ("the end of
times"); 76:1–5 (v. 5a: "lest they die in the last times"; "the end of times" also appears in v. 2).
Interestingly, eschatological language is applied to the end of the first world that occurred at the
time of the Noahic deluge; e.g., preceding Noah's flood was a time of "all lawlessness," which
indicated the "nearness" of the "end" (*2 En.* [A] 71:24–25); see also *1 En.* 108:1–3, which refers
to those "observing the law in the last days," leading up to the great flood.

The Destruction of the Heaven and Earth and a New Creation

On the final day of history God will destroy the entire created order. According to *2 Baruch*, the end of the cosmos is "that time [which] is the end of that which is corruptible and the beginning of that which is incorruptible" (74:1–4). The same book earlier asserts that "the world of corruption" will be "ended" when "the times . . . have been fulfilled" (40:3).[7] When the old earth passes away and "the Mighty One will renew his creation" (chaps. 31–32), there will be abundant fertility throughout the earth (29:1–8; e.g., 29:5a: "the earth will also yield fruits ten thousandfold").[8] And according to *Sibylline Oracles*, directly after the final judgment at the "consummation," "the all-bearing earth will give the most excellent unlimited fruit" for humanity (3:741–745)[9] during a period of peace that will last "to the end of the age" (3:755–756).

The Time of Resurrection

The resurrection of the body will happen only at the very end of the age, when the corruption of all creation would be ended and a new creation was begun. Indeed, resurrection is equivalent to new creation, since the way redeemed humans participate in the new creation is through having transformed newly created bodies. In *Life of Adam and Eve*, God is portrayed as promising to Adam, "I shall raise you on the last day in the resurrection with every man of your seed" ([*Apocalypse*] 41:3); Adam's son is told that "the Sabbath day is a sign of the resurrection, the rest of the coming age" ([*Vita*] 51:2). Earlier in the book, the angel Michael likewise promises that "at the end of times [*ep' eschatōn tōn hēmerōn*] . . . all flesh . . . shall be raised" ([*Apocalypse*] 13:2–3).

The hope is also found generally stated in other early Jewish works. According to Pseudo-Philo, the resurrection will occur "when the years appointed for the world have been fulfilled" (*L.A.B.* 3:10 [see also 19:12–13]). In *4 Ezra* is the prediction that "the heart of earth's inhabitants shall be changed and converted to a different spirit," and "corruption shall be overcome" at "the end of my [God's] world" (6:25–28 [see also 7:26–37]); accordingly, saints in the intermediate state in heaven look forward to "the glory which awaits them in the last days" (7:95 [cf. 7:96]). *Second Baruch* links the hope of resurrection

---

7. See the same thing in the following: *2 En.* [J] 18:6–7; 65:6; *L.A.B.* 3:10 ("when the years appointed for the world have been fulfilled"); *2 Bar.* 83:6 says that everything "will surely pass away" at "the ends of the times," and *2 Bar.* 85:10 says this will happen at "the coming of the times." An eschatological notion is applied to the coming of Noah's flood: *1 En.* 10:2 says that God sent an angel to "reveal to him [the son of Lamech] the end that is approaching: that the whole earth will be destroyed, and a deluge is about to come upon the whole earth, and will destroy all that is on it."

8. It is possible that the abundant fertility occurs before the new creation, but this is improbable in light of the overall context of *2 Bar.* 28–32, which begins with asking the question of where incorruptible people will live "at the consummation of time" (cf. 28:5–7; 29:8).

9. After which a series of descriptions of the fertility are listed in *Sib. Or.* 3:745–750.

with the coming of the Messiah at "the end of times": "When the time of the appearance of the Anointed One has been fulfilled and he returns with glory, . . . then all who sleep in hope of him will rise" (30:1–4).[10]

In like manner, the final resurrection is also spoken of in terms of saints receiving "glory" on the final day. "The full glory does not abide" in the present world, but at "the end of this age" there follows directly "the beginning of the immortal age to come, in which corruption has passed away," when no one will be able "to harm him who is victorious" (*4 Ezra* 7:43[113]–45[115]). Qumran asserts that "the reward" of the "sons of truth" "will be healing, plentiful peace in a long life, fruitful offspring with all everlasting blessings, eternal enjoyment with endless life, and a crown of glory with majestic raiment in eternal light" (1QS IV:6–8). The basis of the saints receiving such a blessing is that such ones "God has chosen for an everlasting covenant and to them shall belong all the glory of Adam" (1QS IV:22–23). In so many words, this refers to the resurrection of the Qumran believers, which will happen at "the appointed end [*qṣ*] and the new creation" (1QS IV:25).

The resurrection of Christ by angelic intervention is considered to have happened "in the last days" (*Mart. Ascen. Isa.* 3:15–18).[11]

Reception of a Glorious Inheritance

Saints will receive an eschatological inheritance. For example, faithfulness will result in "inheriting the . . . endless age that is coming" (*2 En.* 50:2 [so also *2 En.* [J] 66:6–8; cf. *1 En.* 108:1–2]). Likewise, *m. Sanh.* 10.1 asserts that "all Israelites have a share in the world to come," though the "all" is qualified in the following context to refer only to faithful Israelites. This inheritance is sometimes equated with the gaining of immortal life. In this respect, *4 Ezra* 7:95–97 is apt: saints exalted to heaven anticipate "the glory which awaits them in the last days. . . . They have now escaped what is mortal, and shall inherit what is to come," especially the "spacious liberty which they are to receive and enjoy in immortality" (so also *2 Bar.* 48:48–50, and similarly *4 Ezra* 4:26–29). Saints will have "peace in the name of the world that is to become . . . forever and ever and ever," and "dwelling places" and a "portion" together with the "Son of Man" (*1 En.* 71:15–17).

Especially vivid in this respect is *4 Ezra* 8:51–55, which refers to

the glory of those who are like yourself [Ezra], because it is for you that Paradise is opened, the tree of life is planted, the age to come is prepared, plenty is provided, a city is built, rest is appointed, goodness is established and wisdom is provided

---

10. For the hope of resurrection "in the last times" and "the end of times," see also *2 Bar.* 76:1–5; similarly *Liv. Pro.* 3:11–12, which identifies Ezekiel's prophecy of the dry bones to find its fulfillment "in the coming age"; *T. Job* links "the resurrection" with "the consummation of the age."

11. A Christian addition to this Jewish work.

beforehand. The root of evil is sealed up from you, illness is banished from you, and death is hidden; hell has fled and corruption has been forgotten; sorrows have passed away, and in the end the treasure of immortality is made manifest.

Fulfillment of the Patriarchal Promises

God's promise to Abraham, Isaac, and Jacob that Israel would be multiplied, subdue its enemies, possess the land, and bless all the nations is understood to find its fulfillment in the eschatological epoch. The patriarchal promise is tied closely to the idea of eschatological inheritance in the OT and in early Judaism, the latter of which we just noted above. For example, *Jub.* 22:10 says that Isaac "called Jacob and said: 'My son Jacob, may the God of all bless you and strengthen you to do righteousness, and his will before him, and may he choose you and your seed that you may become a people for his inheritance according to his will always.'"[12] In *Lad. Jac.* 1:9–11 it is said that this reiterated patriarchal promise made to Jacob from Gen. 28:11–19 will come to pass "in the last times of the years of completion." Such a fulfillment is indicated in *L.A.B.* 19:2–4, where God's "remembering the covenant that he established with your fathers" is directly linked to "God [who] has revealed the end of the world so that he might establish his statutes."[13]

Restoration of Israel

There is to be a restoration of God's people at the very end of history, which is likely ultimately linked to the patriarchal promises. In *4 Ezra* 13:46 the vision refers to the restoration of the ten tribes of Israel that were led into Assyrian captivity, which will occur in "the last times." Accordingly, Sir. 48:24–25 refers to Isaiah, who prophesied Israel's restoration and "saw the last things [*ta eschata*], and he comforted them that mourned in Zion" about the certainty of their coming restoration.

Restoration of Israel's Temple

At the time of Israel's restoration, there is also to be a restoration of the temple. Tobit 14:4–5 is one of the best-known passages expressing this hope: restored Israelites "shall build a temple, but not like the first, until the time of that age be fulfilled." Comparably, Qumran can also speak of "the house which [he {God} will establish] for [him] in the last days [*b'hryt hymym*]" (4Q174 frgs. 1,

---

12. So also see *Jub.* 22:9, 15, 29, which respectively refer to the eschatological time of fulfillment as "unto all the ages," "for all the ages," and "unto the days of eternity."

13. So also *L.A.B.* 27:8; 28:1–2, which appear to locate the fulfillment of the promised patriarchal "covenant" "in the last days." Also *4 Ezra* 4:27 plausibly alludes to the patriarchal promise: "the age" that "is hastening swiftly to its end" will "bring the things that have been promised to the righteous."

I,21,2:2–3). *Sibylline Oracles*, narrating the future from the perspective of accomplishment, tells of a "blessed man [who] came from the expanses of heaven with a scepter in his hands," clearly the Messiah, who "made a holy temple, exceedingly beautiful in its fair shrine"; God is also seen as the "founder" of this "greatest temple" in the "last time" (5:414–430).[14] And according to *2 Baruch*, before the destruction of the temple, an angel took all the furniture and vessels of the holy of holies and the holy place and hid them in order that they might be "restored" in "the last times" together with the renewed Jerusalem itself (6:5–9).

Extreme Eschatological Lawlessness, False Teaching, or Deception

There will be an increase in doctrinal error and deception during the latter days that lead up to the final judgment of evil and consummation of God's kingdom. The Qumran community, which believed that they were living in the end times, thought that the religious leaders in Jerusalem were false teachers, and that true saints needed to avoid them and resist their influence, lest their very souls be at stake. "In the final days" (*l'ḥryt hymym*) and "in the final time" (*b'ḥryt hqṣ*), "those looking for easy interpretations" and "misdirecting" people will be revealed to all Israel and judged (4Q169 frgs. 3–4, II:2; frgs. 3–4, III:3–5). Similarly, "[the trai]tors in the last days . . . are violator[s of the coven]ant who do not believe" God's inspired interpretation of fulfilled prophecy through the Teacher of Righteousness about "the final generation" (1QpHab II:3–10). And "the last generation" are those who "strayed from the path" and "sought easy interpretations" (CD-A I:12–19); kings of nations "ha[tch idle plots against] the elect ones of Israel in the last days [*b'ḥryt hymym*]" (4Q174 frgs. 1, I,21,2:18–19). The same idea is found in other parts of the early Jewish literature.[15] There will also be "purification of the heart of men of [the Community] . . . [. . .] in the last days [ ]" because of false teaching from Israel's religious leaders, apparently the latter being a means of refinement for the people of truth (4Q177 II:7–13).

Eschatological Wisdom

Those living "in the last days" will need divine "wisdom" in order to discern the signs of the times or not to be deceived by the unique deception and extreme sinful living that are to occur at the end (*4 Ezra* 14:20–22; see also *1 En.* 37:3, which refers to "latter days"). Some "who live on earth in those

---

14. See also *1 En.* 90:28–36 for the building of a huge temple in the eschaton, though no explicit eschatological temporal language is used.

15. This idea of people teaching and practicing lawlessness in the eschaton occurs repeatedly in *Testaments of the Twelve Patriarchs* (*T. Levi* 14:1 [see 14:1–8]; *T. Jud.* 18:1–3; *T. Iss.* 6:1–2; *T. Zeb.* 9:5–9; *T. Dan* 5:4; *T. Gad* 8:2, on which, see the initial section of this chapter for discussion), as well as in *T. Mos.* 7:1–10; *Apoc. El.* 1:13; 4:25–26 (Christian); *Mart. Ascen. Isa.* (3:30–31 ["in the last days"]; 4:1–12; cf. 4:1: at the time of "the completion of the world"); so also *Apoc. Ab.* 29:1–13 (Christian interpolation).

days will not understand that it is the end of times, but everyone who will understand will be wise at that time" (*2 Bar.* 27:15b–28:1a [similarly 25:1–4]). In order not to be deceived, the faithful will have to know God's law and be "observing the law in the last days" (*1 En.* 108:1). Likewise, those who will be of the tribe of Levi "will know the law of God and will give instructions concerning justice and concerning sacrifice for Israel until the consummation of times" (*T. Reub.* 6:8). Consequently, God's true people must be faithful to the law in the midst of wickedness "in the final days" (*b'ḥryt hymym*) in order not to be conformed to ungodliness and its erroneous teachings (1Q28a I:1). One is enabled to be faithful in this manner in the "last days" because "with a strong [hand he {God} turned me aside from walking on the path of] this people" (4Q174 frgs. 1, I,21,2:14–16).[16]

The Coming of the Messiah

One of the most popular hopes was that the Messiah or an equivalent figure would come at the end of time. For example, *4 Ezra* 12:32–34 says that the Messiah would judge the wicked and deliver saints at the "end of days" and the "end." The Messiah's coming would be "in the last days" (*Apoc. Ab.* 29:9–11; 4Q174 frgs. 1, I,21,2:11–12 [*b'ḥryt hymym*]), "at the consummation of time" (*2 Bar.* 29:3, 8; 30:1), or in "the last time" (*Sib. Or.* 5:414–433 [see esp. v. 432]).[17]

The Teacher of Righteousness, the inspired teacher who was so formative for that community's understanding of themselves as the true end-time community of God, was one "who teaches justice at the end of days [*b'ḥryt hymym*]" (CD-A VI:10–11). As such, he was a quasi-messianic figure.

Some of the Christian additions to the Jewish literature identify Christ's first coming to have happened in the eschaton (*Mart. Ascen. Isa.* 9:13, the incarnation of Christ "in the last days"; and *Sib. Or.* 8:456–459, the incarnation of Christ "in the last times") or to occur at "the end time," when he will judge (*Sib. Or.* 8:217–234).[18]

End-Time Suffering and Tribulation

In the end-time epoch directly before the very end of history, God's people will undergo great suffering, including persecution for their faith (see, e.g., *Sib. Or.*

16. Here I follow the translation of the lacuna supplied in Florentino García Martínez and Eibert J. C. Tigchelaar, *The Dead Sea Scrolls Study Edition*, 2 vols. (Grand Rapids: Eerdmans, 2000), 1:353. Here Ps. 1:1 and Isa. 8:11 are applied to the faithful who walk uninfluenced by the wicked in the "last days" (*l'ḥryt [h]ymym*).

17. See also *T. Jos.* 19:1–12; *T. Benj.* 11:2–3, on which, refer to the introductory section of this chapter.

18. Intriguingly, *Sibylline Oracles* views the coming of a Roman ruler to occur "when the end of the time of the age is at hand" (11:270–275). This figure is portrayed as "a prince" who "will be king, a godlike man," a perspective, of course, from the pagan point of view.

5:73–79, where trials occur "in the final time").[19] Humanity will encounter all kinds of horrible trials (*Sib. Or.* 5:447–482) that will occur "in the last time" (5:447) and "at the end" (5:476), such as a massive "swarm of locusts," "a bloody war throwing the world into confusion," and birds that "will devour all mortals." "Many miseries will affect those who inhabit the world in the last times" (*4 Ezra* 8:50).[20] Much of this affliction will be caused by God's enemies in the "last days" (*4 Ezra* 12:23–26), and some of the suffering will be an outcome of internecine fighting among divine enemies "in the last days" (*4 Ezra* 12:28). An end-time opponent will arise "in the last time" who will cause great suffering (*Sib. Or.* 5:361–374 [in this case, the opponent is the supernaturally returning Nero]). Accordingly, God's people will experience "woe . . . dangers . . . distress" in "the last days" (*4 Ezra* 13:16–20). Indeed, all inhabitants of the earth living "at the end of days" and "the end of times" will suffer "many tribulations" and severe torments (*2 Bar.* 25:1–27:5). Likewise, the Qumran community predicts that there will be a "laying waste [of] the land through drought and hunger" in "the last days" (4Q162 II:1). Even true, faithful priests will suffer "at the end of days" (*b'hryt hymym*) (CD-A IV:4–5).[21]

A Christian addition to *Martyrdom and Ascension of Isaiah* (4:1–3) foretells persecution by the antichrist at the time of the "completion of the world."

An Absolute End of Sin and Evil

Judaism believed that there would be an absolute end of sin. For example, *Testament of Levi* affirms that there will be "transgression" that people "may commit until the consummation of the ages," but no sin will be done after that point (10:2). In *4 Ezra* 6:27 it is said that at the time of the final resurrection "evil shall be blotted out, and deceit shall be quenched." Similarly, at the conclusion of "the end of this age" there follows directly "the beginning of the immortal age to come, in which corruption has passed away, sinful indulgence has come to an end, unbelief has been cut off"; at this time no one will be able "to harm him who is victorious" (*4 Ezra* 7:43[113]–45[115]).

Other Ideas Related to the End Times

Among other notions associated with end-time happenings are:

1. "In the last days God will send his compassion on all the earth" (*T. Zeb.* 8:2).
2. God's people will experience eternal rest. According to *4 Ezra* 2:34, this rest will come at "the end of the age," and *L.A.E.* [*Vita*] 51:2 explains

19. Though this could be conceived of as having been inaugurated in Egypt's history at some point during its long demise.
20. See also *4 Ezra* 10:59 ("what the Most High will do to those who dwell on earth in the last days") in light of the following two chapters.
21. Curiously, the trials of humanity's scattering and conflict at the judgment of Babel is said to have happened "in the last days" of the first world (*L.A.B.* 6:1).

that "the seventh day is a sign of the resurrection," which represents "the rest of the coming age."

3. The kingdom will come "at the end of the age" (*4 Ezra* 2:34–35). "At the last years" Adam will "sit on the throne of him who overthrew him" (*L.A.E.* [*Vita*] 47:3).

4. Complete salvation will come to the faithful. For example, those who have persevered through the final end-time trials "shall be saved and see my salvation and the end of my world" (cf. *4 Ezra* 6:25 with 6:13–24).

5. There will be certain signs that the end of the world is near. *Sibylline Oracles* 3:796–807 refers to spectacular signs in the heavens that will occur "when the end of all things comes to pass." "Famine and civil war" will also be warnings that "the end of the world and the last day is near" (*Sib. Or.* 8:88–94). Close family members being hostile to one another also will be a harbinger by which people should "know that the end is near" (*Gk. Apoc. Ezra* 3:11–15). *Sibylline Oracles* 2:154–171 lists further signs that will take place during "the last generation."

6. The eschatological period will last a long time. *Sibylline Oracles* 5:344–350 affirms that "the last time" and "that day will last a long time." In addition, 1QpHab VII:1–17 explains that "the consummation of the era" and "the final age" (mentioned twice) "will be extended and go beyond all that the prophets say, because the mysteries of God are wonderful" (this is stated again a few lines later).

7. Redemption of God's people will occur at the eschaton. In this regard, for instance, 11Q13 II:4, 13 (see the context of II:1–25) says that Melchizedek, apparently an angelic figure, will "free them [the sons of light] from the hand of Belial" "in the last days" (*l'ḥryt hymym*).

8. "The final age" refers to the completion of God's plan for all of history (*2 En.* 33:1–11; see esp. v. 11).

Conclusion

The preceding survey shows that almost all the topics found earlier to be associated with the OT use of "latter days" recur in the early Jewish literature. The ideas of the end-time Spirit and latter-day new covenant have not been found in connection with any latter-day expressions, as in the OT, though it is plausible that further study of the broader contexts where this language appears may yield indirect links with such language. But even if not, apart from formal end-time language, eschatological conceptions of the Spirit and new covenant do occur in this literature.[22]

22. For the latter, see CD-A VI:19; VIII:21; CD-B XIX:33–34; XX:12; for the former, see 1QS IV:3–11; 1QHᵃ VIII:1–13; see also 1QHᵃ VI:13–19; *T. Jud.* 24:1–6.

Some apparently new ideas in conjunction with technical eschatological language are developed in early Judaism, but these do occur elsewhere in Judaism separately from precise eschatological wording. In fact, these apparently "new" Jewish concepts are even implicit in the OT contexts containing latter-day formulas:

1. There will be reception of a glorious inheritance, which is an aspect of the Adamic and patriarchal blessings; the need for eschatological wisdom, which is part of the eschatological scenario of Dan. 11:32–35; 12:3–4, 9–10.
2. There will be an absolute end of sin and evil, which is implied in the OT end-time prophecies of the defeat of evil kingdoms, perhaps especially in Dan. 2:44–45; 8:25; 11:45.
3. End-time eternal rest is not explicit in the OT, but I argued earlier that it is implied in Gen. 1:28; 2:3.
4. That the eschatological period will last a long time is a point made earlier in connection with some OT passages that we observed in which the latter days begin, at least, at the time of Israel's restoration from Babylon. These inaugurated latter days are not culminated in the initial return and building of the second temple but continue on throughout the entire Second Temple period. God's latter-day compassion probably has a close analogue in the "goodness" expressed toward Israel in Hos. 3:5.

The ideas that the final end refers to the completion of God's plan for all of history, and that certain signs indicate that the end of the world is near, appear to be more novel than the ones just mentioned. The latter would be fairly easily deducible from Dan. 11–12, where severe persecution of the faithful and deception within the covenant community directly precede the resurrection of the saints. Furthermore, some of the "day of the LORD" passages in the prophets speak of signs in the heavens betokening or accompanying God's judgment, both of evil nations and of Israel (Isa. 13:10; 24:23; Ezek. 32:8; Joel 2:10, 30–31; 3:15). The eschaton being the completion of the divine decree would also be an understandable biblical-theological deduction from several OT passages (cf. Eccles. 3:1–17 with Isa. 41:4; 44:6–8; 48:12–14; Dan. 7:10; 12:2).

So there is nothing really absolutely new in early Judaism, though there are developments and different emphases.

5

The Eschatological Storyline of the Old Testament in Relation to the New Testament

The New Testament Focus on the Latter Days

As we saw in the OT and early Judaism in the preceding chapters, it should not be astonishing to discover that eschatology is a dominant idea in the NT. In fact, it is not an overstatement to say that to understand NT eschatology, one must have some acquaintance with how the NT authors viewed eschatology or the "end times."[1] This may sound like a surprising proposition, since people in the church often think of the end times as a period that will happen only at the very climax of history. Many biblical scholars are not immune to such a myopic view. After all, can one not have an excellent understanding of the NT without knowing exactly how the world is going to end? Are not questions about the time of the so-called rapture, tribulation, second coming, and millennium secondary to the salvation that Christ accomplished at the cross and through his resurrection? These questions could be answered with a "yes" if the end times were a period coming only at the very final phase of history. Unfortunately, many assume this to be true, so that Christ's death

---

1. On the vagueness of the term "eschatology" and clarification of its definition, see I. Howard Marshall, "Slippery Words I: Eschatology," *ExpTim* 89 (1978): 264–69; for the relation of the term to "apocalyptic," see David E. Aune, "Apocalypticism," *DPL* 25–35; see also Larry J. Kreitzer, "Eschatology," *DPL* 253–69.

and resurrection are events that happened at his first coming and therefore are not eschatological in nature and are not closely connected with those events leading to his second coming.

However, such an understanding of the latter days that views them as arriving only at the very end of history needs rethinking. The phrase "latter days" (and similar phrases) occurs numerous times in the NT and often does not refer exclusively to the very end of history, as we typically think of it. This wording is used frequently to describe the end times as beginning already in the first century. Consequently, a survey of these phrases in the NT as well as a brief overview of the language in the OT, Judaism,[2] and the Apostolic Fathers demand that the popular and even often-held scholarly view be reassessed. What especially needs reevaluation is the approach to NT theology that considers eschatology not as central but merely as one of many topics that together compose an overall theology of the NT. I could widen the following study of the NT to include other conceptual references to eschatology, but the present survey of explicit eschatological terms will be sufficient to make the point.[3]

The following survey of eschatological language in the NT changed my entire perspective on the NT, and I hope that the same will happen with readers of this book.

Eschatological References in the Synoptic Gospels

While we will see in a later chapter how greatly inaugurated eschatology permeates the Synoptic Gospels, actual end-time terminology does not appear much, and when it does, it always refers to the "not yet" aspect, typically with the language of the final "age" (*aiōn*) that is coming. The phrase "end of the age" (*synteleia tou aiōnos*) refers either to the final, coming judgment in the future (Matt. 13:39–40, 49; likely also 24:3) or to Christ's presence that will continue with his people until the end of time (Matt. 28:20). The saints will receive "in the age to come, eternal life" (Mark 10:30 // Luke 18:30), which is also directly linked with "resurrection from the dead" (Luke 20:34–35). The Messiah's "reign" is also said to last "unto the age" or "forever," referring to the unending eschatological period (Luke 1:33). Sometimes there is reference

---

2. The uses in the OT and Judaism have been discussed in the preceding chapters.

3. Here I will not even survey the prolific eschatological references to "day" throughout the NT, which refer typically to the final judgment, final time of salvation, or generally to Christ's final coming (though 1 Thess. 5:2–8 appears to portray an already–not yet perspective of the eschatological "day"). Similarly, the expression "the day of the Lord" is particularly thorny, since in the OT it appears to refer to judgments on Israel (Joel 1:15; 2:1, 11, 31; Amos 5:18, 20; Zeph. 1:7, 14; cf. Mal. 3:2, 5) or on other nations (Isa. 13:6, 9; Ezek. 30:3; Joel 3:14; Obad. 15) that took place within the OT era, whereas in the NT it refers to the final day of judgment in the future via some kind of typological rationale (1 Cor. 5:5; 1 Thess. 5:2; 2 Thess. 2:2; 2 Pet. 3:10; see the phrase in Acts 2:20, where there is debate on the timing of its fulfillment).

to coming signs or events that precede the "end" (*telos*) (Matt. 24:6 [// Mark 13:7; Luke 21:9]; 24:13–14).

Eschatological References in the Gospel of John

Like the Synoptic Gospels, the Gospel of John can speak of the last judgment and the final bodily resurrection as occurring in the future, though he uses the language of "the last day" (*tē eschatē hēmera*). For example, in 6:40 Jesus says, "For this is the will of My Father, that everyone who beholds the Son and believes in Him, will have eternal life, and I myself will raise him up on the last day" (so also 6:39, 44, 54; 11:24; for judgment, see 12:48). Likewise, Jesus refers to resurrection life that will continue "forever" (*eis ton aiōna* ["unto the age"]) or "unto eternal life" (*eis zōēn aiōnion*) (4:14; 6:51, 58). Similarly, when the Messiah comes, he will exist "forever" (*eis ton aiōna*) (12:34), as will his Spirit (14:16).

Unlike the Synoptics, John's Gospel contains formal language that indicates that the latter days have begun with the first coming of Christ. In particular, as we just noted, although Jesus asserts that the resurrection is future, in 5:24–29 he affirms that the resurrection both is coming and has already come, so that the unending eschatological age has already begun:

> Truly, truly, I say to you, he who hears My word, and believes Him who sent Me, <u>has eternal life</u>, and does not come into judgment, but has passed out of death <u>into life</u>. Truly, truly, I say to you, an <u>hour is coming and now is, when the dead will hear the voice of the Son of God, and those who hear will live</u>. For just as the Father has life in Himself, even so He gave to the Son also to have life in Himself; and He gave Him authority to execute judgment, because He is the Son of Man. Do not marvel at this; <u>for an hour is coming, in which all who are in the tombs will hear His voice, and will come forth; those who did the good deeds to a resurrection of life, those who committed the evil deeds to a resurrection</u> of judgment.

Jesus's words about the "hour" of the resurrection are from the well-known resurrection prophecy of Dan. 12:1–2. In particular, verses 28–29 quote Dan. 12:2 (see table 5.1).

Jesus is referring in verses 28–29 to how future physical resurrection will still assuredly occur, just as Daniel prophesied. However, notice that Jesus also clearly refers to the same Daniel prophecy in verses 24–25 and applies it to people presently (or imminently) coming to life ("an hour is coming and *now is*"). Is he saying that those who are presently entering into "eternal life" are only like resurrected beings but are not really resurrected beings because their physical resurrection has not yet occurred, as verses 28–29 say that such a physical resurrection will occur?

Table 5.1

Daniel 12:1–2 (OG)	John 5:24–25, 28–29
	5:24: ". . . he who hears My word, and believes Him who sent Me, has <u>eternal life</u>, and does not come into judgment, but has passed out of death into <u>life</u>.
12:1: "And at that <u>hour</u> . . . 12:2: "Many of <u>those who sleep</u> in the width of the earth <u>will arise</u> [*anastēsontai*] . . . some unto <u>eternal life</u> and others to <u>reproach</u> . . . <u>and to eternal shame</u>."	5:25: ". . . an <u>hour is coming</u> and now is, when the dead will hear the voice of the Son of God, and those who hear will live."
	5:28: ". . . for an <u>hour is coming</u>, in which <u>all who are in the tombs</u> will hear His voice, 5:29: "and <u>will come forth</u>; those who did the good deeds to a <u>resurrection</u> [*anastasin*] of <u>life</u>, those who committed the evil deeds to a <u>resurrection</u> [*anastasin*] of <u>judgment</u>."

Note: Solid underlining represents direct literary allusions, and broken underlining represents conceptual allusions.

Again, it is apparent that an OT prophecy is applied to believers in the present because they are actually beginning to fulfill it. Jesus understands the Dan. 12 prophecy to have begun fulfillment. The most telltale sign of this is Jesus's reference to "hour." Daniel's "hour" (*hōra*) of resurrection (followed by tribulation) and prophecy of "eternal life" is not merely to find fulfillment at the very end of world history (John 5:28) but has begun at Christ's first coming (John 5:25). The phrase "eternal life" is found in the LXX only in Dan. 12:2,[4] so that John 5:24's reference to the same phrase is an allusion to that text. We will also see directly below that John's use of "hour" in an end-time sense derives from the OG of Dan. 8; 11–12, where it is equivalent to explicit end-time expressions in the Hebrew and refers to end-time events (e.g., Dan. 8:17, 19; 11:35, 40). And as we just have seen, in Dan. 12:1–2 it refers to the hour of tribulation followed by resurrection. In fact, the "hour" of Dan. 12:1 OG is further understood as "the hour of the end" in Dan. 12:4 OG.

Daniel's end-time "hour" of resurrection has begun, but it will be completed in the future. How has the final resurrection begun? Must we not "spiritualize" or "allegorize" Daniel's prophecy to say that it can be fulfilled without there being a "physical" fulfillment? I contend, indeed, that Jesus is saying both that this prophecy is beginning fulfillment and that it is beginning "literal" fulfillment. Daniel was predicting not only a physical resurrection but also a spiritual one: he believed that when the body is resurrected, the renewed spirit will be resurrected with it. Thus, he predicted the resurrection of the whole

4. The same phrase is found in 2 Macc. 7:9; 4 Macc. 15:3; and *Pss. Sol.* 3:12 (125 BC to first century AD), which likely themselves allude to Dan. 12:2.

person.[5] What is a bit unexpected about the way Jesus sees it being fulfilled is only the timing of the fulfillment. It is being fulfilled in a *staggered* manner: first, in this age, believers are raised spiritually from the dead, and then beginning in the new eternal age to come their bodies will be raised. Thus, the saints' spiritual resurrection is a beginning literal fulfillment of Daniel's eschatological prophecy of a "spiritual-physical" resurrection.

In light of the Danielic background of John 5:25–28 and its inclusion of reference to the Dan. 7:13 "Son of Man," it is likely that John 12:23 is to be read against the same background: "And Jesus answered them, saying, 'The hour has come for the Son of Man to be glorified.'" Dan. 7:13–14 prophesies that the "Son of Man" will be an end-time eternal king and receive glory from all. The context of John 12:23–34 indicates that this reception of latter-day glory will, ironically, begin at Jesus's crucifixion and later at his resurrection (the same use of "hour" also likely occurs in John 17:1).

There is an eschatological use of "hour" (*hōra*) in 1 John that will have to wait for discussion until we survey the General Epistles below, but because of its significant bearing on the Gospel's usage, I address it very briefly here.[6] In 1 John 2:18 the writer says, "Children, it is the last hour; and just as you heard that antichrist is coming, even now many antichrists have appeared; from this we know that it is the last hour." As we will see in further analysis of this passage, this again, like John 5:25, is a classic "already and not yet" end-time passage that affirms that the later tribulation has begun to break through.

It is in light of this discussion of John 5:24–29 and 1 John 2:18 that uses of "hour" (*hōra*) in John 16 are best understood. The same phrase "an hour is coming" found in 5:25, 28 and 1 John 2:18 appears in 16:2, 25 (likewise 16:4, 21). In fact, even the fuller "already and not yet" phrase found in John 5:25 and 1 John 2:18 (though in altered form) is encountered in 16:32: "Behold, an hour is coming, and has <u>already</u> come, for you to be scattered, each to his own home, and to leave me alone; and yet I am not alone, because the Father is with me." These same syntagmatic expressions tie the uses in John 16 to those in 5:25 and 5:28, as well as with 1 John 2:18. All five uses in John 16 pertain to tribulation for Jesus's followers and thus fit well into the Danielic uses of "hour" in the OG, where they refer to the eschatological "hour" of trial and persecution for faithful Israel.

---

5. Judaism specifically refers to "soul" and body participating in the final resurrection (e.g., *4 Ezra* 7:97–101, alluding to Dan. 12:3; likewise Ps.-Phoc. 103–115; *Apoc. Ezek.*, frg. 1, introduction, in allusion to Ezek. 37:1–14; Isa. 26:19 LXX; implicit in *4 Ezra* 7:32, in allusion to Dan. 12:2; see also *4 Ezra* 7:75, 88–101; for other references, see Josephus, *Ant.* 18.14; *J.W.* 3.374 [perhaps also 2.163]; *Sib. Or.* 4:187–191 [probably also 2:221–226]; *L.A.B.* 3:10; 23:13; *Hist. Rech.* 16:7a; *Pirqe R. El.* 31, 34).

6. Here I am assuming common authorship of John's Gospel and of 1 John (so, e.g., Colin G. Kruse, *The Letters of John*, PNTC [Grand Rapids: Eerdmans, 2000], 9–15). Even if one merely held that 1 John was written by someone in the Johannine circle, the point would still be pertinent.

One other significant eschatological use of "hour" in line with the preceding ones is in John 4:21–24:

> Jesus said to her, "Woman, believe Me, an hour is coming when neither in this mountain nor in Jerusalem will you worship the Father. You worship what you do not know; we worship what we know, for salvation is from the Jews. But an hour is coming, and now is, when the true worshipers will worship the Father in spirit and truth; for such people the Father seeks to be His worshipers. God is spirit, and those who worship Him must worship in spirit and truth."

Here is another classic "already and not yet" end-time formula, which we have observed in John 5:25; 16:32; 1 John 2:18. But what is eschatological about it? First, Jesus is saying that the place for true worship now and in the future is no longer in one location, such as Jerusalem, but rather is extended. But to where is it extended? True worship is any place where the end-time Spirit is or where worship in the sphere of that Spirit takes place: the time has come and will continue when true worshipers will worship the Father in the sphere of the promised Spirit and end-time truth that has come in Christ (4:23; so also 4:24). Thus, to worship "in spirit and truth" is not a reference to "truly sincere" worshipers or worshipers who are "sincere in their spirit about the truth" (in which there is no capitalization), but is a reference to the Spirit, who has come in fulfillment of the OT promises. Accordingly, the first clause of 4:24 should be rendered "God is the Spirit" rather than "God is spirit."[7] "Truth" (*alētheia*) also has an eschatological nuance of fulfillment in light of the same use elsewhere in John, especially when used in relation to typological realities from the OT that are seen as foreshadowing what has come in Christ (note *alēthinos* or *alēthēs* in the following passages: "true light" [1:9]; "true bread" [6:32]; "true food" and "true drink" [6:55]; "true vine" [15:1]). Here God's presence in Israel's localized temple is viewed as foreshadowing God's tabernacling presence in Jesus now and his people later, after his resurrection and the sending of the Spirit.

A reference to the Holy Spirit in John 4:23b and 4:24b would not be unnatural or unusual for John, since outside of John 4, the Greek word *pneuma* occurs twenty-one times, at least seventeen of which refer to the divine "Spirit," two to Jesus's emotional "spirit," and once to the regenerated human "spirit" (John 3:6).[8]

7. For the latter, see D. A. Carson, *The Gospel according to John*, PNTC (Grand Rapids: Eerdmans, 1991), 224–26. Carson asserts that 4:24a should be rendered "God is spirit," referring to the spiritual dimension of God's being. This certainly is possible and does not necessarily negate my point about reference to the eschatological Spirit in 4:23b and 4:24b.

8. Possibly also 6:63 refers to the regenerated spirit: "It is the Spirit who gives life; the flesh profits nothing; the words that I have spoken to you are spirit and are life." But more likely the last clause further explains the first, carrying the notion of "the Spirit that gives life" or "life-giving Spirit." The fact that there is no definite article "the" before *pneuma* in 4:23–24 does not

What further indicates a reference to the divine "Spirit" in John 4:23–24 is that in the narrative flow of the chapter *pneuma* is symbolized implicitly by "living water" (4:10–11; so also 4:14) that quenches spiritual "thirst," and it would be natural for Jesus's use of *pneuma* later in the continuing discussion with the Samaritan woman to refer to God's Spirit. The dialogue about "living water" and quenching spiritual "thirst" in John 4 finds unique correspondence with John 7:37–39, where again "living water" is a symbol for the "Spirit" that quenches "thirst." John 7:38 is an allusion to three OT prophecies (Ezek. 47:1–12; Joel 3:18; Zech. 14:8) about the end-time temple that are beginning fulfillment in Jesus and his followers. One of these prophecies, Zech. 14:8, predicts that "living water will flow out of Jerusalem" and is connected later with all of the city and all of Judah becoming as "holy" as the temple itself (14:20–21). In light of Joel 3:18 and Ezek. 47:1–12, the water will flow out from the back of the temple and affect all of the land of Israel and beyond. Strikingly, the "living water" of John 4:10–11, 14 probably is also an allusion to Zech. 14:8,[9] so that this passage is developed further in the John 7 temple text.[10]

The notion in John 4:23–24 of the expanding geography of the place of the true temple and of true worship in the inaugurated new age is likely a continuation of the earlier narrative about the "living water" from Zech. 14 and is part of the anticipation of John 7:37–39, and thus its roots are in the idea of the expanding temple and its holiness prophesied in Zech. 14 and Ezek. 47, as well as elsewhere in the OT.[11] Specifically, God's special revelatory presence in the form of the Spirit will no longer be located in the holy of holies of Israel's temple but instead will break out of its architectural shackles in the eschaton and spread throughout the earth. The true temple and true place of worship and true worshipers can be found wherever the extending form of God's holy of holies presence in the Spirit goes and among whoever is included in its sphere.[12] Consequently, wherever a true believer is, there also is the Spirit, as John 7:37–39 affirms.

---

militate against its identification as the divine Spirit, since four other instances of clear reference to the divine Spirit also do not have the article "the" (1:33; 3:5; 7:39; 20:22), a stylistic feature elsewhere in the NT, as well as the LXX (note that 1:33 has exactly the same wording as 4:23–24 with the addition of "holy": *en pneumati hagiō* [lit., "in the Holy Spirit"]).

9. The margin of NA²⁷ at John 4:10–11 notes the Zech. 14:8 allusion.

10. Another link between the two passages is the remarkably similar language of "a well of water springing up to eternal life" (4:14) and "from his innermost being will flow rivers of living water" (7:38).

11. On which, see further G. K. Beale, *The Temple and the Church's Mission: A Biblical Theology of the Dwelling Place of God*, NSBT 17 (Downers Grove, IL: InterVarsity, 2004), 192–200, as well as passim for this notion throughout both Testaments.

12. If 4:23b and 4:24b do refer to the believer's regenerated "spirit" and not to the divine "Spirit," which is quite plausible, then my point about the expanding end-time temple and worship here still stands. Carson (*John*, 224–25) sees the possibility that the divine "Spirit" may well be in mind in these two verses.

To sum up, John has an already–not yet understanding of eschatology in which he sees that the latter-day resurrection, Spirit, tribulation, and temple have begun fulfillment but are yet to be consummately fulfilled.

Eschatological References in Acts[13]

Past and Present

The first time the wording "last days" appears in the NT (in canonical order) is Acts 2:17, where Peter explains, "'And it shall be in the last days,' God says, 'that I will pour forth of My Spirit upon all mankind; and your sons and your daughters shall prophesy.'" Here Peter understands that the tongues being spoken at Pentecost are a beginning fulfillment of Joel's end-time prophecy that a day would come when God's Spirit would gift not merely prophets, priests, and kings, but all classes of people in the covenant community would "prophesy" (Acts 2:15–17a; cf. Joel 2:28–29). At the beginning of the Joel 2:28 quotation, Peter substitutes the phrase "in the latter days" (*en tais eschatais hēmerais*) in place of Joel's "after these things" (*meta tauta*). The substitution comes from Isa. 2:2–3 (the only place in the LXX where this exact phrase occurs):[14]

> In the last days
> The mountain of the house of the LORD
> Will be established as the chief of the mountains,
> And will be raised above the hills;
> And all the nations will stream to it.
> And many peoples will come and say,
> "Come, let us go up to the mountain of the LORD,
> To the house of the God of Jacob."

Thus, Peter appears to interpret the Spirit's coming at Pentecost upon the Christian community in fulfillment of Joel also to be the beginning fulfillment of Isaiah's prophecy of the end-time temple, under the influence of which the nations would come. Part of the reason for linking these texts is that the following context of Joel itself is concerned with the establishment of the end time temple (Joel 3:18).[15]

---

13. The following sections on eschatology in Acts, Hebrews, the General Epistles, and the Apostolic Fathers (though not on Paul) use and expand on G. K. Beale, "Eschatology," *DLNTD* 332–37, 341–45.

14. On which, see discussion above of Isa. 2:2; also David W. Pao, *Acts and the Isaianic New Exodus*, WUNT 2/130 (Tübingen: Mohr Siebeck, 2000), 156–59.

15. On which, see further G. K. Beale, "The Descent of the Eschatological Temple in the Form of the Spirit at Pentecost: Part I," *TynBul* 56, no. 1 (2005): 93–99, as well as chap. 18 of this book, for the full argument that the descent of the Spirit at Pentecost was the inauguration of the church as the end-time temple. Interestingly, some LXX manuscripts of Joel 2:28 have *en*

The resurrection marked the beginning of Jesus's messianic reign, and the Spirit at Pentecost signaled the inauguration of his rule through the church (see Acts 1:6–8; 2:1–43).

At significant transitional points in Acts where the gospel is being extended to new regions or ethnic entities, the pouring out of the Spirit is repeatedly mentioned in order to indicate events subsequent to Pentecost that followed in its pattern, perhaps to be considered as "little Pentecosts." These later outpourings continue to demonstrate Christ's exalted reign, but they also indicate that gentiles as well as Jews are accepted by faith and are included as subjects in the Messiah's new kingdom. This is a point implied from Acts 2, where Jews representing all parts of the known gentile world were present at Pentecost. The clearest example of a subsequent outpouring of the Spirit modeled on Acts 2 is Acts 10:34–47, where the Roman soldier Cornelius and his gentile associates believed in Christ, and "the gift of the Holy Spirit [was] . . . poured out on the Gentiles also" (v. 45).

It is unlikely that Acts represents a "de-eschatologizing" by substituting a history of the church for a near expectation of the end.[16] Indeed, Luke sees that the pouring out of the Spirit is a further stage of eschatological fulfillment, which makes the time of the church an eschatological era.[17]

The reason why the coming of the Spirit is perceived in such a highlighted eschatological manner is that one of its purposes was to demonstrate the exalted, heavenly messianic kingship of Jesus, as a result of the resurrection from the dead. This is natural because the Spirit was linked with the future hope of resurrection life in the OT and in Judaism, a link found elsewhere also in the NT (see, e.g., Rom. 1:4; 1 Tim. 3:16).[18] As a consequence of Jesus's resurrection, the eschatological center of gravity had shifted from his ministry on earth to his reign in heaven. The very notion that Jesus had been raised from the dead was a highly charged end-time idea whose roots lay in the OT (Isa. 25:7–8; 26:18–19; Ezek. 37:1–14; Dan. 12:1–2) and postbiblical Judaism (e.g., 2 Macc. 7:9, 14; 1QH[a] XIX:12; *1 En.* 51:1; *2 Bar.* 30:1–3; 50:1–4; *T. Jud.* 25:1; *L.A.E.* [*Apocalypse*] 41:3). Consequently, other references to Jesus's resurrection throughout the book, though not formally linked with technical eschatological terminology as in Acts 2, are eschatological in nature, especially since often they are associated in context with OT hopes and promises

---

tais eschatais hēmerais, probably as a result of a Jewish scribe interpreting Joel by Isa. 2:2 or of a Christian scribe doing the same thing but under the influence of Acts 2:17.

16. As represented by, e.g., L. Sabourin, "The Eschatology of Luke," *BTB* 12 (1982): 73–76.

17. For both sides of the debate, see Beverly R. Gaventa, "The Eschatology of Luke-Acts Revisited," *Encounter* 43 (1982): 27–42; on the problem of the purported delay of Christ's final coming, see further Larry J. Kreitzer, "Parousia," *DLNTD* 872–73.

18. On which, see Geerhardus Vos, "The Eschatological Aspect of the Pauline Conception of the Spirit," in *Redemptive History and Biblical Interpretation: The Shorter Writings of Geerhardus Vos*, ed. Richard B. Gaffin Jr. (Phillipsburg, NJ: P&R, 1980), 91–125.

(see Acts 1:3–11, 22; 3:15, 26; 4:2, 10, 33; 5:30–31; 7:55–56; 9:3–6; 10:40–41; 13:30–37; 17:31–32; 22:6–11; 25:19; 26:6–18, 22–23). Likewise, the resurrection of some Christians probably was identified with Jesus's eschatological resurrection (Acts 9:37–41; 20:9–12; cf. Matt. 27:52–53).

That fulfillment of other latter-day OT prophecies, in addition to that of the resurrection and the outpouring of the Spirit, had been inaugurated certainly was also an indication that the last times had begun (Acts 3:18, 22–26; 4:25–28; 13:27–29, 46–48; 15:14–18; 26:22–23).

Future

In Acts 1:6 the disciples ask Jesus, "Is it at this time You are restoring the kingdom to Israel?" Jesus replies, "It is not for you to know times or epochs which the Father has fixed by His own authority" (1:7) and then promises that the Spirit will come upon them and empower them to witness (1:8). Some commentators understand verses 7–8 as a response that explains that there will be an indefinite delay of the coming of Israel's restored kingdom in its consummated form, but that during the interim period the Spirit will maintain the witness of Jesus's followers.[19] Accordingly, the time of the restoration of the kingdom is equated with the time of Jesus's final coming to conclude history, which is mentioned in the directly following context of verse 11. In addition, Acts 3:19–21 is seen to continue the theme of the future coming kingdom. Along these lines, in those verses the "times of refreshing" and the "times of restoration of all things" are to occur when Jesus returns to conclude history, apparently in the same way as he left at the ascension (cf. 1:11).

Another perspective on Acts 1:6–8, however, is plausible, if not probable. Jesus responds in verses 7–8 to three misunderstandings inherent in the apostles' question in verse 6. First, verse 7 is a response to their wrong assumption that it was proper for them to know the precise time (cf. 1 Thess. 5:1–11) about when the kingdom would be restored to Israel; such knowledge is reserved for the Father alone.

Second, verse 8 appears to be a response to an implicit assumption in the question of verse 6 that future stages of the kingdom would be only physical in their expression. Verse 8 contradicts this assumption. Although some understand the continued response of verse 8 to refer to the notion of a parenthetical period characterized by the Spirit that is not part of the messianic kingdom, it is more likely that the verse asserts that a near-future form of the kingdom is to be "spiritual" in nature ("you will receive *power* [of the kingdom] when the Holy Spirit has come"). This promise, of course, begins fulfillment at Pentecost, which Peter understands to be an escalation of the

---

19. See Anthony Buzzard, "Acts 1:6 and the Eclipse of the Biblical Kingdom," *EvQ* 66 (1994): 197–215.

"latter days" first inaugurated by Jesus, when he himself began to receive the Spirit at his baptism. In fact, "the latter days" were not only the time of the expected outpouring of God's Spirit in the OT and Judaism, but the OT inextricably linked the repeated phrase "latter days" with the prophesied kingdom, so that Peter's reference to the phrase in 2:17 conveys the notion of fulfillment of the foreseen kingdom (e.g., see the discussion and references in the first section of this chapter).

Third, 1:8 appears to be a reply to an apparent ethnocentric presupposition in 1:6 that the nature of the kingdom would be essentially Israelite ethnically and nationally. Jesus's reply is that the kingdom will encompass subjects who lived even "unto the end of the earth," in partial allusion to Isa. 49:6, which refers to Israel's and the nations' restoration (cf. Acts 13:47, which refers back to the conclusion of 1:8, and where the Isa. 49:6 reference is explicit). In addition, the reference in 1:8 to "the Holy Spirit coming upon you" is from Isa. 32:15: "until the Spirit is poured out upon us from on high," a prophecy of Israel's restoration.[20]

Hence, Acts 1:8 affirms what will be an ongoing and progressive fulfillment of the prophecy of the OT kingdom and Israel's restoration, which had already begun establishment in Jesus's earthly ministry.[21] In this light, the apostles' question in 1:6 may also reveal an incorrect eschatological presupposition: Israel's end-time restoration and kingdom would be fulfilled at one point of time at the very end of history. Jesus's response is that the fulfillment is "already and not yet," with the beginning stage of fulfillment being extended before consummation, as Acts 2 and following reveal, but that the apostles in Acts 1 did not understand.

Acts 3:20–21 clearly refers to the future consummation, when Christ comes a final time and achieves "the restoration of all things." Acts 3:19, however, may include an already–not yet notion, especially because of its placement directly following an assertion that God had already "fulfilled" OT prophecy about Christ's suffering: "Therefore repent and return, so that your sins may be wiped away, in order that times of refreshing may come from the presence of the Lord." This verse may be parallel to Acts 2:38: "Repent, and . . . be baptized . . . for the forgiveness of your sins, and you will receive the gift of the Holy Spirit." Likewise, Acts 3:22–26 refers to beginning fulfillments of

---

20. The allusion to Isa. 32:15 is made clearer by recognizing that the very end of Luke's first volume ends with the same allusion: "I am sending forth the promise of my Father upon you, but you are to stay in the city until you will be clothed with power from on high" (Luke 24:49), which Acts 1:4, 8 explicitly develops.

21. See David Hill, "The Spirit and the Church's Witness: Observations on Acts 1:6–8," *IBS* 6 (1984): 16–26, on which the preceding discussion of Acts 1:6–8 is partly based, though Hill denies that Luke has an inaugurated eschatological perspective. For a balanced, already–not yet view of Acts 1:6–8 and of the entire book, see F. F. Bruce, "Eschatology in Acts," in *Eschatology and the New Testament: Essays in Honor of George Raymond Beasley-Murray*, ed. W. Hulitt Gloer (Peabody, MA: Hendrickson, 1988), 51–63.

OT messianic prophecy.[22] Even the reference "until the times of restoration of all things" in 3:21 has an already–not yet notion, since the "restoration" had likely begun with Jesus's coming, his resurrection, and the giving of the Spirit.[23]

An incontestably future reference to a future judgment is Acts 17:30–31, where Paul affirms that people should repent in the present because God "has fixed a day" at the end of history when "he will judge the world in righteousness" through Jesus Christ (likewise Acts 24:25).[24]

Paul also affirms a "hope of the promise" of the final resurrection for the nation Israel in Acts 26:6–7, yet we learn from his letters that even this has been inaugurated in Christ's, the true Israel's, resurrection (as is clear from Acts 13:32–33; 23:6–7; 26:22–24).

Eschatological References in Paul's Writings

Present and Past

Paul says that the OT was written to instruct the Corinthian Christians about how to live in the end times, since upon them "the ends of the ages have come" (1 Cor. 10:11). He refers to Jesus's birth as occurring "when the fullness of the time came" in fulfillment of the messianic prophecies (Gal. 4:4).

22. For further argument in support of this analysis, see W. S. Kurz, "Acts 3:19–26 as a Test of the Role of Eschatology in Lukan Christology," *SBLSP* 11 (1977): 309–23, and sources cited therein; see also Hans F. Bayer, "Christ-Centered Eschatology in Acts 3:17–26," in *Jesus of Nazareth: Lord and Christ*, ed. Joel B. Green and Max Turner (Grand Rapids: Eerdmans, 1994), 236–50.

23. So Bayer, "Christ-Centered Eschatology."

24. On the futurist aspects of eschatology in Acts, see also Anders E. Nielsen, "The Purpose of the Lucan Writings with Particular Reference to Eschatology," in *Luke-Acts: Scandinavian Perspectives*, ed. Petri Luomanen, PFES 54 (Helsinki: Finnish Exegetical Society; Göttingen: Vandenhoeck & Ruprecht, 1991), 76–93; on the already–not yet notion of eschatology in Acts, which has its precedent in Luke's Gospel, see, e.g., E. Earle Ellis, "Present and Future Eschatology in Luke," *NTS* 12 (1965): 27–41; see further Henry J. Cadbury, "Acts and Eschatology," in *The Background of the New Testament and Its Eschatology: Studies in Honour of C. H. Dodd*, ed. W. D. Davies and D. Daube (Cambridge: Cambridge University Press, 1956), 300–321; Kevin Giles, "Present-Future Eschatology in the Book of Acts (I)," *RTR* 40 (1981): 65–71; idem, "Present-Future Eschatology in the Book of Acts (II)," *RTR* 41 (1982): 11–18; Eric Franklin, "The Ascension and the Eschatology of Luke-Acts," *SJT* 23 (1970): 191–200; Fred O. Francis, "Eschatology and History in Luke-Acts," *JAAR* 37 (1969): 49–63; Gaventa, "Eschatology of Luke-Acts" (which also gives a good overview of the history of the debate); see, similarly to Gaventa, Robert H. Smith, "The Eschatology of Acts and Contemporary Exegesis," *CTM* 29 (1958): 641–63; idem, "History and Eschatology in Luke-Acts," *CTM* 29 (1958): 881–901; John T. Carroll, *Response to the End of History: Eschatology and Situation in Luke-Acts*, SBLDS 92 (Atlanta: Scholars Press, 1988), 121–67 (although, see the apparently inconsistent p. 137); see also Andrew J. Mattill Jr., *Luke and the Last Things: A Perspective for the Understanding of Lukan Thought* (Dillsboro, NC: Western North Carolina Press, 1979), which focuses, however, on Luke's near expectation and hope of the end.

Likewise, "the fullness of the time" alludes to when believers were delivered from Satan and sin through Christ's death and resurrection (Eph. 1:7–10; 1:20–2:6), which commenced his own rule over the whole earth (Eph. 1:19–23). Christ's death and resurrection launched the beginning of the latter-day new creation prophesied by Isaiah (cf. 2 Cor. 5:17, "there is a new creation; the old things have passed away; behold, new things have come," with Isa. 43; 65–66); this new creation marks the turning point of the ages, which Paul refers to as "the now" (2 Cor. 5:16) and later formally defines as "the acceptable time" and "the day of salvation" (2 Cor. 6:2).[25] The end-time prophecies of Israel's restoration from exile reach beginning fulfillment in Christ's, the true Israel's, resurrection and in those in the church who identify by faith with him (e.g., 2 Cor. 6:16–18).[26]

In addition, the presence of tribulation in the form of false, deceptive teaching at the church of Ephesus is also one of the signs that the long-awaited latter days had finally come (1 Tim. 4:1; 2 Tim. 3:1). The wording in 2 Tim. 3:1 (*en eschatais hēmerais*) is a general echo of the repeated corresponding phrases "in the latter days" of the LXX.[27] That this idea in 1–2 Timothy is not a reference only to a distant, future time is evident in the recognition that the Ephesian church is already experiencing the latter-day tribulation of deceptive teaching and apostasy (see 1 Tim. 1:3–4, 6, 7, 19–20; 4:7; 5:13–15; 6:20–21; 2 Tim. 1:15; 2:16–19, 25–26; 3:2–9). This understanding of a latter-day tribulation characterized by false teaching and unbelief is in line with the expectation that we observed in Dan. 7–12 and in early Judaism (especially the DSS and *Testaments of the Twelve Patriarchs*).

Future

Paul makes general references to the everlasting eschatological time ("forever," *eis tous aiōnas*) that have a predominantly future focus. God and the Messiah will be "blessed forever" (Rom. 1:25; 9:5) and will receive "glory forever" (respectively Rom. 11:36; 16:27; Gal. 1:5; see also 2 Tim. 4:18 with respect to the "Lord").

The apostle can also refer to the future fulfillment of the latter days. In 1 Cor. 15:24 he says that at "the end" Christ "delivers up the kingdom to the God and Father, when he has abolished all rule and all authority and power." And in 1 Cor. 1:8 he states that God will also "confirm" believers "to the end [*telos*], blameless in the day of our Lord Jesus Christ" (cf. the similar use of *telos* in 2 Cor. 1:13).

---

25. See G. K. Beale, "The Old Testament Background of Reconciliation in 2 Corinthians 5–7 and Its Bearing on the Literary Problem of 2 Corinthians 4:14–7:1," *NTS* 35 (1989): 550–81.

26. Ibid.

27. Although they all, except Isa. 2:2 (*en tais eschatais hēmerais*), begin with the Greek preposition *ep'* instead of *en* and are in the genitive, so that the 2 Timothy phrase is closest to the Isaiah passage.

Eschatological References in Hebrews

Past and Present

The book of Hebrews begins with God, who "in these last days [*ep' eschatou tōn hēmerōn toutōn*] has spoken to us in his son, whom he appointed heir of all things" (1:2). This may be a collective allusion to the near-verbatim case forms of the same repeated phrase (so 16x) that corresponds to the Hebrew OT passages containing "in the latter days" (*bĕ'aḥărît hayyāmîm*), which I discussed earlier in chapter 3. The exact form of this phrase in Heb. 1:2 (though without the final *toutōn* ["these"]) occurs four times in the OT, all of which are translations of the Hebrew "in the latter days" (*bĕ'aḥărît hayyāmîm*) from Num. 24:14; Jer. 23:20; 25:19 (49:39 MT); Dan. 10:14.[28] It may well be that the Num. 24 messianic passage is echoed, since the wording at the end of Heb. 1:2 (the "Son, whom He appointed heir of all things") is an allusion to Ps. 2:7–8 concerning the messianic "Son," who will "inherit" the nations and the "ends of the earth." Interestingly, both Num. 24:14–20 and Ps. 2:8–9[29] use "scepter" (*šēbeṭ* [Num. 24:17; Ps. 2:9]) as an image for the Messiah, who will "crush" the "nations" (Num. 24:17; Ps. 2:9 [LXX: "rule" over them]) and receive them as an "inheritance" (Num. 24:18; Ps. 2:8). That Heb. 1:2 is combining the "latter days" of Num. 24:14 with Ps. 2 is also suggested by 2 Pet. 1:17–19, where an allusion to Ps. 2:7 is followed by an allusion to Num. 24:17.[30]

In this respect, Heb. 1:5–13 cites OT prophecies primarily concerning the messianic son's kingship that have begun fulfillment in Jesus's first advent (see also 5:5; 8:1; 10:12–13; 12:2). Likewise, the portrayal of the ideal Adam's reign as "the Son of Man" from Ps. 8, never completely realized in the OT period, is applied to Christ as the one who finally has started to "fill the shoes" of this exemplary human figure (Heb. 2:6–9). Christ has done what the first Adam and Israel (the corporate Adam) failed to achieve.[31] It is in this sense of Christ's "fulfillment" of end-time prophecy that he is also to be understood as a "son" who was "made [eschatologically] complete" (not "perfected") and has begun to lead and will finish leading his people to their end-time completed salvation (see further 2:10; 5:8–9, 14; 6:1; 7:11, 19, 28; 9:9; 10:1, 14; 11:40; 12:2).[32] In this manner, Christ has decisively defeated the power of the devil and death (2:14), a reality not expected to occur until the eschatological new creation. The writer to the Hebrews can even refer in 9:26 to Christ's mission "to put

---

28. Dan. 10:14 OG contains the reading *ep' eschatou tōn hēmerōn*; Dan. 10:14 TH reads almost identically.

29. Here in mind are both the Hebrew and the Greek texts of Num. 24 and Ps. 2.

30. Among the Qumran texts, 4Q174 frgs. 1, I,21,2:18–21 understands Ps. 2:1–3 to refer to "the end of days," when the nations will oppress "the elect of Israel."

31. For the notion of Israel as a corporate Adam, see N. T. Wright, *The Climax of the Covenant: Christ and the Law in Pauline Theology* (Minneapolis: Fortress, 1992), 21–26.

32. See Moisés Silva, "Perfection and Eschatology in Hebrews," *WTJ* 39 (1976): 60–71.

away sin by the sacrifice of himself" as happening at the "consummation of the ages" (cf. 10:10, 12, 14).

Consequently, as seen elsewhere in the Gospels, Acts, and Paul, Christ's first coming commences the beginning of the end times, which had been prophesied by the OT. This is why the author refers to the beginning fulfillment of Jeremiah's prophecy of a new covenant, which is concluded in Jeremiah and Hebrews with an underscoring of the forgiveness of sin: "I will forgive their iniquity, and their sin I will remember no more" (cf. Jer. 31:31–34 with Heb. 8:8–12; 10:16–17). In line with the end-time tone of Heb. 9:26, Jeremiah's prophecy was also one that was inextricably linked to "latter-day" happenings (cf. Jer. 30:24 ["in the latter days"] with 31:31 ["days are coming"], 31:33 ["after those days"]). Jeremiah 30:24 says that the people of Israel "in the latter days will understand" what is "the intent of his [God's] heart" in expressing his "fierce anger" against them. This appears to be developed in Jer. 31:31–34, where it is said that God will put his "law within them and on their heart," which is based on him "forgiving their iniquity." That is, Israel would understand that the consequence of God's judgment of them is not merely to punish, but ultimately that forgiveness would be extended to them.

The writer of Hebrews says that Jesus's followers have also "tasted the powers" of "the age to come" (6:5), among which, apparently, is "the heavenly gift . . . of the Holy Spirit" (6:4).[33] This is the closest the NT comes formally to identifying the Holy Spirit as a mark of the inbreaking eschatological age (although see also Rom. 8:23; 2 Cor. 1:21–22; Eph. 1:13–14). Even Christians' "hope" of a future consummated salvation is rooted in Christ as already having begun to realize that hope (see 6:17–20).[34] In fact, Christians have already "come to Mount Zion and to the city of the living God, the heavenly [new] Jerusalem" (12:22), so that the expected latter-day city of God has invaded invisibly into the present age in order that saints may now be able to participate in it. Likewise, Christ's priestly work of sacrificing himself has inaugurated the eschatological temple (9:8, 23).[35] Those who spurn Christ's "once for all" sacrifice at the "consummation of the ages" (9:26) cannot be "renewed to repentance," since no other sacrifice will be offered other than the one that they have despised (6:4–6; 10:26–29).[36]

One striking feature of the eschatology of Hebrews, though also a trait of NT eschatology elsewhere, is its two-dimensional nature: it is characterized by vertical

33. See Paul Ellingworth, *The Epistle to the Hebrews: A Commentary on the Greek Text*, NIGTC (Grand Rapids: Eerdmans, 1993), 320. It appears that "the holy gift" is identified in the following clause to be "the Holy Spirit."

34. See further William C. Robinson, "Eschatology of the Epistle to the Hebrews: A Study in the Christian Doctrine of Hope," *Encounter* 22 (1961): 37–51.

35. See L. D. Hurst, "Eschatology and 'Platonism' in the Epistle to the Hebrews," SBLSP 23 (1984): 41–74.

36. See Charles E. Carlston, "Eschatology and Repentance in the Epistle to the Hebrews," *JBL* 78 (1959): 296–302.

and horizontal planes, or spatial and temporal elements. The preceding discussion focused on the temporal aspect that the "end times" had begun in Christ's past work but also the final "end" was still to come in the future. In the light of the spatial perspective, the end-time temple, for example, can be viewed both as a reality in present time that extends spatially from the heavenly dimension into the earthly and also as an invisible spatial dimension different from that of the material, earthly dimension (Heb. 9:1–10:26) because of the work of Christ.[37]

Future

Hebrews refers to the everlasting eschatological period ("forever," *eis ton aiōna*),[38] which has a predominantly future focus, though the present beginning of that period is not out of sight. Jesus's end-time reign (1:8), his priesthood (5:6; 7:17, 21, 24, 28), and his glory (13:21) are everlasting.

There is debate about whether the "rest" of Heb. 3–4 has been inaugurated with Christ's first coming[39] or whether it is a reality only at the final consummation.[40] Both views are supported by viable arguments, though the futuristic conception of the rest is, perhaps, more likely. The emphasis throughout Heb. 3–4, as well as the entire letter, is upon persevering until the end, when the final reward is to be received (3:6, 14). Furthermore, the "rest" is referred to as "a promise" that "remains," meaning that it has not yet been fulfilled (4:1, 6, 9). While it is true that the "rest" is spoken of as being present (4:3: "we enter that rest") and even past (4:10: "the one who has entered his rest"), these uses are best understood as being viewed from a future vantage point.[41] The dominant theme of these two chapters is that in contrast to Israel's failure to enter the "rest" of the promised land after its wilderness sojourn and subsequently in its history, the Jewish Christians addressed in the book of Hebrews are exhorted to persevere in their earthly sojourn so that they will enter the "rest" of the antitypical "heavenly country" (11:16), which the land of Canaan typologically foreshadowed. Only then will the intended Sabbath rest of the new creation be enjoyed.[42]

37. For this notion in Paul's thought, see Kreitzer, "Eschatology."

38. As well as other case forms of the expression.

39. So C. K. Barrett, "The Eschatology of the Epistle to the Hebrews," in Davies and Daube, eds., *Background of the New Testament*, 366–73; Andrew T. Lincoln, "Sabbath, Rest, and Eschatology in the New Testament," in *From Sabbath to Lord's Day: A Biblical, Historical, and Theological Investigation*, ed. D. A. Carson (Grand Rapids: Zondervan, 1982), 197–220.

40. So Richard B. Gaffin Jr., "A Sabbath Rest Still Awaits the People of God," in *Pressing toward the Mark: Essays Commemorating Fifty Years of the Orthodox Presbyterian Church*, ed. Charles G. Dennison and Richard C. Gamble (Philadelphia: Committee for the Historian of the Orthodox Presbyterian Church, 1986), 33–51.

41. Heb. 4:10, e.g., is easily understood in the sense of a Hebrew prophetic perfect, referring to the certainty of a future event by speaking of it as if it had already happened.

42. As noted, this issue of whether the "rest" in Heb. 3–4 is inaugurated or still future is debated. For fuller discussion of the position taken here, see chap. 23 under the heading "New Testament Testimony to the Sabbath."

The coming judgment of unbelievers and apostates at the end of the age is a repeated theme in Hebrews (6:2; 9:27), especially as a warning serving as encouragement to persevere (10:26–31, 36–38; 12:25–29; 13:4).[43] Saints are exhorted to persevere "until the end" (*telos* [3:14; 6:11]). Those who pay heed to the warnings of judgment and the exhortations to continue in faith will receive at the consummation of history full salvation (9:28), their "reward" (10:35; 11:26), and the complete inheritance of what was promised (6:11–12, 17–18; 9:15; 10:23, 34–35; 11:39). The inheritance of the promised land of the new earth is the author's irreducible summary of what true believers will receive at the eschaton (11:9–16; 13:14). God will raise them from the dead so that they will be able to participate in the inheritance (11:35; cf. 6:20). This final inheritance will be indestructible (12:27–28) and eternal. In the new earth, God will be seen, and his presence will be more fully experienced (cf. 12:14). The readers should not be lax about these exhortations, since the final "day" is "near" (10:25).[44]

Eschatological References in the General Epistles

Past and Present

JAMES, 1–2 PETER, JUDE

An indication of the incipient form of the new creation occurs in James 1:18: "As a result of exercising his will, he has given birth to us by means of the word of truth in order that we should be a kind of firstfruit among his creatures." A full-blown allusion to the true temporal nature of the time in which the author and readers live appears in James 5. There, James chastises people for living in ungodly ways and not redeeming the opportunities for doing righteousness in view of the significant time period in which they are presently living: "It is in the last days [*en eschatais hēmerais*] that you have stored up your treasure" (5:3). Because it is already the last period of history, the final "coming of the Lord" and the time of judgment for such unrighteous people are imminent (see 5:7–9).[45]

---

43. See Stanley D. Toussaint, "The Eschatology of the Warning Passages in the Book of Hebrews," *GTJ* 3 (1982): 67–80.

44. For further discussion of an already–not yet notion of eschatology in Hebrews, see Barrett, "Eschatology of the Epistle to the Hebrews"; George W. MacRae, "Heavenly Temple and Eschatology in the Letter to the Hebrews," *Semeia* 12 (1978): 179–99; Clyde Woods, "Eschatological Motifs in the Epistle to the Hebrews," in *The Last Things: Essays Presented by His Students to Dr. W. B. West Jr. upon the Occasion of His Sixty-Fifth Birthday*, ed. Jack P. Lewis (Austin: Sweet, 1972), 140–51.

45. On the problem of imminence mentioned here and elsewhere in Hebrews, the General Epistles, and Revelation, see Kreitzer, "Parousia"; idem, "Eschatology."

Like James, 1 Peter commences with a mention that the latter-day new creation of believers has taken place: God has "caused us to be born again to a living hope through the resurrection of Jesus Christ from the dead" (1:3). Their new birth and consequent "living hope" are integrally linked to Christ's resurrection as a basis. This notion of a new age is developed further in 1:20–21, where Christ's resurrection "from the dead" is portrayed as part of "the end of the times" (*ep' eschatou tōn chronōn*), and where it is through the resurrected Christ that the readers have become believers with a hope. It is through this same resurrection that Jesus has been placed at God's right hand to begin ruling (3:18–19, 21–22). The latter-day Spirit is the agent bringing about the resurrection of Christ (3:18) as well as the resurrection life of his followers (4:6 [whether physically dead or alive]) and their ongoing conduct in the sphere of that life (1:2). Similar to Hebrews, 1 Peter also speaks of Christ's death for sins with the age-turning expression "once for all" (3:18). Not only this, but the final judgment has also been set in motion with the divinely ordained sufferings directed toward the Christian community, which serve to test their faith (4:12–19).

The letter of 2 Peter makes the most far-reaching reference to Christ's kingship by observing that it commenced at the very beginning of his earthly ministry, when he was baptized (1:16–17). Both 2 Peter and Jude remind readers that Christ and the apostles foretold of false teachers who would infiltrate the church community "in the last days" (*ep' eschatōn tōn hēmerōn* [2 Pet. 3:3]) or "in the last time" (*ep' eschatou tou chronou* [Jude 18]). Both letters contend that this expected latter-day tribulation of apostate teaching already has been expressed through the appearance of false teachers who were then attempting to pervert the truth in the very midst of the Christian community (cf. 2 Pet. 3:2–3 with 2:1–22; 3:16–17; cf. Jude 17–18 with 4, 8, 10–13). The precise form of 2 Peter's latter-day expression occurs eleven times in the LXX, so it may echo these uses. To apply the language to false teaching and perversion of the truth is especially in line with my earlier observations about Qumran's use of end-time expressions and early Jewish interpretation of Jacob's eschatological forecast for the tribes of Israel in Gen. 49:1.

The Johannine Epistles

1 John 2:18[46]

The Johannine Epistles reveal an acute awareness that the eschaton has already broken into history. The most notorious expression indicating this is the repeated references to the "antichrist," especially in 1 John 2:18, which I touched on in the earlier discussion of eschatology in John's Gospel: "Children, it is the last hour, and just as you have heard that antichrist is coming,

---

46. This section is a summary of G. K. Beale, "The Old Testament Background of the 'Last Hour' in 1 John 2:18," *Biblica* 92 (2011): 231–54.

even now many antichrists have appeared; from this we know that it is the last hour."

John identifies these antichrists with those who had committed apostasy and left the true church: "They went out from us, but they were not really of us; for if they had been of us, they would have remained with us; but they went out, so that it would be shown that they all are not of us" (1 John 2:19). He further describes them as false teachers and those who are not true believers: "Who is the liar but the one who denies that Jesus is the Christ? This is the antichrist, the one who denies the Father and the Son. Whoever denies the Son does not have the Father; the one who confesses the Son has the Father also" (1 John 2:22–23).

First John 2:18 most directly goes back to Jesus's prophecy of "false Christs": "For false Christs and false prophets will arise and will show great signs and wonders, so as to mislead, if possible, even the elect. Behold, I have told you in advance" (Matt. 24:24–25 [// Mark 13:22]). Paul also predicts the coming of the "man of lawlessness," who will deceive God's people in the final days of history (2 Thess. 2:3–10). Both Jesus's and Paul's prophecies go back to Daniel's prophecy of the end-time opponent who will attempt to deceive God's people (Dan. 7–9; 11–12):

Dan. 7:25 "He will speak out against the Most High and wear down[47] the saints of the Highest One, and he will intend to make alterations in times and in law; and they will be given into his hand for a time, times, and half a time."

Dan. 8:12 And on account of transgression the host will be given over to the horn along with the regular sacrifice; and it will fling truth to the ground and perform its will and prosper.

Dan. 8:23–25 "A king will arise, insolent and skilled in intrigue. His power will be mighty, but not by his own power, and he will destroy to an extraordinary degree, and prosper and perform his will; he will destroy mighty men and the holy people. And through his shrewdness he will cause deceit to succeed by his influence; and he will magnify himself in his heart, and he will destroy many while they are at ease. He will even oppose the Prince of princes."

Dan. 11:30–34 "So he will come back and show regard for those who forsake the holy covenant. . . . By smooth words he will turn to godlessness those who act wickedly toward the covenant, but the people who know their God will display strength and take action. Those who have insight among the people will give understanding to the many. . . . Now when

---

47. Several LXX manuscripts and versions, as well as church fathers, replace "wear out" (*katatribō* [OG], *palaioō* [TH] = Aram. *yĕballē'*) with *planaō* ("deceive"), so that here the end-time opponent is portrayed as "deceiving" the saints.

they fall they will be granted a little help, and many will join with them in hypocrisy."

That Jesus is developing the prophecy of Daniel's latter-day deceiver is apparent from the saturation of other Dan. 7–12 allusions elsewhere in Matt. 24 together with its Synoptic parallels.[48] For example Matt. 24:15, 21 quote the famous "abomination of desolation" and "great tribulation" passages from Daniel. Paul's prophecy likewise contains specific allusions to Dan. 11:31, 36.[49]

Thus, 1 John 2:18–23 is developing Jesus's and Paul's predictions of an end-time opponent that is based on Daniel's earlier prediction.[50] Is John merely comparing the false teachers in his church to the antichrists referred to in Matthew, the "man of lawlessness" predicted by Paul, and to the eschatological deceiver described in Daniel? Is he merely comparing his "last hour" to that of the end-time period referred to in Daniel by Matthew and Paul? If he is, then the antichrists in 1 John are not the fulfillment of Jesus's, Paul's, and Daniel's prophecies but are only compared to the figures in those prophecies. Since there is no explicit fulfillment formula anywhere in the context of 1 John 2, one might conclude that John is only making a comparison. But, if 1 John 2 is describing the beginning fulfillment of Jesus's, Paul's, and Daniel's prophecies, then how could the false teachers depicted in the church to which John is writing be seen as literally fulfilling the prophecy, since the incarnate antichrist is not yet on the scene and since the situation in 1 John is a church composed of Jews and gentiles who are facing deception and not of faithful Jews in the nation of Israel itself, about which Daniel prophesies?

How should we decide this difficult hermeneutical issue? Is John merely making a comparison, or is he depicting the inaugurated fulfillment of Daniel's and Jesus's prophecies? My first answer to this is to respond with a presupposition that is supported by much exegesis of other OT texts in NT texts elsewhere: those with a high view of Scripture should presuppose that the NT interprets the OT contextually and with hermeneutical integrity (even though many in the scholarly guild disagree with such a presupposition). Accordingly, if an OT passage quoted in the NT is a prophecy in its original context, would not a NT author such as John also see it as a prophecy, and would he not see it as beginning fulfillment, if he identifies the prophecy with some reality in his own present time? And even if there is no fulfillment formula, would not John still see it as fulfillment? Possibly

48. On which, see Lars Hartman, *Prophecy Interpreted: The Formation of Some Jewish Apocalyptic Texts and of the Eschatological Discourse Mark 13 par.*, ConBNT 1 (Lund: Gleerup, 1966), 145–74.

49. This is acknowledged by most commentators; see, e.g., G. K. Beale, *1–2 Thessalonians*, IVPNTC (Downers Grove, IL: InterVarsity, 2003), 203–11.

50. John may be dependent on a circulating oral Gospel tradition or on the written Gospel of Matthew, which may have been read orally to and heard by the church to which he is writing.

he could use the OT analogically, but the weight of the prophetic context of the OT passage tilts toward a notion of fulfillment, if there is no clear evidence to the contrary in the NT context (or, if context makes it clear, a NT author could be affirming that an OT prophecy has not been fulfilled yet but assuredly will be in the future). If this is a correct hermeneutical approach, then the prophecies about the antichrist and his deceptive emissaries are beginning fulfillment in some real manner.

Further analysis of 1 John 2, moreover, indicates that John does likely understand that the prophecy in Dan. 7–12, Matt. 24, and 2 Thess. 2 is beginning fulfillment. This is most apparent in the introductory phrase "last hour" in 1 John 2:18: "Children, it is <u>the last hour</u>; and just as you heard that antichrist is coming, even now many antichrists have appeared; from this we know that it is <u>the last hour</u>." The only eschatological uses of "hour" (*hōra*) in all of the OT occur in the "old" Greek (= OG, not TH) of Dan. 8; 11; 12. In every one of these occurrences "hour" (*hōra*) refers not generally to the eschaton but rather to the specific eschatological time when the opponent of God's people will attempt to deceive them. Examples can be found in Dan. 8; 11; 12 (see table 5.2).

Tables 5.2

Daniel 8:17, 19; 11:35, 40; 12:1 MT	Daniel 8:17, 19; 11:35, 40; 12:1 OG (not TH)
8:17b: "Son of man, understand that the vision pertains <u>to the time of the end</u> [*lĕʿet-qēṣ*]."	8:17b: "Son of man, understand, for yet <u>unto the hour of time</u> [*eis hōran kairou*] is this vision."
8:19: He said, "Behold, I am going to let you know what will occur at the final period of the indignation, for it pertains to <u>the appointed time of the end</u> [*lĕmôʿēd qēṣ*]."	8:19: And he said to me, "Behold, I am announcing to you what will occur at the end of the wrath to the sons of your people; for yet <u>unto the hours of time of the end it remains</u> [*eis hōras kairou synteleias menei*]."
11:35: "Some of those who have insight will fall, in order to refine, purge and make them pure until <u>the end time</u> [ʿad-ʿēt qēṣ]; because it is still to come <u>at the appointed time</u> [*lammôʿēd*]."	11:35: "Some of those who have insight will understand in order to cleanse themselves and in order that they be selected out and in order that they be cleansed <u>at the time of the end</u> [*heōs kairou synteleias*]; for <u>the time is unto an hour</u> [*kairos eis hōras*]."
11:40: "<u>And at the end time</u> [*ûbĕʿēt qēṣ*] . . . he will enter countries."	11:40: "<u>And at the hour of the end</u> [*kai kath' hōran synteleias*] . . . he will enter into the country of Egypt."
12:1: "<u>Now at that time</u> [*ûbāʿēt hahî'*] . . . there will be a time of distress."	12:1: "<u>And at that hour</u> [*kai kata tēn hōran ekeinēn*] . . . there will be that day of tribulation."

See also Dan. 10:14.[a]

[a]The Hebrew reads "what will happen to your people in the latter days, for the vision pertains to the days yet." The OG and TH have a literal Greek equivalent for the Hebrew text's "for the vision pertains to the days yet," though some LXX manuscripts (967 and 88-Syh) have "for the hour [Greek] pertains to the days yet." This would mean that "hour" is an epexegesis of the directly preceding "latter days." Underlining shows how the OG translates the precise Hebrew phrase.

These uses reveal that "hour" in the OG of Daniel is part of phrases that are the equivalent of the Hebrew phrase "time of the end" or "end time" or are in parallelism with such a phrase. John's twice-repeated references to the "last hour" (*eschatē hōra*) are close equivalents to these OG uses.[51] Perhaps Dan. 11:40 is closest to 1 John, where the phrase "the hour of the end" occurs.

Thus, 1 John's equivalent use of the "hour" plus "last" is most probably based on the uses in Daniel and is a further indication that what Daniel prophesied is beginning fulfillment in John's own day among his readers.

Additional evidence confirming this idea of fulfillment is the phrase "antichrist is coming, even now many antichrists have appeared" in 1 John 2:18. John then says at the conclusion of the verse that "from this" (*hothen*) "we know that it is the last hour." He says that, according to prophetic expectation, "antichrist is coming," but the abrupt phrase "even now many antichrists have appeared" most probably indicates that this prophetic expectation has begun to be realized. The almost identical "already and not yet" expressions in John's Gospel support this conclusion, especially John 5:25–29, which was discussed above.

John goes on to say a few verses later that this prophecy of the antichrist has started fulfillment not only because his foretold false prophetic helpers are already on the scene, but also because there is a true sense in which the antichrist himself is already present: "Who is the liar but the one who denies that Jesus is the Christ? This is <u>the</u> antichrist, the one who denies the Father and the Son" (1 John 2:22). In what sense can John say that the singular "antichrist" is already here? First John 4:2–3 helps to answer this question: "By this you know the Spirit of God: every spirit that confesses that Jesus Christ has come in the flesh is from God; and every spirit that does not confess Jesus is not from God; this is the spirit of the antichrist, of which you have heard that it is coming, and now it is already in the world." Thus, although the antichrist has not yet come in his incarnate form, his spirit is here, inspiring his false teachers in antithetical parallelism to the work of Christ's Spirit in his true people. Consequently, the prophecy of the antichrist has begun fulfillment in that his spirit has begun to come and inspire his false teachers to do their work of deception. The prophecy has begun literally also in the sense that the prophesied deceptive teachers are working in the covenant community, as they were literally prophesied so to do.

Some would argue that the prophecy cannot be literal because the Daniel prophecies say that the antichrist and his false teachers will infiltrate Israel and defile Israel's temple. How could that be fulfilled literally, since John is referring to the church, not Israel, as the place where the false teaching is occurring? Must this not make the application of the prophetic expectation an analogy; otherwise would not the fulfillment have to be seen as allegorically fulfilled?

---

51. Although in Dan. 8:19; 11:35, 40 *synteleia*, not *hōra*, is used for the actual reference to "end," *hōra* is directly related to it; however, in the manuscript tradition of Dan. 10:14, "hour" directly follows and is synonymous with "last days."

Another possible objection that 1 John 2:18 is not using Daniel with its original contextual idea in mind is that the end-time opponent in Dan. 7–12 is prophesied to persecute God's people, but 1 John has no reference to such persecution. Such an objection, however, appears to assume that all aspects of an OT context must be carried over into the alluding NT passage for there to be a valid allusion. This assumption demands too much. NT authors can refer to parts of an OT context without referring to everything in that context and still intend to allude to that context. Such would seem to be the case with 1 John 2:18 and its immediate context in relation to the contextual use of "hour" in Daniel.

So we have to ask a further question: is it a misappropriation of Scripture to apply to the church a prophecy that was to occur in the land of Israel and among Israelites? The answer to that depends on whether one believes that Jesus is true Israel. If he is, then true Israelites are those who identify with him. This would then not be an allegorical hermeneutic or a wild spiritualizing hermeneutic but rather a recognition of what one might call a "legal representative" hermeneutic, whereby those who are represented take on the literal legal identity of their representative in the same way adopted children take on the name of the family that adopts them even though their bloodline is different from the adoptive family.

But even if one accepts this conclusion about Jesus and the church being true Israel (which I will elaborate on in a later chapter), how could the Daniel prophecies be fulfilled literally, since they speak about the temple being harmfully affected by the false teachers? The church to which John writes is not a literal architectural temple. However, could it be a literal temple in some other sense nevertheless? And if so, how? This matter, too, I will address later (chaps. 18–19).

1 John 3:4

There is further evidence of inaugurated eschatology of Daniel's prophesied latter-day tribulation in 1 John. There are false teachers, little "antichrists," from within the community, who have since departed but are still threatening to deceive Christians about the nature of Christ's person and his commandments (2:22–23, 26; 4:1–6; cf. 2 John 7–11). We have just observed that these deceivers, likely holding to a protognostic form of doctrine, are the corporate embodiment of the beginning fulfillment of the Dan. 7–12 prophecy. As I have argued, Jesus and Paul also further developed the Daniel prophecy (cf. Mark 13; Matt. 24; Luke 21; 2 Thess. 2). And 1 John 3:4 even identifies these false teachers with *the* covenantal "lawlessness" that Daniel prophesied would characterize the deceivers who would arise from within the ranks of the faithful: "Everyone who does *the* sin also does *the* lawlessness, and *the* sin is *the* lawlessness" (in this translation I have emphasized the presence of the Gk. definite articles).

Some commentators view the "lawlessness" of 1 John 2:18 to be an expected eschatological lawlessness, which was expressed in various sources but not derived from any one of these sources.[52] Is it merely coincidental that virtually all the passages cited as expressing the purported broader background of the expected eschatological lawlessness are part of a Danielic tradition or Synoptic tradition, the latter of which we have seen to be saturated with Daniel's eschatology and also standing in the background of 1 John 2:18?[53] But what makes Daniel more prominent as an influence in 1 John 3:4 is that only in the Septuagintal tradition of Daniel is eschatological "sin" equated with eschatological "lawlessness," as in 1 John 3:4. Daniel 12:10 TH describes the end-time lawbreakers thus: "<u>The lawless ones</u> [anomoi] <u>will do lawlessness</u> [anomēsōsin]; and none of <u>the lawless ones</u> [anomoi] will understand"; whereas the OG version reads, "<u>The sinners</u> [hoi hamartōloi] <u>will sin</u> [hamartōsin]; and by no means will <u>the sinners</u> [hoi hamartōloi] understand." In addition, this latter-day lawlessness of Dan. 12:10, which entails lack of understanding, was described earlier in Dan. 11:32 TH thus: "<u>The ones doing lawlessness</u> [hoi anomountes] will bring about a covenant in deceitful ways"; whereas the OG version reads, "<u>In sins</u> [en hamartiais] toward the covenant they will pollute among a hardened people." Here, once again, "the ones doing lawlessness" is parallel in the OG to "sinning" (lit., "in sins"). What is striking about the Septuagintal renderings is that both interpret the individual end-time opponent of the Hebrew text corporately as the false teachers and compromisers who are clearly in mind elsewhere in the Dan. 11 narrative (e.g., vv. 31–32, 34). This is striking in the light of the individual and corporate view of the antichrist in 1 John 2:18–19, 22; 4:1–6.

Accordingly, the LXX tradition equates the prophecy of "the lawless ones doing lawlessness" with "the sinners sinning," just as 1 John 3:4 equates those doing "the sin" with those doing "the lawlessness." This is unique in all the Greek literature of the OT, early Judaism, and early Christianity, including the other parallel expectations of the expected lawlessness noted above (such

52. See I. Howard Marshall, *The Epistles of John*, NICNT (Grand Rapids: Eerdmans, 1978), 176–77; idem, *1 and 2 Thessalonians*, NCB (Grand Rapids: Eerdmans, 1983), 188–90; Stephen S. Smalley, *1, 2, 3 John*, WBC 51 (Waco: Word, 1984), 155; Raymond E. Brown, *The Epistles of John*, AB 30 (Garden City, NY: Doubleday, 1982), 399–400.

53. Brown (*Epistles of John*, 399–400) adduces the following texts anticipating this coming eschatological lawlessness: *T. Dan.* 6:1–6; *Barn.* 4:1–4, 9; 18:1–2; Matt. 7:22; 13:41; 24:11–12; *Did.* 16:3–4; 2 Thess. 2:3–8. Among these, only *T. Dan.* 6:1–6 and Matt. 7:22; 13:41 are unrelated to either the Danielic or the Synoptic tradition (for Danielic influence behind the "lawlessness" in 2 Thess. 2:3, e.g., see Beale, *1–2 Thessalonians*, 206–9). *Barnabas* and *Didache* may well be contemporary with 1 John and thus also be developing, respectively, Daniel and the Synoptic tradition. There is also an end-time opponent prophecy in *Sib. Or.* 3:63–74 (latter part of first century AD or later) in which those deceived by him are called "lawless" (*anomos*). *Apocalypse of Elijah* (AD 150–275) refers to the eschatological fiend as "the son of lawlessness" (1:10; 3:1, 5, 13, 18; 4:2, 15, 20, 28, 31; 5:6, 10, 32) and "the lawless one" (2:41), all ultimately under the influence likely of 2 Thess. 2:3. The use in *Apoc. El.* 4:31 is also linked directly to the end-time "hour" (4:30).

as 2 Thess. 2:3, 7).[54] Therefore, "the lawlessness" in 1 John 3:4 is that expected lawlessness of the end-time opponent and his colleagues (the latter of which Dan. 11:32; 12:10 describe prophetically), which has begun fulfillment in John's community, as, I have argued, in the case of 1 John 2:18. Note that even the definite articles before "sinners" in the OG and before "lawless ones" in TH may be carried over into 1 John 3:4 (even if at first glance this sounds awkward) to underscore that this is not just any sin and lawlessness but rather the specific sin and lawlessness prophesied by Daniel. If all of this is on the right track, then there is a natural link between 1 John 2:18 and 3:4, which is further strengthened in that the "now" in 2:28 and again in 3:2 are likely eschatological, further developing the "now" that occurs for the first time in the letter in 2:18, which is clearly eschatological (as is the "now" in 4:3). In this respect, the notion of "lawlessness" is to be identified with the end-time sin of the "lawless one" of 2 Thess. 2, which likewise has drawn on Daniel.

The upshot is that the readers need to be aware that they are living in the midst of the "great tribulation," which has been expressed among them in the form of false teachers, so that they will not be caught off guard and be deceived.[55] In 1 John 5:16, "the sin leading to death" is best understood in light of this highly charged latter-day context. That is, this "sin" in 5:16 refers to covenant community apostasy, which is either deceiving others or allowing oneself to be deceived by the false teachers, a sign of never truly having belonged to the community of faith and of having experienced spiritual death all along (cf. 2:19).[56]

THE BROADER CONTEXT OF 1 JOHN

From another perspective, Christ's life and death have such a cosmic impact on the world through his followers that it can be said that the old, fallen world of darkness "is passing away" (1 John 2:8, 17 [cf. 2:2, 12–14]). The basis for the cosmic upheaval is that Christ's redemptive work has dealt a mortal blow to the evil ruler of the old age (3:8). Those who identify with Christ's redemptive work also participate in the victory over the devil (2:13–14).

Alternatively, although the old world has begun to disintegrate spiritually, Christ's death and resurrection have also set in motion a new creation, so that

54. It is true that *hamartia* and *anomia* are closely juxtaposed throughout the LXX, but Dan. 11:32 is the only place where the juxtaposition occurs as part of a prophecy of the end-time "sin" and "lawlessness" (Isa. 27:9; 53:5 prophesy about the future, but with respect to Israel's "sin" and "lawlessness" being forgiven).

55. For an expansion of the above sections not only on 1 John 2:18 but also on 3:4, see Beale, "The Old Testament Background of the 'Last Hour' in 1 John 2:18."

56. Although he does not discuss the eschatological context, see David M. Scholer, "Sins Within and Sins Without: An Interpretation of 1 John 5:16–17," in *Current Issues in Biblical and Patristic Interpretation: Studies in Honor of Merrill C. Tenney Presented by His Former Students*, ed. Gerald F. Hawthorne (Grand Rapids: Eerdmans, 1975), 230–46. Scholer argues that "the sin to death" is that committed only by pseudobelievers.

there is an overlap of the old with the new: "The darkness is passing away and the true Light is already shining" (2:8). The resurrection life of the eternal age to come has begun in Jesus's resurrection and in the spiritual resurrection of his followers, who identify with his death and resurrection (see 1:2; 2:17, 25; 3:14; 4:9; 5:11–13, 20, esp. in light of John 5:21–29). It is also the Spirit, prophesied to be poured out in the eschatological age (cf. Joel 2:28–32 in Acts 2:17–18 above), who gives assurance that one truly has entered into the midst of the divine presence that characterizes the new age (3:24; 4:13).

Future

Judgment is also a significant theme in James (2:13; 3:1). On the one hand, people will be judged because of their selfishness, greed, and persecution of the righteous (5:1–9). The day of the final judgment "is at hand" (5:8). On the other hand, those who demonstrate true faith through good works will receive a reward at the last day (1:12; 5:7).

The writer of 1 Peter affirms that a day will come when God will impartially judge all people by their works, whether or not they have lived lives of godly obedience (1:17; cf. 4:17: "it is time for judgment to begin"). Even now God "is ready to judge the living and the dead" (4:5), since "the end of all things has come near" (4:7). In light of this imminent judgment, believers are advised to live circumspectly so as not to be found deserving judgment when it unexpectedly occurs. Intriguingly, the statement "it is time for judgment to begin with the household of God" (4:17) indicates that in some sense the final judgment has been pushed back into the present. Those who are able to persevere in faithfulness will receive definitive "salvation ready to be revealed in the last time" (1:5 [cf. 1:9]), when Christ returns again (1:13) and his followers can fully rejoice in the greater manifestation of his glory (4:13; cf. 5:1). At this "proper time" (5:6) believers "will receive the unfading crown of glory" (5:4), and God will "perfect, confirm, strengthen, and establish" (5:10) for all time those who have persevered to the end (cf. 5:6). Another image of this final reward is that of receiving an "inheritance" that "will not fade away" (1:4 [cf. 3:9]). The believer's "hope" is focused on this goal (3:15). When the final day comes, God's "dominion" will be decisively manifested as being "forever and ever" (4:11; 5:11).

Both the "already" and "not yet" aspects of the latter days in 1 Peter provide a theological framework for better understanding the Christian's ethical obligation.[57]

---

57. See Ronald Russell, "Eschatology and Ethics in 1 Peter," *EvQ* 47 (1975): 78–84; for an already–not yet notion of eschatology in 1 Peter, see E. C. Selwyn, "Eschatology in 1 Peter," in Davies and Daube, eds., *Background of the New Testament*, 394–401.

The notion of the coming final judgment is picked up again in 2 Peter (2:3, 9 ["the day of judgment"]; 3:7)[58] and Jude (6 ["the judgment of the great day"], 14–15). At the time of this judgment "the earth and its works will be burned up" (2 Pet. 3:10). This is likely a literal expectation on the part of the author. The purpose of reflecting on the cosmic conflagration is pastoral and ethical: to encourage saints to be holy so that they might "be found" faithful when the expected judgment day occurs (cf. 2 Pet. 3:11–12 ["the day of God"], 14). In contrast to the ungodly, they will find mercy on that dreadful day (Jude 21). The old creation, which is to be destroyed, will be replaced by "new heavens and a new earth" (2 Pet. 3:13), language reminiscent of Rev. 21:1, though both are based on the new-creational prophecy of Isa. 65:17 and 66:22. At this time, the kingdom that was inaugurated at Jesus's first coming will be established in its completeness (2 Pet. 1:11), and God's people will stand in the immediate presence of his glory (Jude 24). The attribute of glory is an eternal divine characteristic, which is possessed by both the Father (Jude 25) and the Son (2 Pet. 3:18) and will be revealed clearly at the end of time.

First John 2:28 and 4:17a together present the possibility of Christ's final "coming" (*parousia*) occurring at any time, and so readers should persevere ("abide") in their faith, so that when he does come, they will have confidence in obtaining salvation and not be ashamed and find themselves deserving wrath on "the day of judgment." Such perseverance will result in them becoming fully conformed to his likeness when he comes a final time because the faithful will finally be able fully "to see him just as he is" (3:2). Those who maintain this "hope" will be motivated in the present to begin to resemble his holy image (3:3; similarly 4:17b).

Eschatological References in Revelation

The technical vocabulary for the eschatological period ("latter days," etc.) found in most other NT books does not appear in the book of Revelation. Nevertheless, other kinds of terminology are used, and the concepts of inaugurated and consummated eschatology are woven into the fabric of the book throughout.

Revelation expects the final coming of Christ to occur at some point in the near future (e.g., 16:15; 22:7, 12, 17, 20). The fulfillment of the eschatological prophecies is "near" (1:3; 22:10), though interpreters debate whether this refers to inauguration or imminent expectation. The visions of the book parabolically express an expectation of Christ's coming, especially to judge the ungodly.[59] This punishing judgment of the ungodly will last forever (in

---

58. See J. Ramsey Michaels, "Eschatology in 1 Peter III.17," *NTS* 13 (1967): 394–401.

59. E.g., Rev. 6:12–17; 11:15–19; 14:14–20; 17:14; 19:11–21; cf. either Christ or God as the agent of judgment in 6:10–11; 11:11–13; 14:8–11; 16:17–21; 20:9–15; 21:8.

this respect, see variants of *eis tous aiōnas tōn aiōnōn* in 14:11; 19:3; 20:10). Nevertheless, Christ will come also to reward and finally bless his people (11:18; 19:7–9; 21:1–22:5, 12, 14; cf. possibly 7:9–17). At this time he will establish his kingdom in its final, complete, and eternal form (*eis tous aiōnas tōn aiōnōn* in 11:15–17; 22:5; 7:9–17 [?]; cf. 19:1), though it is evident elsewhere that this unending kingdom has already begun (*eis tous aiōnas tōn aiōnōn* in 1:6; 5:13; 7:12 [?]). Directly preceding the last judgment and the full coming of the kingdom will be a tribulation of deception and persecution for God's people (e.g., 11:7–10; 16:12–14; 20:7–9; cf. possibly 3:10; 6:11; 7:14; 13:5–18), as well as a final period of torment for their persecutors (e.g., 16:21; 17:16–17; cf. 3:10). Many of these same future conceptions can be observed in other NT literature.

The book of Revelation also uses *hōra* under the influence of the aforementioned Danielic eschatological uses of *hōra* (3:10; 14:7), as well of Dan. 4:17a LXX, which is employed in 17:12; 18:10, 17, 19 in a typological manner with regard respectively to the time leading up to the last judgment and to the time of the final judgment itself.[60] In particular, the use in 14:7 is significant because it is implicitly related to the demise of the "beast" (see 14:8–11), whose picture in 13:1–11 is constructed from a series of allusions to the eschatological portrayal in Dan. 7.[61]

There are a variety of problems in Revelation that pertain to whether a number of topics and key passages are to be related to inaugurated eschatological realities or only to future eschatological fulfillment at the very end of the present age.[62] Many of these problems are too complex to be addressed here and deserve separate treatment, which I have undertaken elsewhere.[63]

Eschatological References in the Apostolic Fathers

Past and Present

Like the NT, the Apostolic Fathers understand that the blessings of the age to come have begun but have not reached their consummate form. Not uncommon is mention that the age in which the writers were living was also the time of the "last days," which had commenced with the initial coming of Christ (e.g., *2 Clem.* 14:2; *Barn.* 12:9; 16:5). For example, it can be said that

60. On which, see G. K. Beale, *The Book of Revelation: A Commentary on the Greek Text*, NIGTC (Grand Rapids: Eerdmans, 1999), commenting on the texts above.
61. On this last point, see ibid., 728–30.
62. On the problem in general, see A. J. Bandstra, "History and Eschatology in the Apocalypse," *CTJ* 5 (1970): 180–83.
63. G. K. Beale, *John's Use of the Old Testament in Revelation*, JSNTSup 166 (Sheffield: Sheffield Academic Press, 1998). For example, there is debate about whether references to Christ's "coming" in Rev. 1–3; 22 are inaugurated or future. For other such problems, see Beale, "Eschatology," 337–41.

"these are the last times" (Ign. *Eph.* 11:1), that "Christ . . . appeared at the end of time" (Ign. *Magn.* 6:1) or "in the last days" (*Herm.* 89:3), and that Christians have a "foretaste of things to come" (*Barn.* 1:7).

Comparable to the NT also, the Apostolic Fathers held so intensely to the inaugurated aspect of the end times that they even believed that the promised new creation had been set in motion. *Barnabas* 6:13 can say that God "made a second creation in the last days," which was modeled on the first creation: "Behold, I make the last things as the first." Hence, Christians had become "new, created again from the beginning" (*Barn.* 16:8 [cf. 6:11, 14]), likely on the basis that their progenitor himself, Jesus Christ, was the representative "new man" from whom they received their identity (cf. Ign. *Eph.* 20). Such thinking motivated some writers to assert that believers were already participating in the blessings of the garden of Eden (*Diogn.* 12:1–2; *Frag. Papias*, Tradition of the Elders 2). Such a heightened notion of inaugurated eschatology is apparently the basis for the seer's misguided question in *Shepherd of Hermas* concerning whether "the consummation had already arrived" (16:9).

Again, following the lead of NT writers, the Apostolic Fathers see an inextricable link between the beginning phase of the latter-day new creation and the resurrection of saints. Resurrection is the means by which believers become a part of the new creation, first spiritually at conversion, then physically at the end of the age at the final resurrection. Christ brought "the newness of eternal life" (Ign. *Eph.* 19:3) by himself becoming a "new man" (Ign. *Eph.* 20:1), as a result of his own resurrection. The inaugurated and consummated resurrection of Christians occurs because of their identification with Christ's resurrection (see Ign. *Magn.* 9; Ign. *Trall.* 9:2; cf. *1 Clem.* 24:1; Pol. *Phil.* 2:2; *Barn.* 5:6–7). Those who believe in Jesus "will live forever" (*Barn.* 11:11). Conversely, God has also commenced with the destruction of the old creation "for his elect" (*Herm.* 3:4), which is likely best understood as beginning through Christ's own death (i.e., destruction of his old body) and resurrection; the resurrection put an end to the curse of death for God's people (Ign. *Eph.* 19:3; *Barn.* 5:6), so that even when believers die physically, ironically they enter into an escalated phase of their new birth and of their immortality (*Mart. Pol.* 19:2).

There is a link not only between the eschatological new creation and resurrection, but also between the new creation and the notion that the church has become the temple of God (Ign. *Eph.* 15:3; Ign. *Trall.* 7:2; Ign. *Phld.* 7:2; *Barn.* 4:11), though this connection is explicitly made only in *Barnabas* (6:8–19; 16:1–10). The likely reason for associating the two concepts is that the garden of Eden of the first creation was identified by later OT writers as sanctuary-like,[64] and it became natural for NT writers and the early church fathers to make the same connection between the new creation and the temple.

---

64. See Meredith G. Kline, *Images of the Spirit* (Grand Rapids: Baker Academic, 1980), 35–56.

In the OT, the apparent chronology of predicted end-time events placed the final tribulation before the resurrection of the dead and the new creation (e.g., Dan. 11:35–12:12). Now, however, the Apostolic Fathers once again follow the NT in placing the beginning of the final tribulation at the same time as the inaugurated new creation and its attendant blessings (as also in, e.g., Rev. 1:9). The author of *Barnabas* understands that he is living in the "last days," the "age of lawlessness" (4:9), and "the deception of the present age" (4:1 [cf. 18:2]), which is the inception and harbinger of the soon to be fulfilled antichrist prophecy from Dan. 7:7–8, 24 (4:4–6; cf. 2 Thess. 2:3–7; 1 John 2:18, where "lawlessness" is also used and is rooted in Dan. 12:10 TH); that prophecy apparently was to commence more concrete fulfillment imminently, though not necessarily consummately, through the infiltration of false teachers in the church (cf. 4:1, 9–11; 18:1–2). Similarly, *Shepherd of Hermas* contends that "great tribulations" have already been suffered (7:1) that apparently prepare saints for "the coming great tribulation."[65] Likewise, Hermas "escaped a great tribulation" from a satanic beast that was "a foreshadowing of the great tribulation that is coming" (23:4–5).

Future

There are two ages: the present age and the age to come; the former is imperfect, and the latter perfected.[66] The consummation of all things will be in the "age to come" (*Herm.* 24:5; 53:2; *2 Clem.* 6:3–6). *Barnabas* states that at this concluding temporal point there will be a complete new creation: at this time "all things [will] have been made new" (*Barn.* 15:7); the "renewed creation" will be exceedingly fertile (*Frag. Papias* 14). In connection with the preceding context in *Barnabas*, on the basis that "a thousand years are like one day" (Ps. 90:4), *2 En.* 25–33 appeals to the seven days of creation in Gen. 1 and affirms that history will follow the same sevenfold pattern, the consequent reckoning of the historical age being seven thousand years and a following "eighth day," apparently referring to eternity.[67]

Just as an inextricable link has been observed between the inaugurated new creation and the resurrection, so the same connection exists between the final phase of both: "When the righteous will rise from the dead and reign, when creation, too, [is] renewed" (*Frag. Papias* 14). This will be the time of the consummated resurrection (*1 Clem.* 50:4; *2 Clem.* 19:3–4; Pol. *Phil.* 2:2;

---

65. See *Herm.* 6:7; cf. 7:4. For a similar correspondence between a present "great tribulation" and "the great tribulation" to come, see Rev. 2:22; 7:14.

66. Note *2 Clem.* 6:3 ("this age and the one that is coming"); 19:4 ("the present time" and "a time of blessedness"); *Barn.* 10:11 ("this world" and "the holy age to come").

67. For a survey of how Ps. 90 and the days of creation influenced the church fathers of the third and fourth centuries with respect to the duration of world history and the question of chiliasm, see Alfred Wikenhauser, "Weltwoche und tausendjähriges Reich," *TQ* 127 (1947): 399–417.

Mart. Pol. 14:2), eternal life (*Herm.* 24:5; cf. *Barn.* 11:11), and immortality (*1 Clem.* 35:1–4; *2 Clem.* 14:5). Being "saved in the end" is equated with people experiencing "the fruit of the resurrection" (*2 Clem.* 19:3). Interestingly, the tradition purportedly stemming from Papias associates the final resurrection of the righteous with the commencement of the millennial reign of the saints (*Frag. Papias* 3:12; 16).

Believers will enter the final form of God's kingdom at this time (*2 Clem.* 5:5; 11:7; 12:1–2, 6; *Herm.* 89:5, 8; 92:2) and will reign with the Lord (Pol. *Phil.* 5:2). Believers "translated" to "paradise" at death will "remain there until the end of all things, as a prelude to immortality" (*Frag. Papias*, Tradition of the Elders 2 [Irenaeus, *Haer.* 5.5.1.]). When the church throughout the ages "is finished being built, then the end comes" (*Herm.* 16:9). Before this occurs, however, Christians must pass through a final tribulation of deception and persecution that is greater than any earlier trials (*Did.* 16:3–5). For example, *Did.* 16:3 says, "For in the last days the false prophets and corrupters will abound, and the sheep will be turned into wolves, and love will be turned into hate" (cf. also the notion of "*the* coming great tribulation" in *Herm.* 6:7; cf. 7:4).[68] Thus, the phrase "latter days" and its synonyms can refer in context to inaugurated eschatology and to a future period that is the consummation of the latter-day period.

Therefore, the full reward of the true saint lies in the future and must be waited for in the present (*2 Clem.* 20:2–4). This reward, which includes final resurrection of the body, will be given by the Son of God when he comes to draw the present age to its conclusion (*Did.* 16:6–8), though no one knows when this will occur (*Did.* 16:1). Consequently, one must be constantly ready for his coming (*Did.* 16:1; cf. *Herm.* 114:4). Accordingly, "Those who profess to be Christ's will be recognized by their actions. For the work [of true faith] is not a matter of what one promises now, but of persevering to the end in the power of faith" (Ign. *Eph.* 14:2).

There will be final judgment for God's enemies and the unfaithful who are not prepared for Christ's coming (*2 Clem.* 18:2; Ign. *Eph.* 16:2; *Mart. Pol.* 11:2; *Barn.* 19:10). This judgment is imminent and in fact is already on the way (*2 Clem.* 16:3). Continued awareness of the coming judgment serves as the basis of motivation for a believer's upright conduct (*2 Clem.* 18:2; *Barn.* 19:10). Christ himself will execute this judgment (Pol. *Phil.* 2:1; 6:2).

Consequently, there will be both salvific reward and judgment at the conclusion of history (*2 Clem.* 10:3–5; *Barn.* 4:12–14; 21:2–3, 6; *Herm.* 53).[69] Such reward surely will be given to genuine saints "if they continue serving the

---

68. On "great tribulation" in *Shepherd of Hermas*, see Richard Bauckham, "The Great Tribulation in the Shepherd of Hermas," *JTS* 25 (1974): 27–40.

69. For sources discussing patristic eschatology, see J. McRay, "Charismata in Second-Century Eschatology," in Lewis, ed., *Last Things*, 151–68.

Lord to the end" (*Herm.* 104:3). "The possibility of repentance" will continue "until the last day" (*Herm.* 6:5).

As in the NT, so too the Apostolic Fathers have repeated declarations that all glory will go to the Father and to Christ "forever and ever" (with repeated use of *aiōn*; see, e.g., for the former, *1 Clem.* 32:4; 43:6; 45:7, and for the latter, *1 Clem.* 50:7; 58:2; 64:1). These affirmations are oriented primarily to the unending future.

Conclusion

The phrase "latter days" and its synonyms in the NT and the Apostolic Fathers refer in various contexts to inaugurated eschatology and in other contexts to a future period that is the consummation of the latter-day period. Thus, the well-known phrase "already and not yet" is a very apt description of the way that eschatology was understood by the NT writers and the earliest church fathers. How does this dominant eschatological notion relate to the overall storyline of Scripture? The following chapter will attempt to show in more depth how eschatology is related to the Bible's overall storyline.

6

Further Reflections on the Nature
of the Eschatological New Testament Storyline

The NT repeatedly uses precisely the same phrase "latter days" as found in the OT prophecies, though other synonymous expressions are also employed. Many of these uses may be echoes of the OT expression, though I have concluded that some uses appear to be specific allusions to some of the "latter day" OT texts. The eschatological nuance of the phrases is generally identical to that of the OT, except for one difference: in the NT the end days predicted by the OT are seen as beginning fulfillment with Christ's first coming and will culminate in a final consummated fulfillment at the very end of history. All that the OT foresaw would occur in the end times has begun already in the first century and continues on until the final coming of Christ.[1] This means that the OT end-time expectations of the great tribulation, God's domination of the gentiles, deliverance of Israel from oppressors, Israel's restoration, Israel's resurrection, the new covenant, the promised Spirit, the new creation, the new temple, a messianic king, and the establishment of God's kingdom have been set in motion irreversibly by Christ's death and resurrection and the formation of the Christian church. Of course, other eschatological themes will be discussed in this book, but they are subsets of the preceding ones listed. Early Judaism is in line with the eschatological developments of the NT writers, though there is little evidence of inaugurated eschatology, except in the Qumran community. The Apostolic Fathers follow the NT's lead in its "already and not yet" view of eschatological fulfillment of OT prophecy.

This already–not yet eschatological concept may be pictured in the following manner:[2]

1. Although I have earlier qualified this exclusively futuristic assessment of the OT by contending that some of the expressions there later find apparent inaugurated fulfillment still within the OT period itself (e.g., Israel's end-time restoration begins at the time of the return of the remnant from Babylon: see Deut. 4:30; 31:29), these were not "true" inaugurated eschatological fulfillments, since these apparent fulfillments did not involve irreversible conditions.
2. Anthony A. Hoekema, *The Bible and the Future* (Grand Rapids: Eerdmans, 1979), 20.

Christians live between "D-day" and "V-day." D-day was the first coming of Christ, when the opponent was defeated decisively; V-day is the final coming of Christ, at which time the adversary will finally and completely surrender.[3] "The hope of the final victory is so much more the vivid because of the unshakably firm conviction that the battle that decides the victory has already taken place."[4] Anthony Hoekema concludes,

> The nature of New Testament eschatology may be summed up under three observations: (1) the great eschatological event predicted in the Old Testament has happened; (2) what the Old Testament writers seemed to depict as one movement is now seen to involve two stages: the present age and the age of the future; and (3) the relation between these two eschatological stages is that the blessings of the present [eschatological] age are the pledge and guarantee of greater blessings to come.[5]

How does the evidence of the preceding chapter on the prominence of eschatology in the NT and the early church fathers relate to and contribute to past proposals for "centers" of the NT? The following are among the prominent proposals: (1) anthropology; (2) salvation history; (3) covenant; (4) love; (5) Christology; (6) justification; (7) reconciliation; (8) God's kingdom; (9) second exodus/restoration of end-time Israel; (10) mission; (11) God's glory. But, as was the case with the OT "centers," so likewise it is viable to combine many of these main ideas of the NT into a thematic storyline.[6] As I do this, I will attempt to show how eschatology relates to this storyline.

My revised proposal of the main storyline of the OT at the end of chapter 3 was this: *The Old Testament is the story of God, who progressively*

3. Ibid., 21.

4. Oscar Cullmann, *Christ and Time: The Primitive Christian Conception of Time and History*, trans. Floyd V. Filson (Philadelphia: Westminster, 1950), 87.

5. Hoekema, *Bible and the Future*, 21–22.

6. For discussion of many of these "centers," see Gerhard F. Hasel, *New Testament Theology: Basic Issues in the Current Debate* (Grand Rapids: Eerdmans, 1978). Hasel sees that many of these central themes should be combined into a multiplex approach. More recently, see Charles H. H. Scobie, *The Ways of Our God: An Approach to Biblical Theology* (Grand Rapids: Eerdmans, 2003); Frank Thielman, *Theology of the New Testament: A Canonical and Synthetic Approach* (Grand Rapids: Zondervan, 2005), 219–33, and esp. 681–725, both of which give a multiplex perspective, though the former covers a whole-Bible view and not merely the NT.

reestablishes his eschatological new-creational kingdom out of chaos over a sinful people by his word and Spirit through promise, covenant, and redemption, resulting in worldwide commission to the faithful to advance this kingdom and judgment (defeat or exile) for the unfaithful, unto his glory. How does this OT storyline relate to the aforementioned proposed "centers" of the NT and what we have discovered in the preceding chapter on NT eschatology? How should the NT storyline be stated in light of its relation to that of the OT? I propose the following: *Jesus's life, trials, death for sinners, and especially resurrection by the Spirit have launched the fulfillment of the eschatological already–not yet new-creational reign, bestowed by grace through faith and resulting in worldwide commission to the faithful to advance this new-creational reign and resulting in judgment for the unbelieving, unto the triune God's glory.* This statement of the NT narrative line is to be understood from two angles. First, my thesis is that this storyline is the principal generative concept from which the rest of the other major notions in the NT are derived;[7] therefore, second, this idea is the overarching concept or organizing structure of thought within which the others are best understood.

I have stated that it is preferable and more sensitive to the Bible as literature to speak of a "storyline" rather than a single "center." Just as differently proposed centers can be debated, conflicting storylines can also be proposed and debated. Therefore, it is helpful to lay out methodological criteria by which a storyline can be judged to be more probable than another.

Methodological Issues and Problems for Positing a Central Storyline for Biblical Theology

General Methodological Reflections on the Validity of Formulating Centers or Storylines[8]

David Wenham notes two reasons why a search for a "center" in Scripture is important:[9] (1) if a "coherent shape and a center in an author's thought

7. Thielman (*Theology of the New Testament*, 231–32) sees this as one way to understand a "center."
8. This first section of the excursus is a revised summary of an unpublished paper written by my research student Daniel J. Brendsel ("Centers, Plots, Themes, and Biblical Theology," paper presented at the Doctoral Seminar on Theological Interpretation of Scripture, Wheaton College, December 18, 2008). A number of his ideas overlap with mine (indeed, he summarizes and interacts with some of my previously published ideas on this topic). Nevertheless, his methodological essay has helped me to crystallize my own thinking about the viability of attempting to summarize Scripture with one idea, a multiplicity of ideas, or a storyline. Directly before publication of this book Brendsel's paper was published as "Plots, Themes, and Responsibilities: The Search for a Center of Biblical Theology Reexamined," *Themelios* 35, no. 3 (2010): 400–412.
9. David Wenham, "Appendix: Unity and Diversity in the New Testament," in *A Theology of the New Testament*, by George Eldon Ladd, rev. ed. (Grand Rapids: Eerdmans, 1993), 710.

and writing" can be perceived, it will give a better understanding of both the work as a whole and the individual parts (that is, a center has heuristic value); (2) if Scripture consists of books that are ultimately unified by one divine author, then the presumption is that these books will not have "significantly different centers."

A third reason for a search for a "center" can be suggested, which is more of a presupposition for the legitimacy of such a search. In Acts 20:26–27 Paul says to the Ephesian elders that he "is innocent of the blood of all men" because he "did not shrink from declaring . . . the whole purpose of God." Paul summarized God's purposeful activity in salvation history over a three-year period and called it "the whole purpose of God." Exactly what his summary of that purpose was is not clear, but he does call his summary "profitable" (Acts 20:20), "the gospel of the grace of God" (Acts 20:24), and "the kingdom" (Acts 20:25). Thus, Paul appears to see a basic deposit (a heart, a core, a center?), which does not nullify but rather serves the other variegated details of the Bible. This deposit provides an order and illumination of the various biblical details such that when Paul leaves, the Ephesians can reflect further on those details and gain greater clarity about them through the lens of the summarized deposit.[10]

Therefore, seeking a center to Scripture is an attempt to find heuristic lenses for God's people that guide them to understand better the various details of Scripture. Acts 20:26–27 is a biblical rationale for searching for the content of such a center.

D. A. Carson asks pertinently what precisely is meant by a "center": "Does it refer to the most common theme, determined by statistical count, or to the controlling theme or to the fundamental theological presuppositions of the New Testament writers, so far as they may be discerned?"[11] James Hamilton defines a "center" as "the concept to which the biblical authors point as the ultimate reason" for all of God's works, and "the theme which all of the Bible's other themes serve to exposit."[12] Is a "center" to be defined as heart, core, main/controlling theme, ultimate purpose, unifying principle, and so on?

Referring to the "storyline" of Scripture instead of its "center," however, better avoids the critique that one is imposing a foreign system on the biblical data, or that one is not giving an equal voice to every part of Scripture. Carson offers a "plotline" approach to Scripture: "The fact remains that the Bible as a whole document tells a story, and properly used, that story can serve as a metanarrative that shapes our grasp of the entire Christian faith."[13] Likewise, Craig Blomberg asserts,

10. See Brendsel, "Centers, Plots, Themes."
11. D. A. Carson, "New Testament Theology," *DLNTD* 810.
12. James Hamilton, "The Glory of God in Salvation through Judgment: The Center of Biblical Theology?" *TynBul* 57, no. 1 (2006): 61.
13. D. A. Carson, *The Gagging of God: Christianity Confronts Pluralism* (Grand Rapids: Zondervan, 1996), 194.

It is not often asked if it is necessary to reduce that which is couched in story form to a single theme or proposition. Perhaps it is more appropriate to consider how the story might be retold in its simplest form. Treating the Bible as a narrative suggests a model for demonstrating in greater detail the unfolding unity and diversity within Scripture.[14]

Consequently, a search for a storyline or plotline better avoids the difficulties of giving prominence to a single theme or a group of themes, though, as we will see, it does not avoid this problem altogether.

However, there are several objections to summarizing a plotline of the Bible. Summative storylines are also open to the criticism of being reductionistic, and for the same reasons as proposed centers: (1) one can ask why specific ideas or events are chosen and seen to be more conceptually dominant than other events; (2) furthermore, a plotline approach may not be sufficiently representative, since significant portions of Scripture are not narrative (e.g., wisdom literature, apocalyptic, and epistolary material); (3) whatever themes are chosen are the result of interpreters seeing only what they have been culturally conditioned to see, since many believe that all knowledge is culturally conditioned.

All these critiques notwithstanding, a plotline or storyline approach is better than trying to isolate single centers. With respect to the first two objections, which are similar, a storyline is composed of several themes. The fact that a storyline is composed of several themes means that a multiperspectival approach is incorporated into the narrative-line approach and thus indicates one of the clear advantages over a single-center method. And a storyline composed of several themes is likewise preferable to a merely multiperspectival approach, since the latter makes no attempt directly to relate one theme to another, whereas the storyline binds them together in some kind of logical, redemptive-historical, and narratival manner. Nevertheless, the problem remains of why certain events that convey particular themes are chosen over other events and their associated themes.

Although some object that there is no basis for subordinating some things in Scripture to other ideas that are supposedly more comprehensive, the following reasons may be offered to legitimize an attempt to highlight some themes above others. As noted earlier, Scripture itself does this, the prime example being Acts 20. To this can be added Matt. 23:23, where Jesus criticizes the religious rulers for ignoring the "weightier matters of the law." Likewise, the prophets affirm that God desires loyalty, obedience, and knowledge more than

---

14. Craig L. Blomberg, "The Unity and Diversity of Scripture," *NDBT* 66. See likewise Richard B. Hays, "Can Narrative Criticism Recover the Theological Unity of Scripture," *JTI* 2 (2008): 193–211. Hays attempts a thumbnail sketch of how viewing Scripture as a unified and coherent dramatic narrative can contribute to the doing of NT theology (note also therein further secondary sources supportive of this notion).

sacrifice. Micah similarly sums up God's requirements by referring to justice, kindness, and humility, and similarly Jesus summarizes the law by saying that people should love God and neighbor. Thus, Scripture itself "summarizes large swaths of biblical material, and in that summary it prioritizes and 'hierarchalizes,' such that some elements move into the spotlight while others slide to the periphery."[15]

The objection that a historical storyline approach may not sufficiently represent major genres of Scripture (e.g., wisdom literature) does not adequately acknowledge that such genres have woven within them significant links to Scripture's historical plotline.[16] In this connection, James Barr states that "in general, although not all parts of the Bible are narrative, the narrative character of the story elements provides a better framework into which the non-narrative parts may be fitted than any framework based on the non-narrative parts into which the story elements could be fitted."[17] For example, I tried to show in chapter 2 how the biblical wisdom literature fits within that aspect of my proposed storyline concerning the wise rule of an Adam-like king. The same thing could be shown with respect to God's glory in this literature. I will attempt to show how the notions of kingship, new creation, and divine glory are crucial threads throughout NT epistolary and apocalyptic literature.

Other observations in Scripture can result in distinguishing which elements are subordinate to others, especially with respect to which storylines are dominant or broader than others. For example, observing repetition of narratives and identifying climactic points in narratives are at least two criteria that can help in this manner. At times it may be difficult to decide whether one idea is subordinate to another. The ideas that form components of plotline proposals are likely not subordinate to one another. For instance, recall my proposed storyline of the OT: *The Old Testament is the story of God, who progressively reestablishes his eschatological new-creational kingdom out of chaos over a sinful people by his word and Spirit through promise, covenant, and redemption, resulting in worldwide commission to the faithful to advance this kingdom and judgment (defeat or exile) for the unfaithful, unto his glory.* In this statement, on the one hand, "new creation" and "kingdom" are two sides of one redemptive-historical coin and are likely not to be subordinated one to the other, as is also the case with "promise" and "covenant," as well as with "word" and "Spirit." On the other hand, it is likely that God's "glory" is the logical climax and goal of everything that precedes in the idea, so that in this sense it is perhaps a more dominant notion than the other conceptual components of the storyline statement.

15. Brendsel, "Centers, Plots, Themes."

16. In further support of this point, see James Barr, *The Concept of Biblical Theology: An Old Testament Perspective* (Minneapolis: Fortress, 1999), 356. However, I disagree with Barr that "story" in Scripture means that "myth" or "legend" is included (on which, see ibid., 345–61).

17. Ibid., 356.

In response to the second objection, that all interpretations, including proposed centers or plotlines, are culturally conditioned, one can observe that such proposals from different stages of church history overlap.[18] It is surprising how many suggested centers over the past century coalesce around just a few major notions, especially given the different cultures and situations of the various interpreters.[19] Thus, there is "external evidence . . . emphasizing certain themes and items in Scripture not being arbitrary or a practice in imposition,"[20] nor is it merely the expression of a commentator's socially constructed knowledge. In addition, if one acknowledges that Scripture is God's living and written word, then one must leave room for the Spirit to break through our socially constructed knowledge. Accordingly, such a breakthrough will cause us to regrind our interpretative lenses according to God's intended meaning in Scripture so that Christian interpreters may increasingly think God's thoughts after him and not merely rethink the thoughts of other human interpreters.

It is true that no center or cluster of centers or even a storyline has yet been proposed that has proved satisfactory for a decisive majority of scholars.[21] And no such consensus proposal is likely in the future. Neverthless, we have seen that Scripture itself expresses tendencies to hierarchalize its different materials, which provides us an impetus to continue doing our best to do likewise. In light of this excursus, the best way to try to hierarchalize in Scripture is to attempt to formulate a storyline that is composed of various themes that could be considered "central themes" but is organized in a statement of the redemptive-historical purpose of the canon. The storyline proposed above is my attempt to do this respectively for the OT and then for the NT. It especially is based on Gen. 1–3, where one observes a priest-king ruling over an original creation to reflect God's glory, and then subsequent OT history is a process of rebuilding toward a recapitulation of the primeval creational kingdom, as I argued in earlier chapters of this book. We also noted earlier that the book of Revelation concludes with a vision of a restored eschatological Eden and new creation in which kingly conquerors will dwell. Thus, the process of working toward a restoration of the first creational kingdom in the OT is consummated in the NT. Accordingly, the canon has an inclusio: it begins with a pristine creation over which a priest-king rules for God's glory and ends with a new-creational kingdom where a priest-king rules with his followers

18. E.g., Augustine's "city of God" has significant overlap with the "kingdom of God" mentioned in several contemporary works on biblical theology; there is affinity between Thomas Aquinas's "beatific vision" and Jonathan Edwards's view of the beauty and glory of God.

19. See Scobie, *Ways of Our God*, 87.

20. Brendsel, "Centers, Plots, Themes."

21. See Stanley E. Porter, "Is There a Center to Paul's Theology? An Introduction to the Study of Paul and His Theology," in *Paul and His Theology*, ed. Stanley E. Porter, PS 3 (Leiden: Brill, 2006), 1–19. Porter surveys various approaches to finding theological centers proposed for Paul and indicates that this is an example of the same difficulties faced by doing the broader task of a NT theology in which one attempts to find theological unity.

(who are subordinate kings and priests) for God's glory. The storyline with the key components of reestablishing a new-creational kingdom for God's glory is crucial to both Testaments.

More Particular Methodological Reflections on the Validity of Formulating Centers or Storylines with Special Respect to the Storyline Proposed in This Book

Whenever a particular idea is proposed as the key to biblical theology, the issue of validation must be discussed. That is, how are we to judge one proposed "center" to be better than others? As noted in chapter 2 and the preceding section, the very discussion of centers is not felicitous, since such proposals can be reductionistic and overlook other major ideas.

The issue is not as thorny for those who hold a "multiple lens" perspective, but still they must validate why their central themes are more legitimate than other multiple themes proposed. When one center is offered over others, the magnitude of the problem increases, and the burden of proof is on validating that such a proposal is probable. The center that is most comprehensive is to be judged the most probable. As discussed earlier, the present approach is not to propose one central theme but rather to combine a number of them into a central storyline for the OT and then the NT (as understood in light of the OT). This approach attempts to be more sensitive to the Bible as narrative literature, and while there are other genres besides narrative in Scripture, these others still reflect to one significant degree or another a literary storyline.[22] But how does one go about validating that one is more comprehensive than another?

Obviously, such a task demands a book of its own, but here, at least, we can look at four tests of validation. First, the proposed storyline should be related to all other viable centers and suggested storylines, and it needs to be shown that the proposed focus is more overarching than the others, and that the others are logically subcategories of it; this can be done through logical analysis of the nature of the centers themselves and of their relationship to one another.

Second, the proposed plotline must have a textual basis throughout the NT canon and be related to the various major themes of the books of the NT (which may overlap with some of the competing centers or storylines at issue in the preceding test of validation) in order to be adequately and naturally related to the diversity present throughout the NT. If there is a blurring of the lens in some books, it probably is not comprehensive enough; if the lens remains sharp and sheds greater light on the data and meaning of the books than other lenses, it validates itself. If an idea stands in serious tension with any of the major emphases of the NT books or with any of their ethical

---

22. Limits of space do not allow demonstration of this point.

teachings, it becomes less viable.[23] If a hermeneutical lens is a good heuristic device, it will not result in fuzzy thinking or in a reductionistic atomism in which it fails to explain the interrelatedness and complexity of concepts.[24] Thus, a viable storyline must be neither too broad to be useful nor too narrow to be exclusive of other important but subordinate ideas.[25]

Third, a viable storyline must be integrally related to major OT themes,[26] undergirded by a theological worldview or belief system about God's relationship with humanity,[27] and anchored in Christ's death and resurrection.

Fourth, just as is done for the focus storyline, each competing center or storyline must be analyzed thoroughly for its comprehensiveness to see if it perhaps might be the most overarching. This last test of validation would take a number of lifetimes; thus one must be content with depending on the work of scholars who have attempted to demonstrate the viability of some of the competing centers or storylines; likewise, works that have surveyed and evaluated some of the significant centers must also be relied on.[28]

The first, second, and third tests of validation may now be addressed, though, again, only a skeletal outline needing more detailed fleshing out at some later time can be drawn here. With respect to the third criterion, the approach in this book is to attempt to root every aspect of NT theology in the OT, especially the storyline of the new-creational kingdom as the recapitulation of the original creation and kingdom of Gen. 1, but on a grander scale. The recapitulating storyline of the new-creational kingdom theme has been set forth in table form in chapter 2 and is summarized here: (1) chaos of precreation state and creation/commission of Adam as king, followed by fall; (2) chaos of

23. On this way of expressing the issue, see Richard B. Hays, *The Moral Vision of the New Testament: Community, Cross, New Creation; A Contemporary Introduction to New Testament Ethics* (San Francisco: HarperSanFrancisco, 1996), 195.

24. This particular formulation of a criterion for validity was mentioned by Philip Towner ("Response to Prof. Greg Beale's 'The Eschatological Conception of New Testament Theology,'" paper presented to the Tyndale Fellowship Triennial Conference on Eschatology, Swanick, Darbyshire, July 1997; Beale's lecture was subsequently published as "The Eschatological Conception of New Testament Theology," in *"The Reader Must Understand": Eschatology in Bible and Theology*, ed. K. E. Brower and M. W. Elliott [Leicester: Apollos, 1997], 11–52).

25. On this way of stating one of the criteria for validity, see Thielman, *Theology of the New Testament*, 232.

26. This presupposes not only the Jewish roots of early Christianity, but also the necessity that any good NT theology be adequately linked to OT theology.

27. The criterion of "story" as essential to a biblical theology has been emphasized by N. T. Wright, *The New Testament and the People of God* (Minneapolis: Fortress, 1992), esp. 31–80, 121–44, 215–24; as well as by Craig G. Bartholomew and Michael Goheen, "Story and Biblical Theology," in *Out of Egypt: Biblical Theology and Biblical Interpretation*, ed. Craig Bartholomew, et al., Hermeneutics Series 5 (Grand Rapids: Zondervan, 2004), 144–71 and the literature cited therein.

28. Hasel (*New Testament Theology*) and Scobie (*Ways of Our God*), e.g., have offered critiques of most of the competing centers discussed here.

deluge and re-creation/commission of Noah, followed by fall (sins of Noah and his sons); (3) chaos of Egyptian captivity and plagues of de-creation, followed by re-creation (at exodus)/commission of Israel (anticipated by commission of patriarchs), followed by fall (golden calf); (4) chaos of captivity in Babylon and in Israel's own land, followed by re-creation/commission of Jesus the true Israel (in his life, death, and resurrection), followed by no fall of Jesus as last Adam, and by successful consummation of initial re-creation in eternal new heaven and earth.[29] This storyline[30] expresses a worldview rich in theological doctrines.[31] And, as we have seen, the new-creational proposal also is anchored in Christ's life, death, and resurrection.[32]

How does the storyline revolving around the new-creational kingdom fare when it is related to the various major themes of the books of the NT (the second criterion of validation noted above)? Does the lens of this storyline become fuzzy in some books, or does it remain sharp and shed greater light on them? Throughout this book, I relate the storyline of the new creation and kingdom to the subject matter of all the major NT corpuses and books. Although this is not a thorough analysis, it sketches the broad contours of how this question could be answered in more depth. The reader will have to decide whether this broad outline holds promise for further developing

29. The word *palingenesia* ("regeneration, rebirth"), which in Matt. 19:28 refers to the new creation and kingdom that Christ will bring to completion, is used by Philo to refer to the regaining of life (*Cher.* 114; *Post.* 124) and to the renewal of the earth after the cataclysmic flood (*Mos.* 2.65). Josephus employs the same word with reference to the restoration of Israel after the Babylonian exile (*Ant.* 11.66) (so David C. Sim, *Apocalyptic Eschatology in the Gospel of Matthew*, SNTSMS 88 [Cambridge: Cambridge University Press, 1996], 112). These uses by Philo and Josephus reflect that these two significant events in OT history were conceived in early Judaism along the lines of new creation. For the creation themes interwoven into the narrative of Israel's exodus from Egypt (esp. in Exod. 15), see William J. Dumbrell, *Covenant and Creation: A Theology of the Old Testament Covenants* (Nashville: Thomas Nelson, 1984), 100–104.

30. For comparison of this to N. T. Wright's analysis, see the brief discussion at the end of this section of his three levels of covenantal purpose.

31. See, e.g., the sixteen theological concepts elaborated on in the next few paragraphs as previously proposed centers, which can be viewed as facets of the new creation, or of the new re-creation storyline. Barr contends that "story is not theology, but is the 'raw material' of theology," so that theological "axioms guided stories [e.g.] about Abraham or about Moses" (*Concept of Biblical Theology*, 354, 361). While this can certainly be true of various stories in the Bible, others more clearly express theological notions and can be formally summarized in this manner. My formulation of the storyline of the OT above and of the NT directly below contains themes that are more explicitly theological. It is important to underscore, however, that these ideas are biblical-theological, not systematic-theological.

32. See Eugene E. Lemcio, "The Unifying Kerygma of the New Testament," *JSNT* 33 (1988): 3–17; idem, "The Unifying Kerygma of the New Testament (II)," *JSNT* 38 (1990): 3–11. Lemcio contends that "the unifying kerygmatic center to the diverse witness of the NT" is sixfold: (1) God, who (2) sent (according to the Gospels) or raised (according to the rest of the NT witness) (3) Jesus, (4) followed by a response, (5) toward God, (6) which brings benefits. It is significant that according to this scheme, Jesus's resurrection is the core of the post-Gospels message.

the kingdom of the new creation as *the* heuristic device for understanding NT theology.

More elaboration is needed to respond adequately to the first criterion for validation: how do some of the other previously proposed centers or story-lines logically compare to the new-creational kingdom core of my proposed storyline and vice versa? The following proposed centers are the most viable contenders, some of which were mentioned above: kingdom, covenant, promise, salvation, redemption, history of redemption, new exodus, justification, reconciliation, people of God, new temple,[33] life, new Jerusalem/Zion, presence of God, God's glory, and mission.[34] To discuss these even briefly involves some necessary though minimal repetition from earlier parts of the book, and it involves the discussion of the remainder of this book.

Is the story of the movement toward the new-creational kingdom broad enough to encompass organically the rich diversity of major NT thoughts and doctrines that have formed the bases of these other competing centers? Several crucial notions are addressed throughout this book, and there is an attempt throughout to show how they are facets of the new-creational kingdom. These will have to be judged on the merits of the limited discussions elaborated on in this book. Among some of the competing central ideas discussed, the most prominent competitors with that of the new-creational kingdom are the notion of the "kingdom" by itself in the Gospels and of justification and reconciliation in the Pauline Epistles. The kingdom is a major facet of new creation, since Jesus was seen as reinstating the vice-regency that Adam should have successfully carried out in the original creation. But, just as in the first creation, the kingdom is so inextricably linked to new creation, and not more comprehensive than or even synonymous with new creation, that the two should be seen as coequal. This is why I often refer to these two together as the "new-creational kingdom." It is thus best to combine new creation and kingdom together as above as the dominant focus of my proposed storyline.

The images of the "new Jerusalem/Zion" and of the "new temple" in both Testaments allude to the presence of God in the midst of his victorious reign in a new creation,[35] and thus it is best seen to be coequal conceptually with the new-creational reign. However, reconciliation is a serious contender for pride of place in biblical theology, since it could be seen logically to be the goal of the new-creational kingdom: the purpose of restoring creation is that sinful people might be restored to relationship with the Creator (indeed, in 2 Cor. 5:17–21 reconciliation comes right on the heels of the announcement

---

33. Especially as proposed in G. K. Beale, *The Temple and the Church's Mission: A Biblical Theology of the Dwelling Place of God*, NSBT 17 (Downers Grove, IL: InterVarsity, 2004).

34. Especially as proposed in I. Howard Marshall, *New Testament Theology: Many Witnesses, One Gospel* (Downers Grove, IL: InterVarsity, 2004), 717–26.

35. So William J. Dumbrell, *The End of the Beginning: Revelation 21–22 and the Old Testament* (Homebush West, NSW: Lancer, 1985), 1–34.

of "new creation" in Christ). However, the two could also be seen as virtually synonymous: new-creational kingdom involves reconciliation, and the condition of new creation does not cease to exist once reconciliation is accomplished but rather continues to endure along with the state of reconciliation. Yet, on further reflection, we realize that reconciliation is a facet of the new-creational kingdom, inextricably linked to it and a subcategory of it (on which, see further below). So new-creational kingdom is the broad reference to the restoration of the fallen cosmos, within which there is restoration of humanity's vice-regency and reconciliation between God and alienated humans and among alienated humans themselves.

Richard Hays has proposed three focal images that he believes represent the NT's underlying storyline and bring all its texts into clearer focus: "community, cross, and new creation." His broad storyline can be summarized as follows: God has begun to rescue a lost world through Christ's death and resurrection, producing a witnessing community empowered by the Spirit to reenact Christ's loving witness as a sign of and until the consummation of God's redemptive purposes for the world.[36] This is an excellent attempt at reducing the data of the NT to its most basic components within the context of a storyline, but it remains, I think, too vague with respect to how new creation relates to or permeates community and cross and how the latter two realities are eschatological in nature.[37]

The "new exodus" is a major theme in portions of the NT (esp. the Gospels, Pauline Epistles, and Revelation), but this is another metaphor for the new-creational kingdom. The plagues on Egypt that begin the process of the exodus are designed to indicate a de-creation and situation of chaos from which Israel can emerge through the division of water and earth as a new humanity on the other side of the Red Sea.[38] The notion of Israel being part of a new creation is also suggested by Deut. 32:10–11, which describes the exodus as God finding Israel in an "empty" (tōhû) desert and describes his rescue like an eagle "hovering" (rāḥap) over its young; both terms also occur in the initial creation narrative of Gen. 1:2 with reference to the "empty" earth with the Spirit "hovering" over it. Just as Israel was a corporate Adam, as discussed earlier, so Israel's inheritance of the promised land was to be none other than what God had promised to Adam if he had obeyed: full posses-

36. Hays, *Moral Vision of the New Testament*, 193–200.

37. Hays's exegetical and biblical-theological discussions elaborating on "new creation" are few, and what can be found is too brief (see, e.g., ibid., 19–21, 198). Typically, the discussions tend to reflect more generally on the tension of the "already and not yet" and the implications of this tension for NT ethics.

38. Wisdom 19:6 portrays the exodus as a new creation: "For the whole creation was again renewed [*dietypouto* = also "fashioned, formed, framed"] in its own kind anew" (19:18 adds, "for the elements were changed in themselves"). On the nuances of the verb *diatypoō*, see Richard M. Davidson, *Typology in Scripture: A Study in Hermenuetical τύπος Structures*, AUSDDS 2 (Berrien Springs, MI: Andrews University Press, 1981), 132.

sion of the garden of Eden and, by extension, the ends of the earth. This is why the land promised to Israel is also referred to as the garden of Eden (Isa. 51:3; Ezek. 36:35; Joel 2:3; cf. Isa. 65:21–23 LXX). Likewise, if the people of Israel had obeyed as a corporate Adam, they would have inherited their own paradisal garden and, ultimately, the whole earth. But they disobeyed and, like Adam, were disinherited. The episode of the golden calf was the event that recapitulated the fall of Adam.[39]

All this is recapitulated in Israel's history of exile, which is compared to a state of creational chaos, and in the promises of the people's return from exile, which is compared by Isaiah to another exodus. And although the promise of restoration seems to begin fulfillment in the return from Babylonian exile, the significant features of the fulfillment are delayed, since (1) only a remnant and not the whole nation returns, and even this remnant is not faithful; (2) the rebuilt temple does not meet the expectations of the one promised in Ezek. 40–48 (because it is smaller and likely because the divine presence is absent from it); (3) Israel is still under foreign domination, which extends on into the first century AD; (4) there is no new creation in which the land is renovated, nor is there a renewed Zion with a king into which the redeemed return from among the gentiles, nor is there peace between Jew and gentile. The major irreversible features of the restoration promises begin fulfillment in Christ's coming, which is apparent from both Jesus's and Paul's appeals to OT restoration promises beginning fulfillment in their midst. And because the promises of restoration were coined in language of a new exodus, Jesus is seen as launching the realization of those prophecies,[40] and because new exodus is nothing more than initial reinstatement of the primal creation, the NT can also refer to the fulfillment of the promises of restoration from captivity as the fulfillment of new creation.[41]

The proposed centers of "salvation," "redemption," and "justification" are too narrow in focus in comparison to the storyline about the movement toward

---

39. For the events of Israel's sin, judgment, and restoration in Exod. 32–34 being a recapitulation of Adam's sin, fall, and restoration, see Scott J. Hafemann, *Paul, Moses, and the History of Israel: The Letter/Spirit Contrast and the Argument from Scripture in 2 Corinthians 3*, WUNT 81 (Tübingen: Mohr Siebeck, 1995), 227–31. Hafemann also shows that this was, to varying degrees, the view of Judaism.

40. In addition to the relevant segments of N. T. Wright's work already noted, see Willard M. Swartley, *Israel's Scripture Traditions and the Synoptic Gospels: Story Shaping Story* (Peabody, MA: Hendrickson, 1994), 44–153; Rikki E. Watts, *Isaiah's New Exodus in Mark* (Grand Rapids: Baker Academic, 1997), both of which analyze the patterns of second exodus in the Synoptic Gospels.

41. On the dual notion of Christ's death and resurrection as fulfilling both the promises of new creation and the prophecies of Israel's restoration, see G. K. Beale, "The Old Testament Background of Reconciliation in 2 Corinthians 5–7 and Its Bearing on the Literary Problem of 2 Corinthians 4:14–7:1," *NTS* 35 (1989): 550–81; idem, "The Old Testament Background of Rev 3.14," *NTS* 42 (1996): 133–52.

the new-creational kingdom. All three are part of the means used to accomplish the goal of new-creational kingdom: people are saved from their sinful state, so that the wrath of God will not overwhelm them at the final judgment, and they pass through it, so that they can enter the new creation, where God rules. Redemption is a metaphor similar to salvation and plays the same instrumental role in relation to new creation, but it has the nuance of being bought out of slavery to sin and to Satan. Likewise, justification is one of the means used to work toward the new cosmos, but it has overtones of a legal metaphor in which the penalty for sin is viewed as having been paid by a representative on behalf of sinners in the court of God, who also transfers to their credit his own Son's righteousness.[42] In the case of all three—salvation, redemption, justification— Christ is the subject in carrying out the action on behalf of his sinful people.

The proposal of the "history of redemption" as the biblical-theological focal point is variously understood. Its generally accepted definition is God's salvific dealings with his people throughout the entire history, from the fall of Adam until the final consummation, with judgment playing a secondary role. This also fits fairly obviously into the same penultimate position in relation to the new-creational reign as we saw with the ideas of salvation, redemption, and justification, since all of these are solutions to the predicament of sin, which prevents kingship in the new creation from occurring.

"Covenant" has been a prominent idea that several scholars have seen as the central motif of both Testaments. All the various covenants, though not precisely the same in nature, are a penultimate means to accomplishing rule in the new creation, whether one has in mind the so-called covenant of creation or covenant of works made with Adam, or the covenants made with Noah, Abraham, Moses, David, and then the new covenant promised in Jeremiah and inaugurated in the NT.[43] Covenant is the primary means by which God, the suzerain, governs his people, the vassal.

The notion of "promise" has the similar intermediate role of covenant in that covenants are formalizations of earlier salvific promises, though covenants are broader because they include considerations of stipulations and judgment as well. Although both the promise of redemption in Christ and the new covenant are fulfilled consummately in the new heaven and earth, that condition of fulfillment continues eternally. The condition of kingship in the new creation also exists forever.

The proposal of the "people of God" or the "new community" as the central NT concept is one-sided because it does not include sufficient focus on God, Christ, and the Spirit, and it is too general because a number of things can be said to be true of God's people.

---

42. For elaboration of the notion of justification, see the extended discussion in chap. 15 below.
43. For this role of the covenants in relation to creation, see Dumbrell, *Covenant and Creation*, and *End of the Beginning*.

Charles Scobie has mentioned "life" as a theme that has been proposed as the dominant one in the canon. This theme is best understood as virtually synonymous with the idea of resurrection and regeneration, which I discuss later (see chaps. 8–11, 18). Likewise, if one construes life to refer to the manner of life that one lives, then this might fit better under the category of sanctification, likewise analyzed later (see chaps. 25–26). Whichever is the case, it is still a subcategory of new-creational reign, since it is not broad enough to comprehend all the other facets of new-creational reign. If life is understood ultimately as resurrection life of redeemed humanity, it is still not a broad enough concept to encompass the renewed life of the nonhuman creation in the consummated entire new creation.

Likewise, the major notion of the "presence of God" is very close to reconciliation, since people are reconciled to God's presence, which then reconciles them to one another. God's presence, however, is greater than merely being seen as a facet of reconciliation. Indeed, the divine presence is almost synonymous with "God's glory," which can refer to the essence of his attributes and very being. God's glorious presence is not coequal with his rule in a new creation. God, Christ, and the Spirit are the sovereign agents in bringing about new creation, and they rule in the new creation. As mentioned earlier, the images of the new Jerusalem/Zion and the new temple connote the notions of God's presence and active reign.[44] So, in this light, God's glorious presence is part of the core (new-creational reign) of my proposed storyline. The centrality of the covenant community's mission, I have argued, is to be understood primarily through the lens of the extension of the temple of God's presence over the earth, so that the concept of "mission" is perhaps best subordinated to the redemptive-historical idea of the temple. As we will see more clearly at the conclusion of this discussion, God's glory, both his very essence and the glorious praise offered for who he is and what he has done, is the *goal* of the overall storyline that I have formulated.

The consummated eschatological new creation kingship is the overarching reality composed of and integrating, at least, the following distinct elements which were part of the first, prefall creation (Gen. 1–2), but it goes beyond these initial creation elements because now they exist in *escalated* eschatological form with respect to their nature or quality:[45] (1) God's life-giving presence (through his Spirit; chaps. 17–19) and glory (see esp. chap. 28); (2) in his temple (chaps. 18–19), which entails a worldwide commission to humanity (chap. 19); (3) perfected human life (involving resurrection life after the fall; see chaps. 8–11); (4) peace (involving reconciliation after the fall; see chap. 16); (5) restoration of the material cosmos (see chaps. 22, 27); (6) righteousness

44. For this dual idea of temple, see Dumbrell, *End of the Beginning*, 35–76.
45. For discussion of the recapitulated and escalated elements of the final form of the new creation, see G. K. Beale, *The Book of Revelation: A Commentary on the Greek Text*, NIGTC (Grand Rapids: Eerdmans, 1999), 1039–1121, on Rev. 21:1–22:25.

175

(see chaps. 15, 25–26); (7) Sabbath rest; and (8) the original primordial command to "be fruitful and multiply," which Genesis 12:1–3 (and reiterations in following chaps.) transformed into a promise to multiply Abraham's seed, finding its fulfillment in Christ as the true Adamic image and king (chap. 13) and true Israel (chap. 20) and the many sons created through him into God's image (chap. 13) and true Israel (chaps. 20–24), all of whom will be finally perfected in the consummated new cosmos (chap. 27). The elements of God's glorious presence,[46] perfected and righteous human life and rest,[47] are all an integral part of new creation kingship and best not seen as subordinate notions to it. Peace and multiplying seed are subordinate ideas, though peace could be viewed as synonymous with kingship resting. Indeed, all of the other chapter topics are overlapping notions with or facets of the idea of eschatological new-creational kingship, except, of course, the chapter topics on the tribulation and idolatry.

Special comment needs to be made about our chapters on the "Tribulation" (chap. 7) and "Sin as Idolatry" (chap. 12). The reason to include a whole chapter on the eschatological tribulation lies in the notion that it is a recapitulation of the first great trial in Eden, when Satan assaulted Adam and Eve with a bombardment of deception and caused them to "fall." This would be recapitulated again in the eschatological age with Christ, the last Adam, and those identified with him, as especially prophesied in Dan. 7–12. The chapter on idolatry is included to show that the great sin of Adam and Eve in Eden continues to have its effects in humanity.

The preceding chapters (chaps. 2–6) give the foundation upon which the subsequent chapters are based and the seedbed from which these chapters grow. Chapter 2 gives a thumbnail sketch of the thought of Gen. 1–3 and how this is developed in the OT. The reason for starting in this manner is that it is our belief that the very beginning of the Bible has the major seed-form ideas that are developed throughout the OT and on into the New. Then chapters 3–5 first develop the notion of eschatology in the OT, Judaism, and in the NT. These three chapters have been placed at the forefront of the book because they represent the escalated final temporal stage that Adam, Eve, and their progeny should have reached had they been faithful. Chapter 6, the present chapter, has stopped to reflect again on the nature of the biblical storyline as it relates to eschatology.

Therefore, what begins in Gen. 1–3 and is developed throughout the rest of the biblical canon finds its climax in Rev. 21:1–22:5, which recapitulates Gen. 1–3 and portrays the goal that the last Adam and his people have finally attained. Thus, as we said in chapter 2, the biblical material between

46. Here we include all three persons of the Trinity.
47. Note later in the book the discussion of "rest" being an essential aspect of the climactic exercising of absolute end-time kingship (e.g., see chap. 23 under the subheading "Should the Church Keep the Sabbath in the Very Same Way as Israel Did?").

the poles of creation and new creation is to be read not only in the light finally of its origins in Gen. 1–3 but also in view of its goal in Revelation. Consequently, it is the thesis of this book that everything in the biblical canon should be seen to have its roots in Gen. 1–3 and to move toward its final goal in Rev. 21.

It is in this light that our choice of which topics to choose for study in each chapter of this book is not a completely subjective choice but is chosen because it is a prominent idea that we have already observed (see chap. 2) in Gen. 1–3 and is prominent in the final vision of the consummated new creation in Rev. 21–22. The topics of each chapter are, therefore, chosen because they are also major facets of the already and not yet new-creational kingdom (though the tribulation [chap. 7] precedes and prepares for new creation and the sin of idolatry [chap. 12] is what caused the process of working back toward restoration of new creation). Finally, these topics are also chosen because they appear to be developed by the NT in a more major manner than other topics, especially through the use of the OT in the NT. In addition, the majority of the topics on which each chapter elaborates have been viewed by one significant scholar or another in the past two-hundred years (and even before) to be major biblical-theological topics in the NT. In this respect, we have attempted to build on the shoulders of other NT biblical theologians and put their ideas together in choosing the topics that we have.

Finally, the order of these chapter topics in the book (see the table of contents) has been determined by what I perceive to be the order of the elements in our proposed redemptive-historical storyline and the development of the notions in it together with attempting to sort out these topics logically.

Therefore, the upshot of this entire book is that although "eschatology" is used in a variety of ways, I am defining it not merely as the end of redemptive or cosmic history, or the goal of Israel's hopes, or the goal of the individual saint's hopes, but rather as an "already–not yet new-creational reign in Christ," and all other things associated with eschatology are to be understood in inextricable relationship with this notion.[48] The well-known dictum *Endzeit als Urzeit*[49] is on the mark, as is that of *Barn.* 6:13: "Behold, I make the last things as the first things." Eschatology is protology, which means that the goal of all redemptive history is to return to the primal condition of creation from which

---

48. See I. Howard Marshall, "Slippery Words I: Eschatology," *ExpTim* 89 (1978): 264–69. Marshall summarizes nine ways in which the term *eschatology* has been used; he concludes that the core definition must include the idea of the awareness that God's promises have begun to be fulfilled in the present but have not been consummately fulfilled, so that there is still a forward-looking aspect as well.

49. Literally translated as "end-time as prehistory," with the sense of the end-time being like the beginning of time. As far as I am aware, this was first established in scholarship as a significant idea by the work of Hermann Gunkel, *Schöpfung und Chaos in Urzeit und Endzeit: Eine religionsgeschichtliche Untersuchung über Gen 1 und Ap Joh 12* (Göttingen: Vandenhoeck & Ruprecht, 1895), e.g., 367–70.

humankind fell[50] and then go beyond it to a more heightened state, which the first creation was designed to reach but did not. The goal of returning to the primal state of Adam's rule in creation and to an escalation of this state is the engine that runs the entire eschatological program. That all the doctrines or notions of salvation/redemption are thematically subordinate to God's new-creational reign through an earthly representative is evident from recalling that *eschatology precedes soteriology in Gen. 1–3.* That is, had Adam been faithful in ruling over the first creation, he would have received subsequent escalated blessings, which would have been none other than eternal end-time blessings, with the result of God's glory filling the whole earth. I believe that up to the present time, the storyline notion highlighting eschatological new-creational kingship has not been acknowledged adequately as the basis of a NT biblical theology.

Despite my refining of the term "eschatology" as "new-creational reign," one could still ask precisely how I am using the phrase "new-creational reign." (1) Is it employed with the strict idea of the specific apocalyptic notion of the dissolution and re-creation of the entire cosmos, including the resurrection of people? (2) Or does it function as a theological construct in which all eschatological hopes are wrapped up in one theological package? (3) Or does it allude to the general future hope typical of Israel's worldview in which the following are included as the objects of that hope: resurrection, renewal of the cosmos, vindication of Israel, return from captivity, salvation of those believing among the nations, punishment of the wicked nations, and, possibly, other theological themes that need to be linked together? My answer is that I am using the phrase "new-creational reign" broadly with all three senses and thus to refer to the entire network of ideas that belong to renewal of the whole world, of Israel, and of the individual. One could respond to my answer by asking what advantage or gains does such an apparently broad idea have over the general center of the "already–not yet eschatological salvation" (as proposed recently by Caird and Hurst,[51] as well as others).[52]

In further response, I believe, however, that the refinement of "eschatology" in terms of "new-creational reign" advances our understanding of "already–not yet eschatology." But how so? Part of the answer lies in N. T. Wright's view of the three levels of human categories that comprise the notion of election: (1) a cosmic or worldwide level, in which Israel's role was to be an agent in restoring the fallen creation; (2) a national level, in which Israel suffered because of its own sin and needed its own restoration; (3) the individual level, in which an Israelite received forgiveness and restoration symbolically through

50. So Dale C. Allison Jr., *The End of the Ages Has Come: An Early Interpretation of the Passion and Resurrection of Jesus* (Philadelphia: Fortress, 1985), 91.
51. G. B. Caird and L. D. Hurst, *New Testament Theology* (Oxford: Clarendon, 1994).
52. This question was posed by Philip Towner ("Response"), after asking which of the three senses of "new creation" I had in mind.

the sacrificial system, as a small-scale model of the coming restoration of the nation.[53] Not only is election one of the main lenses through which humans were to perceive their experience of the world, but also the notions of monotheism and eschatology form the fundamental structure of OT/Jewish "basic belief."[54] These foundational ideas of election, monotheism, and eschatology were a threefold complex of covenantal concepts that "gave Israel a particular understanding of who precisely she was as a people within the purposes of the creator God."[55]

These three levels of election together with monotheism and eschatology are better viewed within a complex of new-creational kingdom ideas, with the notion of covenant playing a subsidiary role within the complex. This is a sharpening of the understanding of "eschatological salvation," and it explains more precisely how eschatological ideas are interrelated. When it is recalled that eschatology precedes soteriology in Gen. 1–3, it becomes clearer that redemption is a subordinate notion to new-creational kingship, since redemption enables one to regain in the last Adam the position of the first Adam and then to go beyond him in receiving the escalated end-time blessings in the last Adam that the first Adam forfeited. Hence, redemption is subordinate to new-creational kingship, since it is the means toward achieving the goal of new-creational kingship.

Furthermore, this proposal profitably refines the general "eschatology" center, since the central element of the inaugurated new-creational reign is Jesus Christ. On the one hand, this is very specific yet appropriately general along the lines of the biblical concept of "the one and the many" or of "corporate representation."[56] The beginning of the new-creational reign is understood as Christ's life, especially his death, resurrection, and ongoing ascended resurrection existence and rule, so that he is a formative microcosmic model that determines the nature and destiny of people, and the rest of creation, on a macrocosmic scale. What happened to Christ in his life, death, and resurrection contains patterns of things that not only recapitulate earlier OT historical patterns but also embody patterns of things that will happen to his people—for example, with respect to his suffering, resurrection as first fruits, his identity as Son of God (Christians are adopted sons/daughters) and Son of Man (i.e., Adam: Christians become true humanity in Christ), being a light to the nations, reception of the Holy Spirit, keeping of the law,

---

53. Wright, *New Testament and the People of God*, 259–60.

54. Ibid., 262.

55. Ibid.; see also 263–68, 332.

56. For discussion of this concept, see H. Wheeler Robinson, *Corporate Personality in Ancient Israel* (Philadelphia: Fortress, 1980), and the attached bibliography therein; also Aubrey R. Johnson, *The One and the Many in the Israelite Conception of God* (Cardiff: University of Wales Press, 1960). The concept of corporate personality rightly has been qualified by later critics; it is better to speak of corporate solidarity and representation.

restoration or reconciliation to God's presence from death, and his vindication becoming the Christian's justification.[57] The new-creational reign is the NT's hermeneutical and eschatological center of gravity.

I am not maintaining that the storyline revolving around the new-creational reign is the sole key that explains exhaustively why all features appear as they do in the NT. There are cultural, linguistic, sociological, political, and other factors reflected in the NT that apparently have nothing to do with "kingship in the new creation." For example, that the NT was written in Greek resulted not from any theological agenda but rather from the historical particularity in which the writers naturally found themselves. Nor does any theological idea necessarily help to explain why an author might employ an epistolary genre or a historical Gospel genre or an apocalyptic genre (although I have made proposals about this above and will comment a bit more on this directly below). Or writers might express their ideas through sociological lenses unique to the time and commonly accepted (e.g., the Greco-Roman notion of the "household code").[58] A number of background features from which NT authors drew or through which they naturally expressed their ideas, whether Jewish or, especially, Greco-Roman, are in mind here.[59]

On the other hand, one should not be reticent to ask the question about whether certain background ideas were chosen in order to supplement and enrich the theology of a particular writer. For instance, the "book" in Rev. 5 is depicted partly through allusion to the OT and partly against the Roman background of testaments or wills. The allusion to Ezek. 2 carries with it notions of judgment, while the reference to the opening of a Roman seven-sealed will conveys the idea that Jesus has gained for his people an earthly inheritance lost by humanity.[60] Revelation elaborates on this inheritance as none other than receiving a place in the new heaven and earth (21:1–22:5). Likewise, the household code in Ephesians is plausibly referred to because of an overriding concern in the letter about the fragmented condition of fallen humanity, which Christ as the Adamic "household manager" (1:10; 3:9) has begun to put back together, as he has the rest of the creation (1:10). An example in Ephesians of such fragmentation is the separation of Jews and gentiles, which has been breached by Christ's death and resurrection (2:1–3:7); another

---

57. In this respect, I have subsequently discovered Wright's insightful observation: "Paul is telling . . . the whole story of God, Israel and the world as now compressed into the story of Jesus. . . . His repeated use of the Old Testament is designed . . . to suggest new ways of reading well-known stories, and to suggest that they find a more natural climax in the Jesus-story than elsewhere" (*New Testament and the People of God*, 79). I agree with Wright's backward-looking emphasis on the OT, but there is also a forward-looking element that I elaborate on here.

58. Mentioned by Towner, "Response."

59. See, e.g., the works of Abraham J. Malherbe on various Greco-Roman backgrounds, and note the ongoing New Wettstein project published by de Gruyter.

60. The "book" of Rev. 5 carries other connotations; for fuller discussion, see Beale, *Revelation*, 337–49.

example of such fragmentation is the different levels of fractured relationships in the family (= the household), whose healing has also begun for those in Christ (chaps. 5–6 [the household code in Colossians serves a similar role]). Likewise, the question can viably be asked why the NT contains genres such as epistle, history, biography, and apocalyptic. That is, how does the choice of such genres relate to the redemptive-historical concerns of the writers? I think that they do very much relate, but the limits of the present project do not allow further exploration of these interesting and pertinent questions.[61]

Were the NT writers really conscious of having new-creational reign as the core of their storyline and theology? I believe the answer to this question is "yes," to varying significant degrees, since all of them were immersed in an OT/Jewish thought world, which had at its inner ideological core the recapitulating storyline of rule over creation; they understood Jesus to be the key player in the beginning climax of this redemptive-historical storyline, though they drew the connections in different ways and highlighted diverse aspects of it (some emphasizing tribulation, others reconciliation, others kingdom, others mission, and so on). I am now faced, however, with this question: if they did have such a storyline consciously in mind, why did they not make it more explicit, and would they have agreed among themselves that new-creational reign was central? In my view, the NT writers, as early Jewish-Christian leaders, would agree that Jesus plays the crucial role in the initial unfolding of the storyline's creational-kingdom goal, but they would insist on maintaining their own distinct expressions and emphases in formulating their particular versions. Once their unique expressions of how Christ and the church relate to the storyline of creation and kingship are clearly understood, the new-creational reign as the hub around which the storyline revolves can, I believe, be seen to have been present in their minds.

Furthermore, there is no doubt that no NT author wrote with the explicit purpose of producing only a theological understanding of the faith; rather, these authors wrote usually and primarily because of circumstances and problems in the various churches. This does not mean that theology was unimportant to them. Their aim was to solve those problems by appealing to the most germane parts of their underlying theology, so that they express only those parts of their larger theology that were most relevant for addressing the particular circumstances of each situation. This means that we must put pieces of their theological puzzle together. I believe that we have enough of the pieces to put

61. E.g., with respect to the relationship of the origin of the Gospel genre, see Meredith G. Kline, *The Structure of Biblical Authority* (Grand Rapids: Eerdmans, 1972), 172–203. Kline proposes that the Gospel genre is intended to function as a legal witness to the new covenant introduced by Christ somewhat similarly to Exodus, which was a legal witness to the old covenant at Sinai. Likewise, the apocalyptic-prophetic aspect of Revelation's genre has its origin in the same genre of some OT books, and this is inextricably linked to the redemptive-historical message of those books (see Beale, *Revelation*, 37–43).

most of the puzzle together, but we have to speculate about some of the gaps and pieces that they have not given to us. The circumstantial problem is also the cause for their unique theological emphases and expressions. This is one of the main reasons why the biblical writers have not provided us a theology as explicit as we would like, though Romans and Ephesians come close to an attempt to set forth a theology of the cross and resurrection and its implications for living. Likewise, one of the recent trends in Gospel scholarship is to contend that the Gospels were written not because of the circumstances or problems of particular Christian communities but rather for all Christians.[62] If this is on the right track, then the purpose of the Gospels is to set forth a biography of Jesus and his place in the redemptive-historical purposes of God. Likewise, Acts, as the follow-up volume to Luke, should be taken the same way, though with the focus on the role of Jesus's Spirit working through the church on earth in carrying out its worldwide mission of witness.

In summary, the notion of new-creational kingship as the core of the NT storyline may be conceived of as a doctrinally thematic skeleton giving shape to the outer skin, which consists of various other elements not so closely related organically or thematically to the skeletal biblical-theological structure.[63] In light of this "skeleton and skin" metaphor,[64] my analysis contends that the most comprehensive idea of NT theology is best formulated through the following storyline, stated earlier in this chapter: *Jesus's life, trials, death for sinners, and especially resurrection by the Spirit have launched the fulfillment of the eschatological already–not yet new-creational reign, bestowed by grace through faith and resulting in worldwide commission to the faithful to advance this new-creational reign and resulting in judgment for the unbelieving, unto the triune God's glory.*[65]

I have discussed the glory of God earlier, and I want to be clear about its precise role in my proposed storyline. The glory of God is the uppermost goal even within the storyline, since every aspect of the consummated new-creational reign is designed to display the divine glory completely in contrast to

---

62. See Richard Bauckham, ed., *The Gospels for All Christians: Rethinking the Gospel Audiences* (Grand Rapids: Eerdmans, 1998).

63. Or one could think of an umbrella, in which the metal radial ribs provide the basic form, which is covered by the fabric.

64. The aptness of this analogy was suggested by Towner, "Response."

65. See Thielman, *Theology of the New Testament*, 681–725. After an inductive analysis of the NT books corpus by corpus, Thielman distills the following major elements of the NT message: (1) Jesus as the solution to human sin; (2) the response of faith to God's gracious initiative; (3) the Spirit as the eschatological presence of God; (4) the church as the people of God; (5) the consummation; and he concludes that Christ is central to all five of these elements. Marshall (*New Testament Theology*, 717–26), after his inductive study of the NT books, concludes that mission is the unifying theme of the NT, in which the major actors are God, Jesus and his saving work on behalf of sinners through the Spirit, and the faithful response of the church as renewed Israel; this mission will be fully consummated at the end of history.

the partial manifestation of it on earth during preconsummation history (see Num. 14:21; Rev. 21:1–22:5 [e.g., 21:10–11, 23]). God's glory as the zenith of the new-creational reign is natural because it has already been anticipated by the other recapitulating quasi-new creation episodes of the redemptive-historical storyline in the OT.[66] In this respect, God's glory should be seen as the major point of the storyline, since it is the ultimate goal, and new-creational kingship and its expansion are the main means toward achieving that goal. Thus, the substance of this book is focused on the penultimate hub or stepping-stone of the storyline: movement toward the new-creational kingdom. The ultimate goal, then, of this storyline hub is God's glory. Other books have been written on this goal,[67] but this book focuses on the main means to accomplish that goal: the movement toward the kingdom of the new creation. That this is the main stepping-stone to achieving divine glory is evident in that Gen. 1–3 and the last vision of Revelation (21:1–22:5) form an inclusio for all of Scripture (as I argued in chap. 2 under the heading "The Repeated Cosmic Judgment and New Creation Episodes of the Old Testament"). Genesis 1–3 focuses on Adam as a king who was to extend the new-creational kingdom for God's glory but failed, and Rev. 21 concentrates on showing how what Adam should have done is finally brought to pass. Certainly, there are other theological facets of the beginning and end of this scriptural inclusio, but, as I argue throughout this book, the movement toward a new-creational reign for divine glory forms the major contours of it.

One might reasonably wonder if I am disguising the language of a "center" with that of my preference for the terminology of a "storyline" or "plotline," so that the two are ultimately essentially the same. If this were the case, then my methodological criticisms of searches for a center would be applicable to my storyline approach as well. But I believe that the distinction between the two is that the core of the storyline ("new-creational reign") is penultimate to divine glory in the storyline, and the other ideas of the storyline are essential in understanding the movement toward the kingdom of the new creation.

---

66. In this respect, God's glory or great name is viewed as the goal of events such as the exodus, the wilderness wanderings, the conquest of Canaan, the building of the temple, the exile and promised restoration, and Jesus's life and death (so John Piper, *Desiring God: Meditations of a Christian Hedonist* [Portland, OR: Multnomah, 1986], 227–38; Piper demonstrates this from various biblical texts and includes other significant OT and NT events [e.g., the Gen. 1 creation account] in his analysis in order to show that their goal too is the divine glory). This point is so important that it deserves an entire section of discussion, which can be found in the conclusion of this book.

67. E.g., with respect to the NT, see Thomas R. Schreiner, *Paul, Apostle of God's Glory in Christ: A Pauline Theology* (Downers Grove, IL: InterVarsity, 2001); idem, *New Testament Theology: Magnifying God in Christ* (Grand Rapids: Baker Academic, 2008). With respect to glory as the central focus of both Testaments, see Piper, *Desiring God*; Hamilton, "Glory of God in Salvation," 57–84; idem, *God's Glory in Salvation through Judgment: A Biblical Theology* (Wheaton: Crossway, 2010).

Nevertheless, the other parts of the storyline must be kept in mind, lest distortion of its core and its goal occur. Insofar as it is legitimate to perceive a core of a storyline and a goal, then my discussion in distinguishing centers from storylines is at least methodologically plausible. If one still resisted this logic, I would respond by affirming the storyline and leaving it at that, without seeking a core of the storyline. Even in such a case, this book focuses on that part of the storyline that concerns the eschatological movement toward the kingdom of the new creation. And even if my storyline is not accepted as being central, I hope that such readers will appreciate the perspective of the "already–not yet, end-time, new-creational kingdom" and the insights that it has to offer in understanding the NT.

Part 2

The Story
of the Inaugurated
End-Time Tribulation

7

The Eschatological Great Tribulation
Commencing in Jesus and the Church

The last part of chapter 3 attempted to show how the "latter-day" expressions in the OT refer to yet future eschatological conditions that were not fulfilled in the OT epoch. We saw in chapters 5 and 6 that prophecies of the latter days began fulfillment with the first coming of the Messiah and will be consummated at his last coming. The main eschatological notions revealed in the initial survey of unfulfilled conditions in chapter 3 were:

1. a final, unsurpassed and incomparable period of tribulation for God's people by an end-time opponent who deceives and persecutes, in the face of which they will need wisdom not to compromise; afterward they are
2. delivered,
3. resurrected, and their kingdom reestablished;
4. at this future time, God will rule on earth
5. through a coming Davidic king who will defeat all opposition and reign in peace in a new creation over both
6. the nations and
7. restored Israel,
8. with whom God will make a new covenant, and
9. upon whom God will bestow the Spirit, and
10. among whom the temple will be rebuilt.

We also saw that the notions of kingdom, king, and rule over the nations are sometimes developed in connection with the fulfillment of the Adamic-patriarchal promises of blessing. In this connection, Gen. 1–3 reveals that Adam should have reigned as a consummate priest-king in God's perfect image. His inability to perform such a task in the face of satanic trials and deception left open the necessity for another Adam figure to come and accomplish the first Adam's commission.

The purpose of the remainder of this book is to trace out these major eschatological and biblical-theological notions mapped out in chapters 2–3, as well as some associated and subordinate themes. The rationale for this procedure is to set up the major prophetic themes from the OT and then to focus on how these major themes are developed in the NT in terms of their fulfillment. The presupposition for this rationale is that the two Testaments are unified by one divine author, though because of redemptive-historical particularity and progression there is inevitably some diversity that is not always easily reconcilable. Nevertheless, this project is titled *A New Testament Biblical Theology* because it endeavors to investigate the NT's theology in the light of its OT backdrop. This means that my understanding of NT theology is not based solely on an investigation of the NT but is generated also by my prior survey of OT biblical-theological and eschatological ideas, which sets the agenda for what I am going to investigate in the NT.

The subject of eschatological tribulation will be addressed initially in this first of the remaining chapters and bulk of the book, which discuss how different major theological ideas of the NT are facets of my proposed NT storyline: *Jesus's life, trials, death for sinners, and especially resurrection by the Spirit have launched the fulfillment of the eschatological already–not yet new-creational reign, bestowed by grace through faith and resulting in worldwide commission to the faithful to advance this new-creational reign and resulting in judgment for the unbelieving, unto the triune God's glory.* The theme of end-time tribulation to be discussed in this chapter is an attempt to elaborate on that part of this NT storyline concerning Jesus's eschatological "trials."

The topic of tribulation is addressed first because it was the first thing to happen to God's people in the eschatological period, from which they would be delivered and would subsequently experience all the other end-time prophetic promises noted above (as we will see, e.g., according to the prophecies of Dan. 7–12).[1] Tribulation typically is portrayed in the OT and Judaism as

---

1. It is true, however, that there is a sense in which in Daniel and Ezek. 38–39 Israel's end-time oppressors persecute them *after* they have been restored to the land of promise from captivity, which itself was seen as the beginning fulfillment of Israel's latter-day prophecies, as we saw in the earlier discussion of Deut. 4:27–31; 31:29. Interestingly, Deut. 4:29–30 also says that Israel's restoration "in the latter days" will occur out of the midst of its "tribulation" (LXX: *thlipsis*). Thus, there appear to be two stages of eschatological tribulation for Israel from the

happening directly before the other multifaceted aspects of the prophesied new creation and kingdom begin fulfillment.

This prophesied eschatological tribulation likely best fits into the OT pattern of recapitulated chaos, as discussed in chapter 2 (under the heading "The Repeated Cosmic Judgment and New Creation Episodes of the Old Testament") and as formulated in my storyline of the OT: *The Old Testament is the story of God, who progressively reestablishes his <u>eschatological</u> new-creational kingdom <u>out of chaos</u> over a sinful people by his word and Spirit through promise, covenant, and redemption, resulting in worldwide commission to the faithful to advance this kingdom and judgment (defeat or exile) for the unfaithful, unto his glory.* As we have seen and will see later, the element of chaos in the recapitulating OT pattern is expressed in the tribulation of the exodus plagues and in the trials that Israel went through as it went into exile into Babylon (see Isa. 45:18–19; Jer. 4:23–28).[2] The chaos of the exodus plagues, therefore, comes later to be seen as the pattern for the end-time tribulation as portrayed in the plague series of the trumpets and bowls in the book of Revelation. This pattern of end-time trial is also expressed in the inaugurated trials of Jesus's ministry and of the church, which I will discuss in this chapter.

We will also see in the last major section of this chapter that the devilish onslaught of deceptive trials that felled the first Adam in the first creation must be replicated in the end-time. This end-time Adam to come, therefore, must face the same storm of deception. But, unlike the first Adam, the eschatological Adam will withstand the attack and overcome the forces of evil. Likewise, his followers will be subject to this recapitulated tribulation of deception and will also overcome it through their identification with their latter-day leader, who paved the way for them.

The End-Time Tribulation in the Old Testament

The survey of OT "end-time" language in chapter 3 and part of chapter 5 uncovered a few references to the prediction of a coming tribulation for God's people. Ezekiel 38:10–16 prophesies that a northern foe will invade and oppress Israel when the people are "at rest" and "living securely" in their land after returning from exile. Daniel 7–12 places the latter-day trial for Israel at a time after its initial restoration to the land has occurred but before the consummation of all the various prophecies associated with Israel's return from exile (e.g., resurrection and new creation). More precisely, commentators place the trial at the time of the last world kingdom (Dan. 2 also prophesies the defeat

---

OT perspective: (1) the trial from which they are initially restored, and (2) a subsequent trial that will happen after they have been restored for a time.

2. On which, see chap. 27 under the heading "Deception, Trials, Persecution, and Cosmic Breakup as Tribulation."

of the fourth and last antitheocratic world kingdom).[3] The end-time trial of Dan. 7–12 (e.g., 12:1) includes the following:

1. the period of the end-time enemy's deception, which involves his distortion of God's truth, influencing false teachers to arise and infiltrate the covenant community, and fostering of covenant disloyalty;
2. the enemy's persecution of the saints,
3. his desecration of the temple,
4. his opposition to God, and
5. his subsequent final judgment.

I can abbreviate discussion of this OT background about the eschatological tribulation because it was dealt with substantially in the preceding chapter, and I will integrate some of this into the discussion below of Judaism and especially the NT.

The End-Time Tribulation in Early Judaism

We saw in chapter 4 that Judaism anticipated an increase in doctrinal error, false teaching, and deception during the latter days that lead up to the final judgment of evil and consummation of God's kingdom. Likewise, we saw references to Israel committing evil in the eschatological period. In addition, during the end-time period preceding the consummation of history the saints will undergo severe suffering, including persecution for their faith, and humanity will experience all kinds of terrible trials involving wars and convulsions of the natural world.

Second Baruch 25–27 asserts that the final "great tribulations" will consist of convulsions in nature together with a great outbreak of sin or demonic activity.[4] *Fourth Ezra* 5:1–19 affirms the same thing but adds that "the way of truth shall be hidden and the land shall be barren of faith" in a great tribulation.[5] Some texts emphasize only the upheavals of the natural world (*4 Ezra* 9:2–4). The Qumran community foresaw a final eschatological battle between "the sons of light" and the "sons of darkness" in which "it will be a time of suffering for all the people redeemed by God" (1QM 1:11–12 [likewise XV:1]) through which they will be refined (4Q174 frgs. 1, II,3,24,5:1–4a).[6]

---

3. Scholars debate whether this fourth kingdom is Greece or Rome, but for the present purposes it is not necessary to engage in this debate.

4. So also *2 Bar.* 70:2–8; *4 Ezra* 6:24; 15:3–19; 16:18–39, 74; *4 Ezra* 15:3–19 includes persecution of the godly, as do *T. Mos.* 8:1–5; *Gk. Apoc. Ezra* 3:11–16.

5. The following contain the same notions, including a demise of truth and faith: *m. Soṭah* 9.15; *Sib. Or.* 2:154–174; *1 En.* 91:5–9; *4 Ezra* 14:14–18; *b. Sanh.* 97a.

6. See Brant Pitre, *Jesus, the Tribulation, and the End of the Exile: Restoration Eschatology and the Origin of the Atonement*, WUNT 2/204 (Tübingen: Mohr Siebeck; Grand Rapids: Baker

The Already–Not Yet End-Time Tribulation in the New Testament

The latter-day trial as prophesied and in its beginning fulfillment in the NT focuses on deceptive teaching and persecution rather than on the chaos of cosmic destruction, though the consummated form of the tribulation will conclude with all these features.

The Son of Man and the Great Tribulation

I will address the topic of the "Son of Man" in the OT and in the Gospels more fully in a later section dealing with Christology. Nevertheless, the topic must be addressed in part here because it is so pertinent to our present concern of tribulation, especially as Dan. 7 elaborates on this figure.

IDENTIFICATION OF THE SON OF MAN IN DANIEL 7

When I lecture on Dan. 7, I first ask students to read verses 15–28 carefully and silently in class. Before they read, however, I summarize for them verses 1–14: Daniel has a vision of four beasts arising from a windblown sea, one after another. The vision continues with a description of "the Ancient of Days" on his throne (vv. 9–10), then the last beast undergoing judgment (vv. 11–12), and finally "one like a Son of Man" approaching the Ancient of Days' throne and receiving eternal rule over all the earth (vv. 13–14). I then explain to my students that verses 15–28 are the formal interpretation of the vision. Then I say something quite apparently unprofound. I tell them that visionary literature typically has a pattern of vision followed by interpretation, and that the interpretative section interprets the vision; accordingly, I declare to them that verses 15–28 simply interpret the preceding vision. The students sometimes look at me as if I thought I was teaching first-graders. Then I tell them to start reading the interpretative section and to tell me how it interprets the "Son of Man" figure of the vision, since such a key figure in the last part of the vision certainly would be identified in the interpretative section.

After they have finished reading, I ask them to tell me whom the interpretative part of Dan. 7 identifies as the "Son of Man." It is clear that many students have experienced hermeneutical and theological anxiety because they have discovered that the interpretation does not apparently identify the "Son of Man" as an individual messianic figure. The expression "Son of Man" does not even occur in the interpretative section. The anxiety of the students is intense because they, of course, know that Jesus repeatedly identifies himself as the "Son of Man" in all four Gospels. After a few minutes of reflection, some of the students offer an answer about the identification: some timidly and tentatively propose that the "Son of Man" is identified as the "saints of

Academic, 2005). Pitre's survey of the notion of eschatological tribulation in early Judaism is compatible with mine here and earlier in the book but is much more extensive.

the Highest One," referring to faithful Israel. Their reasoning is that the "Son of Man" receiving an "eternal kingdom," found in the vision in verses 13–14, is not mentioned in verses 15–28, but only the "saints" of Israel "receiving the kingdom forever" is found repeatedly:

> **Dan. 7:18** "But the saints of the Highest One will receive the kingdom and possess the kingdom forever, for all ages to come."
>
> **Dan. 7:22** " . . . until the Ancient of Days came and judgment was passed in favor of the saints of the Highest One, and the time arrived when the saints took possession of the kingdom."
>
> **Dan. 7:27** "Then the sovereignty, the dominion and the greatness of all the kingdoms under the whole heaven will be given to the people of the saints of the Highest One; his kingdom will be an everlasting kingdom, and all the dominions will serve and obey him."

I then say, "Yes, you are right. The 'Son of Man' is the saints of Israel." Of course, this question then arises: "What do we make of Jesus's claim in the Gospels that he is the Son of Man?" My answer is that although the interpretative section in Dan. 7 does identify the "Son of Man" with the saints of Israel, there are indications both in the vision itself and in the following explanation that the "Son of Man" is also an individual messianic-like figure. First, the fact that the figure "comes with the clouds of heaven" is a curious portrayal, since elsewhere it is only God who travels on the clouds[7] (indeed, the rabbis sometimes called God the "cloud rider"). This means that the Son of Man is portrayed as a divine being as he approaches the Ancient of Days' throne. One major version of the LXX (the OG) interprets this in the following manner: "Upon the clouds of heaven came one like a Son of Man, and he came as the Ancient of Days" (whereas the Aramaic and the Theodotionic LXX have "he came up to the Ancient of Days"). Thus, the earliest extant interpretation of Dan. 7:13 depicts the Son of Man as a deity like the Ancient of Days.[8]

There is also a part of the interpretation that suggests how both an individual messianic king and the Israelite saints could be the "Son of Man." The four beasts are referred to in verse 17 as "kings" and in verse 23 as "kingdoms," thus apparently distinguishing between individual kings and the kingdoms that they rule and represent, though there is also some kind of identification of these kings together with their kingdoms. Some OT theologians have referred to this kind of relationship as "the one and the many" or "corporate representation," whereby a king, priest, or father represents respectively a kingdom, a nation, a family. Even though the king, priest, or father is, of course, technically distinct

---

7. E.g., 2 Sam. 22:10–12; Job 22:14; Pss. 97:2–5; 104:3; Jer. 4:13; Nah. 1:3.

8. Other early interpretations of Dan. 7:13 in Judaism will be addressed in chap. 13 below on Christology.

from what he represents, each one is corporately identified and represents the kingdom, nation, or family. Such representation means that what is true of the representative is true of the represented. In the case of Dan. 7, the interpretative section refers to the Son of Man as the faithful nation Israel, presumably because he as the individual king of Israel representatively sums up the people in himself. Consequently, certain of his actions become representative of them, and vice versa. Their general identity is also the same. Both can be conceived of as Israel (just as the battle between David and Goliath could be referred to as one between Israel and the Philistines).

There is one last possible hint about an individual Son of Man in the latter part of Dan. 7:27: "Then the sovereignty, the dominion and the greatness of all the kingdoms under the whole heaven will be given to the people of the saints of the Highest One; his kingdom will be an everlasting kingdom, and all the dominions will serve and obey him." A few commentators identify "his" and "him" at the conclusion of the verse as an individual Son of Man from verses 13–14. But, first of all, this presupposes that the figure in verses 13–14 is only an individual. Although this is possible, especially in light of the aforementioned indications of such an individual in Dan. 7, the last part of verse 27 is, at least, ambiguous. The more likely identification is that "his" and "him" refer to the directly preceding antecedent, "the Highest One," or, plausibly, that the singular pronouns reflect a corporate reference to the closely preceding "saints" of verse 27a (see, e.g., RSV, ESV). Thus, the "kingdom" at the end of verse 27 is that of "the Highest One" or of "the saints."

The Son of Man, the Saints, and the Tribulation in Daniel 7

Having identified the "Son of Man" as focused primarily on the saints and secondarily on an individual king, I now can address the issue of the tribulation depicted in Dan. 7. We saw above that three times Daniel prophesies that the saints will receive a kingdom (vv. 18, 22, 27). Verses 21–22 say that Israel will suffer severe trial from the end-time opponent directly before possessing the kingdom: "I kept looking, and that horn was waging war with the saints and overpowering them until the Ancient of Days came and judgment was passed in favor of the saints of the Highest One, and the time arrived when the saints took possession of the kingdom." Verses 23–27 affirm the same thing, as verse 25 highlights: "He will speak out against the Most High and wear down the saints of the Highest One, and he will intend to make alterations in times and in law; and they will be given into his hand for a time, times, and half a time."[9] Verses 17–18 imply the same pattern of the saints' oppression

9. Recall that several LXX manuscripts and versions, as well as church fathers, replace "wear out" (= *katatribō* [OG], *palaioō* [TH] = Aram. *yĕballē*) with *planaō* ("deceive"), so that here the end-time opponent is portrayed as "deceiving" the saints. See the textual apparatus in Joseph Ziegler, ed., *Susanna, Daniel, Bel et Draco*, vol. 14.2 of *Septuaginta* (Göttingen: Vandenhoeck & Ruprecht, 1999).

followed by their reception of the kingdom. If, as I argued above, the saints of Israel are the primary interpretive identification that verses 15–28 give to the "Son of Man" in verses 13–14, then verses 15–28 are portraying that Israel as the Son of Man must go through the end-time trial before receiving the kingdom. Furthermore, if I have been correct in saying that Dan. 7 also, though subtly, identifies the Son of Man as an individual end-time king who represents Israel, then it seems likely that he also must go through the final distress imposed by the eschatological enemy before he receives the kingdom.[10]

The Son of Man's Trial and Kingdom in the Gospels

A fuller study of the Son of Man in the Gospels, as well as in early Judaism, will have to wait for a subsequent chapter. Here I will attend only to those texts in the Gospels that refer to the Son of Man's suffering or apparently ignoble life. There are two types of these sayings, pertaining to Jesus's (1) precrucifixion ministry, and (2) death on the cross.

References to Jesus's Precrucifixion Ministry

First, there are references that pertain to the precrucifixion ministry of Jesus, some of which are:

Matt. 8:20 Jesus said to him, "The foxes have holes and the birds of the air have nests, but the Son of Man has nowhere to lay His head" (// Luke 9:58).

Matt. 11:19 "The Son of Man came eating and drinking, and they say, 'Behold, a gluttonous man and a drunkard, a friend of tax collectors and sinners!' Yet wisdom is vindicated by her deeds" (// Luke 7:34).

Mark 10:45 "For even the Son of Man did not come to be served, but to serve, and to give His life a ransom for many" (// Matt. 20:28).

Luke 19:10 "For the Son of Man has come to seek and to save that which was lost."

Each of these "son of man" references has some degree of linkage with Dan. 7:13. Some of the passages have clearer connections than others, which is evident from noticing the same language in common with Dan. 7:13. In table 7.1, notice the parallel language between Dan. 7:13 and some of the preceding Synoptic expressions.

Although this passage probably focuses on Jesus's death, the reference to his "coming" probably includes his preceding ministry when he began to "serve," which was aimed to culminate in his suffering of death. Whereas the Daniel vision portrays the Son of Man surrounded by an angelic royal

---

10. I first came across this interpretation of the Son of Man in relation to the saints' ordeal in R. T. France, *Jesus and the Old Testament: His Application of Old Testament Passages to Himself and His Mission* (Downers Grove, IL: InterVarsity, 1971), 128–30, though at the time of writing France himself did not hold the view.

Table 7.1

Daniel 7:13 OG	Mark 10:45 (// Matt. 20:28)
"One like a son man came . . . , and all . . . were serving him. . . ."	"For even the Son of Man did not come to be served, but to serve, and to give His life a ransom for many."

host (cf. Dan. 7:9–10) approaching the heavenly divine throne to receive authority over a universal cosmic kingdom, Mark 10:45 depicts Jesus as beginning to fulfill the Daniel prophecy in an apparently different way than prophesied. This probably is an allusion to Dan. 7:13, although it is more debatable whether it is intended to be a mere analogy to the figure in Dan. 7 or a reference to the beginning fulfillment of that prophetic vision. There is no fulfillment formula, and the wording seems to indicate not that Jesus is actually receiving a kingdom during his ministry, but rather that he "serves" them instead of they "serving" him, and he does so through the suffering, which is climaxed by the suffering of death (which is clearly implied). Despite these two factors, it likely is best to take the phrase as indicating inaugurated fulfillment. The reason for this is that many references to OT prophecies that indicate fulfillment do not have fulfillment formulas. Unless evidence of the context demands a mere analogical application of an OT prophecy, the prophetic context of the OT reference should be viewed as carrying over into the NT context, so that fulfillment presumably is in mind. Accordingly, Jesus's present suffering in his ministry and his imminent death would begin to fulfill the Daniel prophecy.

But if the present passage has such fulfillment in mind, how does one explain the use of the Son of Man's coming that apparently differs from that described in Dan. 7? Mark 10:45 views the fulfillment of Daniel to be occurring in a hitherto unexpected manner. That is, Jesus begins to carry out the prophecy by first exercising authority to redeem and thus serves his people by suffering for them to secure their redemption; they subsequently will serve him. Hence, Jesus's coming during his ministry is the beginning of his victorious approach to enthronement pictured in Dan. 7. In this sense, we may refer to it as an inaugurated "ironic" fulfillment of Dan. 7:13–14.

R. T. France rejects attempts to see this verse as an allusion to Dan. 7:13. France refers to C. K. Barrett, who contends that if the saints must undergo suffering and oppression before receiving a kingdom, so must the Son of Man, since he is their representative and is to be identified with them. Therefore, he must also suffer before receiving the kingdom.[11]

---

11. C. K. Barrett, "The Background of Mark 10:45," in *New Testament Essays: Studies in Memory of Thomas Walter Manson, 1893–1958*, ed. A. J. B. Higgins (Manchester, UK: Manchester University Press, 1959), 13–14. For others holding this position, see sources cited in France, *Jesus and the Old Testament*, 128n187.

France proposes arguments against this position. First, he says that nowhere in Daniel is it stated that the Son of Man suffers or is identified with the suffering of the saints. He is identified only with a kingdom. However, supporting Barrett's perspective is that Dan. 7, as we noted earlier, lends itself to some degree of representational identification between the Son of Man and the Israelite saints. If so, the idea of the suffering of the Son of Man must be allowed to be an implied notion in Dan. 7 itself. In this light, Jesus's reference to himself as a suffering Son of Man may not be so unexpected as an initial fulfillment of Dan. 7 as might appear at a first reading.

Second, France points out that even if one grants Barrett's point, vicarious or substitutionary suffering by the Son of Man is neither stated nor implied in Dan. 7. This is true, but the general pattern of suffering leading to a kingdom should still be seen as viable, and the vicarious element seen as a result of combining the redemptive suffering of Isaiah's prophesied Servant (Isa. 53:11–12) with the Dan. 7:13–14 allusion (though it should be recalled that the explicit suffering of "the Messiah" is foretold in Dan. 9:26).

Finally, France contends that Jesus refers clearly to the Dan. 7:13–14 Son of Man in the form of quotations only in application to his postresurrection triumphant exaltation (thus, he sees only seven references by Jesus to Dan. 7:13–14 throughout the Synoptic Gospels). Most commentators would not be so strict as France in limiting the number of Dan. 7:13 references, affirming that there are a number of additional clear allusions. It should be added that it is likewise wrong to rule out an allusion to Isa. 53 in Mark 10:45.

The full Danielic nature of Mark 10:45 has been insufficiently noticed by most commentators. The saying comes in a context where the topic of discussion is rank in the eschatological kingdom (10:37, 40). Jesus says that rank in his kingdom comes in the reverse manner of that in earthly kingdoms—that is, through ironic rule (10:42–44). And all of this is set in a broader "kingdom" context (10:14–15, 23–25; 11:9–10). In 10:45 Jesus applies this ironic concept of the kingdom to himself. Not only is allusion to Dan. 7 apparent in Jesus speaking of the Son of Man's "coming," but also his "serving" others appears, in this context, to be an ironic development of the prophecy in Dan. 7:14 that all the nations would "serve" him.[12]

Now we return to the question of how all this relates to the inauguration of the great end-time tribulation. The prophecy of Dan. 7 concerning

---

12. Mark uses *diakoneō*, whereas the OG has *latreuō* and TH has *douleuō*; however, *diakoneō* could well be a viable rendering of the Aramaic word for "serve" (e.g., note the comparative parallelism of *diakonos* and *syndoulos* in Col. 1:7; 4:7). For interaction with other views on the OT background of Mark 10:45, see France, *Jesus and the Old Testament*, 116–23. Though France was skeptical that Mark 10:45 is an allusion to Dan. 7:13, in his commentary on Mark published decades later he acknowledges a combination of Dan. 7:13 with Isa. 53:10–12 (see R. T. France, *The Gospel of Mark: A Commentary on the Greek Text*, NIGTC [Grand Rapids: Eerdmans, 2002], 419–21).

the suffering of Israel and the kingdom of the Son of Man has begun to be fulfilled in Jesus's ministry and culminates with his death. But the suffering that Daniel predicts would precede the kingdom has been combined with the inauguration of the kingdom itself, so that Jesus is to be viewed as commencing to establish the kingdom in the midst of his own suffering. This highlights the element of ironic fulfillment, which was alluded to earlier. Of course, it is now virtually commonplace among scholars to acknowledge that Jesus inaugurated the kingdom in his earthly ministry, but not as many show sufficient awareness that the eschatological tribulation also began during his ministry, which involved varying degrees of suffering, and that, for Jesus, this suffering was consummated at the cross.[13]

Luke 19:10 is quite similar to Mark 10:45, as is Luke 7:34 (see table 7.2), though the latter deserves some elaboration.

Table 7.2

Daniel 7:13 OG	Luke 7:34; 19:10
"One like a Son of Man came. . . ."	7:34: "The Son of Man has come eating and drinking, and you say, 'Behold, a gluttonous man and a drunkard, a friend of tax collectors and sinners!'"
	19:10: "For the Son of Man has come to seek and to save the lost."

In contrast to Dan. 7, which portrays the Son of Man surrounded by an angelic royal host (cf. vv. 9–10) as he approaches the heavenly divine throne to receive a kingdom, Luke 7:34 depicts Jesus as beginning to fulfill the Daniel prophecy in an apparently different way than prophesied. The wording "the Son of Man has come" is sufficient to recognize an allusion to Daniel, and, as with Mark 10:45, it is best to assume that Luke has in view incipient fulfillment rather than a mere analogy to Daniel's Son of Man. Strikingly, those who surround the coming of the Son of Man are not angels, as in Dan. 7, but rather Jesus's retinue is tax collectors and sinners. Again, this appears to be part of his incognito victorious coming to receive authority over a kingdom, which begins even before his death and resurrection. Although explicit suffering is not mentioned here, his seeming ignoble appearance receives ridicule and condemnation from the religious leaders. Although a number of scholars have thought that the "wisdom" saying in Luke 7:35 was a floating piece of tradition inserted willy-nilly here, it actually fits well: "Yet wisdom is vindicated by all her children." Jesus is one of God's wise children (he is the "Son"), and God's wisdom of turning the world's values on their head is illustrated with him.

13. One of the significant exceptions to this is the study by Pitre, *Jesus, the Tribulation, and the End of the Exile*, which also surveys important earlier works that anticipated his own on this topic.

The wisdom of the world judged him to be an ignoble figure, but in reality he was a faithful son who persevered through suffering and insults while at the same time inaugurating his own kingdom. God's wise way of ironically introducing the kingdom through Jesus was vindicated at Jesus's resurrection and will be at the end of the age by the resurrection of all the saints who have followed in his ironic footsteps.

This ignoble treatment is a part of the end-time tribulation that Jesus began to suffer during his ministry in partial fulfillment of Daniel, recalling again that the Son of Man is identified with the saints of Israel, who were prophesied to suffer.

References to Jesus's Death on the Cross

Jesus's eschatological tribulation that he began to experience during his ministry was consummated for him by his death on the cross. And this is what the second set of suffering "Son of Man" passages focuses on.

Matt. 12:40 "For just as Jonah was three days and three nights in the belly of the sea monster, so will the Son of Man be three days and three nights in the heart of the earth."

Matt. 17:9 As they were coming down from the mountain, Jesus commanded them, saying, "Tell the vision to no one until the Son of Man has risen from the dead" (// Mark 9:9).

Matt. 17:12 "But I say to you that Elijah already came, and they did not recognize him, but did to him whatever they wished. So also the Son of Man is going to suffer at their hands" (cf. Mark 9:12–13).

Matt. 17:22 And while they were gathering together in Galilee, Jesus said to them, "The Son of Man is going to be delivered into the hands of men."

Matt. 20:18 "Behold, we are going up to Jerusalem; and the Son of Man will be delivered to the chief priests and scribes, and they will condemn Him to death."

Matt. 20:28 "Just as the Son of Man did not come to be served, but to serve, and to give His life a ransom for many."

Matt. 26:2 "You know that after two days the Passover is coming, and the Son of Man is to be handed over for crucifixion."

Matt. 26:24 "The Son of Man is to go, just as it is written of Him; but woe to that man by whom the Son of Man is betrayed! It would have been good for that man if he had not been born" (// Mark 14:21; Luke 22:22).

Matt. 26:45 Then he came to the disciples and said to them, "Are you still sleeping and resting? Behold, the hour is at hand and the Son of Man is being betrayed into the hands of sinners" (// Mark 14:41).

Mark 8:31 And He began to teach them that the Son of Man must suffer many things and be rejected by the elders and the chief priests and the scribes, and be killed, and after three days rise again.

Mark 10:45 "For even the Son of Man did not come to be served, but to serve, and to give His life a ransom for many."

Luke 9:22 "The Son of Man must suffer many things and be rejected by the elders and chief priests and scribes, and be killed and be raised up on the third day."

Luke 9:44 "Let these words sink into your ears; for the Son of Man is going to be delivered into the hands of men."

Luke 22:48 But Jesus said to him, "Judas, are you betraying the Son of Man with a kiss?"

Luke 24:7 "The Son of Man must be delivered into the hands of sinful men, and be crucified, and the third day rise again."[14]

Like the earlier references to Jesus's ministry of suffering, each of these "Son of Man" references likely has some degree of linkage with Dan. 7:13, though some scholars would disagree. Jesus represented and embodied the saints of Israel as the Son of Man, and his death on the cross was a fulfillment of Daniel's prophecy of the great end-time trial in which the eschatological fiend would oppress the faithful Israelites and kill many of them (a prophecy implicitly including the individual Son of Man).[15] In fact, the Messiah himself is likely to be included among those who would die in this latter-day persecution, since "the abomination of desolation," directly linked in Dan. 9:26–27 with the Messiah's death, takes place elsewhere in Daniel during the time of the final tribulation, when the evil opponent persecutes and kills the saints (Dan. 11:30–35; 12:10–11; cf. 7:25).[16]

2 Thessalonians 2 and the Great Tribulation[17]

Apparently in Thessalonica, as elsewhere, false teachers were claiming that Jesus's future advent had already happened in some spiritual manner,

14. Also included in this list could be reference to the "Son of Man" being "lifted up" (John 3:14; 12:32, 34), which is likely a double entendre, alluding to lifting up on the cross followed by the lifting up of resurrection and ascension.

15. That the death of saints is included in the final ordeal is apparent from Dan. 8:24; 11:33–35; 12:10; cf. 7:25.

16. With regard to Jesus as the representative Son of Man suffering the great tribulation prophesied in Dan. 7, I have found myself in line with the discussion in Dale C. Allison Jr., *The End of the Ages Has Come: An Early Interpretation of the Passion and Resurrection of Jesus* (Philadelphia: Fortress, 1985), 128–41.

17. For fuller discussion of the following section, see G. K. Beale, *1–2 Thessalonians*, IVPNTC (Downers Grove, IL: InterVarsity, 2003), 199–221.

either by his coming in the person of his Spirit (perhaps at Pentecost) or in conjunction with the final (spiritual) resurrection of the saints. In response, Paul exhorts the church not to be disturbed by such false teaching (so 2 Thess. 2:1–2). Paul summarizes in verse 3 what he has just said in verses 1–2: "Let no one in any way deceive you" (v. 3a). The first reason why they should not be deceived is that Christ will not come back finally until there has "first" come an "apostasy" or "falling away" (*apostasia*) from the faith, primarily within the worldwide community of the church, though the unbelieving world will, no doubt, also be affected (v. 3c). In addition to the sign of "apostasy," a second reason why the readers should not be misled into believing that Christ has already come is that the eschatological appearance of the antichrist must also precede the Messiah's last advent: "the man of lawlessness" first must be "revealed" (v. 3c). Therefore, Christ cannot have come back already, since these two signs have not yet come about in their full form.

In verse 4 Paul develops the prophecy about the antichrist from Dan. 11 (see table 7.3).[18]

Table 7.3

Daniel 11:31, 36	2 Thessalonians 2:3–4
11:31: "Forces from him will arise, desecrate the <u>sanctuary</u> fortress, and do away with the regular sacrifice. And they will set up the abomination of desolation" (see also 9:27; 12:11).	". . . the man of lawlessness . . . who opposes and exalts himself <u>above every</u> so-called <u>god</u> or object of worship, so that he sits in the <u>temple</u> of God, proclaiming himself to be God"[a] (my translation).
11:36: "He will exalt and magnify himself <u>above every god</u> and will speak monstrous things against the God of gods."	

[a]For verbal parallels, see James E. Frame, *A Critical and Exegetical Commentary on the Epistles of St. Paul to the Thessalonians*, ICC (New York: Scribner, 1912), 255.

In addition, the expression "man of lawlessness" (*anthrōpos tēs anomias*) echoes Dan. 12:10–11 TH, which is strikingly similar to Dan. 11:29–34 and refers to the end-time trial as a period when "the lawless ones [*anomoi*] will do lawlessness [*anomēsōsin*]; and none of the lawless ones [*anomoi*] will understand" (i.e., they will mislead or be misled, or both). This doing of lawlessness in Daniel is directly linked to, if not partly explained by, "the time

18. Among those who discern some degree of Daniel influence in 2 Thess. 2:4, see Otto Betz, "Der Katechon," *NTS* 9 (1963): 282–84; F. F. Bruce, *1 & 2 Thessalonians*, WBC 45 (Waco: Word, 1982), 168; I. Howard Marshall, *1 and 2 Thessalonians*, NCB (Grand Rapids: Eerdmans, 1983), 190–91; Charles A. Wanamaker, *The Epistles to the Thessalonians: A Commentary on the Greek Text*, NIGTC (Grand Rapids: Eerdmans, 1990), 246–47; Lars Hartman, *Prophecy Interpreted: The Formation of Some Jewish Apocalyptic Texts and of the Eschatological Discourse Mark 13 par.*, ConBNT 1 (Lund: Gleerup, 1966), 198–205.

that the regular sacrifice is abolished and the abomination of desolation is set up" (Dan. 12:11 [cf. 11:31]) by the end-time enemy *in the temple*.[19]

As we have already seen, according to the prophecy of Dan. 11:30–45, a final enemy of God will attack the covenant community. In addition to persecution, the attack will be in the form of deception: the end-time opponent will execute a subtle attack of deception by influencing with "smooth words" some within the community "who forsake the holy covenant" (v. 30) and "who act wickedly toward the covenant" (v. 32), all of which stands behind Paul's reference to "the apostasy" in verse 3.[20] The fiendish adversary will influence these people to turn to "godlessness" themselves (v. 32), to compromise, and to foster deception and further compromise among others. Daniel says that "many will join with them [the faithful] in hypocrisy" (v. 34), claiming to be faithful, while in fact they are not. This end-time antagonist will appear openly before the community, "exalt and magnify himself above every god" (v. 36), and then meet his end under God's judicial hand (v. 45). Hence, Paul is developing the Dan. 11–12 prophecy in verses 3–4 and following.[21]

Paul has said in verses 3–4 that the readers should not be led astray in thinking that Christ's coming has already happened because the two signs of the final apostasy in the church and the final appearance of the antichrist have not yet occurred.[22] He states emphatically in verse 5 that a third reason why they should not be deceived about this is that what Paul has just told them is not new information. Already Paul had repeatedly told them about the coming apostasy and antichrist: "Do you not remember that while I was still with you, I was telling you these things?" (v. 5). Verses 3–4 were a reminder of what they already knew. The implication of the reminder is that Paul has perceived that the readers were becoming vulnerable to false teaching because they were in the process of forgetting the truth that he had already taught them.

Although Paul has underscored that the final manifestation of the antichrist is in the future, in verses 6–7 he warns them that they cannot relax and let down their guard against his deceptive powers in the present. In fact, Paul

19. So also Dan. 7:25 speaks of Israel's persecutor as opposing God's "law" (see William Hendriksen, *Exposition of I and II Thessalonians* [Grand Rapids: Baker Academic, 1979], 176).

20. Geerhardus Vos, *The Pauline Eschatology* (1930; repr., Grand Rapids: Baker Academic, 1979), 111.

21. This is not the place to attempt to answer the question about whether the satanic figure "takes his seat" in a literal temple of God or whether his deceiving and desecrating activities occur within a physical temple that will be rebuilt at some future point from the time of Paul. This topic will be addressed in chap. 19, dealing with the temple in the NT, where the conclusion will be reached that the church community of Paul's time and at the end of history composes the true temple of God.

22. There is a theological problem of relating 2 Thess. 2:1–4 to 1 Thess. 5:1–8, the former affirming that there are signs presaging Christ's coming, and the latter saying that there are no signs and that Christ's coming will occur unexpectedly for all. For possible resolution of the problem, see Beale, *1–2 Thessalonians*, 143–57, 199–211.

makes the radical statement that they are no safer from deception now than when the antichrist will actually come. Consequently, saints must not suppose that just because the antichrist has not yet come in physical form, he cannot mislead them now.

We saw in verses 3–4 that Dan. 11:30–45 prophesied that a final foe of God would attack the covenant community in the latter days. The attack was to take three forms: persecution, desecration of the temple, and deception through the subversion of divine truth. Paul first says in verse 6 that this antagonist has not yet come in full consummate form because something "restrains him now, so that in his time he may be revealed." The purpose of the restraining force is to hold back the manifestation of the lawless one until it is the right time for his appearance. This also they should know because it is part of the instruction that he had given them during previous visits (so v. 5). There are at least seven identifications of the "restrainer,"[23] though it is likely a good and not an evil force.[24]

Although Paul says that the prophesied "man of lawlessness" has not yet come in full incarnate form, he claims that there is a sense in which he has come: "the mystery [*mystērion*] of lawlessness is already at work" (v. 7). What does Paul mean by this? As with the majority of NT uses of "mystery" (*mystērion*), this one is placed in close connection with an OT reference, this time to Dan. 11 in verse 4. The word elsewhere, when so linked to OT allusions, is used to indicate that prophecy is beginning fulfillment but in an unexpected manner in comparison to the way OT readers might have expected these prophecies to be fulfilled.[25]

The reason why Paul uses the word "mystery" in verse 7 is that he understands the antichrist prophecy from Daniel as beginning to be fulfilled in the Thessalonian church in an enigmatic manner not clearly foreseen by Daniel. The word "mystery" (*mystērion*) occurs with an eschatological meaning only in Dan. 2 (vv. 18–19, 27–30, 47), which points further to allusion to Daniel, in addition to Dan. 11:31, 36, noted above. Daniel says that the final antichrist will appear in full force and openly to all eyes ("to exalt and magnify himself"), when he will attempt to deceive and persecute. Paul sees that although this fiend has not yet come as visibly as he will at the final end of history, he is nevertheless "already at work" in the covenant community through his deceivers, the false teachers. We would expect from Daniel's prophecy that when this fiend's deceivers are visibly on the scene, he would be visibly present as well. The revealed "mystery" in the church at Thessalonica is that the prophecy

---

23. See the excellent summary and evaluation in Marshall, *1 and 2 Thessalonians*, 196–200.

24. For the view that the "restrainer" is the angel Michael, see Beale, *1–2 Thessalonians*, 213–21.

25. See G. K. Beale, *John's Use of the Old Testament in Revelation*, JSNTSup 166 (Sheffield: Sheffield Academic Press, 1998), 215–72, which gives a survey and discussion of all the NT uses of *mystērion*.

of Dan. 11 is starting to be fulfilled unexpectedly, since the devilish foe has not come in bodily form, but he is already inspiring his "lawless" works of deception by his spirit through false teachers (on which, see also 1 John 4:1–3).

Paul is saying that even now the false teachers that have been prophesied by Daniel and Jesus (see, e.g., Matt. 24:4–5, 23–24) are with his readers. This means that the end-time great tribulation prophesied by Dan. 11 has begun in part. The prophecy of the "apostasy" and coming of "the man of lawlessness" (into the temple, as I will argue later)[26] of the new covenant church has started fulfillment.

Indeed, the sign of Jesus's death together with what 1 John 2:18 and 2 Thess. 2:6–7 have said makes it clear that the great tribulation, when the antichrist will come, has already begun to take place.[27] The prophesied antichrist has already begun to enter the covenant community and to defile it. Daniel predicted three telltale marks of the great tribulation: persecution, desecration of the temple, and deception through false teachers within the temple and in the covenant community. It is clear that persecution and deception in the ecclesiological community started in the first century and has continued ever since. The desecration of the covenant community is the entry of the unclean and deceptive spirit of the antichrist into the sacred community of faith, which attempts to alter God's laws. Therefore, the end-time tribulation has been going on throughout the age of the church (for persecutions in Thessalonica, see Acts 17:5–8; 1 Thess. 1:6; 2:14; 3:3–4).

To be sure, this tribulation has not yet reached its climax. There will be an escalation of the present tribulation when *the* incarnate antichrist appears at the end of history (*Apoc. El.* 4:20–23 says that the "son of lawlessness" will severely persecute the saints during this time of trial).[28] At that time, persecution and deception, which formerly have affected only part of the church throughout history, will be present throughout the worldwide church, at which point Christ will return a final time (see Rev. 11:1–13; 20:1–10).

1 John and the Great Tribulation

Earlier we saw that the use of "hour" in the OG version of Dan. 8–12 was a translation of "end-time" language from the Hebrew.[29] I concluded that this repeated reference to the end-time "hour" of trial and deception inspired by the

26. For full argument of this point, see G. K. Beale, *The Temple and the Church's Mission: A Biblical Theology of the Dwelling Place of God*, NSBT 17 (Downers Grove, IL: InterVarsity, 2004), 269–92.

27. Although this was discussed in some depth in the earlier chapter on NT eschatology, I will address it again in the section below on 1 John 2:18.

28. See also *Apoc. El.* 1:10; note also 2:41, "the lawless one will appear in the holy places," which reaffirms the idea of 2 Thess. 2:3–4 (so too *Apoc. El.* 3:5; 4:1–2).

29. See the section on 1 John in chap. 5 under the heading "Eschatological References in the General Epistles."

end-time adversary[30] stands behind 1 John 2:18: "Children, it is the last hour; and just as you heard that antichrist is coming, even now many antichrists have arisen; from this we know that it is the last hour." Thus, although the antichrist has not yet come in his incarnate form at the very end of the age, his "spirit" is here now inspiring his false teachers (1 John 4:3). Consequently, the prophecy of the antichrist has begun fulfillment in that his spirit has begun to come and inspire his false teachers to do their deceiving work. The prophecy has begun literally also in the sense that the prophesied deceptive teachers are working in the covenant community, as they were literally prophesied so to do by Daniel.

This means that the eschatological tribulation began in the first-century church and is not something that will happen only at some climactic point in the future.

We saw in chapter 5 that this sheds light on a significant passage later in 1 John: "Everyone who practices sin also practices lawlessness; and sin is lawlessness" (3:4). Some systematic theologians adduce this passage as a good summary of what "sin" is: it is the transgression of God's law. While this is true, the background of this passage enriches our understanding of it, especially in relation to the beginning of the antichrist prophecies by Jesus and Daniel. We observed in chapter 5 that Dan. 11:32; 12:10 OG equate eschatological "sin" (the *hamartia* word group) with eschatological "lawlessness" (the *anomia* word group), and that 1 John 3:4 likely reflects this equation.[31] Thus, there is more to John's use of "lawlessness" (*anomia*) than it merely being a definition of "sin." Rather, "sin" is being identified as "the iniquity" that is the prophesied and expected state of hostility in the latter days. In addition to the highly charged notion of the already–not yet coming of the antichrist in 2:18, 22, both 2:28 and 3:2–3 continue to focus on latter-day themes, particularly the future, final coming of Christ. Therefore, the equation of "sin" and "lawlessness" in 3:4 continues to ring with end-time associations.

In this regard, Matt. 24:11–12 speaks of the latter days as a time when "lawlessness" (*anomia*) will be multiplied: "love will grow cold"[32] (Matt. 7:22–23; 13:41 may also speak of the same thing). Jewish tradition speaks of the latter days as "the time of the iniquity of Israel" in which there will be a struggle between the angel of peace and Satan (*T. Dan* 6). So, more clearly, *Did.* 16:3–4:

> For in the last days the false prophets and corrupters will abound, and the sheep will be turned into wolves, and love will be turned into hate. For as lawlessness

---

30. Sometimes even the reference "hour of the end" (*hōra synteleias*) is used (Dan. 11:40).

31. See the section on 1 John in chap. 5 under the heading "Eschatological References in the General Epistles."

32. Hartman (*Prophecy Interpreted*, 158, 207) argues that Mark 13 (and parallels) are based on a coherent exposition or mediation on Dan. 7–9, 11–12 (see the full discussion on pp. 145–252). Hartman also proposed that this Danielic "midrash" was developed by Paul in parts of 1–2 Thessalonians (pp. 178–205) and in 1 John (pp. 237–38).

[*anomia*] increases, they will hate and persecute and betray one another. And then the deceiver of the world will appear as a son of God and "will perform signs and wonders," and the earth will be delivered into his hands, and he will commit abominations the likes of which have never happened before.

Barnabas 4:1–6a associates the works of "lawlessness" (*anomia*) with the "deception of the present age" as constituting the fourth kingdom foretold by Daniel:

> We must, therefore, investigate the present circumstances very carefully and seek out the things that are able to save us. Let us, therefore, avoid absolutely all the works of lawlessness lest the works of lawlessness overpower us, and let us hate the deception of the present age, so that we may be loved in the age to come. Let us give no rest to our soul that results in its being able to associate with sinners and evil men, lest we become like them. The last stumbling block is at hand, concerning which the Scriptures speak, as Enoch says. For the Master has cut short the times and the days for this reason, that his beloved might make haste and come into his inheritance. And so also speaks the prophet: "Ten kingdoms will reign over the earth, and after them a little king will arise, who will subdue three of the kings with a single blow." Similarly Daniel says, concerning the same one: "And I saw the fourth beast, wicked and powerful and more dangerous than all the beasts of the earth, and how ten horns sprang up from it, and from these a little offshoot of a horn, and how it subdued three of the large horns with a single blow." You ought, therefore, to understand.

According to Dan. 11–12 and Jesus's view of it, the latter days are to be characterized by rebellion against God in the form of covenant apostasy in terms of denying the true God and in terms of unrighteousness. Jesus repeatedly emphasizes this in Matt. 24:

Matt. 24:4 And Jesus answered and said to them, "See to it that no one misleads you."

Matt. 24:5 "For many will come in My name, saying, 'I am the Christ,' and will mislead many."

Matt. 24:10 "At that time many will fall away and will betray one another and hate one another."

Matt. 24:11 "Many false prophets will arise and will mislead many."

Matt. 24:12 "Because <u>lawlessness</u> is increased, most people's love will grow cold."

Matt. 24:13 "But the one who endures to the end, he will be saved."

Matt. 24:23 "Then if anyone says to you, 'Behold, here is the Christ,' or 'There He is,' do not believe him."

Matt. 24:24 "For false Christs and false prophets will arise and will show great signs and wonders, so as to mislead, if possible, even the elect."

Matt. 24:25 "Behold, I have told you in advance."

Matt. 24:26 "So if they say to you, 'Behold, He is in the wilderness,' do not go out, or, 'Behold, He is in the inner rooms,' do not believe them."

Jesus's forecast itself is based on Dan. 7–12, in particular the following:

Dan. 8:23 "A king will arise, insolent and skilled in intrigue."

Dan. 8:25 "And through his shrewdness he will cause deceit to succeed by his influence; and he will magnify himself in his heart."

Dan. 11:30 "He will be disheartened and will return and become enraged at the holy covenant and take action; so he will come back and show regard for those who forsake the holy covenant."

Dan. 11:32 "By smooth words he will turn to godlessness those who act wickedly toward the covenant, but the people who know their God will display strength and take action."

Dan. 11:34 "Now when they fall they will be granted a little help, and many will join with them in hypocrisy."

Dan. 12:10 "But the wicked [in the covenant community] will act wickedly; and none of the wicked will understand, but those who have insight will understand."

Even Jesus's notion of "lawlessness" (Matt. 24:12) appears to derive from Dan. 11–12.

In light of the above parallels and in view of 1 John 2:18, 22, we see that 1 John 3:4 speaks of the "lawlessness" that was to occur in the latter days, which was to be inspired by the latter-day opponent and spread especially by his false teachers. John identifies the false teachers whom he is combating and particularly their false teaching about Christ as part of the beginning fulfillment of the prophesied lawlessness that was to occur in the community of the saints in the eschaton.

The Relation of 1 John 2–3 and 2 Thessalonians 2

Recalling the antichrist passages of 1 John 2:18, 22; 3:4, we see that 2 Thess. 2 speaks apparently of the same expectation when referring to the future coming of the "man of lawlessness" (*anomia*) in 2:3 or "the lawless one" (*ho anomos*) in 2:8 or "the mystery of lawlessness" (*anomia*) in 2:7. The additional parallels between the two passages show that they have the same eschatological expectation in mind:

1. both have an eschatological context,
2. in which there is deception with respect to the truth (2 Thess. 2:3, 10; 1 John 2:26–27) and apostasy (2 Thess. 2:3; 1 John 2:19);
3. an antichrist figure opposing God (2 Thess. 2:3; 1 John 2:18; 4:3);
4. the word "coming" (*parousia*) (1 John 2:28) is used with reference both to Christ's and the lawless one's future coming (2 Thess. 2:8–9),
5. at which time Christ will destroy him (2 Thess. 2:8), perhaps alluding in part to Dan. 11:45 (1 John 3:8 refers to Christ's inaugurated "destruction of the works of the devil").[33]

The Idea of the Great Tribulation in the Book of Revelation[34]

The well-known phrase "the great tribulation" occurs in Rev. 7:14. The passage is part of a continuing vision shown to John that identifies from whence the saints dressed in white clothing had come: "These are the ones who come out of the great tribulation [*tēs thlipseōs tēs megalēs*], and they have washed their robes and made them white in the blood of the Lamb." The passage focuses on believers who have been persecuted for their faith during the great tribulation. This great tribulation is most often identified only with a coming crisis at the very end of the age, directly before Christ's final coming. Accordingly, of course, some commentators do not believe that the great tribulation has yet begun. However, in order better to understand the nature and timing of this severe trial, it is important to peruse the references to "tribulation" (*thlipsis*) and to other closely related notions in the preceding chapters.

REVELATION 1

Revelation 1 contains the first suggestion of suffering and trial, implied in verse 5, where Christ is said to be "the faithful witness" and "firstborn of the dead." The implication is that his witness was resisted and he was put to death for persevering in that witness, after which he was resurrected and became "ruler of the kings of the earth." Verse 9 is the first mention of suffering by God's people: "I, John, your brother and fellow partaker in the tribulation [*thlipsis*] and kingdom and perseverance which are in Jesus, was on the island called Patmos because of the word of God and the testimony of Jesus."

To reign in this kingdom begins and continues only as one faithfully endures tribulation. This is a formula for kingship; faithful endurance through

33. Note even the similar exhortation in 2 Thess. 2:3 ("let no one in any way deceive you") and 1 John 3:7 ("let no one deceive you"); note in 2 Thess. 2:2–3 that it is a "spirit" that "deceives," as in 1 John 4:1–4. Also compare the stress of "love of the truth" in 2 Thess. 2:10 with that in 1 John 3:18 ("love . . . in truth"); 2 John 1; 3 John 1. For more discussion of 2 Thess. 2:1–12, see Beale, *1–2 Thessalonians*, 198–224.

34. For expanded discussion of the following passages in Revelation, see G. K. Beale, *The Book of Revelation: A Commentary on the Greek Text*, NIGTC (Grand Rapids: Eerdmans, 1999).

tribulation is the means presently to reign with Jesus. Believers are not mere subjects in Christ's kingdom. That John uses the word "fellow partaker" underscores the active involvement of saints, not only in enduring tribulation but also in reigning in the midst of it.[35]

This ironic exercise of rule is modeled on that of Christ who revealed his veiled kingship on earth before his exaltation by enduring suffering and death in order to achieve his heavenly rule (cf. v. 5). Just as Christ ruled in a veiled way through suffering, so do Christians, which argues further against the proposal that saints do not exercise kingship until the final coming of Christ when they are exalted over their enemies. In this light, the threefold self-description in verse 9a is modeled on that of Christ in verse 5a (enduring witness, trial of death, ruler) because John views Christians as identified corporately with Jesus: their kingly endurance through trial is "in Jesus" (*en* can designate both sphere and incorporation with respect to Christ). This corporate identity is the basis for the trials that confront them, as well as for their ability to endure such trials and to participate in the kingdom as kings. If Christ went through the end-time tribulation, so must those who identify with him.

That the "Son of Man" figure is applied to Jesus twice in the space of only seven verses in Rev. 1 (vv. 7, 13) is highly appropriate in light of my study above of Dan. 7, since the Son of Man in Dan. 7 was a corporate representative for the saints with respect to both suffering eschatological trial and to ruling, and this title was uniquely used only by Jesus in the Gospels to indicate his veiled, inaugurated kingship amid the inaugurated suffering of the end-time trial.

Therefore, according to Revelation, when believers endure in their faith, they are said to "have kept the word of My [Christ's] perseverance" (3:10). Like Jesus's beginning kingship, their reign consists in conquering by not compromising their faithful witness in the face of trials (e.g., 2:9–11, 13; 3:8; 12:11), spiritually ruling over the powers of evil that physically oppress them (e.g., 6:8 in relation to 6:9–11), defeating sin in their lives (chaps. 2–3), as well as beginning to rule over death and Satan through their identification with Jesus (1:5–6, 18). Their endurance is part of the process of conquering (see the concluding promise in each of the letters to the seven churches). The tribulation is a present reality (so also 2:9) and will continue among the churches in the imminent future (2:10, 22). If the present reality of the kingdom is eschatological, so is the tribulation. Enduring faith is necessary lest false teaching gain a foothold in the churches or various forms of persecution tempt them to compromise their allegiance to Christ.

Revelation 2

Revelation 2 contains the next reference to tribulation: "I know your tribulation [*thlipsis*] and your poverty (but you are rich), and the blasphemy by those

---

35. See Beale, *Revelation*, 192–96, for the argument that saints are not mere subjects of Christ's messianic kingdom but actually have begun to reign in it.

who say they are Jews and are not, but are a synagogue of Satan" (v. 9). There is not space here to elaborate, but suffice it to say that the Smyrnaean believers were being politically oppressed by their Jewish opponents, who probably were reporting them to the pagan authorities as practicing an illegitimate religion. Such oppression was going to bring suffering for the Christians, as is clear from verse 10: "Do not fear what you are about to suffer. Behold, the devil is about to cast some of you into prison, so that you will be tested, and you will have tribulation [*thlipsis*] for ten days. Be faithful until death, and I will give you the crown of life."

At the end of Rev. 2 the notion of tribulation arises again (vv. 20–23):

> But I have this against you, that you tolerate the woman Jezebel, who calls herself a prophetess, and she teaches and leads My bond-servants astray so that they commit acts of immorality and eat things sacrificed to idols. I gave her time to repent, and she does not want to repent of her immorality. Behold, I will throw her on a bed of sickness, and those who commit adultery with her into great tribulation, unless they repent of her deeds. And I will kill her children with pestilence, and all the churches will know that I am He who searches the minds and hearts; and I will give to each one of you according to your deeds.

If the Jezebel party of false teaching does not repent of their deeds, Christ will bring a "great tribulation" (*thlipsis megalē*) on them, which will be within the lifetime of these people, if they do not repent. Thus, as in 2:10, the trial is imminent, though it is conditioned on repentance; but if it occurs, it would be part of the inaugurated tribulation that had already begun. However, this is the first time that such trial has been viewed as punishment on apostates or unbelievers.

REVELATION 3:10

Though the precise word "tribulation" does not appear in Rev. 3:10, that passage is another reference to the same reality: "Because you have kept the word of My perseverance, I also will keep you from the hour of testing [*peirasmos*], that hour which is about to come upon the whole world, to test [*peirazō*] those who dwell on the earth." That punishment of the ungodly is the focus of the "hour of testing" is apparent when we recognize that the phrase "the ones dwelling upon the earth" is a technical reference throughout Revelation for unbelieving idolaters who suffer under various forms of retributive tribulation (see 6:10; cf. 8:13; 11:10; 12:12; 13:8, 12, 14; 14:6; 17:2, 8). The testing is probably an intensification at some point in the future of the end-time tribulation, which has already been set in motion (as in 1:9; 2:9–10, 22).

That John has in mind a spiritual protection of Christians as they go through tribulation is evident also in that Rev. 3:10 may well be alluding to Dan. 12:1, 10 OG, where "that hour" (*hē hōra ekeinē*) is immediately described as "that day of tribulation" (*ekeinē hē hēmera thlipseōs*), when "many are tested

[*peirazō*] and sanctified and sinners sin." This suggests that the "testing" of
Rev. 3:10 has the double effect of purifying and strengthening believers but of
being at the same time a divine punishment of unbelievers.

REVELATION 7

We return to the well-known passage about "the great tribulation" with
which we began this section, Rev. 7:14: "These are the ones who come out of
the great tribulation [*tēs thlipseōs tēs megalēs*], and they have washed their
robes and made them white in the blood of the Lamb."

Daniel 12:1 is acknowledged as the likely origin for the idea of "the great
tribulation": "There will be a time of tribulation, such tribulation as has not
come about from when a nation was upon the earth until that time" (TH).
That Daniel is in mind is also apparent in that the phrase "great tribulation"
occurs outside Revelation in the NT only in Matt. 24:21 and Acts 7:11 (*thlipsis
megalē*). While there appears to be no OT allusion in Acts 7:11, Matt. 24:21
is part of a fuller explicit reference to Dan. 12:1.[36]

The tribulation in Daniel consists of the eschatological opponent persecuting the saints because of their covenant loyalty to God (see Dan. 11:30–39, 44;
12:10). Some will commit apostasy and also persecute those remaining loyal,
especially by attempting to cause the faithful to forsake their loyalty.[37] The
same idea is involved in the tribulation of Rev. 7, since the seven letters have
revealed a significant segment of the church that is in danger of losing its very
identity as representing the true people of God (Ephesus, Sardis, Laodicea).
Other churches are in the process of seriously compromising their loyalty to
Christ (Pergamum and Thyatira). A similar idea occurs again in Rev. 7:3–8,
where only a remnant among the professing new covenant community on
earth, the church, is given a seal to remain faithful.

The metaphor of "making oneself white" by persevering in faith through
tribulation is found in the OT only in Dan. 11–12. Daniel 11:35 affirms that
oppression and suffering come "in order to refine, purge and make them white
until the end time."[38] The OG of Dan. 11:35 replaces the Hebrew text's phrase
"in order to refine, purge, and make them white [*wělalbēn*] until the end of
time" with "to cleanse [*katharisai*] themselves and in order to be chosen out,
even in order to be cleansed [*eis to katharisthēnai*] until the time of the end,"
which may also stand behind the term "washed" in Rev. 7:14. This change in
Dan. 11:35 pictures the saints cleansing themselves and being cleansed by the

36. See likewise Mark 13:19. 1QM I:11–17 prophesies that God will protect Israelite saints
as they pass through the imminent, unprecedented "time of distress" prophesied in Dan. 12:1,
after which they will be rewarded with eternal blessing (1QM I:8–9).
37. See Dan. 11:32, 34; 12:10. Dan. 11:32 LXX has the Jewish apostates, rather than the evil
pagan king, seducing people to godlessness.
38. So also Dan. 12:10; cf. *ekleukanthōsin* ("they were made white") in Dan. 12:10 TH and
eleukanan ("they made white") in Rev. 7:14.

end-time trial, which is part of God's purpose of election.[39] One LXX version (TH) has "in order to test them by fire, and to choose and in order that they should be manifested at the time of the end" (the implied subject of the first two infinitives must be God because of the decretive nature of the verse).

The reference in Rev. 7 is a fulfillment of the Dan. 11–12 preview of the latter-day tribulation, where the saints are "made white" through the "refining," "purging," and "cleansing" fire of persecution, so that they come out as undefiled and blameless (cf. Rev. 14:4–5). This is yet another way that the saved multitude from the nations are identified as authentic Israel. For it is they who fulfill the Daniel prophecy concerning the tribulation that the remnant of faithful Israel would endure. Consequently, the ideas of the saints "cleansing" or "washing" themselves and of "being made white" are found in the Daniel expectation of the final distress, and this is the most plausible background for the origin of the same two ideas in Rev. 7:14. This confirms further the link seen above with the same context of Daniel.[40]

In view of the fact that John applies the references of *thlipsis* in Rev. 1–2 to first-century realities, and that all of them are related to Daniel, especially "great tribulation" in 2:22, it is probable that Rev. 7:14 refers to "the great tribulation," which has begun and will be consummated in the future (though it is possible that it refers only to the future phase of what has already begun). Elsewhere the NT similarly views this end-time tribulation as having commenced: John 16:33; Acts 14:22; Rom. 5:3; 8:35–36; 2 Tim. 3:12 (in Paul's letters all but two of the twenty-three occurrences of *thlipsis* ["tribulation"] refer to a present reality).

The inaugurated nature of the trial is bolstered by the fact that elsewhere John sees the end-time prophecies of Daniel already beginning fulfillment.[41] This could be supported by viewing the definite article ("*the* great tribulation") in Rev. 7:14 as anaphoric and referring back in part to "a great tribulation" that was to occur imminently in the church of Thyatira in the first century (cf. *thlipsin megalēn* in 2:22).[42] This phrase in 2:22 is also likely an allusion to Dan. 12:1, as in 7:14, since, as we just saw, of the two times the phrase "great tribulation" (*thlipsis megalē*) occurs in the NT outside of Revelation one of

39. Although *eklegēnai* ("choose, select") just as well could be a refining metaphor in the sense of "selected out" as a result of a purifying process.

40. This OT background also is implicit in Rev. 3:4b–5a, where those receiving "white robes" have their names written in "the book of life," a partial allusion to the book of life in Dan. 12:1–2 (see 3:4–5). Richard Bauckham (*The Climax of Prophecy: Studies on the Book of Revelation* [Edinburgh: T&T Clark, 1993] 227–28) has confirmed the presence of the Dan. 11–12 background in Rev. 7:14, highlighting even the parallel of the reflexive nuance of the verbs in Dan. 12:10 and the Revelation text.

41. See 1:1, 13, 19. Note that John 5:24–29 sees the resurrection of the saints predicted in Dan. 12:2 as being inaugurated in Jesus's ministry.

42. Robert L. Thomas (*Revelation 1–7: An Exegetical Commentary* [Chicago: Moody, 1992], 496) makes the same connection but sees both passages as referring to a future, severe stage of trial at the end of history.

these uses (Matt. 24:21) is part of a larger, explicit reference to Dan. 12:1. Since the phrase occurs within Revelation only in 2:22 and 7:14, "the great tribulation" has begun with Jesus's own sufferings and shed blood, and all who follow him must likewise suffer through it.[43] This corporate identification of suffering believers with Jesus is expressed, as we have observed, especially by John's self-identification as a "fellow partaker in the tribulation . . . and endurance in Jesus" in 1:9, as well as by Col. 1:24; 1 Pet. 4:1–7, 12–13 (the Col. 1:24 reference will be discussed subsequently in this chapter).[44]

Other References to Tribulation in the New Testament

Here I list and only briefly discuss other passages, on which further elaboration is prohibited by the scope of the present project.

THE ESCHATOLOGICAL DISCOURSE OF JESUS (MATTHEW 24; MARK 13; LUKE 21)

The so-called eschatological discourse of Matt. 24; Mark 13; Luke 21 predicts a series of end-time trials. There is much debate about whether these trials refer exclusively to events leading up to and including the destruction of Jerusalem in AD 70, or events associated with an attack on Jerusalem directly preceding the final coming of Christ, or events related to Jerusalem's AD 70 crisis that are also typological of the crisis that will occur right before the second coming of Christ.[45]

One observation relevant to earlier discussion in this chapter is that Jesus's discourse is saturated with references to Dan. 7–12 (e.g., Matt. 24:15, 30), including allusions to the prophesied tribulation.[46] Jesus understands this period of suffering to be inaugurated with the suffering of the apostles themselves, which is suggested by the comparison of Mark 13 and John 15 shown in table 7.4.

What Jesus had predicted in Mark 13 to occur in the coming distress, he says, according to John, will happen imminently in the lives of his followers. In this light, it appears to be no accident that the conclusion of John 16 (vv. 32–33) refers to Daniel's eschatological "hour" of tribulation:

Behold, an hour [hōra] is coming, and has already come, for you to be scattered, each to his own home, and to leave Me alone; and yet I am not alone, because the Father is with Me. These things I have spoken to you, so that in Me you

43. Hippolytus, *Comm. Dan.* frg. 3, which explains Dan. 12:1's "time of tribulation" as severe persecution of saints.
44. See further Allison, *End of the Ages.* See likewise H. Schlier, "θλίβω, θλῖψις," *TDNT* 3:145. Schlier sees Rev. 1:9 and 2:9 as beginning stages of "the great tribulation" of Rev. 7:14.
45. There are yet even further views—for example, that throughout the discourse there is a mix of references to AD 70 and to yet distant future events at the very end of the age.
46. There is not enough space to present the evidence here; for a persuasive presentation, see Hartman, *Prophecy Interpreted*, 145–77.

Table 7.4

Mark 13:5–13	John 15:18–16:11
13:13: "You will be <u>hated</u> by all <u>for my name's sake</u>."	15:19: "I chose you out of the world, therefore the world <u>hates</u> you."
13:9: "They will deliver you to councils; and you will be beaten in synagogues; and you will stand before governors and kings <u>for my sake</u>."	15:20–21: "They will persecute you . . . <u>for my name's sake</u>."
13:11: "Do not be anxious beforehand about what you are to say; but say whatever is given you in that hour, for it is not you who speak, but <u>the Holy Spirit</u>."	[15:26–27; 16:7: Jesus will send <u>the Spirit</u> of truth, and he will witness concerning Jesus.]
[13:9–10: The persecution of Christians is a <u>testimony</u> (*martyrion*), and the gospel must first be preached to all the peoples.]	15:27: "You also will <u>testify</u> [*martyreite*]."
13:5: "Take heed that no one leads you astray." (Cf. 13:23: "I have told you all things beforehand.")	16:1: "I have said all this to you to keep you from falling away."
13:9: "You will be beaten in <u>synagogues</u>."	16:2: "They will put you out of the <u>synagogues</u>."
13:12: "Brother will hand brother to death, and father son, and children will rise against parents and <u>kill</u> them."	16:2: "Whoever <u>kills</u> you will think he is offering service to God."

Note: This table is taken from Allison, *End of the Ages*, 60.

may have peace. In the world you have <u>tribulation</u> [*thlipsis*], but take courage; I have overcome the world.

As we saw in the preceding chapter, John 16:32 utilizes an "already and not yet" formula with Daniel's end-time "hour" (*hōra*), like that elsewhere in Johannine literature (John 4:23; 5:25; 1 John 2:18). In addition, the combination of "hour" with "tribulation" may reflect the combination in Dan. 12:1 OG, which refers to the great tribulation. All five uses in John 16 (vv. 2, 4, 21, 25, 32) pertain to tribulation for Jesus's followers and thus fit well into the Danielic uses of "hour" in the OG of Daniel, where they refer to the eschatological hour of trial and persecution for faithful Israel, even unto death (cf. Dan. 11:30–35; 12:10–11 with John 16:2: "An hour is coming for everyone who kills you to think that he is offering service to God").

OTHER PASSAGES ALLUDING
TO AN INAUGURATED ESCHATOLOGICAL TRIBULATION

I have already commented on several passages in the Pastoral and General Epistles that refer to the language of "the latter days" (or synonyms) in explaining that the great trial of the eschaton has begun (see chap. 5), especially with regard to the entrance of satanic deception into the covenant community (1 Tim. 4:1; 2 Tim. 3:1; 2 Pet. 3:2–7; Jude 18–19). Additional passages could be discussed, prominent among which are Rom. 8:17; Phil. 3:10; Col. 1:24; and Eph. 5:16 in relation to 6:13. Colossians 1:24 refers to "the tribulations of the Messiah," which some commentators probably rightly understand to reflect the background of the expected sufferings of the Messiah prophesied in Dan. 7; 9, as well as in Isa. 53, a notion also developed to a small degree in early Judaism (e.g., *4 Ezra* 7:28–29). Paul says that he does his part in participating in and "filling up that which is lacking" in these messianic tribulations, which things the Messiah's people are prophesied to suffer in following after Jesus. When all believers in the Messiah throughout the church age have fulfilled their allotted amount of "tribulations," then none will be left "lacking," the closest parallel of which is found in Rev. 6:11.[47] The same reality presumably is reflected when Rom. 8:17 refers to "suffering with" Christ, and when Phil. 3:10 alludes to "the fellowship of his sufferings."

In Eph. 6:11–13 Paul refers to believers being prepared "to resist in the evil day" (v. 13) "the schemes of the devil" (v. 11). Ephesians 4:14 alludes to such "schemes" being carried out by false teachers in the church. We have already seen in the earlier survey of the final tribulation in the OT and early Judaism that false teachings in association with apostasy was one of the evils predicted to be prevalent in the latter-day community of the saints (e.g., 1QpHab II:5–III:6; *Sib. Or.* 5:74–85; cf. 5:505–516). It appears that the presupposition underlying Paul's exhortation to believers in Eph. 5:16 to "redeem the time because the days are evil" was that the deceptive evils of the end times had begun in his time, and that believers needed to be careful not to be deceived and influenced by such evil.

Besides the few texts discussed earlier in Revelation, a number of others could be addressed, especially from the narratives of the seals, trumpets, and bowls, as well as in part of the interlude section of Rev. 11–13. Since, however, there is much debate about whether any of these tribulations have yet been inaugurated or whether they are all future, I will not discuss this material.[48]

How Is the Already–Not Yet Latter-Day Tribulation Different from the Tribulation That Old Testament Saints Experienced?

How was the suffering of God's people in pre-NT times, especially Israel, different from the eschatological trial launched against Jesus and the church,

---

47. Revelation 6:11: "They were told that they should rest for a little while longer, until the number of their fellow servants and their brethren who were to be killed even as they had been, should be completed." On this, see further Beale, *Revelation*, 394–95.

48. For some detail on this issue, see ibid., passim. I conclude, e.g., that the plagues of the seals, trumpets, and bowls represent an already–not yet eschatology.

which will culminate at his final coming? On the one hand, Israel, for example, suffered both deception and persecution throughout its history. It is true that when OT saints suffered or died for their faith, the pain of their suffering was no less than the pain suffered by NT saints, whether throughout or at the very end of the age. Likewise, the errant teaching of Israel's false prophets was just as fallacious as that of false prophets in the first-century church. So there is truth to the notion that the sufferings and deceptions of former ages are no different experientially from those of believers living in the age of the eschatological tribulation.

On the other hand, according to Dan. 12:1, at the least, the final phase of the tribulation will be worse than anything that has happened before. But the pressing question is how the beginning stage of the tribulation differs from the previous suffering of God's people. It must be remembered that Christ's death was the culmination of the great tribulation for him as representative Israel, suffering the great tribulation prophesied in Dan. 7–12. The inaugurated tribulation for the church is comparable to the tribulation that was commenced during Jesus's ministry, before the severe trial of his death. So how is the inaugurated tribulation of Jesus before his death and of the church before the very end different from previous tribulations for God's people? The basic answer is that the redemptive-historical context of Jesus's and the church's inaugurated suffering makes this trial qualitatively worse.

The NT affirms that the prophecies of the great tribulation prophesied by Dan. 7–12 have begun fulfillment with the coming of Christ and the creation of the church. This means that the eschatological tribulation that has commenced with Christ is worse than earlier kinds of trials in Israel, since Daniel's prophecy itself said that it was to be incomparably worse than former trials of deception and persecution in Israel (Dan. 12:1: "And there will be a time of distress such as never occurred since there was a nation until that time").

Daniel 12:1 is saying that the persecution and deception will be worse than ever before. But, as we have seen, the NT portrays this tribulation as having begun during Jesus's ministry and during the church age, directly following Jesus's resurrection. In this respect, one need only recall the foregoing discussion about "great tribulation" as an allusion to Dan. 12:1 in Matt. 24:21; Rev. 2:22; 7:14, the first applied to the AD 70 destruction of Jerusalem, the second to the church age, and the last to the beginning and end of the age.

So in what sense can the beginning phase of this distress be worse than prior ones?[49] First, since the Daniel prophecy has begun fulfillment, the redemptive-

---

49. First Maccabees 9:27 alludes to "great tribulation" from Dan. 12:1 and says that it began fulfillment when the Greeks militarily oppressed Israel: "And there came about a great tribulation in Israel, such as had not come about since the time that prophets ceased to appear among them" (cf. RSV: "Thus there was great distress in Israel, such as had not been since the time that prophets ceased to appear among them"). This may be seen as a beginning fulfillment of Dan. 12:1, the pattern of which is recapitulated on grander scales in the AD 70 decimation of

historical context of the trials in the Christian age is different from the postfall age of the OT. Although the culmination of Daniel's prophecy has not been fully reached, when the trial will be most severe, there is a sense that Dan. 12:1 has begun fulfillment, so that even the beginning tribulation associated with its fulfillment is to be considered worse than any that has happened in previous ages. Indeed, the Dan. 7–12 prophecy of Israel suffering the end-time distress at the hands of the eschatological antichrist figure began fulfillment in Jesus's life and in his church, and this prophecy was consummated in Jesus's death and will be further consummated in the final attack on the church at the very end of history (Rev. 11:7–10; 20:7–9).

Thus, the trials taking place in the former period are qualitatively different from in the latter. But in what manner are they qualitatively distinct? That the Messiah fulfilled messianic prophecy by entering into history shows that Jesus was a greater king representing his people than any other Israelite king. And, accordingly, the fact that the devil and his forces waged war against Christ indicates a qualitatively greater battle than had ever before occurred in the sense that it was fought against the greatest king of Israel, the God-man, Jesus Christ. Furthermore, that the antichrist has begun to enter into conflict with Jesus's followers (as we have seen in 1 John 2; 4; 2 Thess. 2) also indicates a more significant clash between God's people and unbelievers than any previous one in history. According to OT prophecy, the antichrist was to appear in the end time and be a greater incarnation of satanic evil than any prior figure in history (cf. Dan. 7–12). Although he has not yet appeared in his final incarnate form, as he will at the very end of the age, his "spirit" is present, inspiring false teachers within the church. His presence even in spirit indicates that the battle against the church is an escalated battle in comparison to any before, since the antichrist is an opponent greater than any before.

Revelation 12:7–17 indicates an additional way that Satan's present attack on the believing community is greater than any prior one. In particular, verses 9–10, 12 reveal that Satan's wrath is directed toward the believing community on earth during the interadvent period more than in previous ages:

Jerusalem, the persecution of saints throughout the church age, and the final universal attack against the covenant community directly prior to Christ's last coming. The early Christian text *Shepherd of Hermas* affirms that the tribulation prophesied by Dan. 12:1 that will come in the future is but a continuation of what has already begun. In 7:1 Hermas himself is described as already enduring "great tribulations," as others have also (10:1). And 7:4 asserts that "tribulation comes" on others if they deny the Lord. The same phrase "great tribulation" found in 6:7–8 ("Blessed are you, as many as endure the coming great tribulation"); 7:1 occurs also in 24:4–6, referring to a reality presently experienced by Hermas, which serves as a "type of the great tribulation which is to come." These verses are an allusion not only to the verbal descriptions of Dan. 11:35; 12:10, but likely also to the incomparable "tribulation" of Dan. 12:1, which suggests the likelihood that the earlier references in *Shepherd of Hermas* to the tribulation are also based on Dan. 12:1, as is Rev. 7:14 (see further Beale, *Revelation*, 435, especially for the Greek phrases found in *Shepherd of Hermas* that allude to Dan. 12:1).

Rev. 12:9 "And the great dragon was thrown down, the serpent of old who is called the devil and Satan, who deceives the whole world; he was thrown down to the earth, and his angels were thrown down with him."

Rev. 12:10 ". . . the accuser of our brethren has been thrown down, who accuses them before our God night and day."

Rev. 12:12 "For this reason, rejoice, O heavens and you who dwell in them. Woe to the earth and the sea, because the devil has come down to you, having great wrath, knowing that he has only a short time."

The "place" that the devil lost (Rev. 12:8: "there was no longer a place found for them in heaven") was his hitherto privileged place of accusation, formerly granted him by God. His accusations throughout pre-Christian times were ceaseless. On the basis of the description in Rev. 12:9–12 and the description of Satan in Job 1:6–11; 2:1–6; Zech. 3:1–2, it can be concluded that the devil was permitted by God to have a place in the heavenly court as a barrister to "accuse" God's people of sin. The OT texts portray Satan accusing saints of unfaithfulness, with the implication that they did not deserve God's salvation and gracious blessings (Zech. 3:1–5, 9; cf. *Num. Rab.* 18.21). Implicit also in the accusations was the charge that God's own character was corrupt.

In light of Rev. 12:11 ("they overcame him [the devil] because of the blood of the Lamb"), the accusations mentioned in verse 10 appear to be directed against the illegitimacy of the saints' participation in salvation. The devil's accusation is based on the correct presupposition that the penalty of sin necessitates a judgment of spiritual death and not salvific reward. The charges are aimed against all saints who do not receive the deserved punishment. Until the death of Christ, it could appear that the devil had a good case, since God ushered all deceased OT saints into his saving presence without exacting the penalty of their sin. Satan was allowed to lodge these complaints because there was some degree of truth in the accusations. However, the devil's case was unjust even before the death of Christ, since in part the sins about which he was accusing and for which he wanted to punish people were instigated by his deceptions.

The death and resurrection of Christ have banished the devil from this privileged place and prosecutorial role formerly granted him by God. This is because Christ's death was the penalty that God exacted for the sins of all those who were saved by faith. The sinless Christ vicariously took on himself the wrath that was threatening saints so that they might be delivered from the final wrath to come. This meant that the devil no longer had any basis for his accusations against the saints, since the penalty that they deserved and for which he pleaded had at last been exacted in Christ's death (see also Rom. 3:21–26).

Therefore, since Christ's death and resurrection, a woe is directed to the sphere of earth because the evil "has been cast down" to it. The woe is announced because the devil will now concentrate his efforts on causing chaos among the inhabitants of earth, since he can no longer wreak his threatening havoc in heaven. Rather, the devil's fury is expressed against Christians, as Rev. 12:11, 13–17 makes clear. His destructive work on earth is fueled by his "great wrath" over losing his position in heaven. The devil's lost position in heaven, then, is among the reasons why his attack against saints on earth is greater in the new age than in the old one.

There is also a sense in which the latter-day tribulation of deception and persecution of those in the covenant community is quantitatively greater than that in the OT. In the OT this tribulation was limited to the nation of Israel in the Middle East; in the NT age it occurs in the covenant community scattered throughout the world.

Concluding Biblical-Theological Reflection on the Inauguration of the Latter-Day Tribulation

We saw in the previous section that, indeed, there were continuities between trials for believers in the OT and for those in the NT. There is one other way that the end-time tribulation is not new. It is a replication of the deceptive trial encountered by Adam. The difference now, however, is that the last Adam, Jesus, and his true followers succeed in contrast to the first Adam, who failed and was deceived by the devil.

As we have seen, Jesus experienced selective tribulation throughout his ministry, which climaxed with the absolute tribulation of death at the cross, after which he rose from the dead. Likewise, Christ's followers "follow the Lamb wherever He goes" (Rev. 14:4). The "body of Christ" will suffer tribulation selectively during the church's ministry of the interadvent age. Then, at the close of the age, Christ's followers will endure universal tribulation (i.e., persecution), in which many will die and others will go underground to continue to worship as a church. Thus, the great tribulation has been inaugurated with Jesus and the church.

The specific trial and temptation during the present age is that believers are always undergoing deceptive influence against them not to believe in Christ and his precepts—that is, to commit "covenant community apostasy." The letter of 1 John testifies to this temptation to fall away through the instruction of false teachers (2:18–3:4). On the basis of the warnings about these errant teachers, John exhorts his flock again in 3:7 to "let no one deceive you" (cf. 2:26: "These things I have written to you concerning those who are trying to deceive you"). John puts a stress on love as a love growing out of an understanding of Jesus's person and death (4:1–18). This is what John means when he says "love in truth" (2 John 1; 3 John 1; likewise 1 John 3:18). When Jesus speaks of a "love growing cold" in Matt. 24:12, he likely has in mind those who have lost their love for God and his truth and who are committing apostasy.[50]

That is, Satan's deception of Adam and Eve that characterized the beginning of history has been typologically reproduced, so that Satan's primal deception comes to characterize the end of history, the age of the last Adam, not merely that period directly before Christ's second coming but the time extending from Christ's first coming until his last coming. This reflects the scriptural pattern that God has designed that "the last things be like the first things" (cf. *Barn.* 6:13). That such a redemptive-historical pattern is in mind in parts of the NT is evident in, for example, 1 John, where the following ideas unique to Gen. 3 appear together:

1. mention of "the devil," who "sinned from the beginning," in direct connection with and exhortation not to be "deceived" (3:7–8; cf. Gen. 3:13);
2. mention of "children of the devil" in contrast with "the children of God" and God's "seed" (3:9–10; cf. Gen. 3:15);
3. mention of "Cain, who was of the evil one and slew his brother" (3:12; cf. Gen. 4:1–15).

Paul also testifies to this recapitulated primal satanic deception of the first humans. In Rom. 16:17–20 he says,

> Now I urge you, brethren, keep your eye on those who cause dissensions and hindrances contrary to the teaching which you learned, and turn away from them. For such men are slaves not of our Lord Christ but of their own appetites; and by their smooth and flattering speech they deceive the hearts of the unsuspecting. For the report of your obedience has reached to all; therefore I am rejoicing over you, but I want you to be wise in what is good and innocent in what is evil. The God of peace will soon crush Satan under your feet.

As in the first covenant community in Eden, so again in the believing community in Rome, there is "deception" and a need to be "wise in what is good and innocent in what is evil." If the Roman Christians continue in their faithful "obedience" (Rom. 16:19, 26) and heed Paul's exhortation not to be deceived by the false teachers in their midst, then "the God of peace will . . . crush Satan under your feet," a clear reference to a beginning fulfillment of Gen. 3:15. Genesis 3:15 prophesies that the woman's "seed" will "bruise" the serpent "on the head." No doubt, Paul saw Jesus's death and resurrection as the decisive blow on the serpent's head, but since the devil has yet to be consigned to his eternal prison of punishment, he still "prowls about like a roaring lion, seeking

---

50. Especially since Matt. 24 is saturated with the context of Dan. 7–12, one of the major of themes of which, as we have seen, is false teaching and apostasy (e.g., Dan. 11:30–35).

someone to devour" (1 Pet. 5:8). Thus, Jesus won a "D-day"-like victory over the devil, and the "body of Christ" walks in the wake of that decisive victory in "mopping-up operations" over Satan and his allies, who continue to put up resistance, though the final outcome of "V-day" is inevitable at Christ's final coming. The Roman Christians will participate in these mopping-up operations as a result of Jesus having already defeated Satan, and in this sense they also can be seen as fulfilling the Gen. 3:15 prophecy.

It is against this background of Paul's admonition to the Roman church that his warning to the Corinthians is best understood: "But I am afraid that, as the serpent deceived Eve by his craftiness, your minds will be led astray from the simplicity and purity of devotion to Christ" (2 Cor. 11:3 [in light of 11:4, 13–15]).

Revelation 12:17 also is a partial fulfillment of the promise in Gen. 3:15, where God had prophesied that the individual (messianic) and corporate seed of the woman would fatally bruise the head of the serpent: "The dragon [cf. 12:9: 'the serpent of old'] was enraged with the woman, and went off to make war with the rest of her seed, who keep the commandments of God and hold to the testimony of Jesus." An old Aramaic version of Gen. 3:15 (*Targum Pseudo-Jonathan*) interprets the "seed" corporately: "When the children of the woman keep the commandments of the law . . . they will strike you on the head. But when they forsake the commandments of the law you will . . . wound them in the heels. . . . For them, however, there will be a remedy; and they are to make peace in the end, in the days of King Messiah."[51] In the verses directly following, one of the heads of the beast is depicted as "slain" (13:3) not only because of Christ's work, but also because of his followers' faithfulness, in light of the connection with 12:17 (as well as, secondarily, 12:11). Christ's work of decisively smiting the serpent, as the individual "seed" (lit., the "child" and "son") of the woman, is first recounted in 12:4–5, where the encounter between the two results in Christ's victory over the dragon. The woman's "seed" in 12:17 represents the corporate "seed" who compose, in Paul's language, the "body of Christ." The "woman" in 12:6, 13–17 represents suffering of the "true" covenantal community from the heavenly perspective, and the woman's "seed" in 12:17 represents suffering from the perspective of "the people of God on earth." The point of verses 13–17 is that the one heavenly church being persecuted on earth cannot be destroyed because it is heavenly and ultimately inviolable spiritually, but the many who individually compose the church can suffer physically from earthly dangers.[52] And whenever persecution, deception, and compromise are resisted, the devil is seen as continuing to be defeated (as in Rev. 12:11; Rom. 16:17–20). However, the

51. *Targum Neofiti* is almost identical. Here I am following J. P. M. Sweet, *Revelation* (London: SCM, 1979), 205. See further Beale, *Revelation*, 676–80.
52. See further Beale, *Revelation*, 676–77.

allusion to Genesis shows that the church's persecution is prophetically determined by God's hand, since Gen. 3:15 is a prophecy that the serpent "will bruise" the woman's "seed." This is a prophecy that the first trial of confronting the devil in the garden would be replicated with the last Adam and his seed. The Gen. 3 background also confirms my conclusion that in Rev. 12:15–16 the "serpent" opposes the "woman" once again through not only persecution but also deception, as in the garden of Eden. This is but another instance of the end being modeled on the beginning (see Rev. 12:9 again, where "the ancient serpent" is derived primarily from Gen. 3).

What Difference Does It Make for Christian Living That the Latter-Day Tribulation Has Begun?

I do not always comment at the end of other chapters in this book about contemporary application to Christians, but it is especially warranted here. If it is true that the church age is a recapitulation of the deceptive trial launched by Satan against Adam and Eve, then the patterns of sinful behavior in that primal tribulation should be helpful as warnings not to repeat the same thing. What was the sinful conduct in Eden that is beneficial for the church today to contemplate? To observe Satan's first deception and the response to it can contribute understanding about the nature of the present and future eschatological deception.

1. Satan deceived Adam and Eve into breaking their covenant relationship with God.
2. Part of Satan's deceptive method was to tell Eve that if she did what he said, she could "know" in a much deeper way than before and be much more enlightened (Gen. 3:5).
3. Satan deceived them about their own marriage relationship, so that they did not function as "help meets" (Gen. 2:18, 20 KJV) to help meet each other's need to defend against the devil's attack. One way this occurred was that they did not help each other remember God's word that Satan was opposing, as we will see directly below.
4. Satan deceived them about the lethal danger that he posed. He was able to bring them into dialogue with himself without them realizing how dangerous such an apparently casual conversation like this could be.
5. Satan contradicted God's word in Gen. 2:17, denying the reality of God's coming judgment and saying, "You surely will not die" (Gen. 3:4).
6. Satan made evil seem good, which is a mark of the latter-day antichrist. In particular, he passed himself off as a being who posed no danger, and he made sinful disobedience to God's word appear as a good course of action. He also portrayed God as being motivated by jealousy in commanding them not to eat of the tree (Gen. 3:5).

7. Eve was deceived because she did not know God's word sufficiently or did not esteem it highly enough. Recall that after God put Adam into the garden "for serving [cultivating][53] and guarding" (Gen. 2:15), he gave Adam a threefold statement to remember by which he would be helped to "serve and guard" the garden-temple: God said, "From any tree of the garden [1] you may eat freely; but [2] from the tree of the knowledge of good and evil you shall not eat, [3] for in the day that you eat from it you will surely die" (Gen. 2:16–17). As we observed in an earlier section, when confronted by the satanic serpent, Eve either failed to remember God's word accurately or changed it intentionally for her own purposes. First, she minimized their privileges by saying merely, "We may eat," whereas God had said, "You may eat freely." Second, Eve minimized the judgment by saying, "Lest you die," whereas God said, "You will surely die." Third, she maximized the prohibition by affirming, "You shall not . . . touch" (becoming the first legalist in history), whereas God originally said only, "You shall not eat."[54] If Adam did remember God's word, then he did not trust it, since he did not come to Eve's aid when she failed to recollect the word rightly in the face of the serpent's accusations. Adam and Eve did not remember God's word adequately, and they "fell." When the defense of God's word is taken away, all kinds of satanic lies come to fill the void, the desire to resist temptation breaks down, and sin inevitably occurs.

Jesus Christ, however, knew the word and, by obeying it, established himself as God's true last Adam and true Israel. Recall, in Matt. 4:1–11, when the devil sought to tempt Jesus. With each temptation Jesus responded to Satan by quoting from the OT, from passages in Deuteronomy where Moses rebuked Israel for failing in its task. In contrast to Adam and Eve, Jesus overcame the temptations by knowing and trusting in God's word. These temptations also reflected those that Adam endured, which is apparent in Luke's ending his genealogy of Jesus with "the son of Adam, the son of God" (Luke 3:38), which is followed directly by the temptation narrative (beginning with "and Jesus"), thus portraying Jesus as an Adam figure undergoing temptation. Likewise, the temptations are comparable to those in Eden, involving, for example, the temptations of food (Gen. 3:6; Luke 4:3) and of self-aggrandizement (Gen. 3:6; Luke 4:5–7). Jesus succeeded against exactly those temptations in which Adam and Israel failed because he remembered God's word and obeyed it. We see here again, in the case of the eschatological tribulation,

---

53. For the notion that "cultivating" in Gen. 2:15 carries connotations of "serving," see Beale, *Temple*, 66–70.

54. See Allen P. Ross, *Creation and Blessing: A Guide to the Study and Exposition of the Book of Genesis* (Grand Rapids: Baker Academic, 1988), 134–35. Ross notices these three changes in the original wording of Gen. 2:16–17.

the indebtedness of NT biblical theology to Gen. 1–3, with which I started this study in chapter 2.

Likewise, Jesus's followers "follow the Lamb wherever He goes" (Rev. 14:4), including down the path of facing satanic temptations. The same onslaught of devilish deceptions is directed against the church as was directed against Adam and Eve and Jesus. The same kind of deceptions that entered the garden (note again the deceptions in Eden discussed above) also enter the church today. Like Jesus, his "body of believers" goes through the eschatological trial of deception about various aspects of God's truth, both in the family and in the covenant community, as well as in other areas of life. Through all manner of deception, the evil one attempts to tear us away from our faith in and loyalty to Christ. But we are to identify with Jesus the Messiah in his "faithful witness" (Rev. 1:5) through tribulation, even unto death.

The heart of the matter is this: do Christians know God's word, do they believe it, and do they do it? If not, then the lies of the evil one will slip into our lives and churches ever so subtly. When this happens and the process goes unchecked and uncorrected, then the deceptions begin to pour in like an overflowing river (cf. Rev. 12:15: "And the Serpent poured water like a river out of his mouth after the woman [the church], so that he might cause her to be swept away with the flood"). Do Christian families make God's word the center of their homes? Do pastors set aside sufficient time to study God's word in preparation for Sunday sermons in order to "be diligent to present yourself approved to God as a workman who does not need to be ashamed, accurately handling the word of truth" (2 Tim. 2:15)? If not, then the false teaching of those "who have gone astray from the truth" will make inroads into the church (2 Tim. 2:18).

Some years ago I made an appointment with an oral hygienist to check and clean my teeth, since I had not been for a checkup in a long time. While sitting in the dental chair during a two-minute break in the procedure, I glanced at some pictures on the wall directly opposite me. They pictured the progressive stages of gum disease, from healthy gums all the way to gums that appeared to be rotted. When the hygienist came back in to continue, I asked her where I was located in the series of pictures. She said that my gums were on the road heading toward the set of pictures that depicted the rotted gums. I said, "But my gums feel fine. How can they be diseased, since they don't hurt?" She responded, "That's the genius of gum disease. It doesn't hurt badly until it's too late." The pictures of the stages of gum disease together with her interpretative commentary shocked me into the reality of my condition. Since then, I have brushed my teeth typically twice a day and flossed every day. By so doing, I was able to halt the onset of imminent gum disease and to maintain healthy gums. Sometimes deception and the sin leading from it are like gum disease: we may not feel the spiritual hurt until significant harm has happened. We need God's word to shock us into perceiving the reality of our deception and sin and to spark us back into a healthy relationship with God. God's word can shock us into the reality that there is an inaugurated end-time tribulation, and that its deceptive character in our midst can cause us to be deceived and to undergo spiritual rot and to suffer harm.

Therefore, God's word can jolt us back into the reality of our relation with God whenever we are being lulled to spiritual sleep and into deception. The defense of God's word will keep out the flood of the evil one's lies, which spiritually anesthetize people and keep them in a dazed state, causing them to become desensitized to the destructiveness of sin.

It is at this precise point that believing that "the great tribulation" has partially begun should inspire believers to be even more on guard against sin and satanic deception. If danger from the antichrist is believed to be a reality only for some future generation of saints, then such people now will be more susceptible to the dangerous influence of the antichrist who is already at work in the present age (e.g., 2 Thess. 2:7; 1 John 2:18). If you do not believe that an enemy is present, even though he really is, then you will not worry about protecting yourself from that enemy. Belief in the inaugurated end-time tribulation and antichrist should cause the church to be more vigilant about making sure not to be torn away from trust in Christ and his word. Thus, although it may not always appear that the church is presently suffering the great tribulation, at any given time there are some sectors of it that are indeed doing so, and other sectors are always under the threat.

PART 3

THE STORY OF THE INAUGURATED END-TIME RESURRECTION AND NEW-CREATIONAL KINGDOM AS A FRAMEWORK FOR NEW TESTAMENT THEOLOGY

8

The Old Testament-Jewish View of Resurrection and Resurrection as Inaugurated End-Time New Creation and Kingdom in the Gospels and Acts

The Jewish/OT hope affirmed that the resurrection would occur at the end of history, so that Christ's resurrection was the beginning of the end-times. Recall that the resurrection of the body would occur only at the end of the age, when corruption of all creation would be ended and a new creation was commenced. Resurrection is conceptually equivalent to new creation because the way redeemed humans participate in the new creation is through having transformed, newly created bodies. I will set out to demonstrate exegetically and theologically in this chapter and the next three that this notion of resurrection throughout the NT is equivalent to eschatological new creation and kingship for Christ and all who identify with him.[1] I will labor at some length to demonstrate this idea, since this chapter and the next three are a linchpin for the rest of the book. Indeed, I have argued that Jesus's resurrection as the new-creational kingdom is the core of the NT storyline that I have formulated

1. See Stefan Alkier, *Die Realität der Aferweckung in, nach und mit den Schriften des Neun Testaments*, Neuetestamentliche Entwürf zur Theologie 12 (Tübingen: Narr Francke Attempto Verlag GmbH + Co., 2009), which unfortunately came to my attention too late to interact with in the present book.

in earlier chapters.[2] This is important to establish in this chapter and the next three because the chapters in the remainder of the book will attempt to show that the most important ideas of the NT are facets of the diamond of the "already–not yet, end-time, new-creational kingdom."

The Latter-Day Hope of Resurrection and New Creation in the Old Testament

The first possible hint of resurrection life may be discernible in Gen. 1–3. The promise of death due to disobedience in Gen. 2:16–17 begins to be fulfilled in Gen. 3 when Adam and Eve disobey God's command. Death comes in an inaugurated manner: first the couple are separated from God, suggesting the beginning of spiritual death, which would be followed at a later point by physical death. The promise in Gen. 3:15 of the seed of the woman who would decisively defeat the serpent likely entails also an implicit reversal of his work that introduced death.

In addition, the subsequent clothing of the couple by God indicates a restoration to God, so that the separation of inaugurated death has begun to be overcome in some unseen way (in a spiritual manner). The clothing, we will see later, symbolizes the coming inheritance that Adam and Eve would receive at some point (see chap. 14). Indeed, significant research has revealed that clothing in the ancient Near East and in the OT indicated an inheritance and also a change in status for the person or object being clothed, whether that be idols (as images of the gods), people in general, or kings and priests in particular. Kings especially were clothed in an investiture ceremony as a sign of the new status of their royal authority. And since kings often were considered to be living images of their gods, their clothing probably was seen to reflect this image. Since Adam was to be a priest-king in fulfilling the mandate of Gen. 1:28, after his sin and initial restoration, his destiny was likely to receive clothing appropriate to his kingly office, of which God's clothing him with "garments of skin" was a symbolic down payment of a greater clothing to come. If so, then it "suggests that the reason for mentioning Adam and Eve's nakedness at the end of Gen. 2 is to arouse in the reader an expectation of

---

2. See Peter Stuhlmacher, *Biblische Theologie des Neuen Testaments* (Göttingen: Vandenhoeck & Ruprecht, 1992), 1:175, who says that the early Christian confession of the resurrection came to be the "all decisive" central fact of the NT biblical theology, though he does not relate this to new creation at this point in his discussion. In this respect, Stuhlmacher does not develop throughout his two-volume work this assertion about the all-decisive aspect of the resurrection for biblical theology but rather develops much, much more the significance of the atoning work of Christ. In addition, while Stuhlmacher certainly refers to inaugurated eschatology at points throughout his work, he does not see it as the lens through which to see the various major facets of NT theology. Perhaps he assumes this, though he never makes an explicit statement to this effect.

royal investiture in keeping with man's Gen. 1 status as the ruling 'image of God' on earth."[3]

This clothing not only symbolizes a beginning restoration to God but also probably has to do with a reflection of God's glory,[4] all of which must entail a living relationship with God and will come fully at some future point. Thus, spiritual and physical death will be reversed at some point. The naming of Adam's wife as "Eve ['Life'] because she was the mother of all the living" (Gen. 3:20) further points to this notion that the curse of death was in the process of being removed. The passing on of the Gen. 1:28 commission to various individual and corporate Adam figures, part of whose commission was to bear children of life, likely entails the hope and promise of life and the reversal of the curse of death that would prevent them from carrying out this mandate. This is especially applicable to that final, eschatological "seed" who would finally and completely fulfill the promise of Gen. 3:15 by defeating the serpent, which had been responsible for introducing death.

It is important at this point to note the various expressions of resurrection hope in the OT, where the concept of "latter days" is in mind but not the specific wording: Deut. 32:39 (cf. Exod. 3:6); cf. Job 14:14 with 19:25–26; 1 Sam. 2:6; Pss. 16:9–10; 22:28–29; 49:14–16; 73:24; Isa. 25:7–9; 26:19; 53:10–11; Ezek. 37:1–14; Dan. 12:1–2; Hos. 6:1–3; 13:14.[5]

Scholars debate how early the notion of resurrection came to be expressed in the OT. Many consider Dan. 12:2 to be the clearest expression of an expectation of resurrection in the OT: "And many of those who sleep in the dust of the ground will awake, these to eternal life, but the others to disgrace and everlasting contempt." This event, together with the prior time of tribulation, will happen at "the end time" ('ēt qēṣ [Dan. 12:4]) and "at the end of the days" (lĕqēṣ hayyāmîn [Dan. 12:13]). But even before Daniel there was a clear hope in the future resurrection in Isa. 25:8: God "will swallow up death for all time, and the Lord GOD will wipe tears away from all faces."

Likewise, Isa. 26:19 says, "Your dead will live; their corpses will arise. You who lie in the dust, awake and shout for joy, for your dew is as the dew of the dawn, and the earth will give birth to the departed spirits."[6] Many understand

3. William N. Wilder, "Illumination and Investiture: The Royal Significance of the Tree of Wisdom," *WTJ* 68 (2006): 66. I am dependent on Wilder's article for the significance of investiture with clothing and clothing as symbolizing inheritance, which I find compatible with my discussion of the significance of clothing in Col. 3 in chap. 14 (under the subheading "The Image of the Last Adam in Colossians 1:15–18; 3:9–10") below. Wilder also provides numerous secondary sources on which he partly depends for his discussion.

4. Ibid., 64–69. Wilder shows the close association of clothing with glory in the ancient Near East and in the NT.

5. For discussion of most of the references above, see Colin Brown, "Resurrection," *NIDNTT* 3:261–70, to which I am indebted for some of them.

6. Though higher critics see that these two Isaiah texts are not from Isaiah's hand but are later insertions.

Ezekiel's vision of the "valley of dry bones" and the bones being given flesh and resurrected to be a metaphorical prediction merely of Israel's return from Babylonian exile. Even though Judaism typically understood this passage to be predicting the literal physical resurrection of dead Israelite saints, that appears not to be the primary focus. Nevertheless, while the prophecy is a metaphorical reference to return from exile, an actual idea of resurrection is likely included. Ezekiel 37:1–14 develops the reference to spiritual renewal in 36:26–27 at the time Israel is to be restored to the land. The prophecy of Ezekiel 36:26–35 reads,

> "Moreover, I will give you a new heart and put a new spirit within you; and I will remove the heart of stone from your flesh and give you a heart of flesh. I will put My Spirit within you and cause you to walk in My statutes, and you will be careful to observe My ordinances. You will live in the land that I gave to your forefathers; so you will be My people, and I will be your God. Moreover, I will save you from all your uncleanness; and I will call for the grain and multiply it, and I will not bring a famine on you. I will multiply the fruit of the tree and the produce of the field, so that you will not receive again the disgrace of famine among the nations. Then you will remember your evil ways and your deeds that were not good, and you will loathe yourselves in your own sight for your iniquities and your abominations. I am not doing this for your sake," declares the Lord God, "let it be known to you. Be ashamed and confounded for your ways, O house of Israel!" Thus says the Lord God, "On the day that I cleanse you from all your iniquities, I will cause the cities to be inhabited, and the waste places will be rebuilt. The desolate land will be cultivated instead of being a desolation in the sight of everyone who passes by. They will say, 'This desolate land has become like the garden of Eden; and the waste, desolate and ruined cities are fortified and inhabited.'"

"Living in the land" (v. 28) is a result of God "giving Israel a new heart and a new spirit" (v. 27) and putting his "Spirit within them" (v. 26). This refers to Israel returning to the land and being spiritually regenerated. That Ezek. 37:1–14 refers to the same thing is signaled by the concluding phrase of this visionary section: "I will put my Spirit within you, and you will come to life, and I will place you on your own land," the first phrase being a verbatim repetition of 36:27a, and the last clause a paraphrase of 36:28a ("and you will live in the land"). This parallelism with Ezek. 36 indicates that the prophecy of Israel's resurrection in Ezek. 37 does indicate new creation, but in terms of resurrection of the spirit. And resurrection of the spirit is inextricably linked to resurrection of the body, the latter of which is how the majority of Judaism understood the Ezek. 37 prophecy.[7]

7. See also N. T. Wright, *The New Testament and the People of God* (Minneapolis: Fortress, 1992), 332. Wright likewise sees that the Ezek. 37 prophecy of Israel's resurrection as a metaphorical expression of Israel's return from exile included also the notion of a literal resurrection from the dead.

Even earlier, Hos. 13:14 asserts, "I will ransom them from the power of Sheol; I will redeem them from death. O Death, where are your thorns? O Sheol, where is your sting?" (my translation).[8] And Ps. 49:14–15 says, "As sheep they are appointed for Sheol; death shall be their shepherd; and the upright shall rule over them in the morning; and their form shall be for Sheol to consume, so that they have no habitation. But God will redeem my soul from the power of Sheol, for He will receive me." Accordingly, 1 Sam. 2:6 similarly affirms that "the LORD kills and makes alive; He brings down to Sheol and raises up."

Perhaps the earliest explicit OT reference to resurrection is Deut. 32:39: "See now that I, I am He, and there is no god besides Me; it is I who put to death and give life. I have wounded and it is I who heal, and there is no one who can deliver from My hand."

The prophecies of new creation in Isaiah (43:18–21; 65:17; 66:22) also appear to include the notion of the resurrection in the age to come. The prophecy of new creation in Isa. 43 begins with "Behold, I will do something new" (v. 19) and concludes with "<u>The people whom I formed for Myself</u> will declare My praise" (v. 21). The immediate contexts of the prophecies in Isa. 43 and Isa. 65 imply a notion of resurrection (cf. 43:21). In particular, the description of the conditions of new creation in Isa. 65 suggest the same idea (see vv. 17–23), especially the LXX of verse 22: "For according to the days of the tree of life will be the days of my people; they will long enjoy the works of their labors." The LXX interprets the Hebrew "days of a tree" to be the "tree of life" in Eden, which early Judaism and Christianity believed granted eternal life. The same notion of an unlimited enduring new-creational life among God's people is apparent in Isa. 66:22: "'For just as the new heavens and the new earth which I make will endure before Me,' declares the LORD, 'so your offspring and your name will endure.'" As long as the new creation will exist (which it will eternally) is how long the human offspring of the new creation will live.[9] The Isa. 66 prophecy appears to pick up the earlier resurrection prophecy of Isa. 26:19 (discussed above), where resurrection is described as the earth giving "birth to the departed spirits." The Isa. 66 prediction also apparently picks up on the earlier portrayed Suffering Servant, who will die, yet Isa. 53:10b–11a asserts that the Servant nevertheless "will see his seed, God will prolong his

8. Many commentators see this not as a divine promise to redeem Israel from death but rather as a passage about judgment, though many other commentators do see it as a positive promise. The first two clauses of Hos. 13:14 sometimes are translated as questions, but I prefer to see them as statements of promise. In 1 Cor. 15:54–57 Paul also understands Hos. 13:14 positively as a resurrection promise.

9. Could the LXX use of the future tense of the Greek verb *histēmi* ("your seed *will stand* [*stēsetai*]") for the Hebrew *'āmad* ("stand") suggest further a notion of resurrection? In this respect, note that the Isa. 26:19 prophecy, which is explicit about resurrection, translates the Hebrew "your dead will live" by "the dead *will arise* [*anastēsontai*]," using the future tense of *anistēmi* quite similarly to the use of *histēmi* in Isa. 66:22.

days. . . . As a result of the anguish of his soul, he will see and be satisfied."[10] This is best read to refer to the Servant's recovery from death, and that his recovery will include the production of a "seed," which Isa. 66:22 affirms is God's new people, who will live forever in the new creation.[11]

Thus, it is likely that resurrection was a concept of new creation in the OT. As we will also see, the prophecies of new creation in Isa. 43; 65–66 (especially for Paul) form the basis for Christ's resurrection being the beginning of the new creation, though the NT also sees that these same prophecies will be consummately fulfilled at Christ's final return.[12]

The Eschatological Hope of Resurrection and New-Creational Kingdom in Judaism

Judaism likewise reflects a hope of resurrection,[13] no doubt as a development of the OT idea.[14] The Jewish developments, however, clarify and make explicit repeatedly what is only conceptually expressed in the OT: the resurrection will occur on the last day or at the end time. We saw in chapter 4 that the hope of resurrection is spoken in the same breath with "end time" or equivalent eschatological time references.[15] Likewise, the future promise of the saints' glorious inheritance includes or often is synonymous with their resurrection in the last day (e.g., "the glory which awaits them in the last days . . . they have now escaped what is mortal, and shall inherit what is to come" [4 Ezra 7:95–96]). This inheritance is much more than that of a resurrection body; it involves new life in the context of a new heaven and earth.

It is this last point about resurrection being part of a larger new creation that is found elsewhere in early Judaism. *Second Baruch* 44:12–15 refers to "the new world which does not carry back to corruption those who enter into

---

10. The LXX renders the Hebrew text's "he will see his seed, he will prolong his days" as "your [the Servant's] soul will see a long-lived seed."

11. Some even saw Isa. 43:10 as having its ultimate reference point in the future resurrection at the end of the age (*Gen. Rab.* 95.1; *Midr. Tanh. Gen.* 11.9). It is important to recall at this point that Isa. 65:17 and 66:22 are viewed in Judaism as referring to the final resurrection (see *S. Eli. Rab.* 86; *Pirqe R. El.* 31; *Midr. Ps.* 46.2).

12. See chap. 10 under the heading "Paul's Conception of Death and Resurrection as the Beginning End-Time New Creation: Galatians 5:22–25; 6:15–17" and chap. 16 under the heading "Paul's View of Reconciliation as New Creation and Restoration from Exile."

13. See also Stuhlmacher, *Biblische Theologie*, 1:175–76, for discussion of the hope of resurrection in early Judaism.

14. To supplement the present survey, see J. R. Daniel Kirk, *Unlocking Romans: Resurrection and the Justification of God* (Grand Rapids: Eerdmans, 2008), 14–32. Kirk surveys the function of resurrection in Judaism and also cites other surveys of resurrection in the Jewish literature.

15. E.g., *L.A.E. [Apocalypse]* 13:2–3: "I [God] shall raise you [Adam] on the last day in the resurrection with every man of your seed"; *L.A.E. [Vita]* 51:2: "at the end of times . . . all flesh . . . shall be raised."

its beginning. . . . For those are the ones who will inherit this time . . . and to these is the heritage of the promised time. . . . For the coming world will be given to these." *Jubilees* 1:29 asserts that "the day of the new creation" is the time "when the heaven and earth and all of their creatures shall be renewed," which includes "the elect of Israel" (likewise presumably also *Jub.* 4:26; cf. 5:12). We saw earlier that Qumran also affirmed that at "the appointed end [*qṣ*] and the new creation" (1QS IV:25), the Essene saints would be rewarded with "everlasting blessings, eternal enjoyment with endless life" (1QS IV:7), and "to them shall belong all the glory of Adam" (1QS IV:23).[16] Accordingly, God will "raise the worms of the dead from the dust . . . to renew him with everything that will exist" (1QHᵃ XIX:11–14). Josephus likewise says that to faithful Jews "God has granted to be created [or 'born,' *ginomai*] again and to receive a better life in the revolution of the ages" (*Ag. Ap.* 2.218). Other early Jewish texts could be discussed here (e.g., *Sib. Or.* 4:180–190; 2 *Bar.* 57:2, where "the world which will be renewed" is virtually equated with "the life that will come later"; *L.A.B.* 3:10). Some sectors of early Judaism also believed that God "will make the dead live," when the Messiah would come.[17]

Later Judaism follows suit. For example, *Midr. Tanḥ. Yelammedenu Gen.* 12.3 affirms that the resurrection prophecy of Isa. 25:8 will be fulfilled at the end-time new creation predicted in Isa. 65:17.[18] Also, some of these later texts assert that the resurrection will take place during the time of the Messiah.[19] The above references to the coming of the Messiah and resurrection suggest that the resurrected new creation of saints is a part of the coming Messiah's kingdom.

Early and late Judaism followed and developed the OT notion of the Spirit as the agent of the latter-day resurrection.[20] The LXX of Isa. 57:15–16, which apparently is different from the Hebrew text, also affirms the life-giving role of the Spirit: "This is what the Lord says, the Most High who dwells in the heights for eternity, Holy in the holies is his name, the Lord Most High who

16. For further discussion of resurrection in early Judaism, see Brown, "Resurrection," 272–74, and N. T. Wright, *The Resurrection of the Son of God* (Minneapolis: Fortress, 2003), 129–206.

17. 4Q521 frgs. 2, II:12; see also 2 *Bar.* 30:1–2. The Messiah could be in mind in 4Q521 as the one who resurrects, since the phrase occurs in the midst of an Isa. 61:1 allusion, which depicts the task of the anointed one.

18. So also *Tg. Neof.* Deut. 32:1; *Tg. Ps.-J.* Deut. 32:1; *Pirqe R. El.* 34 equates the Isa. 26:19 prophecy ("your dead shall live") with God's "quickening of the dead and renewal of all things"; cf. *Tg. Mic.* 7:14.

19. With respect to the prophecy of resurrection in Isa. 25.8, see *Exod. Rab.* 20.3; *Eccles. Rab.* 1.4.3; with regard to the same kind of prophecy in Isa. 26:19, see *Midr. Ps.* 18.11; *Eccles. Rab.* 1.7.7; *S. Eli. Rab.* 22. Isaiah 25:8 is viewed as a prophecy in which the Messiah himself will defeat Satan and his allies, who formerly imposed death on humanity (*Pesiq. Rab.* 36.1; almost identically, see *S. Eli. Rab.* 21 [also citing Isa. 25:8]). Other Jewish texts affirm that the resurrection will take place at the time of the coming of the Messiah (e.g., *Pesiq. Rab.* Piska 1.4).

20. See the discussion above of Ezek. 36:26–27; 37:1–14 and compare it with, e.g., 1 *En.* 61:5–7; *b. 'Abod. Zar.* 20b ("the holy spirit leads to eternal life"); *Song Rab.* 1.1.9; *Midr. Tanḥ. Gen.* 2.12; cf. 1 *En.* 49:3, which develops Isa. 11:2.

rests in the holies, who gives patience to the discouraged ones and who gives life to the broken in heart:[21] . . . 'The Spirit will come forth from me, and I [will] have created all breath'" in the new creation.[22]

Reflection on the latter-day resurrection sometimes was developed in connection with the garden of Eden according to the principle that "the last things must be like the first things" (e.g., see Ezek. 36:26–35 above, as well as *Barn.* 6:13: "Behold, I make the last things as the first things").[23]

The emerging importance of the Jewish hope of resurrection may well be reflected in a rabbinic saying recorded in the Babylonian Talmud:

> R. Jacob . . . said: There is no reward for precepts in this world. For it was taught: R. Jacob said: There is not a single precept in the Torah whose reward is [stated] at its side which is not dependent on the resurrection of the dead. (*b. Qidd.* 39b)

The Already–Not Yet Latter-Day Resurrection and New-Creational Kingdom in the Gospels

The Gospels also directly link resurrection with the latter days. The Gospel of John particularly links the end of the age with resurrection:

John 6:39 "This is the will of Him who sent Me, that of all that He has given Me I lose nothing, but raise it up on the last day."

John 6:40 "For this is the will of My Father, that everyone who beholds the Son and believes in Him will have eternal life, and I Myself will raise him up on the last day."

John 6:44 "No one can come to Me unless the Father who sent Me draws him; and I will raise him up on the last day."

---

21. The preceding two phrases are a rendering of the MT's "to make alive the spirit of the crushed and to make alive the spirit of the fallen," which emphasizes the giving of life.

22. The significance of this LXX text for the Spirit's role in new creation will be expanded in chap. 17 under the subheading "The Eschatological Role of the Spirit in Paul's Thought" (on Gal. 5:22–23), which is a summary of a fuller analysis in G. K. Beale, "The Old Testament Background of Paul's Reference to the 'Fruit of the Spirit' in Gal. 5:22," *BBR* 15 (2005): 1–38.

23. In this respect, the Greek fragment from *Testament of Moses* (ca. first century AD) reads, "For . . . from the presence of God his Spirit went forth and the [first] world came into being" (*gar . . . apo prosōpou tou theou exēlthe to pneuma autou kai ho kosmos egeneto*). The fragment is preserved in Gelasius of Cyzicus (fifth century AD), *Collection of the Acts of the Council of Nicea* II. xxi. 7, part of which is also found in Jude 9 ("Michael the archangel, disputing with the devil"). Psalm 103(104):30 LXX also is relevant: "You do send your Spirit, they are created; and you do renew the face of the ground," which refers to God's preservation of the life of the first creation by his Spirit. Likewise, the above Jewish references in *1 Enoch*, the Talmud, the various midrashim, and the LXX show that God's Spirit will again create new beings through resurrection in the end-time new creation.

John 6:54 "He who eats My flesh and drinks My blood has eternal life, and I will raise him up on the last day."

John 11:24 Martha said to Him, "I know that he will rise again in the resurrection on the last day."

John 12:48 "He who rejects Me and does not receive My sayings, has one who judges him; the word I spoke is what will judge him at the last day."

We observed earlier in John 5:24–29 that Jesus refers to the last "hour" of Dan. 12:1–2, one of the well-known resurrection passages of the OT, and that he sees it to have begun fulfillment in a spiritual manner in his ministry and a culminating fulfillment at the very end of time in the physical resurrection of all people.[24] In response to Lazurus's death, Jesus tells Martha, "Your brother will rise again." Martha responds, "I know that he will rise again in the resurrection on the last day," to which Jesus replies, "I am the resurrection and the life; he who believes Me will live even if he dies" (John 11:23–25). Consequently, the fact that Jesus identifies himself presently with resurrection life likewise includes an affirmation that this is to be identified with "the resurrection of the last day," which thus had begun with him. Jesus's raising of Lazarus later in the narrative (John 11:38–44) is another indication that "the resurrection of the last day" had been inaugurated in some way, even though the role of Lazurus's resurrection within the overall storyline of John is to be an anticipation of Jesus's own resurrection, which occurs on a grander scale (since Lazurus presumably died at some later point).[25]

The idea of being "born again" in John 3 is likely tied to the OT concept of resurrection and thus to new creation. Jesus tells Nicodemus that "unless one is born again he cannot see the kingdom of God" (v. 3). Nicodemus responds, asking how can one "enter a second time into his mother's womb and be born," expecting Jesus to give him a negative answer (v. 4). Jesus responds by explaining that the meaning of being "born again" is to be understood as a fulfillment of the prophecy from Ezek. 36 (see table 8.1).

The Ezekiel passage is the only OT text prophesying that in the end time God will put "water" and the "Spirit" on his people in order to create them anew[26] (*Jub.* 1:23–25; 1QS IV:21–24 also reflect this prophecy about end-time renewal). As we noted in the OT section of this chapter, Ezek. 37:1–14 develops

24. See chap. 5 under the heading "Eschatological References in the Gospel of John." Jesus's prediction of his own resurrection in John 2:19–22, though without reference to Dan. 12, is likely to be identified generally with OT resurrection hopes.

25. Not only does Lazarus's resurrection anticipate Jesus's resurrection, but also Lazarus's death anticipates Jesus's death because both deaths are manifestations of God's/Jesus's glory (see John 11:4, 15, 40).

26. See Linda Belleville, "'Born of Water and Spirit': John 3:5," *TJ* 1 (1980): 125–41. Belleville also sees dependence on Ezek. 36 and initially influenced me to see the importance of this OT passage; so similarly D. A. Carson, *The Gospel according to John*, PNTC (Grand Rapids:

Table 8.1

Ezekiel 36:25–27	John 3:5
36:25: "Then I will sprinkle clean <u>water</u> on you, and you will be clean; I will cleanse you from all your filthiness and from all your idols." 36:26: "Moreover, I will give you a new heart and put a new <u>spirit</u> within you; and I will remove the heart of stone from your flesh and give you a heart of flesh." 36:27: "I will put My <u>Spirit</u> within you and cause you to walk in My statutes, and you will be careful to observe My ordinances."	Jesus answered, "Truly, truly, I say to you, unless one is born of <u>water and the Spirit</u> he cannot enter into the kingdom of God."

the spiritual renewal of 36:26–27 that was to occur at the time when Israel was to be restored to the promised land (36:28–35); this is significant because just as in John 3:8 the wind (*pneuma*) is interpreted to be the Spirit (*pneuma*), so Ezek. 37:9, 14 does the same ("Come from the four <u>winds</u> [*pneumatōn*], O <u>wind</u> [*pneuma*], and breathe on these slain, that they may come to life. . . . I will put My <u>Spirit</u> [*pneuma*] within you").[27] As we saw at the beginning of the chapter, the parallelism between chapters 36 and 37 of Ezekiel indicates that the prophecy of Israel's washing with water and new creation by the Spirit in chapter 36 is virtually equivalent to the prediction of resurrection by the Spirit in chapter 37, which we saw was to be understood both as a pictorial portrayal of Israel's return from exile and as a first installment of the full-orbed resurrection from the dead (the latter of which was inextricably linked to physical resurrection).

Jesus appropriately terms the resurrection/new creation of the prophecy in Ezek. 36 as being "born again." Nicodemus asks, "How can these things be?" to which Jesus replies, "Are you the teacher of Israel, and do not understand these things?" (vv. 9–10). Jesus's question indicates that Nicodemus should have known well this prophecy because he is one of the teachers of the OT in Israel. Jesus then says that what he has just told Nicodemus is part of his faithful witness based on sure knowledge, but that it is understandable that Nicodemus has not comprehended such "heavenly things," since he has difficulty in comprehending even earthly things that Jesus has told him (vv. 11–12). Jesus's explanation of the "heavenly things" that he has been discussing since verse 3 continues in verses 13–15:

Eerdmans, 1991), 191–96. The next closest parallel is Isa. 44:3, where the pouring of water on the ground is a picture for God "pouring out my Spirit on your [Israel's] offspring."

27. Perhaps relevant also for John 3's combination of "water," "wind," and "Spirit" are OT passages where the "wind" (*rûaḥ*/*pneuma*) of God blows the "waters" and where "wind" may be associated with God's Spirit: Gen. 8:1–3; Exod. 15:10; 2 Sam. 22:16–17; Pss. 18:15–16; 33:6–7; 147:18. Cf. Isa. 63:11–12, which portrays the first exodus, when God "brought them up out of the sea," "divided the waters," and "put his Holy Spirit in the midst of them."

No one has ascended into heaven, but He who descended from heaven: the Son of Man. As Moses lifted up the serpent in the wilderness, even so must the Son of Man be lifted up; so that whoever believes will in Him have eternal life.

Jesus links his coming resurrection and ascent into heaven with those who believe in him and thus are identified with him and consequently share in his "eternal life,"[28] a phrase we have already seen to refer to the resurrection life prophesied in Dan. 12:2 (see chap. 3). But how is this a continuing explanation of the "heavenly things" that Jesus has just been discussing, especially the concept of being "born again" in the light of its Ezek. 36 background? Just as Ezek. 37 interpreted the washing by water and new creation by the Spirit in Ezek. 36 as resurrection by the Spirit, so Jesus appears to do the same thing: those who believe in him are identified with him and his resurrection and share in his eternal resurrection life, which is a further explanation of what it means to be "born again." Significantly also, the notion of new creation and resurrection in John 3:1–15 is virtually equated with "the kingdom of God" (vv. 3, 5), a near equation that we have observed already elsewhere and will see again. In this connection, the phrase "see/enter the kingdom of God" (3:3, 5) is to be interpreted by participating in God's kingdom at the eschaton by experiencing "eternal resurrection life" (3:15).[29] And all of this is the other side of the coin of the idea of "regeneration," which is the traditional doctrinal notion of being created as a new creature. In light of the discussion so far, regeneration should be viewed as a highly charged eschatological concept.

The notion of the final resurrection became so connected with the time of the end that in Matthew and Luke resurrection represents the "time of the final resurrection" (e.g., Matt. 22:30: "For in the resurrection [i.e., 'at the time of the resurrection'] they neither marry nor are given in marriage, but are like angels in heaven").

Throughout the Gospels, Christ (or others) speaks of his rising again,[30] and he raises the dead as an anticipation of his own resurrection (John 14:19) and as an acted-out parable that he is able to give true life to all those who believe in him.[31] The literary and thematic climax of each of the four Gospels is the resurrection of Christ and the risen Christ's commission to his disciples to continue to advance the kingdom through his continuing presence with them (though missing in Mark's shorter ending). Thus, this notion of resurrection

28. The "lifting up" of the Son of Man is a double entendre, referring to both Jesus's lifting up on the cross and his resurrection.
29. Andreas J. Köstenberger, *John*, BECNT (Grand Rapids: Baker Academic, 2004), 122, following D. A. Carson and G. R. Beasley-Murray.
30. The following words, e.g., are used in this regard throughout the Gospels: *egeirō* (15x) and *anistēmi* (8x).
31. E.g., John 12:1, 9, 17. See N. T. Wright, *The Resurrection of the Son of God* (Minneapolis: Fortress: 2003). Wright thoroughly discusses the material in the NT, including the Gospels, dealing with the physical resurrection of Christ and the hope for the physical resurrection of all believers.

permeates the Gospels, including the resurrection of others besides Jesus.[32] Although the actual phrase "new creation" or synonyms does not occur in the Gospels, the concept is repeatedly conveyed by the multitude of references to resurrection. That resurrection is a "new creation" concept is clear from the simple fact that a resurrected body is a newly created body, and the body that saints will have in order to be part of the consummated, eternal new creation of the whole cosmos is a resurrected body. In this respect, Christ's resurrected body was the first newly created body to pass to the other side of the new creation. The coming new creation penetrated back into the old world through the resurrected, new-creational body of Jesus.[33] Although his postresurrection existence was on this old earth for a time, he ascended to the unseen heavenly dimension of the beginning new creation, which will finally descend visibly at the end of time, when the old cosmos disintegrates (Rev. 21:1–22:5).

The Already–Not Yet Latter-Day Resurrection and New-Creational Kingdom in Acts

Resurrection in the Book of Acts

The ending of Luke's Gospel actually continues as the introduction to his second account in Acts 1:1–11. Accordingly, the narrative of Christ's postresurrection appearances continues. In particular, the introductory section in Acts 1 about the risen Christ's final words expands on Luke 24:46–51:

> And he said to them, "Thus it is written, that the Christ would suffer and rise again from the dead the third day, and that repentance for forgiveness of sins would be proclaimed in His name to all the nations, beginning from Jerusalem. You are witnesses of these things. And behold, I am sending forth the promise of My Father upon you; but you are to stay in the city until you are clothed with power from on high." And He led them out as far as Bethany, and He lifted up his hands and blessed them. While He was blessing them, he parted from them and was carried up into heaven.

Acts 1, expanding on the Lukan ending, is portraying the risen Christ "speaking of the things concerning the kingdom of God" (v. 3), and the disciples

---

32. This occurs approximately 30x. In addition, the expression "eternal life" (about 30x) in John's Gospel also refers to resurrection life in its unending sense (e.g., 5:24–29).

33. This new creation is depicted as beginning even before Christ's resurrection according to John 5:24–29 (on which, see discussion in chap. 5 under the heading "Eschatological References in the Gospel of John") and in *Gos. Thom.* 51: "His disciples said to him, 'When will the repose of the dead come to pass, and when will the new world come?' He said to them, 'That which you are waiting for has come, but for your part you do not recognize it.'" For the concept of new creation throughout John see J. K. Brown, "Creation's Renewal in the Gospel of John," *CBQ* 72 (2010): 275–90.

ask Jesus, "Is it at this time you are restoring the kingdom to Israel?" (v. 6). Elaboration about this question and Jesus's answer will come in a later chapter, but for now it is necessary only to point out that mention of the "kingdom" is directly linked with Jesus's resurrection ministry. That the kingdom about which Jesus and the apostles are speaking is not put off until a distant, final coming of Christ is apparent from Acts 2, where the kingdom is mentioned as having been inaugurated to a greater level than even during Jesus's ministry. In particular, the coming of the promised Spirit at Pentecost is intended to be understood as evidence testifying to how Jesus was raised from the dead (vv. 22–28). The resurrection and ascension of Christ indicate at least two things. First, God has "put an end to the agony of death" (v. 24), so that resurrection is really a process of new creation in that it is an overcoming of a condition of de-creation characterized by bodily "decay" (v. 27). Second, the resurrection fulfills the promise to David "to seat one of his descendants upon his throne" (vv. 30–31). Christ has begun to sit on the throne of the end-time kingdom, which he did not do in his ministry, though he was at that time inaugurating the kingdom. The fuller context of Acts 2:30–36 makes this clearer:

And so, because he was a prophet and knew that God had sworn to him with an oath to seat one of his descendants on his throne, he looked ahead and spoke of the resurrection of the Christ, that he was neither abandoned to Hades, nor did his flesh suffer decay. This Jesus God raised up again, to which we are all witnesses. Therefore having been exalted to the right hand of God, and having received from the Father the promise of the Holy Spirit, He has poured forth this which you both see and hear. For it was not David who ascended into heaven, but he himself says:

"The Lord said to my Lord,
'Sit at My right hand,
until I make Your enemies a footstool for Your feet.'"

Therefore let all the house of Israel know for certain that God has made him both Lord and Christ—this Jesus whom you crucified.

The main point is that Jesus's resurrection and ascension are the beginning of an even more escalated kingship than was commencing in the midst of his ministry. He has now begun to fulfill the messianic prophecy of Ps. 110:1 (cited to indicate fulfillment in Acts 2:34–35). The Spirit is poured out on believers to enable them to witness to this great redemptive-historical accomplishment (Acts 1:8; cf. 1:22; 3:15; 4:33; 13:31). Paul's sermon in Acts 13 also underscores that Christ's resurrection fulfilled the OT prophecy of God, who would install his Messiah as king: "God has fulfilled this promise to our children in that He raised up Jesus, as it is also written in the second Psalm, 'You are My son; today I have begotten You'" (13:33). And, as in Peter's Acts 2 sermon, Jesus's resurrection is viewed also as a fulfillment of a promise to David, especially with respect to transforming death and bodily decay (13:34–36) into an irreversible condition of a newly created body (quoting Isa. 55:3 in Acts 13:34, and Ps. 16:10 in Acts 13:35; see also Acts 13:37–38).

Thus, in the two structurally crucial sermons in Acts 2 and Acts 13 the concepts of new creation through resurrection from the de-creation of death and of kingdom establishment through resurrection are very closely linked, which is especially highlighted by repeated mention of the resurrection of the Messiah (i.e., the eschatological Israelite king) in the Acts 2 account. Therefore, the idea of the new-creational kingdom is underscored by explaining Jesus's resurrection from the dead. The topic of Jesus's resurrection is also an important theme at points throughout the book of Acts (1:22; 3:15, 26; 4:2, 10, 33; 5:30; 25:19).

The next section containing several references to resurrection language is Acts 17. First, speaking in Thessalonica, Paul underscores that Jesus's resurrection is crucial to understanding that he is the Messiah (v. 3). This is understood by Paul's opponents to be a claim that Jesus is "another king," which is to "act contrary to the decrees of Caesar" (v. 7). Again, Jesus's resurrection is inextricably linked to the understanding that he is Israel's king. Then, speaking in Athens, Paul refers to Jesus's resurrection, again directly linking the kingly function of judgment with that of resurrection: "Because He has fixed a day in which He will judge the world in righteousness through a Man whom He has appointed, having furnished proof to all men by raising Him from the dead" (v. 31 [cf. the references to Paul's preaching of Jesus's resurrection in vv. 18, 32]).

After Acts 17 there is only one explicit reference to Jesus's resurrection in the remainder of the book (26:23). There are other references that likely include Jesus's resurrection, but they are generally allusions to the resurrection of all the dead, among which Jesus's is included (23:6; 24:21; 26:8; cf. 23:8). There is also exclusive reference to a future resurrection of all the dead (24:15). In addition, Acts mentions a person being brought back from the dead, presumably as a reflection of Jesus's resurrection and as an anticipation of the future general resurrection (9:40–41). Finally, Acts narrates three times that gentile belief leads to them being given "eternal life" (*zōē aiōnios*).[34] This refers to the resurrection, which is inaugurated spiritually at the inception of the faith experience (11:18 [mentions only "life"]; 13:46 [in contrast to unbelieving Jews], 48) and is consummated physically.

---

34. Recall from the earlier section on eschatology in John (chap. 5) that this same Greek phrase for "eternal life" occurs repeatedly in John as a reference to the resurrection of the dead and sometimes as an allusion, to one degree or another, to Dan. 12:2, where the same exact phrase is found. There are forty-one uses of this phrase in the NT, and though many of them may not be direct allusions to Daniel, they probably have their roots there, as a result of the formative influence of repeated early Christian usage that was explicitly dependent on Daniel. The same phrase "eternal life" occurs elsewhere in the LXX only in the later apocryphal books, likely in allusion to Dan. 12:2 (2 Macc. 7:9; 4 Macc. 15:3; *Pss. Sol.* 3:12).

Altogether, there are about thirty references to resurrection in the book of Acts,[35] showing it to be an important theme in the development of the early Christian movement. In particular, most of the time it refers to Christ's resurrection, which connotes his kingship and existence as a new creature.

The Damascus Road Christophany as a Resurrection Appearance

The most stunning reference to resurrection in all of Acts is the threefold reference to Christ's resurrection appearance to Paul on the Damascus Road (Acts 9; 22; 26). Although the Greek words for "resurrection" are not used in the accounts of chapters 9 and 22, the actual words are used to introduce and summarize the chapter 26 narrative (vv. 8, 22–23). Paul's narrated explanation in Acts 26 of Christ's appearance to him cannot be fully understood without observing and evaluating his use of the OT there (see table 8.2).

Table 8.2

Acts 26	Old Testament (LXX)
26:16a: "stand on your feet"	Ezek. 2:1: "stand on your feet"
26:16–17: "to appoint you"; "delivering you"; "I am sending you" (see also Gal. 1)	Jer. 1: "I send you" (v. 7); "to deliver you" (vv. 8, 19); see also vv. 5, 10 (see also Gal. 1:15: "But when God, who had set me apart even from my mother's womb," alluding to Jer. 1:5 in application to Paul's Damascus Road experience)
26:18: "to open their eyes so that they may turn from darkness to light and from the dominion of Satan to God"	Isa. 42:6b–7: "for a light of the Gentiles to open the eyes of the blind, to bring the bound and them that sit in darkness out of bonds and the prison-house" Isa. 42:16: "I will bring the blind by a way that they knew not, and I will cause them to tread paths which they have not known: I will turn darkness into light for them."
26:23: "to proclaim light both to the Jewish people and to the Gentiles"	Isa. 49:6: "for the covenant of a race, for a light of the Gentiles, that you should be for salvation to the end of the earth"
26:16: "a minister and a witness"	Isa. 43:10: "witness . . . servant" (referring to Israel)

Why does Luke describe Paul's experience through allusion to the calling of the OT prophets Jeremiah and Ezekiel and through the calling of the prophetic Servant of Yahweh in Isaiah?[36] There appear to be at least three reasons. First, Luke wants to portray Christ as speaking as the Lord of the

---

35. These consist of a variety of Greek terms, such as *egeirō* ("raise"), *anistēmi* ("raise up"), *anastasis* ("resurrection"), *zaō* ("live"), *zōē* ("life"), and *gennaō* ("beget").

36. All the above allusions in Acts 26 are often recognized. E.g., the margin of NA[27] notes them, except for Isa. 49:6 in Acts 26:23, which others, however, have recognized, such as F. F. Bruce, *The Book of the Acts*, NICNT (Grand Rapids: Eerdmans, 1954), 494. Bruce also cites the parallel texts Isa. 42:6; 60:3, which may also be in mind in Acts 26:23, though Isa. 49:6 is likely uppermost in mind as a development of Acts 1:8; 13:47. There is more debate about

OT, who gave the prophets their vocation (note in this respect that Jesus is called "Lord"). Second, Luke wants to emphasize the prophetic authority of Paul and that his authority is equal to that of OT prophets; that is, he also is a divine spokesman. Note that all the major prophets of the OT begin their prophetic careers by being commissioned by God through a theophanic vision and verbal communication (although God does not appear in Jeremiah's vision and in the call of the Isaianic Servant). Third, just like these OT prophets, Paul's prophetic function was to preach salvation and, especially, judgment (above all here, note Jeremiah and Ezekiel).

In light of the above parallels, it is probable that Acts 26:13 ("On the way I saw from heaven, greater than the <u>brightness of the sun</u> [*lamprotēta tou hēliou*], <u>a light</u> [*phōs*] <u>shining</u> [*perilampsan*])" is an allusion to Isa. 60:1–3, where there is an emphasis on God's light not only for the "sons" of Jerusalem, but also for kings and gentiles (cf. Acts 9:15). In Isa. 60:1–3 we find the language of "give light" (*phōtizou* [2x]), "light" (*phōs* [2x]), "glory of the Lord" (*doxa kyriou* [2x]), and "brightness" (*lamprotēti* [1x]). Perhaps, we may also add the parallel from Isa. 42:1 ("elect" [*eklektos*]) with Acts 9:15 ("elect vessel" [*skeuos eklogēs*]).

Thus, against the background of Isa. 42; 43; 49, Paul is seen as carrying on the task of the prophesied Isaianic Servant begun by Christ, with whom Paul is corporately identified and by whom Paul is represented (of course, in doing so, Paul is a ministering assistant of the Servant).[37] Like Christ, Paul "opens eyes to turn from darkness" and "shines light to the Gentiles" (cf. esp. Acts 26:23 with 26:18). Christ and Paul are leading the second, new exodus and return from exile prophesied in Isa. 40–66.

This identification with Isaiah's prophesied Servant is also brought out by comparing Luke 2:30–32; Acts 13:47; 26:18, 23 with the most relevant Isaiah passages (see table 8.3).

This also means that Christ and the apostles were the beginning of the new Israel, since Isa. 49:3 affirms explicitly of the Servant in 49:6 that "you are My Servant, Israel." Even the identification of Christ with "glory" in Luke 2:32 may well arise from Isa. 49:3b ("in whom I will show My glory"). In Acts 26:13–18 Jesus is so identified with "light" that "light" probably stands for him.[38] Against the background of Isa. 60:1–3, Jesus is seen as Yahweh, whose light and glory now sets on the new Israel, through which light will be shone to the gentiles:

---

allusion to Isa. 43:10 in Acts 26:16, but in light of the other allusions to nearby Isaiah texts, it falls into place naturally.

37. By this I mean that Paul is not fully identified with the messianic Servant, Jesus, in every way, but that he continues to mediate the message of restoration from exile and of the second exodus, which began to be announced by Christ.

38. So Luke 2:30–32; note likewise Luke 1:78b–79: "The Sunrise from on high [i.e., Christ] will visit us, to shine upon those who sit in darkness and the shadow of death," quoting Isa. 9:2, which is applied to Jesus in Matt. 4:16.

Table 8.3

Isaiah 42:6–7, 16	Isaiah 49:6
42:6b–7: "for a light of the Gentiles to open the eyes of the blind, to bring the bound and them that sit in darkness out of bonds and the prison-house" 42:16: "I will bring the blind by a way that they knew not, and I will cause them to tread paths which they have not known: I will turn darkness into light for them."	"for the covenant of a race, for a light of the nations, that you should be for salvation to the end of the earth"

Luke 2:30–32	Acts 13:47	Acts 26:18, 23
"For my eyes have seen Your salvation [i.e., Christ], which You have prepared in the presence of all peoples, a light of revelation to the Gentiles, and the glory of Your people Israel."	"For so the Lord has commanded us, 'I have placed you as a light for the Gentiles, that you may bring salvation to the end of the earth.'"	26:18 "to open their eyes so that they may turn from darkness to light and from the dominion of Satan to God" 26:23: "that the Christ was . . . to proclaim light both to the Jewish people and to the Gentiles"

> Arise, shine; for your light has come,
> And the glory of the LORD has risen upon you.
> For behold, darkness will cover the earth,
> And deep darkness the peoples;
> But the LORD will rise upon you,
> And His glory will appear upon you.
> Nations will come to your light,
> And kings to the brightness of your rising.

Consequently, the Luke-Acts passages about Jesus and Paul indicate inaugurated fulfillment of the Isaianic prophecies. But why is light underscored in Isaiah? The Isa. 60 passage may represent what is in mind in the other Isaiah prophecies about light. The reference that "darkness will cover the earth, and deep darkness the peoples," likely alludes to Gen. 1:2–4: "And darkness was over the surface of the deep. . . . Then God said, 'Let there be light'; and there was light. And God saw that the light was good; and God separated the light from the darkness." Isaiah 60:1–3 is depicting the coming restoration and redemption of Israel against the background of Gen. 1:2–4. The reason for doing this is that Isaiah understands the future blessing on Israel and the world to be a recapitulation of the first creation, so that Israel's and the nations' salvation is painted as a new creation and emergence from spiritual darkness. The same notion of new-creational light presumably is also in mind in the NT allusions to these Isaiah verses. That the idea of new creation is conveyed in the NT uses is also indicated by Paul's statement in 2 Cor. 4:6: "For God, who said, 'Light shall shine out of darkness,' is the One who has shone in our hearts to give the light of the knowledge of the glory of God in the face of Christ." I will contend in a following chapter that in 2 Cor. 4:4–6 Paul is reflecting partly on Acts 26:18, 23, as well as the closely connected idea of "glory" in Isa. 49:3; 60:1–3 (alluded to also in Luke 2:32), and also Isa. 9:1–2, the only other place where the Greek phrase "light will shine" is used. And, as we have seen and will see again in Paul's writings, Isa. 40–66 combines prophecies of new creation with prophecies of return from exile because the restoration was also to be a new creation.

The Reflection of Old Testament Theophanic Visions in the Three Damascus Road Christophany Reports

Gerhard Lohfink sees a pattern in a number of OT visions that is common to the Damascus Road accounts. He detects the following pattern in Gen. 46:1–4 (cf. esp. Acts 9:4–6); Gen. 31:11–13 (Acts 26:14–16); Gen. 22:1–2, 11–12; Exod. 3:2–13; 1 Sam. 3:4–14:[39]

1. the double vocative,
2. the question of the man, or the man's response,
3. the self-presentation of the one appearing, and
4. the mission.

For example, the pattern is easily observable in Exod. 3:2–10:[40]

1. the double vocative: "Moses, Moses" (v. 4);
2. the response or question of the man: "Here I am" (v. 4) and "Now they [Israel] may say to me, 'What is His name?' What shall I say to them?" (v. 13);
3. the self-presentation of the one appearing: "I am the God of your father, the God of Abraham, the God of Isaac, and the God of Jacob" (v. 6);
4. the commission: "Therefore, come now, and I will send you to Pharaoh, so that you may bring My people, the sons of Israel, out of Egypt" (v. 10 [see also vv. 14–22]).[41]

The same pattern is narrated in Christ's appearance to Paul in Acts 26:

39. Gerhard Lohfink, *Paulus vor Damaskus: Arbeitsweisen der neueren Bibelwissenschaft dargestellt an den Texten Apg 9:1–19, 22:3–21, 26:9–18*, SBS 4 (Stuttgart: Katholisches Bibelwerk, 1966), 53–60.
40. In some cases the pattern is not as easily discernible.
41. Lohfink observes that the same pattern occurs in Jewish apocalyptic writings (e.g., *Apoc. Abr.* 8:2–5; 9:1–5; *Jos. Asen.* 14:6–8; short form; *Jub.* 18:1–2, 10–11; *Apoc. Abr.* 11:4–6; 12:6–7; 14:1–3, 9–10; 19:1–3; 20:1–3; *Apoc. Mos.* 41; *T. Job* 3:1–2.

1. the double vocative: "Saul, Saul" (v. 14);
2. the response or question of the man: "Who are you, Lord?" (v. 15a);
3. the self-presentation of the one appearing: "I am Jesus whom you are persecuting" (v. 15b);
4. the commission: "But get up and stand on your feet; for this purpose I have appeared to you, to appoint you a minister and a witness not only to the things which you have seen, but also to the things in which I will appear to you; rescuing you from the Jewish people and from the Gentiles, to whom I am sending you, to open their eyes so that they may turn from darkness to light and from the dominion of Satan to God, in order that they may receive forgiveness of sins and an inheritance among those who have been sanctified by faith in Me" (vv. 16–18).

The significance of this observable pattern is that Paul is being commissioned as a prophet. Indeed, in the past thirty years or so of Pauline scholarship, the commissioning typically has been the focus, and there has been a rejection of the formerly held view that Paul had a conversion experience on the Damascus Road. But why cannot Paul have been both converted and commissioned as a prophet at the same time? Indeed, the OT prophetic commissioning patterns may also include both notions. For example, it is possible that Moses was converted and commissioned by the theophanic experience at the burning bush (there is not definitive evidence that he was a believer in Yahweh before that time). Likewise, it is even more likely that the prophetic commissioning of Isaiah was executed at the time of his conversion. In Isa. 6 Isaiah says, "Woe is me, for I am ruined! Because I am a man of unclean lips, . . . for my eyes have seen the King, the LORD of hosts" (v. 5). An angelic being then touches his mouth with a burning coal taken from the altar and announces, "Your sin is forgiven" (v. 6–7). Then Isaiah receives his prophetic commission (vv. 8–10). This language points strongly to conversion.

Another important part of the pattern in the repeated OT theophanic-prophetic commissioning narratives is that the one who appears is always the Lord or the angel of the Lord. In Acts 26 the name of Jesus is substituted for God in the "self-presentation" part of the pattern ("I am the God of . . ." [cf. esp. Gen. 31:13; 46:3; Exod. 3:6]): "And the Lord said, 'I am Jesus whom you are persecuting'" (v. 15b). This highlights the deity of Jesus and his divine authority in calling Paul as a prophet.

The Significance of Heaven in the Damascus Road Conversion Narratives

In Acts there are three references to the heavenly source of the revelation to Paul on the Damascus Road: "light from heaven" (*phōs ek tou ouranou* [9:3]); "from heaven a very bright light flashed all around me" (*ek tou ouranou periastrapsai phōs hikanon peri eme* [22:6]); "a light from heaven, brighter than the sun, shining all around me" (*ouranothen hyper tēn lamprotēta tou hēliou perilampsan me phōs* [26:13]). "Heaven" in Acts refers to the sphere of Jesus's inaugurated eschatological reign (cf. 2:30–36; 7:55–56 with 1:8–11). In 1:9 Jesus "was lifted up . . . and a cloud received him" in association with heavenly angels explaining to the onlookers why this was happening. This appears to be a reflection of Dan. 7:10, 13–14,[42] where the prophetic vision foresees a time when "with the clouds of heaven one like a Son of Man was coming, and he came up to the Ancient of Days," surrounded by angels, "and to Him was given dominion, glory, and a kingdom." That Dan. 7 is the background in Acts 1:9 is further indicated by the references in Acts 2; 7 to heaven in conjunction with Jesus's residence there. Jesus's "ascent to heaven" has resulted in him "having been exalted to the right hand of God" and "seated upon his throne" to reign as "Messiah" (2:30–36). The references in Acts 1:9; 2 are then developed further in 7:55–56:

> But being full of the Holy Spirit, he [Stephen] gazed intently into heaven and saw the glory of God, and Jesus standing at the right hand of God; and he said, "Behold, I see the heavens opened up and the Son of Man standing at the right hand of God."

Note the combined mention of "heaven," "glory," and "Son of Man," further telltale reflections of the famous Dan. 7 prophecy of the Son of Man's prophesied kingship, which has been inaugurated by Christ's resurrection and ascension and has its eschatological center of gravity in the heavenly dimension.[43]

The Acts references to Christ being in heaven and Paul's own experience of Christ's revelation to him from that heaven perhaps led Paul also to hold not only that Christ had become heavenly through his resurrection (1 Cor. 15:42–49), but also that by virtue of his exaltation Christ was now in heaven (Eph. 2:6; Phil. 3:20–21; Col. 3:1; 4:1). The NT eschatological center of gravity has moved from the earthly realm (in the Gospels) to the heavenly realm (Acts and Paul). For example, in addition to Acts 1–2; 7, this theme is expressed in Ephesians. The "blessing in the heavenly places in Christ" (1:3) includes Christ commencing

42. Following Wright, *New Testament and the People of God*, 462.

43. This idea of inaugurated eschatological realities having their source in the heavenly realm is similar to some Jewish writings, since in some of the Jewish apocalypses the seers saw aspects of future, end-time salvation as present realities in heaven (see *4 Ezra* 7:14, 26, 83; 13:18; *2 Bar.* 21:12; 48:49; 52:7). The Qumran community held that they were the elect on earth and had begun to experience the heavenly realm (1QHᵃ XI:19–22; see also XIX:10–13; both texts also suggest that the resurrection of the redeemed saint has begun in some way, perhaps spiritually). Note further references in Jewish apocalyptic to the future, end-time benefits of salvation as present realities in heaven: *4 Ezra* 8:52; *2 Bar.* 4:6; *1 En.* 46:3. I am following Andrew T. Lincoln, *Paradise Now and Not Yet: Studies in the Role of the Heavenly Dimension in Paul's Thought with Special Reference to His Eschatology*, SNTSMS 43 (Cambridge: Cambridge University Press, 1981), 101, 149. Lincoln cites these references and the ones above from Jewish apocalyptic and the DSS.

"the heading up of all things . . . in the heavens and . . . on the earth" (1:10). In particular, Christ's resurrection has led to him having been seated at God's "right hand in the heavenly places," and consequently, God "has put all things in subjection under His feet" (1:20, 22), the latter phrase an allusion to Ps. 8:6 (cf. similarly Phil. 3:20–21; Col. 3:1, the former of which views "heaven" as the dwelling place of "the Lord Jesus Messiah"). This is summarized as God making Christ "head over all things" (1:22), likely a further unpacking of the "heading up" reference in 1:10. Ephesians 4:10 appears to develop the same theme ("He who ascended far above all the heavens, so that He might fill all things").

The Dan. 7 and Ps. 8 background in connection with Jesus's beginning kingship in heaven rings with the sound of Adam's beginning kingship in the beginning new creation in Gen. 1–2.[44]

The upshot of this section is that Paul first experienced on the Damascus Road the inaugurated realities of the kingdom of the new creation in heaven, where the resurrected Christ had begun to reign and from where he was revealing himself to Paul.

Conclusion to the Discussion of the Damascus Road Christophany

Christ's resurrection appearance to Paul on the Damascus Road revealed that Christ was eschatological king, and Christ's appearance made Paul a prophet (apostle), an Isaianic servant (participating as a prophetic assistant corporately identified with the Servant in leading the second exodus and restoration from exile), part of end-time Israel (whose call was to witness), a new creation, a Christian, and an apocalyptist. In the following chapters that focus on Paul's writings I will unpack each of these realities that Paul began to experience in order to see that the notion of new creation in connection to kingdom is the integrating core of the other realities just noted, though it is important to see that the second exodus and the return from exile are vitally linked to new creation (which for humans was resurrection existence) and are stepping-stones to it.

Conclusion

I have argued that in the Gospels and Acts Christ's resurrection is so linked to his kingship that the two are two sides of one coin. Resurrection is obviously

44. This notion in Dan. 7 and Ps. 8 will be elaborated on further in chap. 13. In Dan. 7 faithful Israel in corporate identification with the Son of Man is portrayed as an Adam figure (i.e., as "son of Adam") who reigns over the animal kingdoms of the earth, which oppress the saints (so also N. T. Wright, *The Climax of the Covenant: Christ and the Law in Pauline Theology* [Minneapolis: Fortress, 1992], 23). That this depiction is preceded by waters of chaos further aligns Dan. 7 with Gen. 1–2. Similarly, the allusion to Ps. 8 in Eph. 1:22 provides another background of the ideal eschatological Adamic kingship in a new creation (which itself alludes explicitly to Gen. 1:26–28). For Dan. 7:13–14 and Ps. 8 as developments of Gen. 1:28, see chap. 2.

the beginning of new creation, which is clear from considering that the way all redeemed humans will inhabit the eternal new heavens and earth is by being resurrected as new creations themselves and thus taking their part in the new cosmos (for the same notion, see the Christian *Odes. Sol.* 22:7–12; similarly, 33:7–12; *T. Adam* 3:3–4). Jesus's resurrection made him the first to become part of this new creation, though it is more precise to say that he was the beginning of the end-time new creation, which began to be located in heaven directly following his ascension.

Since the resurrection and ascension are the climax of each of the four Gospels and the launching pad of Acts, I also propose that Christ's resurrection as the beginning of the new-creational kingdom is not only the goal of the Gospels and Acts but also the dominant theological framework within which the other major theological concepts of these NT books are to be understood. To put it another way: the resurrection as the expression of the already–not yet new-creational kingdom is the crucial strand of the thread of the Bible's redemptive-historical storyline as it is being woven into the NT witness. Note the restatement of that storyline and the function of resurrection as new-creational kingship in it (underlined): *Jesus's life, trials, death for sinners, and* resurrection *by the Spirit* have launched the fulfillment of the eschatological already–not yet new-creational reign, *bestowed by grace through faith and resulting in worldwide commission to the faithful to advance new-creational reign and resulting in judgment for the unbelieving, unto the triune God's glory.*

This needs some qualification. We will see in the following chapters that Jesus begins to introduce the movement toward the new-creational kingdom by functioning in the role of the end-time Adam, who begins to reverse the curses of the first Adam by doing what he should have done. Jesus begins his decisive defeat of the devil by overcoming temptation in the wilderness and then subjects the demons to his kingship. He also does many miracles of healing, which begins to undo the curses of the fall. Of course, the decisive undoing of the Adamic curses is Jesus's resurrection, which Paul understands to be the "first fruits" of his own people's resurrection in the future. Paul understands Jesus's resurrection as not only reversing the curse of death but also decisively defeating the devil. In fact, we will see in subsequent chapters how Paul and the rest of the NT writers understand that this victory over Satan actually took place. We will also see that those who identify with Jesus in this life begin to experience true, literal resurrection on the spiritual level, which guarantees resurrection on the physical level at the end of the age, which will be a consummate return from the exile of death and the effects of the old, sinful world.

9

Resurrection as Inaugurated End-Time
New Creation and Kingdom in Paul's Writings

This chapter will continue to argue that Christ's resurrection establishes the inaugurated end-time new-creational kingdom. We will see that this core of the NT storyline is prevalent in Paul's thought. Paul refers to the resurrection of Christ and of believers throughout his writings. For example, Paul identified the resurrection of the saints with the end of time in 1 Cor. 15:21–26:

> For since by a man came death, by a man also came the resurrection of the dead. For as in Adam all die, so also in Christ all will be made alive. But each in his own order: Christ the first fruits, after that those who are Christ's at His coming, then <u>the end</u>, when He delivers up the kingdom to the God and Father, when He has abolished all rule and all authority and power. For He must reign until He has put all His enemies under His feet. <u>The last enemy that will be abolished is death.</u>

Why does Paul identify the resurrection of believers with the very end of the age? We have already observed in early Judaism and in the Gospels that resurrection was so linked to the very end of the world that it was almost synonymous with the end, since it was the last event to happen together with judgment, after which the eternal new creation of the age to come would commence.

As in the Gospels, so also especially in Paul's writings, the resurrection of Christ and of believers is mentioned quite often, and, in light of the associations in Judaism and the Gospels, Paul also understands the resurrection to be an

249

inherently end-time notion (the words that Paul uses to speak of resurrection are mainly *egeirō* ["raise"], *anistēmi* ["raise"], *zaō* ["live"], and *zōē* ["life"]).

Resurrection in Romans

In Romans Paul refers to Christ's resurrection repeatedly (4:24–25; 6:9). The introduction to the entire letter refers to the "gospel . . . promised beforehand through His prophets in the holy Scriptures, concerning His Son, who was born of a seed of David according to the flesh, who was declared the Son of God with power by the resurrection from the dead" (Rom. 1:1–4). Thus, the resurrection is seen to be part of the fulfillment of OT prophecy. J. R. Daniel Kirk has even seen the mention of resurrection in the introduction of the letter as an indication that the entire letter is consumed with the notion of Christ's and believers' resurrection.[1] This perhaps goes too far, but Kirk certainly is correct to see that resurrection is one of Paul's preoccupations in Romans.

In Romans Christ's resurrection is sometimes viewed as the basis for believers' resurrection existence that begins in this life (6:4–5, 8–9, which could be taken to indicate the saints' future resurrection). That present resurrection existence is in mind is apparent, since in 6:11, 13 Paul understands the references in 6:4–10 to form the basis for concluding that believers presently should be "alive to God in Christ Jesus" (6:11) and should "present [themselves] to God as those alive from the dead" (6:13).

Consequently, Paul's affirmation of believers' possession of "eternal life" (6:22–23) is likely an already–not yet reality. Hence, saints are not merely like resurrected beings; rather, they actually have begun to experience the end-time resurrection that Christ experienced because they are identified with him by faith. Although Paul can use the language of being in "the likeness of His resurrection" (supplying the ellipsis in 6:5b), he does not mean this in some purely metaphorical way, contrary to what some scholars contend.[2] That he intends to refer to literal resurrection is apparent from observing that he parallels it with being in "the likeness of his death" in 6:5a, which refers to real identification with his death, such that "our old man was crucified with Him" (6:6) and believers have really "died" (6:7–8). Paul does not refer to identification with Christ's death in a metaphorical manner. So likewise believers are in the "likeness" of Christ's resurrection because they actually have begun to be identified with it and participate in it. Of course, they are not fully identified with Christ's resurrection, since he has experienced full physical

---

1. J. R. Daniel Kirk, *Unlocking Romans: Resurrection and the Justification of God* (Grand Rapids: Eerdmans, 2008), 33–55. Kirk's book argues that resurrection pervades the entire book of Romans (see further, e.g., pp. 34, 55, 206, 208).
2. See, e.g., N. T. Wright, *The Resurrection of the Son of God* (Minneapolis: Fortress: 2003), 347.

resurrection life and those identified with him have experienced only inaugurated resurrection life on the spiritual level. Nevertheless, this inauguration is the beginning of true resurrection existence and is not metaphorical only because it is spiritual (as I explained in chap. 5 with respect to John 5:25–29). If saints are only like Christ's resurrection, then Paul's exhortation to them to live as resurrected beings is emptied of its force: if Christians have begun to be end-time resurrected creatures, then they have resurrection power not to "let sin reign in [their mortal bodies] . . . but present [themselves] to God as those alive from the dead" (6:12–13).

The relation of the "indicative" to the "imperative" in Paul's writings has been an issue of some debate. But if the above is a correct analysis of the saints' resurrection life, then the basis of Paul issuing commands to people is that such people have the ability to obey the commands because they have been raised from the dead, are regenerated, and are new creatures who have the power to obey. In fact, in 6:4 Paul refers to this resurrection life with new-creational language: "newness [*kainotēs*] of life" (or "new life"), a cognate of the word *kainos* found in 2 Cor. 5:17; Gal. 6:15 in the well-known inaugurated eschatological expression "new creation," where in both cases it refers to resurrection life.[3] Not coincidentally, one of the early references to resurrection in Romans directly connects resurrection and creation: "God, who gives life to the dead and calls into being that which does not exist" (4:17). This statement is not merely a gnomic saying about God's attributes but likely connects resurrection to new creation (not merely the first creation), since 4:17 prepares for the conclusion that such a God not only can bring life from Sarah's dead womb (4:18–21), but also can, and has, brought Jesus up from the dead (4:24–25).

Thus, Paul does not give commands to live righteously to those outside the community of faith. This is because they do not have this power of the inbreaking age of the new creation, but are still part of the old age (the "old man" [6:6]), in which they are dominated by sin, Satan, and the influence of the world (so Eph. 2:1–3).

Not taking seriously enough the resurrection language applied to the Christian's present experience to designate real eschatological resurrection existence, albeit on the spiritual level, has unintentionally eviscerated the ethical power of church teaching and preaching, since Christians must be aware that they presently have resurrection power to please and obey God. This is why in Rom. 6 and elsewhere Paul employs Christ's latter-day resurrection as the basis for believers' resurrection identity and for his exhortations that they rule over sin.

3. On which, see discussion below in this chapter and the next chapter. *Kainos* also appears in Eph. 2:15; 4:24 with reference to the new creation (on which, see below in this chapter), and in 1 Cor. 11:25; 2 Cor. 3:6 in the phrase "new covenant," which also refers to the beginning of the new age, in allusion to Jer. 31:31–34.

The OT and Judaism looked forward to the new age, when the power of sin would be broken and the final resurrection would occur. For example, as we have seen repeatedly earlier in chapter 8, Ezek. 36:25–29; 37:12–14 affirms,

> Then I will sprinkle clean water on you, and you will be clean; I will cleanse you from all your filthiness and from all your idols. Moreover, I will give you a new heart and put a new spirit within you; and I will remove the heart of stone from your flesh and give you a heart of flesh. I will put My Spirit within you and cause you to walk in My statutes, and you will be careful to observe My ordinances. And you will live in the land that I gave to your forefathers; so you will be My people, and I will be your God. Moreover, I will save you from all your uncleanness. . . .
>
> Therefore prophesy and say to them, "Thus says the LORD God, 'Behold, I will open your graves and cause you to come up out of your graves, My people; and I will bring you into the land of Israel. Then you will know that I am the LORD, when I have opened your graves and caused you to come up out of your graves, My people. I will put My Spirit within you and you will come to life, and I will place you on your own land. Then you will know that I, the LORD, have spoken and done it,' declares the Lord."

Ezekiel 36 speaks of a spiritual renewing ("new heart," "new spirit"), which is spoken of in terms of resurrection in Ezek. 37 ("come up out of your graves," "come to life"). Although the majority of Judaism understood Ezek. 37:12–14 to refer to literal physical resurrection, most contemporary commentators understand Ezek. 37 to refer to Israel's restoration to their land from exile through the metaphor of resurrection, which certainly would include spiritual renewal. Indeed, Ezek. 36–37 is speaking of the resurrection of the dead human spirit, which is carried out by God's Spirit. In this sense, literal resurrection is indeed the subject, but only literal resurrection of the spirit is the focus. Recall that the OT and Judaism envision the resurrection of the whole person—spirit (or soul) and body.[4] Ezekiel focuses on the eschatological resurrection of the former. The resurrection of the body would have been viewed as occurring at the same time as that of the spirit, and this was likely also Ezekiel's implicit perspective. This may be why Judaism almost universally understood Ezek. 37:1–14 to refer to physical resurrection through the instrumentation of the Spirit, since it would have been hard to conceive of spiritual resurrection without the physical.

Paul expresses what much of the OT implies about resurrection and, in particular, what Ezek. 36–37 focuses on: sin is broken by the power of resurrection in the inner person, which Paul sees will be consummated later by corporeal resurrection (Rom. 8:18–23). Paul may even have these Ezekiel chapters in mind, which is apparent from the following observations:[5]

---

4. See the discussion of John 5:25–28 in chap. 5.

5. I have found confirmation for some of the following observations supporting an Ezek. 36–37 background for the notion of resurrection in Rom. 6–8 in Thomas R. Schreiner, *Romans*, BECNT

1. Paul speaks of water baptism as the means to having the "old man" removed and having it replaced with "newness of life" (Rom. 6:3–4), just as Ezek. 36:25–28 is the only place in the LXX that refers to "sprinkling clean water" on people in the end time, which results in a "new heart and a new spirit."

2. Another pointer to Ezek. 36:26 is Rom. 7:4–6. After speaking of believers having been "joined" to "Him who was raised from the dead" (7:4), Paul says that the result is "that we might bear fruit for God" and "serve in <u>newness of the spirit</u> [*kainotēti pneumatos*]." The Ezek. 36 text says that in the end time God will give his people a "new spirit" (*pneuma kainon*) (v. 26; so also Ezek. 11:19).[6]

3. The Ezekiel background may be evident further in Rom. 8, where Paul picks up the resurrection theme again and speaks of it in terms of linking "Spirit" and "life" (8:2 ["Spirit of life," *pneumatos tēs zōēs*], 5–6 ["the mind set on the Spirit is life," *to phronēma tou pneumatos zōē*]).[7] So also Ezek. 37:5 ("Spirit of life," *pneuma zōēs*) is the only passage in the LXX that makes the same linkage in an eschatological context (likewise Ezek. 37:6, 14: "I will give you my Spirit [*pneuma*] and you will live [*zaō*]."[8]

4. Romans 8 and Ezek. 36 are the only texts in biblical literature that contrast unbelieving "flesh" with the human "spirit" that has been renewed by the divine Spirit: note Rom. 8:9–10, "not in the flesh [*sarx*] but in the Spirit . . . <u>the spirit is alive</u> [*pneuma zōē*]" (cf. Rom. 8:4–8, 11), and Ezek. 36:26–27, "I will give you . . . a new spirit . . . and I will remove the stone heart from your flesh . . . and I will put My Spirit within you" (cf. Ezek. 11:19).

5. Just as God's Spirit was to be the agent in raising his people from the dead in the end time (Ezek. 37:1–14), an idea developed also in Judaism,

---

(Grand Rapids: Baker Academic, 1998), 396, 400, 408, 415–16. See also Hans Hübner, *Biblische Theologie des Neuen Testaments*, 3 vols. (Göttingen: Vandenhoeck & Ruprecht, 1990–95), 2:301–6. Hübner likewise lists several continuities but also notes discontinuities between Ezek. 36–37 and Rom. 8:1–17.

6. Likewise *Jos. Asen.* 8:11 expresses a request that God "renew her by your Spirit," which is equated with the expressions "form her anew by your hidden hand" and "make her live again by your life," the first and last clauses apparently being allusions respectively to Ezek. 36:26 and perhaps to Ezek. 37:5 (on the latter, see directly below).

7. In light of Rom. 8:6, the phrase "Spirit of life" in 8:2 is probably best taken as a genitive of apposition ("Spirit which is life"), though it could be a genitive of destination or purpose ("Spirit leading to life").

8. John W. Yates, *The Spirit and Creation in Paul*, WUNT 2/251 (Tübingen: Mohr Siebeck, 2008), 145, makes the same observation. The phrase "spirit of life," referring to the human spirit as a mere part of the preeschatological created order, appears in Gen. 6:17; 7:15; Jdt. 10:13; cf. 2 Macc. 7:22; the same phrase refers to the "living beings" around God's heavenly throne (Ezek. 1:20–21; 10:17). See 2 Macc. 7:23; 14:46 for "life and spirit" being given back to the Maccabean martyrs at the time of their resurrection.

so it is likely the inspiration for Paul's statement in Rom. 8:11: "He who raised Christ Jesus from the dead will also give life to your mortal bodies through His Spirit who dwells in you,"[9] a resurrection that, as we have seen, begins in this life spiritually also through the work of the Spirit (as implied in Rom. 8:13–14). Believers' life through the Spirit's energizing work is modeled after Jesus's own "resurrection from the dead because of the Spirit of holiness" (Rom. 1:4). This is consistent with recalling that Jesus's resurrection, which "declared" him to be the "Son of God" (Rom. 1:4), is also the model for Christians being declared "sons of God" (Rom. 8:14, 19, 23 in the light of 1:4 together with 8:29).

6. Finally, Rom. 8:4 refers to fulfilling "the <u>requirement</u> [*dikaiōma*] of the Law" by those who "walk [*peripateō*] . . . according to the <u>Spirit</u> [*pneuma*]." Strikingly, Ezek. 36:27 refers to God, who "will put My <u>Spirit</u> [*pneuma*] within you and cause you to <u>walk</u> [*poreuomai*][10] in My <u>requirements</u> [*dikaiōma*]." The close connection of these three terms in both texts makes an allusion to Ezek. 36–37 even more probable.[11]

Thus, Paul views Christians in Rom. 6–8 to be the actual beginning fulfillment of the prophesied spiritual resurrection of Israel that was to transpire in the latter days at the time of their restoration from exile. The power of Paul's exhortations for his readers to conquer sin is to assure them that they are part of God's eschatological people who have begun to be raised from the dead spiritually, which is a literal part of and the down payment of the physical resurrection to come. Their spiritual resurrection has restored them from their spiritual exile and alienation from God back into God's presence. Paul would say, on the one hand, that if believers do not "bear fruit," then perhaps they have not experienced the "newness of the Spirit" within them (Rom. 7:5–6). On the other hand, if "by the Spirit" saints "are putting to death the deeds of the body," they can be assured that they "are being led by the Spirit of God" and are obedient "sons of God," to which the "Spirit himself bears witness with their spirit" (Rom. 8:13–16).

Consequently, when Paul speaks of people experiencing "life" (*zōē* [Rom. 8:6, 10]) and "living" (*zaō* [Rom. 8:13]), he is not merely speaking of people existing as Christians in contrast to those who "live" as unbelievers; rather, he is referring to them as actual eschatologically resurrected beings.[12] Again,

---

9. There is a textual problem in Rom. 8:11. For a defense of the conceptual sense of the above translation of Rom. 8:11, see the excursus at the end of this section.

10. By the time of the NT, *peripateō* was the replacement of and equivalent to *poreuomai* (on which, see Yates, *Spirit and Creation*, 144).

11. For this observation, see ibid.

12. This may also be evident from Rom. 14:7–9, where believers are told that "not one of us lives for himself, and not one of us dies for himself," but rather they "live for the Lord, or . . . die for the Lord," which is tied directly to them being "of the Lord," who "died and lived

the reason why Paul issues imperatives in his letters and expects Christian audiences to obey his commands is that they have begun to experience the resurrection of the end time, and they have the moral power of such new creation life to obey and please their Creator. We will return to Rom. 8 again in subsequent chapters on the Spirit and on justification, but the point here has been to focus on resurrection and that believers have begun to experience truly, not metaphorically, the beginning form of end-time resurrection life. This inextricable link between the inaugurated latter-day resurrection and power for Christian "living" can be seen also by observing that Rom. 12:1–2 is a development of Rom. 6:13, 16, 19 (see table 9.1).

Table 9.1

Romans 6:13, 16, 19	Romans 12:1
6:13: "And do not go on presenting the members of your body to sin as instruments of unrighteousness; but present yourselves to God as those alive from the dead, and your members as instruments of righteousness to God."	"I urge you therefore, brethren, by the mercies of God, to present your bodies a living and holy sacrifice, acceptable to God, which is your spiritual service of worship."
6:16: "Do you not know that when you present yourselves to someone as slaves for obedience, you are slaves of the one whom you obey, either of sin resulting in death, or of obedience resulting in righteousness?"	
6:19: "For just as you presented your members as slaves to impurity and to lawlessness, resulting in further lawlessness, so now present your members as slaves to righteousness, resulting in sanctification."	

The "therefore" in Rom. 12:1 indicates that the following is based on the broad themes of the preceding eleven chapters, to which Rom. 6 certainly contributed, so that it should not be surprising to see the link proposed directly above. If Rom. 12:1 is developing Rom. 6 to some degree, which appears likely, then the mention of "presenting your bodies a <u>living</u>, holy sacrifice" is developing the earlier idea of believers existing as eschatologically resurrected beings (6:13: "present yourselves to God as those <u>alive</u> from the dead"), who have already begun to taste of "the powers of the age to come" (Heb. 6:5). On the basis of assuming that his readers partake of this reality and have the infused moral power of those living in the new creation, Paul exhorts them in these two introductory verses of Rom. 12, and in the following chapters, to serve and obey God. That the "living" of 12:1 is new-creational life also in development of 6:4 ("so we too might walk <u>in newness of life</u> [*en kainotēti*

---

again, that He might be Lord both of the dead and of the living." This is strikingly similar to 2 Cor. 5:14–17, where the expression "they who live might no longer live for themselves, but for Him who died and rose again on their behalf" (v. 15) is linked directly not just to Christ's death and resurrection, but to Christ's resurrection as "new creation" (on which, see further the following chapter).

zōēs]") is apparent from 12:2: "And do not be conformed to this world, but be transformed by the <u>renewing of the mind</u> [*tē anakainōsei tou noos*], that you may prove what the will of God is, that which is good and acceptable and perfect." More precisely, in 12:2 Paul sees a progressive new-creational "transformation by the renewing" of believers.

As confident as Paul is in affirming the reality of inaugurated resurrection life, he is just as adamant in underscoring in Rom. 8:18–23 that such life and its concomitant sufferings must eventuate into full physical resurrection life (a notion anticipated in 8:11):

> For I consider that the sufferings of this present time are not worthy to be compared with the glory that is to be revealed to us. For the anxious longing of the creation waits eagerly for the revealing of the sons of God. For the creation was subjected to futility, not of its own will, but because of Him who subjected it, in hope that the creation itself also will be set free from its slavery to corruption into the freedom of the glory of the children of God. For we know that the whole creation groans and suffers the pains of childbirth together until now. And not only this, but also we ourselves, having the first fruits of the Spirit, even we ourselves groan within ourselves, waiting eagerly for our adoption as sons, <u>the redemption of our body</u>.

Paul views the beginning new resurrection life created within the Christian by the indwelling Spirit to be "the first fruits of the Spirit" (v. 23), which is the initial stage of new-creational life that will be consummated physically as a part of a larger newly created cosmos.[13] "First fruits" in the OT were offered to God to indicate that the remainder of what was offered also belonged to God. Such offerings could be animals, but the dominant OT image is that of offering the "first fruits" of crops to signify, at the least, that the remainder of the harvest belonged to God.[14] Paul's use of "first fruits" elsewhere indicates the first of more to come later.[15] Of greatest relevance for our text is 1 Cor. 15:20, 23, where Christ's resurrection is "the first fruits" of more people to be resurrected later. Here in Rom. 8:23 the newly created spiritual being of

13. Many plausibly take "first fruits of the Spirit" in Rom. 8:23 to be an appositional genitive ("first fruits, which are the Spirit"), which is supported further by Eph. 1:13–14: "the Holy Spirit of promise, who is given as a down payment of our inheritance." However, the preceding context of the Spirit in direct linkage with (probably as the agent of) resurrection life (Rom. 8:5–14) points more to a genitive of production ("first fruits produced by the Spirit") or, less possibly, a genitive of source ("first fruits from the Spirit"). For the category of the former, see Daniel B. Wallace, *Greek Grammar beyond the Basics* (Grand Rapids: Zondervan, 1996), 104–6, adducing as an example Eph. 4:3 ("the unity of [produced by] the Spirit").

14. For further support of this idea, see James D. G. Dunn, *Romans 1–8*, WBC 38A (Dallas: Word, 1991), 473.

15. E.g., Rom. 16:5; 1 Cor. 16:15; 2 Thess. 2:13, speaking of the first converts in an area of more to come; cf. Rom. 11:16, where many think that *aparchē* ("first fruits") refers to the promises to the patriarchs, which anticipates more in Israel to be redeemed later.

saints ("the first fruits of the Spirit") is the beginning of a greater physical resurrection existence to come, and it seems even to be conceived as the initial form of the whole new cosmos to come. The thought of 1 Cor. 15:20, 23 is the same as in the Rom. 8 context, where Christ is the bridgehead of the new creation, and especially Christ is said to be the "firstborn" of more to be resurrected later (8:29). His resurrection is also the bridgehead not only of his future resurrected people but also of the entire coming new cosmos, as we will see in Gal. 6:15–16; 2 Cor. 5:14–17; Col. 1:15–20.

The resurrection of God's people in Rom. 8:18–23 appears to be the catalyst in some sense for the rest of the new creation coming into being (cf. v. 19: "the anxious longing of the creation waits eagerly for the revealing of the sons of God"; so also vv. 20–22). Perhaps part of the reason for this is that new creation begins with humanity first and then, at the time it is completed in humanity, the crown of creation, the rest of creation is renewed along with God's people. This has its roots way back in Gen. 1–3, so that Rom. 8 here is depicting a renewal of the creation that was corrupted in Gen. 3.[16] This reinforces the notion observed above in Judaism, the Gospels, and Acts that the resurrection of the saints is part of the broader renewal of all creation, and thus the resurrection of believers itself is essentially new creation. This resurrection overhaul will be a reversal of the corruptible creation in which the incorruptible new creation will last forever, a notion that we have also already observed elsewhere in the OT (e.g., Dan. 12:2–3), Judaism, and the NT.

Paul expresses the everlasting nature of the resurrection in Rom. 2:7: "those who by perseverance . . . seek for . . . immortality, eternal life." In the interim before the saints' consummate resurrection, it is because of Christ' resurrected position that he "intercedes" for his people as they endure trials (8:34–39), which assures them that they will successfully endure such tribulations. Such trials are not to be viewed as punishments for the "elect," since Christ has taken this punishment upon himself and overcome it (8:31–34). Thus, part of the salvific effect of Christ's resurrection (5:10; 10:9) is that his "intercession" for saints and his "Spirit's intercession" ensure that all their trials "work together for good to those who love God" (cf. 8:26–28 with 8:34–39). This also means that no trial whatsoever can separate believers "from the love of God, which is in Christ Jesus," since they have become identified with Christ's death *and resurrection* (8:33–39).

Recalling the close relationship between kingship and new creation, we are not surprised to discover that Paul makes the same link in Romans. Paul's opening statement in 1:3–4 that Christ was "of the seed of David" and was "declared the Son of God with power by the resurrection from the dead"

16. For the Gen. 1–3 background of new creation, which Rom. 8 portrays as occurring through the Spirit in accomplishing the resurrection of Christ and believers, see Kirk, *Unlocking Romans*, 134–53.

identifies Jesus with the expected messianic king; the direct link with God's promise "beforehand through His prophets in the holy Scriptures" (1:2) indicates that Paul views Jesus's sonship as messianic kingship in fulfillment of the OT messianic prophecies of such a "son" from David's line (2 Sam. 7:12–16; Isa. 11:1–5; Jer. 23:5; Ezek. 34:23–24; 37:24).[17] And toward the end of Romans, Paul more explicitly indicates that the Messiah "died and lived again, that He might be Lord both of the dead and of the living" (14:9). Probably for the same reason, 10:9 directly links "Jesus as Lord" with "God raised him from the dead." On the basis that Jesus's resurrection has launched an escalated stage of his messianic rule, so likewise will his people "reign in life through the One, Jesus Christ" (5:17),[18] and even while suffering, they will "overwhelmingly conquer through Him" (8:37).

Excursus The Question of Whether the Spirit Is the Agent of the Already–Not Yet Resurrection in Romans

One of the texts in Romans most clearly depicting the Spirit as the agent of resurrection is 8:11: "But if the Spirit of Him who raised Jesus from the dead dwells in you, He who raised Christ Jesus from the dead will also give life to your mortal bodies through His Spirit who dwells in you." There is, however, a textual problem in this verse: some good manuscripts read "because of his Spirit" (B D F G Ψ 33 1739 1881) instead of "through his Spirit" (ℵ A C), leading Gordon Fee, who prefers the former, to say that nowhere does Paul see the Spirit as the agent of resurrection life for the Christian.[19] Other scholars prefer the reading of "through his Spirit."[20]

Fee's interpretative arguments in favor of the "because" reading could just as well be turned on their head in support of the "through" reading. However, though this is a difficult textual problem, either reading ultimately supports the Spirit as the one bringing about resurrection, since "because of his Spirit" could refer to believers' future resurrection taking place because of the prior presence of the Spirit in them, indicating only the qualification for being resurrected (so Fee), or the idea more likely could be that the Spirit is the cause of the resurrection in the sense of being the one who causes the resurrection to

17. Following Schreiner, *Romans*, 39–40; see likewise Dunn, *Romans 1–8*, 13–14.
18. Whether this is a reference to an inaugurated or future consummated "reign" is not clear here, though elsewhere in Paul's writings and the NT it is an already–not yet concept. Similarly, the same question can be asked about "life from the dead," which will be addressed in chapter 16 (under the subsection "Romans 11") on the relation of resurrection and new creation to reconciliation.
19. See Gordon D. Fee, *God's Empowering Presence: The Holy Spirit in the Letters of Paul* (Peabody, MA: Hendrickson, 1994), 543, 552, 808–9.
20. E.g., Bruce M. Metzger, *A Textual Commentary on the Greek New Testament* (London: United Bible Societies, 1971), 517; the textual notes to the NET at Rom. 8:11; Schreiner, *Romans*, 417. Schreiner, in response to Fee (*God's Empowering Presence*), sees other passages in Paul's letters where the Spirit is viewed as the agent of resurrection life.

occur.[21] Likewise, 1:4 could be taken either way: "who was declared the Son of God with power by the resurrection from the dead, according to the Spirit of holiness, Jesus Christ our Lord." That the Spirit is the agent of resurrection in 8:11 is further pointed to in the light of 7:6 ("newness by means of the Spirit"), 8:13–14, and, above all, the background of Ezek. 37:1–14, which, I have argued, is alluded to in Rom. 6–8 and clearly portrays the Spirit as the agent of the end-time resurrection in its OT context. Furthermore, if being "led by the Spirit of God" in 8:14 begins at the commencement of resurrection life (which continues forever), then the Spirit should be seen here as the one "leading" people "from the dead" at this inceptive moment. The phrase in 8:13, "if by the Spirit you are putting to death the deeds of the body, you will live," views the Spirit as the agent of ongoing resurrection life; therefore it likely includes the commencement of such life. But even if 8:11 does not affirm that the Spirit is the agent of resurrection, the aforementioned texts from Rom. 8 do. Likewise, whether "the Spirit of life" is an appositional genitive ("Spirit which is life") or a genitive of destination or purpose ("the Spirit leading to life"), the Spirit is inextricably linked to resurrection life probably as its cause or source, which is close to agency. The same idea is supported also by other Pauline passages: 1 Cor. 15:45 ("life-giving Spirit"); 2 Cor. 3:6 ("the letter kills, but the Spirit gives life" [in beginning fulfillment of Ezek. 11:19; 36:26–27]); as well 2 Cor. 3:17–18; Gal. 5:25; Titus 3:5. Galatians 6:8 likely also sees the Spirit as the bestower of resurrection life (see also 1 Tim. 3:16; Rev. 11:11). One could also debate this idea in 1 Cor. 15:45; 2 Cor. 3:17–18; 1 Tim. 3:16, but my discussion below argues that these passages are also supportive. Interestingly, later, Judaism affirmed that "the Holy Spirit leads to the resurrection" (*m. Soṭah* 9.15).[22]

Resurrection in 1 Corinthians

All but two of Paul's references to resurrection in 1 Corinthians are in chapter 15:[23]

1 Cor. 15:4 "And that He was buried, and that He was raised on the third day according to the Scriptures."

1 Cor. 15:12 "Now if Christ is preached, that He has been raised from the dead, how do some among you say that there is no resurrection of the dead?"

21. This latter view is also expressed by Geerhardus Vos, "The Eschatological Aspect of the Pauline Conception of the Spirit," in *Redemptive History and Biblical Interpretation: The Shorter Writings of Geerhardus Vos*, ed. Richard B. Gaffin Jr. (Phillipsburg, NJ: P&R, 1980), 102.

22. On which, see further chap. 17 on "The Spirit as the Transforming Agent of the Inaugurated Eschatological New Creation" for the references in Judaism to the Spirit as the instrumentation of resurrection.

23. Those two are 1 Cor. 6:14 ("Now God has not raised the Lord, but will also raise us up through His power"); 9:1 ("Have I not seen Jesus our Lord?").

1 Cor. 15:13 "But if there is no resurrection of the dead, not even Christ has been raised."

1 Cor. 15:14 "And if Christ has not been raised, then our preaching is vain, your faith also is vain."

1 Cor. 15:15 "Moreover we are even found to be false witnesses of God, because we testified against God that He raised Christ, whom He did not raise, if in fact the dead are not raised."

1 Cor. 15:16 "For if the dead are not raised, not even Christ has been raised."

1 Cor. 15:17 "And if Christ has not been raised, your faith is worthless; you are still in your sins."

1 Cor. 15:20 "But now Christ has been raised from the dead, the first fruits of those who are asleep."

1 Cor. 15:21 "For since by a man came death, by a man also came the resurrection of the dead."

1 Cor. 15:29 "Otherwise, what will those do who are baptized for the dead? If the dead are not raised at all, why then are they baptized for them?"

1 Cor. 15:32 "If from human motives I fought with wild beasts at Ephesus, what does it profit me? If the dead are not raised, 'Let us eat and drink, for tomorrow we die.'"

1 Cor. 15:35 "But someone will say, 'How are the dead raised? And with what kind of body do they come?'"

1 Cor. 15:42 "So also is the resurrection of the dead. It is sown a perishable body, it is raised an imperishable body."

1 Cor. 15:43 "It is sown in dishonor, it is raised in glory; it is sown in weakness, it is raised in power."

1 Cor. 15:44 "It is sown a natural body, it is raised a spiritual body. If there is a natural body, there is also a spiritual body."

1 Cor. 15:45 "So also it is written, 'The first man, Adam, became a living soul.' The last Adam became a life-giving spirit."

1 Cor. 15:52 "In a moment, in the twinkling of an eye, at the last trumpet; for the trumpet will sound, and the dead will be raised imperishable, and we will be changed."

Most of the twenty-three references to resurrection in 1 Cor. 15 employ *egeirō* ("raise"), although *anastasis* ("resurrection" [vv. 12–13, 21]) and *zōopoieō* ("to give life" [vv. 22, 36, 45]) also occur. The references to resurrection here can be divided into five major movements of thought as follows:

(1) Christ's resurrection from the grave (vv. 3–11). Some commentators have acknowledged that behind the phrase "He was raised on the third day according to the Scriptures" lies Hos. 6:2: "He will revive us after two days; He will raise us up on the third day, that we may live before Him." If so, and

I think that it is likely,[24] then Paul sees the resurrection prophecy applied to Israel to have begun in Jesus, which may be an anticipation of his later comment in verse 23: "Christ the first fruits, after that those who are Christ's at His coming."

(2) The second movement of thought is that the assumption of the truth of Christ's resurrection necessitates belief in the general resurrection of the dead, which if denied means that the Christian faith is in vain (vv. 12–19).

(3) Third, despite skepticism among some, Christ's resurrection is a fact, which necessitates the resurrection of all who believe in him (vv. 20–23). His resurrection is "the first fruits" of all saints who will be resurrected at the end of the age. As we noted above in Rom. 8, "first fruits" in the OT were given to God to signify that the remainder of what was offered also belonged to God, and that this first part was but the beginning of more to come. So likewise in 1 Cor. 15:20–23, Christ's resurrection is referred to as "first fruits" to show not only that his resurrection is the first of more to come, but also that the additional future resurrections must necessarily come because they actually belong to Christ's resurrection itself; this is the meaning of the phrase "Christ the first fruits, after that those who are Christ's [i.e., those resurrected ones who are part of the remainder of Christ's first fruits resurrection] at his coming" (v. 23).

We have already seen in John 5:24–29 (in chap. 5) that the OT prophesied the last great resurrection as a one-time event, but this is fulfilled in staggered fashion: believers' spiritual resurrection followed later by physical resurrection. Now, Paul portrays another version of this notion of "staggered" resurrection fulfillment: the Messiah is physically raised first, and then later his people are raised physically. Remembering that the OT appeared to prophesy that all of God's people together were to be resurrected as part of one event, Paul views the prophecy of the end-time resurrection to begin fulfillment in Christ's physical resurrection, which necessitates that the saints' subsequent physical resurrection had to happen. In other words, the great event of the final resurrection had begun in Christ, but since that event was not completed in the resurrection of others, the completion of that prophesied event had to come at some point in the future.

(4) The fourth major movement of 1 Cor. 15 comes in verses 24–28. These verses affirm two things will happen at the time of "the end," when the resurrection of the saints finally happens. First, Christ will "deliver up the kingdom to the God and Father" (vv. 24, 28). Second, death "will be abolished," which indicates that the resurrection of the saints will be an irreversible, immortal condition (v. 26). There is also important comment in verses 25–27 about

24. Possibly Matt. 12:40 may be included in the background of Paul's statement: "So will the Son of Man be three days and three nights in the heart of the earth." However, this is a prediction of Jesus's death and not his resurrection, nor is it part of the "Scriptures" of the OT that Paul has in mind.

conditions leading up to the final resurrection: Christ "must reign until He has put all His enemies under His feet." In context, this reign begins at Jesus's resurrection and concludes at the time of the resurrection of his people. This is another instance where Paul directly connects resurrection as new creation with kingship (vv. 36–57 below link resurrection conceptually with new creation).

Paul views Christ's kingship during the interadvent age to be a fulfillment of Ps. 8:6: "For He has put all things in subjection under His feet" (v. 27). We have already seen that Ps. 8 is an "ideal Adam" psalm, which is one of the most explicit developments of Gen. 1:26–28 in all of the OT (see chap. 2). Psalm 8:6 itself is a development of Gen. 1:28: "fill the earth, and subdue it, and rule." Just as there was an enemy (the satanic serpent that could bring "death") to subdue in Eden as a part of the fulfillment of Gen. 1:28, so also Ps. 8:2 links the rule of the ideal Adam with "making the enemy and the revengeful cease." Likewise, Paul probably derives his statement about "abolishing death" as the "last enemy" from both Gen. 1–3 and Ps. 8:2–8. In this light, Paul is already anticipating his later explicit affirmation of Christ as "the last Adam" (v. 45). In this respect, we do not have to wait for the conceptual discussion of resurrection as new creation in verses 36–57, since the Ps. 8:6 reference in verse 27 already compares Christ as the eschatological Adamic king in the new creation to the first Adam, who was to rule in the first creation.

(5) The last significant development of 1 Cor. 15 is in verses 36–57. This segment expands on the implications of the earlier assertion that death "will be abolished" at the time of the consummate resurrection (v. 26). Just as there are relative degrees of glory in other parts of God's creation (vv. 38–41), the same is true of the crown of creation with respect to preconsummation bodies compared to the greater escalated conditions of postconsummation bodies (vv. 42–54), which have more glory and power and possess immortal life of the heavenly world. And just as Christ will complete his ongoing rule at the very end, so at the same time believers will be given "the victory through our Lord Jesus Christ" (v. 57), which should motivate them to live for the Lord during the interim period (v. 58).

In this last section Paul has been intent on comparing the perishable body with the imperishable resurrection body, though at verse 45 he quotes Gen. 2:7 and goes back beyond the first Adam's fallen, mortal body to the time when he had not yet sinned and become susceptible to death: "So also it is written, 'The first man, Adam, became a living soul.' The last Adam became a life-giving spirit." His point seems to be that even the first man did not have a glorious, immortal body like that of Jesus Christ and of those who will be resurrected in "the image of the heavenly" man, Jesus. The apparent point is that the first human was created to reach the goal of such a glorious, imperishable body, *if* he had obeyed God and been faithful in reflecting God's image and carrying out the mandate of Gen. 1:28 (on which I elaborated in the early part of chap. 2). In contrast to the first Adam, who failed because of faithless disobedience, Christ has subdued and obeyed in the way his progenitor should have. Consequently, Christ has inherited that for which humanity was originally destined but failed to reach. Jesus's body was not only a renewed physical body, but it had become a transformed "heavenly," "spiritual," and "imperishable" body.

In addition, Christ became a "life-giving Spirit" (v. 45b), which is an elaboration of Paul's similar earlier statement: "For as in Adam all die, so also in Christ all shall made alive" (v. 22). Christ as the progenitor, head, and "first fruits" of his eschatological people includes him having the ability to give them resurrection life like his own. That Christ had become the life-giving Spirit does not mean that Christ has become only a purely spiritual being or somehow become the Holy Spirit. Rather, the focus is on the notion that through his resurrection he has come to be identified with the life-giving function of the Spirit, and conversely, this is why elsewhere Paul can refer to the Spirit as the "Spirit of Jesus." The Spirit is a separate person from Jesus Christ, though also he is Christ's alter ego. The two have a oneness of function in terms of giving eschatological life, but they are still two distinct persons. The statement in verse 45b, "The last Adam [Christ] became a life-giving Spirit," is likely the equivalent of Acts 2:33, where Jesus was "exalted to the right hand of God, and . . . received from the Father the promise of the Holy Spirit," and then "poured forth" the Spirit on his people at Pentecost and subsequently on others in Acts.[25] We saw in chapter 2 that Christ's escalated resurrection condition is but one among others that Adam and the world would have experienced had he been faithful. Consequently, Christ does not merely return to Adam's prefall condition; rather, he goes beyond it and enables his people also to go beyond it.

The repeated references in verses 45–48 to the contrast between the first Adam in the first prefall creation and the last Adam enhances the notion that Christ's resurrected state is a new-creational state that has transcended the primordial prefall state. Hence, again we see that resurrection and new creation are two sides of one coin or that the former is a subset of the latter.

And again we see that Christ's resurrection as new creation is so closely linked to kingdom and Adam as a king[26] that the notions of resurrection as new creation and kingdom are inextricably linked.

---

25. Although 1 Cor. 15:45 needs much more explanation, there is insufficient space to do so here. For a superb analysis of this thorny verse, see Richard B. Gaffin Jr., "The Last Adam, the Life-Giving Spirit," in *The Forgotten Christ: Exploring the Majesty and Mystery of God Incarnate*, ed. Stephen Clark (Nottingham, UK: Apollos, 2007), 191–231, which I have tried to summarize above.

26. So see 1 Cor. 15:24–27 in connection to "Christ" (which recall means "anointed one" as king) as the last Adam (1 Cor. 15:21–22), which also carries with it the background of kingship in a beginning creation from Gen. 1:26–28 as developed in Ps. 8, which comes to the surface again in 1 Cor. 15:50, 54–57.

Resurrection in 2 Corinthians

References to resurrection are scattered throughout this letter.

References to Resurrection in 2 Corinthians 1–3

The first mention of resurrection occurs in 1:9–10: "Indeed, we had the sentence of death within ourselves in order that we should not trust in ourselves, but in God who raises the dead; who delivered us from so great a peril of death, and will deliver us, He on whom we have set our hope. And He will yet deliver us." God had delivered Paul and his companions from death in order that they would trust not in themselves but in God, "who raises the dead." In fact, their "trust" and "hope" in God in this context are specifically focused on God's ability to raise the dead in the future, which will be the ultimate manner by which God "will deliver" them physically in the future.

Paul soon makes it evident that this future resurrection at the end of the age has already begun (2:14–16):

> But thanks be to God, who always leads us in triumph in Christ, and manifests through us the sweet aroma of the knowledge of Him in every place. For we are a fragrance of Christ to God among those who are being saved and among those who are perishing; to the one an aroma from death to death, to the other an aroma from life to life. And who is adequate for these things?

The "triumph" in which God "leads" Paul and that exudes "the sweet aroma of the knowledge" of God includes "a fragrance of Christ to God among those who are being saved," which Paul further says is "an aroma from life [zōē] to life [zōē]," a probable reference to resurrection life. Here we see a likely link, if not virtual equation, between "being saved" and "life" (it may even be "from [inaugurated resurrection] life to [consummative resurrection] life"). Paul asks about "who is adequate" for being a servant through whom God manifests such "life." He answers this question in 3:5–6:

> Not that we are adequate in ourselves to consider anything as coming from ourselves, but our adequacy is from God, who also made us adequate as servants of a new covenant, not of the letter but of the Spirit; for the letter kills, but the Spirit gives life.

Only God can make his servants "adequate" for this life-giving ministry, which can be effective only through "the Spirit," the "Spirit of the living God" (3:3), who brings people out from under "the ministry of death" and "makes alive" (3:6–7). This is in beginning fulfillment of Ezek. 11:19; 36:26–27; 37:14, which prophesy the spiritual resurrection life of Israel by God's Spirit (to which allusion is made in 2 Cor. 3:3), which would restore them from exile into God's presence.[27] Particularly in mind is Ezek. 37:6, 14 LXX, where God says, "I will put my Spirit into you and you will live" (see also the Hebrew text of 37:5, 14).[28] This latter statement shows further that the "life" of 2 Cor. 2:16 is not a mere general lifestyle reference to people who exist in the present world but rather is a specific allusion to the resurrection life that commences with belief (i.e., "whenever a person turns to the Lord" [2 Cor. 3:16]). This resurrection "transformation" (*metamorphoō*) into the divine "image" that begins with belief and occurs through the Spirit's work continues throughout the Christian's existence (2 Cor. 3:17–18):

> Now the Lord is the Spirit, and where the Spirit of the Lord is, there is liberty. But we all, with unveiled face, beholding as in a mirror the glory of the Lord, are being transformed into the same image from glory to glory, just as from the Lord, the Spirit.

That resurrection existence is in mind in these two verses is apparent in that the combination of "transformation" language together with the use of "image" (*eikōn*) also occurs in 1 Cor. 15:49–54, where it is clear that resurrection transformation is in mind, though there it is the resurrection at the end of the age. In addition, the reference to the "Spirit" as an essential condition for "liberty" (*eleutheria*) also points to resurrection, since the Spirit is similarly seen in Romans as the agent of resurrection, leading to "the freedom [*eleutheria*] of the glory of the children of God" (Rom. 8:21; cf. 8:11, 22–23).

It is important to remember that the purpose of the discussion in 2 Cor. 2:14–3:18 is to underscore the authority of Paul as God's true apostle. Paul does not need "letters of commendation" from human sources, whether the Corinthians or others, to attest to his unique prophetic authority (3:1). Indeed, the very existence of the Corinthians as those who had become Christians through Paul's ministry was telltale evidence to all already that God had worked in them through him as a prophet. Thus, their very existence as Christians was the only "letter from Christ" that was needed to commend Paul's divine authority (3:2–3). And it is not merely their existence as Christians that composes such a "letter"; it is their essential being as those who had begun to experience resurrection life that is the content of this redemptive-historical eschatological "letter" from Christ (and the "letter" is "from Christ" [*Christou*, a genitive of source or agency] because it is Christ's Spirit who raised them from the dead).

27. Note Ezek. 11:19: "And I will give them one heart, and put a new spirit within them. And I will take the heart of stone out of their flesh and give them a heart of flesh"; and Ezek. 36:26–27: "Moreover, I will give you a new heart and put a new spirit within you; and I will remove the heart of stone from your flesh and give you a heart of flesh. And I will put my Spirit within you."
28. Yates (*Spirit and Creation*, 109–13) sees the same allusion in 2 Cor. 3:18.

Thus, early on in 2 Corinthians Paul views the resurrection life of believers to be a major pillar supporting his defense of his apostolic authority, a notion with which he also concludes the letter (on which, see below). The questioning of this authority is what provides the occasion for him to take up his pen to write the letter.

References to Resurrection in 2 Corinthians 4

The transition from death to life is continued in 2 Cor. 4. There the "gospel is veiled . . . to those who are <u>perishing</u>," whose "minds" have been "blinded . . . in order that the light of the gospel of the glory of Christ, who is the image of God, should not shine" upon them (4:3–4). In contrast, God's servants are those who have experienced the light of the new creation: "For God, who said, 'Light shall shine out of darkness,' is the One who has shone in our hearts to give the Light of the knowledge of the glory of God in the face of Christ" (4:6). In view of believers' later identification in 5:14–17 with Christ's resurrection as the beginning fulfillment of OT new-creational prophecies, it is likely evident here that Paul also has in mind new creation as a recapitulation of the light shining in the first creation. The new creation begins in the same way as the first creation: the irresistible light of God irrupts upon the darkness, which anticipates Paul's formal reference to "new creation" in 5:17. Paul presumably understands that the inception of the first creation is a typological foreshadowing of the way the new creation commences.

The phrase "to give the light of the knowledge of the glory of God" may refer not to believers understanding the revelation of Christ but rather to believers who have had light "shone in their hearts" so that they themselves become agents of "giving the light" to others. This may be an autobiographical allusion to Paul's own experience of Jesus's resurrection on the Damascus Road, where God shone light in his heart, which virtually simultaneously became a commission for him to take this light to the nations. If this allusion is correct, then it is another feature pointing to 4:4–6 as a conceptual reference to the revelatory effect of Christ's resurrection as a new creation.[29] The reference to "the glory of Christ" as "the image of God" (4:4) develops the mention of Christians being "transformed into the same image from glory to glory" (3:18), which we saw was inextricably linked to resurrection existence. Could there be a link with Isa. 9:1–2 in the phrase in 4:6, "light shall shine"? The actual phrase appears only in the Greek of Isa. 9:1–2, not in Genesis or in Paul's Damascus Road encounter. The imagery is mostly from Genesis, but the language itself is that of Isaiah. If there is an Isaiah allusion here, it might

29. For elaboration of and support for the ideas in this paragraph, see Seyoon Kim, *The Origin of Paul's Gospel* (Grand Rapids: Eerdmans, 1982), 5–11, 231–33.

be a further way of linking 4:6 with the Isaianic new-creational text in 5:17[30] (to be discussed in the next chapter).

In 4:7–18 Paul elaborates on how this new-creational resurrection existence impacts the ongoing life of saints. God's people have a "treasure in earthen vessels." The likely antecedent of this "treasure" is the possession of "the glory of [the risen] Christ" and his "image" as the progenitor of newly created humanity.[31] The reason why God designed the treasure to be encased in frail human receptacles is that "the surpassing greatness of the power [*dynamis*] will be of God and not from ourselves" (4:7). The reference to "power" is not a nebulous allusion to divine power in general but rather a direct allusion to God's power expressed in raising Christ from the dead. This is apparent from observing that the same word for divine "power" (*dynamis*) together with the notion of human bodily weakness occurs twice later in 2 Corinthians to refer to the power of Christ's resurrection that is designed to work through weak human believers:

And He has said to me, "My grace is sufficient for you, for power is perfected in weakness." Most gladly, therefore, I will rather boast about my weaknesses, that the power of Christ may dwell in me. (12:9)

For indeed He was crucified because of weakness, yet He lives because of the power of God. For we also are weak in Him, yet we will live with Him because of the power of God directed toward you. (13:4)

Significantly, the "power" alluded to in 12:9 is clearly explained in 13:4 to be the "living" resurrection "power of God" in Christ that is the basis of believers "living with Christ."[32] Thus, the same understanding of God's "power" is expressed in 4:7.[33] Such resurrection power demonstrates itself by enabling Christians not to be "crushed" though they are "afflicted," not to "despair" though they are "perplexed," not to be "destroyed" though they are "struck down" (4:8–9). This is another example of how inaugurated eschatological resurrection conveys not merely analogical truth but rather a reality in which Christians participate and is crucial for practical living because it fuels such living.

The reason why such trials do not annihilate Christians is that they are "always carrying about in the body the dying of Jesus, so that the life of Jesus also may

30. This observation comes from my research student Dan Brendsel.
31. See 4:4, which is repeated at the end of 4:6; cf. Col. 2:3, the only other occurrence of "treasure" (*thesaurus*) in Paul's writings, where in Christ "are hidden all the treasures of wisdom and knowledge."
32. In line with Phil. 3:10: "that I may know Him and the power of His resurrection and the fellowship of His sufferings, being conformed to His death."
33. In fact, note that Eph. 1:19–20 uses almost the same Greek phrase (*to hyperballon megethos tēs dynameōs*) as in 2 Cor. 4:7, "the surpassing [greatness] of the power" (*hē hyperbolē tēs dynameōs*) to indicate the power of God demonstrated through Christ's resurrection.

be manifested in our body" (4:10).[34] The comparison here to Christ's "dying" and the "life of Jesus" is not mere analogy. Rather, they are truly and really identified with Jesus's death and resurrection, as I have argued in Rom. 6 and 1 Cor. 15 and will argue again in 2 Cor. 5:14–17.[35] This means that they really have begun to die to the old cosmos through their identification with Christ's death, and they have begun to live in the new order through their union with his resurrection. Although they have not yet physically died and been raised, they have begun to do so in a literal yet nonmaterial sense. And the ironic apostolic ministry whereby Christ's risen life is manifested in the midst of suffering results in others sharing in this eschatological "life" ("So death works in us, but life in you" [4:12]). Paul repeats virtually the same idea in 5:14–15 ("all died . . . so that they might live"); 6:9 ("as dying yet behold, we live"); 7:3 ("I have said before that you are in our hearts to die together and to live together") (see also 3:2–6).

In 4:13 Paul cites the LXX of Ps. 116:10 ("I believed, therefore I spoke") and says that he has "the same spirit of faith" that the psalmist had in making his statement. Following the model of the psalmist, Paul says, "We also believe, therefore we also speak" (4:13b). What do this verse and the appeal to the psalm have to do with Paul's focus in the preceding section on identification with Christ's death and resurrection life, and how does this affect the believer's life? The answer is not hard to find when one looks at the context of the psalm. The content of the psalmist's "I believed" is not merely that he said, "I am greatly afflicted" (that was not hard for him to believe),[36] but that God would deliver him in the midst of his dire trials that are associated with death, which is the major thematic thread running throughout Ps. 116:1–9. In fact, just as Paul has twice contrasted "life" (*zōē/zaō*) with "death" (*thanatos*) in 4:11–12, so also twice the psalmist (in the LXX) makes the contrast between "life" (*zōē/zaō*) and "death" (*thanatos*) (vv. 2–4, 8–9).[37]

Thus, both the psalmist and Paul "believe" that in the midst of afflictions connected to death God gives or preserves life. Because of the progressive

34. Verse 11 virtually reiterates the same thing, and likely so does 6:9 ("as dying yet behold, we live").

35. Note 5:14–15: "One died for all, therefore all died; and He died for all, so that they who live might no longer live for themselves, but for Him who died and rose again on their behalf."

36. The Hebrew text of Ps. 116:10 has "I believed when I said" with the following "I am greatly afflicted" as the content of the speech, whereas the LXX (Ps. 115:1) has "I believed, therefore I spoke," so that the primary content of what is spoken is the preceding two verses: "He has delivered my soul from death. . . . I will be well-pleasing before the Lord in the land of the living" (Ps. 114:8–9 LXX). The ultimate difference of meaning in the wider context is negligible. (The LXX divides the Hebrew psalm into two psalms but the continuity of the context of the one Hebrew psalm continues.)

37. Verses 8–9 of the psalm (Ps. 114 LXX) read, "He has delivered my soul from death [*thanatos*]. . . . I will be well-pleasing [*euaresteō*] before the Lord in the land of the living [*zaō*]," which may anticipate Paul's reference to "pleasing" (*euarestos*) the Lord in connection to resurrection living in 2 Cor. 5:9.

revelatory redemptive work of Christ at "the ends of the ages" (cf. 1 Cor. 10:11; 2 Cor. 1:20), Paul escalates the object of the psalmist's belief into a belief in Christ's resurrection. That is, since the apostle believes in inaugurated resurrection existence, he speaks of such existence (4:7–12). Paul's "faithful speaking" about this initial form of end-time existence leads him to affirm that "He who raised the Lord Jesus will raise us also with Jesus and will present us with you" (4:14).[38] Paul's confidence that believers are already truly participating in Christ's resurrection life as regenerated beings prompts him to conclude that such life will be consummated at the very end in the form of physical regeneration for all. The reason why Paul wants to affirm this resurrection faith is that the spreading of this message about resurrection and its reality will lead to "the giving of thanks . . . to the glory of God" (4:15).

The apostle returns to speaking of incipient resurrection living in 4:16–18 and, as in 3:18, refers to it as transformation:

> Therefore we do not lose heart, but though our outer man is decaying, yet our inner man is being renewed day by day. For momentary, light affliction is producing for us an eternal weight of glory far beyond all comparison, while we look not at the things which are seen, but at the things which are not seen; for the things which are seen are temporal, but the things which are not seen are eternal.

On the basis that believers' latter-day resurrection has begun and will be consummated bodily in the future (4:7–15), Paul concludes ("therefore") that "we do not lose heart" and gives the reason for this courage: "Though our outer man is decaying, yet our inner man is being <u>renewed</u> [*anakainoō*] day by day." This is transformative new-creational language that continues the similar themes not only of 3:18 but also of 4:6, where the "creative light" terminology of Gen. 1:3 is applied to saints.

The only other use of this verb for "renew" (*anakainoō*) in the NT occurs in Col. 3:10, which likely sheds light on the meaning: "And you have donned the clothes of the new man who is being renewed [*anakainoō*] to a true knowledge according to the image of the One who created him." This verse contrasts with the one before it, where believers are said to have "disrobed [themselves of] the old man" (Col. 3:9). The reference is to being corporately identified no longer with the old Adam but rather with the new Adam, Jesus Christ. Paul tells the Colossians that they have only begun to take on this identity, with the result that "the new man . . . is [progressively] being renewed . . . according to the image of the One [who newly] created him," until the final day of the consummation. Ephesians 4:22–24 is an almost identical parallel with Col. 3:9–10 ("putting off the old man" and "donning the clothes of the

---

38. I take the adverbial participle *eidotes* ("knowing") at the beginning of v. 14 to indicate the result of "believing and speaking" in v. 13, though it could be the cause of it or even the explanation of the object of the faith expressed in the preceding verse.

new [*kainos*] man, which according to [the image of] God has been created"). Similarly Eph. 2:15, "that He might create one new man in Him [Christ]," shows that in Ephesians the "new man" exists corporately in Christ, and the "old man" there is likely the antithesis, the old Adam. So likewise, we have previously seen that Rom. 6:4 refers to the saints' resurrection life as "newness of life" and presents its antithesis to be the "old man" who "was crucified" (Rom. 6:6) (cf. Rom. 7:6: "newness of ['from' or 'by'] the Spirit").

In this light, the "renewal" of "the inner man" in 2 Cor. 4:16 is an anticipation of 2 Cor. 5:14–17, where believers' identification with Jesus's resurrection is said to be a "new creation" (*kainē ktisis*), though not yet consummated (the same phrase is applied to believers in Gal. 6:15).[39] Likewise, 2 Cor. 4:16 probably has the same focus, and my earlier proposal that it develops 3:18 and 4:4–6 is further indicated in that in both of these texts "image" and "glory" are spoken of synonymously, so that the reference to "glory" in 4:17 continues the notion.

In 2 Cor. 4:17 Paul gives a second basis for persevering in not "losing heart," and it is an interpretation of the first basis given at the end of 4:16 ("though our outer man is decaying, yet our inner man is being renewed day by day"): "For momentary, light affliction is producing for us an eternal weight of glory far beyond all comparison." The "eternal weight of glory" is in the process of being produced and refers to the glorious image of the "inner new Adamic man" that is being renewed until the final end of history. The renewal takes place, ironically, through persevering faith in the face of trial and bodily weakness. Paul explains in 4:18 that this ongoing, everlasting renewal cannot be seen with human eyes, but only with the eyes of faith.

References to Resurrection in 2 Corinthians 5

In 2 Cor. 5:1–10 Paul continues the focus on resurrection but returns once again to the future bodily raising of the dead and then back again to the inaugurated reality of this eschatological resurrection.

> For we know that if the earthly tent which is our house is torn down, we have a building from God, a house not made with hands, eternal in the heavens. For indeed in this house we groan, longing to be clothed with our dwelling from heaven; inasmuch as we, when we are clothed, shall not be found naked. For indeed while we are in this tent, we groan, being burdened, because we do not want to be unclothed, but to be clothed, in order that what is mortal may be swallowed up by life. Now He who prepared us for this very purpose is God, who gave to us the Spirit as a down payment. Therefore, being always of good courage, and knowing that while we are at home in the body we are absent from the Lord—for we walk by faith, not by sight—we are of good courage,

---

39. We will wait to analyze these two new creation texts in the next two chapters, since they are so significant for our argument.

I say, and prefer rather to be absent from the body and to be at home with the Lord. Therefore we also have as our ambition, whether at home or absent, to be pleasing to Him. For we must all appear before the judgment seat of Christ, that each one may be recompensed for his deeds in the body, according to what he has done, whether good or bad.

The "earthly tent" in verse 1 refers to the believer's mortal body that will eventually suffer corruption (be "torn down"). After death, however, Christians will "have a building from God, a house not made with hands, eternal in the heavens" (v. 1). This refers to their future resurrection and transformation into becoming part of the new "heavens" and earth, which, we will see, is equated with becoming part of the temple of God. The notion of the "clothing" being the final resurrection is clear from verse 4. That Paul has a temple image in view[40] is apparent from the phrase "not made with hands," which virtually everywhere else is a technical way of speaking about the new eschatological temple.[41] In addition, the references to "building" (v. 1), "house" (v. 1), and "dwelling" (v. 2) occur elsewhere in the NT with respect to Israel's temple or the church as the temple.[42]

This introduction of the notion of the temple as part of the explanation of the resurrection may appear surprising at first glance. However, we will see in a following chapter that resurrection as a new creation fits admirably with the idea of the temple. For example, the OT temple was symbolic of the cosmos, including the coming new cosmos, and partly for this reason Christ says that his own resurrection, which we have seen as the beginning of new creation, was the establishment of the end-time temple. Consequently, it would be natural also to identify the believer's resurrection as being part of a temple here in 2 Cor. 5. Portraying the church as the latter-day temple of God anticipates the even more explicit depiction of the same thing not far away in 6:16–18 (on which, see chap. 19 below).

Although the readers will be "swallowed up by [resurrection] life" at the end of the age (2 Cor. 5:4), such "life" was already at "work" in them

40. See E. Earle Ellis, "II Corinthians V.1–10 in Pauline Eschatology," *NTS* 6 (1960): 217–18. Ellis is a leading proponent of the view that Paul has in mind the church as a temple here, though his notion that in 5:1–4 the temple is a present reality is questionable.

41. For discussion of this phrase and like expressions, see G. K. Beale, *The Temple and the Church's Mission: A Biblical Theology of the Dwelling Place of God*, NSBT 17 (Downers Grove, IL: InterVarsity, 2004), 222–27. The relevant texts are Exod. 15:17; Isa. 66:1–2; Dan. 2:34, 45 LXX; Mark 14:58; Acts 7:48–49; 17:24; Heb. 9:11, 24; *Sib. Or.* 4:11; Euripides, *Fragment* 968 (on which, see F. F. Bruce, *The Book of the Acts*, NICNT [Grand Rapids: Eerdmans, 1954], 357). Colossians 2:11 refers to "circumcision made without hands."

42. "Building" (*oikodomē*) refers to Israel's temple (Matt. 24:1; Mark 13:1–2) or to the church as the temple (1 Cor. 3:9; Eph. 2:21); Paul does not use "house" (*oikos*) anywhere else to refer to the temple, though the word has this reference elsewhere in the OT (e.g., 2 Sam. 7:6–7, 13) and the NT (e.g., Luke 19:46; 1 Pet. 2:5); "dwelling" (*oikētērion*) appears outside of 2 Corinthians only in Jude, without reference to the temple, but its synonym (*katoikētērion*), used once by Paul, refers to the church as the temple in Eph. 2:22.

(2 Cor. 4:12). Just as the Spirit is linked to the origin of the resurrection life of faith, not only in Rom. 8 but also in 2 Cor. 4:12–13, so here the Spirit is the "down payment" for the future consummation of resurrection life (2 Cor. 5:5).[43]

The Spirit himself is the beginning evidence of the new creation, wherein is resurrection existence and the abode of the cosmic temple. In 2 Cor. 5:5 Paul says that God, "who prepared us for this very purpose" of receiving resurrection life and becoming a part of the eternal temple, "gave to us the Spirit as a down payment" of these realities. The Spirit is not merely an anticipation or promise of these realities but rather is the beginning form of them, which is what "down payment" clearly connotes in ancient and modern times (a payment of part of a larger sum, the remainder of which is paid later).[44] This is made clearer in 2 Cor. 1:20–22: "the promises of God [from the OT] in Him [Christ] . . . are yes," which means that they have begun fulfillment in Christ's first coming. Paul then says that God "establishes us with you in Christ . . . and gave us the Spirit in our hearts as a down payment." That is, the Spirit is the beginning evidence that the latter-day promises have begun to be realized in Christ and his people, since it is the Spirit who is the agent who causes those who trust in the risen Christ to become identified with him existentially and thus also identified with participating in the beginning fulfillment of those same promises that Christ has begun to fulfill. The Spirit is "the first fruits" of the future "redemption of our body" (Rom. 8:23). Likewise, Eph. 1:13–14 asserts that believers have been "sealed" with the promised Holy Spirit, who is the "down payment" of the full "inheritance" to come at the end of the age.

It is appropriate that the process of resurrection "renewal" (2 Cor. 4:16) is equated with a process of building up glory (4:17), since the temple was the proper place throughout history for the abode of glory, where also the image of God was ideally to abide to reflect the divine glory (as was the case originally with Adam in his Edenic sanctuary).[45] Now, God's glory appropriately resides in Christ, the last Adam and image of God, who perfectly reflects God's glory in the end-time temple, and this glory is reflected among those in Christ, who are now also a part of the new temple. Paul says as much in 1 Cor. 6:19–20: "Or do you not know that your body is a temple of the Holy Spirit . . . ? Therefore glorify God in your body." This glory would perfectly be reflected in the temple of the new creation

43. So also Scott J. Hafemann, *2 Corinthians*, NIVAC (Grand Rapids: Zondervan, 2000), 186–87.

44. In Hellenistic Greek the word *arrabōn* can refer to "an 'earnest,' or a part given in advance of what will be bestowed fully afterwards" (MM 79); e.g., the word can refer to a down payment to someone to perform a commercial task, and after the task is accomplished the remainder of the promised money is paid.

45. On which, see Beale, *Temple*, 81–122.

throughout eternity (e.g., Rev. 21:11; cf. 15:8). Since the new temple that has already sprung into existence is, unlike the old one, "not made with hands," likewise neither can it be seen as the old temple could: "The things which are seen are temporal, but the things which are not seen are eternal" (2 Cor. 4:18; cf. 5:7).

On the basis that the Spirit is the beginning down payment ("therefore," *oun* [5:6]), the Corinthians are to have a "courageous spirit," most likely in not being discouraged and "groaning" (5:2, 4) at the bodily "decay" that has set in and in facing the "afflictions" that confront them (cf. 4:16–17). That is, although they suffer trial on earth, they can receive comfort that they are already experiencing the life of the age to come. Despite this, it is also true that while they are "at home in the body," they are not yet "home" with the Lord (they are "absent [or 'exiled'] from the Lord") (5:6). They have to "walk by faith, not by appearance" in order to act on the unseen reality of the initial form of their resurrection life, which they are to trust will be consummated physically in the future (5:7). An expression of such trust in unseen things results in "good courage" (5:8a), which looks to the even greater though still preconsummate blessing of the intermediate state, which Paul prefers over the earthly state, where resurrection life has begun (5:8b). The apostle apparently sees this interim state as a further escalation of the resurrection condition that has been commenced on earth (as John also likely does in Rev. 20:4).[46] God's people should desire to please him regardless of whichever eschatological condition they find themselves in, since the beginning end-time realities fuel their courage on earth or comfort them in the preconsummate heavenly existence. In other words, the practical exhortation to "please" God is grounded in recognizing already–not yet eschatological realities, especially of resurrection and of the temple, and acting by faith in those unseen realities.

Paul concludes this first paragraph of 2 Cor. 5 with another reference to the future, final resurrection, which provides another basis for why the Corinthians should be motivated to please God: "For we must all appear before the judgment seat of Christ, that each one may be recompensed for his deeds in the body, according to what he has done, whether good or bad" (5:10). There must be a bodily resurrection (all must "appear before . . . Christ") of both the believing and the unbelieving (the latter of which commingle in the covenant community) in order that true saints will be rewarded for their deeds in the body and pseudosaints will be judged for their sinful works done on earth. Both must be resurrected to receive their due in bodily form for what they had committed in their physical bodies. Those who desire to please God in Christ now should be motivated to continue to do so, looking forward to

---

46. On which, see G. K. Beale, *The Book of Revelation: A Commentary on the Greek Text*, NIGTC (Grand Rapids: Eerdmans, 1999), 972–1026.

their reward from their heavenly Father ("Well done, good and faithful servant" [Matt. 25:21, 23]).[47]

In 5:11–13 Paul affirms that on the basis of the preceding point (courageous living through affliction by faith, not by sight, in resurrection reality as a foundation for pleasing God), the readers should evaluate his apostleship by faith and not "appearance," since he himself walks by faith and not sight and perseveres through suffering in order to be pleasing to God.

Then 5:14–17 launches off into another section, as I have already said, once again identifying Christians with Christ's death and resurrection, which explicitly is referred to as a "new creation." Since this section of the letter is so significant for the present book, I will address it independently in the next chapter.

The Reference to Resurrection at the Climax of 2 Corinthians

The last reference to resurrection comes at the end of the book in support of Paul's apostolic authority, which is the main point that Paul wants to demonstrate throughout 2 Corinthians (13:3–4):

> Since you are seeking for proof of the Christ who speaks in me, and who is not weak toward you, but mighty in you. For indeed He was crucified because of weakness, yet He lives because of the power of God. For we also are weak in Him, but toward you we will live with Him because of the power of God.

Just as Christ died in weakness yet lived because of God's power in raising him from the dead, so too Paul and his circle are weak yet "will live" in the midst of the Corinthians with Christ because of the power of God.[48] That Paul is speaking not merely of the final resurrection but rather of the present resurrection life is further apparent from verse 5, where Paul challenges the hearers to "test" themselves about whether "Jesus Christ is in you"—that is, the risen Christ. Thus, the way one evaluates rightly Paul's apostolic authority is not to reject Paul because he appears "weak" according to human standards (cf. 2 Cor. 10:10; 11:6) but instead to discern that he is a prophet who, like Jesus, perseveres courageously through affliction and weakness yet has experienced the resurrecting power of God, which will be completed at Christ's final coming.

47. Here I cannot comment on the nature of the reward, though suffice it now to say that elsewhere Paul affirms that the outcome for true faith at the end of time is salvation, not any "reward" in addition to salvation.

48. Although some understand the future tense "we will live" to refer to the very end of time and the final resurrection, Victor Paul Furnish (II Corinthians, AB 32A [New York: Doubleday, 1984], 568, 571) argues that the future tense "will live" is either a logical future or an imminent future, alluding to Paul's impending visit to the readers (whose translation of v. 4b I have also followed above: "toward you we will live"); alternatively, it could refer to the general future from the time Paul was writing, which would be close to a gnomic future.

Consequently, the already–not yet resurrection is a basis at points throughout the letter and especially at its climax for offering proof of Paul's prophetic authority, which some in the Corinthian church were doubting.

Resurrection in Galatians

Galatians has few explicit references to resurrection, but the concept forms the two bookends of the letter. Galatians is the only NT letter or book that begins in its first verse with a reference to Jesus's resurrection:[49] "Paul, an apostle, not sent from men nor through the agency of man, but through Jesus Christ, and God the Father, who <u>raised Him from the dead</u>" (1:1). The letter concludes with reference to resurrection through the language of "new creation": "For neither is circumcision anything, nor uncircumcision, but a new creation" (6:15). Fuller analysis of this verse must wait for a following chapter, which will elaborate on resurrection as the beginning of the new creation, in fulfillment of Isaiah's prophecies of the coming new cosmos. The point here is that this notion frames the letter, which indicates its importance for an understanding of the entire letter. This is clear in view of the generally acknowledged notion that Paul's epistolary introductions contain the themes to be developed throughout a letter,[50] and that his epistolary conclusions function to summarize the main points of what he has written throughout.[51] The first mention of resurrection in the body of Galatians is 2:19–20:

> For through the Law I died to the Law, that I might live to God. I have been crucified with Christ; and it is no longer I who live, but Christ lives in me; and the life which I now live in the flesh I live by faith in the Son of God, who loved me and delivered Himself up for me.

Although the word "resurrection" (the noun *anastasis* or its verbal form) does not occur, the verb "live" (*zaō*) does, which we have seen in other of Paul's letters to be a synonym for resurrection life. And, as we have also seen repeatedly in Paul's writings, when there is mention of being identified with Christ's death (as here, "crucified with Christ"), the contrast is with "life," an identification with Christ's life, which can be only his ongoing resurrection life (as here, "Christ lives in me . . . I live by faith in the son of God").

---

49. Romans is similar, since Christ's resurrection is mentioned in the introduction at 1:4.

50. For this function in Paul's introductory thanksgivings, see Peter T. O'Brien, *Introductory Thanksgivings in the Letters of Paul*, NovTSup 49 (Leiden: Brill, 1977). Although Galatians does not contain giving of thanks, the introduction there functions similarly as a general preview of the themes to come.

51. See Jeffrey A. D. Weima, *Neglected Endings: The Significance of the Pauline Letter Closings*, JSNTSup 101 (Sheffield: Sheffield Academic Press, 1994), where Galatians is probably to be seen as the clearest example of the thesis set forth by Weima.

The insertion of "now" ("and the life which I now [*nyn*] live in the flesh") is a temporal reference to the end-time turn of the ages that had invaded Paul's own being.[52] This likely expresses part of Paul's understanding that the final resurrection that was prophesied to come at the end of the world had already broken in with Christ's death and resurrection and with all those who are identified with Christ's death and resurrection. The same pattern of the believer's identification with Christ's death and resurrection occurs later in 5:24–25:

> Now those who belong to Christ Jesus have crucified the flesh with its passions and desires. If we live by the Spirit, let us also walk by the Spirit.

To "live by the Spirit" refers to the Spirit as the agent of the life of the new age, which those "who belong to Christ Jesus" possess because they are identified not only with his death but also with his life from the dead. The law cannot be the agent that "makes alive" (3:21), but only the Spirit, who "leads" (5:18) one to "faith in Christ," can produce the fruit of faithfulness and godliness (5:22–23; see also 3:21–22). Ongoing resurrection life occurs "by means of the Spirit" (5:25).[53] And as noted above, Paul finishes the letter by identifying this resurrection life with "a new creation," which again is a contrast with identification with Christ's death in 6:14.

This beginning life of the new end-time epoch will be consummated physically, again by means of the Spirit, at the very end of the present age: "The one who sows to the Spirit shall from the Spirit reap eternal life" (6:8).

In chapter 10 we will look at the rhetorical and ethical function of Paul's references to the inaugurated resurrection and new creation in Gal. 5–6, but here I will reflect briefly on the role that the apostle's allusion to the final resurrection plays. This is seen by observing the two verses following 6:8:

> Let us not lose heart in doing good, for in due time we will reap if we do not grow weary. So then, while we have opportunity, let us do good to all people, and especially to those who are of the household of the faith.

Paul underscores here that Christians should "not lose heart" and "not grow weary" in "doing good" in the present, since their efforts surely will be culminated in final, physical resurrection, just referred to in verse 8. This is very similar to 1 Cor. 15, where the extended elaboration about the final resurrection of saints is the basis for them to "be steadfast, immovable, always abounding in the work of the Lord, knowing that your toil is not in vain in the Lord" (v. 58).

52. The majority of Paul's uses of "now" (*nyn*) indicate the time of the eschatological turn of the ages; e.g., note the most explicit illustrations in Rom. 13:11; 16:26; 2 Cor. 6:2; Eph. 3:5, 10; Col. 1:26; 2 Tim. 1:10; see also John 4:23; 5:25; 1 John 2:18; 4:3.

53. A further indication that the "living" of 5:25 is new-creational life is that the word for "walk" in 5:25 and 6:15–16 is the unusual word *stoicheō*.

The point is that when one knows in the midst of battle that future victory is assured, such assurance causes the imminently victorious combatant to have all the more motivation to fight. It is the same with the Christian's fight against sin and against the various obstacles necessarily faced in this fallen world.

Resurrection in Ephesians[54]

The first mention of resurrection is in 1:20–22:

> . . . which He brought about in Christ, when He raised Him from the dead and seated Him at His right hand in the heavenlies, far above all rule and authority and power and dominion, and every name that is named, not only in this age but also in the one to come. And He put all things in subjection under His feet, and gave Him as head over all things to the church, which is His body, the fullness of Him who fills all in all.

What one first notices is that Christ's resurrection placed him in a position of heavenly rule. This is described as an already–not yet rule ("not only in this age but also in the one to come"). Christ's resurrected kingship is said to be a beginning fulfillment of the ideal eschatological Adam's reign projected in Ps. 8 ("You have put all things under his feet" [8:6]). Psalm 8:6 is a direct development of Gen. 1:26–28. Here Paul identifies Christ's resurrected existence as the rule in a new creation that was anticipated in the psalm. This is striking when we recall, as I began to argue at the beginning of this book with respect to Gen. 1–2 and its development elsewhere in the OT, that kingship and new creation went hand in hand.[55] And we have already observed elsewhere in the NT that Christ's resurrection was identified with his kingdom rule and new creation (recalling that resurrection itself is the essence of new creation for humanity).[56]

Paul goes on in Eph. 2 to identify believers with Christ's resurrection and kingship: God "made us alive together with Christ . . . and raised us up with Him, and seated us with Him in the heavenly places in Christ Jesus" (2:5b–6). Then they are immediately identified as being a new creation in Christ: "We are his creation [poiēma], created [ktizō] in Christ Jesus for good works" (2:10); "in Himself He might make [ktizō] the two into one new man" (2:15b). The "new man" (kainos anthrōpos) is Christ, the new corporate, representative,

---

54. In this book I assume that Paul wrote all the epistles traditionally attributed to him, including, in this case, Ephesians, to which his name is attributed. Since the scope of the present project does not allow space to argue in favor of such Pauline authorship, on this topic, see further D. A. Carson and Douglas J. Moo, *An Introduction to the New Testament*, 2nd ed. (Grand Rapids: Zondervan, 2005).

55. See, e.g., the discussion of Gen. 1–2 and Ps. 8 in chap. 2.

56. See, e.g., chap. 8.

eschatological Adam, with whom believers are identified or unified. This same notion is picked up again later in 4:22–24:

> . . . that, in reference to your former manner of life, you lay aside the old man, which is being corrupted in accordance with the lusts of deceit, and that you be renewed in the spirit of your mind, and put on the new man, which in the likeness of God has been created in righteousness and holiness of the truth.

If it is clear from 2:15 that the "new man" is the believer's position in the corporate representative Messiah, then the same is likely the case in 4:24, though the stress there may be on the side of the saints' existential link to that position. Alternatively, if this is correct, then the "old man" designates, at the least, one's position in the old world and, presumably, one's part in the corporate representative old Adam of that world.[57] The believer's living link to the position of the "new man" is constantly being "renewed" until "the day of redemption," for which Christians have been "sealed" by "the Holy Spirit of God" (4:30). The identification with Christ as a new Adam is further apparent from the fact that Paul says that this "new man . . . in the likeness of God has been created in righteousness and holiness of the truth" (4:24).[58] This is also confirmed from 5:1, where Paul exhorts the readers to "be imitators of God."

The language of "new creation" continues in Eph. 5, where saints are said to have been "formerly darkness, but now you are Light in the Lord; walk as children of Light (for the fruit of the Light consists in all goodness and righteousness and truth)" (5:8–9). Why would Paul use such a contrast between darkness and light in application to Christians? Since Paul had new creation in mind in the preceding context of Ephesians, it is not unnatural to find a contrast of light shining in darkness, patterned after the first creation, where the same contrast occurred. Furthermore, such a contrast is not unexpected here, since we have already seen that in 2 Cor. 4:6 ("Light shall shine out of darkness") Paul applies Gen. 1:3 to people who have come out of the darkness of unbelief into the light of the new creation. And just as 2 Cor. 4 also refers to "the glory of Christ" as the new-creational "image of God" (v. 4), so too the mention of "goodness and righteousness and truth" as a definition of "the fruit of the Light" repeats a reference to the image of God in Eph. 4:24, where the same wording appeared. "Fruit" is also part of that which results inevitably from the shining light in Gen. 1 (see there vv. 11–12, 28–29). Indeed, both Gen. 1:28 and

---

57. Most translations render *anthrōpos* as "self," with the resulting translation of "old self" and "new self." But this neuters the probable redemptive-historical identification with the old Adam and the new Adam that we have seen, the representative "men" respectively of the old and the new creation.

58. The phrase "the likeness of" is not in the Greek but is likely a good expanded translation based on the probable parallel to Col. 3:10, where believers "have put on the new man who is being renewed to a true knowledge <u>according to the image</u> [*kat' eikona*] of the One who created him."

Eph. 5:9 apply the notion of bearing "fruit" in human obedience to God (on which, see discussion of direct allusions to Gen. 1:28 in Col. 1:6, 10 in chap. 14). The atmosphere of the new creation in Eph. 5:8–9 is intensified by the continuation of the same antithesis of darkness and light in 5:11–14:

> Do not participate in the unfruitful deeds of darkness [*skotos*], but instead even expose them; for it is disgraceful even to speak of the things which are done by them in secret. But all things become visible when they are exposed by the light [*phōs*], for everything that becomes visible is light [*phōs*]. For this reason it says,
>
> > "Awake [*egeireō*], sleeper,
> > and arise [*anistēmi*] from the dead [*tōn nekrōn*],
> > and Christ will shine on you."

The suggestion by some that verse 14 is based on a combination of Isa. 26:19; 51:17; 60:1–3 seems likely:[59]

Isa. 26:19 Your <u>dead</u> [*hoi nekroi*] <u>will live</u> [LXX: "rise," *anistēmi*];
Their corpses <u>will rise</u> [*egeirō*].
You who lie in the dust, awake and shout for joy,
For your dew is as the dew of the dawn,
And the earth will give birth to the departed spirits.

Isa. 51:17a Rouse yourself [*exegeirō*]! Rouse yourself [*exegeirō*]!
Arise [*anistēmi*], O Jerusalem.

Isa. 60:1 Arise, shine; for your <u>light</u> [*phōs*] has come,
And the glory of the LORD has risen upon you.

Isa. 60:2 For behold, <u>darkness</u> [*skotos*] will cover the earth
And deep darkness the peoples;
But the LORD will rise upon you
And His glory will appear upon you.

Isa. 60:3 And nations will come to your <u>light</u> [*phōs*],
And kings to the brightness of your rising.

Isaiah 26:19 is a prophecy of the resurrection of Israel, Isa. 51 prophetically exhorts God's people to come out of exile, and Isa. 60 commands end-time

59. See Hans Hübner, *Vetus Testamentum in Novo* (Göttingen: Vandenhoeck & Ruprecht, 1997), 460–61, citing Isa. 26:19; 51:17; Ps. 44:24 and also listing Isa. 60:1–2 as an idiomatic basis for part of Eph. 5:14; so also Peter T. O'Brien, *The Letter to the Ephesians*, PNTC (Grand Rapids: Eerdmans, 1999), 375–76, seeing the same three Isaiah texts (adding also Isa. 51:9; 52:1) as inspiration for the verse. The translations of the Isaiah texts here follow the English rendering of the Hebrew in the NASB, with LXX equivalents inserted at some points.

Israel to "arise, shine" and be restored from exile by reflecting God's eschatological light of the new creation breaking forth into the darkness of the old creation and enlightening gentiles, who had been ensconced in the gloom of the old cosmos. Paul presumably combined these texts and understood that they interpreted one another; the resurrection of the saints at the eschaton is the beginning light of the new creation, when God's people would be restored to him. This Isaiah background is uniquely comparable to Eph. 5:8–14, where God's people in the new creation are to be light shining into the darkness of the old creation with a view to making gentiles a part of the new order. The command in 5:14 refers to those who have begun to experience the light of the risen Christ in the new age in order that they may reflect it to other gentiles who lie in deep gloom (or it refers to those themselves who lie in such gloom to come to the light for the first time). Ephesians 5:8–14 indicates a beginning fulfillment in the church of all three Isaiah prophecies.

The last reference to the concept of resurrection in Ephesians comes in its final verse. Paul refers to the incorruptible new creation of Christians in Christ that would last forever: "Grace be with all those who love our Lord Jesus Christ in incorruption" (6:24).[60] This conclusion is another way of referring to the Christians' beginning spiritual resurrection existence, which is part of the "incorruptible" new creation and will consummate with incorruptible physical resurrection existence.

How does this Ephesians portrayal of being identified with Christ as a resurrected Adam and as part of the new creation affect one's ethical motivation? Paul says that because of such an identification ("therefore," *oun* [4:25]), people should "lay aside" sins such as falsehood, anger, theft, unwholesome and unedifying speech, and "all bitterness and wrath and anger and clamor and slander" (4:25–31). This again exhibits the pattern of the "indicative followed by the imperative."

In this connection we ask again, why does Paul repeatedly explain to his hearers what God has done for them and who they are in Christ before he tells them what they are obligated to do as a subject of the divine king? A basis for ethical motivation is knowing that one has begun to be raised from the dead and has begun to be part of the new creation. Why is the new creation a basis for being able to follow Paul's commands to live godly? It is because without the resurrection power of the new creation, people are unable to obey God's precepts. Augustine said, "Give me the grace to do as you command, and command me to do what you will!" (*Conf.* 10.29), and John Calvin likewise affirmed, "What

---

60. The NASB renders *en aphtharsia* as "with incorruptible love," but its marginal reading is merely "in incorruption," which I use here because it follows the Greek more closely and appears to focus on the incorruptible spiritual existence of resurrected people living in the inaugurated form of the new creation.

God commands by Paul's mouth, He accomplishes inwardly."[61] Unless people are "made alive" and become part of the new creation, they are "dead in transgressions" because they are under the controlling influence of the ungodly world, under the domination of the devil, and are held captive to act only according to their own sinful nature (Eph. 2:1–6). Such "deadness" means that people have neither the desire nor the ability to initiate life with God and to please him.

Those who have begun to experience resurrection life and the new creation have the power to obey God. And when one knows that God is going to give the strength to obey, such knowledge does not lead to inaction but instead creates a desire to do what God wants. Paul knew this from his own experience of God's grace: "But by the grace of God I am what I am, and his grace to me was not without effect. No, I worked harder than all of them—yet not I, but the grace of God that was with me" (1 Cor. 15:10 NIV). He applied the same notion to other Christians (2 Cor. 9:7–8). Knowing that we have the moral power to obey instills in us a desire to comply with God's precepts.[62]

Resurrection in Philippians

In Phil. 1:19–22 Paul first reflects on the resurrection as a result of contemplating his imprisonment for the sake of the gospel:

> For I know that this will turn out for my salvation [or "deliverance"] through your prayers and the provision of the Spirit of Jesus Christ, according to my earnest expectation and hope, that I shall not be put to shame in anything, but that with all boldness, Christ will even now, as always, be exalted in my body, whether by life or by death. For to me, to live is Christ and to die is gain. But if I am to live on in the flesh, this will mean fruitful labor for me; and I do not know which to choose.

There is much debate about whether Paul's use of *sōtēria* ("salvation, deliverance") in verse 19 refers to physical deliverance from prison or spiritual deliverance. Five observations, among others, point strongly to the notion that Paul has in mind his own perseverance in the faith leading to his eschatological salvation.

1. There is a conceptual parallel between 1:12 and 1:19.
2. The "deliverance" will occur regardless of what happens to Paul (1:20b).
3. Philippians 1:19 is an allusion to Job 13:16.[63]

61. John Calvin, *Commentaries on the Epistles of Paul the Apostle to the Galatians, Ephesians, Philippians, Colossians, and 1 and 2 Thessalonians, 1 and 2 Timothy, Titus, Philemon* (repr., Grand Rapids: Baker Academic, 1984), 298.

62. I expand on the relation of the new creation to the indicative-imperative pattern in Paul and elsewhere later in this book (chap. 25).

63. "And this will turn out for my salvation" (LXX), which refers to Job's salvific standing before God; note also the soteriological nuance of *sōtēria* in Phil. 1:28; 2:12.

4. Elsewhere Paul uses "earnest expectation" (*apokaradokia*) and "hope" (*elpis*) to refer to final salvation (see, e.g., Rom. 8:19, 24–25).
5. The combination of "hope" and "shame" is used in the same kind of contexts (Rom. 5:4–5).

Thus, Phil. 1:19 appears to express the same reality as 2 Tim. 4:18, where no hope of physical deliverance in the present life of the old world is in view: "The Lord will rescue me from every evil deed, and will bring me safely to His heavenly kingdom" (cf. 4:6).[64]

Thus, the "salvation" in Phil. 1:19 is not deliverance from jail but rather a spiritually conceived salvation. It is a salvation that is "earnestly expected and hoped for," which puts it in an eschatological category. The "provision of the Spirit of Jesus Christ" is to enable the apostle to be a vessel through which Christ can "be magnified" in his body, whether this be through physical life or death. Recall that elsewhere in the NT this Spirit is sent by the risen Christ (Acts 2:33; 1 Cor. 15:45; Titus 3:5–6; cf. Gal. 4:6), which here is distantly in mind, as we will see. For Paul, "to live" is not to live as ordinary unbelieving humanity; rather, "to live is Christ" (Phil. 1:21). This phrase likely is equivalent to his assertion in Gal. 2:20, "Christ lives in me,"[65] which we have seen includes reference to Christ's resurrection life dwelling in Paul. If so, then the previously mentioned "Spirit" is the agent giving ongoing resurrection life, as we have seen elsewhere in Paul's writings (Rom. 1:4; 8:11, 14; 1 Tim. 3:16; cf. 1 Pet. 3:18). Yet Paul sees that "to die is gain," since apparently it is an escalation of spiritual resurrection existence, when the nonmaterial soul or spirit departs from the old, fallen body and is translated to be in the very heavenly presence of Christ. Although Paul expresses anxiety about which to choose, he prefers death in order to be closer to Christ, but he recognizes that God's will is for him to remain a little longer on earth to minister to God's people (Phil. 1:23–26).

The first explicit reference to Christ's resurrection in Philippians is in 2:9, where his exaltation is mentioned: "God highly exalted Him, and bestowed on Him the name which is above every name." This refers to the ascension that was an escalated phase of Jesus's initial earthly resurrection existence. This is very similar to Eph. 1:20–22, since both passages assert that the outcome of Jesus's resurrection/ascension is to place him "above every name," which in both texts indicates that he is sovereign over all earthly and heavenly powers (over those "who are in heaven and on earth and under the earth"). Again, we have a direct link between resurrection (and hence new creation) and kingship, as we have seen often elsewhere already in Paul's writings.

64. For this analysis of Phil. 1:19, see Moisés Silva, *Philippians*, BECNT (Grand Rapids: Baker Academic, 1992), 76–79.
65. Ibid., 82.

As faithful followers of the exalted Lord and as "children of God," the readers are "to shine as stars in the world, holding fast the word of life, so that in the day of Christ I will have cause to glory because I did not run in vain nor toil in vain" (Phil. 2:15–16). The phrase "word of life" likely conveys the notion of "the word that leads to life" (a genitive of destination); that is, the message about the gospel leads to the possession of resurrection existence, which is eternal life for the one believing.[66] That this "life" indicates resurrection life is apparent from recognizing that the directly preceding clause, "shine as stars in the world," is an allusion to Dan. 12:3 (see table 9.2).

Table 9.2

Daniel 12:3 (OG)	Philippians 2:15
"And the ones understanding will shine as stars of the heaven [*phanousin hōs phōstēres tou ouranou*] and the ones becoming strong in my words [will shine] as the stars of heaven."	"You shine as stars in the world [*phainesthe hōs phōstēres en kosmō*], holding fast the word of life."

Recognizing the Dan. 12:3 allusion is significant because it continues the prophecy about the end-time resurrection from Dan. 12:2: "Many of those who sleep in the dust of the ground will awake, these to everlasting life, but the others to disgrace and everlasting contempt." Daniel 12:3 continues to portray the reward of those who participate in the final resurrection. Perhaps even Paul's reference to "life" echoes the "everlasting life" of Dan. 12:2, which, of course, is eternal resurrection life.[67]

Accordingly, the Philippians are those who have begun to experience the resurrection prophesied in Dan. 12:2, and because they still live in a dark world of "crooked and perverse" people, they need now to "shine as stars" by "holding fast the word leading [others] to resurrection life."[68] Paul's exhortation to "hold fast the word of life, so that in the day of Christ I may have cause to glory" appears to refer to persevering until the final day, when Christ appears at the very end of history and the Philippians are manifested as those who truly had believed Paul's message. This manifestation is evident through their successful passing through the "day" when God "will judge . . . through Christ Jesus"

66. Note that hearing the "word" also leads to "life" for those believing it in John 5:24; Acts 13:46, 48.

67. Indeed, the reference later in Philippians to those "whose names are in the book of life" (4:3) likely is also an allusion to Dan. 12:1–2: "Everyone who is found written in the book will be rescued . . . to [a resurrection of] everlasting life." Psalm 69:28 could also be combined with the Dan. 12:1–2 reference, but the psalm refers to those "blotted out of the book of life." For the combination of Ps. 69:28 and Dan. 12:1–2 for "the book of life" in Rev. 3:5; 13:8; 20:12; 21:27, see Beale, *Revelation*, 278–82, 701–3, 1032–33.

68. This phrase reflects Daniel's "the ones becoming strong in my words will shine as the stars of heaven," which is the OG rendering of the Hebrew, "those who lead the many to righteousness [will shine] like stars."

(Rom. 2:16) and Jesus "will also confirm" them "to the end . . . in the day of our Lord Jesus Christ," when he is finally and fully "revealed" (1 Cor. 1:7–8). It is at this time that Christians, who have begun to be spiritually resurrected, will consummately "attain to the resurrection from the dead" (Phil. 3:11), at the time when Jesus is revealed from heaven and "will transform the body of our humble state into conformity with the body of His glory" (3:21).

The day of the final resurrection is an eschatological beacon shining light back into history and toward which Christians should look for guidance in their earthly pilgrimage (3:10–14):

> . . . that I may know Him and the power of His resurrection and the fellowship of His sufferings, being conformed to his death; in order that I may attain to the resurrection from the dead. Not that I have already obtained it, or have already become perfect, but I press on in order that I may lay hold of that for which also I was laid hold of by Christ Jesus. Brethren, I do not regard myself as having laid hold of it yet; but one thing I do: forgetting what lies behind and reaching forward to what lies ahead, I press on toward the goal for the prize of the upward call of God in Christ Jesus.

Note the order of things in verse 10. Paul wants to know "the power of his resurrection" before "the fellowship of his sufferings." Why? One plausible answer is that the Spirit who raised Jesus has come into and energized his followers and is the power that they must first experience in order to persevere through trial. As they persevere through trial, they are experiencing "the fellowship of his sufferings" and are "being conformed to his death." The final result of persevering through suffering by infused resurrection power is attainment of the final physical resurrection of the dead (v. 11). Although Paul has not obtained such final resurrection, he desires to press on so that he may "lay hold" of it, since that is the purpose for which Christ initially "laid hold" of him on the Damascus Road (v. 12). And though the apostle has not yet experienced this final resurrection, he "reaches forward" to it as a runner does right before the tape at the finish line (v. 13). In fact, the comparison with a runner comes into clearer focus in verse 14: "I press on toward the goal for the prize of the upward call [to resurrection] of God in Christ Jesus." The "prize" is the ultimate possession of the resurrection body, and it is a desire for this that drives Paul in this life to please the Lord.

Resurrection in Colossians

Colossians 1–2

The first reference to resurrection in Colossians occurs in 1:18a, where Christ is said to be the "firstborn from among the dead ones." This means that he is "the beginning" of the new creation "so that He Himself will come to have first place in everything" (1:18b). Those who identify with him[69] also become subsequently born as resurrected beings into the beginning of the new creation. They have been born through being raised from spiritual death to spiritual life by means of being identified with Christ's own resurrection (2:12–13):

> . . . having been buried with Him in baptism, in which you were also raised up with Him through faith in the working of God, who raised Him from the dead. And when you were dead in your transgressions and the uncircumcision of your flesh, He made you alive together with Him, having forgiven us all our transgressions.

Again, as we have repeatedly observed, Christ's resurrection is closely linked to his kingship: "When He had disarmed the rulers and authorities, He made a public display of them, having triumphed over them through Him" (2:15). Although, in light of Col. 2:14, this appears to focus on Christ's death, the "triumph" may include reference to the resurrection.

Colossians 3:1–11

Paul likely viewed the resurrection of believers not in mere metaphorical terms but rather as a true, literal resurrection. Their resurrection, however, is occurring in two stages, first spiritually (3:1) and then physically at the final consummation (3:4). If they are experiencing the beginning of literal resurrection, then they are part of the beginning of the new creation.

After explaining that Christians are identified with Christ's resurrection in 2:12–13, Paul in 3:1 says that on the basis ("therefore," *oun*) of that resurrection status ("if you have been raised up with Christ"), they are to "keep seeking the things above, where Christ is, seated at the right hand of God."

The reference to "Christ . . . seated at the right hand of God" is an allusion to Ps. 110:1 and is an explicit connection between his resurrection and kingship. This allusion occurs often elsewhere in the NT, where it refers to the exalted position of Christ in heaven as a result of the resurrection.[70] Psalm 110:1 says, "The LORD says to my Lord: 'Sit at My right hand, until I make Your enemies a footstool for Your feet.'" The first phrase, "The LORD says to my Lord," seems to indicate that the king being addressed is a divine king,

---

69. Note the readers' "faith in Christ" (Col. 1:4), which has caused them to be identified with Christ ("transferred to the kingdom of His beloved Son" [v. 13]) and even united with him ("in whom" [v. 14]; see vv. 13–14, which are directly linked to Christ as "the image of the invisible God" in v. 15). The theme of their identification with Christ as their representative continues in 1:22, 24, 27, 28; 2:6, 10–13, 19; 3:1, 3–4, 10.

70. See explicit citations in Matt. 22:44; Mark 12:36; Luke 20:42; Acts 2:34–35; Heb. 1:13; see allusions in Matt. 26:64; Mark 14:62; 16:19; Luke 22:69; Rom. 8:34; 1 Cor. 15:25; Eph. 1:20; Heb. 1:3; 8:1; 10:12–13; 12:2; 1 Pet. 3:22. See further David M. Hay, *Glory at the Right Hand: Psalm 110 in Early Christianity*, SBLMS 18 (Nashville: Abingdon, 1973).

whose divinity is pointed to further by his ascription "as a priest <u>forever</u>" (Ps. 110:4, also in direct relation to "right hand" in v. 5). At the very least, David refers to a coming king who is greater than him, since he calls this king "my Lord [Adonai, not Yahweh or Elohim]." This points strongly to the original messianic nature of the psalm, and it is interpreted this way by Jesus (Mark 12:35–37).

Early Judaism applied Ps. 110:1 to pious individuals, human leaders, the future Davidic Messiah, or supernatural beings (the heavenly Melchizedek, Enoch, or the Son of Man). Later Judaism applied the passage to pious individuals or the Messiah.[71] The point of Ps. 110:1 is not merely achievement of a sovereign position of rule; rather, the focus is on the *beginning* achievement of that rule: "Sit at my right hand <u>until I make Your enemies a footstool for Your feet</u>." Psalm 110:2 expands further on this inaugurated rule: "The LORD will stretch forth Your strong scepter from Zion, saying, 'Rule in the midst of Your enemies.'" This fits perfectly into the broad NT notion that Christ commenced his messianic rule during his ministry, death, resurrection, and exaltation. This psalm strikingly shows that the "already and not yet" eschatology was prophesied in the OT itself.

The notion of an inaugurated rule is also appropriate within the immediate context. Colossians 2:10 says that Christ "is the head over all rule and authority"; similarly, 2:15 says that "when He [Christ] had disarmed the rulers and authorities, He made a public display of them, having triumphed over them through it [the cross]." Christ has won the decisive victory over evil angelic powers, which is also how Ps. 110:1 is applied in 1 Cor. 15:25; Eph. 1:20; 1 Pet. 3:22; and possibly Rev. 3:21 (cf. *1 Clem.* 36:5; Pol. *Phil.* 2:1). Although the crucial battle has been won at Christ's cross and resurrection, the enemy is not yet completely defeated. Colossians 1:20 says that God had designed "to reconcile all things to Himself, having made peace through the blood of His [Christ's] cross." This complete reconciliation has not yet been accomplished by the time Paul writes Colossians, which is clear in that Paul has to warn the readers against the detrimental influence of false teachers (2:8, 18–23), who are part of the "authority of darkness" (1:13) and through whom the unseen demonic "rulers and authorities" still work even though they have been decisively defeated.

Consequently, Paul tells readers, "Set your mind on the things above, not on the things that are on the earth" (3:2), in the sense that they are to live on earth in the light of their identification with the resurrected Christ in heaven. This should result in them not being influenced by the false, idolatrous teaching described in 2:8, 18–23, which has its ultimate origin in the old cosmos (the "elements of the world" [2:8, 20]) that is passing away and not from the new cosmos that has broken in through Christ.

71. For use in Judaism, see ibid., 21–33.

The Colossians have died to the old world ("you have died"), and their new, resurrection "life is hidden with Christ," "who is their life" as their resurrected Lord, with whom they are united (3:4–5). The identification with Christ's death and resurrection is a repetition of what has already been affirmed in 2:12–13, 19. The reason for the repetition, which is virtually always the reason that Paul appeals to Jesus's death and resurrection, is to undergird his attempts to move the readers to obey his ethical commands. So in 3:5a, building on 3:1–4, he urges the Christians to "consider the members of your earthly body as dead" to a list of sins that summarizes the readers' former manner of sinful living (3:5b–9a). Then Paul again gives the basis for ceasing from such sinful behavior (3:9b–10):

> . . . since you laid aside the old man with its evil practices, and have put on the new man who is being renewed to a true knowledge according to the image of the One who created him.

This passage will undergo more sustained analysis in a subsequent chapter, where I will argue for the position on these verses taken here.[72] Here I am content to repeat what I have said above. That they have "laid aside the old man" means that they are no longer identified with the old Adam and the fallen, dead world. Instead, they "have put on the new man," which indicates that they have become identified with the resurrected last Adam and the new creation. This interpretation is partly based on translating *anthrōpos* as "man" instead of "self." Each saint is to act like the "new man" of the new age that has penetrated from the future dimension into the present, not like the "old man" of the sinful, old age that is passing away.

Resurrection in 1–2 Thessalonians

In describing the conversion of the Thessalonians, Paul refers to how they "turned to God from idols to serve a living and true God, and to wait for His Son from heaven, whom He raised from the dead, that is Jesus, who delivers us from the wrath to come" (1 Thess. 1:9–10). Later in 1 Thessalonians, the apostle says that those who "believe that Jesus died and rose again" can be assured that deceased saints are identified with Christ now ("the ones sleeping in Jesus" and who are "in Christ") and will be raised physically from the dead at the final coming of Christ (4:14–17):

> For if we believe that Jesus died and rose again, even so God will bring with Him those who have fallen asleep in Jesus. For this we say to you by the word of the Lord, that we who are alive and remain until the coming of the Lord, will not

72. On which, see chap. 25.

precede those who have fallen asleep. For the Lord Himself will descend from heaven with a shout, with the voice of the archangel and with the trumpet of God, and the dead in Christ shall rise first. Then we who are alive and remain shall be caught up together with them in the clouds to meet the Lord in the air, and so we shall always be with the Lord.

At the end, living believers "will be caught up together" in bodily resurrection with their departed brothers and sisters. This is summarized in 5:10: "who died for us, so that whether we are awake or asleep, we will live together with Him." Paul's purpose in saying what he does in 4:14–17 and 5:9–10 is to "comfort" people about those Christians who had died. Paul concludes the letter with a prayer that the Thessalonians would achieve this consummate resurrection: "Now may the God of peace himself sanctify you entirely; and may your spirit and soul and body be preserved complete, without blame at the coming of our Lord Jesus Christ" (5:23). This reminds us that the resurrection (spoken of here as "preservation") is not mere resuscitation of the body but regeneration also of the immaterial sphere of humanity ("spirit and soul"), which began at the moment of first believing.

In 1 Thessalonians Paul focuses on the future reality of resurrection life in the coming age, though there may be one passage where he reflects on the inaugurated reality. At first or even second glance, 3:7–8 does not appear to be alluding to resurrection life, but when seen through the lens of inaugurated eschatology, it has a different look: "Therefore, brothers, in all our distress and persecution we were encouraged about you through your faith. For now we really live, since you are standing firm in the Lord" (NIV).[73] What "really living" means is difficult to say. The phrase represents the NASB and NIV translation of zōmen (lit., "we live"). It is parallel with the preceding mention of "we were encouraged" in verse 7, though it is not synonymous with it. "We really live" may well be an interpretation of what it means to be "encouraged": Paul's anxiety about the readers has now been removed because of the report about their enduring belief ("joy" has the same connotation in v. 9). This could imply, however, that "living" is a mere figure of speech for not being anxious (cf. JB: "now we can breathe again"; NEB: "it is the breath of life to us"). Elsewhere Paul is invigorated by his readers' spiritual growth (Rom. 15:32; 1 Cor. 16:18; 2 Cor. 7:2–3, 13; Philem. 7, 20),[74] but it is not clear how these general parallels shed further light on 1 Thess. 3:8.

The mention of living, however, probably is not figurative but instead refers to actual salvific "life" in relationship with God that is the opposite

73. For fuller analysis of this passage in its context, see G. K. Beale, *1–2 Thessalonians*, IVPNTC (Downers Grove, IL: InterVarsity, 2003), 103–6, of which the present discussion is a summary. It may be that 1 Thess. 5:10 ("we may live together with him") also includes reference to the beginning stage of resurrection (see ibid., 154–55).

74. So I. Howard Marshall, *1 and 2 Thessalonians*, NCB (Grand Rapids: Eerdmans, 1983), 96.

of "death," which is separation from God (Eph. 2:12). How can Paul say that "now he really lives" if he already had spiritual life before? Continuing the thought of 2:17–20, the readers' unflagging persuasion of the truth is a crucial ingredient in Paul's own steadfast fidelity to Christ in carrying on his new life's task of bringing the good news of Israel's Messiah beyond the boundaries of Israel. Paul's salvific life "in Christ" (cf. 1:1; 2:14) is not merely a past reality experienced at his conversion, but rather an ongoing condition, about which he receives confidence because of his renewed knowledge that his recent converts are continuing in the reality of their new life. As evident also in 2:17–20, the successful outcome of their life in Christ is a fruit demonstrating the genuineness of Paul's own life in Christ. The phrase "now we really live" expresses this confidence "<u>since</u> [or 'because'] they are standing firm <u>in the Lord</u>" and have not been moved from their commitment to Christ, as was feared in 3:3–5.[75]

That Paul is speaking about assurance concerning his own salvific life is borne out also by how Paul often uses the same word *zaō* ("live") to indicate true life in the Messiah elsewhere.[76] This life is none other than "life in the resurrected Christ," an inbreaking eschatological resurrection existence, with which many of Paul's other uses are consistent (e.g., Gal. 2:20: "It is no longer I who live, but Christ <u>lives</u> in me"). The nature of Paul's life as resurrection life is suggested also by his use of *zaō* later in 1 Thessalonians: Christ "died for us [and came to life], so that whether we are awake or asleep, we will <u>live</u> together with Him" (5:10). The parallel in 4:14 shows that the present resurrection life of the believer will be consummated on a greater scale in the future ("we believe that Jesus died and rose again," and so we believe that "God will bring with Him [at the final day of resurrection] those who have fallen asleep in Jesus").[77] The phrase "announce the good news [or gospel]" in 1 Thess. 3:6, which describes the report about the ongoing vitality of the Thessalonians' faith, suggests further that Paul had a heightened awareness of his own true existence: to hear of their endurance is a life-imparting gospel experience for him that is crucial to his growth in and assurance of his true resurrection existence in the Messiah.[78] That Paul can say to the Corinthians that "you are in our hearts to die together and to live together" (2 Cor. 7:3) suggests also that

---

75. Although *ean* often is rendered "if," with the sense of probable fulfillment of a condition in the future, the NIV's rendering of *ean* as "since" is good because the context indicates that the present faithful condition of the readers is the logical basis for "really living" (see Wallace, *Greek Grammar*, 696–99).

76. Some eighteen times; his remaining uses typically refer either to various aspects of literal physical life or figuratively to life lived apart from a covenantal relationship with Christ.

77. The two uses of *zaō* in 4:15, 17 appear to refer primarily to the physical existence of Christians.

78. For a similar link to v. 6, see Ernest Best, *The First and Second Epistles to the Thessalonians* (Peabody, MA: Hendrickson, 1972), 143.

believers nourish one another's resurrection life "in Messiah" by means of their ongoing spiritual vitality.[79]

The only apparent reference to resurrection in 2 Thessalonians is in 2:1, where Paul speaks of "our gathering together [*episynagōgē*] to Him" at the time of Christ's final coming. This is likely parallel to 1 Thess. 4:14–17, which portrays God "bringing" believers "together" to be with Jesus at the end time by resurrecting them.

Resurrection in 1–2 Timothy and Titus

The only reference to resurrection in 1 Timothy is in 3:16: "By common confession great is the mystery of godliness: He who was revealed in the flesh, was vindicated by the Spirit, seen by angels, proclaimed among the nations, believed on in the world, taken up in glory." The "vindication by the Spirit" is commonly understood to be a reference to Jesus's resurrection that "vindicated" him from the wrong verdict cast upon him by the human court. And this led to him being "taken up in glory."

The opening verse of 2 Timothy affirms "the promise of life in Christ Jesus." That this is the promise of resurrection life is probable, especially since 1:9–10 speaks of God's "purpose and grace which was granted us in Christ Jesus from all eternity, but now has been revealed by the appearing of our Savior Christ Jesus, who abolished death, and brought life and immortality to light through the gospel." It is this gospel of Christ's death and resurrection that has been entrusted to Paul and Timothy (1:11–14), an entrustment that is also to be passed on to others (2:2), for which Timothy is to be willing to suffer (2:2–7), since Paul himself suffers for this (2:8–9, "Remember Jesus Christ, risen from the dead, descendant of David, according to my gospel, for which I suffer hardship . . ."). Paul repeats again that he "endures" in order that God's elect "may obtain salvation . . . with . . . eternal glory" (2:10), which is explained by 2:11–12: "It is a trustworthy statement: For if we died with him, we shall also live with him; if we endure, we shall also reign with him." Identification with Christ's death and endurance through suffering will result in identification with his resurrection and kingship. Notice once again significantly that resurrection and kingship go together.

This truth about the future resurrection of believers is absolutely crucial to maintain, since it was being denied by some in the church at Ephesus. Hymenaeus and Philetus had "gone astray from the truth saying that the resurrection has already taken place, and thus they upset the faith of some" (2:17–18).

Like 2 Timothy, the letter to Titus begins with "the hope of eternal life, which God, who cannot lie, promised long ages ago" (1:2). As in 2 Tim. 1:1,

---

79. See ibid., 142. Best compares also 2 Cor. 4:11–12.

this presumably is to be identified with the promise of eternal resurrection life. This is suggested further from observing that in Titus 1:3, as in 2 Tim. 1:1, 9–14, where the message of Christ's death and resurrection is entrusted to Paul and Timothy, Paul immediately says that "at the proper time [he] manifested *even* his word, in the proclamation with which I was entrusted . . ." (esp. compare the parallelism of 2 Tim. 1:9–10 and Titus 1:2–3). The repeated mention of the "hope of eternal life" in 3:7 continues the same theme from the introduction.

Finally, Titus 3:5 asserts, "He saved us, not on the basis of deeds which we have done in righteousness, but according to his mercy, by the washing of regeneration and renewing by the Holy Spirit." The reference to "regeneration" (*palingenesia*) refers to a re-enlivening of a person and is conceptually synonymous with the notion of bringing a person back to life. As we have just seen above in Paul's writings (e.g., in the discussion of Rom. 7:4–6) that identification with Christ's resurrection life can be called being "in newness of the Spirit," so also here "regeneration" is referred to as "renewing by the Holy Spirit." Again we find that the Spirit is the agent of the resurrection of the new creation. And, as so often elsewhere in Paul's writings, this resurrection begins in this life spiritually and will be consummated in the full physical resurrection life of the age to come, which Titus 3:7 refers to as "eternal life," of which those now regenerated are "heirs," though this "eternal life" commences in the present.[80] In this light, the traditional theological idea of "regeneration" must be seen as an intensely eschatological idea.

Why Is Resurrection So Prevalent in Paul's Writings?

Richard Gaffin has elaborated on how Christ's resurrection is central to Paul's theology.[81] My survey above bears out Gaffin's assessment. Why is Paul so consumed with the idea of resurrection? One could answer generally that together with Christ's death, the resurrection is a crucial element of early apostolic tradition that was passed on to Paul, after he became a Christian. But there is a more specific reason that Paul's mind is soaked with resurrection. Seyoon Kim has provided the most plausible answer to date.[82]

Kim argues that the Damascus Road Christophany is the reason why Paul's new conceptual world was dominated by Christ's resurrection. Paul's experience with the risen Christ on the way to Damascus was an eschatological event in which he experienced the kingdom and the new creation, two ideas that we have seen are inextricably linked to the resurrection of Jesus and of believers.

80. Paul's letter to Philemon has no mention of resurrection.
81. Richard B. Gaffin Jr., *The Centrality of the Resurrection: A Study in Paul's Soteriology* (Grand Rapids: Baker Academic, 1978).
82. Kim, *Origin of Paul's Gospel*.

This is evident from seeing the Damascus Road Christophany as a resurrection appearance that was the beginning of the "last days." Indeed, Kim persuasively argues that Christ's resurrection appearance on the Damascus Road made such a lasting impact on Paul's mind that it became the central thrust of his thinking in his writings. He argues that Paul's major ideas are colored by this earthshaking event in the apostle's life. In that the resurrection is equivalent to the new-creational kingdom, both came to function as one lens through which he explains all his major ideas. Significant reflections of the Damascus Road event are found throughout Paul's letters, which point to how this life-changing event left its imprint on him. Several contexts in Paul's letters show the indelible imprint of his mind-changing experience (e.g., Rom. 10:2–5; 1 Cor. 9:1; 15:8–10; 2 Cor. 4:4–6; 5:14–17; Gal. 1:13–17; 3:12–14; Phil. 3:6–9; Eph. 3:1–13). These are tips of the resurrection/Damascus Road Christophany iceberg that lie beneath much of Paul's thought.[83]

Christ appeared to Paul (1 Cor. 15:8; Acts 9:17; 26:16), and Paul saw him (1 Cor. 9:1). This was an "untimely birth" for him (1 Cor. 15:8). What kind of birth was this? Probably it was both a conversion and a call to prophetic apostleship, the latter being the focus in 1 Cor. 15:8. It was the same kind of appearance as the other apostles saw (1 Cor. 15:5–11). It is described as an "apocalypse" of Christ to Paul of the exalted Son of God (Gal. 1:12, 16). Since this phrase in Gal. 1:12 ("an apocalypse of Jesus Christ") occurs elsewhere in the NT only in reference to Christ's final coming (1 Cor. 1:7; 2 Thess. 1:7; 1 Pet. 1:7, 13; Rev. 1:1),[84] it suggests that Gal. 1:12 is saying that Christ was revealed to Paul in the form in which he will come at the end of time—his exalted, reigning, resurrected new-creational form. This is a classic example of the eschatological future breaking back into the present, making the present an eschatological time.

Paul received an inner spiritual illumination from this apocalyptic appearance (2 Cor. 4:6), perhaps the same kind as John received in the book of Revelation. In particular, it was a moment of decision in which Paul gave up his own Pharisaic righteousness in order to attain the knowledge and righteousness of Christ (Phil. 3:2–12). There is debate about whether these two passages only refer to Paul's apostolic call. It is likely that they also point to and include a conversion. At this time, Paul was given a knowledge of Christ as "Lord." This was the moment when Paul was transferred to a true knowledge of Christ from false knowledge about the Messiah (2 Cor. 5:16–17; Gal. 3:13; 1 Tim. 1:12–16).[85] That Paul also became a Christian at the time of this

83. The remainder of this section depends for the most part on ibid., 1–71.

84. Although, Rev. 1:1 includes the content of the whole book of Revelation, which includes Christ's final appearing.

85. Of course, those not holding to Pauline authorship of the Pastoral Epistles would not be persuaded by appeal to 1 Tim. 1:12–16, but it is beyond doubt that this passage refers to Paul's Damascus Road encounter with Christ as a conversion.

initial encounter with Christ is further indicated by Isaiah's and Moses's initial theophanic experiences and prophetic commissions, which may well have included also their own conversions (e.g., see Exod. 3; Isa. 6). The relevance of Isaiah's experience is apparent from Acts 28:23–28, where Luke portrays Paul as an agent in carrying out the same hardening ministry to Israel that Isaiah had been commissioned to carry out (according to Isa. 6) in his own generation. And in Rom. 11:8 Paul alludes to Isa. 6:9–10 ("eyes to see not and ears to hear not"), together with Deut. 29:4, in arguing that the hardening of Israel that occurred through Isaiah's ministry continues down to Paul's own day and in the midst of his own ministry to Israel (see Rom. 11:11–25).

The commissioning aspect of Paul's Damascus Road experience is highlighted in 1 Cor. 9:1; 15:1–11, and, of course, as we have seen in the preceding chapter, the call is underscored in the Acts 26 narrative. It was a verbal commission, since it was on a par with the other resurrection appearances to the other apostles. The other apostles also all received their commission through a resurrection appearance of Christ.[86] In this apostolic call Paul saw himself as a latter-day Isaiah and Jeremiah who was to be the Messiah's prophet of light to the nations, which is expressed through allusions to Jer. 1:5 and Isa. 49:1–6 together in Gal. 1:15: "But when God, who had set me apart even from my mother's womb and called me. . . ." No doubt, it took Paul years to understand how to carry out this commission (Gal. 1:15–18).

Four texts in particular from the above merit further analysis at this point, especially in order to observe how important for Paul was his initial vision of the resurrected Christ.[87]

2 Corinthians 4:6

In this text Paul is describing the Christian's typical conversion experience by means of his own. The comparisons in tables 9.3 and 9.4 between 2 Cor. 4 and Acts 26 reveal that Paul is reflecting on his Damascus Road experience in the former passage.

The combined mention of "light" and "glory" as the realm of "God" that "shines" in contrast to "darkness" as the realm where Satan rules reflects Paul's Damascus Road experience.[88] The phrase "shone in our hearts" describes God's objective historical disclosure of the risen Christ that penetrated the inner heart of Paul and caused salvific light to be dispersed into his spiritually dark heart, which had been held captive in Satan's realm. This brought Paul "face-to-face" with Christ. The focus, however, is more on Paul's apostolic ministry

---

86. So Matt. 28:16–20; Luke 24:36–50; John 20:19–23 (cf. here the possible Adam–new creation typology); 21:15, 19; Acts 1:8.

87. Again, analysis of these four texts is based on Kim, *Origin of Paul's Gospel*, 3–32.

88. In the other two Damascus Road accounts in Acts Paul also is said to have seen a heavenly light shining around the risen Christ (9:3; 22:6).

Table 9.3

Acts 26:13, 17–18	2 Corinthians 4:4, 6
26:17–18: . . . *egō apostellō se anoixai ophthal-mous autōn, tou epistrepsai apo skotous eis phōs kai tēs exousias tou satana epi ton theon.*	. . . *en hois ho theos tou aiōnos toutou etyphlōsen ta noēmata tōn apistōn eis to mē augasai ton phōtismon tou euangeliou tēs doxēs tou Christou . . . ho theos ho eipōn; ek*
26:13: . . . *eidon . . . ouranothen hyper tēn lamprotēta tou hēliou perilampsan me phōs* (cf. Acts 22:9).[a]	*skotous phōs lampsei, hos elampsen en tais kardiais hēmōn pros phōtismon tēs gnōseōs tēs doxēs tou theou en prosōpō [Iēsou] Christou.*

[a] In this table and those that follow, solid underlining represents lexical and cognate parallels, and broken underlining indicates close conceptual parallels (and so throughout the remainder of the book).

and commission, which both the preceding (4:1–5) and the following context (4:7–15) indicate. In particular, the purpose of God shining light into Paul's heart was that his apostolic office be used as an instrument through which God illumines others: God "is the One who has shone in our hearts to give the light of the knowledge of the glory of God." God did not shine light into Paul merely to regenerate him but so that he would be one who shines that light to others. Paul says this at this point as part of his ongoing argument to indicate the truth of his apostleship.

2 Corinthians 5:16–17

Here Paul says, "Therefore from now on we recognize no one according to the flesh; even though we have known Christ according to the flesh, yet now we know Him in this way no longer. Therefore if anyone is in Christ, he is a new creation; the old things passed away; behold, new things have come."

I will examine this passage in more depth in the next chapter, but a few comments are appropriate here with respect to its relationship to Paul's own past experience. "To know Christ according to the flesh" means to evaluate him according to a worldly Jewish conception that expected only a military messiah. This is the way Paul had formerly evaluated Jesus, and it is why he had rejected him, since Jesus had not come as a glorious and triumphal messiah of Israel. Again, Paul is setting up his experience and universalizing it to

Table 9.4

Acts 26:13, 17–18	2 Corinthians 4:4, 6
26:17–18: ". . . I am sending you, *to open their eyes* so that they may turn from darkness to light and from the *dominion of Satan* to God."	". . . in whose case the *god of this world has blinded the minds* of the unbelieving so that they might not see the light of the gospel of the glory of Christ. . . . God, who said, 'Light shall shine out of darkness,' is the One who has shone in our hearts to give the light of the knowledge of the glory of God in the face of Christ."
26:13: ". . . I saw on the way a light from heaven, brighter than the sun, shining all around me" (cf. Acts 22:9).	

all true Christians. In fact, his point here is to get the Corinthians to evaluate his apostleship in the same way that they evaluated Jesus: they were professing to believe in Jesus as the Messiah and were thereby not judging Jesus by Jewish standards, as Paul had done in unbelief. But *they were* rejecting Paul because they were evaluating him by worldly standards that were comparable to those that resulted in Israel's rejection of Jesus. Paul is contending that if the Corinthians judge him by the true standard of godly judgment by which they accept Jesus, they will also accept Paul's prophetic authority.

Verses 16–17 affirm that Christ's death and resurrection (see vv. 14–15 and the introductory "therefore" of v. 16 and v. 17) are the end-time turning point from the old to the new age (note the "from now on" in v. 16 and the "new creation" in v. 17). This new age invades a person's life at conversion and did so in Paul's case, when he was also given his apostolic commission. It was at the time when Paul became a "new creation" that he was also "reconciled" to God (v. 18 [Paul likely includes himself in the phrase "God . . . reconciled us to Himself"]). It was on the Damascus Road and in his confrontation with the resurrected Christ that Paul began to experience this reconciliation.

Romans 10:2–4

Paul understands the tragedy of Israel in light of his own conversion. What he says of Israel had formerly been true of himself and corresponds with his autobiographical statement in Phil. 3:4–9 (see table 9.5).

Both the pre-Christian Paul and unbelieving Israel had a "zeal" for God's law, but "not in accordance with knowledge" of the Messiah and the righteousness

Table 9.5

Romans 9:31–32; 10:2–4	Philippians 3:4–9
9:31–32: "But Israel, pursuing a law of righteousness, did not arrive at that law. Why? Because they did not pursue it by faith, but as though it were by works." 10:2–4 "For I testify about them that they have a zeal for God, but not in accordance with knowledge. For not knowing about God's righteousness and seeking to establish their own, they did not subject themselves to the righteousness of God. For Christ is the end of the law for righteousness to everyone who believes."	". . . although I myself might have confidence even in the flesh. If anyone else has a mind to put confidence in the flesh, I far more: circumcised the eighth day, of the nation of Israel, of the tribe of Benjamin, a Hebrew of Hebrews; as to the Law, a Pharisee; as to zeal, a persecutor of the church; as to the righteousness which is in the Law, found blameless. But whatever things were gain to me, those things I have counted as loss for the sake of Christ. More than that, I count all things to be loss in view of the surpassing value of knowing Christ Jesus my Lord, for whom I have suffered the loss of all things, and count them but rubbish in order that I may gain Christ, and may be found in Him, not having a righteousness of my own derived from the Law, but that which is through faith in Christ, the righteousness which comes from God on the basis of faith."

that comes only through him by faith and not works. When Christ appeared to Paul, he received a true "knowledge of Messiah Jesus" (Phil. 3:8) as "the end of the law" (Rom. 10:4). Israel was in the condition that Paul was in before he became a Christian.

Ephesians 3:1–13

This passage underlines the fact that Paul received his apostolic commission to carry the gospel to gentiles, which includes the "mystery" that gentiles are on the same footing with Jewish believers: "The Gentiles are fellow heirs and fellow members of the body, and fellow partakers of the promise in Christ Jesus through the gospel" (v. 6). This likely shows that Jews and gentiles form the continuation of true Israel in the eschatological age, which will not be elaborated on here, since it will be developed later (see chap. 20).

Conclusion

The Damascus Road Christophany constituted both Paul's regenerative understanding of the gospel (as a result of conversion) and his apostolic commission to the gentiles. In this regard, note again Gal. 1:16: (1) "to reveal His Son in me" and (2) "I might preach Him among the Gentiles." This twofold aspect of conversion/commission is reflected in Gal. 2:7: "entrusted with the gospel to the uncircumcised" (cf. Rom. 1:1 ["called as an apostle, set apart for the gospel of God"], 5; see also prologues to Paul's other letters).[89]

The passages surveyed above indicate that the appearance of the resurrected Christ was a fundamental influence on Paul. This influence did not diminish but rather increased throughout the rest of his life because of his further reflection on the experience in the light of four things:

1. the Jewish Scriptures;
2. interpretative traditions based on the Jewish Scriptures;
3. the tradition about Jesus that he received from earliest Christianity;
4. ongoing apocalyptic visions of the ascended Christ.

The residual impression on Paul's mind of the Damascus Road Christophany as a resurrection event and its developed meaning formed a framework within which he typically thought when reflecting on Christian theology and its implications in his letters. Indeed, Christ's resurrection as a new creation was the generative source from which Paul's conception of most of his major theological conceptions arose. We have seen how this is the case with regeneration, and I will argue that it is true also with respect to things such as justification,

---

89. Again, see Kim, *Origin of Paul's Gospel*, 3–27, 57.

reconciliation, sanctification, anthropology, ecclesiology, image of God, the law, the Spirit, Christology, and missiology.

It is indeed a large claim to say that the majority of Paul's doctrines ultimately derive from his continuing reflection on Christ's resurrection as a new creation and escalation of the kingdom that he had already begun to establish. However, I am claiming this idea not as a "center" but rather more as an organic generative influence, as an acorn is to an oak tree.[90] This is the way I conceive pictorially the centrality of the storyline of the NT, which was formulated in earlier chapters: *Jesus's life, trials, death for sinners, and especially resurrection by the Spirit have launched the fulfillment of the eschatological already–not yet new-creational reign, bestowed by grace through faith and resulting in worldwide commission to the faithful to advance this new-creational reign and resulting in judgment for the unbelieving, unto the triune God's glory.* Resurrection as new creation and kingship is a, and I think *the*, fundamental part of this idea. To demonstrate this as the generative source for most of Paul's important notions and those of the NT in general will be the burden of the remaining chapters of this book.

90. I borrowed this metaphor from Richard B. Hays, *The Conversion of the Imagination: Paul as Interpreter of Israel's Scripture* (Grand Rapids: Eerdmans, 2005), 181. Hays uses it to refer to the generative influence of Deut. 32 throughout the book of Romans. Other metaphors for the new-creational resurrection as the shaping influence on Paul's thought are (1) the metal ribs of an umbrella, which provide the basic structure and then are covered by fabric; (2) a skeleton, which gives the shape to the flesh of the body.

10

More-Explicit Pauline Expressions
of Resurrection as Inaugurated End-Time
New Creation and Kingdom

I concluded in the preceding chapter that because of Paul's own experience with the resurrected Christ, the notion of resurrection permeates his writings. We saw that although Paul rarely uses the actual phrase "new creation" or synonyms for it, the concept is repeatedly conveyed by numerous references to resurrection. As we have observed already in the case of the Gospels, the fact that resurrection is a new-creational concept is clear in that a resurrected body is a newly created body, the body that God's people will have as part of the final, eternal new creation. In this respect, Christ's resurrected body was the first newly created body to pass to the other side of the new creation. The coming new creation penetrated back into the old world through the resurrected body of Jesus. This occurs with the followers of Jesus through the work of the Spirit, who is the agent causing the new creation to begin to penetrate their hearts and giving hope for its consummation, which has begun in them (cf. Rom. 8:18–25).

That Paul did sometimes think more explicitly of Christ's resurrection (including the resurrection appearance that he experienced) as an event of new creation is apparent at various significant points in his writings: 2 Cor. 5:17; Gal. 6:15; Col. 1:15–18. It is to these more explicit expressions that we now turn. These texts are mere tips of the iceberg that point to Paul's conception of Christ's and believers' resurrection as new creation being widespread throughout his writings. This is a crucial part of the overall NT biblical-theological storyline, as noted in the preceding two chapters.

Paul's Conception of Resurrection as the Beginning End-Time New Creation: 2 Corinthians 5:14–18

Although I briefly discussed this passage earlier, I now must address it in more depth. In 2 Cor. 5:14–18 Paul says,

> For the love of Christ controls us, having concluded this, that one died for all, therefore all died; and He died for all, so that they who live might no longer live for themselves, but for Him who died and rose again on their behalf. Therefore from now on we recognize no one according to the flesh; even though we have known Christ according to the flesh, yet now we know Him in this way no longer. Therefore if anyone is in Christ, he is a new creation; the old things passed away; behold, new things have come. Now all these things are from God, who reconciled us to Himself through Christ and gave us the ministry of reconciliation.

Verse 14 affirms that believers are identified with Christ's death, so that they are considered to have died to the old world and to their part in the old world. Being in Christ results in having resurrection life and in living such life for him instead of ourselves (v. 15). To live for Christ and not for ourselves is to evaluate things in life differently from the way unbelievers do (v. 16). That is, to live for Christ is to live by his word and not by the word of the world. Now in verse 17 we find out why Christians are to evaluate things in such a radically different way from that of the old, unregenerate world of humanity: "Therefore if anyone is in Christ, he is a new creation; the old things passed away; behold, new things have come." The point is that to live for Christ and not for ourselves is to evaluate differently from people in the old creation precisely because we live in the new creation.

Are the Corinthians experiencing the real beginning of the eschatological prophecies of new creation, or are they merely *like* what those prophecies predicted? In particular, does verse 17 say that Christians are only *like* the end-time new creation, or that they are *a real* beginning of the prophesied new creation? Is the regeneration of Christians merely compared to being like a new creation, or is that regeneration an actual beginning of the end-time new creation? The prophecy in mind specifically is that of the new creation predicted in Isa. 43 and Isa. 65 (see table 10.1).

Although the matter is debated, 2 Cor. 5:17 probably refers to the most famous of Isaiah's prophecies about the coming new creation, as generally acknowledged by commentators.[1] Some would not want to see the prophecies of new creation actually starting fulfillment because Paul does not appear to

---

1. For elaboration of the validity of the allusion to Isa. 43 and 65; 66 in 2 Cor. 5:17, as well as discussion of those not seeing specific allusion to Isaiah, see chap. 16 under the heading "Paul's View of Reconciliation as New Creation and Restoration from Exile." Isaiah 66:22, virtually identical to Isa. 65:17, may also be included in the allusion.

Table 10.1

Isaiah 43:18–19; 65:17 LXX	2 Corinthians 5:17
43:18–19: "Do not remember the first things [*ta prōta*] and the ancient things [*ta archaia*] do not consider. Behold, I create new things [*idou poiō kaina*]."	"If anyone is in Christ, that one is a new creation [*kainē ktisis*]; the ancient things [*ta archaia*] have passed away, behold [*idou*], new things [*kaina*] have come about."
65:17: "For there will be a new [*kainos*] heaven and a new [*kainē*] earth, and by no means will they remember the former things [*tōn proterōn*]."	

be applying the prophecy to the same literal situation that Isaiah had in mind. That is, how could Paul be describing the actual dawning fulfillment of Isa. 43 and 65 when the old earth is still here and Christians still have old, fallen bodies in which they exist? Isaiah, however, predicted a complete renovation of heaven and earth, and that has not yet happened. This is, no doubt, why some are compelled to conclude that Paul is merely comparing believers' re-generated condition with the future new creation, which has not yet begun: believers have left their old condition of unbelief and spiritual deadness and are now spiritually new creatures, but this is not to be understood as being part of Isaiah's prophesied literal new creation. But, those who hold such a futurist position might say, this is not what Isaiah's prophecy had in mind. Accordingly, for Isaiah's prophecies to be literally fulfilled, does not the old earth have to be destroyed to make way for the new creation at Christ's second coming? Furthermore, for believers to be part of the new creation, do they not have to possess newly created and resurrected bodies? Therefore, such commentators would see Paul's allusion to Isa. 43 and Isa. 65 not as an indication of any form of fulfillment but instead only as a pure analogy.

There do appear, however, to be reasons to understand Paul to be saying not that our new creation in Christ is merely like Isaiah's prophecy of the coming new creation, but rather that it actually is the beginning fulfillment of that prophecy. One reason pointing to this assessment is that these are *prophecies* of the new heaven and earth in their OT contexts, and unless it is clear otherwise from the NT context, they should continue to be seen as prophecies either of the future consummation or of the beginning reality of those prophecies that have been inaugurated. That Paul sees Christians fulfilling the Isaiah prophecy is further indicated by his summarizing statement in 2 Cor. 1:20: "For as many as are the promises of God [in the OT], in Him [Christ] they are yes." This is restated in 2 Cor. 7:1: "Therefore, having these promises, beloved, let us cleanse ourselves from all defilement of flesh and spirit." This statement about promises refers most immediately to the temple and restoration promises of the OT (2 Cor. 6:16–18), which Paul saw beginning fulfillment in the church of Corinth. These two references to beginning fulfillment of promises form bookends around 2 Cor. 2–6 and likely refer not merely to the temple prophecies at the end of 2 Cor. 6 but include the other prominent prophetic promises discussed in 2 Cor. 2–5, including "new covenant" and "new creation."

It is probable that the promises that the Corinthians were beginning to fulfill also included Isaiah's promises of new creation, since they were just that—prophetic promises, some of the most famous in the OT. Peter refers specifically to Isa. 65:17 and 66:22 as a promise: "But according to His <u>promise</u> we are looking for new heavens and a new earth, in which righteousness dwells" (2 Pet. 3:13). What Peter sees to be consummately fulfilled in the future heavens and earth, Paul sees as having begun fulfillment. Paul's concluding reference to "new things have come" at the end of 2 Cor. 5:17 highlights this inaugurated fulfillment further. In addition, since the Isaiah prophecies were about the renovation of the entire cosmos, believers' beginning participation in fulfilling these prophecies in 2 Cor. 5:17 indicates that their initial spiritual renewal not only will be completed further in physical resurrection but also is part of a larger coming renovation of the entire fallen creation. This is confirmed from Rom. 8:18–23, where, as we saw, the new spiritual resurrection life of the saints is but an initial stage of their final resurrection and new creation, which is also part of the renewal of the whole cosmos (see chap. 9 under the heading "Resurrection in Romans").

In this light, it appears that we are compelled to conclude that somehow Paul views Isaiah's prophecies of new creation not as mere analogies but rather as beginning to be fulfilled in the Corinthian Christians. But if so, how can his understanding of the way new creation has begun be squared hermeneutically with what Isaiah had in mind? Isaiah had in mind a new physical heaven and earth, and Paul has in mind the new spiritual condition of individual believers. Again, how can we live in the new creation when we still live on the old earth? Does not the old earth have to be destroyed to make way for the new creation at Christ's second coming, and do not believers need to have newly created bodies before they can be in the new creation?

The answer is that the new creation is here in part but not in its completeness, a notion that we have already encountered repeatedly. Indeed, how are God's people going to enter the final form of the physical new creation at the very end of world history? They will enter it by being resurrected bodily. But as we have seen in the use of Dan. 12:2 in John 5, the OT prophets did not merely predict a bodily resurrection but also expected that a renewed human spirit would be part of that resurrection. What is a little unusual in both John 5 and 2 Cor. 5 is that the eschatological resurrection is conceived of as beginning fulfillment in a staggered manner: first the spirit of a person is literally raised from spiritual death in this age, and in the next age that person's body will be raised, in which that person's new spirit will be housed.[2] But it is only the

---

2. Unlike John 5, 2 Cor. 5:14–17 does not explicitly affirm the "not yet" consummate new creation to come, though Paul affirms this at points elsewhere (e.g., Rom. 8:18–23).

timing of the prophecy that occurs a bit unexpectedly; the literal nature of the prophecy is fulfilled according to the literal understanding of the prophet.

Thus, the new creation in 2 Cor. 5:17 has begun spiritually with Christ's resurrection from the dead, but it will be consummated spiritually and physically at Christ's second coming, along with the renewal of the whole cosmos. That "new creation" in verse 17 refers to the beginning resurrection existence of believers is apparent from 2 Cor. 5:14–15:

> For the love of Christ controls us, having concluded this, that one died for all, therefore all died; and He died for all, so that they who live might no longer live for themselves, but for Him who died and rose again on their behalf.

Verse 17 says, "If anyone is in Christ [i.e., in the resurrected Christ], then that one is a new creation." Believers are identified with both Christ's death and his resurrection. This identification is spiritual or unseen, so that believers are viewed as having died to the spiritual penalty of sin and having been spiritually raised. Afterward, at the final day, they shed their old bodies and put on new bodies. Verse 17 identifies Christ's resurrection mentioned in verse 15 to be the beginning of the new creation, of which believers are a part, since they are also identified with Christ's resurrection (as also seen in Col. 1:18; Rev. 3:14). The new creation has even begun physically in the form of Christ's resurrection body, which is the first re-created body of the new creation. Christ is the first one, according to 1 Cor. 15, who has already experienced the consummate resurrection and individual consummate new creation. As such, he is the "first fruits" of all God's people who will be raised at the end of the age. Thus, believers' present identification with Christ's resurrection is identification with new creation, since his resurrection was the very inception of the eschatological new creation.

Note also that in the Isaiah prophecies the emphasis is on the minds of those who become part of the new creation: they think or evaluate things differently because there is a new creation ("Do not call to mind the former things, or ponder things of the past" [43:8]; "The former things will not be remembered or come to mind" [65:17]). The Israelites whom Isaiah was addressing were not to let the thoughts of the old world (idolatry, sins for which they were held in bondage, etc.) dominate their minds. Instead, their minds were to be consumed with thoughts of the new world with new standards of thinking and evaluating. Similarly, Paul likely sees that Christians' new-creational existence in Christ is the basis for them not evaluating things by the standards of the old world: "Therefore from now on we recognize [or 'evaluate'] no one according to the flesh; even though we have known Christ according to the flesh, yet now we know Him this way no longer" (2 Cor. 5:16).[3]

---

3. This analysis of 2 Cor. 5:17 is a contrast with that by Moyer V. Hubbard, *New Creation in Paul's Letters and Thought*, SNTSMS 119 (Cambridge: Cambridge University Press, 2002), 133–87. Hubbard believes that "new creation" in this passage is about only a "soterio-anthropological"

What Difference Does It Make for Christian Living That the Latter-Day New Creation Has Begun?

If believers are merely like a new creation, they might get away with thinking that they really do not have to live and think radically as new creatures. But if Christians are the actual beginning of the end-time new creation, they must act the way new creatures act, which is to live for Christ by viewing all of reality from the perspective of his word and not from the viewpoint of the world. Just as a butterfly cannot return to its cocoon and act like a caterpillar again, so all who are part of the beginning fulfillment of the prophesied new creation in Christ cannot return to being unbelievers and, therefore, will perhaps slowly but surely act like people who have begun to be part of the new creation. It is on the basis that Christians are a new creation that Paul can issue commands to them. That is, they have the power to obey the commands by virtue of the new-creational ability inherent in them.

Do God's people think differently from the way the world thinks? Do they set their mind on the things of the old, fallen world, on the sinful thoughts of the world? Or do they have a desire to read God's word in order to think more like he does? If people have never had a desire to do this, they ought to ask themselves whether they are a new creation. Do sexual images and sexual messages on television and radio and in movies, videos, and magazines bother a Christian? If not, that person ought to ask, "Am I really a new creation?" The saints' desire to read God's word and think like he does

---

and not "soterio-cosmological" reality. It appears that for Hubbard, the "new creation" language is metaphorical only for personal salvation, which is not a part of the cosmological new creation prophesied in the OT. Here there is not enough space to offer significant critique, except for the following: (1) the two categories of "soterio-anthropological" and "soterio-cosmological" are not mutually exclusive and easily overlap; (2) Hubbard does not see allusions to the famous cosmological "new creation" texts of Isa. 65:17 and 66:22 in 2 Cor. 5:17, which I have argued are likely allusions; (3) Hubbard makes no mention of Christ's resurrection in 2 Cor. 5:15, which represents the beginning of the actual new creation, since resurrection is the way humans would participate in the coming new creation; thus, those "in Christ" (v. 17) are part of that beginning new creation. While it is true that they are not bodily part of the new creation, their resurrected spirits have become part of such a new creation, since cosmological resurrection entails resurrection of both spirit and body. Consequently, Hubbard concludes, mistakenly in my view, that 2 Cor. 5:17 is not a part of inaugurated cosmic eschatology. I have the same critique of Hubbard's same conclusion in his chapter about Gal. 6:15 (on which, see discussion below in this chap.). See also Douglas J. Moo, "Creation and New Creation," *BBR* 20 (2010): 39–60: Moo argues in line with my analysis of 2 Cor. 5:17 and Gal. 5:15 (below) and offers the similar critique of Hubbard (see, e.g., pp. 51, 58). For critique of others who hold the same kind of view as Hubbard's but in other "new creation" Pauline passages, see John W. Yates, *The Spirit and Creation in Paul*, WUNT 2/251 (Tübingen: Mohr Siebeck, 2008), e.g., 122–23, 160, 172–73, 176–77. Most recently, see T. Ryan Jackson, *New Creation in Paul's Letters: A Study of the Historical and Social Setting of a Pauline Concept*, WUNT 2/272 (Tübingen: Mohr Siebeck, 2010), esp. 83–114, 115–49. Jackson offers the most sustained and incisive critique of Hubbard's view in 2 Cor. 5:17 and Gal. 6:15. Jackson's analysis of 2 Cor. 5:14–17 offers further in-depth support from various angles of my conclusions about this passage.

and their lack of desire to think like the old world should slowly but surely grow, so that they increasingly become imitators of God (Eph. 5:1) and not imitators of the world.

This is why Paul says in 2 Cor. 5:16 that true believers must evaluate things differently, and that their different evaluation begins "from now on." This "from now on" is a reference to the end times, beginning with Christ's resurrection, which is the beginning of the new creation. That the "now" (*nyn*) in 2 Cor. 5:16 refers to the end-time turn of the ages is apparent from 2 Cor. 6:2, where the same word refers to the beginning fulfillment of another Isaiah prophecy about the end times.[4]

There is a struggle for the Christian's ideological allegiance. Although saints are part of a new creation, it has not yet fully come. Whereas in the future fullness of the new creation there will be no sinful influences (Rev. 21:1–22:5), right now sinful influences still vie for the loyalty of God's people because they still live physically in the old, fallen world, where Satan and evil have not yet been finally destroyed. There is a battle for Christian minds, as 2 Cor. 4:4–6 says that Satan has "blinded the minds of the unbelieving" (v. 4) and tries to put Christians in the fog whenever he can. But this fog begins to dissipate significantly for true believers, who have been transferred out of spiritual darkness and into the light of the new creation: "For God, who said [in Gen. 1:2–4], 'Light shall shine out of darkness,' is the One who has shone in our hearts to give the light of the knowledge of the glory of God in the face of Christ" (v. 6). The effect of being a new creation will be that we will "destroy speculations and every lofty thing raised up against the knowledge of God and we take every thought captive to the obedience of Christ" (2 Cor. 10:5).

Paul's Conception of Death and Resurrection as the Beginning End-Time New Creation: Galatians 5:22–25; 6:15–17

Introduction[5]

Galatians 6:15 is the second most explicit text in Paul's writings about new creation: "For neither is circumcision anything, nor uncircumcision, but a new creation." Discussions of the OT background of "new creation" in verse 15 and its relation to verse 16 ("And those who will walk by this rule, peace and mercy be upon them, and upon the Israel of God") have heretofore been general and have not targeted any particular OT passage. Here I seek to demonstrate four points not sufficiently observed thus far:

4. As we saw in chap. 9, the word "now" (*nyn*) is often used in this way (John 5:25; Rom. 3:26; Eph. 3:5; 1 John 2:18).

5. This section is based on and is a summary of G. K. Beale, "Peace and Mercy upon the Israel of God: The Old Testament Background of Gal. 6,16b," *Bib* 80 (1999): 204–23.

1. Galatians 6:15–16 picks up and develops explicit ideas and metaphors of new creation from Gal. 5:22–26.
2. *Stoicheō* in Gal. 6:16 is a word fraught with "new creation" overtones.
3. The phrase "peace and mercy" has its most probable background in the OT promise of Israel's restoration in Isa. 54.
4. In light of the three preceding points, the "marks" of Jesus on Paul's body in Gal. 6:17 make perfect sense.

The following analysis will also include the relation of Gal. 6:15–16 to the context of the letter in general and, in particular, to the logical development of Paul's argument within chapter 6.

The Eschatological Connection of 6:14–15 with 5:22–26

Galatians 5:22–26 is likely best understood through the lens of the new creation, which is developed even more explicitly in 6:15–16. "The fruit of the Spirit" in 5:22 is a general allusion to the OT promise that the Spirit will bring about abundant fertility in the coming new age.[6] Specifically, uppermost in mind are Isaiah's repeated prophecies that in the new creation the Spirit will be the bearer of plentiful fruitfulness, which Isaiah often interprets to be godly attributes such as righteousness and holiness and trust in the Lord, as well as joy and peace. For example, Isa. 32:15–18a says,

> Until the Spirit is poured out upon us from on high,
> And the wilderness becomes a fertile field
> And the fertile field is considered as a forest.
> Then justice will dwell in the wilderness,
> And righteousness will abide in the fertile field.
> And the work of righteousness will be peace,
> And the service of righteousness, quietness and confidence forever.
> Then my people will live in a peaceful habitation.

Likewise, other texts in Isaiah make the same connection between the eschatological pouring out of the Spirit and the figurative fruits of godly characteristics.[7] The imparting of resurrection life is another way in which the OT understands the Spirit to be an active agent in bringing about the latter-day

6. For expansion of the OT background of "the fruit of the Spirit" and its link to new creation in Gal. 5:22, see chap. 17 under the heading "The Eschatological Role of the Spirit in Paul's Thought."
7. See Isa. 11:1–5, and likewise the similar link between the Spirit and its fruits in Isa. 44:2–4; 61:1, 3, 11; and probably 4:2–4. For fruitfulness as figurative for godly traits in the coming new age, see Isa. 27:6; 37:31–32; 45:8; 51:3; 58:11 (cf. 55:10–13 with 56:3; 60:21; 65:8, 17–22), though the Spirit does not appear in these texts. The eschatological fruitfulness depicted in Joel 2:21–22 is inextricably linked to the pouring out of the Spirit in 2:28–29. See also Hos. 14:2–8; cf. Jer. 17:7–8.

new creation. This end-time role of the Spirit is also generally reflected in Paul's thought, including Galatians, especially in 5:25.

The OT prophesied that the Holy Spirit will be given as a gift at the end of the world, and one of its benefits will be to raise the saints from the dead. The above connection between the Spirit and fertility in the OT and in Gal. 5:22 implies that the Spirit is the imparter of life to God's people (see esp. Isa. 32:15–18a; 44:2–4; 61:1–3, 11; cf. also "life" in Isa. 4:3 with the "Spirit" in 4:4). More explicit is Ezek. 36:26–28, where God's Spirit will be the end-time agent that creates "a new spirit" and new "heart of flesh" so that Israel can "live in the land." Likewise, in Ezek. 37:13–14 God says, "When I have . . . caused you to come up out of your graves. . . . I will put My Spirit within you, and you will come to life," though this is part of a metaphorical depiction of Israel's return from captivity. As discussed earlier in this book, although the Ezek. 37 reference is not as explicit as the one in Ezek. 36, it surely includes the people of Israel's spiritual regeneration when they return to the land and likely implies their physical resurrection as well. Early and late Judaism followed and developed the OT's notion of the Spirit as the agent of the latter-day resurrection.[8]

The first Israelite saint to be raised in the age of the eschaton was Jesus, whom the Spirit set apart at the beginning of his ministry and raised physically from the dead at the end of his ministry (Rom. 1:4; cf. 1 Tim. 3:16). This same Spirit raises people spiritually in the present (Rom. 8:6, 10–16;[9] cf. 6:4–5) and will do so bodily at the second coming (Rom. 8:11). Indeed, Paul understands that the Holy Spirit is what causes believers to be existentially linked with the new world to come, so that they partake of the blessings of the future world through the Holy Spirit.[10]

The notion of the Spirit as an eschatological reality and as being linked with the giving of life appears in Galatians. Writing on eschatology in Galatians, Moisés Silva points out the eschatological nature of the Spirit in 3:2–5, 14; 4:4–6, 29; 5:5, 25; 6:8.[11] One of the clearest expressions of this is tēn epangelian tou pneumatos ("the promise of the Spirit") in 3:14, which refers to the beginning fulfillment of the Abrahamic promise among gentiles. Here the genitive phrase is best understood epexegetically or appositionally: "the

8. E.g., 1 En. 49:3; 61:7; Sib. Or. 3:771; b. 'Abod. Zar. 20b; Song Rab. 1.1.9; Midr. Tanḥ. Gen. 2.12.

9. Here note the combination of "Spirit" (pneuma) with either "live" (zaō) or "life" (zōē).

10. This paragraph and the preceding one are based on Geerhardus Vos, "The Eschatological Aspect of the Pauline Conception of the Spirit," in Redemptive History and Biblical Interpretation: The Shorter Writings of Geerhardus Vos, ed. Richard B. Gaffin Jr. (Phillipsburg, NJ: P&R, 1980), 91–125.

11. Moisés Silva, "Eschatological Structures in Galatians," in To Tell the Mystery: Essays on New Testament Eschatology in Honor of Robert H. Gundry, ed. Thomas E. Schmidt and Moisés Silva, JSNTSup 100 (Sheffield: JSOT Press, 1994), 140–62.

promise which is the Spirit."[12] The Abrahamic promise was, in light of NT revelation, none other than the promise that God's Spirit would create gentiles into his own people by means of his Spirit (cf. 3:16 with 3:26–29). That this is an eschatological fulfillment is underscored by 4:4–6, where "the fullness of the time" is the time when, "because you are sons, God has sent forth the Spirit of His son into our hearts."

Paul's understanding of the Spirit's latter-day function as the creator of a new humanity is apparent from Gal. 4:29; 5:25. Richard Hays[13] and Karen Jobes[14] argue that the quotation of Isa. 54:1 in Gal. 4:27 continues the theme of the fulfillment of the Abrahamic promises among gentiles elaborated on earlier in 3:26–29 (and 4:4–6). The reference to the "barren one" in Isa. 54:1 itself alludes to Sarah and develops further Isa. 51:2 ("Look to Abraham your father, and to Sarah who gave birth to you"), which in turn alludes to the Abrahamic blessing as a basis for the forthcoming prophesied restoration from captivity. Yet Paul does not merely see gentile Christians as the first to fulfill the Abrahamic promise, for in Gal. 3:16 he contends that Christ sums up in himself the true Israelite seed of Abraham in whom gentiles, because of their faith in him, are included.

The striking conclusion is that Christ, as the initial fulfiller of the Abrahamic promise through his death and resurrection, is the one also who first fulfilled the Isa. 54:1 prophecy, and hence he is the "firstborn" child (cf. Col. 1:18; Rev. 1:5) of the "barren woman," Sarah. Thus, Paul "construed the resurrection of Jesus Christ to be the miraculous birth which would transform Jerusalem the barren one into Jerusalem the faithful mother city."[15] According to Gal. 3:16, Jesus is the son or "seed" that God promised to Abraham and is therefore the eschatological son of Sarah. In this respect, "the nation which God promised to bring from Sarah's dead womb and the population of the new Jerusalem prophesied by Isaiah are those people who are born through the resurrection of Jesus, not those who are circumcised."[16] All who identify with Jesus by faith are also part of the fulfillment of Abraham's promised seed, so that in Gal. 4, directly preceding the Isa. 54 citation in verse 27 Paul can refer to "the promise" (v. 23), and immediately following the quotation he can call Christians "children of promise" (v. 28) who have been "born according to the

---

12. So Vos, "Eschatological Aspect," 103. It could, however, be an objective genitive ("[God] promised the Spirit") or an adjectival genitive ("promised Spirit"), or these two could be included in the appositional genitive.

13. Richard B. Hays, *Echoes of Scripture in the Letters of Paul* (New Haven: Yale University Press, 1989), 118–21.

14. Karen H. Jobes, "Jerusalem, Our Mother: Metalepsis and Intertextuality in Galatians 4.21–31," *WTJ* 55 (1993): 299–320.

15. Ibid., 314 (but see passim). Moisés Silva believes that Jobes's view has "much to be said in its favor" ("Eschatological Structures in Galatians," 156).

16. Jobes, "Jerusalem, Our Mother," 316.

Spirit" (v. 29).[17] This is another way of claiming what has already been asserted in 3:26–29, but now the Spirit is underscored, even more clearly than in 3:14 and 4:6, as the agent who causes Abraham's children to come into existence, the same one who raised Jesus from the dead (cf. Rom. 1:4).[18]

The last two references linking the Spirit with life occur in Gal. 5:25; 6:8. The most explicit link occurs in 5:25: "If we live by the Spirit [zōmen pneumati], let us be in line with the Spirit" (my translation). That this refers to the inaugurated resurrection life of a believer is apparent from two observations. First, in 5:24 those who are identified with Jesus (lit., "who are of Christ Jesus") "have crucified the flesh with its passions and desires," which likely refers to their identification with Christ's own crucifixion and its present effects for them. Accordingly, it is natural that, after referring to the believer's identification with Christ's crucifixion, Paul would speak of the believer's identification with Christ's resurrection. Second, 2:19–20 sets a precedent for a crucifixion-resurrection pattern in which the believer is identified with Christ: "For through the Law I died to the Law, so that I might live to God. I have been crucified with Christ; and it is no longer I who live, but Christ lives in me; and the life which I now live in the flesh I live by faith in the Son of God, who loved me and gave Himself up for me."[19]

The discussion so far demonstrates that Gal. 5:22–25 is a highly charged eschatological passage about new creation, which is brought about through the agency of the Spirit. Such an understanding enables us to recognize its eschatological connection to Gal. 6:14–16.

The conclusion of Gal. 6:11–17 sums up one of the major themes, indeed likely the preeminent theme, of the letter: Christ, not the law, is the identity marker of the new people of God.[20] After underscoring his authorship of the

---

17. Cf. Silva, "Eschatological Structures in Galatians," 156.

18. Noting that except for Romans, Galatians is the only letter that at the beginning focuses on Christ's resurrection (1:1), Silva (ibid., 145–46) suggests that its uniqueness may be designed to prepare the way for a better understanding of the Isa. 54 quotation in chap. 4.

19. In Gal. 5:5 Paul says, "For we through the Spirit, by faith, are awaiting the hope of righteousness." This is likely another place where the Spirit is the agent for the new life of Christ, though here the manner of the new life is categorized as "awaiting" the final revelation of divine righteousness. Galatians 6:8 seems to be the only text in the letter referring to an exclusively future reference to the Spirit: the one who identifies with the fleshly mode of existence now will experience corruption at the end, and the one who identifies with the Spirit's mode of existence in the present will inherit "eternal life" at the last day.

20. That 6:11–17 sums up the major themes of Galatians has been argued most trenchantly by Jeffrey A. D. Weima, "Gal. 6:11–18: A Hermeneutical Key to the Galatian Letter," CTJ 28 (1993): 90–107; idem, "The Pauline Letter Closings: Analysis and Hermeneutical Significance," BBR 5 (1995): 177–98. Weima underscores four major themes throughout Galatians that he sees summarized in 6:11–17, but all revolve around the central notion of identification with Christ: (1) boasting in the flesh versus boasting in Christ; (2) avoiding persecution because of identity with Christ versus willingness to be persecuted for identifying with Christ; (3) identifying with circumcision or uncircumcision versus identifying with Christ; (4) the old world versus the new

letter, Paul says that his opponents make circumcision compulsory so they would not "be persecuted for the cross of Christ" (v. 12). The reason ("for," *gar*) why they do not want to be persecuted for the cross is that they would rather boast in the law (e.g., circumcision in the flesh) than in Christ (v. 13). Paul, however, says in verse 14 that he prefers boasting in the cross, with which he has identified by faith; consequently, he no longer has a place in the old "world," since that place has been destroyed (i.e., the world has been "crucified to him," and he has been "crucified to the world"). Verses 15–16 explain why Paul boasts only in the cross: neither circumcision nor uncircumcision matter one whit to God, since they are part of the old world, which is passing away. What does matter, however, is the "new creation," since its inauguration is the new redemptive-historical stage, which has made obsolete the earlier stage characterized by Torah. In the old age, Torah was the epitome of divine revelation, but now its high position has been surpassed in the "new creation," which expresses the zenith of God's revelation in Christ, a revelation only pointed to in the former age of Torah (see, e.g., Gal. 3:23–25). The "new creation" is the other side of the coin of the crucifixion; Jesus's crucifixion was inextricably linked to his resurrection, since the former was necessary for and led to the latter, which Paul understands elsewhere to be a new creation.[21]

Reference to "new creation" in 6:15 is likely an allusion to Isa. 65:17: "I create new heavens and a new earth" (so almost identically Isa. 66:22, and similarly Isa. 43:19),[22] especially since the only other time Paul uses the phrase is an allusion to the same Isaiah text(s).[23] The allusion is also pointed to further by the previous references discussed in this chapter, and I will discuss later (chap. 21) that a new creation prophecy from Isa. 54 is alluded to in Gal. 6:16. Thus, Paul sees the beginning of Isaiah's prophesied new creation to have begun through Christ's death (Gal. 6:14) and his resurrection (the latter of which is assumed in "new creation," to which the context of Galatians also testifies, beginning with 1:1–4 and again toward the end in 6:16).

Part of Paul's point is that his identification with the death of Christ is the actual inception of his separation from the old, corruptible, and sinful world, and it is the precise commencement of the old world's separation from him (v. 14). Paul's separation from the old cosmos means that he has started to be set apart to another world, which in verse 15 he calls a "new creation." Thus,

---

creation, the former focusing on the law and the flesh, the latter on Christ. Hans Dieter Betz says, "The whole argument in the letter leads up to the rule in v. 15" (*Galatians*, Hermeneia [Philadelphia: Fortress, 1979], 321). See also Frank J. Matera, "The Culmination of Paul's Argument to the Galatians: Gal. 5:1–6:17," *JSNT* 32 (1988): 79–91. Matera argues that the last two chapters of Galatians summarize the letter's earlier themes and are the culmination of Paul's overall argument.

21. See G. K. Beale, "The Old Testament Background of Reconciliation in 2 Corinthians 5–7 and Its Bearing on the Literary Problem of 2 Corinthians 4:14–7:1," *NTS* 35 (1989): 550–81.

22. These two Isaiah texts may also be included in the allusion.

23. See Beale, "Old Testament Background of Reconciliation," 553–57.

Christ's death is inextricably linked to the new creation, which necessarily leads to the resurrection of Christ and of believers, which probably is also included in his thought in verse 15, as verse 16 makes probable in light of my discussion following directly in this section and the next. Christ's death in verses 14–15 is explicitly seen to be absolutely vital to the inauguration of new creation, and the resurrection is only implied. Galatians 1:4, speaking of Christ as the one "who gave Himself for our sins so that He might rescue us from this present evil world," expresses virtually the same thing as 6:14–15. Christ's death is the means by which people are delivered out of the old, fallen cosmos.

Therefore, "new creation" in 6:15 together with 6:16 is a way of speaking not only of the effects of Christ's death but also of the resurrection life mentioned in 5:25, both of which underlie Paul's comprehension of how both the Isa. 54:1 prophecy and the Isa. 65:17 "new creation" prophecy began fulfillment. That this is so is apparent from 2:19–20 and, especially, 5:24–25, where mention of crucifixion is directly followed by reference to resurrection life. The same twofold pattern is discernible in 6:14–16, particularly since 5:22–25 also focuses on the theme of new creation. The result of the new creation for its inhabitants in 5:22–25 is their not becoming "boastful, challenging one another, envying one another" (5:26), a negative development of the positive attributes of the "fruit of the Spirit," particularly "peace, patience, kindness, . . . gentleness, self-control" (5:22–23). Thus, the dividing function of the law has been set aside so that it cannot be "against such things" as maintaining peace in the new order (5:23). Likewise, 6:15–16 says that in the "new creation" circumcision, which stands for the dividing function of the law (see below), means nothing, so that the effect on those residing in the new cosmos is "peace and mercy" (6:16), a development of "peace" and "kindness" from 5:22–23, which are traits characteristic of the new creation.

The Use of "Walk" (stoicheō) in Galatians 6:16 as a Term Closely Linked with New Creation

One more crucial eschatological link between the segment of Gal. 5:22–25 and 6:14–16 consists in the common use of *stoicheō* in 5:25 and 6:16,[24] which is often translated as "walk." Galatians 6:16 continues to explain new creation from 6:15. The reference to "this rule" (*kanōn*) at the beginning of verse 16 must refer to the regulating principle of the "new creation" that has just been mentioned in verse 15.[25] Therefore, believers are to "walk" by means of this regulative principle of the new creation, just as earlier they were to "walk by

24. I have found corroboration for this in Matera, "Culmination of Paul's Argument," 88. Matera contends that *stoicheō* in 6:16 "echoes" the earlier use in 5:25, and that the "rule" of 6:16 refers to depending on the Spirit (in 5:25) and not on circumcision.

25. For the use of "new creation" in Judaism in comparison with Gal. 6:15, see Bruce D. Chilton, "Galatians 6:15: A Call to Freedom before God," *ExpTim* 89 (1978): 311–13. See also

means of the Spirit" (5:25).[26] Some translations render *stoicheō* here as "walk" (RSV, NASB, KJV), while some have "follow" (NRSV, NIV, JB), others "take for their guide" (NEB, similarly Moffatt), and still others "live by" (NLT). However, *stoicheō* is a word that appears not to be precisely synonymous with *peripateō*, Paul's usual word for "walk." Oddly, none of the above translations have "be in line (accord or agreement) with," which is the best translation for all the NT uses.[27]

In order to better understand the notion of *stoicheō*, we need to recall the main theme of Galatians. Christ has abolished that part of the law which divided Jews from gentiles so that they could become one. Gentiles no longer need to adapt the signs of Torah and customs of national Israel (such as circumcision, dietary laws, and calendrical regulations) to become true Israelites. They do not need to identify with geographical Israel to become true Israel. They need to identify only with Jesus, the one toward whom Torah pointed all the time (Gal. 2:23–25). They need to be circumcised not in the flesh but rather in the heart by Christ's death, which is their true circumcision, since it cut them off from the old world and set them apart to the new (Gal. 3:1–5; 5:1–6, 11–12; 6:12–15; cf. Col. 2:10–14). They do not need to keep the dietary laws, since they have been definitively cleansed by Christ. The only holiday on the new calendar is the day of resurrection, when they worship.[28] Therefore, the old, fallen world is characterized by the nationalistic identifying expressions of the law, whereas the only identifying sign of the new creation is Christ.

The contrasting nature of the identifying signs of the old and new creations is highlighted by a comparison of Gal. 5:6 and 6:15:

5:6   For <u>in Christ Jesus</u> neither circumcision nor uncircumcision means anything, but <u>faith working in love</u>.

6:15   For neither is circumcision anything nor uncircumcision, but <u>a new creation</u>.

The words underlined in these verses reveal the positive contrast with the sign of circumcision, which belongs to the old world. Significantly, in 5:6 the phrase

---

G. K. Beale, "The Old Testament Background of Rev 3.14," *NTS* 42 (1996): 133–52, especially for uses of Isa. 43:18; 65:16–17 in Judaism.

26. It is possible to translate both 5:25 and 6:16 as "walk in the sphere of" respectively the Spirit or of the new creation, since *kanōn* means "sphere" elsewhere in its only other occurrences in the NT (2 Cor. 10:13, 15, 16; note the variant readings where the word also occurs in Phil. 3:16 [see the NA[27] apparatus], which can viably refer to "sphere"). If this is the idea, then the focus would be on believers now living in the realm of the Spirit and of the new creation.

27. See discussion below; also G. Delling, "στοιχέω, κ.τ.λ.," *TDNT* 7:666–69; BAGD (679) gives this as the first plausible definition.

28. See T. David Gordon, "The Problem at Galatia," *Int* 41 (1987): 32–43. Gordon contends that the main point of Galatians is that gentiles no longer need to identify with the signs of Torah to be a part of the true people of God.

"in Christ Jesus" is actually part of the positive element of the contrast that concludes the verse, so that the resulting sense is: "Neither circumcision nor uncircumcision means anything, but <u>faith in Christ Jesus working through love</u>." This positive contrast in 5:6 is parallel to the positive part of the contrast in 6:15, so that "faith in Christ Jesus" is parallel to, and likely synonymous with, "a new creation." Therefore, the old, fallen world is characterized by the identifying signs of Torah (e.g., circumcision), which segregate the sinful divisions inherent to the fallen creation, whereas the only identifying tag of the new creation is Jesus the Messiah.[29]

Therefore, in this light, the point of Gal. 5:16 is that believers are to live by means of the power of Christ, the beginning of the new creation, and by means of his Spirit, who has been sent to them.

Paul believes that the entire old world, not merely a part of it, has been struck a fatal blow. Of course, the beginning phase of the destruction is primarily focused on the spiritual aspects and their associated national (physical) signs of separation. Paul, however, likely held the view that the culmination of this beginning process would be some kind of radical destruction of the physical cosmos as well, since elsewhere he sees a reestablishment of a physically transformed earth,[30] including physically renovated resurrection bodies (see, e.g., Rom. 8:18–25; 1 Cor. 15:20–58).[31]

In this respect, we should remember that Christ's resurrection, which is the beginning of the new creation, is not merely a spiritual but also a physical reality, so that his physical place in the old world has been destroyed and his place has been transferred into the new world. Similarly, believers have begun to experience spiritual resurrection through the Spirit. And, if they have been resurrected out of the old creation, their spiritual place in that former world has been destroyed, as Paul testifies has happened to him (Gal. 6:14, through "the cross of our Lord Jesus Christ," Paul says, "the world has been crucified to me, and I to the world"). Subsequently, the saints' spiritual resurrection will be consummated in physical resurrection. This same two-step, already–not yet notion is applicable to the destruction of the cosmos. This means that Paul is

29. On the parallelism between Gal. 5:6 and 6:15, see Ulrich Mell, *Neue Schöpfung: Eine traditionsgeschichtliche und exegetische Studie zu einem soteriologischen Grundsatz paulinischer Theologie*, BZNW 56 (Berlin: de Gruyter, 1989), 298–99. Mell also points out the parallel to 1 Cor. 7:19. Betz (*Galatians*, 319) argues here that for the Christian to be in a "new creation" is to be "in Christ," in light of Gal. 2:19–20; 3:26–28; 4:6; 5:24–25.

30. Note 2 Pet. 3:10, 12, where the physical "elements" (*stoicheia*) of the cosmos are destroyed through fire and will be transformed into a "new heavens and a new earth" (3:13). Intriguingly, only two verses later "Paul" and "all his letters" are mentioned (3:15–16), which reflects some conscious link with Pauline tradition.

31. Mell (*Neue Schöpfung*, 316–17, 324) also says that the "new creation" of Gal. 6:15 cannot be a limited reference only to humanity but rather refers primarily to the soteriological transformation of the whole world. He does not, however, develop the idea, nor does he relate it to *stoicheō* or *stoicheia*.

not being figurative when he speaks of the beginning of the destruction of the world and the reconstitution of the new world, since he would have held that the elements that composed the old and the new worlds were actually both spiritual and physical in nature (and even the "spiritual" was a literal reality for Paul). If Paul is indeed alluding to Isa. 65:17 and 66:22 in Gal. 6:15, then this would have enforced his view that the "new creation" of which he speaks is a holistic reference to the entire new cosmos, part of which has begun to be inaugurated through Christ's resurrection and the spiritual resurrection of saints. Even a partial destruction or reconstitution of the elements in either of these worlds is an ontological reality, not a figurative one.

We will have to wait until later (chap. 21) to see that the foregoing conclusions are supported further by recognizing that the reference to "peace and mercy" in Gal. 6:16 is an allusion to Isa. 54:10, which is part of a prophecy that Israel will be blessed in the new creation. Now this prophecy is seen to be applied to the entire church in Galatia.

How Galatians 6:17 Precisely Fits into the Foregoing Analysis

Since "peace" should reign in the new creation (v. 16b), Paul asks that "no one [apparently no so-called brother] cause trouble for me." He explicitly says this is because he bears on his "body the brand-marks of Christ." On the one hand, those who belong to the old age insist on "making a good showing in the flesh" by being identified with the mark of "circumcision," in which they "boast" (v. 13). Since Paul, on the other hand, wants to "boast" only "in the cross of our Lord Jesus Christ," through which he has been "crucified to the world," and since circumcision means nothing anymore (v. 15), Paul wants to be identified with the only mark of the new creation, which is Messiah Jesus himself. Therefore, Paul's statement in verse 17 that he "bears on his body the brand-marks of Jesus" is another way to say that he does not want to be identified by the badge of the old age (circumcision) but wants to be identified with the only sign of the new age: Jesus, and his suffering at the cross.[32]

32. This point is different from that made by many commentators, who usually appeal to the use of *stigma* as a brand or tattoo mark on slaves to show who their owner was (e.g., see Richard N. Longenecker, *Galatians*, WBC 41 [Nashville: Thomas Nelson, 1990], 299–300). If overtones of such a meaning are in mind, they have been shaped by the idea of identification discussed here. James Dunn comes close to my own conclusion, but he does not relate his view of v. 17 to the old and new creations: "Paul . . . sets in contrast an identity defined in terms of circumcision and one focused in the cross of Christ" (*The Epistle to the Galatians*, BNTC [Peabody, MA: Hendrickson, 1993], 347); likewise Donald Guthrie, *Galatians*, NCB (Camden, NJ: Thomas Nelson, 1969), 163; F. F. Bruce, *The Epistle of Paul to the Galatians: A Commentary on the Greek Text*, NIGTC (Grand Rapids: Eerdmans, 1982), 275–76 (also citing 2 Cor. 4:11 in support); Timothy George, *Galatians*, NAC 30 (Nashville: B&H, 1994), 442; Ronald Y. K. Fung, *The Epistle to the Galatians*, NICNT (Grand Rapids: Eerdmans, 1988), 314.

Conclusion

In this section I have contended that Paul's reference to "new creation" in Gal. 6:15–16 is best understood against the background of new-creational passages and themes from Isaiah, which are echoed also earlier in Galatians, especially in 5:22–26. The demonstration of an Isaianic background for the concept of new creation in Gal. 6:15–16 falls in line with Paul's other reference to "new creation" in 2 Cor. 5:17 and John's allusion to new creation in Rev. 3:14, where Isa. 43 and 65–66 stand behind both passages.[33] Galatians 6:14–16 highlights Christ's death as crucial to the very inception of the new creation, though resurrection is certainly included in the concept of new creation. Second Corinthians 5:14–17 also views Christ's death, as well as his resurrection, to be vitally linked to the new creation.

Thus, Gal. 6:15–16 is one of the most explicit places in all of Paul's writings where he speaks of "new creation."[34] These two verses also bring out what is said with other words throughout Galatians. It is my contention that this notion of "new creation" also permeates most of Paul's thinking in one way or another.

Paul's Conception of Resurrection as the Beginning End-Time New Creation: Colossians 1:15–20

Commentators have written about the famous so-called poem of Col. 1:15–20 more than any other particular passage elsewhere in the letter.[35] Here I can give only a brief analysis of the passage.[36] If the conclusion of most scholars that Paul alluded to a preexisting hymn is correct, then Paul has adapted it to fit into the context of what he is writing. Since we do not have the context of the preexisting hymn against which to interpret Paul's use, we must concentrate on how Paul is using the wording in its context. Most directly, verses 15–20

33. As argued in Beale, "Old Testament Background of Reconciliation"; idem, "Old Testament Background of Rev 3.14."

34. As noted earlier, there will be more elaboration of the Isaianic new-creational background (i.e., Isa. 54:10) for Gal. 6:16 in a subsequent chapter (see chap. 21 under the heading "The Beginning Fulfillment of Israel's Restoration Prophecies in the Church according to Paul"). For in-depth analysis of Gal. 6:15–16, see Jackson, *New Creation in Paul's Letters*, 83–114. Jackson's work supports in various ways my study of this passage here.

35. For significant qualifications about this passage being based on a preformed hymn, see Peter T. O'Brien, *Colossians, Philemon*, WBC 44 (Waco: Word, 1982), 32–37.

36. For discussion of the poem and its background and debated meaning, see the bibliography cited in G. K. Beale, "Colossians," in *Commentary on the New Testament Use of the Old Testament*, ed. G. K. Beale and D. A. Carson (Grand Rapids: Baker Academic, 2007), 869–70, and for fuller discussion of 1:15–20, see ibid., 851–55; see also G. K. Beale, *Colossians and Philemon*, BECNT (Grand Rapids: Baker Academic, forthcoming).

are an explanation of the directly preceding verses 13b–14: "the Son of His love, in whom we have redemption, the forgiveness of sins."

The verses of the passage can be broadly divided into two sections: Christ's supremacy over the first creation (vv. 15–17), and Christ's supremacy over the new creation (vv. 18–20). See table 10.2 and 10.3 for portrayals of the parallels of these texts, first in Greek and then in English.

Table 10.2
Preeminence of Christ in the First Creation
and in the New Creation: Colossians 1:15–20

In the First Creation	In the New Creation
v. 15 *hos estin eikōn tou theou tou aoratou*	v. 19 *hoti en autō eudokēsen pan to plērōma katoikēsai*
v. 15 *prōtotokos pasēs ktiseōs*	v. 18 *prōtotokos ek tōn nekrōn*
v. 17 *kai autos estin pro pantōn*	v. 18 *kephalē / archē . . . hina genētai en pasin autos prōteuōn*
v. 16 *hoti en autō ektisthē ta panta en tois ouranois kai epi tēs gēs*	v. 20 *kai di' autou apokatallaxai ta panta eis auton . . . eite ta epi tēs gēs eite ta en tois ouranois*

Note: I am grateful to my former student Tim Sweet for constructing these tables. Fuller parallels can be seen in the complete Greek text of Col. 1:15–20 in N. T. Wright, *The Climax of the Covenant: Christ and the Law in Pauline Theology* (Minneapolis: Fortress, 1992), 104.

Table 10.3
Preeminence of Christ in the First Creation
and in the New Creation: Colossians 1:15–20

In the First Creation	In the New Creation
v. 15 He is the image of the invisible God	v. 19 For it was the Father's good pleasure for all the fullness to dwell in Him
v. 15 the firstborn of all creation	v. 18 He is also the firstborn from the dead
v. 17 He is before all things	v. 18 head / beginning . . . so that He Himself will come to have first place in everything
v. 16 For by Him all things were created, both in the heavens and on earth	v. 20 and through Him to reconcile all things to Himself . . . whether things on earth or things in heaven

1. Just as Christ was already the "image of the invisible God" at the time of the first creation (1:15), so in the beginning of the new creation the "fullness" of deity "dwelt in Him," so that he was the perfect representation of God "in bodily form" (1:19; 2:9).

2. Just as Christ was "the firstborn of all [in the first] creation," so he is the "firstborn" of the new creation through having been raised "from among the dead ones" (1:18). This text is one of the clearest examples in the NT that Christ's resurrection was understood to be the beginning of a new creation of more to come (i.e., of more resurrected ones from the dead to come).

3. Just as Christ existed "before all things" created in the first creation (1:17), so he became the "head" and the "beginning" so that "He Himself will come to have first place among all things" in the new creation (1:18).
4. Just as "all things were created . . . in the heavens and on earth" by Christ in the first creation (1:16), so Christ "reconciled all things to Himself . . . whether things on earth or things in heaven" in the second creation (1:20).

These parallels demonstrate that Paul believed that the last things of the new creation were modeled on the first things of the Genesis creation because the last Adam had finally come and done what the first Adam should have done but did not do. The effects of the obedience and disobedience of the respective Adams had implications not only for humanity but also for the rest of the cosmos.

It is likely that the portrayal of Christ as "the image of God" and "the firstborn of all creation" has an Adamic background, which means that Paul is portraying Christ as a "last Adam" figure, who is the head and supreme ruler of both the first and the second creation, though the evidence and fuller explanation for this will have to wait until a subsequent chapter.[37]

Why has Paul written this introductory portion of Colossians? Most likely it is to get the Colossians to focus on their own identification with Christ as a new creation, which is referred to later in Col. 3:9–11. Through such an identification, the readers are reminded to heed Paul's new-creational teaching and ethic so that they will not be deceived by false teachers who are attempting to get them to abide by rules of behavior that are now outmoded because they are part and parcel of the old, fallen world that is passing away.[38]

Conclusion

This chapter has shown that Paul explicitly thought of Christ's resurrection as the beginning of the latter-day new creation, and the Colossians passage shows that he understood Christ's kingship to virtually overlap with this new creation.

---

37. See chap. 14 under the heading "The Image of the Last Adam in Paul's Writings."
38. For this purpose and fuller discussion, see Beale, *Colossians and Philemon*.

11

Resurrection as Inaugurated End-Time New Creation and Kingdom in the General Epistles and Revelation

What we have found in the preceding chapters in the Gospels and Paul we will find also in the General Epistles and Revelation: Christ's resurrection is the beginning of the end-time new creation and kingdom, which is a significant part of the NT storyline that I have proposed and repeatedly referred to.

The Already–Not Yet Resurrection and New-Creational Kingdom in the General Epistles

Hebrews

Hebrews virtually begins with reference to Jesus's ascension ("He sat down at the right hand of the Majesty on high"), directly after "He had made purification of sins" (1:3b). That God "appointed [Jesus] heir of all things" (1:2) is picked up again in 1:4, where it says that "He has inherited a more excellent name." Verse 3, sandwiched between the two inheritance propositions, refers to Jesus as the exact image of God ("the radiance of His glory and the exact representation of His nature") ruling by his "word of power," having been installed "at the right hand" of God. This is classic Adamic language in verses 1–4, which we have seen so often before in Gen. 1–2 and elsewhere in both Testaments:

1. God's "son" (who is the first Adam) has come "in these last days"
2. as the image of God,
3. as a ruler and
4. inheritor of the earth, and
5. as a new creation (recalling conceptually that ascension is an escalated phase of Christ's resurrection existence [e.g., see Acts 2:31–35]), which is the beginning of new creation.[1]

These Adamic notions are developed explicitly in 2:6–9 in connection again with Jesus's death and position of "glory and honor."

Hebrews 1:5 gives the ground for Jesus as inheritor (in vv. 2, 4) to be the fulfillment of two prophecies: Ps. 2:7 ("You are My Son, today I have begotten You") and 2 Sam. 7:14 ("I will be a father to him, and he will be a Son to Me"). We saw that these were parts of important prophecies that were developing in various ways the theme of Adamic kingship from Gen. 1:26–28.[2] These prophecies do not designate Jesus's birth through Mary but rather his birth as a new creation and enthronement as a king at his resurrection, which is in line with the way Paul is narrated as explaining Ps. 2:7 to be a prophecy of Jesus's resurrection in Acts 13:32–34. The 2 Samuel prophecy is applied to those identified with Jesus in Rev. 21:7, where it includes the notion of ruling (conquering), inheriting, and being God's "sons."

The resurrection demonstrates not only Jesus's kingship but also his priesthood: "We have a great high priest who has passed through the heavens, Jesus the Son of God" (Heb. 4:14). Psalm 2:7, in addition to supporting Jesus's kingly inheritance in Heb. 1:2–4, is adduced to support Jesus becoming "high priest" at the time of his resurrection. Conceptually, this also has an analogue with Gen. 1–2, where we saw that Adam, being a king in God's image, was also a priest. And it is not likely coincidental that the first mention of priesthood in Hebrews is at 2:17, right on the heels of Jesus's portrayal as a "last Adam" figure (cf. 2:6–9). That it was the resurrection that also clearly indicated Christ's eternal priesthood is clear from 7:16–17: Christ "has become [a Melchizedekian priest] not on the basis of a law of physical requirement, but according to

---

1. Theologians have commonly spoken of Christ's "humiliation" (referring to Christ's suffering, death, and burial) and to his state of exaltation (his resurrection, ascension, session at God's right hand during the interadvent age, and his final coming in glory). Christ's resurrection existence continues in escalated glorified stages with the ascension, his reigning at God's right hand, and return in glory (see Wayne Grudem, *Systematic Theology* [Grand Rapids: Zondervan, 1994], 616–20).

2. See chap. 2 under the heading "The Repeated New-Creational Expectation of an Adamic King throughout the Old Testament."

the <u>power of an indestructible life</u>. For it is attested of Him, 'You are a priest forever according to the order of Melchizedek.'" Consequently, Jesus "abides forever" and "holds his priesthood permanently," so that "he always lives to make intercession" for his people (7:24–25).

Now, in Heb. 8, the author puts together formally what has been implied in the preceding chapters: Christ's kingship and priesthood are of a piece and are a result of the ascension: "Now the main point in what has been said is this: we have such a high priest, who has taken His seat at the right hand of the throne of the Majesty in the heavens" (v. 1). That Christ's ascension propelled him as a priest into a new creation is apparent from 9:11: "But when Christ appeared as a high priest of the good things to come, He entered through the greater and more perfect tabernacle, not made with hands, that is to say, not of this creation." He became a priest in a temple of the new creation (cf. similarly 9:24). Again, 10:12–13 underscores the combination of priesthood and kingship in the one person of Jesus: "He, having offered [as a priest] one sacrifice for sins for all time, sat down at the right hand of God,[3] waiting from that time onward <u>until His enemies be made a footstool for His feet</u>."

The last phrase of 10:13 ("until His enemies be made a footstool for His feet") is the fifth time in Hebrews that allusion has been made to Jesus's fulfilling Ps. 110. Once, Ps. 110:1 ("Sit at My right hand, until I make Your enemies a footstool for Your feet") is appealed to (1:13) in order to underscore Jesus's inaugurated kingship, as also here in 10:13. Psalm 110:4 ("The LORD has sworn and will not change his mind, 'You are a priest forever'") is referred to three times (5:6; 7:17, 21) to emphasize Jesus's eternal priesthood. The repeated use of this psalm shows again how the author is so concerned with merging into Jesus's one person the offices of both kingship and priesthood, and his constant appeals to Ps. 110:1, 4 show that this psalm likely was the main influence leading him to merge the two functions into one person.[4] This merging of the two offices is enhanced by the fact that the catena of quotations in Heb. 1 begins and ends with Ps. 2 and Ps. 110, and the two are paired in 5:5–6. In addition, both texts launch the discussion in Heb. 1: Ps. 2:7 is alluded to in verse 2, and Christ "sitting down at the right hand of the Majesty on high" in verse 3 probably alludes to Ps. 110:1.[5]

A more explicit reference to Jesus's commencing a new creation by his ascent as the eschatological priest occurs in Heb. 10:19–21, where Jesus as "a great priest over the house of God" is said to have "inaugurated [or 'renewed']" "a new and living way" into the heavenly sanctuary for his people. This "living

---

3. On which, see also Heb. 12:2.

4. On the basis of Ps. 110, the following Jewish texts also merge the two offices into one figure: *T. Reub.* 6:8–11; *Gen. Rab.* 55.6; *Deut. Rab.* 2.7; *S. Eli. Rab.* 94; *b. Ned.* 32b; the Targum of Ps. 110:4 interprets the one appointed to the eternal priesthood of Melchizedek as one who is "appointed as prince for the world to come."

5. I am grateful to my research assistant Dan Brendsel for these last two observations in Heb. 1.

way" is none other than new resurrection life in the presence of God in his temple, which we have seen earlier in Hebrews was inaugurated at Jesus's resurrection/ascension (4:14; 6:20; 7:16–17; 8:1; 9:11) and to be consummated at his final return. Believers who identify with the resurrected and ascended Jesus as an inaugurated new creation enter into the presence of God in the holy of holies, though they are still not without sin. Their only access to the heavenly new creation, and hence the divine presence, is through Jesus, since only a sinless person can go into the heavenly holy of holies and not be destroyed by the direct presence of the Holy God.

God's preservation of the Abrahamic seed, in the case of delivering Isaac from death, was a "type" of the resurrection of the dead to come, of which Jesus's was the first (Heb. 11:17–19). The last two chapters conclude the epistle with two more references to resurrection. Hebrews 12:23 refers to the "church of the firstborn ones," who are such because they are identified with Jesus, the "firstborn" from the dead.[6] Hebrews 2:10–14 confirms this further, since there Christians are called "many sons" led by "the author [Jesus] of their salvation," and they are referred to as "brothers" of Jesus and "children whom God has given" to Jesus.[7] That in some unseen way the readers of Hebrews "have come" to the heavenly realm ("Mount Zion" and "Jerusalem"), where the "church of the firstborn" exists, must include the notion that they themselves are part of this firstborn congregation. Here, "firstborn" presumably refers to all those who will experience resurrection like their firstborn progenitor, Jesus. It is likely, however, given the prior emphasis in Hebrews to the readers being identified with Jesus's ascended entrance into the heavenly tabernacle, that their firstborn status has been inaugurated through this present identification with his resurrection/ascension, and that such ascended status becomes escalated upon death and exaltation into the heavenly Zion and Jerusalem, among "the spirits of righteous men made perfect" (Heb. 12:22–23).

The readers have been described as those who have entered the "holy of holies" through their forerunner, Jesus (10:19–22; 4:14–16). On the basis of this entrance they can be said to be identified with "Zion and . . . the heavenly Jerusalem" and the other realities in 12:22–23 because the "holy of holies" was the center of all these things.[8] For example, that believers have come to "Mount Zion" and "the heavenly Jerusalem" likely indicates that they have become a part of these localities in that they are citizens of the heavenly Zion and Jerusalem. Believers on earth are identified now with and experience in

6. So Heb. 1:6; cf. "firstborn from the dead" in Col. 1:18; Rev. 1:5; in Rom. 8:29 Paul relates Jesus as "firstborn" to his "brothers."

7. On this connection to 12:23, see Paul Ellingworth, *The Epistle to the Hebrews: A Commentary on the Greek Text*, NIGTC (Grand Rapids: Eerdmans, 1993), 679.

8. For the holy of holies as the centerpiece of the temple, Jerusalem, the promised land, and the entire world, see G. K. Beale, *The Temple and the Church's Mission: A Biblical Theology of the Dwelling Place of God*, NSBT 17 (Downers Grove, IL: InterVarsity, 2004).

some way the heavenly realities of verses 22–23. This identification is apparent from 12:24, which says they also "have come" "to Jesus, the mediator of a new covenant, and to the sprinkled blood [of Jesus]," which is a repetition of the cultic realities with which Hebrews says believers have already begun to be identified in their present earthly existence (e.g., 10:10–14, 19–22).[9] Hebrews 12:24 is the climax of verses 18–24 and thus of the entire epistle.[10] The climactic function of this verse further confirms that the "holy of holies" is the central focus of the heavenly realities mentioned in 12:22–23, since these realities lead up and point to this climax. However, although believers have begun to be identified with the heavenly city (as also in Gal. 4:26: "the Jerusalem above . . . is our mother"), the final form of this "heavenly Jerusalem" is still "to come" (Heb. 13:14; so also Rev. 3:12; 21:2).

The last mention of resurrection in Hebrews comes in 13:20, which is an allusion to Isa. 63:11 LXX (see table 11.1).

Table 11.1

Isaiah 63:11 LXX	Hebrews 13:20
"Where is he that brought up from the sea the shepherd [Moses] of the sheep [Israel]?" (some LXX manuscripts have "the great shepherd").[a]	"God of peace, who brought up from the dead the great Shepherd of the sheep."

[a]Manuscripts 564 Bo Eus. eccl.

Now, Jesus is the greater Moses whom God has delivered from death at the greater exodus, along with his people.[11] And just as the exodus was thought of as a new creation,[12] so it is followed by the even more monumental new exodus and new creation in Jesus's resurrection. Just as the first exodus was to lead to the establishment of the temporary temple (e.g., Exod. 15:17; Isa. 63:18), so Isa. 63:15 ("Look down from heaven and see from Your holy and glorious habitation") and 64:1 ("Oh, that You would rend the heavens and come down") prophesy that the second, end-time exodus (Isa. 63:11) will also lead to God's heavenly sanctuary descending to earth and residing permanently.

9. See also F. F. Bruce, *The Epistle to the Hebrews*, NICNT (Grand Rapids: Eerdmans, 1990), 360.

10. As argued by Ellingworth, *Hebrews*, 81.

11. Even the phrase "the eternal covenant" at the end of Heb. 13:20 occurs approximately six times in the OT to refer to the new, eternal relationship that God will have with his eschatological people at the end-time exodus and final restoration out of sin's captivity (so Isa. 55:3; 61:8; Jer. 32:40; 50:5; Ezek. 16:60; 37:26). Perhaps the reference to "the eternal covenant" in Isa. 61:8 is uppermost in mind because it, like the Isa. 63:11 allusion, is part of a second-exodus prophecy (see Isa. 61:1–3).

12. See further G. K. Beale, "The Eschatological Conception of New Testament Theology," in *"The Reader Must Understand": Eschatology in Bible and Theology*, ed. K. E. Brower and M. W. Elliott (Leicester: Apollos, 1997), 47. Note, e.g., Wis. 19:6 with respect to the first exodus: "For the whole creation was fashioned in its own kind anew."

As Hebrews has recounted in earlier chapters, Jesus has led his people to that heavenly mountain-tabernacle (6:19–20; 9:11–12, 23–24; 10:19–22; 12:22–24).

James

Although James nowhere speaks of Christ's resurrection, the epistle does allude to the believers' resurrection. According to 1:12, the "man who perseveres" and "has passed the test . . . will receive the crown of life, which the Lord has promised to those who love Him." The phrase "crown of life" likely is best translated "the crown, which is life" ("life" being an appositional genitive). The "crown" refers to the ancient runner's reward, which here is none other than resurrection life at the end of the age. Verse 18 indicates that this eschatological life has already begun in the existence of believers: "In the exercise of His will He brought us forth by the word of truth, so that we would be a kind of first fruits among His creatures." God's people begin to participate in the new creation even before their final physical resurrection at the end of the age. "By the exercise of his will," God "brought us forth by the word of truth" at initial conversion, just as he brought forth the first creation in Gen. 1 by his word and by the exercise of his will.[13] James's statement is the conceptual equivalent to Paul's application of Gen. 1:3 to the saints' regeneration in 2 Cor. 4:6: "For God, who said, 'Light shall shine out of darkness,' is the One who has shone in our hearts to give the Light of the knowledge of the glory of God in the face of Christ." The reference to "the exercise of his will" probably alludes also to God's creative activity, since it is typical language used elsewhere of God's absolute freedom and determination in creating (e.g., see Ps. 113:11 LXX [115:3 MT]; Job 23:13; Rev. 4:11).[14]

The designation of believers as "the first fruits among his creatures [or 'creation']"[15] indicates that their eschatological new creation is the first expression of the broader inbreaking of all the rest of the new creation,[16] perhaps another striking similarity to Paul in Romans, where he says that "the anxious longing of the creation waits eagerly for the revealing of the sons of God" in their resurrection bodies (8:19; cf. 8:21), and believers are said already to have "the first fruits of the Spirit" within them (8:23). In James 1 and Rom. 8, just as Adam and Eve were the crown of creation, so the resurrection of saints is

---

13. Note in this respect that Heb. 11:3 similarly asserts that "the worlds were prepared by the word of God," and 2 Pet. 3:5 similarly says, "By the word of God the heavens existed long ago and the earth was formed" (so also Ps. 33:6).

14. Following Ralph P. Martin, *James*, WBC 48 (Waco: Word, 1988), 39, which also lists such uses in Philo.

15. The word *ktisma* elsewhere refers to either the creation or the creatures that have been created, which are part of the creation; see Wis. 9:2; 13:5; 14:11; Sir. 36:14; 38:34; 3 Macc. 5:11; 1 Tim. 4:4; Rev. 5:13; cf. Rev. 8:9 (following Peter H. Davids, *The Epistle of James: A Commentary on the Greek Text*, NIGTC [Grand Rapids: Eerdmans, 1982], 90).

16. So also Martin, *James*, 40.

the decisive event that must happen before the rest of the new creation can come about. It is not clear whether believers as "first fruits" refers to their inaugurated new-creational status or to their final physical resurrection. Nevertheless, since the initial part of James 1:18 refers to their new creation already having come about, it is plausible that "first fruits" (*aparchē*) refers to the same. Romans 8:18–23 lends secondary confirmation to this conclusion, where "first fruits" refers to the beginning resurrection existence of saints, which has come about through the Spirit.[17] James, like Paul, views Christians "as that part of creation first harvested by God as part of the new creation."[18] Those whom God has "brought forth" as newly created "first fruits" will produce "peace" as "the fruit of righteousness" (3:18). As we will see, peace is one of the main conditions resulting from the new creation, which believers will exude as being a part of the new creation.[19]

Against the background of this discussion, it is natural that James would refer to God in 1:17 as "the Father of lights," since "God" or the "Lord" is often referred to as the creator of light, especially the light of the creation.[20] In particular, the name for God in 1:18 is likely an allusion to God's creation of the "lights" or luminaries (Gen. 1:14–16; Ps. 136:7; Ezek. 32:8). In dependence on these OT passages, early Judaism referred to God as "the prince of lights" (CD-A V:17–18; cf. 1QS III:20; 1QM XIII:10).[21] Some commentators try to decide whether James is using the language of "new creation" or simply that of "redemption," sometimes opting for the latter.[22] However, it is likely that James does not distinguish between these, seeing God's redemptive regenerating work in Christians to be the literal beginning of the new creation with more to come. Thus, "divine creation (of the stars in their courses [in v. 17]) is matched by the new creation" in verse 18.[23]

1–2 Peter

1 PETER

In comparison to James, 1 Peter has quite a few references to both Christ's and believers' resurrection.

---

17. The term "first fruits" (*aparchē*) is also twice used in 1 Cor. 15:20, 23 of Christ's resurrection as the beginning phase of the resurrection of all the saints at the very end of the age.

18. Davids, *James*, 90.

19. On the relationship of new creation and reconciliation in Paul's thinking, see further chap. 16 below.

20. For the latter, see Gen. 1:3–5, 14–18; Jer. 31:35 with reference to the light of the first creation, and Isa. 30:26; 60:1, 19–20; 2 Cor. 4:6; Rev. 22:5 with reference to the light of the new creation.

21. Following Martin, *James*, 38.

22. E.g., Martin Dibelius and Heinrich Greeven, *A Commentary on the Epistle of James*, trans. Michael A. Williams, Hermeneia (Philadelphia: Fortress, 1975), 103–7.

23. Martin, *James*, 39.

1 Peter 1

As we have seen elsewhere, the language of being "born" is part of resurrection thought according to 1:3–5:

> Blessed be the God and Father of our Lord Jesus Christ, who according to His great mercy has caused us to be born again to a living hope through the resurrection of Jesus Christ from the dead, to obtain an inheritance which is imperishable and undefiled and will not fade away, reserved in heaven for you, who are protected by the power of God through faith for a salvation ready to be revealed in the last time.

Saints have been "born again to a living hope through the resurrection of Jesus." The language of "born again" indicates new creation, just as Jesus's resurrection can repeatedly convey the notion of him being the "firstborn" (Rom. 8:29; Col. 1:18; Heb. 1:5–6; Rev. 1:5). The language here presumably is applied to believers, since elsewhere Jesus as "firstborn" is identified with people whom he represents as such (Rom. 8:29; cf. Heb. 1:6; 12:23). Peter says that we have been "born again" by means of one primary reality: "through [*dia*] the resurrection of Jesus Christ from among the dead ones" (1:3).[24] How were they "born" through Christ's resurrection? The most straightforward answer is that they were identified and came into union with Christ and with the reality of his resurrection as the "firstborn" when they believed, and that

24. It is possible that in v. 3 the phrase "through the resurrection" modifies the directly preceding "to a living hope" instead of "has caused us to be born again," with the resultant following interpretative translation: "having caused us to be born again to a living hope which is a living hope through the resurrection" (so, e.g., Paul J. Achtemeier, *1 Peter*, Hermeneia [Minneapolis: Fortress, 1996], 95; Thomas R. Schreiner, *1, 2 Peter, Jude*, NAC 37 [Nashville: Broadman, 2003], 62; Peter H. Davids, *The First Epistle of Peter*, NICNT [Grand Rapids: Eerdmans, 1990], 52). The idea is that the resurrection of Christ inspires the "living hope." It is better, however, to see both the prepositional phrases modifying the verbal participle "having caused to be born again" (so also D. E. Hiebert, "Peter's Thanksgiving for Our Salvation," *SM* 29 [1980]: 89; J. Ramsey Michaels, *1 Peter*, WBC 49 [Nashville: Nelson, 1988], 19). The reason for this is that prepositional phrases typically do not modify other prepositional phrases but rather the nearest verbal forms. In addition, the only other time that the phrase *di' anastaseōs Iēsou Christou* occurs in the NT is in 1 Peter itself, where it clearly modifies a verbal form and designates the instrumentality of those baptized being "saved" (3:21). Furthermore, if "resurrection" modified "living hope," then a relative clause would likely be used (as noted above in the interpretative translation of this option), and the repetition of the verb "born anew" in v. 23 clearly is followed by an instrumental sense: "born again through the living and abiding word of God" (following Wayne Grudem, *The First Epistle of Peter*, TNTC [Leicester: Inter-Varsity, 1988], 56). The concept expressed in either case is equally awkward conceptually. Thus, the idea in v. 3 is that God "has caused us to be born again . . . through the resurrection." Leonhard Goppelt (*A Commentary on 1 Peter*, trans. John E. Alsup, ed. Ferdinand Hahn [Grand Rapids: Eerdmans, 1993], 84) and J. N. D. Kelly (*The Epistles of Peter and Jude*, BNTC [Peabody, MA: Hendrickson, 1999], 48) see that both "new birth" and "hope" come about "by the resurrection of Jesus," and John Elliott (*1 Peter*, AB 37B [New York: Doubleday, 2000], 334–35) connects new birth, hope, and salvation with Christ's resurrection.

this identification caused them to be considered to be "born" in resurrection themselves. The conception is quite like that in Rom. 6:4–8 (on which, see discussion in chap. 9). The direct link between "born again" and Christ's resurrection confirms that the verb conveys a resurrection idea, which, as we have seen, is new creation, and in fact the verb in question (*anagennaō*) can be translated, as in several English versions, as "given new birth"[25] (which is supported by 2:2, where "newborn" [*artigennētos*] occurs as a synonym).

They have been "born again" for two goals. First, they have been "born again" in order that they would be characterized as those possessing "a living hope" (1:3). This is not talking of a hope possessed by people who merely physically exist in this world. The adjective "living" probably explains the nature or orientation of the "hope": it is a hope shot through with focus on the final outcome of their present resurrection existence, which is consummate bodily resurrection at the very end of history. The second goal of their new birth is that they would obtain "an inheritance which is imperishable and undefiled and will not fade away, reserved in heaven for you" (1:4). Those who will receive this inheritance are also those "who are protected by the power of God through faith for . . . salvation" (1:5). The inheritance is likely the full completion of their salvation by physical resurrection in a newly created cosmos, an idea again uniquely comparable to Rom. 8:18–25 (see also Eph. 1:13–14). That this is an inheritance in a new creation is evident from the adjectives "imperishable, undefiled, unfading." Revelation 21:1, 4 also underscores the qualitative contrast between the old and the new creation: "I saw a new heaven and a new earth; for the first heaven and the first earth passed away" (v. 1); "there shall no longer be death; there shall no longer be any mourning, or crying, or pain; the first things have passed away" (v. 4b). Many commentators have rightly noted that the background for understanding the "inheritance" in 1 Pet. 1 is the promised land that was to be Israel's inheritance, which it lost because of sin. What commentators have not noticed, however, is that this inheritance has become a foreshadowing of an unlosable inheritance in the new cosmos.[26]

That this "inheritance" and "salvation" focus on new-creational existence "to be revealed in the last time" (1:4–5) is apparent from the conclusion of

---

25. BAGD 58; Achtemeier, *1 Peter*, 94. Philo (*Aet.* 8) also uses the noun form of the word to refer to the Stoic belief in the cyclic conflagration and "rebirth" of the world (*anagennēsis kosmou*, "a reborn world"). Philo also often uses *palingenesia* to refer to the same thing, as well as the renewed earth after the Noahic deluge (on which, see the related note below in this chapter under the subheading "1 Peter 3").

26. The reference to "a fellow heir of the grace of life" (i.e., "grace leading to [resurrection] life" as a genitive of destination) in 3:7 probably refers to the same inheritance here of physical resurrection in a renewed cosmos, as does also 3:9, "you were called . . . that you might inherit a blessing," and this future inherited blessing is referred to believers "loving life and seeing good days" (3:10). The latter wording is part of a quotation from Ps. 34:12–16, which concludes in vv. 20–22 with "[God] keeps all his bones. . . . The LORD redeems the soul of His servants; and none of those who take refuge in Him will be condemned."

chapter 1 in verses 19–25. There the readers are told that Christ "has appeared in these last times for the sake of" them, "who through Him are believers in God, who raised Him from the dead ones" (vv. 20–21). There is a "salvation ready to be revealed in the last time" (1:5), but that last time has been inaugurated in the first coming of the Messiah. The focus of this eschatological commencement is Christ's death and resurrection and glory, since no other aspects of Christ's coming are mentioned. "Who through Him [Christ] are believers in God" is a near conceptual equivalent to the earlier "born again to a living hope through the resurrection of Jesus Christ from among the dead ones" (1:3). Thus, again the notion of the saints' identification with Christ's resurrection is close in mind. In direct connection to 1:20–21 is the affirmation that they "have in obedience to the truth purified [their] souls" and they "have been born again" (1:22–23), and these two realities should result in them having the ability to be "loving one another" (1:22).[27]

The reference to "born again" in 1:23 picks up the same idea of new creation by identification with Christ's resurrection from 1:3 (where the same verb, *anagennaō*, occurs). And, as also in 1:3–4, this new-creational condition is said to be not "perishable but imperishable," since they have been born by "seed" that is the "living and enduring word of God" (v. 23). This was in contrast to the "perishable . . . way of life inherited from your forefathers" (1:18), and it is an implicit continuation of the "imperishable inheritance" mentioned earlier (1:4).

As in James 1:18, the conceptual background here for Peter's "born again" notion is the Gen. 1 account, where God creates all things by his "word," including Adam, the firstborn human (so also Heb. 11:3; 2 Pet. 3:5). The adjective "living" designates God's "word" as possessing life and thus able to give life. Peter supports his statement in 1:23 by appealing to Isa. 40:8: "All flesh is like grass, and all its glory like the flower of grass. The grass withers, and the flower falls off, but the word of the Lord endures forever" (1:24–25a). This is a reference not merely to the never-fading divine word in Isaiah but rather to the wider context of God's coming restoration and new creation, in which God will create realities that will never perish, including his newly formed people, who "will run and not get tired" and who "will walk and not become weary" (in Isa. 40:31).[28]

27. The participles *hēgnikotes* ("having set apart in dedication") and *anagegennēmenoi* ("having been born again") in 1:22–23 function to give the basis for the command to love.

28. Note the new-creational imagery even in Isa. 40:3–4 with respect to God's creative activity in the "wilderness" and "desert," which is expanded more overtly as language of "new creation" in 41:18–20 and esp. 43:18–21, one of the clearest expressions of new creation in all of Isa. 40–66. God is repeatedly referred to as the creator of the first creation in Isa. 40 (vv. 12, 22, 26, 28) in order to affirm his omnipotence in bringing forth a new cosmos. For the central theme of restoration as new creation in Isa. 40–66, see chap. 16 under the heading "Paul's View of Reconciliation as New Creation and Restoration from Exile."

Peter concludes the chapter by applying the Isaiah prophecy of God's creative word to the readers: "And this is the word which was <u>preached</u> [*euangelizō*] to you [as good news]" (here the verb *euangelizō*, used twice in Isa. 40:9, is a continued allusion to and application of Isa. 40 to the hearers). Thus, Isaiah's prophecy of restoration and new creation through God's word has begun fulfillment among Peter's readers. As we have seen earlier (e.g., 2 Cor. 5:13–21), so here the beginning fulfillment of restoration promises is inextricably linked to new creation and resurrection.

1 Peter 2

On the basis ("therefore," *oun* [2:1]) that the Christians are "born again" by God's "living word" (1:23–25) in fulfillment of Isaiah, Peter commands them again, "as newborn ones," to "long for" God's word because they have "put off" all manner of sin from their former life (2:1–2). It is the "living word" that brought them into being as a new creation, and they need to know that it is that same word that will cause them to "grow" as new beings. Peter compares new believers to "newborn" human babies, who need milk to grow. However, they are not infants of the old creation; they are literally "newborn ones" in a literal new creation, and God's word is the essential literal ingredient for the success of their growth.

In 2:4–5 Christians are identified as those "coming to Him [Jesus] as to a living stone," and because of their identification with Christ as a "living stone," they have become "living stones." The mention of "living" refers to Christ as "living" in the sense of being a living, resurrected person, and the saints' identification with him indicates their resurrection status even now (this is in line with the associations of the preceding two uses of the participial form of *zaō* in 1:3, 23). What is the connection between the readers being a new creation in 1:21–2:2 and being part of a temple in 2:4–6? The direct connection of new creation and temple, indeed their equation, is a dominant biblical motif in both Testaments[29] to which 1 Pet. 1–2 testifies again. Israel's temple was symbolic of the cosmos and pointed to the new heaven and earth to come. This is part of the reason why Jesus refers to his resurrection in John 2:19–22 as the raising up of the new temple, since resurrection is a new creation.

1 Peter 3

The most explicit allusion to Christ's resurrection in 1 Peter comes in one of the most difficult passages in the NT, concerning Christ's "proclamation to the spirits in prison, who were once disobedient . . . during the construction of the ark [of Noah]" (3:18–22). The passage begins and ends with reference to Christ's resurrection (vv. 18, 21b–22). Verse 18 says that he was "put to death

---

29. On which, see Beale, *Temple*; also chap. 19 below.

in the flesh, but made alive by the Spirit,[30] by whom also He went and made proclamation to the spirits in prison." It is unlikely that this refers to Christ going to "hell" to preach to unbelievers between his death and resurrection, since the verb "made alive" is most likely a reference to the resurrection[31] and since verses 21b–22 refer to "the resurrection and ascension of Jesus Christ, who is at the right hand of God, having gone into heaven, after angels and authorities and powers had been subjected to Him." Thus, the "proclamation to the spirits in prison" is likely a reference to Christ proclaiming his victory in resurrection and the defeat of all satanic and antagonistic forces as he ascended into heaven.[32]

In 3:20–21 "baptism" is said to be the NT reality that "saves" and "corresponds" to those "brought safely through the water" in Noah's ark. "Baptism" is further defined as "an appeal to God for a good conscience through the resurrection of Jesus Christ."

The rite of baptism, by which a person emerges through and from water, is symbolic of Christ's resurrection, by which he emerged from the tomb and death, with which the baptized person is identified. From this point of identification, believers have a basis for an "appeal to God for a good conscience" because "Christ also died for [their] sins once for all" (3:18), and they now, in imitation of his suffering, "arm themselves also with the same [suffering] purpose" (4:1 [cf. 3:16–18]).[33] This is borne out by the important parallel in Heb. 10:19–24, in which verse 22 is quite striking: "Let us draw near with a sincere heart in full assurance of faith, having our hearts sprinkled clean from an evil conscience and our body washed with pure water" (note also the

30. Michaels (*1 Peter*, 205) is likely correct in saying that "in the Spirit" is a better rendering of the dative *pneumati* because it appears in antithetical parallelism with the dative *sarki* ("in the flesh"), though he acknowledges that there is not only a spheric but also an instrumental sense with the dative *pneumati*: Christ was bodily raised "in a sphere in which the Spirit and power of God are displayed without hindrance or human limitation. . . . Jesus Christ is set free from death."

31. E.g., the verb "make alive" (*zōopoieō*) occurs elsewhere only with reference to "raising the dead" (twice in John's Gospel and seven times in Paul's writings, though Gal. 3:21 may or may not include reference to resurrection life).

32. For a good explication of this view in more detail, see Michaels, *1 Peter*, 194–222, which also discusses other viewpoints and relevant sources supporting them.

33. The same notion appears to be in mind in 2:24: "And He Himself bore our sins in His body on the cross, that we might die to sin and live to righteousness; for by His wounds you were healed." The "living to righteousness" here is likely equivalent to "an appeal to God for a good conscience" in 3:21, since a "good conscience" is inextricably linked to "good behavior" in 3:16. Furthermore, the "living to God," as a result of the preceding mention of Christ's death on the cross and in contrast to "we might die to sin," refers to the believer's resurrection life, which is lived for God; this is strikingly almost identical to Rom. 6:11, 13b, which is linked to "baptism" in 6:3–4: "Even so consider yourselves to be dead to sin, but alive to God in Christ Jesus" (v. 11); "but present yourselves to God as those alive from the dead, and your members as instruments of righteousness to God" (v. 13b).

internal washing in 1 Pet. 1:2, 22, both directly related to Christ's death). The imperative in Hebrews is based on the fact of Christ's death and resurrection. A "good conscience" results from the Spirit's cleansing work in a person who has been identified with Jesus's death and has demonstrated obedience to the gospel.[34] Thus, the baptism of which Peter speaks includes reference to Christ's death but focuses on his resurrection.

Hence, this symbolic emergence in resurrection by believers corresponds to Noah and his family emerging safely through water, which brought death to those outside the ark. Is it coincidental that the emergence of the earth from the water at the conclusion of the Noahic deluge is depicted as a second new creation in the Genesis narrative[35] and was so viewed in early Judaism?[36] In fact, the portrayal of the new ground emerging out of water is found in ancient Near Eastern,[37] OT,[38] and Jewish descriptions of the original creation and the

34. Following Michaels, *1 Peter*, 216.

35. On which, see Derek Kidner, *Genesis*, TOTC (Downers Grove, IL: InterVarsity, 1967), 92–93, 100; Nahum M. Sarna, *Genesis*, JPSTC (Philadelphia: Jewish Publication Society, 1989), 49–51; Claus Westermann, *Genesis 1–11*, trans. John J. Scullion (London: SPCK, 1984), 50–52, 417, 423, 433, 450–51, 457, 462. For various aspects of the Noah narrative as recapitulations of the Adam and creation narrative in Gen. 1–3, see especially Kenneth A. Mathews, *Genesis 1–11:26*, NAC 1A (Nashville: Broadman & Holman, 1996), 350–423, as well as Allen P. Ross, *Creation and Blessing: A Guide to the Study and Exposition of the Book of Genesis* (Grand Rapids: Baker Academic, 1988), 189–205; Warren Austin Gage, *The Gospel of Genesis: Studies in Protology and Eschatology* (Winona Lake, IN: Carpenter Books, 1984), 8–16; John H. Walton, *Genesis*, NIVAC (Grand Rapids: Zondervan), 330–52 (and see further bibliography therein).

36. The term *palingenesia* ("regeneration") refers in Philo, *Mos.* 2.65, and in *1 Clem.* 9:4 to the renewal of the earth after the flood. The Philo context also refers to the earth directly after the deluge as "renewed" (*neas*) and to Noah and his family as "inaugurators of a second cycle" (*Mos.* 2.64–65), "born [*ginomai*] to be the likeness of God's power and image" (*Mos.* 2.65). Philo also uses the word to refer to the Stoic belief in the cyclic conflagration and "rebirth" of the world (*Aet.* 9, 47, 76, 85, 93, 99, 107). As a synonym for these uses, Philo (*Aet.* 8) also uses *anagennēsis kosmou* ("a reborn world"). Philo can also use *palingenesia* to refer to the "rebirth" of a person after death, when the immaterial being is separated from the material (*Cher.* 114). Matthew 19:28 uses the same word for the renewal of the earth in the eschaton, and Titus 3:5 refers to believers "saved . . . by the washing of regeneration [*palingenesia*] and renewing by the Holy Spirit." Indeed, the word *palingenesia* itself can be translated "renewal" (BAGD 752).

37. The beginning of the rule of the Egyptian sun-god (Re) at the start of creation is identified with the emergence of a primeval hill: "Re began to appear as king . . . when he was on the [primeval] hill which is in Hermopolis." See J. B Pritchard, *Ancient Near Eastern Texts relating to the Old Testament* (Princeton: Princeton University Press, 1969), 3–4. Pritchard cites a similar passage about the beginning of creation: "O [divine] Atum-Khepri, thou wast on high on the (primeval) hill; thou didst arise as the *ben*-bird of the *ben*-stone in the *ben*-House [temple] in Heliopolis." Egyptian pyramids were analogues of such primeval hills (ibid., 3). See likewise Richard J. Clifford, *Creation Accounts in the Ancient Near East and in the Bible*, CBQMS 26 (Washington, DC: Catholic Biblical Association of America, 1994), 105–10. Clifford (ibid., 45–46, 62–64) notes similar notions of primeval hills in Sumerian and Mesopotamian cosmogonies.

38. See Beale, *Temple*, 92–93, 148–52. The mountain of Eden, though not depicted as arising from the sea (although cf. Gen. 1), probably represented the place from which the habitable creation was to extend (note the geography in Gen. 2, whereby water flowed out from Eden,

second new creation,[39] the latter commencing after the Noahic deluge.[40] Accordingly, the emergence of the ark out of the flood to rest on Mount Ararat, Christ's emergence from death, and believers' identification with Christ's emergence from death are new-creational depictions. Again, resurrection and new creation are to be understood as two sides of one coin. The allusion to Ps. 110:1 in 1 Pet. 3:22 ("who is at the right hand of God") also indicates that Christ's resurrection is part and parcel with his kingship over all "authorities and powers." Hence, once again we see new creation and kingship to be overlapping realities.

1 Peter 4–5

As with 1 Pet. 3:18–21, there has been much debate about 4:6, especially since one line of interpretation identifies the "dead" as the "spirits" in hell to whom Christ "preached" in 3:18–20. But my interpretation of 3:18–20 disagrees with this view of that contested passage. Accordingly, 4:6 likely refers to Christians who have died, which means that although they have suffered physical or earthly judgment ("judged in the flesh according to unjust human standards"),[41] nevertheless "they may live in the Spirit according to the will

---

apparently in a downward direction, and note that in Ezek. 28:13–16 there is reference to "Eden, the garden of God" as "the holy mountain of God"). Likewise the depiction in Dan. 2 of a stone becoming a mountain and filling the earth represents a similar picture for the end-time new creation, though this stone does not arise out of the sea.

39. Judaism also held that the "world was [started] created from Zion . . . the world was created from its center" when God "cast a stone into the ocean, from which the world then was founded" (*b. Yoma* 54b). This stone became "the foundation stone with which the Lord of the world sealed the mouth of the great deep from the beginning" (*Tg. Ps.-J.* Exod. 28:29), from which new land emerged and spread out until the main land mass of the creation was formed. Interestingly, the stone supporting the holy of holies was thought by later Judaism to be that upon which "all the world was based," since God had begun to create the world from that point in the beginning (*Song Rab.* 3.10.4; *Pirqe R. El.* 35; *Midr. Tanḥ. Yelammedenu* [Exodus] 11.3; so also *Midr. Tanḥ. Lev.* 10, on which, see Joan R. Branham, "Vicarious Sacrality: Temple Space in Ancient Synagogues," in vol. 2 of *Ancient Synagogues: Historical Analysis and Archaeological Discovery,* ed. Dan Urman and Paul V. M. Flesher, StPB 47 [Leiden: Brill, 1995], 325).

40. E.g., the top of Mount Ararat was the first emerging part of the creation that arose after the flood and was the place from which Noah and his family were to spread out to repopulate the earth, of which Philo says "when earth rising from its ablutions showed itself renewed" (*Mos.* 2.64).

41. The judgment could be that of death as a part of God's judgment pronounced on Adam and all his progeny, or it could be the ungodly world's judgment of wrongly accusing Christians and executing wrongful judgments on them. Either view could receive support from 4:17, where it says that "judgment [is] to begin with the household of God . . . first." Three considerations favor the second view (generally following Achtemeier, *1 Peter,* 288–91): (1) 4:14–16 seem to support the latter view, since "suffering as a Christian" there obviously has to do with unjust persecution and judgment by the worldly powers; (2) 3:18 seems to support the same view, since the expression that Christ was "put to death in the flesh" pertains to his unjust punishment by the evil earthly authorities (this is especially so in the light of 2:18–23; 3:16–18); (3) 4:4 speaks of the unbelievers "maligning" Christians.

of God." Just as Jesus was unjustly "put to death in the flesh, but made alive in the Spirit," so true believers unjustly "judged in the flesh" will "live in the Spirit." In the eyes of the world their "death" seemed to be only further validation of the wrong verdict cast on the Christians, but they will be vindicated from the world's verdict by their future resurrection, as was Jesus (cf. 1 Tim. 3:16). The parallelism between 3:18 and 4:6 indicates that believers follow the destiny of their "Chief Shepherd" (5:4), so that after death, they will experience resurrection.[42] From the human vantage point, this eschatological (*telos*) event of final judgment (4:5) and of resurrection (4:6) could happen at any time (it "has come near" [4:7]), and consequently believers must be prepared.

The last chapter of 1 Peter also resonates with the notion of incorruptibility and ultimately resurrection life. That the faithful "will receive an unfading crown of glory" (5:4) recalls 1:4, which referred to their "inheritance which is imperishable and undefiled and will not fade away." The "crown" is the reward for running a race victoriously, and here the crown is the reward of the "inheritance," which, I argued, in 1:4 was resurrection in a new heavens and earth. Those who "entrust their souls to a faithful Creator in doing what is right" (4:19) will inherit such an immortal crown.

2 PETER

The letter of 2 Peter has no direct mention of resurrection, but the idea probably is included in 1:3–4a: "His divine power has granted to us everything pertaining to <u>life</u> [*zōē*] and godliness, through the true knowledge of Him who called us by His own glory and excellence. For by these He has granted to us His precious and magnificent promises." Probably the phrase "everything pertaining to life" includes not merely life on this earth but rather everything concerning life on the new earth, which, of course, would refer to resurrection life. That life of the new world to come is in mind in 1:3–4a is apparent from the mention in verse 4 that the "life" of verse 3 is part of "the promises," and the only other time this precise word for "promise" (*epangelma*) occurs in the NT is in 3:13, which refers to the promise of the coming new creation: "But according to His <u>promise</u> [*epangelma*] we are looking for new heavens and a new earth, in which righteousness dwells." A synonym for "promise" (*epangelia*) also occurs in 3:4, 9, where it refers to the final coming of Christ. Thus, at Christ's last coming God will create a new cosmos, in which his people will not "perish" (3:9) but will find new (resurrection) life and "be found by him in peace, spotless and blameless," so that in the new cosmos "righteousness dwells" (3:13–14). Indeed, "promise" elsewhere refers to the promise of resurrection life or at least includes significant reference to

---

42. It may be that Peter sees that believers' "living in the s(S)pirit" includes their existence immediately after death, though the parallelism with Christ's "made alive in the s(S)pirit" in 3:18 points to the focus being on the saints' physical resurrection.

resurrection (Acts 13:32–34; 26:6–8; 1 Tim. 4:8; 2 Tim. 1:1; Titus 1:2; James 1:12; 1 John 2:25; cf. Heb. 11:17–19). Again we see the close correlation of resurrection with new creation.

That the promised resurrection "life" of 1:3 has already broken in from the future is apparent from Peter's statement in 1:4 that the "promises" enable saints to "become partakers of the divine nature, since [the time that] they have escaped the corruption that is in the world by lust." Their escape from corruption occurred at their conversion and suggests that they have already fled from one world to a new world. They will finally enter that world completely through physical resurrection "to eternal life" at Christ's final coming (Jude 21; cf. 24).

The Johannine Epistles

The first hint of resurrection is in 1 John 2:17: "The world is passing away, and also its lusts; but the one who does the will of God lives forever." There is a real sense in which the old world is passing away, which has already been noted in 2:8: "The darkness is passing away and the true Light is already shining." But in what sense is the "world passing away"? The contrast of light and darkness is common in descriptions of the first creation and of the coming new creation (e.g., for the former, see Gen. 1, and for the latter, see Isa. 60:1–3 [cf. 58:10–11]; John 1:1–10; 2 Cor. 4:4–6; Eph. 5:8–9, 13–14 [the latter of which refers to resurrection]). The "light already shining" in 2:8 must refer to the divine "Light" of 1:5, 7, which has broken in with the revelation of Jesus Christ (1:1–3), which implicitly 2:8 and more explicitly 2:17 express as the irrupting of the new creation into the midst of the old. The latter verse concludes with a contrast of the fading old creation with the inbreaking new: "But the one who does the will of God abides forever." That is, those who are part of God's new creation are not "passing away" but instead "abide forever" in fulfillment of God's "promise" of "eternal life" (2:25).

This promise was made at the "beginning" (2:24) of Jesus's ministry. We must go back to John's Gospel for the context of this promise, since so much in the Johannine Epistles has its roots in that Gospel.[43] The immediate context bears out the relevance of John's Gospel for understanding this promise, since the eschatological use of "hour" in 2:18 ("last hour") is unique to Johannine literature, both the Gospel and Revelation.[44] Furthermore, this eschatologi-

---

43. On which, see Raymond E. Brown, *The Epistles of John*, AB 30 (Garden City, NY: Doubleday, 1982), 34–35, 69–130, 757–59. Note, e.g., the prologue of both books, as well as the themes of light and darkness, truth and falsehood, love and hatred.

44. For the eschatological use of "hour" (*hōra*) in John's Gospel, see chap. 5; also Stefanos Mihalios, *The Danielic Eschatological Hour in the Johannine Literature* LNTS 346 (New York: T&T Clark, 2011). For the uses of "hour" (*hōra*) in Revelation, see G. K. Beale, *The Book of Revelation: A Commentary on the Greek Text*, NIGTC (Grand Rapids: Eerdmans, 1999), on Rev. 3:3, 10; 9:15; 11:13; 14:7, 15; 17:12; 18:10, 17, 19.

cal use in John's Gospel, Revelation, and 1 John 2:18 is based on the unique end-time employment of "hour" (*hōra*) in the book of Daniel.[45] In addition, the "already and not yet" expression in which some of the "hour" uses occur are also unique to John's Gospel and 1 John 2:18. In the earlier analysis of John 5:24–29, we saw that not only does "hour" have a Danielic background, but so does the use of "eternal life," which derives from Dan. 12:2, the only occurrence of the phrase in all of the canonical OT. In particular, I concluded that both "hour" and "eternal life" in John 5:24–29 are an allusion to the LXX of Dan. 12:1–2. In both the Dan. 12 and John 5 passages "eternal life" clearly refers to resurrection life that lasts forever.[46]

That John 5:24 is specifically in mind in 1 John 2:17, 25 is borne out further from 1 John 3:14, where John says that "we have passed out of death into life," a virtual verbal replication of the resurrection saying by Jesus in John 5:24, which appears nowhere else in the NT: "he has passed out of death into life."[47] Thus, 1 John 2:17–18, 25 exhibit the close conjunction of "eternal life" and "hour," much like that in John 5:24–29, so that it is a safe deduction that "eternal life" has the same Dan. 12 background as it does in John 5:24, which is everlasting resurrection life. Such a meaning for 1 John 2:17, 25 enhances the notion of new creation that we have already seen with 2:8, 17, since the resurrection of humans is conceptually the same as human new creation. Thus, the light of the new creation is breaking into the darkness of the old cosmos through the inaugurated resurrection of God's people and the fruit of love that they demonstrate (2:5–11, 17–18, 24–25). In contrast, "Everyone who hates his brother is a murderer; and you know that no murderer has eternal life abiding in him" (3:15). And as also in the Gospel (John 11:24–25),[48] so too in 1 John believers' participation in beginning resurrection existence is because of their identification with Christ, who possesses eternal resurrection life, as stated in 5:11–13:

> And the testimony is this, that God has given us eternal life, and this life is in His Son. He who has the Son has the life; he who does not have the Son of God does not have the life. These things I have written to you who believe in the name of the Son of God, so that you may know that you have eternal life.

Likewise, 5:20 says, "And we know that the Son of God has come, and has given us understanding, so that we may know Him who is true; and we are

45. On which, see the extended discussion in chap. 5 above and in Beale, *Revelation*, on Rev. 3:10; 14:7; 17:12; 18:10, 17, 19.

46. "Eternal life" elsewhere in John's Gospel also can clearly refer to the same thing: 6:40, 47, 54; 10:28, and these uses likely inform the others in 3:15–16, 36; 4:14; 5:39; 6:27; 12:50; 17:2–3.

47. The only difference between the two passages is the singular verb in John and the plural in 1 John.

48. "Martha said to him, 'I know that he [Lazarus] will rise again in the resurrection on the last day.' Jesus said to her, 'I am the resurrection and the life; he who believes in Me will live even if he dies.'"

in Him who is true, in His Son Jesus Christ. This is the true God and eternal life." Consequently, "God has sent his unique Son into the world so that <u>we might live through Him</u>" (4:9b).

John's mention of being "born again" also alludes to the age of the invading new cosmos. He says that the following people "have been born [perfect tense of *gennaō*] from God":

1. "whoever believes that Jesus is the Messiah" (5:1a);
2. those who "do righteousness" (2:29);
3. those who do not commit the "sin" of apostasy from Christ and are the true community of faith (3:9; 5:18);
4. those who love fellow believers (4:7; cf. 5:1b);
5. those who have genuine "faith" and thus "conquer the world" (5:4).

Since the Gospel of John also repeatedly uses the same word (*gennaō*) for the same concept, it is likely again that we must return there to understand better the concept of being "born" (so John 1:13; 3:3–8).[49] In fact, the phrase "begotten from God" occurs only in John 1:13 and repeatedly in 1 John (3:9a, 9b; 4:7; 5:1a, 4, 18a, 18b; cf. 2:29; 5:1b), so that the latter may even be dependent on the former.

The most in-depth elaboration of this notion in John's Gospel is in the well-known exchange between Jesus and Nicodemus in John 3, where the verb occurs eight times. Here I summarize my analysis of this passage from chapter 8. In John 3 Jesus says that one must "be born again" by the Spirit in order to see and enter "the kingdom of God" (vv. 3, 5). Nicodemus responds to Jesus's explanation of this by asking, "How can these things be?" (v. 9). Jesus replies, "Are you the teacher of Israel and do not understand these things?" (v. 10). Nicodemus should have understood what Jesus was saying because, presumably, it came out of the OT, the main source that Nicodemus would have depended on for his teaching. Of particular interest in this respect is Jesus's statement that "unless one is born of water and the Spirit, he cannot enter into the kingdom of God" (v. 5). Several commentators have acknowledged that the source of Jesus's words is Ezek. 36:25–27:[50]

Then I will sprinkle clean water on you, and you will be clean; I will cleanse you from all your filthiness and from all your idols. Moreover, I will give you a new heart and put a new spirit within you; and I will remove the heart of stone from your flesh and give you a heart of flesh. I will put My Spirit within you and cause you to walk in My statutes, and you will be careful to observe My ordinances.

49. The same word designates the similar notion in 1 Cor. 4:15; Gal. 4:24, 29; Philem. 10, and note synonyms for the same idea in James 1:18; 1 Pet. 1:3, 23.
50. See, e.g., D. A. Carson, *The Gospel according to John*, PNTC (Grand Rapids: Eerdmans, 1991), 194–95.

The combined reference to "water" and the "Spirit" is unique in the OT as forming part of a prophecy of Israel's future resurrection life. This is one of the OT passages that earlier we noted as contributing to the prophetic testimony of the resurrection from the dead, and it is expanded in Ezek. 37:1–14, the well-known prophetic vision of the valley of dry bones. The Ezek. 37 vision is generally regarded as a metaphorical depiction of Israel's return from exile through the picture of resurrection. I concluded earlier, however, that it refers to an actual, literal spiritual resurrection of the people of Israel when they return to the land, since it is a development of Ezek. 36:25–27, which clearly coveys the notion of Israel's spiritual renewal at the time of restoration from captivity.[51] Conversely, in the light of Ezek. 37, the prophecy of Israel's spiritual renewal in 36:25–27 can also be understood as a spiritual resurrection and the beginning of participation in the new creation.

It is this prophesied spiritual resurrection of Israel that Jesus is discussing with Nicodemus. Therefore, through the wording of being "born again" John 3 conveys the idea of being raised to new spiritual life in fulfillment of the Ezek. 36 promise. In confirmation of this idea, Jesus immediately discusses his own resurrection and ascent, so that "whoever believes in [identifies with] Him shall not perish, but have eternal life" (John 3:11–16) through partaking in his resurrection life (cf. John 11:23–26).

If, as I have argued, the concept of "born again" has its roots in John's Gospel, especially John 3, then there is likely the idea in 1 John not only of "new spiritual birth," but also that such birth designates entry into the resurrection life of the never-ending new world to come. It is not likely coincidental that the combined notions of "born again" and "enter the kingdom" in John 3 finds a parallel in 1 John 5:4, where "whatever is born of God" is directly linked to "the victory that has overcome the world." At the time of the consummation of this "victory," when Jesus appears a final time, "we will be like Him, because we will see Him just as He is" (1 John 3:2).

Revelation

RESURRECTION AND NEW-CREATIONAL KINGSHIP IN REVELATION 1:5

The resurrection of Jesus Christ is one of the first items mentioned in the introduction of the book of Revelation: "Jesus Christ, the faithful witness, the firstborn of the dead, and the ruler of the kings of the earth" (1:5). Notice once more that Christ's resurrection directly results in his being universal king.

Commentators are no doubt right in seeing Ps. 89:27, 37 as the basis for the statement that Christ is "faithful witness," "firstborn," and "ruler of the kings of the earth," since all three phrases occur there. However, the significance

---

51. E.g., chap. 8 under the heading "The Already–Not Yet Latter-Day Resurrection and New-Creational Kingdom in the Gospels."

of the allusion usually is not discussed. The immediate context of the psalm speaks of David as an "anointed" king who will reign over all his enemies and whose seed will be established on his throne forever (Ps. 88:19–32 LXX; Judaism understood Ps. 89:27 [MT] messianically [*Exod. Rab.* 19.7]). John views Jesus as the ideal Davidic king on an escalated eschatological level, whose death and resurrection have resulted in his eternal kingship and in the kingship of his "beloved" children (cf. 1:5b), which is developed in 1:6. "The faithful witness" is likely also based on Isa. 43:10–13 (see further on 3:14 below).

"The firstborn" refers to Christ's high, privileged position as a result of the resurrection from the dead (i.e., a position with respect to the OT idea of primogeniture, especially in the context of royal succession [Ps. 89:27–37 is developing this idea from 2 Sam. 7:13–16; Ps. 2:7–8]). Christ has gained such a sovereign position over the cosmos, not in the sense that he is recognized as the first-created being of all creation or as the origin of creation, but rather as the inaugurator of the new creation via his resurrection, as we will see that 3:14 explains (on which, see below; cf. the same language and idea in Col. 1:18). Time and again we have seen that resurrection as new creation is an overlapping reality with kingship, and Rev. 1:5 is another example.

Christ's kingship over "the kings of the earth" at this point in the book indicates his rule not over his redeemed people[52] but rather over his defeated enemies, since the almost identical phrase *hoi basileis tēs gēs* ("the kings of the earth") refers typically elsewhere in Revelation to antagonists of God's kingdom (6:15; 17:2; 18:3, 9; 19:19; cf. 16:14). This includes not only the kingdoms and peoples represented by them but also the satanic forces behind these kingdoms. It is possible that Christ's rule in the present will result in the conversion of some of these defeated kings, which may be pictured in 21:24, where "the kings of the earth" stream into the heavenly city.

Resurrection as New Creation in Revelation 3:14

The Rev. 1:5 text is developed later in 3:14, where there is continued allusion to Ps. 89, thus repeating the link between Jesus's resurrection and kingship (see table 11.2).

Table 11.2

Revelation 1:5	Revelation 3:14
the faithful witness	the Amen, the faithful and true Witness
the firstborn of the dead, and the ruler of the kings of the earth	the Beginning of the creation of God

52. Against Paul S. Minear, *I Saw a New Earth: An Introduction to the Visions of the Apocalypse* (Washington, DC: Corpus, 1969), 14; Elisabeth Schüssler Fiorenza, "Redemption as Liberation: Apoc 1:5f. and 5:9f.," *CBQ* 36 (1974): 223.

"The faithful witness" of 1:5 is amplified in 3:14 as "the Amen, the faithful and true Witness," and "the firstborn of the dead" is interpreted to be "the beginning of the [new] creation of God." But 3:14 alludes to some other important OT texts in addition to Ps. 89, and the verse needs some extended discussion because, like Gal. 6:15–16; 2 Cor. 5:17; Col. 1:15–18, this passage is one of the most explicit texts in the NT that interprets Jesus's resurrection as new creation.

The promise of a new creation by the faithful God of Israel in Isa. 65:16–17 ("the God of Amen . . . the God of Amen . . . I create new heavens and a new earth") primarily stands behind the title "the Amen, the faithful and true," as well as behind the concluding "the Beginning of the creation of God." The notion of God and of Israel as "faithful witness" to the new creation in Isa. 43:10–12 forms the background for "witness." These OT allusions are used to indicate that Christ is the true Israel and the divine "Amen, the faithful and true Witness" to his own resurrection as "the Beginning of the [new] creation of God," in inaugurated fulfillment of the Isaianic prophecies of new creation. If relevant Jewish exegetical tradition based on Gen. 1:1 or Prov. 8:22, 30 (or Prov. 8:22 by itself) also was in mind, it would have to be viewed as now being applied to the new creation of the latter days, which is not inconceivable.

Past Views of the Old Testament Background of Revelation 3:14

L. H. Silberman,[53] building on an earlier article by C. F. Burney,[54] argues that the expression "the Amen" in Rev. 3:14 is a mistransliteration of the Hebrew 'āmôn ("master workman"), which is employed to describe Wisdom in Prov. 8:30 and which refers to Torah in the *Midrash Rabbah* on Gen. 1:1. He also argues that the titles in Rev. 3:14, "the faithful and true Witness" and "the Beginning of the creation of God," are drawn respectively from the Hebrew of Prov. 14:25 ('ēd 'ĕmet, "faithful witness") and 8:22 (rē'šît darkô, "beginning of his ways"). To buttress his argument, he shows that the midrash equates the phrase "beginning of his ways" and "master builder," since both are applied to the Torah.[55] Silberman concludes by proposing that Rev. 3:14 must have read in a Hebrew antecedent, "Thus says the Master Workman, the faithful and true witness, the foremost of his creation."

J. A. Montgomery has proposed somewhat similarly that Rev. 3:14 is dependent on Prov. 8:22, 30.[56] In particular, he argues that John in rabbinic fashion changed the vocalization of 'āmôn ("master builder") in Prov. 8:30 to 'āmēn. This then means that John understood wisdom in that passage as

---

53. L. H. Silberman, "Farewell to O AMHN: A Note on Rev. 3:14," *JBL* 82 (1963): 213–15.

54. C. F. Burney, "Christ as the APXH of Creation (Prov. viii 22, Col. i 15–18, Rev. iii 14)," *JTS* 27 (1926): 160–77.

55. Agreeing with Silberman's analysis is L. P. Trudinger, "'O AMHN (Rev. III:14) and the Case for a Semitic Original of the Apocalypse," *NovT* 14 (1972): 277–79.

56. J. A. Montgomery, "The Education of the Seer of the Apocalypse," *JBL* 45 (1926): 73.

the "Amen" and immediately applied it as a title to Christ in Rev. 3:14. In more straightforward fashion than Silberman and Montgomery, others have proposed that Col. 1:18 and Rev. 3:14 are parallel, that both depend directly on Prov. 8:22 and are employed polemically against Jewish-gnostic ideas about Jesus as a mediating power but not as a supreme one.[57] Some have denied any dependence on Col. 1:15, 18 and have seen only a reference to Prov. 8:22, with the emphasis of *archē* being on Christ's temporal priority to the original creation.[58]

Revelation 3:14 as a Reference to the Resurrected Christ and as an Allusion to Isaiah's Prophecies of New Creation

The aforementioned proposal by Silberman and others like it are possible. However, apart from the problems of dating this Jewish tradition, other factors raise questions about the proposal. First, regardless of the relationship of Rev. 1:5 and 3:14 to Col. 1:15–18, both are primarily to be interpreted by their immediate contexts in Revelation. In this respect, 3:14 is designed to be a literary development of Christ's title in 1:5, just as each of the other self-presentations by Christ in the initial part of each letter draws from some saying or description of Christ in chapter 1. It is clear there, as noted above, that Jesus as "faithful witness" and "firstborn of the dead" in 1:5 is related not to the original creation but rather to his ministry, death, and resurrection. The second part of the self-description in 3:14, "the Beginning of the creation of God," is evidently a development of the phrase "firstborn of the dead" in 1:5, which there also immediately follows "the faithful witness."[59]

In contrast to what most commentators think, this is not a reference linking Jesus to the original creation in Gen. 1; it is an interpretation of Jesus's resurrection from 1:5.[60] His resurrection is viewed as being the beginning of the new creation, which is parallel with Col. 1:15b, 18b: compare "firstborn of all creation" (*prōtotokos pasēs ktiseōs*) in Col. 1:15b, which likely refers

---

57. E.g., Colin J. Hemer, *The Letters to the Seven Churches of Asia in Their Local Setting*, JSNTSup 11 (Sheffield: JSOT Press, 1986), 186–87.

58. Traugott Holtz, *Die Christologie der Apokalypse des Johannes*, TUGAL 85 (Berlin: Akademie-Verlag, 1971), 143–47.

59. That this second phrase in 3:14 develops "firstborn of the dead" in 1.5 is evident in that Christ's self-presentations at the beginning of each of the other letters draws on some description of Christ from chap. 1, and since "faithful witness" in 3:14a clearly draws from 1:5a, it seems likely that 3:14b draws from the directly following phrase "firstborn of the dead" in 1:5. The phrase "beginning of the creation of God" in 3:14 does not occur in chap. 1, so it must be viewed as an interpretation of something from that chapter, and "firstborn of the dead" in 1:5 is the most likely and proximate candidate.

60. So likewise only Burney, "Christ as the APXH," 177; S. MacLean Gilmour, "The Revelation to John," in *The Interpreter's One-Volume Commentary on the Bible*, ed. Charles M. Laymon (Nashville: Abingdon, 1971), 952. Martin Rist sees both ideas of original and new creation included ("The Revelation of St. John the Divine [Introduction and Exegesis]," in vol. 12 of *The Interpreter's Bible*, ed. George A. Buttrick [Nashville: Abingdon, 1957], 396).

to the original creation of Genesis, and "the beginning, the firstborn from the dead" in Col. 1:18b (*archē, prōtotokos ek tōn nekrōn*). The latter clause refers to the resurrection as a new cosmic beginning (as evidenced by the link not only with Col. 1:15–17 but also with 1:19–20, 23). This is parallel with 2 Cor. 5:15, 17, where Paul understands Jesus's resurrection as bringing about a "new creation," the latter verse in allusion to Isa. 43:18–19; 65:17 (cf. the linking *hōste* ["so that"]; so also Eph. 1:20–23; 2:5–6, 10).

The conclusion that the title "the Beginning of the creation of God" in Rev. 3:14 is an interpretative development of "firstborn of the dead" from 1:5 is confirmed by the observation that *archē* ("beginning") and *prōtotokos* ("firstborn") generally are related in meaning and especially are used together almost synonymously in Col. 1:18b (*archē, prōtotokos ek tōn nekrōn*) to refer to Christ's sovereign position in the new age, as a result of the resurrection. In addition, the titles of Christ in Rev. 22:13 use *archē* ("beginning") synonymously with *prōtos* ("first"). It is not inconceivable that *hē archē* ("the beginning") could be an interpretative development not only of *ho prōtotokos* ("the firstborn") in 1:5 but also of the immediately following phrase *ho archōn* ("the ruler"). If so, it might be an interpretative pun: *rē'šît* ("beginning") and *rō'š* ("ruler") are based on the same root, and both *archē* (approximately 75x) and *archōn* (approximately 90x) typically translate *rō'š* in the LXX.[61]

Thus, Christ as "firstborn from the dead, and the ruler of the kings of the earth" in 1:5 is interpreted in 3:14 as the sovereign inaugurator of the new creation. Consequently, the title "Beginning of the creation of God" refers not to Jesus's sovereignty over the original creation but rather to his resurrection as demonstrating him to be the inauguration of and sovereign over the new creation. The variant *ekklēsias* ("church") for *ktiseōs* ("creation") is secondary, as it has weak manuscript support (read only by ‫א‬*) and may have been an unintentional misreading of *ktiseōs* (the resulting reading in ‫א‬* is "the beginning of the church"). However, the variant may not have been accidental, since the scribe may well have been trying to conform it to the parallel with Col. 1:15, 18, where Christ as "firstborn of all creation" is interpreted by Christ as "the head of the body, which is the church." At the least, the variant reading would have come to represent an early interpretation of the verse as Christ being the beginning not of the original creation, but of the newly created church or the new age of the church.

Many commentators have concluded that behind the title *ho amēn* stands Isa. 65:16 ("the God of amen ['āmēn]"), although exegetical analysis is rarely adduced in support of the contention, and the Isaianic connection is never related to the idea of the creation in 3:14.

61. For further evidence that *archē* can include both ideas of "beginning" and "sovereign head" in Col. 1:18; Rev. 3:14, and elsewhere, see Burney, "Christ as the ΑΡΧΗ," 176–77; Holtz, *Christologie*, 147.

However, there is weighty evidence that the Isaiah text is the primary source for the titles in Rev. 3:14. Seven lines of evidence support an allusion to Isa. 65:16.

(1) *ho amēn* ("the Amen") is a Semitic equivalent to the Greek "faithful" (*pistos*), as well as "true" (*alēthinos*), which is evident from the LXX's typical translation of verbal and nominal forms of the root *'mn* ("to be faithful") mainly by *pistos*, but also sometimes by *alēthinos*.[62] Therefore, the threefold name could be an independent, expanded translation of Isaiah's "Amen."

(2) Together with Rev. 1:5 (and the allusion there to Ps. 89:37), the textual tradition of Isa. 65:16 and its context represent a sufficient quarry of terms and ideas likely extant in the first century from which the titles of 3:14 could have been derived.[63] First, the Hebrew text refers twice to God as "the God of truth [*'āmēn*]," which is translated in the following three ways by different versions of the Greek OT: (1) *ton theon ton alēthinon* (LXX); (2) *en tō theō pepistōmenōs* (Aquila; Jerome; manuscript 86 has *pepistōmenos*); (3) *en tō theō amēn* (Symmachus; Theodotion has *amēn* for the second "Amen" of Isa. 65:16). Respectively, these three translations refer to God as "true," "faithful,"[64] and as the "Amen."[65]

Against this background, the title *ho martys ho pistos kai alēthinos* ("the faithful and true Witness") in Rev. 3:14 is best taken as an interpretative translation of *'āmēn* ("Amen" = *amēn*) from Isa. 65:16.[66] Perhaps "Amen" is placed first followed by "faithful and true" to show that the latter clause is an interpretative expansion of the Isaianic "Amen."

The formulation could be an independent, amplified rendering of the Isaiah text. Or, similarly, "faithful" from Rev. 1:5 has been taken and now understood in the light of Isaiah's "Amen." "True" has been taken from Rev. 3:7, where it occurred already as a rendering of "faithful" from 1:5, and was added as part of the expansion in 3:14. Yet another possibility is that the different readings of the LXX, Aquila, Symmachus, and Theodotion were already extant in the first century in earlier versional forms or represented prior exegetical traditions on Isa. 65:16, and that the Rev. 3:14 rendering was "sparked off" by and composed under the influence of such prior versions or traditions.

It is difficult to decide whether the enlarged rendering was done independently or dependently. The latter is an attractive possibility because it seems

---

62. See Edwin Hatch and Henry A. Redpath, *A Concordance to the Septuagint and the Other Greek Versions of the Old Testament* (Graz: Akademische Druck- u. Verlagsanstalt, 1954).

63. Cf. 3 Macc. 2:11, where God is referred to as "faithful . . . true" (*pistos . . . alēthinos*).

64. Aquila and Jerome have literally "faithfully," and ms. 86 apparently has "faithful one."

65. If this expresses a liturgical formula, it would still reflect on God's trustworthiness, so that "Amen" would still be applicable to God.

66. So likewise Mathias Rissi, *The Future of the World: An Exegetical Study of Revelation 19.11–22.15*, SBT 2/23 (London: SCM, 1972), 21; H. Schlier, "αμήν," *TDNT* 1:337, though neither cites the above LXX versions in support.

more than coincidental that the four Greek versions of Isa. 65:16 together have virtually the same amplified renderings as that of Rev. 3:14. Whichever is the case, the articulation of the heavenly Christ's name through an exegesis of OT texts has affinities with the practice in Judaism of formulating personal names for angels on the basis of exegeting OT texts.[67]

What strengthens the notion that the three Greek readings existed in some form prior to the second century AD is that the Hebrew *'mn* could be pointed in three possible ways, which correspond at least to two and possibly three of the LXX versional readings and to Rev. 3:14.

(3) "Amen" usually is a response by people to a word from God or to a prayer in both Testaments, and it sometimes refers to Jesus's trustworthy statements in the Gospels. However, an observation underscoring a link between Isa. 65:16 and Rev. 3:14 is that these are the only two passages in the Bible where "Amen" is a name.

(4) The "blessing" of the "God of truth," which is only generally referred to in Isa. 65:16, is precisely understood in the following verse to be that of the new creation that he will bring about: "For behold, I create new heavens and a new earth" (65:17).[68] Similarly, the reference to Jesus as "the Beginning of the creation of God" directly after the Isa. 65:16 allusion ("the Amen, the faithful and true Witness") probably alludes to the prophecy of new creation in Isa. 65:17, which also comes directly after 65:16. Consequently, Christ is viewed to be the beginning of "the *new* creation."

(5) That this section of Isaiah is in mind is also likely because John has been meditating on Isa. 62:2; 65:15 in the nearby context of 2:17; 3:12, in addition to focusing on other related texts of Isaiah in 3:7, 9.

(6) An allusion to Isa. 65:16 is also corroborated by Rev. 21:5, where the one "on the throne" says *idou kaina poiō panta* ("Behold, I make all things new"), a reference to Isa. 43:19; 65:17, and then he refers to this declaration as *hoi logoi pistoi kai alēthinoi eisin* ("these words are faithful and true"). This declaration itself is a development of the earlier allusion to Isa. 65:17 in 21:1 ("And I saw a new heaven and a new earth"). In this light, it is not accidental that in 21:6 God or Jesus is called "the beginning" (*hē archē*). This suggests that the desired consummation of the new creation of 21:1, 5 has already been inaugurated by Jesus's resurrection (in 3:14), since both allude to the very same Isaianic prophecies of new creation. This is further hinted in that of the three times the phrase *pistos kai alēthinos* ("faithful and true") occurs elsewhere in the book, one serves as an introductory affirmation of the truth that God will "make *all* things new" (21:5), and a second (22:6) functions likewise as an

---

67. See Saul M. Olyan, *A Thousand Thousands Served Him: Exegesis and the Naming of Angels in Ancient Judaism*, TSAJ 36 (Tübingen: Mohr Siebeck, 1993).

68. Note also the identity of v. 16 with v. 17 in the parallel phrases of the second line of each verse: "the former troubles are forgotten / the former things shall not be remembered."

emphatic conclusion to the same discussion of the new creation in 21:5–22:5 (although in 21:5 and 22:6 the words are in the plural).[69]

(7) Although the Ps. 89 background behind "faithful witness" is likely carried over from Rev. 1:5 into 3:14, there is an additional OT background for the idea of "faithful witness," especially in the context of the expression in 3:14, which is highlighted there more than Ps. 89:37. The LXX of Isa. 43:10 says, "You [Israel] be my witnesses, and I am a witness, says the Lord God, and my servant whom I have chosen." Likewise, 43:12–13 LXX is parallel with 43:10 and has "You [Israel] are my witnesses, and I am a witness, says the Lord God, even from the beginning [kagō martys legei kyrios ho theos eti ap' archēs]."[70]

What is striking in Isa. 43 LXX is that Israel, God, and the Servant are all called "witnesses." Indeed, the Targum interprets "My servant" as "My servant the Messiah." To what are Israel, God, and the Servant or Messiah to witness? In context, it is evident that they are primarily witnesses to God's past act of redemption at the exodus (43:12–13, 16–19) and, above all, to God's coming act of restoration from exile, which is to be modeled on the former redemption from Egypt. Isaiah 43:18–19 LXX refers to the coming restoration as none other than a new creation: "Do not remember the first things, nor consider the beginning things. Behold, I create new things." Therefore, Israel, God, and the Messiah are to be witnesses of the future restoration and new creation. Isaiah 44:6–8 also says that Israel is a "witness" both to God's past act of creation and his coming deliverance of the nation from exile. Both Isa. 43:10–13 and 44:6–8 also underscore the notion that the witness is against the idols, which cannot compare with the true God and his sovereign acts.

Especially noteworthy is that the witness by Israel, God, and the Servant (Messiah) in Isa. 43:10–13 is to events "from the beginning" (ap' archēs [likewise Isa. 44:8]), which are linked with the future new creation, to which they are likewise to bear witness. This phrase "from the beginning," and like formulations of archē in various contexts of Isaiah in the LXX, refer to the "beginning" at the first creation (40:21; 42:9; 44:8; 45:21; 48:16) or the "beginning" when God created Israel as a nation at the exodus (41:4; 43:9, 13; 48:8, 16; 51:9; 63:16, 19). But the point of saying that God is a "witness . . . still [yet, even] from the beginning" in the LXX of 43:12–13 (kagō martys . . . eti ap' archēs) is to emphasize the witness to God's past acts of redemption as new creations as the basis for his future act of redemption as an escalated new creation. God

---

69. Philip Mauro comes close to suggesting initial fulfillment of the Isa. 65 prophecy of new creation in Rev. 3:14 as a possibility, though his discussion is brief (*The Patmos Visions: A Study of the Apocalypse* [Boston: Hamilton, 1925], 129–30). In 2 Cor. 5:14–17 Paul also understands that the resurrection of Christ inaugurated the new creation prophesied by Isa. 43:19; 65:17 (see G. K. Beale, "The Old Testament Background of Reconciliation in 2 Corinthians 5–7 and Its Bearing on the Literary Problem of 2 Corinthians 4:14–7:1," *NTS* 35 [1989]: 550–81).

70. Although some LXX manuscripts lack *martys* in 43:12, the phrase *legei martys* still could be implied or assumed.

has been a witness to his past acts of creating the cosmos and of creating Israel as a nation at the exodus (which, we have seen, was also conceived of as a new creation),[71] and he will be a witness yet again to another creation.

Therefore, the emphasis lies on Israel, God, and the Servant being "witnesses" to the coming new creation as another "beginning" in the nation's history and in cosmic history. The "witness" of Isa. 43:10, 12 is to be understood as a "true witness" because of the directly preceding contrast with Isa. 43:9, where the "witnesses" (*martyras*) of the nations (= false idols or prophets) are commanded by Isaiah to speak the "truth" (*alēthē*). The word *alēthēs* underscores the exhortation that the witnesses be true. It is not by happenstance that Judaism viewed the witness of Isa. 43:12 as a true witness, since it is explicitly contrasted in the midrashim with those who bear "false witness" (*Lev. Rab.* 6.1; 21.5).

Conclusion

In mind in Rev. 3:14 is not Jesus as the principle, origin, or source of the original creation but rather Jesus as the inaugurator of the new creation. The phrase *tēs ktiseōs* ("of the creation") is best taken as a partitive genitive, although implicit in the idea of *hē archē* may be three ideas: (1) inauguration, (2) supremacy over, and (3) temporal priority. The latter two ideas are apparent from the parallel of Col. 1:18 and especially from Rev. 1:5, where "firstborn from the dead" is directly explained by "ruler of the kings of the earth."[72] The Isa. 43 prophecy of new creation is probably more the focus in the mention of "witness" in 3:14, since it appears to be interpreting the Ps. 89 allusion from 1:5: Jesus as "faithful witness," "firstborn," and "ruler of the kings of the earth" in fulfillment of Ps. 89 is interpreted to be the sovereign divine-human witness to the new creation, of which he is the bridgehead, in fulfillment of Isa. 43.

Some commentators who assume that *tēs ktiseōs tou theou* ("of the creation of God") refers to the original creation do not like the translation of "beginning" for *archē* because they think that it necessitates viewing Jesus as a created being along with the rest of creation.[73] However, seeing the phrase as a reference to the new creation results in the different understanding for which I have argued. No doubt the message about the new creation (21:5) and of the book in general (22:6) is referred to as "faithful and true" because it is from Jesus, who is "faithful and true" (19:9, 11; 3:14; 1:5).

Ernst Lohmeyer has argued that the phrase "beginning of the creation of God" in 3:14 refers to Christ as Lord of the newly created church community

71. E.g., Wis. 19:6.
72. For "beginning" as connoting temporal priority in Jewish and Greek literature, see Holtz, *Die Christologie*, 145–46.
73. See, e.g., George Eldon Ladd, *A Commentary on the Revelation of John* (Grand Rapids: Eerdmans, 1972), 65.

but not of the whole new creation.[74] Codex Sinaiticus could be an early witness to such an interpretation (above, we noted its variant reading, which has Christ as "the beginning of the church"). This is because he interprets 3:14 in light of Col. 1:18, which he understands to pertain only to the creation of the church. However, even if for the sake of argument it is granted that Col. 1 is the only key to interpreting Rev. 3:14, Col. 1:18 should not be limited only to the new church community, since it is linked with the cosmic creation in Col. 1:15–17. The following context of Col. 1:19–20, 23 shows that Paul understands Jesus's position in 1:18 as extending beyond the church to the whole creation. Jesus and the church are the beginning of the new creation but do not exhaust it. In support of Lohmeyer, however, it could also be contended that Jesus is viewed as Lord only of the church because that is the way he is presented in the inaugural vision of Rev. 1:12–20. Certainly, this is partially correct, but as in Colossians, although Jesus and his community are the beginning of the new creation, they do not exhaust it, as Rev. 21:1–5 reveals. Further, it is also clear from Rev. 1 that Jesus is universal king and Lord, especially from 1:5, which is the primary basis for 3:14. It has also been shown that 3:14 has integral links with 21:1, 5, which concern the universal new creation.[75] Thus, resurrection, new creation, and kingship go hand in hand.

RESURRECTION ELSEWHERE IN REVELATION 1–3

The entire section of Rev. 1:13–3:22 is an account of the resurrected Christ, appearing to John (1:13–20), and then through his appearance and communication to John he delivers prophetic messages to the seven churches (2:1–3:22). In the chapter 1 resurrection narrative Jesus is portrayed as the king, priest, and judge, which again links his resurrection with kingship. He is the reigning king, the "Son of Man," who has begun to fulfill the Dan. 7 prophecy of the "Son of Man" who would rule over all the world (Rev. 1:13). His clothing is associated not only with that of a king but also especially with that of a priest (1:13b). The "sword" image also conveys the idea that he is the end-time judge (1:16, in allusion to Isa. 11:4; 49:2), which is clearly applied in this manner in 2:12, 16; 19:15. The Isa. 11:4 allusion indicates that judgment was to be a key function for the coming messianic king (see Isa. 11:1–4), and this finds fulfillment in Jesus, the resurrected messianic king.[76] It is not inappropriate to remember that Adam was the priest-king of the first new creation who was

---

74. Ernst Lohmeyer, *Die Offenbarung des Johannes*, 3rd ed., HNT 16 (Tübingen: Mohr Siebeck, 1970), 38.

75. The above discussion of the OT background of Rev. 3:14 is a summary of G. K. Beale, "The Old Testament Background of Rev 3.14," *NTS* 42 (1996): 133–52. For further discussion of the alternative meanings for *archē*, see Moses Stuart, *Commentary on the Apocalypse*, 2 vols. (Andover, MA: Allen, Morrell & Wardwell, 1845), 2:97–100.

76. For more in-depth analysis of 1:13–16, as well as for everything in the remainder of this chapter, see Beale, *Revelation*.

to pronounce judgment on the serpent.[77] Furthermore, we have seen that Dan. 7:13–14 is one of the OT texts that develop Gen. 1:28, and that "the Son of Man [Adam]" is a development of Adam. The chaotic sea and the hybrid mutant animals arising from it convey a notion of de-creation, which implies a move to an ordered new creation, after their judgment (cf. Dan. 7:22), in the rule of the Son of Man (Dan. 7:13–14) and the saints (Dan. 7:18, 22, 27).[78]

Within this introductory part of Revelation there are specific and explicit references to Jesus's resurrection. Once more, in 1:18 Jesus affirms that kingly sovereignty results from his resurrection: "I was dead, and behold, I am alive forevermore, and I have the keys of death and of Hades." The notion of kingship is underscored by 3:7, which expands on 1:18: Jesus is the one "who has the key of David, who opens and no one will shut, and who shuts and no one opens" (for the idea of sovereign authority, as well as priestly echoes, see Isa. 22:20–23, which is partially quoted in Rev. 3:7).[79] Two more times in the letters of Revelation, Jesus's resurrection is directly linked to his kingship.[80]

The promise in 2:7 to the "overcomer" of "eating of the tree of life" refers to inheriting the eternal life in the new heaven and earth, which is clarified as such by 22:2, 14, 19. In 2:8 Jesus's resurrection from the dead is a demonstration of his attribute of eternity: he is "the first and the last." Because Jesus possesses eternal resurrection life, the one who is "faithful until death," identifying with the pattern of Jesus's own experience, will inherit the same reward that Jesus did, "the crown of life" (i.e., "the crown which is [resurrection] life," a genitive of apposition [2:10]).[81] The crown in part conveys the notion of kingship, which is also the reward that Jesus obtained on his resurrection. Also, 2:11 further explains "the crown of life" to be invincibility to "the second death," which is explained later to be immunity from the final judgment (on which, see 20:11–15; 21:8). This may best be seen as a reward given most fully at the time of physical death but already enjoyed in part, since in 3:11 the Philadel-

---

77. And that Gen. 1–3 may be in mind is suggested by the clear allusion in Rev. 2:7 to eating "of the tree of life which is in the Paradise of God." Genesis 1:28 also has in common with Isa. 11:1–2 the botanical metaphor applied to human growth (note the common verb *prh* in Gen. 1:28 and Isa. 11:1 of the Hebrew, and *auxanō*, read by the LXX in Gen. 1:28 and by Aquila and Symmachus in Isa. 11:1), which could have facilitated the association of the two passages.

78. See chap. 2.

79. On which, see Beale, *Revelation*, 283–85.

80. Revelation 2:27: "as I also have received authority from My Father," as a result of his "overcoming"; 3:21: "I also overcame and sat down with My Father on His throne." In addition, later in the book Jesus is described as a "son, a male child, who is to rule all the nations with a rod of iron; and her child was caught up to God and to His throne" (12:5, in fulfillment of the messianic kingship prophecy of Ps. 2:7–9). That "overcoming" for Jesus is synonymous with his resurrection, see 5:5–6.

81. The very same dual idea is reflected in 3:21: "He who overcomes, I will grant to him to sit down with Me on My throne, as I also overcame and sat down with My Father on His throne." So also 2:26–27. Thus, because Jesus's resurrection results in a position of rule, the resurrection of believers does likewise.

phians are commanded to "hold fast what you have," which is immediately explained to be their "crown."[82]

Again, we find the notion of new creation (expressed in resurrection) to be combined with kingship, a combination that we observed first in Gen. 1–2 and then repeatedly elsewhere in the OT and the NT.

RESURRECTION AS NEW CREATION AND KINGSHIP IN REVELATION 4–5

Chapters 4–5 are pivotal for the entire book of Revelation. Flowing from chapters 1–3, these two chapters are the source from which flow the remaining chapters of the book. The main point of chapters 4–5 is this: God's punitive and redemptive purpose for the world begins to be accomplished through the death and resurrection of Christ, through whose reign God's purpose for creation will be consummately executed and divine glory accomplished. The pastoral purpose of this point is to assure suffering Christians that God and Jesus are sovereign, and that the events that they are facing are part of a sovereign plan that will culminate in their redemption and the vindication of their faith through their own resurrection and the punishment of their persecutors.

Probably the best known mention of resurrection in the entire book comes in 5:5–6:

> And one of the elders said to me, "Stop weeping; behold, the Lion that is from the tribe of Judah, the Root of David, has overcome so as to open the book and its seven seals." And I saw between the throne (with the four living creatures) and the elders a Lamb standing, as if slain, having seven horns and seven eyes, which are the seven Spirits of God, sent out into all the earth.

In 3:21 Christ says, "I also overcame and sat down with my Father on His throne," and the picture and commentary in 5:5–14 likely is an expansion of this. And 3:21 itself is a development of 3:14, which is a part of the pattern of each of the seven letters, where the conclusion to each letter typically is related in some essential way to Christ's self-presentation at the commencement of each letter. In this case, Christ as the witness to the beginning of the new creation in his resurrection (3:14) is interpreted to be the resurrected Lord reigning on his Father's throne in 3:21. Christ's resurrected and ascended status continues as he continues to reign as king throughout the church age. This may be a hint that chapters 4–5 are connected to the theme of new creation. Again, chapter 5 portrays Jesus's resurrection as exalting him to a position of rule over all the cosmos, which he is seen to exercise in various ways throughout the following chapters (chaps. 6–19). In particular, his resurrection leads

---

82. In *Odes Sol.* 20:7 believers are exhorted in the present to "put on the grace of the Lord generously, and come into his Paradise, and make for yourself a crown from his tree"; this crown is both a past and a present reality for the saint (*Odes Sol.* 1:1–3; 17:1; cf. *Mart. Ascen. Isa.* 9:18).

to and continues in his position of kingship and sovereignty, as evident from his possession of the "book" as symbol of God's sovereign rule (5:7) and his identification with God's throne (5:12–13). Consequently, those whom he redeems also share in his kingship and priesthood: "You were slain and did purchase for God with Your blood" people from throughout the earth, "and You have made them to be a kingdom and priests to our God; and they are reigning upon the earth" (5:9–10).[83]

Christ's resurrection and its effects for him and his people with respect to kingship and priesthood in chapter 5 are part of a portrayal of the beginning new creation, as hinted at above. But where does one see new creation in chapter 5? There is perhaps an anticipation of new creation already in chapter 4. The three precious stones in 4:3 are a summary and an anticipation of the fuller list of precious stones in 21:11, 19–20, where the glory of God is revealed, not only in heaven, as in 4:3, but also in consummated form throughout the new creation. There in Rev. 21 the stones and their luminescence are part of the depiction of the new creation (see also 21:18–23). Together with the stones, the rainbow is also an incipient hint that this vision eventually will issue into a new creation on a grander scale than that of Noah's day, recalling that the rainbow was the first revelatory sign of the new creation that emerged after the Noahic flood. Could the presence of the rainbow be the first heavenly sign of the new creation that had been inaugurated in Christ and would be consummated at the end of history?

Where else does the idea of new creation peek through in chapters 4–5? That the new creation is inaugurated with Christ's redemptive work is apparent from 3:14, as I have argued, but it is also discernible from the use of "new" in 5:9 to describe that work. The word "new" (*kainos*) in the phrase "new song" (5:9) is another feature associating Christ's redemptive work with the beginning of a new creation, since

1. the vision of chapter 5 flows out of explicit mention of God's work of creation in 4:11, so it must have something to do with creation;
2. the following hymns in 5:12, 13 about Christ and his redemptive work are explicitly paralleled with the hymn in 4:11 about God's work of creation (see 5:12);
3. of the other six times "new" occurs in Revelation, it describes the coming renovated creation three times in chapter 21 (vv. 1–2, 5), twice it refers to some aspect of the new cosmos (3:12; and 2:17 in the light of 3:12), and once it refers again to the "new song" (14:3);

---

83. In 5:9 we see Christ's priestly activity of presenting himself as a sacrifice and blood offering, which is a development of the same priestly notion in 1:5, which, as in 5:9–10, is also joined with the idea of Christ's kingship and believers' kingship and priesthood (1:6). On this, see Beale, *Revelation*, 190–96, 358–64. For the present tense of "are reigning" instead of "will reign," see the discussion directly below.

4. of the seven times "new song" is mentioned in the OT, four are associated with God's act of creation in connection with his sovereignty and the deliverance of Israel (cf. Pss. 33:1–22; 96:1–13; 149:1–9; Isa. 42:5–13);

5. the "new song" in some of these OT references is related by Judaism to the coming messianic age and the new creation.[84]

It is clear in chapter 5 that the reign is understood as present for Christ,[85] as well as the saints (so 5:10a, esp. in light of 1:6).[86] Accordingly, the kingdom of the new creation has broken into the present, fallen world through the death and resurrection of Christ.

But how does the motif of creation fit into both chapters 4 and 5? God's sovereignty in creation (chap. 4) is the basis for his sovereignty in judgment and in redemption (chap. 5), which elicits the praise of all creatures. The concluding hymns of 4:11 and 5:9–13 bear out this integral link between the two chapters, since these hymns function as interpretative summaries of each chapter.[87] The striking parallelism of the two hymns shows that the former is directly linked to the latter,[88] and the likely link is that the former hymn serves as the basis for the latter.[89]

The parallels show that John intended to draw a very close interpretative relationship between God as creator and as redeemer through his work in Christ. This suggests that the redemption of the Lamb is a continuation of God's work of creation[90] but on a new scale. The creation that had fallen is brought back into relation with its creator either through willing obedience or forced subjection, as the following chapters reveal.[91] The verbal links between the hymns of chapters 4 and 5 also mean that God's control

---

84. *Numbers Rabbah* 15.11; *Midr. Tanḥ. Gen.* 1.32; *b. ʿArak.* 13b; interestingly, *Exod. Rab.* 23.11 applies Ps. 98:1 to the messianic age prophesied in the new-creational text of Isa. 65:16.

85. Although some attempt to argue that the enthronement of Christ in chap. 5 refers to a future enthronement (e.g., directly preceding a purported millennium), it is fairly clear that chap. 5 depicts the ascension of Christ, after his resurrection (on which, see further Beale, *Revelation*, 312–69).

86. The same is likely true for 5:10b ("and they are reigning upon the earth"), though it is possible that the variant reading of the future tense ("they will reign") is original, and if so, then 5:10a and 5:10b would be a classic "already and not yet" expression (on which see discussion in Beale, *Revelation*, 361 64).

87. See Minear, *I Saw a New Earth*, 67; David R. Carnegie, "Worthy Is the Lamb: The Hymns in Revelation," in *Christ the Lord: Studies Presented to Donald Guthrie*, ed. Harold H. Rowden (Downers Grove, IL: InterVarsity, 1982), 250–52.

88. Note especially *axios ei* ("worthy are you") in 4:11a and 5:9 (cf. 5:12), as well as *axios* ("worthy") + *ektisas ta panta* ("you created all things") in 4:11, and *axios* ("worthy") + *pan ktisma* ("all creation") in 5:12–13.

89. See Carnegie, "Worthy Is the Lamb," 248–49.

90. Ibid., 249. The similarity between *ktizō* ("create" [4:11]) and *poieō* ("make" [5:10]) also hints at such an interpretive link.

91. Heinrich Kraft, *Die Offenbarung des Johannes*, HNT 16A (Tübingen: Mohr Siebeck, 1974), 102.

of the whole creation mentioned in 4:11b is specifically accomplished by Christ through his death and resurrection and the Spirit, which results in the commencement of a new creation. Christ's resurrection and kingship, and the ensuing redemption that it accomplished, become the bridgehead of the new creation.

An Overview of Resurrection in Revelation, Especially in Revelation 6–22

The resurrection of believers appears to be depicted in three stages in the book of Revelation. First, implicitly, we have seen that believers on earth are identified with realities that are unique to the resurrected Christ. So, for example, as a result of Christ's resurrection, we have seen that he experienced an escalated form of the earlier kingdom, and believers living on earth presently are likewise identified with this kingdom (e.g., 1:5–6, 9). Or believers' "conquering" is identified with Christ's "conquering" (e.g., see the conclusion to each of the seven letters).

More clearly, a second stage of Christians' resurrected existence is the ascent of their soul to heaven. This is probably depicted in 6:9–11, where those who had been slain are "underneath the altar" in heaven and are rewarded with a "white robe."[92] The depiction in 6:9 of exalted believers as "having been slain" (perfect tense) is a signal identifying them with the "slain" (perfect tense) Lamb of 5:6. This seems to identify them not merely with the Lamb's death but also with the Lamb's resurrection life, which is the greater focus than death in 5:6.[93] That in their postearthly existence they are pictured as clothed in white further identifies them with the Lamb's resurrection existence, since he also was portrayed as clothed in a robe and in white in his kingly resurrection existence in heaven (1:13–14). The difference between them and the Lamb, however, is that although they have experienced a form of resurrection life in the spirit, they have not yet been physically raised.

Almost identical to 6:9–11, 20:4 says that John saw "the souls of those who had been beheaded . . . ; and they came to life" and "sat" on heavenly "thrones," thus experiencing a "resurrection" and escalated kingship (20:6). There is much dispute about the meaning of the "millennium" in Rev. 20, but if the extended argument that I have set forth elsewhere is pointing in the right direction, then verses 4–6 refer to a spiritual resurrection of believers

92. Revelation 14:13 is quite similar: "'Blessed are the dead who die in the Lord from now on!' 'Yes,' says the Spirit, 'so that they may rest from their labors, for their deeds follow with them.'"

93. This identification is highlighted by part of the manuscript tradition of 6:9 (1611ᶜ 2351 𝔐ᵏ syʰ**), which has the secondary addition of *tou arniou* immediately following *dia tēn martyrian* ("on account of the witness of the lamb"); a fraction of the Majority Text tradition also has "Jesus Christ" instead of "the Lamb" (see H. C. Hoskier, *Concerning the Text of the Apocalypse*, 2 vols. [London: Bernard Quaritch, 1929], 2:179).

at the time of physical death throughout the interadvent age.[94] The portrayal of formerly deceased believers before the heavenly throne in 7:14–17 and the believing host in 14:1–5 appear to be parallel to 6:9–11 and 20:4–6, though they probably picture an already–not yet perspective of the resurrected believing host. The twenty-four elders wearing crowns and sitting on thrones in 4:4 may also be exalted saints who represent during the interim age all the people of God and their kingship (though it is possible that they are angelic beings who are representative of the church and its privileged status).

The third way that the resurrection is portrayed is as a final consummative event. The portrayal usually is not directly about physical resurrection, but other closely associated, overlapping ideas of the final state are presented. The most literal depiction comes in 20:12–13, 15:

> And I saw the dead, the great and the small, standing before the throne, and books were opened; and another book was opened, which is the book of life; and the dead were judged from the things which were written in the books, according to their deeds. And the sea gave up the dead which were in it, and death and Hades gave up the dead which were in them; and they were judged, every one of them according to their deeds. . . . And if anyone's name was not found written in the book of life, he was thrown into the lake of fire.

That "the sea" and "death and Hades gave up the dead" so that all were "standing before the throne" refers to the final general resurrection of all people (in line with John 5:28–29; Acts 24:15; Rev. 20:5a), some of whom will be judged in "the lake of fire" and others whose names are "found written in the book of life" will be rewarded with "life." The reference to those "written in the book of life" is an allusion to Dan. 12:1–2: "And at that time your people, everyone who is found written in the book, will be rescued. And many of those who sleep in the dust of the ground will awake, these to everlasting life, but the others to disgrace and everlasting contempt." The "book of life" in 20:15 is best understood as an appositional genitive, "the book which is life," which is clarified earlier in 20:12: "another book was opened, which is of life."[95]

What is it about the "book of life" that spares them and gives them life? The fuller title for the book is "the book of life of the Lamb who has been slain" (13:8 [21:27 has "book of life of the Lamb"]). The added description "of the Lamb" is either a genitive of possession or source (preferably, "the Lamb's book of life"). The "life" granted them in association with the book comes

---

94. On which, see Beale, *Revelation*, 984–1021, which N. T. Wright (*The Resurrection of the Son of God* [Minneapolis: Fortress: 2003], 472–75) finds unconvincing but does not give, in my view, sufficient reasons for his disagreement. For more persuasive criticism of my position, see Grant R. Osborne, *Revelation*, BECNT (Grand Rapids: Baker Academic, 2002), 696–719.

95. The same basic meaning for "the book of life" occurs in 3:5; 13:8; 17:8, which I take to be resurrection life because all are allusions to Dan. 12:1–2.

from their identification with the Lamb's righteous deeds, and especially his death, which means likewise that they are identified with his resurrection life (cf. 5:5–13). They do not suffer condemnation from the evaluative judgment for their evil deeds because the Lamb has already suffered it for them: he was slain on their behalf (so esp. 1:5; 5:9; see further 13:8). The Lamb acknowledges before God all who are written in the book (3:5) and who are identified with his righteousness and his death.[96]

The description in 11:11–12 of the two witnesses is debated. I have contended elsewhere that it refers to the final vindication of God's people, which likely includes actual resurrection, and I am still persuaded of this conclusion:[97]

> And after the three and a half days the breath of life from God came into them, and they stood on their feet; and great fear fell upon those who were beholding them. And they heard a loud voice from heaven saying to them, "Come up here." Then they went up into heaven in the cloud, and their enemies beheld them.

If the two witnesses are not two individual prophets but are figurative for the witnessing church in its prophetic role, then this depiction of resurrection represents their final vindication before the eyes of their persecutors at the very end of the age. The picture of resurrection comes from Ezek. 37:5, 10. Ezekiel 37:1–14 is a prophecy of God's restoration of Israel out of Babylonian captivity. The nation's defeated condition of captivity is likened to dead bodies, of which only dry bones remain. However, their restoration to the land and to God would be like dry bones coming to life. Like the witnesses, Israel is seen as "slain" by persecutors and then coming to life (Ezek. 37:9).

The deliverance in 11:11–12 could be that of literal physical resurrection from the dead. However, while such an idea is probably implied, this appears not to be the focus, since the conquering of the witnesses did not entail all their (literal) deaths. The ascent of the witnesses figuratively affirms a final, decisive deliverance and vindication of God's people at the end of time. This figurative focus is enforced from the Ezekiel prophecy, which uses nonliteral resurrection language to speak of Israel's restoration from captivity. We have seen, however, that this Ezekiel prophecy is not purely figurative, since it does refer to literal spiritual resurrection, which, by implication, will be followed by physical resurrection.[98] It is likely that this is part of the reason why Judaism almost universally understood the Ezek. 37 prophecy to be about physical resurrection.[99]

---

96. It is possible that believers go through the "judgment" of 20:12–13 but are not condemned by it because their works are considered to be "good," because they have been done "in the Lord," which could be implied by 1:9; 14:13 (this could be in line with 2 Cor. 5:10).

97. Beale, *Revelation*, 596–602.

98. On which, see chap. 8.

99. Ezekiel 37:10 was seen this way in *Sib. Or.* 2:221–224; 4:181–182; *Pirqe R. El.* 33; as well as Irenaeus, *Haer.* 5.15.1; so likewise various parts of the Ezek. 37:1–14 vision in *Pesiq. Rab.*

Since Ezekiel prophesies the restoration of an entire faithful nation back to God, John sees the fulfillment in all the faithful of the church, not merely in two faithful individuals. John applies Ezekiel to the restored church because he sees them finally released from their earthly pilgrimage of captivity and suffering. This demonstrates that they are God's true people (cf. Ezek. 37:12–13). Such a final and complete deliverance from bondage must be not only spiritual but also physical. That physical resurrection may well be secondarily in mind is pointed to further by John 5:24–29, where together with clear spiritual and physical resurrection references from Dan. 12:1–2 (vv. 24, 28–29), Ezek. 37 is employed to indicate both an inaugurated (spiritual) resurrection (Ezek. 37:4, 6, 12–14 in v. 25) followed by a consummate (physical) resurrection at the eschaton (Ezek. 37:12 in v. 28: "all who are in the tombs will hear His voice").[100] Similarly, Matt. 27:52 utilizes Ezek. 37:12–13 to describe physical resurrection ("The tombs were opened, and many bodies of the saints who had fallen asleep were raised").[101] And we saw, indeed, that physical resurrection probably was implied in Ezek. 37 itself.

In addition to the depictions in Rev. 11; 20, other pictures of the final state in the new creation imply resurrection. This is especially evident from the account of the new cosmos in 21:1–22:5. The most explicit that this passage gets in this respect is in 21:1–4, where John "saw a new heaven and a new earth; for the first heaven and the first earth passed away." Since the redeemed are later depicted as dwelling in this new cosmos and being a part of it (21:2–4, 6, 24–27; 22:4–5), they presumably also have newly created bodies. This presumption is supported by the fact that the clear allusion to Isa. 65:17 in 21:1, 4 has occurred in 3:14, where, as we saw earlier, it applied to Jesus's resurrection as the beginning of the new creation. Since Jesus's people are clearly designated to be part of the renewed cosmos, also in fulfillment of Isa. 65:17, they likely are also seen to fulfill this prophecy in the way Jesus did (i.e., by physical resurrection). Among God's people in the new order "there will no longer be any death," since death was a part of "the first things" that "passed away" (21:4). Those in the renovated cosmos will be only "those whose names are written in the Lamb's book of life" (21:27), and they are seen to have inherited the promised resurrection "life" of the book[102] (on which, see the discussion above of 20:12–15). This resurrection life enables them to inherit all things that they enjoy in the eternal state (they "will inherit these things"), especially a living relationship with God (21:2–7). "The water of life" that they drink connotes the same thing (22:17).

Piska 1.6; *Gen. Rab.* 14.5; *Lev. Rab.* 14.9; *Deut. Rab.* 7.6; for the same perspective on Ezek. 37:5, see *y. Šeqal.* 3.3ⁱ; *y. Šabb.* 1.3[8.A]ᴸ.

100. This would be even more significant if there is common authorship of John and Revelation.

101. Ezekiel 37:6, 14 is likely also employed in Rev. 20:4, though this passage is highly debated.

102. Recalling that the Dan. 12:1–2 background behind "the book of life" is clearly about resurrection life.

Other texts in Revelation narrating the final state of the redeemed also plausibly imply their resurrection (15:2–4; 19:7–9).[103] In 15:2 in particular, the saints are now "standing" before God's throne in heaven (where the heavenly analogue to the earthly sea exists in 4:6). Perhaps the "standing" (*hestōtas*) includes the idea of resurrection, since this passage is tied in to 4:6; 5:5–9: note the common ideas of the sea as glass associated with fire, the Lamb's and believers' "conquering" (*nikaō*), playing harps, and singing a redemptive song, in the midst of which in Rev. 4–5 is the "standing" (*hestēkos*) of the Lamb (5:6), which expresses his resurrection.[104] This is suggested further by 10:5, 8, if the angelic figure there who "stands on the sea" is to be identified as Christ, being equivalent to the angel of the Lord of the OT.[105]

At the end of Revelation Christians are exhorted to have a share in this consummate resurrection life: "Let the one who wishes take the water of life without cost" (22:17 [cf., almost identically, 21:6; see also 22:14]).[106]

Conclusion

I have labored in this chapter and the preceding three chapters to demonstrate exegetically and biblical-theologically that Christ's resurrection is the beginning of the new creation and kingdom. Christ's resurrected and ascended status continues throughout the interim age, as does also his condition of being a new creation and king. All those who believe in Christ are also identified with Christ's resurrected and new-creational kingly status. This identification begins spiritually in this age and physically in the age to come. The notion of the resurrection as the beginning of the new-creational kingdom and the

103. This is the case in 19:7–9 to the degree that the "marriage" metaphor in this passage is developed in 21:2, which I have just argued is part of new creation and associated resurrection notions.

104. For the same idea of "standing" in 7:9, see further Beale, *Revelation*, 424–28, on the introduction to Rev. 7 (see further on 15:3). In 15:3 two distinct songs are not sung, but only one (note the epexegetical *kai*, "that is," "even"): the saints praise the Lamb's victory as the typological fulfillment of that to which the Red Sea victory pointed (enhanced by the song of Moses also being spoken by Jesus [= Joshua] [cf. Deut. 32:44]). In *Midr. Ps.* 145.1; 149.1 the song by the sea of Exod. 15:1 is linked to the eschatological singing of the saints in the age to come (cf. *Tg. Song of Songs* 1:1; see further Louis Ginzberg, *The Legends of the Jews*, trans. Henrietta Szold, 7 vols. [Philadelphia: Jewish Publication Society, 1909–38], 3:34–35, 6:11). In addition, there are references in later Judaism that affirm that the song of Exod. 15:1 implies the resurrection of the Israelite singers to sing once again in the new age (*b. Sanh.* 91b; *Mek. de Rabbi Ishmael*, Tractate Shirata 1.1–10). This could be a further hint suggesting that Rev. 15:2–3 is a resurrection scene.

105. As argued in Beale, *Revelation*, 537–39, 547–50.

106. See likewise "springs of the water of life" in 7:17. The promises to the "overcomers" at the conclusion of each of the letters likely are already–not yet promises of eternal resurrection life and victorious kingship with God (on which, see Beale, *Revelation*, 223–310).

continuation of this reality throughout the age is foundational to my argument in chapter 6 that the new-creational kingdom and its expansion form the major stepping-stone in the scriptural storyline to accomplishing divine glory. It is important at this juncture to restate the NT storyline that I formulated earlier: *Jesus's life, trials, death for sinners, and especially resurrection by the Spirit have launched the fulfillment of the eschatological already–not yet new-creational reign, bestowed by grace through faith and resulting in worldwide commission to the faithful to advance this new-creational reign and resulting in judgment for the unbelieving, unto the triune God's glory.* This was a revision of my previously formulated OT storyline: *The Old Testament is the story of God, who progressively reestablishes his eschatological new-creational kingdom out of chaos over a sinful people by his word and Spirit through promise, covenant, and redemption resulting in worldwide commission to the faithful to advance this kingdom and judgment (defeat or exile) for the unfaithful, unto his glory.*

These last four chapters are absolutely crucial for understanding the remainder of the book because all that follows is an attempt to demonstrate that all the major notions of the NT are facets of the diamond of Christ's resurrection, which is the beginning of the "already–not yet, end-time, new-creational kingdom."[107]

107. In this respect, see Richard B. Gaffin Jr., *The Centrality of the Resurrection: A Study in Paul's Soteriology* (Grand Rapids: Baker Academic, 1978), 114–34. Gaffin's seminal idea about Christ's resurrection influenced me years ago, and I am trying to expand on it in many ways in this book. Gaffin argues that in Paul's thinking, Christ's resurrection was his "redemption"—i.e., deliverance from death. Furthermore, he argues that "justification, adoption, sanctification, and glorification as applied to Christ are not separate, distinct acts; rather, each describes a different facet or aspect of the *one act*" of having been raised and redeemed from the dead (ibid., 127). When believers are identified with and come into union with the resurrected Christ, they are also identified with these same facets.

PART 4

THE STORY OF IDOLATRY AND RESTORATION OF GOD'S IMAGE IN THE INAUGURATED END-TIME NEW CREATION

12

Sin as Idolatry—Resembling the Image That Is Revered Either for Ruin or for Restoration

The preceding four chapters have elaborated at length on how the NT understands that the end-time new creation and kingdom have begun with Christ's first coming, particularly through his resurrection and the resurrection of those who identify with him. Their resurrection and kingship begins spiritually in this age and is completed physically at the end of history. But now we take a step back to see why people needed to be created anew in Christ. This chapter explains that because of the entrance of sin into history, all people have become idolatrous and either worship themselves or something in this creation instead of the Creator. Thus, instead of resembling God's image as had Adam before the fall, they worship and resemble some image in the creation.[1] In this manner, the image of God in humanity became distorted. The following two chapters after this one narrate how Christ's coming as the new, last Adam began to set right what the first Adam did wrong. Christ's work begins to regain for humanity what was lost: humans begin to be re-created and to reflect the image of God instead of the likeness of fallen creation, a process completed at Christ's final coming. Thus, sin is to be viewed as having its roots in idolatry. Consequently, the focus of this chapter is on the sin of idolatry and not sin in general, since we see that idol worship is the origin of all other sins. Thus, the

---

1. This chapter is a summary of G. K. Beale, *We Become What We Worship: A Biblical Theology of Idolatry* (Downers Grove, IL: IVP Academic, 2008). I am grateful to my research student Mike Daling for helping me to summarize the book.

focus on sin in the statement of my NT storyline is primarily explained in terms of idolatry, although, of course, much more could be said on the topic of sin.

Genesis 1–3 and Idolatry

Adam as the Image and Likeness of the Creator

Although Gen. 3 does not explicitly label Adam and Eve's sin as idolatry, we must investigate further whether a concept of idolatry is present there. When Adam stopped being committed to God and reflecting his image, he revered something else in place of God and resembled his new object of worship. Thus, at the heart of Adam's sin was idolatry.

Adam and Eve, as Gen. 1:28 affirms, were to subdue the entire earth: "God blessed them . . . and said to them, 'Be fruitful and multiply, and fill the earth, and subdue it; and rule over the fish of the sea and over the birds of the sky, and over every living thing that creeps on the earth.'" Genesis 1:27 provides the means by which the commission and goal of verse 28 was to be accomplished: humanity will fulfill the commission by means of being "in the image of God."[2] Part of Adam's reflection of God's image was to reflect God's kingship by being his vice-regent on earth.

Genesis 2 pictures the first couple placed in God's arboreal temple as his image to reflect him. Adam and Eve and their progeny were created to be in God's image in order to reflect his character and glory and fill the earth with it (Gen. 1:26–28).

Just as Adam's son was born according to Adam's "likeness" and "image" (Gen. 5:1–3) and resembled his human father in appearance and character, so Adam was a son of God who was to reflect his divine father's image. This means that the command for Adam to fill, subdue, and rule over the earth indicates that he was to populate the earth, not merely with progeny, but with image-bearing progeny who would reflect God's glory.[3]

Adam's Sin of Idol Worship

Genesis 3 recounts, however, that Adam and Eve sinned and did not reflect God's image. They violated God's command not to eat of "the tree of the

2. The same relationship exists between 1:26a and 1:26b. See William J. Dumbrell, *The Search for Order: Biblical Eschatology in Focus* (Grand Rapids: Baker Academic, 1994), 18–20.
3. On which, see chap. 2. From here on I will usually refer to Adam and not Eve, since Adam was the vice-regent with ultimate responsibility for carrying out the commission in Gen. 1:28 (see Rom. 5:12–19), and he was the high priest in the Edenic sanctuary. I will not attempt to argue this at this point, except to note that, in addition to Rom. 5:12–19, Col. 1:15–19 views Christ as the last Adam with authority over the new creation, which would appear to point to the first Adam as having authority over the first creation. This NT perspective has roots in Gen. 1–3 (e.g., see James B. Hurley, *Man and Woman in Biblical Perspective* [Grand Rapids: Zondervan, 1981]).

knowledge of good and evil." Adam failed in the task with which he was commissioned, which included the failure to keep out of the garden-temple that which was antagonistic to God and unclean. Although Gen. 2–3 does not explicitly say that Adam's task of ruling and subduing was to guard the garden against the satanic snake, the implication is clearly there.[4] Thus, by allowing the snake entrance into the garden, Adam allowed sin, chaos, and disorder into the sanctuary and into the lives of both himself and his wife. Rather than ruling over the serpent and casting it out of the garden, Adam allowed the serpent to rule over him. Instead of wanting to be near God to reflect him, Adam "and his wife hid themselves from the presence of the LORD God among the trees of the garden" (Gen. 3:8 [so also 3:10]).

Rather than extending the divine presence of the garden sanctuary by reflecting it as they and their progeny moved outward, Adam and Eve were expelled from it. It was to be only in the Eden temple where Adam and Eve were to reflect God's rest.[5] Outside the garden, where they were exiled, they could find only wearisome toil (3:19). Consequently, Adam and Eve disobeyed God's mandate in Gen. 1:28, so that they no longer were in close proximity to be able to reflect God's living image in the way they were designed to do, and they were to experience death (Gen. 3:19).

There is no explicit vocabulary describing Adam's sin as idol worship, but the idea appears to be inextricably bound up with his transgression. "Idol worship" should be defined as revering anything other than God. At the least, Adam's allegiance shifted from God to himself and probably to Satan, since he came to resemble the serpent's character in some ways. The serpent was a liar (Gen. 3:4) and a deceiver (Gen. 3:1, 13). Likewise Adam, when asked by God, "Have you eaten from the tree of which I commanded you not to eat?" (3:11), does not answer forthrightly. Adam replies, "The woman whom You gave to be with me, she gave me from the tree, and I ate" (3:12). Adam was deceptively blaming Eve for his sin, which shifted accountability from him to his wife, in contrast to the biblical testimony that Adam, not Eve, was accountable for the fall (e.g., see Rom. 5:12–19). In addition, Adam, like the serpent, did not trust the word of God (with respect to Adam, see 2:16–17; 3:6; with respect to the serpent, 3:1, 4–5). Adam's shift from trusting God to trusting the serpent meant that he no longer reflected God's image but rather the serpent's image.[6]

---

4. On which, see further G. K. Beale, *The Temple and the Church's Mission: A Biblical Theology of the Dwelling Place of God*, NSBT 17 (Downers Grove, IL: InterVarsity, 2004), 66–71, 86–87; Meredith G. Kline, *Kingdom Prologue: Genesis Foundations for a Covenantal Worldview* (Overland Park, KS: Two Age Press, 2000), 54–55, 65–67.

5. For the notion that Eden was a temple, see chap. 19 below.

6. Likewise, Eve's misquotation in Gen. 3:2–3 of God's commandment given in 2:16–17, which Adam did not correct, mirrored the serpent's intended change of the same command in 3:4, "You surely will not die!" which was already implied by the serpent's question in 3:1. For

There also seems to be an element of self-worship in that Adam decided that he knew what was better for him than God did, and that he trusted in himself, a created man, instead of in the Creator. He had likely heard the serpent's tempting words to Eve, "In the day you eat from it your eyes will be opened, and you will be like God, knowing good and evil" (3:5). Then, in 3:22–23a, Adam is cast out of the garden because there was a sense in which the serpent's words came true:

> Then the LORD God said, "Behold, the man has become like one of Us, knowing good and evil; and now, he might stretch out his hand, and take also from the tree of life, and eat, and live forever"—therefore the LORD God sent him out from the garden of Eden, to cultivate the ground from which he was taken.

On the one hand, Adam could become like God and resemble him only by trusting and obeying him. On the other hand, there was a way in which Adam had become like God that was not good; indeed, it was blasphemous. Adam had arrogated to himself the authority to make ethical law, which is a prerogative that belongs to God alone. As I noted earlier, having "the knowledge of good and evil" refers to making judgments. The tree by that name was the place where Adam was to recognize either concurrence with or transgression of God's law (on which, see chap. 2 above). Accordingly, as a priest-king, he was to pronounce judgment on anything not conforming to God's righteous statutes. Adam, however, not only stood by while his covenantal ally, Eve, was deceived by the serpent, but also decided for himself that God's word was wrong and the devil's word was right. In doing so, perhaps Adam was reflecting another feature of the serpent, who had exalted his code of behavior over and against the dictates of God's righteous standard. But, if not, certainly Adam was deciding for himself that God's word was wrong. This is precisely the point where Adam placed himself in God's place—this is worship of the self.

The interpretation of Gen. 3 in Ezek. 28 presents sin as the rearranging of existence around the self, with the result that one attempts to become one's own creator, healer, and sustainer.[7] The notion that Adam was committing

---

elaboration on this, see chap. 2 under the heading "Adam's Commission in the First Creation and the Passing On of the Commission to Other Adam-Like Figures," and toward the beginning of that section. In effect, the serpent's questioning of God's word (3:1) and negation of God's command (3:4) were a nullification of the truthful effect of God's word, and Eve's changes to God's command were a reflection of the serpent's ungodly stance, which also represented a negation of the full truth of that command.

7. Not only does the LXX identify Adam as the glorious figure dwelling in the primeval Eden in Ezek. 28:14, but also it is plausible that the Hebrew text does so as well (as argued by, e.g., Dexter E. Callender Jr., *Adam in Myth and History: Ancient Israelite Perspectives on the Primal Human*, HSS 48 [Winona Lake, IN: Eisenbrauns, 2000], 87–135, 179–89). The metaphor in the Hebrew of Ezek. 28:14a, *'at-kĕrûb mimšaḥ hassôkēk* ("you were the anointed

self-worship appears to be confirmed from Ezek. 28, where there are two successive pronouncements of judgment on the king of Tyre (vv. 1–10, 11–19). The first pronouncement accuses the king of the sin of hubristic self-worship, for which he will be judged. Strikingly, the second pronouncement against the king appears to be against someone in the garden of Eden who had sinned and was cast out. Commentators have variously identified this figure either as a fallen angel (usually Satan) or, much more often, as Adam. Whichever it is (Adam, I think), the king of Tyre's sin and judgment is seen primarily through the lens of the sin and judgment of the figure in Eden instead of his own particular sin, so that this most ancient figure becomes a representative of the king of Tyre, and the latter's sin and judgment is viewed as a kind of recapitulation of the primeval sin. Consequently, all sin includes idolatry.[8] The worship of idols often involves self-worship, since, for example, people worshiped various gods in the ancient world in order to ensure their own physical, economic, and spiritual welfare.[9]

The Old Testament Notion of Becoming like the Images of Idols That Are Worshiped

At various points in the OT the gentile nations or idolatrous Israel is portrayed as "having eyes but not seeing, having ears but not hearing, and having a heart but not understanding." Such depictions are about spiritual, not physical, organs of perception. Whenever the organs of spiritual perception were seen not to be functioning, this might be called "sensory organ malfunction" language. When this language is used, it often refers not just to sin in general, but to one particular kind of sin: idol worship. This can be demonstrated from several passages in the OT.

---

cherub who covers"), could well be understood as a suppressed simile: "you were [like] the anointed cherub who covers," similar to such metaphorical statements as "the LORD is [like] my shepherd" (Ps. 23:1). Two things further point to this figure being Adam in Eden: (1) the king of Tyre is addressed through this representative figure, and it would be more consonant that the representative figure be human and not angelic, since what is represented is human; (2) Ezek. 28:18 says that the sin of the glorious figure in Eden "profaned your sanctuaries," which alludes to Eden as a temple being profaned. The only account that we have that the Eden sanctuary became unclean because of sin is the narrative about Adam in Gen. 2–3, so that the king is being identified with Adam's sin and punishment. Conversely, the Adam figure is sometimes also identified with the king of Tyre and his sin, particularly his sin of exalting himself to be God. In fact, in Ezek. 28 the phrase "your heart was lifted up" (*gābah libbĕkā*) is applied to both the king of Tyre (vv. 2, 5) and Adam (v. 17), as is also the portrayal of being involved in "trade" (vv. 5, 16, 18).

8. Likewise, Ezek. 22:1–16 asserts that Israel's idolatry (vv. 1–4) led the nation to all manner of sins (vv. 5–13), which then led to its judgment (vv. 14–16).

9. G. Ernest Wright, *God Who Acts: Biblical Theology as Recital* (London: SCM, 1964), 25.

Psalm 115 (// Psalm 135)

Perhaps the clearest example of people being described as becoming like the idols that they worship is Ps. 115:4–8 (// Ps. 135:15–18):

> Their idols are silver and gold,
> The work of man's hands.
> They have mouths, but they cannot speak;
> They have eyes, but they cannot see;
> They have ears, but they cannot hear;
> They have noses, but they cannot smell;
> They have hands, but they cannot feel;
> They have feet, but they cannot walk;
> They cannot make a sound with their throat.[10]
> Those who make them will become like them,
> Everyone who trusts in them.[11]

Psalm 115:4–8 (// Ps. 135:15–18) concludes with the climactic thought that those nations that make and worship idols will become like those very idols. Hence, the reader is to deduce that worshipers of idols will be judged by being made to resemble the idols portrayed—that is, having mouths but being unable to speak, having eyes but being unable to see, and so on. The statement in Ps. 135:14 that "the LORD will judge His people" makes this more explicit, introduces verses 15–18, and shows that Israel could be associated with the judgment of verse 18. Thus, the description of the nations (and implicitly Israel) as "having ears but not hearing" and like expressions are best understood as metaphors of idolatry that are applied to the disobedient nations in order to emphasize that they will be punished for their idol worship by being judged in the same manner as their idols: they will be destroyed. An aspect of this pronouncement of judgment also includes the idea that the idolaters had begun to resemble the lifeless nature of their idols. Although idolaters

---

10. The Ps. 135 parallel adds the clause "nor is there any breath at all in their mouth" (v. 17) and omits the following wording of Ps. 115:7: "They have noses but they cannot smell; they have hands but they cannot feel; they have feet but they cannot walk; they cannot make a sound with their throat."

11. Philo (*Decal.* 72–75) uses the words of Ps. 115:5–7 to assert that "the true horror" of idolatry is that idolaters should be exhorted to become as lifeless as the images that they worship, though he thinks that the idol worshipers themselves would abhor such an exhortation and "abominate the idea of resembling them [the idols]," which he believes shows the deeply impious extent of such perverse worship. Philo may reveal the psychological truth that on the conscious level idolaters do not want to resemble what they revere, but in reality that is exactly what happens to people as a punishment for the obstinate worship of lifeless images. Philo elaborates on this punishment in *Spec.* 2.255–256, where he says, again likely in allusion to Ps. 115:8: "And therefore let him too himself [the idolater] be made like unto these works of men's hands. For it is right that he who honours lifeless things should have no part in life, especially if he has become a disciple of Moses and has often heard from the prophetic lips."

thought that they were committing themselves to that which is the source of life and would bless them with life-giving blessings, in reality their idols were lifeless and empty, and would bring only death. Part of the judgment of death was that idolaters would resemble the spiritual lifelessness of their idols. Accordingly, the idolaters are portrayed just like the idols: having physical ears but not spiritual ears, having physical eyes but not spiritual eyes, and so on.

Isaiah 6

This notion of idolaters becoming spiritually like their idols occurs elsewhere. Notice, for example, the resemblance between Isa. 6:9b–10a and Ps. 115:4–6a (// Ps. 135:15–17a) as shown in table 12.1.[12]

Table 12.1

Isaiah 6:9b–10a	Psalm 115:4–6a (// 135:15–17a)
(Cf. Isa. 2:8b, 20b: "they worship the work of their hands"; "their idols of silver and their idols of gold, which they made for themselves to worship")	"Their idols are silver and gold, the work of man's hands."
"Keep on hearing, but do not understand; and keep on seeing, but do not know. Render the hearts of this people fat, and their ears dull, and their eyes dim, lest they see with their eyes, hear with their ears . . . and repent."	"They have mouths, but they cannot speak; they have eyes, but they cannot see; they have ears, but they cannot hear."

When the broader message of Isa. 6:9–10 is surveyed, there appears to be not only a verbal likeness with Ps. 115 (and Ps. 135) but also a comparable contextual function of phraseology. Recall that the idolatry pericope of Ps. 115:4–8 (// Ps. 135:15–18) concludes with the climactic thought that those nations who make and worship idols will become like those very idols. This same principle found in Ps. 115 also occurs in Isa. 6.

Isaiah 6 contains threads that go back to the very beginning of Israel's history, back even to the beginning of history, and threads that go forward into the NT. The fuller context of Isa. 6:8–13 reads as follows:

> Then I heard the voice of the Lord, saying, "Whom shall I send, and
>   who will go for us?" Then I said, "Here am I. Send me!"
> He said, "Go, and tell this people:
> 'Keep on listening, but do not perceive;

12. It is possible that there is an intertextual dependence of Isa. 6 on these two psalms (or one of them) but more likely that, if there is a literary relationship, one or both psalms are developing Isaiah and making the idolatry idea more explicit. There is debate about whether Ps. 115 is late preexilic or postexilic, while most understand Ps. 135 to be postexilic (for a brief convenient listing of positions, see Rikki E. Watts, *Isaiah's New Exodus in Mark* [Grand Rapids: Baker Academic, 1997], 191). Thus, the likelihood is that the two psalms were composed after Isa. 6.

Keep on looking, but do not understand.'
Render the hearts of this people insensitive,
Their ears dull,
And their eyes dim,
Otherwise they might see with their eyes,
Hear with their ears,
Understand with their hearts,
And return and be healed."
Then I said, "Lord, how long?" And He answered,
"Until cities are devastated and without inhabitant,
Houses are without people
And the land is utterly desolate,
The LORD has removed men far away,
And the forsaken places are many in the midst of the land.
Yet there will be a tenth portion in it,
And it will again be subject to burning,
Like a terebinth or an oak
Whose stump remains when it is felled.
The holy seed is its stump."

In verses 5–7 Isaiah, even though sinful, is declared to be forgiven by the grace of God. Isaiah, distraught at being in the holy presence of God, says, "I am a man of unclean lips, and I live among a people of unclean lips" (v. 5). Then a seraph, carrying a burning coal from the altar, comes to Isaiah and touches his mouth with it to symbolize that Isaiah has experienced the forgiving grace of God (vv. 6–7). Isaiah is declared forgiven by the holy God, and Isaiah's life is to be lived to the redounding of the glory of God. After Isaiah is forgiven, God chooses him to address Israel, which is not holy, and so he commissions him as a prophet. Therefore, Isaiah is one who reveres God and resembles his holiness, resulting in Isaiah's restoration and his commission as a prophet (vv. 5–7).

After this, a verdict is pronounced on Israel in verses 8–10. After the call goes out and Isaiah responds (v. 8), Isaiah is commanded to "go" and give a message from God to the people (v. 9). The second and third lines of verse 9 continue with the commission to Isaiah to command that the people misunderstand God's revelation. The phrases "do not perceive" and "do not understand" are part of the command.[13] The imperative is compounded in verse 10, where God again commands the prophet to speak to the people of Israel in such a way that would cause them to be "insensitive" to God's spiritual message of salvation, so that they would not hear, see, or understand spiritually. The intended result of this is that they would not "return" to God from their sin and "be healed." As we will soon see below, the blindness and deafness of Israel in verses 9–10

13. Both of the parallel lines in Hebrew have an imperative followed by a jussive form, which is equivalent to an imperative.

is a description of idol worshipers being judged by being made to reflect the very idols that they worship.

In response to the scorching message of judgment for idolatry in verses 9–10, Isaiah asks God how long this blinding and deafening judgment will last (v. 11b). The answer also gives the effect and the extent of the judgment on Israel: "Until cities are devastated and without inhabitant, houses are without people, and the land is utterly desolate" (v. 11b).

The extent of the judgment continues to be described in verse 12: "The LORD has removed men far away, and the forsaken places are many in the midst of the land." What was implied in verse 11 becomes explicit in verse 12: God will remove the inhabitants of Israel and send them into exile in another land. Israel's physical exile and separation from its promised land indicates its spiritual exile from God, since its land was where God's unique, special revelatory presence dwelled in the temple, which represented God's presence with his people through the priestly mediation and their worship.

The effect of Israel's spiritual and physical destruction and exile is explained in verse 13: "Yet there will be a tenth portion in it, and it will again be subject to burning, like a terebinth or an oak whose stump remains when it is felled. The holy seed is its stump." A remnant will survive ("a tenth portion") of both those who remained from living in the land and from exile. Furthermore, verse 13 indicates that the judgment in verses 9–12 is continuing and reaching a climax in the remaining remnant that will return from captivity. Verse 13 asserts that even the Israelite idol worshipers will be made like their idolatrous symbols, their destiny resembling the destructive end of their own idols, which was a mere "stump" of the formerly beautiful idolatrous tree. The reference to idols in verse 13b functions to identify the cultic nature of the previously mentioned burning trees in verse 13a. As a result, the poetic comparison of Israel's judgment with that of the destruction of the idolatrous trees is heightened. Even in their fallen stump-like condition their idolatrous identity is still not completely erased. The last clause of the verse is the climax to this as the stump image of a destroyed idolatrous tree is now transferred to sinful Israel.[14]

14. Most commentators think that the representation of the remnant as "subject to burning" like trees with a remaining "stump" indicates a purification or refining of faithful Israel. The reference to the "stump" as picturing the "holy seed" is especially seen to support this idea. However, several observations can be made that show this interpretation to be improbable. (1) Elsewhere in Isaiah the picture of oaks and terebinths burning is part of a description of God's destruction of idols. In particular, in 1:29–31 is found the only other use of 'ēlâ ("terebinth") in the book outside 6:13. This unique parallelism is heightened by the observation that b'r ("burn") appears in close relation to 'ēlâ ("terebinth") in both passages. In 1:29–31 these words appear as part of a description of Israel being judged by God because of its idolatry. Indeed, this passage even sees the idolaters becoming spiritually like the idolatrous objects that were worshiped: "For you will be like an oak whose leaf fades away, or as a garden that has no water" (1:30). The remaining uses of 'ēlâ in prophetic literature are in Ezek. 6:13 (cf. 6:3–13) and Hos. 4:13 (cf. 4:12–17), both of which refer to places where idol worship takes

Therefore, what Isaiah was called to do in 6:9–10 was to proclaim God's judgment against Israel for its idolatry. Thus, in verse 9 God, through Isaiah, commands the idolatrous people to become like the idols that they have refused to stop loving. In verse 10 God commands Isaiah to make the people like their idols through his prophetic preaching. This is an example of the *lex talionis*—an eye for an eye. People are punished in like manner to their own sin.

In summary, the expressions in Isa. 6:9–10 describing Israel as, for example, having ears but being unable to hear are best understood as metaphors of idolatry that are applied to the disobedient nation in order to emphasize that it would be punished for its idol worship by being judged in the same manner as its idols: it will be destroyed. Another aspect of this pronouncement of judgment is that the idolaters had begun to resemble the lifeless nature of their idols. That this is the case is further pointed to by 6:13b, which seems best understood as identifying the nation as an idolatrous symbol (or "cultic stump").[15]

---

place. The other word in Isa. 6:13, *'allôn* ("oak"), appears six other times in prophetic genre, three of which are part of a description of idol worship (Isa. 2:13; 44:14; Hos. 2:13). The same application of this "burning terebinth" metaphor likely occurs also in 6:13a, especially because of the proximity of the parallel context in Isa. 2. (2) The Hebrew word *maṣṣebet*, translated as "stump" in the first set of renderings, does not appear to mean "stump" or mere "wood substance" anywhere else in biblical or extrabiblical Hebrew. Elsewhere in the OT it means "a commemorative pillar" (15x), whether memorializing the dead, experiences with Yahweh, or agreements validated by divine witness. The only other meaning is that of "cultic pillar" in the sense of an idolatrous symbol, which accounts for the majority of uses (21x). (The word *maṣṣebet* is an alternative feminine singular form of *maṣṣēbâ*, the former of which occurs only in 2 Sam. 18:18. The word study here includes also the singular form *maṣṣēbâ*, which occurs more often. Both forms are likely to be considered the same Hebrew word.) All other uses in extrabiblical Hebrew, Jewish-Aramaic, and Syriac sources do not extend beyond these semantic bounds. See Samuel Iwry, "*Maṣṣēbāh* and *Bāmāh* in 1Q Isaiah[a] 6 13," *JBL* 76 (1957): 226–27. That such an apparently popular word for cultic pillar during Isaiah's time should have been used to mean "stump" of a tree is unlikely, especially since other more common words for "stump" probably were readily available to the author (cf. *gēza'* in Isa. 11:1; 40:24; Job 14:8; *'iqqār* in Dan. 4:15, 23, 26 [4:12, 20, 23 MT]). (3) The only other occurrence of "holy seed" in the OT is in Ezra 9:1–2, where the phrase is negative and has an idolatrous connotation, which further supports the same notion in Isa. 6:13.

15. For a more in-depth argument for the analysis given so far throughout this chapter on Isa. 6:9–13, see G. K. Beale, "Isaiah VI 9–13: A Retributive Taunt against Idolatry," *VT* 41 (1991): 257–78. The following concur with my conclusion about my idolatry interpretation of Isa. 6: John F. Kutsko, *Between Heaven and Earth: Divine Presence and Absence in the Book of Ezekiel*, BJS 7 (Winona Lake, IN: Eisenbrauns, 2000), 137–38; Gregory Yuri Glazov, *The Bridling of the Tongue and the Opening of the Mouth in Biblical Prophecy*, JSOTSup 311 (Sheffield: Sheffield Academic Press, 2001), 126–58; Watts, *Isaiah's New Exodus*, 191–92; David W. Pao, *Acts and the Isaianic New Exodus*, WUNT 2/130 (Tübingen: Mohr Siebeck, 2000), 106; Edward P. Meadors, *Idolatry and the Hardening of the Heart: A Study in Biblical Theology* (New York: T&T Clark, 2006), 9, 64–65. For further evaluation of my view by commentators, see Beale, *We Become What We Worship*, 63–64n49.

Isaiah elsewhere sees that idolaters are uniquely those people who have ears but cannot hear and eyes but cannot see.[16] Other OT passages outside Isaiah also use this language in close relationship to idolatry.[17]

Exodus 32

According to Exod. 32, directly after the first generation of Israel worshiped the golden calf, Moses describes them in a manner that sounds like they are being portrayed as wild calves or untrained cows: they became (1) "stiff-necked" (32:9; cf. 33:3, 5; 34:9) and would not obey but (2) "were let loose" because "Aaron had let them go loose" (32:25),[18] (3) so that "they had quickly turned aside from the way" (32:8), and they needed to be (4) "gathered together" again "in the gate" (32:26), (5) so that Moses could "lead the people where" God had told him to go (32:34).[19] In 32:8 the expression "they quickly turned aside from the way" is placed directly before the phrase "they have made for themselves a molten calf." Following this, 32:9 portrays the people as "stiff-necked," so that the three descriptions are inextricably linked.[20]

How is Israel's sin of idolatry portrayed in Exod. 32? The description can be seen as using cattle metaphors. Sinful Israel seems to be depicted metaphorically as rebellious cows running wild and needing to be regathered. Is the language just coincidental? The likelihood is that this is a narrative taunt directed against Israel as rebellious cows out of control because they are worshiping a cow. This is pointed to further by the aforementioned three closely juxtaposed phrases "quickly turned aside from the way," "made for themselves

---

16. See Isa. 29:9–14; 42:17–20; 43:8; 44:18. For elaboration of these passages, see Beale, *We Become What We Worship*, 41–48.

17. Virtually the same phenomenon is observable in the following texts: (1) Jer. 5:21 (cf. 5:7, 19); (2) Jer. 7:24, 26 (cf. 7:9, 18, 26, 30–31); (3) Jer. 11:8 (cf. 11:10–13); (4) Jer. 25:4 (cf. 25:5–6); (5) Jer. 35:15; (6) Jer. 44:5 (cf. 44:3–4, 8, 15, 17–19); (7) Ezek. 12:2 (cf. 11:18–21); (8) Ezek. 44:5 (so 40:4a; cf. 44:7–13). All these passages need elaboration, but the aims of the present study do not allow for it. There are some uses of this "sensory organ malfunction" language either where it is unclear whether idolatry is in mind (Isa. 1:3; Jer. 6:10; 17:23; Mic. 7:16; Zech. 7:11–12) or where it is not in mind at all, although the latter category uses atypical malfunction language in comparison with the above surveys. However, almost without exception, the phraseology "having eyes but not seeing" or "having ears but not hearing" in conjunction with other "sensory organ malfunction" language is applied to people who are idolaters.

18. Note elsewhere in the OT the picture of a "calf skipping" or "dancing" (Ps. 29:6, though a different verb than found in Exod. 32:19; 32:25), and note Israel itself acknowledging at the time of exile its having been "chastised like an untrained calf" that needed to "be restored" (Jer. 31:18).

19. Deuteronomy 32:15–18 may also picture Israel as a rebellious cow at the episode of the golden calf and at subsequent acts of idolatry in the land: "But Jeshurun grew fat and kicked" (v. 15a), which is interpreted to be Israel's "forsaking God" (v. 15b), worshiping "strange gods" (v. 16), "sacrificing to demons" and "new gods" (v. 17), and "forgetting the God who gave you birth" (v. 18).

20. In summarizing the episode of the golden calf, Deut. 9 repeats this threefold connection in v. 12 (see also v. 16).

a golden calf," and "stiff-necked" in Exod. 32:8–9.[21] Hosea 4:16 adds to the picture, echoing the event of the golden calf in Exod. 32: "Since Israel is stubborn like a stubborn heifer, can the LORD now pasture them like a lamb in a large field?"[22] (the implied answer is no). Hosea 4:17 then says, "Ephraim is joined to idols; let him alone." The idea emerging from these two verses is that Israel's stubbornness, like a rebellious calf or sheep, is idol worship, which in Hosea often is called calf worship, and is punished by God through "leaving them without a shepherd."[23] First-generation Israel and Hosea's generation had become as spiritually lifeless as the calf idols that they worshiped.

The first generation of Israelites did not literally become petrified golden calves like the one that they worshiped, but they are depicted as acting like out-of-control and headstrong calves,[24] apparently because they were being mocked as having become like the image that represented a spiritually rebellious and ornery calf that they had worshiped. What they had revered, they had come to resemble, and that resemblance was destroying them. The statement in Exod. 32:7 that because of their idolatry the people had "corrupted themselves" further demonstrates the inner spiritual deterioration that had set in and had transformed their inner beings. There is no explicit propositional statement in Exod. 32–34 saying that Israel became like the calf, but the idea appears to be expressed through the narrative genre.

Conclusion

The biblical-theological principle expressed by passages such as Ps. 115, Isa. 6, and Exod. 32 is that what you revere you resemble, either for ruin or

---

21. The Israelites' identification with their idol in Exod. 32 may be enhanced by the later portrayal of Moses making them drink the ground-up powder from the golden calf that he had destroyed (Exod. 32:20). Although the purpose of this act may seem unclear, it may merely "have been to shame them by making their idol become part of them" (so John D. Currid, *A Study Commentary on Exodus*, 2 vols. [Auburn, MA: Evangelical Press, 2000–2001], 2:281–82; along similar lines, see William H. C. Propp, *Exodus 19–40*, AB 2A [New York: Doubleday, 2006], 561). For further discussion of this episode in Exod. 32:20, see interpretations of the narrative of the golden calf in Judaism in Beale, *We Become What We Worship*, 149–60.

22. Among the DSS, CD-A I:13 describes the apostates of their generation with the clause "they are the ones who turn aside from the way," which is a quotation of Exod. 32:8 (or Deut. 9:12, the parallel to the Exodus text): "they turned aside from the way," describing Israel's rebellion in worshiping the golden calf. Then CD-A I:13–14 identifies this with Hos. 4:16: "That is the time of which it was written, 'like a stubborn cow, so Israel became stubborn.'" Thus, this Qumran text understands the rebellion in Exod. 32:8 to be compared to idolatrous Israel running around like cows. This early Jewish interpretation, I believe, unpacks the suggested meaning of Exod. 32:8, though written hundreds of years later.

23. For elaboration of the connection of Hos. 4:16–17 and the original event of the golden calf in Exod. 32, see Beale, *We Become What We Worship*, 99–110.

24. Oxen are commonly depicted as being out of control (Exod. 21:28–29, 32, 35–36; 23:4; Deut. 22:1) or running loose when they are wild and untrained (Num. 23:22; 24:8; Deut. 33:17; Job 39:9–10; Pss. 29:6; 92:10).

restoration. Isaiah wanted to revere the Lord's image and reflected his holiness, resulting in restoration, whereas Israel revered idols and reflected their spiritual lifelessness and image, resulting in ruin.

Idolatry in Romans 1[25]

Paul's epistles have several references to idolatry, though the one most relevant for our purposes is Rom. 1.[26] This passage reveals that Paul's thinking about idolatry is deeply saturated with some of the very same OT texts and ideas discussed already, including the motif that the idol worshiper becomes like the idol worshiped.

Romans 1:20–28 is Paul's most explicit elaboration on idolatry:[27]

> For since the creation of the world His invisible attributes, His eternal power and divine nature, have been clearly seen, being understood through what has been made, so that they are without excuse. For even though they knew God, they did not honor Him as God or give thanks, but they became futile in their speculations, and their foolish heart was darkened. Professing to be wise, they became fools, and exchanged the glory of the incorruptible God for an image in the form of corruptible man and of birds and four-footed animals and crawling creatures. Therefore God gave them over in the lusts of their hearts to impurity, so that their bodies would be dishonored among them. For they exchanged the truth of God for a lie, and worshiped and served the creature rather than the Creator, who is blessed forever. Amen. For this reason God gave them over to degrading passions; for their women exchanged the natural function for that which is unnatural, and in the same way also the men abandoned the natural function of the woman and burned in their desire toward one another, men with men committing indecent acts and receiving in their own persons the due penalty of their error. And just as they did not see fit to acknowledge God any longer, God gave them over to a depraved mind, to do those things which are not proper.

25. For the use in Judaism of the theme of becoming like the idol that one worships, see Beale, *We Become What We Worship*, 141–60.

26. Numerous NT passages deserve attention because of their relation to the concept of idolatry, including Matt. 13:13–15; Mark 4:12; Luke 8:10; John 12:40; Acts 28:26–27; Rom. 11:8; 1 Cor. 2:9; Rev. 9:20 (all of these quote Isa. 6:9–10 or related texts). Although many of these are pertinent to the present discussion, space limitations prohibit full treatment.

27. Paul's survey of the history of idolatry includes all humanity who have turned from God to worship something else, which would seem to include Adam and Eve (whom 1:20–21 appears to include in its purview): "For since the creation of the world His invisible attributes . . . have been clearly seen, . . . so that they are without excuse. For even though they knew God, they did not honor Him as God." There is debate about this among commentators. Douglas Moo, e.g., notes commentators on both sides of the issue, though he himself is unconvinced about an Adamic background (*The Epistle to the Romans*, NICNT [Grand Rapids: Eerdmans, 1996], 109).

This introductory section to Romans affirms that idol worship is the root sin of all other sins. When one turns from trust in God to trust in some part of God's creation, then the "heart" becomes "darkened" and all manner of sins follow from this, as Paul has begun to elaborate in verses 24–28, which is continued in verses 29–32.[28] Thus, Paul sees idolatry to be the root of and the essence of sin.[29]

In Rom. 1 the essential nature of idolatry is explained to be "exchanging the glory of the incorruptible God for an image" (v. 23), "exchanging the truth of God for a lie" (v. 25a), and "worshiping and serving the creature rather than the Creator" (v. 25b). The fitting punishment for malfunction in worshiping God is malfunction in other relationships, which includes homosexuality, lesbianism, disobedience to parents, and all kinds of dysfunctional relationships with others (vv. 24–32). Likewise, the *lex talionis* judgment ("the punishment must fit the crime") for "not honoring God" (v. 21) is "that their bodies would be dishonored among them" (v. 24); similarly, the penalty for not "approving to have God in their knowledge" is, fittingly, that God "gave them over to an unapproved mind" (i.e., a mind not approved by God) (v. 28).

The punishment itself is that the idol worshipers' unnatural relationships with others resemble their unnatural relationship with God. Because they have "suppressed the truth" of God, they have also suppressed knowledge and reflection of the attributes of his "divine nature" (vv. 18–20). As a result, they fail to acknowledge and to reflect God's nature and attributes, and instead they mirror the corruptible nature of the creation (vv. 21–25). Thus, they are not righteous like God but rather are "unrighteous" (vv. 18, 29a), not "wise" as reflectors of God's wisdom but "foolish" (v. 22), not truthful but filled with "deceit" (v. 29), not good but "inventors of evil" (v. 30), not loving but "unloving" (v. 31), and not merciful but "unmerciful" (v. 31).

The Old Testament Background of Psalm 106 in Romans 1:23–25

The description of idolatry among the gentiles in this passage is portrayed with the wording of Israel's idolatry in Ps. 106:20. There it is said that the Israelites "exchanged" the object of true worship, "their glory"—that is, the

---

28. So also Wis. 14:12: "For the idea of making idols was the beginning of fornication, and the invention of them was the corruption of life"; Wis. 14:27: "For the worship of idols not to be named is the beginning and cause and end of all evil" (see the context of Wis. 13:1–16:1); *L.A.B.* 44:6–10 says that every one of the Ten Commandments are broken by committing some form of idolatry (on which, see further Frederick J. Murphy, "Retelling the Bible: Idolatry in Pseudo-Philo," *JBL* 107 [1988]: 279–81).

29. In line with Thomas R. Schreiner, *Romans*, BECNT (Grand Rapids: Baker Academic, 1998), 88. I am especially grateful to my student Mike Daling for highlighting this idea for me.

glorious Lord—for an idolatrous image. This is a conscious use of Scripture by Paul.[30] The passage in the psalm is an allusion to the episode of the golden calf. By referring to the idolatry of the golden calf, Paul wants to anticipate his charge of idolatry against Israel that will come (Rom. 2:22), which is part of his mounting argument that gentiles and Jews are equally sinful and equally worthy of condemnation (Rom. 3:9–20). Implicit also is the notion that even Israel, who was to play the role of a corporate Adam in functionally reflecting God's image, has malfunctioned in that role.[31] That Paul has the episode of the golden calf in mind is evident also from the parallel language in Rom. 1:25, "they exchanged the truth of God for a lie," which echoes Jewish tradition about the episode.[32]

Through using this example from Israel's history, Paul has tapped into the context of the first formal sin in Israel's existence as a nation. I explained above that Exod. 32 portrays its sin of worshiping the molten calf in language describing rebellious cattle in order to convey the idea that Israel had become like the object of its worship. Sinful Israel was mocked by being depicted metaphorically as rebellious cows running around and needing to be regathered because it had become as spiritually lifeless as the calf that it was worshiping.

Psalm 106:20 says that Israel "exchanged" the object of true worship (its "glory"), which was the glorious Lord, for an idolatrous image. The phrase "they exchanged their glory for the image of an ox" appears to be thickly packed, probably including exchanging the object of their worship but also the glorious character of the true God for identification with the character of another god. Later Jewish interpretations of Ps. 106:20 took it in just this way.[33] Later Jewish interpreters understood that the worshipers of the golden calf resembled that idol.[34]

---

30. For the validity of the Ps. 106 allusion, see Morna D. Hooker, *From Adam to Christ: Essays on Paul* (Cambridge: Cambridge University Press, 1990), 73, 76, 82–83, where she also says that the allusion "is generally accepted" (cf. the NA[27] margin at Rom. 1:23). For others who see this allusion, see Beale, *We Become What We Worship*, 205–6.

31. On which, see further Beale, *Temple*, 81–121.

32. Philo says of Moses's reaction to the calf idolatry that he "marveled at the sudden apostasy of the multitude and [how] they had exchanged [*hypoallassō*] so great a lie [*pseudos*] for so great a truth [*alētheia*]" (*Mos.* 2.167) (also cited in Moo, *Romans*, 112); the Greek words in brackets are the very same words that Paul uses in Rom. 1:25. Actually, Philo has the obverse of what Paul says ("they exchanged the truth of God for a lie"), but yielding the same idea. On Jewish traditions about the golden calf, see Scott J. Hafemann, *Paul, Moses, and the History of Israel: The Letter/Spirit Contrast and the Argument from Scripture in 2 Corinthians 3*, WUNT 81 (Tübingen: Mohr Siebeck, 1995), 227–31.

33. For substantial argument in favor of these two ideas in Ps. 106:20, see Beale, *We Become What We Worship*, 86–92. Instead of mere "glory," some LXX manuscripts of Ps. 106:20 have "his glory" and others "the glory of God" (the latter of which Paul may actually be dependent on), while the Targum has "the glory of their Lord."

34. See ibid., 149–60.

The Old Testament Background of Jeremiah 2 in Romans 1:21–26

Furthermore, part of Paul's description in Rom. 1:18–24 appears also to come from Jer. 2. The possibly combined allusion to Jer. 2:11 suggests further that Ps. 106:20 indicates the exchange of the nation's identification with and reflection of that glory in which it participated in its worship of the true God.

Jeremiah 2:11 says, "Has a nation changed gods, when they were not gods? But My people <u>have changed their glory</u> for that which does not profit." Other nations never denied their own gods but would add others to their pantheon. The rhetorical point is that Israel is even worse than other nations in its idolatry because it really did exchange worship of the true God for the false. Jeremiah 2:11 itself may be an allusion to Ps. 106:20, since Jeremiah's point is to say that Israel's sin of idolatry in his own day is but a continuation of that same sin that began at the inception of the nation's existence (see 2:2–3). Indeed, Paul's reference in Rom. 1:21 to the idol worshipers having "become empty/vain [*emataiōthēsan*]" is based on a second reference to Jer. 2: "What injustice did your fathers find in Me, that they went far from Me and <u>walked after vanity</u> [*tōn mataiōn* = idols] and <u>became vain</u> [*emataiōthēsan*]?" (v. 5).[35]

The vast majority of OT commentators understand that the Israelites "changing their glory" in Jer. 2:11 refers only to changing God as the object of their reverence for another god. In light of the close connection to 2:5, however, verse 11b may also include the idea of Israel changing the "glory" of God that it reflected in its worship of him for the inglorious, vain likeness of other gods, which it came to reflect: "They walked after vanity [idols] and became vain." Jeremiah 2:7b–8 continues this theme of walking after idols: "And My inheritance you made an abomination. . . . and the prophets prophesied by Baal and <u>walked after things that did not profit</u>." As a result, God "will yet contend" against Israel (v. 9), since this idolatry is even unattested by the nations surrounding Israel (v. 10: "See if there has been such a thing [among the nations] as this"; i.e., the nations have never exchanged worship of the true God for a false one). Consequently, the inextricable link between verses 5–10 and verse 11 points to the Israelites' "changing their glory" in the latter verse to include the notion that they reflected the likeness of their idols instead of God's glorious likeness and image.[36]

This understanding of Jer. 2.11 is pointed to further by the possibility that it is an allusion to Hos. 4:7: "I will change their glory into shame." The "change of glory" in Hosea probably refers to God's ironic punishment of

---

35. NA²⁷ lists a third allusion to Jeremiah, "everyone is foolish [*emōranthē*]" (10:14) in Rom. 1:22, "they became foolish [*emōranthēsan*]," both of which concern idolaters becoming foolish. This third allusion suggests further that Jeremiah is within Paul's purview.

36. See C. F. Keil, *The Prophecies of Jeremiah*, trans. David Patrick and James Kennedy, K&D (repr., Grand Rapids: Eerdmans, 1968), 1:57. Keil sees that the "change of glory" includes reference to both God and his glory; e.g., he understands "the glory" to be that "in which the invisible God manifested His majesty in the world and amidst His people."

Israel by causing it to reflect and share in the empty glory of its idols rather than God's glory. This idea of Hos. 4:7 is emphasized further in that the rest of the chapter (vv. 10–19) explicitly identifies Israel's sin as that of idolatry. This idolatry climaxes with the identification of the Israelites as the "stubborn heifer" that they worship (v. 16) and to which they "join" themselves (v. 17). This is further paralleled to a harlot and the man with whom she has intercourse (they become "one," though illicitly [v. 18]).

Thus, Hos. 4:7, developed in Jer. 2:11, demonstrates that Jeremiah includes a reference to an ironic penalty of Israel becoming like the corruptible glory of the idols that it worships. We have already seen that this is suggested in the immediate context of Jer. 2:11, which repeatedly mentions other kinds of *lex talionis* punishments, especially where Israel had "walked after vanity and became vain."

Conclusion to the Old Testament Background of Romans 1:21–26

The OT allusions in Rom. 1:23–25 may be summarized as shown in table 12.2.

Table 12.2

Old Testament Texts	Rom. 1:25b, 23a
Ps. 106:19–20: "They made a calf . . . and they worshiped [*prosekynēsan*] a molten image. Thus they exchanged their glory for the image [*ēllaxanto tēn doxan autōn en homoiōmati*] of an ox that eats grass."	1:25b: "They worshiped and served [*esebasthēsan kai elatreusan*] the creature."
	1:23a: "They exchanged the glory [*ēllaxan tēn doxan*] of the incorruptible God for an image in the likeness [*en homoiōmati eikonos*] of corruptible [*phthartou*] man and of birds."
Jer. 2:11b: "But My people have changed their glory [*ēllaxato tēn doxan autou*] for that which does not profit [*ex hēs ouk ōphelēthēsontai*]" (cf. vv. 20–28).	
	Cf. also Rom. 1:24: "Therefore God gave them over in the lusts of their hearts to impurity, so that their bodies would be dishonored [*atimazesthai*] among them";
Hos. 4:7: "I will change their glory into dishonor [*tēn doxan autōn eis atimian thēsomai*]"ᵃ (cf. vv. 8–18).	Rom. 1:26a: "For this reason God gave them over to dishonorable [*atimias*] passions."

Note: Solid underlining represents the same words and cognates, and broken underlining represents conceptual parallels.
ᵃThe Hebrew verb (*'āmîr*) is more explicit in reading "I will change," though the Greek word can have this meaning.

Therefore, Rom. 1:21a, "they did not honor Him as God or give thanks," is a positive way of speaking of the negative act of idol worship and prepares the way for the following phrase in 1:21b, "but they became vain in their speculations," which is an allusion to Jer. 2:5 ("they went after vain things [idols] and became vain").[37] Accordingly, Paul appears to follow Jeremiah's notion that Israel became as vain and empty as the idols that it worshiped.

37. See Richard H. Bell, *No One Seeks for God: An Exegetical and Theological Study of Romans 1.18–3.20*, WUNT 106 (Tübingen: Mohr Siebeck, 1998), 24–25, 94; A. J. M. Wedderburn,

Thus, Ps. 106:19–20 and, though perhaps less clearly, two allusions to Jer. 2 are present in Rom. 1, which indicate that Israel became like the idols that it worshiped.[38] It appears that Paul's shortening of Jer. 2:5 to "and they became empty" in Rom. 1:23 still carries with it the notion of people becoming as corruptible as their corruptible idols. Indeed, the idea of "exchanging" divine glory for that of idols includes the thought, suggested above, that Israel gave up "the opportunity to bask in the glory of the immortal God" and to have "direct contact with God's awesome presence."[39] The implication is that they would bask in and reflect the nature of that which they were substituting for God. Consequently, Paul is affirming in Rom. 1:23 both that humanity changed the object of its worship and that this entailed a change in its nature. It is the converse of the positive notion mentioned elsewhere in Paul's writings—for example, 2 Cor. 3:18: "But we all, with unveiled face beholding as in a mirror the glory of the Lord, are being transformed into the same image from glory to glory, just as from the Lord, the Spirit"[40] (see also 1 Cor. 15:48–49 for both the negative and the positive aspects of reflecting, respectively, the first Adam and the last Adam). Thus, one of the elements of Rom. 1:23 is that people become like that which they worship.[41] Peter Stuhlmacher accordingly con-

"Adam in Paul's Letter to the Romans," in *Papers on Paul and Other New Testament Authors*, vol. 3 of *Studia Biblica 1978: Sixth International Congress on Biblical Studies, Oxford, 3–7 April 1978*, ed. E. A. Livingstone, JSNTSup 3 (Sheffield: JSOT Press, 1980), 414. Both argue for the presence of an allusion to Jer. 2:11.

38. Allusions to Gen. 1–3 may also be detected. If this is the case in Rom. 1:23, then the idea of either reflecting or not reflecting God's glorious image is enhanced in the verse (cf. *Gen. Rab.* 11.2; *b. Sanh.* 38b, which affirm that Adam ceased reflecting God's glory when he sinned). Douglas Moo (*Romans*, 109), though unpersuaded of an Adamic background here, acknowledges two proposed allusions to Gen. 1–3 in Rom. 1:23: (1) the threefold portrayal of the animal world ("birds and four-footed animals and crawling creatures"); (2) the pairing of "image" (*eikōn*) and "form" (*homoiōsis*) reflects Gen. 1:26: "Let Us make man according to Our image [*eikōn*], according to Our likeness [*homoiōsis*]." To these may be added three more: (1) Adam and Eve were the first idolaters in that they shifted their loyalty from God to the serpent, a crawling creature, whose deceitful character they came to represent, since they started lying immediately after their fall in Gen. 3:10–13; (2) the combined ideas that the idolaters had "knowledge" and falsely pursued "wisdom" may also reflect Gen. 3:5–6 ("knowing good and evil . . . the tree was desirable to make one wise"); (3) the fact that Paul makes allusion to the event of the golden calf (via Ps. 106:20) may fall well in line with Adamic echoes, since Jewish tradition frequently associated Israel's sin of idolatry at Sinai with that of Adam's fall (on which, see James D. G. Dunn, *Romans 1–8*, WBC 38A [Dallas: Word, 1991], 61; see also Hafemann, *Paul, Moses, and the History of Israel*, 228–29). But see Mark A. Seifrid, "Unrighteous by Faith: Apostolic Proclamation in Romans 1:18–3:20," in *The Paradoxes of Paul*, vol. 2 of *Justification and Variegated Nomism*, ed. D. A. Carson, Peter T. O'Brien, and Mark A. Seifrid (Grand Rapids: Baker Academic, 2004), 117–18. Seifrid, unconvincingly in my view, sees no echoes in Rom. 1 of Adam from Gen. 1–3, citing others in support. Hooker (*From Adam to Christ*, 73–84) sets forth a cumulative case for the probability of allusion to Adam in Rom. 1:18–25, which is a persuasive rejoinder to Seifrid and others.

39. Moo, *Romans*, 108–9.

40. So Bell, *No One Seeks for God*, 130–31; Wedderburn, "Adam," 418.

41. So Bell, *No One Seeks for God*, 130–31; Wedderburn, "Adam," 418.

cludes his discussion of Rom. 1:18–21 likewise: "Whoever follows after that which is nothing, becomes nothing himself (Jer. 2:5)!"[42]

The Reversal from Reflecting the Image of Idols to Reflecting God's Image in Paul's Thought

We have just seen in Rom. 1 that a malfunction in one's relationship with God (i.e., idolatry) brings the corresponding punishment of a malfunction in one's relationship with other humans (e.g., homosexuality, lesbianism, disobedience to parents, etc.). It has also been proposed that Paul's thought indicates the concept that people become spiritually lifeless like the idols that they venerate. However, Scripture also emphasizes that there is a reversal to this condition.

Just as Paul starts the first part of Romans speaking of perverted worship, he starts the last part of the book discussing proper worship. That Paul intends to present 12:1–2 as the antithesis to 1:18–28 is apparent from the use of the same terms used oppositely or the use of actual antonyms (see table 12.3).

Table 12.3

Romans 1:18–28	Romans 12:1–2
v. 24: "that their bodies would be dishonored among them"	v. 1: "present your bodies a living and holy sacrifice, acceptable to God"
v. 25: "they worshiped and served the creature rather than the Creator"	v. 1: "your spiritual service of worship"
v. 25: "they worshiped and served the creature rather than the Creator"	v. 2: "And do not be conformed to this world, but be transformed by the renewing of your mind [in God]"[a]
v. 28: "just as they did not approve [it proper] to have God in their knowledge, God gave them over to a disapproved mind [a mind not approved by God]"	v. 2: "be transformed by the renewing of your mind, so that you may approve what the will of God is"

Note: Solid underlining designates the same words or cognates in Greek; broken underlining represents uniquely parallel ideas.
[a]That the renewing is in the sphere of the newness of Christ's resurrection state is apparent from the links to Rom. 6, where the newness of Christ's resurrection is explicitly spoken of: (1) "presenting" oneself to sin or to God; (2) "living" before God; (3) living in a "holy" or "sanctified" manner (so Michael B. Thompson, *Clothed with Christ: The Example and Teaching of Jesus in Romans 12.1–15.13*, JSNTSup 59 [Sheffield: Sheffield Academic Press, 1991], 78–80).

This combination of words together with the ideas that they express is rare in Paul's writings.[43] First, Paul is exhorting Christians to present their "bodies"

42. Peter Stuhlmacher, *Paul's Letter to the Romans: A Commentary*, trans. Scott J. Hafemann (Louisville: Westminster John Knox, 1994), 36.
43. Note that the only other place the phrase *ta sōmata hymōn/autōn* occurs is 1 Cor. 6:15 (though cf. Rom. 8:11: *ta thnēta sōmata hymōn*).

in religious "service" to God instead of participating in idolatrous liturgical "service" in which their "bodies" become dishonored because they present them immorally to others of the same sex. Second, instead of "worshiping and serving the creature rather than the Creator," Paul wants his hearers to "not be conformed to the world, but be transformed by the renewing" of their minds. Third, in contrast to the idolaters who do "not approve" with their "mind" God-ordained worship, God wants his people to "approve" with their "mind" what God's will is for them.[44]

Romans 12:2 itself is also a development of 8:28–29:

> And we know that God causes all things to work together for good to <u>those who love God,</u> to those who are called according to His purpose. For those whom He foreknew, He also predestined to become <u>conformed to the image of His Son</u>, so that He would be the firstborn among many brethren.

Thus, to be "transformed [*metamorphoō*] by the renewing of your mind" in 12:2 is the virtual equivalent of "becoming conformed [*symmorphos*] to the image of [God's] son" in 8:29.[45] Of the eight uses of "image" (*eikōn*) in Paul's writings, only two appear in Romans (1:23; 8:29). This suggests that the image of God's son to which Christians are becoming conformed in Rom. 8 is the antithesis to the worldly "image" that unbelieving humanity had exchanged in place of God's glory in Rom. 1. The deduction that can be made from this is that those who are not "loving God" (8:28) and, consequently, not being "conformed to the image of God's Son" are loving some other earthly object of worship and, consequently, being conformed to that earthly image. It is clear from the intended antithesis between Rom. 1 and 12 that if one is not committed to the Lord, then, by default, one is devoted to the world, and such devotion causes one to "become conformed to [like] the world."[46] It is equally

---

44. See Thompson, *Clothed with Christ*, 81–86, which has the most developed discussion of the antitheses and years ago initially inspired my own thoughts on the links. Subsequently, see Seyoon Kim, "Paul's Common Paranesis (1 Thess. 4–5; Phil. 2–4; and Rom. 12–13): The Correspondence between Romans 1:18–32 and 12:1–2, and the Unity of Romans 12–13," *TynBul* 62 (2011): 109–39, who independently of Thompson has made essentially the same observations about the link between Rom. 1:18–32 and 12:1–2.

45. This equivalence is further inidicated by the combination of "renewal" and "image" in Col. 3:10: "You have put on the new man who is being <u>renewed</u> to a true knowledge <u>according to the image</u> of the One who created him" (so also Eph. 4:22–24). Similarly, 2 Cor. 3:18 affirms that those who want to be near the Lord will take on his likeness: they will "behold as in a mirror the glory of the Lord" and be "transformed [*metamorphoō*] into the same image from glory to glory, just as from the Lord, the Spirit."

46. Elsewhere Paul underscores that it is in Christ that people begin to be transformed into God's image (Rom. 8:28–30; 12:2; 2 Cor. 2:17; 4:4) in connection to fulfillment of prophecies from some of the Isaianic contexts that describe the reversal of this type of judgment (e.g., see the use of Isa. 9:1 in 2 Cor. 4:4; Isa. 43:18–19; 65:17 in 2 Cor. 5:17; Isa. 52:11 in 2 Cor. 6:17; Isa. 43:6 in 2 Cor. 6:18). This process of transformation into the divine image will be completed at

clear, however, that the reversal of the spiritually vacuous state incurred through idolatry is becoming conformed to the "image of God's Son." This further confirms that 1:21–25 refers not only to idolatry but also to resembling the idols that are worshiped. Thus, whichever image one reveres (God's or the world's) one resembles, either for ruin or for redemptive restoration.

The Reversal from Reflecting the Image of Idols to Reflecting God's Image in the Gospels

I could have addressed the issue of idolatry as it is depicted in the Gospels. However, the notion, though there, is not as explicit as in Paul's writings.[47] Nevertheless, the background of Isaiah's restoration prophecies in the Gospels does assume a background of God's people coming out of idolatry and being re-created by God. The Gospels, therefore, convey a distinct interest in the reversal from people reflecting the images of the world's idols to reflecting God's image. Directly after the quotation of Isa. 6:9–10 in Matt. 13:14–15, Jesus says, "But blessed are your eyes, because they see; and your ears, because they hear." This, in 13:11, is stated to be the result of a divine gift: "To you it has been granted to know the mysteries of the kingdom of heaven" (so also Luke 8:10). Luke 10:21–24 expands on its earlier reference to Isa. 6:9–10 in 8:10 and on what we see in Matt. 13:16–17, underscoring that the reversal of spiritual blindness and deafness into spiritual "seeing and hearing" is purely the gift of God.[48]

> At that very time He rejoiced greatly in the Holy Spirit, and said, "I praise You, O Father, Lord of heaven and earth, that You have hidden these things from the wise and intelligent and have revealed them to infants. Yes, Father, for this was well-pleasing in Your sight. All things have been handed over to Me by My Father, and no one knows who the Son is except the Father, and who the Father is except the Son, and anyone to whom the Son wills to reveal Him." Turning to the disciples, He said privately, "Blessed are the eyes which see the things you see, for I say to you, that many prophets and kings wished to see the things which you see, and did not see them, and to hear the things which you hear, and did not hear them."

Jesus's view about God or himself being the only giver of sight and hearing to the spiritually blind and deaf is closely related to the book of Isaiah. In Isaiah, it is God who has caused Israel to become like its idols, and it is God who will bring it out from under their idolatrous anesthesia. Whereas the

---

the end of history, when Christians will be resurrected and fully reflect God's image in Christ (1 Cor. 15:45–54; Phil. 3:20–21).

47. See the section on the Gospels in Beale, *We Become What We Worship*, 160–83.

48. See also Matt. 11:25–27.

Israelites "formed" their idols and worshiped them and came to resemble their spiritually deaf and blind images, God, the only real image maker (cf. Gen. 1:26–27), could reverse this condition and "form" them to reflect his true image, so that they would be able spiritually to see and hear.[49] Thus, the only legitimate images on earth are humans who are reflecting God's image.

In Isa. 6 it is only by God's gracious initiative that the prophet could be transformed from being like the idolatrous people into one who reflects God's holy image. However, the book of Isaiah indicates that others would likewise be transformed. This is made explicit in 29:9–16, 18. First, Isa. 29:9–10, in partial beginning fulfillment of 6:9–10, says,

> Be delayed and wait,
> Blind yourselves and be blind;
> They become drunk, but not with wine,
> They stagger, but not with strong drink.
> For the LORD has poured over you a spirit of deep sleep,
> He has shut your eyes, the prophets;
> And He has covered your heads, the seers.

Verses 11–14 elaborate further on unbelieving Israel's spiritual blindness, which resembles its Egyptian idols' spiritual blindness. But then v. 18 shows there will be a reversal in Israel's idolatrous character when "the deaf will hear . . . and out of their gloom and darkness the eyes of the blind will see."[50]

Furthermore, Isaiah makes the contrast between men "forming" (*yāṣar*) idols and God "forming" (*yāṣar*) Israel.[51] Isaiah 44 especially highlights the contrast between God as the true "former" (vv. 2, 21, 24) and the idol makers as sinful "formers" of false images. Verses 9–17 go into elaborate detail about how people manufacture or "form" (vv. 9–10, 12) idols. Then, abruptly, the idol makers and the worshipers are said to be those who "do not know, nor do they understand, for He has smeared over their eyes so that they cannot see and their hearts so that they cannot comprehend" (v. 18 [likewise

---

49. Also, Acts 17 narrates Paul's speech to the Athenians about their idol worship and how they needed to turn from their many idols to the true God. Toward the conclusion of Paul's address (vv. 30–31) he exhorts the Athenians to repent of their idolatry. Those who believed Paul's preaching turned from their idols to trust in God, to be restored to him, and to be like him, since now they had truly become "his offspring [family]" (v. 28). This is the main point of Acts 17, since it represents the final and climactic response to the entire Mars Hill narrative. See also Pao, *Acts and the Isaianic New Exodus*, 181–216.

50. Further Isaianic prophecies that suggest restoration from the blinding and deafening judgment seen in 6:9–10 include 32:3–4; 42:6–7.

51. E.g., Isa. 43 repeatedly refers to God "forming" Israel to reflect his "glory" and "praise" (vv. 1, 7, 21) and says that no true god could have been "formed," since Yahweh is the only God (v. 10). The idol worshipers are "people who are blind, even though they have eyes, and . . . deaf, even though they have ears" (v. 8), but end-time Israel will be "formed" by God as a part of the coming new creation (vv. 18–21).

vv. 19–20, 25]). Then, in direct contrast, God says to Israel, "I have <u>formed</u> you, you are My servant" (v. 21), so that "in Israel He shows forth His glory" (v. 23 [likewise 49:3]) at the time of its restoration (vv. 24, 26–28). God is the potter who re-*forms* his sinful people, trans-*forming* them from reflections of earthly idolatrous images and remaking them into his image, so that they will reflect him and his glorious light as they spread throughout the earth as his emissaries and agents through which God shines his light and re-forms others into his image (cf. Isa. 49:6).

That Jesus has in mind this kind of restoration context from Isaiah is also apparent from Matt. 11:2–15:

> Now when John, while imprisoned, heard of the works of Christ, he sent word by his disciples and said to Him, "Are you the Expected One, or shall we look for someone else?" Jesus answered and said to them, "Go and report to John what you hear and see: the blind receive sight and the lame walk, the lepers are cleansed and the deaf hear, the dead are raised up, and the poor have the gospel preached to them. And blessed is he who does not take offense at Me." As these men were going away, Jesus began to speak to the crowds about John, "What did you go out into the wilderness to see? A reed shaken by the wind? But what did you go out to see? A man dressed in soft clothing? Those who wear soft clothing are in kings' palaces! But what did you go out to see? A prophet? Yes, I tell you, and one who is more than a prophet. This is the one about whom it is written,
>
> > 'Behold, I send My messenger ahead of You,
> > Who will prepare Your way before You.'
>
> Truly I say to you, among those born of women there has not arisen anyone greater than John the Baptist! Yet the one who is least in the kingdom of heaven is greater than he. From the days of John the Baptist until now the kingdom of heaven suffers violence, and violent men take it by force. For all the prophets and the Law prophesied until John. And if you are willing to accept it, John himself is Elijah who was to come. He who has ears to hear, let him hear."

When John the Baptist asks if Jesus is "the Expected One," Jesus responds by appealing to Isa. 35:5–6 ("the blind receive sight and the lame walk . . . and the deaf hear"), which is part of a prophecy of Israel's restoration (Isa. 35:1–10). That this "sight" and "hearing" include spiritual as well as physical restoration is evident from the end of Matt. 11:5, where there follows a quotation from Isa. 61:1, another restoration prophecy: "The poor have the gospel [good news] preached to them." The Isa. 61:1 prophecy also concludes with a promise that the blind will see.[52] Interestingly, Isa. 35:2 says that the restored Israelites "will see the glory of the LORD," and Isa. 61:3 develops this theme by affirming that

---

52. Isaiah 61:1 LXX continues and elaborates on the sensory organ of sight: "to bind up the brokenhearted, to proclaim liberty to captives and <u>recovery of sight to the blind</u>." This appears to include spiritual blindness. The LXX's phrase "recovery of sight to the blind" here is a slight interpretation of the Hebrew text's "opening of the eyes to those who are bound" (for this sense

they will "be given glory instead of ashes . . . [and] a garment of glory instead of a spirit of weariness."[53] The phrase "he who has ears to hear, let him hear" in Matt. 11:15 clearly develops the earlier "sensory organ" language in terms of spiritual hearing. Spiritual perception is needed to discern Jesus's true identity (as emphasized in Matt. 11:6) and John the Baptist's identity. The idea is that Israel's newly restored organs of perception will also allow it to perceive and thus to reflect the glory of God himself instead of reflecting the image of the sinful creation.

Conclusion

The point of this chapter has been to underscore that, on the one hand, trust in idols "formed" by humans results in spiritual blindness and deafness, as a reflection of the idols themselves. It is idolatry that leads to all other sins committed by humans. On the other hand, trust in God as the only legitimate "former" of images results in humans being "formed" into something that is uniquely able to reflect God's glorious image. Being re-created in God's image leads to increasing righteousness. The only hope in being delivered from reflecting the spiritually lifeless images of the world is to be re-created or re-formed by God into an image that reflects God's living image, which results in spiritual life and ethical fruit. God has the ability to bring Israel and the nations out from their idolatrous darkness and deep sleep by restoring them and re-creating them in his image again, as Isa. 29 affirms, replanting in them eyes to see and ears to hear his true word. This restoration will include a new creation that for humans means resurrection of the whole person, first spiritually and then physically. It is this restoration of God's image that we now turn to in the next two chapters.

---

of the Heb. *pĕqaḥ-qôaḥ*, see David J. A. Clines, ed., *The Dictionary of Classical Hebrew*, vol. 6 [Sheffield: Sheffield Phoenix Press, 2007], 749).

53. This is the LXX's interpretative rendering of the Hebrew text's "giving them a garland instead of ashes . . . [and] the mantle of praise instead of a spirit of fainting."

13

The Inaugurated End-Time Restoration of God's Image in Humanity

The Old Testament and the Synoptic Gospels

The Creation of Humanity in the Image of God and Humanity's Fall

In the preceding chapter I discussed how human beings had sinned and come to distort the image of God in themselves and to reflect the idolatrous image of the fallen creation. I briefly elaborated on how humanity could be transformed from reflecting the image of idols to reflecting God's image in the way that he had designed. Here it is necessary to go into more detail about how the marred image of God in humanity can be set right.

There has been much discussion throughout the history of the church concerning the precise definition of "the image of God in humanity." The Reformed confessions associate the image of God with the "knowledge, righteousness, and holiness" that Adam had in the prefall state (the Shorter Catechism, question 10; so virtually identically the Heidelberg Catechism, question 6). This image is then understood to have been marred or distorted as a result of the "fall" of Adam. Many today still define the image of God quite similarly to that of the Reformed confessions. The emphasis is on an ontological definition—that is, what the image is in the being of a person. The definition typically revolves around the spiritual, moral, and intellectual aspects of humanity in distinction to the animal world.

The problem in giving a precise definition of the image of God is that Scripture never explicitly defines what the "image" or "likeness" of God in humanity is. In chapter 2 we saw that Gen. 1:26–28 said that humanity was to function as the image of God as a vice-regent, representing God's rule on earth. And we saw that sin caused a distortion in the image, so that humanity could not reflect God in the way for which it was designed. Adam did not rightly discern between good and evil in the garden, which led to his failure to rule over the serpent. God's command to Adam not to eat "from the tree of the knowledge of good and evil" (Gen. 2:17) was an expression that Adam was to have a moral awareness.[1]

Thus, the restoration of this image in humanity must entail the necessity of "true knowledge" to discern between good and evil and to function adequately in reflecting God's image. Accordingly, Col. 3:10 says that the believer in Christ has been "renewed to a true knowledge according to the image of the one who created him," and Eph. 4:24 affirms similarly that the Christian "according to God [i.e., according to God's image] has been created in righteousness and holiness of the truth." It therefore likely is legitimate to read this back into Gen. 1:26 and to conclude, as do the Reformed confessions, that the image of God in our first parents consisted of possessing the moral attributes of "knowledge, righteousness, and holiness" of God. But to conclude this, one must put Colossians and Ephesians together and assume also that Eph. 4:24 is referring to God's image. I think that this is a legitimate inference, but it is more a biblical-theological inference than an exegetical one.

Although the aforementioned inference about the divine image likely is correct, the text of Gen. 1:26–27 does not express such a definition. In fact, these verses do indicate that the divine image is not something that humans are in themselves but rather something that humans do in reflection of what God does:

> Then God said, "Let Us make man in Our image, according to Our likeness; and let them rule over the fish of the sea and over the birds of the sky and over the cattle and over all the earth, and over every creeping thing that creeps on the earth." God created man in His own image, in the image of God He created him; male and female He created them.

If there is any hint about how humanity has been created "in the image of God," it is that Adam and Eve were to reflect God's image by "ruling" over the creation, apparently in reflection of God as the ultimate ruler. The next verse, Gen. 1:28, points further to the image being something that humans do rather than something that they are: "God blessed them; and God said to them, 'Be fruitful and multiply, and fill the earth, and subdue it; and rule over the fish of the sea and over the birds of the sky and over every living thing that moves on the earth.'" Thus,

---

1. Also, God's repeated declaration that the creation was "good" (Gen. 1:4, 10, 12, 18, 21, 25, 31) was likely something that Adam himself was also to recognize about the creation.

any definition of God's image in humanity at this point would need to explain it as functional rather than ontological; that is, the emphasis in explaining the divine image is that it is something that humans do rather than what they intrinsically are. Genesis 1:28 expands on the function of ruling mentioned in 1:26: they are not only to "rule," but also to "be fruitful and multiply, and fill the earth, and subdue it." I discussed this matter in chapter 2, and here I refer the reader back to the beginning of that chapter for further elaboration.[2]

In chapter 2 I noted that Adam's role in Eden is part of the initial carrying out of the mandate given to him in Gen. 1:26–28. Just as God, after his initial work of creation, subdued the chaos, ruled over it (1:1–10, in the first three days of creation), and further created and filled the earth with all kinds of animate life (1:11–25, in the final three days of creation), so Adam and Eve, in their garden abode, were to reflect God's activities in Gen. 1 by fulfilling the commission to "subdue" and "rule over all the earth" and to "be fruitful and multiply" and "fill the earth" (1:26, 28).[3] Even God's "resting" at the end of his creative work (2:2–3) was to be reflected in an inaugurated manner by God's placement of Adam to reside in the garden instead of the outermost uninhabitable area outside the garden.[4] And, it appears, God intended an even greater "rest" for Adam had he been faithful.

In particular, Adam was to begin to subdue and rule over the creation by cultivating the garden (2:15), by naming the created animals (2:19–20) in reflection of God's naming the parts of creation, and by "guarding" the garden from the entrance of unclean things, such as serpents. Just as God's subduing and ruling activity expressed his intellect, wisdom, and volition, so the same probably was reflected in Adam's same activity—for example, his naming of the animals.

In addition, Adam was to create and fill the earth with his creation (cf. Gen. 2:24; 4:1–2), just as God had created and filled the earth in Gen. 1. This "filling," as I argued in chapter 2, was not merely filling the earth with physical offspring but rather with image-bearers who reflect God's glory. It is probable that humanity's first parents were equipped with the ontological aspects of the divine image (e.g., "knowledge, righteousness, and holiness") in order to obey

2. See chap. 2 under the heading "Adam's Commission in the First Creation and the Passing On of the Commission to Other Adam-Like Figures."

3. Following Warren Austin Gage, *The Gospel of Genesis: Studies in Protology and Eschatology* (Winona Lake, IN: Carpenter Books, 1984), 27–36. I am indebted to Gage for the threefold functional notion of the divine image and its relation to the NT, both of which are elaborated on below. There is debate about whether Gen. 1 depicts God first creating the chaos from nothing or portrays the chaos already present before God's work of creation; here, I assume the former, traditional view but cannot lay out the arguments due to limits of space.

4. In this respect, note the second verb in Gen. 2:15: "Then the Lord God took the man and put him into the garden of Eden." The English "put" is a translation of the Hiphil (causative) form of the Hebrew word typically translated as "to rest" (*nûaḥ*), which could be rendered here as "he caused to rest in the garden."

the divine command of Gen. 1:28 and to reflect God's activities in Gen. 1 in their own activities. After the fall there would be unbelieving image-bearers in the marred image of God, who would be the physical offspring of believing or unbelieving parents. That is, some who had no relationship with God and were in the same distorted image as was Adam before he was restored to God (in Gen. 3:20–21) could come back into an inaugurated saving knowledge of God under the influence (dare we say "witness"?) of other redeemed image-bearers. Thus, postfall humanity, especially the redeemed remnant, was likewise equipped with the ontological aspects of the divine image in order to be enabled to obey functionally the divine command of Gen. 1:28 and to begin to reflect God's activities in Gen. 1 in its own activities.

Hence, in the divine command of Gen. 1:28 humanity is commissioned as God's image to imitate God's own threefold activity observed in his creation of the earth. In this respect, Adam was to be God's vice-regent, ruling in his stead on the outpost of earth. This can be understood through the ancient Near Eastern practice of kings who sometimes set up images of themselves in territories over which they ruled but in which they typically were not present. Their image in such a region indicated that though absent, they nevertheless ruled there. The same was the case with Adam, a living image of Yahweh the king, who was set up by God on the territory of earth to show that God was the ultimate ruler of the world.

Humanity's labor of subduing the earth, however, became wearisome and vain (Gen. 3:17–19; Eccles. 1:2–3; Rom. 8:19–23); instead of subduing, Adam became subdued by the creation itself (a serpent). Instead of creating and filling the earth with children bearing God's image of glory, he created and filled it with offspring bearing their own inglorious sin and ultimately reflecting the image of the fallen created order. Eve's labor of filling the earth became sorrowful (Gen. 3:16). After their fall, Adam and Eve and their progeny were unable to fulfill the divine mandate of Gen. 1:28 and thus to reflect the image of God in the way for which they were originally designed.[5] Even after their reintroduction into knowing God personally again, they were not in a position to fulfill the original divine mandate in the consummate way that God had intended.

Brief Overview of Jewish Expectations of an Eschatological Adam Who Would Reflect God's Image[6]

Judaism believed that the prefall state would be restored at the end of time. At this time, a messiah was to come to inaugurate a new exodus after the pattern of the first exodus, led by Moses. This coming new exodus was sometimes thought of as a new creation. Likewise, the Jews of Qumran hoped that they

5. See Gage, *Gospel of Genesis*, 27.

6. For the following survey of Jewish expectations, I am indebted to Seyoon Kim, *The Origin of Paul's Gospel* (Grand Rapids: Eerdmans, 1982), 187–91.

would be the latter-day community to be restored with the "glory of Adam" (1QS IV:23; CD-A III:20; 1QHᵃ IV:15; see also 1QHᵃ XVI:4–14a). Also, the Books of Adam express an expectation that Adam would be resurrected at the end of the age, though not as a messianic figure.[7]

In addition, the OT and Judaism viewed history in terms of some select representative figures. We have already seen in chapter 2 that Adam, Noah, Abraham, Isaac, and Jacob were heads of their progeny. In particular, the last four of these people were seen as having received the mantle of Adam's commission. In later Judaism the failure of Adam is contrasted with Abraham, Moses, and Elijah, and especially the Messiah, who are viewed as reversing the wrongs of Adam for humanity. In *Deut. Rab.* 11.3 there is an argument between Moses and Adam about who is greater. Moses contends that he is greater because he retains the luster of face that Adam had lost. The idea in context is that the image of God was restored at the giving of the law at Sinai and then lost again at the episode of the golden calf, so that the ultimate restoration was to occur at the time when the Messiah would finally come. The Messiah was to take away the curse of Adam on humanity and restore the prefall conditions (*T. Levi* 18:10–14). Similarly, there is the oft-repeated statement in later Judaism that the six things that Adam lost would be restored in the messianic age: his luster (equivalent to the divine glory and image), his immortality, his height, the fruit of the earth and trees, and the luminaries (e.g., *Gen. Rab.* 12.6; *Num. Rab.* 13.12). On the one hand, there are statements in the rabbinic literature that imply that the divine image was lost at the time of Adam's fall (*Gen. Rab.* 8.12; *Num. Rab.* 16.24; *Deut. Rab.* 11.3). On the other hand, there are assertions that even after Adam's primal sin, humanity still retained God's image (especially with respect to morality) and was still to be seen as the crown of creation (e.g., *b. B. Bat.* 58a; *Lev. Rab.* 34.3; *Gen. Rab.* 24.7; *Mek. Exod.* 20.16).

These different perspectives may not be mutually exclusive, since some Jews could have reckoned that some aspects of God's image had been lost but others retained. Perhaps the rabbis thought that the image of God was diminished or distorted but not lost by Adam's sin.[8]

The Story of Jesus as the End-Time Adam of the New Creation Who Unswervingly Reflected God's Image and Led the Way to Restoring This Image in Humanity (in the Synoptic Gospels)

In order to begin to understand how the image of God is restored in humanity, we must begin with the first coming of Christ. Throughout the NT Christ

7. E.g., *L.A.E.* [*Apocalypse*] 13:2–3: "I [God] shall raise you [Adam] <u>on the last day</u> in the resurrection with every man of your seed."

8. So Kim, *Origin of Paul's Gospel*, 260–62.

is portrayed in various ways as the last Adam, who has come to do what the first Adam failed to do and to represent his eschatological progeny in doing so. In particular, we will see that Christ came to subdue and rule, to multiply and create and to fill, and to rest in the way that God originally designed that humanity should have done in the first place. In so doing, he was introducing in decisive manner the beginning of the latter-day new creation and kingdom. Not only did he recapitulate what the prefall Adam should have done as king in the first creation of Eden, but also he went beyond that in his faithfulness and obedience to succeed in the task at which Adam had failed. Accordingly, as an absolutely righteous last Adam, Jesus reflected God's image completely and obtained the eschatological blessings and glory for succeeding in this task, which Adam never received. All those who identify with Christ as the last Adam also benefit from these blessings, especially the blessing of having the glorious image of God restored in them.

Therefore, an examination of Jesus as the last Adam in the Synoptic Gospels is one way of obtaining *conceptually* the evangelists' picture of him as the flawless image of God on earth. This task, as we will see, is easier in the case of Paul, since he uses explicit language of "Adam" and "image" of God in application to Christ and believers, which the Gospels do not use. Nevertheless, I believe that we can trace conceptually in Jesus's ministry the functional aspects of ruling, multiplying, and resting, which have their roots in the threefold functions that Adam was originally designed to carry out in reflection of God's same threefold activities in Gen. 1. What especially will become evident and is the focus in the following study is the portrayal of Jesus as an eschatological Adam inaugurating the kingdom of the new creation. Although the functions of multiplying spiritual children and resting are not highlighted as much as Christ's Adamic rule in a new creation, they are present.

This chapter is not a thorough survey of the Synoptic Gospels. The focus will be on Matthew, with references to Mark and Luke where they supplement Matthew. One reason for focusing on Matthew is to try to show how one would go through a Gospel to study one biblical-theological theme. The theme is that of Christ as the end-time Adam inaugurating a new-creational reign, which I believe is vitally linked to Christ as the image of God, a notion that Paul picks up on explicitly. The portrayals of Christ as an Adam figure in Matthew have significant overlap with depictions also in Mark and Luke.

This may be one of the most controversial chapters of this book, since I am discussing a significant amount of the Synoptic material under the conceptual category of Jesus restoring the functional image of God. This is an unusual move for a theology of the NT. However, recall that this book is not a "theology of the New Testament" but rather a "biblical theology of the New Testament." I believe that the Synoptic material, especially about the kingdom, fits well into this conceptual category of Jesus restoring the functional image of God in inaugurating the kingdom of the new creation for Israel and for humanity. Such a categorization of Jesus's ministry fits with my prior for-mulation of the storyline of the NT (see, e.g., chaps. 5–6): *Jesus's life, trials, death for sinners, and resurrection by the Spirit have launched the fulfillment of the eschatological already–not yet new-creational reign, bestowed by grace through faith and resulting in worldwide commission to the faithful to advance this new-creational reign and resulting in judgment for the unbelieving, unto God's glory.* I have contended that the "kingdom of the new creation" is the major stepping-stone of the storyline in accomplishing divine glory. And, as we saw in chapter 2 and elsewhere, Adam's establishment of the kingdom of the first creation would have been one of the central ways in which he reflected the functional image of God. The same is true of Jesus in doing what the first Adam should have done.

The attempt, then, in this section is to place over our interpretative eyes the lens of Jesus as a new regal Adam who introduces the latter-day new creation. I have already set forth in the overview of the OT in chapter 2 four major new-creational episodes of the OT: the first creation in Gen. 1–2, the second new creation of the Noahic epic, Israel's exodus from exile in Egypt, and Israel's restoration from exile in Babylon. We also saw there that Noah served as a second Adam figure, and that Israel's purpose of being delivered from exile was to serve as a kind of corporate Adam. All four of these new-creational and Adamic episodes will be used as lenses through which to look at Jesus in Matthew and elsewhere in the Synoptics. Somewhat like people who have sunglasses that flip over their regular glasses, we will try to put on four sets of biblical-theological sunglasses that flip over our interpretative lenses, each with a different redemptive-historical tint. Sometimes one new-creational lens will enlighten how Matthew is attempting to depict Jesus, and sometimes another will shed light, and sometimes two of these lenses at once can clarify how the Gospel writer is trying to portray Jesus.

There will be particular focus on the promise of Israel's restoration as a new creation in the Synoptic Gospels because it is inextricably linked with Jesus as a true Adam and true Israel (i.e., a representative of Israel, which was a corporate Adam) and thus with Jesus being in God's consummate image and paving the way to restore that image for others. Thus, the directly following brief discussion focuses on Israel's restoration hopes, but only ultimately as these hopes are linked to the promise of a restored new humanity in a new creation, finally fully reflecting God's image.

The Problem of the Timing of the Fulfillment of the Restoration Promises to Israel

Before we begin to look at Matthew and the other Synoptic Gospels, the question must be addressed about how many of the prophetic promises of Israel's eschatological restoration had been fulfilled during the so-called intertestamental period, leading up to NT times. This question is important to answer because it will help to explain the particular problem that the Gospels are attempting to address. I was tempted somewhat to answer this question in chapter 3, and here again I am tempted to do so. However, full discussion of this will be put off until later chapters. Nevertheless, the brief answer to the question is that in a true eschatological sense the restoration promises had not been fulfilled up until and through the first century AD.

It is true that the promise of restoration appeared to begin incipient fulfillment in the return from Babylonian exile, since Jeremiah had prophesied that after seventy years of captivity Israel would return to the land (Jer. 25:11–12; 29:10). But all the other restoration prophecies were not fulfilled at this time, so that the physical return of some from Judah and Benjamin, though prophesied by Jeremiah, was ultimately a hollow eschatological restoration fulfillment. Some commentators believe that significant fulfillment of these prophecies continued to be delayed when Israel rejected Jesus, so that the fulfillment was put off until directly before and after his final return. Others believe that the restoration prophecies truly began fulfillment at Christ's first coming, but that Jesus's followers and the church established after his ascension were not true Israel. Still others affirm that the prophecies began true fulfillment, and that Jesus's followers and the church were part of true Israel. In later chapters I will argue for this third view, and here I will assume it, though some of these arguments will begin to some degree already in this chapter. It is through the lens of this third perspective that the fulfillment of Jeremiah's above restoration prophecy is best understood. This topic of Israel's restoration is important because, as I argued earlier in chapter 2, Israel was a corporate Adam, and thus its restoration is vitally connected to the restoration of the entire creation, including alienated humanity, as I will continue to contend. We also saw in the preceding chapter that Isaiah prophesied that God would re-form redeemed Israel and humanity into his image at the time when he would restore Israel to himself.

The Beginning of Matthew and of the Other Gospels Introduces Christ as the End-Time Adam Inaugurating the New Creation

Matthew's genealogy begins in 1:1 with *biblos geneseōs*, which can be translated as the "book of the genealogy" or the "book of beginning" or the "book of genesis." Genesis 2:4 LXX has *biblos geneseōs*: "This is the book of the generation [or 'the book of the genesis'] of heaven and earth, when they came about, in the day in which God made the heaven and the earth." Likewise Gen. 5:1–2 LXX has "This is the book of generation [*biblos geneseōs*] [some render it as 'genealogy'] of man [i.e., Adam] in the day in which God made Adam, according to the image of God he made him. Male and female he made them, and blessed them; and he called their name Adam in the day in which he made them." Then follows the first genealogy in the Bible, beginning with Adam and ending with Noah at the end of Gen. 5.

These are the only two places in the entire OT where the phrase *biblos geneseōs* occurs. Matthew's expression thus appears to be an intentional allusion to these two statements early in the book of Genesis. The point is that Matthew is narrating the record of the new age, the new creation, launched by the coming, death, and resurrection of Jesus Christ.[9] And, since Matthew is narrating a genealogy of Jesus, it is likely that the Gen. 5:1 reference is uppermost in mind, and that Jesus is being painted with the genealogical brush of Adam. And just as Adam created others "in his own likeness, according to his image" (Gen. 5:3), so would Christ.[10]

There is also mention of the Holy Spirit in conceiving Jesus (Matt. 1:18–20), who is the beginning of the new creation. Just as the Spirit was mentioned in Gen. 1:2 in bringing about the creation, so Matt. 1:18, 20 says, "Now the generation [*genesis*] of Jesus Christ was in this manner. . . . that which is begotten [*gennēthen*] in her is from the Holy Spirit." This seems to focus even more on Jesus as the new Adam, as the beginning of the new creation.

Matthew's genealogy (Matt. 1:1–17) also rings with gentile echoes, pointing subtly to Jesus's mission as one that not only focuses on Israel but also on the world. Mention of Abraham at the beginning of Matthew's genealogy is crucial because of the gentile thread woven throughout it: the mention of the four gentile women (Tamar, Rahab, Ruth, and Bathsheba).[11] Usually, women are not mentioned in genealogies, but the presence of these women suggests that Jesus's mission is not merely to Israel but is to extend beyond to the nations, to the ends of the earth.

The gentile mission of Jesus becomes more explicit in Matt. 2:1–12, in the narrative of the magi from the gentile east, who are attracted to the star's light and want to come to "worship" Jesus (v. 2). Their presentation of gifts from their "treasures" of "gold and frankincense" is the beginning fulfillment of Isaiah's prophecy in 60:3, 5–6, 10–11, 14 (cf. 49:23). There, in the eschatological future, a great "light" will "shine" in Israel, "and nations will come to your light, and kings to the brightness of your rising" (v. 3); "the wealth of nations will come" to Israel, and the nations "will bring gold and frankincense" (vv. 5–6), and they "will come bowing" to Israel (v. 14). Matthew has combined a new-creational idea (light shining to overcome darkness) with a passage

---

9. W. D. Davies and Dale C. Allison Jr., *A Critical and Exegetical Commentary on the Gospel according to Saint Matthew*, 3 vols., ICC (Edinburgh: T&T Clark, 1988–97), 1:149–53.

10. For further support of this conclusion about the Genesis background of Matt. 1:1, see Jonathan T. Pennington, "Heaven, Earth, and a New Genesis: Theological Cosmology in Matthew," in *Cosmology and New Testament Theology*, ed. Jonathan T. Pennington and Sean M. McDonough, LNTS 355 (London: T&T Clark, 2008), 39–40, though his use of the language of *mythos* in connection to this to describe Matthew's worldview is not a felicitous choice (see p. 40).

11. Bathsheba may be included because she was married to a gentile Hittite, Uriah.

that speaks of restoration from captivity, thus enhancing the previous birth narrative as an event of new creation. This finds its consummate fulfillment in the new heaven and earth: there will be a glorious "luminary" (Rev. 21:11), and "the nations will walk by its light, and the kings of the earth will bring their glory into it" (Rev. 21:24), "and they will bring the glory and the honor of the nations into it" (Rev. 21:26).[12]

The introductory link of "Jesus Christ" to Abraham in the first verse of Matthew's genealogy (1:1) enforces the notion of the worldwide concern, especially given that this Gospel ends with the commission "to make disciples of all the nations" (28:18–20):

> And Jesus came up and spoke to them, saying, "All authority has been given to Me in heaven and on earth. Go therefore and make disciples <u>of all the nations</u>, baptizing them in the name of the Father and the Son and the Holy Spirit, teaching them to <u>observe all that I commanded you</u>; and lo, <u>I am with you always</u>, even to the end of the age."

Matthew 28:18 portrays Jesus as the Son of Man saying, "All authority has been given to Me in heaven and on earth." This is an allusion to the prophecy of Dan. 7:13–14 LXX, where it is said of the "Son of Man" that "authority was given to him, and all the nations of the earth . . . [were] serving him." On the basis of this authority, Jesus then gives the well-known commission, "Therefore, as you go, disciple all the nations, baptizing them . . . teaching them to keep all things which I commanded you; and behold, <u>I am with you</u> all the days until the end of the age." Notice that Jesus uses the same divine accompaniment formula that God used in the later applications and reiterations of Adam's commission to the patriarchs and Israel to subdue and rule over the earth, upon which I elaborated in chapter 2. Christ's presence with his followers will enable them to fulfill "the great commission" to rule over and fill the earth with God's presence, which Adam, Noah, and Israel had failed to carry out.

In this respect, Jesus is a "last Adam" figure, and this is partly why he implicitly identifies himself with Daniel's "Son of Man" in issuing the universal commission to his followers in 28:18: he is the "son of Adam," the equivalent to Daniel's "Son of Man," finally accomplishing what the first Adam should have and what Daniel predicts the messianic end-time Adam would do. Recall that Dan. 7:13–14 was among the reiterations of the Gen. 1:28 commission, and, furthermore, the same passage portrays the Son of Man as heading up Israel's end-time kingdom and also depicts him as a latter-day Adam figure ("the son of Adam") and as a king over all the beasts and people of the earth. In addition, we observed in Dan. 7 several allusions and echoes of the first

---

12. For a discussion of the allusions to Isa. 60 in these verses in Revelation, see G. K. Beale, *The Book of Revelation: A Commentary on the Greek Text*, NIGTC (Grand Rapids: Eerdmans, 1999).

creation in Gen. 1, so that Dan. 7 also serves as a *new-creational* kingdom prophecy. These resonances, to one degree or another, stand in the background of the concluding verses of the Gospel of Matthew.[13]

As we just observed above, even the divine accompaniment formula ("I am with you") occurs in Matt. 28:20 to indicate how the disciples will be empowered to carry out the commission. The reference to "all the nations" (*panta ta ethnē*) is an echo of Gen. 22:18 (likewise Gen. 18:18), again one of the repetitions of Gen. 1:28. The reminiscence of the Abrahamic promise returns to the theme found in the first verse of Matthew's Gospel (1:1), "that the blessings promised to Abraham and through him to all peoples of the earth (Gen. 12:3) are now to be fulfilled in Jesus the Messiah."[14]

Thus, even at the beginning and then again at the end of his Gospel, Matthew portrays Christ as the son of Adam, or the Son of Man, who has begun to do what the first Adam should have done and to inherit what the first Adam should have inherited, including the glory reflected in God's image. Matthew 19:28 indicates that the new creation begun in Jesus (see above on Matt. 1:1) will be consummated by Jesus as the "Son of Man [Adam]" at the time of the "regeneration" (*palingenesia*) of the cosmos:[15] "And Jesus said to them, 'Truly I say to you, that you who have followed Me, in the regeneration when the Son of Man will sit on His glorious throne, you also shall sit upon twelve thrones, judging the twelve tribes of Israel.'"

The other Gospels have some general similarities to Matthew's new-creational beginning, though his initial focus on allusion to Adam in Matt. 1:1 is unique to him. Instead of beginning with David and Abraham and working down toward the time of Jesus like Matthew, Luke's genealogy begins with the time of Jesus and works back to Adam, with which it ends: "the son of Adam, the son of God" (Luke 3:38). The purpose is to identify Jesus as the last Adam, the Son of God.[16] As I will comment further below, one reason that Luke does this is that he wants his readers to view Jesus as an Adam figure in his directly following wilderness temptation (Luke 4:1–13). For his part, Mark starts his Gospel with "The beginning [*archē*] of the gospel of Jesus Christ" (Mark 1:1 [cf. *en archē* in Gen. 1:1 LXX]). Directly following his opening statement, Mark (1:2–3) refers to the introduction of Isaiah's prophecies of a second exodus:

> As it is written in Isaiah the prophet:
> "Behold, I send My messenger ahead of You,
> Who will prepare Your way;

13. For an amplification of the ideas in this paragraph, see the relevant discussion in chap. 2 above.

14. D. A. Carson, *Matthew 13–28*, EBC (Grand Rapids: Zondervan, 1995), 596. Gen. 12:3 LXX has "all the tribes of the earth."

15. On which, see Pennington, "Heaven, Earth, and a New Genesis," 40–43.

16. See S. Craig Glickman, *Knowing Christ* (Chicago: Moody, 1980), 55–58.

> The voice of one crying in the wilderness,
> 'Make ready the way of the Lord, make his paths straight.'"

Although there is no attempt by Mark to depict Adamic notions, the reference to Jesus's prophesied forerunner, John the Baptist, through the lens of Isaiah's prophesied second exodus also resonates with new-creational ideas. In this respect, we have seen that the exodus from Egypt was already considered a new creation in the OT and Judaism, and Isaiah's expectations of a new exodus in Isa. 40–66 are intertwined with hopes of new creation.[17]

In the light of the beginnings of Matthew, Mark, and Luke,[18] it should not be surprising that the prologue of John's Gospel also begins with explicit new-creational allusions (1:1–13):

> In the beginning was the Word, and the Word was with God, and the Word was God. He was in the beginning with God. All things came into being through Him, and apart from Him nothing came into being that has come into being. In Him was life, and the life was the light of men. The Light shines in the darkness, and the darkness did not comprehend [overtake] it. There came a man sent from God, whose name was John. He came as a witness, to testify about the Light, so that all might believe through him. He was not the Light, but he came to testify about the Light. There was the true Light which, coming into the world, enlightens every man. He was in the world, and the world was made through Him, and the world did not know Him. He came to His own, and those who were His own did not receive him. But as many as received Him, to them he gave the right to become children of God, even to those who believe in His name, who were born, not of blood nor of the will of the flesh nor of the will of man, but of God.

This introduction shows Jesus to be deity (v. 1) and that he was the creator of the cosmos in the very beginning (vv. 2–3, 10b). Verse 4 begins to show him to be the commencement of another new creation at his incarnation: he was the source of "life" and the creative "light" (v. 4) that "shines in the darkness." And just as the first light in Gen. 1 was not swallowed up by the darkness, so Jesus as the "light" was not dimmed by the surrounding darkness (v. 5). Consequently, as the first light in Genesis shone irresistibly in the world, Christ's light "enlightened" people as he came into the world (vv. 5–9). As he came into

17. See Rikki E. Watts, *Isaiah's New Exodus in Mark* (Grand Rapids: Baker Academic, 1997), 53–90. Watts contends that Mal. 3:1, though quoted before Isa. 40:3 in Mark 1:2–3, fits well into the idea of a second exodus in Isa. 40:3, especially because Mal. 3:1 itself alludes to Exod. 23:20, a text of the first exodus, which also speaks of a forerunner preparing the way for Israel after the nation came out of Egypt. Thus, Mal. 3:1 serves as an interpretative aid to Isa. 40:3, which becomes more understandable when it is discovered that Isaiah's prophecies of a second exodus, as Watts argues, are prevalent throughout Mark's Gospel.

18. Adamic or new-creational references do not come until the end of Luke 3, whereas in Matthew such references come earlier, but there are allusions to the Abrahamic covenant in Luke 1:55, 72–73.

the world as the source of the new creation, most of his own people (Israel) did not accept him (v. 11), but to those who did receive him "he gave the right to become children of God," because such receiving on their part indicated that they had been born of God (vv. 12–13). In line with the preceding context, verses 11–12 appear to indicate that just as in the beginning God created the world and Adam, his "firstborn" child,[19] so now Christ as the source of "life" and creative "light" (this time identified not with Adam but rather with God), begins the second creation by creating and multiplying "children" again.

Thus, the beginnings of each of the Gospels in various ways elicit concerns about new creation in connection to the recounting of the beginning of Christ's life or ministry.

Jesus as Both the End-Time Adam and the End-Time Israel Who Restores the Kingdom to God's People

In this section I will continue to discuss Christ as an Adamic figure, but also I will present an analysis of him as summing up true Israel in himself. Many might think that including the Gospels' portrait of Jesus as true Israel in a chapter on "the image of God" is a category confusion. However, I have already argued that Israel was intended as a corporate Adam figure, as evident, for example, in that the commission applied to Adam in Gen. 1:28 is reapplied to the patriarchs, to historical Israel, and to prophecies about eschatological Israel. This earlier argument must be kept in mind in this section. Recall also that Gen. 1:28 is a functional definition of how Adam was to be in the image of God. The very names for Jesus, "Son of God" and "Son of Man," were also names for Israel, which alluded to their corporate Adamic role. We will see also that it is difficult to make a distinction between Jesus as Adam and Jesus as Israel in some Gospel narratives because the two notions are intertwined. The reason for the intertwining is that the notion of Israel in the OT also carried with it at significant points the notion of an Adamic role. Thus, Jesus comes as the eschatological Adam, and true Israel, who will functionally reflect God's image (e.g., ruling, producing children for God)[20] in a way that the first Adam did not.

Jesus as the Danielic Son of Man (Adam)

The title "Son of Man" appears in all the Gospels (about 80x). Although the title is used often, it is never used by others about Jesus but used only by

---

19. Recall the discussion in chap. 2, where it was noted from a comparison of Gen. 1:26–27 with Gen. 5:1–3 that to be created in the likeness and image of God was to be created as a child of God.

20. For this notion, e.g., see again John 1:12–13, discussed briefly above. For the idea of Jesus summing up true Israel in himself in Matt. 1–4, see Joel Kennedy, *The Recapitulation of Israel*. WUNT 2/257 (Tübingen: Mohr Siebeck, 2008).

Jesus himself. Only once is there any suggestion that the audience might have been uncertain about its meaning (John 12:34). Today, however, scholarship is in disarray over what Jesus meant by this title. Here I cannot do justice to the immense and complicated discussion that has been generated by this title. Many say that the title is a creation of the later church, but the fact that, with one exception (Acts 7:56), the use of this title disappears completely from the NT after Jesus's death suggests that the term was original with him.[21] If it were the creation of the church, we would expect to encounter it in the NT Epistles.

Jesus's self-reference as "the Son of Man" is one of the main ways he indicates that he has begun to inaugurate the eschatological kingdom. To demonstrate this, the OT context of Dan. 7:13, where the "Son of Man" reference occurs, must be reviewed, and then a survey of the clearest allusions to Daniel's Son of Man in the Gospels and its significance there will also be discussed. The point here is not to launch a major study of Jesus as the Son of Man, but merely to show some connections between Jesus, Daniel's Son of Man, and Adam, as well as the significance of these connections.[22]

The Daniel 7 Context of the Son of Man

The expression "son of man" is sometimes an exclusively human reference in the OT (e.g., Ezekiel; Ps. 8). In Ps. 8 it is a human reference combined with a royal office (see vv. 4–9). But Dan. 7:13 is the most likely source of the "son of man" phrase as used by Jesus in the Gospels. Daniel 7 begins the visionary section, but it is a repetitive parallel to Dan. 2.

The Visionary Section (7:1–15)

There is a vision of four beasts appearing in succession and exercising an increasingly oppressive power, until at last "the Ancient of Days" sits in judgment over them, and they are judged. Then "one like a Son of Man" comes with the clouds of heaven to the Ancient of Days and is given an everlasting dominion over all peoples.

The Interpretive Section (7:16–28)[23]

The four beasts are interpreted to be four successive empires (vv. 17, 23). But how does this section identify the Son of Man? At first glance, one might say that he is not identified, since the Son of Man is not mentioned in the

21. Reference to the Dan. 7 "one like a son of man" occurs, but not as a title, in Rev. 1:13; 14:14.

22. For a more extensive study that interacts with relevant secondary sources, see James D. G. Dunn, "The Danielic Son of Man in the New Testament," in vol. 2 of *The Book of Daniel: Composition and Reception*, ed. John J. Collins and Peter W. Flint (Leiden: Brill, 2001), 528–49. Dunn's conclusions are somewhat different from mine, though he does see significant influence of the Dan. 7 "Son of Man" on Jesus's use of the expression at significant points in the Synoptic Gospels.

23. This section is a rehearsal of an earlier section on the Son of Man in Daniel 7 (on which, see chap. 7 under the heading "The Already–Not Yet End-Time Tribulation in the New Testament."

following interpretative section. However, verses 16–28 are the interpretation of the visionary section of verses 1–15, and for there to be no interpretation of the climax of the vision in verses 13–14, which is the Son of Man and his coming kingdom, would be quite unlikely. Daniel 7:13–14 says that the Son of Man "was given dominion," which was an "everlasting dominion" and a "kingdom . . . which will not be destroyed." Likewise, verse 18 says that the "saints" of Israel will "possess the kingdom forever," verse 22 that the "saints took possession of the kingdom," and verse 27 that this will be an "everlasting kingdom." Thus, it is very likely that the interpretative section of the vision identifies the "Son of Man" figure with end-time Israel, "the saints of the Most High" (vv. 18, 22, 27), who are first oppressed by the fourth kingdom and then vindicated and exalted to dominion over all powers through God's judgment.

Therefore, the keynote is vindication and exaltation of the Son of Man in the vision and of the saints of Israel in the interpretative section: the inauguration of the Son of Man's kingdom is Israel's kingdom, which supersedes the human kingdoms that previously opposed God and oppressed his people. It should also be noted that the "coming" of the Son of Man in verse 13 is a coming to God in heaven to receive authority, not a coming to earth. In Dan. 7, is the "Son of Man" figure merely a personification of the "saints of the Most High," or is he an individual "ruler"? The first answer that we have been led to by the interpretative section is that he is identified with Israel.

Part of the key to understanding the figure is the Hebrew conception of corporate headship or representation,[24] whereby an individual (usually a king, priest, or father) represents others and thereby sums them up in himself. That the Son of Man was so conceived is evident from the fact that the beasts represent kings who represent their respective empires (peoples), and there is clear parallelism between the role of the beasts and the Son of Man. For example, all four beasts are interpreted in verse 17 as "kings" (*malkîn*, from *melek*), and in verse 23 the fourth beast is described as "a . . . kingdom" (*malkû* [or "royalty, reign"]).[25] Therefore, this suggests that the Son of Man is both an individual and also a representative for a community.[26]

24. For this concept, see H. Wheeler Robinson, *Corporate Personality in Ancient Israel* (Philadelphia: Fortress, 1980); Aubrey R. Johnson, *The One and the Many in the Israelite Conception of God* (Cardiff: University of Wales Press, 1960). However, it is better to speak of corporate solidarity and representation rather than corporate personality. For significant qualifications on the concept, see Joshua R. Porter, "The Legal Aspects of the Concept of 'Corporate Personality' in the Old Testament," *VT* 15 (1965): 361–80; John W. Rogerson, "The Hebrew Conception of Corporate Personality: A Re-Examination," *JTS* 21 (1970): 1–16; Stanley E. Porter, "Two Myths: Corporate Personality and Language/Mentality Determinism," *SJT* 43 (1990): 289–307.

25. Though it is possible that "kings" in v. 17 is figuratively the equivalent of "kingdoms" in v. 23 (so BDB 110).

26. In my understanding of Dan. 7 here I have followed mainly R. T. France, *Jesus and the Old Testament: His Application of Old Testament Passages to Himself and His Mission* (Downers Grove, IL: InterVarsity, 1971), 169–71.

This dual identification of the "Son of Man" figure is important for our understanding of Jesus's use of the phrase. That the Son of Man is a representative individual is pointed to also by verse 13, where he comes "with the clouds of heaven." Elsewhere in the OT only one figure rides on the clouds, and that is Yahweh. This suggests that the Son of Man is a divine figure coming to receive kingly authority from God in heaven. The earliest interpretation of Dan. 7:13 makes this view even more explicit. Whereas one LXX version (TH) literally translates Dan. 7:13 ("one like a Son of Man . . . came up to the Ancient of Days"), another version (OG) has "one like a Son of Man . . . came [there] as the Ancient of Days." Perhaps such a rendering may have been partly influenced by Dan. 3:25, where the heavenly being in the furnace with Daniel's friends was called one "like the son of *the* gods." Some scholars think that the variant reading in the OG of Dan. 7:13 is an accidental scribal error, but others believe that the Greek translator was interpreting the Son of Man as a divine figure, which could well have been an attempt to draw out the association of the Son of Man coming "with the clouds of heaven" with God's depiction elsewhere.

THE USE OF DANIEL'S SON OF MAN IN THE SYNOPTIC GOSPELS TO INDICATE THE ALREADY–NOT YET ESCHATOLOGICAL KINGDOM

There are three kinds of "Son of Man" sayings in the Synoptic Gospels:

1. those that refer to aspects of Jesus's earthly, prepassion ministry;
2. those that refer to Jesus's death;
3. those that refer to Jesus's future coming in glory.

The clearest references to Jesus as the Son of Man from Dan. 7:13 come in the third category, where there are quotations of Dan. 7:13 (Matt. 24:30; Mark 13:26; 14:62; Luke 21:27). However, it is likely better to see most of these third-category references fulfilled not at the very end of history but rather in AD 70 at the destruction of Jerusalem, in which the Son of Man's coming would be understood as an invisible coming in judgment, using the Roman armies as his agent.[27] The reference in Matt. 25:31 to "the Son of Man" who will "come in His glory" and "sit on His glorious throne" is not a quotation

---

27. The design of this chapter does not allow for argumentation of this view; for a persuasive argument of the quotation in Mark 13, see France, *Jesus and the Old Testament*, 227–39. If this view is correct, it may be that the AD 70 coming of Christ in judgment as portrayed by the Synoptics is a typological foreshadowing of his final coming in judgment. However, the traditional view that the coming of the Son of Man in the Synoptic eschatological discourse refers to Christ's final coming certainly is plausible. This issue is a thorny one that still deserves much more study. Surely, there is abundant testimony to Christ's final coming to conclude history elsewhere in Acts, Paul's writings, and the rest of the NT.

of but rather an allusion to Dan. 7:13–14,[28] which clearly is applied to the very end of the age at Christ's final coming.

Many scholars do not see Dan. 7 behind the "Son of Man" references in the Synoptics, except where it is part of a quotation. However, scholars are increasingly recognizing that a number of the references outside of the quotations are indeed allusions to Dan. 7:13. These allusions typically have reference to the "Son of Man" who "comes," which appears to be sufficient wording to recognize an allusion to the "Son of Man" who "comes" in Dan. 7:13, though other wording from Dan. 7:13–14 is sometimes found in combination with the "Son of Man."[29] Some of these allusions also refer to Christ's post-ascension coming in the future (e.g., Mark 8:38).[30] Many of these allusions come in the sayings about Jesus's earthly ministry.

Mark 10:45[31]

One of the most significant of these "Son of Man" sayings with respect to his earthly mission is in Mark 10:45 (see table 13.1).

Table 13.1

Daniel 7	Synoptic References
7:13: "I kept looking in the night visions, and behold, with the clouds of heaven one like a <u>Son of Man</u> was <u>coming</u>, and <u>he came</u> up to the Ancient of Days and was presented before him." 7:14: "And to Him was given dominion, glory and a kingdom, that all the <u>peoples, nations and men of every language might serve Him</u>. His dominion is an everlasting dominion which will not pass away; and His kingdom is one which will not be destroyed."	Mark 10:45 (// Matt. 20:28): "For even the <u>Son of Man</u> did not <u>come</u> to <u>be served</u>, but <u>to serve</u>, and to give His life a ransom for many."

28. Note that Dan. 7:13–14 (MT) says, "One like a Son of Man was coming. . . . And to him was given dominion, glory and a kingdom." Likewise, see Matt. 19:28, which probably is an allusion to the same Daniel passage.

29. Dunn ("Danielic Son of Man," 529–30) sees that three key elements from Dan. 7:13 in some cases are enough to recognize a clear allusion (e.g., "Son of Man" + "coming" + "on/ with the clouds"), though he says that when only "Son of Man" + "coming" occurs, "the case for literary dependence is less clear."

30. Though here Jesus may be looking forward imminently to inaugurating the fulfillment of the kingdom prophesied in Daniel in Mark 9 at the Mount of Transfiguration (cf. esp. 9:3, 7, 9; note reference to Jesus's future resurrection in v. 9) and probably continuing especially through the resurrection and ascension and perhaps even up through the destruction of Jerusalem. See likewise Matt. 10:23, which has "you will not finish going through the cities of Israel until the Son of Man comes," which may refer to Christ's resurrection or ascension or, perhaps, his AD 70 coming.

31. This subsection on Mark 10:45 and the following one on Luke 7 and 19 are summaries of an earlier discussion but are included here again because they are so important for understanding part of the Danielic background for the "Son of Man" in the Synoptics (see chap. 7 under the heading "The Already–Net Yet End-Time Tribulation in the New Testament").

Nowhere in Dan. 7 is it stated explicitly that the Son of Man suffers (i.e., "gives his life"), but as we have seen, he is identified with the suffering of the saints in Dan. 7:15–27. Thus, if representational identification is granted at all between the Son of Man and saints, then the idea of suffering for the Son of Man must be allowed as viable in Dan. 7. While it is true that a vicarious, substitutional suffering by the Son of Man is not found in Dan. 7, two observations are noteworthy: (1) the general pattern of suffering leading to a kingdom should still be seen as viable, and (2) the vicarious element is a development resulting from combining Isa. 53:10–12 with Dan. 7. In the first clause of Mark 10:45 Jesus refers to Dan. 7:13–14 and applies it to the purpose of his earth ministry.[32]

The full Danielic nature of Mark 10:45, however, typically goes unnoticed. The saying comes in a context in which the topic of discussion is rank in the eschatological kingdom (10:37, 40). Christ says that rank in his kingdom comes in the reverse manner of that in earthly kingdoms: not in outward triumph over people but rather through humble suffering for people—that is, through ironic rule (vv. 42–44; note the broader "kingdom" context in Mark 10:14, 15, 23–25; 11:9–10).

In Mark 10:45 Christ applies this ironic principle of the kingdom to himself. Besides the close contextual relation of "kingdom" to the "Son of Man," allusion to Dan. 7:13–14 is evident through the use of the phrase "he has come."[33] In addition, the idea that Christ came not to "be served" but rather "to serve" appears in this context to be an ironic development of Dan. 7:14: all nations were prophesied to serve him, but before this could happen, Christ reveals that he must first "serve" them during his earthly ministry and at the cross (as the last phrase of v. 45 affirms).[34]

Therefore, Mark 10:45 (// Matt. 20:28) is the application of a Dan. 7:13–14 allusion to Jesus's preresurrection ministry. Christ has begun to participate in fulfillment of the prophesied reign of Dan. 7:13–14, but the first stage of this fulfillment occurs in an unexpected and ironic manner. It may not appear to the world's eyes that Jesus is beginning to fulfill this prophecy, but those with ears to hear and eyes to see can perceive that he is indeed doing so.[35]

32. France (*Jesus and the Old Testament*, 128–30) sees no reference at all to the suffering of the "Son of Man" in conjunction with the "saints" in Dan. 7, though I have not found his objections ultimately persuasive.

33. Although this is stated negatively in the first phrase in v. 45 ("did not come to be served"), the next phrase assumes its positive use ("but [he came] to serve").

34. Here Mark uses *diakoneō* for "serve," whereas the OG has *latreuō* and TH has *douleuō*; however, *diakoneō* could well be a viable rendering of the Aramaic word for "serve" and can be synonymous with either of the renderings in the two LXX versions (note the comparative parallelism of *syndoulos* and *diakonos* in Col. 1:7; 4:7; see also Rom. 15:25–27; 2 Cor. 8; 9:12 [cf. with 2 Cor. 8:19–20], where the *diakoneō* and *leitourgeō* word groups appear to stand in parallel).

35. For interaction with other views on the OT background of Mark 10:45, see France, *Jesus and the Old Testament*, 116–23. For an in-depth discussion of the combined influence of Dan. 7

Luke 7:34–35; 19:10

Similar to Mark 10:45 is Luke 19:10: "For the Son of Man has come to seek and to save that which was lost." Again, we have the essential core of the Dan. 7:13 wording ("Son of Man" + "has come"), and, as in Mark 10:45, the Dan. 7:13 allusion is applied to Christ's earthly ministry, perhaps including his crucifixion. Accordingly, Christ begins to fulfill the prophecy of the Son of Man's foretold kingship through suffering, which is implicit in the saying of Luke 19:10, though his beginning kingly authority is veiled to the eyes of the world.

Luke 7:34–35 (// Matt. 11:19) is especially interesting in line with Mark 10:45 and Luke 19:10: "The Son of Man has come eating and drinking, and you say, 'Behold, a gluttonous man and a drunkard, a friend of tax collectors and sinners!' Yet wisdom is vindicated by all her children." The same core allusive wording to Dan. 7:13 is found ("Son of Man" + "has come") and, again, applied to Jesus's earthly ministry. The prophecy of the Son of Man's reception of authority in Dan. 7:13–14 is placed in the context of heaven, where he comes before God's throne, which is surrounded by myriad heavenly hosts (Dan. 7:9–10, 13). Thus, one would expect that when the prophecy begins fulfillment, this majestic angelic retinue surrounding the Son of Man will be present. However, his only retinue at the beginning of the fulfillment is "tax collectors and sinners," the very people he came to save, who would eventually "serve" him (Dan. 7:14). Some might conclude that this could not be a fulfillment of Dan. 7. Nevertheless, God's "wisdom" turns the world's wisdom upside down and "vindicates" (Luke 7:35) that, in fact, God has seen fit that the Dan. 7:13 prophecy be fulfilled in this veiled way in contrast to human expectations. Accordingly, the world's misfits are deemed the fittest to become the Son of Man's court that surrounds him in the commencement of his beginning reception of Daniel's kingdom authority.

Thus, in Mark 10:45, Luke 19:10, and Luke 7:34–35 Jesus begins to exercise the eschatological authority of the foreseen Dan. 7:13 kingdom by coming as a suffering person in order to serve and save sinners that they might then become his kingdom subjects subsequently to serve him. Jesus sees his fulfillment of Dan. 7 in terms of an unexpected, ironic enthronement approach to God's throne taking place during his entire earthly ministry rather than momentarily (as might appear to be the case in Dan. 7) and occurring through inglorious suffering rather than through a glorious and majestic investiture.

Matthew 9:6; 28:18

In Matt. 9:6 (// Mark 2:10) Jesus decides to a heal a crippled man "in order that you [the scribes] may know that the Son of Man has authority on earth to forgive sins." Again, there is an essential connection between

---

and Isa. 53 on Mark 10:45, see Seyoon Kim, *"The 'Son of Man'" as the Son of God*, WUNT 30 (Tübingen: Mohr Siebeck, 1983), 38–60.

this saying and that of Dan. 7:13–14 OG: "One like a Son of Man . . . was given authority, and all the nations of the earth . . . were serving him." There are three elements of commonality: "Son of Man" + "authority" + all "the earth."[36] As in the above Synoptic passages, the prophesied Son of Man's kingdom authority over the earth is viewed as beginning to be realized through Christ's authority to forgive sin, which is demonstrated by the healing miracle.

Matthew 28:18 may develop this further: "And Jesus came up and spoke to them, saying, 'All authority has been given to Me in heaven and on earth.'" Although the expression "the Son of Man" does not occur here, the clause "all authority has been given to Me in heaven and on earth" is reminiscent of Dan. 7:14 OG, where "to him [the Son of Man] was given authority," which was to begin in heaven (note 7:13: "He came with the clouds of heaven" and approached God's throne in heaven to receive the authority elaborated on in 7:14). In addition, Dan. 7:14 says that his authority was also to extend over "all the nations of the earth."[37] As a result of his resurrection, Jesus proclaims to his disciples that he has gained universal authority over all creation. Matthew 9:6 indicates that this authority had begun to occur even earlier, though such authority has now reached an escalated stage.

CONCLUSION ON THE SON OF MAN IN THE SYNOPTICS

Both formal quotations and allusions to the prophecy of Dan. 7:13–14 indicate Jesus's beginning fulfillment of the Son of Man's reign through his suffering, his deliverance of his people from sin, his defeat of Satan and demons, his death, his resurrection, and his judgment of Israel in AD 70. His rule will be consummated at the end of time when he returns to execute final judgment. I suggest that even when other Dan. 7 allusions are not combined with the "Son of Man" title, Dan. 7:13 is not completely out of mind.

The application of the Dan. 7 "Son of Man" to Jesus also carries with it echoes of an Adamic eschatological rule. As noted earlier in this section, we saw in chapter 2 that Dan. 7:13–14 is among a number of other reiterations ultimately of the Adamic commission of Gen. 1:28,[38] though most directly an allusion to the Gen. 22:17–18 prophecy of an end-time king in Abraham's line, which is also one of the Adamic reiterations. The link is especially evident because Gen. 22:17–18 is the only repeated Adamic promise that also contains "possessing the gate of your enemy," a major theme likewise in Dan. 7 concerning the Son of Man and the Israelite saints. Also the Son of Man's rule of sea beasts (portraying the enemy) reflects Adam's original commission to

36. Kim ("The 'Son of Man,'" 89–90) also sees the parallel of Mark 2:10 against the same Dan. 7 background.
37. France (Jesus and the Old Testament, 142–43) also sees the allusion to Dan. 7.
38. For the full survey of passages and discussion, see under the subheading "The Passing On of Adam's Commission to His Descendants" in chap. 2.

do the same. The allusion to the Adamic commissions, especially Gen. 22:18, in Dan. 7 is further confirmed by the fact that the precise phrase "all the nations of the earth" (*panta ta ethnē tēs gēs* [Dan. 7:14 OG])[39] occurs only five other times in the OT, four of which are among the repetitions of Adam's commission in Gen. 1:28 (esp. Gen. 22:17–18; 26:4, as well as Deut. 28:10; Josh. 4:24). Daniel 7:13–14 may also allude partly to Ps. 8:5–8: both refer to the (1) "son of man," (2) as a ruler over all creation, (3) and particularly over sea beasts. If this is the case, then the Adamic association of Dan. 7:13–14 is enhanced, since Ps. 8:5–8 is one of the clearest developments of Gen. 1:28 in all of the OT. Some even see a direct allusion to Gen. 1:26, 28 (1:26: "rule . . . over all the earth") in Dan. 7:14 ("to him was given dominion" over "all the nations of the earth").[40]

If these Adamic associations are present in Dan. 7:13–14, then Jesus's repeated application of the Danielic Son of Man to himself is another example of the numerous connections between Adam and Jesus that we have already seen in this chapter. In this case, the link highlights Jesus's Adamic kingship.

Jesus as the Adamic Son of God

The purpose here, as with the matter of the Son of Man above, is not to do a full study of Jesus as "the Son of God" in the Gospels but rather to discuss how this title might relate to the connections between Jesus and Adam and Israel that we have seen above.

SONSHIP IN RELATION TO ADAM

The expression "son of God" has an OT background. Adam was conceived of as a "son of God," though that exact phrase is not used in Gen. 1–3. In Gen. 1:26 Adam and his wife are said to have been created "in the likeness" and "according to the image" of God. As we have observed earlier in this chapter and in chapter 2, Gen. 5:1–2 reiterates the image language of Gen. 1:26 by referring to Adam having been "created" in the "likeness of God," and then Gen. 5:3 applies this language to the notion of sonship:

> This is the book of the generations of Adam. In the day when God created man, He made him <u>in the likeness of God</u>. He created them male and female, and He blessed them and named them Man in the day when they were created. When Adam had lived one hundred and thirty years, he became the father of a son <u>in his own likeness, according to his image</u>, and named him Seth.

39. The OG here clarifies what the Aramaic conveys conceptually (the latter of which has "all the peoples, nations, and men of every tongue").

40. Joyce G. Baldwin, *Daniel*, TOTC (Leicester: Inter-Varsity, 1978), 143, 150. See also N. T. Wright, *The Climax of the Covenant: Christ and the Law in Pauline Theology* (Minneapolis: Fortress, 1992), 23.

In Gen. 5:3 Adam is said to have "become the father of a son <u>in his own likeness, according to his image</u>." This is virtually identical to Gen. 1:26. The point of the wording in Gen. 5:3 is clearly that for Seth to be "in the likeness, according to the image" of Adam indicates that he has been born from Adam, reflects Adam's nature, and is Adam's son. This is "sonship" language. The explicit sonship notion of this language in Gen. 5:3 should inform our understanding of the same wording in Gen. 5:1–2, which refers back to Gen. 1:26. If so, then this language in Gen. 1:26 indicates that Adam is a son of God.

The next occurrence of the idea of divine sonship is in Gen. 6:2–4, where "the sons of God" are mentioned twice. Lack of space prevents discussion of this controverted passage here.[41] The notion of divine sonship occurs again in Exodus, where for the first time God refers to Israel as his son: "Thus says the LORD, 'Israel is My son, My firstborn. So I said to you, "Let My son go that he may serve Me"'" (Exod. 4:22–23). Elsewhere Israel is likewise said to be God's "son" (Ps. 2:7;[42] Hos. 11:1; Wis. 18:13; *Pss. Sol.* 18:4) or "firstborn" (Deut. 33:17; Ps. 89:27;[43] Jer. 31:9; *Jub.* 2:20; *4 Ezra* 6:58; Sir. 36:17 [36:11 LXX]; *Pss. Sol.* 18:4).

Why was Israel called God's "son" or "firstborn"? Later Jewish literature says that "Adam was the world's firstborn" (*Num. Rab.* 4.8).[44] We have seen that the concept of Adam being a son of God is deducible from the book of Genesis itself by comparing Gen. 1:26 with Gen. 5:1–3. The likely reason that Israel was referred to as God's "son" or "firstborn" is that the mantle of Adam had been passed on to Noah and then to the patriarchs and their "seed," Israel. In chapter 2, I discussed in some depth the way that the OT constantly reiterates Adam's commission from Gen. 1:28 and applies it to Israel. Thus, the commission given to Adam as God's son is passed on to Israel, so that Israel also has inherited the position of being God's son. This idea was understood early in Jewish thought: Isaac gives Jacob the following blessings in *Jub.* 22:13: "May the Most High God give thee all the blessings wherewith he has blessed me and wherewith he blessed Noah and Adam; may they rest on the sacred head of thy seed from generation to generation for ever."[45] This appears to be a better reason than any other offered for why Israel is repeatedly called God's "son" and "firstborn."

We have seen also that Israel was equated with the "Son of Man" in Dan. 7, which meant in part that Israel was prophesied to be an eschatological "son

41. Some see this as referring to angels, others to a royal class of humans.
42. Here applied to the coming eschatological king of Israel.
43. Here applied to the coming eschatological Davidic king of Israel.
44. See further references in this respect in Louis Ginzberg, *The Legends of the Jews*, trans. Henrietta Szold, 7 vols. (Philadelphia: Jewish Publication Society, 1909–38), 1:332 (and see note 89 therein).
45. Note likewise, though negatively stated, *Pesiq. Rab Kah.* Piska 15.1: "As with Adam, said God, so with his children: I brought them into the Land of Israel, I gave them commands, but they transgressed My commands."

of Adam" led corporately by an Adamic king. Likewise, Ps. 8:4 referred to this ideal end-time king as the "son of Adam." Psalm 80:17 refers to the whole nation also as "the son of Adam": "Let Your hand be upon the man [Israel] of Your right hand, upon the son of man whom You made strong for Yourself." The Qumran community believed that their own community was beginning to fulfill end-time promises originally intended for the first Adam. In 4Q418 frg. 81 (= 4Q423 8 + 24?) God is said to be "your portion and your inheritance among the sons of Adam, [and over] his [in]heritance he has given them authority" (line 3). Thus, the members of the Qumran community are those who are the true "sons of Adam" to whom God has given authority over an "inheritance." It is also said that God "has placed you . . . as a firstborn" (line 5). Those who "inherit the earth" will "walk" in an "eter[nal] plantation" (lines 13–14), likely referring to the whole earth as a large Eden.[46] They "shall fill[47] [apparently the earth] and . . . be satiated [or 'satiate themselves'] with the abundance of good" (line 19). This description of the community reflects the commission to Adam in Gen. 1:26, 28, which the Qumran community believed it had begun to fulfill.

When one then comes to the Gospels and finds Jesus being repeatedly called "the Son of God," this probably should be understood in light of the OT and Jewish background of Adam and Israel being conceived to be God's son. It is a reference to Jesus being and doing what the first Adam and Israel should have been and should have done. He is not only a completely obedient human son but also a divine son, since he is fully obedient.

The last verse of Luke 3 is the tip of this iceberg of thought, where Jesus's genealogy is concluded with "Seth, the son of Adam, the son of God." This confirms further my analysis of Gen. 5:1–3, where I noted that Seth's being in the "likeness" and "image" of Adam reflects the language of sonship, and that this indicated that Adam's being in the "likeness" and "image" of God reflects the same language. It is important that Luke ends the third chapter of his Gospel with this reference, since, as we will see later in this chapter, the directly following narrative places Jesus as "the Son of God" in the wilderness

---

46. A closely related passage in 4Q475 is apparently the most explicit Qumran text affirming that the earth will become Eden and that Israel or its end-time king will inherit it as a "son": after all sin has been extinguished from the earth, "all the world will be like Eden, and all . . . the earth will be at peace for ever, and . . . a beloved son . . . will . . . inherit it all" (lines 5–6).

47. The word rendered "fill" here is a Niphal stem (and imperfect) in Hebrew and could be rendered passively ("be filled") or, as I prefer, actively (for the former translation, see Michael O. Wise, Martin G. Abegg Jr., and Edward M. Cook, *The Dead Sea Scrolls: A New Translation* [New York: HarperCollins, 2005], 387; for the latter, see Florentino García Martínez, *The Dead Sea Scrolls Translated: The Qumran Texts in English*, trans. Wilfred G. E. Watson, 2nd ed. [Grand Rapids: Eerdmans, 1996], 391, which seems to take it also with an imperatival sense). The more active use may be classified as a reflexive benefactive ("fill for yourself") or as roughly equivalent to an active Piel or Hiphil (on which, see Bruce K. Waltke and M. O'Connor, *An Introduction to Biblical Hebrew Syntax* [Winona Lake, IN: Eisenbrauns, 1990], 388–94).

being tempted with the same temptations that Adam and Israel had experienced, but succeeding where they failed.

In the light of the foregoing discussion, it is evident that "Son of God" and "Son of Man" are both sometimes references to inheriting an Adamic position and obligation and promised blessings for obedience. In this regard, it is unlikely to be coincidental that "Son of Man" and "Son of God" seem to be used interchangeably in early Judaism and in the Gospels.[48]

We saw above that Dan. 7:13 OG says that "the Son of Man . . . came as the Ancient of Days," indicating that he was also a divine being. "Son of God" would be a very appropriate title for the OG's view of the divine "Son of Man." And, in fact, we also saw that the heavenly being in the furnace in Dan. 3 was called one "like the son of the gods," which may have influenced the OG rendering of Dan. 7:13. Other parts of early Judaism also understood the Dan. 7 "Son of Man" as the "Son of God." 4Q246 (sometimes referred to as 4QpDanA) is an interpretative paraphrase of Dan. 7, including Dan. 7:13–14, which interprets "the Son of Man" as "the Son of God" and "the son of the Most High" (in the following, underlining represents interpretative paraphrases of parts of Dan. 7):[49]

4Q246 I:1 [. . . a spirit from God] rested upon him, he fell before the throne. [= Dan. 7:13]

4Q246 I:2 [. . . O ki]ng, wrath is coming to the world, and your years

4Q246 I:3 [shall be shortened . . . such] is your vision, and all of it is about to come unto the world.

4Q246 I:4 [. . . Amid] great [signs], tribulation is coming upon the land.

4Q246 I:5 [. . . After much killing] and slaughter, a prince of nations

4Q246 I:6 [will arise . . .] the king of Assyria and Egypt

4Q246 I:7 [. . .] he will be ruler over the land

4Q246 I:8 [. . .] will be subject to him and all will obey [= Dan. 7:14]

4Q246 I:9 [him. Also his son] will be called The Great, and be designated by his name.

4Q246 II:1 He will be called the Son of God, they will call him the son of the Most High. [= Dan. 7:13] But like the meteors

4Q246 II:2 that you saw in your vision, so will be their kingdom. They will reign only a few years over

4Q246 II:3 the land, while people tramples people and nation tramples nation

48. The following is a summary of the seminal though brief study by Kim, "The 'Son of Man,'" 1–37.

49. For further discussion of the links between Dan. 7 and 4Q246, see ibid., 20–22.

4Q246 II:4 <u>until the people of God arise; then all will have rest from warfare.</u>

4Q246 II:5 <u>Their kingdom will be an eternal kingdom</u> [= Dan. 7:14, 18, 27] and all their paths will be righteous. <u>They will judge</u> [Dan. 7:22]

4Q246 II:6 the land justly, and all nations will make peace. Warfare will cease from the land,

4Q246 II:7 and all the nations shall do homage to them. The great God will be their help,

4Q246 II:8 He Himself will fight for them, putting peoples into their power,

4Q246 II:9 overthrowing them all before them. <u>God's rule will be an eternal rule</u> [= Dan. 7:27] and all the depths of [the earth are His.]

Despite the partially fragmented text, the crucial observation is that where Dan. 7:13 has "one like a Son of Man" this Qumran paraphrase has "the Son of God" and "the son of the Most High." Likewise, the late first-century apocalypse *4 Ezra* refers to the vision of "the form of a man" (13:1–3), which clearly refers to the Dan. 7:13 "Son of Man"; then, in the following interpretative section of the vision, the "man" is called repeatedly "my [God's] Son" (*4 Ezra* 13:32, 37, 52).[50] Similarly, though in later Judaism, *Midr. Ps.* 2.7 interprets Ps. 2:7 ("You are My Son") corporately by "the children of Israel" who "are declared to be sons" elsewhere in Scripture. Two of the Scriptures adduced to support this are Exod. 4:22 ("Israel is My son, My firstborn") and Dan. 7:13 concerning the "Son of Man."

The Gospels also interchange references to Jesus as "the Son of Man" with "the Son of God." The clearest illustrations of this are Mark 8:38 (cf. 9:7); 14:61–62; Matt. 16:13–17; John 1:49–51; 3:14–18; 5:25–27. Similarly, Rev. 1:13 portrays Jesus as appearing as "one like a son of man," and then 1:14 describes him with a description of the Ancient of Days from Dan. 7:9: "His head and His hair were white like wool." Then Rev. 2:18 introduces Jesus from the initial vision in 1:13–15 but calls him "the Son of God," again seeing this as an equivalent to "one like a son of man" in 1:13.

The probable reason for equating these two titles for Jesus is their virtual synonymy in the OT and Judaism. Adam was a "son of God," and Israel, inheriting Adam's mantle, was thus a "son of God" and "son of man [Adam]." Likewise the eschatological king of Israel prophesied in Dan. 7 was understood to be both "son of man" and "son of God," who would corporately represent his people, so that they could be called a corporate "son of man" and "son of God."

Thus, these two titles for Jesus underscore his essential Adamic identity, yet we have seen that in Dan. 7 the figure is also understood as a divine figure.

50. Kim (*"The 'Son of Man,'"* 27–29) also mentions other Jewish apocalyptic visions that refer to heavenly figures both as "a man" and as a "son of God" or "firstborn."

The further theological significance of this for Jesus's mission is, according to Seyoon Kim, that

> with "the 'Son of Man,'" Jesus designated himself in reference to the heavenly figure who appeared to Daniel "like a son of man" . . . in a vision. Understanding the figure to be the inclusive representative of the ideal people of God, or the Son of God representing the sons of God, Jesus saw himself destined to realize the heavenly counsel revealed to Daniel in advance and create the eschatological people of God. So, as "the 'son of Man'" (= the representative of the ideal people of God), Jesus understood his mission. . . . *In short, with "the 'Son of Man,'" Jesus intended discreetly to reveal himself as the Son of God who creates the new people of God (the children of God) at the eschaton, so that they may call God the creator "our Father."*[51]

If Kim's conclusion is correct, then even the Son of Man's function in creating children may be in mind, which reflects one of the key ways that Adam was to function in reflecting God's image in Gen. 1:28.

Jesus as Latter-Day Israel and Son in Matthew 2[52]

Matthew portrays Jesus to be recapitulating the history of Israel because he sums up Israel in himself. Since Israel disobeyed, Jesus has come to do what it should have, so he must retrace Israel's steps up to the point where it failed and then continue to obey and succeed in the mission that Israel should have carried out. The attempt by Herod to kill the Israelite infants and the journey of Jesus and his family into Egypt and back to the promised land follows the same basic pattern of Israel of old. This pattern is expressed by appeal to Hos. 11:1, where Matthew says that the trip to Egypt and back is the fulfillment of Hosea's prophecy, "Out of Egypt have I called my son" (Matt. 2:15). Jesus's journey out of Egypt is identified with Israel's from out of Egypt.

The reference to Hos. 11:1 being fulfilled in the early experience of Jesus has caused much debate. The verse in Hosea is a mere historical reflection, but Matthew clearly understands it as a direct prophecy that is fulfilled in Christ. Some have viewed this as an erroneous interpretation by Matthew, who somehow understood Hos. 11:1 to be a prophecy when it was only a historical reflection on the original exodus. Others have understood Matthew to be employing a faulty hermeneutic used elsewhere in Judaism, which Christians cannot emulate, but nevertheless the interpretative conclusion is divinely inspired. Thus, the interpretative procedure is wrong, but the Holy Spirit caused the conclusion to be right and authoritative. Still others see the interpretative procedure not to be wrong but as so unique that Christians

---

51. Ibid., 99.

52. This section is based on a paper I delivered at the Affinity Theological Studies Conference in Hoddesdon, Hertfordshire, England, February 2–4, 2011, and will appear in a forthcoming publication in more detailed form.

today dare not practice the same procedure in approaching other similar OT passages that merely narrate a historical event.

Usually such conclusions are made because Matthew (and other NT writers) is being judged by what is often called a "grammatical-historical" interpretative method. There are, however, other approaches to interpreting Scripture that have hermeneutical viability and integrity. For instance, could it be that Matthew is intentionally not doing "grammatical-historical exegesis" but rather is employing a kind of biblical-theological approach? It appears that Matthew is interpreting Hos. 11:1 in light of its relation to the entire chapter in which it is found and, we will see, in light of the entire book. In Hos. 11, after alluding to Israel's exodus from Egypt (v. 1), the prophet briefly narrates the history of the nation in its land. The people did not respond faithfully to God's deliverance of them from Egypt and to his prophetic messengers exhorting them to be loyal to God, and they worshiped idols, despite the grace that God had shown to them (vv. 2–5). Consequently, God will judge them for their lack of repentance (vv. 6–7). Nevertheless, the judgment will not be absolute because of God's compassion on the nation (vv. 8–9). God's compassion is said to express itself through future restoration of his people, who "will walk after the LORD" and "come trembling from the west. They will come trembling like birds from Egypt, and like doves from the land of Assyria," so that God "will settle them in their houses" in their land (vv. 10–11).

Thus, in the end time there will be a restoration of Israel from several lands, including "Egypt."[53] In fact, even the lion imagery describing God leading Israel out of Egypt is an allusion to the first exodus, where God is said to lead Israel out of Egypt, and the people or the king are compared to a lion (see table 13.2).

Table 13.2

Numbers 23–24	Hosea 11:10–11
23:22a: "God brings them <u>out of Egypt</u>, He is for them like the horns of the wild ox."	"He will roar <u>like a lion</u>; indeed He will roar and His sons . . . will come trembling like birds <u>from Egypt</u>. . . ."
23:24: "Behold, a people rises <u>like a lioness</u>, and <u>as a lion</u> it lifts itself; it will not lie down until it devours the prey, and drinks the blood of the slain."	
24:8: "God brings him <u>out of Egypt</u>, He is for him like the horns of the wild ox."	
24:9a: "He couches, he lies down <u>as a lion</u>, and <u>as a lion</u>, who dares rouse him?"	

53. Some commentators say that "Egypt" is metaphorical for Assyria, but the "west" is also mentioned here, which seems to point to a restoration from a number of lands. Such a restoration from multiple lands appears to be supported also by other OT prophecies (e.g., Isa. 11:11: "The Lord will again recover the second time . . . the remnant of His people . . . from Assyria, Egypt, Pathros, Cush, Elam, Shinar, Hamath, and from the islands of the sea"; Isa. 11:15–16 likewise foresees Israel's future return from both Egypt and Assyria; cf. Isa. 49:12; 60:4–9).

The Numbers passages together with Hos. 11:11 are the only places in the OT where there is the combined mention of (1) God bringing Israel "out of Egypt" and (2) of either the deliverer or the delivered being compared to a lion. In Num. 23 the people are compared to a lion, and in Num. 24 the king leading Israel is compared to a lion,[54] though it is possible that this describes God. The exact identification of the lion in Hos. 11:10 is somewhat difficult. It is also possible that the lion in Hos. 11 is this future prophesied king, but it appears to continue a description of God himself.[55] Nevertheless, in both Numbers passages God is said to be "for them [or 'him'] like the horns of the wild ox," so that the directly following lion description (also a metaphor of power) may likewise be applied to the people and the king because they are identified with their God, who is the one giving ultimate power for deliverance. This ambivalence may be reflected also in Hos. 11:10. Nevertheless, in light of Israel and its king being likened to a lion in Num. 23–24, God appears to be the one compared to a lion in Hos. 11 because of the corporate identification between Israel and its God and because God is the one who brings Israel "out of Egypt" in both Numbers texts.

Thus, the main point or goal of Hos. 11:1–11 is the accomplishment of Israel's future restoration from the nations, including "Egypt."[56] The overall meaning of Hos. 11 is to indicate that God's deliverance of the Israelites from Egypt, which led to their ungrateful unbelief, is not the final word about God's deliverance of them; though they will be judged, God will deliver them again, even from "Egypt." The chapter begins with the exodus from Egypt and ends with the same exodus from Egypt, the former referring to the past event and the latter to a future event. The pattern of the first exodus at the beginning of Israel's history will be repeated again at the end of Israel's history in the end time. It is unlikely that Hosea saw these two exoduses to be accidental or coincidental or unconnected similar events. Hosea appears to understand that Israel's first exodus (Hos. 11:1) was to be recapitulated at the time of the nation's latter-day exodus.

The mention of a first exodus from Egypt outside of Hos. 11:1 occurs elsewhere in Hosea, and a future return from Egypt seems to be implied by

54. That the individual king of Israel is referred to is evident from "his king" and "his kingdom" in Num. 24:7, the pronouns "him" in 24:8, and the blessing and cursing in 24:9, which refers to the king. In addition, Num. 24:9a itself is an allusion to the prophecy of the eschatological king from Judah in Gen. 49:9: "Judah is a lion's whelp. . . . He couches, he lies down as a lion, and as a lion, who dares rouse him up?"

55. For discussion of these allusions in Hos. 11, see John H. Sailhamer, "Hosea 11:1 and Matthew 2:15," *WTJ* 63 (2001): 87–96. These descriptions in Num. 23–24 may be descriptions of Israel's recent exodus from Egypt, or they may be prophetic descriptions of a future exodus from Egypt. The allusion to Gen. 49:9 in both Numbers texts may suggest that the latter is the case. Or, there may be a mixture of the two views.

56. Hosea 11:12, concerning Israel's deception and rebellion, is actually the beginning of the negative narrative continued throughout Hos. 12.

repeated prophecies of Israel returning to Egypt in the future (see table 13.3), while Hos. 1:10–11 and 11:11 are the only texts explicitly affirming a future return from Egypt (though, as we have seen, several texts in Isaiah are also explicit about this).

Table 13.3

First Exodus from Egypt	Future Return to Egypt (implying a future return from Egypt)
Hos. 2:15b: "And she will sing there as in the days of her youth, as in the day when she came up from the land of Egypt." [Although, this passage compares the first exodus with a future exodus.]	Hos. 7:11: "So Ephraim has become like a silly dove, without sense; they call to Egypt, they go to Assyria."
	Hos. 7:16b: "Their princes will fall by the sword because of the insolence of their tongue. This will be their derision in the land of Egypt."
	Hos. 8:13b: "Now he will remember their iniquity, and punish them for their sins; they will return to Egypt."
Hos. 12:13: "But by a prophet the LORD brought Israel from Egypt, and by a prophet he was kept."	Hos. 9:3: "They will not remain in the LORD's land, but Ephraim will return to Egypt, and in Assyria they will eat unclean food."
	Hos. 9:6: "For behold, they will go because of destruction; Egypt will gather them up, Memphis will bury them. Weeds will take over their treasures of silver; thorns will be in their tents."
	Hos. 11:5: "They will return to the land of Egypt."[a]

[a]Some translations and commentators prefer the rendering "They will *not* return to the land of Egypt," a debate we cannot here enter into.

If one were to have asked Hosea if he believed that God was sovereign over history and that God had designed the first exodus from Egypt as a historical pattern that foreshadowed a second exodus from Egypt, would he not likely have answered yes? At least, this appears to be the way Matthew understood Hosea, especially using the language of the first exodus from Hos. 11:1 in the light of the broader context, especially of Hos. 11,[57] whose main point and goal is the end-time exodus from Egypt. What better language to use for Hosea's prophecy of the second exodus and the beginning of its fulfillment in Jesus than the language already at hand describing the first exodus? This is a short step away from saying that the first exodus was seen by Hosea and, more clearly, by Matthew as a historical pattern pointing to the reoccurrence of the same pattern later in Israel's history. In this respect, Matthew's use of Hos. 11:1 may also be called "typological" in that he understood, in light of the entire chapter 11 of Hosea, that the first exodus in Hos. 11:1 initiated a historical process of sin and judgment to be culminated in another, final exodus (Hos. 11:10–11).

57. And in light of the hopes of the first exodus and implied second exodus elsewhere in the book.

But there is more. The application of what was applied to the nation in Hos. 11:1 to the one person, Jesus, also may have been sparked by the prophecy of the king of Israel coming out of Egypt in Num. 24, which appears to be echoed in Hos. 11:10–11. Numbers itself applies the very same lion imagery to the people (23:24) as to the king (24:9). The potential to apply corporate language to the individual is also suggested by Hos. 1:10–11, where the people of Israel will be called "sons of the living God" at the time of their future restoration, which will be led by "one leader." Even the statement at the end of 1:11, "And they will go up from the land," is a reference to going up from the "land" of Egypt,[58] especially since it is an allusion to Exod. 1:10 and Isa. 11:16.[59] After all, what sense does it make that this refers to the land of Israel, since at the end time Israel was to be restored *to its land*, and to describe this as Israel "going up from the land" would be, at best, exceedingly odd. If this is a reference to Israel's future return from Egypt, it fits admirably with the hope expressed in Hos. 11:10–11 (and other such implied references noted above), and it would specifically affirm that such a future exodus would be led by an individual leader (the Hebrew reads lit., "one head"). Such a return led by an individual leader appears to be further described in Hos. 3:5 as a latter-day Davidic king: "Afterward the sons of Israel will return and seek the LORD their God and David their king; and they will come trembling to the LORD . . . in the last days." This image of "trembling" to describe the manner in which the Israelites approach God when they are restored is parallel to the description of the manner of their restoration in Hos. 11:10–11, where

58. In Hosea the Hebrew word for "land" (*'ereṣ*) refers to Israel (7x), Egypt (5x), earth (2x), Assyria (1x), and the wilderness of Israel's sojourn (1x). However, the idea of "going up from the land" occurs only in 1:11 (2:2 MT) and 2:15 (2:17 MT): the former text has "they will go up from the land" (*wĕʿālû min-hāʾāreṣ*), and the latter has "she [Israel] went up from the land [ʿālōtâh mēʾereṣ] of Egypt," the latter referring to Israel's first exodus. This identifies the two passages, suggesting that 1:11 is a reference to Israel "going up from the land" of Egypt at the time of its future restoration.

59. What confirms that the expression in Hos. 1:11 refers to "going up from the land" of Egypt is that it is an allusion to either Exod. 1:10 or Isa. 11:16, which have *ʿālâ + min + ʾereṣ* in the expression "they [or 'he' = Israel] went up from the land [of Egypt]" (though Judg. 11:13 and esp. 19:30 are nearly identical to Isa. 11:16). Fifteen other times in the OT the same Hebrew wording is used but refers to God causing Israel to "go up from the land" (Exod. 3:8; 32:4, 8; Lev. 11:45; Deut. 20:1; 1 Kings 12:28; 2 Kings 17:7, 36; Ps. 81:10; Jer. 2:6; 7:22; Amos 2:10; 3:1; 9:7; Mic. 6:4); five times the expression is used with reference to Moses doing the same thing (Exod. 32:1, 7, 23; 33:1; Num. 16:13). It is possible that the expression in Hos. 1:11 (2:2 MT) is a collective allusion to all these references, which would only enforce a reference to "going up from the land" of Egypt in the Hosea passage. Derek Drummond Bass has proposed that Exod. 1:10 is the allusion in Hos. 1:11 (2:2 MT) ("Hosea's Use of Scripture: An Analysis of His Hermeneutics" [PhD diss., Southern Baptist Theological Seminary, 2008], 128–29). Isaiah 11:16 may be uppermost in mind, since it is the only other reference using this wording that refers to Israel's future restoration and uses it in conjunction with restoration from "Assyria," which Hos. 11:11 also does together with restoration from Egypt (note the similar combination of Egypt and Assyria in Hos. 7:11; 9:3; 12:1).

also they "will come trembling from the west . . . trembling like birds from Egypt" (though a different Hebrew verb is used for "trembling"). This may point further to Hosea's biblical-theological understanding that when Israel comes out of Egypt in the future (according to both 1:11 and 11:10–11), it will indeed be led by an individual king, which enhances further why Matthew could apply the corporate national language of Hos. 11:1 and apply it to an individual king, Jesus. Could Matthew not have had such a biblical-theological reading of Hosea?

Interestingly, the reference to the restoration of "the sons of the living God' in Hos. 1:10 has its closest parallel in the NT in Matt. 16:16, where Peter professes that Jesus is "the Messiah, <u>the Son of the living God</u>." This may well be an allusion to Hos. 1:10[60] by which Jesus is seen as the individual kingly son leading the sons of Israel, whom he represents.[61] Such an identification of this individual son with the corporate sons is likely the reason that Matt. 2:15 applies the corporate "son" reference of Hos. 11:1 to the individual Jesus. If this kingly nuance stands in the background, then, there is a faint echo of Israel's Adamic kingly role.[62]

There is one last rationale for understanding how Matthew can take what applied to the nation in Hos. 11:1 and apply it to the individual Messiah. Duane Garrett analyzed the use of Genesis in Hosea and found that repeatedly the prophet alludes to descriptions in Genesis of the individual patriarchs and other significant individuals in Israel's history. Sometimes these are good portrayals, and sometimes bad. The prophet applies these descriptions to the nation of his day. For example, the iniquity of Israel in the present involves its following the same pattern of disobedience as that of Adam (Hos. 6:7) or Jacob (Hos. 12:2–5), and the promise made to the individual Jacob to "make your seed as the sand of the sea, which is too great to be numbered" (Gen. 32:12 [cf. Gen. 15:5; 22:17, addressed to Abraham]) is now reapplied and addressed directly to the nation Israel: "Yet the number of the sons of Israel will be like the sand of the sea, which cannot be measured or numbered" (Hos. 1:10). Similarly, the Valley of Achor, where Achan and his family were taken to be executed for his sin (Josh. 7:24–26), is taken by Hosea and reversed to indicate that God would reverse Israel's judgment of defeat and exile, and Israel would not be exterminated for its sin but rather would have a hope of redemption (Hos. 2:15). Instead of going from the one to the many, Matthew

---

60. This allusion is proposed by Mark J. Goodwin, "Hosea and 'the Son of the Living God' in Matt. 16:16b," *CBQ* 67 (2005): 265–83.

61. The only other occurrence of "sons" together with "living God" occurs in early Jewish literature, though not as close to the wording of Hos. 1 and Matt. 16: Add. Esth. 16:16 ("sons of the Most High, the most mighty living God"); 3 Macc. 6:28 ("sons of the almighty and living God of heaven").

62. Especially given the Gen. 1–3 allusions in Hosea—e.g., 2:18; 4:3; 6:7 (though contested); 10:8; and other allusions elsewhere to Genesis (on which, see directly below).

goes from the many (Israel) to the one (Jesus), but he utilizes the same kind of "one and many" corporate hermeneutical approach to interpreting and applying prior Scripture as did Hosea.[63]

Therefore, Matthew contrasts Jesus as the "Son" (2:15) with the "son" in Hosea (11:1). The latter, who came out of Egypt, was not obedient and was judged but would be restored (11:2–11), while the former did what Israel should have done: Jesus came out of Egypt, was perfectly obedient, and did not deserve judgment but suffered it anyway for guilty Israel and the world in order to restore them to God. Hence, Jesus did what Israel should have done but did not do.[64] This use of Hos. 11:1 also is an example of how important exodus patterns were to Matthew and the other NT writers in understanding the mission of Jesus and the church, as we will continue to see.

Jesus as Israel and God's Son Elsewhere in Matthew: The Baptism of Jesus, His Wilderness Testing, and Other Aspects of His Earthly Ministry

The Baptism of Jesus

John the Baptist fulfills the first prophetic announcement of Israel's restoration in Isa. 40–66: "For this is the one referred to by Isaiah the prophet when he said, 'The voice of one crying in the wilderness, "Make ready the way of the Lord, make His paths straight"'" (Matt. 3:3 [cf. 3:1–4]).

John baptizes Jesus in the Jordan River, along with other Israelites (Matt. 3:5–6, 13–17). What is the significance of the water? Why is it apparently so important that Jesus be baptized by water in a river, along with other Jews, at the inception of his ministry? The answer seems ready at hand, if one is sensitive to OT precedents. Just as Israel was led by Moses and had to go through the sea at the exodus to enter the promised land, and just as the second generation had to do the same thing at the Jordan River under Joshua's leadership, as a miniature second exodus, so again, now that Israel's restoration is imminent through Jesus, true Israelites must again identify with the water and the Jordan and their prophetic leader in order to begin to experience true restoration.[65]

This is also in fulfillment of the prophecies of Israel's restoration as a second exodus through water (Isa. 11:15; 43:2, 16–17; 44:27–28; 50:2; 51:9–11), especially through rivers (Isa. 11:15; 42:15; 43:2; 44:27; 50:2). The picture of a separation of waters in conjunction with mention of God's Spirit and of God

---

63. See Duane Garrett, "The Ways of God: Reenactment and Reversal in Hosea" (inaugural address for the installation of Duane Garrett as professor of Old Testament at Gordon-Conwell Theological Seminary, South Hamilton, MA, fall 1996). See also Bass, "Hosea's Use of Scripture."

64. Here I am following Peter Enns, *Inspiration and Incarnation: Evangelicals and the Problem of the Old Testament* (Grand Rapids: Baker Academic, 2005), 134, although I understand Matthew's hermeneutical approach differently.

65. I first heard this connection made by Joel White, a former student, and then later by N. T. Wright.

placing people in a new land seems to go all the way back to Genesis. Gen. 1:2 refers to "the Spirit [*rûaḥ*] of God hovering over the face of the waters," and 1:9 says, "Then God said, 'Let the waters below the heavens be gathered into one place, and let the dry land appear'; and it was so." Then Adam and his wife are made in God's image to rule over, multiply upon, and fill the dry land of the earth (Gen. 1:26–28).

The same pattern occurs with Noah, where toward the end of the deluge, Gen. 8:1–3a affirms that "God caused a wind [*rûaḥ*, often rendered as 'Spirit'] to pass over the earth, and the water subsided. . . . And the water receded steadily from the earth." Then Noah and his family were able to live on the dry land again. Could the dove descending over the water at Jesus's baptism even echo the dove over the waters of the Noahic flood, which indicated also that waters were dividing from dry land, so that the new humanity could dwell on it and fulfill the commission originally given to Adam (on which, see Gen. 9:1, 6–7)?[66] The later events of the exodus from Egypt and a second time through the Jordan[67] and the prophecies of a future exodus are all also associated with and virtually equated with a new creation because apparently they are seen to some degree as recapitulations of the initial dividing of waters and placement of humanity on dry land in Gen. 1.[68] For example, note Exod. 15:8, 16: "At the blasting wind [*rûaḥ*, often rendered 'Spirit'] of Your nostrils the waters were piled up, the flowing waters stood up like a heap; the deeps were congealed in the heart of the sea. . . . Until Your people pass over. . . ."[69]

66. From a narrative-critical perspective, the Hebrew verb for "hovering" in Gen. 1:2 has been observed by several scholars to be an avian metaphor, since the same verb (*rāḥap*) is used in Deut. 32:11: "Like an eagle that stirs up its nest, that hovers over its young, He spread His wings and caught them, He carried them on His pinions." This perhaps associates the Gen. 1:2 image with that of the dove hovering over the chaotic waters toward the end of the Noahic flood.

67. In 2 Kings 2:8–15 Elijah divides the waters of the Jordan and walks on dry land, and, after receiving the divine spirit that had been on Elijah, Elisha does the same thing. The reference in v. 9 to "a double portion of your [Elijah's] spirit [*rûaḥ*] be upon me" and the fulfillment in v. 15 ("the spirit of Elijah rests upon Elisha") most likely refer to the divine spirit that had empowered Elijah's ministry, and now the same spirit was empowering Elisha's prophetic task. This is pointed to further by v. 16, where the prophets say, "The Spirit of the Lord has taken him [Elijah] up," presumably referring to the divine spirit that had characteristically empowered Elijah as a prophet throughout his ministry. This, then, is a recapitulation on a small scale of Israel's second exodus through the Jordan, which itself was a smaller-scale repetition of the first exodus through the Red Sea. The apparent purpose of the episode in 2 Kings 2 is to identify both Elijah and Elisha as prophets like Moses and Joshua in leading Israel's restoration back to worship of Yahweh in the midst of the nation's capitulation to Baal worship, so that even before Matthew's application of this exodus motif to Jesus, it had also been applied to Elisha, perhaps serving as a precedent for the later use in the NT.

68. Note, e.g., *Exod. Rab.* 21.8: "If I made dry land for Adam, who was only one [citing Gen. 1:9] . . . how much more ought I to do so on behalf of a holy congregation [Israel at the exodus]?"

69. English translations differ about whether *rûaḥ* should be translated as "Spirit" or "wind" in Gen. 1:2, though most prefer the former. However, all the translations that I consulted translated *rûaḥ* in Gen. 8:1 and Exod. 15:8 respectively as "wind" and "blast." The likely narratorial

This would fit with the imagery of Israel's restoration as a new exodus because the exodus itself was an act of new creation (as I contended in chap. 2), and the prophecies of the second exodus from Babylon are similarly portrayed as a new creation (as I also argued in chap. 2).[70]

Jesus's baptism signifies not only the beginning of a new exodus but also a new creation, since he has come to reverse the curses of the fall (through his healings, cross, and resurrection), the first act of which is to defeat the devil during the wilderness temptations, to which both Adam and Israel had succumbed. After his baptism, Jesus steps directly into the land of promise to begin his new creation/exodus mission after his baptism, which, as we will see later, is but a foreshadowing of the ultimate promised land of the new creation. Thus, Christ begins to rule over the powers of evil in beginning fulfillment of the Adamic commission to rule and subdue and in contrast to the first Adam, who was ruled over and subdued by the serpent.

It may be discernible that Matt. 3:16–17 most reflects Isa. 63:11–15a; 64:1, which look back to the first exodus as a pattern anticipating a similar deliverance to occur in Israel's eschatological future (see table 13.4).

The unique elements shared by these passages are that of God's people going through water with the presence of the Holy Spirit and that Spirit subsequently leading them onto land and into the wilderness at a major redemptive-historical episode.[71] This explicit connection between the Spirit bringing Israel out of

___

intention to portray the conclusion of the flood and the exodus narratives as a recapitulation of the creation narrative would invite the reader to make a comparison between the Spirit's hovering over the primal watery chaos and God's wind over the watery chaos of the Noahic deluge and the Red Sea waters. Second Samuel 22:16–17 (// Ps. 18:15–16) is quite similar to Exod. 15:8, 16, though now the scenario is applied figuratively to God's deliverance of David from his enemies. The dividing of the waters at the Jordan under Joshua's leadership does not mention the presence of God's Spirit or wind, but the ark of the covenant is placed in the midst of the Jordan and is the cause of the splitting of the waters; the ark represents there God's very presence (Josh. 3:10: "By this you will know that the living God is among you" [see also 3:11, 13]).

70. Later Judaism held that both the new creation of the postdiluvian world and of the exodus were modeled on the first creation when God separated the waters and made dry land that would be habitable for the first family (so *Mek. de R. Ishmael*, Beshallaḥ 3.10–22, which directly correlates in this manner Gen. 1:9–10 and Israel's promised restoration in Isa. 51:9–10). *Leviticus Rabbah* 27.4 and *Eccles. Rab.* 3.15 assert that making the sea into dry land is one of the things that God will do when he renews the world in the future. *Zohar* 1.4b affirms that God has "pledged himself to swallow up all the waters of the creation . . . on that day when all the nations shall assemble against the holy people, so that they shall be able to pass on dry land." In addition, *Apoc. El.* 5 says that part of the tribulation leading up to the "new heaven and a new earth" (v. 38) will be the drying up of waters from the earth: "The earth will be dry. The waters of the sea will dry up. . . . We went to the deep places of the sea, and we did not find water" (vv. 9, 14).

71. The LXX of Isa. 63:11 says that God "brought up from the earth the shepherd [singular] of the sheep," which shifts the focus to the individual Moses in more correspondence to the individual Jesus. In both Isa. 63 and Matt. 3 Israelites are in the water along with the "shepherd(s)." See Watts, *Isaiah's New Exodus*, 102–8; his arguments for the same Isaiah background in Mark

Table 13.4

Isaiah 63:11–15a; 64:1	Matthew 3:16–17; 4:1
Isa. 63:11–15a: "Then His people remembered the days of old, of Moses. Where is He who brought them up out of the sea with the shepherds of His flock? Where is He who put His Holy Spirit in the midst of them, who caused His glorious arm to go at the right hand of Moses, who divided the waters before them to make for Himself an everlasting name, who led them through the depths? Like the horse in the wilderness, they did not stumble; as the cattle which go down into the valley, the Spirit of the LORD gave them rest. So You led Your people, to make for Yourself a glorious name. Look down from heaven and see from Your holy and glorious habitation; where are your zeal and your mighty deeds?" Isa. 64:1a: "Oh, that You would rend the heavens and come down."	Matt. 3:16–17: "After being baptized, Jesus came up immediately from the water; and behold, the heavens were opened, and he saw the Spirit of God descending as a dove and coming upon him, and behold, a voice out of the heavens said, 'This is My beloved Son, in whom I am well-pleased.'" Matt. 4:1: "Then Jesus was led up by the Spirit into the wilderness to be tempted by the devil."

the waters and onto land ("who led them through the depths . . . in the wilderness" and "the Spirit of the LORD gave them rest" [Isa. 63:13–14]) is now related to a latter-day exodus. This expresses a somewhat similar end-time exodus hope found elsewhere in the OT.[72]

In addition, behind "This is My beloved Son" in Matt. 3:17 stands Ps. 2:7 ("You are My Son, today I have begotten You"), possibly together with echoes of Israel being God's "son" (Exod. 4:22; Hos. 11:1; Jer. 31:9; Wis. 18:13; *Pss. Sol.* 17:27).[73] "My beloved Son, in whom I am well-pleased" in Matt. 3:17 alludes to Isa. 42:1, which is made even clearer later in Matt. 12:18–21 (where Isa. 42:1–4 is formally quoted), which begins with "Behold, my servant [child], whom I have chosen; my beloved[74] in whom my soul is well pleased; I will put my Spirit upon him." In this connection, the following observation highlights

---

1:9–11 for the most part apply here also to the same Matthean version of Jesus's baptism. The influence in Matthew may even be a bit clearer, since Matt. 3:16 uses *anoigō* ("to open"), not Mark 1:10's *schizō*, in line with *anoigō* in Isa. 63:19 LXX (64:1 in the English text).

72. E.g., (1) Isa. 11:1–5 alludes to a messianic leader on whom "the Spirit of the LORD will rest," and then 11:10 refers to the same figure, who apparently will be involved in restoring not only the nations but also Israel according to the pattern of a second exodus (see esp. 11:11, 15–16, the latter of which mentions dividing water so that people can "walk over dry-shod"); (2) Isa. 43:2, 16–17, which refer to Israel being delivered by going through the waters, are bounded broadly by reference to the "Spirit," who will empower God's Servant to deliver the people (42:1) and enable God's people themselves to experience restoration (44:3–5). Similar to Isaiah, Ezek. 36:25–27 says that at the time of the latter-day restoration, God will "sprinkle clean water" on Israel and "put his Spirit within" them, so that they "will live in the land" (36:28), which will "become like the garden of Eden" (36:35 [cf. 37:14]). See also Isa. 51:9–11.

73. Watts, *Isaiah's New Exodus*, 113–14.

74. "Beloved" here and in Matt. 3:17 is not part of Isa. 42:1 itself but probably has been added under the influence of "beloved" (forms of *agapaō*) in Isa. 41:8–9; 44:2, where Israel the Servant respectively is referred to as "the seed of Abraham whom I loved" and "beloved Israel" (though some, like Watts [*Isaiah's New Exodus*, 113], doubt this).

an intention in Matt. 3:17 to associate Jesus as a representative of Israel: the words "beloved" (*agapētos* [and related verb forms]) and "well-pleased" (*eudokeō*) are not found in the Greek version of Isa. 42:1, though they could be viable renderings of the Hebrew. But, even if these words were not part of the Isa. 42:1 allusion, they would likely best be seen as woven into the allusion because elsewhere in the OT they form concepts together with "son" (*huios*) that are applied to Israel. All of this enhances the appeal to the new-exodus passage of Isa. 42:1.[75]

There is debate about whether the Servant prophecies in Isa. 40–53 refer to an individual or to a group of faithful Israelites. However, together with the Ps. 2 reference to the individual "Son" and the echoes to corporate Israel, it seems best to see Jesus being identified with both: he is the individual royal son who represents the true sons of Israel, and this appears to be the way Isa. 42:1 is being used, especially since the Servant Songs of Isa. 49:1–8 and 52:11–53:12 are best construed in the same way.[76] Jesus as the individual king who sums up Israel in himself is the one being introduced as the restorer of wayward Israel, in fulfillment of Ps. 2 and especially the new-exodus restoration prophecy of Isa. 42:1. This is a highly appropriate way to identify Jesus at the inception of his ministry and is not inconsistent with the royal conception of the first Adam.

In conjunction with this OT pattern of the exodus and, as we saw earlier, new creation, that Jesus's baptism was part of his work "to fulfill all righteousness" (Matt. 3:15) seems to allude to the fact that he came to set right what Israel and Adam had done wrong; he was coming successfully to obey, in contrast to Israel's former disobedience, as well as that ultimately of Israel's progenitors, Adam and Noah. "By his baptism Jesus affirms his determination to do his assigned work"[77] as God's "servant" in restoring Israel and being a light to the nations (note the reference to Abraham in Matt. 3:9, which continues the subtheme of Jesus's mission, which includes salvation of the gentiles).

Therefore, "all righteousness" refers to Jesus's obedience to God's will and commandments throughout his ministry as the eschatological Adam and Israel, culminating with his obedience of suffering at the cross. His obedience formally begins with the baptism and the immediately following test in the

75. Here I am following in general ibid., 116–17.

76. In Isa. 49:1–8 the "Servant," who is called "Israel" (v. 3), has the goal of restoring "Israel" (v. 5), which then is qualified as "the preserved ones of Israel" (i.e., the remnant) (v. 6). Thus, Isa. 49:1–6 prophesies that "Israel" will restore the remnant of "Israel," meaning that the former Israel is either a tiny remnant that restores a larger remnant or an individual called "Israel" who restores the remnant. It is likely that Isa. 49 and Isa. 53 see this Servant, Israel, not to be a small righteous group but rather an individual who represents the nation, which is borne out by the NT uses and applications of the Servant prophecies. Neither Isaiah nor any other OT prophet can be seen to be this individual, since he never fulfilled the mission of Isa. 49:3–6 or Isa. 53.

77. D. A. Carson, *Matthew 1–12*, EBC (Grand Rapids: Zondervan, 1995), 108.

wilderness. In doing so, he was fulfilling all the prophecies and types and other ways in which the OT looked forward to him.

Likewise also, part of the significance of the baptism is that he is identifying with humanity's sin, for which he will atone and for which he is the representative who will work complete eschatological righteousness for them.

The Wilderness Testing of Jesus

Jesus "fasted forty days and forty nights" in the wilderness during his temptation by Satan. This episode echoes Israel's forty years in the wilderness. If so, the forty years figuratively are reduced to days.[78] However, a perhaps better and more specific background is Exod. 24:18; 34:28 (also Deut. 9:9–11), where Moses was on Mount Sinai (located in the wilderness) for "forty days and forty nights" and "did not eat bread or drink water." He repeated this again when he received the Ten Commandments on Sinai a second time (Deut. 10:9–10).[79] Moses was a representative of Israel at Sinai[80] when he received the law. As true Israel and a latter-day Moses, Jesus is the micro-Israel who has replaced the macronational Israel. Each response by Jesus to Satan is taken from a response

78. The rationale for this could be Num. 13–14, where Israel's representatives spied out the land of promise for forty days (13:25), and the majority gave a negative report to not enter the land, which the Israelites accepted. God's punishment for this was that "according to the number of days which you spied out the land, forty days, for every day you shall bear your guilt a year, even forty years, and you will know My opposition" (14:34). Accordingly, Jesus would be doing in the land what Israel should have done: enter it and conquer the powers of evil.

79. After Moses smashed the two tablets that he had received at Sinai, he prayed for "forty days and nights" that God would not destroy Israel (Deut. 9:18, 25). So also Elijah, modeled after Moses, fasted for "forty days and forty nights" in journeying to Sinai to behold another divine theophany (1 Kings 19:8). First Kings 19:4–8, where Elijah is aided by an angel in the wilderness, may be included in the background of Mark 1:12–13, where Jesus is ministered to by angels in the wilderness (see Richard J. Bauckham, "Jesus and the Wild Animals [Mark 1:13]: A Christological Image for an Ecological Age," in *Jesus of Nazareth—Lord and Christ: Essays on the Historical Jesus and New Testament Christology*, ed. Joel B. Green and Max Turner [Grand Rapids: Eerdmans, 1994], 8; Bauckham sees only the 1 Kings 19 background for the "forty days" in Mark 1:12–13). In addition, 1 Kings 17:3–6 shows ravens in a harmonious relationship with Elijah, providing for him. Likewise, the rain fell "forty days and forty nights" during the flood (Gen. 7:4, 12), during which Noah and his family were preserved in the safety of the ark. The notion of preparations for a new creation in Gen. 7 may be echoed in the preparations of Jesus's inauguration of a new creation in his ministry through his prior perseverance in the wilderness. This background may be in the peripheral vision here in view of the possible Noahic background for the hovering dove at the baptism of Jesus suggested above.

80. That Moses was a representative of Israel at Sinai is apparent in that he functioned as a high priest at the top of the mountain temple, where the ark was created and where he experienced the theophanic presence of God, as Israel's later high priests also could enter the holy of holies in the presence of the ark and God's theophanic presence (for Sinai as a tripartite mountain temple, see chap. 19). In addition, Moses's representative role for Israel is suggested by Exod. 32:10 (as well as Deut. 9:14), which says that God wanted to destroy Israel and "make of you [Moses] a great nation." Thus, Moses potentially was to be the head and progenitor of a new people of God.

by Moses to Israel's failure in the wilderness (Deut. 8:3 in Matt. 4:4; Deut. 6:16 in Matt. 4:7; Deut. 6:13 in Matt. 4:10). Jesus resists the same temptations to which Israel succumbed.

The reason, however, that Luke's genealogy ends with "Adam, the son of God" (Luke 3:38) and is directly followed by Jesus's temptation narrative is to identify Jesus as an end-time Adam, the true Son of God, resisting the temptations to which Adam and Eve had succumbed. That Eden's temptations are in mind may be suggested by Mark's comments that after Jesus successfully endured the temptations in the wilderness, "he was with the wild beasts, and the angels were ministering to him" (Mark 1:13). This may be pointed to further by the prophetic vision that humanity was to dwell peaceably with antagonistic animals at the time of the new creation (Isa. 11; 43; 65), which was also understood to overlap with the end-time exodus:

> Isa. 11:6–9 And the wolf will dwell with the lamb,
>> And the leopard will lie down with the young goat,
>> And the calf and the young lion and the fatling together;
>> And a little boy will lead them.
>> Also the cow and the bear will graze,
>> Their young will lie down together,
>> And the lion will eat straw like the ox.
>> The nursing child will play by the hole of the cobra,
>> And the weaned child will put his hand on the viper's den.
>> They will not hurt or destroy in all My holy mountain,
>> For the earth will be full of the knowledge of the LORD as the waters
>>> cover the sea.

> Isa. 43:20 "The beasts of the field will glorify Me,
>> The jackals and the ostriches,
>> Because I have given waters in the wilderness
>> And rivers in the desert,
>> To give drink to My chosen people."

> Isa. 65:25 "The wolf and the lamb will graze together,
>> And the lion will eat straw like the ox;
>> And dust will be the serpent's food
>> They will do no evil or harm in all My holy mountain," says the Lord.

The Isa. 43 and 65 passages are explicitly linked to the new creation (see Isa. 43:18–19; 65:17), and the verbal parallel of Isa. 11:6–9 and 65:25 points to the same reality in the former passage. Likewise, both the Isa. 11 and 43 texts are directly connected to second-exodus portrayals (see 11:11, 15–16; 43:16–17). Strikingly, the segment quoted above from Isa. 11 is bounded by extended reference to the messianic leader of the new creation and of the second exodus, "the shoot . . . from the stem of Jesse" (11:1–5) and "the root of Jesse" (11:10). Isaiah 11:6–9 is a continuation of the eschatological depiction of verses 1–5 but focuses on the conditions of animal and human harmony in the new creation. Then verses 10–16 continue the theme of harmony in the new cosmos but now focusing on the peace among the formerly antagonistic people groups of gentiles and Jews, who find mutual peace in resorting to "the root of Jesse" (the Messiah) (v. 10). Thus, Isa. 11:6–16 places the messianic leader of Israel's future restoration together with the wild beasts. Likewise, Isa. 43:20 places Israel in the wilderness together with the wilderness "beasts" (*thērion* in the LXX, the same word, in the plural, as in Mark 1:13), which "glorify" ("bless" in the LXX) God because of his restoration blessings that he bestows on Israel in the eschaton. If Isa. 65 is echoed, then perhaps it is not irrelevant to notice that it alludes to Gen. 3 in predicting a recapitulation of Edenic conditions in the coming new cosmos: "For [as] the days of the tree of life, [so] shall be the days of my people" (Isa. 65:22 LXX and Tg., both alluding to Gen. 3:22); "dust will be the serpent's food" (Isa. 65:25, alluding to Gen. 3:14). Thus, links with Adam and Eden again seem within view in Isaiah's prophecy of new creation.[81]

The defeat of the devil in the wilderness may also be viewed secondarily to be Jesus's first act of conquering the latter-day "Canaanites in the promised land" as true Israel. One might question whether this idea is present in the temptation account, since the major theme, as we noted above, is that of Jesus resisting temptations to sin to which Israel surrendered. The theme of temptation certainly is highlighted in that each of the three OT citations from Deuteronomy refers to the manner in which Israel should have responded to its temptations but did not. However, a closer inspection of each of the Deuteronomy contexts reveals the goal of God's desire for the people of Israel to remain faithful in the face of their temptations: they would "go in and possess the good land which the LORD swore" to give "by driving out all your enemies from before you" (Deut. 6:18–19).[82] It is plausible that Jesus had in mind this common purpose of each of the three contexts.

Consequently, Jesus's victory over temptation appears to have prepared him to conquer the one who was the ultimate satanic prince of the Canaanites and of all wicked nations[83] and to conquer the land in a way that Israel had not been able to do. His very resistance to these satanic allurements was the very

81. Bauckham ("Jesus and the Wild Animals") likewise sees that the main background of Mark 1:13 is Isa. 11 and 65 (though he also mentions Job 5:22–23). However, he is doubtful that there is a "new Adam Christology" in Mark 1:13, even though he acknowledges allusions to Gen. 2–3 in both Isaiah passages.

82. Likewise, Deut. 6:13 is directly followed by a description of what will happen if Israel follows other gods in the land: God "will wipe you off the face of the land"—Israel will not possess it. Part of the introduction to Deut. 8:3 is "Be careful to do [the law] that you may live and multiply, and go in and possess the land which the LORD swore to your forefathers" (Deut. 8:1).

83. This idea perhaps is supported by the fact that the devil is elsewhere referred to in the Gospels as "Beelzebul" (Matt. 10:25) or "Beelzebub," variant names for deities associated with the god Baal in Canaan (e.g., note "Baalzebub" in 2 Kings 1:2–3, 6, 16, referring to the Philistine

beginning of his defeat of the devil. Jesus's ministry of casting out demons continues his holy warfare as the true Israel. His exorcisms were an expression of his incipient, though decisive, defeat of Satan, who had brought creation into captivity through his deception of Adam and Eve. This is perhaps part of the significance of the parable of the binding of the strong man (Matt. 12:29 // Mark 3:27). By casting out the devil and his forces, Jesus was accomplishing the latter-day defeat of Satan that Adam should have accomplished in the first garden.[84] In Matt. 4:6 the devil tries to tempt Jesus by quoting Scripture, saying,

> If You are the Son of God, throw Yourself down [from the pinnacle of the temple]; for it is written, "He will command His angels concerning You"; and "On their hands they will bear You up, so that You will not strike your foot against a stone."

This is a quotation of Ps. 91:11–12. Psalm 91:13, however, goes on to say that the righteous one cared for by the angels "will tread upon the lion and the cobra, the young lion and the serpent you will trample down." This verse may allude to the great Gen. 3:15 promise "He shall bruise you on the head, and you shall bruise him on the heel."[85] Jesus's refusal to follow Satan's advice during the wilderness temptations was the beginning victory over Satan prophesied in the psalm. Matthew likely intends to some degree that the reader be aware of this broader context of the psalm, which, together with the three Deuteronomy contexts above, further reveals the theme of Jesus's victory over opposition.[86]

---

god, apparently translated as "lord of the flies"). See further Theodore J. Lewis, "Beelzebul," *ABD* 1:638–40.

84. Dan G. McCartney, "*Ecce Homo:* The Coming of the Kingdom as the Restoration of Human Viceregency," *WTJ* 56 (1994): 10. McCartney also mentions that Jesus's proclamations of the kingdom are expressions that the vice-regency lost with the first Adam was now being announced, and his power over nature was another example of exercising the dominion over the earth as God's vice-regent, which the first Adam should have exercised. See also Meredith G. Kline, *Kingdom Prologue: Genesis Foundations for a Covenantal Worldview* (Overland Park, KS: Two Age Press, 2000), 65–67. Kline makes the suggestive observation that "the tree of the knowledge of good and evil" in Gen. 2 refers to Adam's duty to discern between good and evil, so that when the serpent entered the garden, Adam was to judge the serpent as an evildoer. Kline supports this partly by adducing other texts that refer to a discerning between "good and evil" as the exercise of "a legal-judicial kind of discrimination" (Isa. 5:20, 23; Mal. 2:17), such as "a king engaged in rendering judicial decisions" (2 Sam. 14:17; 1 Kings 3:9, 28).

85. Artur Weiser sees Ps. 91:13 alluding to "the cultic [creation] myth . . . of the god killing a dragon and as a sign of his victory over the monster putting his foot on its neck," which he then sees as applicable to OT saints (*The Psalms: A Commentary*, trans. Herbert Hartwell, OTL [London: SCM, 1962], 612). It is interesting that Weiser sees an allusion to a great primal episodic reference, but my view differs in that I see it as an echo of Gen. 3:15, which I consider to represent real primeval history.

86. The comment about "ministering angels" in Mark 1:13 as a concluding comment to Jesus's condition immediately after his wilderness testing suggests further that he was the promised one of Ps. 91:11–12 (and cf. 91:13).

Luke's quotation of Ps. 91:12 in his version of the temptation account also has the following context of the psalm in mind, since only a few chapters later he actually alludes to Ps. 91:13 in Luke 10:19: "Behold, I have given you authority <u>to tread on serpents</u> [*patein epanō opheōn*] and scorpions, and over all the power of the enemy, and nothing will injure you" (Ps. 90:13 LXX [91:13 MT] has "You will tread[87] on the asp and basilisk, and <u>you will tread</u> [*katapatēseis*] on the lion and the dragon"). It is helpful to see the larger context of the verse in Luke 10:17–20:

> The seventy returned with joy, saying, "Lord, even the demons [*daimonion*] are subject to us in Your name." And he said to them, "I was watching Satan fall from heaven like lightning. Behold, I have given you authority to tread on serpents and scorpions, and over all the power of the enemy, and nothing will injure you. Nevertheless do not rejoice in this, that the spirits are subject to you, but rejoice that your names are recorded in heaven."

Among the dangerous forces in the psalm, in verse 6 of the LXX, is the "demon" (*daimonion*), which is the word used in Luke 10:17 in parallelism with "serpents and scorpions" in Luke 10:19. The immediately surrounding context of verse 13 of the psalm also repeatedly highlights protection from evil (vv. 3–7, 10–11, 14), which is the thought in Matthew's and Luke's quotation of Ps. 91:12 in the account of Jesus's temptation and also at the end of Luke 10:19 ("nothing will injure you"). For example, verses 5–6 of the psalm (LXX) affirm, "You will not be afraid of terror by night . . . nor of the evil thing . . . and the demon." The statement in Luke 10:17–19 includes not only the powers of evil in general but also Satan, since the preceding verse has "I was watching Satan fall from heaven like lightning." What precise event during Jesus's ministry this "fall" of Satan refers to is debated by commentators, but probably it is best to follow George Ladd's view that "it is the entire mission of Jesus which brings about Satan's defeat."[88]

Nevertheless, it is probable that Jesus's resistance to the devil in the wilderness is the very first instance of his decisive victory over Satan, since it is the first event that the Gospels record of Jesus's encounter with evil and successful resistance to it. This is also suggested by the fact that directly after Jesus's successful resistance to the devil, both Matthew and Luke narrate the beginning of Jesus's ministry, which includes announcement of the inauguration of the kingdom and beginning fulfillment of messianic OT prophecies. Also, both Jesus's wilderness trial and the subsequent launch of his ministry are under the guidance of the "Spirit" (see Luke 4:1, 18). The likely connection between

---

87. Here the LXX has *epibēsē* ("you will sit"), but one Greek OT version (Symmachus) has *patēseis* ("you will tread").

88. George Eldon Ladd, *The Presence of the Future: The Eschatology of Biblical Realism* (Grand Rapids: Eerdmans, 1974), 157.

the two sections is that the temptation narrative is probably seen implicitly as Jesus's first victory over Satan, which then unleashes the positive accomplishment of his mission, including continued subjugation of evil, satanic powers.

The victorious aspect of this encounter with Satan in the wilderness is enhanced by Luke's connection of Jesus with Adam (Luke 3:38–4:1) and the Ps. 91:12 quotation, when seen in light of its following context and in light of the use of Ps. 91:13 in Luke 10:17. The connection with Adam may be hinted at in Luke 10:19 not only by the allusion to Ps. 91:13 but also by an echo of Gen. 3:15 included along with it. This is also suggested by the parallel text in *Testament of Levi* (second century BC), which has almost the same wording as Luke 10:19. Note again Luke's wording, "<u>I have given you authority</u> [*dedōka hymin tēn exousian*] <u>to tread on serpents</u> [*tou patein epanō opheōn*] and scorpions," in comparison with that in *Testament of Levi*, "<u>He will give authority</u> [*dōsei exousian*] to his children <u>to trample upon</u> [*tou patein epi*] the evil spirits," which refers to a messianic priest who is prophesied to come and also to "remove the threatening sword against Adam, and he will give to the saints to eat from the tree of life" (*T. Levi* 18:10–12). Here the allusion to "trampling upon the evil spirits" is likely an allusion to Gen. 3:15 because of the other clear allusions to Gen. 3 in the immediate context. Likewise, *T. Sim.* 6:6 uses the noun form of "trampling" in the same manner in direct connection again to mention of Adam: the Lord "by himself will . . . save Adam. Then all the spirits of error will be given over to being trampled under foot." Again, the mention of Adam makes likely another allusion to Gen. 3:15 here, as in *Testament of Levi*. Both references in the *Testaments of the Twelve Patriarchs* (second century BC) point further to the parallel of Luke 10:17–19 having within its purview the same Gen. 3:15 reference, all three of which seem to be interpreting the "bruising of the head" of the serpent as "trampling him underfoot." They likely do not borrow from one another but rather reflect a broader understanding of how Gen. 3:15 was understood in early Judaism and Christianity.

Other Aspects of Jesus's Earthly Ministry in Relation to His Role as an End-Time Adam

Jesus's victory over Satan in the wilderness launched his subsequent successful ministry. After defeating the devil in the promised land, Jesus again is seen as beginning to fulfill Isaiah's promises of Israel's restoration (Matt. 4:12–16). Consequently, Jesus begins to regather the tribes of Israel by beginning to call his twelve apostles (Matt. 4:18–22), who represent the microcosmic true Israel under their leader Jesus—that is, Yahweh, though Jesus is also portrayed as a latter-day Moses.[89]

89. See Dale C. Allison Jr., *The New Moses: A Matthean Typology* (Minneapolis: Fortress, 1993).

The restoration that Jesus was introducing involved various kinds of healings, which were prophesied to occur when Israel would undergo true end-time restoration to God (Matt. 4:23–25; 11:4–6; cf. Isa. 32:3–4; 35:5–6; 42:7, 16). Jesus's healings also represented the restoration of creation from the fallen condition of the world. The physical (and spiritual) curses of the fall were beginning to be removed by Jesus, as he was reestablishing the new creation and kingdom, which Adam should have established. Seen within the framework of the new creation, Christ's miracles of healing not only inaugurated the end-time kingdom but also signaled the beginning of the new creation, since the healings were a beginning reversal of the curse of the old, fallen world.[90] The miracles were a sign of the inbreaking new creation, where people would be completely healed. Those whom he healed, and especially raised from the dead, foreshadowed his own resurrection and then, ultimately, their own final resurrection. Christ's resurrection was the first fruits of all believers. They, like him, would be raised with perfected, restored bodies at the very end of the age when the new world would finally be ushered in (see Matt. 19:28–29; for Paul, see 1 Cor. 15:20). The repeated and dominating notion of the kingdom in the Gospels is one of the main ways by which the evangelists express ideas about the new creation.

The resurrection of Jesus is a further development of the new creation (e.g., Matt. 27:57–28:15). Resurrection is a full-blown new-creational notion, since, as we have repeatedly noted, the way the righteous were to enter in and become a part of the new heavens and earth is through God re-creating their bodies. Jesus's claim "All authority has been given to Me in heaven and on earth" (Matt. 28:18) alludes to Dan. 7:13–14, which prophesied that the "Son of Man" (i.e., "son of Adam") would be "given authority, glory and sovereignty" forever.[91] Then, as we noted at the introduction of this chapter, he immediately gives the disciples the so-called Great Commission: "Go therefore and make disciples of all the nations . . . teaching them . . . ; and lo, I am with you always" (Matt. 28:19–20). This edict not only continues the allusion to the Dan. 7 prophecy (v. 14: "that all the peoples, nations, and men of every language might serve him") but also, as discussed earlier in this chapter, is itself a renewal of the Gen. 1:26–28 commission to Adam.

Jesus as the Adamic Son Who Represents Those Who Identify with Him as Sons

Accordingly, Jesus came to reflect God's image, which the first Adam and the corporate Adam, Israel, were to do but did not. He ruled and subdued the powers of evil and creation itself through his word and miraculous powers;

---

90. See Ridderbos, *Coming of the Kingdom*, 65, 115, who speaks only briefly and in passing of Christ's healing miracles as "restoration" of creation, and as a "renewal" and "re-creation."

91. See also France (*Jesus and the Old Testament*, 142–43), who also sees the allusion to Dan. 7.

he increased and multiplied people who followed him, so that they became his true family and sons and daughters of God. This chapter has focused on Jesus's reflection of the image through his subduing and ruling activity in inaugurating a new creation. That aspect of the Adamic image in Gen. 1:28 of "increasing and multiplying" and "filling the earth" with progeny is not as clearly expressed in the Gospels as it perhaps is elsewhere in the NT (e.g., in Paul's writings), which to some degree will be addressed in the next and subsequent chapters.

Nevertheless, it is fitting to analyze briefly a few passages that could bear upon this theme in the Synoptic Gospels. Matt. 12:46–50 reads,

> While He was still speaking to the crowds, behold, His mother and brothers were standing outside, seeking to speak to Him. Someone said to Him, "Behold, Your mother and Your brothers are standing outside seeking to speak to You." But Jesus answered the one who was telling Him and said, "Who is My mother and who are My brothers?" And stretching out His hand toward His disciples, He said, "Behold My mother and My brothers! For whoever does the will of My Father who is in heaven, he is My brother and sister and mother."

Here Jesus redefines a true Israelite as "whoever does the will of My Father" (the parallel in Luke 8:21 has "who hear the word of God and do it"). Jesus's true family consists of those who trust in him, not those who are related to him by blood. Because Jesus is restoring not only Israel but also all of creation, including gentiles (Matt. 15:21–28; 21:40–44), the true people of God no longer can be marked out by certain nationalistic badges that distinguish one nation from another. Therefore, in order to become a true Israelite and part of Jesus's real family, one no longer needs to keep all the specific requirements of Israel's law that marked Israel out as Israel in contrast to the rest of the nations: laws of circumcision, diet,[92] the temple, the Sabbath, and so on.

Jesus is redefining the true Israel, the true people of God, by saying that loyalty to him is the mark of a faithful Israelite. People no longer must possess the badges of old national Israel in order to be part of the true, new Israel. Almost identically, Jesus says in Matt. 10:34–39 (cf. Luke 14:26) that members of the true family of God are not those who belong to a particular bloodline but rather those who put faith in and have ultimate loyalty to him:

> Do not think that I came to bring peace on the earth; I did not come to bring peace, but a sword. For I came to set a man against his father, and a daughter against her mother, and a daughter-in-law against her mother-in-law; and a man's enemies will be the members of his household. He who loves father or mother more than Me is not worthy of Me; and he who loves son or daughter more than Me is not worthy of Me. And he who does not take his cross and

92. On which, see Matt. 15:11–20; Mark 7:18–23.

follow after Me is not worthy of Me. He who has found his life will lose it, and he who has lost his life for my sake will find it.

The same essential point is made elsewhere in Matt. 3:9; 19:29; Luke 11:27–28:

Matt. 3:9 "And do not suppose that you can say to yourselves, 'We have Abraham for our father'; for I say to you that from these stones God is able to raise up children to Abraham" (cf. Luke 3:8).

Matt. 19:29 "And everyone who has left houses or brothers or sisters or father or mother or children or farms for My name's sake, will receive many times as much, and will inherit eternal life" (cf. Luke 18:29).

Luke 11:27–28 While Jesus was saying these things, one of the women in the crowd raised her voice and said to him, "Blessed is the womb that bore You and the breasts at which You nursed." But he said, "On the contrary, blessed are those who hear the word of God and observe it."[93]

You do not have to be of the bloodline of Abraham to be his true child, nor do you have to move to Israel geographically to become an Israelite; you merely have to move to Jesus, true Israel, and embrace him. As we will see, this applies to the temple (Jesus is the temple), circumcision (in him we have been circumcised [Col. 2:11]), and the Sabbath rest (true, ultimate rest is found in him forever, not merely physical rest on the seventh day). This issue of what are the essential identification badges of membership in the true people of God will be taken up in greater length in a following chapter on the relation of the OT law to Jesus and his followers in the new epoch instituted by him (see chap. 26).

The main point here is that Jesus is now the locus and the originator of the true community of faith for both believing Jews and gentiles. The true family of God has its source in identification with Jesus Christ, who is their progenitor. Conceptually, this notion seems to fit suitably within that aspect of Jesus's ministry as the last Adam, who was to reflect the divine image by creating a people to live in and fill the earth. Accordingly, Jesus is the one in whom the eschatological family finds its ultimate source and whose task was to create a new family of God, which should have been part of the task of the first Adam. Along these lines, Jesus's appointment of the twelve apostles represented not only a reconstitution of the new Israel around himself, which was to grow exponentially, but also the creation of a new people to live in a new creation.

The word "sons" is appropriately applied to Jesus's followers because it is associated with reflecting the heavenly Father's image. Sons reflect the likeness

---

93. On these passages from Matt. 10; 19; Luke 11, I have followed N. T. Wright, *Jesus and the Victory of God* (Minneapolis: Fortress, 1996), 401–3.

of their fathers in various ways. Matthew 5:9 says, "Blessed are the peacemakers, for they shall be called sons of God." Jesus elaborates further on this in Matt. 5:44–48:

> But I say to you, love your enemies and pray for those who persecute you, so that you may be sons of your Father who is in heaven; for He causes His sun to rise on the evil and the good, and sends rain on the righteous and the unrighteous. For if you love those who love you, what reward do you have? Do not even the tax collectors do the same? If you greet only your brothers, what more are you doing than others? Do not even the Gentiles do the same? Therefore you are to be perfect, as your heavenly Father is perfect.

Like Jesus, his followers are to show benevolence to their enemies in order to reflect God's benevolence that he shows to evil people. Thus, they are "to be complete" or "perfect" as is their Father (i.e., they are to aspire toward the end-time goal of the law, which the Father perfectly reflects).[94] If they do not reflect him in this manner, then they will have no reward in the heavenly kingdom. Jesus expands this same idea when, in Luke's Gospel, he appears to clarify that the "reward" of Matt. 5:46 is being considered a "son" by God: "But love your enemies, . . . and your reward will be great, and you will be sons of the Most High" (Luke 6:35). Then Jesus adds, "Be merciful, just as your Father is merciful" (Luke 6:36). In the coming age, saints cannot "die any more, because they are like angels, and are sons of God, being sons of the resurrection" (Luke 20:36). Since an intrinsic characteristic of God is to have endless life, when he imparts such life to his people at the end of the age, they can be called his "sons" because they share in and reflect the life of God himself.[95] But there is more. Since Christ was declared "the Son of God as a result of the resurrection from the dead" (Rom. 1:4), so his people are called the same by their resurrection[96] because of the identification with him by faith (see further Rom. 8:14–24, 29). That this is not an eisegetical parallel to Luke 20 is evident in that Jesus himself is called "Son of God" elsewhere in Luke (1:35; 4:3, 9, 41; so likewise 1:32; 3:22; 8:28; 9:35; 10:22; 22:70), including the directly preceding context (20:13, though the precise phrase is "beloved son").

Similarly, Jesus refers to his followers becoming "sons of light" when they "believe in the light" (i.e., believe in Jesus as the revelation of God). That is, when they identify with Jesus, they reflect him and his revelatory truth. Perhaps

94. Following Carson, *Matthew 1–12*, 161.

95. So Luke Timothy Johnson, *The Gospel of Luke*, SP 3 (Collegeville, MN: Liturgical Press, 1991), 318. That the attribute of divine life is in mind in Luke 20:36 is pointed to further by the directly following reference to Exod. 3:6 in Luke 20:37; Exod. 3:6 is further expanded in 3:14–15, where self-existence is predicated to be intrinsic to God's being, directly followed again by the threefold reference to Yahweh being the God of Abraham, Isaac, and Jacob.

96. Ibid.

426

"children of God" has a similar connotation of God's people bearing a family resemblance to him (see John 1:12; 11:52).

What is the basis for Jesus's followers becoming sons of God? We saw earlier in this chapter that Jesus understood himself to be the Son of Man of Dan. 7, who was also the Son of God, and as such he was the inclusive representative of the true eschatological people of God, who by identification with him become the sons of God. In Jesus as the Son of Man, believers come to regain the position of true sons of Adam and sons of God. Hence, they regain in Jesus, the Son of Man (Adam), the eschatological image of Adam. As we will see in the next chapter, concerning Paul's view of this concept, Christians are positionally in heaven fully identified with Christ as the last Adam and the image of God, yet in their lives on earth this image, which has begun to be restored in them, has not yet been completed, but it will be at the final resurrection of the saints.

Conclusion and Summary: Jesus as End-Time Adamic King of Israel's Eschatological Kingdom Who Recovers the Image of God

I have addressed the idea of the "kingdom" in the Synoptic Gospels through explaining Jesus as the Son of Man and in other ways. In the preceding part of this chapter, however, there has been perhaps more emphasis on Jesus as the eschatological Adam, who has recovered the image of God and introduced the new creation. We have seen that just as the first Adam was commissioned to be a king in the living image of God, so Christ is a king. In fact, we saw in the initial study of Gen. 1–3 (chap. 2) that Adam's rule was to be a functional expression of being in the image of God. Thus, Jesus's beginning exercise of kingship in the Synoptic Gospels is conceptually related to his functional reflection of the divine image. This connection to Adam is made in various ways, as we saw earlier in this chapter. The preceding discussion traced the theme of Adam and the new creation at significant points in the Synoptic Gospels, so that it is likely that the notion of the kingdom in the Synoptics is linked conceptually with the original kingly purpose of Adam, who would reflect God and his rule on earth as a faithful vice-regent. Accordingly, the kingdom in the Synoptics is an aspect of Jesus as an eschatological Adam and one who is introducing the new creation. For example, as noted earlier in this chapter, Jesus's miracles of healing and demonic expulsion illustrate his rule over Satan and over nature and represent in part a reversal of the original curse on the first Adam for his disobedience; this curse affected the rest of humanity, since Adam was its representative.

The reason why Jesus reflects both the OT figures of Adam and Israel is, as we observed earlier, that Israel and its patriarchs were given the same commission as was Adam in Gen. 1:26–28. Consequently, it is not an overstatement to understand Israel as a corporate Adam who had failed in its "garden of Eden,"[97] in much the same way as its primal father had failed in the first garden. For these reasons, we recall once again that one of the reasons why Jesus is called "Son of God" is that this was a name for the first Adam (Luke 3:38; cf. Gen. 5:1–3) and for Israel (Exod. 4:22; Hos. 11:1). Recall yet again also that the divine image that Adam was to reflect was expressed more in functional than in ontological terms: Adam was to reflect God's actions in Gen. 1 of subduing and ruling over creation, creating, and filling the world with his creation. Accordingly, Adam was to "rule and subdue," "be fruitful and multiply" (i.e., increase the human progeny of the creation), and "fill the earth" with image-bearers who reflect the divine glory. We even saw that the language of "sonship" in Gen. 5:1–3 was essentially descriptive of someone who was in the "likeness" and "image" of his father, so that Adam himself was to be considered a "son" of God because he too was created in the "image" and "likeness" of God (Gen. 1:26; 5:1).

Likewise, the expression "Son of Man" from Dan. 7:13 refers to end-time Israel and its representative king as the son of Adam who is sovereign over beasts (recall that the Son of Man takes over the kingdoms of former evil empires portrayed as beasts). Understandably, against this background, it is natural that "Son of Man" became one of Jesus's favorite ways to refer to himself.

Thus, Jesus Christ is the son of Adam, or the "Son of Man," who has begun to do what the first Adam did not do and to inherit what the first Adam did not inherit, including an end-time glory that was a consummate reflection of God's image. But he is also the true, end-time Israel, to which the applications of the Dan. 7 Son of Man to Jesus also point strongly, since the Adamic language of "Son of Man [Adam]" is interpreted in Dan. 7 itself first to be the saints of Israel. However, as we saw earlier in this chapter, a careful reading of Dan. 7:13 reveals that the Son of Man is also an individual divine king who corporately represents Israel. We also saw earlier in this chapter and in chapter 2 that Dan. 7 has multiple allusions to Gen. 1, which enforces the notion of an Adamic background. In this regard, at the risk of being overly repetitive, I want to underscore once again that since the nation Israel bore the mantle of Adam (the Gen. 1:28 commission was repeatedly applied to Israel), it was considered to be a corporate Adam and was also functionally to reflect God's image (see chap. 2). *This identification is a crucial linchpin for the biblical-theological conclusions in this chapter and in others to come.* Hence, Jesus's two roles as the last Adam and true Israel are two sides of one redemptive-historical coin.

Therefore, Jesus came as the end-time Adamic Son of God, representing corporate Israel, and in doing so he was doing what the first Adam should have done in completely obeying God. And in this, he was inaugurating the

---

97. Note again OT texts where Israel's promised land is called the "garden of Eden" (Gen. 13:10; Isa. 51:3; Ezek. 36:35; Joel 2:3).

kingdom of the new creation. And in doing so, he was restoring the functional image of God for those whom he represented. In that Jesus himself was the model Adam, and hence the perfect image of God as the first Adam should have been, all those who trust in and follow Jesus are identified with him as the end-time royal Adam and eschatological image of God.

In the next chapter, we will see how this theme of the divine image is picked up and developed in Paul's thinking.

Excursus 1 Other Eschatological Aspects of the Inaugurated End-Time Kingdom in the Synoptic Gospels

The Synoptic Gospels especially highlight Jesus as Israel's king who is inaugurating the latter-day kingdom. There has been much good discussion of this idea in Jesus's ministry.[98] Here the purpose is to do a thumbnail sketch of Jesus as the ruler over the end-time kingdom as this has been developed by others. The aim is to summarize some of these previous studies and to relate them to the eschatological themes that we have been studying so far in this chapter.[99]

A number of references to the "kingdom" in the Synoptics are not clear with respect to whether they refer to the inaugurated kingdom or the future, final form of the kingdom.[100] Nevertheless, there are some significant references in which a time frame can be more clearly discerned, and to these we turn. The "kingdom" is never given a clear definition in the Synoptic Gospels. Therefore, the best way to understand the idea of the kingdom is against the background of Israel's prophesied kingdom in the OT,[101] as well as the background of the Adamic kingship in Gen. 1–3, the latter of which I have already elaborated upon. We saw in this chapter and earlier in the book that the coming of the end-time kingdom would bring not only defeat of Israel's enemies by a coming leader but also a restoration of Israel to the land and to God, when there would be a new temple and the outpouring of God's Spirit (chaps. 3–5). It is this kingdom that Jesus sees beginning to be inaugurated in his midst. As George Ladd has said, the kingdom that Jesus was inaugurating involved, first, God's inbreaking

98. See Peter Stuhlmacher, *Biblische Theologie des Neuen Testaments*, vol. 1 (Göttingen: Vandenhoeck & Ruprecht, 1992), chaps. 5–8 for a good discussion of the various features of the kingdom of God in Jesus's ministry.
99. See, e.g., Herman Ridderbos, *The Coming of the Kingdom*, trans. H. de Jongste, ed. Raymond O. Zorn (Philadelphia: P&R, 1962); Thomas R. Schreiner, *New Testament Theology: Magnifying God in Christ* (Grand Rapids: Baker Academic, 2008), 41–79; Ladd, *Presence of the Future*. In particular, see Ridderbos, *Coming of the Kingdom*, xi–xxxiv, and Ladd, *Presence of the Future*, 3–42, for good overviews of the twentieth-century debates in New Testament scholarship about eschatology in the Synoptic Gospels, especially concerning the following perspectives: the noneschatological spiritualizing, the "consistent" eschatological (exclusively futuristic interpretation), the "realized" eschatological, and the already and not yet.
100. See, e.g., Matt. 5:19–20; 6:10, 33; 9:35; 13:19; Mark 4:30; 9:1; 10:14; Luke 1:33; 4:43; 6:20.
101. See Schreiner, *New Testament Theology*, 45, 49.

rule in the midst of people and, second, a reign over a realm, all of which will be consummated at the very end of history.[102]

An Overview of the Time Frame of the End-Time Kingdom in the Synoptic Gospels

D. A. Carson has summed up well the already–not yet framework of the kingdom that Jesus introduced, especially with respect to parables that explain the kingdom.[103] His study is limited to Matthew, though his conclusions have validity for the time scope of the kingdom in Mark and Luke. The aorist passive verb *hōmoiōthē* ("has become compared to," in Matt. 13:24; 18:23; 22:2) and the future passive verb *homoiōthēsetai* ("will become compared to," in Matt. 7:24, 26; 25:1) do not mean "to be likened to" or "to be compared with" but more precisely "to become like" or "to be like." The aorist passive verb refers to the past inaugurated kingdom, and the future passive to the not-yet-consummated kingdom.[104]

These two passive verb forms frame the eschatological time scope of the kingdom parables that they introduce. However, there are present-tense references in other parables about the kingdom that employ the noun form of the above verbs in introducing other parables: "the kingdom of heaven is like [*homoia estin*]" (Matt. 13:31, 33, 44, 45, 47; 20:1). Consequently, Carson argues that the present-tense expressions focus not on the present or future kingdom but rather on its organic wholeness (13:31, 33), its intrinsic worth (13:44, 45), its essentially gracious nature (20:1).[105] While this is the significance of the present-tense introductions, such a significance still has temporal boundaries. That is, it is a description of the entire kingdom, which has begun in the recent past, is ongoing in the present, and will be consummated in the future. Furthermore, it is significant that the other two classes of kingdom sayings refer explicitly to the past and future forms of the kingdom (employing the aorist and future verbs), and it appears suitable to have kingdom parables that relate to the present, ongoing form of the kingdom. Thus, while the parables of the kingdom introduced by "it is like" refer to the organic nature of the kingdom in its entirety, the focus may well be on the nature of the present inaugurated form of the kingdom (at least this is likely included in the references).

Therefore, these three introductory formulas for the parables focus on the conceptual relation between the already and the not yet forms of the end-time kingdom, which has been recently introduced through Jesus and his ministry.[106]

---

102. Ladd, *Presence of the Future*, 122–48.

103. D. A. Carson, "The *homoios* Word-Group as Introduction to Some Matthean Parables," *NTS* 31 (1985): 277–82.

104. The aorist passive is sometimes used and rendered as "what it [the kingdom] has become like"; likewise, the future passive is found in the rendering of "what it [the kingdom] will be like" (for the passive of *homoioō* like this, see Acts 14:11; Rom. 9:29; Heb. 2:17).

105. Some would call this a "gnomic present" use of the verb, where it is not so much time that is being indicated, but rather a general timeless fact or state of being.

106. The study by Carson contradicts the idea that "kingdom of heaven" is all future in Matthew and only references to the "kingdom of God" in Matthew have to do with the present

The Inaugurated, Unexpected, and Transformed Nature of the End-Time Kingdom

Classic examples of the inaugurated aspect of the kingdom are not hard to find. At the very beginning of Jesus's "preaching the kingdom of God" he announced, "The time is fulfilled and the kingdom of God is at hand; repent and believe in the gospel" (Mark 1:14–15). The time of the OT kingdom prophecies was beginning fulfillment. Similarly, at the very beginning of Jesus's preaching ministry according to Luke's Gospel, Jesus entered the synagogue in Nazareth and "stood up to read. And the book of the prophet Isaiah was handed to Him. And He opened the scroll" (Luke 4:16–17). He then read from Isa. 61:1–2: "The Spirit of the Lord is upon Me, because He anointed Me to preach the gospel to the poor. He has sent Me to proclaim release to the captives, and recovery of sight to the blind, to set free those who are oppressed, to proclaim the favorable year of the Lord" (Luke 4:18–19).

After reading this portion of Isaiah, Jesus said, "Today this Scripture has been fulfilled in your hearing" (Luke 4:21). This portion of Isaiah read by Jesus was part of a broader prophecy of Israel's end-time restoration from captivity, during which all the nations would be subservient to Israel. Jesus was indicating that this prophecy had begun through the very inception of his ministry. He is the one on whom is "the Spirit of the Lord," who was bringing "good news to the afflicted" and proclaiming "liberty to captives" and "freedom to prisoners" (Isa. 61:1). His defeat of Satan in the wilderness (Luke 4:1–13) had enabled his fulfillment of Isa. 61 to commence, a defeat that was further demonstrated by Jesus's power over demons (Luke 4:33–37). Thus, true and ultimate spiritual release and freedom could be announced to Israel, who was still captive in its sin, even though a remnant had returned physically from Babylonian exile.[107] The great expected latter-day restoration was beginning through Jesus, a restoration that was inextricably linked to Israel's kingdom prophecies.

Perhaps one of the most striking features of Jesus's kingdom is that it appears not to be the kind of kingdom prophesied in the OT and expected by Judaism. Part of the reason for the unexpectedness is that the kingdom had begun but was not consummated, and this lack of consummation was to continue on indefinitely. This stands in contrast to OT prophecies of the latter days whose events were predicted to occur all at once at the very end of history. This unexpectedness is perhaps most explicitly expressed in Jesus's parables about the kingdom in Matt. 13. After Jesus tells the parable of the sower and soils, his disciples ask him why he "speaks to them [the crowds] in parables" (v. 10). Jesus begins by responding, "To you it has been granted to know the mysteries of the kingdom of heaven, but to them it has not been given" (v. 11).

The reference to "mystery" (*mystērion*) in verse 11 is sandwiched between the telling of the parable of the soils and the explanation and is part of the larger interlude of verses 10–17. This interlude introduces not only the interpretation

---

form of the kingdom (which contradicts the thesis of Margaret Pamment, "The Kingdom of Heaven according to the First Gospel," *NTS* 27 [1981]: 211–32).

107. Below (chaps. 16, 20) I will explore in more depth how Israel's return from exile had begun through Jesus's coming and ministry as this is depicted in the Synoptic Gospels and Acts.

of the soils parable but also a number of other parables about the kingdom in verses 24–52. The point of the interlude is to underscore the purpose of the parables.

Verses 11–17 give reasons supporting this initial response about speaking in parables in order to communicate the "mysteries of the kingdom." The crucial word in the initial response to the disciples' question is "mysteries," which George Eldon Ladd has briefly explained against the background of Dan. 2: he says that "mystery" in Dan. 2 refers to a divine revelation about eschatological matters that is hidden from human understanding but then is revealed by God himself to the prophet, and he sees "mystery" having the same general idea in Matthew and the rest of the NT.[108] The OT, and especially Dan. 2, prophesied that the kingdom would come visibly, crush all opposition, judge all godless gentiles, and establish Israel as a kingdom ruling over all the earth. The mystery is the revelation that "in the person and mission of Jesus . . . the kingdom which is to come finally in apocalyptic power, as foreseen in Daniel, has in fact entered into the world in advance in a hidden form to work secretly within and among men."[109]

The background of the Dan. 2 mystery and kingdom is further discernible in the following additional affinities with the kingdom in Matt. 13: (1) both mysteries have an eschatological association (note "in the latter days" in Dan. 2:28); (2) both refer to the hidden unexpected interpretation of a divine message (recall that Daniel's interpretation of the giant statue in the king's dream would have been surprising to the king because it includes his own judgment); (3) both refer to people (at least in part) who do not understand the significance of the message (likely the king [despite the subsequent interpretation] and certainly his errant interpreters) in contrast to the faithful remnant of Daniel and his friends (compare those who will understand and those "outside" who will not understand in Matt. 13:11–12); (4) both have an end-time focus on God's defeat of evil world kingdoms and the establishing of an eternal kingdom associated with heaven (cf. Dan. 2:44 with Matt. 13:40–42, 49–50); (5) this defeat is accomplished by a choice stone (though not found in Matt. 13, cf. Dan. 2; 4 *Ezra* 13 with Matt. 21:42–44; Luke 20:18). In light of all the above parallels, Matt. 13:11's reference to "mystery" and the directly following parables about the mystery of the kingdom should be seen as a beginning ironic, unexpected fulfillment of the Dan. 2 mystery/kingdom prophecy. This fulfillment of the Dan. 2 prophecy is delineated in the following survey of the kingdom parables in Matt. 13 (vv. 24–52).

In addition to the Dan. 2 background for "mystery," the Isa. 6 quotation in Matt. 13:14–15 further explains Jesus's initial response to the disciples,[110] as do the following parables in Matt. 13, which contain OT allusions. Ladd explains how these parables in Matt. 13:24–52 explain the hidden or unexpected fulfill-ment of the beginning form of the prophesied OT kingdom (note the explicit

---

108. Ladd, *Presence of the Future*, 223–24; likewise A. E. Harvey, "The Use of Mystery Language in the Bible," *JTS* 31 (1980): 333.

109. Ladd, *Presence of the Future*, 225.

110. The limits of the present study prevent analysis of the Isa. 6 quotation.

notion of hiddenness in vv. 33, 44):[111] whereas the OT and Judaism expected the kingdom to come with a one-time "bang" of external manifestations of power and forcibly impose itself on people, Jesus's kingdom comes first in an inaugurated manner and instead concerns internal decisions of the heart to receive or not receive the message of the kingdom (parable of the soils). Consequently, the growth of the kingdom cannot be gauged by eyesight, since it grows invisibly (parable of the leaven).[112] In contrast to apparent OT expectations of the kingdom and that of Judaism, final judgment has not yet come, so the righteous and the wicked are not yet separated from each other but rather continue to coexist until the very end of history (parable of the tares of the field). The completed form of the kingdom is not established immediately and universally, as expected, but instead starts out tiny and then, after a process of growth, fills the world (parable of the mustard seed). Although the kingdom appears hidden, it is to be desired like a treasure or a priceless pearl.[113] Jesus's begins to express his rule by ruling over invisible enemy forces (the devil and his demonic minions) instead of defeating the visible physical forces of Israel's enemy, Rome.

Ladd's analysis of mystery in Matt. 13 is astute and convincing. The reason for the unexpected, invisible nature of the kingdom is that in the inaugurated stage the heavenly kingdom is breaking into the old, fallen world. When the very end comes, the entire world will be transformed into a new cosmos where the physical and spiritual realms completely overlap and form one reality.

Other Examples of the Unexpected and Transformed Presence of the Inaugurated Eschatological Kingdom

Matthew 11: John the Baptist, Jesus, and Entrance to the Kingdom

Matthew 11:11–13 affirms that the kingdom has come and brought new revelation:

> Truly I say to you, among those born of women there has not arisen anyone greater than John the Baptist! Yet the one who is least in the kingdom of heaven is greater than he. From the days of John the Baptist until now the kingdom of heaven suffers violence, and violent men take it by force. For all the prophets and the Law prophesied until John.

Verse 11 states that John the Baptist was the last official representative of the OT age, and that during that age there was none greater than he. But in

---

111. On which, see Ladd, *Presence of the Future*, 229–42.

112. Similarly, in Luke 17:20–21 Jesus is questioned about when God's kingdom will come, and he explains, contrary to the Pharisees' expectations, that the kingdom is already here but in an invisible manner: "Now having been questioned by the Pharisees as to when the kingdom of God was coming, He answered them and said, 'The kingdom of God is not coming with signs to be observed; nor will they say, "Look, here it is!" or, "There it is!" For behold, the kingdom of God is <u>in your midst</u>'" (or "among you" or "within you").

113. Ladd, *Presence of the Future*, 229–42.

the new age of the kingdom even the least are greater than John because "it was a greater thing to hear the good news and to receive the healing and life of the messianic salvation than to be a prophet as great as John the Baptist"[114] (esp. in light of Matt. 13:16–17). This is true because the OT promised that the blessings of the age to come would be infinitely greater than those of the OT age (so, e.g., Joel 2:28; Ezek. 39:29).

This view of Matt. 11:11 is supported from the following: (1) verse 11 contrasts those in the kingdom with John; (2) verse 12 says that since the days of John something is happening that has to do with the kingdom of God; (3) verse 13 says that an age has ended with John—the age of the law and the prophets. Therefore, John brought to an end the law and the prophets; since John, a new era has begun, and this era is called the "kingdom of heaven."[115]

Matt. 11:12 is particularly thorny: "From the days of John the Baptist until now the kingdom of heaven suffers violence [or 'makes its way powerfully'], and violent men take it by force." The verb *biazetai* (NASB: "suffers violence") can be understood in different ways,[116] but probably it is best to understand the verb as being not in the passive but in the middle voice: "the kingdom of heaven <u>exercises its force</u>" (or "makes its way powerfully"), and "violent men take it by force" refers to the positive powerful, radical reaction needed by those who desire to enter the kingdom.[117]

This view receives further support from Luke 16:16, which probably is a parallel that interprets Matt. 11:12: "The good news of the kingdom of God is preached, and every one enters it violently."[118] Luke uses *euangelizetai* instead of Matthew's *biazetai*, which results in the following sense: the power of the kingdom is expressed through the preaching of the kingdom—that is, Christ's words as well as his deeds—which requires a radical response from those who want to follow Christ and enter into the present kingdom.

Indeed, Matt. 11:2–6 supports the view of an inaugurated kingdom: John expresses uncertainty about whether Jesus is the expected Messiah because Jesus

---

114. Ibid., 201.

115. Ibid., 199–201.

116. Some take *biazetai* as a passive verb (such as "suffers violence"). Accordingly, some see that the passive refers to (1) the repentance aroused by Jesus, who would "drag" the eschatological kingdom from heaven and compel its coming; or (2) zealots trying to seize the kingdom and compel its coming; or (3) a battle between evil spirits and God's kingdom—i.e., evil spirits attacking the kingdom. The last two views understand the kingdom to suffer violence in the persons of its servants when they are persecuted or when enemies try to keep people from entering the kingdom.

117. The main objection to this view is that *biastai* in v. 12b must be taken negatively as "violent men," and therefore so too must the preceding verb *biazō* be negative and viewed as indicating actions against the kingdom. However, there are not enough uses in the NT to discern a developing pattern of the verb *biazō* or the noun *biastēs* typically being used in a negative or a positive manner. Since Jesus used radical metaphors involving physical violence to describe the positive reaction of men to the kingdom, it is consistent that *biastai* could be among these metaphors (cf. Matt. 10:34–39; 13:44; Luke 14:26). To paraphrase this view: "The kingdom of heaven acts powerfully and requires a powerful reaction."

118. Following the translation of Ladd, *Presence of the Kingdom*, 164.

apparently was not accomplishing the consummative judgment and bringing the kingdom as expected. Jesus tells John's disciples to report that he is the Messiah, but that he is introducing the kingdom in an unexpected way (vv. 6, 15, 19). It is because of this that people might be tempted to stumble over Jesus (v. 6), and one needed spiritual ears not to stumble (v. 15).[119]

Jesus's Kingship over Satan and His Demonic Forces

Jesus's beginning rule over Satan's kingdom is expressed vividly in Matt. 12:24–29:

> But when the Pharisees heard this, they said, "This man casts out demons only by Beelzebul the ruler of the demons." And knowing their thoughts Jesus said to them, "Any kingdom divided against itself is laid waste; and any city or house divided against itself will not stand. If Satan casts out Satan, he is divided against himself; how then will his kingdom stand? And if I by Beelzebul cast out demons, by whom do your sons cast them out? For this reason they will be your judges. But if I cast out demons by the Spirit of God, then the kingdom of God has come upon you. Or how can anyone enter the strong man's house and carry off his property, unless he first binds the strong man? And then he will plunder his house."

The focus here is on Jesus's continued response in verse 28 to the Pharisees who had accused him of casting out demons by the power of Satan. In verse 28 Jesus says that he "casts out demons by the Spirit of God," which is evidence that "the kingdom of God has come [*ephthasen*] upon you." Verse 29 is a metaphor of what Jesus is doing with Satan's kingdom as he is introducing his own kingdom: he is in the process of defeating the rule of Satan (the parallel of Luke 11:21–22 emphasizes the idea of conflict even more).

In a similar vein, Luke 10:17–19, discussed earlier in this chapter but relevant here also, reflects Jesus and his followers' defeat of the powers of evil:

> The seventy returned with joy, saying, "Lord, even the demons are subject to us in your name." And he said to them, "I was watching Satan fall from heaven like lightning. Behold, I have given you authority to tread on serpents and scorpions, and over all the power of the enemy, and nothing will injure you."

The basis for Jesus's followers having authority over the dominion of evil powers is Jesus's own defeat of Satan (v. 18). Jesus's victory over Satan in verse 8 may have occurred at the temptation (Matt. 4; Luke 4), or it may be a proleptic vision (prophetic past) referring either to the cross or the second coming. I agree with Ladd that Jesus saw in the successful mission of the seventy evidence of the defeat of Satan and the inauguration of God's kingdom

---

119. This overall discussion of Matt. 11:2–6, 11–13 is a distillation of Ladd, *Presence of the Future*, 158–66.

(cf. Luke 10:9, 11). Probably Jesus's reference in verse 18 is to the effect of his entire ministry, culminating in the cross and resurrection as his final individual victory over Satan.[120]

Jesus as Messianic King

Throughout this chapter, there has been reference to Jewish expectations of a Messiah and some reference to Jesus being the fulfillment of those expectations. This topic deserves further discussion here, though the parameters of the book do not allow lengthy elaboration. No doubt the Jewish expectations of a Messiah are based, at least in part, on the OT prophecies of a Messiah. Among such classic texts are Isa. 9:6–7, Mic. 5:2–5, and Ps. 110:1–4. Daniel 9:25–26 predicts the coming of the "Messiah," who "will be cut off" (the LXX renders this "will be destroyed"). It would appear plausible to identify the "Messiah" of Dan. 9 with the "Son of Man" of Dan. 7:13. It is likely that the earliest Christian community would have viewed this prophecy of Dan. 9 to have been fulfilled in Jesus's death at the cross, though Dan. 9 is never explicitly identified in this manner.

We will see later (chap. 22 under the heading "The Expected Universalization of the Old Testament Land Promises within the Old Testament Itself") that Ps. 72:17 is a development of the reiterated Gen. 1:28 commission and is applied to the coming end-time king, who will rule the entire world, though the word Messiah does not appear there (see likewise Zech. 9:9–10). Similarly, we will also see there that in Ps. 2 God promised the "Messiah" (Ps. 2:2, 7) to "give the nations as your inheritance and the ends of the earth as your possession" (2:8). The language of "inheritance" and "possession" allude to the partriarchal promises to give Israel the land of Canaan. As we have seen, these patriarchal promises are also linked to the reiterated Gen. 1:28 commission.

Accordingly, the messianic promises in these psalms are linked to a coming king who will participate in fulfilling the commission to Adam, a commission that we have seen is repeated in the Pentateuch and elsewhere in the OT (see chap. 2 under the subheading "The Passing On of Adam's Commission to His Descendants"). This conclusion would be enhanced if the Dan. 7 "Son of Man [Adam]" is to be identified with the "Messiah" of Dan. 9.

Jesus is referred to as the Messiah or Christ throughout the Gospels. These identifications of Jesus as the Messiah would appear to be linked, at least some of the time and to some degree to the above OT expectations of the messianic king as one who would rule the earth, thus fulfilling the expectations to which the first Adamic king did not attain. Recall especially the discussion at the

120. On which, see Ladd, *Presence of the Future*, 157. John places Jesus's victory over Satan at the cross (John 12:31–33; 16:11; cf. 16:33). Note the connection of Jesus's victory over Satan in John 12:31–33 with the inauguration of the kingdom in the nearby preceding context (John 12:13, 15, 23).

beginning of this chapter[121] with respect to the phrase "The book of the genealogy of Jesus Christ [Messiah]" in Matt. 1:1. We found that there are only two places in the entire Old Testament where the phrase *biblos geneseoœs* ("Book of the genealogy") occurs: Gen. 2:4 and 5:1–2, both in connection to Adam, especially Gen. 5:1 ("This is the book of generation of Adam"). Matthew's expression thus appears to be an intentional allusion to these two statements early in the book of Genesis, especially the latter. Since Matthew is narrating a genealogy of Jesus, we concluded that it is likely that the Gen. 5:1 reference is uppermost in mind and that Jesus as the "Messiah" is being painted with the genealogical brush of Adam.[122]

Excursus 2 Jesus as the Messianic King and the Last Adam/Son of Man and Son of God, Who Restores the Divine Image in John's Gospel

I believe that the conclusions in this chapter about Jesus as the messianic king and especially the Last Adam/Son of Man, Son of God, and true Israel who restores God's image in humanity would not be changed if we also pursued exploration of these topics in John's Gospel. Nevertheless, the evidence for our conclusions would be enhanced and further illuminated by such an investigation of the Gospel of John. Unfortunately, the limits of the present book do not allow the kind of study we would like to conduct, including an interaction with the literature written on this topic.[123]

121. See under the earlier subheading "The Beginning of Matthew and of the Other Gospels Introduces Christ as the End-Time Adam Inaugurating the New Creation."

122. See Stuhlmacher, *Biblische Theologie*, vol. 1, chaps. 9 and 12, for further discussion of Jesus as "Messiah," where also Jewish background for a Messiah is discussed, as is the relation of Jesus as "Messiah" in relation to the "Son of Man." Likewise, see ibid., chap. 14, for a good concise discussion of Jesus's titles of "Lord," "Christ," and "Son of God."

123. See, e.g., Schreiner, *New Testament Theology*, 226–29, who concludes that John says substantially the same things about the Son of Man as in the Synoptics, though with distinctive language; likewise, see Donald Guthrie, *New Testament Theology* (Leicester: Inter-Varsity Press, 1981), 282–90, who says John's view of the Son of Man is in substantial agreement with that of the Synoptics, though it contributes some features that draw out more explicitly what is in the Synoptics. Similarly, George Eldon Ladd, *A Theology of the New Testament* (Grand Rapids: Eerdmans, 1974), 246, concludes that John "supplements but does not contradict the Synoptic tradition." John's presentation of Jesus as the "Son of God" does have more distinctiveness than in the Synoptics, especially with respect to the focus on Jesus's self-consciousness that he is God's son, but this "makes explicit what was implicit in the Synoptics (ibid., 247; so likewise Guthrie, *New Testament Theology*, 312).

14

The Inaugurated End-Time Restoration of God's Image in Humanity

Paul, Hebrews, and Revelation

Having already reviewed the threefold aspect of the Adamic commission and some of the most relevant Jewish background concerning Adam's glory and image at the beginning of the previous chapter, we may now examine Paul's understanding of God's image in relation to the coming of Christ and the effect on his people. And, as with the Synoptic Gospels in the preceding chapter, Paul sees that Jesus came to do what the first Adam should have done. That is, Jesus's establishment of the new creation and kingdom had to be done by reflecting the functional image of God. In so doing, Jesus represents his people, so they too can be formed into God's end-time image. This notion, as in the preceding chapter, continues to develop the penultimate part of my proposed biblical-theological storyline of new creation and kingdom building.

Paul is the only NT author who explicitly says that Christ is in the image of God and is an eschatological Adam,[1] and at least once he makes both statements together.

The Image of the Last Adam in Paul's Writings

The Image of the Last Adam in 1 Corinthians 15

First Corinthians 15:45–54 is the only passage in which Paul mentions both Jesus as "the last Adam" and as being in an "image." There are many

---

1. Although, as we will see below, Heb. 1–2 comes very close to expressing the same thing.

difficulties in this passage, but the intent here is to focus on Christ as the one who regains the original image of Adam and transforms his people into that image. The relevant section begins in verse 35, where questions about the manner and nature of the resurrection are raised. The beginning of the answer refers to a contrast to glorious and inglorious realities in creation (vv. 36–41). Verses 42–44 directly apply these contrasting creational realities to the contrast between corruptible human bodies and incorruptible ones, which have been raised from the dead. Verses 45–50 give as the apex of this contrast the antithesis between the first Adam and the last Adam:

> So also it is written, "The first man, Adam, became a living soul." The last Adam became a life-giving spirit. However, the spiritual is not first, but the natural; then the spiritual. The first man is from the earth, earthy; the second man is from heaven. As is the earthy, so also are those who are earthy; and as is the heavenly, so also are those who are heavenly. Just as we have borne the image of the earthy, we will also bear the image of the heavenly. Now I say this, brethren, that flesh and blood cannot inherit the kingdom of God; nor does the perishable inherit the imperishable.

There is, at least, an antithetical comparison between the two figures in this passage in its context of 1 Cor. 15 (see table 14.1).

Table 14.1

First Adam	Last Adam
death results (v. 22)	life results
perishable body results (v. 42)	imperishability results
dishonor results (v. 43a)	glory results
weakness results (v. 43b)	power results
natural body results (v. 44)	spiritual body results
"cannot inherit kingdom of God" (v. 50)	

The comparison[2] may even verge into a typological connection: the first Adam was a foreshadowing counterpart to the last Adam (Rom. 5:14 even uses *typos* ["type"] of the first Adam, "who is a type of him who was to come"). There is debate about whether typology is primarily analogy or whether it includes a prefigurative element. I have argued elsewhere that the latter is the case.[3] This

2. I recollect having seen this comparison somewhere, but I have not been able to locate it. See David E. Garland, *1 Corinthians*, BECNT (Grand Rapids: Baker Academic, 2003), 733–34, which contains a similar table that is conceptually unpacked quite similarly in the paragraph that follows it (I thank Seth Ehorn, one of my research students, for finding the Garland reference).

3. For the debate, see the articles by David L. Baker, G. P. Hugenberger, and Francis Foulkes in *The Right Doctrine from the Wrong Texts? Essays on the Use of the Old Testament in the New*, ed. G. K. Beale (Grand Rapids: Baker Academic, 1994).

appears to be fitting for the passage at hand.[4] Adam's death-bringing sin ultimately necessitated its reversal in another Adam, who would perform a life-giving act.[5] And just as the earthy, corruptible progeny are like their corruptible parent, Adam, so also are those who are related to the heavenly last Adam (vv. 47–49). The climaxing statement of these last three verses affirms that although redeemed people have "borne the image of the earthy [the first Adam]," they "will also bear the image of the heavenly [the last Adam]" (v. 49).

Thus, there is a clear reference in verses 45–49 to Christ as an eschatological Adam and to those who will bear his "image."[6] It is through Christ becoming a "life-giving Spirit" that he transforms his people into his image. The point is not that he becomes ontologically transformed into a purely "spirit being"; rather, in his physically resurrected condition, which certainly is transformed in comparison to preresurrection bodies, he becomes functionally identified with the Spirit, who raised him from the dead (Rom. 1:4). This functional identification with the Spirit enables him to perform the eschatologically transforming work of the Spirit, who is raising people from the dead. The notion is very similar to Acts 2:32–33, where by virtue of his resurrection Christ pours forth the Spirit and transforms people at Pentecost.[7]

The following discussion of believers being "changed" (vv. 51–52) because they will "put on" (or "don the clothes of") the incorruptible (vv. 53–54) is a further elaboration of being transformed into the image of the imperishable last Adam (as we will see in the discussion below on Col. 3:9–10). The clothing image probably begins in verse 49, where the notion of "bearing the image"

4. On which, see G. K. Beale, "Did Jesus and His Followers Preach the Right Doctrine from the Wrong Texts? An Examination of the Presuppositions of the Apostles' Exegetical Method," *Themelios* 14 (1989): 89–96. Two indicators point to the prefigurative element here. (1) "For since by a man came death, by a man also came the resurrection of the dead" (v. 21). This is given as the reason (*gar*, "for") why v. 20 affirms that Christ had been raised from the dead as "the first fruits of those who are asleep." That is, Christ was raised from the dead as the progenitor of a resurrection race *because* the first Adam died and brought death to his progeny. (2) A "first" Adam implies the necessity of a second or "last" Adam (some have said in this connection that protology implies eschatology). Verse 45 appears to draw out the logic in this second point, especially if the concluding clause about the "last Adam" is seen to be part of Paul's attempt to unpack the original thick meaning of Gen. 2:7. In this respect, the introductory "it is written" may introduce not only the clause about the first Adam but also the one about the last Adam. If so, then Paul saw Adam in Gen. 2:7 as a type of the last Adam (on this line of argumentation, see Richard B. Gaffin Jr., *The Centrality of the Resurrection: A Study in Paul's Soteriology* [Grand Rapids: Baker Academic, 1978], 79–82).

5. Anthony Thiselton reaches a similar conclusion and says that "the 'old' creation *requires* not merely 'correction' but a new beginning in new creation" (*The First Epistle to the Corinthians: A Commentary on the Greek Text*, NIGTC [Grand Rapids: Eerdmans, 2000], 182) (my italics). See also Gaffin, *Centrality of the Resurrection*, 82n14, following Geerhardus Vos.

6. Thiselton (*First Epistle to the Corinthians*, 1289–90) sees v. 49 to be an anticipation of Rom. 8:29 ("For those whom He foreknew, He also predestined to become conformed to the image of His Son, that He would be the firstborn among many brethren").

7. Gaffin, *Centrality of the Resurrection*, 85–92.

really connotes "wearing the image" (much as one wears a coat of arms or badge).[8] This discussion of Christ and his people coming to be in the end-time image of God through resurrection is another way to speak of new creation, since the new creation will be an incorruptible and imperishable state. The fallen image of the first Adam is rectified through the resurrection of Christ, which, as we have seen repeatedly, is a synonymous notion with new creation. In fact, Christ does not merely regain the fallen image of God in Adam; he restores it to an eschatological stage beyond which the first Adam experienced (i.e., a stage of incorruptibility).[9]

It is unlikely a coincidence that, just as we saw in Gen. 1–2, Adam was created in God's image to function as a king advancing God's kingdom in a new creation, so Paul speaks about Christ and those with his image as being in the kingdom of a new creation through resurrection existence. In particular, the clear implication of verse 50 is that the resurrection of Christ's people will cause them to inherit the kingdom, whereas Christ's resurrection is explicitly described earlier as the event that inaugurates his kingdom in the present, which will be consummated at the resurrection of all "those who are Christ's at His coming" (vv. 20–28). The first Adam also had a confrontation with an enemy in which he lost and consequently suffered death, whereas in 1 Cor. 15 the last Adam gains victory over his enemies, and the ultimate enemy, death (vv. 25–27, 54–57). Believers who identify with Christ's resurrection share in this victory (vv. 54, 57). In the midst of the earlier discussion of Christ's resurrection inaugurating the kingdom (v. 27), it is natural that Paul cites Ps. 8:7 LXX (8:6 MT) ("For he has put all things in subjection under his feet"), which is the clearest elaboration of Gen. 1:26–28 in all of the OT. Adam's sin resulted in his toil being in vain (Gen. 3:17–19), but the Christian's "immovable" identification with the last Adam results in the "toil" not being "in vain" (1 Cor. 15:58).

The 1 Cor. 15 passage thus gives us a genuinely striking antithetical counterpart to the first Adam of Gen. 1–3. This is a prime example of how Paul's understanding of the image of God regained in Christ is a facet of the establishment of the new-creational kingdom. Although Rom. 5:12–21 does not mention the image of God or of Adam, it is quite similar to 1 Cor. 15:45–50 in its contrast of Christ with the first Adam, who is a "type of Him [Christ] who was to come" (Rom. 5:14). The first Adam disobeyed and as a representative brought condemnation to all, whereas the last Adam obeyed and as a

8. Thiselton, *First Epistle to the Corinthians*, 1289–90. For the clothing imagery in vv. 49–54 and the notion that v. 49 refers to "wearing" the restored Adamic image of God, which is the transformed resurrection existence on a more escalated level than even that of the first Adam before the fall, see also Jung Hoon Kim, *The Significance of Clothing Imagery in the Pauline Corpus*, JSNTSup 268 (London: T&T Clark, 2004), 197–200. For virtually the same metaphorical "clothing" language used of the image of God, see the discussion of Col. 3:9–10 below.

9. On this notion, see again Gaffin, *Centrality of the Resurrection*, 82n14.

representative brought justification to all who believe in him. There may be some connection with the concept of the image of God in Rom. 6:4–6, which certainly is logically and thematically linked to the preceding discussion in chapter 5. Romans 6:4–6 reads,

> Therefore we have been buried with Him through baptism into death, so that as Christ was raised from the dead through the glory of the Father, so we too might walk in newness of life. For if we have become united with Him in the likeness of His death, certainly we shall also be in the likeness of His resurrection, knowing this, that our old man was crucified with Him, in order that our body of sin might be done away with, so that we would no longer be slaves to sin.

In verse 4 believers are identified with Christ's death in order that they might "walk in newness of life," thus resembling Christ, who "was raised from the dead through the glory of the Father." This is explained in verse 5 as being "united with Him in the likeness [*homoiōma*] of his death" and "of his resurrection." Verse 6 says that identification with Christ means that "our old man" (i.e., the former identification with the old Adam) was destroyed in Christ, so that the new existence is described as "newness of life" (v. 4), which is identification with Christ (which Rom. 5 has identified as the converse of the old Adam or, by implication, the new Adam) in his resurrection existence.

Believers' identification with and "likeness" to Christ here appears to be developed later in Rom. 8:29: "For those whom He foreknew, He also predestined <u>to become conformed to the image of His Son, that He would be the firstborn among many brethren</u>." In Rom. 8:12–30 the language of Christians being in Christ's "image" (8:29), possessing "sonship" (8:14–15, 19, 23), and having "glory" (8:17–18, 21, 30) strongly echoes the Gen. 1 creation narrative. As we saw in chapter 2, Adam was God's son created in his image to reflect his glory.[10] The thought packed into Rom. 8:29 is the following: in being resurrected, Christ was declared to be the Son of God (Rom. 1:4), who, as the last Adam, fully represents God's image and reflects his glory, and believers are in union with the resurrected Christ and thus also reflect God's (and Christ's) image and glory and become adopted sons.[11] That "glory" and "image" are virtually synonymous here is in line with such synonymity elsewhere in Paul's writings (1 Cor. 11:7; 2 Cor. 3:18; 4:4), elsewhere in the NT (Heb. 1:3), the OT (Ps. 106:20), and Judaism (Philo, *Spec.* 4.164; 4Q504 frg. 8, I:4).[12]

---

10. Here I follow J. R. Daniel Kirk, *Unlocking Romans: Resurrection and the Justification of God* (Grand Rapids: Eerdmans, 2008), 135, 137, 139, 141–43, 148–49, which has reminded me of the connections between Gen. 1 and Rom. 8.

11. So also ibid., 143.

12. Cf. also Rom. 3:23; *L.A.E.* [*Vita*] 12:1; 16:2; 17:1; *L.A.E.* [*Apocalypse*] 20:2; 21:6, where "glory" is used by itself but is equivalent to the image of God; note, e.g., *L.A.E.* [*Apocalypse*] 20:2: "You [the serpent] have deprived me [Eve] of the glory with which I was clothed."

The Image of the Last Adam in Colossians 1:15–18; 3:9–10

The so-called poem of Col. 1:15–20 has received more attention from commentators than any other passage in the epistle. I will address this passage first and Col. 3 afterward. Here I can give only a brief analysis of Col. 1:15–18 and some of the main lines of past interpretation.[13] If the conclusion of most scholars is correct that here Paul is alluding to a preexisting hymn, then Paul has adapted it to fit into the context of what he is writing.[14] Since we do not have the context of the preexisting hymn against which to interpret Paul's use, we must concentrate on how Paul is using the wording in its context. As we investigate the hymn, we will see how its themes are developments of the preceding context. Most directly, verses 15–20 are an explanation of the directly preceding verses 13b–14: "the Son of His love, in whom we have the redemption, the forgiveness of sins."[15]

The verses can be broadly divided into two sections: Christ's supremacy over the first creation (vv. 15–17) and Christ's supremacy over the new creation (vv. 18–20), which I discussed at the end of chapter 10.

> He is the image of the invisible God, the firstborn of all creation. For by Him all things were created, both in the heavens and on earth, visible and invisible, whether thrones or dominions or rulers or authorities—all things have been created through Him and for Him. He is before all things, and in Him all things hold together.
>
> He is also head of the body, the church; and He is the beginning, the firstborn from the dead, so that He Himself will come to have first place in everything. For it was the Father's good pleasure for all the fullness to dwell in Him, and through Him to reconcile all things to Himself, having made peace through the blood of His cross; through him, I say, whether things on earth or things in heaven.

13. For further discussion of the poem and its background and meaning, see Peter T. O'Brien, *Colossians, Philemon*, WBC 44 (Waco: Word, 1982), 31–32; N. T. Wright, *The Epistles of Paul to the Colossians and to Philemon*, TNTC (Grand Rapids: Eerdmans, 1986), 63–80; John M. G. Barclay, *Colossians and Philemon: A Commentary*, NTG (Sheffield: Sheffield Academic Press, 1997), 56–68; Michael Wolter, *Der Brief an die Kolosser, der Brief an Philemon*, ÖTK (Gütersloh: Mohn, 1993), 70–71; James D. G. Dunn, *The Epistles to the Colossians and to Philemon: A Commentary on the Greek Text*, NIGTC (Grand Rapids: Eerdmans, 1996), 83–104; Hans Hübner, *An Philemon, an die Kolosser, an die Epheser*, HNT 12 (Tübingen: Mohr Siebeck, 1997), 55; for a convenient bibliography on the hymn, see Petr Pokorný, *Colossians: A Commentary*, trans. Siegfried S. Schatzmann (Peabody, MA: Hendrickson, 1991), 56–57; Eduard Lohse, *A Commentary on the Epistles to the Colossians and to Philemon*, trans. William R. Poehlmann and Robert J. Karris, ed. Helmut Koester, Hermeneia (Philadelphia: Fortress, 1975), 41.

14. For significant qualifications about this passage being based on a preformed hymn, see O'Brien, *Colossians, Philemon*, 32–37.

15. The remainder of this section on Colossians is a slight revision of G. K. Beale, "Colossians," in *Commentary on the New Testament Use of the Old Testament*, ed. G. K. Beale and D. A. Carson (Grand Rapids: Baker Academic, 2007), 851–55, 865–68.

AN ADAMIC BACKGROUND FOR THE PORTRAYAL OF CHRIST: "THE IMAGE OF GOD"

A number of commentators rightly understand that the reference to Christ as the "image of the invisible God" (Col. 1:15) is, at least in part, an allusion to Gen. 1:2: "God created man in his own image, in the image of God he created him" (LXX: "God made man according to the image of God"). Paul's language here is virtually identical with his reference elsewhere to "man" being in "the image and glory of God" (1 Cor. 11:7, where clear allusion is made to Gen. 1:27).[16] Paul's thought may have been led to this reference, not only because of the repeated allusion to Gen. 1:28 in the preceding context (Col. 1:6, 10) but also because of the mention of "Son" in verse 13: the relative pronoun "who" (*hos*), like that in verse 14 ("whom," *hō*), has its antecedent in "the Son of His love" in verse 13. Sonship, as we noted earlier, is sometimes inextricably linked to the Gen. 1 notion of God's image. For example, as we have already observed in earlier chapters, Gen. 5:1–4 implies that Adam's being in God's image means that Adam was God's son, since when Adam's son was born, Adam was said be the "father of [a son] in his own likeness, according to his image" (Gen. 5:3).

Early Judaism sometimes closely associated the notions of Adam's sonship and his being in God's image, sometimes even referring to his being the image of the "invisible" God. *Life of Adam and Eve [Apocalypse]* (ca. AD 100) refers to God as Adam's "unseen Father" because "he is your image" (35:2–3). Philo (*Plant.* 18–19), who stresses only the aspect of the "image," also underscores that Adam was created "to be a genuine coinage of that dread Spirit, the Divine and Invisible One," and that he "has been made after the image of God [Gen. 1:27], not however after the image of anything created."[17] As a second Adam figure, Noah is viewed as being given the original Adamic commission from Gen. 1:28 and, accordingly, is said to be "born to be the likeness of God's power and visible image of the invisible [*eikōn tēs aoratou*] nature" of God (Philo, *Mos.* 2.65[18] [cf. Col. 1:15: *eikōn tou theou tou aoratou*]).

Paul either independently interprets the OT notion of the Adamic image along the same lines as does Judaism or he follows the interpretative trajectory begun in earlier Judaism. Either way, he sees that Christ was the image of God before creation and still is God's image, though now this has been functionally enhanced in a redemptive-historical manner. Christ has come in human

---

16. On 1 Cor. 11:7, see Gordon D. Fee, *First Epistle to the Corinthians*, NICNT (Grand Rapids: Eerdmans, 1987), 515.

17. Likewise, Philo says, "the invisible Deity stamped on the invisible soul the impress of Itself, to the end that not even the terrestrial region should be without a share in the image of God" (*Det.* 86–87).

18. This is my translation; the LCL edition has "born to be the likeness of God's power and image of his nature, the visible of the Invisible."

form and accomplished that which the first Adam did not; consequently, as the divine and ideal human, Christ reflects the image that Adam and others should have reflected but did not.

A clear link to Gen. 1:26–27 in Col. 1:15 is also indicated in that precisely the same phrase "who is the image of God" occurs in 2 Cor. 4:4, where it probably is referring to Christ as the pristine image of that which the first Adam should have been, since 4:6 ("Light shall shine out of darkness") cites Gen. 1:3 in further explanation of 4:4.[19] Furthermore, as in Col. 3:10, so also 2 Cor. 3:18 refers to Christians becoming "transformed" into this "image." Also strikingly similar to Col. 1:15 is Rom. 8:29, which echoes Gen. 1:27 (note the allusion to Gen. 3:17–19 in Rom. 8:20): Christ is both "the image" (to which believers become "conformed") and the "firstborn." Within the context of Col. 1:15–17, Christ's preexistence certainly is being affirmed, though the focus in verse 15a is on his present condition of being the divine image and being firstborn ("he is the image").[20]

Hence, the stress in this first phrase of Col. 1:15 is on Christ as the incarnate revelation of the invisible God. This incarnational revelatory emphasis is also pointed to by Col. 1:12–14, where the exodus redemption background has been applied to God's redemption of people through his Son. Indeed, verse 15 continues to describe the "Son," who accomplished redemption and forgiveness for his people.[21] Likewise, 1 Cor. 15:45–49 portrays Christ possessing the heavenly image of the last Adam, which Christians will fully reflect at his final parousia. To see Col. 1:15 primarily against the background of Genesis is a line of interpretation followed by many commentators, though a few strongly resist it.[22] However, it is difficult not to see "image" in Col. 1:15 having the same background and meaning as "image" in Rom. 8:29; 2 Cor. 4:4; 1 Cor. 15:45–49.

But even if the thought here is only of Christ being in God's image before creation began, the identification with being the ideal Adam still holds: if the exalted Christ was the full expression of God's image, then he had always been the divine image. Hence, "the one who can be described in Adamic language (Gen. 1:27) can also be held to have existed before Adam

19. Philippians 2:6–7, where it is said that Christ "existed in the form of God . . . and coming about in the likeness of men," apparently has the same significance as 2 Cor. 4:4.

20. Many commentators believe that the figurative portrayal of Wisdom in Judaism and in Prov. 8:22–27 (as "the beginning of His way" prior to the creation) lies behind Col. 1:15–17. For discussion of this possible background, see Beale, "Colossians," 855, 857. There, I contend that such a background is not necessarily mutually exclusive of a Gen. 1 Adam background, though others are adamant that only the Wisdom background is in mind and not Adam in Genesis.

21. So also N. T. Wright, *The Climax of the Covenant: Christ and the Law in Pauline Theology* (Minneapolis: Fortress, 1992), 109.

22. See, e.g., Jean-Noël Aletti, *Saint Paul, Épître aux Colossiens: Introduction, traduction et commentaire*, EBib 20 (Paris: Gabalda, 1993), 94–116.

and to have been on the side of the Creator as well as on the side of the creation."[23] This pattern appears to be present in Phil. 2:6–7, where Christ is said to have "existed in the form of God" before his incarnation, and then he "came to be in the likeness of men," both phrases of which many commentators now view to have an Adamic identification.[24] N. T. Wright has noted that it is appropriate that Christ in his preincarnate divine state could be said to be God's image, since the task of the ideal man who would represent Israel and save the world is one that the OT also attributes to God; indeed, the glorious authority of the ideal man (in fulfillment of Gen. 1:26–28; Ps. 8; Dan. 7:13–14) is (according to Isa. 45) thoroughly suitable for God himself.[25] It may well be that describing Christ's preincarnate condition with the word "image" is a way to portray him "as being, so to speak, a potential man."[26] Just as 2 Cor. 8:9 can refer to the preexistent Messiah by his subsequent incarnate name "Lord Jesus Christ," so is the case with calling the preexistent Christ the human "image" of God, "much as we might say 'the Queen was born in 1925'"[27] or "'the Prime Minister studied economics at Oxford.'"[28]

It seems best, then, to see Christ as God's "image" in Col. 1:15 to point to his sonship and incarnate "revealing of the Father on the one hand and his pre-existence on the other—it is both functional and ontological."[29] Nevertheless, as we will see, the notion of Christ's preexistence is also in mind because the remainder of Col. 1:15–17 indicates that Christ's existence at the beginning of the first creation is in mind. The same dual concept occurs in John 1:1–18; Phil. 2:6–11; Heb. 1:2–2:9.

But in the unlikely event that an Adamic Gen. 1 background is not in mind in Col. 1:15, the second part of the passage (1:18), affirming Christ's role in the new creation, would likely make the point that he is the new Adam and, by implication, represents the divine image the way the first Adam should have. This is pointed to further by Col. 3:10–11 (on which, see below), where Christ is probably portrayed as being the image of the "new man," according to which believers are being renewed. If there is a link between 1:15 and 3:10, which is likely, then understanding the Adamic nature of the image in 1:15 naturally follows.

23. Andrew T. Lincoln, "Colossians," *NIB* 11:597.
24. See, e.g., Wright, *Climax of the Covenant*, 56–98 (esp. 57–62, 90–97).
25. Ibid., 95.
26. Ibid. This is a conclusion that Wright makes about Christ being in "the form of God" in Phil. 2:6.
27. Ibid., 116.
28. Ibid., 98.
29. O'Brien, *Colossians, Philemon*, 44, though "ontological" does not necessarily exclude "functional." It is better here to refer to Christ's existence at the time of the "first creation" and at the time of the "new creation," which includes functional, ontological, and temporal categories.

AN ADAMIC BACKGROUND FOR THE PORTRAYAL OF CHRIST: "THE FIRSTBORN"

The reference directly following in the second line of Col. 1:15 to Christ as the "firstborn [*prōtotokos*] of all creation" highlights and explains further the idea that he was an Adamic figure, in God's image and the "son" of God. The OT repeatedly asserts that the firstborn of every Israelite family gained authority by virtue of being given the inheritance rights. This notion was projected back on the first Adam by early Judaism, since Adam was the firstborn of all human creation.[30] By a similar application, Christ is the last Adam, who is the firstborn, not only of all humanity in the new creation (on which, see on Col. 1:18 below) but also of "all [things in the old] creation."

Even Israel was called God's "firstborn" (*prōtogonos*).[31] The reason why the nation was given this name probably is that the nation was given the same mandate (Gen. 1:28) as Adam and Noah, the latter a second Adam figure. Accordingly, as we have observed repeatedly, Israel was a corporate Adam figure that was to accomplish the same purposes as Adam. Colossians 1:15 shows Christ summing up the purposes of both OT figures, thus being a ruler in the way Adam and Israel were to have been in reflecting God's image (see Gen. 1:28).

Thus, it is understandable that Ps. 88 LXX (89 ET) referred to the coming eschatological messianic king of Israel as having God as his "father" and being "firstborn [*prōtotokos*]" and inheriting a position "higher than the kings of the earth," with a "throne" that lasts "forever" (Ps. 88:27–29, 36–37 LXX).[32] "Firstborn" in Col. 1:15 probably includes allusion to this psalm passage.[33] Paul affirms that Christ is the fulfillment of the psalm prophecy. Later Judaism understood that Ps. 88 could refer to the coming eschatological king on analogy with Exod.

---

30. See, e.g., *Num. Rab.* 4.8, where the reason that "firstborn" Israelites were redeemed by Levites and received the "birthright" is because "Adam was the world's firstborn" who served as a priest, as did his representative progeny until the Levites were established.

31. Accordingly, Israel was "likened to a firstborn [*prōtogonos*]" (Sir. 36:17 [36:11 LXX]); Israel was also God's "firstborn, only begotten" (*4 Ezra* 6:58), his "beloved son and . . . firstborn" (*Pss. Sol.* 13:9), and "a firstborn son, an only child" (*Pss. Sol.* 18:4). So also Philo, *Fug.* 208: "Israel, the son free-born and first-born" [*prōtogonos*], though this refers to Jacob, who is called "Israel," and is Israel's progenitor, who corporately represents and embodies the subsequent nation Israel. See Robert W. Wall, *Colossians and Philemon*, IVPNTC (Downers Grove, IL: InterVarsity, 1993), 67–68. Wall sees both the law of primogeniture and Israel as firstborn as part of the background for Paul's expression.

32. See J. B. Lightfoot, *Saint Paul's Epistles to the Colossians and to Philemon*, rev. ed., CCL (Grand Rapids: Eerdmans, 1961), 147. Lightfoot also cites the parallel of Heb. 12:23, "church of the firstborn," which likely connotes the church being in an exalted position of inheriting eschatological blessings.

33. See T. K. Abbott, *A Critical and Exegetical Commentary on the Epistles to the Ephesians and to the Colossians*, ICC (New York: Charles Scribner's Sons, 1905), 210; also seeing an echo of the psalm are E. K. Simpson and F. F. Bruce, *Commentary on the Epistles to the Ephesians and the Colossians*, NICNT (Grand Rapids: Eerdmans, 1957), 194; O'Brien, *Colossians, Philemon*, 43.

4:22, where God says of the nation, "Israel is my son, my firstborn" (*Exod. Rab.* 19.7, the context of which primarily identifies the patriarch Jacob with "Israel," who then is compared by analogy to the coming Messiah). In this respect, there also may be some kind of underlying connection in Ps. 88 with Adam as a firstborn king over the earth. What points further to a Ps. 88 allusion is the use of *christos* twice in the psalm (88:39, 52 LXX) to refer to Israel and the use of the verbal form (*chriō*) to refer to David and, implicitly, to the coming Davidic seed who will be the eschatological representative king of the nation (see 88:20–29, 35–37 LXX). Although "Christ" as a name does not occur in the poem of Col. 1:15–20, it does appear repeatedly in the nearby context (1:1–4, 7, 24, 27–28).[34]

The additional reference to Christ as "before all things" (Col. 1:17a) further highlights his role as "firstborn" of all creation (Col. 1:15). The three descriptions for Christ in verses 15–17 ("image of God," "firstborn," "before all things") are thus different ways to refer to Christ as an end-time Adam, since they were common ways of referring to the first Adam or to those who were Adam-like figures and were given the first Adam's task, whether this be Noah, the patriarchs, or the nation of Israel. And just as Adam's temporal priority was not the main point of his purpose but contributed to his ultimate design to be a world ruler, so these names in Colossians were not intended merely to indicate Christ's temporal priority to the old creation but primarily underscored his sovereignty over it.[35] The pretemporal connotation indicates not that Christ was the very first part of the creation but rather that he was "born before it,"[36] which places Christ as separate from the rest of the creation; Christ's separateness from creation is underscored by the affirmation that he is the Creator.[37]

It is this point of world sovereignty that Ps. 88 LXX (89 ET) underscores about the "firstborn" messianic king. In particular, "I will make him firstborn" in Ps. 88:28 LXX (89:27 ET) is directly followed by the phrase "higher than the kings of the earth," showing, at the least, that the two notions of temporal priority

34. Similarly, Philo strikingly refers to the highest ranking angelic figure (one "who holds the eldership among the angels, an archangel as it were") as "God's First-born . . . 'the Beginning' . . . the Man after His image . . . that is Israel", and people who want to be represented by this angelic figure can become "sons of God" (citing Deut. 14:1; 32:18) and "sons of His invisible image . . . [who] is the eldest-born image of God" (*Conf.* 145–147 [see also Philo, *Somn.* 1.215; *Agr.* 51; *Conf.* 62–63]). The angel probably was conceived to be Israel's heavenly representative.

35. Likewise the significance of "firstborn" Israelites was that they gained authority over the household and inheritance, and each of Philo's references to the highest-ranking angel called "firstborn" also emphasizes this (except for *Somn.* 1.215).

36. Rightly according to C. F. D. Moule, *The Epistles of Paul to the Colossians and to Philemon*, CGTC (Cambridge: Cambridge University Press, 1957), 76, in the sense of the "eternal generation of the son."

37. E. F. Scott, *The Epistles of Paul to the Colossians, to Philemon and to the Ephesians*, MNTC (London: Hodder & Stoughton, 1948), 21.

and sovereignty are inextricably linked, if not the latter being a further explanation of the former.[38]

This position of authority is also grounded in the acknowledgment that Christ is the sovereign Creator of the world (Col. 1:16, where an introductory *hoti* occurs) and sovereignly maintains its ongoing existence (1:17b). Therefore, Christ perfectly embodies the ruling position that Adam and his flawed human successors should have held. He is, at the same time, the perfect divine Creator of all things, who is separate from and sovereign over that which he has created, which is especially underscored by the phrase "all things have been created through him and for him" at the end of 1:16.[39]

As is widely recognized, while Col. 1:15–17 refers to Christ's sovereignty over the first creation, 1:18–20 affirms his sovereign position in the second, new creation that has been launched. In this respect, the identical title of "firstborn" is reapplied in order to indicate again Christ's rule over the new order by virtue of his resurrection from the dead (v. 18c). His priority in the new creation entails his kingship over it (for relevant parallels, see Heb. 1:2–5; 2:5–9). Once again we find the notion of Christ's resurrection being the beginning of the new creation and also indicating his kingly sovereignty over it.

The reasons given for Christ's position of rule in the new age are stated in Col. 1:19–20: (1) he is the full expression of God (amplified in 2:9 as "the fullness of Deity dwells in bodily form"), and (2) he has inaugurated the process of bringing creation back into harmonious relation to itself and to God (i.e., "reconciling"). Paul portrays Christ as both God and end-time Adam in the flesh in order to affirm that "Jesus fulfills the purposes which God had marked out *both* for himself *and* for humanity."[40] The design for humanity originally reaches its completion in the last Adam. The first Adam's failure left a gap of needed obedience for humanity to reach its eschatological completion, so that even the first Adam's disobedience typologically pointed to another Adam's obedience.

The Image of the Last Adam in Colossians 3:9–10

On the basis ("therefore," *oun* [v. 5]) of believers' identification with Christ's death and resurrection (3:1–4), Paul exhorts them to live like resurrected new creatures and not like those who belong to the old world (3:5–4:6). In 3:9–10 Paul says,

> Do not lie to one another, since you laid aside the old man with its evil practices, and have put on the new man who is being renewed to a true knowledge according to the image of the One who created him.

38. As suggested by Theodore of Mopsuestia, cited in Abbott, *Epistles to the Ephesians and to the Colossians*, 211; likewise, Rev. 1:5, also alluding to Ps. 88:27–29, 36, highlights that Christ's resurrection has placed him in a position of rule.

39. On the latter, see Dunn, *Epistles to the Colossians and to Philemon*, 90–91.

40. Wright, *Paul to the Colossians and to Philemon*, 70–71.

The Genesis 1 Background of "the Image of God" in Colossians 3:10

The first clear OT allusion in this segment appears in 3:10. Paul describes true Christians as those who "have donned the clothes of the new man [*anthrōpos*, implied by v. 9] who is being renewed to a true knowledge <u>according to the image of the one who created him</u> [*kat' eikona tou ktisantos auton*]."[41] The allusion is related to the earlier allusion to Gen. 1:16–17 in Col. 1:15 (Christ as "the image of the invisible God"), as well as to the repetition of the allusion to Gen. 1:28 in Col. 1:6, 10, which depict Christians as beginning to fulfill the "multiply and bear fruit" part of the Gen. 1 commission to Adam (e.g., 1:6: "in all the world also it is constantly bearing fruit and increasing").[42] Thus, Gen. 1:26–28 is in Paul's mind at points throughout this epistle.

Genesis 1:26–28 is a reference to Adam and Eve as the crown of creation, created in God's image to be God's vice-regents over the world and to multiply their progeny as divine image-bearers. The likelihood is that the Genesis passage focuses on humanity being functional reflectors of God's image, though the ontological aspect of the image may secondarily be in mind.[43]

The point in Col. 3:10 is that believers who have begun to be identified with Christ's resurrection[44] are those who have begun to be identified with the new creation in Christ. The creation of humanity in God's image in order to rule and subdue and to be fruitful and multiply (Gen. 1:26–28) is now applicable not only to Christ but also to his people, since he and they have entered into the sphere of the new creation and have begun to do what Adam failed to do. Here the tone is on new creation in the divine image, but ruling is not far away (cf. 3:1), nor is the notion of multiplying (1:6, 10). It may be

---

41. This is a reference to Gen. 1:26–27: "Then God said, 'Let Us <u>make man in Our image</u>. . . .' God <u>created man in His own image, in the image of God He created him</u>" (e.g., cf. v. 27b: *ton anthrōpon kat' eikona theou epoiēsen auton*; while Paul uses *ktizō* for "create," the LXX of Gen. 1:26–27 uses *poieō*, though Aquila, Symmachus, and Theodotion do use *ktizō* in v. 27). See NA²⁷ margin; Lohse, *Epistles to the Colossians and to Philemon*, 142; Joachim Gnilka, *Der Kolosserbrief*, HTKNT (Freiburg: Herder, 1980), 188; note also the allusion to the same Genesis passage in Col. 3:10. So also Lightfoot, *Epistles to the Colossians and to Philemon*, 215–16; A. T. Robertson, *Paul and the Intellectuals: The Epistle to the Colossians*, rev. and ed. W. C. Strickland (Nashville: Broadman, 1959), 503; Simpson and Bruce, *Epistles to the Ephesians and the Colossians*, 272; Norbert Hugedé, *Commentaire de L'Épître aux Colossiens* (Geneva: Labor et Fides, 1968), 175–77; G. B. Caird, *Paul's Letters from Prison: Ephesians, Philippians, Colossians, Philemon*, NClarB (London: Oxford University Press, 1976), 205, calling it a "quotation"; Arthur Patzia, *Colossians, Philemon, Ephesians*, GNC (San Francisco: Harper & Row, 1984), 61; Lincoln, *Ephesians*, 644; Margaret MacDonald, *Colossians and Ephesians*, SP 17 (Collegeville, MN: Liturgical Press, 2000), 138, 146.

42. See further the discussion on Col. 1:6, 9 in this and other respects in Beale, "Colossians," 842–46.

43. See ibid.

44. That is, they "have donned the clothes of the new man," who is the resurrected Christ.

important to recall that part of "ruling and subduing" in Gen. 1:26–28 was to "be fruitful and multiply and fill" the earth not only with literal but also, after the fall, spiritual children who would join Adam in reflecting God's image and in his kingly dominion over the earth. This idea fits quite well with believers' identification with Christ's resurrection and sovereign kingship in 3:1, which is part of the basis for the paraenetic section beginning in 3:5 and continuing with 3:10.

Thus, believers have become identified with Christ (the new man) and are no longer identified with the "old man" (3:9–10).[45] On this basis, Paul exhorts them to stop being identified with the traits of the former life in the "old man/ Adam" and instead to be characterized by those of the new life in the last Adam. Accordingly, the image in which they are being renewed is Christ's image, especially in light of the link back to 1:15–16, and "the one having created" them in this image is God.[46] However, its image here may simply be God's image, in which the new humanity is created, and their creation in Christ's image specifically may be secondarily in mind.

Even the reference to being "renewed to a true knowledge [epignōsis]" in 3:10 may echo the Genesis context, where "knowledge" was at the heart of the fall (cf. Gen. 2:17: "From the tree of the knowledge of good and evil you shall not eat").[47] Humanity's "failure to act according to their knowledge [epignōsis] of God by not acknowledging him in worship was the central element in Paul's earlier analysis of the human plight."[48]

Related to this is the observation that the second allusion to Gen. 1:28 in Col. 1, "bearing fruit . . . and increasing," is directly appended by "in the knowledge [epignōsis] of God" (v. 10). This further connects being in God's image with knowing him and his will, since Gen. 1:28 is part of the functional manner in which humanity was to reflect the divine image. Adam and his wife's "knowledge" of God also included remembering God's word addressed to Adam in Gen. 2:16–17, which Adam's wife failed to recall and which Adam failed to acknowldge in Gen. 3:2–3.

Being "renewed unto a knowledge of the image" of God will ensure that the Colossian believers are not being "deluded with persuasive argument" (2:4) and "taken captive through . . . empty deception" (Col. 2:8) in the way Adam and Eve were through the serpent's deceptive speech.[49]

---

45. Consequently, the participles in 3:9–10 that are often translated "putting off" and "putting on" are not imperatives, which would be a very rare use of the participle; rather, they are to be understood indicatively, describing a present reality.

46. Following Hugedé, *Colossians*, 177; David M. Hay, *Colossians*, ANTC (Nashville: Abingdon, 2000), 126; Daniel Furter, *Les Épîtres de Paul aux Colossiens et à Philémon*, CEB (Vaux-sur-Seine: Edifac, 1987), 173.

47. Following Dunn, *Epistles to the Colossians and to Philemon*, 221–22.

48. Ibid., 222; followed by MacDonald, *Colossians and Ephesians*, 138.

49. The last time "knowledge" was used in Colossians was not coincidentally in this context of deception in 2:2–3 (*epignōsis* followed by *gnōsis*).

The Genesis 3 Background of Paul's "Clothing" Metaphors

The portrayal of stripping off old clothing and donning new clothing in Col. 3:9–10 may reflect a background of changing clothes in relation to the rite of baptism (so several commentators), though this is uncertain.[50] Also, the portrayal of putting on and putting off garments, though widespread in antiquity, is likely not the background here.[51]

More plausibly, in light of the two allusions to the divine "image" and "knowledge" in 3:10 from Gen. 1–3, the references to clothing in 3:9–10 may be an allusion to Gen. 3. Genesis 3:7 says that directly after their sin, Adam and Eve tried to cover their sinful nakedness by their own autonomous efforts: "They sewed fig leaves together and made themselves loin coverings." However, in an apparent expression of their beginning restoration to God after the fall (esp. in light of 3:20), Gen. 3:21 says, "The LORD God made garments of skin for Adam and his wife, and clothed [endyō] them." The clear implication is that their first suit of clothes was taken off and replaced by divinely made clothing, indicating that the self-made clothing was associated with their alienated condition and sinful shame (Gen. 3:7–11) and was an insufficient covering for those who have begun to be reconciled to God.[52]

Likewise, Col. 3:9–10 refers to believers who have "stripped off the clothes [ekdyō] of the old [sinful] man" and "clothed yourselves [endyō] with the new man," which indicates their inaugurated new-creational relationship with God.[53] The imagery is not precisely "laying aside" and "putting on," the usual rendering of the English translations, but rather is sartorial language. They have laid aside the clothes of the first Adam (the "old man"), in which they could not come into God's presence, and have clothed themselves with the last Adam (the "new man"), in whom they have been "renewed."[54] By donning their new clothing, they have begun to return to God and will do so

---

50. The custom of changing clothes as a part of the custom of baptism is not attested until after the middle of the second century AD (on which, see Lincoln, *Colossians*, 643), though Lev. 16:23–24 may have influenced the later practice.

51. Even the parallels of the initiation into the Isis mysteries and of gnosticism are post–first century, belong to a different realm of ideas, and have no literal verbal parallels with taking off and putting on a person versus clothing (on which, see O'Brien, *Colossians, Philemon*, 189).

52. That Adam's and Eve's "loin coverings" were not proper attire to wear in God's holy presence is clear from the fact that "they hid themselves from the presence of the LORD God" and still considered themselves "naked" (Gen. 3:8–10); this view of the clothing in Gen. 3:8 is also taken by *Sib. Or.* 1:47–49.

53. The NRSV and NLT also have apparel metaphors: "You have stripped off . . . and have clothed yourselves" (cf. similarly NJB, NET); for closely parallel wording, see Eph. 4:22–24; similarly *Barn.* 6:11–12, which also quotes Gen. 1:26, 28.

54. Likewise seeing a contrast between the figures of the first Adam and the last Adam are John Calvin, *Commentaries on the Epistles of Paul the Apostle to the Philippians, Colossians, and Thessalonians* (repr., Grand Rapids: Baker, 1999), 211; Simpson and Bruce, *Ephesians and Colossians*, 272–74; Herbert M. Carson, *The Epistles of Paul to the Colossians and Philemon*, 2nd ed., TNTC (Grand Rapids: Eerdmans, 1966), 84; O'Brien, *Colossians, Philemon*, 190–91.

consummately in the future.[55] Hence, one is either in the position of the old, fallen first Adam, the corporate "embodiment of unregenerate humanity," or in the new, resurrected last Adam, the corporate "embodiment of the new humanity."[56]

Some early Jewish and Christian writings express the belief that Adam and Eve were clothed in glorious garments before the fall, lost that glory, and then wrongly tried to cover their inglorious shame with fig leaves. Some also held that the new set of clothes given to Adam and Eve in Gen. 3:21 actually possessed some degree of glory or designated Adam the first high priest or pointed to a greater inheritance of the final glorious clothing of immortality. The first and third notions may lie behind the clothing imagery in Col. 3:10. Others also believed that the glorious clothing that the devil possessed as a holy angel before his fall was given to Adam and Eve.[57]

In Col. 2:11 believers' old clothing is referred to as "the body of the flesh," which was "unclothed" (*apekdysis*) in contrast to their new condition, which Paul characterizes as "made without hands" (*acheiropoiētos*)—that is, divinely created by causing them to be "raised" and "made alive with Christ" (2:12–13).[58] This is consistent with the use elsewhere of "handmade" to refer to sinful, idolatrous, and corruptible realities of the old world in contrast to an already–not yet new-creational reality of "made without hands."[59] This also fits with the notion that Adam and Eve's first set of clothes were handmade, whereas the second set were divinely created, made without human hands.

Early Christian tradition also understands the removal of old clothing and putting on of new clothing to represent a new, converted condition in a new creation of a latter-day Eden.[60] *Life of Adam and Eve [Apocalypse]* 20:1–5 (Jewish, ca. AD 100–200) expresses the belief that after Adam had lost "the

---

55. So likewise Ralph P. Martin, *Colossians and Philemon*, NCB (repr., London: Oliphants, 1974), 107; Wright, *Paul to the Colossians and to Philemon*, 138; both also see a contrast between identification with the old Adam and the new Adam.

56. O'Brien, *Colossians, Philemon*, 190–91. The latter side of the identification is made clear by Rom. 6:5–11; 13:14; Gal. 3:27.

57. For Jewish references supporting the statements in this paragraph, see G. K. Beale, *Colossians and Philemon*, BECNT (Grand Rapids: Baker Academic, forthcoming). E.g., for Adam's lost glorious clothing, see the Armenian version of *L.A.E.* 44(20):1, 4–5; 44(21): 1–2.

58. For "flesh" being equivalent to the old age characterized as uncircumcision, see Beale, "Colossians," 860–62.

59. E.g., handmade temples of the old age (Mark 14:58; Acts 7:48; 17:24; Heb. 9:11, 24) in contrast to the new, eschatological temple, which is equivalent to God's dwelling in the new creation with his resurrected people (Mark 14:58; 2 Cor. 5:1). On the further significance of the contrast between "handmade" and "made without hands," see G. K. Beale, *The Temple and the Church's Mission: A Biblical Theology of the Dwelling Place of God*, NSBT 17 (Downers Grove, IL: InterVarsity, 2004), 152–53, 309–12, 375–76.

60. E.g., *Odes Sol.* 11:10–14; *Mart. Ascen. Isa.* 9:6–18; likewise *T. Levi* 18:10–14; *Apoc. El.* 5:6; *4 Ezra* 2:33–48; *Gos. Truth* 20.28–34; so also the following Jewish texts, though without mention of Eden: *Jos. Asen.* 14:12[13]–15[17]; 15:5[4]–6[5]; *Apoc. Ab.* 13:14; *2 En.* 22:8–10.

righteousness with which [he] had been clothed [*endyō*]," he made for himself "skirts" (*perizōma*) from a fig tree to "cover" his nakedness and shame, and at his death he was clothed with divinely given garments, indicating his beginning restoration to God (see also the Armenian version *L.A.E.* 48[40]:2–3, 5b–6; see chaps. 47–48 [*Vita*]).[61]

This Jewish and early Christian background, especially the Adamic Genesis and eschatological uses, are very similar to Paul's use of Gen. 3 and enhance the presence of an allusion to the Gen. 3 clothing in Col. 3:9–10 and even its inaugurated application. This is apparent in that the majority of the most relevant aforementioned texts related to Gen. 1–3 or new creation also speak of a new spiritual or redemptive-historical status inaugurated but not consummated for the people of God, especially speaking in terms of resurrection, new

61. These garments probably represented a new status of redeemed life that would consummate in resurrection (*L.A.E.* [*Apocalypse*] 28:1–4; 43:1–4). The removing of old clothes and the putting on of new clothes in the OT represents forgiveness of sin (Zech. 3:4–5) or the new eschatological relationship that the people of Yahweh were to have with him after their restoration from Babylon (Isa. 52:1–2; 61:3, 10). Also, new clothes were donned by people when they were installed into positions of rule in the OT (e.g., Joseph in Gen. 41:41–44; Eliakim in Isa. 22:21; Daniel in Dan. 5:29), as well as in the ancient Near East in general. On this, see William N. Wilder, "Illumination and Investiture: The Royal Significance of the Tree of Wisdom," *WTJ* 68 (2006): 51–70. Wilder shows that clothing in the ancient Near East, OT, Judaism, and the NT often represented the new status of a person, often in connection to a new status of a ruling position.

Indeed, the precise wording of "clothe" (*endyō*) followed by "unclothe" (*ekdyō*) occurs in Isa. 52:1–2 together with resurrection imagery: "Awake, awake, clothe [*endyō*] yourself with strength, O Zion, and clothe yourself with glory. . . . Shake yourself from the dust, rise up . . . ; unclothe [*ekdyō*] yourself of the band around your neck, O captive daughter of Zion." Likewise, the very same wording of "unclothe" (*ekdyō*) followed by "clothe" (*endyō*) represents various priestly or high priestly statuses (Num. 20:26, 28; Ezek. 44:19; see also Lev. 16:23–24; *m. Yoma* 3.4, 6; 7.4 [Hebrew equivalent]) or represents the change from a former condition to a new status (*T. Zeb.* 4:10; Jdt. 10:3–4; cf. 16:7–9), particularly that of a deliverer (Jdt. 10:3–4; *L.A.B.* 27:12 [though not in Greek]), a ruler (1 Macc. 10:62), or new salvific condition (*Odes Sol.* 11:10–11 [also not in Greek]). Particularly striking is the reference in Judaism, again with *endyō* + *ekdyō*, to the removing of old clothes and donning of new ones (Bar. 5:1–4, alluding to Isa. 61:3, 10). Generally, Judaism understood that a change from one set of clothes to more glorious clothing represented a change of relationship (*Jub.* 31:1–2; *L.A.B.* 40:6) or especially status, whether with respect to being a priest (Josephus, *J.W.* 5.236; *2 En.* 71:21–22; cf. Sir. 45:6–10; 50:11; 4Q213b 4–6; *T. Levi* 8:2–7) or a leader (*L.A.B.* 20:2–3). Similarly, *Shepherd of Hermas* refers to believers getting rid of evil desires and "clothing" (*endyō*) themselves with virtuous desires (44:1; 61:4; 106:3).

Most of the above OT, Jewish, and early Christian uses refer not only to a new status but also to one that entails an inheritance, whether this is the inheritance of eternal life with God and of rule in a new creation (the focus of the texts associated with Gen. 1–3) or more general eschatological blessings or privileges of a new office (priesthood or rulership). Even in the ancient Near East or in the OT, to receive a robe from a parent or to be disrobed by a parent indicated respectively inheritance and disinheritance. On this, see Gordon P. Hugenberger, *Marriage as a Covenant: Biblical Law and Ethics as Developed from Malachi*, VTSup 52 (Leiden: Brill, 1994), 198–99. Hugenberger also has developed the notion of clothing as symbolic of inheritance at points in the OT and the NT (on which, see his "A Neglected Symbolism for the Clothing of Adam and Eve (Gen. 3:21)" [paper presented at the Annual Meeting of the Tyndale Fellowship, July 1996]).

creation, or incorruption. Paul himself elsewhere expresses virtually the same sartorial contrast in relation to Adam and Christ with regard to "inheriting" glorious clothing at the consummation (most clearly in 1 Cor. 15:50–54). Is it coincidental that references to believers' "inheritance" from God occur in the context of Colossians (1:12; 3:24), one of which is sandwiched between an allusion to Gen. 1:28 (in 1:10b) and Gen. 1:26–27 (1:15)?[62] Virtually the same clothing metaphor occurs in Gal. 3:27 and is even more closely linked to gaining an "inheritance" (Gal. 3:29).

Paul appears to be using the Gen. 3 "clothing" language analogically: believers are seen to have discarded the clothes of the old, fallen Adam and have been clothed with the attire of the last Adam, with which Adam himself was proleptically clothed to indicate his restored relationship with God. "Having donned the clothes of the new man" in Col. 3:10 is directly explained as "being renewed to a knowledge of the image of God." The clothing metaphor is one of the ways believers are referred to as regaining the image of God.

Why does Paul portray Christ as the last Adam and as the image of God in Col. 1, and why does he depict Christians as identified with Christ as the last Adam, the image of God and the "new man," in Col. 3? Most likely it is to get the Colossians to focus on their own identification with Christ as a new creation and his apostolic teaching so that they will not be deceived by false teachers who are attempting to get them to abide by rules of behavior that are now outmoded because they are part and parcel of the old, fallen world that is passing away.[63]

The Image of the Last Adam in 2 Corinthians

In 2 Cor. 3–4 Paul says that when people "turn to the Lord, the veil is taken away" (3:16). When this occurs, "all, with unveiled face beholding as in a mirror the glory of the Lord, are being transformed into the same image from glory to glory, just as from the Lord, the Spirit" (3:18). Those who trust in Christ come back into close relationship with God and begin to reflect the glory of his image. In fact, "glory" and "image" are virtually synonymous in verse 18, as they also are in 1 Cor. 11:7 (man "is the image and glory of God"). The mention of "Christ" in verse 14 is the most probable antecedent for "Lord"

---

62. For many of the Jewish references in this section on clothing, I am indebted to my research students Ben Gladd and, especially, Keith Williams, whose survey and listing of references to clothing in Judaism (the latter with respect to his research related to Gal. 3:27) alerted me to study the various contextual uses of several of these references and their relationship to Col. 3. After finishing this section, I learned of Jung Hoon Kim, *The Significance of Clothing Imagery in the Pauline Corpus*, JSNTSup 268 (London: T&T Clark, 2004), which made all these same essential points about the "clothing" background of Col. 3:9–10 on the basis of most of the same biblical, Jewish, and Christian texts.

63. On this, see Beale, "Colossians," 860–63, and fuller discussion in Beale, *Colossians and Philemon*.

in verses 16–18, so that it is Christ's glory and image into which believers are being transformed. This is most likely referring to the first Adam, who ceased to reflect God's glory after his sin. Thus, he did not lose the divine image altogether, but it did become distorted by losing the glorious aspect of that image.

That this is Paul's view is also borne out by texts such as Rom. 3:23: "For all have sinned and are lacking[64] the glory of God."[65] We saw in the earlier chapter on sin as idolatry that Rom. 1:18–25 had its partial background in Adam and Eve's fall in Eden, where "they exchanged the glory of the incorruptible God for an image" of idols. This meant that they ceased to reflect God's glorious image but reflected the vanity of idols. I discussed earlier in this chapter that Judaism also saw that Adam and Eve lost the glory of God when they sinned (*L.A.E.* [*Apocalypse*] 20:1–5).[66] So Adam's sin caused him to lose the glorious reflection of God. Romans 3:23, in developing Rom. 1, likely refers to Adam's effect on all fallen humanity, who also had failed to reflect God's glory. Romans 3:24 says this glory is regained in Christ, and Rom. 5:12–19 more explicitly sees Christ as the last Adam reversing what the first Adam did.

The argument of 2 Cor. 3 has climaxed with believers being transformed into the glorious image of Christ, and 4:1–6 continues that idea. On the basis of this climactic point (note the "therefore" in 4:1), Paul says in 4:1 that having this "ministry" of conveying the gospel message leading to transformation to Christ's image causes him not to "lose heart." Instead, he "commends" himself to the consciences of others as a truthful proclaimer of God's word (4:2). In particular, this commendation is based on "the manifestation of truth," which in context is the revelation of Christ's image and glory, into which those receiving Paul's message are transformed. But this manifestation through Paul's preaching is "veiled to those perishing, in whose case the god of this age has blinded the minds of the unbelieving, so that the light of the gospel of the glory of Christ, who is the image of God, might not shine [on them]" (vv. 3–4). Whereas those "with unveiled face" who believe "behold the glory of the Lord" (3:18) and "are being transformed into the same image," those disbelieving and under a "veil" do not behold "the glory of Christ, who is the image of God" (4:4). Thus, 4:4 is the converse of 3:16–18 and again virtually equates Christ's "glory" with his "image."

Thus, it is through Paul's message that the light of Christ's image transforms its recipients (3:16–4:2), despite the fact that the devil blinds some, so that they

---

64. For the meaning of "lack" for the Greek *hystereō*, see BDAG 1043–44.

65. Likewise, see Rom. 8:18, 21; Phil. 3:21. See also C. Marvin Pate, *The Glory of Adam and the Afflictions of the Righteous: Pauline Suffering in Context* (Lewiston, NY: Mellen Biblical Press, 1993), 67–89, where he cites Jewish sources that held that Adam had lost his glory through his sin but that this glory would be regained in the eschaton.

66. This Jewish text says that Eve "was estranged from her glory with which she was clothed"; one chapter later, Eve confesses that her and Adam's sin "brought us down from great glory" (*L.A.E.* [*Apocalypse*] 21:2).

cannot see or be transformed by Christ's glorious image (4:3–4). The apostle gives two reasons why he commends his apostolic message to others. The first reason is in verse 5: "For we do not preach ourselves but Christ Jesus as Lord, and ourselves as your bond-servants for Jesus's sake." That is, he commends himself not as the content of his message or center of attention but only as a messenger though whom Christ is preached. The second reason he commends his ministry is that through his message God shines new-creational light through Paul to others so that they will see "the Light of the knowledge of the glory of God in the face of Christ" (v. 6). That is, Paul elaborates on 3:16–4:2 by saying that through his message people can perceive "the glory of Christ, who is the image of God" (4:4) and be transformed by it.

The transformational nature of 4:6, "For God, who said, 'Light shall shine out of darkness,' is the One who has shone in our hearts," comes from its OT background in Gen. 1:3, to which he refers. Just as God irresistibly caused light to flood into the darkness of the first creation, so has he begun to do so with blinded humans in the new creation. That the OT prophecies of new creation are seen as commencing in 4:6 is apparent a little later from 5:17: "Therefore, if any one is in Christ, that one is a new creation; the old things passed away; behold, new things have come." There is a string of new-creational references to Christ's resurrection life and renewal that provides one of the links between 4:6 and 5:17 (see 4:7, 10–12, 14, 16–18; 5:1–4, 14–15). The OT context of the Gen. 1:3 reference in 4:6 also points further to the idea of the image of Christ and of God in 3:18 and 4:4 having its background in Adam as the image of God in Gen. 1:26–27. It is in Christ that one now becomes transformed to God's image and glory, the same glory that the first Adam had reflected but lost in Gen. 3 (recall that the loss of glory distorted the image of God in Adam but did not destroy it).

It is apparent that one of the main ways that Paul sees believers becoming conformed to the last Adam's image in the present stage of the inaugurated eschaton is through suffering in imitation of Jesus. Just as Jesus's own life was characterized by suffering climaxed with final physical resurrection, so do his people follow this pattern. This idea of suffering as an important instrument through which one is transformed into the Messiah's suffering and glorious image is found in 2 Cor. 4:4–5:6, though it is seen elsewhere in Paul's writings.[67]

Significant References to the Image of God Elsewhere in Paul's Writings

Some see significant reference to Adam in Phil. 2:5–11:

> Have this attitude in yourselves which was also in Christ Jesus, who, although
> He existed in the form of God, did not regard equality with God a thing to be

---

67. This notion of suffering in relation to the divine image in Paul's writings deserves further development, which the limitations of the present study do not allow. C. Marvin Pate (*Glory of Adam*) has developed this notion in Paul's writings more than anyone else.

grasped, but emptied Himself, taking the form of a bond-servant, and being made in the likeness of men. Being found in appearance as a man, He humbled Himself by becoming obedient to the point of death, even death on a cross. For this reason also, God highly exalted Him, and bestowed on Him the name which is above every name, so that at the name of Jesus every knee will bow, of those who are in heaven and on earth and under the earth, and that every tongue will confess that Jesus Christ is Lord, to the glory of God the Father.

N. T. Wright represents many in saying that verses 6–11 are shot through with references and echoes to Adam. Wright says that such references are a virtual certainty, and that there is wide agreement that this passage is an example of "Adam-christology."[68] He offers the following primary arguments in favor of this, which have an overall cumulative effect:

1. A common theme is shown of Christ's obedience unto death in Rom. 5:12–21; Phil. 2:6–11, the former of which explicitly refers to Christ as an Adam figure.
2. There is a link with 1 Cor. 15:20–28 (which cites the Adamic Ps. 8:6 [8:7 LXX] in v. 27) in the reference to Christ's exaltation in Phil. 2:10–11 (in light of the echoed themes in Phil. 3:20–21).
3. The theme of lordship and exaltation in Phil. 2:9–11 carries overtones of Gen. 1:27–28.
4. "The theme of a humiliated and then exalted figure who is given great authority and power alongside the one God of Jewish monotheism reminds us irresistibly of Daniel 7."[69]
5. The phrases "made in the likeness of men" (v. 7b) and "being found in appearance as a man" (v. 8a) reflect the "image of God" language of Gen. 1:26–27.

I am open to seeing Adamic allusions in the Philippians passage, but there is no clear verbal allusion to any OT Adamic passages, whether Gen. 1 or Ps. 8. The only clear allusion is to Isa. 45:23 in Phil. 2:10–11, which is not an Adamic passage. Wright (and others) actually are appealing to unique ideas, not verbal expressions, in Phil. 2 that they believe likely can be traced back only to Adamic passages. This certainly is possible, and it is viable to attempt to argue this way, but it is not as clear as other references to Adam elsewhere in Paul's writings (e.g., Rom. 5:12–21; 1 Cor. 15:20–28, 45–49). Rather than positing clear thematic allusions, it may be better to see a more subtle Adamic background. That is, this background is not explicitly expressed

68. Wright, *Climax of the Covenant*, 58–59 (for the fuller argument, see pp. 57–62, 87–98). See likewise Pate, *Glory of Adam*, 185–91, also citing numerous scholars who hold to various versions of an Adamic background for Phil. 2:6–11.

69. Wright, *Climax of the Covenant*, 58.

by Paul because he may have merely presupposed the network of associations with Gen. 1–3,[70] since he was such a deep and experienced reader of the OT Scriptures. This would not exclude a semantic link with OT Adamic texts, but Paul may have been unconscious of such links or did not intend his readers or hearers to pick up on them. In either case, recognition of the OT echoes and the enrichment of meaning they carry might well disclose Paul's underlying or implicit presuppositions, which undergird the foundation for the explicit statements in the Phil. 2 passage.

So what is the significance of the underlying Adamic associations, if they are present at all?[71] Although Wright focuses too much on explicit allusions to or echoes of Adam, his conclusions about the significance of these echoes can equally be seen as the foundation underlying his explicit statements about Christ in the text:

> Adam, in arrogance, thought to become like God; Christ, in humility, became human. . . .

> Christ's obedience is not simply the replacement of Adam's disobedience. It does not involve merely the substitution of one sort of humanity for another, but the solution of the problem now inherent in the first sort, namely, sin. The temptation of Christ was not to snatch at a forbidden equality with God, but to cling to his rights and thereby opt out of the task allotted to him, that he should undo the results of Adam's snatching.[72]

Wright goes on to conclude that Christ's exaltation not only alludes to Isa. 45:23 but also echoes Gen. 1:26–28; Ps. 8:4–8; Dan. 7:14, which refer to the final position of the obedient man's glorious exaltation, which "is thoroughly appropriate for God himself," as the Isa. 45:23 allusion bears out.[73] I would rather say that the significance of the Isaiah allusion is Paul's way of identifying Christ with Yahweh and his glorious eschatological exaltation prophesied by Isaiah. Paul understands that Christ's resurrection and ascension are the inaugurated fulfillment of that prophecy. The network of possible OT Adamic associations throughout the passage undergirds the previous portrayal in Phil. 2:6–8 of Christ as one in the human image of God who had come to redeem humanity. It was necessary that he bear the human image of God in order to redeem those who reflected the fallen and distorted image and to restore them

---

70. See Moisés Silva, "Philippians," in Beale and Carson, eds., *Commentary on the New Testament Use of the Old Testament*, 843. Silva sees "an undeniable network of associations between Phil. 2 and Gen. 1–3."

71. See Gordon D. Fee, *Pauline Christology: An Exegetical-Theological Study* (Peabody, MA: Hendrickson, 2007), 372–93. Fee, citing others in support, doubts that there are any allusions to Adam in Phil. 2:6–8.

72. Wright, *Climax of the Covenant*, 91–92.

73. Ibid., 95.

to God's image, which Phil. 3:21 more explicitly develops. The conclusion that identifies Christ with Yahweh picks up on the earlier reference to Christ's divine preexistence in 2:6.[74] It is important to point out that Christ's resurrection and ascension led to his kingly sovereign status (Phil. 2:9–11), and the continuation of that ascended resurrection state overlaps with his kingship and new-creational Adamic image.

One other passage merits discussion of Paul's understanding of the Adamic image of God. We noted in an earlier chapter how in Rom. 1 idolatry reflects the image of the creation instead of the Creator. Then we saw in Romans the reversal of that process, whereby "renewal" (12:1–2) in Christ causes one to begin to be "conformed to the image of His Son, that He would be the firstborn of many brethren" (8:29). Again, the reference to both "son" and "firstborn" conjures up Adam language (as we saw above in the discussion of Colossians), so that the image distorted in Adam becomes regained in Christ, a "last Adam" figure. The connection with the first Adam is also apparent because we also saw that Rom. 1:19–25 included allusion to Adam's sin. As we have seen above, at the end of the age Christ will complete the process of creating his people in his eschatological image, when he "will transform the body of our humble estate into conformity with the body of His glory" (Phil. 3:21).[75] As in Rom. 8:29, so in Phil. 3:21, in the light of Phil. 2, Christ's followers become conformed to the image of their Lord.

The discussions in Phil. 2 and Romans further point to the fact that Paul's mind was saturated with eschatology. Christ has come in the image of God to restore fallen humanity into that image. He is identified as an Adam figure, along with his redeemed people, because God "makes the last things like the first things" (*Barn.* 6:13). That the eschatological age is commencing with Christ's first coming is evident in that he and his people are viewed as restarting history in the way it originally started, being in the divine Adamic image (Christ's people being in the restored image), as was the first man, who started the age of the first creation in Gen. 1–2. This time, however, a successful consummation to the irreversible inauguration of this new age is guaranteed by divine decree.

Conclusion to the Image of God in Paul's Writings

Jesus is the end-time Adam, who perfectly reflects the image of God in the new creation, which he inaugurated by his life, death, and resurrection. Those who believe in Christ, the last Adam, begin to be transformed into the image of God. Why does Paul underscore this idea repeatedly and more explicitly than any other NT author? The most likely reason is that this conception of

---

74. For a good discussion of the relation of Christ's divine preexistence to his humanity, see ibid., 90–98.

75. Philippians 3:21 probably develops the reference to Christ himself, who "existed in the form of God . . . and [was] made in the likeness of men" (Phil. 2:6–7).

Christ as the image of God and last Adam was grounded in the appearance of Christ to Paul on the Damascus Road.[76] There Paul saw the risen and exalted Messiah as reflecting the divine image, and, after subsequent reflection, Paul concluded from this that Jesus was the expected latter-day messianic Adam, who would possess God's glorious image and enable others to regain the glory of this image. One of the pieces of evidence that Paul derived this view from his experience at the Damascus Road Christophany is that he makes allusions to the Christophany in the midst of discussing the image of Christ. This is most clearly seen in the parallels between 2 Cor. 4:4–6 and Acts 26, the last of three accounts in Acts narrating Paul's Damascus Road encounter with the risen Christ (see tables 14.2 and 14.3).

Table 14.2

Acts 26:13, 17–18	2 Corinthians 4:4, 6
26:17–18: egō apostellō se anoixai ophthalmous autōn, tou epistrepsai apo skotous eis phōs kai tēs exousias tou satana epi ton theon. . . .	4:4: . . . en hois ho theos tou aiōnos toutou etyphlōsen ta noēmata tōn apistōn eis to mē augasai ton phōtismon tou euaggeliou tēs doxēs tou Christou.
26:13: hemeras mesēs kata tēn hodon eidon . . . ouranothen hyper tēn lamprotēta tou hēliou perilampsan me phōs. . . . (cf. Acts 22:9).	4:6: ho theos ho eipōn; ek skotous phōs lampsei, hos elampsen en tais kardiais hēmōn pros phōtismon tēs gnōseōs tēs doxēs tou theou en prosōpō [Iēsou] Christou.

Note: In both tables, lexical and cognate parallels are indicated by solid underlining, and close conceptual parallels by broken underlining.

Table 14.3

Acts 26:13, 17–18	2 Corinthians 4:4, 6
26:17–18: "I am sending you, to open their eyes so that they may turn from darkness to light and from the dominion of Satan to God. . . ."	4:4: ". . . in whose case the god of this world has blinded the minds of the unbelieving so that they might not see the light of the gospel of the glory of Christ, who is the image of God."
26:13: "At midday . . . I saw on the way a light from heaven, brighter than the sun, shining all around me. . . ." (cf. Acts 22:9).	4:6: "God, who said, 'Light shall shine out of darkness,' is the One who has shone in our hearts to give the Light of the knowledge of the glory of God in the face of Christ."

The cumulative effect of the parallels points strongly to the interdependence of the two accounts (whether Paul's narration is very close to Luke's or Luke's is dependent on Paul's).[77] Thus, it is likely that Paul's discussion of

76. The most thorough argument for this is given by Seyoon Kim, *The Origin of Paul's Gospel* (Grand Rapids: Eerdmans, 1982), 137–268.
77. "The god of this world has blinded the minds" in 2 Cor. 4 is parallel to "darkness . . . the dominion of Satan" in Acts 26; "glory" in 2 Cor. 4:13 is parallel to the "light" in Acts 26; "to give the light" in 2 Cor. 4:6 is parallel to "to open their eyes" in Acts 26, to which "they might not see" in 2 Cor. 4:4 is a contrast.

Christ as the end-time image of God is rooted in his perception of the resurrected Jesus as being in God's image on the Damascus Road. This further enhances the thesis that the resurrected Christ is the eschatological Adam in God's image, and so also those identified with Christ have the same position because they have begun to be transferred into the new creation through inaugurated resurrection.

The Restoration of the Image in Hebrews against the Old Testament and Jewish Background

Hebrews 1:3 is a clear reference to Jesus being in God's image: "the radiance of His glory and the exact representation of His nature." The preceding and following contexts support this by directly associating it with ideas that we have seen in Paul's thinking also to be associated with Christ as the image of God. Hebrews 1:2 says that Jesus is God's "Son, whom He appointed heir of all things," which is an allusion to Ps. 2:7–8: "He said to Me, 'You are My Son. . . . Ask of Me, and I will surely give the nations as your <u>inheritance</u>, and the very ends of the earth as your possession.'"[78] This allusion anticipates the clear quotation of Ps. 2:7 in Heb. 1:5, only two verses later, where again the "son" referenced in the psalm is seen to be fulfilled in Jesus. The combined ideas of sonship and inheritance in both Ps. 2:7 and Heb. 1:2 have a definite Adamic ring, which is enhanced by Christ also being called "firstborn" in Heb. 1:6,[79] a name that Paul, as we have seen, inextricably links to Adam and Christ as the last Adam, as well as to Christ as divine Wisdom.[80] While the Wisdom background is in

78. See, e.g., Harold W. Attridge, *The Epistle to the Hebrews*, Hermeneia (Philadelphia: Fortress, 1989), 40.

79. See my discussion of Gen. 1–3 in chap. 2. Strikingly close to Heb. 1:2–6 is the Qumran text 4Q418 frg. 81 [= 4Q423 8 + 24?]), which connects Israel's "sonship" and "firstborn" status with Adam's "inheritance" of the entire world and with the eschatological time when God's "splendor" and "beauty" would be expressed (see the translation in Florentino García Martínez and Eibert J. C. Tigchelaar, *The Dead Sea Scrolls Study Edition*, 2 vols. [Grand Rapids: Eerdmans, 2000], 2:871–73). A closely related passage in 4Q475 asserts that after all sin has been extinguished from the earth, "all the world will be like Eden, and all . . . the earth will be at peace for ever, and . . . a beloved son . . . will . . . inherit it all" (following ibid., 2:957). See also 1QH IV:14–15, where God will give Israel's "seed" (*zr'*) "all the glory of Adam as an inheritance [along with] long life." CD-A III:19–20 also speaks of the faithful receiving in the future "all the glory of Adam" (on which, see further Beale, *Temple*, 156).

80. We have seen this same combination of ideas (son, image, firstborn) in Paul's thinking to be associated with the personification of wisdom in Prov. 8 and early Judaism (Beale, "Colossians," 855), and commentators probably rightly point out this wisdom background in Heb. 1:3 (e.g., Hugh Montefiore, *A Commentary on the Epistle to the Hebrews*, BNTC [London: A&C Black, 1964], 36–37; F. F. Bruce, *The Epistle to the Hebrews*, NICNT [Grand Rapids: Eerdmans, 1990], 47–48; Attridge, *Hebrews*, 42–43; Luke Timothy Johnson, *Hebrews*, NTL [Louisville: Westminster John Knox, 2006], 68–70]).

mind here, as possibly in Col. 1:15–18, it appears also to carry with it an Adamic background.[81] This is apparent in that the commission of Gen. 1:26, 28, which included "ruling over . . . all the earth," was applied to the patriarchs with the language of "possess the gate of their enemies" and imparting a blessing to "all the nations of the earth" (Gen. 22:17–18), the latter of which is directly connected with being "given all these lands" (Gen. 26:3–4).[82] This is obvious "inheritance" language. Psalm 2:8 is likely a partial development of the reiteration of Gen. 1:26, 28 in the patriarchal promises, perhaps especially Gen. 22:17–18 and Ps. 72:17, where an individual king is promised to have sovereignty over all the nations of the earth.[83] Like Heb. 1:2, Rom. 4:13 explicitly applies these promises to the whole earth (Abraham "would be heir of the cosmos"), and Heb. 11:13–16 applies these promises to the entire new cosmos, where Gen. 22:17 is not coincidentally cited as partial support (perhaps together with Gen. 32:12). Also in this connection, Heb. 6:12–17 quotes the Abrahamic promise from Gen. 22:17, a promise in which the readers of Hebrews have hope, in direct linkage to what Jesus has begun to accomplish. Both these references in Heb. 6 and 11 are likely developments of this introductory statement in Heb. 1:2, especially since the same verb for "inherit" (*klēronomeō*) together with

81. See Harald Sahlin, "Adam-Christologie im Neuen Testament," *ST* 41 (1987): 30. Sahlin sees that "the radiance of his glory" in Heb. 1:3 alludes to Gen. 1:27 and also the description of Wisdom in Wis. 7:25–27, which he sees also to be inspired by Gen. 1:27.

82. See likewise Gen. 12:3; 13:16; 15:5; 28:14; see further in chap. 2.

83. William Lane (*Hebrews 1–8*, WBC 47A [Dallas: Word, 1991]), following H. Langhammer, has come closest to making this observation, noting a striking similarity between Abraham's change of name and his "appointment" as "father of many nations" in Gen. 17:5 and Christ being "appointed heir of all things" and "inheriting a more excellent name" (Heb. 1:2, 4), both in direct connection to Ps. 2:7–8; Paul Ellingworth (*The Epistle to the Hebrews: A Commentary on the Greek Text*, NIGTC [Grand Rapids: Eerdmans, 1993], 94–95) makes a similar observation ("Christ has now received from God a possession which was only promised and looked forward to by people in Old Testament times") and links it to the inheritance of the promised land. We have also seen how the ideal eschatological king of Ps. 72:17 ("Let men bless themselves by him; let all nations call him blessed") will be a specific fulfillment of the promised seed who would bless the nations from Gen. 22:17–18. Psalm 2:7 is part of this OT interpretative tradition, which, like Ps. 72:17, applies the patriarchal promise to an end-time king, who will "inherit" and "possess" the nations (developing also Gen. 22:17–18, where the Hebrew of v. 17 can be rendered as "your seed shall possess [*yāraš*] the gate of their enemies," or the verb *yāraš* can be rendered as "inherit"). Psalm 2 may be exploiting these two nuances of the Hebrew word by referring to both "inheritance" and "possession" in parallelism to each other. The dual use of the Greek *klēronomia* ("inheritance") and *kataschesis* ("possession"), used in the LXX of Ps. 2:8, also occurs in combination elsewhere to refer to the idea of "inheritance" in connection in one way or another to the promised land (Num. 35:8; 36:3; Ezek. 46:16, 18; see also Ezek. 44:28). Likewise, the Hebrew *naḥălâ* ("inheritance") and *'ăḥuzzâ* ("possession"), both also found in the Hebrew of Ps. 2:8, occur together elsewhere and refer to the notion of "inheritance" in direct linkage to the promised land (Num. 22:7; 32:32; 35:2, 8; Ezek. 44:28; 46:16, 18). Other combinations in Hebrew and Greek where words for "inheritance/possession" occur with respect to the promised land are found in Deut. 25:19; 26:1; Judg. 2:6; Ezek. 36:12.

the noun form (*klēronomos*) are used in both 1:2–4 (both in application to Ps. 2:7–8) and 6:12, 17.[84]

The Adamic tone of Heb. 1:2–3 is also indicated by the links between Christ in chapter 1 and the extensive quotation of the ideal Adam of Ps. 8 in Heb. 2:5–9, which is applied to Christ. These links show that the Ps. 8 quotation is a further explanation of who Christ is in chapter 1.[85] Psalm 8 is the clearest and most elaborate interpretation of Gen. 1:26–28 in all of the OT, and its application to Christ explicitly makes him the fulfillment of the ideal end-time Adam.

Thus, again, Christ is portrayed as possessing the eschatological "glory" of Adam "and the exact representation" of God, and he has achieved the ruling position that the first Adam lost. In this position he is also able to "bring many sons to glory" (Heb. 2:10), so they will be identified with and enjoy the benefits of his Adamic position. The overt eschatological nature of Heb. 1:1–6 (indeed of the whole book) is introduced by 1:2, where it says that God has revealed these things through Christ "in these last days." We saw in chapter 3 that the exact form of this phrase (*ep' eschatou tōn hēmerōn toutōn*, though without the final *toutōn* ["these"]) occurs four times in the OT, all of which are translations of the Hebrew "in the latter days" (*bĕʾaḥărît hayyāmîm*) from Num. 24:14; Jer. 23:20; 25:19 (49:39 MT); Dan. 10:14.[86] It appears that the Num. 24 messianic passage may be uppermost in mind, since the wording at the end of Heb. 1:2 (the "Son whom He appointed heir of all things") is an allusion to Ps. 2:7–8 concerning the messianic "son" who will "inherit" the nations and the "ends of the earth." Both Num. 24:14–20 and Ps. 2:8–9[87] use "scepter" (*šēbeṭ* [Num. 24:17; Ps. 2:9]) as an image for the Messiah, who will "crush" the "nations" (Num. 24:17; Ps. 2:9), "rule" over them, and receive them as an "inheritance" (Num. 24:18; Ps. 2:8). This enhances the eschatological nature of Heb. 1:2.

Christ's inheritance and his being in the divine image overlap with his ascended position of kingship (Heb. 1:3b, 13 in allusion to Ps. 110:1). Thus, again, his continued resurrection existence,[88] which we have seen is new creation, is part and parcel with his kingship, inheritance, and being in the image of God.

---

84. Johnson (*Hebrews*, 67) also sees that the combination of "son" with "inheritance" in Heb. 1:2 is closely associated with the promise of the land inheritance to Abraham, and he cites Heb. 6:13–14 in this connection.

85. Note the following links between Heb. 1 and the Ps. 8 quotation in Heb. 2:5–9: (1) the application of "glory" to Christ (1:3), Adam (2:7), and again to Christ (2:9); (2) ruling expressed with the image of enemies being under the king's feet (1:13 [which develops 1:3b]; 2:8); (3) Christ's ruling position being better than the position of angels (1:4; 2:5); (4) "all things" (*ta panta*) being subjected to Christ's rule (1:3; 2:8a, 8b; see also 2:10, where the phrase pertains to that over which God is sovereign).

86. Daniel 10:14 OG contains the reading *ep' eschatou tōn hēmerōn*; Dan. 10:14 TH reads almost identically.

87. Here in mind are both the Hebrew and Greek texts of the Numbers and Ps. 2 texts.

88. Christ's resurrection is also indicated in Heb. 1:5a, where the Ps. 2:7 citation ("Today I have begotten You") refers to Christ's ongoing resurrection state (i.e., his ascended state), as it

The Restoration of the Image in the Book of Revelation

I argued in an earlier work that in Revelation a "mark" on the forehead and hand identifies one with commitment to the beast, and a different mark also distinguishes the followers of the Lamb (see Rev. 13:16–14:1).[89] These marks connote that the followers of Christ and the followers of the beast are stamped with the image (= character) of their respective leader.[90] Each group also bears the "name" of its respective leader (whether of the beast or of the Lamb and God). We also saw that to bear or reflect the name of someone is to reflect that person's character. I argued that this is likely the conceptual way that Revelation conveys the idea of fallen humans bearing the image of fallen and deceived humanity and of God's people regaining and being in the image of Christ and the Father (see Rev. 14:1). Thus, one resembles what one reveres, either for ruin or for restoration. Those who bear Christ's "new name" (Rev. 2:17; 3:12) show that they have entered into an eschatological marriage relationship with God through Christ, and that they become one with him and so share in the attributes of his image and reflect him. In this respect, God and the Lamb's "name" is written on "their forehead" as they are pictured being completely restored to the reestablished garden of Eden in the new creation, where "there will no longer be any curse" (see Rev. 22:1–5). They thus regain the position that Adam lost and are escalated into an even greater closeness to God that will never be lost. They "will see his face" and so reflect the glorious light of that face (cf. Rev. 21:10–11; 22:4–5) and consequently reflect his image as originally intended.

Conclusion: The Restoration of the Image of God in the New Testament

Christ has come as the end-time Adam to do what the first Adam should have done and to reflect his Father's image perfectly and to enable his people to have that image restored in them. In so doing, Christ is restarting history, which is a new-creational age to be successfully consummated at his final coming.

---

does in Acts 13:33, though there it refers to the inception of the resurrected state of Jesus (the phrase "You are My Son" from Ps. 2:7 is applied also to Jesus at his baptism [Matt. 3:17; Mark 1:11; Luke 3:22], but the language of "today" and "begetting" is omitted). For various interpretations of the phrase in Heb. 1:5a and for his own conclusion, in line with my view here, see Ellingworth, *Hebrews*, 113–14; see likewise Ben Witherington, *Letters and Homilies for Jewish Christians: A Socio-Rhetorical Commentary on Hebrews, James and Jude* [Downers Grove, IL: IVP Academic, 2007], 126).

89. For elaboration of the following paragraph, see G. K. Beale, *We Become What We Worship: A Biblical Theology of Idolatry* (Downers Grove, IL: IVP Academic, 2008), 254–64.

90. For *charagma* meaning not only "mark" or "stamp" but also "image," see BDAG 1077.

PART 5

THE STORY OF SALVATION AS INAUGURATED END-TIME NEW CREATION

15

The Inaugurated Latter-Day Justification

This chapter will discuss the redemptive-historical story of salvation primarily through the lens of the "already and not yet" notion of justification. Salvation will be looked at in light of justification as the end-time righteousness that was to be characteristic of the new creation, especially in connection to the death and resurrection of Christ and the saints' identification with Christ's death and resurrection. Thus, in addition to the idea of the image of God discussed in the preceding two chapters, I will argue that justification also is best understood as a facet of the new creation introduced by Christ's death and especially his resurrection. Consequently, this chapter will focus on that part of my proposed NT storyline that deals with Christ's death and resurrection for his people as an all-important element in the building of the kingdom of the new creation.

Justification as the Attribution[1] of the Representative Righteousness of Christ to Believers

It is appropriate to begin with a definition of justification.[2] The following definition comes from the opening statement on "Of Justification" in Article 11

---

1. For the use of the word "attribution" to explain "imputation," see Mark A. Garcia, "Imputation and the Christology of Union with Christ: Calvin, Osiander, and the Contemporary Quest for a Reformed Model," *WTJ* 68 (2006): 219–51. Garcia first explains the model of "christological attribution," which he sees to be the key to understanding "soteriological [or justifying] attribution" as it relates to union with Christ. That which is true of one of the natures is attributed to the entire person of Christ. The humanity and deity of Christ, and the qualities unique to these natures, should be kept distinct. Yet the two natures inseparably belong to the person of Christ. What is said to be true of one nature is, by means of the reality of the unity of the person, understood to be true of the entire person and, hence, in some way true of the other nature (ibid., 245). Soteriological attribution is understood on analogy with christological attribution. "The distinctive righteousness of Christ, which is proper to him alone, is 'attributed' to believers *only within* and *because of* the reality of their union with him. This 'attributed' righteousness, proper to Christ alone, is ours 'improperly' but truly because of the reality of the union" (ibid., 246). Thus, "imputation is the *attribution* to the believer of the righteousness which is proper to Christ and yet truly the personal possession of the believer within the context of his union with Christ, the 'foundation' for this attribution" (ibid., 246).
2. For a broad overview of debates about the meaning of justification and its significance for Paul in the mid- to late twentieth century, see Peter T. O'Brien, "Justification in Paul and Some

of the Westminster Confession of Faith, which has been highly influential in the Protestant Reformed tradition:

> Those whom God effectually calleth, he also freely justifieth: not by infusing righteousness into them, but by pardoning their sins, and by accounting and accepting their persons as righteous; not for any thing wrought in them, or done by them, but for Christ's sake alone; not by imputing faith itself, the act of believing, or any other evangelical obedience to them, as their righteousness; but by imputing the obedience and satisfaction of Christ unto them, they receiving and resting on him and his righteousness by faith; which faith they have not of themselves, it is the gift of God.

Introduction

Today there is debate about imputation and its relation to "justification by faith." Many Protestants still view the imputation of Christ's representative "active and passive obedience" to be fundamental to understanding justification by faith. Nevertheless, many others have expressed skepticism about "positive imputation" or the so-called imputation of righteousness achieved by the "active obedience" of Christ. Given a choice between the imputed "active obedience" of Christ and that of his "passive obedience," some scholars believe that only the latter can be supported scripturally. D. A. Carson has recently described well the current varying perspectives on this issue:

> For many Protestants today, the doctrine of imputation has become the crucial touchstone for orthodoxy with respect to justification. For others, imputation is to be abandoned as an outdated relic of a system that focuses far too much attention on substitutionary penal atonement and far too little attention on alternative "models" of what the cross achieved. For still others, including N. T. Wright, imputation should be abandoned, even though (he maintains) everything that Reformed theologians want to preserve under that rubric he thinks he preserves under his much larger categories. And for still others, such as Robert Gundry, what is to be rejected is certainly not every aspect of imputation, but affirmations of the imputed righteousness of Christ.[3]

Thus, the traditional doctrine of the imputation of Christ's active obedience in relation to justification is presently being reevaluated and debated.[4] This

Crucial Issues of the Last Two Decades," in *Right with God: Justification in the Bible and the World*, ed. D. A. Carson (Grand Rapids: Baker Academic, 1992), 69–81.

3. D. A. Carson, "The Vindication of Imputation: On Fields of Discourse and Semantic Fields," in *Justification: What's at Stake in the Current Debates*, ed. Mark A. Husbands and Daniel J. Treier (Downers Grove, IL: InterVarsity, 2004), 46–47. Carson names representative scholars holding each position listed.

4. Besides N. T. Wright, I especially have in mind the debate between Robert H. Gundry and Thomas C. Oden in *Books and Culture*: Gundry, "Why I Didn't Endorse 'The Gospel of Jesus Christ: An Evangelical Celebration' . . . Even Though I Wasn't Asked To," *Books and Culture*

issue is not merely a debate between scholars; it has raged among members of some of the evangelical Presbyterian denominations.[5]

Here I cannot survey the permutations of this doctrine since the time of the Reformation and describe how widespread in Protestant circles this traditional doctrine was. Nevertheless, I think it fair to say that it was widespread and even the dominant view, though not all held to it.[6]

In this chapter I hope to make a small contribution to this debate. In the initial section of this chapter I will first discuss briefly the passages most typically proposed to favor the crediting, or "attributing," of Christ's righteousness to believers. Second, I will survey the expectations for Adam's obedience as it is stated in Gen. 1–2, as it is restated and reapplied to others in the early and later chapters of Genesis, and then repeated and reapplied at other points subsequently in the OT. Third, I will briefly look at two passages in the NT, 1 Cor. 15 and Eph. 1–2, where Christ is portrayed as a "last Adam" figure with the language of the OT expectations and how his status as such an eschatological and new-creational figure relates to believers in Christ. Ephesians 1–2 especially is a text that, to my knowledge, has not played a significant role in the discussion of justification. The remaining bulk of the chapter will address the "already and not yet" end-time aspect of justification, especially in relation to Christ's death and, above all, his resurrection.

Texts Traditionally Adduced to Support the Imputation of Christ's Active Obedience to Believers

Four texts traditionally adduced to support this doctrine are Rom. 5:15–19; 1 Cor. 1:30; 2 Cor. 5:21; Phil. 3:9. All, in my view, support the concept of

---

7, no. 1 (2001): 6–9; Oden, "A Calm Answer to a Critique of 'The Gospel of Jesus Christ: An Evangelical Celebration,'" *Books and Culture* 7, no. 2 (2001): 1–12, 39; Gundry, "On Oden's Answer," *Books and Culture* 7, no. 2 (2001): 14–15, 39. Note also the exchange between D. A. Carson and Robert Gundry at the Wheaton Theology Conference of 2004: for the written form of Gundry's address, see "The Non-imputation of Christ's Righteousness," in Husbands and Treier, eds., *Justification*, 17–45. See also John Piper, *Counted Righteous in Christ: Should We Abandon the Imputation of Christ's Righteousness?* (Wheaton: Crossway, 2002); idem, *The Future of Justification: A Response to N. T. Wright* (Wheaton: Crossway, 2007). Piper argues for the traditional Reformed view and in the latter work negatively evaluates the position of Wright.

5. See E. Calvin Beisner, ed., *The Auburn Avenue Theology, Pros and Cons: Debating the Federal Vision* (Ft. Lauderdale, FL: Knox Theological Seminary Press, 2004), which represents the debates among some evangelical Presbyterians in the United States.

6. For a survey of those in the Reformed tradition who have affirmed that imputation is a part of a proper understanding of justification, see Heinrich Heppe, *Reformed Dogmatics Set Out and Illustrated from the Sources*, trans. G. T. Thompson, rev. and ed. Ernst Bizer (London: Allen & Unwin, 1950), 548–51; Benjamin B. Warfield, *Biblical and Theological Studies*, ed. Samuel G. Craig (Philadelphia: P&R, 1952), 262–69; Michael F. Bird, "Incorporated Righteousness: A Response to Recent Evangelical Discussion concerning the Imputation of Christ's Righteousness in Justification," *JETS* 47 (2004): 253–56; the last two works also cite some in the Protestant tradition who have not held to imputation.

Christ's righteousness being passed on representatively to those who believe in him.[7] Here my purpose is to review briefly what I think are viable texts supporting the notion of the attribution of Christ's righteousness to saints.

Although Rom. 5:15–19 focuses on Christ's death as the "one act of righteousness" that resulted in "justification," it is plausible that this one act serves as the climax of the obedience of his whole ministry, so that his entire life of righteousness may secondarily be in mind also.

Second Corinthians 5:21 has the same focus as Rom. 5:15–19 with the same implications: "He made Him who knew no sin to be sin on our behalf, so that we might become the righteousness of God in Him." This affirms that Christ was identified with an alien guilt and suffered a punishment that he did not deserve.[8] The verse says that the purpose of this is that the sinners for whom Christ bore the punishment would "become the righteousness of God in Him [Christ]." This means that they would thus be considered "not guilty" and not deserving the punishment even though they had been sinful. However, to "become the righteousness of God in Christ" apparently involves more than a "not guilty" status; it also means being identified with "the righteousness of God," not just in the dead Christ but explicitly in the risen Christ, so that some positive aspect of Christ's righteousness is attributed to believers. Some contend that this passage has nothing to do with Christ's own righteousness that represents his people, since it speaks of "the righteousness of God." But this is "the righteousness of God in Christ." Thus, Christ himself reflects God's righteousness, and that righteousness is attributed to believers "in Christ." We will see in this chapter that this at least entails being identified with God's righteous vindication of Christ and thus Christ's own vindicated position of resurrection that had

---

7. For recent discussion of these passages, among others, in this respect, see Piper, *Counted Righteous in Christ*, 52–119.

8. The phrase "He made Him to be sin [*hamartia*]" should likely be rendered "He made Him to be a sin offering," since the singular *hamartia* often has this meaning in the OT (e.g., see multiple such uses in Leviticus and Numbers). That this is Paul's meaning in using the word is apparent in that, although he uses the word often in his epistles, he never uses it in the way he does here, since elsewhere it refers to moral transgression, but here does not (otherwise he would be viewing Christ as a sinner). That the word means "sin offering" is probable also because Paul is likely alluding to Isa. 53:10, where the Servant is said to "render Himself as a guilt offering." The LXX translates the Hebrew "guilt offering" (*'āšām*) as *hamartia*. The allusion is pointed to further by the fact that this Isa. 53 context is the only place in the OT where it is prophesied that a prophetic leader of Israel would not be guilty of sin (53:9) yet would bear the punishment of the sin of others (53:4–6, 8, 12), together with employing the idiom of "sin" to mean "sin offering," in order to redeem them and declare them righteous (53:11). Such an allusion to Isa. 53 paves the way for the allusion to Isa. 49:4 in 2 Cor. 6:1 ("not to receive the grace of God in vain") and for the quotation of Isa. 49:8 in 2 Cor. 6:2. For further support of the Isa. 53 allusion, see G. K. Beale, "The Old Testament Background of Reconciliation in 2 Corinthians 5–7 and Its Bearing on the Literary Problem of 2 Corinthians 4:14–7:1," *NTS* 35 (1989): 559–60; Scott J. Hafemann, *2 Corinthians*, NIVAC (Grand Rapids: Zondervan, 2000), 247–48.

overturned the world's guilty verdict on him and demonstrated him to have been righteous in his earthly life.

Some dispute that Phil. 3:9 is a text that affirms the imputation of Christ's righteousness to saints because it speaks of "the righteousness which comes from God [not Christ] on the basis of faith." Accordingly, as with 2 Cor. 5:21, it is argued that this refers to God's righteousness, and therefore Christ's own righteousness is not to be seen here as attributed to believers. I think that a viable and sufficient response to this is to say that on the basis of faith in Christ, God declares believers righteous, and that this is "not a righteousness of my own derived from the Law" but rather one that comes because saints have given up their flawed righteousness "for the sake of Christ" (3:7) and in order to "gain Christ" (3:8 [which likely would include Christ's righteousness]) and to be "found in Him" (3:9a [Would this not also include being identified with Christ's own righteousness?]).

Accordingly, the "righteousness which comes from God" is mediated to believers by their identification and unity with the righteous Christ. The Christ with whom they are identified is the one who "became obedient to the point of death" (Phil. 2:8), so that his people being "found in him" likely are identified with that obedience, which reached a climax at the cross. "The righteousness which comes from God" is contrasted with "not having a righteousness of my own derived from the Law," so that this is a positive righteousness with which Paul the believer is now identified. And, as in 2 Cor. 5:21, it is God's righteousness with which one is identified, which likely itself is also to be identified with Christ, since Paul is given this status because he has "gained Christ" and is "found in" Christ (Phil. 3:8–9). To say that God's righteousness in this passage is not also identified with Christ (and then believers) would be a very thin descriptive view. As we will see later God has declared Jesus righteous (i.e., vindicated), and this is a righteous status that Jesus himself possesses, and those in union with him share in Christ's justified (vindicated) status.

The text that I see as the strongest affirmation of the positive imputation of Christ's righteousness to believers is 1 Cor. 1:30: "But by His doing you are in Christ Jesus, who became for us wisdom from God, and righteousness and sanctification [or 'holiness'], and redemption." Believers' identification and union with Christ means that "in him" they are considered to have the same (perfect) wisdom, righteousness, holiness, and redemption that Christ had.[9] This does not mean that believers possess these attributes in their personal existence on earth; rather, they are represented by Christ as having become these things for them because of their positional identification of unity with

---

9. It is perhaps best to translate v. 30 interpretatively as "But by his doing you are in Christ Jesus, who became to us wisdom from God, *that is* righteousness and sanctification and redemption," so that these last three realities are appositional to what "wisdom" is (so G. D. Fee, *The First Epistle to the Corinthians*, NICNT [Grand Rapids: Eerdmans, 1987], 85–86. This does not, however, have significant affect on the following discussion.

him (i.e., they "are in Christ"). The "for us" (*hēmin*) in the verse refers to their position "in Christ Jesus" and identification with his attributes being on their behalf or for their benefit.[10]

Objectors to this analysis find it hard to see how Christ was personally redeemed in the same way believers are to be seen as redeemed. They argue that the verse speaks of Christ redeeming people but not of he himself being redeemed from sin on their behalf as their representative, for it would be un-Pauline and heterodox to conceive of Christ himself being redeemed from sin, even as a representative for his people. Then it is argued that neither should the references to wisdom, righteousness, and holiness in the verse be taken in a representative manner. Such a view would, of course, undercut 1 Cor. 1:30 as a text that supports the positive reckoning of Christ's righteousness to the Christian. The verse would merely refer to believers becoming wise, righteous, sanctified, and redeemed through Christ, the first three attributes being godly traits that should increasingly characterize the lives of true believers but are not completely attained because of one's position in Jesus, who is unfailingly complete in these qualities.

A word study of the Greek word for "redemption," however, resolves this apparent problem. The word for "redemption" in 1 Cor. 1:30 is *apolytrōsis*, which is part of the "redemption" word group (*lytroō, lytrōsis*). Except for the verb *lytroō* ("redeem"), the other forms occur little in the LXX. One of the prominent uses of the verb is that of referring to God delivering Israel from the oppression of Egypt (about 15x), though the notion of delivering individuals from various forms of oppression is found (about 15x), as well as deliverance from the oppression of Babylon (about 5x). Although there are some uses where "redeem" involves delivering people from or out of their sin, the above uses refer only to deliverance from oppression, not from their own sin. In light of the LXX background, it would seem to be a very normal usage in 1 Cor. 1:30 for "redemption" to refer to deliverance from oppression, especially in the case of Christ. It would refer to his deliverance, indeed salvation, from death and bondage to the powers of evil by his resurrection.

Particularly interesting is Isaiah's use of "redemption" in 63:4 to speak of Israel's redemption from the oppression of enemy nations, and especially the verb "redeem" in 63:9 ("He redeemed them"), referring to God's deliverance of Israel at the exodus; this thought is continued in 63:11, "Where is He who brought up from the sea with the shepherd of His flock?" referring to God's deliverance of Moses from the Egyptian army and the flooding sea. This is striking because Heb. 13:20 alludes to Isa. 63:11 and applies that redemptive deliverance from the Red Sea to Christ's deliverance from death by resurrection:

10. For *hēmin* as a dative of advantage in 1 Cor. 1:30, see, e.g., Anthony C. Thiselton, *The First Epistle to the Corinthians: A Commentary on the Greek Text*, NIGTC (Grand Rapids: Eerdmans, 2000), 191.

"Now the God of peace, who brought up from the dead the great Shepherd of the sheep. . . ." Paul's own uses of this "redemption" word group refer not only to deliverance from sin (Rom. 3:24; Eph. 1:7; Col. 1:14; Titus 2:14) but also to deliverance from death through resurrection (Rom. 8:23; and likely Eph. 1:14; 4:30).[11]

Thus, it is not problematic to see that Christ was "redeemed" (i.e., delivered from death by resurrection), and that his full and absolute deliverance represented the deliverance from death for those who believe in him and are positionally found "in him." What also points to all the attributes of 1 Cor. 1:30 being completely true of saints because of their identification with Christ is that the "holiness" (*hagiasmos*) mentioned there is likely a development of the first mention of it in 1:2: "to the church of God which is at Corinth, <u>to those who have been made holy</u> [*hēgiasmenois*] in Christ Jesus." Some might want to argue that Christ's becoming "holiness" (or "sanctification") for us refers to an actual holiness that is partially and progressively worked out in people during the present age, not to an imputed or perfected positional reality.[12] Some think that the same thing is true of "wisdom" and "redemption." If so, the reference to "righteousness" would seem to be parallel and refer to a righteousness that is worked out in believers partially and progressively, not to the perfect righteousness of Christ. This is, for example, the objection of N. T. Wright, who says that if 1 Cor. 1:30 speaks of the perfect righteousness of Christ imputed to the believer, then "we must also be prepared to talk of the imputed wisdom of Christ; the imputed sanctification of Christ; the imputed redemption of Christ."[13] The use of the perfect tense in 1 Cor. 1:2, however, refers to an act in the past that has been fully completed with the effects of that act continuing on into the present.[14] Both verses have the believers positioned "in Christ Jesus," and verse 2 sees the saints as having been already fully sanctified or considered completely holy, even though on earth each one is still very sinful, as the remainder of the letter will elaborate.

11. For expansion of this notion of the resurrection as the redemption of Christ, see Richard B. Gaffin Jr., *The Centrality of the Resurrection: A Study in Paul's Soteriology* (Grand Rapids: Baker Academic, 1978), 114–16.

12. So Piper (*Counted Righteous in Christ*, 86), who would affirm this about "holiness" in 1 Cor. 1:30 yet still holds that "righteousness" refers to a positional or imputed righteousness; if so, the series of terms in this verse does not refer to parallel positional or imputed concepts, contrary to the argument being set forth here. Accordingly, the idea would be that believers have unity with Christ, and that some aspects of that unity are positionally representative or imputational while others have a direct effect on believers' actual living of life on earth. I agree with this concept, though I see no need to appeal to it in 1 Cor. 1:30.

13. N. T. Wright, *What Saint Paul Really Said: Was Paul of Tarsus the Real Founder of Christianity?* (Oxford: Lion Publishing, 1997), 123.

14. The present effects of the past act being either the fully sanctified positional condition of the saints or the beginning but partial effects of actual holiness in their lives (though the former is more probable).

Therefore, it is natural to take the reference in 1:30 to Christ becoming "holiness" for the saints in the same way. That is, 1:30 explains that the saints became fully sanctified (1:2) because Christ was perfectly holy, and their position "in him" as their representative caused them to be considered entirely holy. We have also seen that it is natural to take "redemption" (i.e., redemptive deliverance) in the same way, and there is no reason not to take "wisdom" likewise. That is, Christ is the perfect expression of divine wisdom, and those identified with Christ are represented by this wisdom (which, as we have seen elsewhere, is a part of Adam Christology in that Christ is the ultimate eschatological wise man that Adam should have been).[15] Accordingly, such a view of "righteousness" also fits well into this. In fact, *hagiazō*, the verbal form of "holiness," occurs in 1 Cor. 6:11 together with *dikaioō*, the verbal from of "righteousness," and both refer to a completed act on behalf of the saints: "Such were some of you; but you were washed, but you were sanctified, but you were justified [or "declared righteous"] in the name of the Lord Jesus Christ and in the Spirit of our God." Just as they were completely and definitively "washed," so were they likewise completely "sanctified" and justified." All the attributes mentioned in 1:30 have found complete and perfect eschatological expression in Christ, and this complete latter-day expression of these things in Christ is attributed to believers, who positionally share in these things by virtue of their union with Christ. So, for instance, ethical perfection was to be achieved only in the new creation, and since Christ has inaugurated such complete "holiness," it is attributed to believers even though they have not yet achieved it.

This notion of believers being represented by these attributes of Christ is enhanced by the first part of 1:30, which says that it was "by His [God's] doing" (*ex autou*, "because of him" or "from him") that they "are in Christ Jesus," and because they are "in" him, they positionally share in his perfect traits that are listed. This notion of God's causative action in placing them in Christ probably is a development of the immediately preceding references to their election in 1:26–28. Thus, they are to boast not of their own abilities (vv. 29, 31) but rather of the positional benefits that come from their representation by Christ and his flawless abilities.

Some object to the idea that these attributes are those of Christ, since 1:30 says that these are characteristics "from God." Accordingly, it has been argued

---

15. On which, see chap. 2, where I discuss Adam and wisdom, as well as chap. 14, where I discuss Christ as a wise Adam figure in Col. 1:15–18; see also Seyoon Kim, *The Origin of Paul's Gospel* (Grand Rapids: Eerdmans, 1982), 258–60. Paul identifies Christ as "the last Adam" in 1 Cor. 15:45, and in 15:46–54 speaks of this last Adam's image in relation to the believers' final reflection of that image, which may have some degree of relevance for the present discussion. In this latter respect, see Benjamin L. Gladd, *Revealing the* Mysterion: *The Use of* Mystery *in Daniel and Second Temple Judaism with Its Bearing on First Corinthians*, BZNW 160 (Berlin: de Gruyter, 2008), e.g., 267–69, who contends that the divine "mystery" in 1 Corinthians is used as a reference to divine wisdom as a polemic against the Corinthians worldly wisdom, and this includes the reference to "mystery" in 1 Cor. 15:51, which is inextricably linked there to the image of Adam discussion.

that "the righteousness that Christ becomes for us is not his own righteousness, but God's."[16] This is a specious objection, since the full thought is that "Christ Jesus . . . became for us wisdom <u>from</u> God, and righteousness. . . ." So of course this is the righteousness of God, but Christ is fully identified with God's righteousness and hence possesses it, and thus so are believers fully identified with God's righteousness as it has been fully expressed in Christ, which is also Christ's righteousness. As seen above, this is also similar to the thought involved in Phil. 3:9, where being "found in him [Christ]" and "not having a righteousness of my own" results in being identified with "the righteousness which comes from God," and is expressed in Christ. We saw the same notion in 2 Cor. 5:21. In fact, this analysis of 1 Cor. 1:30 points further to the likelihood of my earlier conclusion that in 2 Cor. 5:21 and Phil. 3:9 the "righteousness of God" is identified with Jesus himself, and then his righteousness is attributed to saints.

Therefore, 1 Cor. 1:30 is best taken to be supportive of the notion that saints are represented by the perfect righteousness of Christ and are considered fully righteous as he is.[17] This is the righteousness fit only for the eternal new creation of the end time. I believe that Rom. 5:15–19; 1 Cor. 1:30; 2 Cor. 5:21; Phil. 3:9, traditionally adduced for the positive imputation of Christ's righteousness, stand as such, but much more can be said in favor of the doctrine. To this we now turn.

The Expectations for Adam's Obedience and the Application of These Expectations to Other Adam-Like Figures and Finally to Christ

It is important to review at this point the discussion of Gen. 1:28 from chapter 2 because I will argue that this is an important background for

16. Gundry, "Why I Didn't Endorse," 7.
17. Consistent with this conclusion, David Garland says that "righteousness" is a legal reference to "the state of having been aquitted and sharing Christ's righteous character" (*1 Corinthians*, BECNT [Grand Rapids: Baker Academic, 2003], 80]); so too Thiselton (*First Epistle to the Corinthians*, 193), who also points out that the verbal form is used elsewhere in the book only in a declarative legal sense of "count righteous" or "acquit." Likewise, Gordon Fee says that "righteousness" is more a forensic than ethical term that "highlights the believer's undeserved stance of right standing before God" (*First Epistle to the Corinthians*, NICNT [Grand Rapids: Eerdmans, 1987], 86). Thiselton's (*First Epistle to the Corinthians*, 190–95) understanding of being "in Christ Jesus" and of the four attributes with which saints are identified in 1 Cor. 1:30 as referring to a complete or definitive status because of "corporate solidarity," and not a referring to "private Christian existence," is consistent with my analysis here. Early testimony to this notion comes from *Diognetus* (late second century AD): "In whom was it possible for us, the lawless and ungodly, to be justified, except in the Son of God alone? O the sweet exchange, O the incomprehensible work of God, O the unexpected blessings, that the sinfulness of many should be hidden in one righteous man, while the righteousness of one should justify many sinners!" (9:4–5).

understanding Christ's justifying work. The commission of Gen. 1:26–28 involved the following elements, especially as summarized in verse 28:

1. God blessed them;
2. be fruitful and multiply;
3. fill the earth;
4. subdue the earth;
5. rule over all the earth.

It also appears that God's making of Adam in his "image" and "likeness" is what is to enable Adam to carry out the particular parts of the commission. As an image-bearer, Adam was to reflect the character of God, which included mirroring the divine glory. Together with the prohibition in Gen. 2:16–17, the essence of the commission was that of subduing and ruling over the earth and filling it with God's glory, especially through glorious image-bearing progeny. I explained in more detail in chapter 2 what this commission entailed and what escalated eschatological blessings Adam would have received had he obeyed. The essence of this reward was an irreversible and eternal incorruptibility of physical and spiritual life, which would be lived in an incorruptible cosmos that was free from any evil or sinful threat.

Adam, however, failed in the task with which he was commissioned. We also saw in chapter 2 a long list of OT passages indicating that Adam's commission was passed on to other Adam-like figures (e.g., Noah, the patriarchs, Israel), but all of them failed to carry out the commission. Beginning with the patriarchs, however, the repeated Adamic commission was combined with a promise of a "seed" who would "bless" the nations, thus suggesting that the commission would finally be fulfilled at some point by the seed. Failure would continue until there would arise this seed, a "last Adam," who would finally fulfill the commission on behalf of humanity.

The restatements of the Gen. 1 Adamic commission beginning with Abraham are put in terms either of a promise of some positive act that will occur or of some command that is to lead to positive obedience. Both the promissory and the imperatival reiterations pertain to the seed's positive "multiplying and increasing," "spreading out," actual conquering and possessing or inheriting. In this light, would it not be odd if the NT never spoke of the last Adam, Jesus, in the same positive terms? Now, it is true that the NT conceives of part of Christ's obedience to the mandate of Adam to be his obedience to death. This is certainly, at the least, what Rom. 5:12–17; Phil. 2:5–11; Heb. 2:6–10 speak about. Jesus did not only what the first Adam should have done but also much more: he even became obedient to death on behalf of his people on the road to his great victory of resurrection and exaltation.

It should be admitted that Paul, for example, speaks more about Christ's so-called passive obedience of death than he does his own active obedience in redeeming people. Nevertheless, in addition to the above references to the attribution of Christ's righteousness to saints, there are some places in the NT where Jesus as the last Adam is portrayed without reference to his death but instead is viewed as having done what Adam should have done. For example, I analyzed Christ's temptation in the wilderness (Matt. 4:1–11; Luke 4:1–13) in terms of Christ being both a last Adam and a true Israel figure (i.e., corporate Adam) who obeys at just the points where Adam and Israel disobeyed (see chap. 13).

Likewise, Paul sometimes portrays Christ as a last Adam who has received the victorious position and reward of glorious and incorruptible kingship, apparently as a result of having accomplished all the requirements of obedience that were expected of the first Adam, especially conquering and possessing. In 1 Cor. 15:27 and Eph. 1:22 Paul says that Christ has fulfilled the Ps. 8:6 ideal that was expected of the first Adam: "He [God] has put all things in subjection under His [Christ's] feet." The concluding phrase in Eph. 1:23, "Him who fills all in all," is applied to Christ here and likely reflects "fill the earth" in Gen. 1:28, which was part of the original commission to Adam. In 1 Cor. 15:45 Paul explicitly refers to Christ as the "last Adam," who has achieved the escalated blessing of incorruptibility that the first Adam failed to obtain. Both the 1 Corinthians and the Ephesians passages identify believers with either Christ's incorruptible blessings (1 Cor. 15:49–57) or his position of all things being in subjection to him (Eph. 2:5–6). The same implications are expressed in Heb. 2:6–17, though there it is Christ's death that is highlighted and the resurrection is muted (though cf. Heb. 2:9: "crowned with glory and honor").

Paul views Christ himself as having decisively fulfilled the Adamic commission of Ps. 8; this likely entails Paul's belief, in light of the context of Ps. 8, that Christ himself, individually and flawlessly, ruled, subdued, multiplied spiritual progeny (though this element is missing in Ps. 8), and filled the earth with God's glory, as fully as one human could in one lifetime. This is an inaugurated eschatological idea, since Christ's faithful obedience as the last Adam is the only thing that could have led to the reward of being propelled into the new creation and kingship in that creation. That is, his resurrected body was the literal beginning of the latter-day new creation and his obedient reign in that new creation, which is what was expected of the first Adam but never obtained by him. As believers are identified with Christ's heavenly position of resurrection and kingly exaltation, they also are identified with his reward of exalted kingship in the new creation and the faithful obedience that continues to characterize that new-creational kingship, an obedience that is the climax of his victorious obedience on earth that led up to the heavenly reward. This represents a breaking in of the future new creation into the present. It is not a completed new creation, since believers are not personally on earth perfectly obedient kings, nor have they personally experienced their full reward of consummate resurrection as they will at the very end of the age. Nevertheless, they are identified with Christ as the last Adam, who was completely obedient.

This notion of Christ doing what Adam should have done and achieving the glorious blessed position that Adam should have inherited and then having believers identified with this glorious position is close conceptually to and suggestive of the idea of attributing Christ's positive obedience to believers.[18]

Justification in Relation to Death and Resurrection as an Already–Not Yet Latter-Day Reality

In the preceding section I mainly discussed, albeit briefly, Christ's representative faithful obedience as the last Adam and his reward of entering into the new creation as an inaugurated eschatological concept. The goal of the rest of this chapter is to continue to comment on the eschatological nature of justification, especially with respect to how the inaugurated phase as an end-time reality relates to how it is to be consummated. Accordingly, I will focus more on the future nature of justification. This section is not an exhaustive essay on the nature of justification in general but rather a discussion of how the eschatological death of Christ, and especially his resurrection—and the resurrection of believers represented by Christ—helps us to better understand both the "inaugurated eschatological phase" and the "consummated eschatological phase" of justification. In this section I will continue to argue in favor of the imputation of Christ's positive righteousness to the believer through focusing on how the believer is identified with Christ's resurrection, though the justifying nature of Christ's death and the believers' identification with it will also be addressed.

The Inaugurated Eschatological Nature of Justification

My preceding discussion of Christ as the righteous last Adam and his representation of saints provides a good example of the eschaton breaking into history. Christ's role as the resurrected last Adam indicates that another new creation has begun and broken into the old age of the fallen creation. The notion that complete righteousness could be achieved by a human was something reserved for humans only in the eternal new creation. This has begun in Christ and vicariously through him for his people.

THE CROSS OF CHRIST BEGINS THE ESCHATOLOGICAL JUDGMENT

The other side of the coin of this inaugurated eschatology about Christ's representative righteousness is that the final judgment that was to occur at the

---

18. See Peter Stuhlmacher, *Biblische Theologie des Neuen Testaments*, vol. 2 (Göttingen: Vandenhoeck & Ruprecht, 1999), 15–16, who views the concept of justification being taken up in Eph. 2:1–10, though the actual language of justification is not used.

very end of history has been pushed back into history at the cross of Christ. This is expressed in Rom. 3:21–26:

> But now apart from the Law the righteousness of God has been manifested, being witnessed by the Law and the Prophets, even the righteousness of God through faith in Jesus Christ for all those who believe; for there is no distinction; for all have sinned and fall short of the glory of God, being justified as a gift by His grace through the redemption which is in Christ Jesus; whom God displayed publicly as a propitiation in His blood through faith. This was to demonstrate His righteousness, because in the forbearance of God He passed over the sins previously committed; for the demonstration, I say, of His righteousness at the present time, so that He would be just and the justifier of the one who has faith in Jesus.

God in his "forbearance" had "passed over the sins previously committed," which sins, according to OT and Jewish expectation, would be punished in the last great judgment. This great judgment, however, has begun to be executed upon the Messiah on behalf of his people (v. 25) before the watching world, which shows that despite delaying judgment for a time, God does punish sin and is vindicated as righteous. This is the case even though the judgment that Jesus suffers is on behalf of those who believe (vv. 22, 26). Thus, the eschatological judgment has begun in Jesus, but it will be consummated in the judgment of unbelievers at the very end of the age, directly preceding the establishment of the new creation. Hence, the final judgment is staggered for "all the world," which is "accountable" to God for its sin (Rom. 3:19): the sin of believers is judged first in Christ's death in the first century, and unbelievers suffer this judgment in their own persons at the climax of history.

Further confirmation that Rom. 3 is speaking of the eschatological judgment that commences with Jesus on behalf of the faithful is apparent in the inclusio consisting of end-time temporal language that frames verses 21–26. Verse 21 starts with "now" (*nyni*), and verse 26 contains the same form of the word but in expanded form, "the present [now] time" (*tō nyn kairō*). The first "now" of verse 21 highlights that the "righteousness of God" has recently been "manifested" and was prophetically "witnessed" to by the OT, and it indicates that this righteousness is part of prophetic eschatological fulfillment (which is pointed to further by the similar statement in Rom. 16:25–26). The "now," therefore, indicates the commencement of latter-day expectations. Likewise, "the present [now] time" of verse 26 is also linked to a climax of the demonstration of the righteousness of God in contrast to the past period of redemptive history when "God passed over the sins previously committed."

While there are varying uses of "now" in the NT (a logical use, a reference to mere present time, etc.), the eschatological use of "now" to demarcate the beginning of an age in contrast to a former old age occurs elsewhere in Paul's writings and the NT. Paul combines "now" with "time" six other times, most of them clearly in connection to latter-day contexts.[19] The use of "now" by itself can often have the same temporal association.[20] Thus, Paul's use of an eschatological "now" in Rom. 3:21, 26 fits naturally into his other such uses and underscores an inaugurated eschatological context for understanding justification.

INAUGURATED JUSTIFICATION IN RELATION TO CHRIST'S REDEMPTION AND PROPITIATING DEATH AT THE CROSS

This section continues exploration and discussion of Rom. 3:21–26, especially with focus on how Paul's references to "propitiation" and "redemption" in verses 24–25 relate to "being justified" in verse 24:

> . . . being justified as a gift by His grace through the redemption which is in Christ Jesus; whom God displayed publicly as a propitiation in His blood through faith. This was to demonstrate His righteousness, because in the forbearance of God He passed over the sins previously committed.

First, a word about the preceding context of Romans is necessary. Romans 1:18–3:8 leads to the conclusion that both unbelieving Jews and gentiles are "under sin" (3:9), and that "by works of the Law no flesh will be justified in His sight" (3:20),[21] since "through the Law comes the knowledge of sin" (3:20)

---

19. The use in Rom. 8:18 indicates the part of the time period when resurrection existence for God's people is beginning (8:10–11), as is their experience of the end-time Spirit (8:5–17, 22–23); Rom. 13:11–12a is fairly straightforward in this respect: "Do this, knowing the time, that it is already the hour for you to awaken from sleep; for now salvation is nearer to us than when we believed. The night is almost gone, and the day is near"; 2 Cor. 6:2 refers to the present time when the latter-day Isaiah prophecy about God helping his servant was beginning realization (Isa. 49:8), which continues the earlier reference to the "now" of the inaugurated resurrection life and new creation, when proper evaluative judgments about Christ will be made (5:14–18); the "now" of 2 Thess. 2:6 is the same time when "the mystery of lawlessness is already at work," which is a beginning fulfillment of the end-time opponent prophecy of Dan. 11:36 (for the discussion of resurrection and the Spirit in Rom. 8, see chap. 9; for further discussion of 2 Cor. 5:14–6:2, see chaps. 10, 16; for additional discussion of 2 Thess. 2, see chap. 7); the uses in Rom. 11:5 and 2 Cor. 8:14 are not explicitly eschatological but are susceptible of such a meaning.

20. The more obvious examples of this use of "now" (*nyn*) are Rom. 16:25–26; Eph. 3:5, 10; Col. 1:26; outside of Paul's writings, see John 4:23; 5:25; 12:31; 1 John 2:18; 4:3; with respect to the alternate form of "now" (*nyni*), see Rom. 7:6; 1 Cor. 15:20; Eph. 2:13; Col. 1:22; outside of Paul's writings note Heb. 9:26: "Otherwise, He would have needed to suffer often since the foundation of the world; but now once at the consummation of the ages He has been manifested to put away sin by the sacrifice of Himself."

21. The "works of the Law" should not be seen only as effort by preconverted believers to fulfill the law; it also includes works of the law done by believers in their postconversion experience. This is apparent from, e.g., Rom. 4:6–8, which cites Ps. 32:1–2: "Just as David also speaks of the blessing on the man to whom God credits righteousness apart from works: 'Blessed are those whose lawless deeds have been forgiven, and whose sins have been covered. Blessed is the man whose sin the Lord will not take into account.'" This refers to the works of a believing

and not righteousness. This leads to the conclusion that "all the world may become accountable to God" (3:19). In contrast (*nyni de*, "but now"), 3:21 then asserts that "the Law and the Prophets witnessed" that "apart from the Law the righteousness of God" comes. This righteousness comes "through faith in Jesus Christ for all who believe" (3:22). Paul then again states the reason why righteousness must come from faith in Christ and not through one's own attempt to fulfill the law: "For all have sinned and [therefore] fall short of the glory of God" (3:23). But despite this fact,[22] 3:24 underscores that such sinners can still be "justified as a gift by His grace." Paul's use of "justified" (*dikaioō*) has been shaped by the OT, especially the LXX, and has the notion of "being declared righteous" and not "being made righteous" (in an ethical manner).[23] The entire tenor of the preceding context, beginning back at 1:17 and climaxing with 3:20, underscores that all humans stand condemned and are deserving of God's wrath because of their sin. Therefore, the notion of "justified" in 3:24 must concern primarily the prior verdict of condemnation and wrath and must indicate that those believing in Christ are now declared legally in the right and no longer in a position of condemnation.[24] This legal declaratory notion of justification also gains support from Paul's synonymous expression "the man to whom God credits [or 'reckons'] righteousness apart from works" (4:6 [so also 4:3, 5, 9–11, 22–24]).[25]

Consequently, "justification" is a forensic, legal term for Paul and specifically here in Rom. 3:25. Accordingly, Paul affirms in 3:19–24 that sinful people under condemnation are "declared" (not "made") righteous through faith in Jesus Christ. This justification in 3:24 is "a gift" (or "free")[26] and is applied

---

person (David), which Paul says cannot justify a person. Likewise, the same notion appears to be conveyed in Titus 3:5–7.

22. "Being justified" in 3:24 appears to be an adverbial participle apparently indicating a concessive idea in relation to 3:23: "all [the ones believing] [cf. v. 22] have sinned and fall short of the glory of God, though they are justified."

23. The LXX consistently renders the Hebrew *ṣādaq* with *dikaioō* in a legal declaratory sense, "pronounce/declare righteous"; even the Hiphil verb throughout the OT is not causative ("make righteous") but rather declarative ("declare righteous") (see G. Schrenk, "δικαιόω," *TDNT* 2:212–14). That this is Paul's idea throughout Rom. 3–6 in his use of the word is illustrated from his quotation of Ps. 51:4 in 3:4: "that You <u>may be justified</u> in your words." The Hebrew behind the LXX's *dikaioō* is the Qal stem of *ṣādaq*, which clearly also has the notion of "declare righteous" and not "make righteous."

24. For the relevance of the preceding context of Romans in relation to justification and propitiation in 3:25, see Leon Morris, *The Apostolic Preaching of the Cross* (Grand Rapids: Eerdmans, 1955), 167–70.

25. The idea of faith being reckoned as righteousness in Rom. 4:3, 5, 9–11, 22–24 connotes the sense of faith *in Christ's redemptive work* being reckoned as righteousness, as 3:25 and 4:24–25 make clearer. For further discussion of the legal declaratory notion of "justify" in the NT, see below under the subheading "The Meanings of *Dikaioō*."

26. The Greek word *dōrean* could be translated as "for nothing" (Gen. 29:15; Exod. 21:2, 11; Isa. 52:3; John 15:25; Gal. 2:21) or "freely" or "without a cause" (Pss. 35:7; 109:3; 119:161; Lam. 3:52), as sometimes in the LXX, which highlights even more that justification is by divine grace.

"by his [God's] grace." Thus, those being justified contribute nothing to their justification, though they receive it passively through faith, which too is a gift (see, e.g., Rom. 4:16; 9:16; Eph. 2:8–9). The cause of their justification is not from within themselves but rather is God's "free grace." Christ's penal death accounts believers not guilty and not worthy of condemnation, and they are credited with Christ's righteousness.[27]

"Redemption" in Romans 3:24

In the remainder of Rom. 3:24 and in 3:25 Paul explains the means by which justification comes about: through "redemption" and "propitiation." First, Paul says that "being justified" comes through "the redemption which is in Christ Jesus." The word "redemption" (*apolytrōsis*) means merely "release" or "release by a cost or price." Some prefer the former because the same word is used of Israel's redemption from Egypt, which appeared to entail no cost. In addition, some contend that the word in the LXX generally does not have the idea of "ransom by a price."[28] Furthermore, and in line with this, it is argued that the word used elsewhere in the NT does not carry any notion of "release by cost" or "ransom."

However, some contend that "release by a cost" is apparent in Paul's thought. First, "release by a price" is the consistent meaning of the *lytron* ("redemption" or "ransom") word group (of which *apolytrōsis* is a part) in Hellenistic Greek (e.g., referring to the release of slaves by a price).[29] Second, that "release by a price" is in mind is apparent from the observation that humans have received justification "freely" (without cost to themselves), though the following wording of 3:24 indicates that there was a cost to someone else (i.e., Christ). Third, even the exodus redemption could be conceived of as involving the cost of shedding the Passover lamb's blood, especially when seen in the light of it becoming typological of Christ's shed blood. So, for example, 1 Cor. 5:7 says that "Christ our Passover has been sacrificed," and this is still likely not out of mind when Paul says a little later, "For you have been bought with a price" (1 Cor. 6:20) (see similarly the application of the exodus redemption in the reference to Exod. 19:5; Deut. 14:2 in Titus 2:14, which is introduced by "who gave Himself for us"). Similarly, 1 Pet. 1:18–19 clearly connects the background of the exodus redemption with the blood of Christ, which was the cost of redemption for believers: "knowing that you were not redeemed [*lytroō*] with perishable things like silver or gold from your futile way of life inherited from your forefathers, but with precious blood, as of a lamb unblemished and spotless, the blood of Christ."

---

27. This latter point about positive imputation is not in mind in Rom. 3:24–25, though I discussed it earlier in this chapter and will elaborate on it more in the remainder of this chapter in connection with Christ's resurrection and believers' identification with that resurrection.

28. This is disputed by Morris, *Apostolic Preaching of the Cross*, 12–20.

29. See ibid., 22–26.

A fourth piece of evidence indicating that Paul thinks of Christ's redemption as a release from a penalty or debt by a cost is found in 1 Tim. 2:6. There, Christ is the one "who [as a 'man,' v. 5] gave Himself a ransom [*antilytron*][30] for all," which conveys the concept of a price paid. The price was Christ's death. This itself likely is built from Mark 10:45 (// Matt. 20:28): "The Son of Man did not come to be served, but to serve, and to give His life a ransom [*lytron*] for many." Mark 10:45 is an allusion to Isa. 53:12 ("He poured out Himself to death . . . ; He Himself bore the sin of many"), along with echoes of Isa. 53:10–12. Paul is likely aware of this Isaiah background in alluding to Mark (or the pre-Synoptic tradition on which Mark depended). Throughout Isa. 53 the Servant suffers and offers himself as a substitute for the penalty of Israel's guilt in order to redeem and justify Israel. In this light, the mention of Christ serving in Mark 10:45 likely echoes the Servant figure in Isa. 53:11, as does 1 Tim. 2:6.[31]

When "redemption" (*apolytrōsis*) is used elsewhere, it is directly linked to Christ's blood ("redemption through his blood" [Eph. 1:7]) or his forgiveness.[32] The passage in Col. 1:14 also reflects the background of Israel's exodus from Egypt.[33] In light of the uses in 1 Cor. 6; 1 Pet. 1; 1 Tim. 2, these uses in Eph. 1 and Col. 1 also appear to refer to Christ's blood (i.e., his death) as the cost of the redemption.[34]

In light of the usage of the "redemption" word group in the NT, especially by Paul, it appears plausible that the phrase "through the redemption which is in Christ Jesus" in Rom. 3:24 refers to Christ's death as the price of the release of believers from under the condemnation of God. This becomes probable because the next phrase, "whom God displayed publicly as a propitiation in His blood

30. The word *antilytron* is not used elsewhere in the NT and does not appear in the LXX, Josephus, Philo, Apostolic Fathers, Greek Pseudepigrapha, or NT Apocrypha, so primarily 1 Tim. 2 and the other forms of the word in the NT provide the context for determining its meaning. The form *lytron* occurs in Matt. 20:28; Mark 10:45: "The Son of Man did not come to be served, but to serve, and to give His life a ransom [*lytron*] for many."

31. Following R. T. France, *The Gospel of Mark: A Commentary on the Greek Text*, NIGTC (Grand Rapids: Eerdmans, 2002), 420–21. France discusses the Isaiah background for Mark 10:45 and also hears an echo of the Mark text in 1 Tim. 2:6.

32. Ephesians 1:7 reads, "In Him we have redemption through His blood, the forgiveness of our trespasses" (cf. Col. 1:20); note also *apolytrōsis* in Col. 1:14, which likely includes reference to his "blood" (Col. 1:20, 22).

33. On which, see in detail G. K. Beale, "Colossians," in *Commentary on the New Testament Use of the Old Testament*, ed. G. K. Beale and D. A. Carson (Grand Rapids: Baker Academic, 2007), 848–50.

34. The same is the case with Heb. 9:15: "since a death has taken place for the redemption of the transgressions" (see the preceding context of v. 14, where "the blood of Christ" appears as an anticipatory reference to Christ's death in v. 15). The reference to "redemption" in several passages alludes to the yet future redemption of believers through resurrection (Rom. 8:23; Eph. 1:14; 4:30, where "cost" is not uppermost in mind).

[i.e., death]" (Rom. 3:25),[35] is an explanation of what the redemption involves. Some grammarians even refer to the Greek construction "in his blood" or "by means of his blood" to be a dative construction indicating price.[36] The key issue here is that Christ had to give something for the redemption of people to occur, and what he gave was his life, which is essentially the cost of redemption.

Christ as the "Mercy Seat" in Romans 3:25

I must discuss the reference to "propitiation" in Rom. 3:25 before attempting to explain more precisely how this "redemption" in 3:24 is the means by which justification is accomplished. The phrase "whom God displayed publicly as a propitiation [*hilastērion*] in His blood" is crucial for understanding the nature of the redemption and, thus, the justification. The word *hilastērion* has been highly debated during the past century. Some want to see it involving a notion of "propitiation": the forgiveness of the penalty of sin by means of a substitute who assumes the penalty (e.g., KJV, NASB, ESV, HCSB). Others prefer the idea of "expiation": the forgiveness or sending away of sin by Christ's death but without a penal substitutionary notion, though also without any explanation of how sin is sent away (e.g., RSV). The NET has "mercy seat." Some translations are ambiguous and have translations such as "sacrifice of atonement" (NRSV, NIV) or "sacrifice for reconciliation" (e.g., NJB). I believe that the best translation is "mercy seat" (not an adjective but rather a neuter singular accusative noun), which refers to the golden lid of the ark of the covenant.[37] This is its meaning in the only other use of *hilastērion* in the NT (Heb. 9:5). The same Greek word occurs twenty-eight times in the LXX and almost always refers to the lid of the ark of the covenant—that is, the mercy seat (also always there a neuter singular noun).[38]

---

35. See Morris, *Apostolic Preaching of the Cross*, 117–24. Morris shows that the vast majority of the ninety-eight uses of "blood " in the NT refer to death, and the several places where Christ's "blood" in particular is mentioned, his death is meant. "Blood" here in Rom. 3:25 more likely modifies not "faith" but rather "mercy seat" ("set forth as a mercy seat in his blood").

36. See, e.g., BDF §219(3), which contends that *en* + the dative (*en tō autou haimati*) is to be understood as "at the price of his blood" (so also the same comment about the very similar expression in Rev. 5:10).

37. The phrase "whom [*hon*] God displayed as a mercy seat [*hilastērion*]" is a double accusative in which "whom" (Christ) is the proper object, and "mercy seat" is the complement of the object, both together functioning like a predicate nominative in which the complement further defines or predicates something about the object "whom" (Christ) (Daniel B. Wallace, *Greek Grammar beyond the Basics* [Grand Rapids: Zondervan, 1996], 184–87).

38. Only five times does the word clearly not refer to the mercy seat in the holy of holies. Five times in Ezekiel (43:14, 17, 20) it refers to the larger ledge of the altar of burnt offering in the courtyard of the end-time temple. There, it seems that the reason for referring to the "mercy seat" as part of the altar of burnt offering is that there is no holy of holies or ark of the covenant in Ezekiel's picture of the latter-day temple (though 43:14 distinguishes between a "small mercy seat" and "a great mercy seat" located on the one altar). The LXX translator appears to have transferred the function of the lid of the ark of the covenant to the major ledge of the altar of burnt offering. The only place in all of the LXX where *hilastērion* does not refer to a cultic

It is likely that Paul is referring to the mercy seat in the holy of holies, since he has introduced this paragraph by saying that the declaration of righteousness that he is about to speak has been "witnessed by the Law and Prophets" (Rom. 3:21). Thus, the background for *hilastērion* must come from within "the Law and the Prophets" and not from the pagan use of the word, which typically referred to a gift to propitiate (to bring about the favor of) the gods. It was on the mercy seat that blood was sprinkled by the high priest annually on the Day of Atonement. Since it is probable that this is Paul's allusion, perhaps alluding specifically to the use in Lev. 16,[39] it is important to study the meaning of the mercy seat and of the sacrifice there on the Day of Atonement, which entails also an analysis of the meaning of the Hebrew word for "atone, make atonement" (*kipper*) and the corresponding noun form "ransom" (*kōper*), of which word group the "mercy seat" (*hilastērion* = *kappōret*) in Hebrew is a part.

The close connection of "atone, make atonement" and "mercy seat" occurs in Lev. 16:11–19,[40] where Aaron is to "sprinkle blood" on the "mercy seat" in order "to make atonement" for "himself and for his household" as well as for "the sons of Israel." This atoning is also said to be "for the holy place," "for the tent of meeting," and for "the altar" (vv. 16–18), though the latter is made outside the holy of holies in the holy place. It is apparent that the atonement also effects consecration, since, as seen in vv. 16–18, atonement is made "for the holy place" and "for the tent of meeting," presumably to cleanse and to consecrate it (as the atonement at the courtyard altar also does in Lev. 16:19). The presupposition is that human sin has in some way defiled (perhaps disabling the function of) the temple, so that it needs cleansing to become functional again.[41] Leviticus 16:33 then summarizes and says that atonement is made for all these people groups and objects of the temple. Likewise, in Ezek. 43:14–27 "mercy seat" occurs five times, and "make atonement" once. The atonement is made by sprinkling blood on the altar (including the mercy seat), so that the altar will be "cleansed" (43:20, 22–23, 26) and "consecrated" (43:26).

The meaning of the Hebrew verb *kipper* ("atone, make atonement") is debated. Some prefer the notion of "ransom," which is a payment that delivers a guilty party from a just punishment by the offended party and appeases the

place is 4 Macc. 17:21–22, where it refers to the small group of Maccabean martyrs who were "a ransom for the sin of our nation. And through the blood of those devout ones and their death as an expiation/propitiation [*hilastērion*], divine Providence preserved Israel." But even here, the rendering "the mercy seat of their death" is most literal and may refer to their death as the figurative cultic place where substitutionary wrath was carried out, much like that in Rom. 3:25.

39. So also Thomas R. Schreiner, *Romans*, BECNT (Grand Rapids: Baker Academic, 1998), 192.

40. Where "make atonement" occurs four times, and "mercy seat" four times.

41. See Robert Jewett, *Romans*, Hermeneia (Minneapolis: Fortress, 2007), 287.

offended party, thus restoring peace to the relationship.[42] Others prefer the idea of "purify," since this is sometimes seen to be the effect of the "atoning" (e.g., Lev. 16:33a; Ezek. 43:20–26). In reality, in all the contexts where the verb occurs it is very difficult to choose one idea over another, since one notion may be the focus while another is implied or echoed secondarily. So why does the verb *kipper* appear in contexts both of major impurity (where no apparent sin has occurred) and of inadvertent sin? "The answer, briefly stated, is that inadvertent sins and major impurities share this in common: both endanger (requiring ransom) and both pollute (requiring purification). The verb [*kipper*] occurs in both contexts because it refers to [*kōper*]-purgation, with the blood of the sacrifice serving both to ransom and to purify."[43]

Accordingly, the mercy seat is the place where the atonement is made. It is the place where punishment is carried out (represented by the substitutionary animal's blood) and where cleansing occurs by means of the blood. God's presence is above the mercy seat, and there he accepts the twofold atonement. It is apparent that the atonement also effects consecration through cleansing, since, as seen above in Lev. 16:16–18, atonement is made "for the holy place" and "for the tent of meeting" (so also 16:33).[44] Yet Lev. 16 also equally says that this atonement at the mercy seat is for Aaron, his family, and all Israel (vv. 11–15, 33). Even the scapegoat that "shall bear on itself all their [Israel's] iniquities" and was to be sent into the wilderness (vv. 21–22) is the corollary to the dead goat's blood sprinkled on the mercy seat, and it conveys the notion of a substitutionary figure, likely bearing the nation's punishment.[45]

How does this background help us to understand Rom. 3:25? The two viable OT notions of atonement at the mercy seat are those of "ransom" and "cleansing," though notions of "consecration" are likely included with "cleansing." Does Paul have in mind all these ideas? The context of Rom. 3:25, as I

---

42. The acceptance of this payment completely depends on the choice of the offended party, and the payment is a lesser punishment than was expected originally. Among relevant texts with this meaning, see Exod. 21:28–32; 30:11–16; Num. 35:30–34; Ps. 49:7–8.

43. Jay Sklar, "Sin and Impurity: Atoned or Purified? Yes!" in *Perspectives on Purity and Purification in the Bible*, ed. Baruch J. Schwartz et al. (London: T&T Clark, 2008), 31. My discussion above on the twofold ransoming and purifying aspect of atonement is based on Sklar's article. Sklar's convincing article is based on his published dissertation: *Sin, Impurity, Sacrifice, Atonement: The Priestly Conceptions*, HBM 2 (Sheffield: Sheffield Phoenix Press, 2005). For a recent survey of atonement and theories of atonement in the OT, see Christian A. Eberhart, "Atonement. I. Old Testament/Hebrew Bible," in vol. 3 of *Encyclopedia of the Bible and Its Reception*, ed. Hans-Josef Klauck et al. (Berlin: de Gruyter, 2010), 23–31. The benefit of Sklar's view is that he is able to put together formerly competing theories of atonement. See likewise David Peterson, "Atonement in the Old Testament," in *Where Wrath and Mercy Meet: Proclaiming the Atonement Today*, ed. David Peterson (Carlisle, UK: Paternoster, 2001), 5–15, following Sklar and others.

44. We likewise saw that atonement of the mercy seat in Ezek. 43:14–26 also brought about cleansing and consecration.

45. Following Peterson, "Atonement in the Old Testament," 14–15.

labored to demonstrate earlier, primarily focuses not on the need for cleansing or consecration but rather on the fact that sinful humanity deserves God's condemnatory wrath. Thus, Paul is drawing on that aspect of atonement at the mercy seat dealing with ransom by means of the blood of a penal substitute (hence the suitability of mentioning Christ's blood only a few words later in Rom. 3:25).[46] Christ is now the place where God's penal wrath is poured out for sinful humans, who deserve the condemnation. What was done in the old temple in the secrecy of the holy of holies is now "displayed publicly." Part of the core of the temple, the mercy seat of the ark, is identified with Jesus, likely portrayed as the beginning of the eschatological temple,[47] to which the old temple ark pointed (so that, perhaps, there is a nuance of Christ as the atonement, which consecrates the new temple).[48] Likewise, the animal sacrifice, the blood of which was sprinkled on the mercy seat, pointed to the greater sacrifice of Christ. God's presence above the old ark has also broken in as a part of the new temple, so that he is the one who is revealing or "displaying publicly" the new covenant fulfillment to which the mercy seat and its sacrifice pointed.[49] This fits with the overall purpose of the Levitical sacrifices to

46. For good responses to some of the major objections to viewing *hilastērion* as a reference to the mercy seat in Exodus, Leviticus, and Numbers, see Schreiner, *Romans*, 193–94.

47. Paul may see the mercy seat as not merely the core of the temple but as a metonym: it is a key part of the temple that represents the whole temple.

48. With regard to focus on Jesus's identification with the mercy seat being a revelation of the new temple, I am grateful to Daniel P. Bailey, "Jesus as the Mercy Seat: The Semantics and Theology of Paul's Use of *Hilasterion* in Romans 3:25," *TynBul* 51, no. 1 (2000): 155–58, which is a summary of his dissertation of the same title. See likewise, Wolfgang Kraus, *Der Tod Jesu als Heiligtumsweihe: Eine Untersuchung zum Umfeld der Sühnevorstellung in Römer 3,25–26a*, WMANT 66 (Neukirchen-Vluyn: Neukirchener Verlag, 1991). Kraus argues, partly on the basis of Lev. 16, that the mercy seat was the place where atonement was carried out to dedicate the temple of God's presence, which implies that the mercy seat itself represented the temple. He then sees Jesus to be the mercy seat, who as the eschatological place of atonement consecrates the new temple, representing God's presence. Kraus does not appear to acknowledge that atonement at the mercy seat in Leviticus is made for all the people but rather highlights the notion of temple consecration, which I think is an omission because Paul in the context of Rom. 3 highlights humanity deserving wrath, and the mercy seat solves that problem. Notions of "consecration" do not appear to be dominant or, at least, are not mutually exclusive of atonement for humanity. However, Kraus's view of the mercy seat as representing the new temple is a good insight. See Daniel P. Bailey, review of *Der Tod Jesu als Heiligtumsweihe*, by Wolfgang Kraus, *JTS* 45 (1994): 247–52, likewise criticizing Kraus for emphasizing primarily the consecration notion of Lev. 16. I am grateful to Bailey for alerting me to Kraus's work and helping me gain a better understanding of it.

49. But contra Charles Talbert (*Romans*, SHBC 24 [Macon, GA: Smyth & Helwys, 2002], 113), the mercy seat is not to be equated precisely with the presence of God, since that presence was directly above the mercy seat (LXX of Exod. 25:22; Lev. 16:2; Num. 7:89). Accordingly, unlikely is Talbert's conclusion that the main point of Jesus being a mercy seat is to indicate that he is the revelatory presence of God. Philo (*Mos.* 2.95–96) says that the mercy seat is "a symbol . . . of the gracious power of God," probably expressing the notion that God's mercy is shown through the provision of the mercy seat as a place of atonement for Israel's sins.

keep Israel as a set-apart people for God (Exod. 19:5–6) and to allow God to continue to dwell in his tabernacle among them (Exod. 29:38–46).[50]

Conclusion to Romans 3:24–25

In summary, we saw earlier that "the redemption which is in Christ Jesus" is the means by which justification is carried out. The following mention of Christ as a "mercy seat" either further explains "redemption" or is a further explanation of how justification is executed. It is hard to decide which is in mind, but since the mercy seat in this passage is drawing on that aspect of atonement in the OT dealing with ransom, it is more probable that the mercy seat further explains redemption, which we saw also has overtones of ransoming by a price. Accordingly, Paul is saying in Rom. 3:24–25 that God's declaration of righteousness and of being not guilty, applied freely by grace, comes through redemptive release from condemnation through Christ, which itself comes by Christ suffering the wrathful punishment of sin as the substitute for sinful people and as the revelation of the new temple mercy seat.[51] It is on the basis that Christ has suffered the wrath due his people that Paul can say that believers "will be saved from the wrath of God through him [Christ], the wrath that unbelievers will suffer" (Rom. 5:9; also 1 Thess. 1:10).

This notion of redemptive penal substitution in Rom. 3:25 as part of the means of accomplishing justification is borne out later by Rom. 4:24–25 in explaining the significance of the believer's justification through Christ's death and resurrection:

> But for our sake also, to whom it [righteousness] will be credited, as those who believe in Him who raised Jesus our Lord from the dead, <u>He who was delivered over because of our transgressions</u>, and was raised because of our justification.

The phrase "was delivered over because of our transgressions" alludes to Isa. 53:12 LXX: "he was delivered over because of their sins." Isaiah 53 is one OT passage that speaks most clearly of the end-time Servant, who will suffer the punishment that the Israelites deserve in order to deliver them salvifically (see esp. vv. 4–11), and in particular to "justify" them (v. 11).[52]

---

50. On this overall purpose, see Peterson, "Atonement in the Old Testament," 3.

51. Bailey ("Jesus as the Mercy Seat," 157) makes the plausible proposal that Rom. 3:24–25 alludes partly to Exod. 15:13 LXX: "You have led in your <u>righteousness</u> [*dikaiosynē*] this your people, whom you have <u>redeemed</u> [*lytroō*]; in your power you have summoned them into your <u>holy abode</u>" (and v. 17 expands on the "holy abode" by referring to it as the "prepared dwelling place that you made, . . . a sanctuary . . . that your hands prepared").

52. Adolf Schlatter (*Romans: The Righteousness of God*, trans. Siegfried S. Schatzmann [Peabody, MA: Hendrickson, 1995], 118) sees the Isaiah allusion and Paul's use of it as development of Jesus as the mercy seat in Rom. 3:25; similarly, N. T. Wright ("Romans," *NIB* 10:475) sees allusion to Isa. 53:6, 12 in Rom. 4:25, "summing up the entire train of thought from 3:21."

Conceptual connections between Rom. 3:25 and the Isa. 53 allusion in Rom. 4:25 can be observed in at least four ways. First, the Suffering Servant was to "render Himself as a <u>guilt offering</u> [*'āšām*]" (Isa. 53:10) as a "sheep" or "lamb" (Isa. 53:7), which is likely a development of the repeated mention of the guilt offering of animals, including lambs,[53] in Leviticus and Numbers, as well as in Ezek. 40–44.[54] The Servant appears to be interpreted as the grand eschatological guilt offering to avert wrath coming on Israel's sinful guilt, to which the guilt offerings in Leviticus and Numbers pointed.[55]

This connection points to the notion that both the Levitical guilt offerings and the Servant in Isa. 53 are also a development of the Passover lamb's blood, which averted the wrath of the angel of death.

A second link between Rom. 3:25 and 4:25 may be seen between the Servant's work and that of Leviticus and Numbers. Isaiah 53 repeats that the Servant took on Israel's sins: "He bore our griefs" and "He carried our sorrows" (v. 4), "He will bear their iniquities" (v. 11), and "He Himself bore the sin of many" (v. 12). Leviticus uses some of the same phraseology either of sinful people who will "bear [*nāśā'*] their iniquity ['*āôn*]" (about 10x) or "sin (*ḥēṭĕ'*)" (about 5x) or a sacrificial animal that will "bear [*nāśā'*] iniquity ['*āôn*]" (Lev. 10:17; 16:22). The Servant appears to be interpreted as the consummative Levitical sin-bearer for Israel, a similar notion that we saw in Rom. 3:25.

A connection between the Levitical sacrifices and Isa. 52–53 may be seen, which hints at a further conceptual link between Rom. 3:25 and 4:25. Isaiah

---

Other commentators who see an Isa. 53:12 allusion in Rom. 4:25 include Schreiner, *Romans*, 243; F. F. Bruce, *The Epistle of Paul to the Romans*, TNTC (Grand Rapids: Eerdmans, 1963), 118–19, C. E. B. Cranfield, *A Critical and Exegetical Commentary on the Epistle to the Romans*, 2 vols., ICC (Edinburgh: T&T Clark, 1975), 1:251–52; Jewett, *Romans*, 342; the latter three probably rightly include Isa. 53:6 LXX as part of the allusion ("the Lord gave him up for our sins"). Peter Stuhlmacher (*Paul's Letter to the Romans: A Commentary*, trans. Scott J. Hafemann [Louisville: Westminster John Knox, 1994], 71, 75) also sees allusion to Isa. 53:11 and 53:12, as I do (if so, Paul is likely alluding to a mixed text, since the LXX of v. 11 apparently has the Servant being justified, whereas the MT has the sinful people being justified); so also Cranfield, *Epistle to the Romans*, 1:251–52; Douglas J. Moo, *The Epistle to the Romans*, NICNT (Grand Rapids: Eerdmans, 1996), 288, the latter, though, more tentative about Isa. 53:11. See also James D. G. Dunn, *Romans 1–8*, WBC 38A (Dallas: Word, 1988), 241. Dunn sees the description of the Suffering Servant throughout Isa. 53 being alluded to in Rom. 4:25.

53. For guilt offerings specifically of lambs, see Lev. 5:6; 14:12–13, 17, 21, 24–25, 28; Num. 6:12; and for rams, see Lev. 5:15–16, 18–19; 6:6; 19:21–22.

54. The word *'āšām* rendered as a "guilt offering" occurs some thirty-five times in Leviticus, Numbers, and Ezekiel; it also appears in this manner four times in 1 Sam. 6:3–17, where it refers to a guilt offering that the Philistines need to make for capturing the ark of the covenant in order to avert the wrathful plague that had come among them.

55. The word *'āšām* can also be translated merely as "guilt," and in noncultic contexts it refers almost without exception to guilt that leads to judgment (see, e.g., the noun form in Gen. 26:10; Ps. 68:22 [68:21 ET] and the verbal form in Gen. 42:21; 2 Chron. 19:10; Pss. 5:11 [5:10 ET]; 34:22 [34:23 ET]; Isa. 24:6; Jer. 2:3; Ezek. 22:4; Hos. 5:15). These noncultic uses indicate the likelihood that the cultic uses also entail that the guilt offerings avert some form of judgment.

52:15 says that the Suffering Servant will "sprinkle many nations" as a part of his mission to redeem his people. The Hebrew word used for "sprinkle" (*nāzâ*) is the typical word used in Leviticus and Numbers to describe "sprinkling" blood on people and various parts of the temple for a sin offering to ransom from guilt (in context, see Lev. 4:6, 17; 5:9) or for cleansing with a view to consecration (likewise see Exod. 29:21; Lev. 6:27; 8:30; 14:7, 51; Num. 19:4), although, as seen earlier, it is likely that both sin offering for ransom from guilt and cleansing/consecration are in mind to varying degrees in these uses. Three of these uses occur in the aforementioned crucial passage Lev. 16:14–19 with respect to sin offering both for ransom from guilt and for cleansing/consecration. In light of the preceding two observations (the lamb as a guilt offering and the bearing of iniquity) that also connect Isa. 53 with the Levitical sacrifices, the Servant here in Isa. 52:15 apparently is to be seen as one who performs an end-time sacrificial sprinkling for the nations, to which the Levitical sprinklings pointed.[56]

A fourth observation pointing to a conceptual connection between Rom. 3:25 and 4:25 is that the Targum of Isa. 53:5 says that God "will build the sanctuary which was . . . handed over for our inquities," the last phrase of which is an interpretative paraphrase of the Hebrew of 53:5, affirming of the Servant that "he was crushed for our iniquities."[57] Thus, God's building of an end-time temple is directly linked to the Servant's suffering and the notion of being handed over for iniquities (wording very similar to Rom. 4:25a).[58] Likewise, I have argued that the suffering of Jesus in Rom. 3:25 entailed the setting forth of a new temple by God.

Except for the element of the temple, this conclusion about Rom. 3:24–25 has been reached by many others previously, but I have arrived at it by traveling a rather different exegetical and biblical-theological route in the OT.

The remainder of this chapter focuses more on the resurrection in relation to justification than on Christ's death. The reason for this, on the one hand, is that Christ's death has been discussed much more in relation to justification and how that death was suffered by Christ so that sinners could be justified as not guilty. On the other hand, the resurrection has received relatively little discussion in relation to justification. The remainder of this chapter seeks to remedy this.

The Resurrection of Christ Inaugurates the Eschatological Vindication

In addition to justification through Christ's death as an inaugurated latter-day judgment on behalf of saints, I want to focus on another inaugurated

---

56. Perhaps also in the background is the same use of "sprinkle" (*nāzâ*) but sprinkling with "water" or "oil" for cleansing/consecration (Lev. 8:11, 30; 14:16, 27; Num. 8:7; 19:18–21).

57. Bruce (*Romans*, 119) observes the similarity between the wording of Rom. 4:25a and the Targum of Isa. 53:5.

58. Although in the Targum the Servant who suffers is the nation Israel.

aspect of justification. We have seen clearly in earlier chapters that resurrection is one of the most highly charged eschatological concepts in the NT. Here the focus is on a particular aspect of the resurrection: the resurrection that was to occur at the very end of the world has begun in Jesus's bodily resurrection. Jesus's own resurrection was an end-time event that "vindicated" or "justified" him from the wrong verdict pronounced on him by the world's courts. The vindication of God's people against the unjust verdicts of their accusers was to happen at the eschaton,[59] but this has been pushed back to Christ's resurrection and applied to him. All those who believe in Christ are identified with his resurrection that vindicated him to be completely righteous, and this identification vindicates and declares them to be completely righteous.

1 Timothy 3:16

Particularly pertinent to the issue of Christ's justification is 1 Tim. 3:16:

> By common confession, great is the mystery of godliness:
> He who was revealed in the flesh,
> Was vindicated [declared righteous, *dikaioō*] by the Spirit,
> Seen by angels,
> Proclaimed among the nations,
> Believed on in the world,
> Taken up in glory.

The phrase "was vindicated by the Spirit" refers to the Spirit's raising of Christ from the dead (as in Rom. 1:4), which was a vindication against the wrongful verdict[60] issued against him by the sinful human court and a declaration of his righteousness.[61] Geerhardus Vos says in this connection,

> Christ's resurrection was the de facto declaration of God in regard to his being just. His quickening bears in itself the testimony of his justification. God, through suspending the forces of death operating on Him, declared that the ultimate,

---

59. As prophesied by Isa. 40–53, discussed later in this chapter. For resurrection functioning as vindication of God's people in Dan. 12:1–2 and in 2 Maccabees, as well as elsewhere in Judaism, see J. R. Daniel Kirk, *Unlocking Romans: Resurrection and the Justification of God* (Grand Rapids: Eerdmans, 2008), 15–24, 93–96.

60. For the unjust verdict against Christ, see Matt. 27:24; Mark 15:4, 14; Luke 23:24; John 18:29–31; 19:4; Acts 13:27–29; 1 Tim. 6:13. For the unjust accusation that Jesus was a "deceiver," see Matt. 27:63; John 7:12; Justin Martyr, *Dial.* 69, on which see Stuhlmacher, *Biblische Theologie*, 1:147, who also discusses the Jewish background against which such accusations were made.

61. For persuasive elaboration on this point, see Gaffin, *Centrality of the Resurrection*, 119–22. See also Kirk, *Unlocking Romans*, 222, in agreement with Gaffin and citing others in broader agreement. Acts 13:27–30 likely refers to the same vindication but without the technical language of "justification."

the supreme consequence of sin had reached its termination. In other words, resurrection had annulled the sentence of condemnation.[62]

Acts 17:31

Acts 17:31 expresses a similar notion: "Because He has fixed a day in which He will judge the world in righteousness through a Man whom He has appointed, having furnished proof to all men by raising Him from the dead." The proof that God will judge the world on the last day by his appointed human agent is that this agent of judgment has been raised from the dead. That is, the logic appears to presuppose that Christ's resurrection has demonstrated him to be just and, therefore, one who will exercise justice at the last judgment.

Isaiah 50

This thought of eschatological vindication by God against an unjust verdict has precedence in Isaiah. For example, the Servant Song in Isa. 50 portrays the Servant as having been obedient to God's call to suffer unjust persecution (vv. 4–6) and unjust accusation (vv. 8–9) from which he will be vindicated by God (vv. 7–11) and be seen as truly righteous. In this respect, verses 8–9 affirm, "He who vindicates [*dikaioō*] Me is near; who will contend with Me? . . . Who is he who condemns Me?" God helps the Servant (vv. 7, 9) to overturn the false condemnation, thus vindicating his Servant in the latter days.

Isaiah 53

The well-known Suffering Servant passage of Isa. 53 makes the same point conceptually, and the LXX specifies that God will "justify [*dikaioō*] the just one [the Servant]"[63] from the wrongful legal persecution that he will suffer (cf. v. 11 with vv. 7–9, 12), showing him to be absolutely righteous after all. This vindication consists in causing the Servant to enjoy victory even after and despite his own death (vv. 10–12; e.g., v. 12a: "I will allot Him a portion with the great, and He will divide the booty with the strong"). Although he would die (vv. 5, 8–9), he would be given this victory, which includes seeing life after his painful death: "He will see His seed [LXX: "long-lived seed"], He will prolong His

---

62. Geerhardus Vos, *The Pauline Eschatology* (1930; repr., Grand Rapids: Baker Academic, 1979), 151.

63. The Hebrew at this point has "the Righteous One, My Servant, will justify the many," in place of which the LXX has *dikaiōsai dikaion*, which is best rendered as "to vindicate [justify] the just one" (so Lancelot C. L. Brenton, *The Septuagint with Apocrypha: Greek and English* [1851; repr., Peabody, MA: Hendrickson, 1986]; likewise almost identically, Albert Pietersma and Benjamin G. Wright, eds., *The New English Translation of the Septuagint* [New York: Oxford University Press, 2007]). Although it is possible to render the Greek as "the just one to justify," it would be awkward and not in line with the parallelism of the preceding two infinitives. The LXX here probably is interpreting the Hebrew by saying that the one who will justify will himself be justified, which may be inspired by the preceding Servant passage in Isa. 50:8 ("He who vindicates Me is near").

days. . . . He will see [light]"[64] (vv. 10–11). Although this portion of Isa. 53:10–11 is not cited in the NT, it would doubtless have understood this victory to be resurrection, since so much of the surrounding context of Isa. 53 concerning the Servant's suffering is alluded to and applied to Christ throughout the NT. Since Isaiah says elsewhere that the Spirit was to be the empowering agent of the Servant's ministry (11:2; 42:1; 48:16; 61:1), it is not unreasonable to think that this Spirit would play a role in vindicating this ministry.

This all comes very close to what 1 Tim. 3:16 has said above. First Timothy 3:16 possibly alludes to Isa. 53:11 (LXX, or Isa. 50:8),[65] but even if it does not, Isaiah still stands as a precedent even before the time of Paul for thinking that the Messiah's "justification/vindication" would consist, at least partly, in his recontinuation of a prosperous life after his death.[66]

The Meanings of Dikaioō

Just above we discussed the meaning of "justify" (*dikaioō*) in relation to Christ's death in Rom. 3:24–25. It is fitting at this point that a further comment be made about the possible meanings of *dikaioō*, especially as it is related to Christ's resurrection. In addition to our earlier discussion, it is important to note that the standard lexicon of the Greek NT gives the following ranges of meaning:

1. "to take up a legal cause, show justice, do justice, take up a cause";
2. "to render a favorable verdict, vindicate";
3. "to cause someone to be released from personal or institutional claims that are no longer to be considered pertinent or valid, make free, pure";
4. "to demonstrate to be morally right, prove to be right."[67]

All the uses by Paul can be reduced to "vindicate" or "declare righteous," both referring to rendering a favorable verdict, which represents the essence of the above fourfold range of meaning. This translation is as applicable to Christ in 1 Tim. 3:16 as it is to believers. The obvious difference is that the resurrection vindicates Christ's innocence, thus overturning the unjust verdict against him. However, the saints were justly accused of sin and guilt and sentenced

---

64. 1QIsaᵃ, 1QIsaᵇ, and 4Q58 add "light" after "he will see": "he will see light." The LXX has almost identically "to show him light."

65. See Stuhlmacher, *Biblische Theologie*, 2:22, who notes that, while the MT of Isa. 53:11 has the "Servant" who "will justify the many," the LXX has God as the one who "justifies the just one [the Servant] who serves many well," which then leads into the installation of the Servant into his victorious position (Isa. 53:12). In this light, Stuhlmacher views the LXX rendering as an allusion in 1 Tim. 3:16.

66. The same observation from Isa. 53:11 is made by Michael F. Bird, "Justification as Forensic Declaration and Covenant Membership: A *Via Media* between Reformed and Revisionist Readings of Paul," *TynBul* 57, no. 1 (2006): 115.

67. BDAG 249.

to death, but they have been vindicated by Christ's work, declaring them not guilty and righteous because he suffered the penalty of death due them and has provided them with his own righteousness, *which has been vindicated by his own resurrection*. This last point about Christ's righteousness in connection to his resurrection being attributed to saints needs more substantiation, which I will attempt to do in the following sections.

Michael Bird has likewise rightly focused on Christ's vindication from a wrong verdict by resurrection with which believers are identified: "Thus, believers are justified only for the reason that they share a corporate solidarity with the justified Messiah and what is true of him is true of God's people,"[68] because they are "in-Christ,"[69] though, as noted above, unlike Christ, they deserved the guilty verdict.

Romans 4:25

The relation between the believer and Christ's resurrection as a "justifying" event is reflected in Rom. 4:25:

> . . . He who was delivered over <u>because of</u> [*dia*] our transgressions, and was raised <u>because of</u> [*dia*] our justification.

Some commentators understand the dual use of *dia* to be identical ("because of"), while others understand the first *dia* to be causal ("because of") and the second as final or purposive ("for the sake of," "with a view to"). Some commentators suggest that Christ's resurrection is mentioned after the reference to Christ's vicariously dying for sins because his resurrection was confirmation that his penal death on behalf of sinners was effective, since he himself was no longer bound by the penalty of death.

Although the last clause of this verse has been debated because of its apparent vagueness, Richard Gaffin gives probably the most persuasive assessment of it. He argues that the solution is to do justice to both sides of the parallelism within the context of Paul's broader theology. Jesus's dying "on account of our transgressions" identified him with believers in the punishment due those transgressions. Correspondingly, Christ's resurrection "on account of our justification" identifies him with saints in the verdict of justification, which was due for his establishing of righteousness. But what precisely is the content of his establishment of righteousness? Gaffin answers, keeping in mind that Jesus's resurrection is the focus of his solidarity with the saints in justification. He says that "the unexpressed assumption in Rom. 4:25b is that Jesus's resurrection is his justification."[70] Accordingly, when believers are identified with Christ's resurrection, which

---

68. Bird, "Justification as Forensic Declaration," 115.
69. Ibid., 120.
70. Gaffin, *Centrality of the Resurrection*, 123.

justified him, they also are justified[71] and declared to be just as righteous as he was.

The Future Consummated Eschatological Nature of Justification in Relation to Resurrection

To understand better the believers' inaugurated vindication, we must also look at how it is related to the very end of the age and their own resurrection. The following represents the "not yet" aspect of justification of the Christian, which remains to be consummated in the future. I will argue in the remainder of this chapter that there are three aspects of future, end-time justification:

1. public demonstration of justification/vindication through the final, bodily resurrection;
2. justification/vindication of the saints through public announcement before all the world;
3. public demonstration to the entire cosmos of believers' justification/ vindication through their good works.

These three aspects may be depicted as shown in table 15.1.

Table 15.1

Action	Means	Location
justification/vindication	bodily resurrection of believers	publicly displayed
justification/vindication	God's announcement	publicly announced before all the world
justification/vindication	good works exhibited by bodily resurrected believers	publicly demonstrated before the entire cosmos

The Final Resurrection as Justification/Vindication of the Saints

God's people are vindicated from the sentence of condemnation due their sin when they believe during the age leading up to Christ's final return.

THE BELIEVER'S VINDICATION IS DEFINITIVE

On the one hand, this vindication is once for all and definitive. It is definitive in the sense that saints are declared from God's perspective not guilty because

71. Gaffin acknowledges that his point was anticipated by, among others, Heinrich Heppe, who, citing Rom. 4:25 in support, says, "Just as by giving the Son to death the Father actually condemned all our sins in him, the Father also by raising Christ up from the dead, acquitted Christ of our sin-guilt and us in Christ. . . . So Christ's resurrection is our righteousness, because God further regards us in the perfection in which Christ rose" (*Reformed Dogmatics*, 499).

Christ suffered the penalty of their sin. And, just as definitively, they are also declared righteous because Christ achieved representative righteousness for them in his resurrected person and was completely vindicated from injustice (showing that he had been righteous all along), a vindication with which the saints are also identified. Consequently, they are declared to have the same righteousness (by imputation or attribution) that Christ possessed throughout his life and still possesses.

THE BELIEVER'S VINDICATION IS INCOMPLETE

On the other hand, there is a sense in which this vindication is not completed, especially in that the world does not recognize God's vindication of his people. Just as happened to Jesus, the ungodly world has judged the saints' faith and obedience to God to be in the wrong, which has been expressed through persecution of God's people. As was the case with Christ, so with his followers: their final resurrection will vindicate the truth of their faith and confirm that their obedience was a necessary outgrowth of this faith.[72] That is, although they had been declared righteous in God's sight when they believed, the world continued to declare them guilty. Their physical resurrection will be undeniable proof of the validity of their faith, which had already declared them righteous in their past life.

This follows the pattern of Christ's own vindication from the unjust verdict pronounced against him. He had already been perfectly innocent during his earthly life of persecution leading up to death and before his vindicating resurrection. Likewise, saints will have been already declared as completely righteous by God before their deaths and their resurrection, the latter of which will vindicate that their prior justified status was in fact true despite the world's verdict about their faith. Of course, the vindication of their righteous status is different in one important respect from the vindication of Christ's righteous standing: they were originally guilty of sin, and their vindication is not a defense of their own innate righteousness but rather is their identification with Christ's righteousness (which has been attributed to them) and a vindication that the works that they performed through the Spirit, while not being perfect, were faithful deeds and not evil, as the world had judged them.

Romans 5:18b

The link between the saints' justification and their final resurrection is also expressed in Rom. 5:18b: "Through one act of righteousness there resulted justification leading to life[73] for all men." This refers to the notion that those

---

72. For a similar argument, see Kirk, *Unlocking Romans*, 221.

73. It is not unusual to take the phrase "justification of life" in Rom. 5:18 as a genitive of result (e.g., Douglas J. Moo, *Romans 1–8*, WEC [Chicago: Moody, 1991], 355, citing others in support). Accordingly, this is borne out by Rom. 5:21b: "even so grace would reign through righteousness to eternal life through Jesus Christ our Lord."

who are truly justified will receive resurrection life, which begins spiritually in the present (Rom. 8:6, 10–11) and will be completed with physical regenerated life in the future (Rom. 8:11, 13, 23). This "life" is not merely a necessary consequence of justification; it also demonstrates that the one resurrected has already in the past age been justified. It is especially the final form of bodily resurrection that is the final vindication of true justifying faith, the reality of which the world and the powers of evil have denied. The final resurrection shows that the saints were in the right after all in placing their justifying faith in Christ and living in obedience to him, and it shows the world to have been in the wrong.

Romans 1:4; 8:14–23

Christ's physical resurrection according to Rom. 1:4 was a "judicially constitutive declaration of sonship":[74] Christ "was declared the Son of God with power by the resurrection from the dead, according to the Spirit of holiness, Jesus Christ our Lord." Although he already had the status of "Son of God," the resurrection demonstrated this climactically and definitively and signaled the beginning of the new eschatological aeon.[75] Acts 13:27–41 indicates that Christ's resurrection proved that he was God's "Son" and overturned the unjust verdict on him, including the refusal to acknowledge him as such. The ruling authorities of Jerusalem "did not recognize" him and thus "condemned" him (v. 27), "though they found no ground for putting him to death" (v. 28). This wrongful verdict was overturned by God "raising up Jesus," which fulfilled Ps. 2:7: "You are My Son; today I have begotten You" (v. 33). Jesus's resurrection vindicated him against the unjust verdict of Israel's leaders and of Pilate (vv. 27–28), showing that he was God's true Son after all.

In the same manner as Christ in Rom. 1:4 (and Acts 13:27–41), Christians gain the status of "adopted sonship" in Christ when they believe in and become identified with him as God's Son (Rom. 8:14–17; Gal. 4:4–7; Eph. 1:5, 14). Yet it is also clear from Rom. 8:19–23 that this sonship is only a beginning phase for saints:

For the anxious longing of the creation waits eagerly for the revealing of the sons of God. For the creation was subjected to futility, not willingly, but because of

74. Gaffin, *Centrality of the Resurrection*, 118. Gaffin explains the forensic nature of the declaration in Rom. 1:4.

75. See Geerhardus Vos, "The Eschatological Aspect of the Pauline Conception of the Spirit," in *Redemptive History and Biblical Interpretation: The Shorter Writings of Geerhardus Vos*, ed. Richard B. Gaffin Jr. (Phillipsburg, NJ: P&R, 1980), 104–5. Vos sees that the phrase "by the resurrection from among the dead ones" in Rom. 1:4 designates a contrast between two ages: "The resurrection is characteristic of the beginning of a new order of things, as sarkic birth is characteristic of an older order of things"; just as Jesus derived his earthly sonship "according to the flesh," "from the seed of David," so the resurrection marks a new position of sonship.

> Him who subjected it, in hope that the creation itself also will be set free from its slavery to corruption into the freedom of the glory of the children of God. For we know that the whole creation groans and suffers the pains of childbirth together until now. And not only this, but also we ourselves, having the first fruits of the Spirit, even we ourselves groan within ourselves, waiting eagerly for our adoption as sons, the redemption of our body.

Here is it evident that although believers already experience an official status of sonship in Christ because of the Spirit's work in raising them spiritually from the dead (Rom. 8:9–10; cf. 8:23), such sonship has not been revealed publicly to the cosmos (Rom. 8:18–19). However, a time will come when their sonship is declared climactically and consummately through the physical resurrection of their bodies, as verse 23 emphatically asserts (though note also 8:11). This follows the pattern of Jesus's own legal declaration of sonship by his physical resurrection in Rom. 1:4,[76] which is enhanced by recalling that the process of adopted sonship in the Greco-Roman world was an essentially legal procedure. This sonship of God's people will be demonstrated physically and publicly in a way as never before, which is underscored by verse 19 ("the revealing of the sons of God") and verse 21 ("the freedom of the glory of the children of God"). This consummative declaration of sonship further identifies them with Jesus and further demonstrates that they already have been justified by Christ.

Thus, the demonstration of adopted sonship by the final resurrection represents a similar trend of thought as that of the vindication of the legally just status of the believer by the resurrection.[77]

Romans 8:29–30

Romans 8:29–30 also suggests the very close link between justification and resurrection:

> For those whom He foreknew, He also predestined to become conformed to the image of His Son, so that He would be the firstborn among many brethren; and these whom He predestined, He also called; and these whom He called, He also justified; and these whom He justified, He also glorified.

76. For this link between the legal declaration of Christ's sonship through resurrection and the declaration of believers' sonship through their resurrection, see Gaffin, *Centrality of the Resurrection*, 118.

77. Vos, *Pauline Eschatology*, 152. See also Heppe, *Reformed Dogmatics*, 552–53. Heppe discusses the very close link between justification and sonship; e.g., he says, citing Heidegger, "This concession of the right to life [that comes through justification] really coincides with adoption and is none otherwise distinguished from it than that in justification eternal life is viewed as a due, in adoption as an inheritance; and in the former case God sustains the role of a judge, in the latter that of a Father" (p. 552). For the close linkage of justification to sonship but not an equation of the two, see John Gill, *A Body of Doctrinal Divinity* (London: M. & S. Higham, 1839), 518–19.

The linking together here of sonship (v. 29) and justification and glorification (v. 30) supports the notion that justification leads to glorification. The glorification in 8:30 probably should be understood in light of 8:17–18, 21, since this is the last time Paul has mentioned "glory" (3x). There, reference to glory clearly refers to the glory of saints' final resurrection bodies (as clarified by vv. 21–23). Thus, though "glorification" is placed directly after "justification" without any statement about their precise relation, it is likely that verse 30 includes the notion that justification will result in the final glorification of saints in their resurrection bodies. Another way to say this is that the glorious final resurrection of true saints is an eschatological declaration leading necessarily from their prior justified status.[78]

Romans 8:32–34

There remains one more relevant passage to discuss, which follows right on the heels of Rom. 8:17–30. The text is Rom. 8:32–34:

He who did not spare His own Son, but delivered Him over for us all, how will He not also with Him freely give us all things? Who will bring a charge against God's elect? God is the one who justifies; who is the one who condemns? Christ Jesus is He who died, yes, rather who was raised, who is at the right hand of God, who also intercedes for us.

The crucial wording for our purposes comes in verses 33–34, which allude to the Greek version of Isa. 50:8 (table 15.2).

Table 15.2

Isaiah 50:8 LXX	Romans 8:33–34
"For he who has justified [ho dikaiōsas] me draws near. Who is the one condemning[a] [tis ho krinomenos] me? . . . Who is the one condemning [tis ho krinomenos] me?"	"God is the one who justifies [ho dikaiōn]; who is the one condemning [tis ho katakrinōn]?"

[a]For rendering krinō as "condemn, judge, pass judgment, punish, contend," see Johan Lust, Erik Eynikel, and Katrin Hauspie, Greek-English Lexicon of the Septuagint, 2 vols. (Stuttgart: Deutsche Bibelgesellschaft, 1996), 2:267–68.

It is probable, as a number of commentators think,[79] that the Romans text clearly refers to the Isaiah text, which is validated by the fact that nowhere else in the LXX does the verb "justify" (indeed, in the participial form) occur

78. It seems too in the directly following verses (8:31–34) that mention of Christ's death *and resurrection* as the basis for believers' exemption from condemnation is significant (on this, see the directly following discussion). Kirk (*Unlocking Romans*, 154) reaches a similar conclusion about the significance of Rom. 8:30–34.

79. E.g., Bruce, *Romans*, 169; Cranfield, *Epistle to the Romans*, 1:437–38; Dunn, *Romans 1–8*, 503; Brendan Byrne, *Romans*, SP 6 (Collegeville, MN: Liturgical Press, 1996), 276. See also Jewett, *Romans*, 541; Ernst Käsemann, *Commentary on Romans*, trans. and ed. Geoffrey W.

in syntactical relation to "who is the one condemning?" The verb *dikaioō*, rendered above as "justify," can just as easily be translated "vindicate."[80]

This part of the Servant Song from Isa. 50 was discussed just above with respect to the vindication of Jesus being prophesied by Isaiah. We saw that the Servant was obedient to the divine call to suffer unjust persecution (vv. 4–6), as well as unjust accusation (vv. 8–9), though he would be vindicated by God (vv. 7–11) and viewed as being in the right after all. I concluded that Jesus's resurrection was the means that God used to vindicate him in overturning false and unjust condemnation.

Now, however, Paul applies this prophecy about the Servant's vindication to believers! What was prophesied of the Servant's vindication now becomes true of the believers' vindication. The likely reason for this application is that Christ, as the Servant, represented his people by his obedience through wrongfully imposed suffering in the face of false accusation and condemnation followed by vindication. Whereas Christ's vindication occurred through his resurrection, that of believers occurs through both his resurrection and his death. That both are in view as the basis of their justification/vindication is apparent in that the mention of their justification and lack of condemnation in verses 33b–34a is sandwiched between references to Christ's death and resurrection. Verse 32 refers to God who "delivered Him over for us all," and also asks, "How will He not also with Him freely give us all things?" This giving of "all things" because they are "with Him" certainly includes reference to their identification with the resurrected Christ, through whom comes all future blessings of the new creation, which has been inaugurated by Christ's resurrection.[81] Verse 34b repeats this double reference to Christ's death and resurrection: "Christ . . . died . . . [and] was raised" and "is at the right hand of God," which is a further explanation of how they are identified

---

Bromiley (Grand Rapids: Eerdmans, 1980), 248. Both Jewett and Käsemann cite others who see a clear reference to Isa. 50:8, though they themselves are tentative about hearing even an echo.

80. See Lust, Eynikel, and Hauspie, *Greek-English Lexicon*, 2:115.

81. The question "Will He not also with Him freely give us all things?" likely includes the final resurrection hoped for in Rom. 8:18–25, and this directly relates probably to not being condemned in the future, as well as the present, the latter of which is the emphasis of vv. 30–34. Strikingly, Byrne (*Romans*, 276) says that when v. 32 is seen in the light of the following lists (vv. 35–39) and particularly in view of 1 Cor. 3:21–23, where the apostle says that "all things are yours" with a focus on inheritance of the coming world, then "all things" in Rom. 8:32 likely refers to the physical inheritance of the earth (already anticipated in Rom. 4:13). This inheritance belongs to Christians as "fellow heirs with Christ" (Rom. 8:17; cf. "with Him [Christ]" in v. 32), and Rom. 8:17b–23 sees such heirship focused on the obtaining of resurrection bodies in a new creation (so likewise see *ta panta* in 2 Cor. 5:17–18, though underscoring inaugurated eschatology with specific reference to the "new creation," which has been launched through Christ's resurrection). So also Dunn (*Romans 1–8*, 502), who sees all the coming new creation to be in mind. So similarly, Cranfield (*Epistle to the Romans*, 1:436–37), though he finally sees Rom. 5:10 as the closest parallel, where "saved by His life" is the focal point, which is a reference to being saved by his resurrection life.

"with Him" in verse 32. This shows further that the giving of "all things" in verse 32 includes believers' identification with the benefits of Christ's resurrected and ascended position of rule at God's right hand.[82]

> God "delivered Him over for us all" . . . (v. 32a)
> "How will He [God] not also with Him [the resurrected Christ] freely give us all things?" (v. 32b)
>
> > "It is God who justifies. (v. 33b)
> > Who is to condemn?" (v. 34a)
>
> "Christ . . . died . . . (v. 34b)
> [and] was raised" and "is at the right hand of God." (v. 34c)

The significance of this dual mention of Christ's death and resurrection before (v. 32) and after (v. 34b) mention of God's justification/vindication of saints and their noncondemnation (vv. 33–34b) is that the guilty verdict of the world against them and the world's unjust persecution of them has begun to be overturned in Christ's suffering and condemnation on their behalf; furthermore, their already–not yet identification with Jesus's resurrected status as the obedient Servant, which has overturned the world's guilty verdict on him, has begun to overturn the world's verdict against them, a guilty verdict especially expressed through the persecution described in 8:35–39. In contrast to persecution by the world and Christians being "put to death all day long" (8:35–36), the final bodily resurrection of the saints represents the climactic stage of their vindication against the world's unrighteous evaluation of them. That the saints' physical resurrection at the eschaton is in mind here is evident from the expression "will He [God] not also with Him [the resurrected Christ] freely give us all things" (8:32), which, as noted above, continues the theme of the redemption of the body from 8:17–25. At this time when they receive "immortality" and "eternal [resurrection] life," they will also be "glorified" and given "honor" before those who had unrighteously mistreated and shamed them (2:7, 10; 8:30).[83]

That neither "angels nor principalities . . . will be able to separate" believers "from the love of God" in Christ (Rom. 8:38–39) indicates that Satan and his angelic hosts are among those who had maliciously treated and wrongly accused Christians and whose slander will be nullified at the vindication of the final resurrection. No one, including Satan, can "bring a charge against God's elect" now (Rom. 8:33 [see also Rev. 12:7–10]) or on the last day. The consummation

82. I am grateful to my research student Mitch Kim for the essence of this paragraph, which came from an unpublished doctoral seminar paper at Wheaton College Graduate School in April 2008.

83. See Bird, "Justification as Forensic Declaration," 122, with which I have found significant agreement here on the significance of Rom. 8.

of this inability to accuse God's faithful ones is likely included in Rom. 16:20: "The God of peace will soon crush Satan under your feet." At this time, the devil will be "thrown into the lake of fire and brimstone" (Rev. 20:10), which means that he will have no prosecuting or condemnatory function in the final judgment. It is not coincidental that Rev. 20:11–15 (to be addressed below) is a picture of the judgment at the final resurrection, in which not only is Satan conspicuously absent but also those raised whose names are "written in the book of life" will be exempted from the judgment narrated there.

The final bodily resurrection of the saints vindicates them before the onlooking world in that it is an "enfleshing" or "incarnation"[84] of their prior spiritual identification with Christ's vindicating resurrection. This identification with Christ's vindicating resurrection was neither seen nor recognized by the ungodly powers during the preconsummation age but nevertheless declared them to be fully righteous because they were identified with the righteousness that Christ was proved to have had. That is, spiritual resurrection that is visible only to the eyes of faith (2 Cor. 4:6–11, 16–18) will become visible in the consummated form of physical resurrection (2 Cor. 4:14; 5:1–5) to all eyes, which is foundational to people being judged favorably by Christ at the end[85] and vindicated before those who had judged them unjustly and persecuted them.

2 Corinthians 4:16

Second Corinthians 4:16 presents a significant paradigm for understanding this notion of initial invisible justification and later visible justification: "Therefore we do not lose heart, but though our outer man is decaying, yet our inner man is being renewed day by day." In light of this, the believer has a two-sided existence: the "inner man," which is the unseen immaterial aspect, and the "outer man," the visible bodily aspect. Accordingly, although 2 Cor. 4:16 refers to the progressive resurrection renewal, we may speak more broadly and say that the identification of believers with Christ's resurrection in this age (discussed earlier in this section) pertains to the believer's "inner man," and therefore that initial resurrection identification and existence are the beginning evidence of justification. The granting of spiritual life is an overturning of the verdict of spiritual death in that the believer has been delivered from the execution of that death verdict. But although Christians have been declared not guilty from the entire penalty of sin, spiritual and physical, they have not yet been delivered from the physical death penalty of sin that has been carried out on them, the decaying effects of which they still live under. What this means is that their physical resurrection is the final overturning of the death penalty, the actual verdict of which they had already been declared as having been justified from. This removing of the execution of the physical death

---

84. Bird (ibid.) uses this word in referring to the resurrection being "the incarnation of the justification of the saints."

85. On this subject, see further discussion of 2 Cor. 4:6–5:10 below.

penalty is a final part of the eschatological, two-stage, already–not yet effects of justification: (1) resurrection of the "inner man" followed by (2) resurrection of the "outer man."[86] Richard Gaffin refers to this double justification as "justified by faith" and "yet to be justified by sight."[87] In that the complete overturning of the death penalty lies still in the future, there is a sense in which the full justification/vindication from that penalty is also still yet to be carried out, though this carrying out is ultimately an effect of the earlier declaration of justification from the complete penalty of sin that comes by faith. Table 15.3 attempts to express this twofold justification.

Table 15.3

Justification by faith	resurrection of the "inner man"	declared innocent of the penalty of sin
Justification by sight	resurrection of the "outer man"	delivered from the penalty of sin's effects on the body, vindicated from the world's wrong verdict

An illustration here may be helpful. A man has been wrongfully convicted of a crime and has begun to serve a jail sentence. When new evidence has been adduced to demonstrate his innocence, the court nullifies the former verdict and declares him not guilty. However, because of the necessary administrative paperwork, the actual release of the prisoner does not take place for another three weeks. Thus, the prisoner's justification occurs in two stages: (1) the court's announced verdict of "not guilty" and (2) the subsequent bodily release from the prison, which was a punishment of the former guilty verdict that was decisively overturned three weeks earlier, the full effects of which are now carried out.[88]

The Final Resurrection and Good Works in Connection to the Justification/Vindication of the Saints

We have seen that believers' bodily resurrection is a visible, consummative, end-time manifestation of their end-time, unseen, presently justified status. "Good works" are part of this final "manifestive justification." A few texts speak of a future end-time justification of Christians. For example, Rom. 2:13 says, "For it is not the hearers of the Law who are just before God, but the doers of the Law will be justified."[89] Paul also repeatedly speaks of believers

86. Romans 8:10–11, 23 refers to the same kind of two-stage process (following Richard B. Gaffin Jr., *By Faith, Not by Sight: Paul and the Order of Salvation* [Waynesboro, GA: Paternoster, 2006], 86).
87. Ibid., 88.
88. For the ideas in the last two paragraphs I am indebted to Gaffin (ibid., 86–92).
89. This refers to a future justification (to which the context of Rom. 2:3–10, 15–16 strongly points) and likely not, as some hold, to a principle that if people are to be justified by keeping the law, it is by a perfect doing of the law.

appearing "before the judgment seat" of God or Christ (Rom. 14:10, 12; 2 Cor. 5:10). James 2:14–26 also speaks of the close link between justification and good works (e.g., v. 14: "a man is justified by works and not by faith alone"). This text is also likely focusing on a final justification at the end of time.[90]

How can believers be said to be judged by works and yet be justified by faith? There is much more to be said than can be elaborated on here about believers' righteous works in connection to this consummate, manifestive stage of justification. The directly following discussion is just the beginning of an answer to that question, which will be addressed in more depth later in the conclusion to this chapter.

It may be surprising to some to learn that it is not uncommon in the Reformed tradition to speak of what has been called variously a "twofold justification," or a past justification by faith and a subsequent justification by works, or a "first justification" and a "second justification."[91] A mundane illustration may help to clarify. In the United States, some large discount food stores require people to pay an annual fee to have the privilege of buying food at their store. Once this fee is paid, the member must present a card as evidence of having paid the fee. The card gets the members into the store, but it is not the ultimate reason that the person is granted access. The paid fee is the ultimate reason, the card being the evidence that the fee has been paid. We may refer to the paid fee as the "necessary causal condition" of store entrance and to the evidential card more simply as a "necessary condition."[92] The card is the external manifestation or proof that the price has been paid, so that both the money paid and the card issued are necessary for admittance, but they do not have the same conditional force for gaining entrance. We may call the paid fee a "first order" or "ultimate" condition and the card a "second order" condition.[93]

---

90. There is no space to demonstrate this here, but see Douglas J. Moo, *The Letter of James*, PNTC (Grand Rapids: Eerdmans, 2000), 134–36, 144; see also idem, *The Letter of James*, TNTC (Grand Rapids: Eerdmans, 1985), 99–101. For further analysis of the James 2 passage, see toward the end of this chapter.

91. For a helpful discussion, see Heppe, *Reformed Dogmatics*, 562–63. See also John Owen, *Justification by Faith* (Grand Rapids: Sovereign Grace Publishers, 1971), 137–52. Owen sees two stages: (1) an absolute justification at the inception of faith and (2) persevering in the justified condition by exercising faith in Christ as the advocate who makes petition to the Father that his propitiatory death render forgiveness for ongoing sins. See also Francis Turretin, *Institutes of Elenctic Theology*, vol. 2, trans. George Musgrave Giger, ed. James T. Dennison Jr. (Phillipsburg, NJ: P&R, 1994), 685. Turretin sees multiple temporal phases of justification: (1) the justified state of the believer at the inception of faith; (2) the pardon of particular sins during the course of the saint's life, based on the prior and ongoing justified condition; (3) the declaration of this justification made immediately after death; and (4) publicly later on the last day—"an adjudication of the reward, in accordance with the preceding justification."

92. In this respect, Jonathan Edwards proposes "a distinction between causal conditionality and non-causal conditionality" (Samuel T. Logan, "The Doctrine of Justification in the Theology of Jonathan Edwards," *WTJ* 46 [1984]: 32).

93. For the latter category, see ibid., 38.

Likewise, Christ's justifying penal death is the price paid "once for all" (Heb. 9:12; cf. 9:26–28),[94] and the good works done within the context of Christian faith become the inevitable evidence of such faith at the final judicial evaluation. Christ's work is the "necessary causal condition" for justification, and the believer's works are a "necessary condition" for it. Jonathan Edwards helpfully referred to Christ's work as "causal justification" and the believer's obedience at the end of the age as "manifestive justification."[95] This manifestive evidence not only is part of a judicial process but also becomes evidence that overturns the wrong verdict of the world on believers' faith and works done in obedience to Christ. This is not to say that *dikaioō* should be translated as "rendering legal demonstration," but that it has the notion of "vindicate," which in this context is based on the presence of good works.

Of course, good works are only part of this final "manifestive justification," since, as we have also seen, the believers' resurrection also forms part of this consummative eschatological manifestation. A full-orbed discussion of "good works" in relation to justification cannot be set forth here or even later in the conclusion of this chapter. Accordingly, the following discussion is limited to the link of such works to the saints' resurrection. In particular, the following passages reveal an inseparable connection between believers' bodily resurrection and their final judgment according to works. I believe that this connection sheds further light on the question of how believers can be said to be judged by works (e.g., 2 Cor. 5:10) and yet be justified by faith.

2 Corinthians 4:6–5:10

This passage closely links the saints' final resurrection and their judgment according to works. As noted briefly earlier, the spiritual resurrection in the present age, not recognized in the eyes of the world (2 Cor. 4:6–11, 16–18), will become manifest in the final form of bodily resurrection (2 Cor. 4:14; 5:1–5). Particularly important here is 2 Cor. 5:1–10.

> For we know that if the earthly tent which is our house is torn down, we have a building from God, a house not made with hands, eternal in the heavens. For indeed in this house we groan, longing to be clothed with our dwelling from heaven, inasmuch as we, having put it on, will not be found naked. For indeed while we are in this tent, we groan, being burdened, because we do not want to be unclothed but to be clothed, so that what is mortal will be swallowed up by life. Now He who prepared us for this very purpose is God, who gave to us the Spirit as a pledge. Therefore, being always of good courage, and knowing

---

94. Though by stressing Christ's justifying death here, I do not mean to exclude his imputed obedient life and justifying resurrection as part of this once-for-all justification.

95. Logan, "Doctrine of Justification," 39. Or one could refer to this as "internal justification," which is seen or recognized only by God and the believing community, and "external justification," which manifests the internal verdict through the believer's works to all the world at the eschaton.

that while we are at home in the body we are absent from the Lord—for we walk by faith, not by sight—we are of good courage, I say, and prefer rather to be absent from the body and to be at home with the Lord. Therefore we also have as our ambition, whether at home or absent, to be pleasing to Him. For we must all appear before the judgment seat of Christ, so that each one may be recompensed for his deeds in the body, according to what he has done, whether good or bad.

On the basis of ("therefore," *oun* [5:6]) the consummate resurrection elaborated upon in verses 1–5, believers are to be of "good courage" (v. 6), "for [in the present age]," verse 7 asserts, "we walk by faith, not by sight" (in recognizing our present spiritual resurrection and especially its inevitable final expression in bodily resurrection). Thus, both verses 1–5 and verse 7 give the basis for being of "good courage" in verse 6, which is confidence in the fact of resurrection, particularly as this is realized bodily in the future. Then verse 8 repeats being "of good courage," which, again, is based on verses 1–5 concerning the coming resurrection. Such courage is necessary in the face of affliction (2 Cor. 4:7–12, 16–17). Verse 9 continues the argument by affirming that on the basis of (*dio*, "therefore") being of good courage (vv. 6, 8) because of confidence in the coming bodily resurrection (vv. 1–5), believers should strive "to be pleasing to Him [God]." Courage inspired by confidence in the coming resurrection motivates one to be pleasing to God: since God will act favorably on behalf of believers by raising them from the dead, they should now be motivated to show their gratitude by doing those things that are pleasing to him.[96] Verse 10 gives a further reason that Christians should want to please God: "because" (*gar*) they must all appear (in resurrected bodies) before the bar of the divine law court "so that each one may be recompensed" for good or bad deeds. They should be motivated to please God by doing good deeds because they will be called to account for how they live.

A point not often observed in this passage is that pleasing God, and thus doing good works, is ultimately based not only on the confidence in future resurrection but also on the fact that resurrection existence has already begun. Accordingly, it is out of the renewing power of such inaugurated resurrection existence (so 2 Cor. 4:16), which shows identification and solidarity with Christ's resurrection existence now (2 Cor. 4:10–11; 5:14–15) and proleptically on the last day (2 Cor. 4:14), that the desire to please God and do good works arises.

In this light, Paul believed that true believers who are truly identified with Christ's resurrection now and will be identified with his bodily resurrection at the last great assize will "appear" or "be manifested" before the "judgment seat" *in resurrection bodies*. In light of the broader context of Paul's thought,

---

96. The same rationale is straightforwardly given in 2 Cor. 4:14–15, though there the language of "giving thanks" is expressed instead of being "pleasing."

we see that such people will be judged not on whether their deeds have been perfect but rather on whether they have borne the fruit of good works in keeping with and as a result of their resurrection existence and union with Christ's resurrected person.[97] Thus, what is being evaluated is the character (i.e., the "in Christ" resurrection character) from which the works arose.[98] This is further apparent in that Paul's reference to believers' future "building from God . . . not made with hands" with which they are "longing to be clothed" (2 Cor. 5:1–4) is none other than their resurrection body: they want "to be clothed, so that what is mortal may be swallowed up by life" (5:4) and "not be found naked" (5:3). Thus, in light of 5:1–4, 5:10 includes the notion that what "clothes" a person is good deeds pleasing to God, inextricably linked to and arising from the person's resurrection character, which is manifested bodily[99] on the last day. And, since they are "manifested before the judgment seat of Christ," the resurrected Christ himself acknowledges their resurrection identification with him (see also 1 Cor. 15:22–23) and evaluates them and their works positively.

This means that believers are first resurrected immediately before being "recompensed for their deeds." Recall from earlier in this chapter that Paul elsewhere sees believers' resurrection to be part of their justification, vindicating them from the wrong verdict declared on them by the world and vindicating them from the penalty of bodily death resulting from their own sin against God. Thus, believers "appear" as already openly justified in their resurrection bodies immediately preceding their examination before "the judgment seat of Christ." In this respect, the last judgment for believers, which is according to works, is "reflective of and further attesting their justification that has been openly manifested in their bodily resurrection."[100] In addition, we noted earlier that believers begin to be in Christ's restored image during the present age and consummately and perfectly so at the final resurrection.[101] This means that as they appear before the judgment seat in their resurrected body, they are also now in the perfect image of the last Adam and in union with him, which further includes a testimony to their righteous, obedient character. Such righ-

---

97. So also Kirk, *Unlocking Romans*, 224, 226.

98. In this respect, in 2 Cor. 5:10 the change from the plural "deeds" (*ha* [lit., "what things"]) to the singular "good or bad" (*agathon eite phaulon*) appears to suggest that "conduct will be judged as a whole," so that it is not distinct acts but rather character that will be punished or rewarded (following Murray J. Harris, *The Second Epistle to the Corinthians: A Commentary on the Greek Text*, NIGTC [Grand Rapids: Eerdmans, 2005], 407–8).

99. Just as Christ's resurrection life had begun to be "manifested" (aorist passive of *phaneroō*) spiritually through the saints while they are in their earthly bodies (2 Cor. 4:10–11), so it will be fully "manifested" (again, aorist passive of *phanerō*) in their resurrection bodies at the end of the age (2 Cor. 5:10).

100. Gaffin, *By Faith*, 99–100.

101. For the former, see 2 Cor. 3:18, and for the latter, see 1 Cor. 15:45–54; see also Rom. 8:29, which includes both.

teous obedience begins during the interadvent age, which is actually a part of what it means to begin to be in Christ's image during that age.[102]

In contrast, others who profess to have been identified with Christ's resurrection but who do not bear such fruit will "be found naked"—that is, not found resurrected "in Christ" and lacking new, life-bearing works. As a consequence, they will "fail the test" of this judicial evaluation (2 Cor. 13:5; cf. 1 Cor. 11:19) because they have "received the grace of God in vain" (2 Cor. 6:1) and, consequently, are still "yoked together with unbelievers," are in "fellowship with darkness," are characterized by "lawlessness" (2 Cor. 6:14), and are identified with the devil (2 Cor. 6:15; 11:13–15).[103] Such people will suffer judgment with the world of unbelievers because they have "disguised themselves as servants of righteousness, whose end shall be according to their deeds" (2 Cor. 11:15), since such deeds reveal their true, unbelieving character (see also Matt. 7:15–23).[104]

This means that 2 Cor. 5:10 is not about Christ distributing differing awards to Christians, all of whom are "saved," according to their differing works. Rather, some will be found to be true, resurrected, fruit-bearing believers, while others will not. With respect to the latter group, it is suitable to refer to this passage as expressing the notion of a future "manifestive justification or vindication" through judgment. A very similar idea is expressed in 1 Cor. 3:13: "Each man's work will become manifest [*phaneros*]; for the day will show it because it is to be revealed with fire, and the fire itself will test the quality of each man's work." This refers to some who are saved and others who will be judged at the eschaton.[105]

1 Corinthians 4:3–5

This future "manifestive justification" also occurs in 1 Cor. 4:3–5. Although the text lacks reference to resurrection, it is included for discussion here because it employs formal "justification" language in connection to manifesting what was formerly invisible and unknown:

> But to me it is a very small thing that I may be examined by you, or by any human court; in fact, I do not even examine myself. For I am conscious of nothing against myself, yet I am not by this acquitted [justified]; but the one who examines me is the Lord. Therefore do not go on passing judgment before the time, but wait until the Lord comes who will both bring to light the things

102. In this paragraph I am indebted to Gaffin, *By Faith*, 99–101.

103. Although 2 Cor. 11:13–15 refers specifically to the false Jewish Christian teachers, it may be applicable to those in the Corinthian church who follow and thus identify with them (cf. 2 Cor. 11:3–4).

104. For the connection of the "clothing" with good "deeds" in 2 Cor. 5:1–4, I have generally followed Hafemann, *2 Corinthians*, 217.

105. For elaboration of 1 Cor. 3:10–17 along these lines, see Fee, *First Epistle to the Corinthians*, 143–45.

hidden in the darkness and disclose the motives of men's hearts; and then each man's praise will come to him from God.

Part of the problem in the Corinthian church was that some were not evaluating Paul to be an authoritative apostle (1 Cor. 1:11–12; 3:3–4; 4:9–13; 9:3).[106] Although some in the church and even a "human court" may conclude that Paul did not bear the true marks of a divine prophet (v. 3a), he would not attempt to defend himself from such negative evaluations in order to be seen as "justified/vindicated" (*dikaioō*) (vv. 3b–4a). Instead, Paul says, "The one who examines me [truly] is the Lord" (v. 4b), and definitive justification/vindication comes only from him. But it is clear that Paul is referring to a justification/vindication that occurs when "the Lord comes" on the last day (v. 5). At this time, the Lord will "disclose the motives of men's hearts" so that what formerly was not seen clearly will be. Then Christ will examine such motives and find them wanting or deserving "praise."[107] In the context, Paul has himself in mind (and secondarily the apostolic circle together with all genuine believers), so that the upshot of 1 Cor. 4:3–5 in context is that Paul's motives will be vindicated as being truly suitable to those of a prophetic servant of God and true believer (as also in 1 Thess. 2:2–4), in contradiction to worldly forces that have rejected him as a true divine messenger, and "praise will come to him from God." Others' motives will be revealed as bad, and they will suffer final judgment (2 Cor. 11:13–15).[108] This passage, then, focuses on the motives behind works, which again puts the spotlight on the character of a person being examined on the last day (i.e., the true believer is found to "belong to Christ" [1 Cor. 3:23]) and not merely the person's

106. See Fee, *First Epistle to the Corinthians*, 161–62; Richard B. Hays, *First Corinthians*, IBC (Louisville: John Knox, 1997), 65–66. Both see that the Corinthians were in the process of accusing Paul of ill motives in his ministry.

107. Actually, Paul mentions only that "praise" will come, though probably he is looking here only at the reward of good motives and assuming that judgment for bad motives will also occur. However, Thiselton (*First Epistle to the Corinthians*, 344) maintains that "praise" (*epainos*) has the general idea of "recognition," which would include both a positive and a negative evaluation, though Paul uses the word only positively in his other eight uses of it.

108. In 1 Cor. 4:1–5 the thread of 3:9–17 is picked up again, but space allows me only to summarize my view of the latter text. The person building is the Christian leader or minister, the building is the temple founded on Christ, the materials built on the foundation (= "each man's work") are those Christians who are brought to faith and/or shepherded by the ministers (so 1 Cor. 9:1), the work that remains is those shepherded saints who end up finally redeemed (and, implicitly, resurrected), the burned-up work is the lives of those shepherded who suffer final judgment at the end, though the minister "himself shall be saved." Accordingly, Paul concludes, "If any man [any confessing believer] destroys/corrupts [see 6:18–19] the temple of God, God will destroy him" in final judgment (3:17). For further elaboration of 1 Cor. 3:9–17, see G. K. Beale, *The Temple and the Church's Mission: A Biblical Theology of the Dwelling Place of God*, NSBT 17 (Downers Grove, IL: InterVarsity, 2004); along similar lines, see Fee, *First Epistle to the Corinthians*, 142–45.

outward works. This is virtually the same as what I concluded about 2 Cor. 5:10 in its context.

Again, final justification makes visible the justified character "in Christ" that was not visible to unbelieving eyes during the interadvent age.

REVELATION 20:11–15

This is another important passage concerning the judgment by works in relation to the Christian's standing at the final judgment. Sometimes the saints' identification with Christ's death and resurrection at the time of final judgment is stressed so much that they are viewed as being excluded from being judged "according to their works" in the way that unbelievers are so judged. Revelation 20:11–15 is a classic expression of judgment according to deeds.

> Then I saw a great white throne and Him who sat upon it, from whose presence earth and heaven fled away, and no place was found for them. And I saw the dead, the great and the small, standing before the throne, and books were opened; and another book was opened, which is the book of life; and the dead were judged from the things which were written in the books, according to their deeds. And the sea gave up the dead which were in it, and death and Hades gave up the dead which were in them; and they were judged, every one of them according to their deeds. Then death and Hades were thrown into the lake of fire. This is the second death, the lake of fire. And if anyone's name was not found written in the book of life, he was thrown into the lake of fire.

That John sees "the dead, the great and the small, standing before the throne" presupposes that the last, great resurrection of both the unrighteous and the righteous has finally taken place (in light of Rev. 20:5; cf. Dan. 12:2; John 5:28–29; Acts 24:15). The Lamb standing before a throne in 5:6, expressing resurrection existence, reinforces the same idea here in 20:11–15, where verse 13 makes clear that resurrected people are standing before God's throne.

The clauses "books were opened" and "another book was opened, which is the book of life" combine allusion to Dan. 7:10 ("the books were opened") and Dan. 12:1–2 ("everyone who is found written in the book will be rescued . . . to everlasting life"). The point of "the books" in Dan. 7 is to focus on the evil deeds of the end-time persecutor(s) of God's people, for which he (and they) would be judged. The book mentioned in Dan. 12:1 also concerns the end of time, but it is an image of redemption. Those "written in the book" will be given resurrection life, while those excluded from the book will suffer final judgment. Therefore, the vision in Rev. 20:11–15 gives assurance that the prophesied final judgment and redemptive resurrection will occur. The opening of the book in 5:1–9 referred partly to the inauguration of judgment, but the image there connoted more broadly the decree involving all facets of judgment and redemption during the era preceding Christ's final return and culminating at the end of history. The judgment at the end is what is highlighted here in 20:12, although final salvation is secondarily included.[109] As in 13:8; 17:8, the "book of life" is introduced to bring attention to those excluded from it, although, of course, it includes reference secondarily to those who have been included in the book.

The phrase "the dead were judged" reveals the focus on judgment and shows 20:11–15 to be an amplification of the earlier, shorter account of final judgment in 11:18 (where also occurs the almost identical phrase "the time [came] for the dead to be judged"). Even though 11:18 also focuses on judgment of the wicked, included there too is the "reward" to God's "bond-servants the prophets and the saints and those who fear [God's] name." Strikingly, the same phrase "the small and the great" refers to all classes of believers in 11:18 and to all classes of unbelievers in 19:18, so that the same wording in 20:12 may be an all-inclusive reference to both believers and unbelievers. The basis (*kata*, "according to") for judgment of the impious is the record of their evil deeds having been "written in the books." The record books are metaphorical for God's memory, which never fails and at the end provides the account of the misdeeds of the wicked that is presented before them.

In 20:15, as in 20:12–14, the note of final judgment is rung once more for emphasis. Anyone whose name "was not found written in the book of life . . . was thrown into the lake of fire." This implies that all who are found written in the "book of life" are spared from the judgment, which 3:5 and 21:27 make explicit: "I will not erase his [the overcomer's] name from the book of life" (3:5); "those [overcomers] whose names are written in the Lamb's book of life" (21:27). This implication that those written in the "book of life" do not go through the same judgment process as the ungodly is warranted by the positive form of the statement in Dan. 12:1 LXX: "All the people will be saved [i.e., resurrected], <u>whoever is found having been written in the book</u>."

What is it about the "book of life" that spares true saints? The fuller title for the book is "the book of life <u>of the Lamb having been slain</u>" (13:8 [cf. 21:27: "book of life of the Lamb"]). The added description is a genitive of either possession or source. The "life" granted them in association with the book comes from their identification with the Lamb's righteous deeds (note how the Lamb is "worthy," qualifying him "to open the book" in 5:4–9 [cf. 5:12]), especially identification with his death on their behalf, which means likewise that they are identified with his resurrection, which "overcame" death (cf. 5:5–13). They do not suffer judgment for their evil deeds because the Lamb has already suffered it for them: he was slain on their behalf (so esp. 1:5; 5:9;

109. For full OT and Jewish background on the two books in Revelation, see G. K. Beale, *The Book of Revelation: A Commentary on the Greek Text*, NIGTC (Grand Rapids: Eerdmans, 1999), on 3:5; 13:8; 17:8; 20:12, 15.

see further 13:8). The Lamb acknowledges before God all who are written in the book (3:5) and who are identified with his righteousness (i.e., worthiness), his death, and his resurrection life.

That believers' identification with the Lamb's resurrection life is also intended by their inclusion in the book is obvious from three facts: (1) the very name of the book, the "book of life" (on which, see 3:5; 13:8; 17:8; 21:27); (2) the Dan. 12:1–2 allusion, "everyone who is found written in the book will be rescued" and "will awake to everlasting life"; (3) the Lamb who is worthy to "open the book," also an allusion to Dan. 7:10; 12:1–2, has been "slain" but is able to possess "the book" because of his "standing" in resurrection existence (5:5–9).[110] The inevitable conclusion is that the saints written in the book are identified with the Lamb's resurrection life.

At the end, God recognizes those who have taken refuge in the Lamb and have been recorded in the book for an inheritance of eternal resurrection life. While we have seen that Paul can conceive of true believers going through a kind of judgment according to works, Revelation gives another perspective on this by saying that saints' works and unbelievers' works are not evaluated in the same way. Rather, true saints are evaluated according to their placement in the "book of life," which identifies them with the Lamb's perfect worthiness, his penal death and resurrection on their behalf. Thus, those who have "their faith in Jesus" and "who die in the Lord . . . may rest from their labors, for their works [erga] follow with them" (14:12–13). Consequently, any evaluation of their works on the last day can be done only as they are already viewed as identified with the risen Lamb and their works done "in the [risen] Lord." I reached this same conclusion with respect to the Pauline "judgment according to works" passages. The Pauline texts focus more on evaluation of the believers' works, and the Revelation texts more on identification with Christ's worthiness, death, and resurrection.

Conclusion

Initial justification and final justification (or twofold justification) are grounded in believers' union with Christ, the former coming by faith and the latter through the threefold demonstration of (1) the bodily resurrection, (2) God's public announcement to the cosmos, and (3) evaluation by works. So far in this chapter I have been able to develop only the first and third points, the aspect of resurrection and to some degree how good works relate to resurrection and, hence, justification. This, in part, is a classic example of "already and not yet" eschatology. In particular, we have seen throughout this book so far that Christ's resurrection and believers' identification with that resurrection are the beginning of the end-time new creation. In this chapter I have tried to demonstrate that

---

110. However, for the difference between the book in 5:2–9 and the books in 20:12, 15, see ibid., on those verses.

Christ's resurrection and believers' identification with it are the justification/vindication of both Jesus and his people. In this respect, justification is not just an eschatological notion but also a facet of the end-time new creation.

What Douglas Moo has said about James 2 is also a good summary of what I have said so far in this section:

> The believer, in himself, will always deserve God's judgment: our conformity to the "royal law" is never perfect, as it must be (vv. 10–11). But our merciful attitude and actions [= good works] will count as evidence of the presence of Christ within us. And it is on the [ultimate] basis of this union with the [resurrected] One who perfectly fulfilled the law for us that we can have confidence for vindication at the judgment.[111]

Moo's comment serves as a good transition to the last section of this chapter, which focuses even more directly on the subject of good works in relation to justification.

The Saints' Final Eschatological Justification/Vindication through Public Demonstration of Their Good Works

From the time of the early church there has been discussion about how justification by faith relates to a final judgment by works, to which even the believer is said to be subject. In the preceding section I discussed works in connection to resurrection and judgment; in this section I address further the subject of works in relation to justification. The following views summarize more recent alternative interpretations, which are representative of earlier perspectives on this issue.

Various Interpretations about How Justification Relates to a Final Judgment by Works

Before listing various interpretations of how justification relates to a final judgment by works, I should note that one approach to the question is to say simply that the two are ultimately irreconcilable because Paul is inconsistent in his thinking.[112] Although some see this solution as persuasive, it does not deal sufficiently with how the apparently contrary views of Paul relate to each other.

Others, however, see that justification and final judgment by works are reconcilable. Several different solutions have been offered.[113] Justification and good works can be viewed as compatible in the following ways:

111. Moo, *James* (1985), 99.
112. See, e.g., William Wrede, *Paul*, trans. Edward Lummis (London: Philip Green, 1907), 77–78.
113. The following list of alternative interpretations is based on Dane Ortlund, "Justified by Faith, Judged according to Works: Another Look at a Pauline Paradox," *JETS* 52 (2009):

1. Justification by faith and justification (or judgment) of the believer by works is hypothetical, especially in a text such as Rom. 2:13. That is, there are two ways to be justified, by faith or by works, the latter of which can be accomplished only by being perfect, and therefore sinful humanity can receive justification only by faith.[114]
2. Justification or judgment by works must be appreciated through understanding Paul's rhetorical purposes,[115] which differ depending on the circumstances and audiences to which he is responding. For example, some readers who lacked assurance of their salvation needed the message of justification only by faith through grace, while other readers who were overconfident and had a false sense of security about their salvation needed to be told they would face a judgment by works. Accordingly, in this view, how justification by faith and judgment according to works go together theologically is not altogether clear.[116]
3. Judgment according to works for saints occurs as a distribution of differing rewards for differing degrees of faithful service at the very end of time and, therefore, subsequent to their having been justified by faith.[117]
4. Final justification and acquittal is based only on works.[118]
5. Justification and judgment are grounded in the believer's union with Christ, the former coming by faith, and the latter being an evaluation of works that necessarily arise from the true faith-union with Christ and by means of the Spirit's empowerment.[119]

323–39. I will indicate only one or two representative scholars for each position, though each has permutations that cannot be elaborated on here.

114. See, e.g., Frank Thielman, *Paul and the Law: A Contextual Approach* (Downers Grove, IL: InterVarsity, 1994), 172–74 (n42 gives other alternative interpretations of Rom. 2:13).

115. On which, see Neil Elliott, *The Rhetoric of Romans: Argumentative Constraint and Strategy, and Paul's Dialogue with Judaism*, JSNTSup 45 (Sheffield: JSOT Press, 1990), 221–27.

116. See, e.g., Nigel M. Watson, "Justified by Faith: Judged by Works—An Antinomy?," *NTS* 29 (1983): 214–20.

117. See, e.g., George Eldon Ladd, *A Theology of the New Testament*, rev. ed. (Grand Rapids: Eerdmans, 1993), 612; Paul Barnett, *The Second Epistle to the Corinthians*, NICNT (Grand Rapids: Eerdmans, 1997), 273–77.

118. Chris VanLandingham, *Judgment and Justification in Early Judaism and the Apostle Paul* (Peabody, MA: Hendrickson, 2006).

119. See, e.g., Piper, *Future of Justification*, 184–86. This view is compatible with Klyne R. Snodgrass, "Justification by Grace—to the Doers: An Analysis of the Place of Rom. 2 in the Theology of Paul," *NTS* 32 (1986): 72–93. Snodgrass holds that justification excludes "legalistic works" done to earn salvation but includes an evaluation of imperfect works done that are inspired by grace. This view also possibly could be consistent with N. T. Wright's position, which, in my view, is ambiguous but could be summarized as justification by faith being a polemic against ethnocentric divisions in the early church, which included works as contributing to final acquittal (see, e.g., N. T. Wright, *Paul: In Fresh Perspective* [Minneapolis: Fortress, 2005], 111–14). How Wright precisely relates justification by faith alone to a final judgment by works is unclear. For an evaluation of Wright's multifaceted notions about justification, see Piper, *Future of Justification*, which has a convenient survey of Wright's discussions on justification.

Limitations of space prohibit evaluation of all these alternatives here. The following discussion is most reflective of the last option, with which I most agree.

Justification and Final Judgment Based on the Christian's Faith-Union with Christ

Justification and final judgment have their foundation in the believer's union with Christ. Justification occurs by faith alone, and judgment happens on the basis of an examination of works, which are the fruit of the genuine faith-union with Christ and are empowered by the Spirit. The following discussion focuses on the meaning of judgment at the eschaton according to works for people already justified by faith alone.

Relevant Pauline Texts

There are a few texts in the NT where people are said to be justified by works. A well-known one is Rom. 2:13:

For it is not the hearers of the Law who are just before God, but the doers of the Law will be justified.

There are two dominant interpretations of this verse. Some understand the future tense ("will be justified") not to refer to future time but rather to express the principle that if people are to be justified by keeping the law, it is by a perfect doing of the law: this is "the standard that must be met if a person is to be justified."[120] Others believe that Rom. 2:13 refers to the final judgment when those who are believers in Christ have "good works," though not perfect, and consequently "will be justified" on the basis of those works.[121] Those who reject this view and prefer the first do so on the basis that Paul typically uses the verb *dikaioō* to refer not to vindication at the final judgment but rather to the "verdict of acquittal pronounced by God," which comes only through human faith (although, as we have seen, the verb is used in the future manner in 1 Cor. 4:4).

The first view certainly is viable from the vantage point of Pauline usage, but the immediate context, especially Rom. 2:3–10, appears to focus on the

---

In addition to Piper for a negative evaluation of Wright's positions on this issue, see Peter T. O'Brien, "Was Paul a Covenantal Nomist?," in *The Paradoxes of Paul*, vol. 2 of *Justification and Variegated Nomism*, ed. D. A. Carson, Peter T. O'Brien, and Mark A. Seifrid (Grand Rapids: Baker Academic, 2004), 249–96. For evaluation of various alternative positions on the relation of works to justification, see also O'Brien, "Justification in Paul," 89–95 (O'Brien himself would identify with the fifth view listed above).

120. Moo, *Romans*, 144.

121. Representative of this position are Cranfield, *Epistle to the Romans*, 1:154–55; Snodgrass, "Justification by Grace."

last judgment (accordingly, note the underlined phrases below) as the occasion for "the doers of the law" being "justified" in verse 13. Rom. 2:3–10 reads,

> But do you suppose this, O man, when you pass judgment on those who practice such things and do the same yourself, that you will escape the judgment of God? Or do you think lightly of the riches of His kindness and tolerance and patience, not knowing that the kindness of God leads you to repentance? But because of your stubbornness and unrepentant heart you are storing up wrath for yourself in the day of wrath and revelation of the righteous judgment of God, who will render to each person according to his deeds: to those who by perseverance in doing good seek for glory and honor and immortality, eternal life; but to those who are selfishly ambitious and do not obey the truth, but obey unrighteousness, wrath and indignation. There will be tribulation and distress for every soul of man who does evil, of the Jew first and also of the Greek, but glory and honor and peace to everyone who does good, to the Jew first and also to the Greek.

These verses focus not only on the time of final judgment but also on the time of reward for those who "do good" (vv. 7, 10). Verse 6 ("who will render to each person according to his deeds") seems best interpreted in this context to mean that there will be a judicial evaluation of the works of all people; some will be found wanting and be judged, others will be found to have good works and not be judged but will receive life. Accordingly, with this preceding context in mind, it seems best to understand Paul's statement in verse 13, "the doers of the Law will be justified," to refer to the final judgment when those who have faith in Christ and possess good works, though not perfect, will be "justified" or "vindicated" on the basis of those works. This idea of judgment by works, though without the language of "justification/vindication," is also reflected later in Rom. 14:10, 12:

> But you, why do you judge your brother? Or you again, why do you regard your brother with contempt? For we will all stand before the judgment seat of God. . . . So then each one of us will give an account of himself to God.

And 2 Cor. 5:10 affirms the same thing, though again without the terminology of "justification/vindication."[122]

> For we must all appear before the judgment seat of Christ, so that each one may be recompensed for his deeds in the body, according to what he has done, whether good or bad.

It is likely that the same notion of standing before God's judgment seat in resurrected bodies, as we have seen in 2 Cor. 5:10, is assumed in Rom. 14:12–14.

122. On which, see further elaboration earlier in this chapter under the subheading "2 Corinthians 4:6–5:10."

518

If so, for the true believer, the "account" that one gives to God is given by one who has just experienced redemptive bodily resurrection, and the deeds of that person are seen as works directly connected to being related to the resurrected Christ.

THE TEXT OF JAMES 2

The well-known text of James 2:14–26 supports the same notion that we have just seen in Paul's thinking:

> What use is it, my brethren, if someone says he has faith but he has no works? Can that faith save him? If a brother or sister is without clothing and in need of daily food, and one of you says to them, "Go in peace, be warmed and be filled," and yet you do not give them what is necessary for their body, what use is that? Even so faith, if it has no works, is dead, being by itself. But someone may well say, "You have faith and I have works; show me your faith without the works, and I will show you my faith by my works." You believe that God is one. You do well; the demons also believe, and shudder. But are you willing to recognize, you foolish fellow, that faith without works is useless? Was not Abraham our father justified by works when he offered up Isaac his son on the altar? You see that faith was working with his works, and as a result of the works, faith was perfected; and the Scripture was fulfilled which says, "And Abraham believed God, and it was reckoned to him as righteousness," and he was called the friend of God. You see that a man is justified by works and not by faith alone. In the same way, was not Rahab the harlot also justified by works when she received the messengers and sent them out by another way? For just as the body without the spirit is dead, so also faith without works is dead.

There is not enough space here for a thorough discussion of this thorny text, but the following is a summary of what I see it to be affirming about justification. A typical Roman Catholic view and some Protestant perspectives understand that it is not faith alone that justifies, but that works are of the same importance in justifying the believer. That is, having faith in Christ's death and resurrection and doing good works are equally the basis for establishing a saving relationship with God and for being in right standing with God. Accordingly, the passage is seen either to contradict Paul or to clarify him.

But there is another view that is equally plausible and, I believe, more probable. The key is how James 2:14–26 is connected to the preceding and following context. In 1:10–11 there is what appears to be an allusion to the last judgment ("the rich man in the midst of his pursuits will fade away"). Then 2:9–13 focuses on being a "transgressor of the law," for which final judgment will come (v. 13: "For judgment will be merciless to one who has shown no mercy"). Verse 14 then asks the question of whether a person with faith but no works can be saved from this final judgment ("Can that faith save him" from this final judgment?). The verse immediately following 2:14–26 also mentions judgment for sin: "teachers . . . will incur a stricter judgment" (3:1). The reference in 3:6 to the "tongue . . . set on fire by hell" likely also refers to this judgment. The theme of judgment is continued later in the epistle: God "is able to save and destroy" (4:12), and 5:1–9 warns those who oppress others that "the coming of the Lord is near" (v. 8) and that "the Judge is standing right at the door" (v. 9), references respectively to the imminent expectation of the end and to the judgment to come at the end. Verse 12 also warns people not to "fall under judgment."

In light of the context, it is unlikely that James 2:14–26 mainly addresses the issue of how to establish a right standing with God in this life but instead is concerned primarily with how faith and works relate to the final judgment at the end of one's life. The main point is that genuine faith will produce and thus be accompanied by good works; otherwise it is "dead." Such faith is not genuine and alive but rather is a kind of empty belief like that which is held by "the demons" (v. 19), a sort of purely cognitive recognition of who God is without a desire to trust and to obey.

Therefore, the reference to being "justified" by works together with faith in verses 21–24 probably has this final, eschatological meaning. Previously I discussed the range of meanings for *dikaioō* and concluded that in Paul's writings the translation "vindicate" is preferable,[123] in the sense of both (1) vindicating persons from the guilty verdict on their sin and thus establishing a relationship with God through Christ during this age, and (2) vindicating such people before God's judgment seat at the end of the age against the wrongful verdict pronounced by the world (i.e., against the world's unjust verdict concerning the wrongness of believers' faith and of God's prior verdict of acquittal upon them). This second aspect of vindication is in view in Matt. 12:36–37, where Jesus says,

> But I tell you that every careless word that people speak, they shall give an accounting for it in the day of judgment. For by your words you will be justified, and by your words you will be condemned.

Not only do both James and Matthew have in mind future justification/vindication at the last judgment, but also both introduce this topic by reference to good works (James 2:14–17) or good fruit (Matt. 12:33; see likewise Matt. 25:31–46).

An objection to this understanding of justification/vindication in James as happening at the future judgment could be that verses 21–25 refer to Abraham and Rahab as having been "justified," which seems to place their justification in the past and not in the future; furthermore, verse 24 says that a person "*is* justified," which seems to say that this justification happens throughout the

---

123. The context of the Gen. 22:12 reference in James 2:21 does give plausibility to translating this as "proved righteous." See Ralph P. Martin, *James*, WBC 48 (Waco: Word, 1988), 91–95. Martin renders v. 21, e.g., as "proved righteous [as demonstrated] by his deeds" (p. 91).

time leading up to the end of history. The best way to view this is to see that they were vindicated not only by faith but also by the evidence of the works that they did. The context of the reference to Abraham's offering of Isaac from Gen. 22 supports this interpretation. In Gen. 22:12 the voice from heaven says to Abraham, "For now I know that you fear God, since you have not withheld your son, your only son, from Me." Abraham's obedience indicated to God that he had true vindicating faith, and this obedience thus vindicated the verdict about the truthful reality of that vindicating faith. If there had been no good works, then Abraham would not have received the declaration of vindication; that would have been the case because the lack of works would have indicated that he possessed no genuine justifying faith.[124]

James's focus, however, on vindication at the final judgment is hard to deny in the light of the preceding and following context of 2:14–26, so that the text must be interpreted in this light. Accordingly, Abraham's submission to God's command about Isaac is to be seen as representative of the many good works performed by the patriarch, which had such an eschatologically vindicating function,[125] as we just saw above. The same, then, is true in the case of Rahab. James 2:24 formulates a universal principle on the basis of the example of Abraham: "You see that a man is justified by works and not by faith alone." Notice the plural "works" here, which confirms that it was the many good works of Abraham's whole life that vindicated the true nature of his faith over against any negative evaluations of his faith. Thus, the works of a person's *entire life* are taken into consideration. It is true that the beginning good works of a person are of a vindicating nature, as with Abraham. However, once this holistic perspective on a person's life of works is discerned and it is placed in the preceding and following context of final judgment in James, then it becomes natural to understand that James's broader focus is on good works done throughout a person's life that will receive God's final vindicating approval at the end of the age that can "save" a person from final condemnation (2:14, which introduced our focus paragraph of vv. 14–26).[126]

Consequently, *dikaioō* in James 2:21–24 affirms "that the ultimate vindication of the believer in the judgment is based on, or at least takes into account, the things that a person has done."[127] James is contending that one can have the right kind of faith (i.e., a faith that produces results) and not so much that good works should be added to belief.[128] Such a faith that inspires fruitful

124. Following Martin, *James*, 94.

125. See Moo, *James* (2000), 136.

126. The use of "save" elsewhere in James also appears to be used in this final eschatological manner (1:21; 4:12; 5:20, on which see Moo, *James* [1985], 101).

127. Moo, *James* (2000), 134–35. Moo's discussion of James 2:14–26 has helped to shape my thinking on it. See similarly Martin, *James*, 82–101.

128. Moo, *James* (2000), 144.

works (so James 2:22) will vindicate the validity of one's authentic justifying faith at the last judgment.

The Public Demonstration of the Saints' Final Eschatological Justification/Vindication by Announcing It before All the World

Whereas the announcement of the believer's justification/vindication in the present age is directed only to the community of the church, this announcement of the church's final vindication is made publicly to the cosmos at the very end (cf. Rom. 2:13–16). Although Paul does not actually use the language of "justification" to make this precise point, the book of Isaiah does. One of the most striking instances of this is Isa. 45:22–25:

> Turn to Me and be saved, all the ends of the earth;
> For I am God, and there is no other.
> I have sworn by Myself,
> The word has gone forth from My mouth in righteousness
> And will not turn back,
> That to Me every knee will bow, every tongue will swear allegiance.
> They will say of Me, "Only in the LORD are righteousness and
>   strength."
> Men will come to Him,
> And all who were angry at Him will be put to shame.
> In the LORD all the offspring of Israel will be justified and will glory.

This is a striking passage because verse 24 says "only in the LORD are righteousness and strength," and this is followed up by the statement that "Israel will be declared righteous." All humanity will bend the knee, whether by faith or by force, and in this cosmic context God's people will be seen by all as "vindicated" by God, whereas others "will be put to shame." This is a context of which Paul would have been aware, since he clearly alludes to Isa. 45:23–24 in Phil. 2:10–11.

Isaiah 53:11 is another Isaianic text that prophesies the justification/vindication of Israel in the eschaton, though the NT views it to have an already–not yet fulfillment: "My Servant will justify the many, as He will bear their iniquities" (cf. Acts 3:13; Rom. 5:19).[129] In response to the announcement of the Servant's work and his being "exalted," "kings will shut their mouths on account of Him" (Isa. 52:13, 15), and they will "see" and "understand" what

129. The NA[27] margin lists these texts as alluding to Isa. 53:11, which I think is likely, but if not, it is quite clear that other references to the Isa. 53 passage are understood by the NT to have begun fulfillment in Christ's first coming (e.g., 1 Pet. 2:22–25).

previously had not been seen or understood.[130] This will happen climactically at the very end of history.

Isaiah 54, like Isa. 45, also pictures the final eschatological phase of the vindication of God's people. In Isa. 54:14–15, 17 God declares,

> In <u>righteousness</u> you will be established;
> You will be far from oppression, for you will not fear;
> And from terror, for it will not come near you.
> If anyone fiercely assails you it will not be from Me.
> Whoever assails you will fall because of you. . . .
> No weapon that is formed against you will prosper;
> And every tongue that accuses you in judgment you will condemn.
> This is the heritage of the servants of the LORD,
> And their <u>vindication</u> is from Me.

It is true, however, that Isa. 54:13 ("all your sons will be taught of the LORD") is understood by Jesus to have begun fulfillment in his ministry (John 6:45), so that even Isa. 54:14–17 might therefore conceivably be understood to have an inaugurated fulfillment (though these verses are not referred to anywhere in the NT).

At the very end of time, God's people, in both their justifying faith and resulting righteous actions, will be acknowledged before all to have been in the right all along.[131]

Conclusion: The Nature of Justification/Vindication in Its Future Consummated Eschatological Phase in Relation to the Inaugurated Phase

So far, I have discussed three aspects of future justification/vindication: it occurs through (1) final resurrection, (2) public demonstration of the good works of God's people at the very end in direct connection with their bodily resurrection, and (3) public demonstration by announcing it before the entire cosmos. The question that arises is how this threefold justification/vindication at the end of

130. This likely refers to a response of both belief and unbelief in the Servant's work, the latter of which is especially made explicit in Isa. 53:1, which has an already–not yet application (for the "already" application, see John 12:37–41).

131. *Diognetus* 5:14 alludes to 2 Cor. 6:8–10, which gives a series of descriptions of how the world views believers in contrast to how God views them. One of the descriptions is based specifically on the phrase "by evil report and good report" (2 Cor. 6:8b), which is phrased as "they are slandered, yet they are vindicated." Paul's "good report" (*euphēmia*) is expressed as "they are vindicated" (*dikaiountai*). Here the time scope pertains to the present life of Christians, so that this later Christian author understood that the unjust verdict pronounced by the world was to be seen as having already been overturned, though those outside the community of faith do not yet recognize this.

history expressed particularly by the "judgment according to works" passages relates to people being justified by faith in the midst of history. Is the verdict of justification at the inception of faith an incomplete verdict? One answer to this is that the penalty of sin borne by Christ declares people not guilty, and their good works complete the positive side of their justification by declaring them or making them righteous (what is often considered a typically Roman Catholic approach but also found in some Protestant circles). This would mean not that Christ's actual obedience is transferred to his people to declare them righteous, but that their own obedience contributes to the declaration of them to be righteous or contributes to the making of them to be righteous at the end. Thus, according to this view, both Christ's death and believers' obedience work together as causes of justification.[132]

Another, I think better, version of the "not yet" aspect of justification/vindication is that believers in this age are declared both not guilty because of Christ's substitutionary punishment and fully righteous because of the transferral of his perfect righteousness to them;[133] then at the end of the age, the good works of saints (which are imperfect) justify/vindicate that they were truly justified by Christ in the past. Accordingly, this final form of justification is not on the same level as the justification by faith in Jesus, though it is linked to it. Good works are the badge that vindicates the saints in the sense of declarative proof that they have been truly already justified by Christ. The good works demonstrate not only the prior true justified status of a person but probably also the injustice of the world's verdict in rejecting such works as a witness to Christ, often resulting in political persecution. On the one hand, good works are absolutely necessary at the last eschatological judgment in order to demonstrate and thus vindicate that someone has truly believed in Christ and been justified, with the result that this person is allowed entrance into the eternal kingdom of the new creation. On the other hand, such works do not in and of themselves cause one to gain entrance into the eternal kingdom, but such entrance is granted because these good works are seen as the inevitable external badge of those who have internal justifying faith. So there is a sense in which the initial eschatological verdict in justification is incomplete, but

132. It should be remembered, however, that there are permutations within the Roman Catholic view. Recall, for example, that Augustine held to the view described above, but he believed that believers' justifying obedience was completely a result of divine grace, whereas the Roman Catholic tradition since Augustine has more commonly held to some kind of significant synergism whereby the believer does perform some obedience apart from the inward working of God's grace.

133. Admittedly, texts in support of this latter view are few (e.g., 1 Cor. 1:30; 2 Cor. 5:21; Phil. 3:8–9). However, there is a broader biblical-theological and systematic-theological rationale for this notion, which I have repeatedly tried to explicate in the preceding part of this chapter. For example, believers' identification with the resurrected Christ entails their identification with him as the one vindicated as truly innocent throughout his life leading up to his unjust condemnation to death, so that believers are also identified with his vindicated status of complete innocence and righteousness.

only in the sense that it is a verdict known only by God and the community of the faithful, but at the end this verdict will be announced to the whole world. On the one hand, the making known of the verdict at the end both by God's universal proclamation and by manifestation through resurrection and works completes the earlier announcement of the verdict. On the other hand, someone's right standing before God because of Christ's work is completed at the point of that person's initial faith.

Therefore, initial justification and consummative justification (or twofold justification) are grounded in believers' union with Christ (both his death and his resurrection), the former coming by faith and the latter through the threefold demonstration of the bodily resurrection, evaluation of works,[134] and public announcement to the cosmos.

It is important to reiterate that Christ's death and resurrection are the beginning of new creation. Therefore, since justification/vindication comes

134. A recent trend of interpretation proposes that "faith" is equivalent to "faithfulness" or "faithfully performed good works" (this seems to be the position of Wright, "Romans," *NIB* 10:420). This is based sometimes on Gal. 5:6: "For in Christ Jesus neither circumcision nor uncircumcision means anything, but faith working through love." Accordingly, the idea proposed is that faith manifests itself in love, which means that love itself is a form of faith. The conclusion is then drawn that to be "justified by faith" means to be justified by one's attitude of trust together with good works, such as love, which are really just "concretized faith." See, e.g., Norman Shepherd, *The Call of Grace: How the Covenant Illuminates Salvation and Evangelism* (Phillipsburg, NJ: P&R, 2000), 50–52. Shepherd sees that part of the definition of saving faith is obedience to God's commands. John Piper (*Future Justification*, 204–6) has cogently responded to this perspective on Gal. 5:6. His argument deserves more in-depth summary, but essentially he says that the middle voice *energoumenē* ("working") in the Galatians text does not have the idea of faith extending itself in the form of love, so that faith and love are not ultimately the same thing. In addition, the participle (*energoumenē*) without the article following a noun (*pistis*) without the article is best understood as having an attributive function: "faith, which through love becomes effective."

There is another problem in defining "good works" as a form of faith. Throughout the NT "faith" and "works" are contrasted. Such a contrast is simple evidence that the two are not the same reality. A great burden of proof would be required to argue persuasively that this contrast can be reduced almost to the vanishing point. See, e.g., Rom. 3:28. Is it plausible that Paul would affirm that "works of the law" done by a believing heart justify someone? Paul's reference to the works of David and Abraham (which include postconversion works) in Rom. 4, which is linked to "works of the law" in Rom. 3:28, argues that works done by believers do not contribute toward justification. Likewise, Titus 3:5, 7 ("He saved us, not on the basis of deeds which we have done in righteousness . . . being justified by His grace") seems to include in its purview works of righteousness by a saint that cannot avail for salvation. This appears also to be the view among some of the Apostolic Fathers: e.g, *1 Clem.* 32:3–4: "All, therefore, were glorified and magnified, not through themselves or their own works or the righteous actions which they did, but through his will. And so we, having been called through his will in Christ Jesus, are not justified through ourselves or through our own wisdom or understanding or piety or works which we have done in holiness of heart, but through faith, by which the Almighty God has justified all who have existed from the beginning; to whom be the glory for ever and ever. Amen." Of course, much more needs to be said on this issue, but the limits of the present project prohibit it.

through Christ's death and resurrection, justification is a facet of the end-time new creation. Brief comment is needed on precisely how Christ's death is a part of the new creation, since Paul does not usually connect it to the new creation as he does with resurrection. However, Paul does do so in Gal. 6:14–15 (which I discussed in chap. 10):

> But may it never be that I would boast, except in the cross of our Lord Jesus Christ, through which the world has been crucified to me, and I to the world. For neither is circumcision anything, nor uncircumcision, but a new creation.

Part of Paul's point is that his identification with Christ's death is the very beginning of his separation from the old, fallen world, and it is the beginning of the fallen world's separation from him (v. 14). His separation from the old world can only mean that he has begun to be set apart to another world, indeed, a "new creation" (v. 15). Thus, Christ's death is the very inception of the new creation, which is completed by Christ's resurrection and the resurrection of believers, which is likely also in mind in verse 15, as verse 16 makes probable (and as I argued in chap. 10). This notion of Christ's death as the very inception of new creation is likely implied in other references that Paul makes to Christ's death.[135]

<hr/>

135. I have not addressed the issues revolving around various versions of the so-called "New Perspective," which would have been relevant to do, but due to the magnitude of the issue, the limitations of the present project do not allow for sufficient discussion of it in this chapter or other chapters. Nevertheless, the issue is important, and I have addressed it in G. K. Beale, "Review of D. A. Carson, P. T. O'Brien, and M. A. Seifrid, eds. *Justification and Variegated Nomism*, vol. 2: *The Paradoxes of Paul* (Grand Rapids: Baker Academic, 2004)," in *Trinity Journal* 29 NS (2008), 146–49. See also the above-mentioned work by Carson, O'Brien, and Seifrid, *Justification and Variegated Nomism*, vol. 1: *The Complexities of Second Temple Judaism* (Grand Rapids: Baker Academic, 2001). For a summary of Carson's view, see D. A. Carson and Douglas J. Moo, *An Introduction to the New Testament* (Grand Rapids: Zondervan, 2005), 375–85. The literature on this subject is also massive and cannot be summarized and evaluated adequately within the confines of this book.

16

Inaugurated Latter-Day Reconciliation as New Creation and Restoration from Exile

This chapter will discuss the redemptive-historical story of salvation primarily through the lens of reconciliation, which itself will be understood through the inaugurated OT promises of restoration from exile and the new-exodus deliverance from exile. Reconciliation as return from exile represents a part of the OT expectation of the beginning of the new creation. Other aspects of salvation could be looked at, but justification (from the preceding chapter) and reconciliation have been chosen to illustrate the overall approach that I am taking throughout this book with respect to how the "already–not yet, end-time, new-creational kingdom" enhances our perspectives on the major traditional doctrines or notions in the NT. Accordingly, this chapter, like the preceding one, will focus on that part of the NT storyline that deals with Christ's death and resurrection for his people as an all-important element in the building of the kingdom of the new creation.

As I have tried to show throughout previous chapters, when one thinks of NT biblical theology, a crucial consideration is the relation of the OT to the NT. In studying the biblical theology of reconciliation, therefore, one might think that there is a clear OT background that could shed significant light on the NT doctrine. There is, however, no Hebrew word for "reconciliation" in the OT, and there is general agreement that Paul obtained this word not primarily from the Jewish but mainly from the Greco-Roman world. While the *katallassō/diallassomai* word group is found in the LXX and Josephus, it is found also in Classical, Hellenistic, and Koine writings. The use of the word group in these writings has been well documented.[1]

---

1. On which, note the various sources cited in the section below on Paul.

This chapter will first study the explicit uses of the term "reconciliation" in the NT and then widen its scope to include conceptual references to the idea of reconciliation. Since the actual terms for "reconciliation" in connection to Christ's redemptive work occur only in Paul's writings, I will first address his understanding of this concept and then look at other parts of the NT.

Paul's View of Reconciliation as New Creation and Restoration from Exile

Even though there has been much discussion about the formulation of the doctrine of reconciliation, there have been few proposals that there is any precise OT background for this notion in Paul's thinking.[2] Although proposals that Paul derives his understanding of reconciliation from any specific OT background are rare, there have been some more general suggestions along these lines.[3] That such a background has not been looked into more is perhaps due to a too narrow view of establishing parallels on a semantic basis often in exclusion of conceptual considerations.

Contrary to the apparent near consensus, there appears to be a specific OT background in some of the key passages where Paul explicitly discusses reconciliation. These crucial passages are 2 Cor. 5:14–21 and Eph. 2:13–17. After one determines the background and meaning of reconciliation in these two passages, Paul's other "reconciliation" texts (Rom. 5:1–6:11; 11:11–31; Col. 1:15–22) should be analyzed in their respective contexts, and then the relation of these texts to 2 Cor. 5 and Eph. 2 should also be discussed.[4]

"Reconciliation" in 2 Corinthians 5:14–21

Explicit words for "reconciliation" are found in greater number in 2 Cor. 5:14–21 than any other in Paul's letters (here the verb and noun for "reconciliation," respectively *katallassō* and *katallagē*, occur 5x).

For the love of Christ controls us, having concluded this, that one died for all, therefore all died; and He died for all, so that they who live might no longer live

---

2. One exception is Otfried Hofius, "Erwägungen zur Gestalt und Herkunft des paulinischen Versöhnungsgedankens," *ZTK* 77 (1980): 186–99, arguing that 2 Cor. 5:18–21 is based on Isa. 52–53; see also G. K. Beale, "The Old Testament Background of Reconciliation in 2 Corinthians 5–7 and Its Bearing on the Literary Problem of 2 Corinthians 4:14–7:1," *NTS* 35 (1989): 550–81. Note also Mark Gignilliat, *Paul and Isaiah's Servants: Paul's Theological Reading of Isaiah 40–66 in 2 Corinthians 5.14–6.10*, LNTS 330 (London: T&T Clark, 2007). Gignilliat affirms much of my proposed background and especially the methodological consideration in both my article and Hofius for both lexical and conceptual parallels (I thank Dan Brendsel for reminding me of this source).

3. See, e.g., Peter Stuhlmacher, *Das Evangelium von der Versöhnung in Christus* (Stuttgart: Calwer, 1979), 44–49.

4. The limitations of the present discussion allow for analysis primarily of 2 Cor. 5 and secondarily Eph. 2.

for themselves, but for Him who died and rose again on their behalf. Therefore from now on we recognize no one according to the flesh; even though we have known Christ according to the flesh, yet now we know Him in this way no longer. Therefore if anyone is in Christ, he is a new creature; the old things passed away; behold, new things have come. Now all these things are from God, who reconciled us to Himself through Christ and gave us the ministry of reconciliation, namely, that God was in Christ reconciling the world to Himself, not counting their trespasses against them, and He has committed to us the word of reconciliation. Therefore, we are ambassadors for Christ, as though God were entreating through us; we beg you on behalf of Christ, be reconciled to God. He made him who knew no sin to be sin on our behalf, so that we might become the righteousness of God in Him.

I have tried to demonstrate in the preceding chapters of the present project that various NT notions are tied in one way or another to the idea of the "already and not yet" eschatological new creation. Paul's understanding of reconciliation likewise has such a connection. This passage was discussed in chapter 10 only in connection to new creation, but now the task is to explore the link between new creation and reconciliation in this passage. Paul links reconciliation in some way with the idea of the new creation in 2 Cor. 5:17–21, in which is found his most intense and longest excursus on the subject of reconciliation. Although some commentators have acknowledged this apparent linkage on the exegetical level, none have been able to offer sufficiently specific reasons about how reconciliation and new creation are conceptually related in this passage.[5] Yet there does appear to be a specific conceptual relationship. In particular, the overarching thesis of this discussion is to show that Paul understands both "new creation" in Christ as well as "reconciliation" in Christ (2 Cor. 5:17–21) as the inaugurated fulfillment of Isaiah's and the prophets' promise of a new creation in which Israel would be restored into a peaceful relationship with God, and that this theme actually extends through to the beginning of 2 Cor. 7.[6]

Brief discussion of the broader literary context merits initial consideration in order to discern the function of this text in Paul's overall argument. The

5. See, e.g., the helpful albeit general discussions of F. C. Hahn, "Siehe, jetzt ist der Tag des Heils," *EvT* 33 (1973): 244–53; Peter Stuhlmacher, "Erwägungen zum ontologischen Charakter der *kaine ktisis* bei Paulus," *EvT* 27 (1967): 1–35; idem, *Versöhnung, Gesetz und Gerechtigkeit: Aufsätze zur biblischen Theologie* (Göttingen: Vandenhoeck & Ruprecht, 1981), 133–34, 238–39; Hofius, "Erwägungen zur Gestalt und Herkunft," 188; Ralph P. Martin, *Reconciliation: A Study of Paul's Theology* (Atlanta: John Knox, 1981), 108; idem, *2 Corinthians*, WBC 40 (Waco: Word, 1986), 149–53, 158; Hans-Jürgen Findeis, *Versöhnung, Apostolat, Kirche: Eine exegetisch-theologische und rezeptionsgeschichtliche Studie zu den Versöhnungsaussagen des Neuen Testaments (2 Kor, Rom, Kol, Eph)*, FB (Würzburg: Echter, 1983), 157–64, 176.

6. For a fuller analysis of Paul's use of the OT and his flow of argument in 2 Cor. 2:14–7:6, see Beale, "Old Testament Background of Reconciliation."

motivation for Paul writing 2 Corinthians is the readers' rejection of him as God's true apostle for the gospel (cf. 3:1; 5:12; 10:10; 11:6–8, 16–18; 13:3, 7). Paul's purpose throughout the letter, then, is to demonstrate the authenticity of his divine apostleship so that those questioning it would fully reaffirm it. His claim of apostleship cannot be proved according to worldly standards of evaluation (note *kata sarka* ["according to the flesh"] in 5:16; 10:3–7) but only by means of perceiving that Paul's authority and spiritual power are present because of the past work that God has accomplished through him among the Corinthians[7] and because of his perseverance through suffering and weakness, which is characteristic of his life in Christ (cf. 4:7–12, 16–18; 6:3–10; 10:2–7; 12:7–10; 13:3–7).[8] In light of this overall purpose, the literary unit of 5:14–21 is best understood as functioning to strengthen Paul's argument that the readers should accept him as God's apostle, and the precise language of reconciliation is employed to underscore emphatically this idea of acceptance. That is, the Corinthians' reconciliation with Paul will also be their reconciliation with God and Christ, since Paul is the legal ambassador of both (cf. 5:20). And if they understand their past reconciliation rightly, they will respond to Paul's message favorably. This same theme continues in 6:1–7:6.

In 5:17 Paul states that one effect (*hōste*, "consequently" or "so that") that Christ's death and resurrection (vv. 14–15) have on the readers is that they are a new creation: "If anyone is in Christ, he is a new creature [or 'there is a new creation']; the old things have passed away; behold, new things have come about." In the context of the argument, the idea of the new creation is already implicit in the mention of Christ's death and resurrection of verses 14–15, as we have observed throughout previous chapters that Christ's resurrection is another way of speaking of new creation. Therefore, the theme of new creation here also provides the basis for Paul's exhortation in verse 16 (on which, see further below). Thus, in verse 16 he exhorts the readers not to evaluate his claim of apostolic authority according to the unbelieving, fleshly standards of the old world, which for the readers have passed away. They are part of a new creation in the resurrected Christ and consequently should evaluate all things by the spiritual standards of the new world.

Paul draws from Isaiah in explaining the reality of the readers' part in the new creation. Although the wording of 5:17 is not a verbatim quotation of any OT text, it has unique parallels traceable to Isa. 43:18–19 and likely to Isa. 65:17 (see table 16.1).[9]

---

7. So Scott J. Hafemann, "'Self-Commendation' and Apostolic Legitimacy in 2 Corinthians: A Pauline Dialectic?," *NTS* 36 (1990): 66–88.

8. The same point has been made by Scott J. Hafemann, *Suffering and Ministry in the Spirit: Paul's Defense of His Ministry in II Corinthians 2:14–3:3* (Grand Rapids: Eerdmans, 1990), 58–87.

9. Among relevant Jewish texts, the next closest parallels are *1 En.* 91:16; 1 QH[a] V:11–12, which also contrast the old creation with the new creation; the former text has only a generally

Table 16.1

Isaiah LXX	2 Corinthians 5:17
Isa. 43:18–19: "Do not remember the first things [ta prōta], and the ancient things [ta archaia] do not consider. Behold, I create new things [idou poiō kaina]."	"If anyone is in Christ, that one is a new creation [kainē ktisis]; the ancient things [ta archaia] have passed away, behold [idou], new things [kaina] have come about."
Isa. 65:17: "For there will be a new [kainos] heaven and a new [kainos] earth, and by no means will they remember the former things [tōn proterōn]."	

Note: Solid underlining represents the same words and cognates; broken underlining represents conceptual parallels.

Especially striking is the contrast, found nowhere else in pre-NT literature outside of Isaiah, between "the ancient things" (*ta archaia*) and "new things" (*kaina*), which is connected by the word "behold" (*idou*) plus "creation" vocabulary.

Commentators have generally acknowledged Paul's allusion to Isaiah, especially Isa. 43:18–19; 65:17. Victor Paul Furnish, however, is representative of a few in seeing 2 Cor. 5:17 as generally dependent only on the concept of creation in apocalyptic Judaism.[10] Furnish adds that "the roots of the apocalyptic idea go back to Isa. 65:17–25 (cf. Isa. 42:9; 43:18–19; 48:6; 66:22)."[11] Peter Stuhlmacher understands this apocalyptic tradition as having been based on Isa. 43 and 65.[12] If the roots of the notion in Jewish apocalyptic go back to Isaiah, it certainly is viable to conceive of the same background for Paul's idea.[13] Surprisingly, there appears to have been no specific attempt to link the generally acknowledged Isaiah background in 2 Cor. 5:17 precisely with the following discussion of reconciliation in verses 18–21. Only a general linkage is made between "new creation" and "reconciliation" in the sense that God's reconciliation of humanity in Christ has begun to reverse the alienation introduced at the fall, and a return to the peaceful conditions of the original creation has been inaugurated in the eschatological age of the new

parallel contrast, while the latter is so filled with lacunae that its original wording is questionable. For "new creation," see also *Jub.* 1:29; 4:26; *Sib. Or.* 5:212.

10. Victor Paul Furnish, *II Corinthians*, AB 32A (New York: Doubleday, 1984), 314–15.
11. Ibid., 315.
12. Stuhlmacher, "Erwägungen zum ontologischen Charakter," 10–13, 20.
13. Among those viewing either Isa. 43:18–19 or 65:17 (or 66:22), or both, as the basis for 2 Cor. 5:17, see Stuhlmacher, "Erwägungen zum ontologischen Charakter," 6; Hans Windisch, *Der zweite Korintherbrief*, 9th ed., KEK 6 (Göttingen: Vandenhoeck & Ruprecht, 1970), 189; R. V. G. Tasker, *The Second Epistle of Paul to the Corinthians*, TNTC (Grand Rapids: Eerdmans, 1958), 88; Martin, *2 Corinthians*, 152; F. F. Bruce, *1 and 2 Corinthians*, NCB (Greenwood, SC: Attic Press, 1971), 209; Seyoon Kim, *The Origin of Paul's Gospel* (Grand Rapids: Eerdmans, 1982), 18n2.

creation in Christ.[14] I can only suppose that there has been no discussion of the recognized links with Isaiah because commentators perhaps view Paul as merely using Isaiah's words to convey his own new thought that is foreign to the OT context. The remainder of this discussion will try to show that this view, though possible, is improbable.

If Paul does have the context of Isaiah in mind, then in what manner is he developing this OT context in verse 17, and how do verses 18–21 logically flow out of the thought of verse 17? Of course, it is conceivable that Paul's discussion of reconciliation in these verses is a separate and new subject unrelated to "new creation" in verse 17 to which Paul is now turning his attention, but this is unlikely, as is borne out by the majority of the literature on this text.

The primary text to which Paul alludes in verse 17 is Isa. 43:18–19. The context of these two verses refers to God's promise that a time will come when he will cause the Israelites to return from Babylonian exile and to be restored to their land in Israel (Isa. 43:1–21). Isaiah 43:18–19 is an exhortation to Israel that it reflect no longer on its past sin, judgment, and exile but rather on God's promise of restoration. This is a reiteration of the theme of Isa. 43:1–13, which also expresses a promise of restoration not only back to the land but also into a relationship with Yahweh as Israel's creator, redeemer, savior, and king (cf. 43:1, 3, 7, 10–11). Israel was to be God's "servant," "chosen" to be restored so that it "may know and believe Me and understand that I am He" (43:10). Furthermore, Israel's promised restoration is referred to as both an imminent redemption (43:1; cf. v. 14) and creation (43:6–7). In this context, Yahweh's role as Israel's "creator" (43:1) is accentuated, as he is portrayed as the one who "created," "formed," and "made" the nation for his "glory" (43:7). The point of this emphasis on God as creator is to focus not on the first creation or primarily the first exodus, when the nation was initially created, but rather on the re-creation of the nation through restoring it from exile to its homeland, as Isa. 43:3–7 makes clear. Isaiah 43:14–21 repeats the same idea, where Yahweh again refers to himself as Israel's "creator" (vv. 15, 21), "redeemer" (v. 14), and "king" (v. 15), and the restoration from exile (vv. 14–17) is described with "new creation" language. The Israelites are exhorted not to reflect on their former condition of exile, when they experienced divine wrath (43:18; cf. 65:16b–19), but rather on God's imminent new creation of them as his "chosen people," whom he "formed" for himself (43:19–21). This coming restoration is further highlighted as a new creation through describing Israel's return with paradisical imagery: "beasts . . . jackals and ostriches" glorify God because of the water that he has caused to gush forth in the desert for the sake of his returning people (43:19–20). This second creation is also referred to as a second exodus (43:2, 16–17).

14. E.g., Martin, *2 Corinthians*, 149–53; Philip E. Hughes, *Paul's Second Epistle to the Corinthians*, NICNT (Grand Rapids: Eerdmans, 1967), 201.

It may well be the case that Isa. 65:17 is also included in Paul's allusion. If so, the emphasis on restoration as a new creation would be even stronger, since this is the point of Isa. 65:17–25 in its context (cf. Isa. 60:1–65:25; 64:8–65:16; see also 66:19–23).

Indeed, Isa. 43:18–19 is but one of a series of pericopae in the so-called Book of Consolation (Isa. 40–55) that explains the restoration of exiled Israel as a new creation or at least integrally associate the two concepts of restoration and creation.[15] Isaiah 60:15–22; 65:17–25; 66:19–24 continue the same thematic emphasis. God's act of new creation as restoration is also described outside of chapter 43 as his "redemption" of Israel[16] and as a new exodus.[17]

Moreover, Isa. 40–66 describes Israel's exile as an expression of divine "wrath" (51:20; 60:10), "anger" (47:6; 51:17, 22; 54:8; 57:16–17; 64:5, 9), "forsakenness" (49:14; 54:6–7; 62:4), "rejection" (54:6), "hiddenness" (54:8; 57:17; 59:2; 64:7), and consequent "separation" between God and the nation (59:2). All these texts assume that sin or iniquity is the cause of Israel's forsaken condition, and this cause is sometimes explicitly stated for the sake of emphasis (50:1; 51:13; 57:17; 59:1–15; 64:5–9). God's restoration of Israel from this estrangement is described not only as a redemptive new creation but also as a time when the nation will "not be forsaken" (62:12) and will be reunited with God (45:14) and "know" him (43:10) because of his gracious initiative in regathering it (54:6–8; 57:18). And God will "wipe out their transgressions" (43:25) and free them from the bondage resulting from sin (42:6–9; 49:8–9) by the sacrificial death of the Servant, who becomes the guilt offering for the people (53:4–12). Therefore, the return from exile is a period in which there is a cessation of anger and in which "peace" is reestablished between the nation and its God (cf. 48:18; 52:7; 57:19). This is a peace that results from and is characteristic of the new creation, modeled on the original paradisical conditions.[18] In fact, in the context of Isa. 43, restoration and new creation are to be viewed as brought about through the payment of a ransom (43:3–4) and the forgiveness of sins (43:22–25). The vicarious suffering of the Servant in Isa. 53 probably has the same function.

In addition, Isa. 60:10 is noteworthy because the Hebrew word *rāṣôn* ("pleasure, favor") is rendered by the Targum's equivalent term *raʿăwāʾ* ("pleasurable

---

15. Isaiah 40:28–31; 41:17–20; 42:5–9; 44:21–23, 24–28; 45:1–8, 9–13, 18–20; 49:8–13; 51:1–3, 9–11, 12–16; 54:1–10 (note v. 5); 55:6–13. See Carroll Stuhlmueller, *Creative Redemption in Deutero-Isaiah*, AnBib 43 (Rome: Biblical Institute Press, 1970), 66–98, 109–61, 193–208; William J. Dumbrell, *The End of the Beginning: Revelation 21–22 and the Old Testament* (Homebush West, NSW: Lancer, 1985), 97–100.

16. Isaiah 44:1–8; 44:24–45:7; 54:1–10. See Stuhlmueller, *Creative Redemption*, 112–34, 196–208.

17. Isaiah 40:3–11; 41:17–20; 44:24–28; 51:1–13; 52:7–10; see also 43:16–21. See Stuhlmueller, *Creative Redemption*, 66–73, 82–94; Dumbrell, *End of the Beginning*, 15–18, 97.

18. See Isa. 26:11–19; 27:1–6 (cf. Targum); 32:15–18; 45:7–8 (cf. Targum); 45:18–25 (Symmachus); 55:12 (MT); 60:15–22; 66:12–14, 19–23.

acceptance"), which refers elsewhere to God's "pleasurable acceptance" (Isa. 1:11, 15; 56:7; 60:7) and specifically to "pleasurable acceptance" in the sense of restoration from exile (Isa. 34:16–17; 60:10; 62:4; 66:2). The LXX (in the version of Symmachus) of Isa. 60:10 renders the Hebrew *rāṣôn* with *diallagē*, which refers likewise to God's acceptance of Israel by restoring it as "reconciliation": "For on account of my wrath I smote you, and on account of reconciliation I loved you." These general OT lexical associations in Isaiah, together with Isa. 43 and 65, may be suggested as part of the possible origin of Paul's use of the *katallassō* word group in 2 Cor. 5:18–20 (and elsewhere in his letters) to express divine acceptance or reconcilation.[19] That such a lexical background is in mind is plausible because Isa. 49:8 also uses the Hebrew *rāṣôn*, a text from which Paul explicitly quotes in 2 Cor. 6:2 (on which, see below).

Therefore, the complex of ideas in 2 Cor. 5:14–21 can already be seen in Isa. 40–66. In light of the thematic overview of Isa. 40–66, it is plausible to make this proposal: *"reconciliation" in Christ is Paul's way of explaining that Isaiah's promises of "restoration" from the alienation of exile have begun to be fulfilled by the atonement and forgiveness of sins in Christ.* Separation and alienation from God because of sin have been overcome through the divine grace expressed in Christ, who has restored believers into a reconciled relationship of peace with God. Paul's point in 2 Cor. 5:14–21 is that if the Corinthians are truly partakers of the new creation and of a reconciled relationship with God (vv. 14–19), then they should behave like reconciled people (v. 20). They have been acting like people alienated from God, since they have questioned the divine authority of Paul's apostleship. If this alienation between Paul and his readers continues, it will also be an alienation from God, since Paul represents God's authority and it is actually God who is "making an appeal" through him (5:20; cf. 2:14–17; 3:6; 6:7; 10:8; 13:3). There is to be a connection between their identity as reconciled people and their behavior as such people. Therefore, Paul appends an imperative of *katallassō* ("be reconciled" [v. 20]) after his previous four uses of the participial and nominal forms, which may connote the reality of the readers' participation in such a reconciled condition (vv. 18–19).[20] Nevertheless, the first-person plurals ("us," *hēmin*) in verses 18b and 19b probably have primary reference to Paul and his circle,[21] to whom God has given the ministry to announce reconciliation to the audience.

19. Although Paul uses only the *katallassō* word group, it is synonymous with the *diallassō* word group, so that the latter could have sparked off the former in Paul's mind.

20. Paul may also be calling for unbelievers among the professing readers to be reconciled, as 2 Cor. 13:5 may bear out.

21. But the first-person plural "us" (*hēmas*) in v. 18a could well include the readers; there is occasional ambiguity over the precise reference of the first-person plural pronoun in 2 Corinthians (e.g., 1:21–22; 3:18; 5:4–10, 16, 21; 6:16a; 7:1).

Furthermore, it was evident from the above overview of Isa. 40–66 that 43:18–19 (and perhaps 65:17) is but part of a broader theme of that segment that concerns a promise that Israel's restoration from exile is to be a redemptive new creation brought about by the payment of a ransom and the forgiveness of sins. This was to result in a cessation of divine wrath and in a peaceful relationship between Yahweh and the people. Paul alludes to Isa. 43:18–19 and 65:17 in order to link this Isaianic promise with the work of Christ. Christ's death and resurrection are the beginning fulfillment of this promise. As in the case of the Isaianic Servant's mission and in line with Jewish interpretative tradition, Paul explains the atonement not only as a negative means of doing away with sin but also as resulting in the reuniting and renewing of sinful people with God, which amounts to a new creation.[22]

This is clear, as we observed earlier in this chapter, in that Paul understands the "new creation" of 2 Cor. 5:17 to be a direct effect (*hōste*, "consequently," or "so that") of Jesus's "death for all" mentioned in verse 15. Verse 17 also concludes that, in addition to Christ's death, his resurrection (also mentioned in v. 15) is a new creation, "so that" as one is identified with this resurrection, one also becomes a part of the new creation.[23] Therefore, the idea of the new creation is already anticipated in the mention of both the death and especially the resurrection in verse 15, both of which Christians have been identified with. It is significant to highlight again that not only the resurrection but also the death of Christ relates partly to the notion of new creation in that it represents that beginning part of the old world (with which the earthly Christ was identified) that began to be destroyed (the whole of which would be consummately destroyed at the very end of the age) and thus paved the way for the new creation first manifested in Christ's resurrection. We have also seen in Gal. 6:14–16 (see chap. 10) that Christ's death is the very inception of the "new creation" in that it separates believers from the old, fallen world, and the old world from them (which begins spiritually in this age): through the "cross . . . the world has been crucified to me, and I to the world" (v. 14). This means that believers are not in some neutral territory in being identified with Christ's death but rather are in the initial sphere of the "new creation" (v. 15). The same is true in 2 Cor. 5:14–17. There is a parallel with Christ's death itself where, immediately after his death and for three days before his resurrection, he was in "paradise" (Luke 23:43).

As also noted earlier, the word "consequently" (*hōste*) in 2 Cor. 5:16 in dependence on verse 15 shows that a result of the readers being part of such a new creation through identification with Christ's death and resurrection is

22. For possible Jewish backgrounds linking the Day of Atonement and new creation, see Kim, *Origin of Paul's Gospel*, 17nn1, 4.

23. As we have seen in earlier chapters, Christ's resurrection is also viewed as the beginning of the new creation elsewhere in the NT (see Col. 1:15–16, 18; Eph. 1:20–23; 2:5–6, 10; Rev. 1:5; 3:14).

that they will evaluate Paul's apostleship according to the spiritual standards of the new creation (or new age [note "now," *nyn*])[24] and no longer by means of the fleshly standards of the fallen creation (if "indeed" they really are "in Christ" [2 Cor. 13:5]).

Therefore, in verses 18–21 Paul does not shift his thinking to a new, unrelated topic. In these concluding four verses Paul makes clear what lies beneath the surface of his new creation allusion to Isaiah in verse 17. Christ's death for human sin (2 Cor. 5:14–15, 21) has removed the condition of separation between God and sinful people, and, against the Isaiah background, both his death and resurrection can be viewed as inaugurating true Israel, the church, into the presence of God. We suggest that just as Christ, the true Israel,[25] was separated from the Father because of his vicarious death on behalf of his people (vv. 14–15, 21) and was restored from the exile of death to a relationship with God by means of the resurrection, so likewise is the church restored from the exile of sinful alienation through corporate identification with Christ. Therefore, in the light of the OT background, to say that the church is a new creation because of Christ's resurrection (v. 17) is also to speak of the church as being "restored" or "reconciled" to God from its former exile and estrangement (vv. 18–20).[26] Simply put, Paul understands both "new creation" in Christ as well as "reconciliation" in Christ (2 Cor. 5:18–20) as the inaugurated fulfillment of Isaiah's promise of a new creation in which Israel would be restored to a peaceful relationship with Yahweh. And Israel's exile in Isaiah is seen as representative of humanity's alienation from God, since Paul is applying Isaiah's message for Israel predominantly to gentiles.

The two concepts of new creation and reconciliation are explicitly linked in 2 Cor. 5:18a by the phrase "and all these things [*ta de panta*] are from God, who reconciled us to himself through Christ." The "new things" (*kaina*) of the "new creation" (v. 17) are seen as having their creative source in God, who has brought the new world (*ta panta*) into being and "reconciled" people to himself through Christ (v. 18a). The phrase *ta de panta* ("and all these things") functions as a reference to the new creation and in doing so likely also summarizes the preceding thought of verses 14–17.[27] The phrase "through Christ" can have no reference here other than Christ's death and resurrection

---

24. It may not be coincidental that Paul uses *nyn* here to designate the beginning of the new age, since Isa. 43:18–19, which we have seen is alluded to in 2 Cor. 5:17, uses the same word to indicate the beginning period of the prophesied new creation: Isa. 43:19 LXX says, "Behold, I will make new things which now [*nyn*] will spring forth."

25. For elaboration on Christ being "true Israel," see chaps. 20–21 (esp. the beginning of chap. 20).

26. See J. R. Daniel Kirk, *Unlocking Romans: Resurrection and the Justification of God* (Grand Rapids: Eerdmans, 2008), 30–31. Kirk shows that resurrection was a facet of Israel's restoration in both Ezek. 37 and Dan. 12, as well as in Judaism.

27. See Windisch, *Der zweite Korintherbrief*, 191.

(vv. 14–15). This means—and it bears repeating—that both the death and the resurrection of Christ are the means to the "new creation" (v. 17), and likewise both are a means to "reconciliation" (vv. 18–21). The two ideas of new creation and reconciliation, then, are almost overlapping concepts for Paul, as for Isaiah. To be propelled into the eschatological new creation is to enter into peaceful relations with the Creator, although, as I have argued throughout this book, reconciliation is a facet of the larger diamond of the new creation. Nevertheless, the point is that they are of a piece with one another and are organically linked.

So far, the argument about Paul's view of reconciliation is based entirely on the suggested Isaiah background of 2 Cor. 5:17. Indeed, if Otfried Hofius's argument that Isa. 53 stands behind 2 Cor. 5:18–21 can be sustained, then the links with Isaiah are even stronger.[28] In 2 Cor. 5:18–21 he discerns a twofold pattern of a "reconciliation act" and a "reconciliation word," which he sees as based on the portrayal of the Servant's salvific role in Isa. 52:13–53:12 and the proclamation of Israel's coming salvation in Isa. 52:6–10. In addition, he adduces a number of specific conceptual parallels between Isa. 53 and 2 Cor. 5:21.

Hofius's proposal should be judged as plausible with respect to 2 Cor. 5:21 because the combined ideas of a sinless penal substitute, the imputation of sin to a sinless figure to redeem a sinful people, and the granting of righteousness are uniquely traceable to Isa. 53:4–12. As we observed earlier, Isa. 53 functions in the argument of Isaiah as explaining the means that Yahweh will employ to restore Israel, and Paul seems to have recognized this. It is likely no coincidence that Paul has combined allusions to Isa. 43 and Isa. 53, since, as Werner Grimm has shown, references to these two chapters had already been utilized together by the Gospel writers.[29] This exegetical tradition may have influenced Paul to combine the same two OT contexts.

Although I believe that the argument could stand on its own up to this point, a consideration of the following context of 2 Cor. 6 lends confirming evidence to my proposal that reconciliation is Paul's way of referring to the Corinthian church's end-time restoration as true Israel.[30] Paul repeatedly refers in 2 Cor. 6 to OT references prophesying Israel's restoration from exile and applies them to the Corinthian church. The quotation of Isa. 49:8 in 6:2 and the catena of OT references in 6:16–18 are good examples of this, though there are similar OT allusions that could be mentioned and are included in table 16.2.

28. See Hofius, "Erwägungen zur Gestalt und Herkunft," 196–99.

29. Werner Grimm, *Weil Ich dich liebe: Die Verkündigung Jesu und Deuterojesaja*, ANTJ 1 (Bern: Herbert Lang, 1976), e.g., 254, 267 (and p. 275 of the second edition).

30. For in-depth elaboration attempting to demonstrate that the church is eschatological Israel, see chaps. 20–21 below.

Table 16.2

Old Testament	2 Corinthians 5:17–6:18
Isa. 43:18–19 // 65:17	5:17
Isa. 53:9–11	5:21
Isa. 49:8	6:2
Ps. 118:17–18 (117:17–18 LXX)	6:9
Isa. 60:5 (Ps. 119:32 [118:32 LXX])	6:11b
Isa. 49:19–20	6:12
Lev. 26:11–12	6:16b
Ezek. 37:27	6:16b
Isa. 52:11	6:17a
Ezek. 11:17; 20:34, 41	6:17b
2 Sam. 7:14; Isa. 43:6; 49:22; 60:4	6:18

The OT reference in 6:2 and, almost without exception, the six generally agreed on OT references in verses 16–18 refer in their respective contexts to God's promise to restore exiled Israel to its land. This observation is crucial in tracing Paul's argument because it allows us to view verses 16–18 as a continuation of the restoration promises to Israel quoted by Paul in 6:2 and even earlier in 5:17, which were utilized as prooftexts to support Paul's appeal for the Corinthians to be reconciled.[31]

"Reconciliation" in Ephesians 2:13–17

The conclusions about 2 Cor. 5:14–21 are corroborated by Eph. 2:13–17:

But now in Christ Jesus you who formerly were far off have been brought near by the blood of Christ. For He Himself is our peace, who made both groups into one and broke down the barrier of the dividing wall, by abolishing in his flesh the enmity, which is the Law of commandments contained in ordinances, so that in Himself He might make the two into one new man, thus establishing peace, and might reconcile them both in one body to God through the cross, by it having put to death the enmity. And He came and preached peace to you who were far away, and peace to those who were near.

In verse 13 and verse 17 the restoration promise of Isa. 57:19 is respectively alluded to and then quoted to explain the conception of "reconciliation" found in verse 16 (on which, see table 16.3). In the original context, "those far away" refers to the restoration of the Israelite exiles in captivity, and "those near" refers to the people still living in the land who would be reconciled with the returning exiles. The former are now identified as believing gentiles, and

31. For an expanded discussion of the OT restoration texts to which Paul alludes in 2 Cor. 6:1–7:2, see Beale, "Old Testament Background of Reconciliation," 550–81. For discussion of the OT prophecies of the temple in connection to Israel's restoration promises cited in 2 Cor. 6:16–18, see chap. 19 below.

the latter as ethnic Israelite believers in general. As in 2 Cor. 5–7, so here the church(es) to which Paul is writing is understood to be the beginning fulfillment of Isaiah's restoration promises.

This reconciliation of Jew and gentile is also referred to as "creating the two in one new man," which is a continuation of the new creation theme begun in Eph. 2:10 ("we are His creation [*poiēma*], created in Christ Jesus"). Indeed, this new creation has come about through Christ's death and, especially, resurrection (cf. Eph. 1:20–23; 2:5–6), as is also clear in 2 Cor. 5:14–17. That this is the case is evident from the likelihood that the phrase "we are His creation, created in Christ Jesus" in Eph. 2:10 is parallel to the phrase in verse 15b, "in Himself He might create the two into one new man," so that the "new man" is none other than the resurrected Christ. That the concepts of new creation in verse 15b, reconciliation in verse 16, and the OT promise of restoration in verses 17–18 are virtually synonymous in Eph. 2 is indicated by their literary parallelism: (1) each speaks of the "two" (Jew and gentile) existing in one organism ("one new man," "one body," "one Spirit"); (2) each refers to the primary activity resulting in "peace" or the dissolving of enmity; (3) each appears to be in purpose clauses dependent on the *hina* ("so that") of verse 15b.[32] The mention of "peace" (vv. 14, 15, 17), being "brought near" (v. 13), and "putting to death the enmity" (v. 16) is essentially equivalent to the concept entailed in being "reconciled" (v. 16). The threefold literary parallelism in verses 15–18 focuses on a reconciliation of hostile humans, gentiles and Jews. The gentiles are reconciled from their former "separation from Christ," "exclusion from the commonwealth of Israel," and separation from "the covenants of promise" and from God (2:11). Thus, the reconciliation is not only between hostile people groups but also between sinful humanity and God, both of which are summed up well in verses 15–16: "so that in Himself He might . . . reconcile them both in one body to God through the cross."

Consequently, in this passage, much as in 2 Cor. 5:14–21, the three notions of new creation, reconciliation, and Israel's restoration are virtually synonymous. However, there is a significant difference: Christ is the subject of the reconciling activity in Eph. 2, whereas God is the subject in 2 Cor. 5.[33] Christ "made both groups into one and broke down the barrier of the dividing wall, . . . so that in Himself He might make the two into one new man, thus establishing peace, and might reconcile them both in one body to God through the cross, by it having put to death the enmity" (Eph. 2:14–16). Christ's reconciliation of people to himself and to one another is the beginning fulfillment of the promise of Israel's restoration from Isa. 57:19 (see table 16.3).

32. This is the case even though the introductory verb in v. 17 is an indicative and the previous two are subjunctives. The reason for the difference in mood may well lie in the author's intention to employ the Isa. 57:19 citation in vv. 17–18 both as a parallel with v. 15b and v. 16 and as a concluding parallel with the same Isa. 57:19 allusion in v. 14, thus forming an inclusio.

33. Following Stanley E. Porter, "Peace, Reconciliation," *DPL* 699.

Table 16.3

Isaiah 57:19 LXX	Ephesians 2:17
". . . creating the praise of the lips. <u>Peace, peace to him who is far and to him who is near.</u>"	"And He came and preached peace to you who were far away, and peace to those who were near."

The quotation from Isa. 57:19 is introduced with the words of Isa. 52:7, which also prophesies Israel's restoration and underscores Paul's allusion to Isaiah's restoration expectation: "the feet of <u>one preaching glad tidings of peace</u>." Note that "peace" is inextricably linked to "reconciliation" in the Eph. 2 passage, so that "peace" is almost synonymous with "reconciliation."

This beginning fulfillment of Isaiah's promised restoration is also seen to be the beginning time of new creation, when God would "create" alienated humanity "into one new man" (Eph. 2:15).[34] However, as we have observed above, Christ is the subject of this new creation and of reconciliation, so that what the OT foresees that God would do in this respect, Christ does. This identification of Christ doing what the OT prophesied that God would do is one of the many ways that Paul indicates the deity of Christ.

Another point of similarity between Eph. 2 and 2 Cor. 5–7 is that the emphasis of reconciliation is on both the restoration of alienated human relationships and the reconciliation of alienated people to God.

"Reconciliation" in Other Pauline Passages

The same combination of reconciliation language with OT notions of restoration and the idea of the new creation found in the 2 Corinthians and Ephesians passages is probably also present in the contexts of Rom. 5:1–6:11;[35] 11:11–31; Col. 1:15–22. The limits of the present discussion preclude substantial analysis of these passages, but some comment is called for.

ROMANS 5

Romans 5:10–11 mentions reconciliation three times:

> For if while we were enemies we were reconciled to God through the death of His Son, much more, having been reconciled, we shall be saved by His life. And not only this, but we also exult in God through our Lord Jesus Christ, through whom we have now received the reconciliation.

34. See Robert H. Suh, "The Use of Ezek. 37 in Eph. 2," *JETS* 50 (2007): 715–33. Suh argues that the Ezekiel text is the framework for the argument in Eph. 2. If so, it would highlight the theme of return from exile in the Isaiah texts, since Ezekiel depicts return from exile through the image of resurrection of the dead (on which, see resurrection from the dead in Eph. 2:1–6). However, I am unconvinced of this thesis.

35. We will see in chap. 25 below that Rom. 6:1–11 is shot through with notions of new creation.

It is clear here that "reconciliation" refers to people being restored through Christ's death from a state of hostility into a peaceful relationship with God. The implicit idea is that Christ experienced God's hostility and wrath at the cross so that those who believe in Christ and become identified with his death are considered to have also experienced God's eschatological wrath, so that they can now come into a peaceful relationship with him (note Rom. 5:1: "Therefore, having been justified by faith, we have peace with God through our Lord Jesus Christ").[36] This implication is anticipated in Rom. 5:6–9:

> For while we were still helpless, at the right time Christ died for the ungodly. For one will hardly die for a righteous man; though perhaps for the good man someone would dare even to die. But God demonstrates His own love toward us, in that while we were yet sinners, Christ died for us. Much more then, having now been justified by His blood, we shall be saved from the wrath of God through Him.

After concluding the first section of Rom. 5 with a threefold emphasis on reconciliation in verses 10–11, Paul opens the next section with an extended contrast between the sin and death introduced by the first Adam and the righteousness and life introduced by the last Adam (vv. 12–19). But how are these notions of reconciliation and of contrast between the two Adams linked? Christ's death leading to past justification and reconciliation and to future consummate salvation (vv. 6–10) is the reason "we exult in God through our Lord Jesus Christ," especially since it is through him that "we have now received the reconciliation" (v. 11). This exultation because of reconciliation is the main point toward which Paul has been aiming since verse 1. So our question about the link between verses 6–11 and verses 12–19 can be refined by asking specifically how exulting in God because of reconciliation relates to the contrast of the two Adams.

The answer begins to be found in the initial part of verse 12: "for this reason" (*dia touto*). That is, exulting in God because of reconciliation (v. 11) is what launches Paul off into the contrast of the two Adams, which climaxes with the goal of verses 12–21: "So that, as sin reigned in death, even so grace would reign through righteousness to eternal life through Jesus Christ our Lord" (v. 21). The connection, then, between these two segments in Rom. 5 is that Paul's repeated elaboration of reconciliation at the end of the first segment leads him in the second to expound on the final result of reconciliation: "so grace would reign through righteousness to eternal life through Jesus Christ our Lord" (v. 21). Recall that earlier we saw that this "eternal life" is resurrection life of the new creation. In working toward the ultimate life-giving effect of reconciliation, Paul also goes to the very origin of humanity's "sin" that is

---

36. Note again the very close conceptual relationship of "peace" and "reconciliation" between Rom. 5:1 and 5:10–11.

at first only generally stated (v. 8) and has led to humanity having the status of "enemies" (v. 10) and deserving "wrath" (v. 9). The origin of that sin and enmity is now identified to be the original sin of the first Adam, which brought death, which is contrasted with the last Adam, who performed righteousness and brought "eternal life" (v. 1).

Consequently, Paul understands the peaceful relationship with God that is brought by "reconciliation" in verses 9–11 to be a restoration from not merely the divine "wrath" due to sin but from the very wrath introduced by the first Adam's sin. Romans 5:12–21 identifies that wrath as "death" (vv. 12, 14–15, 17) and "condemnation" (vv. 16, 18). Christ, the last Adam, suffered that "death" and "condemnation" for us (vv. 6–10) so that humans could be in a peaceful relationship with God (v. 1) and consequently experience "righteousness to eternal life through Jesus Christ our Lord" (v. 21). This "eternal life" is the life that should have been experienced by the first Adam in the first creation but now can be experienced through identification with the last Adam, who is the beginning of the new creation.

Thus, whereas in 2 Cor. 5 and Eph. 2 reconciliation is viewed as part of the beginning of the new creation and the beginning fulfillment of prophecies about Israel's restoration from the wrathful state of exile, in Rom. 5 reconciliation is seen to be restoration from the hostile state of exile introduced by the first Adam and overcome by the last Adam. But, similar to the 2 Corinthians and Ephesians texts, Rom. 5 connects reconciliation with the last Adam's work of reintroducing the life of the first creation and even going beyond that to the guarantee that this life will be eternal.

Romans 11

The remaining reference to reconciliation in Romans is in 11:15: "For if their [Israel's] rejection be the reconciliation of the world, what will their acceptance be but life from the dead?" This text is part of a discussion in Rom. 11 about Israelites returning to a salvific relationship with God from their present condition of being "hardened" and "blinded" (vv. 7–10), as well as of being cut off from God (vv. 17–21). The time of Israel's "rejection" of the Messiah was the time when greater numbers of gentiles were finding "reconciliation" with God. This reconciliation is likely to be understood in light of Paul's earlier elaboration of reconciliation in 5:10–11, just analyzed above. But what is interesting is that Paul concludes 11:15 by speaking of Israel's "acceptance" of the Messiah, and that this is equivalent to (or leads to) it having "life from the dead." Romans 11:15 parallels "rejection" with "acceptance," and the second parts of the two clauses put "reconciliation" in parallel with "life from the dead." Thus, "reconciliation" and "life from the dead" appear to be roughly synonymous or overlapping concepts in some way. Such a rough equation is not surprising in light of what we saw in 2 Cor. 5, Eph. 2, and Rom. 5, where reconciliation is inextricably linked with Christ's resurrection life of the new creation. The precise connection between reconciliation and new-creational life in all these texts, then, probably is that the former leads to the latter. However, that the two are overlapping conditions is apparent in that the initial act of reconciliation continues on as an everlasting condition in the eternal new creation.

Colossians 1

The last passage to discuss that contains the terminology of reconciliation is Col. 1:15–22. In chapter 10 I discussed Col. 1:15–18 with regard to Christ being identified as an end-time Adam figure (e.g., being in "the image of God" and being "firstborn of all creation") and his resurrection being the beginning of the new creation: "He is the beginning, the firstborn from the dead, so that He Himself will come to have first place in everything" (v. 18). Note how the last three verses (vv. 20–22) in 1:15–22 highlight the very close link between Christ as an eschatological Adam and commencement of the new creation in the preceding verses and Christ's reconciling work. Colossians 1:15–22 reads,

> He is the image of the invisible God, the firstborn of all creation. For by Him all things were created, both in the heavens and on earth, visible and invisible, whether thrones or dominions or rulers or authorities—all things have been created through Him and for Him. He is before all things, and in Him all things hold together. He is also head of the body, the church; and He is the beginning, the firstborn from the dead, so that He Himself will come to have first place in everything. For it was the Father's good pleasure for all the fullness to dwell in Him, and through Him to reconcile all things to Himself, having made peace through the blood of His cross; through him, I say, whether things on earth or things in heaven. And although you were formerly alienated and hostile in mind, engaged in evil deeds, yet He has now reconciled you in His fleshly body through death, in order to present you before Him holy and blameless and beyond reproach.

Again, as in 2 Cor. 5, Eph. 2, and Rom. 5, new creation, resurrection, and reconciliation are very closely related. Likewise, as in the Eph. 2 and Rom. 5 passages, "peace" is a virtual synonym with "reconcile." Colossians 1:19 explains why Christ should "come to have first place in everything" (v. 18) of the new creation. Several commentators have observed that the wording of "well-pleased" and "dwell" in verse 19 is based on the LXX of Ps. 67:17–18 (68:16–17 MT) (see table 16.4).[37]

The psalm says that "God was well-pleased to dwell in" the temple on Zion. Jesus is now identified with this OT temple. We will see in a later chapter

---

37. See esp. G. K. Beale, "Colossians," in *Commentary on the New Testament Use of the Old Testament*, ed. G. K. Beale and D. A. Carson (Grand Rapids: Baker Academic, 2007), 855–57, which surveys commentators who hold this view and other possible relevant OT backgrounds.

Table 16.4

Psalm 67:17–18 LXX (68:16–17 MT)	Colossians 1:19
"God <u>was well-pleased</u> [*eudokēsen*] <u>to dwell</u> [*katoikein*] <u>in it</u> [*en autō* {the temple in Zion}]. . . . The Lord will dwell [there] forever . . . <u>in the holy place</u> [*en tō hagiō* {= Heb. *qōdeš*}]."[a]	"<u>In him</u> [*en autō*] all the fullness of deity <u>was well-pleased</u> [*eudokēsen*] <u>to dwell</u> [*katoikēsai*]." (Or, "In Him He was well-pleased for all the fullness to dwell.")

[a]Most translations render *qōdeš* as "holy place" or "sanctuary" (KJV, NIV, HCSB, NJB, NLT, RSV, NRSV, ESV; so also *3 En.* 24:6–7), though a few translate it as "holiness" (e.g., NASB, NEB).

(chap. 19) that other parts of the NT also understand that Christ is the temple of the divine presence. In particular, here God's dwelling in the architectural temple on Zion now finds its fuller expression in God's dwelling in Jesus as his end-time temple. Jesus, as an individual, eschatologically instantiates and typologically fulfills all that the OT temple represented. However, as we will see in a subsequent chapter (again, chap. 19), during the interadvent age the church is built as a part of the temple on the foundation of Christ. Then at the final consummation the process of building the temple is completed.

The reason (*hoti*, "for" [v. 19]) that Christ should "come to have first place in everything" (v. 18b) of the new creation is that he is the escalated form of God's holy of holies presence on earth, and as such a perfect or full expression of that presence (so note the significance of "all the fullness"), he himself is God. We will also see that the idea of Christ as the temple is a new-creational one (e.g., John 2:19–22 portrays Christ's resurrection as the establishment of the true temple). Thus, it is understandable that Christ as the beginning of God's new-creational temple, from which the temple would grow throughout the inaugurated end-time age, would naturally place him as the inception of the new creation. Christ is the theological-geographical point from which the rest of the new creation spreads. This therefore well explains why Christ should "come to have first place in everything" (v. 18b) of the new creation.

But how does Christ as the full expression of God's tabernacling presence in the new creation relate to the repeated focus on "reconciliation" in Col. 1:20–22? Verse 20 begins with the ambiguous connector "and" (*kai*). It is possible that verse 20 introduces a new topic unrelated to verse 19. More likely, however, the phrase "and through Him to reconcile all things to Himself" refers to Christ as God's tabernacling presence on earth through whom God reconciles believers to himself. When people believe in Christ and are identified with him, they enter into the temple of God's presence and are "reconciled" there with him and have "peace." This link between verses 19 and 20 is pointed to by 2:9–10:

> For in Him all the fullness of Deity dwells in bodily form, and in Him you have been made full, and He is the head over all rule and authority.

Commentators have generally recognized that Col. 2:9 is a verbal parallel and conceptual development of 1:19: "For in him all the fullness of God was pleased to dwell" (NRSV). This is significant because 2:10, "and in Him you have been made full," is clearly a result of 2:9. That is, Jesus's divine fullness has resulted in believers being "made full." It is not my purpose here to elaborate on the precise meaning of believers being "made full," but I would say that believers experience an already–not yet eschatological fullness in Christ. Now, if 2:10 is the direct result of 2:9, then it is more plausible that the repeated emphasis on reconciliation in 1:20–22 is the result of the fullness of deity tabernacling in Christ in 1:19.

As in Rom. 5, so too in Col. 1:20 Christ's death is the means by which reconciliation comes.[38] The mention of God "making peace" is synonymous with the directly preceding reconciliation in verse 20. The "blood" may be a continued reflection of the temple idea in verse 19, since the OT temple is the place where bloody sacrifices were offered so that the people could avert God's wrath. Human "alienation" from and "enmity" against God have been overcome by this reconciling work, so that now a state of peace has come about. Again, as in Eph. 2:14–16 and in contrast to 2 Cor. 5 and Rom. 5, Christ is the subject of "reconcile": "He has now reconciled you in His fleshly body" (Col. 1:22a).[39] Since God is clearly the subject of "reconcile" in verse 20 and Christ the subject in verse 22, Christ's identification with God as the reconciler is highlighted even more than in Eph. 2. He is God's tabernacling presence on earth, the true temple, to which people may come and be reconciled to God and Christ.

Therefore, Col. 1:15–22 closely weaves together the notions of new creation, resurrection, and reconciliation, as well as the new temple. That the new temple in Christ should be the place of reconciliation may not be surprising, since both 2 Cor. 5–6 and Eph. 2 also closely associate the temple with reconciliation (see 2 Cor. 6:16–18; Eph. 2:20–22). The temple was the place in the OT where God would "make his face shine" on people and thus "give them peace" (Num. 6:25–26). And in the eschatological restoration of Israel

38. In 1:20, it is an already–not yet notion that Christ has come "to reconcile all things . . . whether the things upon earth, whether the things in the heavens": the inaugurated stage of this reconciliation applies to those who believe in Christ in this age, but the consummated stage involves Christ reconciling all alienated realities by force (though this latter point about the consummated form of reconciliation is debated, it is beyond the present purposes to pursue this issue further).

39. It is possible that the subject of the reconciling activity in Col. 1:22 is God, but more likely it is Christ, for three reasons: (1) Christ is the subject of the main clauses in 1:15, 17, 18; (2) Christ plays a key role in reconciliation even in 1:19–20; (3) divine functions are attributed to Christ in 1:15–20, and the structure of 1:21–22 is inextricably linked to these preceding verses (so Porter, "Peace, Reconciliation," 698). The parallel of Eph. 2:16a also points to Christ being the subject of the reconciling in Col. 2:22. Nevertheless, one must admit that the pronoun references in Col. 1:20–22 are somewhat difficult to identify.

God "will make a covenant of peace," which will include the temple being the place where "My dwelling place also will be with them; and I will be their God, and they will be My people" (Ezek. 37:26–27 [the latter verse is cited in 2 Cor. 6:16b]). Ephesians 2:20–22 is especially interesting in regard to Col. 1:18–22 because it speaks of Christ as "the foundation" of the temple from "whom the whole building . . . is growing into a holy temple" (Eph. 2:21).

"Peace" as a Reconciliation Concept in Paul's Thought

We have already seen that "peace" expresses the concept of reconciliation in Eph. 2, Col. 1, and probably also in Rom. 5. Paul uses "peace" often elsewhere in his epistles, and they likely to one degree or another mostly express the notion of reconciliation with God. For example, repeated expressions of "peace from God" in the introductions to Paul's epistles likely contain this notion.[40] There is a broad OT background for many of these occurrences of "peace." In the OT "peace" for the Israelite came through sacrifices, and for Paul "peace" comes from God through the sacrificial work of Christ. What the OT sacrifices temporarily and partially achieved has been completely accomplished by Christ's peacemaking sacrifice.[41]

Conclusion for Reconciliation as New Creation and Restoration from Exile in Paul's Thought

We have seen in several passages that the new creation and Christ's resurrection are so closely related to the concept of reconciliation that the latter is to be seen as one of the essential conditions, and even a facet, of the new creation (Rom. 5; 2 Cor. 5; Eph. 2; Col. 1). Furthermore, in these passages reconciliation was seen to be the beginning fulfillment of the OT expectation of the new creation or an escalated recapitulation of the first creation.

In addition, in light especially of the foregoing discussion of 2 Cor. 6 and Eph. 2, the idea of reconciliation is to be understood as the fulfillment of the OT promises of Israel's restoration. Hence, Paul views Christ's death and resurrection as the basis of humanity's reconciliation in inaugurated fulfillment of the prophetic promises concerning restoration into the new creation. These promises have begun fulfillment, but they have not been consummated.

40. See Rom. 1:7; 1 Cor. 1:3; 2 Cor. 1:2; Gal. 1:3; Eph. 1:2; Phil. 1:2; Col. 1:2; 2 Thess. 1:2; 1 Tim. 1:2; 2 Tim. 1:2; Titus 1:4; Philem. 3. Porter ("Peace, Reconciliation," 699) observes that there is little evidence of Greek Jewish letters employing "peace" in their superscriptions, so that it is unlikely that Paul's use reflects merely an introductory epistolary stylistic convention that lacks theological meaning. Thus, Paul's very use of it likely reflects some degree of the notion of reconciliation and peaceful relations with God that he develops elsewhere in the body of some of his letters.

41. See Stanley E. Porter, "Peace," NDBT 682–83. Porter has observed this connection between the sacrificial system of the OT and Christ's sacrifice.

By faith, people identify with and partake of the ultimate exile of death in Christ and his resurrection as the beginning of the new creation, which includes reconciliation and peace with God. Through Christ's redemptive actions he represented the nation in himself and so began to fulfill the OT's hopes for the restoration of Israel by reconciling his people to God. And, as we have seen, this OT background is utilized to enforce Paul's argument in 2 Cor. 5–6 that the readers need to be restored or reconciled to Jesus as God's authoritative representative, which amounts to a reconciliation to God himself.

But what could have motivated Paul to conceive of reconciliation through Christ's death and resurrection as the initial realization of the prophetic hopes of restoration, especially those from Isa. 40–66? Such a question can be difficult because it necessitates speculation about an author's wider context of thought that is not expressed in what was written. The overall analysis of this discussion, however, will become more convincing if a cogent answer can be given to this question.

In Acts 26:14–18 the author of Luke-Acts narrates Paul's account before Agrippa of the commission that the risen Christ gave to him on the Damascus Road. In 26:18 there is common acknowledgment that clear reference is made to Isa. 42:6–7, 16 in explaining the essence of Paul's commission: "to open their eyes so that they may turn from darkness unto light and from the dominion of Satan to God."[42] This Isaiah text that speaks of the commission that Yahweh gave to the Servant to restore exiled Israel is now applied by the risen Christ to Paul's apostolic commission. Consequently, it is plausible to suggest that this commission to Paul from Christ provided the foundation and spark for the development of Paul's subsequent understanding and explanation of reconciliation as the inaugurated fulfillment of Isaiah's and the OT's restoration promises. It likewise also accounts best for Paul's self-identification with the Isaianic Servant in 2 Cor. 6:2. The close contextual association of Isaiah's Servant allusions in Acts 26:18 and 26:23, which are applied respectively to Paul and Christ, manifest an idea of corporate representation or solidarity.

In this connection, the fact that many scholars have seen 2 Cor. 5:16 as an allusion to Paul's Damascus Road experience is not a coincidence. Likewise, many commentators have seen the same allusion in 2 Cor. 4:4–6, so that 5:16 may continue what was begun in chapter 4. This may be confirmed further by the common use of creation imagery in the midst of both the purported allusions, which points to Paul's understanding of his initial encounter with Christ as an event that was part of an inaugurated new creation (which, I have argued, is itself inspired by the associations of restoration with a new creation in Isa. 40–66). Therefore, his discussion of reconciliation as starting

42. Cf. Isa. 42:6–7, 16: "I will appoint you . . . as a light to the nations, to open blind eyes, to bring out prisoners from the dungeon and those who dwell in darkness from the prison" (vv. 6–7); "I will lead the blind. . . . I will make darkness into light before them" (v. 16).

to fulfill the OT promises of restoration in 5:18–7:4 develops naturally out of this reflection on the Damascus Road Christophany together, no doubt, with the early Christian tradition about Jesus. In like manner, argument about reconciliation in connection with new creation and the OT restoration hope in Eph. 2:13–17 also may come to mind because in the immediately following context there is a recollection of the Damascus Road experience.[43] Therefore, part of Paul's understanding of reconciliation was influenced by his understanding about his own reconciliation to God through Christ on the Damascus Road.[44]

Could it be that Paul's repeated references to "grace and peace" in his epistolary superscriptions and to "peace" in his conclusions were so formulated because of his understanding of "peace" and "reconciliation" in the passages examined above so far in this chapter? Are these mere thoughtless stylistic expressions at the beginning and end of his epistles? It is likely that these references still have in mind God's grace in forgiving people their hostility and sins against him.[45]

The Concept of Reconciliation as the Inaugurated Fulfillment of New Creation and of Israel's Restoration from Exile Prophecies Elsewhere in the New Testament

The purpose in this section is simply to cite the work of other scholars who, I believe, have argued cogently that even whole books of the NT outside of Paul's writings are dominated by the idea of Isaiah's prophecies of Israel's restoration that have begun fulfillment. This is important for the present chapter because my contention has been that the concept of reconciliation is viewed by Paul to be the beginning fulfillment of Israel's restoration prophecies. The remainder of this chapter will discuss how the OT notion of restoration as God's eschatological acceptance of his people occurs outside Paul's writings, even though actual words for "reconciliation" do not occur in these places.

The Synoptic Gospels and Acts

The expression of this hope of restoration, which includes a significant element of the notion of reconciliation, has been observed to occur in other parts of the NT outside Paul's writings. Moreover, it has been argued that the concept of restoration, especially from Isa. 40–66, forms the framework

43. See Eph. 3:2–11; cf. likewise Col. 1:23, 25, although there is no explicit reference to OT restoration texts.
44. On which, see further Kim, *Origin of Paul's Gospel*, 311–15.
45. Porter, "Peace, Reconciliation," 699.

for books such as Mark,[46] Luke,[47] Acts,[48] and 1 Peter.[49] This means that the notion of reconciliation also occurs in these books, since, as we have seen, this notion is an essential theme included within the broader idea of restoration, as it is developed in Isa. 40–66. In Mark and Acts, for example, Jesus is identified with Yahweh coming to restore his people to him from sinful separation. Both books also view Christ's death and resurrection playing a central role in bringing about this restored relationship. Further, both Mark and Luke-Acts appeal to Isa. 40:3 at their beginnings (Mark 1:3; Luke 3:4): "A voice is calling, clear the way for the Lord in the wilderness; make smooth in the desert a highway for our God." In fact, part of Isa. 40:3 becomes a repeated theme in both Mark and Acts, where "way" is repeatedly mentioned later in Mark and becomes a name for the Christian movement in Acts. Appeal to Isa. 40:3 early in both books underscores the programmatic nature of Isaiah's restoration prophecies and that they are beginning fulfillment. The immediate context of Isa. 40:3 is a good example of how inextricably linked Isaiah's restoration prophecies are with ideas of reconciliation to and acceptance by God. Isaiah 40:1 prophesies that end-time Israel will be "comforted" by God because "her iniquity has been removed," with the result that "like a shepherd . . . in His arm He will gather the lambs and carry them in His bosom" and "will gently lead the nursing ewes" (Isa. 40:11).

With respect to Luke-Acts, Max Turner has commented explicitly about the significance of the "restoration from exile" background there in relation to the theme of reconciliation. In particular, he sees that the restoration hopes have reached their climax by Acts 15. He sees these realized hopes to be expressed in a community "forgiven of sins," a freedom to "serve God . . . without fear," and "in a messianic community of reconciliation and 'peace'"[50] and of "unity."[51] Notice the repeated reference to the "Spirit" in this Acts 15:1–25 narrative and that it climaxes with "peace" and a unified consensus among the representatives of the early church (15:30–33).

I will delay laying out a summary of the arguments in favor of the pervasive idea of restoration in the Synoptics and Acts until a subsequent chapter (see chap. 20). Suffice it to say now that the concept of reconciliation as a part of the beginning fulfillment of the OT hopes of Israel's restoration that we have observed in Paul's writings can be found elsewhere in the NT.

---

46. Rikki E. Watts, *Isaiah's New Exodus in Mark* (Grand Rapids: Baker Academic, 1997).

47. Max Turner, *Power from on High: The Spirit in Israel's Restoration and Witness in Luke-Acts*, JPTSup 9 (Sheffield: Sheffield Academic Press, 1996).

48. David W. Pao, *Acts and the Isaianic New Exodus*, WUNT 2/130 (Tübingen: Mohr Siebeck, 2000); Turner, *Power from on High*. For an elaboration of Turner's study of this subject in both Luke and Acts, see the next chapter.

49. Mark Dubis, *Messianic Woes in First Peter: Suffering and Eschatology in 1 Peter 4:12–19*, SBL 33 (New York: Peter Lang, 2002), 46–62.

50. Turner, *Power from on High*, 419.

51. Ibid., 455.

Revelation

Although discussion of other NT books that pertain to the OT hope of restoration (and to which the idea of reconciliation is linked)[52] will be delayed until a later chapter, the book of Revelation is of such significance for this topic that it needs mention here. So far in this chapter the focus has been on the inaugurated aspect of restoration as it relates to a return from the exile of unbelief and judgment and reconciliation to God. Now, as we explore Revelation, the focus shifts to the consummation of restoration.

Revelation understands that Christians, while having begun to be restored to God through Christ,[53] are still in a continuing exile under Babylonian oppression (e.g., 18:2–4; 19:2). Accordingly, the section in the book that most clearly pictures the consummate restoration of true Israel (= the church) from exile in Babylon (= the world) is in 21:1–22:5. We will see again that restoration of God's people conceptually overlaps with the NT notion of reconciliation, though Revelation does not use the actual word "reconciliation" for this notion. In particular, this last vision of Revelation pictures the pilgrim people of God as having finished their journey through exile in the world and having been restored to God and Christ in the end-time temple, which is equated with the new Jerusalem, the restored garden of Eden, and the new creation.[54]

In Rev. 21:1–8, the first literary segment of this last vision, there are some significant allusions to OT restoration passages that entail the concept of reconciliation with God. Most overtly, 21:2 alludes to Isa. 52:1–2; 61:10 LXX, which refer to end-time Israel coming back to God as a bride comes to her new husband: "And I saw the holy city, new Jerusalem, coming down out of heaven from God, made ready as a bride adorned for her husband." The appended description of "new" to the "holy city, Jerusalem" is partly derived from Isaiah. Isaiah 62:1–2 refers to "Jerusalem" being "called by a new name" at the point of its end-time glorification. This new name is then explained in Isa. 62:3–5 to signify a new, intimate marriage relationship that Israel will have with God. This picture of an intimate marriage is enhanced further by reference to Isa. 61:10 LXX, which similarly says, "He adorned me with ornaments

52. On which, see Dubis, *Messianic Woes*.
53. See G. K. Beale, *The Book of Revelation: A Commentary on the Greek Text*, NIGTC (Grand Rapids: Eerdmans, 1999), 285–89, on 3:8–9.
54. I cannot demonstrate this equation here, but I have attempted to do so in G. K. Beale, *The Temple and the Church's Mission: A Biblical Theology of the Dwelling Place of God*, NSBT 17 (Downers Grove, IL: InterVarsity, 2004), and this will be summarized in a later chapter. See also the fuller exegetical analysis of Rev. 21:1–22:5 in Beale, *Revelation*, 1039–1121, of which the remainder of this chapter is a summary. In addition see the following works, which are consistent with and supplement the following discussion of the use of the OT in Rev. 21:1–22:5: Jan Fekkes III, *Isaiah and Prophetic Traditions in the Book of Revelation: Visionary Antecedents and Their Development*, JSNTSup 93 (Sheffield: Sheffield Academic Press, 1994), 226–76; David Mathewson, *A New Heaven and a New Earth: The Meaning and Function of the Old Testament in Revelation 21.1–22.5*, JSNTSup 238 (Sheffield: Sheffield Academic Press, 2006).

as a bride." Both Isaiah texts assume Israel's former estrangement from God and highlight the reuniting of the people with their God.

Revelation 21:3 also indicates that the exile of God's people will be over, since "the tabernacle of God is among men, and He will dwell among them, and they shall be His people, and God Himself will be among them." The expression of the completed communion between God and redeemed humanity is formulated in the language of several repeated OT prophecies. These prophecies, among which Ezek. 37:27 and Lev. 26:11–12 are foremost, predict that a final time of restoration will come when God himself will "tabernacle in the midst" of Israel and when Israelites will "be to him a people" and he will "be their God." The context in Leviticus threatens a disruption of exile from God's tabernacling presence (26:37–38), after which God will restore the people into his presence in their land (26:40–45). The Ezekiel passage applies the words of divine tabernacling from Lev. 26:11–12 to the time after the nation's estrangement from God and to its return into his presence at some future point. Revelation 21:3 is picturing this final, future point of restoration to God's presence.

Revelation 21:4 continues the theme of returning to a harmonious relationship with God: "And He will wipe away every tear from their eyes; and there will no longer be any death; there will no longer be any mourning, or crying, or pain; the first things have passed away." That God "will wipe away every tear from their eyes" alludes to the future fulfillment of Isa. 25:8 LXX: "God has taken away every tear from every face." The initial part of Isa. 25:8 says that the removal of tears is part of a comfort because "death," which formerly "prevailed" during Israel's captivity, will be done away with. In mind in Isa. 25 and, thus, in Rev. 21:4 is the resurrection of the redeemed (note Isa. 25:8: "He will swallow up death for all time" [cf. Isa. 26:19]). In addition to the end of death, Rev. 21:4 declares also that "there will no longer be any mourning, or crying, or pain." This continues to reflect Isaiah's expectation that in the future Israel will be safeguarded against its earlier "pain and grief and groaning," which will have fled (Isa. 35:10; 51:11 LXX). Again, there is an appeal to OT passages to indicate that the Israelites return from exile will result in a close relationship with God; indeed, God will tenderly comfort them from their former pains.

In addition to the OT allusions just observed in 21:2–4, there is repeated and explicit reference in the same literary section to new creation:

Rev. 21:1 "Then I saw a new heaven and a new earth; for the first heaven and the first earth passed away."

Rev. 21:4b "The first things have passed away."

Rev. 21:5 "Behold, I am making all things new."

Therefore, this question cries out: How do the restoration allusions from the OT (that convey reconciliation notions) examined so far in Rev. 21:2–4 relate to these expressions of new creation? The answer comes from recalling that all three statements of new creation are allusions to Isaiah's prophecies of new creation: Rev. 21:1 = Isa. 65:17 // 66:22; Rev. 21:4b = in part Isa. 43:18 + 65:17b; Rev. 21:5 = Isa. 43:19, perhaps together with Isa. 65:17. We saw at the beginning of this chapter in the discussion of 2 Cor. 5:17 that these same three predictions of new creation from Isaiah are but three among a series of predictions in other sections of Isa. 40–55, which explain the restoration of exiled Israel as a new creation or at least integrally associates the two concepts of restoration and creation. More specifically, we also observed that each of these three Isaiah texts is part of a broader theme of their respective segments that concerns a promise that Israel's restoration from exile is to be a redemptive new creation brought about by the payment of a ransom and the forgiveness of sins. This was to result in a cessation of divine wrath and exile and in a peaceful relationship between Yahweh and the people, which results from and is characteristic of the new creation, modeled on the original paradisical conditions. I concluded that in the 2 Cor. 5:14–6:18 passage Paul's repeated use of "reconciliation" language was part of his interpretation of his quotation of and allusion to OT restoration texts. For him, "reconciliation" was the equivalent of saying that the hopes of restoration had begun. Although Rev. 21 does not use "reconciliation" language, the same kind of conceptual notion of a return into God's gracious presence appears to be at work. The very same Isaiah texts are appealed to and combined with restoration promises about God's intimate presence with his people, a presence that has a healing effect.

The remainder of this last vision in Revelation bears out this theme of restoration to God's very presence. Revelation 21:9–27 pictures the people of God as a glorious city shaped in the form of a temple (i.e., a cubic holy of holies).[55] First, the "bride" (vv. 2, 9), the church, is portrayed as a temple, which is apparent from observing the various allusions to Ezekiel and their specific uses in John's final vision. My present purposes do not necessitate a detailed listing and discussion of all the allusions to Ezekiel and other OT texts in this passage, which I have done elsewhere.[56] Nevertheless, a brief overview of allusions to Ezekiel's vision of the end-time temple and city can be found in table 16.5.

Table 16.5

Revelation 21:1–22:5	Ezekiel
God's tabernacling (21:3)	43:7 (+ 37:27 and Lev. 26:11–12)
Prophetic commission formula (21:10)	40:1–2 and 43:5 (+ 2:2; 3:12, 14, 24; 11:1)
God's glory (21:11)	43:2–5

55. The Rev. 21:1–22:5 vision portrays the new creation to be equated with a city in the shape of a temple and that is garden-like. For elaboration of this equation, see Beale, *Temple*; also chap. 19 below, which summarizes the book.

56. See Beale, *Revelation*, esp. 1030–1117.

Revelation 21:1–22:5	Ezekiel
Twelve city gates at four points of the compass (21:12–13)	48:31–34 (+ 42:15–19)
Measuring of parts of the temple-city (21:15)	40:3–5 (and throughout chaps. 40–48)
"Four-cornered" shape of the city, measured by "length and width" (21:16)[a]	45:1–5 (+ 40:5; 41:21; 48:8–13 + Zech. 2:2; 1 Kings 6:20)
Illuminating glory of God (21:23)	43:2, 5 (+ Isa. 60:19)
Living waters flowing from the temple (22:1–2a)	47:1–9 (+ Gen. 2:10; Zech. 14:8; and possibly Joel 3:18)
A tree with "fruit" and "leaves for healing" on either side of a river (22:2b)	47:12

Note: This table is based on Beale, *Revelation*, esp. 1030–1117, where there is further discussion of each allusion.
[a]Although Revelation's temple-city is more precisely "cubic" and Ezekiel's temple is square, the terminology in describing the dimensions of both is even identical in some cases (on which, see further ibid., 1073–76).

Given the many parallels between the Revelation and Ezekiel passages, John's temple-city resembles many of the features of Ezekiel's. Why? It is because this last vision of Revelation is the fulfillment of what Ezekiel prophesied. This assessment is based not only on the many similarities between the two and actual allusions to Ezekiel, but also on my argument that Ezek. 40–48 itself is a prophecy of an eschatological temple (with which most OT commentators would agree), which was to be one of the essential features of Israel's final restoration. John's eschatological temple-city scene thus depicts that of Ezekiel's eschatological vision. If Rev. 21:1–22:5 is the fulfillment of Ezekiel's prophecy, this means that Ezekiel's temple is to be consummately established in the eternal new heaven and new earth, which is the setting of John's final vision. That God's people are identified with Ezekiel's temple also indicates that they have immediate access to God's glorious presence, which Ezekiel said would completely fill the eschatological temple and the entire world (Ezek. 43:1–5; cf. Rev. 21:11, 23).

In addition, the corporate people of God are depicted as having the position of the high priest in the holy of holies in Rev. 22:4: "They will see His face, and His name will be on their foreheads." In the old cosmos God's presence was primarily located in the temple of Israel and in heaven during the postresurrection era. In the interadvent period of the church, though Christians had greater access to the Spirit's presence than before, the eschatological fullness of Father, Son, and Holy Spirit was not yet revealed to them. Now the divine presence fully permeates the eternal temple and dwelling place of the saints, since "they will see His face," a hope expressed by OT saints (Pss. 11:4–7; 27:4).[57] All in the community of the redeemed are considered to be priests serving in the temple and are privileged to see God's face in the new holy of

57. Cf. Ps. 42:2; see also *4 Ezra* 7:98; *T. Zeb.* 9:8, both of which are Jewish pseudepigraphical texts.

holies, which now encompasses the entire temple-city. The assertion that "His name will be on their foreheads" intensifies the notion of intimate fellowship with God. It is beyond coincidence that God's name was written on the high priest's forehead in the OT. He was the only one allowed entrance into God's very presence in the holy of holies once a year. The entire assembly of saints will have this position in the coming new order. This expresses further the high priestly nature of God's new people and thus their unhindered relationship with God. Nothing from that old, fallen world will be able to hinder the saints from unceasing access to the full divine presence.

One final image needing to be discussed is the association of the garden of Eden with believers in the new creation in Rev. 22:1–3:

> Then he showed me a river of the water of life, clear as crystal, coming from the throne of God and of the Lamb, in the middle of its street. On either side of the river was the tree of life, bearing twelve kinds of fruit, yielding its fruit every month; and the leaves of the tree were for the healing of the nations. There will no longer be any curse; and the throne of God and of the Lamb will be in it, and His bond-servants will serve Him.

The picture of water, river, "the tree of life," and the declaration that there will be no more "curse" recalls the garden of Eden, where Adam and Eve walked in the very presence of God but were cursed and exiled from the garden and God's presence because of their sin. Now, the whole body of the redeemed from all ages are viewed as returning to that garden, though it is one in which no curse can ever be present again, and one that will endure forever.

The point of this identification of God's people with the temple, the high priest, and the garden of Eden is to show the saints' intimate relationship with God, which is unhindered by any of the old-world obstacles that formerly restrained full communion with God. Thus, the purpose of the temple vision in this section is very close to the idea of reconciliation or returning from exile or alienation to a full and close relationship with God.

However, there is something in Revelation's final vision of restoration that differs from Paul's view in Rom. 5, 2 Cor. 5, Eph. 2, and Col. 1, which I discussed earlier in the chapter. On the one hand, Paul views reconciliation as the inaugurated fulfillment of the OT restoration prophecies about Israel. On the other hand, as alluded to at the start of this section, Revelation pictures those who have already begun to be restored to God through Christ but continue to be in exile in the "Babylonian" system of this old world. Although they have begun to return to a redeemed relationship with God, they do not have complete, consummate communion with him because of their continuation in the exile of the fallen world and of their own fallen bodies. This exile prevents full enjoyment of God's presence because of persecution, the believers' own ongoing imperfections, and their own sinful bodies. These impediments still cause partial alienation from full communion with God. Thus, God's wrath on the believer has been taken by Christ, and the inaugurated effect is that spiritual alienation from God has begun to be dissipated; the full effect of Christ's death and resurrection, however, will be felt only at the very consummation, when the full spiritual and physical curses of the fall will be removed. The concluding vision of Revelation portrays the pilgrim people of God coming to the end of their exilic journey and being restored to full and unobstructed fellowship with the Creator. The obstacles of their past journey prohibiting unencumbered intimacy with God will be removed in the new heaven and earth: "And He will wipe away every tear from their eyes; and there will no longer be any death; there will no longer be any mourning, or crying, or pain; the first things have passed away" (21:4). The essence of this restoration for the saints is that their bodies and souls have been removed from the old world through resurrection and placed in a new-creational environment.[58]

Consequently, the finale of Revelation paints the picture of the consummation of the restored and reconciled community in its glorified and resurrected state, which has made it fit for experiencing unimpeded relationship with God.

---

58. The part of the new creation on which John focuses in 21:2–22:5 is that of redeemed and resurrected saints. This is apparent in that this vision is primarily dominated by various figurative portrayals of the glorified community of believers. Second, John 3:14 has indicated that the allusion to the prophecy of new creation in Isa. 43:18–19 and 65:17 has begun to be fulfilled in the physical resurrection of Christ. In line with this, the very same Isaiah allusions in 21:1, 4–5 are applied to the saved community and plausibly refer to that community in its resurrected and glorified state. However, that the new creation includes more than the resurrected community is apparent from the wording of "new <u>heaven</u> and new <u>earth</u>" (v. 1) and "I create <u>all things</u> new" (v. 5).

PART 6

THE STORY OF THE WORK OF THE SPIRIT IN THE INAUGURATED END-TIME NEW CREATION

17

The Spirit as the Transforming Agent of the Inaugurated Eschatological New Creation

The purpose of this chapter is to study the divine Spirit not in all of his various roles but rather with a focus on his eschatological function, especially in the NT, particularly with respect to the giving of resurrection life. In line with the argument of the book and the core of the proposed NT storyline so far, we will see again that the Spirit is best understood as a key agent in bringing about the inbreaking eschatological new creation and kingdom.

The Old Testament Role of the Spirit as a Life-Transforming Agent

God's Spirit began to transform the chaos that existed at the beginning of Gen. 1: "The earth was formless and void, and darkness was over the surface of the deep, and the Spirit of God[1] was moving over the surface of the waters" (Gen. 1:2). Presumably, the Spirit's work in Gen. 1:2 was continued through the creative word of God that ordered and brought about the fertile creation that is narrated in Gen. 1. Later in the OT, Job says, "The Spirit of God has

1. Some English translations have "wind of God" instead of "Spirit of God" (e.g., NRSV, NJPS). Commentators also differ: Gordon Wenham (*Genesis 1–15*, WBC 1 [Waco: Word, 1987], 16–17) prefers "wind of God," and Bruce Waltke (*Genesis* [Grand Rapids: Zondervan, 2001], 60) prefers "Spirit of God" (and appeals to other commentators for more in-depth arguments in favor of this translation).

made me, and the breath of the Almighty gives me life" (Job 33:4). Reference to the Spirit having "made me" does not indicate creation from nothing but rather speaks of the initial creation of Job's life in the womb, as a result of human sexual relations. The ensuing statement, God "gives me life," may be a restatement of the first line, or it may allude to the Spirit's maintaining of Job's life in the womb and throughout his human existence. Likewise, in Ps. 104:30 the psalmist affirms to God with respect to all nonhuman living creatures in the sea and on land, "You send forth Your Spirit, they are created." The verse goes on to say of God, "You renew the face of the ground." The verse primarily concerns God's preservation of all animal and vegetative life, which is really a continual creative process. God's Spirit also equips particularly called people to carry out specific tasks in service to the people of Israel, whether it be prophesying, leading, or other special roles.[2]

There are several references to the eschatological work of the Spirit in the OT. First, the Spirit is prophesied to be the creator of new life in the age to come, just as the Spirit had created life in the first creation. Ezekiel 36:26–27 affirms this:

> Moreover, I will give you a new heart and put a new spirit within you; and I will remove the heart of stone from your flesh and give you a heart of flesh. I will put My Spirit within you and cause you to walk in My statutes, and you will be careful to observe My ordinances.

The Spirit will transform unbelievers into the people of God by removing "the heart of stone" and giving them "a heart of flesh," that is, giving them "a new heart" and "a new spirit." The preceding and following context of Ezek. 36 indicates that this will occur in end-time Israel, when God will restore them from unbelief and exile and cause them to live in the transformed land of promise. Ezekiel 37:1–14, a passage that I have already extensively quoted and discussed,[3] expands on this promise. Verses 1–10 give the picture of God putting "breath" (or "spirit" or the "Spirit") into bones and causing flesh and sinews to grow on the bones to raise up the dead bones and form them into new people. The interpretation of the picture is given in verses 11–14: the bones represent spiritually dead Israel, living in exile ("graves") outside the land (v. 11). God will raise the people of Israel from spiritual death (v. 12a), breathe into them and give them spiritual "life"

---

2. See Exod. 31:3; 35:31; Num. 11:17, 25, 29; 24:2; 27:18; Deut. 34:9; Judg. 3:10; 6:34; 11:29; 13:25; 14:6, 19; 15:14; 1 Sam. 10:6, 10; 11:6; 16:13; 19:20; 2 Sam. 23:2; 1 Kings 18:12; 22:24; 2 Kings 2:16; 1 Chron. 12:18; 2 Chron. 15:1; 20:14; 24:20; Neh. 9:20, 30; Pss. 51:11; 143:10; Mic. 3:8; about ten times the book of Ezekiel refers to the Spirit commissioning Ezekiel as a prophet.

3. See chap. 8 (under the heading "The Already–Not Yet Latter-Day Resurrection and New-Creational Kingdom of the Gospels"); chap. 9 (under the heading "Resurrection in Romans").

through his "Spirit" (v. 14), and restore them from spiritual and physical exile back into the land (v. 12b) so that they willl "know" that it is God who has performed this (vv. 13, 14b).

Ezekiel 37:5, 9 allude to Gen. 2:7 (see table 17.1).

Table 17.1

Genesis 2:7 LXX	Ezekiel 37:5, 9 LXX
"And God formed the man of dust of the earth, <u>and breathed into the</u> [kai enephysēsen eis to] face of him the <u>breath of life</u> [zōēs], and the man became a <u>living</u> [zōsan] soul."	37:5 "Thus says the Lord God to these bones, 'Behold, I *will* bring upon you the <u>breath of life</u> [zōēs].'" 37:9: "Then he said to me, 'Prophesy to the breath, prophesy, son of man, and say to the breath, "Thus says the Lord God, 'Come from the four winds, O breath, <u>and breathe upon these</u> [kai emphysēson eis tous] slain, and <u>let them live</u> [zēsatōsan].'"'"

Note: For the purpose of later comparison with NT parallels, I use the LXX for the textual comparisons above (where the wording is more closely parallel than in the Hebrew; solid underlining represents lexical parallels and dotted lines less close parallels). The Hebrew parallels are sufficient to recognize the allusion (e.g., note the common use of the noun/verbal form of "live" [hyh] and of the verb "breathe" [nph]). Commentators who have observed the allusion include C. F. Keil, *Prophecies of Ezekiel*, vol. 2, K&D (repr., Grand Rapids: Eerdmans, 1970), 117–18; Joseph Blenkinsopp, *Ezekiel*, IBC (Louisville: John Knox, 1990), 173; Daniel I. Block, *The Book of Ezekiel: Chapters 25–48*, NICOT (Grand Rapids: Eerdmans, 1998), 360, 379; Ian W. Duguid, *Ezekiel*, NIVAC (Grand Rapids: Zondervan, 1999), 69; Robert W. Jenson, *Ezekiel*, BTCB (Grand Rapids: Baker Academic, 2009), 281–83.

The significance of the allusion is that Israel's coming to life through God's inbreathing is a recapitulation of God's first act of breathing into Adam and giving him life. Following the two-stage formation of the creation of the first man in Gen. 2:7, Ezek. 37 likewise depicts two stages of the creation of restored Israel: first the formation of bodies, and then God breathes life into them.[4] This, then, is a recapitulated new-creational theme, affirming that Israel's future resurrection will be part of an act of new creation.[5]

That Ezek. 37:1–14 refers to the same thing as Ezek. 36:25–27 is made clearer by the wording "I will put My Spirit within you, and you will come to life, and I will place you on your own land" (37:14a), the first phrase being a verbatim repetition of 36:27a, and the last clause a paraphrased rendering of 36:28a ("and you will dwell in the land"). This parallelism of the two chapters indicates that the prophecy of Israel's washing with water and new creation by the Spirit in Ezek. 36 is virtually equivalent to the prediction of resurrection by the Spirit in chapter 37, which we saw earlier (chap. 8 above) was to be understood as a first installment of the full-orbed resurrection from the dead. The fact that Israel as a newly created corporate Adam will live in a renewed land that is like "the garden of

4. So Keil, *Prophecies of Ezekiel*, 117–18; Block, *Book of Ezekiel*, 379.

5. For a good discussion of the Spirit in relation to new creation in the OT, especially with respect to how Gen. 2:7 is developed in subsequent OT books, including Ezek. 37, see John W. Yates, *The Spirit and Creation in Paul*, WUNT 2/251 (Tübingen: Mohr Siebeck, 2008), 24–41.

Eden" (Ezek. 36:35) makes even more prominent the parallel with the first Adam's creation.

Most commentators understand the Ezek. 37 passage to be a metaphor for Israel's restoration to the land, but there is more that needs to be underscored: this is also a prophecy that when God brings Israel back to the land, he will also regenerate Israel spiritually. The likely implication of this is that at some later point he will complete this spiritual enlivening by performing a physical enlivening—physical resurrection.[6]

In addition to Ezekiel, Isaiah predicts that the Spirit will also be the agent of life and fertility in the latter-day new creation: "until the Spirit is poured out upon us from on high, and the wilderness becomes a fertile field, and the fertile field is considered as a forest" (Isa. 32:15). Likewise, in Isa. 44:3–5 God affirms,

> For I will pour out water on the thirsty land
> And streams on the dry ground;
> I will pour out My Spirit on your offspring
> And My blessing on your descendants.
> And they will spring up among the grass
> Like poplars by streams of water.
> This one will say, "I am the LORD's";
> And that one will call on the name of Jacob;
> And another will write on his hand, "Belonging to the LORD,"
> And will name Israel's name with honor.

These texts are significant, but further explanation must wait until we study some of the uses of "Spirit" in the NT against the background of these Isaiah texts. Other eschatological uses of "Spirit" in Isaiah and some of the other prophets, while sometimes also being directly associated with new-creational life,[7] primarily refer to a special equipping of the messianic servant to carry out his mission[8] or to the Spirit's work among God's people to accomplish their restoration,[9] while at the same time giving them the ability to prophesy like the prophets of old (Joel 2:28–29).

---

6. Ezekiel 37:14 is underscored and amplified by 39:28–29: after restoring Israel, God "will have poured out [His] Spirit on the house of Israel."

7. Isaiah 11:1–9; 34:16–35:10.

8. Isaiah 11:2; 42:1; 48:16; 61:1.

9. Isaiah 34:16; 59:21; Zech. 12:10. Both Hag. 2:5 and Zech. 4:6 refer to God's "Spirit" in empowering Israel to build the second temple in Jerusalem as a part of what appeared to be the continuing restoration from Babylon, which would issue into the consummate eschatological restoration and final new creation. But Israel was disobedient (note, e.g., the implications of Zech. 6:15), and thus the climactic end-time restoration did not come with the building of the second temple.

The Role of the Spirit as a Life-Transforming Agent in Judaism

As in the OT, Judaism viewed the Holy Spirit to be the agent creating eschatological life.[10] One of the earliest references to this notion occurs in *Testaments of the Twelve Patriarchs*: "And he shall give to the saints to eat from the tree of life, and the Spirit of holiness shall be on them" (*T. Levi* 18:11). The close connection between "the tree of life" and "the Spirit of holiness" probably shows an association of the Spirit[11] with the notion of life regained that had been lost in the first Eden.[12] And just as God "gave life to all things" at the beginning of his creation, so his Spirit "renews" and "forms anew" to "make alive again," which leads to "eternal life for ever (and) ever" (*Jos. Asen.* 8:10–11).[13] In particular, early and later Judaism also reflect on the Genesis depiction of God's breathing into Adam "the breath of life" (Gen. 2:7) and connect it with the Spirit and new creation, especially the Spirit as the agent bringing about the new creation.[14] Some of the early church fathers made a similar comparison of the Spirit (e.g., hovering over the waters) as the agent of the first creation, with the Spirit re-creating humans as a new creation in Christ.[15]

10. As in the OT, the "Spirit" in Judaism can also be referred to as the transformer of life; e.g., the Spirit was the agent of creation in Gen. 1: "Let all your creatures serve you, for you spoke, and they were made. You sent forth your Spirit, and it formed them; there is none that can resist your voice" (Jdt. 16:14). So also *2 Bar.* 23:5.

11. However, the translation in James H. Charlesworth, *The Old Testament Pseudepigrapha*, 2 vols. (New York: Doubleday, 1983–85), 2:795, has a lowercase "spirit," indicating that this is not God's Spirit, though the context favors the Spirit of God: e.g., in *T. Levi* 18:7 "the Spirit of understanding and sanctification shall rest upon him [the Messiah]" likely indicates the Holy Spirit (in light of the allusion to Isa. 11:1–2 there, although Charlesworth also renders that with a lowercase *s*), so that the parallel in 18:11, "the Spirit of holiness shall be upon them," likely also refers to the divine Spirit, since the Spirit there comes from the Messiah.

12. Note also *1 En.* 61:7, which refers to those who "were wise . . . in the spirit of life." This may merely refer to those who possessed a regenerated human spirit or to those who possessed a life created by God's Spirit. In addition, *Apoc. Mos.* 43:5 says, "Holy, holy, holy is the Lord, in the glory of God the Father, for to Him it is meet to give glory, honour and worship, with the eternal life-giving Spirit now and always and for ever. Amen." But since this is placed in brackets by R. H. Charles (*The Apocrypha and Pseudepigrapha of the Old Testament*, 2 vols. [Oxford: Clarendon, 1913], 2:154), it appears to be a later addition, the date of which is hard to determine. Although the following are not eschatological, they appear relevant: *1 En.* 106:17 refers to those who in the prediluvian epoch were "given birth" "not of the Spirit but of the flesh"; *T. Ab.* 18:11: "And God sent a Spirit of life into the dead, and they were made alive again" (though Charlesworth [*Old Testament Pseudepigrapha*] does not capitalize "spirit").

13. In this text the language is applied to the conversion of Joseph's Egyptian wife. *Fourth Ezra* 16:61 says of the creation of Adam that God "formed man, and put a heart in the midst of his body, and gave him breath and life," and that "the Spirit of the Almighty God" made all things (Charlesworth [*Old Testament Pseudepigrapha*] does not capitalize "spirit" here).

14. On which, see Yates, *Spirit and Creation*, 42–83.

15. On which, see Oskar Skarsaune, *In the Shadow of the Temple: Jewish Influences on Early Christianity* (Downers Grove, IL: InterVarsity, 2002), 341–44.

The Spirit is especially seen to be the agent of the eschatological resurrection of the dead. The Mishnah says, "The shunning of sin leads to saintliness, and saintliness leads to [the gift of] the Holy Spirit, and the Holy Spirit leads to the resurrection of the dead" (*m. Soṭah* 9.15).[16] *Song Rabbah* 1.1.9 also develops this tradition and supports the concluding mention of resurrection by appeal to Ezek. 37:14: "'Saintliness leads to the Holy Spirit. . . . The Holy Spirit leads to the resurrection,' as it says, 'And I will put My Spirit in you and you will live.'"

The Spirit would also enable those living in the Qumran community to understand eschatological events happening in their midst, which had formerly been a "mystery":

1QH[a] XX:11a–12 "And I, the Instructor, have known you, O my God, by the Spirit which You gave me, and I have listened faithfully to Your wondrous counsel by Your Holy Spirit."

1QH[a] XX:13 "You have opened within me knowledge in the mystery of Your insight, and a spring of [Your] strength [. . .]"[17]

Paraphrasing Isa. 11:2, which prophesied that the Spirit would equip the Messiah in his work, especially of judgment, is *1 En.* 49:2–4:

The Elect one stands before the Lord. In him dwells the Spirit of wisdom, the Spirit which gives thoughtfulness, the Spirit of knowledge and strength. . . . He will judge the secret things.[18]

I alluded briefly above to the context of new creation in which Isa. 11:2 was set.[19] *Testament of Levi* 18:7–11, part of which was noted above, understands

---

16. Almost identically, and presumably dependent on the earlier mishnaic tradition, see also *b. 'Abod. Zar.* 20b.

17. So also 1QH[a] XVII:32; 1QS III:7, 4Q444 frg. 1, 1 (following the translation in Michael O. Wise, Martin G. Abegg Jr., and Edward M. Cook, *The Dead Sea Scrolls: A New Translation* [New York: HarperCollins, 2005]). The eschatological context of these passages is assumed to be implicit in light of the highly eschatological nature of the Qumran community.

18. Although Charlesworth (*Old Testament Pseudepigrapha*) does not capitalize "spirit" in this text, in light of Isa. 11:2, as in *T. Levi* 18:11, it is likely a reference to the divine Spirit. The statements in *1 En.* 61:11; 62:2 are similar and are to be understood as references to the divine Spirit. See also 1QS V:24–25 (in the translation by A. Dupont-Sommer, *The Essene Writings from Qumran*, trans. G. Vermes [Oxford: Blackwell, 1961]); *Pss. Sol.* 17:35–38; *Tg. Isa.* 11:1–4; *Midr. Pss.* 72.3, which likewise allude to Isa. 11:2 to refer to the Spirit equipping the Messiah to execute judgment. See similarly *Midr. Tanḥ. Gen.* 9.13; *b. Sanh.* 93b, which generally attribute "the Spirit of the Lord" to the Messiah in the coming age.

19. Note Isa. 11:1–5 in direct connection to the prophecy of new creation in 11:6–10. Genesis 1:28 also has in common with Isa. 11:1–2 the botanical metaphor applied to human growth (note the verb *prh* in the Hebrew text of Gen. 1:28; Isa. 11:1, and the Greek verb *auxanō*, read by the

Isa. 11:2 explicitly in this manner. The coming Messiah will possess "the Spirit of understanding and sanctification" (an allusion to Isa. 11:2) that will enable him to judge justly (18:9b)[20] and to "open the gates of paradise; he shall remove the sword that has threatened since Adam, and he will grant to the saints to eat of the tree of life. The Spirit of holiness shall be upon them." Thus, the Spirit of the Messiah will enable him to re-create the conditions of Eden and to pass on his Spirit to his people, who, as a result, will be "holy" (or "sanctified") like him and also dwell in this new creation.

Similar to the *Testament of Levi* passage is *T. Jud.* 24–25. There, "a star from Jacob" will "arise" (24:1 [allusion to the messianic prophecy of Num. 24:17]), and "upon him" the Father will "pour out the Spirit" (24:2). Then the Messiah "will pour out the Spirit of grace" on his followers (24:3). In his possession of the Spirit and his impartation of it to people, the Messiah is termed "the fountain for the life of all humanity" (24:4). This is part of what it means for him to "save" them (24:6), which entails them being "resurrected to life" (25:1). As in *Testament of Levi*, we find the Spirit being directly related to the new life of the age to come.

We saw in our survey of the Spirit in the OT that Ezek. 36:26–27; 37:14 predict that the Spirit will be the agent by which, respectively, God's people will become a new creation and God will raise them from the dead. Several Jewish texts appeal to Ezek. 37:14 in affirming that the Spirit will be placed in people at the end time and will raise them to new life.[21] Ezekiel 37:14 also is applied to the giving to Adam of new life "in the time to come" (*Gen. Rab.* 14.8).[22] Sometimes Ezek. 36:26 ("I will remove the heart of stone from your flesh") is explained as being carried out by the future coming of the Spirit prophesied in Joel 2:28 ("I will pour out my Spirit on all flesh").[23] The "new heart" and "new spirit" prophesied by Ezek. 36:26 are also explicitly viewed as a part of the creation that will be "renewed in the time-to-come" (*Pesiq. Rab Kah.* Piska 22.5a), which will be brought about by God's Spirit (Ezek. 36:27; cf. similarly *Midr. Ps.* 73.4).

LXX in Gen. 1:28 and by Aquila and Symmachus in Isa. 11:1). *Genesis Rabbah* 8.1 asserts that Gen. 1:2 ("and the Spirit of God hovered") is equivalent to Isa. 11:2 ("the Spirit of the LORD will rest upon him"), both of which refer to the creation of Adam.

20. Again Charlesworth (*Old Testament Pseudepigrapha*) does not capitalize "spirit." Likewise see *Pss. Sol.* 17:37; 18:7, which also allude to Isa. 11:2 and, in the context of chaps. 17–18, view the Spirit as equipping the Messiah to judge and establish a consummated kingdom for Israel. Later Judaism also applied Isa. 11:2 to the Messiah (*Gen. Rab.* 2.4; 97 [New Version]; *Ruth Rab.* 7.2).

21. See *Midr. Tanḥ. Gen.* 2.12; *Midr. Tanḥ. Gen.* 12.6; *Midr. Tanḥ. Yelammendenu Exod.* 10; *Gen. Rab.* 96.5; *Exod. Rab.* 48.4; *Song Rab.* 1.1.9; *Pesiq. Rab.* Piska 1.6.

22. Likewise, similar appeal is made to Ezek. 36:26 (*Midr. Exod.* 41.7); God's Spirit will also give life to "the children of Adam . . . in the world to come" (Ezek. 36:26–27, according to *Midr. Tanḥ. Lev.* 7).

23. See *Midr. Ps.* 14.5, citing the Joel 2:28 passage directly after Ezek. 36:26.

The Role of the Spirit as an Eschatological Life-Transforming Agent in the New Testament

The Eschatological Role of the Spirit in the Synoptic Gospels

Earlier, I presented a view of Jesus as one in the likeness of Adam, indeed as the last Adam, who was introducing a new creation (see chap. 13). The portrayal of various episodes of new creation in the Synoptic Gospels was sometimes understood to be the fulfillment of prophecies of new creation, or of Isaianic prophecies of a new exodus, or of OT prophecies of Israel's restoration from Babylonian captivity. The OT promise of a new, latter-day exodus also expressed new creation, since the original exodus was viewed as a new creation, and its recapitulation in another, later exodus would be another new creation. Likewise, the appeal to restoration texts from Isaiah also conveyed notions of new creation.[24] Restoration and new creation were inextricably linked in Isaiah itself, so that restoration from captivity was also viewed as restoration back into God's presence in a new creation, the kind of presence that the first Adam enjoyed. This material bears repeating here because a number of Synoptic texts that were discussed in this connection also contained references to the work of the Spirit, so that the Spirit is to be seen as the restorer of the new creation, the new exodus, and the restoration from captivity.

A few examples from the earlier discussion will well express this role of the Spirit in the Synoptics. We saw that Matt. 1:1's reference to *biblos geneseōs* can be translated the "book of the genealogy," or the "book of beginning," or the "book of genesis." We also saw that the only two places in the LXX where the same phrase occurs is Gen. 2:4 and 5:1–2, respectively referring to the accounts of the creation of the cosmos and of the creation of Adam and his descendants. Jesus's genealogy is then given in Matt. 1:1b–17, followed by two references to the Holy Spirit, who is said to have caused Jesus's conception in Mary's womb (Matt. 1:18, 20). Matthew speaks of "the generation [*genesis*] of Jesus Christ" in terms of "that which is begotten [*gennēthen*] in her is from the Holy Spirit" (Matt. 1:18, 20). I reached the conclusion that Matthew alludes to the Genesis expression to indicate that the genealogy, climaxing with Jesus's birth, is the very beginning of the new age, the new creation. In the same manner that the Spirit was sovereignly present at the very beginning of the first creation (Gen. 1:2), so also the same Spirit is active at the inception of the new world, which is Jesus's birth.[25] Thus, although Jesus's life, death, and resurrection were the main events narrated in the Gospels by which the kingdom and the new creation broke in through Jesus, his own birth is seen by Matthew as the very inception of this irruption.

---

24. On which, see chap. 16 under the subheading "'Reconciliation' in 2 Corinthians 5:14–21."
25. Wilf Hildebrandt, *An Old Testament Theology of the Spirit of God* (Peabody, MA: Hendrickson, 1995), 197.

The same kind of conclusion has been reached by Max Turner about Jesus's birth narrative in Luke 2:26–35. He says that, in the context of Luke 1–2, the birth narrative indicates that Israel's restoration "has already decisively begun in the Spirit's conception of the messianic son of God (1:35)—an act of new creation power which simultaneously foreshadows Israel's New Exodus renewal (cf. the allusion to Isa. 32:15–20)."[26] The prophecy of Isa. 32:15, which we have seen is about Israel's eschatological restoration into conditions of new creation, is applied to Jesus's very conception, likely indicating that this is the actual beginning fulfillment of that OT promise.

Right on the heels of the birth narrative in Matthew, Matt. 2:1–11 narrates the visit of the magi from the east who come to "worship" Jesus (2:2), having been led by the light of a magnificent star. They bring "treasures" of "gold and frankincense." I concluded earlier that this was the incipient fulfillment of Isa. 60. There, a "light" will "shine" over a "deep darkness" that "will cover the earth" (vv. 1–2), and "nations will come to your light, and kings to the brightness of your rising" (v. 3); "the wealth of nations will come" to Israel, and the nations "will bring gold and frankincense" (vv. 5–6), and they "will come bowing" to Israel (v. 14). Isaiah 60 has combined a new-creational idea (light shining to overcome darkness) with the notion of restoration from captivity, and Matthew's placement of such an allusion directly after the new-creational birth narrative makes good sense because it fits well with the Isaiah background. It should be no surprise that the final fulfillment of Isa. 60 is pictured in the closing vision of Revelation to be in the new heaven and new earth, where a "luminary" (21:11) will appear, and "the nations will walk by its light, and the kings of the earth will bring their glory into it" (21:24), "and they will bring the glory and the honor of the nations into it" (21:26).

The role of the Spirit in depicting Jesus fulfilling the OT hopes of restoration was noted in the account of Jesus's baptism (Matt. 3:13–17, citing most explicitly the restoration promise of Isa. 42:1).[27] Here I cannot rehearse all the evidence of the earlier discussion, but it can be said that the Spirit's descent on Jesus is to equip him to carry out the prophecies of new-exodus restoration, which are also connected to prophecies of new creation. I argued that it is likely beyond coincidence that the Spirit in connection to water being separated from land was instrumental in the first creation, the Noahic restoration, and the exodus, and was to be key in Israel's future restoration. Jesus's work is the apex to which these earlier patterns pointed.

Similarly, the Spirit's guidance of Jesus "into the wilderness" in the directly following section of Matthew is probably still a reflection of the

26. Max Turner, *Power from on High: The Spirit in Israel's Restoration and Witness in Luke-Acts*, JPTSup 9 (Sheffield: Sheffield Academic Press, 1996), 162.
27. Psalm 2:7 probably also is included secondarily in the allusion.

Spirit's work in leading Jesus to restore the people of God in a new exodus through the wilderness. I noted, in the earlier study of this, the common unique elements shared by Isa. 63:11–64:1 and Matt. 3:16–4:1: (1) God's people passing through water in the presence of the "Holy Spirit," and then (2) that "Spirit" subsequently "leading" them onto land and (3) into the "wilderness" at a major redemptive-historical episode. The LXX of Isa. 63:11 says that God "brought up from the earth the shepherd [singular] of the sheep," which shifts the focus from God leading the people (as in the Hebrew text) to the leading of the individual Moses, in greater correspondence to the individual Jesus.[28]

I also contended earlier that Jesus's healings represented the inauguration of both Isaiah's restoration prophecies and the new creation.[29] The fullest quotation of a restoration prophecy occurs in Matt. 12:18–21, which cites Isa. 42:1–4 and includes the reference to God saying, "I will put My Spirit upon him." This quotation develops further the brief allusion to the same Isa. 42 passage in the account of Jesus's baptism, where the "Spirit of God descended upon" Jesus. Earlier, in Matt. 11:3–5, where Isa. 35:5–6 is quoted in part, Matthew had said that Jesus's healings represented the ongoing fulfillment of Isaiah's expectations of Israel's return from exile.[30] The extensive quotation from Isa. 42 in Matt. 12 now amplifies the Isa. 35 allusion in Matt. 11:3–5, especially since this quotation in Matt. 12 is explicitly said to be partly "fulfilled" through Jesus's healings (12:15–17: "He healed them all. . . . This was to fulfill what was spoken through Isaiah the prophet"). In addition, Jesus's healings directly precede (12:9–15) and follow (12:22) the quotation, showing its fulfillment also to be directly linked to healings. These healings are explicitly said to be done by means of the Spirit working through Jesus: "But if I cast out demons by the Spirit of God, then the kingdom of God has come upon you" (12:28), developing further the reference to "I will put my Spirit upon him" at the beginning of the Isa. 42 restoration citation a few verses earlier. Thus, Jesus's healing ministry was a fulfillment of Israel's end-time restoration prophecies and was performed through the work of the eschatological Spirit.

Similarly, Luke portrays Jesus with some of the same OT background that Matthew employs, receiving the Spirit at his baptism (3:21–22), being "led

---

28. See Rikki E. Watts, *Isaiah's New Exodus in Mark* (Grand Rapids: Baker Academic, 1997) 102–8, in which the arguments for the same Isaiah background in Mark 1:9–11 for the most part apply here also to the Matthean version of Jesus's baptism. The influence in Matthew may even be a bit clearer, since Matt. 3:16 uses *anoigō* ("to open") instead of Mark 1:10's *schizō* in line with *anoigō* in the LXX of Isa. 63:19 (64:1 MT).

29. On which, see chap. 13.

30. See the use of Isa. 35:5–6 there, which itself is linked to the Spirit's eschatological work in Isa. 34:16, especially the work of producing the fertility of the coming end-time creation (so Isa. 35:1–2).

about by the Spirit in the wilderness" (4:1), and beginning his ministry by the power of the Spirit, which Luke supports by an extensive quotation of Isa. 61:1–2 in 4:18–19:[31]

> The Spirit of the Lord is upon Me, because He anointed Me to preach the gospel to the poor. He has sent Me to proclaim release to the captives, and recovery of sight to the blind, to set free those who are oppressed, to proclaim the favorable year of the Lord.

That the prophecy of Isa. 61 is being fulfilled in Jesus to bring both spiritual and physical restoration is apparent in that soon after its citation Luke describes a series of healings, which include casting out demons and healings from various diseases (4:33–41). Recall that it is "the Spirit of the Lord" from Isa. 61:1 who gives Jesus "authority" and "power" to begin to do this restorative work of new creation (see Luke 4:32, 36). Again, it is the Spirit who is the energizer of the life of the new creation.[32]

But what does the Spirit's restoring work through Jesus have to do with new creation and the life of the age to come? I have argued that the physical and spiritual curses of the fall are starting to be taken away by Jesus. The healings were signs of the inbreaking new creation, which were not the complete healing of people's bodies, since they would still die due to the effects of the fall. Nevertheless, these wonders foreshadowed Jesus's own complete healing in resurrection and the time when his followers will be completely healed. These miracles are a sign that the painful consequences of the first Adam's sin upon creation are being removed to make way for a new creation, which is climaxed by the healing of Jesus himself at his own resurrection. This resurrection, Paul says, was the first fruits of the rest of redeemed humanity, who would be raised because Christ was first raised (1 Cor. 15:20–24) as the progenitor of the new creation (1 Cor. 15:39–57). Accordingly, if this is so, then the Spirit is also to be viewed as instrumental in this movement toward the life of the new creation.

In sum, the Synoptic Gospels present Jesus as empowered by the Spirit to begin to fulfill the OT prophecies of Israel's restoration that were also tied in to the fulfillment of the prophecies of the new creation.

The Eschatological Role of the Spirit in John

At least five passages in the Gospel of John merit discussion concerning the Spirit as the eschatological life-giver: 3:1–15; 4:7–26; 6:63; 7:37–39; 20:21–23.

31. See Turner, *Power from on High*, 190–212. Turner discusses much of the same background for these accounts in Luke that we saw above lying behind the same narratives in Matthew.
32. For discussion of the Spirit's key role in Luke of performing through Jesus the beginning fulfillment of the prophecies of new exodus and restoration, see ibid., 140–266.

The text most clearly affirming that the Spirit gives life is John 6:63: "It is the Spirit who gives life; the flesh profits nothing; the words that I have spoken to you are spirit and are life." This is likely a reference to the Spirit as the agent of the resurrection, since the already–not yet resurrection has been repeatedly referred to in the immediately preceding context through the language of both "resurrection" and "life" (6:39–40, 44, 47, 51, 53–54, 58). The next prominent example, John 3:1–15, concerns the well-known conversation between Jesus and Nicodemus on the subject of being "born again." I analyzed this text earlier (chap. 8), finding that Jesus explains that being "born again" is to be understood as a fulfillment of the prophecy from Ezek. 36. This is the only OT passage that prophesies that in the end-time God will create his people anew by putting on them "water" and the "Spirit." In addition, we saw that Ezek. 37:1–14 refers to the same thing as Ezek. 36:25–27 and develops the latter passage, which is evident by their shared wording about God bringing people to life by putting his Spirit within them (Ezek. 36:27; 37:9, 14). Thus, the parallelism of the two Ezekiel chapters indicates that the prophecy of Israel's washing with water and new creation by the Spirit in chapter 36 is virtually equivalent to the prediction of resurrection by the Spirit in chapter 37. This explains why Jesus refers to being "born of water and the Spirit," compares the "Spirit" to "wind" (as in Ezek. 37:1–14), and concludes the conversation with Nicodemus by referring to "eternal life." Jesus sees that the notion of being "born again" in the inbreaking new age is the beginning fulfillment of the Ezek. 36–37 prophecy[33] that the Spirit would create God's new people by resurrecting them.

The third passage to be discussed concerning the Spirit giving life is John 7:37–39:

> Now on the last day, the great *day* of the feast, Jesus stood and cried out, saying, "If anyone is thirsty, let him come to Me and drink. He who believes in Me, as the Scripture said, 'From his innermost being will flow rivers of living water.'" But this He spoke of the Spirit, whom those who believed in him were to receive; for the Spirit was not yet given, because Jesus was not yet glorified.

There are some ambiguities in this passage and some important OT background concerning the temple, but these issues are not essential for my point here,[34] which is merely to observe that there is general consensus that the

---

33. D. A. Carson, *The Gospel according to John*, PNTC (Grand Rapids: Eerdmans, 1991), 194–98, arrives at the same conclusion about the Ezek. 36–37 background to John 3:1–15.

34. On which, see G. K. Beale, *The Temple and the Church's Mission: A Biblical Theology of the Dwelling Place of God*, NSBT 17 (Downers Grove, IL: InterVarsity, 2004), 196–98; for the broader notion of Jesus and the church as the beginning fulfillment of the end-time temple expectations from the OT, see ibid., passim; and also chap. 19 below.

"water" in verse 38 is representative of the Holy Spirit. Verse 39 makes this explicit: "But this [i.e., 'will flow rivers of living water'] he spoke of the Spirit." Verse 38 literally reads "rivers of the water of life." This may also be translated as "rivers of living water"[35] or, just as plausibly, "rivers of water causing life,"[36] but even if the former is preferable, the "water" is seen to have the attribute of "life," which would be not far from the latter idea. In light of the OT background, where waters were to flow out of the end-time temple, Jesus is seen as the beginning of that temple, sending forth his Spirit to give life. However, this point has been argued elsewhere, and the limits of the present discussion do not allow further elaboration.[37]

In light of "water" representing the Spirit that gives "life" in John 7, we may conclude that the same thing is in mind when Jesus earlier tells the Samaritan woman that he is the source of "living water" that will "spring up to eternal life" for those drinking (4:10–14). The John 7 passage expands and interprets the John 4 text.

One last passage concerning the Spirit and life deserves discussion, John 20:21–23:

> So Jesus said to them again, "Peace be with you; as the Father has sent Me, I also send you." And when He had said this, He breathed on them and said to them, "Receive the Holy Spirit. If you forgive the sins of any, their sins have been forgiven them; if you retain the sins of any, they have been retained."

That Jesus is the source of water (= the Spirit) that engenders life may be implied from verse 22, where the resurrected Christ "breathed on them [the disciples] and said to them, 'Receive the Holy Spirit.'" It is no coincidence that, as some commentators have observed, this act of breathing echoes Gen. 2:7, where God "breathed" (*emphysaō*, the same Greek word as in John 20:22) into Adam "the breath of life, and Adam became a living being."[38] In the preceding verse (v. 21), Jesus says, "As the Father has sent Me, I also send you." This is an episode similar to the Great Commission in Matt. 28:18–20, which we have seen in another connection is plausibly to be understood as a renewal of the commission given to Adam.[39] The allusion to Gen. 2:7 suggests that Jesus is empowering his followers not with physical life, as with Adam, but with spiritual empowerment to do what Adam

---

35. Taking *zōntos* as an adjectival genitive.

36. Taking *zōntos* as a genitive of product.

37. See Beale, *Temple*, 196–98, where the background texts Ezek. 47:1–12; Joel 4:18; Zech. 14:8 are briefly discussed.

38. See, e.g., Herman Ridderbos, *The Gospel according to John: A Theological Commentary*, trans. John Vriend (Grand Rapids: Eerdmans, 1997), 643 (he also includes echo of Ezek. 37:5; Wis. 17:11); Andreas J. Köstenberger, *John*, BECNT (Grand Rapids: Baker Academic, 2004), 575.

39. For elaboration of this last point, see Beale, *Temple*, 169, 175–77.

and others had failed to do. The twelve apostles are commissioned as the representative bridgehead of the new humanity, the new Israel.[40] Pentecost (see Acts 2:1–21) shows this bridgehead expanding further with a greater outpouring of the Spirit.

John 20:22 appears to be a development of the promise of the Spirit from John 7, since this is the first time the language of "receiving the Spirit" in application to Jesus's followers has occurred since John 7:39 ("But this He spoke of the Spirit, whom those who believed in Him were to receive"). The link with John 7 is suggested further in that John 7:39 affirmed that the Spirit would not be given until Jesus had been glorified ("For the Spirit was not yet given, because Jesus was not yet glorified"). One might be able to say that Jesus's glorification had begun with the resurrection,[41] even though his full glorification at his ascension had not yet happened (or alternatively, the resurrection, at least, was the beginning of a process inextricably linked to the glorification at the ascension).[42] Just as God's breathing into Adam made him alive and a part of the first creation, so Jesus's breathing into the disciples the Spirit might well be considered an act incorporating them into a stage of new creation,[43] which Jesus had inaugurated already by his resurrection.[44] As such beings of the new age, they are to announce the life-giving forgiveness that can come only from Christ (John 20:23), the center and foundation of the new creation. Here again, therefore, we see the Spirit as the transformer of people into the life of the new creation.

40. This is indicated further if the "inbreathing" is an allusion also to Ezek. 37:9, where the same Greek verb (*emphysaō* ["breathe into"]) as in Gen. 2:7 and John 20:22 is used in portraying the creation of end-time Israel. Ezekiel 37:9 likely itself alludes to Gen. 2:7, as I argued at the beginning of this chapter.

41. That the resurrection was an inaugurated reality of the promise of Jesus's glorification in John 7:39 may be further pointed to by the fact that God even glorifies Jesus at his crucifixion (12:23, 28; 13:31; 17:1, 5), though these texts might even implicitly have in mind the resurrection, especially 17:1, 5 in light of the context of the Farewell Discourse (13:31–17:26). How much more glory would he receive at his resurrection.

42. Though it needs to be reiterated that Jesus's glorification was inaugurated at the cross (e.g., John 12:23–33; 13:31–32), so that Jesus's death and resurrection are inextricably linked in bringing about Jesus's glorification (on which, esp. with respect to Jesus's glorification beginning at his death in John 12:32, see Richard Bauckham, *Jesus and the God of Israel: God Crucified and Other Studies on the New Testament's Christology of Divine Identity* [Grand Rapids: Eerdmans, 2008], 47–49).

43. See G. R. Beasley-Murray, *John*, WBC 36 (Waco: Word, 1987), 380–81. Beasley-Murray recognizes the new-creational significance of this passage on the basis of allusion not only to Gen. 2:7 but also to Ezek. 37:9–10, which prophesies Israel's eschatological resurrection at the time of its restoration (and which develops earlier reference to an end-time "garden of Eden" for Israel from Ezek. 36:35).

44. Thus, the disciples are not being "born again by the Spirit" for the first time; they are OT saints who are being transformed into an escalated redemptive-historical stage of resurrection and new-creational life.

The Eschatological Role of the Spirit in Acts

We have seen in previous chapters and will see again in a following chapter (chap. 20) that both the Gospel of Mark and the book of Acts are saturated with the idea that the great restoration prophecies about Israel's return from captivity have begun in Jesus and his followers. We have also already seen how important this concept is for Paul's understanding of reconciliation in Christ (see chap. 16). However, Acts is the concern here. Although I will wait until chapter 20 to lay out the most significant evidence that restoration from exile is a significant notion in Acts, here I will discuss some of this background for Acts. One point that I wish to make here is that the role of the Spirit in Acts is often directly connected to the beginning fulfillment of Isaiah's prophecies of restoration from exile. This has been argued most cogently for Luke-Acts by Max Turner.[45] In particular, Turner argues that in Luke-Acts the "Spirit is the power of Israel's restoration, cleansing and purging her as the messianic people of God" and "transforming" Israel to be "the Servant of Isa. 49."[46]

For Luke, Turner builds on the work of David Moessner and Mark Strauss. Moessner, building on others, contends that Luke's travel narrative (10:1–18:4), introduced by the transfiguration of Jesus (9:28–36), has been heavily shaped by the picture of Moses and the exodus in Deuteronomy. The point of this influence is that Luke is indicating that Jesus is a new Moses and is inaugurating a new exodus in order to restore eschatological Israel.[47] Strauss, building partly on Moessner, concludes that the more dominant influence in Luke is the new-exodus themes from Isa. 40–66.[48] For Strauss, Luke was significantly influenced by Isaiah's model of a "Davidic king who (like Moses) leads an eschatological new exodus of God's people through suffering as the servant of Yahweh," though he does not go so far as to say that this is "*the* controlling theme of Luke's work."[49] The Isa. 61:1–2 quotation in Luke 4:17–19 and its interpretation in 4:20–21 and the following context view Jesus to be the Isaianic prophet who was to carry out salvation, which Isaiah itself conceived to be a new exodus.[50] Luke regards the Spirit as energizing all the main categories of Jesus's liberating ministry that are narrated in the rest of his Gospel.[51] While not rejecting Moessner's work, Turner agrees with Strauss's proposal of a "fundamentally Isaianic paradigm" for Luke,[52] which he believes is most

---

45. Turner, *Power from on High*.
46. Ibid., 455.
47. See David P. Moessner, *Lord of the Banquet: The Literary and Theological Significance of the Lukan Travel Narrative* (Minneapolis: Fortress, 1989).
48. Mark L. Strauss, *The Davidic Messiah in Luke-Acts: The Promise and Its Fulfillment in Lukan Christology*, JSNTSup 110 (Sheffield: Sheffield Academic Press, 1995), 275–305.
49. Ibid., 304.
50. Ibid., 226, 245, 341–42.
51. Ibid., e.g., 341.
52. Turner, *Power from on High*, 245–49; see also 428–29.

explicitly expressed by Luke 4:18–21, which connotes "the Spirit-anointed Soteriological Prophet [who] inaugurates the 'New Exodus.'"[53] Thus, the Spirit is the agent who transforms the old age into the epoch of the end-time restoration and the new exodus, which also is the new creation, since, as we have seen, Isaiah's prophecies of new-exodus restoration are inextricably linked to new creation prophecies.

After examining in Luke the dominating theme of restoration and new exodus, which is executed through the Spirit, Turner turns to the development of the same theme in Acts. First, he underscores how Acts 1 is programmatic for the entire book, especially verse 8 through its multiple allusions to Isaiah's restoration prophecies (see table 17.2).[54]

Table 17.2

Isaiah LXX	Acts 1:8
32:15: "<u>Until the Spirit shall come upon you from on high</u>, and Carmel [= Heb., 'wilderness'] shall be desert, and Carmel shall be counted for a forest."	"But <u>you will receive power when the Holy Spirit has come upon you</u>."
43:10a: "<u>You be my witnesses</u>, and I too am a <u>witness</u>, says the Lord God, and my servant whom I have chosen: that you may know, and believe."	(Cf. Luke 24:49: "And behold, <u>I am sending forth the promise of My Father upon you</u>; but you are to stay in the city <u>until you are clothed with power from on high</u>"; Luke 1:35: "The angel answered and said to her, '<u>The Holy Spirit will come upon you, and the power</u> of the Most High will overshadow you; and for that reason the holy Child shall be called the Son of God.'")
43:12b: "'<u>You are my witnesses</u>,' declares the Lord, 'And I am the Lord God'" (likewise Isa. 44:8).	
49:6b: "I have given you . . . for a light of the Gentiles, that you should be for salvation <u>to the end of the earth</u>."[a]	"And <u>you shall be My witnesses</u> both in Jerusalem, and in all Judea and Samaria, and <u>even to the end of the earth</u>."

[a]Note the formal citation of Isa. 49:6 at the literary transition of Acts 13:47: "I have placed you as a light for the Gentiles, that you may bring salvation <u>to the end of the earth</u>."

Turner rightly concludes that the point of these allusions is to affirm the beginning fulfillment of Isaiah's prophecies of kingdom restoration in a partial positive answer to the question in verse 6 ("Lord, is it at this time you are restoring the kingdom to Israel?"). Thus, verse 8 is not a response indicating a complete delay in the realization of the kingdom promises, though it is not clear when Luke sees that these prophecies will be consummated. The fact that this is a promise made to the "twelve disciples" (cf. Acts 1:15–26) enhances their role as the nucleus of true Israel, which is commencing the carrying out of the Isaianic predictions.[55]

53. Ibid., 249.
54. This point I will reiterate in a later chapter in summary of the work by David Pao (see chap. 20).
55. Turner, *Power from on High*, 300–302.

The upshot of Acts 1:8, then, is that "the Spirit will come upon the disciples as the power of Israel's cleansing and restoration," an idea that is heightened by John the Baptist's similar promise in Luke 3:16 and is reiterated in Acts 1:5, 8.[56] Another indication of the Spirit's metamorphosing function in 1:8 is the parallel with Luke 1:35 and Luke 24:49 (see table 17.2), of which Acts 1:8 is a development. Indeed, both the Luke 1 and Luke 24 texts also allude to Isa. 32:15, as does Acts 1:8. These parallels between Jesus's conception and the disciples' anticipated reception of the Spirit at Pentecost suggest "that Pentecost involves elements of Israel's new creation or new birth through the Spirit (Luke 1:35), as well as empowering."[57]

In addition to Turner's conclusions about the transformative nature of the Spirit's work within an Isaianic framework,[58] this role of the Spirit in Luke 1:35; 24:49; Acts 1:8 is also underscored by the context of the prophecy in Isa. 32:15–18:[59]

> Until the Spirit is poured out upon us from on high,
> And the wilderness becomes a fertile field,
> And the fertile field is considered as a forest.
> Then justice will dwell in the wilderness
> And righteousness will abide in the fertile field.
> And the work of righteousness will be peace,
> And the service of righteousness, quietness and confidence forever.
> Then My people will live in a peaceful habitation,
> And in secure dwellings and in undisturbed resting places.

In contrast to the land's unfruitful condition (Isa. 32:10–14), in the future the Spirit will come upon Israel and create abundant fertility (v. 15). However, this fertility appears to go beyond mere material abundance to include spiritual fecundity. Not only will the Spirit create literal plants, crops, and trees in the field, but also the Spirit will produce spiritual fruits in the fields: "Justice will dwell in the wilderness, and righteousness will abide in the fertile field" (v. 16). The "task" or "work" (which presumably is viewed as being performed by God's Spirit in the "fertile field" [cf. v. 16]) results in "righteousness" and will also produce "peace," "quietness," and confidence" (v. 17). Thus, the traits mentioned in verse 17–18 appear also to be additional by-products of the Spirit's cultivating work.

56. Ibid., 297–301. Note Luke 3:16: "As for me, I baptize you with water; but One is coming who is mightier than I, and I am not fit to untie the thong of His sandals; He will baptize you with the Holy Spirit and fire"; and Acts 1:5: "For John baptized with water, but you will be baptized with the Holy Spirit not many days from now."

57. Ibid., 434 (see also p. 437). Turner qualifies this statement earlier by saying that "Luke does not spell out his pneumatology, like Paul, in terms of the fulfilment of Ezekiel 36, and new creation" (ibid., 352).

58. On which, see ibid., 346–47 (see also p. 455).

59. Turner (*Power from on High*, 345) makes a point similar to this.

Likewise, the allusion in Acts 1:8 to Isa. 43's repeated reference to Israel as an end-time "witness" (43:10, 12; see also 44:8) is likely to be seen as empowered by the "Spirit" that is "poured out" to transform the dry land into that which is fruitful and to regenerate Israel to bear spiritual fruit (Isa. 44:3–5). In addition, the following context of Isa. 43:10–12 indicates that Israel's "witness" is not only to the uniqueness of Israel's one God (note in this respect, vv. 10–15) but also to the forthcoming new exodus (vv. 16–17), which is none other than a new creation. Isa. 43:18–19 says,

> Do not call to mind the former things,
> Or ponder things of the past.
> Behold, I will make something new [LXX: "new things"],
> Now it will spring forth;
> Will you not be aware of it?
> I will even make a roadway in the wilderness,
> Rivers in the desert.

The nearby context of the Isa. 32 and Isa. 43 allusions in Acts 1:8 contributes to understanding the transformative nature of the Spirit in bringing about restoration and the new exodus.

Turner also plausibly proposes that Acts 2 pictures Jesus in an ascended position of eschatological kingship, ruling and restoring Israel by means of the agency of the Spirit (vv. 30–36). The remainder of Acts is a development of the Spirit as the power of the ascended Messiah in restoring Israel to himself and God.[60] It is important to underscore that it is Jesus's resurrected and ascended position that is the basis for his rule by means of the Spirit. This basis of resurrection is elaborated on in some depth in Acts 2:23–34. Christ could not "be held in death's power" (2:24). He first "received from the Father the promise of the Holy Spirit" and then "poured forth" the Spirit on those who believed (2:33). He was restored from death to life and propelled into God's heavenly presence. This restoration by resurrection would be the way he would restore others to God through the working of the Spirit. The Spirit that marked him out as the ascended Lord (and raised him from the dead [Rom. 1:4]) was "poured out" on his followers to identify them with his position of resurrected kingship, though they remained on earth. Again, we see that resurrection in close linkage to the Spirit as new creation that inaugurated Jesus's kingship and his resurrected new-creational state continues in his ongoing reign as end-time king.[61]

In reality, the Spirit descending in fiery tongues was an inbreaking of the heavenly sphere (where the resurrected Jesus reigned) into the earthly sphere,

---

60. See ibid., 306, 314–15, 418–21.

61. Especially keeping in mind the question in Acts 1:6 and the prophecies of new creation in Isaiah that are connected to the Acts 2 narrative about Jesus, particularly Isa. 32:15 (alluded to in Luke 24:49 and Acts 1:8, which is seen to be fulfilled in Acts 2).

providing a heavenly eschatological lifeline imparting power to earthly believers to spread Christ's kingdom on earth. "The Spirit was the eschatological gift *par excellence*, and possession of the Spirit would be *the* mark of one who belonged to the messianic community of the last days."[62] The Spirit as an eschatological identifying mark is indicated by the fact that Acts 2:17 says that reception of the Spirit was a beginning fulfillment "in the last days" of the Joel 2 prophecy. Accordingly, the resurrected Christ's sending of his Spirit on people, not only in Acts 2 but also in subsequent chapters, identifies them with the resurrected Jesus and thus as resurrected people. Thus, all the various functions later in Acts are functions of the Spirit of the resurrected Jesus. Hence, "the Risen Lord Himself encounters His people in this gift of His" Spirit, and accordingly, "the Spirit becomes parallel to the Risen Lord, Luke 12:12/21:15; Acts 10:14/19; 16:7."[63]

The point of this section on Luke and Acts 1:8 and their allusions to the restoration prophecies from Isaiah is that Christ's resurrection from death represents his restoration to life and his propulsion into the Father's heavenly presence, resulting in his pouring out of the Spirit from heaven. Christ's death, resurrection, reception and giving of the Spirit comprise a beginning fulfillment of Israel's restoration prophecies (e.g., Joel 2:28–32).[64] In doing so, he summed up and represented true Israel in receiving the promise of the Spirit. That is, just as it was prophesied of Israel, Luke 24:46–51; Acts 1:8; 2:31–34 presuppose that Christ begins to fulfill the prophecies by being the first to be restored to God from death by resurrection and being the first to receive the Spirit (Acts 2:31–33), which he then bestowed on others.[65] Jesus's sending of his Spirit incorporates people into true end-time Israel, and this is the beginning of the fulfillment of the restoration promises for people in Acts 2 and then throughout Acts. Turner sees the restoration promises continuing to be developed later in Acts, especially in, for example, 3:19–25; 15:15–21,[66] though not in specific allusion to the Isaiah background but rather alluding to other OT precedents.[67]

62. James D. G. Dunn, "Spirit, New Testament," *NIDNTT* 3:699.
63. Eduard Schweizer, "πνεῦμα," *TDNT* 6:405–6, saying this in connection to Luke 24:49; Acts 2:33.
64. Luke 24 directly links Christ's resurrection (24:46) and his ascension (24:51) with the restoration promise of Isa. 32:15 about the Spirit (Luke 24:49), on which we have already elaborated just above. In addition, Luke 24:48 links Christ's resurrection to the Isa. 43:10, 12 allusion ("you [Israel] are witnesses"), another restoration prophecy.
65. Although Jesus is identified with Israel, his sending of the Spirit in Acts 2:33 identifies him with God, whom Joel 2:28 prophesies will send the Spirit upon Israel.
66. Turner, *Power from on High*, 308–15. However, Turner sees that by Acts 15 Luke understands the restoration promises as "largely fulfilled through the Christ event and the inauguration of the messianic community and fellowship" (ibid., 419). But the theme continues after Acts 15 until the end of the book, as we will see from a later summary (in chap. 20) of David Pao's book *Acts and the Isaianic New Exodus*.
67. However, in light of the discussion so far about Acts in this chapter, other "Spirit-filling" or "Spirit-reception" passages elsewhere in Acts are also likely to be understood to some degree

Thus, Acts portrays the Spirit to be the key agent in bringing about restoration for God's people.

The Eschatological Role of the Spirit in Paul's Thought[68]

I discussed the Spirit's role as eschatological life-giver in an earlier chapter on the idea of already–not yet resurrection in Paul's thought (chap. 9). There is no need to repeat this material here, since all the relevant references concerning the Spirit in relation to resurrection were covered there.[69] I concluded that Christ's resurrection as the inaugurated new creation was the generative influence on Paul's other major theological ideas. When one goes back and reads that chapter, it also becomes apparent how often Paul understands that the means by which Christ's resurrection and the resurrection of his people take place is through the agency of the Spirit. Consequently, again, as in the Gospels and Acts, one finds that the Spirit is the instrument by which resurrection and thus new creation come about. Hence, Paul views "the Spirit as the life of the new *ktisis*."[70] This role of the Spirit is an essentially eschatological concept, and Paul elaborates on it more than any other NT writer.

In the earlier chapter on the end-time resurrection in Paul's thinking, I only very briefly discussed the three metaphors of "down payment," "seal," and "first fruits." These three metaphors are classic expressions of Paul's already–not yet understanding of eschatology, especially of how the resurrection has begun and will be consummated in the future. Although some commentators have seen that the metaphors pertain to eschatological realities, usually their integral connection to eschatological resurrection realities is not recognized.[71]

We saw in 2 Cor. 5:1–10 that the Spirit himself is the beginning evidence of the new creation, wherein is resurrection existence.[72] In 2 Cor. 5:5 Paul says

---

in the specific light of Isaiah's "return from exile" prophecies (see Acts 4:8, 31; 6:3; 7:55; 8:15, 17; 9:17; 10:44–45, 47; 11:15–16, 24; 13:9, 52; 15:8; 19:2, 6).

68. For a general and brief introductory survey of the Spirit's relation to eschatology in Paul, see Neill Q. Hamilton, *The Holy Spirit and Eschatology in Paul*, SJTOP 6 (Edinburgh: Oliver & Boyd, 1957). For more substantial studies of the subject, see Geerhardus Vos, "The Eschatological Aspect of the Pauline Conception of the Spirit," in *Redemptive History and Biblical Interpretation: The Shorter Writings of Geerhardus Vos*, ed. Richard B. Gaffin Jr. (Phillipsburg, NJ: P&R, 1980), 91–125; Gordon D. Fee, *God's Empowering Presence: The Holy Spirit in the Letters of Paul* (Peabody, MA: Hendrickson, 1994), 804–26. Fee has a good study of the eschatological contrast of "flesh" and "Spirit," the former representing the old, fallen world, and the latter the inbreaking new creation.

69. See esp. the crucial section on Romans.

70. Schweizer, "πνεῦμα," *TDNT* 6:416.

71. E.g., Fee (*God's Empowering Presence*, 806–7) rightly sees the metaphors to be dealing generally with eschatology but does not relate them to the already–not yet eschatological resurrection.

72. See chap. 9 under the subheading "References to Resurrection in 2 Corinthians 5." For similar statements concerning the Spirit, see Eph. 1:14; Rom. 8:23.

that God, "who prepared us for this very purpose" of receiving resurrection life and becoming a part of the eternal temple (5:1–4), "gave to us the Spirit as a down payment" of these realities. The Spirit is not merely an anticipation or promise of these realities but rather is the beginning form of them, which is what "down payment" clearly connotes in ancient and modern times (a payment of part of a larger sum, the remainder of which is paid later).[73] Although the readers will be "swallowed up by [resurrection] life" at the end of the age (2 Cor. 5:4), such "life" was already at "work" in them (2 Cor. 4:12). The Spirit is the "down payment" for the future consummation of resurrection life (5:5),[74] because he imparts the beginning of such life in the present, as we will see more clearly below.

Paul makes this clearer in 2 Cor. 1:20–22. He says that "the promises of God" (from the OT) "are yes" in Christ, which means that they have begun fulfillment in Christ's first coming. Paul then says that God "establishes us with you in Christ . . . and gave us the Spirit in our hearts as a down payment." That is, the Spirit is the beginning evidence that the latter-day promises have begun to be realized in Christ—the resurrected Christ—and his people. This is because the Spirit is the agent who causes those who trust in the risen Christ to become identified with him positionally and existentially as the risen Christ and thus also identified with participating in the beginning fulfillment of those same promises that Christ has begun to fulfill. That God "sealed us" means that "he gave the Spirit in our hearts as a down payment" (v. 22). What does it mean that God through the Spirit "establishes" people together "in Christ"? They have come into union with the resurrected Christ. At least part of what it means is that among the "promises of God" that have begun fulfillment "in Christ" (v. 20) and in which believers participate is the already–not yet latter-day resurrection, on which Paul has just elaborated in the directly preceding context of 2 Cor. 1:9–10:

> Indeed, we had the sentence of death within ourselves so that we would not trust in ourselves, but in God who raises the dead; who delivered us from so great a peril of death, and will deliver us, He on whom we have set our hope. And He will yet deliver us.

Paul is not likely speaking merely of deliverance from the threat of physical death during his missionary journeys. Rather, the recent deliverance from

---

73. In Hellenistic Greek the word *arrabōn* can refer to "an 'earnest,' or a part given in advance of what will be bestowed fully afterwards" (MM 79); e.g., the word can refer to a down payment given to someone to perform a commercial task, and after the task is accomplished the remainder of the promised money is paid.

74. For further discussion supporting the notion that the future resurrection is the focus in 2 Cor. 5:1–10, though linked to inaugurated spiritual resurrection, see chap. 9 (under the subheading "References to Resurrection in 2 Corinthians 5") and chap. 15 (under the subheading "2 Corinthians 4:6–5:10").

physical death in Asia was either a shadow or an object lesson of the resurrection life that Christ had already received (alluded to in the wording "God who raises the dead") and that they "hoped" they would fully receive in the future ("He on whom we have set our hope. And He will yet deliver us").[75]

Thus, the "seal" and "down payment" in 2 Cor. 1 are the Spirit's beginning impartation of the OT eschatological promises of God, including that of inaugurated resurrection life that believers share with Christ. That resurrection is among the realities imparted to believers by the Spirit in 2 Cor. 1:22 is further pointed to by the fact that in the directly following chapters Paul repeatedly depicts the Spirit as the agent of such resurrection life (e.g., 3:6, 18; 4:11–12; cf. 4:16; 5:14–17). The Spirit is a "down payment" (2 Cor. 1:22; 5:5) in that he imparts, among other things, inaugurated end-time resurrection existence in the present, and such a "down payment" (2 Cor. 1:22; 5:5) means that the fuller resurrection life will come in the future. A "seal" (usually a wax impression attached to a document) could be used in the ancient world to indicate ownership, authenticity, or protection.[76] Here the Spirit's presence and work probably indicate the authentic identifying mark of the reality that the Corinthian believers have begun to be true partakers of the eschatological promises, which include not only resurrection but also such promises as that of the Spirit itself, the new covenant (3:6), the image of God (3:18; 4:4–6), new creation (5:17), restoration (5:18–7:4), and the temple (6:16).

The terms "seal" and "down payment" also appear together, probably with the same notion as in 2 Cor. 1:22, similarly in Eph. 1:13–14: "You were sealed in Him by the Holy Spirit of promise, who is given as a down payment of our inheritance, with a view to the redemption of God's own possession." Again, the Spirit is the agent bringing people into union with the resurrected Christ: "sealed *in him* by the Holy Spirit," who himself is part of the end-time promise. One of the goals of the Spirit's work is "redemption." When Paul speaks of "redemption" (*apolytrōsis*), he, as so often elsewhere in his eschatology, refers to it in two end-time stages: spiritual redemption from sin's penalty (i.e., forgiveness) in the present (Rom. 3:24; Eph. 1:7; Col. 1:14),[77] and redemption from sin's corrupting effect on the body through future resurrection (Rom. 8:23: "waiting eagerly for . . . the redemption of our body"). The only other future uses of the word "redemption" (*apolytrōsis*) occur in Eph. 1:14; 4:30. The likelihood is that these refer to the consummation of deliverance from sin's penal effects on the body and thus to resurrection of the body.

75. On which, see Scott J. Hafemann, *2 Corinthians*, NIVAC (Grand Rapids: Zondervan, 2000), 64–65.

76. See, e.g., BDAG 980–81, with respect to both the verbal and the noun forms of the word.

77. The word *apolytrōsis* also appears with reference to the past and ongoing present in 1 Cor. 1:30, where it refers to believers being identified with Christ's deliverance from death (on which, see chap. 15 under the heading "Justification as the Attribution of the Representative Righteousness of Christ to Believers").

The inaugurated spiritual deliverance of forgiveness is first stated in Eph. 1:7, and the consummate physical deliverance in 1:14. The reference to "the redemption of God's own <u>possession</u>" in 1:14 further points to the full bodily deliverance of those whom God has begun to possess as his own (recalling that part of the meaning of "sealed" in 1:13 is to indicate ownership). Paul's only other references to the word "possession" (*peripoiēsis*) refer respectively to final resurrection and to being called to possess Christ's glory, which probably includes allusion to the glorious resurrection bodies of saints.[78] The future reference of this "redemption" is clarified further in Eph. 4:30: the "Holy Spirit" is the one "in whom you were sealed unto the day of redemption." Thus, Eph. 1:13–14 and 4:30 assert that believers have been "sealed by the Holy Spirit of promise," whose regenerating presence is the "down payment" of the full physical regeneration, which is the "inheritance" to come at the end of the age. The mention of "the Holy Spirit of promise" in 1:13 underscores that this is a fulfillment of the OT promise of the Spirit surveyed earlier in this chapter.

The last already–not yet metaphor, "first fruits" (*aparchē*), occurs in Rom. 8:23. Many understand "the first fruits of the Spirit" to be an appositional genitive ("the first fruits, which are the Spirit"),[79] but the context points more to a genitive of production ("first fruits produced by the Spirit") or, possibly, a genitive of source ("first fruits from the Spirit").[80] Accordingly, "first fruits" would be the beginning fruit of the new creation produced by the Spirit that expresses itself in the spiritual resurrection of the believer.

In the OT "first fruits" were offered to God to indicate that the remainder of what was offered also belonged to God. Such offerings could be animals, but the dominant image is that of offering the "first fruits" of crops to signify that the remainder of the harvest belonged to God.[81] Paul's use of "first fruits" elsewhere indicates the first of more to come later.[82] Of most relevance for the Rom. 8 text is 1 Cor. 15:20, 23, where Christ's resurrection is "the first fruits"

---

78. First Thessalonians 5:9 refers to Christians being "destined for" the future goal of "possessing [*peripoiēsis*] salvation," which in v. 10 is defined as the goal "that we should live together with [Christ]," referring to final resurrection life; 2 Thess. 2:14 refers to the goal "that you may possess [*peripoiēsis*] the glory of our Lord Jesus Christ," which refers to ultimate eschatological glorification in Christ.

79. This is supported further by Eph. 1:13–14: "the Holy Spirit of promise, who is given as a down payment of our inheritance."

80. The preceding context of the Spirit in direct linkage with (probably as the agent of) resurrection life (8:5–14) points more to a genitive of production or a genitive of source ("first fruits from the Spirit"). For the category of the former, see Daniel B. Wallace, *Greek Grammar beyond the Basics* (Grand Rapids: Zondervan, 1996), 104–6, adducing as an example Eph. 4:3 ("the unity of [produced by] the Spirit").

81. So James D. G. Dunn, *Romans 1–8*, WBC 38A (Dallas: Word, 1988), 473, on which see for further support of this idea.

82. E.g., Rom. 16:5; 1 Cor. 16:15; 2 Thess. 2:13, speaking of the first converts in an area of more to come; cf. Rom. 11:16, where many think that the word *aparchē* refers to the promises to the patriarchs, which anticipate more in Israel to be redeemed later.

of more people to be resurrected later. In this light, in Rom. 8:23 the believer's new resurrected spiritual being ("the first fruits") created by the Spirit is the beginning of a greater physical resurrection existence to come, and, in the light of Rom. 8:18–23, it seems even to be conceived of as the initial form of the whole new cosmos to come. The thought of 1 Cor. 15:20, 23 is also in mind in the Rom. 8 context, where Christ is the bridgehead of the new creation, and especially Christ is said to be the "firstborn" of more to be resurrected later (Rom. 8:30).[83]

The three metaphors of "seal," "down payment," and "first fruits" provide insight into Paul's already–not yet eschatological understanding of the Spirit's work, especially in connection to the Spirit bringing about new-creational life in people. The metaphors revolve around the idea that the Spirit is the present evidence of future realities, especially resurrection, and therefore provide assurance of the consummation of these realities.[84] The Spirit is not preparatory for future end-time existence or only a guarantee of it, but is the very beginning of that existence; as Geerhardus Vos says from a theological perspective: "The Spirit's proper sphere is according to the world to come; from there He projects Himself into the present."[85]

Although I analyzed 1 Cor. 15:45 earlier,[86] it is fitting to summarize that study here. The verse says, "So also it is written, 'The first man, Adam, became a living soul.' The last Adam became a life-giving Spirit." This does not mean that Christ became only a spiritual being or became the Holy Spirit. More probably the notion is that Christ came to be identified with the life-giving function of the Spirit. It is likely for this reason that Paul sometimes calls the Spirit "the Spirit of Jesus." The Spirit is the alter ego of Christ, though he is a separate person. The two have a oneness of function in terms of giving eschatological life, but they are two distinct persons. The reference to Christ becoming a "life-giving Spirit" probably is the equivalent to Acts 2:33, where Peter reports that Jesus was "exalted to the right hand of God," and "having received from the Father the promise of the Holy Spirit," he then "poured forth" the Spirit on his people at Pentecost and subsequently on others in Acts.[87] Acts 2:17 says that the Spirit had been poured out "in the last days" in

---

83. See Joel White, *Die Erstlingsgabe im Neuen Testament*, TANZ 45 (Tübingen: Francke Verlag, 2007), 189–95. White sees that "first fruits" in Rom. 8:23 is an intertextual allusion made by Paul to his earlier reference to Christ as "the first fruits of the ones sleeping" in 1 Cor. 15:20. This would confirm that "first fruits" in the Romans text refers to the beginning of resurrection existence (though White plausibly contends that it refers to Christ as the first fruits and not the believer's beginning spiritual resurrection existence).

84. Following the similar conclusion in Fee, *God's Empowering Presence*, 806.

85. Vos, "Eschatological Aspect," 103 (see also p. 102).

86. See chap. 9 under the subheading "Resurrection in 1 Corinthians"; see also the excursus "On the Possible Goal of the Prefall Adam Experiencing Full Security from Death" in chap. 2.

87. Much more explanation is needed for 1 Cor. 15:45, but the limits of space forbid it here. Further elaboration of this passage can be found in earlier chapters, just noted, though this

fulfillment of Joel, and this formally identifies Christ's pouring forth of the Spirit in 2:33 as eschatological, which his resurrection enhances, since the OT and Judaism expected the resurrection to occur at the eschaton. That Christ is called "the last [*eschatos*] Adam" in 1 Cor. 15:45 also enhances the eschatological function of Christ being a "life-giver." The first Adam should have been a progenitor of spiritually and physically living children, but instead he bore children destined for death; the last Adam performs this task by giving such life that is incorruptible in the new, eternal creation.

James Dunn has noted that the Spirit in Paul's thinking cannot be understood apart from his relationship with the risen Christ, which underscores the eschatological and new-creational overtones of the Spirit's work:

> The Spirit for Paul has been constitutively stamped with the character of Christ. Christ by his resurrection entered wholly upon the realm of the Spirit (Rom. 1:4; cf. 8:11). Indeed, Paul can say that Christ by his resurrection "became life-giving Spirit" (1 Cor. 15:45). That is to say, the exalted Christ is now experienced in, through and as Spirit. Christ now cannot be experienced apart from the Spirit: the Spirit is the medium of union between Christ and the believer (1 Cor. 6:17); only those belong to Christ, are "in Christ," who have the Spirit and in so far as they are led by the Spirit (Rom. 8:9, 14). Conversely, the Spirit is now experienced as the power of the risen Christ—the Spirit now cannot be experienced apart from [the risen] Christ.[88]

But there is another vantage point from which Paul's idea of the life-giving role of the Spirit can be viewed that has not yet been given due attention, the Spirit is the producer of new-creational fruit. To this we now turn.

THE SPIRIT AS THE PRODUCER OF NEW-CREATIONAL ETHICAL FRUIT

This section focuses briefly on the OT background of Gal. 5:22–23: "But the fruit of the Spirit is love, joy, peace, patience, kindness, goodness, faithfulness, gentleness, self-control; against such things there is no law."

Paul refers to "the fruit of the Spirit" and then enumerates several examples of these fruits ("love, joy, peace, patience," etc.). Until recently, commentators had not seen OT or Jewish background for this well-known image, but now some have proposed such a background. Walter Hansen has proposed that Isaiah and a few other OT passages form the background. In adducing a reference to Isa. 32:15–17 and Joel 2:28–32, Hansen says that "the promise of the Spirit and the promise of moral fruitfulness in God's people are connected in the Old Testament," and the reference in Gal. 5:22 "is probably

---

discussion is a brief summary of Richard B. Gaffin Jr., "The Last Adam, the Life-Giving Spirit," in *The Forgotten Christ: Exploring the Majesty and Mystery of God Incarnate*, ed. Stephen Clark (Nottingham, UK: Apollos, 2007), 191–231.

88. Dunn, "Spirit, New Testament," *NIDNTT* 3:703.

drawn from the imagery of the Old Testament."[89] Also briefly, and almost identically, John Barclay has made the same claim, though with a little more emphasis on Isa. 32.[90] In addition, James Dunn has suggested with respect to Gal. 5:22 that "if Paul intended to invoke the imagery of fruit-bearing Israel (classically Isa. V.1–7), his point would be that the fruit for which God looked in Israel was being produced (only) by those (Galatian Gentiles included) who walked by the Spirit."[91] Sylvia Keesmaat locates the background more generally in the covenant blessings of Leviticus and Deuteronomy (e.g., Lev. 26:4; Deut. 7:12–17), as well as the promises of restoration in the prophets, wherein fruitfulness for Israel is foreseen.[92] Most recently, Moisés Silva has proposed that Paul's "reference to the fruit of the Spirit (especially peace) in 5:22 appears to derive from Isa. 32:14–15."[93]

Beyond these five brief comments, standard commentaries on Galatians and other related literature, as far as I have surveyed, have not proposed such an OT background for "the fruit of the Spirit." Also, the recent proposals mentioned above have been made only briefly, with no attempt to substantiate the suggestions. Indeed, as they stand, the proposals look promising but need further substantiation. For example, each of the OT passages proposed as background either mentions only the "Spirit" and does not actually include explicit reference to "fruit" (in the LXX [karpos] or the MT) or lacks references to both the "Spirit" and "fruit" (e.g., in Isa. 5:1–7, though, as in Isa. 32, the concept of "fruit" is connoted).[94]

The purpose of this section is to explore whether the intuitions of these recent commentators is correct, though to consider this point I will primarily adduce and analyze passages in Isaiah other than those already proposed. In particular, I will contend that "the fruit of the Spirit" in Gal. 5:22 and its manifestations appear to be a general allusion to Isaiah's promise that the

89. G. Walter Hansen, *Galatians*, IVPNTC (Downers Grove, IL: InterVarsity, 1994), 178.

90. John M. G. Barclay, *Obeying the Truth: A Study of Paul's Ethics in Galatians*, SNTW (Edinburgh: T&T Clark, 1988), 121. In addition, he cites Isa. 5:1–7; 27:2–6; 37:30–32 in more distant connection, along with a number of other OT passages outside of Isaiah that he "presumes" formed collective imagery with which "Paul was familiar."

91. James D. G. Dunn, *The Epistle to the Galatians*, BNTC (Peabody, MA: Hendrickson, 1993), 308. For a similarly brief proposal, adducing Isa. 11:1–5; 32:13–18; 44:2–4; 61:3, 11; 65:17–22, see G. K. Beale, "The Eschatological Conception of New Testament Theology," in *"The Reader Must Understand": Eschatology in Bible and Theology*, ed. K. E. Brower and M. W. Elliott (Leicester, UK: Apollos, 1997), 31.

92. Sylvia C. Keesmaat, *Paul and His Story: (Re)Interpreting the Exodus Tradition*, JSNTSup 181 (Sheffield: Sheffield Academic Press, 1999), 207–8. For the hope in the prophets, she cites primarily Isa. 27:6; Jer. 31:12; Ezek. 17:23; 34:27; 36:8; Amos 9:14; Zech. 8:12.

93. Moisés Silva, "Galatians," in *Commentary on the New Testament Use of the Old Testament*, ed. G. K. Beale and D. A. Carson (Grand Rapids: Baker Academic, 2007), 810.

94. Although, manuscript 91 of Isa. 5:7 LXX includes a variant reading, "I expected it [the 'plant' of Israel] to make fruit [karpos]," instead of "I expected it [the 'plant' of Israel] to bring forth justice."

Spirit will bring about abundant fertility in the coming new age. I will argue that uppermost in mind are Isaiah's repeated prophecies (not only Isa. 32 but also and especially Isa. 57) that in the new creation the Spirit will be the bearer of plentiful fruitfulness, which Isaiah often interprets to be godly attributes such as righteousness, patience, peace, joy, holiness, and trust in God, traits either identical or quite similar to those in Gal. 5:22–23.

The General Old Testament Background of Galatians 5:22, Especially in the Greek Old Testament

We begin with a passage mentioned by Hansen, Barclay, and Silva, which, I think, is merely "the tip of the iceberg." Isa. 32:15–18 says,

> Until the Spirit is poured out upon us from on high,
> And the wilderness becomes a fertile field
> And the fertile field is considered as a forest.
> Then justice will dwell in the wilderness,
> And <u>righteousness</u> will abide in the fertile field.
> And the work of <u>righteousness</u> will be <u>peace</u>,
> And the service of <u>righteousness</u>, quietness and <u>confidence</u> forever.
> Then my people will live in a <u>peaceful</u> habitation,
> And in secure dwellings and in undisturbed resting places.

Here I will only summarize this passage, since it was discussed earlier in this chapter in the section on Acts and even earlier briefly in chapter 10.[95] In the coming end-time restoration the Spirit will come upon Israel and create abundant fertility (v. 15) and spiritual fruitfulness (vv. 16–18).

Likewise, other texts in the Greek version of Isaiah make the same connection and sometimes exhibit an even closer or more explicit link between the eschatological pouring out of the Spirit and the figurative fruits of godly characteristics. The closest such parallel is Isa. 57:15–19.

The Specific Relation of the Greek Old Testament Background, Especially Isaiah 57 to Galatians 5:22

In the early OT Greek textual tradition of Isa. 57:16–21[96] God prophesies that his "Spirit [*pneuma*] will go forth from" him, and he will "create" (57:16b LXX)[97] and produce spiritual "fruit" (*karpos*) in the godly. In the immediate

---

95. On which, see the section there on Gal. 6:15–17 (under the subheading "The Eschatological Connection of 6:14–15 with 5:22–26").

96. Together with the mainline or eclectic LXX (as given by J. Ziegler's edition of the Göttingen LXX of Isaiah), this textual tradition includes the so-called OT Greek revisions by Aquila, Symmachus, and Theodotion, and other allies. For discussion of how these versions of the LXX often witness to pre-Christian Greek readings, see G. K. Beale, "The Old Testament Background of Rev 3.14," *NTS* 42 (1996): 139–40.

97. It is not so clear that it is God's Spirit that is in mind in the Hebrew text of Isa. 57:16b, though it could well be.

context this fruit is directly construed to be the fruit of "peace" (*eirēnē* [v. 19]) and the by-product of "patience" (*makrothymia* [v. 15]) and "joy" (*chairō* [v. 21]) among God's restored people.[98] Others perhaps have not noticed the possibility of this background because of failure to focus on the potential significance of the variant LXX traditions in this passage and to perceive that this is one of the most highly charged eschatological "Spirit" passages in all of the LXX of Isaiah, the latter of which I have labored to argue elsewhere.[99]

The LXX reading of "fruit" in Isa. 57 probably existed before and during Paul's time, and, together with the words surrounding it that are in common also with Gal. 5:22, it may now be seen as, at least, part of the likely quarry from which he drew some of the crucial terms to compose his famous "fruit of the Spirit" passage in Gal. 5:22–23: "But the fruit of the Spirit is love, joy, peace, patience . . ." (*ho de karpos tou pneumatos estin agapē, chara, eirēnē, makrothymia . . .*).[100]

The only two places in the entire scriptural tradition of the OT and the NT where the combination of the five Greek words for "Spirit," "fruit," "peace," "patience," and "joy" occurs are Isa. 57:15–19 and Gal. 5:22. Enhancing this is that "God sending forth the Spirit" is also close at hand in Galatians (4:6) and uniquely similar (even in comparison to Luke 1:35; 24:49; Acts 1:8) in all of the NT to "the Spirit will go forth from me" in Isa. 57:16.

Thus, the viability of this passage's influence on Paul stands on the following:

1. We know that Paul read and was quite familiar with both the Hebrew and the Greek versions of Isaiah (esp. Isa. 40–66).
2. Paul actually quotes from the OT Greek of Isa. 57:19 in Eph. 2:17[101] and cites Isa. 54:1 LXX in Gal. 4:27.
3. The combined wording of Gal. 5:22 is uniquely common to Paul and Isa. 57.
4. Similarly, the concept of "spiritual fruit" occurs in these two passages, as well as often in other Isaianic passages, where reference to God's

98. It certainly is possible that all of these elements were not merely represented in early Septuagintal tradition but actually occurred in a "mixed text" no longer extant. On this possibility, see Moisés Silva, "Old Testament in Paul," *DPL* 633, giving as an example Isa. 10:22–23 in Rom. 9:27–28, which combines unique readings from Codex A and Codex B. It is equally possible that here Paul is combining two LXX traditions. For the same phenomenon, note Justin Martyr with respect to Dan. 7:9–14, where he combines the Old Greek and Theodotion (on which, see H. B. Swete, *An Introduction to the Old Testament in Greek* [Cambridge: Cambridge University Press, 1902], 421–22).

99. See G. K. Beale, "The Old Testament Background of Paul's Reference to the 'Fruit of the Spirit' in Gal. 5:22," *BBR* 15 (2005): 1–38.

100. This section on the OT background of Gal. 5:22 is a summary of Beale, "Paul's Reference to the 'Fruit of the Spirit,'" which attempts to demonstrate this thesis in depth.

101. Even if one were not to hold to Pauline authorship of Ephesians, it stands in early Pauline tradition.

Spirit also occurs, which confirms the Isaianic connection, as we will see below.[102]

That this is not merely a formal parallel but rather a material one is also borne out by the observation that the notion of the Spirit creating fruit that is spiritual in character is unique to the book of Isaiah in the OT and to Gal. 5 in the NT. When this common notion is then seen to be in an eschatological context in both Isaiah and Galatians,[103] the concept becomes even more unique. In particular, both passages are closely linked to contexts that have to do with new creation. In fact, the LXX phrase in Isa. 57:15–16 explicitly expresses this new-creational theme: God will come down from his heavenly abode and be "the one giving life to the crushed of heart: . . . for my Spirit will go forth from me, and I [will] have created all breath." In Isa. 57 the Spirit is the agent by which God creates new life.[104]

There are likewise further hints of a fecund new creation in Gal. 5:22–25, especially when seen against an Isaianic background. Galatians 5:22, 25 say, after mention of "the fruit of the Spirit," that "fruitful" people who "live by the Spirit" will "walk by the Spirit." The type of life mentioned in verse 25 is best understood as resurrection living. This appears to reflect an end-time role of the Spirit in raising the dead, which is also reflected elsewhere in Galatians, as well as generally elsewhere in Paul's writings and in the OT, as we have seen earlier in this chapter.

In Gal. 6:15 "new creation" probably is a way of speaking of the resurrection life through the Spirit mentioned in 5:25, both of which should be seen as beginning not only with Christ's death (6:14) but also with his resurrection. In addition to other connections, the significant link between 5:25 and 6:16 also consists in their use of the word *stoicheō* for "walk," where in both cases the default word for "walk" (*peripateō*) could easily have been used (e.g., Gal. 5:16) rather than the rarer word *stoicheō* ("keep in step with" or "line up with").[105] Moyer Hubbard has rightly argued with regard to 5:25, as well as the earlier references to the Spirit and the concept of life, that

since the Galatians have received the Spirit (3:3, 14; 4:6), have been "made alive" by the Spirit (3:21–22 with 3:14 and 5:25), have been "begotten" by the Spirit

102. Even if the LXX reading "fruit" in Isa. 57:18 postdates the first century, which is unlikely, it shows that the Hebrew of Isa. 57:18 had the potential to be interpretatively rendered into Greek in such a manner.

103. Note in the broader context of Galatians reference to being delivered "from this present evil age" (1:4), to the coming of "the fullness of the time" (4:4), and to a "new creation" (6:15).

104. See Rodrigo J. Morales, *The Spirit and the Restoration of Israel*, WUNT 2/282 (Tübingen: Mohr Siebeck, 2010), 155–59, who agrees with my view that the language of the Isa. 57 passage has shaped Paul's language in Gal. 5:19–23, especially with respect to the fruits of the Spirit, and he builds on my argument, thus enhancing its probability.

105. For further discussion of the link between Gal. 6:22–25 and 6:15–16, see the earlier chapter on resurrection in Paul (chap. 10).

(4:29), "live" by the Spirit (5:25), "walk" by the Spirit (5:16, 18, 25), and have become "children" and "heirs" through the Spirit in their hearts (4:6–7), Paul argues that the law and circumcision are no longer relevant. This entire chain of reasoning is perfectly summarized under the heading "the motif of transformation," and succinctly recapitulated in the phrase, "neither circumcision nor uncircumcision, but *new creation!*"[106]

In this respect, 5:25 and 6:15 also develop the introduction to the epistle (1:1: "God . . . who raised [Jesus] from the dead") and the pattern of crucifixion and resurrection seen in 2:19–20; 5:24–25.

CONCLUSION TO GALATIONS 5:22

"The fruit of the Spirit" in Gal. 5:22 and its manifestations appear to be a general allusion to Isaiah's promise that the Spirit would bring about abundant fertility in the coming new age. Uppermost in mind are Isaiah's repeated prophecies (esp. Isa. 32 and, above all, Isa. 57) that in the new creation the Spirit will be the bearer of plentiful fruitfulness, which Isaiah often interprets to be godly attributes such as righteousness, patience, peace, joy, holiness, and trust in God, traits either identical or quite similar to those in Gal. 5:22–23. Thus, the Spirit is the agent who creates the fruit of the new creation in God's people, which is also likely to be viewed as connected to and a development of Paul's new-creational concept of "first fruits" in Rom. 8:23. The Spirit first raises the saints from the dead spiritually and then creates these fruits in them.

Paul's rhetorical effect and thematic emphasis are increased by the readers being able to situate themselves as those who are part of the dawning eschatological promises of new creation made to Israel, and hence they are true Israelites who play a significant role in this cosmic redemptive-historical drama. If they are really part of this drama, then they will pay heed to Paul's exhortations.

The Eschatological Role of the Spirit in the General Epistles and Revelation

There are few explicit references to the Spirit as the agent of resurrection in the remainder of the NT. One possibility is 1 Pet. 3:18: "For Christ also died for sins once for all, the just for the unjust, so that he might bring us to God, having been put to death in the flesh, but made alive in the spirit [*pneumati*]." There is debate about whether the word *pneumatos* here refers to the

---

106. Moyer V. Hubbard, *New Creation in Paul's Letters and Thought*, SNTSMS 119 (Cambridge: Cambridge University Press, 2002), 229 (see also p. 235). It is unclear, however, why Hubbard did not include the reference to the "Spirit" and "life" in Gal. 6:8. Hubbard's attempt to limit "transformation" of the "new creation" in Gal. 6:15 to the anthropological, thus excluding the cosmic, does not seem feasible.

divine Spirit or the renewed human spirit of Jesus. A proper understanding of Christology would indicate that it is not Jesus's personal spirit that was "made alive," since that could never die. Rather, the verse likely speaks to two spheres of Christ's existence, the earthly sphere and the eschatological sphere—that is, the sphere of the Spirit. Here the Spirit is not explicitly seen to be the means of Christ's resurrection, but since his resurrection existence is viewed to place him into the reality of the end-time new-creational sphere of the Spirit,[107] this idea may be implied.[108] This implication may be suggested also by references elsewhere in which Paul understands the Spirit to be the explicit agent of Christ's resurrection (Rom. 1:3–4; 1 Tim. 3:16), especially since these texts also contrast "flesh" and "spirit"[109] and perhaps reflect hymns, which could also have affected Peter.

There is also a likely reference to the Spirit as the life-giver in Rev. 11:11–12. Whatever precise event is being depicted in this text, it is one that vindicates the "two witnesses" (who represent the church)[110] and their message before the eyes of the unbelieving world. Here I cannot elaborate on all the aspects of these two verses that deserve attention, but I have addressed this elsewhere.[111] After the death of the two witnesses is narrated, Rev. 11:11–12 speaks of their revival of life:

> But after the three and a half days, the breath of life from God came into them, and they stood on their feet; and great fear fell upon those who were watching them. And they heard a loud voice from heaven saying to them, "Come up here." Then they went up into heaven in the cloud, and their enemies watched them.

In verse 11, "the breath of life from God came into them, and they stood on their feet" is based on Ezek. 37:5, 10:

Ezek. 37:5 "Thus says the Lord GOD to these bones, 'Behold, <u>I will cause breath to enter you that you may come to life</u>.'"

Ezek. 37:10 "So I prophesied as He commanded me, and the breath came into them, and they came to life and stood on their feet, an exceedingly great army."

---

107. Karen Jobes, *1 Peter*, BECNT (Grand Rapids: Baker Academic, 2005), 242.

108. That Christ's resurrection probably is in mind is indicated by 1 Pet. 3:21–22.

109. See J. N. D. Kelly, *The Epistles of Peter and Jude*, BNTC (Peabody, MA: Hendrickson, 1969), 151. Kelly cites these parallels, especially with respect to the contrast of "flesh" and "spirit," and understands the contrast similarly to the way I do. Although in 1 Tim. 3:16 the phrase *en pneumati* could be rendered "in the Spirit" or "by means of the Spirit," perhaps there is an intentional ambiguity in both the 1 Timothy and the 1 Peter passages to include both notions of means and sphere. Likewise, some translations do not capitalize *pneuma* ("spirit"), as is the case also in 1 Pet. 3:18.

110. On which, see G. K. Beale, *The Book of Revelation: A Commentary on the Greek Text*, NIGTC (Grand Rapids: Eerdmans, 1999), 572–608.

111. Ibid., 596–602.

The Revelation passage is particularly difficult. Does the depiction of being raised from the dead refer to an actual resurrection or to a figurative portrayal of a resurrection? The problem is partly solved by the observation of most commentators that Ezek. 37:5, 10 are part of a metaphorical picture of Israel's end-time restoration from Babylonian captivity. But we saw earlier[112] that Ezek. 37:1–14 was not merely metaphorical for Israel's restoration back to the land, but that this restoration included a literal spiritual regeneration. This spiritual rebirth develops further the reference to spiritual renewal in Ezek. 36. In this connection, we saw that "living in the land" (36:28) is a result of God giving Israel "a new heart" and "a new spirit" (36:26) and putting his "Spirit" within the people (36:27). This refers to Israel returning to the land and being spiritually regenerated. That Ezek. 37:1–14 refers to the same thing is signaled by the climactic phrase of that section, "I will put My Spirit within you and you will come to life, and I will place you on your own land" (37:14), the first phrase being a verbatim repetition of 36:27a ("I will put My Spirit within you"), and the last clause a paraphrased rendering of 36:28a ("and you will dwell in the land"). This parallelism with Ezek. 36 points to the likelihood that the prophecy of Israel's resurrection in Ezek. 37 does indicate a literal aspect of resurrection, which is resurrection of the spirit—that is, renewal of the heart by means of God's Spirit.

But Rev. 11:11–12 appears to portray more than a "spiritual" resurrection. We know from other NT texts (1 Cor. 15:52; 1 Thess. 4:16–17), as well as Revelation itself (20:12–15; and probably 21:1–5), that God's people will be vindicated at the very end of the age,[113] as was Christ, by physical resurrection (see on 20:12–15; 21:1–22:5). In this light, although the exegetical point of Rev. 11:11–12 is to convey a symbolic depiction and to underscore the figurative meaning of prophetic vindication and validation, these other passages in Revelation and the NT indicate that the precise form of vindication will be through physical resurrection. Interestingly, Judaism sometimes understood Ezek. 37:1–14, alluded to in Rev. 11:11, as a prophecy of the future, final physical resurrection.[114] As may be the case in these Jewish interpretations of the prophecy of resurrection in Ezek. 37, John appears to understand the spiritual resurrection in that chapter to find its consummate form in physical resurrection, which also comes about through the agency of the Spirit.

---

112. Chapter 8 (the section on the OT notion of resurrection and the section on John). See also the beginning part of this chapter.

113. For the temporal setting of Rev. 11:3–13 being that of the very end of the interadvent age, see Beale, *Revelation*, 596–608.

114. E.g., *Sib. Or.* 2:221–225; *Gen. Rab.* 13.6; 14.5; 73.4; 96.5; *Deut. Rab.* 7.6; *Lev. Rab.* 14.9; cf. 4 Macc. 18:18–19; see also, from early Christianity, *Odes Sol.* 22:8–9.

Conclusion

The point of this chapter was to underscore that the role of the Spirit was to be the eschatological life-giver, enabling people to enter into the resurrection life of the new creation. There are, in addition to the Spirit's role in giving end-time life, other aspects of the eschatological activity of the Spirit, but these will be covered in subsequent chapters, where the subject is combined with other important biblical-theological ideas.[115]

---

115. E.g., the church as the temple (chap. 18), gentiles becoming part of the eschatological people of God (chaps. 20–21), and the Spirit and the law (chap. 26).

18

The Commencement of the Spirit's Building of Believers into the Transformed Temple of the End-Time New Creation

The preceding chapter discussed the eschatological role of the Spirit, especially in his life-giving capacity in resurrecting and thus transforming people so that they can become part of the latter-day new creation. The present chapter focuses on what those who have been raised to life by the Spirit have become: the newly created people of God are the eschatological temple of God. The next chapter (chap. 19) will step back and trace the broader outlines of how the temple in the OT relates to that in the NT. The following chapters will discuss this new people, the church, as the beginning fulfillment of the prophesied restoration of true Israel, which enters into the new creation (chaps. 20–21). Then the issue of how the land promises of the OT relate to the NT age will be addressed (chap. 22). After that comes an examination of the distinguishing marks of the church that uniquely reflect the new creation (chaps. 23–24), followed by two more chapters on the idea of Christian living as a facet of eschatological new creation (chaps. 25–26). The concluding two chapters (chaps. 27–28) will summarize and reflect theologically on the earlier chapters of the book. All these chapters attempt to explain their topics as facets of the end-time new creation in Christ the king. In this and the following aforementioned chapters we will continue to see how the new-creational kingdom core of the NT storyline is developed.

Let us now proceed to see how God's people in the new age first began to be the end-time temple of God.

The Link between the Story of the Church and That of the Spirit: The Spirit's Descent at Pentecost as the Eschatological Temple to Transform People into the Temple[1]

Introduction

Although the Gospels narrate to some extent Jesus's establishment of himself as the end-time temple (e.g., John 2:19–22), and the NT elsewhere refers to the church as the latter-day "temple" or "temple of the Holy Spirit" (e.g., 2 Cor. 6:16), there is no explicit mention of the decisive time when the church was first founded as the eschatological temple. Furthermore, the Gospel of Luke (and Matthew) narrates a keen interest in Israel's earthly temple, with respect to its proper and improper use,[2] and then predicts its destruction. In contrast to Matthew, Mark, and John, who mention the replacement of Israel's temple by Christ's rebuilding of a new temple through his resurrection (Matt. 26:61; Mark 14:58; 15:29; John 2:19–22), Luke never tells the reader who or what will replace the temple.

The purpose of this section is to explore the possibility that in Acts 2 Luke narrates the initial establishment of the church as the latter-day temple in escalated continuation of the true temple of God.[3] In particular, I will argue that God's heavenly tabernacling and theophanic presence began to descend on his people at Pentecost in the form of the Spirit, thus extending the heavenly temple down to earth and building it by including his people in it. This will be shown through analysis of various OT and Jewish allusions and backgrounds, which in their original contexts are integrally connected with the temple. Some of these allusions and backgrounds have more validity than others, but I hope to adduce a cumulative argument that carries a sufficient degree of persuasiveness to undergird the proposal. Although the words "temple" or "sanctuary"

---

1. This chapter is based on revision of G. K. Beale, "The Descent of the Eschatological Temple in the Form of the Spirit at Pentecost: Part I," *TynBul* 56, no. 1 (2005): 73–102; idem, "The Descent of the Eschatological Temple in the Form of the Spirit at Pentecost: Part II," *TynBul* 56, no. 2 (2005): 63–90. Those articles were an attempt to substantiate in much more depth an argument, apparently never previously proposed, set forth earlier in G. K. Beale, *The Temple and the Church's Mission: A Biblical Theology of the Dwelling Place of God*, NSBT 17 (Downers Grove, IL: InterVarsity, 2004), 201–15, the thesis of which is well expressed in the title of this section.

2. In this respect, Luke and Matthew refer to the temple often (e.g., 22x *hieron*, *naos*, and *oikos* are so used, while Mark makes 15 such references, and Acts makes 25, though the latter never applies *naos* to Israel's temple).

3. I am grateful to Desmond Alexander for drawing my attention to the relation of Luke's Gospel to Acts 2 on this topic.

or synonyms are not used in Acts 2,[4] the contention of this chapter is that the concept of the descending heavenly temple is woven throughout and forms part of the underlying meaning of the narrative.

A number of commentators have understood that the fiery coming of the Spirit is a theophany, but no one, as far as I am aware, has suggested that an eschatological temple is in mind in Acts 2. I am proposing that Acts 2 depicts not merely a theophany but instead a theophany in a newly inaugurated eschatological temple, whereby the heavenly temple is being extended to earth in a greater way than it had been to the holy of holies in Israel's temple. It is true, of course, that the theophanic presence could be perceived in the OT as operating not in connection to the heavenly or earthly temple. Nevertheless, often the OT depicts theophanies either in the heavenly or earthly temple, and this was the place where the divine presence was considered to be located, until the destruction of the Solomonic temple. Indeed, the theophanic presence was the essence and center of Israel's tabernacle and temple.

Thus, the proposal that Acts 2 is not simply a theophany but rather one in the context of a new temple is in keeping with the typical temple theophanies of the OT, though at Pentecost this begins to happen on an escalated eschatological level. The fact that several OT texts prophesy that the end-time theophanic presence will be revealed to God's people in a newly expanded, nonarchitectural temple strengthens the claim that this is exactly what Acts 2 portrays as beginning (see Isa. 4:2–6; 30:27–30; Jer. 3:16–17; Zech. 1:16–2:13; cf. Ezek. 40–46; *Sib. Or.* 5:414–432). In light of Matthew's, Mark's, and John's view that Christ himself was the escalated end-time continuation of the true temple, the temple narrative of Acts 2 should be seen as a continuation of Christ's temple-building work through the Spirit.

Tongues of Pentecost as a Theophany of a Latter-Day Sinai Sanctuary

First, I will attempt to establish the Sinai background (which, to a significant extent, is a summary of the work of others), and then I will endeavor to show how it relates to the notion of the new temple.

The appearance of "tongues as of fire" (Acts 2:3) is an expression of the coming Spirit that reflects a theophany. But more can be said: it appears to be a theophany associated with the descending divine presence of the heavenly temple. A number of considerations point to this.

The report that "there came from heaven a noise like a violent rushing wind" (Acts 2:2), and that there appeared "tongues as of fire" calls to mind the typical theophanies of the OT. God appeared in these theophanies with thunderous noise and in the form of fire. The first great theophany of the OT was at Sinai, where "God descended on it in fire" and appeared in the midst

---

4. Although note the use of "house" (*oikos*) in Acts 2:1, on which there will be comment below.

of loud "voices and torches and a thick cloud" and "fire."[5] Sinai was the model theophany for most later similar divine appearances in the OT, and to some degree God's coming at Sinai stands in the background of the Spirit's coming at Pentecost.[6]

Deuteronomy 33:2 refers to God, who "came from Sinai," and "at his right hand there was a fiery law[7] for them," which is equated with God's "words" that Israel "received" (Deut. 33:3). The phrase "like fire" (*hōsei pyros*) in Acts 2:3 may have been partially influenced by Exod. 24:17 LXX: "The appearance of the glory of the LORD was like a burning fire [*hōsei pyr phlegon*] on the mountain top" (similarly 19:18).

This aspect of God's fiery theophanic presence in the Sinai depiction and the way it was developed in early Judaism are similar to Pentecost, when people saw "tongues as of fire" being distributed (Acts 2:3). In this regard, Philo, the well-known first-century Jewish commentator, gave a description of God's appearance at Sinai that is strikingly similar to the language of Acts 2: God's revelation came "from the midst of the fire that streamed from heaven" as a "voice" (*phōnē*) being like a "flame" (*pyr* and *phlox*) that "became a dialect [*dialektos*] in the language familiar to the audience," which caused "amazement" (*Decal.* 46).[8] In addition, Philo says that God at Sinai made an "invisible sound" to have "shape," and that became "flaming fire [*pyr*]" that was "sounded forth like the breath [*pneuma*] through a trumpet [that was] an articular voice [*phōnē*] so loud that it appeared to be equally audible to the farthest as well as the nearest" (*Decal.* 33). Furthermore, Philo also says that at the Sinai event the "new miraculous voice was set in action and kept in flame [*ezōpyrei*] by the power of God which breathed [*epipneousa*] upon it" (*Decal.* 35). Philo's rendering is not that far removed from the aforementioned Exodus account, where "voices" is closely linked to "torches" of fire: "all the people saw the voices [*haqqōlōt*] and the torches [*hallappîdim*]" (Exod. 20:18).[9] Elsewhere Philo describes God's "voice" at Sinai (again citing the LXX of Exod. 20:18)

5. E.g., Exod. 19:16–20; 20:18 LXX; *L.A.B.* 11:5 adds that at Sinai "winds . . . roared," and Philo says that there was a "rush of heaven-sent fire" (*Decal.* 44), which is comparable to the Acts 2:2 imagery of "a noise like a violent rushing wind"; Josephus says there were "blustering winds . . . lightning" (*Ant.* 3.80).

6. So Jeffrey J. Niehaus, *God at Sinai: Covenant and Theophany in the Bible and Ancient Near East* (Grand Rapids: Zondervan, 1995), esp. 371. Niehaus's work traces the biblical-theological development of the Sinai theophany throughout both Testaments.

7. This is the reading of some manuscripts of the Samaritan Pentateuch (fifth century BC), the Qumran copy of Deut. 33:2, the Vulgate, as well as 𝕭 (a sixteenth-century Hebrew manuscript). Other Hebrew manuscripts and versions have "flashing lightning" (*'ēšědāt*) rather than "fiery law" (*'ēš dāt*). The reading "fiery law" at least has ancient attestation, even if considered not to be the original reading.

8. This parallel is noted by several commentators; note the identical wording in Acts 2:3, 6.

9. The LXX has "All the people saw the voice [*tēn phōnēn*] and the torches [*tas lampadas*]," which Philo (*Decal.* 46–47) cites in support.

as "light" and to be "shining with intense brilliance" (*Migr.* 47).[10] Sectors of Judaism also spoke of God's revelation at Sinai as being "in the holy tongue" (*b. Soṭah* 42a on Exod. 19:19), "given in fire,"[11] and "prophecy."[12]

Jewish interpretative tradition on Exod. 19 held that the fiery voice or tongue was "divided" in its application to people from all nations who heard it but rejected it and were judged. Often God's fire-like voice is said to be divided into "seventy tongues" or "languages."[13]

The Jewish tradition and the comparable phenomenon in Acts 2 both probably go back, at least to some degree, to earlier Jewish interpretations of OT passages, especially Exod. 20:18a, pertaining to the revelation of the law at Sinai.[14] The repeated comment that the Sinai revelation was divided into "seventy languages" identifies it with the division of humanity's one language into seventy languages at Babel, perhaps implying that these Jewish commentators viewed Sinai as a continuing judgment on the nations. This resembles the mention of "tongues being divided" in Acts 2:3, echoing the traditional way of referring to the nations spreading out from Babel as the nations being "divided."[15]

In fact, while one could think that Luke's account of Pentecost may contain no direct references from the Sinai theophany,[16] there is even further evidence that indicates various kinds of links and even more indirect allusions than I have shown above to indicate that Luke was not merely aware of Jewish commentaries about Sinai but was directly reflecting on the Exodus descriptions of the Sinai theophany itself in his depiction of Pentecost.[17]

All these parallels suggest that Luke was intending to some degree that his readers have in mind God's revelation to Moses at Sinai as a backdrop for understanding the events leading up to and climaxing at Pentecost. I have

10. On which, see A. J. M. Wedderburn, "Traditions and Redaction in Acts 2:1–13," *JSNT* 55 (1994): 36–37; Max Turner, *Power from on High: The Spirit in Israel's Restoration and Witness in Luke-Acts*, JPTSup 9 (Sheffield: Sheffield Academic Press, 1996), 283–84. Both have drawn out the parallels between Philo's portrayal of Sinai and Acts 2 more than most who have observed the parallel significance.

11. E.g., *Tg. Exod. Neof.* 1; *Tg. Ps.-J.* 20:1–3. In this respect, God's flaming revelatory words at Sinai can be appealed to in order to explain why a "flame [of fire] was burning round" a rabbi when he was "expounding Scripture" (*Lev. Rab.* 16.4); i.e., the rabbi stands in the prophetic tradition that originated with Moses at Sinai; so identically *Ruth Rab.* 6.4 (= *Eccles. Rab.* 7.8.1; *Midr. Song of Songs* 1.10.2; likewise *y. Ḥag.* 2.1).

12. *Midrash Tanḥuma Gen.* 8.23; *Exod. Rab.* 28.6; *Tg. Ps.* 68:34.

13. Cf. Jewish interpretative tradition on Exod. 19 with Acts 2:3: *Midr. Ps.* 92.3; *b. Šabb.* 88b; *Midr. Tanḥ. Exod.* 1.22; *Exod. Rab.* 5.9; 28.6 (though the latter does not mention "fire").

14. N. Neudecker, "'Das ganze Volk die Stimmen . . .': Haggadische Auslegung und Pfingstbericht," *Bib* 78 (1997): 329–49.

15. E.g., *3 En.* 45:3 refers to this as the "division of tongues"; so likewise Deut. 32:8; *L.A.B.* 7:3, 5; *Sib. Or.* 3:105; 8:4–5; 11:10–16.

16. Though Acts 2:3 may be an exception.

17. On which, see further Beale, "Eschatological Temple: Part I," 78–82.

adduced several lines of evidence in favor of a Sinai/Pentecost identification. Some of the arguments in favor of this interpretation may not stand on their own, but they take on more persuasive strength when viewed in light of the other lines of evidence. Although some scholars have doubted any presence of a Sinai background,[18] the overall weight of the cumulative arguments points to its probability. Indeed, as A. J. M. Wedderburn has concluded, "It is hard to maintain that all these parallels are purely coincidental—that surely stretches credulity too far."[19]

The upshot of all these affinities of Acts 2 with the Sinai revelation is to compare them with an observation not made thus far: I have argued elsewhere that Exod. 19 and Exod. 24 portray Sinai as a mountain temple or tabernacle in which God's revelatory presence dwelled, an identification made by several OT commentators.[20] If this conclusion is correct, it contributes to the other evidence throughout this essay that the theophany at Pentecost also may be understood as the irrupting from heaven into earth of a newly emerging temple.[21] In support of this thesis is a hitherto unobserved parallel in Philo (in commenting on Exod. 24:1b) where Moses is said "to enter a dark cloud [on Sinai] and to dwell in the forecourt of the palace/temple[22] of the Father," where God's appearance is referred to as "the tongues of flame"[23] (*QE* 2.28); a few sections later (*QE* 2.33), Philo interprets the sacrifices offered by Moses in Exod. 24:6 to be not only a "sacred offering" but also a "sacred unction [*chrisma*] . . . in order that (men [including Israel at Sinai]) may be inspired to receive the holy spirit [*to hagion pneuma*]."[24]

This is quite similar to Acts 2:3, "there appeared to them tongues as of fire," and 2:38b, "you will receive the gift of the Holy Spirit." These extrabiblical texts show that Luke in Acts 2 was viewing the Sinai theophany in a way similar to ancient Jewish interpreters. Although Acts was not necessarily dependent on the Jewish depictions, that the latter viewed Sinai in these

18. On which, see Turner, *Power from on High*, 279–80, 284–85. Turner is in agreement with my argument and cites others in favor, as well as those against it.

19. Wedderburn, "Traditions and Redaction," 38. However, Wedderburn unpersuasively says that Luke was unaware of these parallels because he was merely and unreflectively using an earlier Christian Pentecost tradition containing them.

20. For a summary of which, see the excursus "Sinai as a Temple" below.

21. In Ezek. 1:13 "torches [*lampas*]" of fire from which God's "voice of speech" emanates (Ezek. 1:24) also is part of a heavenly temple scene partially allusive to the Sinai theophany.

22. Ralph Marcus's translation has only "palace" (*Philo, Supplement II: Questions and Answers on Exodus*, LCL [London: Heinemann, 1953], 69); for the rendering "palace/temple," see Peder Borgen, "Moses, Jesus, and the Roman Emperor: Observations in Philo's Writings and the Revelation of John," *NovT* 38 (1996): 151. For further substantiation of the rendering of "temple" in the Philo reference, see Beale, "Eschatological Temple: Part I," 83n27.

23. This last phrase, "the tongues of flame," is Marcus's (*Philo, Supplement II*, 69) paraphrastic rendering of the Armenian's more literal "sparks of rays."

24. The bracketed Greek represents Marcus's (ibid., 73–74) suggested Greek equivalents of the Armenian.

terms lends support for seeing a Sinai background to Luke's depiction of the Pentecost event. Both Acts and Judaism were likely similarly interpreting the aforementioned passages in Exodus and Deuteronomy that describe the fiery Sinai theophany.

Some Christians wonder about the helpfulness of Jewish interpretations of the OT for understanding the OT and the NT. Do we not often use commentaries on the Bible by contemporary writers in order to better understand the biblical text? Sometimes we find such commentaries helpful in providing a perspective on a text that sheds new light and helps us to understand the text in a much more coherent manner.

Earlier Jewish interpretation of the OT functions comparably to modern commentaries. Should we not also make use of this ancient commentary material, such as early Jewish interpretations of OT texts, themes, and so on? Such Jewish commentary material has the same potential use (and misuse) as do contemporary commentaries, though they also have the potential of picking up early oral interpretative tradition that may actually stem from OT times. We have seen above and will continue to see in the remainder of this chapter that there are some early Jewish interpretations of the temple and of the OT that shed helpful light on what is going in Acts 2.

"Tongues of Fire" and Comparable Depictions in the Old Testament as a Theophany from a Heavenly Sanctuary

Sinai is the only background that portrays the image of speech in the midst of fire. The actual phrase "tongues as of fire" occurs in two OT passages. The first is Isa. 30:27–30:

v. 27 "Behold, the name of the LORD comes from a remote place; burning is His anger and dense is His smoke; His lips are filled with indignation and His tongue is like a consuming fire;

v. 28 His breath is like an overflowing torrent, which reaches to the neck, to shake the nations back and forth in a sieve, and to put in the jaws of the peoples the bridle which leads to ruin.

v. 29 You will have songs as in the night when you keep the festival, and gladness of heart as when one marches to the sound of the flute, to go to the mountain of the LORD, to the Rock of Israel.

v. 30 And the LORD will cause His voice of authority to be heard, and the descending of His arm to be seen in fierce anger, and in the flame of a consuming fire in cloudburst, downpour and hailstones."

This passage refers to God in the following manner: "descending," apparently from his heavenly temple, which is pointed to further by observing that it is located far away ("a remote place" and "the mountain of the LORD"); in addition, God appears in "dense . . . smoke . . . his <u>tongue like a consuming fire</u>,"[25] and his breath [*rûaḥ* = Spirit] like an overflowing torrent . . . in the flame of a consuming fire"; and "the LORD will cause his voice of authority to be heard." "The name of the LORD" (Isa. 30:27) elsewhere refers to God's presence located far away and "high above all nations . . . above the heavens" (Ps. 113:4); "Mount Zion" (cf. Isa. 30:29) was understood to be "in the far north" (Ps. 48:2); and God's throne was viewed to be far above in the heavens (Ps. 113:4–6; cf. Isa. 14:13). Also, God's presence in his heavenly temple is viewed to be in a very high place and thus geographically separated and far from the earth.[26] So also in the Isa. 30 passage, it is significant that God's theophanic presence comes from a "remote place" (v. 27), *which verse 30 locates in heaven.*

Isaiah 30:27–30 clearly alludes to the prototypical Sinai theophany.[27] The theophany is directly associated with "the mountain of the LORD" (v. 29c), from or to which his fiery, storm-like presence appears to descend (v. 30). This is significant because the same expression "the mountain of the LORD" elsewhere in Isaiah refers to God's eschatological temple.[28] The reference to God's "breath" (*rûaḥ*) in Isa. 30:28 may merely be an anthropomorphism for God's word in parallelism to the body parts of "lips" and "tongue" in verse 27c–d, or it could be in parallelism with "the name of Yahweh" in verse 27a. If the latter, then it may best be rendered as "Spirit."

Likewise, a "tongue of fire"[29] occurs as an emblem of judgment in Isa. 5:24–25 and may be an abbreviated scene of theophanic judgment from the heavenly temple like Isa. 30,[30] since it also makes allusion to the Sinai theophany (e.g., cf. "the mountains quaked" in 5:25).[31]

25. Theodotion's version of the LXX reads the Hebrew here as *hē glōssa autou hōs pyr esthion* ("his tongue like a consuming fire"), but the eclectic LXX (Rahlfs edition) omits "tongue" and reads "and the anger of his wrath will devour as fire," which interprets the Hebrew of God's "tongue" as "the anger of his wrath."

26. Deuteronomy 26:15; Pss. 18:6–13; 102:19; Isa. 57:15–16 LXX; 63:15; 64:1; Jer. 25:30; Mic. 1:2–3; cf., implicitly, Pss. 80:1, 14; 92:8; 97:9; 113:4–6; 123:1.

27. Niehaus, *God at Sinai*, 307–8.

28. Isaiah 2:3: "Come, let us go up to the mountain of the LORD, to the house of the God of Jacob"; cf. 2:2: "the mountain of the house of the LORD"; see similarly 11:9; 27:13; 56:7; 57:7, 13; 65:11.

29. The Hebrew text has "tongue of fire," and the LXX versions of Theodotion, Aquila, and Symmachus have the Greek equivalent (*glōssa pyros*).

30. In addition to the common image of a "tongue of fire," note also the partly identical language of "burning anger" (Isa. 5:25; 30:27).

31. For the allusion to Sinai, see Niehaus, *God at Sinai*, 308. The directly following heavenly temple scene in Isa. 6 involves fiery images of God's presence resulting both in blessing (v. 6) and in judgment (v. 13). Strikingly, *Tg. Isa.* 6:6 interprets the Hebrew text's "burning coal in his [the angel's] hand" as "in his mouth there was a speech," and the burning coal touching Isaiah's mouth in 6:7 of the Hebrew is interpreted as "the words of my prophecy in your mouth." This could point further to Isa. 5:24–25 being associated with a divine judgment coming from the heavenly temple.

The "tongue like a consuming fire" in both Isaiah texts connotes God's judgment and could be different from the same image in Acts 2 ("tongues as of fire" [glōssai hōsei pyros]), since there it appears to be a sign only of blessing. However, that the same flaming image even in Acts may also allude to both blessing and judgment is apparent from the Sinai backdrop, where the fiery theophany was associated with both blessing (the giving of the law) and judgment (for those entering too close to the theophany or rebelling [cf. Exod. 19:12–24; 32:25–29]).[32] We will see below that the background of the Joel 2 quotation in Acts 2 confirms a dual blessing/cursing theme. Consequently, Isaiah's linking of "tongues of fire," "Spirit," and "word" to God's descending theophanic presence from a heavenly temple (esp. Isa. 30), all against a Sinai background, has striking affinities to Acts 2 and points further to the same links in Acts 2.

"Tongues of Fire" and Comparable Depictions in Judaism as a Theophany from a Heavenly Sanctuary

Some early Jewish writings possibly show some awareness of or are inspired by the OT image of "tongues of fire" associated with a divine theophany in a heavenly or earthly temple. The phrase "tongues of fire" also occurs in these Jewish passages. Perhaps these Jewish references provide parallels to the "tongues as of fire" in Acts 2:3, which helps us to better understand what the imagery is about.

One astonishing parallel to the fiery tongues in Acts 2:3 is 1 En. 14:8–25, where the phrase "tongues of fire" occurs. In this passage, Enoch ascends in a vision to the heavenly temple, apparently the reflection of or model for Israel's earthly tripartite temple. Enoch comes to the wall of the outer court that was "surrounded by tongues of fire," and he "entered into the tongues of fire" (14:9–10). He then enters through the holy place and is able to peer into the holy of holies, which was "built with tongues of fire" (14:15).[33] Likewise, in 1 En. 71:5 Enoch sees a temple-like "structure built of crystals; and between those crystals tongues of living fire."

Thus, the "tongues of fire" in 1 En. 14 and 71 form part of the heavenly temple and contribute to the overall effect of the burning theophany in the holy of holies, where "the flaming fire was around about him [God], and a great fire stood before him" (14:22). In the "structure built of crystals" (71:5) the saints, together with the "Son of Man" (71:17), will have "their dwelling places" (71:16), a plural reference found elsewhere for angels "dwelling" in

32. In this respect, Philo (QE 2.28) comments explicitly that "the tongues of fire burn" those coming too close to the Sinai theophany but "kindle . . . with vitality" those who obediently maintain the appropriate distance (following the translation in Marcus, Philo, Supplement II, 69).

33. The Greek glōssais pyros ("tongues of fire") from 1 En. 14:9, 15 (as well as the almost identical 14:10) is virtually the same as glōssai hōsei pyros ("tongues as of fire") in Acts 2:3.

smaller "temples" within the larger heavenly temple (*Apoc. Zeph.* A) and typically used of the OT temple on earth (with its multiple sacred precincts and
sections).[34] Furthermore, when Enoch ascended into the heavenly sanctuary
in *1 En.* 71, he "cried with a great voice by the Spirit[35] of the power, blessing,
glorifying, and extolling" (v. 11), which again places the work of the Spirit in
the context of the heavenly temple constructed of "tongues of fire."

What could such a heavenly scene have to do with the earthly scene of
Pentecost depicted in Acts 2? On the one hand, it is possible that the wording
"tongues of fire" in *1 Enoch* is a mere coincidental parallel to Acts 2. On the
other hand, the contextual usage of the wording there may have some overlap
with the use of the same phrase in Acts 2. The *1 Enoch* passages perhaps are
creative developments of the aforementioned Exodus Sinai references or of
the texts from Isa. 5 and 30, as well as especially of Ezek. 1, which themselves
are developments of imagery from the Sinai theophany. For example, in *1 En.*
14:18 the "lofty throne—its appearance . . . like crystal and its wheels like the
shining sun; and [I heard?] the voice of the cherubim" clearly is a condensed
version of Ezek. 1:21–26.[36] Similarly, commentators have recognized that
1 En. 71:1–17 has been woven throughout with OT references from Ezek. 1
and Dan. 7, as well as the earlier vision of *1 En.* 14:8–15:2.[37]

In the light of these *1 Enoch* texts, could it be that the descent of the Holy
Spirit at Pentecost "from heaven" in the form of "tongues of fire" is to be conceived of as the beginning descent of God's temple from heaven in the form of
his tabernacling presence? It is unlikely that Acts 2 depends on *1 En.* 14, but
both passages probably are interpreting the Isa. 5 and 30 passages similarly
and thus showing that "tongues of fire" were considered to be a description of
God's presence in the heavenly temple. Since the heavenly temple is pictured
in the *1 Enoch* texts as being partly constructed by "tongues of fire," it might
be appropriate that the descent of that temple in Acts be pictured with the
same imagery. Thus, it may be perceivable that just as the heavenly temple was
composed of "tongues of fire," within which God's Spirit was active, the new
temple on earth (God's people vivified by the Spirit) that had descended from

---

34. E.g., with regard to the tabernacle, cf. Lev. 21:23; and with reference to the temple, cf.
Pss. 43:3; 46:4; 84:1–4; 132:5, 7; Ezek. 7:24; Jer. 51:51.

35. Most translations refer to "spirit" apparently as Enoch's human spirit, but "the spirit
of power" would be a bit strange in this respect, especially since the divine "Spirit" has been
used for the first time in the Similitudes in 67:10 ("Spirit of the Lord"), followed by 68:2 ("the
power of the Spirit") and 70:2 ("chariots of the Spirit") (though the uses in 49:3 and 61:11 may
also well refer to the "Spirit," since they are allusions to Isa. 11:2), the use in 71:11 being almost
identical to the divine reference in 68:2.

36. Other OT passages probably alluded to are Dan. 7:9–10 (in *1 En.* 14:19–20); Isa. 6:1 (in
1 En. 14:18a).

37. On which, see G. K. Beale, *The Use of Daniel in Jewish Apocalyptic Literature and in
the Revelation of St. John* (Lanham, MD: University Press of America, 1984), 109–11, and
sources cited therein.

heaven was depicted as beginning to be built with the same fiery image. This suggestion may gain force when seen in the light of the other observations throughout this section, which point from different angles to Pentecost as a phenomenon expressing the divine theophanic presence in the temple, often against the backdrop of the Sinai theophany.

In addition, the DSS interpret the high priest's Urim and Thummim to have shone gloriously with "tongues of fire" (1Q29 frg. 1, 3; frg. 2, 3). The Urim and Thummim were two stones placed in a pouch in the high priest's breastplate (Exod. 28:30; Lev. 8:8). He was to carry them "when he enters the holy place . . . before the LORD continually" (Exod. 28:29–30). These stones were likely one of the means by which God's prophetic revelation came. Apparently, they were cast by the priest or drawn out of the pouch ceremonially, and the way they came out revealed a yes-or-no answer to the question at hand. Qumran (1Q29; 4Q376) understands the Urim and Thummim to have shone with "tongues of fire" when God gave the prophetic answer in the midst of his theophanic cloud to the high priest's question about whether a prophet was true or false.[38] In a similar vein, Jewish tradition referred to the Urim and Thummin as "the Lights" (*Pesiq. Rab.* Piska 8; cf. *Tg. Ps.-J.* Exod. 28:30).

Therefore, once more we have the "tongues of fire" as a phenomenon occurring within the "holy of holies" or, more probably, the "holy place" of the temple as an expression of God's revelatory presence.[39] This time, however, it is the earthly and not the heavenly temple that is the focus, though it should be remembered that the holy of holies was viewed as the extension to earth of God's presence in the heavenly temple.[40] Even more striking is that the "tongues" in the Qumran text are an occurrence not merely of God's revelatory presence but of his prophetic communication.[41]

This is, of course, what happens at Pentecost: not only are the "tongues as of fire" a manifestation of God's presence in the Spirit, but that presence also causes the people to "prophesy" (as Acts 2:17–18 later makes clear). And the location from which God's Spirit descends at Pentecost appears to be not only generally "from heaven" but from the heavenly holy of holies or temple,

---

38. It is possible that in mind here are not the Urim and Thummim but rather the two stones on either shoulder of the high priest.

39. Some believe that the square pouch containing the Urim and Thummim symbolized the square shape of the holy of holies (on which, see Beale, *Temple*, 39–41).

40. Recall that the ark of the covenant was referred to as the "footstool" of God, who was viewed as sitting on his heavenly throne (see 1 Chron. 28:2; Pss. 99:5; 132:7–8; Lam. 2:1; cf. Isa. 66:1). *Leviticus Rabbah* 21.12 likewise affirms that "when the Holy Spirit rested upon Phineas [the priest], his face flamed like torches about him," and this is explained by Mal. 2:7: "For the lips of a priest should keep knowledge . . . ; for he is the angel of the LORD of hosts." Thus, strikingly, the priest's exposition of the law expressed through his "lips" is compared to a "flame like torches." Note similarly *2 En.* [J] 1:5: "from their [angels *from the heavenly temple?*] mouths fire was coming forth" (likewise *2 En.* [A] 1:5).

particularly when seen in light of the descriptions in the OT Sinai theophany, Isa. 5 and 30, and the later developments of these images in *1 En.* 14 and 71 and in Qumran. Acts 2 appears to be developing these OT images in the same way as *1 Enoch* and Qumran.

Thus, all these passages together collectively contribute from various vantage points to a picture in Acts 2 that resembles something very like God's fiery theophanic presence as a new heavenly temple extending from heaven and descending on his people and making them a part of it.[42]

Pentecost as a Fulfillment of Joel's Prophecy of the Spirit

Peter explains the theophanic episode of tongues in Acts 2:1–12 to be an initial fulfillment of Joel's prophecy that God would "pour out" his "Spirit upon all flesh," and that all classes of people in the covenant community would "prophesy" (Joel 2:28–29). At the beginning of the Joel 2:28 quotation, Peter substitutes the phrase "in the latter days" (*en tais eschatais hēmerais*) in place of Joel's "after these things" (*meta tauta*). The substitution comes from Isa. 2:2 (the only place in the LXX where this precise phrase occurs):[43] "In the last days [*en tais eschatais hēmerais*] the mountain of the house of the LORD will be established as the chief of the mountains, and will be raised above the hills; and all the nations will stream to it." Thus, Peter appears to interpret the Spirit's coming in fulfillment of Joel to be also the beginning fulfillment of Isaiah's prophecy of the end-time mountain temple, under the influence of which the nations would come.

In the Mosaic era, only prophets, priests, and kings were bestowed with the gifting function of the Spirit to serve, often in the temple (e.g., priests) or sometimes in conjunction with the temple (i.e., kings and prophets). Joel and Acts have in mind not primarily the regenerating function of the Spirit but rather the function that would enable people to serve in various capacities. Joel foresaw a time, however, when everyone in Israel would be given this gift. That Joel 2 and Acts 2 may have in mind gifting for service in connection in some way with the new temple is apparent in that Joel's prophecy develops the earlier text of Num. 11.[44]

In Num. 11 Moses desires that God give him help to bear the burden of the people whom he was leading (vv. 11, 17 [cf. Exod. 18:13–27]). God responds by telling Moses to gather "seventy men from the elders" and "bring them

---

42. For commentators who have seen the relevance of Isa. 5; 30; *1 En.* 14; 71; 1Q29 for Acts 2, though no relation to the heavenly temple, see Beale, "Eschatological Temple: Part I," 91n49.

43. On which, see David W. Pao, *Acts and the Isaianic New Exodus*, WUNT 2/130 (Tübingen: Mohr Siebeck, 2000), 156–59.

44. On Joel's development of Num. 11:1–12:8, see Raymond B. Dillard, "Intrabiblical Exegesis and the Effusion of the Spirit in Joel," in *Creator, Redeemer, Consummator: A Festschrift for Meredith G. Kline*, ed. Howard Griffith and John R. Muether (Greenville, SC: Reformed Academic Press, 2000), 87–93.

to <u>the tent of meeting</u>, and let them take their stand there with you. Then I will come down and . . . will take of the Spirit who is upon you, and will put Him upon them" (vv. 16–17). Moses obeys God: "He gathered seventy men of the elders . . . and stationed them <u>around the tent</u>. Then the LORD came down in the cloud . . . and took of the Spirit who was upon him [Moses] and placed Him upon the seventy elders. And when the Spirit rested upon them, they prophesied" (vv. 24–25). They then stopped prophesying, but two elders at another location continued to prophesy. When Joshua hears about this, he asks Moses to stop them. Moses declines, replying, "Would that all the LORD's people were prophets, that the LORD would put His Spirit upon them" (vv. 26–29).

Accordingly, Joel 2 transforms Moses's prophetic wish into a formal prophecy. Peter quotes Joel's prophecy to show that in his day it was finally beginning fulfillment in Pentecost. The Spirit's gifting, formerly limited to leaders helping Moses and imparted to them at the tabernacle, is universalized to all of God's people from every race, young and old, male and female. That the Spirit's gifting in Acts 2 was connected in some way to the temple is apparent from Num. 11, which notes twice that the "seventy elders" received the Spirit as they were gathered around the "tent" (i.e., the tabernacle). In fact, that in Acts 2 "tongues as of fire . . . rested [lit., 'sat'] on each one" and "they were all filled with the Holy Spirit and began to speak with other tongues" (vv. 3–4 [explained to be "prophesying" in vv. 17–18]) appears to be a specific allusion to Num. 11:25: "When the Spirit rested upon them, they prophesied."[45]

Interestingly, later Judaism compares the Num. 11 text about the Spirit from Moses resting on the elders "to a candle that was burning and at which many candles were kindled."[46] Furthermore, Num. 11:25 says that God "took of the Spirit who was upon him [Moses] and placed Him upon the seventy elders." Likewise, Acts 2:33 refers to Jesus as first "having received from the Father the promise of the Holy Spirit" and then having "poured forth" the Spirit upon those at Pentecost.[47] In this respect, Jesus may be a second Moses figure.

45. See similarly Num. 11:29, which NA[27] cites as an allusion for Acts 2:18b ("I will in those days pour forth of My Spirit and they shall prophesy"). Together with Num. 11:25, Acts 2:3b–4a also may allude to Num. 11:26, where the "Spirit rested upon" some of the elders "and they prophesied" (see also Num. 11:17, 29; similarly, NA[27] proposes that Acts 2:3 alludes to Num. 11:25). There is some evidence in the textual tradition of Num. 11:26, 29 for the reading of "Holy Spirit" in line with the same phrase in Acts 2:4 (see John W. Wevers, ed., *Numeri*, vol. 3.1 of *Septuaginta* [Göttingen: Vandenhoeck & Ruprecht, 1982], 167–68). Likewise, *Tg. Neof.* Num. 11:17, 25–26 reads "Holy Spirit."

46. *Numbers Rabbah* 15.19; so also *Num. Rab.* 13.20; likewise Philo (*Gig.* 24–25), who says the Spirit from Moses in the same Numbers passage was comparable to a "fire" that "kindle[s] a thousand torches."

47. See I. Howard Marshall, "Acts," in *Commentary on the New Testament Use of the Old Testament*, ed. G. K. Beale and D. A. Carson (Grand Rapids: Baker Academic, 2007), 531.

Even the prophesying of the "seventy" in Num. 11 may have links with the people prophesying in Acts 2. We saw above that the Sinai theophany tradition in Judaism is related to the seventy nations dispersed at Babel, and I have noted elsewhere that some commentators see the list of nations represented at Pentecost (Acts 2:9–11) to be an abbreviated allusion to the seventy nations of the earth in Gen. 10.[48] The "seventy" in Num. 11 may also have some such connection. It may even be apparent that the Acts narrative is a further development of Luke's earlier narration of Jesus's sending of the "seventy" select Israelites to symbolize a beginning witness to the "seventy" nations of the world (Luke 10:1–12).[49] Thus, the links between the seventy nations represented in Acts 2 and the "seventy" of Num. 11 may not be coincidental. Judaism also combined the Num. 11 text with Joel 3:1 (2:28 ET) to speak about the blessings "in the world-to-come" (*Midr. Ps.* 14.6; *Num. Rab.* 15.25).

One final observation about Joel is relevant for the temple theme in Acts 2. The expression "the sun and moon grow dark" in Joel 2:10 occurs again in Joel 3:15a and likewise probably refers to the same reality as in Joel 2:31: "the sun will be turned into darkness and the moon into blood." In Joel 3:16–18 the appearance of God comes from "Zion" and is in the "holy mountain" and is inextricably linked to "the house of the LORD."[50] Joel 3 clarifies what Joel 2 may already have implied twice about the origin of revelatory cosmic destruction, since in 3:17 it also occurs in connection with "Zion My holy mountain."[51] The emphasis on God's "tabernacling" presence in the temple at the end of Joel 3 is also expressed through the twice-repeated phrase "Yahweh tabernacles [*šōkēn*] in Zion" (3:17, 21). Again, we have one more indication that theophanic revelation connected with Joel 2:30–31 comes from or appears in the end-time temple, suggesting further that the theophany in Acts 2 also comes from the heavenly sanctuary.

A study by Craig Evans suggests that the sanctuary from the last chapter of Joel may be within the peripheral vision of Luke (or Peter).[52] In this respect, he has argued that the entire context of the book of Joel (including the last chapter) appears to be in Luke's peripheral vision: in addition to the quotation of Joel 2 in Acts 2:17–21, other allusions and echoes from throughout Joel can be detected throughout Acts 2:1–40 (though Evans does not specifically mention the sanctuary reference from Joel).

Marshall argues that Num. 11:25, 29 was a "model" for Luke's description of "the descent of the Spirit on the people and their consequent speech."

48. See Beale, "Eschatological Temple: Part I," 86.

49. Following James M. Scott, *Paul and the Nations: The Old Testament and Jewish Background of Paul's Mission to the Nations with Special Reference to the Destination of Galatians*, WUNT 84 (Tübingen: Mohr Siebeck, 1995), 162–63.

50. The Targum here (= Joel 4:16–18) reads "sanctuary of the Lord."

51. Cf. Joel 2:1 ("Zion . . . My holy mountain") and 2:2–11; likewise 2:31 and 2:32 ("Mount Zion").

52. Craig A. Evans, "The Prophetic Setting of the Pentecost Sermon," *ZNW* 74 (1983): 148–50.

Other Well-Recognized Old Testament Allusions in Acts 2 and Their Connection to the Temple

Apart from the above evidence adduced so far in this chapter, it is important to comment on the other usually well-recognized OT quotations and allusions throughout Acts 2:1–40, which thus far I have not discussed. The purpose of commenting on these other well-known references is to assess how they may or may not relate to the temple theme that I have traced in the preceding part of this chapter. These references are

1. 1 Kings 8:6–13 // 2 Chron. 7:1–3 in Acts 2:2–3
2. Ps. 132:11 in Acts 2:30
3. Ps. 68:18 (67:19 LXX; 68:18 MT) in Acts 2:33–34
4. Ps. 118:16 (117:16 LXX) in Acts 2:32–33a
5. Ps. 110:1 (109:1 LXX) in Acts 2:34–35
6. Ps. 20:6a (in Acts 2:36)
7. Isa. 57:19 in Acts 2:39
8. Joel 2:32 (3:5 LXX) in Acts 2:21, 39

At the end of this chapter (in excursus 2) these allusions, of which there are at least eight, will be summarized and included in a survey of the entire evidence of this chapter. We will see that the majority of these OT allusions are directly linked in their original contexts to either the earthly, the heavenly, or the eschatological temple (though Ps. 110:1 is linked only to priesthood). Consequently, part of the OT contextual meaning of these references is bound up with the notion of the temple. Is it coincidental that Luke, almost without exception, refers to these other OT references that are integrally bound up with a larger narrative framework focusing on the temple? Why would he do this? I think that the best explanation is that he was depicting the descent of the end-time temple at points throughout Acts 2, the strongest evidence of which has been laid out in the substance of this chapter so far.

Conclusion

I have argued from various angles that Acts 2 portrays the descent of the heavenly end-time temple of God's presence upon his people on earth. They are included in and constructed to be part of God's temple, not with physical building materials, but by being included in the descending presence of his tabernacling Spirit. The lines of evidence adduced in favor of this thesis have only indirectly and implicitly supported it. The design of this chapter has been to adduce a number of lines of argumentation, some stronger than others, that form a cumulative argument that points to the plausibility, I think probability, of the presence of a temple portrayal in Acts 2:1–40. In one way or another, most of the OT allusions and background ideas in Acts 2, together with traces of Jewish tradition, are inextricably linked to notions or portrayals of the temple in their respective contexts. Much of this evidence is implicit, but there is more explicit influence that has been discussed.[53]

The Gospels note to some degree that Jesus began to lay the foundation for the new temple, and other NT books refer to the church as the continuation of the end-time temple in identification with him. Nowhere, however, does the NT give an obvious and straightforward account of the critical moment when the church was established as the temple. Matthew, Mark, and John note the replacement of the temple by Christ. However, Luke, who in his first volume expressed much interest in the temple, including prophecy of its destruction, never narrates who or what will replace the temple. This section has attempted to propose that although Acts 2 has no explicit words mentioning a "temple" or "sanctuary," Luke portrays there conceptually and indirectly, through his cumulative use of OT texts, the decisive time when God first began to build his people into his eschatological temple of the Holy Spirit.

This is a similar conclusion to that reached by I. Howard Marshall about Acts 7: "In the light of the undeveloped typology that we have already observed in this speech, it seems to me very probable that Stephen envisaged its [Israel's second temple] replacement by the new house of God composed of his people."[54] Richard Bauckham has also persuasively argued that the quotation of Amos 9:11–12 in Acts 15 is further evidence of the inaugurated end-time temple.[55] Thus, here I have contended that the decisive establishment of the church as the eschatological temple was introduced by Luke in Acts 2, further developments of which Luke draws out in Acts 7 and 15, though the space limits of this chapter prevent me from adducing additional evidence in support of Marshall's and Bauckham's conclusions for Acts 7 and 15.[56]

Zechariah 4 (in comparison with 6:12–13) and Hag. 2:5–10 assert that God's Spirit will be the energizing force in constructing the eschatological temple,[57] the latter text saying in the LXX that "the choice portions of all the nations

---

53. E.g., the use of 1 Kings 8:6–13 // 2 Chron. 7:1–3 in Acts 2:2–3; the "tongues as of fire" in Acts 2 is probably an allusion to Isa. 30; 1 En. 14; 71 (perhaps together with Isa. 5 and the Qumran references to "tongues of fire"); the use of 1 Kings 8:6–13 and 2 Chron. 7:1–3 in Acts 2:2–3 about the temple is also explicit (on which see the excursus on Old Testament Allusions at the end of this chapter).

54. Marshall, "Acts," 571.

55. Richard Bauckham, "James and the Jerusalem Church," in *The Book of Acts in Its Palestinian Setting*, ed. Richard Bauckham, vol. 4 of *The Book of Acts in Its First Century Setting*, ed. Bruce W. Winter (Grand Rapids: Eerdmans, 1995), 452–62.

56. For more in-depth discussion, see Beale, *Temple*, 216–44.

57. Precisely, these two passages refer to the temple to be established after the end-time restoration from captivity, which from one perspective could have been the second temple, but since that temple never met the conditions prophesied, the prophecies of Zechariah and Haggai would still await eschatological fulfillment.

will come" in conjunction with the building effort. Although these passages are not referred to in Acts 2, this second chapter of Luke's second volume seems to be the most suitable NT text for seeing these two OT prophecies as beginning conceptual fulfillment.[58]

Luke's rhetorical goal for readers would be for them to realize that they are a part of the end-time temple and that their evangelistic efforts are crucial in the further building and expansion of that temple. It should be recalled that it was Jesus's resurrection as a new creation and enthronement as king that launched his sending of the Spirit to commence the establishment of his people as the end-time temple. The idea of the temple, therefore, is an important facet of the diamond of the "already–not yet, end-time, new-creational kingdom."

Excursus 1   Sinai as a Temple

At the beginning of this chapter I referred to Sinai as a mountain temple, and here I lay out the evidence for this idea.

First, Sinai is called "the mountain of God" (Exod. 3:1; 18:5; 24:13), a name associated with Israel's temple on Mount Zion.[59]

Second, just as with the tabernacle and temple, Mount Sinai was divided into three sections of increasing sanctity: the majority of the Israelites were to remain at the foot of Sinai (Exod. 19:12, 23), the priests and seventy elders (the latter functioning probably as priests) were allowed to come some distance up the mountain (Exod. 19:22; 24:1), but only Moses could ascend to the top and directly experience the presence of God (Exod. 24:2). In this respect, God told Moses to "set bounds about the mountain and consecrate it" (Exod. 19:23), since if anyone except the seventy elders, Aaron, or Moses "touched" the mountain, he or she would "be put to death" (Exod. 19:12). This is language uniquely reserved elsewhere for the tabernacle:[60] "And when Aaron and his sons have finished covering the holy objects and all the furnishings of the sanctuary, when the camp is to set out, after that the sons of Kohath shall come to carry them, so that they may not touch the holy objects and die. These are the things in the tent of meeting which the sons of Kohath are to carry" (Num. 4:15).[61] So holy was the entire apparatus of the tabernacle that even if "regular priests" directly handled any part of it, they would die.

58. Perhaps Mal. 3:1–3 also could be included.

59. E.g., note "mountain of the LORD" as a virtual synonym for "house of God" in Isa. 2:2–3; Mic. 4:2.

60. A thought inspired by Otto Betz, "The Eschatological Interpretation of the Sinai-Tradition in Qumran and in the New Testament," *RevQ* 6 (1967): 94–95, 106.

61. See also Lev. 7:20–21; 22:1–9; for a positive version of Num. 4:15, see Exod. 30:29: "You shall consecrate them [the tabernacle and its contents]; whatever touches them shall be holy" (for the consecration of these cultic objects, see also Exod. 29:36–37, 44; 40:9–10; Lev. 8:11; 16:19).

Third, just as an altar was in the outermost section of the temple, so an altar was built at the lowest and least sacred part of Sinai. Furthermore, at this altar Israel "offered burnt offerings and sacrificed young bulls as peace offerings to the LORD. And Moses took half the blood and . . . sprinkled [it] on the altar" (Exod. 24:5–6). This is language of "sacrifice" often found elsewhere almost always in connection with the tabernacle or temple.[62]

Fourth, not only does the top part of Sinai approximate the holy of holies because only Israel's temporary "high priest," Moses, could enter there, but also it was the place where God's theophanic "cloud" and presence "dwelt" (Exod. 24:15–17).[63] Significantly, the only other times in all of the OT that God's presence is spoken of as a "cloud dwelling" is with respect to God's presence above the tabernacle (Exod. 40:35; Num. 9:17–18, 22; 10:12). Even the verb "to dwell" (*šākan*) could be rendered "to tabernacle," and the word "tabernacle" (*miškān*) is the noun form of this verb (which is used with the verb in three of the four preceding texts). So also, 1 Kings 8:12–13 says that God "would dwell in the thick cloud" in the temple completed by Solomon. Furthermore, the two "tablets of stone" containing the Ten Commandments and the "ark of wood" in which they were placed were created at the top of Sinai (Deut. 10:1–5), just as later they found their place in the inner sanctum of the temple, once again in God's presence.

Fifth, earlier in Exodus God's presence at Sinai was depicted as a "cassia tree [*sēneh*] [or 'bush'] burning with fire, yet the cassia tree was not consumed" (Exod. 3:2). In light of the parallels already adduced, this unconsumed burning tree may be the proleptic equivalent to the lampstand-like tree in the holy place on Mount Zion, whose lamps burned continually.[64] Correspondingly, the ground around the burning tree is called "the place" of "holy ground" (Exod. 3:5). The correspondence of this small area at Sinai with the later "holy place" is seen from the only other uses of "holy place" in Hebrew, four of which refer to the section of the sanctuary directly outside the "holy of holies" (Lev. 7:6; 10:17; 14:13; 24:9), and the remaining two refer to the temple in general (Ezra 9:8; Ps. 24:3).

In light of the association of Sinai as a temple, it may not be accidental that Rev. 11:19 later alludes to the theophanic phenomena at Sinai in describing the opening of the heavenly holy of holies at the end of history, when "the ark of his covenant" will be revealed ("there were flashes of lightning and sounds and peals of thunder"). The earliest (160 BC) and clearest example of Judaism's identification of Sinai as a sanctuary is *Jub.* 8:19: "And he [Noah] knew that the Garden of Eden was the holy of holies and the dwelling of the Lord. And Mount Sinai (was) in the midst of the desert and Mount Zion (was) in the

---

62. Wherever the expressions "burnt offerings" and "peace offerings" (about 50x, almost always in this order) occur together (outside Exod. 20; 24), sometimes in combination with "altar" (or otherwise the "altar" is implied), either the tabernacle or the temple is the typical location.

63. For Moses as a "high priest," see Philo, *Mos.* 2.75.

64. Gordon Hugenberger mentioned this idea to me in a private communication in the spring of 1999. I have also found this view proposed by Tremper Longman III, *Immanuel in Our Place: Seeing Christ in Israel's Worship* (Phillipsburg, NJ: P&R, 2001), 57.

midst of the navel of the earth. The three of these were created as *holy places*, one facing the other" (my italics).

Indeed, others have observed that the building of the tabernacle itself appears to have been modeled on the tripartite pattern of Sinai.[65]

Excursus 2 Overview of Old Testament Allusions and Associated Jewish Background in Acts 2 Discussed in This Chapter, Which Are Directly Set in or Related to a Temple Context

Old Testament (or Judaism)	Acts
(1) The tower of Babel, an idolatrous temple, and judgment of tongues leading to confusion (Gen. 11:1–9).	Reversal of Babel at the Jerusalem temple by creating tongues leading to a unified understanding (Acts 2:3–8, 11).
(2) Division of humanity into seventy nations/tongues from the idolatrous temple of Babel (Gen. 10–11).	The beginning unification of humanity at the Jerusalem temple, with an abbreviated allusion to the seventy nations from Gen. 10–11 (Acts 2:9–11).
(3) God's revelation to Israel at Sinai and portrayal of God's descending presence there, sanctifying it as a sanctuary through storm-like fire and his fiery revelatory voice (Exod. 19–20) (described by Philo as a "voice" being like a "flame" that "became a dialect"; later Judaism viewed God's fiery voice as being divided into seventy tongues for the nations).	By using many of the same words and phrases describing the Sinai theophany, Luke depicts God's revelation to believers at Pentecost and the portrayal of God's descending presence there in the Spirit, establishing a new community (i.e., spiritual sanctuary) composed of his people, through storm-like fire and his revelatory voice like "tongues as of fire" (Acts 2:1–6).
(4) Related to the preceding point, the ascent of Moses to the Sinai sanctuary directly preceded the giving of the law at Sinai.	The ascension of Jesus to heaven (and its sanctuary?) directly preceded the revelation at Pentecost (Acts 2:33–35).
(5) The phrase "tongues as of fire" occurs in the following OT and early Jewish texts to describe a theophanic appearance or revelation either coming from or being in the heavenly or earthly temple: Isa. 5:24–25; 30:27–30, 1 En. 14:8–25; 71:1–17; 1Q29. Sometimes it is a theophany of blessing or of judgment, appearing to people in heaven or on earth.	The descent of the Holy Spirit at Pentecost "from heaven" in the form of "tongues as of fire" is to be conceived as the descent of God's tabernacling presence (from his heavenly temple?), so that the heavenly realm (temple?) extends to include saints on earth.

65. After writing the rough draft of this section, I have found the following scholars among those who have argued this on the basis of many of the same observations made above: Nahum M. Sarna, *Exodus*, JPSTC (Philadelphia: Jewish Publication Society, 1991), 105; Mary Douglas, *Leviticus as Literature* (Oxford: Oxford University Press, 1999), 59–64; Peter Enns, *Exodus*, NIVAC (Grand Rapids: Zondervan, 2000), 391, following Sarna.

Old Testament (or Judaism)	Acts
(6) Prophecy of the Spirit in Joel 2:28–32 (3:1–5 MT), which alludes to Sinai theophany imagery and has partial parallel in Joel 3:15–17, which concludes with an explicit prophecy of the end-time temple (3:18).	Joel 2:28–32 is quoted in Acts 2:17–21.
(7) "In the last days the mountain of the house of the LORD will be established as the chief of the mountains . . . ; and all the nations will stream to it" (Isa. 2:2:).	Peter substitutes the Isa. 2:2 language of "in the last days" for Joel's "after this" in order to interpret Joel 2 not merely as an eschatological promise but as one about the latter-day temple to which all nations (represented at Pentecost) would eventually stream (Acts 2:17).
(8) The "seventy elders" received the Spirit as they were gathered around the "tent" (i.e., the tabernacle); in particular, "When the Spirit rested upon them, they prophesied. . . . [Moses said,] 'Would that all the LORD's people were prophets, that the LORD would put his Spirit upon them'" (Num. 11:25, 29). Early and later Judaism compared the Spirit of prophecy on Moses and the elders to a fire that kindled other fires.	"Tongues as of fire . . . rested [lit., 'sat'] on each one" (representatives from the "seventy nations"), and "they were all filled with the Holy Spirit and began to speak with other tongues" (Acts 2:3–4 [explained to be "prophesying" in 2:17–18]). The validity of the Num. 11 allusion is enhanced by the fact that Joel 2:28 itself alludes to the same Numbers text. In addition, the narrative in Num. 11 alludes to the experience of the seventy elders at the Sinai theophany (Exod. 24), which should not be surprising, since the Sinai theophany is also developed in Joel 2 and Acts 2.
(9) At the tabernacle, God "took of the Spirit who was upon him [Moses] and placed Him upon the seventy elders" (Num. 11:25).	Jesus first "having received from the Father the promise of the Holy Spirit," then "poured forth" the Spirit upon those at Pentecost (Acts 2:33).

The Significance of Other Old Testament Allusions in Acts 2, Not Explained in This Chapter, Which Are Directly Set in a Temple Context

(10) When Moses finished constructing the tabernacle, "the cloud covered the tent of meeting, and the glory of the LORD filled the tabernacle" (Exod. 40:34–35); when Solomon finished building his temple, "the cloud filled the house of the LORD . . . [and] the glory of the LORD filled the house of the LORD," in addition to fire descending (1 Kings 8:6–13; 2 Chron. 7:1–3). This is followed by praise from the onlookers.	In narrating an inauguration of a new heavenly temple on earth, Acts 2:2–3 appears to include the Exod. 40 and 1 Kings texts in its quarry of OT allusions: "There came from heaven a noise like a violent rushing wind, and it filled the whole house. . . . And there appeared to them tongues of fire distributing themselves." This is followed by praise from the onlookers.
(11) "Pangs of death" set in direct connection with deliverance coming from the heavenly temple (Ps. 18:4–6 [17:5–7 LXX]; so also 2 Sam. 22:6).	"Pangs of death" (Acts 2:24).

(12) "The LORD has sworn to David . . . : 'Of the fruit of your body I will set on your throne'" (Ps. 132:11). This continues the earlier line of thought: "Let us go into His dwelling place; let us worship at His footstool. Arise, O LORD, to your resting place, You and the ark of Your strength. Let Your priests be clothed with righteousness, and let Your godly ones sing for joy" (132:7–9); and in 132:14 God says, "This is My resting place forever; here I will dwell, for I have desired it." Cf. 2 Sam. 7:12–13 to which Ps. 132:11 alludes: "I will raise up your seed after you, who will come forth from your bowels, and I will establish his kingdom. He shall build a house for My name, and I will establish the throne of his kingdom forever."

"And so, because he [David] was a prophet and knew that God had sworn to him with an oath to seat of the fruit of his loins upon his throne . . ." (Acts 2:30).

(13) "Having ascended unto the height, . . . you received gifts" (Ps. 68:18 [67:19 LXX; 68:19 MT]).

Targum Ps. 68:19: "You ascended . . . , you gave gifts to the sons of men."

The conclusion of Ps. 68:18 ("that the LORD God may tabernacle there") locates the verse in a sanctuary context, since the preceding verse supports a Sinai/sanctuary location: "The chariots of God are myriads, thousands upon thousands; the LORD is among them at Sinai in the sanctuary" (68:17 [my translation]), where "the LORD will tabernacle forever" (68:16c)

"[Jesus] having been exalted . . . , having received . . . the promise [v. 38: "gift"] of the Holy Spirit. . . . For it was not David [but Jesus] who ascended into the heavens" (Acts 2:33–34).
Christ "poured forth" (= "gave") the gift of the Spirit (Acts 2:33b).

(14) "The right hand of the Lord has raised me up" (Ps. 117:16 LXX [118:16 ET]).

The concluding section of the psalm (118:19–29), which shows the psalmist's vindication, is set in the context of the temple.

"This Jesus God raised up" (Acts 2:32); "Therefore [Jesus], having been exalted to the right hand of God . . ." (Acts 2:33a).

(15) "The LORD says to my Lord: 'Sit at My right hand until I make Your enemies a footstool for Your feet'" (Ps. 110:1 [109:1 LXX]).

Cf. Ps. 110:4: "The LORD has sworn . . . , 'You are a priest forever,'" which suggests a temple context in which a priest functions.

"The Lord said to my Lord, 'Sit at My right hand, until I make Your enemies a footstool for Your feet'" (Acts 2:34b–35a).

(16) "Now I know that the LORD saves His messiah" (Ps. 20:6a [19:7a LXX]) (this salvation is to come from the heavenly temple [20:1–2, 7b]).

"Therefore . . . know for certain that God has made Him both Lord and Messiah" (Acts 2:36).

(17) "Peace, peace <u>to him who is far and to him who is near</u>" (Isa. 57:19) (preceded by "I [God] dwell on a high and holy place" in 57:15).	"For the promise is for you and your children and for all who are far off" (Acts 2:39).
(18) "<u>Everyone who calls on the name of the Lord shall be saved</u>; for in Mount Zion and in Jerusalem shall the saved one be as the Lord has said, and they that have glad tidings preached to them, <u>whom the Lord has called</u>" (Joel 3:5 LXX [2:32 ET; 3:5 MT]).	"Everyone who calls on the name of the Lord will be saved" (Acts 2:21). ". . . as many as the Lord our God will call to Himself" (Acts 2:39).
Note the clarifying parallel of 2:28–32 in 3:15–18, the latter set in a temple context.	

Relationships within the New Testament

Luke 3:16 (cf. Matt. 3:11) records John the Baptist proclaiming, "I baptize in water," but that one will come after him who "will baptize you with the Holy Spirit and fire" (with allusion to the eschatological tabernacling prophecy of Isa. 4:4 and, possibly, Isa. 30:27–28a).	The coming of the Spirit in the form of "tongues as of fire" is the fulfillment of John the Baptist's prophecy (Acts 2:1–4, 17, 33), which itself includes allusion to Isa. 4:4; 30:27–30.

Note: The first comparison and the comparisons beginning with (10) in this table have not been summarized in this chapter but are discussed respectively in Beale, "Eschatological Temple: Part I," 75–76; idem, "Eschatological Temple: Part II," 77–79.

19

The Story of the Eden Sanctuary, Israel's Temple, and Christ and the Church as the Ongoing Transformed Eschatological Temple of the Spirit in the New-Creational Kingdom

In the preceding chapter I concluded that God's people began to be transformed into the eschatological temple when the Spirit descended from the heavenly temple to earth and formed people to become a part of this temple. This Spirit-formed temple was launched through Christ's resurrection, ascension, and enthronement, which immediately led him to send the Spirit to continue to build the temple. In this regard, again we see the Spirit and its work of temple-building to be directly linked to new creation through its direct connection with Christ's resurrection and kingship.

I examined some of the OT antecedents for the temple notion in Acts 2, but this chapter relates more broadly the Acts 2 incident to the temple in the OT and the NT. In the NT we see Christ as the temple, the church as a temple, and the consummate form of the temple in the eternal new creation. In essence, this chapter is an attempt to sketch a biblical theology of the temple[1] and to relate it to the main theme of this book: already–not yet eschatology,

---

1. This chapter is a minor revision of G. K. Beale, "Eden, the Temple, and the Church's Mission in the New Creation," *JETS* 48 (2005): 5–31.

particularly as this relates to Christ's resurrection as the beginning of the new-creational kingdom. We will see that the idea of the temple is almost synonymous with the new creation.

Perhaps a bit surprisingly, I begin by looking at the consummated temple in the last vision of the book of Revelation and working backward from there to the very beginning of the canon in Genesis. This last apocalyptic vision in Rev. 21:1–22:5 uses prophetic passages such as Ezek. 37:27; 40–48; Isa. 54:11–12 and also alludes back to the garden of Eden. For example, Ezek. 40–48 predicts what many would say is a literal end-time temple, and Rev. 21 alludes repeatedly to Ezek. 40–48 but does not appear to be depicting a literal architectural temple. Since many do not see Rev. 21 to be a "literal" interpretation of Ezek. 40–48, some believe that the Ezekiel prophecy is compared to and not fulfilled in the new creation. Others believe that Ezekiel is being fulfilled but in an allegorical or spiritualized manner. But is it possible that John, the writer of Revelation, is indicating that Ezekiel will be fulfilled in the new cosmos and fulfilled in a "literal" manner, so that somehow John has hermeneutical integrity in the way he uses Ezekiel? We could ask the same question about the prophecies from Ezek. 37 and Isa. 54 in relation to Rev. 21. My belief is that John neither compares the Ezekiel prophecy to the conditions of the future new creation nor allegorizes it, but he sees it to be "literally" fulfilled there.

To try to demonstrate this, I need to look at Revelation and, especially, the OT background, not merely of Ezekiel but of the temple generally in the OT. In so doing, I will try to summarize my book *The Temple and the Church's Mission*[2] and bring to bear some of its main lines of argumentation to shed light on the problem that I have posed here.[3] That earlier study proceeded from the OT and then discussed by canonical order the topic of the temple in the NT books, but the following discussion will be less discrete.

So, we begin by considering the last vision of Revelation, which presents a problem. Why does John see "a new heaven and a new earth" in Rev. 21:1 and yet in 21:2–22:5 see only a city that is garden-like and in the shape of a temple? He does not describe all the contours and details of the new creation, only an arboreal temple-city. Note that the dimensions and architectural features of the city in these verses are, to a significant extent, drawn from Ezek. 40–48, which is a prophecy of the dimensions and architectural features of a future

---

2. G. K. Beale, *The Temple and the Church's Mission: A Biblical Theology of the Dwelling Place of God*, NSBT 17 (Downers Grove, IL: InterVarsity, 2004). The precursor to the book is found in G. K. Beale, "The Final Vision of the Apocalypse and Its Implications for a Biblical Theology of the Temple," in *Heaven on Earth: The Temple in Biblical Theology*, ed. Simon J. Gathercole and T. Desmond Alexander (Carlisle, UK: Paternoster, 2004), 191–209, which is based on a lecture delivered at the annual meeting of the Biblical Theology Group of the Tyndale Fellowship of Biblical Research at Tyndale House Library, Cambridge, in July 2001.

3. Indeed, every part of the following discussion is treated in more detail in the book, which should be consulted by readers who want more substantiation of various points.

temple (so 21:2, 10–12; 21:27–22:2);[4] the precious stones forming the foundation in 21:18–21 reflect the description not only in Isa. 54:11–12 but also of Solomon's temple, which also was overlaid with gold and whose foundation was composed of precious stones: compare respectively 1 Kings 6:20–22 together with 5:17 and 7:9–10, and the dimensions given in Rev. 21:16 ("its length and width and height are equal"), which is based on the dimensions of the holy of holies in 1 Kings 6:20 (where the "length . . . width . . . and height" of the holy of holies are equal).

How can we explain the apparent discrepancy that John saw a new heaven and a new earth in 22:1 and then saw only a garden-like city in the shape and structure of a temple in the remainder of the vision? Why does John not see a full portrayal of the new heaven and earth (valleys, mountains, forests, plains, stars of the sky, etc.)? It is possible, of course, that he merely first sees the new world and then sees a city in one small part of that world, and within the city he sees features of a garden and a temple. But this is not likely the solution because he seems to equate the "new heaven and new earth" with the following description of the "city" and the "temple."

This equation is evident from the following considerations. First, it is probable that the vision of Rev. 21:2 interprets the initial vision of the new heaven and new earth, and that what John hears in verse 3 about the tabernacle is the interpretation of verses 1–2. Thus, the new heaven and new earth are interpretatively equated with the new Jerusalem and the eschatological tabernacle. This pattern of visions interpreting one another or being interpreted by a following saying, prayer, or song occurs elsewhere in the book[5] and is a feature generally of apocalyptic genre. Second, Rev. 22:14–15 says that only the righteous "enter" the city but that the unrighteous (cf. 22:11) remain perpetually "outside" the city. This does not likely depict unbelievers dwelling directly outside the city's walls but within the new creation. More probably it pictures the impious dwelling entirely outside the new creation, since no unrighteousness can exist in the conditions of the consummate new creation (see, e.g., 2 Pet. 3:13, which, like Rev. 21:1, alludes to Isa. 65:17; 66:22). This implies that the city's limits, therefore, correspond exactly to the boundaries of the new creation. Similarly, Rev. 21:27 affirms that "nothing unclean, and no one who practices abomination and lying, shall ever come into [the city]." What further confirms the city's equation with the new creation is Rev. 21:8, where the same category of unrighteous people are said to exist in "the lake that burns with fire and brimstone, which is the second death." The lake of fire and the second death, of course, cannot be in the new creation (see 21:4), so this places the same category of people in 22:15 outside the new creation,

---

4. For a fuller description and discussion of the use of Ezek. 40–48 in Rev. 21:1–22:5, see Beale, *Temple*, 346–54.

5. See G. K. Beale, *The Book of Revelation: A Commentary on the Greek Text*, NIGTC (Grand Rapids: Eerdmans, 1999), at Rev. 5:5–6, 7–13; 21:1–3.

which is also outside the new city and, as I proposed above, the new temple, since no uncleanness could enter Israel's temple.[6]

The equation of the new creation in 21:1 with the following visions of a city that is temple-shaped and garden-like seems problematic. Some might attribute the apparent oddness of equating the new cosmos to a garden-like city in the form of a temple to the irrational nature that visions and dreams can have, though this would be hard to accept for a vision that John claims has its origin in God (cf. 21:9 with 1:1; 22:6). Also, how does this vision relate to Christians and their role in fulfilling the mission of the church, which has been narrated earlier in Revelation?

To solve the problem of this strange equation of the new creation and new Jerusalem with the temple and the garden, we need to look at the purpose of the temple in the OT and how this purpose relates to the NT conception of the temple. It becomes evident in pursuing this task that the first tabernacle and temple existed long before Israel happened on the scene. Indeed, it is apparent that the first sanctuary is discernible from the very beginning of history.

The Garden of Eden Was a Temple in the First Creation

The first sanctuary was in Eden. But how could we possibly know this? There was no architectural structure in Eden, nor does the word "temple" or "sanctuary" occur as a description of Eden in Gen. 1–3. Such a claim may sound strange to the ears of many. A number of scholars recently have argued this from one angle or another.[7] The following nine observations, among others that I do not have space to mention, show that Eden was the first holy sanctuary.

First, the temple later in the OT was the unique place of God's presence, where Israel had to go to experience that presence. Israel's temple was the place where the priest experienced God's unique presence, and Eden was the place where Adam walked and talked with God. The same Hebrew verbal form (Hithpael) used for God's "walking back and forth" in the garden (Gen. 3:8) also describes God's presence in the tabernacle (Lev. 26:12; Deut. 23:14 [23:15 MT]; 2 Sam. 7:6–7; Ezek. 28:14).[8]

Second, Gen. 2:15 says God placed Adam in the garden "to cultivate it and keep it." The two Hebrew words for "cultivate" and "keep" (respectively, ʿābad and šāmar) usually are translated "serve" and "guard." When these two words

---

6. On 21:27 and its resonance with uncleanness in association with the new temple, see ibid., 1101–2.

7. For a good overview of these works, see Richard M. Davidson, *Flame of Yahweh: Sexuality in the Old Testament* (Peabody, MA: Hendrickson, 2007), 47–48.

8. The precise Hithpael form used in Gen. 3:8 is a participle (*mithallēk*), which is the precise form used in Deut. 23:14 (23:15 MT); 2 Sam. 7:6. Outside these three uses, the Hithpael participial form occurs in only five other passages, which have nothing to do with the tabernacle or temple.

occur together later in the OT, without exception they have this meaning and refer either to Israelites serving and guarding/obeying God's word (about 10x) or, more often, to priests who serve God in the temple and guard the temple from unclean things entering it (Num. 3:7–8; 8:25–26; 18:5–6; 1 Chron. 23:32; Ezek. 44:14).[9] Adam also is portrayed as wearing priestly attire in Ezek. 28:13. Some identify this figure as Satan, but that this figure is Adam is pointed to by the description in Ezek. 28:13. The jewels that are said to be his "covering" in Ezek. 28:13 are uniquely listed in Exod. 28:17–21, which describes the jewels on the ephod of Israel's high priest, who is a human and not an angel. Either the Ezekiel list is an allusion to the human priest's bejeweled clothing in Exod. 28 or Exod. 28 has roots in an earlier tradition about Adam's apparel, which is represented by Ezekiel.[10] Furthermore, since Ezek. 28:11–19 is addressed to a figure standing behind "the king of Tyre" (v. 11), who has sinned like the human king, it is more likely that the figure in Eden is also human.[11]

Therefore, Adam was to be the first priest to serve in and guard God's temple. When Adam fails to guard the temple, by sinning and admitting an unclean serpent to defile the temple, he loses his priestly role, and the two cherubim take over the responsibility of guarding the garden temple: God "stationed the cherubim . . . to <u>guard</u> the way to the tree of life" (Gen. 3:24). Their role became memorialized in Israel's later temple when God commanded Moses to make two statues of angelic figures and station them on either side of the ark of the covenant in the holy of holies in the temple. Like the cherubim,

9. See Meredith G. Kline, *Kingdom Prologue: Genesis Foundations for a Covenantal Worldview* (Overland Park, KS: Two Age Press, 2000), 54. Kline sees that only the guarding has any priestly connotations, particularly with respect to the priestly guarding of the temple from the profane (e.g., he cites Num. 1.53, 3.8, 10, 32; 8:26; 18:3–7; 1 Sam. 7:1; 2 Kings 12:9; 1 Chron. 23:32; 2 Chron. 34:9; Ezek. 44:15–16; 48:11).

10. Nine of twelve jewels in Ezek. 28 overlap with those in Exod. 28. In the LXX, eleven of the jewels in Ezekiel overlap with the Greek version of Exod. 28 (though the Greek of Ezekiel has a total of fourteen jewels).

11. As we noted in chap. 12 under the heading "Genesis 1–3 and Idolatry," there are additional indications that this figure in Eden is Adam. Not only does the LXX clearly identify Adam as the glorious figure dwelling in the primeval Eden in Ezek. 28:14 (as does the Targum in Ezek. 28:12), but also it is plausible that the Hebrew text does so as well (as argued by, e.g., Dexter E. Callender Jr., *Adam in Myth and History: Ancient Israelite Perspectives on the Primal Human*, HSS 48 [Winona Lake, IN: Eisenbrauns, 2000], 87–135, 179–89). The phrase in the Hebrew of Ezek. 28:14a, *'at-kĕrûb mimšaḥ hassôkēk* ("you were the anointed cherub who covers"), could well be understood as a mere metaphor, which is a suppressed simile: "you were [like] the anointed cherub who covers," similar to metaphorical statements such as "the LORD is [like] my shepherd" (Ps. 23:1). What further points to this figure being Adam in Eden is that Ezek. 28:18 says that the sin of the glorious figure in Eden "profaned" Eden. The only account that we have that Eden became unclean because of sin is the narrative about Adam in Gen. 2–3. See also Daniel I. Block, *The Book of Ezekiel: Chapters 25–48*, NICOT (Grand Rapids: Eerdmans, 1998), 115; Manfred Hutter, "Adam als Gärtner und König (Gen 2:8, 15)," *BZ* 30 (1986): 258–62. For later Jewish traditions referring to the jewels of Ezek. 28 as "coverings" or "canopies" for Adam and Eve, see Beale, *Revelation*, 1087–88.

Israel's priests were to "keep watch" (the same word as "guard" in Gen. 2:15) over the temple (Neh. 12:45) as "gatekeepers" (2 Chron. 23:19; Neh. 12:45).

Third, the "tree of life" itself probably was the model for the lampstand placed directly outside the holy of holies in Israel's temple: it looked like a small tree trunk with seven protruding branches, three on one side and three on the other, and one branch going straight up from the trunk in the middle.

Fourth, that the garden of Eden was the first temple is also suggested by the fact that Israel's later temple had wood carvings that gave it a garden-like atmosphere and likely were intentional reflections of Eden. According to 1 Kings, there was "cedar . . . carved in the shape of gourds and open flowers" (6:18); "on the walls of the temple round about" and on the wood doors of the inner sanctuary were "carvings of cherubim, palm trees, and open flowers" (6:29, 32, 35); beneath the heads of the two pillars placed at the entrance of the holy place were carved "pomegranates" (7:18–20).

Fifth, just as the entrance to Israel's later temple was to face east and be on a mountain (Exod. 15:17 [Zion]), and just as the end-time temple of Ezekiel was to face east (Ezek. 40:6) and be on a mountain (Ezek. 40:2; 43:12), so the entrance to Eden faced east (Gen. 3:24) and was situated on a mountain (Ezek. 28:14, 16).

Sixth, the ark in the holy of holies, which contained the law (which led to wisdom), echoes the tree of the knowledge of good and evil (which too led to wisdom). The touching of both the ark and this tree resulted in death.

Seventh, just as a river flowed out from Eden (Gen. 2:10), so the postexilic temple (*Let. Aris.* 89–91) and the eschatological temple in both Ezek. 47:1–12 and Rev. 21:1–2 has rivers flowing out from the center (likewise Rev. 7:15–17 and, probably, Zech. 14:8–9).[12] Indeed, Ezekiel generally depicts latter-day Mount Zion (and its temple) with descriptions of Eden in an attempt to show that the promises originally inherent in Eden would be realized in the fulfillment of his vision.[13] Fertility and rivers are also descriptions of Israel's temple in Ps. 36:8–9:

> They drink their fill of the abundance of Your house [temple];
> And You give them to drink of the river of Your delights [lit., "the river of Your Edens"].
> For with You is the fountain of life;[14]
> In Your light we see light [perhaps a play of words on the light from the lampstand in the holy place].

12. Later Judaism understood that from "the tree of life" streams flowed (*Gen. Rab.* 15.6; *2 En.* [J] 8:3, 5).

13. Jon D. Levenson, *Theology of the Program of Restoration of Ezekiel 40–48*, HSM 10 (Cambridge, MA: Scholars Press, 1976), 25–53.

14. Levenson (ibid., 28) sees this phrase as an allusion to the "flow [that] welled up from the earth and watered the whole surface of the soil" from which Adam was created in Gen. 2:6–7.

Jeremiah 17:7–8 also compares those "whose trust is the LORD" to "a tree planted by the water, that extends its roots by a stream," with the result that "its leaves will be green" and it will not "cease to yield fruit" (cf. Ps. 1:2–3). Then 17:12–13 refers to "the place of our [Israel's] sanctuary" and virtually equates it with "the fountain of living water, even the LORD."[15]

Eighth, like Israel's later temple, the garden of Eden may be discerned to be part of a tripartite sacred structure. In this respect, also in connection with the presence of water, it may even be discernible that there was a sanctuary and a holy place in Eden corresponding roughly to that in Israel's later temple. The garden should be precisely viewed as not itself the source of water but rather as adjoining Eden, since Gen. 2:10 says "a river flowed out of Eden to water the garden."

Therefore, in the same manner that ancient palaces were adjoined by gardens, "Eden is the source of the waters and [is the palatial] residence of God, and the garden adjoins God's residence."[16] Similarly, Ezek. 47:1 says that water would flow out from under the holy of holies in the future eschatological temple and would water the earth around. Similarly, in the end-time temple of Rev. 22:1–2 there is portrayed "a river of the water of life . . . coming from the throne of God and of the Lamb" and flowing into a garden-like grove modeled on the first paradise in Gen. 2, as is much of Ezekiel's portrayal.

If Ezekiel and Revelation are developments of the first garden-temple, which later I will argue is the case, then Eden, the area where the source of water is located, may be comparable to the inner sanctuary of Israel's later temple and the garden adjoining the holy place.[17] Even aside from these later biblical texts, Eden and its adjoining garden formed two distinct regions. This is compatible with my further identification of the lampstand in the holy place of the temple with the tree of life located in the fertile plot outside the inner place of God's presence. Additionally, "the bread of the presence," also in the holy place, which provided food for the priests, appears to reflect the food produced in the garden for Adam's sustenance.[18]

I would add to this that the land and seas to be subdued by Adam outside the garden were a third distinct region roughly equivalent to the outer court of Israel's subsequent temple, which is, indeed, symbolic of the land and seas throughout the entire earth.[19] Therefore, one may be able to perceive an

15. Among other commentators, Callender (*Adam in Myth and History*, 51–52) esp. cites Ps. 36 and Jer. 17 as examples of Israel's temple being likened to Eden.

16. John H. Walton, *Genesis*, NIVAC (Grand Rapids: Zondervan, 2001), 167, citing others also for sources showing that ancient temples had adjoining gardens.

17. Discussion of the distinction between Eden and its garden is based on ibid., 182–83.

18. So ibid., 182.

19. I will argue this later in this chapter. For discussion of other commentators who, in various ways, have identified the garden of Eden with a temple or sanctuary, see Terje Stordalen, *Echoes of Eden: Genesis 2–3 and Symbolism of the Eden Garden in Biblical Hebrew Literature*,

increasing threefold gradation in holiness from outside the garden proceeding inward: the outermost region surrounding the garden is related to God and is "very good" (Gen. 1:31) in that it is God's creation (= the outer court); the garden is a sacred space separate from the outer world (= the holy place), where God's priestly servant worships God by obeying him, by cultivating and guarding; Eden is where God dwells (= the holy of holies) as the source of both physical and spiritual life (symbolized by the waters).

Ninth, in the light of these numerous conceptual and linguistic parallels between Eden and Israel's tabernacle and temple, it should not be unexpected that Ezek. 28 refers to "Eden, the garden of God . . . the holy mountain of God" (vv. 13–14, 16) and also alludes to it as containing "sanctuaries" (v. 18), which elsewhere is a plural way of referring to Israel's tabernacle (Lev. 21:23) and temple (Ezek. 7:24; so also Jer. 51:51). The plural reference to the one temple arose probably because of the multiple sacred spaces or "sanctuaries" within the temple complex (e.g., courtyard, holy place, holy of holies).[20] It is also probable, as we saw above, that Ezek. 28:14 views the glorious being who had "fallen" to be Adam. Thus, Ezek. 28:16 is also referring to Adam's sin: "You sinned; therefore, I have cast you as profane from the mountain of God [where Eden was]." That Ezek. 28:13 pictures Adam dressed in bejeweled clothing like a priest (alluding to Exod. 28:17–20) corresponds well to the reference only five verses later to Eden as a holy sanctuary. Ezekiel 28:18 probably is the most explicit place in canonical literature where the garden of Eden is identified as a temple and Adam is viewed as a priest.

All these observations together point to the likelihood that the garden of Eden was the first sanctuary in sacred history. Not only was Adam to "guard" this sanctuary, but also he was to subdue the earth, according to Gen. 1:28: "And God blessed them. . . . 'Be fruitful and multiply, and fill the earth, and subdue it; and rule over the fish of the sea and over the birds of the sky, and over every living thing that creeps on the surface.'" As he was to begin to rule over and subdue the earth, he was to extend the geographical boundaries of the garden until Eden extended throughout and covered the whole earth. This meant the presence of God that was limited to Eden was to be extended throughout the whole earth. God's presence was to "fill" the entire earth.

In this respect, John Walton observes that

> if people were going to fill the earth [according to Gen. 1], we must conclude that they were not intended to stay in the garden in a static situation. Yet moving out of the garden would appear a hardship since the land outside the garden

---

CBET 25 (Leuven: Peeters, 2000), 307–12. Stordalen (ibid., 457–59) offers further evidence in support of the identification.

20. There were even smaller sacred areas in the temple complex—e.g., of Solomon's temple (1 Chron. 28:11) and of the second temple (1 Macc. 10:43). Philo refers to the holy of holies as "the Holies of Holies" (*Leg.* 2.56; *Mut.* 192) or "the innermost places of the Holies" (*Somn.* 1.216).

was not as hospitable as that inside the garden (otherwise the garden would not be distinguishable). Perhaps, then, we should surmise that people were gradually supposed to extend the garden as they went about subduing and ruling. Extending the garden would extend the food supply as well as extend sacred space (since that is what the garden represented).[21]

The intention seems to be that Adam was to widen the boundaries of the garden in ever-increasing circles by extending the order of the garden sanctuary into the inhospitable outer spaces. The outward expansion would include the goal of spreading the glorious presence of God. This would be accomplished especially by Adam's progeny born in his image and thus reflecting God's image and the light of his presence, as they continued to obey the mandate given to their parents and went out to subdue the outer country until the Eden sanctuary covered the earth. At this early point, we can already see a beginning answer to the initial question about why Rev. 21:1–22:5 equates the new cosmos with the garden-like temple: that was the original universal design of the Eden sanctuary. But we must trace the development of Gen. 1–2 throughout Scripture before making final conclusions.

As we know, Adam was not faithful and obedient in subduing the earth and extending the garden sanctuary, so that not only was the garden-temple not extended throughout the earth, but also Adam himself was cast out of the garden and no longer enjoyed God's presence and lost his function as God's priest in the temple.

After Adam's fall and expulsion from the garden-temple, humankind became worse and worse, and only a small remnant of the race was faithful. God eventually destroyed the whole earth by flood because it had become so thoroughly wicked. Only Noah and his immediate family were spared. As a result, God started the creation of the world over again.

It is possible that God started building another temple for his people to dwell in and to experience his presence during Noah's time.[22] Noah and his sons, however, were not faithful and obedient, so that if God had begun another temple-building process, it was immediately stopped because of the sin of Noah and his sons. They followed in Adam's sinful footsteps. In fact, Noah's "fall" is reminiscent of Adam's, as both sinned in the context of a garden. According to Gen. 9:20–21, "Noah began farming and planted a vineyard. And he drank of the wine and became drunk," and this led to further sin by his sons.

After the disobedience of Noah and his family, God started over again and chose Abraham and his descendants, Israel, to reestablish his temple.

21. Walton, *Genesis*, 186.
22. That this is plausible is apparent from the affinities of Noah's altar-building and associated activities with that of the subsequent similar patriarchal activities, which can actually be viewed as inchoate or small-scale temple-building (on which, see further in the following section).

Adam's Commission as a Priest-King to Rule and Expand the Temple Is Passed On to the Patriarchs

As we will see, after Adam's failure to fulfill God's mandate, God raised up other Adam-like figures to whom his commission was passed on. We will find that some changes in the commission occurred as a result of sin entering into the world. Adam's descendants, like him, however, would fail. Failure would continue until there arose a "last Adam," who would finally fulfill the commission on behalf of humanity.

I argued in chapter 2 that Adam's commission was passed on to Noah, to Abraham, and to his descendants. The following references in Genesis are a sample of what was elaborated on earlier in more detail:

Gen. 1:28 <u>God blessed them</u>; and God said to them, "<u>Be fruitful and multiply, and fill the earth</u>, and <u>subdue it; and rule</u> over the fish of the sea and over the birds of the sky, and over every living thing that moves on the earth."

Gen. 9:1, 7 And <u>God blessed Noah and his sons</u> and said to them, "<u>Be fruitful and multiply, and fill the earth</u>. . . . <u>Be fruitful and multiply; populate the earth abundantly and multiply in it</u>."

Gen. 12:2–3 "And I will make you a great nation, and <u>I will bless you</u>, and make your name great; and so you shall be a blessing; and <u>I will bless those who bless you</u>, and the one who curses you I will curse. And in you <u>all the families of the earth</u> will be blessed."

Gen. 17:2, 6, 8 "I will establish My covenant between Me and you, and <u>I will multiply you exceedingly</u>. . . . <u>I will make you exceedingly fruitful</u>. . . . I will give to you and to your descendants after you, the land of your sojournings, all the land of Canaan."

Gen. 22:17–18 "Indeed <u>I will greatly bless you, and I will greatly multiply your seed</u> as the stars of the heavens and as the sand which is on the seashore; and your seed shall possess the gate of his [singular pronoun] enemies. In your seed <u>all the nations of the</u> earth shall be blessed, because you have obeyed My voice."

Gen. 26:3 "Sojourn in this land and I will be with you and <u>bless you</u>, for to you and to your descendants I will give all these lands, and I will establish the oath which I swore to your father Abraham."

Gen. 26:4 "<u>I will multiply your descendants</u> as the stars of heaven, and will give your descendants all these lands; and by your descendants <u>all the nations of the earth shall be blessed</u>."

Gen. 26:24 The LORD appeared to him the same night and said, "I am the God of your father Abraham; do not fear, for I am with you. <u>I will bless you, and multiply your descendants</u>, for the sake of my servant Abraham."

Gen. 28:3–4 "May <u>God Almighty bless you and make you fruitful and multiply you</u>, that you may become a company of peoples. May He also give you the blessing of Abraham, to you and to your descendants with you; that you may possess the land of your sojournings, which God gave to Abraham."

Gen. 28:13–14 "I will give it [the land] to you and to your seed. <u>Your seed will also be like the dust of the earth</u>, and you will spread out to the west and to the east . . . ; and in you and in your seed shall <u>all the families of the earth be blessed</u>."

Gen. 35:11–12 God also said to him, "I am God Almighty; <u>be fruitful and multiply</u>; a nation and a company of nations shall come from you, and <u>kings shall come forth from you</u>. The land which I gave to Abraham and Isaac, I will give it to you, and I will give the land to your descendants after you."

Gen. 47:27 Now Israel lived in the land of Egypt, in Goshen, and they acquired property in it and were fruitful and became very numerous.

In fact, the same commission given to the patriarchs is restated numerous times in subsequent OT books both to Israel and the true eschatological people of God. Like Adam, Noah and his children failed to perform this commission. God then gave the essence of the commission of Gen. 1:28 to Abraham (Gen. 12:2–3; 17:2, 6, 8, 16; 22:18), Isaac (Gen. 26:3–4, 24), Jacob (Gen. 28:3–4, 14; 35:11–12; 48:3, 15–16), and to Israel (see Deut. 7:13 and Gen. 47:27; Exod. 1:7; Ps. 107:38; Isa. 51:2, the latter four of which state the beginning fulfillment of the promise to Abraham in Israel).[23] Recall that the commission in Gen. 1:26–28 involves the following elements, especially as summarized in 1:28: (1) "God blessed them"; (2) "be fruitful and multiply"; (3) "fill the earth"; (4) "subdue" the "earth"; (5) "rule over . . . all the earth."

The commission is repeated to, for example, Abraham: "I will greatly <u>bless you</u>, and I will greatly <u>multiply your seed</u> . . . ; and <u>your seed shall possess the gate of their enemies</u> [= 'subdue and rule']. In your seed all the nations

23. This was first brought to my attention by N. T. Wright, *The Climax of the Covenant: Christ and the Law in Pauline Theology* (Minneapolis: Fortress, 1992), 21–26, on which the above list of references in Genesis is based. Wright sees that the command to Adam in Gen. 1:26–28 has been applied to the patriarchs and Israel; he also cites other texts where he sees Gen. 1:28 applied to Israel (Exod. 32:13; Lev. 26:9; Deut. 1:10–11; 7:13–14; 8:1; 28:63; 30:5, 16). I have subsequently discovered that the same observation is made by Jeremy Cohen (*"Be Fertile and Increase, Fill the Earth and Master It": The Ancient and Medieval Career of a Biblical Text* [Ithaca, NY: Cornell University Press, 1989], 28–31, 39) in dependence on Gary Smith ("Structure and Purpose in Genesis 1–11," *JETS* 20 [1977]: 307–19), both of whom include Noah. For the notion that the blessings conditionally promised to Adam are given to Israel, see also William J. Dumbrell, *The Search for Order: Biblical Eschatology in Focus* (Grand Rapids: Baker Academic, 1994), 29–30, 37, 72–73, 143.

of <u>the earth</u> shall be <u>blessed</u>" (Gen. 22:17–18).[24] God expresses the universal scope of the commission by underscoring that the goal is to "bless" "all the nations of the earth." It is natural, therefore, that in the initial statement of the commission in Gen. 12:1–3 God commands Abraham, "Go forth from your country. . . . And so you shall be a blessing. . . . And in you all the families of the earth will be blessed."

Commentators, however, apparently have overlooked something interesting: the Adamic commission is repeated in direct connection with what looks like the building of small sanctuaries. Just as the Gen. 1:28 commission was initially to be carried out by Adam in a localized place, enlarging the borders of the arboreal sanctuary, so it appears to be no accident that the restatement of the commission to Israel's patriarchs results in the following: (1) God appears to them (except in Gen. 12:8; 13:3–4); (2) they "pitch a tent" (LXX: "tabernacle"); (3) on a mountain; (4) they build "altars" and worship God (i.e., "calling on the name of the LORD," which probably included sacrificial offerings and prayer)[25] at the place of the restatement; (5) the place where these activities occur often is located at "Bethel," meaning the "House of God" (the only case of altar-building not containing these elements or linked to the Gen. 1 commission is Gen. 33:20). The combination of these five elements occurs elsewhere in the OT only in describing Israel's tabernacle or temple.[26]

Therefore, although "occasions for their sacrifices were usually a theophany and moving to a new place,"[27] there seems to be more significance to the construction of these sacrificial sites. The patriarchs appear also to have built these worship areas as impermanent, miniature forms of sanctuaries that symbolically represented the notion that their progeny were to spread out to subdue the earth from a divine sanctuary in fulfillment of the commission in Gen. 1:26–28. Although the patriarchs constructed no buildings, these sacred spaces can be considered to be sanctuaries along the lines comparable to the first nonarchitectural sanctuary in the garden of Eden, particularly because a tree often is present at these sites. It will also be important to recall later that

---

24. Notice that the ruling aspect of the commission is expressed to Abraham elsewhere as a role of "kingship" (Gen. 17:6, 16), and likewise with respect to Jacob (Gen. 35:11).

25. Augustine Pagolu, *The Religion of the Patriarchs*, JSOTSup 277 (Sheffield: Sheffield Academic Press, 1998), 62.

26. The combination of "tent" (*'ōhel*) and "altar" (*mizbaḥ*) occurs in Exodus and Leviticus only with respect to the tabernacle and associated altar (e.g., Lev. 4:7, 18). "Altar" (*mizbaḥ*) and "house" (*bāyit*) occur 28x in the OT with reference to the temple and its altar. Rarely do any of the words in these two combinations refer to anything other than the tabernacle or temple. The building of these worship sites on a mountain may represent part of a pattern that climaxes in Israel's later temple built on Mount Zion (the traditional site of Mount Moriah), which itself becomes a synecdoche referring to the temple. I do not mean that "tent" in the patriarchal episodes is equivalent to the later tabernacle, but that it resonates with tabernacle-like associations because of its proximity to the worship site.

27. Pagolu, *Religion of the Patriarchs*, 85.

a holy piece of geography or a sacred area can be considered a true sanctuary or temple even when no architectural building is constructed there.

Thus, these informal sanctuaries in Genesis pointed to Israel's later tabernacle and temple from which Israel, in reflecting God's presence, was to branch out over all the earth. The patriarch's commission, like Adam's in Gen. 1:28 in connection to Gen. 2, also involved the building of a temple.

That these miniature sanctuaries adumbrated the later temple is also suggested by the fact that "before Moses the altar was the only architectural feature marking a place as holy," and that later "altars were incorporated into the larger [structural] sanctuaries, the tabernacle and the temple."[28] The small sanctuary in Bethel also became a larger sanctuary in the northern kingdom of Israel, though it subsequently became idolatrous and was rejected as a true shrine of Yahweh worship (see Amos 7:13; cf. 1 Kings 12:28–33; Hos. 10:5).

The result of Abraham, Isaac, and Jacob building altars at Shechem, between Bethel and Ai, at Hebron, and near Moriah was that the terrain of Israel's future land was dotted with shrines. This pilgrim-like activity "was like planting a flag and claiming the land"[29] for God and Israel's future temple, where God would take up his permanent residence in the capital of that land. All these smaller sanctuaries pointed to the greater one to come in Jerusalem.

The preparations for the reestablishment of a larger-scale tabernacle, and then temple, began at the exodus, where again God brought about chaos in creation on a small scale and delivered Israel to be the spearhead for his new humanity. Upon them was placed the temple-building commission originally given to Adam.

Israel's Tabernacle in the Wilderness and Later Temple Were a Reestablishment of the Garden of Eden's Sanctuary

What appeared implicit with the patriarchs and with Moses at Sinai becomes explicit with Israel's tabernacle and temple. First Chronicles narrates David's preparations for building the temple that Solomon will accomplish. David's preparatory actions include all the same elements found with the fivefold small-scale temple building activities of Abraham, Isaac, and Jacob, which confirms that their building activities were, indeed, miniature versions of, or pointers to, a later sanctuary. (1) David begins the preparations on a mountain (Mount Moriah). (2) David experiences a theophany (he sees "the angel of the Lord

---

28. Tremper Longman III, *Immanuel in Our Place: Seeing Christ in Israel's Worship* (Phillipsburg, NJ: P&R, 2001), 16. Some commentators acknowledge that some of these patriarchal episodes involve the construction of small sanctuaries, but they do not associate them with Israel's later large-scale temple (so, e.g., H. C. Leupold, *Exposition of Genesis*, 2 vols. [Grand Rapids: Baker Academic, 1942], 2:781, 918, with respect to Gen. 28 and 35).

29. Longman, *Immanuel in Our Place*, 20 (similarly, Pagolou, *Religion of the Patriarchs*, 70).

standing between earth and heaven" so 1 Chron. 21:16; 2 Chron. 3:1). (3) At this site "David built an altar to the Lord . . . ;" (4) "and offered burnt offerings . . . and he called to the Lord" (1 Chron. 21:26). (5) Furthermore, David calls the place "the house of the Lord God" (1 Chron. 22:1) because this is the site of Israel's future temple to be prepared by David and built by Solomon (1 Chron. 22; 2 Chron. 3:1). Now we can see more clearly that the altar building activities of the patriarchs were constructions of small-scale sanctuaries that find their climax with the larger-scale construction of Israel's temple.

The following considerations show that Israel's tabernacle and then temple were another new temple of another new creation.

The dwelling place of God among Israel is explicitly called a "tabernacle" and then a "temple" for the first time in redemptive history. Never before had God's unique presence with his covenant people been formally called a "tabernacle" or "temple."[30] We have seen how, nevertheless, the garden of Eden had essential similarities with Israel's temple, which shows that Israel's temple was a development of the sanctuary implicit in Gen. 2.

Something else that is true of the Eden temple, not yet mentioned, is that it served as a little earthly model of God's temple in heaven that eventually would encompass the whole earth. This is seen most clearly in Israel's temple in the following ways.

Psalm 78:69 says something amazing about Israel's temple: God "built the sanctuary like the heights, [he built the sanctuary] like the earth which He has founded forever."[31] This tells us that in some way God modeled the temple to be a little replica of the entire heaven and earth. Yet, in Isa. 66:1 God says, "Heaven is My throne, and the earth is My footstool. Where then is a <u>house</u> you could build for Me?" God never intended that Israel's little localized temple last forever, since, like the Eden temple, Israel's temple was a small model of something much bigger: God and his universal presence, which could never eternally be contained by any localized earthly structure.

Israel's tabernacle and temple were a miniature model of God's huge cosmic temple that was to dominate the heavens and earth at the end of time. That is, the temple was a symbolic model pointing not merely to the present cosmos but also to the new heaven and earth that would be perfectly filled with God's presence. That it was a miniature symbolic model of the coming temple that would fill heavens and earth is evident from the following figurative features

30. Though we have seen that Jacob calls the worship site in Gen. 28:10–22 "the house of God" (v. 17), "Bethel" (v. 19), and says that the stone that he erected there "will be called God's house" (v. 22).

31. Likewise, God tells Moses, "Let them construct a sanctuary for Me, that I may tabernacle among them. According to all that I am going to show you [on the mountain from heaven], as the pattern of the tabernacle [that you see in heaven] . . . , just so you shall construct it" (Exod. 25:8). Cf. Exod. 25:40: "See that you make them after the pattern for them, which was shown to you on the mountain."

of the three sections of the temple: the holy of holies, the holy place, and the outer courtyard.

(1) The holy of holies represented the invisible heavenly dimension, the holy place represented the visible heavens, and the outer courtyard represented the visible sea and earth, where humans lived.

(2) That the holy of holies represented the invisible heaven where God and his angels dwelled is suggested by the following:

a. Just as the angelic cherubim guard God's throne in the heavenly temple, the statuette cherubim around the ark of the covenant and the figures of the cherubim woven into the curtain that guards the holy of holies reflect the real cherubim in heaven who stand guard around God's throne.

b. The fact that no image of God was in the holy of holies and that it "appeared" empty further points to it representing the invisible heaven.

c. The holy of holies was the place where the heavenly realm extended down to the earthly; this is why the ark of the covenant was called God's "footstool"; God was pictured as sitting on his throne in heaven with his invisible feet on the ottoman of the ark of the covenant.

d. The holy of holies was cordoned off by a separating curtain, which indicates its separateness from the holy place and the outside courtyard, additionally pointing to its symbolism of the invisible heavenly dimension that was separated from the physical.

e. Even the high priest, who could enter only once a year, was prohibited from viewing the light of God's glorious presence by an incense cloud, which underscores again the separateness of this most holy inner space as representing the holy invisible heavenly sphere. The incense cloud itself may have had a further association with the clouds of the visible heaven, which itself pointed to the invisible heaven.

(3) That the holy place likely represents the visible heavens that are still separated from the earth is apparent from the following:

a. The curtains of the holy place were blue, purple, and scarlet, representing the variegated colors of the sky, and figures of winged creatures were woven into all the curtains throughout the tabernacle, enforcing the imagery of the visible heavens.

b. The lampstand had seven lamps on it, and in Solomon's temple there were ten lampstands; thus, if people were to peer into the holy place, they would see seventy lights, which against the darker setting of the curtains of the tabernacle and temple would resemble the heavenly light sources (stars, planets, sun, and moon).

c. This symbolism is enhanced by observing that the Hebrew word for "light" (*māʾôr*) is used ten times in the Pentateuch for the lamps on the lampstand, and the only other place in the Pentateuch where the word occurs is five times in Gen. 1:14–16, where it refers to the sun, moon, and stars. The tabernacle appears to have been designed to represent the creative work of God, who, as Isa. 40 says, "stretches out the heavens like a curtain and spreads them out like a tent to dwell in, and "who has created these *stars*" to hang in this heavenly tent (Isa. 40:22, 6); likewise Ps. 19:1–5 says that in "the heavens" God "placed a tent for the sun." Plausibly, this is the reason why the holy place was covered with gold (1 Kings 6:20–21), on the ceiling, floor, and walls; the sheen of the precious metal possibly was intended to mimic the reflection of the stars of heaven (as was true in ancient Near Eastern temples, esp. in Egypt).

d. Perhaps because of this biblical evidence, the seven lamps on the lampstand in the holy place were understood by first-century Jews (particularly Josephus and Philo) to represent the seven light sources visible to the naked eye of the ancient person, underscoring that this second section of the temple symbolized the visible heavens.[32] Later Judaism equated the seven lamps on the lampstand with the "lights in the expanse of heaven" mentioned in Gen. 1:14–16 (so *Tg. Ps.-J.* Exod. 40:4; *Num. Rab.* 15.7; 12.13).[33] Furthermore, the first-century Jewish historian Josephus, who had firsthand acquaintance with the temple, said that the outer curtain of the holy place had needlework on it of stars, representing the heavens.[34]

(4) The courtyard probably represents the visible sea and earth. This identification of the outer court is suggested further by the OT description, where the large metal washbasin and the altar in the temple courtyard are called respectively the "sea" (1 Kings 7:23–26) and the "bosom of the earth" (Ezek.

---

32. Josephus, *Ant.* 3.145; *J.W.* 5.217; Philo, *Her.* 221–225; *Mos.* 2.102–105; *QE* 2.73–81; Clement of Alexandria, *Strom.* 5.6.

33. For example, one Jewish paraphrase (*Targum Pseudo-Jonathan*) of Exod. 39:37 interpreted the seven lamps on the lampstand "to correspond to the seven planets that move in their orbits in the firmament day and night." For the seven lamps as symbolic of the planets or heavenly lights, see Mircea Eliade, *The Myth of the Eternal Return*, trans. Willard R. Trask (London: Routledge & Kegan Paul, 1955), 6–17; Othmar Keel, *The Symbolism of the Biblical World: Ancient Near Eastern Iconography and the Book of Psalms*, trans. Timothy J. Hallett (New York: Crossroad, 1985), 171–76; Leonhard Goppelt, "τύπος κτλ," *TDNT* 8:256–57; for oil lamps symbolizing planets in Mesopotamia and Egypt, see Leon Yarden, *The Tree of Light: A Study of the Menorah, the Seven-Branched Lampstand* (Ithaca, NY: Cornell University Press, 1971), 43.

34. Josephus says that the "tapestry" hanging over the outer entrance into the temple "typified the universe" and on it "was portrayed a panorama of the heavens" (*J.W.* 5.210–214). The same may have well been the case with the outer part of the curtain separating the holy of holies from the holy place since, also according to Josephus, all the curtains in the temple contained "colours seeming so exactly to resemble those that meet the eye in the heavens" (*Ant.* 3.132). That such may be the case could also be evident from the observation in Exodus that all the curtains of the temple were woven of materials that resembled the variegated colors of the sky.

43:14 [the altar also likely was identified with the "mountain of God" in Ezek. 43:16]).[35] The altar was also to be an "altar of earth" (in the early stages of Israel's history) or an "altar of [uncut] stone" (Exod. 20:24–25), thus identifying it even more with the natural earth. Thus both the "sea" and the "altar" appear to be cosmic symbols that may have been associated in the Israelite mind respectively with the seas and the earth[36] (enhancing the water imagery were the ten smaller washbasins, five on each side of the holy place [1 Kings 7:38–39]). The symbolic nature of the "bronze sea" is indicated by the fact that it was seven feet high and fifteen feet in diameter, holding ten thousand gallons of water, and would not be convenient for priestly washing (in this respect, the ten waist-high washbasins would have been the ones for daily practical cleansings). The arrangement of the twelve bulls "entirely encircling the sea" and the "lily blossom" decorating the brim also seem to present a partial miniature model of land and life surrounding the seas of the earth (2 Chron. 4:2–5). The twelve bulls also supported the washbasin and were divided into groups of three, facing to the four points of the compass, which could well reflect the four quadrants of the earth.[37] That twelve oxen were pictured holding up the "sea" and designs of lions and oxen were on the washbasin stands points further to an "earthly" identification of the outer courtyard (though cherubim were also depicted on the stands). That the outer court was associated with the visible earth is also intimated by the fact that all Israelites, representing humanity at large, could enter there and worship.

The cumulative effect of these observations is that Israel's temple served as a little earthly model of God's temple in heaven that eventually would encompass also the whole earth. Specifically, the inner sanctuary of God's invisible presence would extend to include the visible heavens and earth. This is why the latter two sections in the temple of the holy place and courtyard are symbolized respectively as the visible sky and earth, to show that they will be consumed by God's holy of holies presence.

35. See Jon D. Levenson, *Creation and the Persistence of Evil: The Jewish Drama of Divine Omnipotence* (San Francisco: Harper & Row, 1988), 92–93. Translations of Ezek. 43:14 typically have "from the base on the ground," but literally it is "from the bosom of the earth [or ground]"; among the reasons for associating "the altar hearth" (lit., "Ariel" [*'ărîēl*]) of Ezek. 43:16 with "the mountain of God" is Levenson's observation that the same mysterious word "Ariel" occurs in Isa. 29:1, where it refers to "the city where David camped" and is equated by synonymous parallelism to "Mount Zion" (cf. Isa. 29:7a with 29:8h), so that it resonates with "mountain" imagery (on the ambivalent meaning of the Hebrew word, see BDB 72).

36. On Solomon's "bronze sea" representing the primordial sea or waters of Eden, see Elizabeth Bloch-Smith, "'Who Is the King of Glory?' Solomon's Temple and Its Symbolism," in *Scripture and Other Artifacts: Essays on the Bible and Archaeology in Honor of Philip J. King*, ed. Michael D. Coogan, J. Cheryl Exum, and Lawrence E. Stager (Louisville: Westminster John Knox, 1994), 26–27. Some see it representing the primeval chaos waters that were overcome at creation.

37. Levenson, *Creation*, 92–93; see likewise idem, *Sinai and Zion: An Entry into the Jewish Bible* (San Francisco: Harper & Row, 1987), 139, 162.

When a school or business or church decides to expand and build a new building, typically an architect makes an actual model of the proposed structure. A church that I attended decided to build a new building. The church hired an architect, who made a model of the new complex: there was a parking lot with shrubs that surrounded the big church building, and the roof of the building was cut off in order to show what the actual rooms would look like. Such architectural models do not function only as models; they point to a bigger task, creating a bigger structure in the future.

Israel's temple served precisely the same purpose. The temple was a small-scale model and symbolic reminder to Israel that God's glorious presence would eventually fill the whole cosmos, and that the cosmos, not merely a small architectural structure, would be the container for God's glory. This probably was to serve as a motivation to the Israelites to be faithful witnesses to the world of God's glorious presence and truth, which was to expand outward from their temple.

The temple was a symbol to Israel of the task that God wanted it to carry out. The same task that Adam (and likely Noah) should have carried out but did not, Israel was to execute: to "multiply and fill the earth and subdue it" (Gen. 1:28) by expanding the local boundaries of the temple (where God's special revelatory presence was) to include the entire earth. That is, Israel was to spread God's presence throughout the whole earth. Interestingly, the land of promise, the land of Israel, was repeatedly called the "garden of Eden" (cf. Gen. 13:10; Isa. 51:3; Joel 2:3; Ezek. 36:35), partly perhaps because Israel was to expand the limits of the temple and of its own land to the ends of the earth in the way that Adam should have. That this was Israel's ultimate task is apparent from a number of OT passages prophesying that God will finally cause the sacred precinct of Israel's temple to expand and first encompass Jerusalem (Isa. 4:4–6; 54:2–3, 11–12; Jer. 3:16–17; Zech. 1:16–2:11), then the entire land of Israel (Ezek. 37:25–28), and then the whole earth (Dan. 2:34–35, 44–45; cf. Isa. 54:2–3).

Similarly, as we have seen, God gave to Israel the same commission that he gave to Adam and Noah. For example, to Abraham, the progenitor of Israel, God said, "I will greatly bless you, and I will greatly multiply your seed . . . ; and your seed shall possess the gate of their enemies" (Gen. 22:17).[38] Interestingly, Gen. 1:28 becomes both a commission and a promise to Isaac, Jacob, and Israel.

Israel, however, did not carry out this great mandate to spread the temple of God's presence over the whole earth. The contexts of Isa. 42:6 and 49:6 express that Israel should have spread the light of God's presence throughout the earth, but it did not. Exodus 19:6 says that Israel collectively was to be

---

38. See also Gen. 12:2–3; 17:2, 6, 8; 28:3; 35:11–12; 47:27; 48:3–4; on Noah's commission, see Gen. 9:1, 7.

to God "a kingdom of priests and a holy nation" going out to the nations and being mediators between God and the nations by bearing God's light of revelation. Instead of seeing the temple as a symbol of their task to expand God's presence to all nations, the Israelites wrongly viewed it as symbolic of their election as God's only true people and as an indication that God's presence was to be restricted to them as an ethnic nation. They believed that the gentiles would experience God's presence primarily through judgment.

Thus, God sent them out of their land into exile, which Isa. 45 compares to the darkness and chaos of the first chaos before creation in Gen. 1 (cf. Isa. 45:18–19). So God started the process of temple-building all over again, but this time he planned that the local spiritual boundaries of all the past temples of Eden and Israel would be expanded finally to circumscribe the boundaries of the entire earth. How did this occur?

Christ and His Followers Are a Temple in the New Creation[39]

Christ is the temple toward which all earlier temples looked and that they anticipated (cf. 2 Sam. 7:12–14; Zech. 6:12–13). Christ is the epitome of God's presence on earth as God incarnate, thus continuing the true form of the old temple, which actually was a foreshadowing of Christ's presence throughout the OT era. Jesus's repeated claim that forgiveness now comes through him and no longer through the sacrificial system of the temple suggests strongly that he was taking over the function of the temple, and in fact the forgiveness that he now offered was what the temple had imperfectly pointed to all along. Indeed, the ultimate redemptive-historical purpose of the temple sacrifices was typologically to point to Christ as the ultimate sacrifice of himself, which he would offer for the sins of his people as a priest, at the cross, and in the eschatological temple. In this respect, Christ repeatedly refers to himself in the Synoptic Gospels as the "cornerstone" of the temple (Mark 12:10; Matt. 21:42; Luke 20:17). John 1:14 says that he became God's "tabernacle" in the world.

John 2:19–21 reports this exchange between Jesus and Jewish leaders: "Jesus answered them, 'Destroy this temple, and in three days I will raise it up.' The Jews then said, 'It took forty-six years to build this temple and will You raise it up in three days?' But he was speaking of the temple of his body." It is important to recognize that the Jews thought that he was speaking of the physical temple that he had just cleansed, since the subject of the directly preceding verses is his unusual activity in the temple (2:14–17). Accordingly, the Jews were asking Jesus to adduce a sign to demonstrate his authority in cleansing the temple (2:18). But Jesus was referring to himself as the temple: "He was speaking of the temple of His body" (2:21). He would be the end-time

---

39. For the development of the temple theme in Judaism that has been traced so far above in the OT, see Beale, *Temple*, 45–50, 154–67.

temple-builder by raising it up in the form of his body, in line with OT prophecies that predicted that the Messiah would build the latter-day temple (again,
see 2 Sam. 7:12–14; Zech. 6:12–13).[40]

As alluded to earlier in this section, Jesus began to take over the function
of the old temple during his ministry, so that when he was crucified, he as the
temple was being "destroyed." In addition, the "raising up" of the temple in
"three days" is an obvious reference to his resurrection (John 2:22a: "When
He was raised from the dead, His disciples remembered that He had said
this"). Again, we see the notion of new creation expressed in this, since we
have seen repeatedly that new life and resurrection are none other than new
creation. In addition, relevant for this John 2 passage is my earlier observation
in this chapter that the OT temple symbolized the entire creation and pointed
forward to the entire new creation. In this light, Christ's reason for referring
to his resurrection as a "raising up" of the temple is that the purpose of the
old temple all along was to point symbolically toward the time when God's
special revelatory presence in the old temple would break out of the holy
of holies and fill the entire new creation as his cosmic temple. Accordingly,
Christ's precrucifixion life began to fulfill this (see John 1:14), and especially
his resurrection as the beginning of the new creation is the initial escalated
fulfillment of the symbolic purpose of Israel's temple: the new creation has
begun in Christ, so that he is God's tabernacling presence of the new creation,[41]
which is to expand further until it is completed at the very end of the age in
the whole cosmos becoming the temple of God's consummate presence.

Incidentally, if Jesus is what the temple prophetically pointed to all along,
then it is doubtful that we can think of a possible future physical temple as any
more than a secondary fulfillment, though even this is unlikely. Indeed, 2 Cor.
1:20 says, "For as many as are the [OT] promises of God, in Him [Christ]
they are yes." Christ is the major beginning fulfillment of the prophecies of
the end-time temple.

Will there yet be another architectural temple built right before or after
Christ comes back a second time in fulfillment of OT prophecy? Christian
scholars disagree about this. But if there is going to be another physical temple
built at that time, it should be seen not as the primary fulfillment of the
prophecy of the end-time temple but rather as part of the ongoing fulfillment,
alongside Christ as the fulfillment. To focus only on a future physical temple
as the fulfillment would be to ignore that Christ at his first coming began to
fulfill this prophecy, and that he will completely fulfill it in the eternal new
creation. So even if there is to be a future physical temple built in Israel, it
will point only to Christ and God as the temple in the eternal new creation,

40. So also Judaism held that the Messiah would build the coming temple (e.g., *Tg. Isa.* 53:5
[as an interpretation of the messianic Servant's work]; *Num. Rab.* 13.2).

41. See *Pirqe R. El.* 1, which interprets the new creation prophecy of Isa. 43:16 ("Behold, I
will do a new thing") to refer to the raising up and renewal of the future temple.

pictured in Rev. 21:22. Therefore, to focus only on a future physical temple as the fulfillment is like focusing too much on the physical picture of the temple and not sufficiently on what the picture ultimately represents, which is Christ as the true temple.

During my first year of doctoral study in England, my fiancée and I were corresponding across the ocean quite a bit. I had a picture of her that she had given me. I endearingly looked at it often. Perhaps I even hugged the picture. Now, after thirty-two years of marriage, if she came into our den and saw me looking only at that picture day after day and never looking at her, she would rightly conclude that my focus was wrong. I no longer need the picture because I now have the embodiment in my wife of everything to which her picture pointed.

Likewise, Israel's temple was a symbolic shadow pointing to the eschatological "greater and more perfect tabernacle" (Heb. 9:11) in which Christ and the church would dwell and would form a part.[42] If so, it would seem to be the wrong approach for Christians to look in hope to the building of another temple in Jerusalem composed of earthly "bricks and mortar" as a fulfillment of the OT temple prophecies. Is it too dogmatic to say that such an approach confuses the shadow with the end-time substance? Would this approach not seek to possess the cultic picture alongside the true christological reality to which the picture points (on which, see Heb. 8:2, 5; 9:8–11, 23–25)? And would it not posit a retrogression or reversal in the progress of redemptive history? Although it is possible to agree with the overall approach of this chapter and still hold to some expectation of an architectural temple, to do so would be inconsistent.

A Brief Case Study of 2 Corinthians 6:16–18

We saw in the preceding chapter that the commencement of the church becoming the eschatological temple was at Pentecost. Subsequent to Pentecost, when people believe in Jesus, they become a part of Jesus and the temple, since Jesus himself is the locus of that temple. According to Eph. 2:20–22, believers are then "built on the foundation of the apostles and prophets, Christ Jesus Himself being the cornerstone, in whom the whole building, being fitted together is growing into a holy temple in the Lord [Jesus], in whom you also are being built together into a dwelling of God in the Spirit." In this regard also the Christian's identification with the temple is affirmed by the following:

---

42. In this respect, Heb. 9:9 says that the old, physical tabernacle and temple were a "symbol" or were "figurative" (*parabolē*) for the eschatological temple in which Christ has begun to dwell, which is the "true" (*alēthinos*) temple (Heb. 8:1–2); see further Heb. 9:6–28. See Paul Ellingworth, *The Epistle to the Hebrews: A Commentary on the Greek Text*, NIGTC (Grand Rapids: Eerdmans, 1993), 439–42.

1. 1 Cor. 3:16: "Do you not know that you are a temple of God and that the Spirit of God dwells in you?"
2. 1 Cor. 6:19: "Do you not know that your body is a temple of the Holy Spirit who is in you?"
3. And 2 Cor. 6:16b: "For we are the temple of the living God" (likewise 1 Pet. 2:5; Rev. 3:12; 11:1–2).

The 2 Cor. 6 text needs further elaboration with respect to the question of whether it indicates fulfillment of the OT end-time temple prophecies, since the two texts in 1 Corinthians do not explicitly cite any supporting OT texts. Some commentators speak of the temple in 1 Corinthians only as a metaphor: the church is merely "like" a temple, but it is not part of the beginning fulfillment of the eschatological temple prophecies from the OT.[43] Others contend that Paul compares the church to a temple because he understands it to be the inaugurated fulfillment of the expected latter-day temple, even though the church is not an architectural reality. The problem, as just noted, is that there are no clear references to any OT temple passages in the two 1 Corinthians texts. Also, in the case of 2 Cor. 6:16–18, where there are such references, there is still some ambiguity because there is no introductory fulfillment formula either at the beginning or the ending of the passage.

Is Paul also thinking of the temple in 2 Cor. 6:16–18 to be among the initial fulfillments of OT prophecy, or is he merely saying that the church at Corinth is like a temple but is not the fulfillment of the latter-day prophecies about the temple? We need to look further at this passage in order to shed more light on this question.

Paul's most explicit reference to believers being identified as a temple is 2 Cor. 6:16a: "For we are the temple of the living God; just as God said." Paul cites several texts from the OT to support this declaration, the first of which is a prophecy of the future temple (see table 19.1). This is a combined allusion to Leviticus and Ezekiel, both of which are a prediction of a coming end-time temple.

43. See Gordon D. Fee, *First Epistle to the Corinthians*, NICNT (Grand Rapids: Eerdmans, 1987), 147. Fee expresses a perhaps not atypical tentativeness: the notion that the eschatological temple is in mind in 1 Cor. 3 "is possible, though by no means certain," and yet he says in a footnote that such an end-time view "is probably correct." See also John R. Levison, "The Spirit and the Temple in Paul's Letters to the Corinthians," in *Paul and His Theology*, ed. Stanley E. Porter, PS 3 (Leiden: Brill, 2006), 189–215. Levison consistently refers to Paul's metaphorical use of the temple image in 1–2 Corinthians, and though acknowledging various OT prophetic backgrounds for some of Paul's uses, he does not see that the Corinthians actually are a redemptive-historical temple of God's Spirit in fulfillment of Israel's eschatological prophecies. For him, the church is only like a temple.

Table 19.1

Leviticus 26:11–12; Ezekiel 37:26–27	2 Corinthians 6:16b
Lev. 26:11–12: "I will make My dwelling among you. . . . I will also walk among you and be your God, and you shall be My people."	"I will dwell in them and walk among them; and I will be their God, and they will be My people."
Ezek. 37:26–27: "I . . . will set My sanctuary in their midst forever. My dwelling place also will be with them; and I will be their God, and they will be My people" (cf. Exod. 29:45).	

Paul appends to the Leviticus-Ezekiel prophecy additional allusions to the OT promises that a temple will be rebuilt when Israel returns from Babylonian captivity, first from Isaiah, and then from Ezekiel (see table 19.2).

Table 19.2

Isaiah 52:11; Ezekiel 11:17; 20:41 LXX	2 Corinthians 6:17
Isa. 52:11: "Depart, depart, go out from there, touch nothing unclean; go out of the midst of her, purify yourselves, you who carry the vessels of the Lord."	"'Therefore, come out from their midst and be separate,' says the Lord. 'And do not touch what is unclean;
Ezek. 11:17 LXX: "I will welcome them [MT: 'you']."	and I will welcome you.'"
Ezek. 20:34, 41 LXX: "I will welcome you."[a]	

[a]Perhaps also echoed are the following passages that also refer to God "welcoming" Israel back from restoration: Jer. 23:3; Mic. 4:6; Zeph. 3:19–20; Zech. 10:8, 10, the second two of which have in mind also a return to the temple (cf. Mic. 4:1–3, 7–8; Zeph. 3:10–11).

Isaiah prophetically exhorts not future Israelites in general to "depart" from Babylon, but specifically priests who carry the holy "vessels" of the temple that Nebuchadnezzar had taken from Solomon's temple and had kept in Babylon during the captivity. They are to return the vessels to the temple when it is rebuilt. When Ezekiel repeatedly speaks of God "welcoming" Israel back from captivity, the restoration of the temple is in mind. For example, Ezek. 20:40–41 LXX says, "For on my holy mountain, on my high mountain . . . will I accept you, and there will I have respect for your first fruits, and the first fruits of your offerings, in all your holy things. I will accept you with a sweet-smelling savor . . . and I will welcome you from the countries wherein you have been dispersed." When God will "welcome" Israel back, it will bring offerings to the temple on Mount Zion.

Intriguingly, Ezek. 11:16 says that when the Israelites were in captivity, God "was a sanctuary for them a little while in the countries where they had gone." This assertion is made in direct connection with Ezek. 10:18, in which "the glory of the Lord departed from the threshold of the temple" in

Jerusalem (similarly, Ezek. 11:23). It probably is not coincidental that God's glorious presence departed from the temple and then is said to be with the faithful remnant in some veiled manner, who have gone into captivity. His presence would return with the restored people and would once again take up residence in another temple. It is clear that this did not occur in the second temple built after Israel's return in the way it was prophesied to be at the time of restoration. The fact that the "sanctuary" in Ezek. 11:16, in which God was to be present among his people in exile, is a nonarchitectural sanctuary is likely part of the hermeneutical rationale by which Paul can apply the OT temple prophecies throughout 2 Cor. 6:16–18 to the people of God in Corinth as God's sanctuary.

Paul's last allusion supporting his contention that the Corinthians are "the temple of the living God" is to 2 Sam. 7:14 (see table 19.3).

Table 19.3

2 Samuel 7:14	2 Corinthians 6:18
"I will be a father to him and he will be a son to Me."	"'And I will be a father to you, and you shall be sons and daughters to Me,' says the Lord Almighty."

The 2 Samuel text is primary, but "son" has been expanded into "sons and daughters" under the influence of three Isaianic texts that foretell the restoration of Israel's "sons and daughters" (Isa. 43:6; 49:22; 60:4), the last of which includes in its context the promise that Israel will again worship at a restored temple (Isa. 60:7, 13). The 2 Samuel prophecy is concerned with the future king and temple: "He [the coming king] shall build a house for My name, and I will establish the throne of his kingdom forever" (2 Sam. 7:13). Most commentators agree that this prophecy in 2 Sam. 7 was not finally fulfilled in Solomon and his temple or in Israel's second temple.

Thus, here in 2 Cor. 6:16–18 we have a staccato rattling off of temple prophecies by Paul. Is Paul saying that the Corinthian church has begun to fulfill these prophecies, or is he merely saying that the church is like what these OT passages prophesy about the temple?

In answering this, should not those with a high view of Scripture begin with the presupposition that the NT interprets the OT contextually and with organic hermeneutical continuity, though many in the scholarly guild disagree with such a presupposition? Accordingly, if an OT passage quoted in the NT is a prophecy in its original context, would not a NT author such as Paul also see it as a prophecy, and would he not see it as beginning fulfillment if he identifies the prophecy with some reality in his own present time? And even if there is no fulfillment formula, would not Paul still see it as fulfillment? Possibly, he could use the OT text analogically, but unless there is clear evidence to the contrary in the NT context, the weight of the prophetic context of the OT passage tilts toward a notion of fulfillment.[44] If this is a correct hermeneutical approach, then the prophecies about the temple in 2 Cor. 6:16–18 probably should be taken as beginning true fulfillment in some way in the Corinthian church.

But let us look further at the preceding context of 2 Cor. 6 to see if this tentative conclusion can be confirmed. One of the most theologically pregnant statements in all of Paul's writings occurs in 2 Cor. 1:20a: "For as many as are the promises of God, in Him [Christ] they are yes." The "promises" certainly refer to OT promises that began fulfillment in Christ. But which promises are in mind? Perhaps all of God's prophetic promises are implied, but the ones uppermost in Paul's mind are those that he addresses in the following context of the epistle, particularly in 1:21–7:1. Surely among the prophetic promises that Paul has in mind is that of the new covenant, on which he elaborates in chapter 3. That both 1:20 and 7:1 refer to "promises" plural (the latter introduced with "therefore") is one of the signposts that it is this section within which Paul expounds prophetic fulfillment of more than merely one prophecy. As is well known, the establishment of a new temple was prophesied to be part of Israel's restoration (e.g., Ezek. 37:26–28; 40–48).

Some commentators apparently do not link 2 Cor. 7:1a directly to the preceding verses at the end of chapter 6 (perhaps they do not do so unconsciously because of the chapter break in English and Greek Bibles). But the "therefore" (oun) in 7:1 underscores that foremost among the promises that Paul has in mind in the first six chapters are those of the temple prophecies, since these appear repeatedly in the directly preceding verses (2 Cor. 6:16–18): "Therefore, having these promises. . . ." Christ initially fulfilled the temple promise (cf. 1:20), and the readers participate in that fulfillment also, as they are ones "having these promises" (7:1). The reason why they and Paul fulfill the same promise that Christ does is that God "establishes us with you in Christ" by "sealing" believers and giving the "Spirit in our hearts as a down payment" (1:21–22). As Paul says in 1 Corinthians, the church is "a temple of God" in which "the Spirit of God dwells" (3:16 [cf. 6:19]). They have only begun to fulfill the eschatological expectation of the temple, but a time will come when they will perfectly realize that hope.

Are the Corinthians literally the beginning of the end-time temple prophesied in Lev. 26; Isa. 52; Ezek. 37? Some might agree that Paul understands the church to be the beginning fulfillment of the temple prophecies but maintain that Paul allegorizes, since OT authors would have had in mind a physically conceived architectural structure as a temple and not people composing a temple. Others, in order to avoid casting Paul as an allegorizer, conclude that he is only making a comparison. Accordingly, they would not see actual beginning fulfillment here because it is obvious to them that the Corinthian church

---

44. Or, if context makes it clear, a NT author could be affirming that an OT prophecy has not been fulfilled yet but assuredly will be in the future.

is not what the OT temple prophecies had in mind, since these prophecies are understood in physical architectural terms. However, we have already seen above that Paul probably is viewing the church as a real and true fulfillment of various temple prophecies, which had already begun to be nonarchitecturally conceived in the OT itself. Consequently, it is possible to take Paul's words about fulfillment literally and yet still understand that he had in mind a literal fulfillment that would not have been outside the literal scope of the prophets' authorial intention. Accordingly, Paul is not allegorizing, nor is he merely making an analogy between a temple idea and that of Christians; rather, he is saying that Christians are indeed the real beginning fulfillment of the actual prophecy of the end-time temple.[45]

Building on what has been said so far, I think that it is appropriate to come full circle and refocus attention on the problem with which this chapter began: how are the OT temple prophecies to be understood in Rev. 21:1–22:5? In other words, how are these prophecies of the temple to be consummately fulfilled?

The Problem of John Seeing a New Creation in Revelation 21:1 and Then Seeing in the Remainder of the Vision Only a City in the Form of a Garden-Like Temple

The mystery of Rev. 21–22, I believe, is significantly clarified by my preceding survey of the purpose of temples in the OT and the NT. The new heaven and the new earth in Rev. 21:1–22:5 are now described as a temple because the temple, which equals God's presence, encompasses the whole earth because of the work of Christ. At the very end of time, the true temple will come down completely from heaven and fill the whole creation (as Rev. 21:1–3, 10; 21:22 affirm). Revelation 21:1 commences, as we have seen, with John's vision of "a new heaven and a new earth" followed by his vision of the "new Jerusalem, coming down out of heaven" (v. 2), and then he hears a loud voice proclaiming that "the tabernacle of God is among men, and He will tabernacle among them" (v. 3). As noted in the initial discussion of this chapter, it is likely that the second vision in verse 2 interprets the first vision of the new cosmos, and that what is heard about the tabernacle in verse 3 interprets verses 1–2. If so, the new creation of verse 1 is identical to the new Jerusalem of verse 2, and both represent the same reality as the tabernacle of verse 3.

Consequently, the new creation and the new Jerusalem are none other than God's tabernacle. This tabernacle is the true temple of God's special presence portrayed throughout chapter 21. It is this cultic divine presence, formerly limited to Israel's temple and then the church, that will fill the whole earth and heaven and become coextensive with it. Then the eschatological goal of

---

45. For a similar point about 2 Cor. 6:16, see Edmund P. Clowney, "The Final Temple," *WTJ* 35 (1972): 185–86.

the temple of the garden of Eden dominating the entire creation will be finally fulfilled (so 22:1–3).[46]

Why does Rev. 21:18 say that the temple-city will be pure gold? It is because the entire holy of holies and holy place of Israel's temple, which were paved with gold on the walls, floor, and ceiling (so 1 Kings 6:20–22; 2 Chron. 3:4–8), have been expanded to cover the whole earth. This is why the three sections of Israel's old temple (holy of holies, the holy place, and the outer courtyard) are no longer found in the Rev. 21 temple: God's special presence, formerly limited to the holy of holies, has now extended out to encompass the entire visible heavens and the whole earth, which the holy place and the court respectively symbolized. This is also why Rev. 21:16 says that the city was "square," indeed, cubic: the holy of holies was a cubic shape (1 Kings 6:20). In addition, that the entire creation has become the holy of holies is evident from Rev. 22:4. Whereas the high priest, who wore God's name on his forehead, was the only person in Israel who could enter the holy of holies once a year and stand in God's presence, in the future all God's people will have become high priests with God's "name on their foreheads" and standing not one day a year but forever in God's presence.[47] It is God's people who have continued to extend the borders of the true temple throughout the church age, as they have been guided by the Spirit, as a result of the Father's plan expressed in the redemptive work of the Son, who also consummates the temple-building process. This notion of expanding the temple worldwide finds striking similarity in the Qumran community, who were to honor God "by consecrating yourself to him, in accordance to the fact that he has placed you as a holy of holies [over all][48] the earth, and over all the angels" (4Q418 [= 4Q423 8 + 24?] frg. 81, 4).[49]

Hence, the two outer sections of the temple have fallen away like a cocoon from which God's holy of holies presence has emerged to dominate all creation. What kind of use of the OT in the NT is this? Could John be allegorizing? At first glance, to equate the new cosmos with a garden-like city in the shape of

46. In striking likeness, 4Q475 5–6 affirms that the earth will become Eden: after all sin has been extinguished from the earth, "all the world will be like Eden, and all . . . the earth will be at peace for ever, and . . . a beloved son . . . will . . . inherit it all."

47. In this respect, note that God's throne is also now in the midst of God's people (22:1, 3), whereas previously the holy of holies (or, more specifically, the ark therein) was the "footstool of God's heavenly throne," and only the high priest could come before that footstool (Isa. 66:1; Acts 7:49; cf. Ps. 99:5).

48. The Hebrew-English edition by Florentino García Martínez and Eibert J. C. Tigchelaar (*The Dead Sea Scrolls Study Edition*, 2 vols. [Grand Rapids: Eerdmans, 2000]) rightly fills the lacuna with "over all" because of the following parallelism with "over all the angels" (lit., "gods"), though in García Martínez's earlier English edition he did not do so and gave an otherwise quite different translation, which does not reflect the Hebrew as well as the later translation.

49. Similarly, 4Q511 frg. 35 says, "God makes (some) hol[y] for himself like an everlasting sanctuary. . . . And they shall be priests" (lines 3–4). As such, their task is to "spread the fear of God in the ages" (line 6).

the holy of holies seems to be a superb example of allegory or wild spiritualization. In light of my argument so far, however, this appears unlikely. But could this be mere comparison of the OT texts about the temple to conditions in the new creation? Yes, this is at least the case. Could the use be direct prophetic fulfillment or typological fulfillment? Although some specific OT references in Rev. 21:1–22:4 could fall into one or the other of these categories,[50] the overall view of the temple in Revelation and the allusions to particular OT temple texts are not best described by any one of these categories. Rather, the usage might best be described as completion or fulfillment of intended design (i.e., intended design of the OT temple). In this sense, I think we can refer to this as "literal" fulfillment.

These OT writers prophesying the temple in the new creation are comparable in a sense to people from another planet in a spaceship some distance from the earth. They can see with the naked eye only the earth and its different shading, representing clouds, seas, and land masses. They radio back to their home planet and describe what they see from this distance. When, however, their spaceship approaches closer to the earth and begins to descend into the atmosphere over, say, New York City, they are able to make out the rivers, forests, valleys, and particularly the city, buildings, houses, streets, cars, and people. Both the distant and the close-up views are "literal." The close-up view reveals details that someone with only a distant view could not have seen. The close-up view even offers what looks like a different reality from the one seen from the distant vantage point. Nevertheless, both are "literal" depictions of what is actually there.

Similarly, the literal picture of OT prophecy is magnified by the lens of NT progressive revelation, which enlarges the details of fulfillment in the beginning new world that will be completed at Christ's last advent. This does not mean that OT prophecy is not fulfilled literally, but the literal nature of the prophecy from the OT vantage point becomes sharpened and the details clarified, indeed, magnified. The above illustration breaks down a bit, since I believe that OT prophets also got occasional glimpses of the "close-up" view, which, when put together, were like fragmentary pieces of a jigsaw puzzle in uncompleted form. Most of the visions that they had were of the "far-away" view.

We can say that much of what they saw was the "far-away" perspective, which then becomes sharpened by the details of the progressive revelation unveiled in the fulfillment of the redemptive-historical plan and shows how the formerly seen "close-up" visionary pieces fit into the whole of the new age. As the revelation progresses toward the "planet" of the new creation, meanings of earlier biblical texts become enlarged and magnified. Thus, later biblical

---

50. E.g., directly prophetic fulfillment is indicated by Lev. 26:12; Ezek. 37:27 in Rev. 21:3; Ezek. 40–48 throughout John's vision; Isa. 54:11–12 in Rev. 21:19–20; indirect typological fulfillment is expressed by 1 Kings 6:20 in Rev. 21:16.

writers further interpret prior canonical writings in ways that amplify earlier texts. These later interpretations may formulate meanings of which earlier authors may not have been exhaustively conscious, but that do not contravene their original organic intention. This is to say that original meanings have "thick description,"[51] and fulfillment often "fleshes out" or gives a close-up view of prophecy with details of which the prophet could not as clearly see from far away.

Accordingly, my contention is that not only does Christ fulfill all that the OT temple and its prophecies represent, but also he is the unpacked meaning for which the temple existed all along.[52] Christ's establishment of the temple at his first coming and the identification of his people with him as the temple, where God's tabernacling presence dwells, is a magnified view of the beginning form of the new-creational temple. Revelation 21 is the most highly magnified picture of the final form of the temple that we will have this side of the consummated new cosmos. Like the far-away and close-up views of the earth, such a view of the temple should not be misconceived as diminishing a literal fulfillment of the OT temple prophecies.

We must acknowledge that there do appear to be some end-time prophecies describing what would seem to be a future physical, structural temple, yet we must still ask how Paul in 2 Cor. 6:16–18 and John in his final vision can identify Christ, God, and the church as the fulfillment of such prophecies. It is important also to observe that some prophecies of an end-time temple foresee a nonarchitectural structure. Hence, there are temple prophecies that appear to refer to the establishment of a future architectural temple building and others that seem to depict a nonarchitectural structure.[53] With respect to the latter, on the one hand, some prophecies understand that the temple was to extend over all of Jerusalem (Isa. 4:5–6; Jer. 3:16–17; Zech. 1:16–2:13), over all of the land of Israel (Ezek. 37:26–28; similarly Lev. 26:10–13), and even over the entire earth (Dan. 2:34–35, 44–45), and Rev. 21:1–22:5 sees that the entire cosmos has become the temple. On the other hand, Dan. 8; 11–12, as well as Ezek. 40–48 and other texts, appear to prophesy a physical temple building that will exist in one particular geographical location in the end time.[54]

51. For further elaboration of this concept, see Kevin J. Vanhoozer, *Is There a Meaning in This Text? The Bible, the Reader, and the Morality of Literary Knowledge* (Grand Rapids: Zondervan, 1998), esp. 284–85, 291–92, 313–14, where "thick description" is discussed.

52. To paraphrase Clowney, "Final Temple," 177.

53. Some of the prophecies of a structural temple include passages where no initial establishment of a temple is mentioned but the existence of a latter-day temple is noted or assumed (e.g., Dan. 8:11–13; 11:31).

54. If the detailed prophecy of Ezek. 40–48 is jettisoned as such a prediction, then other, much less descriptive prophecies usually placed in such a category wane in significance. However, see Charles L. Feinberg, "The Rebuilding of the Temple," in *Prophecy in the Making*, ed. Carl F. H. Henry (Carol Stream, IL: Creation House, 1971), 109. Feinberg sees Ezek. 40–48 as a reference to a physical structure and, because of its detail, as determinative in defining the other briefer

How can these texts be harmonized? This is a classic biblical-theological problem. But could it not be that some texts predicting an architectural temple represent a "far-away" view of the future temple, whereas others portraying an expanding temple represent a "close-up" view of the end-time sanctuary?

To explain some of the "far-away" views of the temple (e.g., Ezek. 40–48) hermeneutically, another illustration may be helpful. A father promises in 1900 to give his son a horse and buggy when he grows up and marries. During the early years of expectation, the son reflects on the particular size of the buggy he would like, its contours and style, its beautiful red-leather seat, and also the size and breed of horse that would draw the buggy. Perhaps the father even had knowledge from early experimentation elsewhere that the invention of the "horseless carriage" was on the horizon, but he coined the promise to his son in familiar terms that the son could readily understand. Years later, say in 1925, when the son marries, the father gives the couple an automobile, which has since been invented and mass-produced.

Is the son disappointed in receiving an automobile instead of a horse and buggy? Is this a figurative or a literal fulfillment of the promise? In fact, the essence of the father's word has remained the same: a convenient mode of transportation. What has changed is the precise form of transportation promised. The progress of technology has escalated the fulfillment of the pledge in a way that earlier could not have been conceived of fully by the son when he was young. Nevertheless, in light of the later development of technology, the promise is viewed as "literally" and faithfully carried out in a greater way than could have earlier been apprehended.

The substantial essence of the new temple is still the glory of God; however, that glory is no longer confined within a material building but instead is revealed openly to the world in Christ and his subsequent dwelling through the Spirit in the worldwide church as the temple. The progress of God's revelation has made the fulfillment of apparent prophecies of an architectural temple even greater than originally conceived by finite minds. This is what Hag. 2:9 appears to express: "The latter glory of this house will be greater than the former." Such an escalation from an architecturally conceived temple to a nonarchitectural one is also pointed to by some OT precedents that already understood that a temple could exist without there being an architectural reality. Two examples are the garden of Eden, called a "sanctuary" (Ezek. 28:13–18), and Mount Sinai, understood to be a mountain temple, after which the tabernacle was modeled.[55]

---

prophecies about the temple as also foreseeing physical structures. In response to such a local specifically architectural view, see Beale, *Temple*, chap. 11, where I argue for a figurative view in Ezekiel itself and discuss its use in Rev. 21:1–22:5. In the NT, some see that 2 Thess. 2:4 is the clearest prophecy of a future temple-building (in response to which, see Beale, *Temple*, chap. 8).

55. Note also temple prophecies already mentioned above that contain nonarchitectural depictions, most of which are prophetic: Isa. 4:5–6; Jer. 3:16–17; Ezek. 11:16; 37:26–28 (similarly Lev. 26:10–13); Dan. 2:34–35, 44–45; Zech. 1:16–2:13.

Above all, in John's portrayal of the consummated condition of the new heavens and earth in Rev. 21:22, he says, "I saw no temple in it, because the Lord God, the Almighty, and the Lamb are its temple." Whereas the container for the divine glory in the OT often was an architectural building, in the new age this old physical container will be shed like a cocoon and the new physical container will be the entire cosmos. The ultimate essence of the temple is the glorious divine presence. If such is to be the case in the consummated form of the cosmos, would this not begin to be the case in the inaugurated phase of the latter days? The glorious divine presence of Christ and the Spirit among his people compose the beginning form of the eschatological temple.

Thus, we see temple prophecies such as Ezek. 40–48; Isa. 54; Ezek. 37 fulfilled in the Rev. 21:1–22:5 vision in the sense that this vision prophetically depicts the time when the intended universal cosmic design of OT temples, including that of Eden, will be completed or accomplished. In this light, these prophecies are not merely analogical to the new creation or allegorized by John; they are "literally" fulfilled.

The Ethical Imperative of Being the Eschatological Temple of God's Presence Is to Expand That Temple

Christ, as the last Adam and true priest-king, perfectly obeyed God and expanded the boundaries of the temple as a new creation from himself to others (in fulfillment of Gen. 1:28). In this respect, note that at the climax of the last vision of Revelation God's throne is also now in the midst of God's people (Rev. 22:1, 3), whereas previously the holy of holies (or, more specifically, the ark therein) was the "footstool of God's heavenly throne," and only the high priest could come before that footstool (Isa. 66:1; Acts 7:49; cf. Ps. 99:5). As we saw above, now all are high priests and victorious "overcomers" (Rev. 21:7), who "will reign forever and ever" with Christ and God in the eternal cosmic temple of the new creation (Rev. 22:5). The Rev. 21:1–22:5 vision portrays that what Exod. 15:17–18 prophesied about God's eternal reign in Israel's temple will finally be realized:

> You will bring them and plant them in the mountain of Your inheritance, the place, O LORD, which You have made for Your dwelling, the sanctuary, O LORD, which Your hands have established. The LORD shall reign forever and ever.

These inextricably linked themes of kingship, priesthood, temple, and new creation, as we have seen in this chapter, have their primary roots in and are a consummate development of the same constellation of themes in Gen. 1–2.

We are meant to continue that task of sharing God's presence with others until the end of the age, when God will bring the task to completion, and the whole earth will be under the roof of God's temple, which is to say that God's presence will fill the earth in an unprecedented way. This cultic task of expanding the presence of God is expressed strikingly in Rev. 11. There, the church is portrayed as a "sanctuary" (vv. 1–2), as "two witnesses" (v. 3), and as "two lampstands" (v. 4), the last image, of course, being an integral feature of the temple. Two witnesses were needed in the OT for a valid witness in court, and there are only two churches that are faithful among the seven in Rev. 2–3. The "two witnesses" and "two lampstands" thus indicate that the mission of the church as God's temple is to shine its lampstand-like light of effective witness into the dark world. The mention that the witnessing church is also "two olive trees" (v. 4) indicates its priestly and kingly status:[56] the exercise of their witness is also how the church exercises it mediatorial priesthood and kingly reign. In surprisingly similar fashion, this mission is expressed in 1 Pet. 2:4–5, where Peter calls Christ a "living stone" in the temple, and his people are "living stones . . . being built up as a spiritual house." Furthermore, as they are "being built up" and thus expanding, they are a "holy/royal priesthood" (1 Pet. 2:5, 9, alluding to Exod. 19:6) and are to "proclaim the excellencies of him who has called you out of darkness into his marvelous light" (1 Pet. 2:9). As in Rev. 11; 21:1–22:5, so also in 1 Pet. 2 the notion of God's people exercising their roles as kings and priests in the end-time temple highlights again that the idea of temple is an essential facet of the new-creational kingdom.

Ephesians 2:20–22 asserts that the church has "been built upon the foundation of the apostles and prophets, Christ Jesus Himself being the cornerstone, in whom the whole building, being fitted together, is growing into a holy temple in the Lord, in whom you are also being built together into a dwelling of God in the Spirit." The church is growing and expanding in Christ throughout the interadvent age (cf. Eph. 4:13–16) so that God's saving presence and "the manifold wisdom of God might now be made known" even "in the heavenly places" (Eph. 3:10). And it is through the church's exercise of its gifts (Eph. 4:8–16) that this expansion takes place.[57] Such gifts are given

---

56. That the "two olive trees" represent a priestly and kingly figure is apparent because this is an allusion to Zech. 4, where they represent a priestly figure and kingly figure (see Beale, *Revelation*, 576–77).

57. Note the closely parallel wording in Eph. 2:21–22, "in whom the whole building, being fitted together, is growing . . . in the Lord . . . you also are being built together," and 4:15–16, "we are to grow . . . into Him . . . from whom the whole body, being fitted . . . together . . . causes the growth . . . for the building up of itself." The latter text appears to develop the former on the temple (I am grateful to one of my research students, Brandon Levering, for this insight). Also the Ps. 68:18 quotation in Eph. 4:8, which introduces the list of gifts, is part of a context in which God defeated Israel's enemies and dwelled in his temple in Zion (Ps. 68:17–19 [67:18–20 LXX; 68:18–20 MT]), a text applied to Christ as the temple in Col. 1:19 (see G. K. Beale, "Colossians," in *Commentary on the New Testament Use of the Old Testament*, ed. G. K. Beale and

because all believers, both Jew and gentile, are priests in the end-time temple, as the OT prophesied (Isa. 56:3–7; 61:6; 66:18–21). The various gifts enable them to exercise their eschatological priestly position.

How do we first experience God's tabernacling presence? We do so by believing in Christ, that he died for our sin, rose from the dead, and reigns as the Lord God. God's Spirit comes into us and dwells in us in a way similar to the way that God dwelled on his throne in the sanctuary of Eden and Israel's temple.

How does the presence of God increase in our lives and our churches? How was this to happen with Adam? It was to occur by Adam's trust in God and his word. Likewise, God's presence will become increasingly manifest to us as we grow by grace in our belief in Christ and his word and by obeying it.

Do we come to God's word habitually, as did Jesus, so that we will be strengthened increasingly with God's presence in order to fulfill our task of spreading that presence to others who do not know Christ?

God's presence grows in us by our knowing and obeying his word, and then we spread that presence to others by living our lives faithfully in the world. For example, a persevering and joyous faith in the midst of trial is an amazing witness to the unbelieving world. In so doing, the members of the body of Christ during the interadvent period "follow the Lamb wherever He goes" (Rev. 14:4) as a walking tabernacle during his epoch on earth. We are to realize that the church's place in the eschatological redemptive-historical story is that of being the inaugurated temple, which is designed to expand and spread God's presence throughout the earth. This is that part of the biblical storyline in which the role of Christian "witness" and "mission" is to be understood. Believers are images of God in his temple who are to reflect his presence and glorious attributes in their thinking, character, speech, and actions. And, from another angle, just as sacrifices were made in the OT temple and Christ sacrificed himself at the cross in the beginning of the end-time temple, so Christians sacrifice themselves in the end-time temple by suffering when they do not compromise in their witness. By so doing, God's powerful presence manifests itself through their sacrificial weakness (e.g., see 2 Cor. 4:7–18; 12:5–10). It is this reflection of God's glorious presence that extends out through Christians and imbues others who do not know God, so that they come to be part of this expanding temple.

A few summers ago, my wife and I bought a rose of Sharon bush and planted it on the north side of our house. The bush was supposed to grow to about six feet high and four feet wide and to have flowers. After a few months, however, we noticed that our bush was not growing at all, though it began to produce

---

D. A. Carson [Grand Rapids: Baker Academic, 2007], 855–57). This enhances the link with the temple in Eph. 2:20–22. The psalm quotation in Eph. 4:8 appears to be typologically applied to Christ. Could the gifts in 1 Cor. 12 also be linked to the church as a temple in 3:16–17; 6:15–19? Unfortunately, there is no space to explore this question here.

buds. The buds, however, never opened into full flowers. The problem was that our bush was not getting enough sunlight. If we did not transplant it, the bush would neither grow to normal size nor produce flowers. Likewise, we as the church will not bear fruit and grow and extend across the earth in the way God intends unless we stay out of the shadows of the world and remain in the light of God's presence—in his word and prayer and in fellowship with other believers in the church, always reminding ourselves of our unique place in God's historical story. The mark of the true church is an expanding witness to the presence of God: to our families, to others in the church, to our neighborhood, to our city, the country, and ultimately the whole earth.

May God give us grace to go out into the world as his extending temple and spread God's presence by reflecting it until it finally fills the entire earth, as it will, according to Rev. 21. The prophet Jeremiah says that in the end-time people "will no longer say 'the ark of the covenant of the LORD' [in Israel's old temple]. And it will not come to mind, nor will they remember it, nor will they miss it, nor will it be made again" (Jer. 3:16–17), for the end-time temple encompassing the new creation will be so incomparable to the old temple.

Conclusion

The prophecy of the latter-day temple begins in Christ's first coming and the church through God's special revelatory presence, the essence of the old temple, which has broken out of the old temple. Christ was the first expression of this divine presence that had left the old temple, and then his Spirit indwelling the church was the continuing ongoing expression of the beginning latter-day temple. All along, the symbolic design of the temple was to indicate that God's "holy of holies" presence would eventually fill the entire cosmos, so that the cosmos, instead of a small physical house, would be the container of this glorious presence. Again, the timing of the fulfillment of this prophecy is somewhat unexpected. It is not fulfilled all at once but rather begins with Christ and then his Spirit indwelling the church. We saw that the Corinthian church was part of this inaugurated indwelling. Then, at the climax of all history, the inaugurated indwelling presence of God completely fills the entire cosmos, which appears to have been the design of the Ezek. 40–48 temple prophecy all along.

Thus, the essence of the temple, the glorious presence of God, sheds its OT architectural cocoon by emerging in Christ, then dwelling in his people, and finally dwelling throughout the whole earth. Thus, again, we see a major NT idea, Christ and the church as the end-time temple, to be another facet of the already–not yet new creation.

This particular study of the use of the OT in the NT is an example of what may be the case with other difficult uses of the OT in the NT where "literal" fulfillment does not seem to be indicated. That is, the more we do exegesis and biblical theology in both Testaments, the better we will see how NT authors play their part in a consistent and organic interpretative development of OT passages.

How does the notion of the expanding temple of God's presence fit into the NT storyline that I formulated in earlier chapters? *Jesus's life, trials, death for sinners, and especially resurrection by the Spirit have launched the fulfillment of the eschatological already–not yet new-creational reign, bestowed by grace through faith and <u>resulting in worldwide commission to the faithful to advance this new-creation reign</u> and resulting in judgment for the unbelieving, unto the triune God's glory.* We have seen in the preceding section of this chapter that the temple is an organic aspect of the kingdom of the new creation. Accordingly, the imperative to expand God's tabernacling presence throughout the world is the main way that the "worldwide commission to the faithful" (a crucial part of the storyline just noted above) is to be carried out.

I wish to conclude, however, by focusing on the main point of this chapter for the church: the task of the church in being God's temple, so filled with his presence, is to expand the temple of his presence and fill the earth with that glorious presence until God finally accomplishes this goal completely at the end of time. This is the church's common, unified mission. May we, by God's grace, unite around this goal.

PART 7

THE STORY OF THE CHURCH AS END-TIME ISRAEL IN THE INAUGURATED NEW CREATION

20

The Church as the Transformed and Restored Eschatological Israel

The Presuppositional Basis for the Church Being True Israel

This chapter and the next one will argue at major points that the salvation of the church and its ongoing existence is to be conceived of as the inaugurated restoration of end-time Israel, which, as we have seen throughout and will again, is a part of the latter-day new creation (esp. in Isa. 40–66 and the NT's reflection on that segment of Isaiah). In this respect, these two chapters will also develop that part of the storyline of God's people being faithful in their new-creational existence. We will see that gentiles, who form the majority of the church, are viewed as part of the restoration of latter-day faithful Israel. Before elaborating on the church as the fulfillment of Israel's restoration promises, I must discuss the scriptural approach to understanding how gentiles could become part of true eschatological Israel along with a remnant of ethnic Jewish believers.

I have discussed elsewhere several hermeneutical and theological presuppositions underlying the exegetical approach of Jesus and NT writers.[1] Two of these presuppositions are important for understanding how Christ and the church can be viewed as the inaugurated fulfillment of God's promises of Israel's end-time restoration from captivity. The first presupposition is the

---

1. G. K. Beale, "Did Jesus and His Followers Preach the Right Doctrine from the Wrong Texts? An Examination of the Presuppositions of the Apostles' Exegetical Method," *Themelios* 14 (1989): 89–96.

notion of corporate solidarity or representation or identification, sometimes known as the concept of "the one and the many."[2] In the OT, the actions of kings and prophets represented the nation Israel, and fathers represented families. The many people represented by the one king, prophet, or father were looked upon as if they had done the righteous or the sinful deed done by the representative, so that the many also received the condition of blessing or of judgment that came upon the individual for the deed. One of the best illustrations of this concept is the sin and punishment of the first Adam, which is seen by Paul to be representative of all humanity, so that all humanity is seen to have committed Adam's sin and thus to be deserving of the punishment of that sin. In antithesis, Christ, the last Adam, performed an act of righteousness that resulted in resurrection life, which was representative for believing humanity, so that they were viewed as having done the righteous act and thus as deserving of resurrection life.

The second presupposition, following from the first, is that Christ is the true Israel, and as true Israel, he represents the church as the continuation of true Israel from the OT. Christ came to do what Israel should have done but failed to do. Those who identify by faith with Christ, whether Jew or gentile, become identified with him and his identity as true eschatological Israel. This identification takes place in the same way that we have seen in earlier chapters in which people are identified by faith with Jesus as God's Son, and so they become "adopted sons of God." Likewise, in the same way that we have seen that people become identified by faith with Christ as being in the eschatological image of God, so they begin to regain that image. We saw in chapter 13 that reference to Jesus as "the Son of God" is another way of referring to him as Israel, since this was one of the names by which Israel was called in the OT.[3] And we likewise saw that his title "Son of Man" is yet another way of alluding to him as Israel (Dan. 7:13 in the context of Dan. 7; Ps. 80:17).

It is important to recall that Jesus's titles "Son of Man" and "Son of God" reflect respectively both the OT figures of Adam and Israel. This is because, as we have seen earlier, Adam and Israel are two sides of one coin. Israel and its patriarchs were given the same commission as was Adam in Gen. 1:26–28.[4] Consequently, it is not unwarranted to understand Israel as a corporate Adam who had failed in its "garden of Eden,"[5] in much the same way as its primal

2. For brief elaboration of the scriptural evidence for this presupposition and the second one, see ibid., 90, 95.

3. Note God's "son" in Exod. 4:22–23; Deut. 14:1; Isa. 1:2, 4; 63:8; Hos. 1:10; 11:1, and God's "firstborn" in Exod. 4:22; Jer. 31:9; the coming Messiah of Israel was also known as God's "firstborn" (Ps. 89:27; cf. "son" in Ps. 2:7).

4. On which, see chap. 19 under the heading "Adam's Commission as a Priest-King to Rule and Expand the Temple Is Passed On to the Patriarchs."

5. Note, again, OT texts where Israel's promised land is called the "garden of Eden" (Gen. 13:10; Isa. 51:3; Ezek. 36:35; Joel 2:3).

father had failed in the first garden. In this respect, it is understandable that one reason why Jesus is called "Son of God" is that this was a name for the first Adam (Luke 3:38; cf. Gen. 5:1–3) and for Israel (Exod. 4:22; Hos. 11:1), who was also called a "firstborn" (Exod. 4:22; Jer. 31:9). The Messiah was also prophesied to be a "firstborn" (Ps. 89:27). Likewise, the expression "Son of Man" from Dan. 7:13 refers to end-time Israel and its representative king as the son of Adam who is sovereign over beasts.[6] Thus, God had designed that the nation of Israel be a corporate national Adam who was to represent what true humanity should be like (see, e.g., Deut. 4:6–8). Unfortunately, Israel proved to be unfaithful just like Adam.

This discussion has significance for understanding what it means for the predominantly gentile church to be seen as the continuation of true Israel. It means that being identified with true Israel is neither a narrow parochial identification nor one that erases gentile identity. Rather, the church is also identified with what it means to be true Adam, especially in its identification with Jesus, the true Israel and last Adam. Consequently, for the church to be the beginning of true end-time Israel is to begin to be identified with the original purposes of Adam, true humanity, which Christ has fulfilled.

Therefore, it is important to maintain that the church is not merely like Israel but actually is Israel. This is most in keeping with the original purposes of Israel itself and why the OT prophesies that in the eschaton gentiles will become a part of Israel and not merely be redeemed people who retain the name "gentiles" and coexist alongside but as a separate people from redeemed ethnic Israel. These OT prophecies did not envision that gentile converts to Israel would have their complete gentile identity erased, but neither did these prophecies foresee that redeemed gentiles would exist alongside as a separate people but separate from redeemed Israelites. Rather, these converted gentiles would come to be identified with Israel and Israel's God. Such eschatologically converted gentiles would become identified with Israel as had gentiles in the past, such as Rahab, Ruth, and Uriah. Their gentile identity was not eradicated, but they came to have a greater identity as true Israelites.

The one difference, however, between converted gentiles of the past and those in the future eschaton, which is revealed more clearly in the NT (e.g., Eph. 2:12, 19; 3:4–6), is that the latter did not have to move to geographical Israel, be circumcised and worship at the temple, obey the food laws and observe the holy days, and follow other laws distinguishing national Israel from the nations.[7] Rather, in the end-time period gentiles identify with Jesus, true Israel, and become part of the temple in him and are circumcised by his death and are made clean in him. In the new age, Jesus, as true Adam/Israel, is the

6. Recall that in Daniel the "Son of Man" takes over the kingdoms of former evil empires portrayed as beasts; likewise Ps. 80:17 refers to Israel as "the son of man," a royal figure.

7. During the Israelite theocracy, it seemed to be the rule that gentiles who converted to Israel's faith would move to Israel, though there may have been exceptions.

only ultimate identification tag that transcends gentile identification marks or the old nationalistic Israelite identifying marks of the law.

This way of understanding how gentiles can become part of true end-time Israel is an OT mystery that has been revealed in the NT. This is why Paul says in Eph. 3:3–6 that the "mystery" (*mystērion*) is that "the Gentiles are fellow heirs and fellow members of the body, and fellow partakers of the promise in Christ Jesus through the gospel" (v. 6). What is the essence of the "mystery" in Eph. 3? It was not as clear in the OT that when the Messiah came, the theocracy of Israel would be so completely reconstituted that it would continue only as the new organism of the Messiah (Jesus), the true Israel. In him Jews and gentiles would be fused together on a footing of complete equality through corporate identification.[8] Some commentators have seen the mystery consisting of complete equality, but as far as I can determine, none have apparently underscored the basis for such equality lying in the one person "Christ Jesus" as the true Israel, since there can be no distinguishing marks in him but only unity.

That the subject of gentiles being now related to Israel is in mind in Eph. 3:6 is also apparent from 2:12, where gentiles who do not believe are viewed as separated from the following three realities, which are put in synonymous parallelism: (1) "separate from Christ," (2) "alienated from the commonwealth of Israel," and (3) "strangers to the covenants of promise." To be separate from Christ (Messiah) is to be separated from Israel and from participation in the promises given to it, and Eph. 3:6 presents gentiles as sharers both in the Israelite Messiah and in the "promises," which must be the same as the promises of 2:12. That gentiles can be considered true Israel is apparent in that the Isa. 57:19 prophecy of Israel's restoration can have begun fulfillment partly in gentiles who believe in the directly preceding context (so Eph. 2:17), and that they can be seen as a part of Israel's inaugurated end-time temple in 2:20–22, also in the directly preceding context.[9] The "as" (*hōs*) in 3:5 (the

8. Similarly William Hendriksen, *Exposition of Ephesians* (Grand Rapids: Baker Academic, 1967), 153–55. Hendriksen's comments have helped to clarify my own conclusion, though he is not clear about whether Christ is the "new organism" or the church. F. F. Bruce (*The Epistles to the Colossians, to Philemon, and to the Ephesians*, NICNT [Grand Rapids: Eerdmans, 1984], 314) says that the mystery is that the complete lack of discrimination between Jew and gentile was not foreseen. Robert L. Saucy ("The Church as the Mystery of God," in *Dispensationalism, Israel and the Church: The Search for Definition*, ed. Craig A. Blaising and Darrell L. Bock [Grand Rapids: Zondervan, 1992], 149–51) says that a secondary nuance of the Eph. 3 mystery indicates unanticipated fulfillment in the sense that gentiles are being saved, though Israel's salvation is being set aside for the most part, and in the sense that the OT expected only one age of fulfillment, but Ephesians pictures two such ages. I find neither of these notions present in Eph. 3, though the latter idea could be involved but not the focus, especially as nuanced by an "already and not yet" notion (on which, see below).

9. The cumulative force of the argument in this section points in the opposite direction of the view of Saucy ("Church as the Mystery of God"), who contends, among other things, that the "mystery" has nothing to do with gentiles becoming a part of true Israel.

mystery of Christ "<u>as</u> it has now been revealed") is comparative, indicating partial but not full revelation of the mystery in the OT.[10]

Therefore, this is not an entirely new revelation; it is one with organic links to the OT, and one that is made clearer in the NT revelation. Therefore, the notion of Christ as true Israel and believing Jews and gentiles in Christ composing true end-time Israel makes good sense of the meaning of the "mystery" in Eph. 3.[11] The fact that the great majority of uses of "mystery" (*mystērion*) elsewhere in the NT indicate beginning end-time fulfillment of the OT, often in an unexpected manner,[12] points to the same beginning unexpected latter-day fulfillment here.[13] This unexpected fulfillment involves an alteration in understanding the timing of the fulfillment: from the OT vantage point, it appeared that fulfillment would occur all at once, but the dawn of the eschatological age in Christ reveals that the fulfillment is inaugurated for an unspecified but long period and then completely fulfilled at the very end of the age. But there is another aspect of the unexpected fulfillment that was a mystery from the OT vantage point. The beginning fulfillment involves an actual transformation of how the fulfillment would have been formerly understood. In the case of Eph. 3, as noted just above, gentiles become part of true Israel not by making pilgrimage to geographical Israel and taking on the unique signs of theocratic Israel, but rather by making pilgrimage to Jesus, the true Israel, and identifying with him as the ultimate mark of being part of true Israel.[14]

Consequently, it is not an allegorical or spiritualizing hermeneutic by which the predominantly gentile church is to be identified with Israel" but it is what we might call a "legal representative" or "corporate" hermeneutic that underlies this identification of the church. This second presupposition of Christ as true Israel and the church as true Israel is critical to understanding why OT

10. In contrast to Charles C. Ryrie, "The Mystery in Ephesians 3," *BSac* 123 (1966): 29, who contends that *hōs* has a "declarative force" of only adding additional information, or that it has the notion of "but." Both senses would be very rare meanings of the word and therefore bear the burden of proof. The usual use of the word and the OT background in Eph. 2–3 together are difficult hurdles for such a view to overcome.

11. This section is partly based on G. K. Beale, *John's Use of the Old Testament in Revelation*, JSNTSup 166 (Sheffield: Sheffield Academic Press, 1998), 243–45 (for the fuller analysis of "mystery" in Eph. 3, see pp. 242–46).

12. On which, see ibid., 215–72.

13. I discussed this kind of use of "mystery" in Matt. 13:10–11 (see chap. 13 under the excursus heading "The Inaugurated, Unexpected, and Transformed Nature of the End-Time Kingdom") and in 2 Thess. 2:3–7 (see chap. 7 under the heading "The Already–Not Yet End-Time Tribulation in the New Testament"), and I will do so again later with respect to marriage and the use of Gen. 2:24 in Eph. 5:32 (see chap. 26 under the heading "Marriage as a Transformed New-Creational Institution in Ephesians 5").

14. Chapter 22 will discuss Jesus as the beginning fulfillment of the land promises made to Israel. Here we are concerned only to view Jesus as the corporate representative of true Israel. The two notions of Jesus being the inauguration of the land promises and being the corporate representative of end-time Israel are not incompatible.

promises of eschatological restoration are applied to Christ and the church in the NT, and why both are considered to be the inaugurated end-time fulfillment of the prophesied restoration of Israel. They do not merely resemble what restored Israel was to be; they are the actual beginning of eschatological restored Israel. In particular, the idea is that Jesus as the individual messianic king of Israel represented the true continuing remnant of Israel, and all those identifying with him become a part of the Israelite remnant that he represents.

The Old Testament Notion of Gentiles Becoming Latter-Day True Israel as Background for the New Testament Presupposition That the Church Is True Israel

The idea that the Messiah would represent latter-day Israel and that the gentiles would become part of true end-time Israel is not merely a NT presupposition; it has its roots in the OT itself.

Isaiah 49

Isaiah 49 is among the clearest statements in the OT that in the latter days the Messiah would sum up true Israel in himself. Isaiah 49:3–6 reads,

> He said to me, "You are My Servant, Israel,
> In whom I will show My glory."
> But I said, "I have toiled in vain,
> I have spent my strength for nothing and vanity;
> Yet surely the justice due to me is with the LORD,
> And my reward with my God."
> And now says the LORD, who formed me from the womb to be His Servant,
> To bring Jacob back to Him, so that Israel might be gathered to Him
> (For I am honored in the sight of the LORD,
> And my God is my strength),
> He says, "It is too small a thing that you should be My Servant
> To raise up the tribes of Jacob and to restore the preserved ones of Israel;
> I will also make you a light of the nations,
> So that My salvation may reach to the end of the earth."

Here the Servant is called "Israel": "And He [the LORD] said to me, 'You are My Servant, Israel, in whom I will show My glory" (v. 3). And his latter-day mission is "to raise up the tribes of Jacob and to restore the preserved ones of Israel" (v. 6). Now, the Servant cannot be the entire nation of Israel, since the sinful nation cannot restore itself, nor can the Servant be a faithful remnant of the nation, since the remnant is still sinful, and it would be redundant to say that the remnant's mission was to restore the remnant (which the "preserved ones" refers to in v. 6). Some have identified the Servant with Isaiah the prophet, but there is no indication that he ever accomplished such a mission, especially as further elaborated on in Isa. 53, and especially since he was also still sinful (as was even the faithful remnant) and needed the healing mission explained there. Thus, the Servant in Isa. 49:3 is best understood to be an individual messianic Servant who would restore the remnant of Israel.

But how is the notion of the messianic Servant summing up true Israel relevant to gentiles becoming true Israel in the eschaton? Since this Servant was to be the summation of true Israel, all who wanted to identify with true Israel, whether Jew or gentile, would have to identify with him (which is the implication of Isa. 53).[15] The OT never makes explicit this connection between the individual true Israel, the Servant (or Israel's end-time king), and gentiles who identify with him, but I believe that this is implicit. As we will see, the NT does make it explicit, as I have already begun to suggest in the discussion of Eph. 3 above. The remaining discussion in this section will focus on OT prophecies about how in the latter days converted gentiles will be identified as true Israelites.

Psalm 87

Psalm 87 speaks of gentiles being "born" in Zion in the eschaton, so that they are considered as native-born Israelites:

> A Psalm of the sons of Korah. A Song.
> His foundation is in the holy mountains.
> The LORD loves the gates of Zion
> More than all the other dwelling places of Jacob.
> Glorious things are spoken of you,
> O city of God. Selah.
> "I shall mention Rahab [Egypt] and Babylon among those who
>   know Me;
> Behold, Philistia and Tyre with Ethiopia: 'This one was born there.'"
> But of Zion it shall be said, "This one and that one were born in her";
> And the Most High Himself will establish her.
> The LORD will count when He registers the peoples,
> "This one was born there." Selah.
> Then those who sing as well as those who play the flutes shall say,
> "All my springs of joy are in you."

The "glorious things" spoken of "Zion," the "city of God" (vv. 2–3) include that the gentile nations will be considered to have been "born there" (v. 4). The reference to "there" in verse 4, where the nations are born, refers to "Zion"

---

15. Note the Servant's work of redeeming both gentiles (Isa. 52:15) and Israelites (Isa. 53:4–12).

and the "city of God" in verses 2–3. In verse 6 "the LORD will count when He registers the peoples" refers to a final, end-time accounting of the gentile peoples who "know Him" (v. 4) and who are considered true eschatological Israelites because they have been "born there" (v. 6b)[16] in "Zion" (vv. 2, 5), the "city of God" (v. 3). Thus, people who have their national and ethnic origins among gentile nations will nevertheless be viewed as true end-time Israelites or true citizens of Zion because that is the place of their spiritual birth.[17]

Isaiah 19

Isaiah 19 affirms a strikingly similar idea. Isaiah 19:18–25 reads,

> In that day five cities in the land of Egypt will be speaking the language of Canaan and swearing allegiance to the LORD of hosts; one will be called the City of Destruction. In that day there will be an altar to the LORD in the midst of the land of Egypt, and a pillar to the LORD near its border. It will become a sign

16. So also *Midr. Ps.* 87.7 interprets Ps. 87:6 to refer to "the nations who bring the children of Israel" out of exile as "belonging with Israel."

17. See likewise A. A. Anderson, *The Book of Psalms*, NCB (Grand Rapids: Eerdmans, 1972), 2:621–22; Mitchell Dahood, *Psalms*, 3 vols., AB 16, 17, 17A (Garden City, NY: Doubleday, 1964), 2:300; Thijs Booij, "Some Observations on Psalm LXXXVII," *VT* 37 (1987): 16–25; Marvin E. Tate, *Psalms 51–100*, WBC 20 (Dallas: Word, 1990), 389; James Luther Mays, *Psalms*, IBC (Louisville: John Knox, 1994), 281–82; Craig C. Broyles, *Psalms*, NIBC (Peabody, MA: Hendrickson, 1999), 350–51; Samuel Terrien, *The Psalms: Strophic Structure and Theological Commentary*, ECC (Grand Rapids: Eerdmans, 2003), 622–23; Yohanna I. Katanacho, "Investigating the Purposeful Placement of Psalm 86" (PhD diss., Trinity International University, 2006), 150–54; John E. Goldingay, *Psalms*, 2 vols., BCOTWP (Grand Rapids: Baker Academic, 2007), 2:635–41; Christl M. Maier, "Psalm 87 as a Reappraisal of the Zion Tradition and Its Reception in Galatians 4:26," *CBQ* 69 (2007): 473–86. See also J. J. Stewart Perowne, *The Book of Psalms*, 2 vols. (Andover, MA: W. F. Draper, 1876), 2:134.

However, some think that Ps. 87 is a reference to exiled Jews from the gentile nations listed, who are enrolled in Zion: so Hans-Joachim Kraus, *Psalms 60–150*, trans. Hilton C. Oswald, CC (Minneapolis: Fortress, 1993), 187–88; James Limburg, *Psalms*, WestBC (Louisville: Westminster John Knox, 2000), 295–96; Erich Zenger, "Zion as Mother of the Nations in Psalm 87," in *The God of Israel and the Nations: Studies in Isaiah and the Psalms*, ed. Norbert Lohfink and Erich Zenger, trans. Everett R. Kalin (Collegeville, MN: Liturgical Press, 2000), 123–60; J. A. Emerton, "The Problem of Psalm 87," *VT* 50 (2001): 183–99, esp. 197; Frank Lothar Hossfeld and Erich Zenger, *Psalms 2: A Commentary on Ps. 51–100*, trans. Linda M. Maloney, ed. Klaus Baltzer, Hermeneia (Minneapolis: Fortress, 2005), 382.

A few commentators see that the gentile nations are being registered in Zion, but these commentators are ambiguous about whether these gentiles are also considered to be actual children of Zion or equivalent to natural-born Israelites: so Artur Weiser, *The Psalms: A Commentary*, trans. Herbert Hartwell, OTL (London: SCM, 1962), in loc; Charles A. Briggs, *A Critical and Exegetical Commentary on the Book of Psalms*, 2 vols., ICC (Edinburgh: T&T Clark, 1986–87), 2:240–41. See also Robert Davidson, *The Vitality of Worship: A Commentary on the Book of Psalms* (Grand Rapids: Eerdmans, 1998), 287–88. Davidson sees that the psalm could refer to Jews born in different countries being identified with Zion or to gentiles identifying with Zion as their spiritual home.

and a witness to the LORD of hosts in the land of Egypt; for they will cry to the LORD because of oppressors, and He will send them a Savior and a Champion, and He will deliver them. Thus the LORD will make Himself known to Egypt, and the Egyptians will know the LORD in that day. They will even worship with sacrifice and offering, and will make a vow to the LORD and perform it. And the LORD will strike Egypt, striking but healing; so they will return to the LORD, and He will respond to them and will heal them. In that day there will be a highway from Egypt to Assyria, and the Assyrians will come into Egypt and the Egyptians into Assyria, and the Egyptians will worship with the Assyrians. In that day Israel will be the third party with Egypt and Assyria, a blessing in the midst of the earth, whom the LORD of hosts has blessed, saying, "Blessed is Egypt My people, and Assyria the work of My hands, and Israel My inheritance."

This is another text speaking of the latter-day restoration of the nations, particularly Egypt and Assyria. Egypt and Assyria could be seen as not becoming a part of Israel, even though they are salvifically restored. The reason for this is the mention that "Israel will be a third party with Egypt and Assyria," all three of whom are to be a "blessing in the midst of the earth" (v. 24). However, there also appears to be indication that the Egyptians will be identified as Israelite Semites, since verse 18 says that they "will be speaking the language of Caanan," which is directly linked in the next phrase to "swearing allegiance to the LORD of hosts." Thus, the sworn allegiance to God is seen as being inextricably linked with speaking in the Hebrew tongue, a likely way to connote that such allegiance indicates that one is to be reckoned as a native Israelite. In addition, that Egypt is also called "My people" adds to this impression, since "My people" (*'ammî*) virtually without exception occurs elsewhere with reference to God's people Israel (e.g, in Isaiah, outside of 19:25, "my people" refers to Israel every other time [25x]). Similarly, the expression that Assyria is "the work of My hands" may have the same connotation, since the phrase "work of My hands" (or virtual equivalents with different pronouns) occurs only four times elsewhere in Isaiah, three of which refer to Israel as God's work.[18]

Isaiah 56

Isaiah 56 develops this theme of gentile identification with Israel further. At the time of Israel's eschatological restoration (v. 1), gentiles are exhorted in the following manner: "Let not the foreigner who has joined himself to the LORD say, 'The LORD will surely separate me from His people [Israel]'" (v. 3). Neither will the Israelite eunuch be separated from the Lord (v. 4). Whereas

18. The fourth reference is in Isa. 5:12, which refers to the mighty "deeds of the LORD," as also is the case in Ps. 143:5. The phrase, or virtual equivalents, appears four times elsewhere in Job and Psalms, however, referring never to a nation but to the new resurrected condition of a human (Job 14:15), to all of human creation (Job 34:19), or to the entire creation in general (Ps. 19:1; 102:25).

formerly eunuchs were excluded from worship in the temple (Deut. 23:1) and from the priesthood, now they will have free access to the temple (v. 5). Likewise, although gentile proselytes were not excluded from temple worship, they were excluded from being priests, since that was reserved for men from the tribe of Levi. In the time of Israel's restoration, however, gentile converts ("the foreigners who join themselves to the Lord") will be able "to minister to [the Lord]" by "their burnt offerings and their sacrifices . . . on [the Lord's] altar" in the "house" (i.e., the temple) (vv. 6–7). Although the Hebrew verb for "minister" (*šārat*) can refer to someone ministering outside Israel's temple, it refers to Israelite priests ministering in the temple in at least seventy-five of the some one hundred times it is used in the OT. That gentiles in Isa. 56:6–7 are considered to be ministering as priests is apparent from the clear fact that they are doing so in God's "house" (mentioned three times in v. 7). Furthermore, their ministering by "burnt offerings" and "sacrifices" on God's "altar" is also the manner in which Israel's priests are sometimes portrayed when described by the same verb "minister" (*šārat*).[19]

Isaiah 66

The notion of gentiles becoming Israelite priests serving in God's end-time temple is developed further in Isa. 66:18–21. This important passage is quite difficult to interpret. Therefore, I ask for the reader's patience to follow me through the tangled web of this text. Isa. 66:18–21 reads as follows:

> "For I know their works and their thoughts; the time is coming to gather all nations and tongues. And they shall come and see My glory. I will set a sign among them and will send survivors from them to the nations: Tarshish, Put, Lud, Meshech, Rosh, Tubal and Javan, to the distant coastlands that have neither heard My fame nor seen My glory. And they will declare My glory among the nations. Then they shall bring all your brethren from all the nations as a grain offering to the Lord, on horses, in chariots, in litters, on mules and on camels, to my holy mountain Jerusalem," says the Lord, "just as the sons of Israel bring their grain offering in a clean vessel to the house of the Lord. I will also take some of them for priests and for Levites," says the Lord.

The eschatological restoration of faithful Israel has been focused on in Isa. 66:7–14, though 66:14b–18a prophesies that there will also be judgment of unfaithful, idolatrous Israelites at the same time. Then 66:18b–21 turns the focus to the ingathering of the nations. The last part of verse 18 says that God will gather the nations, so that they will come to see his glory, which is a signpost that the book of Isaiah is ending similarly to the way it began in

---

19. With respect to this verb linked to "burnt offerings," see 2 Chron. 24:14; 31:2; Ezek. 44:11; concerning the verb linked to "sacrifices," see Ezek. 46:24; with regard to the verb in connection to the "altar," see Exod. 28:43; 30:20; Num. 3:31; 4:14; Ezek. 40:46; Joel 1:13; 2:17.

2:2–4, where there is a forecast that the nations will stream into Jerusalem at the eschaton to learn of God's ways.

There is some ambiguity in Isa. 66:19 concerning the identity of "them" in the first part of the verse: "I will set a sign among them and will send survivors from them to the nations." The probable identification is the faithful in Israel who are left ("survivors") after God's purging judgment of ungodly Israelites, and who have begun to be restored immediately subsequent to that judgment, all of which has just been described in verses 7–18a. The identity of "them" in verse 19 must be faithful Jews who have begun to experience restoration, and who now go to the nations to announce God's news of restoration to those nations. Thus, the "they" who "will declare My glory among the nations" (v. 19b) are also restored Israelites. Verse 20 is crucial for understanding the flow of thought for verses 18b–21.

Verse 20a says, "Then they shall bring all your brothers from all the nations as a grain offering to the LORD." The "they" are likely the restored Israelite "survivors" whose mission it will be to go "to the nations" and "declare My glory among the nations" (v. 19).[20] But who are "your brothers" in verse 20?

The "brothers" either are other Israelites who are restored by the Israelite missionaries or are those gentiles from the nations who respond positively to the message about God's glory by the Jewish missionaries. Most of the time the word "brother" (*'āḥ*) refers to brothers of the same bloodline or of the same ethnicity, which here would favor the identification of Israelites. The likelihood, however, is that the "brothers" in this passage are the restored gentiles, since this is the main point in the flow of thought so far in verses 18b–19 (note, e.g., the focus on "gathering all nations" in v. 18 and "declaring glory among the nations" in v. 19). This identification is also apparent from a second observation: nowhere in all of the book of Isaiah or in the prophets is there any mention of Israelites restoring other Israelites, although, as we have seen at the beginning of this chapter and will see again, there is the notion of an "individual Israel" restoring the remnant of Israel (e.g., Isa. 49:2–6; 53).[21] But the idea in verse 20, if the "brothers" are Israelites, would be a remnant of faithful Israelites (plural) restoring other Israelites (plural). And even if in Isa. 49 and 53 Israelites (plural) were to be seen to be restoring other Israelites (which is unlikely), that thought has not been so far raised in Isa. 66.

A third observation also suggests that "your brothers" are gentile converts. Verse 20 ends with a metaphorical comparison: the Israelite missionaries bringing in converts from the nations are compared to "the sons of Israel [who] bring their grain offering in a clean vessel to the house of the LORD."

20. The "they" possibly could refer to gentiles from the nations who have responded to the message declared by the Jewish missionaries at the end of v. 19.

21. The idea of the "one and the many" that later enabled Paul to identify himself with the Isa. 49 Servant (Acts 13:47; 2 Cor. 6:2) opens the possibility within Isaiah itself of Israelites being commissioned to restore other Israelites.

Here "the sons of Israel" represent the whole nation, not a part of the nation, who are separate from the "grain offering" that they bring to the temple. So likewise, it would seem to be more in keeping with the metaphor that the Jewish "survivors" sent to the nations represent all the redeemed of Israel, and therefore that the "brothers" are the converted nations, who are like an offering brought to the temple. The apostle Paul understood the "grain offering" metaphor at the end of Isa. 66:20 in just this way: he says that he is "a minister of Christ Jesus to the Gentiles, ministering as a priest the gospel of God, that my offering of the Gentiles may become acceptable" (Rom. 15:16). Paul compares the bringing in of the gentiles in the first part of Isa. 66:20 to an offering to God in the last part of that verse.[22]

That the "brothers" of Israelites should be identified with gentile believers is not a strange notion in the OT prophets, since we have seen in Isaiah itself that restored gentiles would become identified with Israel and considered fellow Israelites, which is close to the notion of "brother." In the end time gentiles would begin to speak in the Hebrew tongue and would be considered to be "My [God's] people," an expression almost always reserved for Israel (cf. Isa. 19:18, 23–25). And they will be priests in the temple, who can never be "separated from God's people," Israel (cf. Isa. 56:3, 6–7). Virtually the same point about the phrase "My people" is made in Zech. 2:11: "Many nations will join themselves to the LORD in that day and will become <u>My people</u>" (on which, see further directly below). Zechariah 8:23 develops this notion from Zech. 2: "In those days ten men from all the nations of every language will grasp the garment of a Jew, saying, 'Let us go with you, for we have heard that God is with you.'" Similarly, Ezek. 47:22 is very close to the point we see that Isa. 66:20 is making about gentiles being "brothers" of Israelites at the time of the eschatological restoration: gentile "aliens . . . who bring forth sons in your [Israel's] midst . . . shall be to you [Israel] as the native-born among the sons of Israel" (see further directly below). Comparably, we have also seen above in Ps. 87 that various gentile nations will be considered to have been born in Zion at the consummation of the times. If gentiles are considered to be born in Jerusalem at the denouement, then they can also be considered to be eschatological brothers with believing ethnic Israelites.

If it is correct to understand that the "brothers" of Isa. 66:20 are gentile converts, then verse 21 is naturally also applied to these gentile believers: "I [God] will also take some of them for priests and for Levites." It would not seem to make good sense to say that God would take converted Jews to be priests and Levites, since priests and Levites already come from Israel and would have been among Israelites gathered from the nations. Perhaps one could argue that in the end-time restoration God will appoint Levitical priests from tribes other than Levi, though this notion is not found in any other prophecy

22. The NA[27] margin lists Isa. 66:20 as an allusion in Rom. 15:16.

about Israel's restoration. It is also possible that verse 21 pictures the whole Israelite nation as having the position of priesthood in development of Isa. 61:6 (which itself appears to develop Exod. 19:6). The problem with this view is that verse 21 says that only a part of the purported returning Diaspora Jews will be made into priests, not the whole of them.

More likely, God will make gentiles from the nations to be Levitical priests, which probably is another of the various ways to indicate that the nations become identified as Israelites in the latter days. This passage, then, appears to be a further development of the only two other earlier places in Isaiah where converted gentiles are gathered to God's end-time temple (2:2–4) and will serve in that temple as "priests" (56:3, 6–7).[23]

Zechariah

As noted above, we have seen that one of the rare uses of "My people" also occurs in Zech. 2:11, at the time of Israel's eschatological restoration (vv. 9–10): "Many nations will join themselves to the LORD in that day and will become <u>My people</u>. Then I will dwell in your midst, and you will know that the LORD of hosts has sent Me to you." Calling the "many nations" by the name of "My people," as we have seen, is extremely rare, since almost always this is a name reserved for Israel (the phrase occurs three other times in Zechariah [8:7, 8; 13:9], always referring to Israel).[24] Accordingly, again the likelihood is that the nations in Zech. 2:11, who have made pilgrimage to Israel (see 2:12; 8:22–23), are considered to have become converts to Israel, so that they take on Israel's typical name of "My people."

Ezekiel 47

Likewise, Ezek. 47, also mentioned briefly above, understands that at the final restoration of Israel, gentiles will be considered to be part of the nation. Ezekiel 47:21–23 reads,

> "So you shall divide this land among yourselves according to the tribes of Israel. You shall divide it by lot for an inheritance among yourselves and among the aliens who stay in your midst, who bring forth sons in your midst. And they shall be to you as the native-born among the sons of Israel; they shall be allotted an inheritance with you among the tribes of Israel. And in the tribe with which the alien stays, there you shall give him his inheritance," declares the Lord GOD.

That gentile "aliens" are considered a formal part of the nation Israel is indicated by the fact that the nation is commanded to "divide this land among

---

23. See the following excursus, where the recent history of diverse interpretations of Isa. 66:21 is given, some identifying the "priests and Levites" with gentiles, and others with Jews.
24. And note "His people" in Zech. 9:16, which also refers to Israel.

yourselves according to the tribes of Israel," which included giving the "alien" an "inheritance," since these aliens were to be considered "as the native-born among the sons of Israel." It is possible that since verse 22 says the sons of the alien were to be considered "as" (or "like") native-born Israelites, they were not considered to be actual Israelites. However, the best context for understanding this is the precedent of how gentiles became converts to the faith of Israel in the OT epoch. When people such as a remnant of the Egyptians who went with Israel out of Egypt (Exod. 12:38, 48–51), or Rahab (Josh. 6:25; cf. Matt. 1:5) or Ruth (Ruth 1:16; 4:10; cf. Matt. 1:5) converted to the faith of Israel, they were considered members of the nation of Israel, *just as much as was a native-born Israelite.* The same is likely the case here in Ezek. 47. According to the principle that "the last things will be like the first things," the eschatological condition of the "alien" in Ezek. 47:22 ("and they [aliens] will be unto you as a native [*wĕhāyû lākem kĕʾezrāḥ*] among the sons of Israel") appears to echo the condition of the alien at the very inception of Israel's history according to Exod. 12:48 ("and he [the alien] will be as a native [*wĕhāyâ kĕʾezraḥ*] of the land").[25] Ezekiel 47:22–23 is introduced by the statement "You shall divide this land among yourselves according to the tribes of Israel" (v. 21). Then verses 22–23 describe members of the tribes of Israel to be ethnic Israelites, and those who are nonethnic members of the tribes are also mentioned and are also considered to be true tribal members,[26]

---

25. Note that, as in Exod. 12:48, so also Ezek. 47:21–22 has directly in mind Israel's "land." Leviticus 19:34 may be included in the echo: "The alien who resides with you shall be to you as the native among you, and you shall love him as yourself."

26. The Hebrew word *gēr*, rendered in Num. 19:34 and Ezek. 47:22–23 as "alien," can be translated as "sojourner" or, better, "resident alien" and is used often in the OT (as is the verbal form *gwr*). When applied to people coming from outside Israel to reside there, it can indicate either someone in the process of converting to Israel or someone who has converted, who then is to obey all of Israel's laws just as all Israelites are to do (Exod. 12:49; Lev. 18:26; 24:22; Num. 15:15)—e.g., circumcision (Exod. 12:48), Sabbath (Lev. 16:29), diet (Lev. 17:15), offerings (Num. 15:14), blasphemy (Lev. 24:16; Num. 15:30), and Passover (Num. 9:14). Accordingly, Num. 15:15 says, "There shall be one statute for you and for the resident alien who sojourns with you . . . ; as you are, so shall the alien be before the LORD." There is some ambiguity as to whether the OT use of the word "alien" (= *gēr* in Ezek. 47:22) for someone who resides in Israel indicates a full, legal member of Israel. Part of the ambiguity may be resolved by recognizing that becoming a "resident alien" was a process completed by the sign of circumcision, after which the person had equal rights with fellow Israelites. There were two distinct classes of "aliens" in Israel: those who remained only temporarily in the land were termed "foreigners" (designated by *nēkār*) and those who remained longer or permanently in the land were called "sojourners" or, better, "resident aliens" (designated by *gēr*). Exodus 12:43–49 is a classic example of the distinction. Circumcision was the sign that the "resident alien" now held membership in the community of Israel, both sociologically and religiously. Most of the material in the present note follows K. Kuhn, "προσήλυτος," *TDNT* 6:728–29. Although he says that the "resident alien" is "wholly accepted into the religious constitution of the Jewish people," he qualifies this by saying that this person "sociologically . . . retains his ancient [foreign] position and is not fully equivalent to the Israelite citizen" (p. 729), a conclusion that does not appear warranted.

since they get an inheritance of part of Israel's land just like the native born do.[27]

What makes the status of "aliens" (gērîm) in Ezek. 47:22 even more to be an Israelite status is that at the very beginning of the nation's establishment even those who were ethnic members of Israel were also considered to be "aliens" (gērîm). In this respect, Lev. 25:23 says, "The land, moreover, shall not be sold permanently, for the land is Mine; for you [Israelites] are but aliens [gērîm] and sojourners with Me." Therefore, native-born Israelites are considered "resident aliens" and have been given the right by God to share in the land, and they do not own it. Ultimately, they are tenants.[28] Ezekiel 47:22 is saying precisely the same thing about foreigners and their share in Israel's land in the eschaton.

Conclusion

The above texts indicate that the OT prophesied at various points that when gentiles would be converted in the latter days, they would come to Israel and become Israelites.

Excursus 1 The Interpretation of Isaiah 66:21 in Recent Literature

Isaiah 66:21 says, "'I will also take some of them for priests and for Levites,' says the LORD." It appears that the vast majority of commentators/scholars in the past fifty years take the referent of "some of them" (mêhem) in Isa. 66:21 not to be Jews but rather to be gentiles (see table 20.1).

A few commentators explain the reference as being to both Jews and gentiles. These could be listed under the "gentiles" column below in that they view the statement in the same surprisingly universalistic sense of opening the doors of the priesthood to gentiles: Miscall,[29] VanGemeren,[30] and Webb[31] (Watts might also be listed here, but he is vague).[32]

---

27. See likewise D. Kellermann, "גוּר," TDOT 2:448. Similar to Ezek. 47:21–23 is Josh. 8:33, where "all Israel" is described as "standing on both sides of the ark . . . the alien as well as the native . . . just as Moses the servant of the LORD had given command at first to bless the people of Israel." Thus, "all Israel" is described as being composed of "the alien as well as the native." The same thing is expressed in Deut. 29:9–14.

28. For further elaboration, see Bruce K. Waltke, An Old Testament Theology: An Exegetical, Canonical, and Thematic Approach (Grand Rapids: Zondervan, 2007), 542–43.

29. Peter D. Miscall, Isaiah, Readings (Sheffield: JSOT Press, 1993), 148.

30. Willem VanGemeren, "Isaiah," in Evangelical Commentary on the Bible, ed. Walter A. Elwell (Grand Rapids: Baker Academic, 1989), 514.

31. Barry Webb, The Message of Isaiah: On Eagles' Wings, Bible Speaks Today (Downers Grove, IL: InterVarsity, 1996), 251.

32. John D. Watts, Isaiah 34–66, WBC 25 (Waco: Word, 1987), 365; cf. 362.

Table 20.1

"Some of them" (*mêhem*) in Isaiah 66:21 = Jews	"Some of them" (*mêhem*) in Isaiah 66:21 = Gentiles
• Berges 1998	• Barker 2003
• Clifford 1988	• Beyer 2007
• Croatto 2005	• Blenkinsopp 2003
• Gardner 2002	• Bonnard 1972
• Grogan 1986	• Breuggemann 1998
• Höffken 1998	• Childs 2001
• Rofé 1985	• Davies 1989
• Snaith 1967	• Goldingay 2001
	• Hailey 1985
	• Herbert 1975
	• Kidner 1994
	• Knight 1985
	• Koenen 1990
	• Koole 2001
	• McKenna 1994
	• McKenzie 1968
	• Motyer 1993
	• Oswalt 1998
	• Penna 1964 (cited by Koole 2001)
	• Sawyer 1986
	• Schoors 1973 (cited by Koole 2001)
	• Scullion 1982
	• Sekine 1989
	• Smith 1995
	• Westermann 1969
	• Whybray 1975
	• Wodecki 1982
	• Wolf 1985
	• Young 1972

Although the sampling is small, among older commentaries (pre-1960) there seems to be more balance between those who see the referent of verse 21 as Jews and those who see it as gentiles (see table 20.2).

James Muilenburg notes the interpretive difficulty and leaves the matter undecided.[33] Among still older commentators, we could add John Calvin, who takes the verse as referring to gentiles; T. K. Cheyne also lists Gesenius and Ewald as representatives of the second column below (i.e., gentiles).[34] Jan Koole notes that medieval Jewish exegetes typically view the verse as referring to Jews.[35]

33. James Muilenburg, "The Book of Isaiah: Chaps. 40–66," in vol. 5 of *The Interpreter's Bible*, ed. G. A. Buttrick (New York: Abingdon, 1956), 772.
34. T. K. Cheyne, *The Prophecies of Isaiah*, 6th ed., 2 vols. (London: Kegan Paul, Trench, Trübner, 1898), 2:131.
35. Jan L. Koole, *Isaiah III/3: Chapters 56–66*, trans. Antony P. Runia, HCOT (Leuven: Peeters, 2001), 525.

Table 20.2

"Some of them" (*mêhem*) in Isaiah 66:21 = Jews	"Some of them" (*mêhem*) in Isaiah 66:21 = Gentiles
• Box 1908	• Alexander 1847
• Dennefeld 1952 (cited by Koole 2001)	• Cheyne 1898
• Dillmann 1898	• Cowles 1869
• Duhm 1892	• Delitzsch 1949
• Kessler 1956–57 (cited by Koole 2001)	• Feldmann 1926 (cited by Koole 2001)
• Kissane 1943	• Nägelsbach 1871
• König 1926 (cited by Koole 2001)	• Ridderbos 1950–51
• Slotki 1957	• Skinner 1917
• Volz 1932	
• Wade 1911	

One's reading of the previous verse (v. 20) seems to dictate the identification of those taken for priests and Levites in 66:21, particularly the identification of the phrase "your brothers" (*'ăḥêkem*) in verse 20. The majority of commentators think that the phrase "some of them" (*mêhem*) in verse 21 refers to a group taken from these "brothers."[36] Claus Westermann and Joseph Blenkinsopp view verse 20 as a late gloss attempting to correct or mitigate the universalistic tone of verses 18–19, 21.[37]

Those in favor of viewing verse 21 as referring to gentiles typically appeal to the universalistic tone of the surrounding context (esp. vv. 18–19); thus, to understand the reference as being to Israelites would be anticlimactic.[38] Isaiah 56:1–8 (the generally agreed-upon introduction to the so-called Third Isaiah) is cited as preparing one for this very concept. Some suggest that it would be unnecessarily redundant to promise Israelites, some of whom were likely already Levites, that they would be taken as Levites upon their return to the land.[39] Homer Hailey seems to draw attention to the "also," indicating that God would supply gentile representatives in addition to the Israelite priests and Levites.[40] Koole notes that the verb "I will take" (*lāqaḥ*) used in verse 21 "does not fit with a rehabilitation of those who are already members of this class."[41] While John McKenzie thinks

36. Though see, e.g., P. A. Smith, *Rhetoric and Redaction in Trito-Isaiah: The Structure, Growth, and Authorship of Isaiah 56–66*, VTSup 62 (Leiden: Brill, 1995), 168. Smith sees the "brothers" as Jews, and those selected for priests and Levites as gentiles.

37. Claus Westermann, *Isaiah 40–66*, trans. D. M. G. Stalker, OTL (Philadelphia: Westminster, 1969), 423, 426; Joseph Blenkinsopp, *Isaiah 56–66*, AB 19B (New York: Doubleday, 2003), 311, 315.

38. So, e.g., Derek Kidner, "Isaiah," in *New Bible Commentary: 21st Century Edition*, ed. D. A. Carson et al. (Downers Grove, IL: InterVarsity, 1994), 670; Koole, *Isaiah III/3*, 525; R. N. Whybray, *Isaiah 40–66*, NCB (Grand Rapids: Eerdmans, 1975), 291.

39. E.g., Franz Delitzsch, *Biblical Commentary on the Prophecies of Isaiah*, trans. James Martin, 2 vols., K&D (Grand Rapids: Eerdmans, 1949), 2:513; Whybray, *Isaiah 40–66*, 291–92.

40. Homer Hailey, *A Commentary on Isaiah, with Emphasis on the Messianic Hope* (Grand Rapids: Baker Academic, 1985), 528; see also Koole, *Isaiah III/3*, 525; Westermann, *Isaiah 40–66*, 423.

41. Koole, *Isaiah III/3*, 525.

the concept is unparalleled in the OT,[42] Margaret Barker suggests that foreigners had once served in the temple (citing 1 Chron. 9:2, in which the "temple servants" [*nĕtînîm*] are taken by some to be foreigners),[43] and T. K. Cheyne draws a general, unspecified connection to the ending of Zechariah.[44]

Those who take verse 21 as referring to Jews generally understand the verse as subverting the Jerusalem monopoly on the priesthood and thus functioning as a promise that time spent sojourning in foreign lands does not disqualify one from priestly ministry.[45] Often appeal is made to Isa. 61:5–6 as establishing the future hope that gentiles would be merely servants of the Israelites, and Israelites alone would be taken for priests.[46] According to G. H. Box, "The idea of *priests* being taken from the Gentiles is too bold a one to be ascribed to Trito-Isaiah."[47] Finally, J. Severino Croatto suggests a rather unique understanding of the "survivors" (*pĕlêṭîm*) in Isa. 66:19 as referring not to those Israelites surviving the judgment of God described in the earlier verses, who are then sent out for missionary service, but rather to the "escaped-to-the-nations" (i.e., Diaspora Jews), who are summoned to return to Jerusalem. The emphasis of the whole passage, according to Croatto, is not missional and universalistic but instead particularistic and focused on the unification and exaltation of the nation of Israel. Thus, to take verse 21 as referring to the selection of gentiles for priests and Levites would undermine the "kerygmatic and theological center of the text."[48] Blenkinsopp, though seeing verse 21 as referring to gentiles, interprets verse 20 in a way that corresponds with Croatto's interpretation. In verse 20 (a late corrective interpolation, according to Blenkinsopp) gentiles provide only the necessary materials (i.e., "repatriated Israelites") for proper priestly service; Israelites alone are conceived of in verse 20 as valid priests.[49]

42. John L. McKenzie, *Second Isaiah*, AB 20 (Garden City, NY: Doubleday, 1968), 208.

43. Margaret Barker, "Isaiah," in *Eerdmans Commentary on the Bible*, ed. James D. G. Dunn and John W. Rogerson (Grand Rapids: Eerdmans, 2003), 541.

44. Cheyne, *Prophecies of Isaiah*, 2:131.

45. E.g., Ulrich Berges, *Das Buch Jesaja: Komposition und Endgestalt*, HBS 16 (Freiburg: Herder, 1998), 531; Richard J. Clifford, "Isaiah 40–66," in *Harper's Bible Commentary*, ed. James L. Mays (San Francisco: Harper & Row, 1988), 596; J. Severino Croatto, "The 'Nations' in the Salvific Oracles of Isaiah," *VT* 55 (2005): 157; Anne E. Gardner, "The Nature of the New Heavens and New Earth in Isaiah 66:22," *ABR* 50 (2002): 18; Edward J. Kissane, *The Book of Isaiah* (Dublin: Browne & Nolan, 1943), 2:327; Alexander Rofé, "Isaiah 66:1–4: Judean Sects in the Persian Period as Viewed by Trito-Isaiah," in *Biblical and Related Studies Presented to Samuel Iwry*, ed. Ann Kort and Scott Morschauser (Winona Lake, IN: Eisenbrauns, 1985), 212; G. W. Wade, *The Book of the Prophet Isaiah* (London: Methuen, 1911), 420–21. Note, however, the query by Joseph Alexander: "But why should mere dispersion be considered as disqualifying Levites for the priesthood?" (*Commentary on the Prophecies of Isaiah*, 2 vols. [1847; repr., Grand Rapids: Zondervan, 1970], 2:478).

46. Croatto, "'Nations' in the Salvific Oracles," 158; Peter Höffken, *Das Buch Jesaja: Kapitel 40–66*, NSKAT 18/2 (Stuttgart: Katholisches Bibelwerk, 1998), 253; cf. also the statements concerning the role of gentiles in v. 21 made by Blenkinsopp, *Isaiah 56–66*, 315.

47. G. H. Box, *The Book of Isaiah* (London: Pitman, 1908), 357.

48. Croatto, "'Nations' in the Salvific Oracles," 158.

49. Blenkinsopp, *Isaiah 56–66*, 315.

My interpretation in the body of the discussion above falls in line with identifying the "priests" and "Levites" in verse 21 as gentiles, which is supported by the majority of commentators from the twentieth and twenty-first centuries noted above.

The New Testament Notion of Latter-Day True Israel

In various ways the NT identifies the church with Israel.

Names and Images of Israel That the New Testament Applies to the Church[50]

In surveying the various ways that the NT describes the church as Israel, the pressing hermeneutical question will be why it does so. Is it merely to portray the church as being like Israel but not, in reality, the continuation of true Israel? Or are such portrayals intended to indicate that the church really is the continuation of true Israel? In light of the biblical presuppositions about Israel and gentiles in the eschaton just discussed, the natural conclusion is that the following Israelite names and images for the church indicate that the church is actually considered to be true end-time Israel, composed of believing ethnic Jews and gentiles. The concluding major section of this chapter and the excursus to this chapter will attempt to offer further evidence of this by showing that Israel's restoration prophecies have begun fulfillment in the predominantly gentile church. Most of the following names and images come from Paul, though others come from elsewhere in the NT.

PAUL

Christians as the Beloved of God, Elect, and the Church

God calls Israel his "beloved" (Deut. 32:15; 33:12; Isa. 44:2; Jer. 11:15; 12:7;[51] Pss. 60:5 [59:7 LXX]; 108:6 [107:7 LXX]).[52] This is likely the best background against which to understand why Paul calls the church at Thessalonica those "beloved by God" (1 Thess. 1:4).[53] The combination of God's "love" for and "election" of Israel in the OT is likely the best background for Paul's fuller

---

50. In this section I have been greatly helped by the broad outline of Charles D. Provan, *The Church Is Israel Now: The Transfer of Conditional Privilege* (Vallecito, CA: Ross House, 1987), 3–46. Provan surveys many of the names and images of Israel that are applied to the church. Although the exegetical evidence adduced may differ at significant points, I have worked within his general framework.

51. The LXX of these texts uses the perfect passive participle of *agapaō* ("to love") in referring to God's love for Israel.

52. The LXX of these texts uses the substantive adjective *agapētoi* ("beloved").

53. Note that here Paul uses the same perfect passive participle of *agapaō* ("to love") as used in the LXX passages mentioned above.

expression in 1 Thess. 1:4, "knowing, brothers beloved by God, your election."[54] In addition, in the nearby context of 1 Thess. 1:1 Paul refers to "the church [*ekklēsia*] of the Thessalonians." "Church" is a word that he uses often in referring to other assemblies of Christians in other cities to which he writes. The word *ekklēsia* could be used in the Greek world to refer to an officially called group of citizens, but in the LXX it describes Israel being either assembled for worship or not assembled (see the LXX of Deut. 23:2–3; 31:30; 1 Sam. 17:47; 1 Chron. 28:8; Neh. 13:1). Paul likely derives the term from its OT usage. These names for the church are likely not mere metaphors for what the church is like but rather are portrayals of the church as the continuation of the OT people of God, the true Israel.[55] This conclusion is especially likely in light of Paul's OT and Jewish upbringing and background, and it is a conclusion that likely is applicable to Paul's other uses of *ekklēsia*.

Another important reference to Christians as God's "beloved" is Rom. 9:25: "I will call those who were not My people, 'My people,' and her who was not beloved, 'Beloved.'" This text quotes from the prophecy of Hos. 2:23. In Hosea this was a prophecy of the salvation of Israel, when the nation would be restored, but Paul applies it to gentiles. This application is clear from Rom. 9:24, which refers to those "whom [God] also called, not from among Jews only, but also from among Gentiles," and then the Hosea quotation is adduced in verse 25 to support the notion that the Hosea prophecy is being applied to gentiles. I will argue later that this is not a mere analogical comparison of Hosea's prophecy to gentiles but rather is a beginning fulfillment of it.

Christians as Sons of God, Abraham's Seed, Israel, Jerusalem, Circumcised Jews

We saw earlier in chapter 13 on the image of God that Jesus referred to himself as both "Son of God" and "Son of Man" because both names alluded to his role as the last Adam. Jesus had come to do what Adam should have done and to enable fallen humans to reflect the image of God in the way they were originally designed to do. We also saw that these names for Jesus were also names for Israel, since the commission of Adam in Gen. 1:26–28 had been passed on to Israel (see chap. 13 under the heading "Jesus as Both the End-Time Adam and the End-Time Israel Who Restores the Kingdom to God's People" and the subheading "Jesus as the Adamic Son of God"). In particular, as was noted at the beginning of this chapter, Israel was repeatedly referred

54. In both 1 Thess. 1:4 and the OT *agapaō* and *eklegomai* occur in direct connection (in the OT see Deut. 4:37; 10:15; Pss. 46:5; 77:68; Isa. 41:8; 44:2), though in 1 Thess. 1:4 the noun form *eklogē* appears. See also Col. 3:12, where "elect" and "beloved" also refer to the church.

55. In this paragraph I am following Jeffrey A. D. Weima, "1–2 Thessalonians," in *Commentary on the New Testament Use of the Old Testament*, ed. G. K. Beale and D. A. Carson (Grand Rapids: Baker Academic, 2007), 871–72.

to as God's "son(s)" (Exod. 4:22–23; Deut. 14:1; Isa. 1:2, 4; 63:8; Hos. 1:10; 11:1)[56] and "firstborn" (Exod. 4:22–23; Jer. 31:9), and the coming Messiah of Israel was also known as God's "firstborn" (Ps. 89:27).

Believers' identification with Jesus, the summation of true Israel (as argued earlier in the chapter) and the Son of God, is likely the best reason why they are called "sons of God."[57] Since Jesus is God's "son," so are those identified with him, though they are called "adopted sons" because they are not natural sons like Jesus but rather are adopted into the family of God (Gal. 4:4–7).

The notion of Christians being part of God's Israelite family is expressed well in Galatians. This idea is based on the notion that there is one Messiah, who is identified with Israel and represents his people (which we have found above in Isa. 49). Paul views Christ to be the summation of true Israel and understands all, whether Jew or gentile, whom Jesus represents to be true Israel. Galatians 3:16, 26, 29 expresses this concept as shown in table 20.3.

Table 20.3

Galatians 3:16	Galatians 3:26, 29
"Now the promises were spoken to Abraham and to his seed. He does not say, 'And to seeds,' as referring to many, but rather to one, 'And to your seed,' that is, Christ."	3:26: "For you are all sons of God through faith in Christ Jesus." 3:29: "And if you belong to Christ, then you are Abraham's seed, heirs according to promise."

Here Paul sees Christ to be the fulfillment of the promised Abrahamic seed, and then all who identify with him by faith are viewed to be "sons of God" (v. 26) and also "Abraham's seed, heirs according to the promise"—that is, also in fulfillment of the promise. It is important to remember that in the OT mentions of the "seed of Abraham" refer repeatedly and only to the people of Israel and not to gentiles, though the Israelite Abrahamic seed was to bless gentiles (e.g., Gen. 12:7; 13:15–16; 15:5; 17:8; 22:17–18; 26:4; 32:12). The same is true in Judaism. The identification in Gal. 3:29 that both believing "Jew and Greek" (3:28) are "Abraham's seed" is, then, a reference to them as the continuation of true Israel. Again, in Gal. 4:28 Christians are said to be "like Isaac, . . . children of [the Abrahamic] promise."

Consequently, new-covenant believers are children of "the Jerusalem above," who is their "mother," so that they are considered to have been born in the true Jerusalem (Gal. 4:26, 31) and thus to be true Jerusalemites.[58] In saying this, Paul may have been influenced by Ps. 87, which, as we saw earlier,

56. On the Deuteronomy and Isaiah references, see Provan, *The Church Is Israel Now*, 6.

57. Paul's reference to the Roman Christians as "sons of God" and "children of God" likely expresses the same idea (Rom. 8:14–19). Note likewise "children of God" in Phil. 2:15.

58. The same essential point is made in Heb. 12:22: "But you have come to Mount Zion and to the city of the living God, the heavenly Jerusalem." Likewise, saints in the OT epoch were said to be "sons" of Jerusalem (Ps. 149:2; Isa. 51:17–18; Lam. 4:2).

prophesied that gentiles were to be born in end-time Jerusalem and were to be sons of their mother, Jerusalem. Following quite naturally on the heels of Paul's identification of Christians with Jerusalem is the conclusion of Gal. 6:16. After Paul says "neither is circumcision anything nor uncircumcision, but a new creation" (v. 15), he says regarding "those who will walk by this rule" of no ethnic divisions in the new creation, "peace and mercy be upon them, that is, upon the Israel of God" (my translation). Thus, both Jewish and gentile Christians are called "the Israel of God," an identification virtually the same as in Gal. 3:29, where both are called "Abraham's seed." Some commentators, however, see that "peace and mercy" are pronounced here first on gentile Christians and then on Jewish Christians. This view of Gal. 6:16 is possible but improbable. Commentators are increasingly recognizing the identification of both Christian gentiles and Jews as "Israel" in 6:16, especially since one of the main points of the earlier part of the epistle is that there are no longer any ethnic distinctions between God's people.[59] Consequently, Paul concludes the letter by saying that believing Jews and gentiles are the true "Israel of God" (Gal. 6:16).

It is with this background in mind that one can better understand why Paul refers to first-generation Israel as the "fathers" of the Corinthian Christians (1 Cor. 10:1), in contrast to unbelieving Israel as "Israel according to the flesh" (1 Cor. 10:18). For the same reason, Paul can call gentiles "fellow citizens" with Jewish "saints," since believing gentiles now are no longer "excluded from the commonwealth of Israel" (Eph. 2:12, 19). And just as Israelites often were called "Jews" even in pre-NT times (e.g., 15x in Ezra–Nehemiah) and were "circumcised" (e.g., Gen. 17:10–14, 23–24), so too the gentile who trusts in Jesus is considered to be "a Jew who is one inwardly" and who possesses true "circumcision . . . which is of the heart" (Rom. 2:26–29). In contrast to unbelieving Jews, whom Paul calls "the false circumcision," the Philippian Christians "are the true circumcision" (Phil. 3:2–3), since in Christ Christians "were also circumcised with a circumcision made without hands" (Col. 2:11).

We will also see in this chapter that Israel's original commission to be "a kingdom of priests" from Exod. 19:6 is placed on the shoulders of the church by 1 Peter and Revelation.

Christians as Part of the End-Time Temple of God

Chapter 19 has already laid out the evidence for this identification in Paul's writings, but it is a significant identification that should be mentioned here (see, e.g., 1 Cor. 3:10–17; 6:19; Eph. 2:20–22).[60]

59. In the next chapter I attempt to substantiate this in some depth (see chap. 21 under the subheading "Galatians"); see also G. K. Beale, "Peace and Mercy upon the Israel of God: The Old Testament Background of Gal. 6,16b," *Bib* 80 (1999): 204–23.

60. On which, see further G. K. Beale, *The Temple and the Church's Mission: A Biblical Theology of the Dwelling Place of God*, NSBT 17 (Downers Grove, IL: InterVarsity, 2004), 245–92.

Christians as the Bride of Christ

Israel was the wife of Yahweh in the OT (Isa. 54:5–6; Ezek. 16:32; Hos. 1:2), but Israel became a harlot (e.g., Ezek. 16). Paul refers to the church as the bride of Christ in 2 Cor. 11:2; Eph. 5:25–27. We will see later in this chapter that the book of Revelation also pictures the church as the bride of Christ in fulfillment of Israel's restoration prophecies from Isaiah.

Christians as a Vineyard or Cultivated Field

Israel was sometimes referred to as God's "vineyard" or "cultivated field" in the OT. The well-known vineyard parable of Isa. 5:1–7 refers to Israel and concludes by explicitly saying that "the vineyard of the Lord of hosts is the house of Israel." Likewise, Jer. 12:10 refers to Israel as "my [God's] vineyard . . . my field . . . my pleasant field" (so likewise Ezek. 19:10).[61]

Jesus's vineyard parable is also relevant background to be considered in relation to Paul's view of the church as a vineyard to be discussed directly below. The vineyard parable of Isa. 5 is explicitly developed by Jesus in Matt. 21:33–41 and applied to Israel (cf. the Synoptic parallels in Mark 12:1–12; Luke 20:9–19). Jesus says the "vine-growers" (Israel's leaders) had not listened to the vineyard owner's servants (the prophets), who admonished them to be faithful stewards by giving the owner his share of the produce. In addition, the vine-growers harshly treated these messengers (the prophets) and then killed the vineyard owner's son (Jesus). As a result, Jesus says that the vineyard owner (God) "will bring those wretches to a wretched end, and will rent out the vineyard to other vine-growers, who will pay him the proceeds at the proper seasons" (Matt. 21:41). Jesus then interprets this to mean that "the kingdom of God will be taken away from you [Israel] and given to a people, producing the fruit of it" (21:43).[62]

In 1 Cor. 3 Paul refers to himself as a "planter" and Apollos as a waterer of the seed of God's word, but he states that neither he nor Apollos could cause any growth of that seed (3:5–8). Such growth is caused only by God and not by his agents (3:6b–7). Verse 9 refers to the Corinthians as "God's cultivated field" or "God's vineyard."[63] While it is possible that Paul is developing Jesus's

---

61. The Hebrew text reads literally, "your mother [Israel] was like a vine in your blood," which the NASB, NRSV, and ESV render as "your mother [Israel] was like a vine in your vineyard," apparently taking "blood" as a metaphor for wine and then by association a "vineyard." The LXX has "your mother was like a vine/vineyard" (*ampelos*).

62. Even if Jesus did not specifically have in mind Israel as a vineyard from Isa. 5, he would, at least, have been referring to the common association between Israel and the vineyard imagery in the OT and Jewish tradition.

63. The word *geōrgion* can plausibly be rendered "cultivated field" or "vineyard" (e.g., see the LXX of Gen. 26:14; Prov. 6:7; 9:12; 24:5; though in Prov. 24:30 [Rahlfs edition]; 31:16 it is equated with a "vineyard"). Interestingly, the word *geōrgos* occurs repeatedly in the Synoptic Gospels with reference to those who take care of a "vineyard" (often translated "vinedressers" or "vine growers" [e.g., Luke 20:9–16]). BDAG (196) defines *geōrgos* as "one who is occupied in agriculture or gardening."

vineyard parable of Isa. 5,[64] it is more likely that this is a conceptual parallel with that parable. In the parables of both Isa. 5 and 1 Cor. 3 there is the notion of God as the ultimate planter of a vineyard and of God providing its fertile environment, followed by destructive judgment (for the judgment in 1 Cor. 3, see vv. 13–15).[65] All this is implicit in Jesus's development of the Isa. 5 parable, though the concluding element of final judgment is explicit there also. And just as Paul directly connects this agricultural image to the temple in verses 11–12, 16–17, so does the Jewish interpretation of the vineyard parable in Isa. 5 and the conclusion to the parable in Matt. 21:42–45.[66]

For the purposes of the present section it is sufficient to conclude that Paul, possibly in subtle development of Jesus's vineyard parable, portrays the church as "God's vineyard." This probably derives to some degree from the OT prophets' depiction of Israel as God's vineyard.

Christians as Part of an Olive Tree

Israel (Isa. 17:6; Jer. 11:16; Hos. 14:6), ideal individuals in Israel (Ps. 128:3), and Israel's leaders (Judg. 9:8–9; Ps. 52:8; Zech. 4:3, 11–12) are depicted repeatedly as an "olive tree" (LXX: *elaia*).[67] Personified Wisdom, who chose Israel as her dwelling, likewise is referred to as a "beautiful olive tree" (Sir. 24:14), and Israel's high priest as an "olive tree laden with fruit" (Sir. 50:10).

In Rom. 11:17, 24 Paul refers to gentiles as a "wild olive tree" being "grafted into" the cultivated "olive tree" (*elaia*) of Israel. This probably continues the general image of Israel as an olive tree from the OT. Gentiles are now seen to be identified as part of this Israelite olive tree and thus a part of the continuation of true Israel.

Christians as Redeemed from Iniquity and a Special People for God

In light of the foregoing, it is quite natural for Paul to apply to the church one of the well-known epitaphs of Israel. In Titus 2:14, he says that Christ "gave himself for us in order that he might redeem us from all lawlessness and purify <u>for himself a special people</u> [*heautō laon periousion*], zealous for good deeds." The phrase "you shall be to him (or 'me') a special people" (*autō* [*moi*] *laon periousion*) is repeated throughout the Pentateuch (LXX):

Exod. 19:5 "And now if you will indeed hear my voice and keep my covenant, <u>you will be to me a special people</u> above all nations."

<hr/>

64. On which, see David Wenham, *Paul: Follower of Jesus or Founder of Christianity?* (Grand Rapids: Eerdmans, 1995), 204–5.

65. For the argument that these verses indicate judgment of unbelievers (though considered to be part of the church community) rather than a sifting out of a genuine believer's bad from good works, see, e.g., Beale, *Temple*, 245–52.

66. On which, see ibid., 245–52.

67. Exceptionally, people outside Israel are compared to an "olive tree" (Job 15:33; Isa. 24:13).

Exod. 23:22 "If you will indeed hear my voice, and if you will do all the things I will charge you with, and keep my covenant, <u>you shall be to me a special people above all nations</u>."

Deut. 7:6 "And the Lord your God chose you <u>to be to him special people beyond all nations</u> that are upon the face of the earth."

Deut. 14:2 "For you are a holy people to the Lord your God, and the Lord your God has chosen you to be <u>a special people to himself</u> of all the nations on the face of the earth."

Deut. 26:18 "And the Lord has chosen you this day that <u>you should be to him a special people</u>, as he said, to keep his commands."

Paul's allusion to this Israelite epitaph is further observable from the inextricable link in every OT case with Israel's obedience, which is likely summarized by Paul's concluding reference to "zealous for good deeds." Paul's Israelite epitaph is further enhanced by the fact that in Titus 2:14 he fronts it with another allusive description of Israel: "that he might redeem us from all lawlessness," referring to Ps. 130:8 ("He will redeem Israel from all his lawlessness"). Unlike the historical description of Israel in the Exodus and Deuteronomy passages listed above, this one from the psalm is a prophecy, which Paul apparently sees to be finding its inaugurated fulfillment in the church.

It is important to mention in this connection that when Paul uses "people" (*laos*) and applies it to both Jewish and gentile Christians, it has significant redemptive-historical significance. This word in the LXX predominantly refers to Israel as a people, especially as they are God's people (e.g., Exod. 19:4–7; Deut. 4:6; 32:9, 36, 43, 44). The LXX use of "people" (*laos*) typically is a translation of the Hebrew 'am ("people").[68] Other people groups outside Israel are referred to usually by the word "nations" (*ethnē*) and hardly ever by "people" (*laos*).[69] Paul can apply "people" (*laos*) to the church, composed of both Jews and Greeks, and in so doing, he sees the church as the eschatological continuation of true Israel.[70] For example, he quotes from prophecies about Israel's restoration that use this word for "people" to refer to Israel and applies them to the church.[71]

---

68. On which, see H. Strathmann, "λαός," *TDNT* 4:34–37.

69. On which, see Deut. 7:1, 6, 7, 14, 16, 19, 22.

70. See Leonhard Goppelt, *Typos: The Typological Interpretation of the Old Testament in the New*, trans. Donald H. Madvig (Grand Rapids: Eerdmans, 1982), 140–51.

71. E.g., see the use of Hos. 2:23 and 1:10 in Rom. 9:25–26; and Lev. 26:12 and Ezek. 37:27 in 2 Cor. 6:16. See likewise the use of OT references using "people" (*laos*) in Heb. 8:10; 10:30; and cf. Heb. 4:9; 13:12. Strathmann ("λαός," *TDNT* 4:54–55) well notes that sometimes *laos* refers not to a nationalistic Israelite people group but rather generically to a "crowd, population"; however, his attempt to explain that the NT uses this word figuratively to apply to a new people, the church, which goes beyond the LXX use, is somewhat unclear. It is true that the NT use here is a development from the LXX, which used the word for all Israelites, true believers

The main purpose here is to summarize some of the most significant places elsewhere outside of Paul's writings that quote from various OT descriptions of Israel and applies them to the church.

Christians as the Bride of Christ

In addition to Paul's reference to the church as the bride of Christ, the book of Revelation repeatedly refers to the same thing. In so doing, Revelation ties this name directly back to OT prophecies about God marrying Israel again in the end times.

Revelation 21:2 says, "And I saw the holy city, new Jerusalem, coming down out of heaven from God, made ready as a bride adorned for her husband." Revelation 21:9–10 develops the picture further by referring to "the bride, the wife of the Lamb . . . the holy city, Jerusalem." The new world that 21:1 portrays as replacing the old is now called "the holy city, new Jerusalem." Part of the language comes from Isa. 52:1b, "Jerusalem, the holy city," which promises a time when God's people will no longer suffer from captivity but will be restored forever to God's presence (Isa. 52:1–10). The Isa. 52:1b allusion anticipates the directly following marital imagery of Rev. 21:2b ("adorned for her husband") with similar metaphors, which occur in Isa. 52:1a: "Clothe yourself in your strength, O Zion; clothe yourself in your beautiful garments." This implicit marriage portrayal of Isa. 52:1a is developed by Isa. 61:10, which itself, as we will see, forms the explicit basis for the nuptial picture concluding Rev. 21:2.

The appended description of "new" to the "holy city, Jerusalem" is also derived from Isaiah. Isaiah 62:1–2 refers to "Jerusalem," which "will be called by a new name" at the time of its end-time glorification, when Israel is finally restored from captivity. This new name is then explained in Isa. 62:3–5 to signify a new, intimate marriage relationship between Israel and God. Therefore, it is not accidental that the remainder of Rev. 21:2 adduces a marriage metaphor to explain the significance of "new Jerusalem." Already in Rev. 3:12 identification with Christ's "new name" has been seen to be essentially the same as identification with "the name of . . . God" and "the name of . . . the new Jerusalem." All three refer to the intimate, latter-day presence of God and Christ with their people, as expressed in 22:3–4; 14:1–4.[72] Likewise, 21:3 infers the same idea from the "new Jerusalem" and

---

and unbelievers, but it still retains the idea of "Israel" as a name for God's true people. Here the discussion about how the OT itself viewed that gentiles would be redeemed by becoming part of Israel needs to be recalled from the first section of this chapter. And the evidence about the presuppositions concerning Jesus and all believers as "true Israel" in that same initial segment points to the OT view.

72. See G. K. Beale, *The Book of Revelation: A Commentary on the Greek Text*, NIGTC (Grand Rapids: Eerdmans, 1999), 255, 293, which discusses the "new name" that is applied to the church in Rev. 2:17; 3:12 and is derived from Isa. 62:5; 65:15, prophesying that the "new

the following marriage picture: "Behold, the tabernacle of God is among men, and He will tabernacle among them, and they shall be His people, and God Himself will be among them."

The marital imagery in the OT contexts of the prior two Isa. 52 and 62 allusions comes to the fore at the end of Rev. 21:2: the city is now seen "as a bride adorned for her husband." This is a third straight allusion to the same context of Isaiah. Speaking in prophetic perfect style, Isa. 61:10 LXX personifies Zion: "He adorned me with ornaments as a bride" (Isa. 62:5 also uses "bride" as a metaphor for the people of Israel). Isaiah says in the remaining five lines of the same verse that there will be rejoicing by those whom God will clothe at the period of Israel's end-time restoration. The literal meaning of the metaphorical clothing is explained to be "salvation" and "righteousness," resulting in deliverance from captivity. The phrases in Isaiah about the bridegroom and bride being clothed are adduced not to underscore the activity of Israel in accomplishing any part of its salvific righteousness but rather to emphasize further what the reception of the coming salvation and righteousness from God will be like: it will be like a new, intimate marriage relationship in which bride and bridegroom celebrate in festive apparel. The same point is metaphorically affirmed in Rev. 21:2 and abstractly stated in 21:3.

Revelation 19:7–8 has already alluded to the same passage to make the similar point about God's intimacy with his redeemed people: "his bride has made herself ready. And it was given her to clothe herself in fine linen, bright and clean." This clarifies further that the bride is a metaphor for the saints. To be "made ready as a bride adorned for her husband" (Rev. 21:2) conveys the thought of God's preparation of his people for himself. Throughout history God is forming his people to be his bride, so that they will reflect his glory in the ages to come (so Eph. 5:25–27), which the following context of Rev. 21 develops (cf. 2 Cor. 11:2).

The three Isaiah prophecies about Israel's final redemption in Rev. 21:2 find fulfillment in the church. This is also corroborated from 3:12, which identifies both Jewish and gentile Christians in the church of Philadelphia with the "new Jerusalem." This is confirmed further by 21:10–14, which figuratively identifies the names of Israel's tribes and the names of the apostles as part of the structure of "the holy city, Jerusalem, coming down out of heaven from God," which itself is equated with "the bride, the wife of the Lamb" (21:9).[73]

---

name" means that Israel will have a new eschatologically intimate relationship with God (and, as noted above, in Isa. 62:3–5 it is portrayed as a new marriage relationship: just as a wife took on the new name of her husband, so will be the case for Israel in the future).

73. For further elaboration of the passages discussed in Revelation in this section, see ibid., at the verses cited.

Christians as a Kingdom of Priests

In Exod. 19:6 God says to Israel, "You shall be to Me a kingdom of priests," which likely meant that as a whole nation they were to serve as kingly mediators of divine revelation between God and the unbelieving nations (see also Isa. 43:10–13). They were not faithful in this witnessing task. Therefore, God raises up a new priest-king, Jesus, and those identified with him are a "kingdom of priests," as expressed by 1 Pet. 2:9; Rev. 1:6; 5:10, which clearly allude to Exod. 19:6.

My comments here will address only Rev. 1:6,[74] since an understanding of this text will be sufficient for understanding the notion of the church being a "kingdom of priests" in the other two texts. Christ's death and resurrection (1:5) established a twofold office, not only for himself (cf. 1:13–18) but also for believers. Their identification with his resurrection and kingship means that they too are considered to be resurrected and exercising rule with him as a result of his exaltation: he is "the ruler of the kings of the earth" (1:5), and he made them "to be a kingdom, priests" (1:6 [cf. 5:10: "kingdom and priests"]). Not only have they been made to be a part of Christ's kingdom and his subjects, but also they have been constituted kings together with Christ (note the active aspect of their ruling in 5:10, which probably refers to both the present and the future). They also share his priestly office by virtue of their identification with his death and resurrection, since Jesus's shedding of his "blood" (1:5) also suggests his priestly function.[75]

Precisely how the church is to exercise these priestly and kingly functions is not yet explicit in Revelation, but it will not be surprising to find that the answer lies in understanding how Christ himself functioned in these two offices. He revealed God's truth by mediating as a priest through his sacrificial death and uncompromising "faithful witness" to the world, and he reigned as king, ironically, by conquering death and sin through the defeat at the cross and subsequent resurrection (1:5). Believers spiritually fulfill the same offices in this age by following his model (cf. 14:4), especially by being faithful witnesses through suffering (1:9) and thus mediating Christ's priestly and royal authority and message to the world.[76]

Christians as Lampstands and Olive Trees

Revelation 11:4 says that the "two witnesses" who "will prophesy" (v. 3) are "the two olive trees and the two lampstands that stand before the Lord of

---

74. In Rev. 1:6, the phrase *basileian, hiereis* ("kingdom, priests") is based on the similar phrase in Exod. 19:6 LXX (*basileion hierateuma* [cf. MT]). There is some ambiguity about whether this phrase in Exodus is to be understood as a "royal priesthood" or a "priestly kingdom," but the difference is not significant, since both can include reference to kingly and priestly elements (see further discussion of Rev. 1:6 in ibid., 192–96, where also secondary sources are cited in support).

75. OT priests accomplished sanctification and atonement for Israel by sprinkling the blood of sacrificial animals (see Exod. 24:8; Lev. 16:14–19).

76. See likewise Beale, *Revelation*, on 1:6 (pp. 192–96), 1:9 (pp. 200–202), as well as 2:13 (pp. 247–48), where Antipas is called a "faithful witness" (secondary sources are cited in support).

the earth." As Rev. 1:20 makes clear, "lampstands" refer to the church, and that is the meaning of the "lampstands" in Rev. 2:1, 5.

The two pictures of olive trees and lampstands together with the concluding clause of verse 4 come from Zech. 4:14 (cf. 4:2–3, 11–14). In Zechariah's vision the lampstand represented the second temple (the lampstands are an essential part of the temple that likely represents the whole temple in Zech. 4). Zechariah 4:9 says that Zerubbabel had laid the foundation of the second temple. On either side of the lampstands was an olive tree, which provided the oil to light the lamps. The olive trees are interpreted to be "the anointed ones who are standing before the Lord of the whole earth" (v. 14). "The anointed ones" (lit., "the sons of richness") apparently refer to Joshua, the high priest, and Zerubbabel, the king, or to prophetic leaders of Israel.

I am content here merely to note that the description of Rev. 11:4 is another of the ways that the church is identified with Israel. There will not be further elaboration here, since this refers specifically to Christians being identified with a part of Israel's temple (e.g., the lampstands), and I dedicate two chapters (chaps. 18–19) to this notion.[77]

Conclusion

Some of the above Israelite images applied to the church are allusions to particular OT texts, while others have no specific literary point of contact with the OT, though they are derived from within the orbit of general OT usage. The images and names of Israel that are applied to the church discussed in the preceding section are but a sampling of the most significant examples in the NT. These names and images are applied to the church probably because the church is seen as the latter-day continuation of Israel, especially in light of the presuppositions about Israel and the church discussed in the initial section above and in light of the following study of Israel's restoration prophecies finding inaugurated fulfillment in the church. The foregoing discussion has also revealed the interesting observation that sometimes unbelieving ethnic Jews are seen not to be a part of true Israel.[78]

The remainder of this chapter and the next will look consecutively at how the Gospels, Acts, Paul, the General Epistles, and Revelation understand that Israel's eschatological restoration has begun and how (esp. from the perspective of Revelation) it will finally be completed.

---

77. For further explanation of Rev. 11:4 and its OT background in Zechariah, see ibid., 576–79. For the debate about the identity of the two witnesses in Rev. 11:3–4, see ibid., 572–82, where the conclusion is drawn that the witnesses represent the church.

78. E.g., Rom. 2:25–29; 1 Cor. 10:1, 18; Phil. 3:2–3; also note Rev. 2:9; 3:9, where it is said that unbelieving Jews "say they are Jews and are not."

The Transferral of the Stewardship of the Kingdom by Old Testament Israel to the End-Time New People of God (Matthew and Luke)

Having surveyed in the preceding sections the notions of the church as true end-time Israel as an introduction to this chapter, I will now directly address the main topic of this chapter: the followers of Jesus and the emerging church as the beginning fulfillment of Israel's restoration promises. The Gospels of Matthew and Luke portray Jesus repeatedly warning Israel that if they reject him, God will reject them as the true people of God and decisively judge them. Jesus begins to announce God's rejection of the nation and their impending destruction in Luke 19:41–44:

> When he approached Jerusalem, He saw the city and wept over it, saying, "If you had known in this day, even you, the things which make for peace! But now they have been hidden from your eyes. For the days will come upon you when your enemies will throw up a barricade against you, and surround you and hem you in on every side, and they will level you to the ground and your children within you, and they will not leave in you one stone upon another, because you did not recognize the time of your visitation."

Luke 21 reiterates and expands on this prediction of Jerusalem's judgment (vv. 20–24), specifically the destruction of the temple.[79] That this destruction will also indicate a judgment of rejecting ethnic national Israel as God's true people is expressed in Matt. 21. After telling most of the parable of the vineyard (21:33–40), the point of which is to explain Israel's rejection of him, Jesus concludes by eliciting this response from his listeners: "He [God] will bring those wretches to a wretched end, and will rent out the vineyard to other vine-growers who will pay him the proceeds at the proper seasons" (21:41). That is, Israel is no longer receptive and obedient to God's revelation and, as a result, has not borne spiritual fruit. Because of this, God will entrust this stewardship to "other vine-growers," which most likely represents the gentiles. The supporting reason that Jesus offers for his statement in verse 41 is the quotation from Ps. 118:22 in verse 42:

> Jesus said to them, "Did you never read in the Scriptures,
> 'The stone which the builders rejected,
> this became the chief cornerstone;
> this came about from the Lord,
> and it is marvelous in our eyes'?"

In verse 43, which interprets the conclusion of the parable in verse 41, again the psalm quotation is seen as the supporting reason for Israel's rejection from

---

79. In Luke 21:6 Jesus says, "As for these things [the temple] which you are looking at, the days will come in which there will not be left one stone upon another which will not be torn down."

being God's steward: "Therefore I say to you, the kingdom of God will be taken away from you and given to a people, producing the fruit of it." This verse interprets the conclusion of the parable (see v. 41 above): Israel's stewardship of God's kingdom will be taken away from it, and the gentiles will be given the stewardship. But how does the psalm quotation offer a supporting reason for this transferral of kingdom stewardship?

The quotation from Ps. 118:22 refers to a righteous sufferer whom God delivered from oppressors. As a result of his deliverance, he enters through the "gate of the Lord," which is likely the gate of the temple courtyard, in light of the following references in the psalm to the figure being blessed "from the house of the LORD" (v. 26) and to binding "the festival sacrifice with cords to the horns of the altar" (v. 27). Thus, the mention of the rejected cornerstone in Ps. 118:22 probably refers to part of the foundation of the temple as a metaphor for the righteous sufferer who has been oppressed not only by the nations (v. 10) but also likely by those within the covenant community (metaphorically portrayed as temple "builders" who "rejected" him as the "chief cornerstone"). This pious victim, then, is likely a kingly figure in Israel's history, perhaps David himself, who had been oppressed both by the nations round about as well as by those within Israel. Therefore, the point of the psalm quotation is that rejection of Jesus as the "cornerstone" of the temple ("the stone which the builders rejected") is equivalent to rejection of Jesus as the true temple ("this became the chief cornerstone"), which is in the process of being built. Whereas the cornerstone in the psalm probably was a metaphor for a king who was seen to be crucial to the existence of the temple, here it is likely more than merely figurative and is an actual reference to Jesus, the king of Israel, becoming the foundation stone of the new temple.[80]

Thus, the transferral of kingdom stewardship also includes transferral of stewardship of the new temple, centered not in an architectural sphere anymore but now in Jesus and all who identify with him. Matthew 21:41, 43 say that this new form of the kingdom (and by implication of the temple) will be the gentiles, though we know from elsewhere that a remnant of ethnic Jewish believers will also identify with Jesus and join with the gentiles as the new form of the kingdom and temple, which is the church. As further explanation of verse 43, Jesus says in verse 44, "And he who falls on this stone will be broken to pieces; but on whomever it falls, it will scatter him like dust." Some commentators have rightly noticed that this second statement about a stone also has an OT background, this time from Dan. 2:34–35:[81] "A stone

80. See Craig L. Blomberg, "Matthew," in *Commentary on the New Testament Use of the Old Testament*, ed. G. K. Beale and D. A. Carson (Grand Rapids: Baker Academic, 2007), 74. Blomberg acknowledges early Judaism uses of Ps. 118:22 as referring to the cornerstone of the temple.

81. E.g., Joseph A. Fitzmyer, *The Gospel according to Luke (X–XXIV)*, AB 28A (Garden City, NY: Doubleday, 1985), 1282, 1286; John Nolland, *Luke 18:35–24:53*, WBC 35C (Dallas: Word,

was cut out without hands, and it struck the statue . . . and crushed [it]," and it "became like chaff from the summer threshing floors; and the wind carried them away." The statue in Daniel represented the evil world empires that oppress God's people, and the stone symbolized God's kingdom of Israel that would destroy and judge these unbelieving kingdoms. Now, unbelieving Israel has become identified with pagan kingdoms and is portrayed as being judged along with them by also being "broken to pieces" and "scattered like dust."

Thus, Jesus sees Israel as becoming indistinguishable from the ungodly nations and accordingly judged in the very same way. That is, Israel as a nation will no longer exist as God's true covenant people, just as the pagan nations to be judged at the eschaton will no longer exist. Remember also that the "stone" of Daniel's statue, after smashing the colossus, representing the evil kingdoms, "became a great mountain and filled the whole earth." Jesus identifies himself with Daniel's stone that smashes the ungodly nations, which also includes here Israel, which is seen as being allied with these nations. That an aspect of the new form of the kingdom in this passage is the temple, centered in both Jesus and a new "people producing fruit," is further indicated by the fact that the parable of the vineyard from Isa. 57, to which Jesus alludes in the directly preceding context, was interpreted by early Judaism to represent Israel's temple.[82]

That Jesus identifies himself with the cornerstone of the new temple is pointed to further by how in Dan. 2 the stone that struck the statue and then "filled the earth" represented the foundation stone of the temple. That foundation stone grew and grew until it expanded to cover the entire earth.[83] A further indication that Israel identified itself with the nations instead of God's true Israel, Jesus, is seen in Pilate's question to the Jews, "Shall I crucify your King?" to which the chief priests responded, "We have no king but Caesar" (John 19:15). This develops the earlier statement by the Jewish crowd addressing Pilate, "If you release this man [Jesus], you are no friend of Caesar; everyone who makes himself out to be a king opposes Caesar" (John 19:12). In the parallel in Matt. 27:25, the Jews respond to Caesar by saying, "His blood be on us and our children," another radical expression of disassociating themselves from Jesus as the center of the newly emerging Israel, kingdom, and temple.

Jesus's beginning act of reconstituting a new Israel with himself as its head is expressed in Luke 6:12–13, where he goes up to the mountain and chooses twelve disciples from among a larger group of disciples. This likely reflects

---

1993), 953, 955; Darrell L. Bock, *Luke 9:51–24:53*, BECNT (Grand Rapids: Baker Academic, 1996), 1604–5. See also Craig A. Evans, *Mark 8:27–16:20*, WBC 34B (Dallas: Word, 2001), 445. Evans sees Christ's claim in Mark 14:58 to "build another [temple] made without hands" to be an allusion to Dan. 2:44–45. Some manuscripts omit Matt. 21:44, though probably it is original, but even if not, Luke 20:18 includes it without any manuscript variants to the contrary.

82. See Beale, *Temple*, 185–86; Blomberg, "Matthew," 72.

83. For elaboration on this, see Beale, *Temple*, 144–53, 185–86.

the new Mount Sinai, where Jesus begins to start Israel's history over again by choosing twelve people, who represent the beginning stage of the reconstituted people of God.[84]

The notion of restoration in Matthew and in Luke has been covered more briefly respectively in chapters 16 (under the heading "The Concept of Reconciliation as the Inaugurated Fulfillment of New Creation and of Israel's Restoration from Exile Prophecies Elsewhere in the New Testament") and 17 (under the heading "The Role of the Spirit as an Eschatological Life-Transforming Agent in the New Testament").[85] So here we turn to Mark and again to Luke to survey this subject, which will further fill out the Synoptic view on it. There will also be a discussion of the same topic in Acts.

The Beginning End-Time Fulfillment of Israel's Restoration Prophecies among Jesus's Followers and the Church according to Mark, Luke, and Acts

Although the Gospels do not directly refer to the church, it is important to see them portraying Jesus as establishing a new-covenant community that Acts and the rest of the NT see to be the beginnings of the emerging church. Mark, Luke, and Acts understand that Israel's restoration prophecies have begun fulfillment in Jesus, his followers, and the early Christian church. My attempt to argue this will be primarily in an excursus at the end of this chapter, where I will summarize two books that I think have argued well in demonstrating the inaugurated fulfillment of Israel's restoration promises in these biblical books.

In addition to the significant arguments of the excursus on this subject, there are several passages in Luke-Acts on which I especially want to focus.

The Use of Isaiah 42 and 49 in Luke-Acts and the Implications for Jesus and His Followers Being True Restored Israel

Some contend that when gentiles become believers in Acts, they become part of the beginning fulfillment of Israel's restoration prophecies. Despite this acknowledgment, these commentators argue that the gentile Christians do not come to be considered end-time Israel but instead exist alongside Israelite believers and continue in their primary identification as gentiles, albeit redeemed gentiles.[86] However, it has been the contention of this chapter that the equal footing that gentiles share with Jewish believers is to be understood as gentiles becoming

---

84. For expansion of this, see R. T. France, "Old Testament Prophecy and the Future of Israel: A Study of the Teaching of Jesus," *TynBul* 26 (1975): 53–78.

85. See there the summary of Max Turner's work on the Spirit in relation to Luke's understanding of restoration.

86. For this viewpoint, see the excursus at the end of this chapter.

true end-time Israel. Accordingly, I have argued that the church, composed of believing Jews and gentiles, is the commencing fulfillment of the prophecies of Israel's restoration. This idea is apparent in Acts. In this respect, having discussed at the beginning of this chapter the Servant of Isa. 49 as eschatological Israel, the citations of this prophecy in Luke-Acts will be examined in table 20.4.

Table 20.4

Isaiah 49; 42	Isaiah 49:3, 6 in Luke-Acts
49:3: "He said to me, 'You are My Servant, Israel, in whom I will show My glory.'"	**With Application to Christ:**
49:5–6: "And now says the LORD, who formed Me from the womb to be His Servant, to bring Jacob back to Him, so that Israel might be gathered to him (for I am glorified in the sight of the LORD, and My God is My strength), He says, 'It is too small a thing that You should be My Servant to raise up the tribes of Jacob and to restore the preserved ones of Israel; I will also make You a light of the nations so that My salvation may reach to the end of the earth.'"	Luke 2:32: "a Light of revelation to the Gentiles, and the glory of Your people Israel."
	Acts 26:23: "that the Christ was to suffer, and that by reason of His resurrection from the dead He would be the first to proclaim light both to the Jewish people and to the Gentiles."
	With Application to Paul (and Others):
	Acts 13:47: "For so the Lord has commanded us, 'I have placed You as a Light for the Gentiles, that You may bring salvation to the end of the earth.'"
--	--
Isa. 42:6b–7: "And I will appoint you as a covenant to the people, as a light to the nations, to open blind eyes, to bring out prisoners from the dungeon and those who dwell in darkness from the prison."	Acts 26:18: "to open their eyes so that they may turn from darkness to light and from the dominion of Satan to God,[a] that they may receive forgiveness of sins and an inheritance among those who have been sanctified by faith in Me."
See also 42:16, which includes the phrase "I will make darkness into light before them."	

[a]Broken underlining indicates conceptual and not lexical parallels.

The quotations in Luke 2:32 and Acts 26:23 are applied to Christ's mission, which is seen as a fulfillment of the Servant Israel's mission in Isa. 49:1–6. Then Acts 13:47 views Paul and his colleagues to be fulfilling the same prophecy. It is likely the presupposition that the one Christ, Israel the Servant, represents Paul and his special prophetic messengers, so that they also take on what is true of him functionally, which is the mission of Israel to be a light to the nations. In the very same manner, the Servant prophecy of Isa. 42:6–7 is put on the shoulders of Paul in describing his mission as Christ's apostle in Acts 26:18.[87]

87. Paul's identification with the Servant Israel and his mission is pointed to further by reference to Paul being "a servant and a witness" (Acts 26:16) in carrying out the Servant's mission, a double designation also used in describing Israel's mission in Isa. 43:10: "you are My witnesses . . . and My servant." There, however, the commission is clearly Israel's as a nation (taken over by the individual Servant in Isa. 49:1–6), and the word for "servant" (*hupēretēs*) in Acts 26:16 is

The Calling of Israel in Exodus and Deuteronomy and Its Application to the Church in Acts 15:14

Acts 15:14 is also an important text in regard to the question of whether the church was considered to be restored Israel in Acts. This text is part of an introduction to the restoration prophecy of Amos 9:11–12 in Acts 15:16–18, which James interprets to be beginning fulfillment in the church.[88] In Acts 15:14 James summarizes Peter's earlier testimony about gentile salvation from verses 7–11 by alluding to a well-known and repeated OT expression for Israel's original calling that he applies to believing gentiles (see table 20.5).

Table 20.5

Exodus and Deuteronomy LXX	Acts 15:14
Exod. 19:5: "You will be to me a special people from all the nations."	"Simeon has related how God first concerned himself about taking from among the nations a people for his name."[a]
Exod. 23:22: "You will be to me a special people from all of the nations."	
Deut. 14:2: "The Lord God chose you to become to him a special people from all of the nations" (= almost identically Deut. 7:6).	

[a]See Jacques Dupont, "ΛΑΟΣ ΈΞ ΈΘΝΩΝ," *NTS* 3 (1956): 47–50. Dupont sees this wording of Acts 15:14 to be an Israelite formula based on the Exodus and Deuteronomy texts shown in this table.

The application of the expressions from the Exodus and Deuteronomy texts to gentiles in Acts 15:14 would, at the very least, be an analogical application of the formula for Israel's calling in the OT to the calling of the nations, so that the nations certainly are like Israel. But as I argue throughout this chapter, the application is likely more than mere analogy; it is a further pointer to the believing nations' actual identity: they have become part of the true end-time people of God, the eschatological Israel. The phrase at the end of the Amos 9:12 quotation in Acts 15:17, "all the Gentiles who are called by My name," is very similar to the expression in 15:14 ("a people for His name") and likely a development of it. In fact, wherever the "people called by [God's] name" expression occurs in the OT outside of Amos 9:12, it refers only to Israel.[89] We saw earlier in this chapter that most of these same OT texts stood behind

---

different from that in the Greek of Isaiah (*pais*) though a synonym. Paul's identification with the Servant is likely best to be understood as him being a kind of prophetic assistant to that figure.

88. Unfortunately, there is not space to discuss all the complexities of the Amos quotation and its use here. On this, see Beale, *Temple*, 232–44.

89. Deuteronomy 28:10; Isa. 43:7; Jer. 14:9; 15:16 (though this text applies to Jeremiah as a prophet to Israel); Dan. 9:19; Joel 3:5 (2:32 ET); Bar. 2:15 are the only places in the LXX where "call" (*epikaleō*) + "name" (*onoma*) is used in this type of expression. Likewise, note that the only such uses in the LXX of "call" (*kaleō*) + "name" (*onoma*), where God's name may be implicitly referred to, are applied to Israel (Isa. 43:1; 45:3–4; 62:2; 65:15).

the wording of Titus 2:14 ("to purify for Himself a special people"), where I drew the same conclusions being drawn here. Outside of Acts 15:14, whenever Acts mentions "people" (*laos*) to designate a people group, the group is always Israel (Acts 4:10, 27; 13:17; 26:33; 28:26–27). This is also consistent with the observation that Paul uses "people" in the same way.[90] As someone has said, "If someone sees a bird that looks, quacks, waddles, and feels like a duck and in the NT is called a duck—then the creature so described is, indeed, a duck!"[91]

The Inaugurated Fulfillment of the Prophesied Spirit of Joel 2:28–32 in Acts 2:16–21

Another passage in Acts that should be discussed in connection to the relationship of Israel's restoration hopes to the church is the use of Joel 2:28–32 in Acts 2:16–21 (see table 20.6).

Table 20.6

Joel 2:28–32	Acts 2:16–21 (italics = OT quotation)
"It will come about after this that I will pour out My Spirit on all mankind; and your sons and daughters will prophesy, your old men will dream dreams, your young men will see visions. Even on the male and female servants I will pour out My Spirit in those days. I will display wonders in the sky and on the earth, blood, fire and columns of smoke. The sun will be turned into darkness and the moon into blood before the great and awesome day of the LORD comes. And it will come about that whoever calls on the name of the LORD will be delivered; for on Mount Zion and in Jerusalem there will be those who escape, as the LORD has said, even among the survivors whom the LORD calls."	"But this is what was spoken of through the prophet Joel: '*And it shall be in the last days,*' God says, '*that I will pour forth My Spirit on all mankind; and your sons and your daughters shall prophesy, and your young men shall see visions, and your old men shall dream dreams; even on My bondslaves, both men and women, I will in those days pour forth of My Spirit and they shall prophesy. And I will grant wonders in the sky above and signs on the earth below, blood, and fire, and vapor of smoke. The sun will be turned into darkness and the moon into blood, before the great and glorious day of the Lord shall come. And it shall be that everyone who calls on the name of the Lord will be saved.*'"

It is not necessary for the present purposes to attempt a full exposition of this Joel passage in Acts 2. Rather, the focus will be on whether the Joel prophecy prophesies about Israel alone, or the gentiles alone, or Israel and the gentiles, with the gentiles maintaining their identity as gentiles as a separate people from Israel. Then, with the same questions in mind, I will analyze how Luke sees the Joel prophecy to have begun fulfillment.

Joel's prophecy is about the salvation of the faithful remnant of Israel in the end-time. In particular, Joel 2:28–29 indicates that God's Spirit will be distributed to all within the covenant community in some manner greater than before. This probably is referring not to the regenerating aspect of the Spirit

---

90. On which, see my discussion on Paul in the next chapter.
91. Provan, *The Church Is Israel Now*, ii.

but rather to the gifting aspect. Formerly in Israel, prophets, priests, and kings were gifted by the Spirit to carry out their particular roles, but Joel 2 indicates that in the eschatological future there will be a democratization in the distribution of this gifting aspect of the Spirit. In particular, verses 28–29 appear to be making formal Moses's earlier wish in Num. 11:29: "Would that all the LORD's people were prophets, that the LORD would put His Spirit upon them."[92]

A major question, however, concerns the meaning of "all flesh" (*kol-bāśār*), upon which the Spirit is to be poured out. Most commentators see it referring to all within the covenant community who "call upon the name of the LORD" (cf. Joel 2:32). Walter Kaiser, however, sees it as a reference to all classes of people throughout the world, including both Jews and, especially with a major focus, gentiles. Kaiser makes this conclusion on the basis that "all flesh" (*kol-bāśār*) in the OT seldom refers to Israel and most of the time refers to "all humankind." He notes that the phrase occurs thirty-two times, twenty-three of which refer to "all humankind" or to "Gentiles."[93]

Kaiser's statistics need some revision. The phrase "all flesh" occurs approximately forty times,[94] nineteen of which refer to "all humankind," seven to all animals, six to all humans and all animals, and five to all in Israel.[95] The latter references to Israel are especially interesting and relevant because all occur in contexts where Israel is in mind, which we will see is also the case in Joel 2:28–32 (see Jer. 12:12; 45:5; Ezek. 20:48 [21:4 MT]; 21:4–5 [21:9–10 MT]). For example, with respect to the latter category, Jer. 12:12 is part of an announcement of coming judgment on Israel: "On all the bare heights in the wilderness destroyers have come, for a sword of the LORD is devouring from one end of the land even to the other; there is no peace for all flesh." The "all flesh" here refers not to all people throughout the world but rather to all humans living in Israel. Therefore, context must always determine which use is in mind.

The context of Joel 2:28 (3:1 MT) favors "all classes within Israel" who call on the name of the Lord. This is because Joel 2:28–32 is a continuation of the narrative about Israel's future restoration that began at 2:18. In this respect, the identification of the second-person pronouns ("your") in 2:28–29 in relation to the same pronouns in 2:19–27 needs careful study. This pronoun is used ten times in 2:18–27, and each time it clearly refers to Israel. The same pronoun is found three times in 2:28 ("your sons . . . your old men . . . your young men").

---

92. See Raymond B. Dillard, "Intrabiblical Exegesis and the Effusion of the Spirit in Joel," in *Creator, Redeemer, Consummator: A Festschrift for Meredith G. Kline*, ed. Howard Griffith and John R. Muether (Greenville, SC: Reformed Academic Press, 2000), 87–93. See also my earlier discussion of this in chapter 18 under the subheading "Pentecost as a Fulfillment of Joel's Prophecy of the Spirit."

93. Walter C. Kaiser, *The Uses of the Old Testament in the New* (Chicago: Moody, 1985), 96–98.

94. See N. P. Bratsiotis, "בָּשָׂר," *TDOT* 2:319, 327–28.

95. The remaining uses are not relevant to the present discussion.

The direct continuation of the "your" in 2:28 is most naturally identified with Israel, as in 2:19–20, 23–27. In addition, since there appears to be no major break between 2:18–27, the "all flesh" probably refers to all within Israel, just like the uses of "all flesh" that we saw above in Jeremiah and Ezekiel.[96]

That "Israel" is the only focus in 2:28–32 is also apparent because this section is a recapitulation of 2:18–27. The first indication of this may be the introductory "after this" (*'ăḥărê-kēn*) in verse 28. This phrase usually refers to what follows coming subsequently in time with what has preceded (in prophetic literature see, e.g., Jer. 21:7; 49:6). Exceptionally, the phrase can introduce events that recapitulate events in the directly preceding verse (e.g., Isa. 1:24–25 in relation to v. 26, which is introduced by "after this"). Furthermore, very similar phrases can have the function of introducing a recapitulation. For instance, "after those days" in Jer. 31:33 is clearly introducing events that cover the same time as verse 31, which is introduced by "days are coming." Likewise, Dan. 2:28 refers to "the latter days" of Nebuchadnezzar's vision, and verse 29 refers to the very same period by the phrase "after this" (Aram. *'ăḥărê dĕnâ*, virtually identical to the phrase in Joel 2:28). Thus, if context warrants, the phrase in Joel 2:28 could well be introducing verses that cover the same temporal territory as in verses 18–27. That this recapitulative use of the phrase or very similar phrases occurs in such highly charged eschatological contexts as that of Jer. 31:31–33 and Dan. 2:28–29 is suggestive for the end-time context of the phrase in Joel 2:28–32.

In this respect, the climax of Joel 2:18–27 is in verse 27, where the prior description of Israel's restoration in terms of extreme fertility (vv. 21–25) is interpreted to mean that God is "in the midst of *Israel*" and is the one blessing it in this end-time scenario. Similarly, the climax of the 2:28–32 passage is in verse 32, where a remnant of Israelites will "call on the name of the LORD" and "will be delivered . . . on *Mount Zion*," with the obvious implication that God is there present as the one delivering them. This is further supported by the later recapitulation of 2:31 in 3:15–17, where again "the sun and moon" become dark (as in 2:31), followed by "the LORD being a refuge . . . and a stronghold to the sons of Israel," and concluded by "then you [Israel] will know that I am the LORD your God, dwelling in Zion, My holy mountain" (which is similar to both 2:27 and 2:32). Joel 3:18 then says that the result of God being present with Israel is abundant fertility (likely recapitulating 2:21–26). Thus, it is fairly clear that 3:15–18 recapitulates both 2:18–27 and 2:28–32, which increases the likelihood that the latter also recapitulates 2:18–27. An additional observation enhances

---

96. Kaiser (*Old Testament in the New*) argues further that the mention of "male slaves and female slaves" in v. 29 supports the idea of "all mankind"—i.e., a reference to gentiles throughout the world. But, in accord with the contextual idea that Israel is still in mind in 2:28–32 in continuation of 2:18–27, this reference to "slaves" more probably connotes slaves in the community of Israel, including both Israelite slaves and gentile slaves, all of whom are part of the community of Israel.

the idea that verses 28–32 cover the same end-time ground of the directly preceding section. Isaiah repeatedly understands that God's pouring out of the Spirit results in a "fertile field" and "righteousness" and "peace" (Isa. 32:15–18) and in the fruitfulness of God's people in the midst of physical fertility (Isa. 44:3–4; cf. 43:18–21). In fact, Isa. 44:3–4 interprets "I will pour out water on the thirsty land" with "I will pour out My Spirit on your seed." The very close connection of God bringing about material fertility in Israel in Joel 2:21–25 with that of God's pouring out of the Spirit in verse 28 suggests the same connection here in Joel as in these Isaiah passages. The material fertility of verses 21–25 is but an outer indication of the spiritual fertility that will happen to Israel under God's hand of blessing, which is likely expressed by 2:28. As is clearly the case with the aforementioned Isaiah prophecies, so also the Joel prophecy is likely to be viewed as taking place at the time of Israel's eschatological restoration.

All of what I have said is aimed at contending that Joel 2:28–32 is still focused only on Israel and is a prophecy for Israel. This conclusion is enhanced further by the fact that the repeated prophecies throughout the prophets that the Spirit will come in the end time are never for gentiles but only for *Israel*. In addition to Isa. 32:15; 44:3, the following texts underscore the prophecy of the coming of the Spirit to be fulfilled only in Israel: Isa. 11:2; 42:1; 48:16; 59:21; 61:1; Ezek. 36:27; 37:14; 39:29; Zech. 4:6; 12:10.[97] Of these texts, four, like Joel, include reference to the "pouring out of the Spirit" (Isa. 32:15; 44:3; Ezek. 39:29; Zech. 12:10). Again, all of these are restoration prophecies, which points to the same thing in Joel. That the salvation in Joel 2:28–32 is taking place in Israel is made explicit by the phrase in verse 32 that deliverance will occur "on Mount Zion and in Jerusalem." Judaism also understood Joel 2:28–32 to be a prophecy only for Israel.[98]

How is Joel 2 being used and understood in Acts 2? There are some variations between the wording of the Joel text and its quotation in Acts 2,[99] but

97. Of these references, the following refer to the Spirit being given to Israel's end-time leader: Isa. 11:2; 42:1; 48:16; 61:1; Zech. 4:6. The remaining verses listed above refer to the Spirit coming on the nation Israel, though most probably to be interpreted as a remnant of Israel.

98. (1) *Deuteronomy Rabbah* 6.14 combines Ezek. 36:26 and Joel 3:1 and interprets both as referring to God who "will cause My divine presence to rest upon you." (2) In *Lam. Rab.* 2.4.8 and 4.9.14 Joel 3:1 is combined with Zech. 12:10 and Ezek. 36:29, all being summarized as "pourings" for good. (3) Cf. *Midr. Ps.* 138.2, where Joel 3:1 is to occur after the wicked have been judged and the temple rebuilt, when there will be spiritual renewal. (4) *Midrash Psalm* 14.6 combines Joel 3:1 with Ezek. 36:26, emphasizing renewal and restoration, and the following texts are also combined with it: Deut. 5:29 ("Oh that they had such a heart in them, that they would fear me and keep all my commandments always"); Num. 11:29 ("Would that all the LORD's people were prophets"). Likewise, *Tan. d. El.* 4.19 combines Joel 3:1 and Ezek. 36:26 to underscore renewal in the latter days. Some Jewish texts do say that all Israel will prophesy (*Midr. Tanh.* 10.4). Exceptionally, *Eccles. Rab.* 2.8.1 identifies Joel 3:2 as referring to gentile salvation.

99. For the variations in wording, see I. Howard Marshall, "Acts," in *Commentary on the New Testament Use of the Old Testament*, ed. G. K. Beale and D. A. Carson (Grand Rapids: Baker Academic, 2007), 589–93.

only one change is very significant: the change from "after this" (LXX: "after these things") in Joel to "in the latter days." Interestingly, that was the meaning of "after this" in Dan. 2:28–29 and of the very similar phrase in Jer. 31:31–33, which confirms that Peter read Joel 2:28 not necessarily as temporally following Joel 2:18–27 but instead referring to the general end-time period that the former passage also covers. Perhaps even more significant is that the changed wording of "in the last days" (*en tais eschatais hēmerais*) in Acts 2:17 occurs in the LXX only in Isa. 2:2, so that Peter is likely alluding to that OT passage. I argued earlier (chap. 18 under the subheading "Pentecost as a Fulfillment of Joel's Prophecy of the Spirit") that the fiery descent of the Spirit indicates the beginning descent of the end-time temple and the commencement of when God's people began to be incorporated into the latter-day temple. Thus, it should not be surprising that Peter refers to Isa. 2:2, since the phrase there introduces a prophecy of Israel's restored latter-day temple to which converted gentiles will make pilgrimage (vv. 3–4). Isaiah 2:2–4 reads:

> Now it will come about that in the last days the mountain of the house of the LORD will be established as the chief of the mountains, and will be raised above the hills; and all the nations will stream to it. And many peoples will come and say, "Come, let us go up to the mountain of the LORD, to the house of the God of Jacob; that He may teach us concerning His ways and that we may walk in His paths." For the law will go forth from Zion and the word of the LORD from Jerusalem. And he will judge between the nations, and will render decisions for many peoples; and they will hammer their swords into plowshares and their spears into pruning hooks. Nation will not lift up sword against nation, and never again will they learn war.

This likely would have been understood from Isaiah's perspective that the gentiles will convert to the faith of Israel and will stream in and become Israelites in every way, as converted gentiles such as Rahab, Ruth, and Uriah earlier had done. Likewise, we have seen in the introductory part of this chapter that later Isaiah himself prophesies that gentiles will become identified as Israelites in the end-time,[100] and they will become "ministering" priests in the latter-day temple (Isa. 56:3, 6–7). In particular, they will become "Levitical priests" (Isa. 66:18–21). The NT, and in the present case Acts 2, as well as the following chapters of Acts, reveal that gentiles need not move geographically to Israel to become true Israelites and be circumcised and abide by food laws and the other distinguishing nationalist tags of Israel's law. Rather, they need only move to Jesus and be spiritually circumcised in him (Col. 2:11–13) and become clean in him (cf. Col. 2:16 with Acts 11:5–18; 15:9), for he is now the only "tag" that one needs to possess to be identified with end-time Israel, since he sums up Israel in himself.

---

100. Isaiah 19:18, 23–25; see also Ps. 87; Ezek. 47:21–23; Zech. 2:11.

However, I am getting ahead of myself a bit. The allusion to Isa. 2:2 in Acts 2:17 implies that gentiles become identified with Israel. However, in Acts 2 the first people who come to faith and are incorporated into the spiritual temple are Jews from Palestine and the Disapora, as well as proselytes, so that Joel 2 is first fulfilled in Jews and gentile proselytes identified with Israel (Acts 2:5–11). The description in Acts 2:5–11 of the nations from which these people come appears to be an abbreviated list of the seventy nations from Gen. 10–11, which resulted from the scattering of people at the tower of Babel.[101] The significance of this is that it is a further hint that these people groups present at Pentecost represent the gentile lands from which they come, so that the blessing of the Spirit that they experience also represents the application of this blessing to those gentile areas. The fulfillment of the Joel 2 prophecy then becomes explicitly fulfilled also in the gentiles in Acts 10:44–48 (the account is repeated in 11:15–18).[102] There, gentiles who believe have "the gift of the Holy Spirit . . . poured out on" them. In response, "all the circumcised believers" witnessing this "were amazed." Why? It is most likely because they had thought that the promise of Joel was only for Israel, which I have argued was, indeed, the very intent of Joel 2. So the question that faces us now is this: does the pouring out of the Spirit mean that gentiles can receive the Joel promise without becoming Israelites, or is the definition of a true Israelite being understood more broadly than before?

Commentators answer this in different ways. In an effort to say that gentiles do not become identified with Israel but nevertheless receive Joel's promise of the Spirit, appeal often is made to Acts 11:18, where the Jews conclude, "Well then, God has granted to the gentiles also the repentance that leads to life" (likewise appeal can be made to Peter's similar testimony in Acts 15:7–11). However, the thesis of this entire chapter is that when gentiles believe in Christ, they become identified with him, who is true Israel, and as they become identified with him, they are called "little messianic ones" (*christianoi*, i.e., Christians [see Acts 11:26]). This latter view seems more plausible because Joel 2 is so explicit about being a prophecy *only for Israel*. This latter view would explain how gentiles could be part of the fulfillment of this prophecy about Israel without trying to explain in some other way how gentiles could

101. See James M. Scott, "Luke's Geographical Horizon," in *The Book of Acts in Its Graeco-Roman Setting*, ed. David W. J. Gill and Conrad Gempf, vol. 2 of *The Book of Acts in Its First Century Setting*, ed. Bruce W. Winter (Grand Rapids: Eerdmans, 1994), 483–544; idem, *Paul and the Nations: The Old Testament and Jewish Background of Paul's Mission to the Nations with Special Reference to the Destination of Galatians*, WUNT 84 (Tübingen: Mohr Siebeck, 1995), 162–80. Scott argues this on the basis of similarities not only to Gen. 10 but also to early Jewish lists that are linked to Gen. 10 (see also his discussion of the history of the various proposed identifications). Scott's argument was anticipated by M. D. Goulder, *Type and History in Acts* (London: SPCK, 1964), 152–59.
102. Acts 19:6 recounts another incident in which the Spirit comes upon gentiles in Ephesus.

fulfill it and not be identified with Israel.[103] In addition, we have seen in the introductory part of this chapter that the OT repeatedly prophesied that gentiles would convert to become identified with Israel in the latter days. My approach explains how that could be so in light of gentiles being identified with Jesus as the continuation of the remnant of true Israel.

In this regard, it is interesting to ask the question of who, precisely, begins to fulfill the Joel 2 prophecy. The answer is not those who first spoke in tongues upon whom the Spirit was poured out. Rather, Jesus was the very first person to fulfill the Joel prophecy, according to Acts 2:33: "Therefore having been exalted to the right hand of God, and *having received from the Father the promise of the Holy Spirit,* He has poured forth this which you both see and hear." Verses 34–35 then explain that Jesus's ascension has demonstrated him to be both "Lord and Messiah"—that is, king of Israel. Those, then, who identified with him as the king of Israel are represented by him and are considered Israelites, whether they are ethnic Jews or gentile proselytes, as in Acts 2, or are gentiles believing in Jesus who formerly may not even have been proselytes, as in Acts 10–11. Consequently, the Joel 2 prophecy is not diluted or stretched beyond its original hermeneutical boundaries as a prophecy for Israel. Just as was prophesied in Joel 2:32 twice that only a "remnant" (lit., "escaped ones" and "survivors") of Israel would fulfill the prophecy, so it is first fulfilled in the remnant of one, Jesus the Messiah, who represented all other Jews who first believed in Acts 2–6, and who also were a remnant in Israel at the time. This initial fulfillment is then followed by other Jews and gentiles becoming identified with Jesus as the Israelite remnant further fulfilling Joel's prophecy.

In this respect, it should be remembered that the Acts 2 episode of the Spirit's coming is a fulfillment also of Acts 1:8 (as discussed in chap. 17 under the heading "The Role of the Spirit as the Eschatological Life-Transforming Agent in the New Testament"): "But you will receive power when the Holy Spirit has come upon you; and you shall be My witnesses both in Jerusalem, and in all Judea and Samaria, and even to the remotest part of the earth." This

---

103. E.g., some try to explain that the Joel prophecy is merely analogically applied to gentiles and not fulfilled, so that gentiles are not seen as Israel fulfilling the Israelite prophecy of Joel. But this seems to be special pleading because if a full quotation from a clear OT prophecy is applied to something or someone in the NT, the default understanding is that fulfillment is being indicated (and here Peter even says, "This is what was spoken through the prophet Joel"). An analogical use is always possible, but it is not the natural first reading of an OT prophecy applied to a present situation, and therefore it would need to be argued from evidence in the context. Others might see that Joel 2 is fulfilled among gentiles, but that they are still not considered to be part of Israel, on the basis that someone can inherit something from someone else but not have to be of the same family bloodline in order to get the inheritance (perhaps the inheritance comes through adoption, whereby the child's name is not legally changed). In this respect, see the next chapter with regard to this notion of inheritance and the modern illustration of "Johnny Smith."

connection between 1:8 and Acts 2 is important because 1:8 itself is a promise that alludes to some of the great restoration promises of Israel (see table 20.7).

Table 20.7

Isaiah	Acts 1:8
32:15: "Until the Spirit is poured out upon us from on high, and the wilderness becomes a fertile field, and the fertile field is considered as a forest."	"But you will receive power when the Holy Spirit has come upon you [which continues Luke 24:49: "And behold, I am sending forth the promise of my Father upon you; but you are to stay in the city until you are clothed with power from on high"];
43:10a–b: "'You are My witnesses,' declares the LORD, 'and My servant whom I have chosen, so that you may know and believe Me.'"	and you shall be My witnesses both in Jerusalem, and in all Judea and Samaria, and
43:12b: "'So you are My witnesses,' declares the LORD, 'And I am God'" (so also 44:8).	
49:6b: "I will also make You a light of the nations, so that My salvation may reach to the end of the earth."	even to the end of the earth" (recall the formal citation of Isa. 49:6 at the literary transition of Acts 13:47, "I have placed You as a light for the Gentiles, that You may bring salvation to the end of the earth," which confirms the Isa. 49 reference in Acts 1:8).

We saw in the earlier discussion in chapter 17 that these combined allusions affirm the beginning fulfillment of Isaiah's prophecies of kingdom restoration as part of a positive answer to the apostles' question in Acts 1:6 ("Lord, is it at this time You are restoring the kingdom to Israel?"). Thus, the response in verse 8 does not indicate a complete delay in the realization of the kingdom promises but rather signifies an inaugurated fulfillment, which is about to occur (in Acts 2). Recalling that this is a promise made to the twelve apostles (cf. Acts 1:2, 15–26) enhances their role as the nucleus or representative beginning remnant of true Israel, which is commencing the carrying out of the Isaianic predictions, and which reaches an even higher fulfillment stage in Acts 2. As we have seen above, the Joel 2 prophecy of the pouring out of the Spirit to restore end-time Israel is parallel with other prophetic texts prophesying the same thing about Israel, including Isa. 32:15. Therefore, the coming of the Spirit in Acts 2 is seen as a fulfillment of both Joel 2 and Isa. 32, all of which enhances the Israelite nature of the fulfillment, since these two prophecies are about Israel's restoration in their respective contexts.[104] Also, it is worth mentioning that the light-bearing Servant of Isa. 49:6, alluded to in Acts 1:8, is referred to as "my Servant Israel" in Isa. 49:3, which is too contextually close

104. At the least, even if Isa. 32:15 is not explicitly alluded to in Acts 1:8, it is likely echoed, since the wording is so similar and it is conceptually the same as Joel 2:28.

to not have had some degree of influence on Luke in conceiving of Jesus as the "Servant Israel."

Conclusion

The argument that the NT identifies the church as the true end-time Israel has been made in this chapter from a number of different angles. First, the OT prophesies that gentiles will become Israelites in the latter days. Second, the NT directly refers to the church as "the seed of Abraham" and "the Israel of God," in addition to attributing numerous descriptions of Israel from the OT to the church. Mark, Luke, and Acts also view Israel's restoration prophecies to begin fulfillment in Jesus, his followers,[105] and the emerging church. The theological basis of the church being identified as true Israel is to be found in its identification with Jesus, the true Israel, who represents the church.

Thus, the salvation of the church is depicted as the end-time restoration of Israel. This is a facet of inaugurated eschatology in general and an aspect in particular of the latter-day new-creational kingdom, since we have seen in earlier chapters that Israel's restoration was inextricably linked to the latter-day new creation and reign of Israel and its Messiah. Inaugurated eschatology, especially as the beginning of new creation and its spread, is the core of the penultimate part of the NT storyline that I been proposing throughout the book: *Jesus's life, trials, death for sinners, and especially resurrection by the Spirit <u>have launched the fulfillment of the eschatological already–not yet new-creational</u> reign, bestowed by grace through faith and <u>resulting in worldwide commission to the faithful to advance this new-creational reign</u> and resulting in judgment for the unbelieving, unto the triune God's glory.*

Excursus 2 The Beginning End-Time Fulfillment of Israel's Restoration Prophecies among Jesus's Followers and the Church according to Mark, Luke, and Acts

The purpose of this excursus is to summarize two books that have argued cogently that Mark, Luke, and Acts understand Israel's restoration prophecies to have begun fulfillment in Jesus, his followers, and the early Christian church in Acts.

The Inauguration of Israel's Restoration Prophecies in the Gospel of Mark

In *Isaiah's New Exodus in Mark*, Rikki Watts has argued persuasively that the restoration prophecies of Isa. 40–66, understood as announcements of a second

105. Matthew witnesses to the same thing, but lack of space has precluded discussion of this.

exodus, form the framework for Mark's understanding of the ministry of Jesus, especially as these prophecies have been inaugurated.[106] One does not have to agree with every aspect of his argument to appreciate the overall cumulative effect of the various kinds of evidence that he adduces in favor of his thesis.[107]

Only some of the major ideas of Watts's book will be highlighted here.[108] Watts argues in chapter 3 that the OT quotations in Mark 1:2–3 about Israel's restoration as a second exodus provide the conceptual framework for Mark's overall narrative:

> As it is written in Isaiah the prophet,
> "Behold, I send my messenger before your face, who will prepare
>   your way;
> The voice of one crying in the wilderness,
> 'Make ready the way of the Lord,
> Make his paths straight.'"

Verse 3 ("The voice of one crying . . .") is a citation of Isa. 40:3, which is part of the opening prophetic announcement of Israel's restoration in Isa. 40–66. Intriguingly, however, verse 2 ("Behold, I send . . .") is a combined reference to Mal. 3:1 and Exod. 23:20.[109] The Exodus text speaks of God's sovereign guidance of Israel's way to the land at the first exodus, and Malachi, utilizing the Exodus language, foresees another exodus, when God's way will be prepared to come in judgment upon Israel. Both Isa. 40:3 and the Exodus/Malachi references are said to be from Isaiah ("as it is written in Isaiah the prophet"). The Exodus/Malachi references are utilized as interpretations of Isaiah and thus are subordinated to Isaiah to indicate that Isaiah's second-exodus restoration expectations are the dominant OT influence throughout Mark. The programmatic nature of the Isaianic restoration and second-exodus idea for Mark is further suggested by the first verse of the Gospel: "The beginning of the gospel of Jesus Christ, the Son of God. As it is written in Isaiah the prophet. . . ." That is, the Isaiah expectation is viewed to be the first and primary explanation of Mark's "gospel." The actual historical narrative begins in verse 4, after the introductory programmatic statement of verses 1–3.

In chapter 4 of his book Watts explains that John the Baptist is the fulfillment of Malachi's prophecy that Elijah will prepare the way of God's new-exodus coming (Mal. 4:5), which is to be understood as an introductory filling out of the broader Isaianic new-exodus/restoration expectation. Accordingly, the very word "gospel" ("good news") in Mark 1:14–15 (cf. also 1:1) expresses Isaiah's

---

106. Rikki E. Watts, *Isaiah's New Exodus in Mark* (Grand Rapids: Baker Academic, 1997).

107. As some book reviews have also concluded; see, e.g., reviews by Joel Marcus (*JTS* 50 [1999]: 222–25) and Sharon E. Dowd (*JBL* 119 [2000]: 140–41), though Nick Overduin (*CTJ* 37 [2002]: 131–33) remains skeptical about the probability of Watts's argument.

108. I have tried to follow the essence of Watts's own summary of his book in his introduction and conclusion, expanding here and there.

109. Likely Mal. 3:1 alludes to the Exodus text, and Mark appears to include both in his reference.

idea of Yahweh's inbreaking reign spoken of in Isa. 52:7: "How lovely on the mountains are the feet of him who brings good news, who announces peace and brings good news . . . and says to Zion, 'Your God reigns!'" This announcement of the beginning kingdom is signaled by the heavens being split and the Spirit descending (Mark 1:10; cf. Isa. 63:11–64:1). The voice from heaven at Jesus's baptism (Mark 1:11) declares him to be the true "Servant Israel" (Son of God).[110]

Chapter 5 of Watts's work argues that Mark's Gospel has a threefold structure: (1) Jesus's mighty ministry in Galilee and beyond (1:16–8:21/26); (2) Jesus's leading his "blind" disciples along the "way" (8:22/27–10:45/52); and (3) Jesus's climactic coming to Jerusalem (10:46/11:1–16:8). This threefold structure reflects the Isaianic structure of exodus and restoration, where (1) Israel is delivered from bondage by God as its warrior and healer; (2) God leads the "blind" along the "way" of the new-exodus deliverance; and (3) Israel finally arrives in Jerusalem.

In Mark's first section Jesus's healings of the blind, deaf, dumb, and lame are signs of the inaugurated restoration of the new exodus (in fulfillment of Isa. 29:18; 35:5–6, on which, see chap. 6 of Watts's book). The exorcism miracles in the same section appear to be regarded as the epitome of Jesus's powerful works, which is evident from their repeated mention and structural prominence (1:21–28, 34, 39; 3:3ff., 15, 22ff.; 5:1–20; 6:13; 7:24–30; 9:14–29). In this respect, it is striking that when Jesus comments on the significance of the exorcisms, he does so by appealing to Isaiah's prediction that God would be a warrior for Israel against its enemies in the process of delivering it from captivity (see table 20.8).

Table 20.8

Isaiah 49:24–25 LXX	Mark 3:27
49:24: "Will any one take spoils from a giant? And if one should take a man captive unjustly, shall he be delivered?" 49:25: "For thus says the Lord: If one should take a giant captive, he will take spoils, and he who takes them from a mighty man will be delivered. For I will plead your cause, and I will deliver your children."	"But no one can enter the strong man's house and plunder his property unless he first binds the strong man, and then he will plunder his house."

On the one hand, the captives in Isaiah were in captivity to Babylon, and Babylon's power was represented by its idols. On the other hand, in Mark it is the unclean spirits and demons who are the ultimate oppressors, and who probably were understood to be the ultimate power behind idols. Accordingly, Jesus's releasing people from the power of demons by casting them out appears to be how Mark understands part of the beginning fulfillment of Isaiah's prophecy of release from exile and Babylonian bondage. In this manner and others in Mark, Jesus as deliverer and restorer of Israel

---

110. Alluding to Isa. 42:1: "Behold, My Servant, whom I uphold; My chosen one in whom My soul delights. I have put My Spirit upon Him." Woven into this Isa. 42 allusion is reference also to the Davidic messianic Son of God foretold in Ps. 2:7: "You are My Son."

is identified with God as Isaiah's prophesied agent of restoration. This is a very high Christology, since Jesus is identified with Yahweh, whom Isaiah prophesied would restore Israel.

Chapter 7 of Watt's book contends that the Beelzebul controversy in Mark 3:22–30 represents the decisive rejection of Jesus by Jerusalem's leaders (they have "blasphemed against the Holy Spirit") and echoes the rebellion against God's Spirit during the first exodus, as described in Isa. 63:10: "But they rebelled and grieved His Holy Spirit; therefore, He turned Himself to become their enemy; He fought against them." Just as God became an enemy to the rebellious Israelites in the wilderness, so he has become an enemy to those rejecting Christ and accusing him of blasphemy. This episode results in the division within Israel and judgment of the nation, which begins to be carried out through Jesus's parables, in fulfillment of Isa. 6:9–10 (cited in Mark 4:11–13). Mark's only other narrative of confrontation between Jesus and the leaders "from Jerusalem" before his final coming to Jerusalem is portrayed similarly to the earlier confrontation. This again is seen as a fulfillment of another prophecy from Isaiah, which itself develops Isa. 6:9–10.[111]

Watts's eighth chapter focuses on the second major section of Mark, the so-called way section. This segment is framed by this Gospel's only "sight" miracles, which correspond to the theme of blindness in this section. Jesus's leading the uncomprehending "blind" and "deaf" disciples along the "way" calls to mind God's leading the "blind" of Israel in the new-exodus "way" in fulfillment of Isa. 42:16: "I will lead the blind by a way they do not know, in paths they do not know I will guide them. I will make darkness into light before them." Even the faithful remnant being restored by Jesus, represented by his disciples, is blind and deaf, as seen in Mark 8:17–18:

And Jesus, aware of this, said to them, "Why do you discuss the fact that you have no bread? Do you not yet see or understand? Do you have a hardened heart? Having eyes, do you not see? And having ears, do you not hear? And do you not remember?"

Even the disciples are part of the hardened lump of Israel, as already suggested by Mark 6:52: "For they had not gained any insight . . . , but their heart was hardened." However, in contrast to the application of Isa. 6:9–10 to unbelieving Israel in Mark 4, now Jesus reframes the quotation by making it into a question that anticipates Mark 7:18: "Are you so lacking in understanding also?" Reshaping the Isa. 6 quotation into a question likely indicates that the faithful remnant, though still affected by blindness, is slowly but surely undergoing restoration by following Jesus. The miracles of the blind being healed occur at the beginning (8:22–26) and the end (10:46–52) of the "way" segment in order to symbolize the disciples' unspiritual condition and that they are in

111. On which, see Mark 7:5–13 and the quotation of Isa. 29:13 there in connection to Isa. 29:9–10.

the process of undergoing spiritual restoration.[112] This inclusio evokes Isaiah's picture of God leading the blind along the path of restoration through the Servant's work (cf. Isa. 42:1 with 42:16, 18–20).

In this same middle segment of Mark, Jesus's predictions of his suffering and death are understood to be the means by which the Isaianic new-exodus restoration will be carried out, since Isa. 53 foresaw that the messianic Servant Israel would be the key agent under God's hand in executing the new exodus by his redemptive death (see Mark 10:45).

The last exegetical chapter of Watts's work discusses Jesus's cursing of the fig tree and cleansing of the temple as calling to mind the implicit threat in the introductory Malachi reference (Mark 1:2) and in the introductory portrayal of John the Baptist as Elijah. Also, Jesus's rejection and death reflects the Suffering Servant of Isa. 53.

In conclusion, Watts argues that the following pieces of evidence in favor of the dominance of Isaiah's second exodus and restoration have a cumulative effect:

1. It was a literary convention in works of antiquity to employ introductory sentences to summarize the conceptual framework of the writing. Mark appears to have followed this convention in 1:1–3 by starting out with an Isaianic new-exodus restoration passage.

2. Relevant for Mark is the modern sociological observation that in times of internal conflict or of uncertainty a group's reflection on its founding moment is critical for its own self-understanding. The founding moment for Israel was the exodus, which not only shaped its national identity but also influenced prophets to use it as the model for a new exodus in prophesying Israel's restoration from Babylon. Accordingly, it is not coincidental that several emerging groups within Israel described their movements in the language of the new exodus, including emergent Christianity that styled itself as the "way" of the new exodus.[113]

3. Since Isaiah is the best-known prophet of Israel's restoration, it is natural that Mark would portray Jesus's restoration of people to God by appealing to this prophet, especially to Isa. 40–66.

4. Mark's threefold outline reflects Isa. 40–66's outline of the coming restoration.

5. Mark's repeated appeal to Isaiah by citation, allusion, and unique theme further points to this Gospel being saturated with Isaiah's second-exodus and restoration background.

Watts especially highlights the first two points above because they form the basis upon which the original contribution of this book is argued.

---

112. Especially note the narration of the miracle in 8:22–30 immediately following the application of the Isa. 6 quotation to the disciples in 8:17–21.
113. See the summary in Watts, *Isaiah's New Exodus*, 3–4.

As his opening editorial citation indicates, Mark's fundamental herme-neutic for interpreting and presenting Jesus derives from two sources: A) a positive schema whereby Jesus' identity and ministry is presented in terms of Isaiah's New Exodus . . . ; and B) a negative schema by which Jesus' rejection by the nation's leaders and his action in the Temple is cast in terms of the prophet Malachi's warning; a warning which itself concerned the delay of the Isaianic New Exodus. . . . This dual perspec-tive of salvation and judgment—both within the context of the [Isaianic New Exodus]—seems to provide the fundamental literary and theological structure of Mark's Gospel. This is not to deny the presence of other concerns (e.g. discipleship, Mark 13) or OT themes (e.g. Son of Man Christology), but instead suggests only that they [are] presented within the larger literary and theological scheme proposed herein.[114]

Watts's work contributes further evidence for the view of such scholars as C. H. Dodd[115] and Francis Foulkes[116] that the citation of or allusion to OT passages in the NT are indicators of broader hermeneutic frameworks, story-lines, or the larger immediate literary context of the OT passage referred to.

Thus, Mark's portrayal of Jesus and his followers beginning to fulfill Isaiah's prophecies of Israel's second exodus and restoration further identifies the early Christian movement with eschatological Israel. As we will see in the next sec-tion, the book of Acts understands what began in Jesus's ministry to be the beginning of the early church itself. Hence, in this way, the roots of the church are identified as the beginning fulfillment of Isaiah's second-exodus prophecies.

The Restoration of Israel as a Second Exodus Fulfilled in Jesus, His Followers, and the Church according to Luke-Acts

As argued above, prophetic hopes for restoration include the idea of reconcilia-tion to and acceptance by God. In this connection, David Pao, in his book *Acts and the Isaianic New Exodus*, argues that the foundational story of Israel's exodus as transformed by Isaiah (esp. Isa. 40–55) is a hermeneutical paradigm by which Luke provides a "meaningful and coherent 'history' in his structur-ing" of diverse traditions concerning the early development of the Christian movement.[117]

Chapter 1 of Pao's work surveys various approaches to the study of Acts and past works that focus on the use of the OT (esp. Isaiah) in Luke-Acts.

---

114. Ibid., 4.

115. C. H. Dodd, *According to the Scriptures: The Sub-Structure of New Testament Theology* (London: Nisbet, 1952).

116. Francis F. Foulkes, *The Acts of God: A Study of the Basis of Typology in the Old Testa-ment* (London: Tyndale, 1958).

117. David W. Pao, *Acts and the Isaianic New Exodus*, WUNT 2/130 (Tübingen: Mohr Siebeck, 2000), 249. For a good summary of the entire thesis, see pp. 249–50. For a review, including critique, see G. K. Beale, review of *Acts and the Isaianic New Exodus*, by David W. Pao, *TJ* 25 (2004): 93–101.

While some have emphasized the significance of Isaiah and especially Isaiah's new exodus and restoration in Mark and Luke's Gospel, none have yet attempted to explore the possibility that the Isaianic new exodus is important for Luke's second book. Pao sets out to argue that Isaiah's second exodus is the hermeneutical framework for understanding the whole book of Acts. In doing so, he builds especially on the prior work of Mark Strauss[118] and, above all, of Rikki Watts.[119]

Pao's conclusion in the first chapter includes a proposal that his reconstruction of Luke's employment of Isaiah is plausible within the literary and historical context. Pao offers five considerations to support this point:

1. the heavy use of Isaiah in Christian works around the same period;
2. the possibility of Luke's audience being "God-fearers" because of his focus on synagogues;
3. the mention in Acts itself of training new Christian converts in OT Scripture;
4. the extensive use of scriptural citations, allusions, and patterns elsewhere in Acts;
5. Luke's Isaianic program being understandable granted the assumption that he had a wide audience in mind, and that some in that audience would have been able to recognize the use of allusions to Isaiah's exodus and restoration.

These points are important because a number of scholars contend that NT writers were not concerned that readers pick up on their OT references (much less a contextual use of such references), partly because the educational level of typical Greco-Romans would not have enabled them to read Greek (or Hebrew), much less to appreciate references to the LXX in oral form.

In chapter 2 of his monograph Pao develops the significance of the citation from Isa. 40:3–5 that appears at the commencement of Jesus's public ministry in Luke 3:4–6:

> As it is written in the book of the words of Isaiah the prophet,
> "The voice of one crying in the wilderness,
> 'Make ready the way of the Lord,
> Make his paths straight.
> Every ravine will be filled,
> And every mountain and hill will be brought low;
> The crooked will become straight;
> And the rough roads smooth;
> And all flesh will see the salvation of God.'"

---

118. Mark L. Strauss, *The Davidic Messiah in Luke-Acts: The Promise and Its Fulfillment in Lukan Christology*, JSNTSup 110 (Sheffield: Sheffield Academic Press, 1995).
119. Watts, *Isaiah's New Exodus*.

Pao contends that this citation from Isaiah provides the key interpretative framework within which the remainder of Luke-Acts is to be understood. The best expression of this new-exodus paradigm is "way" terminology (derived primarily from Isa. 40:3) in Acts as a name for the nascent Christian movement, polemically identifying the church as God's true people in the midst of rejecting Israel. Isaiah 40:3 reads, "A voice is calling, 'Clear the way for the LORD in the wilderness; make smooth in the desert a highway for our God.'" "The Way" as a name for the Christian church occurs six times in Acts (Acts 9:2; 19:9, 23; 22:4; 24:14, 22). In Isa. 40 "the way" is the way of Israel's restoration, so that the very name of the church embodies the idea that the church was participating in the beginning fulfillment of Isaiah's restoration prophecies. The various motifs found in the prologue to Isa. 41–55 (Isa. 40:1–11) are developed extensively throughout the following chapters of Isaiah and in Acts.

In chapter 3 Pao discusses the use of Isaiah's restoration promises in Luke 4:16–30 (Isa. 61:1–2 + 58:6) and 24:44–49 (Isa. 49:6). He contends that both passages are programmatic for the Acts narrative. But even within the book of Acts Pao finds evidence that Isaiah is used programmatically from the very beginning. In Acts 1:8 there are at least three allusions to Isaiah: "But you will receive power when the Holy Spirit has come upon you; and you shall be My witnesses both in Jerusalem, and in all Judea and Samaria, and even to the end of the earth." Behind "when the Holy Spirit has come upon you" stands Isa. 32:15 ("the Spirit is poured out on us from on high"); "you will be my witnesses" alludes to Isa. 43:10, 12 ("you are My witnesses"); "unto the end of the earth" is inspired by Isa. 49:6 ("I will also make You a light of the nations so that My salvation may reach to the end of the earth"). Again, all three Isaiah allusions are part of restoration prophecies in Isaiah, thus highlighting the theme of the restoration of Israel at the very beginning of Acts.

In addition, three apparent geographical references in Acts 1:8 ("in Jerusalem, and in all Judea and Samaria, and even to the end of the earth") are theopolitical, designating the three phases in the new-exodus program of Isaiah: respectively, (1) the dawning of salvation upon Jerusalem, (2) the restoration of Israel, and (3) the mission to the nations. The commencement of carrying out the last leg of this redemptive-historical plan is highlighted in Acts 13:47 (a major literary hinge in the book), where the last phrase of Acts 1:8 ("to the end of the earth," an allusion to Isa. 49:6) is picked up again, this time as part of a full quotation of Isa. 49:6: "For I have placed You as a light for the nations, that You may bring salvation to the end of the earth." Thus, this passage, which is subtly alluded to in Luke 24:47 ("to all the nations") and Acts 1:8 ("unto the end of the earth"), finally appears appropriately in full-blown form.

Chapter 3 of Pao's book concludes with an analysis of the quotation of Isa. 6:9–10 at the end of Acts (28:26–27). The quotation underscores theocratic Israel's rejection of God's prophetic work of restoration through Christ and his apostolic prophets. Placing this quotation at the end of Acts creates a literary-theological reversal: Isaiah begins with the quotation of 6:9–10, and the book ends with the salvation of gentiles; Acts reverses this pattern.

Pao elaborates on Isaiah's understanding of the restoration, which is built around six crucial themes that play a significant role in the first half of Acts.

(1) The prophesied reconstitution of Israel begins fulfillment in Luke-Acts with the establishment of the twelve apostles, who represent the regathered twelve tribes. The choosing of Matthias to recomplete the circle of twelve apostles continues this theme of Israel's inaugurated end-time restoration begun in Luke and relaunches it for Acts. The reference of the witness to "Samaria" following "Jerusalem" and "Judea" and preceding "the end of the earth" (i.e., gentiles) probably also expresses the reconstitution of Israel's two former kingdoms, the southern and the northern, as one. (2) Likewise, the mention that at Pentecost there were gathered "Jews . . . from every nation under heaven" (2:5 [cf. 2:9–11]) is best related to Isaiah's repeated prophecy of the ingathering of dispersed exiles. Additional references to (3) the coming of the Spirit (chap. 2), (4) the initial repentance of multitudes in Israel (e.g., 2:41–47; 5:14; 6:1, 7; 11:24; 12:24), (5) the rebuilding of the Davidic kingdom (15:13–18), and (6) the inclusion of outcasts among God's true people (like the Ethiopian eunuch [8:26–39]) further reflect Isaiah's restoration prophecies. In this respect, Pao concurs with other scholars (e.g., N. T. Wright, Craig Evans, and James Scott) that Israel's exile was viewed by significant sectors of Judaism as continuing into the first century, and that this well explains Luke's emphasis on the inauguration of Isaiah's restoration promises in the coming of Jesus and the Spirit.

Pao elaborates on the major theme of the Isaianic "word of God" in chapter 5 of his book. He argues that the repeated phrase "the word of God" or "the word of the Lord" (over 20x, plus other variants with "word") has its roots in Isaiah's new-exodus paradigm. The stress in Acts on the journeying of the powerful word in creating a community based on the word is especially underscored at crucial literary transitions in the book (e.g., 6:7; 12:24; 19:20). This emphasis reflects the key role of God's mighty word in effecting restoration in Isaiah, especially from Isa. 2:3, and its developments in Isa. 45:22–24; 55:10–11.[120] Despite opposition, the word makes its way and accomplishes its goal of creating the church community, which, in contrast to the Jewish establishment, is identified as the true heir of Isaiah's new-exodus and restoration promises.

In chapter 6 of Pao's book the polemic against idolatry becomes the focus. Pao surveys the anti-idol polemic in Isa. 40–55 and finds it inextricably linked to a polemic against the nations opposing Israel (e.g., 40:18–24; 41:4–10; 44:9–20; 46:1–13). Isaiah highlights Yahweh's sovereignty over against that of the idols and the nations who trust in the idols. Isaiah's anti-idol polemic finds most explicit expression in Acts 17, where specific allusions to Isa. 40–55 occur. Less explicit expressions of the polemic are found elsewhere in Acts: God's powerful word and incomparable sovereignty are established through the judgment of people who are making competitive divine claims (e.g., Simon in 8:4–24, Herod in 12:20–23, and Elymas the magician in 13:10–11). These episodes are linked to the notion that just as idolatry is refuted, so the antagonism of the nations is overcome. This is based on Isaiah's notion that the idols represented the purported power of the nations. The irresistible sovereignty of the risen Jesus

---

120. Note Isa. 2:3, "For out of Zion shall go forth instruction, and the word of the LORD from Jerusalem" (NRSV), which, Pao asserts, "becomes a summary statement of the word in Acts" (*Acts and the Isaianic New Exodus*, 159).

is included in the polemic, which identifies Jesus with Yahweh of Isaiah's new exodus. It should be added here that the idol polemic was crucial to Isaiah's restoration prophecies, since the polemic showed that God, in contrast to helpless idols, was sovereign to prophesy and to carry out Israel's restoration from Babylon, the land of captivity, and idols. Accordingly, this notion of Jesus's ability to restore his people is likely included in the idol polemic in Acts.

Pao's seventh chapter begins with a discussion of the tension between Isaiah's prophecies of Israel's salvation and judgment of the nations, on the one hand, and the salvation of the nations, on the other hand. Pao concludes that both are significant themes in Isaiah that should not be played off against each other. Nevertheless, he acknowledges that the saved nations will in some way submit to redeemed Israel. Pao concludes that gentiles are "accepted as part of the people of God," but he contends that they are "accepted in the New Exodus of Acts as Gentiles," who exist "alongside the people of Israel."[121] He says that there is, in contrast to or in development of Isaiah's picture, a transformation of this dual hope of the salvation of both Israel and the nations in Acts: not only are the nations included in the new-exodus program of fulfillment and put on an equal footing with saved Israelites, but also gentile salvation becomes the focus and drives the narrative's movement in Acts 13–28.

I would add here, as noted earlier in this chapter, in significant contrast to Pao's assessment, that the equal footing that gentiles share with Jewish believers is better understood as gentiles becoming true end-time Israel. Consequently, the church, composed of believing Jews and gentiles, is the commencing fulfillment of the prophecies of Israel's restoration.

Conclusion

The books by Watts and Pao on Mark and Luke-Acts show how saturated these NT books are with the notion that the end-time second exodus prophesied in Isa. 40–66 was already being fulfilled. Believing Jews and gentiles compose the true Israel that is participating in this second exodus.

---

121. Ibid., 239.

21

The Church as the Transformed and Restored Eschatological Israel (Continued)

The Beginning Fulfillment of Israel's Restoration Prophecies in the Church according to Paul

I discussed in an earlier chapter the notion that the latter-day promise of Israel's restoration was understood by Paul to have begun fulfillment in the church and was sometimes understood explicitly by him to be God's reconciliation in a new creation of alienated people to himself (see chap. 16). In the same chapter we also saw that the inaugurated fulfillment of Israel's restoration promises in the Gospels and Acts at times also reflects the concept of divine reconciliation of people estranged from God. Now we will look at other Pauline expressions that view the restoration prophecies of Israel as having begun realization in the church. The conclusion from this evidence will be that the church is not merely like Israel but is actually the continuation of true end-time Israel, the faithful people of God. This conclusion is strengthened when seen together with the introductory discussion in the preceding chapter concerning the presuppositions in both Testaments about gentiles and end-time Israel, as well as Israelite names, images, and prophecies applied to the church. The notion of the eschatological and new-creational aspect of restoration should be kept in mind as the framework of discussion in this chapter, though its focus will be on the former: the conception of the church as eschatologically restored Israel.

There is so much evidence in Paul's writings on the topic of the already–not yet fulfillment of the restoration promises that here I can give only a thumbnail sketch of some of the most pertinent material in the canonical order of the Pauline Epistles.[1] I hope that this sketch will show how one can understand other restoration prophecies found in Paul's writings that are not addressed here.

Romans[2]

ROMANS 9:24–26

The first relevant passage is Rom. 9:24–26:

> . . . even us, whom He also called, not from among Jews only, but also from among Gentiles. As he says also in Hosea, "I will call those who were not My people, 'My people,' and her who was not beloved, 'Beloved.' And it shall be that in the place where it was said to them, 'You are not My people,' there they shall be called sons of the living God."

Here Paul quotes from Hos. 2:23 and 1:10.[3] In each case the prophecy is about the restoration of Israel from captivity. At the time of the end-time restoration, Israel will again be faithful and be called "my people" and "beloved" and "sons of the living God," whereas formerly in sin and rebellion in captivity Israel was called "not God's people" and "not beloved." What is striking in Rom. 9:25–26 is that not only Jews but also gentiles, "whom God also called" (v. 24), are seen to be the beginning fulfillment of these two restoration prophecies from Hosea.

There is debate about whether this is merely an analogical application of the Hosea restoration prophecies to the church, since it is composed primarily of gentiles and the original prophecies were about the restoration of only Israel. Therefore, it could well be asked: would it not be a spiritualization, or perhaps even an allegorization, of the prophecies to view the predominantly gentile church as the main part of the fulfillment? Those who answer this in the affirmative consequently opt for an analogical use of Hosea 1–2 and would see no notion of fulfillment. In further support of a purely analogical view is the introductory *hōs* ("as") in verse 25, which some argue introduces the Hosea references merely as

---

1. Other additional relevant data in Paul on this topic will be footnoted along the way. Also, unfortunately, limitations of space in this section allow for little consideration of allusions to OT restoration texts, and so primarily quotations will be addressed.

2. For a good and certainly more thorough discussion of many of the OT restoration prophecies in Rom. 9–11, see J. Ross Wagner, *Heralds of the Good News: Isaiah and Paul in Concert in the Letter to the Romans*, NovTSup 101 (Leiden: Brill, 2001).

3. For variations in Paul's quotation of Hos. 2:23 and 1:10 from that of Hosea, see Thomas R. Schreiner, *Romans*, BECNT (Grand Rapids: Baker Academic, 1998), 527; Mark A. Seifrid, "Romans," in *Commentary on the New Testament Use of the Old Testament*, ed. G. K. Beale and D. A. Carson (Grand Rapids: Baker Academic, 2007), 647–48.

comparisons to the salvation of gentiles in Paul's time.[4] Often such an analogical perspective entails a belief that the Hosea prophecies will be fulfilled at some future eschatological time in the salvation of a majority of ethnic Israelites (an interpretation commonly given of Rom. 11:25–26).

However, the *hōs* ("as") is not always a strict indicator of a mere comparison; it can include a comparison of a NT situation to an OT prophecy that is beginning fulfillment. That this is likely the function in verse 25 is apparent because virtually the same word (*kathōs*, "just as") is used only three verses later in verse 29 ("And just as Isaiah foretold . . .") to introduce the beginning fulfillment of Isaiah's prophecy that only a remnant of Israel will be saved in the time of final restoration.

Furthermore, that gentiles can be seen as an actual part of the beginning fulfillment of Hosea[5] is made viable by evidence that I presented in the preceding chapter and the thread of argumentation throughout that chapter. In particular, the OT prophesies that at the end-time restoration of Israel the messianic Servant will be viewed as the summation of true Israel (Isa. 49:3), and that gentiles will also stream in and be redeemed by becoming identified as Israelites. In addition, the NT (esp. Paul) views Jesus to be true Israel (the "seed of Abraham") and Jewish and gentile Christians together in Christ also to be true Israel (Gal. 3:16, 26–29). I discussed other evidence in the NT that testifies to the same things (e.g., true circumcision being of the heart and not of the flesh, with which gentiles are identified [Rom. 2:25–29]), so that the church can even be called explicitly "the Israel of God" (Gal. 6:16 [on which, see later in this chapter]). In the light of such notions, Paul likely views not only believing Jews but also Christian gentiles to be the beginning literal fulfillment of Hosea's prophecy of Israel's restoration: since gentiles believe in Jesus, true Israel, they become identified as true Israelites. The fact that Hos. 1–2 is applied also to "Jews" in Rom. 9:24 poses no problem for them being the beginning fulfillment of the prophecy, since the prophecy was about Israel. Thus, it seems unlikely that Hosea is analogically applied to Jews here. In addition, to say that somehow the prophecy is fulfilled by Jews and merely analogically applied to gentiles would be a convoluted and inconsistent conclusion. But if there is a rationale, as I have given above, that supplies a viable hermeneutical reason for viewing gentiles as part of end-time Israel, then both "Jews" and "Gentiles" in Rom. 9:24 can both be seen as the inaugurated fulfillment of Hos. 1–2.

The immediate context points in this direction, since already in Rom. 9:6 Paul has said that "they are not all Israel who are descended from Israel," which focuses on a distinction within ethnic Israel of true believers from those who

---

4. See Douglas J. Moo, *The Epistle to the Romans*, NICNT (Grand Rapids: Eerdmans, 1996), 613, citing some scholars who affirm this view.

5. Schreiner (*Romans*, 528) concurs with this conclusion and cites others in agreement.

do not believe. Even though this verse focuses on a distinction within ethnic Israel, it leaves the door open for others being considered as part of true Israel, even though they may not be ethnic Israelites. Such an open-door view of 9:6 is pointed to strongly by Rom. 2:25–29 (noted just above). Furthermore, that the presupposition of gentiles being part of true Israel underlies Rom. 9:25–26 is also pointed to by the immediate context of Hos. 1:10. In Hos. 1:11 Israel's restoration is described as led by a "head": "They will appoint for themselves one head [leader], and they will go up from the land." This likely refers to an end-time leader who will rule over Israel during the latter-day restoration.[6] This is supported further by Hos. 3:5, which refers to "David their king," who plays a role in Israel's "return" in "the last days." Thus, Paul's contextual purview likely included the notion of a messianic deliverer who would lead the restoration, with whom end-time Israel would be identified. Paul's application of the prophecy, not only to Jews but also to gentiles, suggests that he sees gentiles to be identified with this messianic leader, which the OT and the NT elsewhere identify as an individual representative for eschatological Israel.[7]

Paul's application to gentiles of the Hos. 1:10 name for Israel, "they shall be called sons of the living God," appears most likely to be sparked by his earlier reference in Rom. 1:4 to Jesus as "declared the Son of God."[8] This reference probably is the intratextual basis for calling Christians "sons of God" in 8:14, 19 (and "sons" in 8:15, 23),[9] especially in light of connecting their sonship to resurrection (as in 1:4) and in light of the shorter references to Jesus as God's "Son" in the immediate context (8:3, 29, 32). That Christians are called "sons of God" because they are identified with Jesus as "the Son of God" is apparent not only from the connections just noted; 8:29 draws out why this identification is made: "For those whom He foreknew, He also predestined to become conformed to the image of His Son, so that He would be the firstborn among many brethren." Thus believers are called "sons of

---

6. The Targum of Hos. 2:2 interprets this reference to be "one head from the house of David."

7. Such a view by Paul of the relation of Israel's "head" to the nation would have been fueled even further, if Paul had any knowledge of the use of Hos. 1:10 by Matthew. The reference to the restoration of "the sons of the living God" in Hos. 1:10 has its closest parallel in the NT in Matt. 16:16, where Peter professes that Jesus is "the Messiah, the Son of the Living God." This may well be an allusion to Hos. 1:10 by which Jesus is seen as the individual kingly son leading the sons of Israel, whom he represents. Such an identification of this individual son with the corporate sons probably is why Matt. 2:15 applies the corporate "son" reference of Hos. 11:1 to the individual Jesus. On Matt. 16:16 as an allusion to Hos. 1:10, see Mark J. Goodwin, "Hosea and 'the Son of the Living God' in Matt. 16:16b," *CBQ* 67 (2005): 265–83 (for further discussion of this allusion, see chap. 13 under the subheading "Jesus as the Adamic Son of God," concerning the conception of Christ as the image of God in Matthew).

8. And note the abbreviated reference to Jesus as "Son" in Rom. 1:3, 9; 5:10; 8:3, 29.

9. See Robert Jewett, *Romans*, Hermeneia (Minneapolis: Fortress, 2007), 601. Jewett also sees the Rom. 9:28 reference to "'sons of the living God' reminiscent of Paul's claim in 8:14 and 19," as well as in 8:15, 23, that Christians are sons of God.

God" likely because they are "brothers" of Christ, who is the "firstborn" "Son of God." Christians, however, are "adopted sons" (*huiothesia* [8:15, 23]) of God through their identification with Christ as the original "Son." In this status, Christians continue the line of true Israel from the OT, when Israel was also called "adopted sons" (*huiothesia* [9:4]). In this respect, as we saw in the preceding chapter, in the OT Israel was named "firstborn" and God's "son."[10]

All this seems to be, at least to some degree, behind Paul's packed rationale for referring to gentiles as eschatologically restored Israelites, whom Hosea prophesied would be "called sons of the living God."[11]

ROMANS 9:27–29

Romans 9:24–26 focuses on believing gentiles as part of the fulfillment of Israel's restoration hopes, and verses 27–29 refocus on a remnant of believing ethnic Israelites who also are part of that fulfillment:

> Isaiah cries out concerning Israel, "Though the number of the sons of Israel be like the sand of the sea, it is the remnant that will be saved; for the Lord will execute His word on the earth, thoroughly and quickly." And just as Isaiah foretold, "Unless the Lord of Sabaoth had left to us a posterity, we would have become like Sodom, and would have resembled Gomorrah."

Verses 25–26 have developed the reference in verse 24 to the "calling" of gentiles, and verses 27–28 return to develop verse 24's allusion to the "calling" of

10. Note, e.g., God's "son" in Exod. 4:22–23; Deut. 14:1; Isa. 1:2, 4; 63:8; Hos. 1:10; 11:1, and God's "firstborn" in Exod. 4:22–23; Jer. 31:9; the coming Messiah of Israel was also known as God's "firstborn" (Pss. 2:7; 89:27).

11. There are other possible rationales for seeing Hos. 1–2 as a prophecy including gentiles. When Hosea refers to Israel as "not my people" (1:9; 2:23), Israel is seen to be identified with gentiles. This is made explicit at points later in the book where, e.g., Israel is identified with Sodom and Gomorrah (an identification made also in Isa. 1:9–10; 3:9; Jer. 23:14; Lam. 4:6; Ezek. 16:46–56). Accordingly, if in Hosea God promised to restore Israel, who had become equivalent to a gentile nation, would not the promise imply the restoration of other gentile nations? The answer appears to be yes in light of the clear allusion in Hos. 1:10 to Gen. 32:12 (these are the only two Abrahamic promise statements that include the following two phrases: the Israelite seed being "as the sand of the sea" that "cannot be numbered"). Genesis 32:12 explicitly refers back to Gen. 28:14, which speaks of Jacob's "seed" being "like the dust of the earth" and says that "in your [Jacob's] seed shall all the families of the earth be blessed." In this light, this allusion in Hos. 1:10 (if the contexts of Gen. 28:14 and 32:12 are in mind), which refers to Israel's multiplication after being restored, suggests that such a restoration will include the blessing of the nations, and thus their restoration. Some think that the allusion in Hos. 1:10 is to Gen. 22:17–18, though the wording there does not come close to Gen. 32:12; however, the idea is the same: Israel's multiplication leads to the blessing of the nations.

It is also possible that since the prophecy of Hos. 1:10 has in mind northern Israel (see vv. 4–9), and that since in Paul's day northern Israel no longer existed but was a gentile land (Samaria), people from Samaria who were becoming Christians were seen to be part of the fulfillment of Hosea's prophecy.

Jews. Two texts from Isaiah are quoted, Isa. 10:22–23 and 1:9, which indicate that at the eschaton only a remnant of Israel will be saved. This is a further explanation of Paul's earlier statement in Rom. 9:6: "But it is not as though the word [promise] of God has failed." Paul here responds to the thought current among his Jewish contemporaries that the majority of Israel would be restored to God in the latter days. Paul begins his answer by saying in the second part of verse 6 that not all ethnic Israelites are true spiritual Israelites, and he goes on in verses 7–13 to show that a remnant principle has been at work, at least, from the time of Abraham. In verses 27–28 he adds to the argument begun in verse 6 that OT prophecy, as illustrated by Isaiah, always predicted that only a remnant of Israel would be saved in the last days, after God's refining judgment.[12]

ROMANS 10:11–13

For the Scripture says, "Whoever believes in him will not be put to shame." For there is no distinction between Jew and Greek; for the same Lord is Lord of all, abounding in riches for all who call on Him; for "Whoever will call on the name of the Lord will be saved."

Verse 11 is a quotation of Isa. 28:16, which is placed in a context of an announcement of judgment on unbelieving Israel at some future point (on which, see Isa. 28:9–22). Isaiah 28:16 is the only positive verse in this context in that it expresses a blessing on those who "believe" in God's provision of refuge ("a costly cornerstone for the foundation") in the midst of the judgment. The one "who believes in it will not be disturbed" (according to the Hebrew text), the last phrase of which the LXX, followed by Paul, interprets as not being "put to shame." All of this takes place "in Zion," so that Isa. 28:16 refers to some Israelites who will "believe" in the midst of judgment on the nation.

Verse 12 offers a reason why all those who believe will not be ashamed: there is "no distinction between Jew and Gentile," so that whatever person from either ethnic group believes will not be ashamed in the day of judgment. This is a reiteration of Rom. 3:22, though there the lack of distinction lies in the fact that both groups are equally sinners (3:22b–23a: ". . . for all those who believe; for there is no distinction; for all have sinned"). And the reason why there is now "no distinction" between these two ethnic groups is that "the same Lord is Lord of all" humanity, "calling" whom he will from either group, which is a development of 9:24 ("whom He also called, not from among Jews only, but also from among Gentiles").

---

12. For more thorough discussion of the OT allusions in Rom. 9:25–29, see Wagner, *Heralds of the Good News*, 78–117. However, I disagree with some of his conclusions. E.g., Wagner sees Paul referring to the remnant concept in Rom. 9 to anticipate a salvation of a much larger segment of the nation "ultimately" at the very end of time in 11:25–26, though at the same time, he says, enigmatically, that the remnant concept continues through the latter passage (see pp. 276–98).

The reason why God "abounds in riches for all who call upon Him" (10:12b) is found in the prophecy of Joel 2:32, which Paul quotes in 10:13: "Whoever will call on the name of the Lord will be saved." As we saw in chapter 18 and chapter 20, Joel 2:28–32 is a prophecy about the restoration and salvation of Israel "on Mount Zion and in Jerusalem" in the end times (Joel 2:32). I went to great lengths in the preceding chapter in the discussion of Joel 2:28–32 in Acts 2 to explain that the Joel text was a prophecy only for Israel, not for gentiles. Yet we saw that the way Luke applied this prophecy to gentiles later in Acts indicates that they were being identified with and incorporated into the emerging eschatological remnant of Israel. The same conclusions about Joel 2 in Acts 2 is likely true about Rom. 10:13,[13] especially since we have seen in the above Pauline passages in this section and in the introduction of this chapter the same idea: when gentiles believe, they do not retain an independent status as redeemed gentiles; they are seen to be gentiles converting to the faith of Israel, and although their gentile ethnicity is not erased, they gain a greater identity as part of Israel because they identify with Jesus, the summation and representative of true Israel.

Romans 11:25–26

This passage is too problematic and controverted to receive adequate discussion within the limited space of this book. In fact, a fully satisfactory interpretation of this text still awaits an entire monograph. In particular, there is much debate about whether verse 26 prophesies that the majority of ethnic Israel will be saved at the very end of the age. Consequently, I think that one's overall view about whether gentiles are to be identified as true Israel should be based not on this passage alone but on other passages, both in the OT and in the NT. Indeed, I believe that this passage has nothing to do with gentile redemption but rather is about the salvation of a remnant of ethnic Israel.[14]

13. See the discussion about Joel 2 in Acts 2 in chap. 20 under the subheading "The Inaugurated Fulfillment of the Prophesied Spirit of Joel 2:28–32 in Acts 2:16–21."
14. For examples of the direction of my own approach to the passage, see O. Palmer Robertson, "Is There a Distinctive Future for Ethnic Israel in Romans 11?," in *Perspectives on Evangelical Theology: Papers from the Thirtieth Annual Meeting of the Evangelical Theological Society*, ed. Kenneth S. Kantzer and Stanley N. Gundry (Grand Rapids: Baker Academic, 1979), 209–27; Ben L. Merkle, "Romans 11 and the Future of Ethnic Israel," *JETS* 43 (2000): 709–21; Anthony A. Hoekema, *The Bible and the Future* (Grand Rapids: Eerdmans, 1979), 139–47. These sources argue that "all Israel" in Rom. 11:26 refers not to a mass conversion of ethnic Israel at the very end of the church age but rather to the entire remnant of ethnic Israel who are redeemed throughout the interadvent age until the very end of time. Other commentators, such as John Calvin, argue similarly but contend that "all Israel" consists of both gentiles and Jews. Many commentators argue that Rom. 11:26 does prophesy that the majority of Israel will be saved at the very end of the interadvent era (e.g., John Murray, *The Epistle to the Romans*, 2 vols., NICNT [Grand Rapids: Eerdmans, 1965], 2:96–100; Robert L. Saucy, *The Case for Progressive Dispensationalism: The Interface between Dispensational and Non-Dispensational Theology* [Grand Rapids: Zondervan, 1993], 250–63).

2 Corinthians

One of Paul's clearest references to an OT restoration promise is in 2 Cor. 6:1–2:

And working together with Him, we also urge you not to receive the grace of God in vain—for He says, "At the acceptable time I listened to you, and on the day of salvation I helped you." Behold, now is "the acceptable time," behold, now is "the day of salvation."

In 6:1 Paul picks up his thought from 5:20. In 5:20 Paul has defined his role as God's ambassador to be an office whereby God is "making an appeal through us," and the opening expression of 6:1 ("and working together with Him, we also urge") continues a description of this role. That is, since it is through Paul's ambassadorial office that God exhorts the readers to be reconciled (5:20), Paul logically views himself and his apostolic circle also as "working together with God" in exhorting the readers to be reconciled or to behave as reconciled people. However, rather than using the language of "reconciliation" as the object of the exhortation as in 5:20, Paul exhorts them "not to receive the grace of God in vain [eis kenon]" (6:1). Paul's reference to "grace" here focuses on "the ministry of reconciliation" (5:18) and "the word of reconciliation" (5:19) that God had committed to him to preach to the Corinthians, which probably was an essential part of Paul's broader apostolic ministry to the gentile world. Indeed, Paul's use of "grace" (charis) in 2 Cor. 1–5 refers primarily not to a work of divine grace in the readers but rather to the manner in which Paul presented the gospel in word and deed (1:12, 15; 4:15), as is also the case elsewhere in his writings. Second Corinthians 6:1b contains typical language used by Paul when he reflects on whether his labor of proclaiming the gospel to gentiles has had salvific effect.

Therefore, in 6:1 Paul is directly developing the thought of 5:18–20 by emphasizing that his exhortation for the readers to be reconciled should not be heard in vain, since it is from God himself (5:20). Indeed, there should not be an unfruitful response to this imperative, since the readers already claimed to be partakers of this reconciling "grace of God" (cf. 5:14–15, 18–19).

Now, in 6:2 Paul appeals to Isa. 49:8 in order to establish further (note the "for" or "because") his claim to be a legitimate divine spokesman of the message of reconciliation. We noted in an earlier chapter that Isa. 49:8 is part of a section in Isaiah that closely associates the restoration of exiled Israel with a theme of new creation (cf. 49:8–13),[15] and so its appearance here as a reinforcement of 2 Cor. 5:17–21 is not surprising. In fact, Isa. 49:8 is an explicit reference to Israel's restoration: the first part of the verse (quoted by Paul) is in synonymous parallelism with the second part. That is, the "favorable

---

15. See chap. 16 under the subheading "'Reconciliation' in 2 Corinthians 5:14–21."

time" and the "day of salvation" (v. 8a) are explained to be the time of coming restoration: "And I will keep You and give You for a covenant of the people, to restore [*lĕhāqîm*] the land, to make them inherit the desolate heritages" (v. 8b). Isaiah 49:8 is a repetition of the promise of restoration mentioned only two verses earlier, where the role of the "Servant" was not only "to raise up the tribes of Jacob and to restore [Heb. *lĕhāšîb*; Gk. *synachthēsomai*] the preserved ones of Israel" but also to extend salvific restoration "to the ends of the earth" (49:6). Isaiah 49:8 is Yahweh's answer to the Servant's future protestation of despair over the apparent failure of his mission to restore Israel (see 49:4–5). His efforts of restoration seemed to have been "in vain" (*kenōs*) and to have resulted "in vanity" (*eis mataion*) and "in nothing" (*eis ouden*) (v. 4). The answer in verse 8, which is a continuation of verse 6, is that although the Servant's work of restoring Israel has appeared largely to be in vain and has caused him to be despised and abhorred (v. 7a), it has a significant effect on some in Israel ("the preserved ones" or remnant [49:6a, 8b MT]), and especially with respect to the nations (49:6b). Although the majority of Israel apparently would reject the Servant's efforts at restoration (49:4–6a, 7a), God would cause such efforts to have a cosmic effect, the salvation of the gentiles (Isa. 49:6b).

Thus, Isa. 49:8 is a divine reaffirmation of the Servant's calling to restore Israel (and the nations) by promising him that God will make his efforts fruitful despite apparent failure. Isaiah 49:9 portrays the Servant attempting to restore Israel to its land: "Saying to those who are bound, 'Go forth,' to those who are in darkness, 'Show yourselves'" (cf. 49:8–9), language similar to that in 2 Cor. 6:14–18.

In radical fashion, Paul applies to himself a prophecy of the Isaianic Servant in order to identify himself with that figure.[16] He is in some way the fulfillment of the righteous "Servant, Israel" (Isa. 49:3), who was to proclaim restoration to sinful Israel. In line with the prophetic portrayal, Paul has proclaimed reconciliation to the gentile, Corinthian church, which is the fulfillment of the latter-day promises of the restoration of Israel. Many in the church at Corinth, however, apparently are not responding because they are questioning the very legitimacy of Paul as God's spokesman. Although the readers claim to have begun to partake of the eschatological promises of restoration to God, they are in danger of forfeiting these blessings if they continue to reject Paul as the official, divine messenger of reconciliation, since to do so is also to reject Jesus. Hence, although Paul's ministry appears to be on the verge of being received "in vain" (*eis kenon* [cf. Isa. 49:4]), he appeals to Isa. 49:8 in order to authenticate his legitimacy as an apostolic servant of restoration and to

---

16. Though Murray Harris disagrees and says that "when Paul cites Isa. 49:8 he is thinking primarily of the Corinthians' experience, not his own" (*The Second Epistle to the Corinthians: A Commentary on the Greek Text*, NIGTC [Grand Rapids: Eerdmans, 2005], 461).

demonstrate that his ministry will bear fruit. According to the contours of the original OT context, the quotation shows that God himself will aid Paul in this ministry in order to express a divine reaffirmation of his calling to proclaim reconciliation (cf. 2 Cor. 6:2: "I listened to you . . . I helped you"). The period in which Paul sees this help and reaffirmation being offered is referred to as *kairos dektos*, usually translated as "acceptable time." However, because of the following parallel expression *hēmera sōtērias*, the phrase *kairos dektos* is best translated as "time of acceptance," referring to the end-time period when God's offer of acceptance or "restoration-reconciliation" is extended to exiled Israel and the nations.

Indeed, as we also have seen earlier,[17] the Hebrew text's reference to "pleasure, favor" (*rāṣôn* [LXX: *dektos*]) is rendered in Isa. 49:8 by the Aramaic equivalent in the Targum (*r'w'*), which is further explained by the paraphrase "I will receive your prayer." The Aramaic equivalent also refers elsewhere in *Targum Isaiah* to God's "pleasurable acceptance" (Isa. 1:11, 15; 56:7; 60:7) and specifically to such "pleasurable acceptance" in the sense of restoration from exile (Isa. 34:16–17; 60:10; 62:4; 66:2). Accordingly, 2 Cor. 5:17–6:2 shows that Paul's understanding of reconciliation is a result of his meditation on the Isaianic restoration context (as may also be the case in 6:3–7:1, as I will argue below).

Therefore, the quotation from Isa. 49:8 and Paul's comment on it in 2 Cor. 6:2b focus primarily on the eschatological period of prophetic fulfillment (cf. the *nyn* ["now"] twice in 6:2) when the servant, Paul, is given divine authority and reaffirmation in his work. It is also a call for the readers to accept this reaffirmation and to be reconciled, in the sense of "making complete" their profession to be partakers of the OT promises of restoration (cf. 2 Cor. 13:5, 9b, 11a).

It may seem unusual that Paul would apply to himself a prophecy that the early Christian community probably would have applied to Christ. However, this is not without precedent. In Luke 2:32 and Acts 26:23 Jesus is viewed as the fulfillment of Isa. 49:6 (cf. Isa. 42:6), while in Acts 13:47 and 26:18a Paul is identified as the fulfillment respectively of Isa. 49:6 and 42:7. The rationale for these dual identifications lies probably in the conception of corporate representation already found in the OT and elsewhere in Paul's writings and the NT, which may well lie behind the Pauline expression of "the Christ who speaks in me" (2 Cor. 13:3; cf. 2:14–17; 12:9, 19). And it is this same idea of corporate representation that allows Paul to understand how the very context of the Isa. 49 Servant could apply to him without distorting the way that he thought it may have been intended originally. Furthermore, in that he was continuing the mission of Jesus, the Servant, he could easily apply this Servant prophecy to himself, though he would not consider himself equivalent to Jesus as the Servant.

Therefore, Paul views the Corinthians as receiving the promises of Isa. 40–66 concerning the redemption of the gentiles that was to occur together with

---

17. See chap. 16 under the subheading "'Reconciliation' in 2 Corinthians 5:14–21."

Israel's salvation. And from this perspective, Paul's use is consistent with that of the context of Isaiah. However, Paul's apparent new development is to view Jewish and gentile Christians together in the Corinthian church as authentic Israelites when they are redeemed. That Isa. 49:8 is part of a restoration prophecy directed to the Servant's restoration of Israel, not the nations, is apparent in that after the beginning of Isa. 49:8, which Paul quotes ("in a favorable time . . . in a day of salvation"), the specific role of the Servant's work is directed toward the restoration only of Israel: "And I will keep You and give You for a covenant of the people [Israel], to restore the land, to make them [Israel] inherit the desolate heritages." And the directly following context continues to focus only on Israel's restoration. Isaiah 49:9–17 reads,

> Saying to those who are bound, "Go forth,"
> To those who are in darkness, "Show yourselves."
> Along the roads they will feed,
> And their pasture will be on all bare heights.
> They will not hunger or thirst,
> Nor will the scorching heat or sun strike them down;
> For He who has compassion on them will lead them
> And will guide them to springs of water.
> I will make all My mountains a road,
> And My highways will be raised up.
> Behold, these will come from afar;
> And lo, these will come from the north and from the west,
> And these from the land of Sinim.
> Shout for joy, O heavens! And rejoice, O earth!
> Break forth into joyful shouting, O mountains!
> For the LORD has comforted His people
> And will have compassion on His afflicted.
> But Zion said, "The LORD has forsaken me,
> And the LORD has forgotten me."
> Can a woman forget her nursing child
> And have no compassion on the son of her womb?
> Even these may forget, but I will not forget you.
> Behold, I have inscribed you on the palms of My hands;
> Your walls are continually before Me.
> Your builders hurry;
> Your destroyers and devastators will depart from you.

Indeed, the remainder of chapter 49 (Isa. 49:18–26) continues with an exclusive focus on Israel's restoration.[18] Thus, if Paul has Isaiah's immediate context in

18. Although it is true that the LXX alters Isa. 49:8b to make it refer to the restoration of the gentiles and not of Israel. Since, as we have just seen, the entire context from 49:9–26 has exclusive focus on the salvation of Israel and not the nations (as the LXX also has), it is still likely that Paul sees 49:8 in light of this following context. But even if Paul has the LXX of 49:8 in mind,

mind, which is likely in view of the Isa. 49:3 "in vain" allusion in 2 Cor. 6:1, then he views himself in the role of the Servant (likely as a prophetic representative of Jesus the Servant), whose task is to restore Israel, which now is composed of a remnant of Jews and a majority of gentiles.

But what is the explanation for this development of applying an Israelite prophecy to a community composed mostly of gentiles? I have addressed this repeatedly earlier but will briefly reiterate here. First, the prophets, including Isaiah, primarily define eschatological Israel not along ethnic, nationalistic lines but rather in a religious or theological manner, according to their covenant loyalty to Yahweh (e.g., Hos. 1:10–11; 2:23), since we have seen that Isaiah himself views the salvation of gentiles to involve them becoming identified with true end-time Israel.[19] Paul may well be applying this prophetic view as a rationale legitimizing his application of Israel's promises to gentiles, as he does in Rom. 9:24–26 in citing Hos. 1:9–10 and 2:23. Therefore, the church is the true Israel insofar as it is now receiving the prophetic promises intended for Israel in the OT. Furthermore, this rationale may have been enforced by Paul's understanding that Christ summed up Israel in himself and hence represented true Israel in a legal, corporate fashion (cf. Isa. 49:3, 6 and Luke 2:30–32; Acts 26:23). Whether Jew or gentile, those who identify with Christ by faith are considered part of genuine Israel, receiving the promises that he inherited as the true Israel (2 Cor. 1:20–21). We have seen the same kind of application of Israelite restoration prophecies to gentiles in Rom. 9:24–26, probably on the same basis.

Therefore, Paul's appeal in 2 Cor. 5:20 to "be reconciled to God" is reemphasized in 6:1–2, where "it is no less emphatically stated that the apostles are serving God in extending it."[20] And this reemphasis of reconciliation in 6:1–2 is expressed through the citation of a prooftext from Isa. 49 concerning a promise of restoration to Israel. Since 6:1–2 is a continuation of the initial appeal to the Corinthians to be reconciled in 5:20, it must be seen as part of that appeal. This appeal itself in 5:20–6:2 is based on the reality of reconciliation as a new creation and the fact that the apostles (e.g., Paul) have been appointed as the official ambassadors to proclaim this reality

---

it is likely, in light of the overall context of my discussion of 2 Corinthians in this section, that he still sees Israelites partaking of the covenant promised to Israel. Note in particular that in Isa. 49:8 the LXX changes the Hebrew text's "I will give you for a covenant of the people" to "I have given you for a covenant of the nations." "Covenant" (*diathēkē*) in the LXX typically refers to God's covenant with Israel in Isaiah (Isa. 24:5; 33:8; 42:6 [?]; 54:10; 55:3; 56:4; 59:21; 61:8). Isaiah 56:6, however, explains that gentiles can participate in God's "covenant" with Israel, which there is described partly, as we saw in the preceding chapter, as gentiles becoming ministering priests in the temple. Indeed, the LXX's change of Isa. 49:8b to refer to gentiles and not Israel might represent an interpretation that views gentiles to be participating in Israelite salvation.

19. So Isa. 19:18, 24–25; 56:3–7; 66:18–21; see likewise Ps. 87; Ezek. 47:21–23; Zech. 2:11 + 8:20–23.

20. Victor Paul Furnish, *II Corinthians*, AB 32A (New York: Doubleday, 1984), 352.

(5:17–19). The focus of the appeal in 5:20–6:2 is that the readers accept Paul as a legitimate divine legate in the extension of the appeal, since to reject the messenger of reconciliation is to reject the God who reconciles. Consequently, Isaiah's promises of Israel's restoration are foundational to the argument of 5:17–6:2.

We should see 2 Cor. 6:3–10 as a continuation of the appeal begun in 5:20 because it offers further support for the appeal, although in this section Paul offers no OT quotations in support but instead the integrity of his faithful lifestyle in the midst of suffering. Thus, there is nothing in Paul's conduct that can be a basis for rejecting his message.

Now in 6:11–13 Paul reissues the appeal of 6:1–2 concerning reconciliation to himself as God's authoritative ambassador, although again the technical language of "reconciliation" is not employed. Accordingly, Paul utilizes metaphors of reconciliation to summarize the tension between himself and his readers: Paul has made overtures to reconcile through his message, actions, and attitude ("our mouth is open to you, . . . our heart is opened wide" [v. 11]), but the readers have begun to shut Paul and his proclamation out of their hearts ("you are restrained in your own affections [toward us]" [v. 12]). In verse 13 Paul appeals to the readers to accept his reconciling overtures ("now in a like exchange . . . open wide to us also").

Although some think that verses 14–16a are an abrupt change of topic, they fit right into the flow of thought in the preceding context:

> Do not be bound together with unbelievers; for what partnership have righteousness and lawlessness, or what fellowship has light with darkness? Or what harmony has Christ with Belial, or what has a believer in common with an unbeliever? Or what agreement has the temple of God with idols?

These commands to separate from various aspects of the ungodly world have to do with believers' relationships with those who are not true Christians. But how does this relate to the preceding context? This is not a general exhortation to separate from the world; rather, Paul likely has in mind that the readers are to separate from the world by not evaluating Paul's apostleship according to the unbelieving standards of the world, as the preceding context has also focused upon. Paul likely did not consider the unbelieving world that he refers to in 6:14–15 to be that which lay only outside the confines of the church, but instead viewed it as a force within the church (cf. 13:5) against whose influence believers needed to be on guard. Far from being an interruption, 6:14–7:2 anticipates the main opposition to be elaborated on in chapters 10–13. A certain type of Jewish Christian opponents are in the process of infiltrating the church and doing what the Judaizers did in Galatia by opposing Paul's authority and preaching another type of Jesus than Paul preached (so 2 Cor. 11:1–4, 13–15, 20–23; Gal. 1:6–8). They are trying to win the congregation to their teaching while Paul is absent. In 2 Cor. 6:14–7:2 Paul shows that the situation is so serious that their very salvation is at stake. Those who are influenced to resist Paul's authority are also resisting his gospel and thereby are bringing into question their very standing as part of God's true people (cf. 13:5). This section of chapter 6 also anticipates the continuing problem of worldly behavior among some in the congregation (12:20–21), which probably is related in part to the false teachers' influence, but not necessarily exhaustively so. Continued participation in the sins noted in 12:20–21 would also mean rejection of the apostle's authority, since he had already commanded the Corinthians in the past to cease such behavior.

Therefore, "unbelievers" (apistoi) in 2 Cor. 6:14 is to be understood generally as emphasizing the worldly, unbelieving standards of evaluating Paul's authority used by the false apostles and those under their influence, as well as by some among the readers who were not repenting of sins of which Paul had earlier convicted them. This warning about evaluating Paul's apostleship in such a worldly manner is likely a development of the same thought from 5:16 (cf. kata sarka, "according to the flesh").

This contextual analysis is confirmed by 7:2, which further explains that the way the readers are to "cleanse" themselves (7:1) is by accepting Paul as God's apostle ("making room" for him), being "reconciled" to Paul and ultimately to God. Second Corinthians 7:1–4 is a conclusion of a section stretching back to 5:17. The most important observation for this overall discussion is that the section of 6:16b–7:1b together with 5:17–19 and 6:2 are based on OT prophetic hopes of Israel's restoration and serve as the foundation for the imperatival segments of 5:20; 6:1, 13–16a; 7:1–2. Paul's statements in 7:3–4, 7 express his confidence that since the readers have begun to participate in these end-time restoration promises, they will respond positively to his exhortation to continue to be part of the fulfillment of such promises.

Now in verses 16b–18 Paul adduces a catena of OT quotations and allusions.

> Just as God said,
>
>> "I will dwell in them and walk among them;
>> And I will be their God, and they shall be My people.
>
> Therefore, come out from their midst and be separate," says the Lord.
>
>> "And do not touch what is unclean;
>> And I will welcome you.
>> And I will be a father to you,
>> And you shall be sons and daughters to Me,"
>
> says the Lord Almighty.

How do these OT references fit into the flow of argument so far up through verses 16a? When viewed in their OT contexts, these references are seen to be associated not only with hopes of restoration and God dwelling among the people in a temple[21] but also with prohibitions concerning idolatry, judgments on idolaters, and promises to deliver the Israelites from idolatry when they are restored.[22] I have already discussed the quotations from Leviticus, Ezekiel, and Isaiah concerning the temple,[23] but these temple references are part of wider promises concerning the reestablishment of the temple as a part of Israel's restoration. The mentioning of "welcome" at the end of verse 17 comes from God's promise to welcome Israel back to the land (Ezek. 11:17; 20:34, 41), and the reference to "sons and daughters" refers to God's regathering of Israel's sons and daughters prophesied in Isa. 49:22; 60:4.[24] Thus, the chain of OT references continues the theme of Israel's promised restoration that is beginning fulfillment among the Corinthians.

Interestingly, when the broader context was examined, beginning at 2 Cor. 5:17 and going up through 6:18, we saw in chapter 16 several OT references, almost all of which are restoration prophecies about Israel.[25] I will restate these OT references here because they are so important to my argument. This shows Paul's dominant concern with this inaugurated end-time notion (see table 21.1).[26]

Table 21.1

Old Testament	2 Corinthians 5:17–6:18
Isa. 43:18–19 // 65:17	5:17
Isa. 53:9–11	5:21
Isa. 49:8	6:2
Ps. 118:17–18 (117:17–18 LXX)	6:9
Isa. 60:5 (Ps. 119:32 [118:32 LXX])	6:11b
Isa. 49:19–20	6:12
Lev. 26:11–12	6:16b
Ezek. 37:27	6:16b
Isa. 52:11	6:17a
Ezek. 11:17; 20:34, 41	6:17b
2 Sam. 7:14; Isa. 43:6; 49:22; 60:4	6:18

The climax of the already–not yet restoration discussion occurs in 2 Cor. 7:1: "Therefore, having these promises, beloved, let us cleanse ourselves from

21. See Lev. 26:11; 2 Sam. 7:2–7, 12–13; Ezek. 37:26–28; 20:40; cf. Ps. 118:17–18, 22–23, 26–27; Isa. 52:11d.
22. See Lev. 26:1, 30; 2 Sam. 7:23; Ezek. 11:18, 21; 20:28–32, 39; 37:23; and probably Isa. 52:11 is to be understood in this general manner.
23. On which, see chap. 19 under the subheading "A Brief Case Study of 2 Corinthians 6:16–18."
24. An allusion to 2 Sam. 7:14 in v. 18a introduces these allusions, though it is not a restoration promise but rather is woven in here with such promises.
25. For a list of these OT references and discussion, see chap. 16 (under the subheading "'Reconciliation' in 2 Corinthians 5:14–21").
26. Here I repeat the table of OT allusions from chap. 16 (under the subheading "'Reconciliation' in 2 Corinthians 5:14–21"). Only Ps. 118:17–18 in 2 Cor. 6:9 and 2 Sam. 7:14 in 2 Cor. 6:18 do not directly concern restoration.

all defilement of flesh and spirit, perfecting holiness in the fear of God." I have already provided significant discussion about why these OT references are not merely applied analogically to the church but are actually beginning fulfillment,[27] but the conclusion that these references are inaugurated Israelite restoration promises is formalized and made clear when Paul concludes, "Therefore, having these promises. . . ." This is a repetition of almost the same formula from 1:20: "For as many as may be the promises of God [in the OT], in Him [Christ] they are yes." The two inaugurated promise statements appear to form an inclusio around 1:21 up through 6:18. This likely means that the "promises" in 7:1 refer not only to Israel's restoration and temple promises of 6:16–18 but also to the other new creation (5:17)[28] and restoration references throughout 5:21–6:12.[29] This likely also includes the promises of the Spirit (1:22), new covenant (3:3, 6), and resurrection (3:6; 5:14–15), all of which are connected to OT restoration hopes.[30] Indeed, the word "promise" (*epangelia*) occurs about fifty times in the NT (about 23x in Paul's writings), most of which refer to the patriarchal promises, though some specifically refer to the OT promises of the Spirit,[31] resurrection,[32] and new covenant.[33]

Thus, in 2 Cor. 5:14–7:1 Paul sees that Israel's various eschatological restoration promises have begun fulfillment in the predominantly gentile church, further pointing to the church as the latter-day covenant community of Israel.

Galatians

Probably the clearest restoration prophecy in Galatians is the citation of Isa. 54:1 in Gal. 4:27, which needs to be set in its immediate context of 4:21–31:

> Tell me, you who want to be under law, do you not listen to the law? For it is written that Abraham had two sons, one by the bondwoman and one by the free woman. But the son by the bondwoman was born according to the flesh, and the son by the free woman through the promise. This is allegorically speaking,

27. See chap. 19 under the subheading "A Brief Case Study of 2 Corinthians 6:16–18."

28. For Paul's notion of new creation as part of the fulfillment of Isaiah's restoration promises, see chap. 16 (under the subheading "'Reconciliation' in 2 Corinthians 5:14–21"), where we saw that Isa. 40–55 explains the restoration of Israel as a new creation or integrally associates the two concepts.

29. For a fuller analysis of Paul's use of the OT and his flow of thought in 2 Cor. 2:14–7:6, see G. K. Beale, "The Old Testament Background of Reconciliation in 2 Corinthians 5–7 and Its Bearing on the Literary Problem of 2 Corinthians 4:14–7:1," *NTS* 35 (1989): 550–81.

30. In this respect, (1) for the Spirit, see the above discussion of Joel 2 in Acts 2 and the other OT promises of the Spirit; (2) for the new covenant, see Jer. 31:31–33; (3) for resurrection, see Ezek. 37:1–14, and discussion of it in chaps. 8 and 17; other restoration texts include reference to resurrection—e.g., Isa. 25:7–8; 26:19; see also Dan. 12:1–2.

31. Luke 24:49; Acts 1:4; 2:33; Gal. 3:14; Eph. 1:13.

32. Acts 26:6–8; 2 Tim. 1:1; 1 John 2:25.

33. In connection to this, see Heb. 9:15–17.

> for these women are two covenants: one proceeding from Mount Sinai bearing children who are to be slaves; she is Hagar. Now this Hagar is Mount Sinai in Arabia and corresponds to the present Jerusalem, for she is in slavery with her children. But the Jerusalem above is free; she is our mother. For it is written, "Rejoice, barren woman who does not bear; break forth and shout, you who are not in labor; for more numerous are the children of the desolate than of the one who has a husband." And you brethren, like Isaac, are children of promise. But as at that time he who was born according to the flesh persecuted him who was born according to the Spirit, so it is now also. But what does the Scripture say? "Cast out the bondwoman and her son, for the son of the bondwoman shall not be an heir with the son of the free woman." So then, brethren, we are not children of a bondwoman, but of the free woman.

As Paul wonders and is perplexed about whether his gospel-bearing message among the Galatians had been received in vain among them (4:8–20), he appeals to the OT. If the readers are tempted to believe that by "faith plus works" (i.e., "to be under law") one can achieve salvation (v. 21), Paul directs their attention to the true meaning of the law that is most relevant for them. He recalls for them that Abraham had two sons, one not regenerate ("born according to the flesh") and the other regenerate ("the son [born] . . . through the promise"). Their respective mothers were likewise in the same spiritual condition (vv. 22–23; for the same kind of analysis of Abraham's and Isaac's children, see Rom. 9:7–13). Accordingly, these two mothers, Hagar and Sarah, who have their own children, represent two covenants. One covenant leads to slavery to the law and death for her children (represented by Sinai), and the other covenant to freedom and life for the other woman's children (represented by the heavenly Jerusalem) (vv. 24–26).

Now in verse 27 Paul quotes Isa. 54:1 to give a reason why "the Jerusalem above is free" and has living children in the present (v. 26). Who are the two women ("the desolate" and "the married") in Isa. 54:1? Isaiah elsewhere portrays Jerusalem as cursed (64:10) and as a blind and deaf city that has been a "rebel from birth" (48:1–11). This unregenerate Jerusalem probably is what is represented by the woman "who has a husband" (i.e., who claims to be married to Yahweh but is a spiritual whore).[34] This unfaithful Jerusalemite woman will not bear living children, but the apparently barren Jerusalem, like Sarah, will bear children of life. Isaiah views the latter woman to be typologically pointed to by Sarah, as evident from 51:2–3: those "who seek the LORD" at the time of the coming restoration are to

> Look to Abraham your father
> And to Sarah who gave birth to you in pain;

---

34. So Isa. 57:3 refers to Jerusalem's or Israel's children as "offspring of an adulterer and a prostitute."

When he was but one I called him,
Then I blessed him and multiplied him.
Indeed, the LORD will comfort Zion;
He will comfort all her waste places.
And her wilderness He will make like Eden,
And her desert like the garden of the LORD;
Joy and gladness will be found in her,
Thanksgiving and sound of a melody.

Formerly barren Sarah, instead of Hagar, was the one through whom the promise and blessing of life passed. Sarah is now set as the one who corresponds to and points to Israel's revival of life from exile, which will result in "joy and gladness." The command in Isa. 54:1 for the "barren one" to "rejoice" (*euphrainō*) and to "break forth" in joyful shouting develops the "joy [*euphrosynē*] and gladness" of Sarah's eschatological children who are to be restored (51:3), which is elaborated on in the remainder of chapter 54. Paul is saying that this end-time restoration of Jerusalem's living children is "now" happening (Gal. 4:25), and that end-time mother Jerusalem has now come into being and borne her children (4:26).[35]

Thus, Gal. 4:22–27 develops further the contrast between true Israel and false Israel. The true believers in Galatia, "like Isaac, are children of promise" (v. 28), continuing the typology of Sarah and Isaac in relation to end-time Israel, whom the believing Galatians have begun to form a part in fulfillment of the Isa. 54:1 prophecy. And, as at the time of Ishmael and Isaac, when the one "born according to the flesh persecuted him born according to the Spirit, so it is now also" (v. 29). This refers to the Christian Judaizers, together with the Judaism that they represent, who persecute the true people of God, Christian believers.[36]

The key and climactic phrase expressing the complete distinction between the two groups and the final disinheritance of physical Israel by God is in Gal. 4:30: "Cast out the bondwoman and her son, for the son of the bondwoman shall not be an heir with the son of the free woman." Just as Ishmael was born only "according to the flesh" and was an unbeliever, so the present unbelieving Israel is in the same condition and, like Ishmael, would not be the one through whom God's blessing of spiritual life would flow; in fact, they would be disinherited. The church, on the other hand, is the true Israel and seed of Abraham (Gal. 3:16, 29) and is beginning to fulfill the Isa. 54:1 restoration

35. For a fuller analysis of Isa. 54:1 in Gal. 4:27, see Moisés Silva, "Galatians," in *Commentary on the New Testament Use of the Old Testament*, ed. G. K. Beale and D. A. Carson (Grand Rapids: Baker Academic, 2007), 808–9, aspects of which have influenced my own reading, particularly of Isaiah's view of an unbelieving and a believing Jerusalem.

36. It is unnecessary to explore what kind of persecution Christians suffered under the Judaizers or the precise identification of the latter (e.g., whether they are from within the Galatian church or from the outside).

prophecy, being identified as spiritual descendants of Isaac and children of the end-time restored Jerusalemite woman (v. 31). Since Christ has already been identified as "Abraham's seed" (3:16) together with Christians as "Abraham's seed" (3:29), and since Isa. 54:1 directly follows the great Suffering Servant passage, applied to Christ throughout the NT, it is likely that Paul sees Christ as the firstborn, end-time Jerusalemite, with whom others can identify and also become new Jerusalem's children.[37]

The conclusion of the argument about true end-time Israel in Galatians comes at 6:15–16:

> For neither is circumcision anything, nor uncircumcision, but a new creation. And those who will walk by this rule, peace and mercy be upon them, and upon the Israel of God.

I have discussed this passage and its OT background in some depth elsewhere, so here I will give only a summary.[38] In verse 16b some commentators want to take "peace and mercy be upon them" as a reference first to the gentile church but see the ensuing phrase "and upon the Israel of God" as an allusion to the believing Jewish segment of the church. However, it is probable that "the Israel of God" refers to the whole church (gentile and Jew) for the following reasons:

1. This fits the contextual theme of the whole epistle of Galatians (see esp. 3:7–8, 26–29; 4:26–31).
2. Paul's primary point in 6:15 is to emphasize the lack of any kind of racial distinctions in the church and to highlight the fact that the church is a unified new creation, which is likely an allusion to Isa. 43:19; 65:17; 66:22, which predict a new creation and which Paul has had in mind in 2 Cor. 5:17. Thus, the entire church at Galatia is part of the initial fulfillment of Isaiah's prophecy of new creation.
3. The "rule" of 6:16 probably refers to believers always living in light of the fact that there are no distinctions of race, gender, and so forth in the membership of the church, the new Israel.
4. There has been no reference in the letter to a part of the church designated as the physically Israelite redeemed part.
5. Furthermore, the phrase in 6:16, *eirēnē ep' autous kai eleos* ("peace and mercy be upon them"), likely is a further development of the use of Isa 54:1–10, to which Paul has appealed in 4:27. For in Isa. 54:10 LXX God says to Israel, "Neither shall my mercy [*eleos*] fail you, nor shall the covenant of your peace [*eirēnē*] be at all removed." Isaiah 54:7–8 LXX

---

37. This is similar to an observation made by Silva ("Galatians," 809) that he derived from Karen Jobes.

38. G. K. Beale, "Peace and Mercy upon the Israel of God: The Old Testament Background of Gal. 6,16b," *Bib* 80 (1999): 204–23.

further emphasizes this: "With great mercy [*eleos*] I will have compassion upon you [*eleeō*]. . . . With everlasting mercy [*eleeos*] I will have compassion [*eleeō*] upon you." And in Isa. 54:5 is found the idea that Israel is God's latter-day creation, and therefore he is God of Israel: "For it is the Lord who made [*ho poiōn*] you, . . . he is the God of Israel." Therefore, the parallels of Isa. 54:10 with Gal. 6:15–16 appear to be clear, so that an allusion is recognizable.[39] Hence, the conclusion is that *kai* of 6:16 (often translated here as "and") is best translated by "even": "peace and mercy be upon them, even the Israel of God." Thus, both gentile and Jewish believers are identified as the fulfillment of the Isa. 54 prophecy about "peace and mercy" being on the one people of God, end-time Israel. The gentile Christians are part of this fulfillment of the restoration prophecy of Isa. 54. The *kai* signals a further explanation of the preceding "them": the whole church is the inheritor of this prophecy as the true spiritual Israel.

The significance of Isa. 54 for Gal. 6:15–16 is that just as it was applied to the church in Gal. 4, as the beginning fulfillment of the Israelite restoration prophecy, so it is here also. And, of course, the point of it in Gal. 4 was to show that the majority of physical Israel was rejected, and that the predominantly gentile church was the new inheritor as the true latter-day Israel. The point is basically the same in Gal. 6:15–16 as in Gal. 4:21–31.

It has been argued, however, that, since the common meaning for *kai* is "and," and since the word "Israel" elsewhere in the NT always refers to the ethnic nation, the burden of proof rests on those who maintain that *kai* in Gal. 6:16 is appositional and refers to both gentile and Jewish Christians.[40]

39. See the earlier discussion of Gal. 6:15–16 in connection to the idea of the church being part of the end-time new creation (chap. 10); see esp. Beale, "Peace and Mercy," where other possible allusions are discussed as being in mind in Gal. 6:16 together with Isa. 54:10 (Ps. 84:10–11 LXX [85:9–10 ET]; Jer. 16:5, which also prophesy Israel's restoration). Outside these passages, the combination of "peace" and "mercy" in such close proximity does not occur elsewhere in the LXX.

40. E.g., S. Lewis Johnson, "Paul and the 'Israel of God': An Exegetical and Eschatological Case Study," in *Essays in Honor of J. Dwight Pentecost*, ed. Stanley D. Toussaint and Charles H. Dyer (Chicago: Moody, 1986), 181–96. For others following a position similar to Johnson's, see his own discussion and Richard N. Longenecker, *Galatians*, WBC 41 (Nashville: Thomas Nelson, 1990), 274. Johnson (p. 188) even agrees with Ellicott's contention that it is unlikely that Paul ever employs *kai* in "'so marked an explicative sense.'" A number of grammars, however, acknowledge the explicative or epexegetical sense of *kai* as an explicit category of usage in the NT and Paul. BAGD (393), e.g., even prefixes its entry of the "explicative" *kai* (expressed as "and so, that is, namely") with "often" (including the subcategory of "ascensive" ["even"]), citing Rom. 1:5; 1 Cor. 3:5; 15:38 as Pauline examples (see also p. 392, I.d). Intriguingly, Maximilian Zerwick (*Biblical Greek: Illustrated by Examples* [Rome: Scripta Pontificii Instituti Biblici, 1963], 154) cites apposition ("that is") as an explicit category for *kai* and then cites Gal. 6:16 as the lone Pauline example (though followed by a question mark). Likewise BDF 229 (§442.9) (citing, e.g.,

In response, Charles Ray has applied to Gal. 6:16 the linguistic rule for *kai* formulated by Kermit Titrud: though *kai* occurs numerous times in the NT (about nine thousand) with various meanings, instead of assuming that the most common meaning applies (which is "generally connective"), one should opt for that meaning "which contributes the least new information to the total context" (a principle sometimes referred to as "the rule of maximal redundancy"). In particular, Titrud maintained that in view of the rule of maximal redundancy, if apposition is a viable option for *kai*, then it should be seriously considered.[41] This means that the overall context of Galatians must be considered in identifying "Israel" in 6:16. To identify "Israel" with only the Christian segment of the ethnic nation would be introducing a new idea into the letter: whereas Paul throughout has underscored unity among redeemed Jews and gentiles, it would seem to be not just a new thought, but quite an odd one, to underscore at the end a blessing on gentile and Jew separately.[42] Ultimately, immediate context must decide the meaning of the use of any word.

Here, as in 2 Cor. 5:14–7:1, it needs to be emphasized that the church in fulfilling Israel's end-time restoration prophecies is also fulfilling Isaiah's prophecies of new creation.

Ephesians

Paul cites another restoration prophecy in Eph. 2:17. The immediate context is, of course, important. Verses 13–18 read,

1 Cor. 12:15; 15:38); Nigel Turner, *Syntax*, vol. 3 of *A Grammar of New Testament Greek*, ed. J. H. Moulton (Edinburgh: T&T Clark, 1963), 334–35 (citing, e.g., Rom. 1:5; 8:17); Alexander Buttmann, *A Grammar of the New Testament Greek* (Andover, MA: W. F. Draper, 1873), 401 (citing 1 Cor. 3:5; 15:38). See also Rom. 5:14. Approximately 80x in the NT *kai* has the appositional meaning in the construction article + substantive + *kai* + substantive, which is known as the Granville Sharp Rule (see Daniel B. Wallace, *Greek Grammar beyond the Basics* [Grand Rapids: Zondervan, 1996], 270–77). Even among the first descriptions of usage in LSJ (857) is the following: "to add a limiting or defining expression." Herbert Smyth says that "copulative *kai* often has an intensive or heightening force" with the sense of "namely" (*Greek Grammar* [Cambridge, MA: Harvard University Press, 1920], 650 [§2869]).

41. See Kermit Titrud, "The Function of *kai* in the Greek New Testament and an Application to 2 Peter," in *Linguistics and New Testament Interpretation: Essays on Discourse Analysis*, ed. David Alan Black (Nashville: Broadman, 1992), 240, 248, 255. Titrud gives numerous examples throughout the essay of the appositional *kai* in the NT.

42. So Charles A. Ray Jr., "Identity of the 'Israel of God,'" *TTE* 50 (1994): 105–14. Ray's conceptual analysis is good, though it may not be precisely accurate to refer to this particular case as an example of "the rule of maximal redundancy" in light of the way the phrase was originally formulated in linguistic discussion (on which, see Moisés Silva, *Biblical Words and Their Meaning: An Introduction to Lexical Semantics* [Grand Rapids: Zondervan, 1983], 153–56); nevertheless, the principle of "the rule of maximal redundancy" appears to be generally applicable to Gal. 6:16. For a full range of the various possible identifications of "the Israel of God," see Frank J. Matera, *Galatians*, SP 9 (Collegeville, MN: Liturgical Press, 1992), 233.

But now in Christ Jesus you who formerly were far off have been brought near by the blood of Christ. For He Himself is our peace, who made both groups into one and broke down the barrier of the dividing wall, by abolishing in His flesh the enmity, which is the Law of commandments contained in ordinances, so that in Himself He might make the two into one new man, thus establishing peace, and might reconcile them both in one body to God through the cross, by it having put to death the enmity. And He came and preached peace to you who were far away, and peace to those who were near; for through Him we both have our access in one Spirit to the Father.

Earlier I addressed this passage and much more briefly the use of it in the OT (chap. 16 under the subheading "'Reconciliation' in Ephesians 2:13–17"). But this text is so significant for my argument in this chapter that a resummary is in order and also some expansion on the OT allusions in this passage. Throughout the passage is the repeated theme of gentiles coming from the separation of alienation to closeness to God through Christ (vv. 13, 16, 17–18), as well as them coming into close fellowship with Jewish Christians (vv. 15–16, 18).[43] Christ's work of nullifying the harmful and separating effects of the law[44] (vv. 14–15a) has three aims:

1. "in order that <u>he should create</u> the <u>two</u> [Jew and gentile] <u>into one new man</u>" (v. 15);
2. "[in order that] <u>he should reconcile</u> the <u>two in one body</u>" (v. 16);
3. "[in order that], after he came, <u>he [could] preach peace to you who were far away, and peace to those who were near</u>" (v. 17), which means "that through him we <u>both have access in</u> the sphere of <u>one Spirit</u> to the Father" (v. 18).[45]

There is a parallelism between these three purpose clauses: "create," "reconcile," and "preach peace," though not synonymous, are generally parallel and thus closely related concepts. The three repeated references to two groups that have become united or "one" are more precisely synonymous. This suggests that the three purpose clauses are speaking about the same basic notion of people coming together through Christ in relationship to God. Accordingly, the notions of "create," "reconcile," and "preach peace" have to do in this context with uniting Jews and gentiles together in coming into relationship with God through Christ.

Strikingly, verse 17 quotes Isa. 57:19, which is a restoration promise addressed to Israel: "Peace upon peace to those who are far and to those who are near."[46]

43. Here I will not address the question of the "dividing wall" and "the law of commandments" in vv. 14–15, as I will focus on it in a later chapter.

44. Here is in mind both separation from God and gentile separation from Israel.

45. Solid underlining highlights the verbal parallels and broken lines highlight the parallel phrases of Jewish-gentile unity.

46. Paul is likely citing the LXX here rather than the MT.

The wording of "he preached peace" at the beginning of Eph. 2:17 seems also to allude to Isa. 52:7 ("one preaching peace"), which prophesies that in the future one will come who will be God's special messenger in announcing Israel's restoration. Both Isaiah texts are prophecies of Israel's (not the gentiles') restoration. One more indication of the Israelite focus is apparent from observing in the OT elsewhere that the language of people being "far" and others "near" is always used of Israelites, some who are in the land of Israel and others farther away from the land (so 2 Chron. 6:36; Isa. 33:13; Ezek. 6:12; Dan. 9:7).[47] In addition, the only other possible allusion to Isa. 57:19 in the NT, Acts 2:39, views "all who are far off" likely to be Jews living in the Diaspora.

The allusion to Isa. 57:19 in Eph. 2:17 has already been anticipated in verse 13 (those "who formerly were far off have been brought near"), so that the Isaiah reference forms bookends around this literary unit of verses 13–18 (with vv. 17–18 forming the last subunit). The significance of these bookends is that the entire passage should be viewed broadly as having to do with the beginning fulfillment of the Isa. 57:19 restoration prophecy. Also noteworthy is that the parallelism of the verbs "create," "reconcile," and "preach peace" and their resulting broad conceptual overlap indicates an earlier notion[48] that Paul's views of reconciliation and of the inaugurated fulfillment of restoration prophecies are very closely related, if not virtually synonymous. That is, people coming back into relationship with God from alienation is tantamount to Israel's beginning restoration from exile. We saw this in 2 Cor. 5:14–6:2, where also, strikingly, we observed that the beginning fulfillment of Isaiah's prophecy of new creation was almost the other side of the coin of the inaugurated restoration promises there, both of which were also inextricably linked to Paul's understanding of reconciliation.

The main point to be highlighted here is that Isa. 52:7 and 57:19 were prophecies about Israel's restoration, not that of the nations, so here the gentiles, together with a remnant of Jewish believers, are viewed as being restored as end-time Israel, a notion seen repeatedly throughout this chapter and the preceding one. In particular, "those who are near" in this passage are Jews, though still in exile spiritually in their land, and "those who are far" are gentiles, viewed as exiled Israelites outside the land. The rationale for why gentiles can be seen this way I also have repeatedly discussed earlier.

It is also likely not coincidental that in the very next paragraph (Eph. 2:19–22), after mention of new creation, reconciliaton, and restoration from exile,

---

47. It is possible that the Isa. 33:13 passage refers to both Jews, who are near, and gentiles, who are far away, esp. in light of Isa. 33:12 ("the peoples will be burned"). However, besides 33:12, the rest of the entire context of 33:1–16 is either about the blessing or the judgment of Israel.

48. See chap. 16 under the subheadings "'Reconciliation' in 2 Corinthians 5:14–21" and "'Reconciliation' in Ephesians 2:13–17," the latter of which also discusses Eph. 2:17 in its immediate context.

Paul refers to gentiles and Jews forming a temple, since we saw the same phenomenon in 2 Cor. 5:14–7:1 of believers forming a temple, after mention of their reconciliation and after mention that they had begun to fulfill prophecies of new creation and restoration. The reason for this is partly that Isaiah had predicted that at the time of Israel's restoration believing gentiles would also become identified with Israel and become priests in the temple alongside Jews (Isa. 56:3–7; 66:21) in a new creation (Isa. 65:17; 66:22).

The Beginning Fulfillment of Israel's Restoration Prophecies in the Church according to the General Epistles and Revelation

Hebrews

The book of Hebrews repeatedly mentions the "new covenant." This is an allusion to the "new covenant" prophecy in Jer. 31:31–34. In light of its preceding context (Jer. 30:1–31:29), Jeremiah's new-covenant prophecy was part of what was to happen to Israel as a part of its end-time restoration. The present purposes do not allow for a thorough study of Hebrews' use of Jeremiah's new covenant, so the focus here will be on whether it has begun to be fulfilled, and, if so, the nature of its fulfillment. The new covenant of Jer. 31:31–34 is alluded to repeatedly throughout Heb. 8–10 and is quoted most fully in 8:7–10:

> For if that first covenant had been faultless, there would have been no occasion sought for a second. For finding fault with them, He says,
>
>> "Behold, days are coming, says the Lord,
>> When I will effect a new covenant
>> With the house of Israel and with the house of Judah;
>> Not like the covenant which I made with their fathers
>> On the day when I took them by the hand to lead them out of the land
>>   of Egypt;
>> For they did not continue in My covenant,
>> And I did not care for them, says the Lord.
>> For this is the covenant that I will make with the house of Israel
>> After those days, says the Lord:
>> I will put My laws into their minds,
>> And I will write them on their hearts.
>> And I will be their God,
>> and they shall be My people."

Hebrews 10:16 quotes Jer. 31:33 again, and then verse 17 adds a quotation from Jer. 31:34: "And their sins and their lawless deeds I will remember no more."

THE VARIOUS INTERPRETATIONS OF JEREMIAH'S "NEW COVENANT"

There is much discussion about how Hebrews understands Jeremiah's new covenant. Five positions are taken on the matter:

1. There are two new covenants, one for the church (not foreseen by Jeremiah) and one for Israel.
2. Jeremiah's new-covenant prophecy will be fulfilled only in the majority of ethnic believing Israel in a future millennium.
3. Jeremiah's new-covenant prophecy is only analogically applied to, not fulfilled in, the church but will be literally fulfilled only in ethnic Israel in the future or in the so-called millennium.[49]
4. Jeremiah's new-covenant prophecy is truly fulfilled in the church, but the church is not considered true Israel, even though the church is inheriting the promises of true Israel, which still leaves room for fulfillment in ethnic Israel in the future.[50]
5. Jeremiah's new-covenant prophecy is fulfilled in an already–not yet way in the church as true Israel, with no future fulfillment in ethnic Israel at the end of the age, except as such Israelites believe in Christ and become a part of the church throughout the interadvent age up until the end.[51]

The first position is self-evidently improbable because it is very difficult to explain how Jeremiah's prophecy, which Hebrews clearly has in mind throughout, could be understood as referring to two different new covenants. The second view has been touched on in earlier chapters, where I noted several places in the OT where the final redemption of Israel will not be of the entire nation but only of a remnant of ethnic Jews.[52] Indeed, I will argue further that nowhere in the OT is it prophesied that the majority of ethnic Israel will be saved in the eschatological age (see "Conclusion" below). This is particularly the case in Jer. 31, where in light of Jer. 31:7 ("O LORD, save Your people, the remnant of Israel") restored Israel of 31:31–34 should be identified not with the whole nation, but only with a remnant. The third view, the analogical perspective, I also have discussed repeatedly in earlier sections. I observed that

---

49. For these first three views, which typically are representative of various dispensational interpreters, see Hans K. LaRondelle, *The Israel of God in Prophecy: Principles of Prophetic Interpretation*, AUMSR 13 (Berrien Springs, MI: Andrews University Press, 1983), 114–23. LaRondelle cites these various commentators and then gives his own critique.

50. This is the typical progressive dispensational view.

51. Although some who hold this last view still see a future salvation of the majority of ethnic Israel at the final coming of Christ, they understand that ethnic Israelites are incorporated into the church, the true Israel, at the climax of the church age.

52. See, e.g., chap. 20 under the subheading "The Inaugurated Fulfillment of the Prophesied Spirit of Joel 2:28–32 in Acts 2:16–21," with respect to Joel 2:28–32; see earlier in this chapter (under the subheading "Romans") for a discussion of the use of Isa. 10:22–23 and Isa. 1:9 in Rom. 9:27–29.

if a NT writer quotes an OT prophecy and applies it to a present reality (such as the church's contemporary situation), then the default response is to see the prophecy as beginning fulfillment unless other factors in the immediate context make it clear that the prophecy is merely being analogically applied. In addition, if there are features in the context that indicate fulfillment, then the conclusion about fulfillment is enhanced. Such features, indeed, are observable in Heb. 8–13. First, Jesus is seen as beginning to fulfill this new covenant prophecy in 8:6:

> But now He has obtained a more excellent ministry, by as much as He is also the mediator of a better covenant, which has been enacted on better promises. (Cf. 12:24)

Likewise, note 9:15–17:

> For this reason He is the mediator of a new covenant, so that, since a death has taken place for the redemption of the transgressions that were committed under the first covenant, those who have been called may receive the promise of the eternal inheritance. For where a covenant is, there must of necessity be the death of the one who made it. For a covenant is valid only when men are dead, for it is never in force while the one who made it lives. Therefore even the first covenant was not inaugurated without blood. (Cf. 13:20)

In addition, similar inaugurated statements are made about believers in the church, who are said to have begun to be partakers of the new covenant:

Heb. 9:15 "For this reason He is the mediator of a new covenant, so that, since a death has taken place for the redemption of the transgressions that were committed under the first covenant, those who have been called may receive the promise of the eternal inheritance."

Heb. 10:29 "How much severer punishment do you think he will deserve who has trampled under foot the Son of God, and has regarded as unclean the blood of the covenant by which He was sanctified, and has insulted the Spirit of grace?"

Heb. 12:22–24 "But you have come to Mount Zion and to the city of the living God, the heavenly Jerusalem, and to myriads of angels, to the general assembly and church of the firstborn who are enrolled in heaven, and to God, the Judge of all, and to the spirits of the righteous made perfect, and to Jesus, the mediator of a new covenant, and to the sprinkled blood, which speaks better than the blood of Abel."

After quoting Jer. 31:33–34 fully for the second time in Heb. 10:16–17, the author concludes, "Now where there is forgiveness of these things, there is no longer any

729

offering for sin" (10:18). The forgiveness of sin promised in the new-covenant prophecy ("Their sins and their lawless deeds I will remember no more" [Jer. 31:34]) has now been accomplished (note also Heb. 9:28: "Christ was sacrificed once to take away the sins of many people" [NIV]; see likewise 10:1–14).

Therefore, two alternative viewpoints remain viable for understanding the new covenant prophesied by Jeremiah. One is that the Jer. 31 prophecy was actually fulfilled in the church, but this does not make the church true end-time Israel. Rather, the boundaries of fulfillment have been widened or transcended to include gentiles,[53] who inherit Israel's blessings but still remain distinct from Israel.

A second plausible view is that the Jer. 31 prophecy has begun to be fulfilled in the church because the church is identified with and has become the inauguration of end-time Israel.

THE NEW COVENANT OF JEREMIAH AS BEGINNING FULFILLMENT IN CHRIST AND THE CHURCH, WHICH IS TRUE ISRAEL

The last two interpretative alternatives are more plausible than the first three. But which of these two is preferable? The second is preferable. I have argued throughout this book, beginning especially in chapter 20, that the inaugurated fulfillment of Israel's restoration prophecies in Christ and the church indicates the likelihood that both are eschatological Israel. I have argued this for the following reasons:

1. As noted above, when a prophecy is quoted and applied to people in the NT, the default response is to presume that the prophecy is beginning fulfillment and is not merely analogically applied to or compared to the people. Entailed with this is that the thrust of the prophecy should be viewed as beginning fulfillment, and if the prophecy is about end-time Israel, then the fulfillment should be seen to be occurring among people who are eschatological Israel.

2. This default presumption could be countermanded by material from the nearby context that presents evidence to the contrary. In the present case, such evidence is lacking. In fact, contextual evidence points in the direction of supporting this presumption. Again, it is important in this respect to cite Heb. 12:22–24:

   But you have come to Mount Zion and to the city of the living God, the heavenly Jerusalem, and to myriads of angels, to the general assembly and church of the firstborn who are enrolled in heaven, and to God, the Judge of all, and to the spirits of the righteous made perfect, and to Jesus, the mediator of a new covenant, and to the sprinkled blood, which speaks better than the blood of Abel.

53. On which, see F. F. Bruce, *The Epistle to the Hebrews*, NICNT (Grand Rapids: Eerdmans, 1990), 194–95.

This is a description of Christians as latter-day Israelites: having "come to Mount Zion . . . the heavenly Jerusalem," who then are described as the "church of the firstborn,"[54] and to "Jesus the mediator of a new covenant." Since the other realities in which Christians have begun to participate are distinctive Israelite realities, so likewise is it probable that Jeremiah's new covenant is an additional description of an end-time Israelite reality in which the Christians partake.

The logic of the two views above is plausible and similar but nevertheless distinct. However, throughout this book and especially in chapter 20[55] and earlier in this chapter, I have preferred the view that the OT prophesies and the NT affirm that gentiles in the end-time will become Israelites by believing. The conclusion of this chapter will continue to give reasons in support of this preference.

THE CONTEXT OF THE JEREMIAH 31 NEW COVENANT AND ITS USE IN HEBREWS

The Nature of the Newness of the New Covenant

It is now appropriate to sketch briefly the broad lines of how to describe more precisely the nature of the Jer. 31 promise and how it was fulfilled. The following outlines an approach that needs to be more fully developed elsewhere, since limitations of space do not allow for such an elaboration here. The main difference between the new (or second) covenant and the old (or former or first) one is that the first covenant did not last and was abrogated (Israel "broke" the covenant [Jer. 31:32]; the covenant was not "faultless" [Heb. 8:7]). In contrast, the fulfillment of the new covenant will never be abrogated, so that what begins to be fulfilled in it will come to final, consummate completion for eternity. In this respect, Jesus's redemptive work "has become the guarantee of a better covenant" (Heb. 7:22 [cf. 8:6]) because it will be in force "eternally" (God "brought up from the dead" Jesus "through the blood of the eternal covenant" [Heb. 13:20]).[56] Thus, the main difference between the two covenants is that the first was temporal and was abrogated, and the second is eternally valid.[57]

But can we be more precise about how the new covenant is fulfilled in relation to the old covenant? Some believe that Jeremiah promises that the fulfillment of the new covenant will bring about the following for the first time:

54. Recall here the LXX use of *ekklēsia*, which referred repeatedly to the congregation of Israel and now is applied to the redeemed people of God in the new age, as we saw earlier in this chapter.
55. On which, see, e.g., discussion of Ps. 87; Isa. 19:18, 23–25; 49:3–6; 56:3, 6–7; 66:18–21; Ezek. 47:21–23; Zech. 2:11. See also Gal. 3:16, 29; 6:16, as well as in chap. 20 under the subheading "Names and Images of Israel That the New Testament Applies to the Church."
56. Likewise, Jer. 32:40 says the new covenant would be an "everlasting covenant."
57. E.g., Jer. 32:40 says that in the latter-day "everlasting covenant" God "will not turn away from them [Israel], to do them good."

1. It "individualizes the saving knowledge of God," so that each person has a "personal and immediate" relationship with God (Heb. 8:11).
2. It internalizes God's law in the heart of people.
3. It definitively and absolutely forgives sin.[58]

These need some qualification. In whatever way we try to specify how the new covenant is fulfilled, it is a secure conclusion that the difference between the old and the new covenants is that the latter is eternally irrefragable, whereas the former not only could be nullified but also was inherently imperfect.

The above three aspects of fulfillment are generally true, but they need elaboration. For example, the Sinai covenant also included an individual's saving knowledge of God and the notion that the law would be within a person's heart by faith and would issue in true, faithful obedience (see, e.g., Pss. 51:10, 17; 73:1, 13;[59] and throughout Ps. 119).[60] There was a faithful remnant beginning at Sinai and throughout Israel's history who experienced individual salvific status and who had the law written on their heart. And we can assume that the remnant of true believers living under the Sinai covenant would be eternally redeemed on the basis of the Abrahamic promises that are developed and fulfilled in the new covenant. So the two aspects of individualizing a saving knowledge of God[61] and the law being in the heart are not new aspects of the new covenant; rather, they represent continuities between the two covenants. The new covenant of Jeremiah did not promise salvation to the majority of ethnic Israel but only to a future faithful remnant. In fact, the preceding context of Jer. 31 says that restored Israel of the future, who would experience the new covenant, is only a remnant: "O LORD, save your people, the remnant of Israel" (Jer. 31:7). Likewise, God's gracious initiative in establishing a relationship with Israel at Sinai overlaps with the new covenant, since God will again exercise a gracious initiative toward Israel.[62]

58. So LaRondelle, *Israel of God*, 115. Likewise, see William J. Dumbrell, *Covenant and Creation: A Theology of the Old Testament Covenants* (Nashville: Thomas Nelson, 1984), 172–85; idem, *The End of the Beginning: Revelation 21–22 and the Old Testament* (Homebush West, NSW: Lancer, 1985), 86–95. Dumbrell concludes the same thing from the OT prophetic perspective of Jer. 31, though he understands the aspect of God putting the law into people's hearts to represent continuity (pp. 80–81).

59. The passages from Pss. 51 and 73 are cited by Dumbrell, *Covenant and Creation*, 180.

60. E.g., Ps. 119:10–11: "With all my heart I have sought You. . . . Your word have I treasured in my heart, that I might not sin against You."

61. Jeremiah 32:40 underscores this: "I will make an everlasting covenant with them . . . ; and I will put the fear of Me in their hearts so that they will not turn away from Me."

62. On this point, see Dumbrell, *Covenant and Creation*, 177. Note also Ezek. 16:60, which indicates some kind of significant continuity with the new covenant: "Nevertheless, I will remember My covenant with you in the days of your youth [i.e., at Sinai], and I will establish an everlasting covenant."

The Newness of the New Covenant as a Democratization of the Priestly Position of Teaching and Especially Knowing God's Revelatory Truths

It is probably not the aforementioned two aspects of individualizing salvation and internalizing the law in the heart that Jeremiah's new covenant focuses on anyway (though many scholars think so), since these were elements of the Sinai covenant, as we just saw above. While it is true that the language of Jer. 31:33–34 is a bit vague, and the aspects of individualizing salvation and internalizing the law may be included in the purview of Jer. 31, its focus appears to be in another direction. Verse 34 draws out what is in mind in verse 33's reference to God's "putting the law in the heart" of end-time Israel: "They will not <u>teach again</u>, each man his neighbor and each man his brother, saying, 'Know the LORD,' <u>for they will all know Me, from the least of them to the greatest of them.</u>" As far as I am aware, there is no reference in the OT to Israelites generally teaching other Israelites. A survey of the typical Hebrew word for "teach" (*lāmad*) shows that there are some references to parents teaching their children in the sphere of the family (e.g., Deut. 4:10; 11:19; Song 8:2), but otherwise the references to teaching outside the family refer often to God directly teaching Israel or individuals through his revelatory word (e.g., Deut. 4:1; Jer. 32:33)[63] or often to a specially called person or official group of teachers commissioned to teach Israel (e.g., Deut. 4:1, 5,14; 6:1; 31:19).[64] These teachers could be Moses, David, Ezra, authors of OT books, a class of specially appointed teachers, or the Levitical priests (Moses and Ezra also functioned as priests).

Accordingly, part of the newness of Jeremiah's covenant seems to be a democratization of the teaching office ("from the least to the greatest" in Israel) in the latter days, so that every Israelite will be in the knowledgeable position of the priests (and likely also prophets) and thus will have no need to be taught by any leaders or caste of priests. There is no longer need for a caste of priests telling the people, "Know the LORD," because, God says, "They will all know Me" (Jer. 31:34). This knowledgeable condition results from God's revelation of his law in their hearts (Jer. 31:33). The likely reason for this democratization is that in the new age all will have more access to revelation than did even the teaching priests and prophets of the former age.[65]

63. About 20x. Likewise there are occurrences of the Hebrew word with God indirectly teaching (about 6x).

64. About 13x. The same Hebrew word is used to indicate indirect teaching by the same general group (about 8x). See synonyms of *lāmad*, where priests are the special class of teachers in Israel (Deut. 24:8; 33:10; 2 Chron. 35:3; Neh. 8:9).

65. Accordingly, this is quite similar to Matt. 11:11, where Jesus says that although John the Baptist was the greatest prophet of the OT, "the one who is least in the kingdom of heaven is greater than he." This is because one who has witnessed the full revelation of Christ has a greater prophetic revelatory stance than the prophets of the former age, who only prophesied about and looked forward to the messianic age of fulfillment. Jesus's thought in 11:11–14 is

The emphasis here is not so much on the actual role of teaching as on the re-velatory position of knowledge that every believer will now have that formerly was unique to the priests (and prophets). If this is correct, then this passage is making virtually the same point about democratization that we saw earlier in Joel 2:28–29, though the latter focuses on the democratization of the Spirit in placing all in the covenant community in the revelatory position of the prophet (on which, see chap. 20 under the subheading "The Inaugurated Fulfillment of the Prophesied Spirit of Joel 2:28–32 in Acts 2:16–21"). Although degrees of knowledge, maturity, and experience among Christians remain, there is no longer, in regard to knowing revelation, a basic categorical distinction between priests/prophets and the rest of God's people in the new-covenant community.[66]

In addition to the revelation of God's law in the heart, there is a second reason for this democratization, which is stated at the end of Jer. 31:34: "I will forgive their iniquity, and their sin I will remember no more." Because God will decisively forgive the sin of Israel in the future, there will be no need for mediation by human priests to offer sacrifice and to teach other Israelites about the intricacies and need of the OT sacrificial system. Also in mind is that forgiven Israelites will be in an intimate relationship with God, such that they have access to revelation and to God's presence that previously only the priests and prophets of the former epoch had. In the new era all of God's people will have more exposure to divine revelation and the divine presence than did even the priests and prophets of old. Thus, consummative forgiveness wipes away the need for a particular class of human priests to minister to the rest of the people.[67] Such decisive forgiveness is also a new feature of the new covenant, since the sacrificial system of the Sinai covenant could not bring final forgive-ness and eschatological "perfection" or "completion" of the believer, as Heb. 9:9–10:18 repeatedly affirms.[68] But even with this new-covenant fulfillment,

developed in 13:17: "For truly I say to you that many prophets and righteous men desired to see what you see, and did not see it, and to hear what you hear, and did not hear it."

66. For the same point about the use of Jer. 31 in 1 John 2:27, see D. A. Carson, "1–3 John," in *Commentary on the New Testament Use of the Old Testament*, ed. G. K. Beale and D. A. Carson (Grand Rapids: Baker Academic, 2007), 1065–66.

67. See also Dumbrell, *Covenant and Creation*, 182. Dumbrell sees more of a focus on the democratization of the office of prophets than that of priests.

68. Limitations of space prohibit in-depth elaboration of how forgiveness of sin through sacrifice in the OT differs precisely from the forgiveness of the new covenant. Certainly Leviticus repeatedly asserts that forgiveness comes through sacrifice (e.g., 4:20, 26, 31, 35; 5:10, 13, 16, 18; 6:7; 19:22). But however one explains the precise nature of this forgiveness and its partial effectiveness in the old covenant, it is clear that Hebrews sees such forgiveness as incomplete and temporary, since only Christ's sacrifice brought perfect or "complete" forgiveness that "perfected" the believers' sinful condition. The usual approach is to understand that the former repeated animal sacrifices were typological foreshadowings of Christ's once-for-all sacrifice, and, as Heb. 11:40 suggests, faithful OT saints received final forgiveness on the basis of Christ's sacrifice, to which the animal sacrifices pointed (e.g., see John Calvin, *Commentaries on the Epistle of Paul the Apostle to the Hebrews* (repr., Grand Rapids: Baker Academic, 1984), 199–233. Ezekiel

the inaugurated stage likely refers to Jesus's sacrifice of forgiving sins so that those forgiven are considered positionally forgiven (i.e., through identification with Christ and his representative work), though they are still existentially not without sin. Such final and complete personal cleansing of sin will come at the consummate stage of the Jeremiah fulfillment, when saints will receive resurrected bodies and souls.[69]

This notion that the Jeremiah passage has in mind the democratization of the priestly class is pointed to further by the close affinity between Lev. 26:9–12 and Jer. 31:31–33 (see table 21.2).

Table 21.2

Leviticus 26:9–12	Jeremiah 31:31–33
v. 9: "So I will turn toward you and make you fruitful and multiply you, and I will confirm My covenant with you. v. 10: You will eat the old supply and clear out the old because of the new.[a] v. 11: Moreover, I will make My dwelling among you [LXX: "I will set my covenant among you"], and My soul will not reject you. v. 12: I will also walk among you and be your God, and you shall be My people."	v. 31: "'Behold, days are coming,' declares the LORD, 'when I will make a new covenant with the house of Israel and with the house of Judah, v. 32: not like the [old] covenant which I made with their fathers in the day I took them by the hand to bring them out of the land of Egypt, My covenant which they broke, although I was a husband to them,' declares the LORD. v. 33: 'But this is the covenant which I will make [= Lev. 26:9] with the house of Israel after those days,' declares the LORD, 'I will put My law within them and on their heart I will write it; and I will be their God, and they shall be My people.'"

[a]The "old" and the "new" here refer to fruitfulness with respect to grain, so that with the coming eschatological covenant (v. 9) there will be an abundance of new grain in contrast to the stored old grain (that grain is in mind is clear from Lev. 25:22, on which, see Baruch A. Levine, *Leviticus*, JPSTC [Philadelphia: Jewish Publication Society, 1989], 184). The same kind of abundant fruitfulness is part of Jeremiah's new covenant, as is evident from the preceding context (31:4–5, 12, 24–28). The point of commonality in this respect is the concept of replacing old things with new things (on the affinity of Lev. 26 and Jer. 31 here I have followed Alan C. Mitchell, *Hebrews*, SP 13 [Collegeville, MN: Liturgical Press, 2007], 172).

These are the only two passages in the OT that have in common (1) the placement of a "covenant into Israel," (2) a contrast of "old" and "new" inextricably linked to the renewal of a covenant and the new end-time conditions accompanying such a covenant, and (3) the concluding formula "I will be your/their God, and you/they will be My people."[70] Thus, the Jeremiah passage appears to be echoing the Leviticus text. What is striking about this is

---

16:60–63 asserts that the future "everlasting covenant" will result in God completely having "forgiven you [Israel] for all that you have done."

69. Such final "perfection" or "completion" of believers' interior being at the consummation is pointed to by Heb. 9:9 and 12:23, which respectively speak of believers' "conscience" and "spirit" being perfected.

70. The only other place in the OT where "covenant" occurs with this concluding formula is Exod. 6:5–7, and it may be that Lev. 26:9–12 is developing the earlier expression.

that the primary expression of the new-covenant blessing in Lev. 26 is that God will establish his tabernacle (i.e., temple) with Israel (v. 11) in order to be present among them (v. 12).[71] Significantly, the Hebrew phrase "I will make My dwelling among you" (v. 11) is interpreted by the LXX as "I will set my covenant among you." For the Greek translator, God's promise to place his tabernacle amid the Israelites is part and parcel with setting his covenant among the people. Of course, all this does is emphasize what the Hebrew text has already said: God's confirmation of an end-time covenant (v. 9) will result in the establishment of a tabernacle (vv. 11–12).

Quite significant in this connection is that Ezek. 37:23–27 also contains reference to (1) the "my people"/"their God" formula (vv. 23, 27), and (2) the "everlasting covenant" that is explained in that context as an everlasting tabernacle: "I will set My sanctuary in their midst forever" (v. 26), "My dwelling place also will be over them" (v. 27), and "when My sanctuary is in their midst forever" (v. 28). I have shown elsewhere that this passage from Ezek. 37 probably is an allusion to Lev. 26:11–12. Thus, we have the Ezekiel text carrying on the Leviticus prophecy about an end-time covenant being expressed primarily as God's making of a tabernacle and setting it among Israel, and Ezekiel highlights this connection even more than does Leviticus.[72] Ezekiel's "everlasting covenant" is very close to Jeremiah's language of a "new covenant," and the Lev. 26 background of both brings them even closer together to suggest that they are in a mutually interpretative relationship.

Consequently, if Jeremiah has in mind the Leviticus text (in light of Jeremiah's affinity with Ezek. 37), the notion of God's establishment of a tabernacle appears to be implicit in Jeremiah with the making of a future covenant.[73] This would help explain the priestly democratization that I perceive in Jer. 31 and have noted above. The point would be that in the end-time covenantal conditions all people will function as priests in the tabernacle, being in God's direct presence. New covenant and end-time tabernacle thus go hand in hand. This would also explain better than any other proposal that I have encountered the fact that the directly preceding context of the Jeremiah quotation in Heb. 8:8–12 is about the new tabernacle in which Christ dwells as a new priest in

71. For further explanation and confirmation of this, see G. K. Beale, *The Temple and the Church's Mission: A Biblical Theology of the Dwelling Place of God*, NSBT 17 (Downers Grove, IL: InterVarsity, 2004), 110–11.

72. For the connection between the Lev. 26 and Ezek. 37 texts, see ibid.

73. Among the repeated formulas of "You/they will be my people, and I will be your/their God," only four are linked to covenant (Exod. 6:5–7 and Lev. 26:9–12). A third and a fourth occurrence are in Ezek. 37:23–28, where the formula appears twice and especially the "everlasting covenant" is expressed by "I will set My sanctuary in their midst forever" (v. 26), "My dwelling place also will be over them" (v. 27), and "when My sanctuary is in their midst forever" (v. 28). Ezekiel 11:20 also connects the formula to God's dwelling with Israel (see Ezek. 11:16–20) but not to covenant. The other occurrences of the formula are in 2 Sam. 7:24; 1 Chron. 17:22; Jer. 7:23; 24:7; 30:22; 32:38; Ezek. 14:11; 34:30; Hos. 1:9; Zech. 8:8.

contrast to the old, flawed temple. The Jeremiah quotation is introduced to support this perspective of the old and new temples in Heb. 8:1–5 as a part of the old and new covenants.

Of course, the book of Hebrews tells us that Jesus is a new priest according to the order of Melchizedek who offered himself as a sacrifice "once for all," doing away with the need for fallible human priests and their temporary, ineffective sacrifices (see Heb. 7–10). By doing so, Christ made all former priestly functions and sacrifices in Israel obsolete. Some may respond that this interpretation of priestly democratization in Jer. 31:33–34 is not self-evident, but it is striking that the use of Jer. 31:31–34 in Hebrews is situated in contexts that mention Christ's superior priestly ministry and definitive sacrifice that make the OT priestly and sacrificial system obsolete (see 8:8–12; 10:16–17). For example, 10:14 forms part of the introduction to the quotation of Jer. 31:33–34 in verses 16–17 in this way: "For by one offering [Christ] has perfected for all time those who are sanctified." Likewise, 10:18 interprets God's no longer remembering sin (10:17) with "Now where there is forgiveness of these things, there is no longer any offering for sin." In addition, 10:19 concludes further that believers can now "have confidence to enter the holy place by the blood of Jesus." He is the "great [high] priest," and all believers genuinely participate in the sphere of the heavenly tabernacle, suggesting that they have some connection to a priestly status (10:19–22). At the very least, all believers are now represented in heaven by Jesus, the priest, so in some sense they participate in or are associated with his priestly status in the heavenly temple (10:19–20).[74]

Concluding Comments on the Nature of the Fulfillment of the Prophesied Democratized Priesthood from Jeremiah 31

In this regard, it is also quite significant to mention the use of the *teleioō* word group, which is usually translated throughout Hebrews as "to perfect" or "perfect." The uses refer not to moral perfection or development but rather to eschatological completion, especially the fulfillment of what the priestly system pointed to, which was access to God in the latter-day temple. In fact, the verb *teleioō* and its noun forms[75] in Hebrews have the connotation of "complete" or "completion" and are close in meaning to "consecrate" or "set apart" (i.e., "sanctify," which is a typical rendering of the Gk. *hagiazō*).[76] Hebrews at this point has been influenced by the background of Exodus and Leviticus, where "fill the hand" is an idiomatic expression of priestly consecration and is translated by the Greek OT as "fill/complete the hand." The verb by itself

---

74. Dumbrell (*Covenant and Creation*, 178) also believes that one of the discontinuities between the two covenants is that whereas Israel's unbelief broke the covenant with God, in the new covenant both parties will be faithful and do nothing to sever the relationship.

75. See in Hebrews *teleios* (5:14; 9:11), *teleiotēs* (6:1), *teleiōtēs* (12:2), and *teleiōsis* (7:11).

76. Note also in Hebrews the related noun forms *hagiasmos* and *hagiotēs*.

conveys the meaning of "consecrate" a priest, and the noun *teleiōsis* refers to priestly "ordination."

According to Hebrews, Jesus reached such end-time completion as a Melchizedekian priest (5:9; 7:28; likewise 2:10 in relation to 2:16–17). The priests of the old covenant could not mediate in a way that could bring God's people eschatological access ("completion") to the inner sanctuary of the old, physical temple (7:11, 19; 9:9), which pointed to the eschatologically "completed" sanctuary in heaven (9:11). Jesus's priestly sacrifice, however, made believers "complete" by causing them to "approach" God's tabernacling presence and reach eschatological access to the holy of holies in the true temple in heaven (10:1, 14).[77] Consequently, such people whom Christ has brought to eschatological "completion" (12:2) can be called "complete" ones (5:14), and the whole gathering of redeemed saints at the latter-day Mount Zion is also thus referred to as "the spirits of the righteous made complete" because of Jesus's priestly mediation (12:22–24). This means that OT saints could not be "completed" apart from those who would live in the age of fulfillment and could not have full redemptive-historical access to God until the fulfillment of the eschaton came[78] (11:40).[79] Therefore, the common use of the *teleioō* word group in Hebrews, which connotes priestly consecration, is applied to both Christ and Christians. The upshot of this discussion is that all believers presently have positional access to God's heavenly sanctuary through Christ's priestly work, and thus they also have a kind of position of priestly consecration in identification with him. This at least means that they have access to the heavenly sanctuary that only the high priest formerly had, though even he did not have the access Christians now have in Christ. It is in this sense that we can speak of a democratization of the OT priestly office or position for new-covenant believers.

This end-time priestly access to God in his temple is probably the same concept expressed by the apocalyptic vision of Rev. 22:4: "And they will see His face, and His name will be on their foreheads." This pictures believers having reached their consummate access to God in the end-time temple; they

---

77. Here note the various verbs used for believers being able to "approach" God throughout Hebrews, which in virtually every context has to do with approaching God's presence in the heavenly temple through Jesus's mediatorial work (see 4:16; 7:19, 25; 10:1 [though negative, it points to positive approaching in the context of 10:1–22], 19–22; 12:18, 22 [esp. in light of 12:23–24]). The use in 11:6 is the only one whose immediate context is not cultic.

78. This final full access to God begins in the inaugurated end-time age but is consummated at the very end of the age.

79. The preceding analysis of the meaning of the *teleioō* word group in Hebrews with respect to the dual notion of eschatological completion together with priestly consecration is based on Moisés Silva, "Perfection and Eschatology in Hebrews," *WTJ* 39 (1976): 60–71; S. M. Baugh, "Covenant, Priesthood, and People in Hebrews" (online: http://baugh.wscal.edu/PDF/NT701/NT701_Hebrews_CPP.pdf), also dependent on Silva. See also Scott D. Mackie, *Eschatology and Exhortation in the Epistle to the Hebrews*, WUNT 2/223 (Tübingen: Mohr Siebeck, 2007), 189–96.

are now in the position of the high priest, who had God's name written on the turban on his forehead. "The privilege of consecration to be acceptable in the immediate presence of God, formerly reserved only for the high priest, is now granted to all God's people."[80]

Not coincidentally, this notion of end-time completion of saints, giving them greater access to God in the true temple, occurs as an introduction to the second quotation of Jer. 31:33–34 in Heb. 10 (see 10:14). This results in the fulfillment of the Jeremiah prophecy in that believers now have access to God's presence in the heavenly temple, which they never had before. Hebrews 10:19–22 reads,

> Therefore, brethren, since we have confidence to enter the holy place by the blood of Jesus, by a new and living way which he inaugurated for us through the veil, that is, His flesh, and since we have a great priest over the house of God, let us draw near with a sincere heart in full assurance of faith, having our hearts sprinkled clean from an evil conscience and our bodies washed with pure water.

Their identification with Jesus as a priest likely identifies them in some way with his priesthood. He is the "great priest," and they share his priestly status and have access to the end-time sanctuary because of his mediatorial work on their behalf. Thus, this connection with believers even experiencing some kind of eschatological completion as consecrated priests with access to the heavenly temple supports the view that Jeremiah's new-covenant prophecy included a notion of all of God's people in the new age having some kind of priestly status.[81]

Some contend that the fallible nature of the old covenant lay only in the fact that Israel "broke the covenant" (Jer. 31:32) and "did not continue in [God's] covenant" (Heb. 8:9).[82] Israel's breach of the covenant did occur, but it is not the only reason that the covenant could not continue in force forever. In light of the intrinsic inadequacies of the old priesthood and sacrificial

---

80. G. K. Beale, *The Book of Revelation: A Commentary on the Greek Text*, NIGTC (Grand Rapids: Eerdmans, 1999), 1114.

81. Likely, this end-time completion notion of the *teleioō* word group secondarily implies the moral perfection of saints' characters at the end-time in light of the contextual uses in Hebrews in connection with forgiveness (also in light of 11:1–17 and the "perfection" of the conscience in 9:9).

82. So Donald A. Hagner, *Hebrews*, NIBC (Peabody, MA: Hendrickson, 1990), 122–23. Hagner contends that the old covenant was not eternally enduring only because of Israel's lack of belief and obedience; otherwise, there was nothing inherently or systemically fallible about it. Likewise, Scott J. Hafemann (*2 Corinthians*, NIVAC [Grand Rapids: Zondervan, 2000], 133–36) sees that the only problem with the fallibility of the old covenant was Israel's disobedience and unfaithfulness. His argument, like Hagner's, seems to assume that the new covenant would be fulfilled in a majority of ethnic Israel who would not break the covenant as the majority of the nation had so done earlier at Sinai. However, as already seen earlier in this section, Jer. 31:7 says only a "remnant" would experience the new covenant.

system noted just above, which was part of the old covenant, that covenant had to be viewed as temporary and not eternally valid, and it prepared the way to the eternally valid covenant that Christ brought about. In fact, even if there had been no human disobedience, the inherent weaknesses of the priestly and sacrificial aspects of the old covenant would have necessitated a new covenant.[83] The systemically temporary nature of the Sinai covenant is also suggested in 2 Cor. 3:5–7, which appears to indicate that even before Israel's sinful response to the Sinai covenant, that covenant was designed not to give life but rather to "kill" and be a "ministry of death." If so, then this enhances all the more the preparatory nature of the old covenant for the eternal new covenant of life.

CONCLUSION ON THE USE OF THE JEREMIAH 31 NEW-COVENANT PROPHECY IN HEBREWS

The upshot of this long section on Hebrews is that the church has begun to fulfill the Jer. 31 prophecy of restoration and of the new covenant. Consequently, it is likely that the church is understood to be the eschatological Israel experiencing the blessings of the new covenant. These blessings revolve primarily around everyone in the new-covenant community experiencing the revelatory position that in the OT only priests had experienced.

1 Peter

The letter of 1 Peter touches on the beginning fulfillment of Israel's restoration promises in the church, but these are most clearly expressed in its identification with Christ as the foundation stone of the end-time temple and believers as stones of the temple built upon him. First Peter 2:4–7a reads,

> And coming to Him as to a living stone which has been rejected by men, but is choice and precious in the sight of God, you also, as living stones, are being built up as a spiritual house for a holy priesthood, to offer up spiritual sacrifices acceptable to God through Jesus Christ. For this is contained in Scripture: "Behold, I lay in Zion a choice stone, a precious cornerstone, and he who believes in Him will not be disappointed." This precious value, then, is for you who believe.

However, those who reject Christ are rejecting him as the reconstitution of the temple and forfeit their part as priests in that temple (2:7b–8). I will not elaborate further on Christ and the church as the temple, since I have discussed earlier how both begin to fulfill the eschatological temple promises. As we

---

83. On which, see William L. Lane, *Hebrews 1–8*, WBC 47A (Dallas: Word, 1991), 211. Lane sees the Jer. 31:31–34 quotation to indicate "the imperfect and provisional character of the old covenant and its institutions (8:6–13)." See likewise Bruce, *Hebrews*, 193–94.

saw, the building of the latter-day temple was to occur in conjunction with other restoration promises and was one of the telltale signs that the restoration was commencing. Because believers are identified with Christ as the "living [foundation] stone" of the temple, they also are "living stones" in the temple. The specific reference to "living" shows that the "living" resurrected Christ represents his people, so they are "living" resurrected beings as well.[84] Accordingly, the church not only forms part of this temple but also continues the role of true Israel, as stated in 2:9–10:

> But you are a chosen race, a royal priesthood, a holy nation, a people for God's own possession, so that you may proclaim the excellencies of Him who has called you out of darkness into His marvelous light; for you once were not a people, but now you are the people of God; you had not received mercy, but now you have received mercy.

I have already discussed above some of the OT background of the references in the preceding quotation (see chap. 20). The phrase "chosen race" (*genos eklekton*) is from Isa. 43:20 LXX, which prophesies that Israel will be restored into a new creation (Isa. 43:18–19). The phrase "so that you may proclaim the excellencies of him" is derived from the directly following verse after Isa. 43:20: they will "tell of my excellencies" (Isa. 43:21 LXX), though Peter has paraphrased it more likely by the LXX of Isa. 42:12 ("they will announce his excellencies"). These expressions from Isa. 42–43 are part of restoration prophecies and are prophecies of new creation (particularly 43:18–21), which were to occur at the time of Israel's restoration. The phrase "a royal priesthood, a holy nation, a people for God's own possession" comes from Exod. 19:5–6 LXX: "You will be to me a special people . . . a royal priesthood and a holy nation" (which is virtually equivalent to Exod. 23:22). God gives these names to Israel to designate who it was and how it was to function. Now, Peter's Christian readers are those who are seen to be part of the restored Israel of the latter days, who have begun to fulfill the prophecies of the temple and of the new creation and to function as priests in the temple (a notion quite similar to the point made above in the section on Hebrews). It is important to notice that along with the notions of temple, priesthood, and new creation, the idea of the believers being a kingdom is included: they are a "royal priesthood" (1 Pet. 2:9), which carries over from Exod. 19:6 the idea not only of priesthood but also of kingship.[85] I have shown repeatedly thoughout this book that the ideas of eschatologi-

---

84. On this point, see Karen Jobes, *1 Peter*, BECNT (Grand Rapids: Baker Academic, 2005), 148–49.

85. For the notions of both kingship and priesthood, see Beale, *Revelation*, 192–95, in discussion of Rev. 1:6, which makes the very same allusion to Exod. 19:6 and likewise applies it to the church.

cal resurrection, new creation, temple, and kingship are inextricably linked and are facets of one another.

In 1 Pet. 2:10 the prophecies of Hos. 1:9 and 2:23 are applied to the church, the same two prophecies that Paul applied to Jews and gentiles in Rom. 9:25–26. Because I have already elaborated on how Paul uses these OT texts, I will not rehearse that here, except to say that Peter probably is using them in the same way: to indicate that the church is beginning to fulfill Hosea's eschatological restoration prophecies about Israel.[86] In that earlier discussion I argued that the underlying presupposition for Paul applying prophecies of Israel's restoration to the church is that Christ was true Israel, who represents the church as true Israel, so that the church too can be identified as true Israel. That presupposition has come closer to the surface here, since 1 Pet. 2:10 follows right on the heels of the church being called "living stones" of the temple because it is identified with Christ as the "living stone" of the temple. That identification probably carries over also to the notion of Christ first fulfilling the prophecies of Israel being restored (by being raised from the dead), which applies also to the church in corporate relationship to him.

Revelation

In chapter 16 I explored how "reconciliation" is one way that Paul discusses the beginning fulfillment of the hope that God would restore Israel to close fellowship with him. I noted that Paul can also express ideas of reconciliation without using the technical "reconciliation" language. I also looked at the Gospels and Acts and observed that the concept of reconciliation is likewise to be found in discussions of how the promises of Israel's end-time restoration had begun to be fulfilled in Jesus and his followers. I concluded that chapter by looking at the final vision of Revelation, which foresees the consummation of the restoration promises and interweaves them with the concept of reconciliation. Thus, I direct the reader back to this discussion for the notion of restoration in Revelation. There are other places in Revelation where this concept could be discussed (e.g., 7; 14:1–4; 20:1–6). Interestingly, Revelation sees ancient "Babylon the Great" typologically to represent the entire ungodly world, so that the church, which has begun to be restored from spiritual exile, still lives in a situation of physical exile on this earth (e.g., 17:1–7; 18:1–5), and even the church's spiritual restoration has not been consummated. This consummate restoration will occur at the final resurrection, when the church will be delivered completely from exile on the old earth. This is compatible with what I observed repeatedly in earlier chapters, that resurrection as new creation was also the way that God's saints come out of exile and are restored to God.

---

86. For discussion of the OT allusions in 1 Pet. 2:4–10, see Jobes, *1 Peter*, 144–64.

Conclusion: Theological Reflection on the Application of Restoration Promises to Jesus, His Followers, and the Church

The OT restoration prophecies discussed in this and the preceding chapter were chosen because they are representative of the way other OT prophecies of Israel's restoration are used in the NT. Among these, the "new covenant" passage of Jer. 31 is a classic example. This prophecy is best understood in the broader restoration context of chapters 29–31. Jeremiah 29–31 elaborates on what will happen when the people of Israel return to the land. Much more was to occur than merely a physical return to the land of Israel. For example,

1. God will "restore the fortunes" of the nation (29:14; 30:3, 18);
2. "the city will be rebuilt . . . and the palace will stand on its rightful place" (30:18; 31:4);
3. God will raise up another king like David for them (30:9; cf. 30:21; indeed, a Messiah, according to Ps. 2:7–9; Dan. 7:13; Hos. 3:5);
4. there will be unending rejoicing (31:4, 7, 12–13);
5. there will be a new covenant, unlike the one made with Israel at Sinai (31:31–33), in which there would be no need for a teaching caste of priests, since all would equally know God in the same way (31:34a);
6. there will be a definitive forgiveness of their sin that had never happened before (31:34b; so also Isa. 53:3–12);
7. God will be their God, and they will be his people.

This segment of Jeremiah contains even more descriptions, not listed here, of the glorious expectations that were inextricably linked to Israel's return to the land.

The prophesied return to the land was fulfilled, but it was only a remnant of Judah and Benjamin, not the majority of the tribes, who actually returned. However, it was never part of the restoration prophecies that the majority of the ethnic nation would return to God in the land. Although a number of commentators understand that the OT prophesied that the vast majority of ethnic Israel would be restored, there is evidence that points the other way, to a hope only for a remnant of Israel to return.[87] In fact, as we saw earlier in

---

87. The majority of references to how many in Israel would be restored indicate a remnant (Isa. 1:9; 4:2–3; 10:20–22; 11:11–12; 37:31–32; Jer. 31:7b; Obad. 17), although some references speak to the "whole house" of Israel being restored (Ezek. 20:40; 37:11; likewise "house of Israel" in Jer. 31:31–34 is often taken this way). However, in the context of each of these passages there is a qualification that only a remnant would be restored, so the "whole house" or "house" of Israel actually refers to the whole remnant and not to the entirety or even majority of the ethnic nation. For example, Ezek. 20:35–38 qualifies v. 40 ("the whole house of Israel"), saying that just as God caused the rebellious first generation not to enter the land, so it will be again at the time of the restoration (e.g., note v. 38: "And I will purge from you the rebels and those who transgress against Me; I will bring them out of the land where they sojourn, but they

the discussion of Jeremiah 31, the Jeremiah prophecy announces hope for the restoration by proclaiming, "O LORD, save Your people, the remnant of Israel" (31:7b), which should be taken as a qualification of who will be restored in 31:31–34. The preceding context of Jeremiah says that God would "gather" this remnant "from all the nations and from all the places where I have driven you" (29:14) and "from the remote parts of the earth" (31:8). Such a thorough restoration of the remnant appeared to take place at the time of the return after seventy years in Babylon, but all the other marvelous things prophesied above by Jer. 31 to occur together with the restoration did not happen.

Does this mean that Jeremiah's prophecy was not fulfilled and that Jeremiah was a false prophet? There is no evidence that Israel's subsequent prophets ever drew such a conclusion about Jeremiah or his prophecy about Israel's return. The likely reason for this is that his prophecy was seen to have begun fulfillment at the end of the seventy years, but the fulfillment was not consummated, and there remained a hope that all the other aspects of the restoration prophecies, indeed the majority of the restoration prophecies, would be realized at some future point.

In addition to the aforementioned things prophesied by Jeremiah that were not fulfilled, other prophecies that other prophets said would occur in association with the restoration to the land were not fulfilled. Like so many of Jeremiah's prophecies, significant features of the fulfillment of prophecies by other prophets were delayed. Some of the significant unfulfilled prophecies interconnected with that of Israel's return to the land are the following:

1. peace between Jews and gentiles (Isa. 11:1–12; 66:18–23);
2. a rebuilt temple bigger than any other, with God's presence in it (Ezek. 40–48);
3. Israel no longer under foreign domination (Ps. 2:1–9; Isa. 2:4; Dan. 2:31–45);
4. a new creation (Isa. 65:17; 66:22);
5. a great outpouring of the Holy Spirit upon Israel (Isa. 32:15; Ezek. 39:29; Joel 2:28);
6. miracles of healing (e.g., Isa. 35:5–6);
7. a great mass of redeemed gentiles streaming into Israel (Isa. 2:3–4);
8. the resurrection of Israel (Isa. 26:11–19; Ezek. 37:1–14).[88]

---

will not enter the land of Israel"). Thus, the "whole house of Israel" in Ezek. 20:40 refers to a remnant of Israel, which is left after its end-time purging. Ezekiel 37:11 likely should be taken in the same way because the restoration theme is continued there. The reference in Ezek. 39:25 and 39:29, where respectively God "restores" "the whole house of Israel" and "pours out his Spirit on the house of Israel," is likely best understood in the light of Ezek. 20:18–40, where the same restoration theme occurs together with the "whole house of Israel" that is defined as the entirety of the remnant.

88. On the Ezek. 37 text being an actual resurrection prophecy of Israel's regenerated spirit, see my analysis above (chap. 20 under the heading "The Old Testament Notion of Gentiles Becoming Latter-Day True Israel as Background for the New Testament Presupposition That the

None of these expectations came about when the tiny remnant of Israel returned to the land, though for a time it appeared that the expectations might be realized, since Israel did start rebuilding Jerusalem and the temple. The rebuilt city and temple, however, never reached the magnitude that the prophecies had envisioned. The reason for this lack of fulfillment was Israel's faithlessness and disobedience (see Neh. 1:6–9). For example, Zech. 4 prophesies the rebuilding of the eschatological temple, as does Zech. 6:12–14, but Zech. 6:15 asserts that the rebuilding activities that Israel performed on its return to the land would not come to successful fruition because they could take place only if the Israelites "completely obey the LORD your God," which they did not.

Consequently, when Israel returned from Babylon, the restoration prophecies could be seen as beginning fulfillment, but nothing more. The motor of fulfillment started, but it quickly stalled and broke down. Although Israel was back in the land, the majority of the other restoration promises did not come about. Consequently, irreversible eschatological conditions of restoration did not take place. This imperfect restoration itself would become typological of one still to take place in the future.

There is much debate today among Jewish and NT scholars about whether Judaism and the NT reflect belief that Israel was still in exile.[89] A balanced assessment is that Judaism itself was divided over whether Israel was still in exile in the first century AD, despite being back physically in the land. I think that the most plausible analysis is that although the nation was physically back in the land, it remained in spiritual exile, as well as physical exile, since it was still dominated by hostile foreign powers, and the majority of the restoration prophecies had not yet been fulfilled. This appears to be the testimony of the latter parts of the OT itself. Although the people of Israel had returned to the land, they had continued to sin by intermarrying with the foreigners around them (Ezra 9–10). In part of the confession of Israel's sin in Neh. 9:36 we find that the people still believe that they are oppressed "slaves" in exile: "Behold, we are slaves today, and as to the land which You did give to our fathers to

---

Church Is True Israel," and chap. 17 under the heading "The Old Testament Role of the Spirit as a Life-Transforming Agent").

89. In favor of the notion of Israel still in exile, see N. T. Wright, *The New Testament and the People of God* (Minneapolis: Fortress, 1992), 268–72, 299–338; idem, *Jesus and the Victory of God* (Minneapolis: Fortress, 1996), xvi–xvii, 126–29, 428–30; James M. Scott, "Restoration of Israel," *DPL* 796–805; Thomas R. Hatina, "Exile," in *Dictionary of New Testament Background*, ed. Craig A. Evans and Stanley E. Porter (Downers Grove, IL: InterVarsity, 2000), 348–51. Others, such as Peter O'Brien ("Was Paul a Covenantal Nomist?," in *The Paradoxes of Paul*, vol. 2 of *Justification and Variegated Nomism*, ed. D. A. Carson, Peter T. O'Brien, and Mark A. Seifrid [Grand Rapids: Baker Academic, 2004], 285–86, 294), deny the notion while rightly emphasizing that there is not an exclusive focus on national concerns about Israel. For a balanced presentation of the issue, see Douglas J. Moo, "Israel and the Law in Romans 5–11: Interaction with the New Perspective," in Carson, O'Brien, and Seifrid, eds., *Paradoxes of Paul*, 204–5.

eat of its fruit and its bounty, behold, we are slaves on it." Likewise, in Ezra 9:9 they say, "For we are slaves; yet in our bondage our God has not forsaken us" (cf. Neh. 5:5). Early Judaism held that Israel's real restoration had not yet happened, despite the return from Babylon generations earlier (e.g., Tob. 14:5–7). Likewise, the Qumran community believed that up until their time, though living in the land, Israel was still in exile.[90]

The NT favors the notion that Israel was still in exile, since in the Gospels and elsewhere restoration prophecies are understood as beginning fulfillment in Christ and the church. The redemptive-historical motor of fulfillment, which had been stalled and had broken down for about four hundred years, was rebuilt, revved up, and put into high gear with the coming of Jesus. That is, the major features of the restoration promises begin fulfillment in Christ's coming, which is apparent, in particular, from both Jesus's and Paul's appeals to OT restoration promises beginning fulfillment in their midst. All the above restoration prophecies are viewed as beginning decisive fulfillment in Christ, whether it concerns prophecies about the Messiah, the eschatological kingdom, the end-time temple, the Spirit, new creation, or promises about healing, definitive forgiveness of sin, resurrection, defeat of evil rulers, or unity between Jews and gentiles. In 2 Cor. 1:20 Paul affirms, "For as many as are the [OT] promises of God, in Him [Christ] they are yes," in terms of beginning fulfillment. In 2 Corinthians Paul especially has in mind the eschatological restoration prophecies of the coming of the Spirit (1:21–22; 3:6, 8, 18), of Jeremiah's new covenant (chap. 3), new creation (5:17), and the end-time temple (6:16–7:1). And indeed, in a text that I have appealed to several times already, 2 Cor. 7:1, Paul says that the Corinthians presently possess or "have these promises." Paul also has in mind, especially in Rom. 9–11, the Deut. 32 framework of (1) God's election and care of Israel; (2) Israel's rebellion; (3) God's judgment, including exile; (4) God's final deliverance and vindication of Israel; and (5) the invitation to gentiles to join in Israel's redemption. Since God's restoration of Israel had not yet happened during the Second Temple period, its exile continued up through to the time of Christ, when the decisive deliverance began to happen.[91]

90. See, e.g., 1QS VIII:13–14, which quotes Isa. 40:3 ("In the wilderness prepare the way of. . . . Make straight in the desert a highway for our God"). Isaiah 40:3 is used as a basis to exhort faithful Qumran saints to depart from "the habitation of perverse men" (i.e., Jerusalem) (A. Dupont-Sommer, *The Essene Writings from Qumran*, trans. G. Vermes [Oxford: Blackwell, 1961], 92). In Isaiah the passage was an exhortation to come out of exile in Babylon, so that now first-century Jerusalem appears to replace Babylon as the place of exile (see likewise 1QS IX:19–20 for the same Isa. 40:3 reference used in the same way). Other texts in early Judaism indicating a continuing exile after the return from Babylon are CD-A I:3–11; Tob. 14:5–11; Bar. 3:6–8; 2 Macc. 1:27–29, on which, in addition to other references, see Wright, *New Testament and the People of God*, 268–72; Scott, "Restoration of Israel," 796–99, the latter discussing evidence in Judaism that the exile had completely ended and a strong stream of tradition that believed that it has not ended.

91. On which, see Scott, "Restoration of Israel," 800–805.

In light of this preceding discussion of the exile and restoration and its beginning fulfillment in Christ and the church, we can refocus on the Gospels, Acts, and Paul. Because the promises of restoration in the Gospels were coined in the language of "new exodus," Jesus is seen as launching the realization of those prophecies.[92] And since, as we have repeatedly seen, new exodus is nothing more than recapitulation of the primal creation, the Gospel writers and other NT witnesses can also refer to the fulfillment of the promises of restoration from captivity as the fulfillment of new creation in Jesus, his followers, and the first-century church, which had been prophesied in Isa. 40–66.[93] It is in this way that the portrayal of the church as restored Israel fits into the core part of the storyline concerning new creation. And the idea of the kingdom is not out of sight, since, as we have seen in earlier chapters, at the time of Israel's restoration its kingdom was to be reestablished by an end-time messianic leader (see, e.g., chap. 3 under the heading "The Latter Days in the Old Testament").

At this point, we must pause to consider three different responses to Jesus's coming in relation to whether the restoration prophecies began to reach decisive and irreversible fulfillment in his ministry. First, some do not see them finding significant fulfillment in Jesus until directly before, during, and after his final coming in a millennial kingdom. This position is known as "classical dispensationalism." Second, the modified position of "progressive dispensationalism" understands that significant fulfillment occurred in Jesus's first coming, but that the church experienced this fulfillment and not the nation Israel, and that Israel as a nation will experience the fulfillment later at the time of Christ's last coming, especially in a millennial kingdom. Although the church begins to fulfill Israel's prophecies, the church is not to be viewed as "Israel." Thus, progressive dispensationalists, like classical dispensationalists, maintain that there is a distinction between the church and Israel, and that the majority of ethnic Israel will be saved at the end of the age.

The progressive dispensational rationale for the church fulfilling these end-time prophecies to Israel, though not being considered eschatological Israel, is found in the following illustration.[94] Let us say that little Johnny Smith, who is

92. In addition to the relevant segments of N. T. Wright's work noted already, see Willard M. Swartley, *Israel's Scripture Traditions and the Synoptic Gospels: Story Shaping Story* (Peabody, MA: Hendrickson, 1994) 44–153; Rikki E. Watts, *Isaiah's New Exodus in Mark* (Grand Rapids: Baker Academic, 1997), both of which analyze the second-exodus patterns in the Synoptic Gospels.

93. On the dual notion of Christ's death and resurrection as fulfilling both the promises of new creation and the prophecies of Israel's restoration, see G. K. Beale, "The Old Testament Background of Reconciliation in 2 Corinthians 5–7 and Its Bearing on the Literary Problem of 2 Corinthians 4:14–7:1," *NTS* 35 (1989): 550–81; see also idem, "The Old Testament Background of Rev 3.14," *NTS* 42 (1996): 133–52.

94. Progressive dispensationalism is difficult to summarize because of the permutations of belief among scholars who claim this view. Thus, I am sure that not all progressive dispensationalists would want to embrace the following illustration, though I first heard it from a scholar who aligns himself with this school of thought. For representative discussions, see Saucy, *Progressive*

six years old, lives next door to my wife and me. Tragically, his parents die in a car crash, and my wife and I have Johnny come to live with us, though he does not change his name. We come to love him, and I decide to will part of my estate to him, as well as to my three biological children. When I die, Johnny receives part of my estate, but this does not make him an "ethnic" Beale. He receives part of my estate as Johnny Smith, and my children by birth receive part of my estate as Beales. Likewise, the church inherits the promises made to Israel, but they remain gentiles without being considered Israelites. A remnant of ethnic Israelites will believe in Christ during this time, and their inheritance of the promises will be as a part of the church. When Christ returns a final time, the majority of ethnic Israelites will also believe in him and so inherit the same promises as the church, but they will do so as ethnic Israelites and not as part of the church's fulfillment.[95]

A third view, in contrast to the two forms of dispensationalism, is that the fulfillment happened with the initial advent of Jesus, who as true Israel began to realize the promises. The church then participates in this fulfillment as the continuation of true Israel through its identification by faith with Jesus as the continuation of authentic Israel. According to this view, all that remains to be fulfilled is the consummation of these prophecies in a new heaven and earth, which will occur at Christ's final coming.

An illustration that can clarify this perspective is similar to that given above for progressive dispensationalism. Let us say again that little Johnny Smith lives next door to my wife and me. Tragically, his parents die in a car crash, and my wife and I legally adopt Johnny, and he comes to live with us with his name changed to "Johnny Beale." We come to love him, and since he is legally reckoned among our true children, I will part of my estate to him, as well as to my three biological children. When I die, Johnny receives part of my estate, and he receives it because legally he is a Beale child, as are my other children, though they are also "ethnic" Beales.

Likewise, the church inherits the promises made to Israel because it has been "adopted" by God, and its members are legally "adopted sons" and represented by Jesus Christ, the true Israel. Any ethnic Israelites who believe in Jesus are also considered to be true Israel and a part of the church, though it is not their bloodline that makes this so but rather their faith in Christ. This will be true

---

Dispensationalism; Craig A. Blaising and Darrell L. Bock, *Progressive Dispensationalism* (Grand Rapids: Baker Academic, 1993). Unfortunately, there is not space here to enter into a robust evaluation of this viewpoint, although I can say that the arguments in previous chapters and especially in the preceding chapter and the present one about the church being true Israel stand in conflict with progressive dispensationalism. The same is true about the following chapter on Israel's land promises beginning fulfillment in Christ and the church.

95. This will occur at the end of the so-called great tribulation at the final coming of Christ. I maintained earlier in this chapter that I have found no place in either of the Testaments that espouses a hope for the salvation of a majority of ethnic Israel at the very end of the age.

of all believers throughout the interadvent age, until Christ comes a second time to destroy the old cosmos and create a new one in which the prophecies that began fulfillment in him and in the church will be consummated.

Both illustrations about Johnny Smith are understandable, and they work as far as they go. The crucial question, of course, is this: which illustration does the data of the NT point to the most? The thesis of this chapter and book is that Jesus, summing up Israel in himself, begins to inherit the prophecies made to Israel, and that all who identify with him become adopted as true Israel (which, recall, is a corporate Adam) and, accordingly, inherit the promises as such. To identify the church as Israel is not a narrow or parochial identification, since, as I noted in earlier chapters, Israel itself as a "son of God" and "son of Adam" was a corporate Adam who was to represent true humanity on earth. And recall that Jesus's titles "Son of God" and "Son of Man" were Israelite and Adamic names. Accordingly, Christ as true Israel and the last Adam represents the church, so that the church becomes true eschatological Israel and part of the end-time Adam.[96] Thus, far from being a narrow name, "true Israel" really is a name that connotes true humanity.

96. On Israel and Christ as Adam figures, see the first part of chap. 13.

22

The Relationship of Israel's Land Promises to the Fulfillment of Israel's Restoration and New Creation Prophecies in Christ and the Church

One cannot think of Israel's restoration promises without thinking also of Israel's promised land. The two were inextricably linked most of the time by the OT prophets. At the time of their restoration from Babylonian exile, Israel was to be returned to the land, where they would build a massive temple and come into intimate fellowship with God, as well as experience other concomitant promises (which I have summarized in chap. 19).

But a problem arises when we try to discover in the NT how this land promise could have begun fulfillment in Christ and the church. When Christ comes and performs his saving and restorative work, he does not return believing people to a physical land as a mark of their redemption. Nor is there mention of Christians returning to Israel's promised land when the NT portrays the church as beginning to fulfill Israel's restoration promises. Such land promises appear absent. Redeemed people do not go to a geographical place to be redeemed; rather, they flee to Christ and God for their salvific restoration. Some texts, such as Matt. 5:5; Rom. 4:13, speak of Christ's followers as those who will inherit the earth (cf. Eph. 6:2–3).[1] There is also reference to Christians who will experience the "rest" that Israel should have experienced

1. The significance of this passage will be elaborated later in this chapter.

in the promised land, but here the "rest" is the focus, and the land of Israel appears to be typological of a rest that is spiritual. Likewise, Heb. 11:13–16 says that Abraham's ultimate hope was not in a literal land on the old earth but rather in a "city" that was "heavenly." However, none of these references appear to be related clearly to the promises of Israel's return to the promised land on this present earth. Furthermore, what references there are to the land in the NT seem to be spiritualized.

Thus, this is a hermeneutical problem in relating the OT promises to the NT. Have the land promises faded from a view of literal, physical fulfillment only to be realized in some spiritual way, so that at best these older promises were typological for inheriting spiritual salvation in Christ?

My contention in this section is that the land promises will be fulfilled in a physical form, but that the inauguration of this fulfillment is mainly spiritual until the final consummation in a fully physical new heaven and earth. The physical way that these land promises have begun fulfillment is that Christ himself introduced the new creation by his physical resurrection. In this connection, we will see that the Abrahamic promises concerning the land are promises to his "seed," referring ultimately to Israel's inheritance of the land. This explanation will be in line with the overall thrust of this book, that "as many as are the [OT] promises of God, in Him [Christ] they are yes" (2 Cor. 1:20). We have looked already at many of these promises and found that even in their OT context they included not only a physical dimension but also a spiritual one. And we have seen that these promises have begun spiritually and will be consummated physically in the final new creation. This two-stage fulfillment can be termed an "installment fulfillment," wherein we have seen that even the initial spiritual stage is "literal" in that the OT promise also had a literal spiritual dimension. For example, we saw that the promise of resurrection in the OT includes a person's spirit also being resurrected along with the body, though the NT sees this spiritual resurrection occurring first. Accordingly, this chapter will attempt to show that the land promises and their fulfillment are a crucial part of the storyline dealing with Jesus's resurrection as the already–not yet end-time new creation.

First, we will look at the most relevant passages about the land promises in the OT, and then I will direct attention to a reassessment of the NT evidence.

The Expected Universalization of the Old Testament Land Promises within the Old Testament Itself

The very inception of a land promise begins in Gen. 1–2. I have argued in my book *The Temple and the Church's Mission* (which is summarized in chap. 19) that Eden was a garden sanctuary and Adam was its high priest. Temples in the ancient world had images of the god of the temple placed in them. Adam was that image, placed in the Eden temple. His task was to "fill the earth" with God's glory as a divine image-bearer along with his progeny as image-bearers (this seems to be the implication of Gen. 1:26–28). Thus, he was to expand the borders of Eden, wherein was God's presence, and he and his progeny were to expand these borders until they circumscribed the entire earth, and so God's glory would thus be reflected throughout the entire earth through the image-bearers.[2]

The commission to Adam and Eve to multiply their offspring and to rule, subdue, and "fill the earth" was passed on to Noah and then repeatedly to the patriarchs and Israel. Consequently, the mantle of Adam's responsibility was placed on Abraham and his seed, Israel, so that they were considered to be a "corporate Adam." The nation was designed to represent true humanity. Starting with the patriarchs, the commission was mixed with a promise that it would be fulfilled at some point in a "seed," but Israel failed to carry out the commission. Thus, the promise was continually made that an eschatological time would come when this commission would be carried out in Israel. That part of the commission to expand Eden to cover the whole earth also continued, but now Israel's land became conceived of as Israel's Eden.[3] This description of Israel's land being like Eden was enhanced by the repeated descriptions of the "land flowing with milk and honey"[4] and luscious fruit (e.g., Num. 13:26–27; Deut. 1:25; Neh. 9:25).[5]

The key to understanding why Israel was to expand the borders of its land to cover the earth rests in the fact that Israel was a corporate Adam, and just as he was to expand the borders of Eden, wherein was the divine presence, so Israel was to do the same. In particular, Eden was not a mere piece of land but was the first tabernacle, which Adam was to expand. Likewise, Israel's land was to expand because at its center in Jerusalem was the temple, in which was the holy of holies, where God's presence dwelled. I discussed in chapter 19 (under the heading "Israel's Tabernacle in the Wilderness and Later Temple Were a Reestablishment of the Garden of Eden's Sanctuary") that Israel's temple symbolized the unseen and seen heavens (respectively the inner sanctuary and the holy place) and the earth (the courtyard). The purpose of the symbolism was to point to the end time, when God's special revelatory presence would break out of the holy of holies and fill the visible heavens and the earth. Accordingly, there are prophecies that describe how God's presence will break out from the holy of holies, cover Jerusalem (Isa. 4:4–6; Jer. 3:16–17; Zech. 1:16–2:11), then expand to cover all of Israel's land (Ezek. 37:25–28), and

---

2. For the full argument, see G. K. Beale, *The Temple and the Church's Mission: A Biblical Theology of the Dwelling Place of God*, NSBT 17 (Downers Grove, IL: InterVarsity, 2004).
3. As it is so called at several points in the OT: Gen. 13:10; Isa. 51:3; Ezek. 36:35; Joel 2:3.
4. This verbatim phrase occurs 14x in the Pentateuch and 5x elsewhere in the OT.
5. This notion is also enhanced by the rich descriptions of the abundantly fertile land of Canaan given in Deut. 8:7–9; 11:9–15.

finally cover the entire earth (Isa. 54:2–3; Dan. 2:34–35, 44–45). Strikingly, the passages from Jer. 3; Isa. 54; Dan. 2 make explicit allusions either back to the patriarchal promises or to Gen. 1:28 in discussing the expansion of the land. From the perspective of the OT writers, it is difficult to know whether this complete expansion was envisioned to occur through military means or through other, more peaceful ways (e.g., through the nations voluntarily bowing to Israel and its God). We know, at least, that Israel was to expand its beginning possession of the promised land through military means (cf. Deut. 9:1; 11:23; 12:29; 18:14). Yet other texts foresee a more peaceful means in the eschaton whereby the nations throughout the earth become subject to Israel (e.g., Amos 9:11–12; Isa. 2:3–4; 11:10–12), with the possible implication of Israel possessing their lands.

It is this expansive temple-land theology that underlies other prophecies of the universal expansion of Israel's land. Strikingly, though not in connection with the temple, at the time of the final resurrection of the dead (Isa. 26:16–19), which will coincide with the resurrected inhabiting the new creation, Isa. 26:15 prophesies, "You have increased the nation, O LORD, You have increased the nation, You are glorified; You have extended all the borders of the land." Thus, the allusion to Gen. 1:28 ("increase and multiply" and "fill the earth"), as it has no doubt been refracted through the Abrahamic promises, leads to the expansion of Israel's land. Amazingly, this cosmic expansion is directly linked to Israel's end-time resurrection, suggesting that the fulfillment of the Gen. 1:28 commission to expand occurs through the resurrection of people. This pattern of multiplying and filling the earth is the same one that we have observed in Gen. 1:28 and Gen. 2, where the commands in Gen. 1:28 are to be concretely carried out by expanding the Eden sanctuary. And we have observed this same Gen. 1–2 pattern in Israel's promised expansion over the earth and the expansion of the Jerusalem temple.

The notion of Israel's borders being expanded to cover the earth not only is implied in Isa. 26:18–19 ("deliverance for the earth" [see esp. the LXX] and "the earth will give birth to the departed spirits") but also is explicitly stated in Isa. 27:2–6. In this passage Israel is portrayed in the eschaton as a "vineyard of delight" (like the garden of Eden)[6] that God will protect and with which he will be at "peace"; this vineyard will expand to cover the whole earth: "In the days to come Jacob will take root, Israel will blossom and sprout; and they will fill the face of the earth with fruit" (Isa. 27:6). This echoes "be fruitful . . . and fill the earth" of Gen. 1:28.

Thus, the Abrahamic promises represent a major development from Gen. 1–2 in the anticipations for the expansion of Israel's land. Since my conclusion concerning Gen. 1–2 is that the sacred land of Eden was to be

---

6. Interestingly, the participial form of the noun for "delight" (ḥemed) occurs in descriptions of Eden in Gen. 2:9; 3:6.

enlarged to cover the entire creation, it would not be surprising to see this theme developed in the promises to the patriarchs. And indeed, this is exactly what we find. Although the initial form of the Abrahamic promise relates only to Canaan, it is placed in a global context: "all the families of the earth will be blessed" (Gen. 12:1–3). The next restatement (Gen. 13:14–17) still has the boundaries of Canaan in view, but it adds that God will make "your seed as the dust of the earth, so that if anyone can number the dust of the earth, then your seed can also be numbered" (13:16). This may be taken figuratively, so that the Israelite descendants will be quite numerous but still fit within the boundaries of the promised land. But because it is eschatological in nature, it is more likely that, while still figurative, it refers to a number of Israelites so large that they could not fit in the land.[7] If the latter is the case, then this passage suggests what has been explicitly stated in some of the above passages about Israel's end-time universalistic expansion. This idea also fits with the Gen. 1–2 idea of expanding the sacred space of Eden until Adam and Eve's progeny "fill the earth."

Subsequent developments of these patriarchal promises in the OT make more explicit the suggestive nature of the universalizing aspect of these promises. For example, Ps. 72:17 ("And let men bless themselves by him; let all nations call him blessed") develops the promise of Gen. 22:18 ("In your seed all the nations of the earth shall bless themselves").[8] This is significant because the one being blessed is the end-time Israelite king (the individualized seed of Abraham)[9] who will "rule from sea to sea, and from the river to the ends of the earth" (Ps. 72:8). This is an explicit widening of the original borders of the promised land, which had been set "from the Red Sea to the sea of the Philistines, and from the wilderness to the River [Euphrates]" (Exod. 23:31).[10] This is summarized in Gen. 15:18 as "from the river of Egypt as far as the great river, the river Euphrates." The psalm begins with the "river" (apparently of Egypt) but substitutes "the ends of the earth" for the "river Euphrates." Again, the patriarchal promise relating to Israel's land is universalized by the psalm. Zechariah 9:10 quotes from Ps. 72:8, developing the same idea about

7. The same idea is implied by Gen. 15:5 ("Count the stars, if you are able to count them. . . . So shall your seed be") and 22:17–18 ("I will greatly multiply your seed as the stars of the heavens, and as the sand which is on the seashore"). Genesis 28:14 directly connects multiplication to blessings for the whole earth: "Your seed shall also be like the dust of the earth, and you shall spread out to the west and to the east and to the north and to the south; and in you and in your seed shall all the families of the earth be blessed" (almost identical is Gen. 26:3–4).

8. For a persuasive argument that Ps. 72:17 alludes to Gen. 22:18, see C. John Collins, "Galatians 3:16: What Kind of Exegete Was Paul?," *TynBul* 54, no. 1 (2003): 75–86.

9. For the argument that the "seed" in Gen. 22:17b–18 is an individual kingly seed who represents the corporate "seed" (in 22:17a), see ibid., 84–86.

10. The only other place in the OT where the double mention of "sea" occurs together with "river" plus a geographical region is Deut. 3:16–17, which describes the borders of the land to be granted to the Reubenites and the Gadites.

Israel's eschatological king: "And His dominion will be from sea to sea, and from the River to the ends of the earth."

Psalm 2 is also similar to Ps. 72. God's promise to the Messiah (Ps. 2:2, 7) is to "give the nations as Your inheritance and the ends of the earth as Your possession" (2:8). The wording of "give an inheritance" (*nātan* + *naḥălâ*) in Deuteronomy is a typical expression used in God's promise of giving the land of Canaan to Israel (e.g., Deut. 4:21, 38; 12:9; 15:4; 19:10; 21:23; 24:4; 25:19; 26:1; 29:8). Likewise "possession" (*'ăḥuzzâ*) refers to Israel inheriting the land of promise (Gen. 17:8; Num. 32:32; Deut. 32:49). Here in Ps. 2 God's promise of the land of Canaan as a possession is extended to the "ends of the earth." And as in Ps. 72, the promise is made to an individual end-time Israelite king under whose rule the original boundaries of the promised land will be widened to cover the whole earth.

The Expected Universalization of the Old Testament Land Promises in Judaism

Perhaps not surprisingly, Judaism sometimes interpreted the Abrahamic land promises universally (*Mek. Beshallah* 25.27 on Exod. 14:31). Likewise, *Jub.* 32:16–19 reflects on Jacob's embryonic temple-building episode (Gen. 28:12–22), a development of the earlier Abrahamic promises, and makes it even more explicit that this was a temple construction: "Jacob planned to build up that place and to build a wall around the court and to sanctify it and to make it eternally holy for himself and his sons after him" (*Jub.* 32:16). *Jubilees* 32:18b–19 says, "Kings will come from you [Jacob]," and "they will rule everywhere that the tracks of mankind have been trod. And I [God] shall give to your seed all of the land under heaven and they will rule in all nations as they have desired. And after this all of the earth will be gathered together and they will inherit it forever." This is an interpretation of Gen. 28:14: "Your descendants will also be like the dust of the earth, and you will spread out to the west and to the east and to the north and to the south; and in you and in your descendants shall all the families of the earth be blessed." In addition, Gen. 28:14 is also interpreted by Isa. 54:2–3 as referring to Israel's land as being expanded beyond its borders into the nations of the world.

Likewise, in direct development of the Abrahamic promises, *Jub.* 19:15–25 refers to the uncountable patriarchal seed as "filling the earth" (vv. 21–22) and "serving to establish heaven and to strengthen the earth and to renew all of the lights which are above the firmament" (v. 25). Strikingly, Abraham's end-time seed will themselves be instrumental in establishing the new heavens and earth, not just filling the old borders of Israel's promised land. *Jubilees* 22 also refers to the Abrahamic blessings, which had already come on Adam and Noah (v. 13), being passed on to Jacob and his seed, which includes the promise that Jacob would "inherit all of the earth" (v. 14).[11]

Sirach 44:21 also describes Abraham's seed as those who will inherit the earth:

> Therefore the Lord assured him [Abraham] by an oath that the nations would be blessed through his posterity; that he would multiply him like the dust of the earth, and exalt his posterity like the stars, and cause them to <u>inherit from sea to sea and from the River to the ends of the earth.</u>

Significantly, the concluding phrase of this passage appears to quote Ps. 72:8 (or Zech. 9:10),[12] which applies the same universal cosmic wording to the latter-day Israelite king that here is applied to the corporate seed.

Thus, both the OT and Judaism viewed Israel's land promises as containing within themselves a notion that the boundaries of the promised land would be expanded to encompass the entire earth.

The Expected Universalization of the Old Testament Land Promises in the New Testament

Future References

All the explicit references to Israel's promised land in the NT refer in various ways to the final consummation of these promises in a new cosmos.

Matthew 5:5

Matthew 5:5 appears to be the first NT reference to Israel's land promise being understood to refer to the whole earth: "Blessed are the humble, for they shall inherit the earth." The verse is an allusion to Ps. 37:11: "But the humble will inherit the land." "Inherit the land" is a repeated phrase and notion in the psalm (vv. 3, 9, 18, 22, 29, 34). The inheritance of the land is placed in an eschatological context—for example, "their inheritance will be forever" (v. 18), and "the righteous will inherit the land, and dwell in it forever" (v. 29). In addition, the "wicked" will be decisively cut off, so that they will not inherit the eternal land (vv. 9–11, 28).

It is unlikely that Jesus is referring merely to Israel's promised land in Matt. 5:5. He appears to be interpreting the eternal land inheritance of the psalm through the lens of the other universalized OT land promises discussed above. What points further to such an interpretation is the parallel in the beatitudes that those "blessed" will inherit "the kingdom of heaven" (Matt. 5:3, 10).

---

11. *First Enoch* 5:7 speaks of the "elect" of the antediluvian generation as those who "shall inherit the earth."

12. See the discussion of Ps. 72:8 in the preceding section.

Thus, "earth" in verses 5 is parallel with "kingdom of heaven" in verses 3, 10, so that the "earth" here is wider than the promised land's old borders and is coextensive with "the kingdom of heaven." This is likely a way to say that the "blessed" will inherit the new heaven and earth and not some mere ethereal heavenly realm.

A striking parallel to this idea in Matt. 5 is found in *m. Sanh.* 10.1: "All Israelites have a share in the world to come, for it is written, <u>Thy people also shall be all righteous, they shall inherit the land forever; the branch of my planting, the work of my hands that I may be glorified.</u>" The "world to come" refers to the new creation, which Israelites will inherit. This statement is supported by appeal to Isa. 60:21:

> Then all your people will be righteous;
> They will possess the land forever,
> The branch of My planting,
> The work of My hands,
> That I may be glorified.

In the context of Isa. 60:21, the "land" refers to the "city of Zion" (v. 14), its "gates" (vv. 11, 18), and the "land" of Israel (v. 18). Isaiah 65:17–18 and 66:20–22 inextricably link end-time Jerusalem with the coming new creation. That Israel will "possess the land forever" (in the second line of Isa. 60:21) must refer to the initial mention of the "world to come" and not merely the localized promised land. Thus, this mishnaic passage sees that the "land" that Israel will inherit is bound up with the entire new creation.

ROMANS 4:13

This verse says, "For the promise to Abraham or to his descendants that he would be heir of the <u>world</u> was not through the Law, but through the righteousness of faith." Here the word is not *gē* (as it is in Matt. 5:5), which can mean "land" or "earth," but *kosmos*, which indicates the entire earth, often including the starry heavens. Paul's statement here is a straightforward universalization of the Abrahamic land promises. The rationale underlying Paul's worldwide view is most probably the various OT texts observed above in which Israel's promise of the land was viewed to concern the whole world (e.g., Ps. 2:8; 72:8; Isa. 26:19; 27:6; 54:2–3). And we saw that these passages themselves were allusions back to the Abrahamic land promises or back to Gen. 1:28 (in the case of Isa. 27:6).[13]

---

13. Ephesians 6:1–3 is similar to Matt. 5. There Paul says children should obey and honor their parents, "so that it may be well with you, and that you may live long on the earth." This is part of a quotation of Exod. 20:12, which promises obedient children that they "may live long in the land" of Israel's promised inheritance in Canaan. Paul clearly universalizes it, which is not surprising, since he so straightforwardly does so in Rom. 4:13. Paul's reference to the earth

Hebrews 11:8–16

By faith Abraham, when he was called, obeyed by going out to a place which he was to receive for an inheritance; and he went out, not knowing where he was going. By faith he lived as an alien in the land of promise, as in a foreign land, dwelling in tents with Isaac and Jacob, fellow heirs of the same promise; for he was looking for the city which has foundations, whose architect and builder is God. By faith even Sarah herself received ability to conceive, even beyond the proper time of life, since she considered Him faithful who had promised. Therefore there was born even of one man, and him as good as dead at that, as many descendants as the stars of heaven in number, and innumerable as the sand which is by the seashore. All these died in faith, without receiving the promises, but having seen them and having welcomed them from a distance, and having confessed that they were strangers and exiles on the earth. For those who say such things make it clear that they are seeking a homeland [*patris*]. And indeed if they had been thinking of that country from which they went out, they would have had opportunity to return. But as it is, they desire a better country, that is, a heavenly one. Therefore God is not ashamed to be called their God; for He has prepared a city for them.

Again, the Abrahamic land promise is viewed as having reference ultimately not to the land of Canaan (they were not "thinking of that country from which they went out" [v. 15]) but rather to "the city which has foundations" (v. 10), a "heavenly one" and "a city prepared for them" (v. 16), which is their ultimate "homeland" (v. 14). This city is "Mount Zion . . . the city of the living God, the heavenly Jerusalem" (Heb. 12:22), "for here we do not have a lasting city, but we are seeking the city which is to come" (Heb. 13:14). This coming "city" is not a mere localized city; it is equivalent to the coming "homeland" (Heb. 11:14). And this "homeland" is none other than the entire coming new earth,[14] which is confirmed from considering the concept of the new creation in relation to the eschatological new Jerusalem in Rev. 21:1–22:5.[15]

---

here probably refers to the new eternal earth. The fifth commandment, originally referring to long life in the promised land, appears to be typologically applied to Christians living long on the new earth (in the light of Eph. 1:14; 4:30, which likely include reference to the final resurrection of saints and their resurrected life in the age of consummation).

14. Hebrews 3–4 may also be relevant to consider in connection to Heb. 11. Here the "rest" that Joshua could have given Israel and that later generations of Israel could have received is carried over and promised to the readers of Hebrews, which, if they persevere in faith, they will receive as an eschatological reward of inheritance.

15. Much of the above discussion of the "land" throughout the OT and the NT is a summary of Mark Dubis, "The Land in Biblical Perspective" (paper presented at the Annual Meeting of the Evangelical Theological Society, Valley Forge, PA, November 17, 2005), particularly the discussions of the Abrahamic promises concerning the implications of an innumerable multitude; Ps. 2; Ps. 72; the Jewish texts (though the elaboration of these passages is mine); Matt. 5; Rom. 4; 8 (directly below); Heb. 1 (directly below); Heb. 3–4; 11; and Rev. 11:15 (though elaboration is mine). The rest is based on my own work, including sections from Beale, *Temple*, which is also summarized in chap. 19.

REVELATION 21:1–22:5

At the beginning of chapter 19 I posed a question about why the concluding vision of Revelation portrayed the new creation (21:1, 5) as a temple (21:3 [more precisely, a holy of holies; see vv. 16–18]), as a city (21:2, 10–27), and as a garden of Eden (22:1–3). At first glance, this looks like bizarre apocalyptic allegory or spiritualization. But I took pains to show that John is combining at least three OT promises into one. First, the original plan for the garden of Eden in Gen. 1–2 was that its borders would be expanded worldwide by Adam. Second, Eden was also a garden temple that Adam, the high priest, was to expand to cover the entire cosmos. Third, some of the eschatological promises of the city of Jerusalem portrayed it as expanding to cover the whole land of Israel and even the entire earth. The expansion was to occur because God's special presence in Jerusalem's temple was to break out of the holy of holies and spread over the city, and then the temple-city was described in places as spreading out to cover the promised land, and then the promised land widened out to include all the earth.[16]

Accordingly, John's portrayal of the entire new creation as a city, a temple, and a garden is exactly what the OT in various places anticipated. Thus, the original design of Eden as a garden-temple (and of Israel's later temple as a recapitulated model of the Eden tabernacle) and the city, Jerusalem, is pictured as being fulfilled in this final apocalyptic vision.[17] God's intent all along was to make the entire creation his holy of holies and his dwelling place. This is much related to Israel's universalized land promises. We saw earlier in this chapter that the promised land was to cover the earth, and we have seen that the likely reason for such prophecies in the OT was that Israel was a corporate Adam whose land was the new Eden, and that its design was just like Eden's: to be expanded over the entire earth by its faithful people. As the holy of holies, patterned also after Eden, was to expand to cover the city of Jerusalem, then the temple-city would widen to cover the land, and, finally, the temple-land would be amplified to surround the earth. The original Eden, Israel's old temple, old land, and old city, never reached the universal goal for which they were designed. As such, they became imperfect typological realities pointing forward to a time when these would again become eschatological realities, whose design would reach their final goal.

16. See also W. D. Davies, *The Gospel and the Land: Early Christianity and Jewish Territorial Doctrine* (Berkeley: University of California Press, 1974), 150–54. Davies says that in both the OT and Judaism the temple, Jerusalem, and Israel's land were inseparable realities in that the temple could be seen as the quintessence of Jerusalem and Jerusalem could be viewed as an extension of the temple, and Jerusalem became the quintessence of the land and the land an extension of Jerusalem; thus, the hope for each of these three things became absorbed into one another.

17. The mention in Rev. 14:1 of "Zion" in the picture of the Lamb and his saints "standing on Mount Zion" is virtually interchangeable with the "new Jerusalem" in Rev. 21 and has the same future, consummative notion.

I will not rehearse the exegetical evidence for this view of Rev. 21–22, since it was summarized above in chapter 19.[18]

One other text in Revelation prophesies that the whole world will become the inheritance of Christ: "The kingdom of the world has [will] become the kingdom of our Lord, and of his Christ; and he will reign forever and ever" (11:15). Not coincidentally, this text is an allusion to Ps. 2:2, 8, which, we have seen just above, predicted that Israel's Messiah would inherit the whole world in fulfillment of the original intent of Israel's land promises.

"Already and Not Yet" References to the Land Promises

Mention of the inauguration of the fulfillment of Israel's land promises is not directly stated, but the biblical-theological notion of it is likely present. On a conceptual level, since the land promises are fulfilled consummately in the new heavens and earth, and since Jesus's resurrection launched an inception of the new creation (e.g., 2 Cor. 5:17), then it is in Jesus as the bridgehead of the new creation that the land promises also begin realization.

HEBREWS 1:2

Hebrews 1:2 shows that at Jesus's first coming, God "spoke to us in His Son, whom He appointed as inheritor of all things, through whom He also made the world." That the "all things" includes a reference to the world (implicitly in renewed form)[19] is likely for two reasons: (1) it is directly followed by "the world," which may have some kind of link to the "all things"; (2) the statement in Heb. 1:2 is an allusion to Ps. 2:7–8, discussed earlier in this chapter: "You are My <u>Son</u>. . . . I will surely give the nations as Your <u>inheritance</u>, and the very ends of <u>the earth as Your possession</u>." Thus, according to Heb. 1:2, "in these last days"—that is, at Jesus's first coming—Jesus has appeared as God's "Son," and God during that time "appointed [Jesus] heir of all things." The likely time of this appointment to inherit the earth as God's Son was at Christ's resurrection, perhaps on analogy with Rom. 1:4: Jesus was "declared with power to be the Son of God by the resurrection of the dead." I have argued in depth in earlier chapters that this resurrection is the beginning of the new creation, which brings this Rom. 1 text close to Heb. 1:2. Accordingly, Heb. 1:2 explains that the inception of the land promise, which Ps. 2:8 extends to the whole world, has begun in Christ, at least by formal legal appointment in history. Since Jesus's resurrection is the beginning of the new creation,[20] as noted

---

18. Which, I want to reiterate, is itself a summary of Beale, *Temple*, where much more in-depth exegetical evidence is adduced throughout.

19. An implicit reference to a renovated world may be pointed to further in Heb. 1:10–12 and 12:26–28.

20. Note that *Midr. Ps.* 2.9 interprets Ps. 2:7 ("Today I have begotten You") to mean "I must create the Messiah—a new creation." The Talmud (*b. Sukkah* 52a) understands Ps. 2:7 to be a

at various points throughout the NT, the consummative cosmic land promises begin in his resurrection as the emerging hillock of the coming renovation of the world (on which, note Heb. 13:20: "God . . . who brought up from the dead the great Shepherd of the sheep . . . Jesus our Lord").

ROMANS 8

In a preceding section we saw that Rom. 4:13 affirmed that Abraham was said to "be heir [*klēronomos*] of the world" (see the antithesis of this in 4:14, where the same word "heir" is used). Romans 8:17 develops this reference: "and if children, heirs [*klēronomoi*] also, heirs [*klēronomoi*] of God and fellow heirs [*synklēronomoi*] with Christ, if indeed we suffer with Him so that we may also be glorified with Him." The link between 4:13–14 and 8:17 is evident in that these are the only passages in Romans where this Greek word for "heir" occurs. Of what are believers "heirs" in Rom. 8? Verses 18–23 answer:

> For I consider that the sufferings of this present time are not worthy to be compared with the glory that is to be revealed to us. For the anxious longing of the creation waits eagerly for the revealing of the sons of God. For the creation was subjected to futility, not willingly, but because of Him who subjected it, in hope that the creation itself also will be set free from its slavery to corruption into the freedom of the glory of the children of God. For we know that the whole creation groans and suffers the pains of childbirth together until now. And not only this, but also we ourselves, having the first fruits of the Spirit, even we ourselves groan within ourselves, waiting eagerly for our adoption as sons, the redemption of our body.

The final bodily resurrection of believers is expressed in verse 19 ("revealing of the sons of God") and verse 23 ("the redemption of our body"). Likewise, "the glory" to come upon Christians is another way of speaking of this last resurrection (vv. 18, 21). Their physical resurrection through the Spirit will occur in the same way that Christ's resurrection happened (see 8:11). This resurrection is seen as the linchpin of the consummate renewal of the entire creation (vv. 19, 21), so that the physical resurrection is another way of talking about the final stage of the new creation of Christians. Thus, at least part of what they will inherit as "heirs" is a resurrection body that is part of the new creation, which is the key to how the rest of creation "will be set free from its slavery to corruption" (v. 21). That they are heirs also of the entire creation is suggested by 8:32, where the saints' identification with Christ means that God will "with Him [Christ] freely give us all things."

The reference to "heirs" in Rom. 4:13–14 and Rom. 8:17 likely indicates that the future hope of the believers' bodily resurrection and of the renewal

---

reference to the coming resurrection of the Messiah. Psalm 2:7 elsewhere in the NT is viewed to be fulfilled in Christ's resurrection (Acts 13:33).

of the cosmos is rooted in the promise that Abraham and his seed would be "heir of the world." A further link with the promise to Abraham is his belief that he would have a "seed," which entailed a belief in God, "who gives life to the dead and calls into being that which does not exist" (Rom. 4:17). In fact, Rom. 4:17 and 8:11 are the only two places in all of Paul's writings where the combination of "give life" (*zōopoieō*) and "dead" (*nekros*) appear: "He who raised Jesus from the <u>dead</u> will also <u>give life</u> to your mortal bodies" (Rom. 8:11). This points further to 8:11, 18–23 being a development of 4:13–14, 17. Thus, Abraham's faith that his seed would inherit the world included a faith in God's ability to raise the dead, an idea that is eschatologically developed in Rom. 8.[21]

This longed-for future resurrection has already begun in an unseen but nevertheless real way, since the Spirit has entered into believers and has begun end-time renovation of their inner beings: "Though the body is dead because of sin, yet the spirit is alive because of righteousness" (Rom. 8:10 [cf. 8:6, 13]). Believers now have "the first fruits of the Spirit." That is, the Spirit has begun the work of resurrection and new creation within them even before the final bodily resurrection.[22] Accordingly, the land promises, which were expected to have a universal scope in the OT, are seen by implication in Rom. 8 to begin in Christ, the heir (cf. Gal. 3:16–18), and also in believers who identify with his resurrection and become heirs (cf. also Gal. 3:29) and begin to experience part of their new-creational inheritance through their resurrection existence.

Ephesians 1:13–14

In Him, you also, after listening to the message of truth, the gospel of your salvation—having also believed, you were sealed in Him with the Holy Spirit of promise, who is given as a down payment of our inheritance, with a view to the redemption of God's own possession, to the praise of His glory.

This passage contains the language that the OT uses to refer to Israel's inheritance of the promised land. Ephesians 1:3–14 sets redemption in Christ against the backdrop of Israel's redemption:

1. God chose Israel to be sons (e.g., Deut. 4:37; 10:15; cf. Eph. 1:3–6);
2. God redeemed Israel by means of the Passover lamb's blood (e.g., Exod. 15:13; Deut. 15:15; cf. Eph. 1:7–12);
3. the Spirit worked among the people of Israel and brought them to begin to inherit the promised land (e.g., Neh. 9:20; Isa. 63:14 + Deut. 3:28; 4:38; 15:4; cf. Eph. 1:13–14).

21. It is likely not coincidental that, as we observed earlier in this chapter, Isa. 26:15–19 linked the fulfillment of the "multiplying and increasing" of Gen. 1:28 through its reiterations in the patriarchal promises to the resurrection of the dead in the eschaton.

22. On this inaugurated aspect of resurrection, see chap. 9, esp. under the heading "Resurrection in Romans."

The reference in Eph. 1:13–14 to the Spirit as "a down payment of our inheritance [*klēronomia*]" likely echoes the promised inheritance of the promised land, which Israel never completely possessed (note that *klēronomia* is repeatedly used in the LXX of the Pentateuch to refer to Israel's land of inheritance). That Christians have begun to possess this inheritance is apparent from Eph. 1:11: "we have obtained an inheritance." This is confirmed further from 1:13–14, which says that the possession of this inheritance is evident from believers having been "sealed in Him [the resurrected Christ] by means of the Holy Spirit of promise," who is "a down payment of our inheritance." That is, the Spirit himself is viewed as the very beginning of this inheritance and not just a guarantee of the promise of its coming. The Spirit, who would be present fully throughout the future new cosmos, has entered in part into believers, so that they have begun to obtain the inheritance of the new earth. The Spirit's presence in believers likely also included reference to their beginning resurrection, since, as we have seen earlier, the Spirit was the agent of resurrection. If so, part of the inheritance that saints are receiving in the present is their beginning participation in resurrection existence, which will be consummated at the end of time in the final form of the new creation of their bodies in the midst of a newly created cosmos.[23] This is parallel to Rom. 8:23, where saints have "the first fruits of the Spirit," which at least includes the Spirit's work of producing in them incipient resurrection life, which we saw earlier in this chapter was part of what they will inherit more fully at the end of time.

COLOSSIANS 1:12–14

. . . giving thanks to the Father, who has qualified us to share in the inheritance of the saints in Light. For He rescued us from the domain of darkness, and transferred us to the kingdom of His beloved Son, in whom we have redemption, the forgiveness of sins.

This segment of Col. 1 forms part of the prayer begun in verse 9. Paul begins by praying that the readers will be "filled" with God's wisdom so that they "will walk in a manner worthy of the Lord, to please Him in all respects" (v. 10a). This goal is to be reached by means of "bearing fruit . . . and increasing in the knowledge of God" and being "strengthened with all power, . . . giving thanks to the Father" (vv. 10b–11). Verses 12b–14 give the reason for the thanksgiving, which is rooted in the language of Israel's exodus and subsequent inheritance of the promised land.

While there is not likely one OT passage in mind about the exodus and land inheritance, the broad tradition describing Israel's exodus appears to have influenced the wording of Col. 1:12–14, which is a pattern that we just observed

---

23. This is also part of the idea included in Eph. 4:30: "in whom [the Spirit] you were sealed for the day of redemption."

in Eph. 1:13–14. "In Christ" the believers "have redemption" (*apolytrōsis*) (Col. 1:14), and they have been "delivered from" (*rhyomai* + *ek*) bondage to evil (Col. 1:13). Likewise, Israel had been "delivered from" bondage of Egypt and "redeemed" (see *rhyomai* + *ek* and *lytroō* in Exod. 6:6 LXX).[24] Interestingly, the second-exodus prophecies of Israel's deliverance from exile also employ the terminology of "redemption" (Isa. 44:22, 23, 24; 51:11; 52:3; 62:12; cf. 41:14; 43:1, 14).

In addition, prophecies of the second exodus use the language of "bringing [Israel] out of darkness" (*skotos*).[25] These prophecies also picture Israel as being restored from the "darkness" (*skotos*) of exile into "light" (*phōs*) (Isa. 9:2 [9:1 LXX]; 42:6b–7, 16; 58:10; 60:1–3), which may be a development of the contrasting "darkness" (*skotos*) and "light" (*phōs*) that was part of the narrative of the first exodus (Exod. 10:21–23; 14:20). The Israelites deliverance from Egypt also had qualified them to become "saints" (*hagios*) (Exod. 22:31 [22:30 LXX]; Lev. 11:44–45; 19:2; 20:7, 26; 21:6; Num. 15:40; 16:3) and to receive a "share of the inheritance" in Canaan. Indeed, the combination of "share" and "inheritance" (*meris* + *klēros*) appears fifteen times in this respect in the LXX of Numbers, Deuteronomy, and Joshua (often with respect to the Levites, who had "no portion" or "inheritance" in the land as did the other tribes [e.g., Deut. 10:9]).

Just as the Israelites had been "delivered from" Egyptian slavery, had become "saints," and then the tribes received "a share of the inheritance" in the promised land, so likewise the church was "delivered from" (*rhyomai* + *ek*; *apolytrōsis*) a greater bondage than that of Egypt (satanic "darkness," *skotos*) and became "qualified . . . for a share" in a greater "inheritance of the saints in light" (*meris* + *klēros* + *hagios* + *phōs*).[26] This inheritance was none other than "the kingdom of [God's] beloved Son" (Col. 1:13).

What inspired Paul's application of exodus imagery to the church's salvation? Presumably, he sees the people of God in Christ as undergoing an exodus like Israel's out of Egypt but on an escalated scale (beginning spiritually in this age and consummated with physical resurrection). Paul was likely also directed to such an application because of Isaiah's second-exodus prophecies, which utilized and developed some of the same language as the first exodus. Elsewhere in his epistles Paul views prophecies of Israel's second exodus and restoration to the land as having begun fulfillment in Christ's first coming

24. See also Deut. 7:8; 13:5 (13:6 LXX); 2 Sam. 7:23; 1 Chron. 17:21; Ps. 106:10 (105:10 LXX); Add. Esth. 13:16 (4:17g LXX [Rahlfs edition]); cf. Deut. 24:18; ten other times the LXX uses *lytroō* to refer to Israel's redemption out of Egypt; so also Exod. 14:30 (*rhyomai* + *ek*). Several commentators also see Israel's deliverance from Egypt as background.

25. See also Ps. 107:10–14 (106:10–14 LXX), where in v. 2 the synonym for "lead" is "redeem" (*lytroō*); Isa. 42:7; cf. 42:16; 49:9.

26. Several commentators also see the phrase "share in the inheritance" in Col. 1:12 to have its background in the allotment of land to Israel in Canaan.

and in the formation of the earliest Christian churches.[27] Additionally, Paul's awareness of OT restoration themes is apparent from his description of his own call in terms of second-exodus language of Isa. 42:7, 16 (noted above) together with wording uniquely similar to Col. 1:12–14: "to open their eyes so that they may turn from darkness to light and from the dominion of Satan to God, that they may receive forgiveness of sins and an <u>inheritance</u> among those who have been sanctified by faith in [Christ]" (Acts 26:18). In fact, it is possible that Paul is reflecting on this aspect of his call in Col. 1:12–14. Note here that the notion of "inheritance" in Acts 26:18 is included in Paul's commission to be an agent in carrying out the new exodus.

Paul uses the exodus images either analogically or, more likely, typologically; if the latter, then Israel's redemptive historical pattern of deliverance from Egypt and receiving an inheritance in the promised land prefigured that of eschatological Israel, the church.[28] Paul does not appear to be the only one of his time to have conducted such a typological exegesis. Early Judaism applied the promise of Israel's "share of the inheritance" in Canaan to an eternal, end-time reward, which was likely also done according to a typological rationale.[29] Paul seems to see the promised inheritance of Canaan to have its end-time inaugurated fulfillment in those who believe in Christ and thus are "in him" (Col. 1:14), so that they "have been raised up with Christ, . . . where Christ is, seated at the right hand of God" (Col. 3:1). As in the case of Acts 2, the geography of David's eschatological throne (at God's "right hand" [v. 34]) is in heaven in Christ, with whom believers are identified. This throne will find its ultimate place of real estate in the consummated new cosmos, so that this is not an allegorizing or wild spiritualizing of the end-time land promises of the OT. If so, then the reference to parts of the fulfillment of the

27. See G. K. Beale, "The Old Testament Background of Reconciliation in 2 Corinthians 5–7 and Its Bearing on the Literary Problem of 2 Corinthians 4:14–7:1," *NTS* 35 (1989): 550–81; James M. Scott, *Adoption as Sons of God: An Exegetical Investigation into the Background of* ΥΙΟΘΕΣΙΑ *in the Pauline Corpus*, WUNT 2/48 (Tübingen: Mohr Siebeck, 1992), 167–71, 179; Sylvia C. Keesmaat, "Exodus and the Intertextual Transformation of Tradition in Romans 8:14–30," *JSNT* 54 (1994): 29–56. Indeed, Paul has just made a combined allusion in Col. 1:9 to significant events associated with the first and the second exodus (respectively Exod. 31:3 and Isa. 11:2 [cf. 11:3–16]). In the preceding two chapters especially I have labored to make this point about the beginning fulfillment of Israel's restoration prophecies in the church.

28. In support of a typological use and qualifications of such a use, see G. K. Beale, "Colossians," in *Commentary on the New Testament Use of the Old Testament*, ed. G. K. Beale and D. A. Carson (Grand Rapids: Baker Academic, 2007), 848–50, on which this section on Col. 1:12–14 has been based.

29. E.g., James Dunn (*The Epistles to the Colossians and to Philemon: A Commentary on the Greek Text*, NIGTC [Grand Rapids: Eerdmans, 1996], 76–77) adduces 1QS XI:7–8 (God "has given them an inheritance in the lot of the saints") as a striking parallel to Col. 1:9–12; similarly 1QH[a] XIX:11b–12; note also Wis. 5:5 ("his inheritance is among the saints"); *T. Ab.* [A] 13:13 (on which, see Petr Pokorný, *Colossians: A Commentary*, trans. Siegfried S. Schatzmann [Peabody, MA: Hendrickson, 1991], 52, including additional references).

land promises (in this case, the geography of the throne of David and Israel's "share" in the "inheritance") that never were fulfilled in the OT epoch are not merely typological but rather are fulfilled in an ultimate straightforward manner in the literal land of the new cosmos, which is the new Jerusalem, new Israel, new temple, and new Eden. This consummate fulfillment will occur after the destruction of the old heavens and earth (Rev. 21:1–5). What Israel never achieved, the church in the resurrected Christ has begun to attain and will consummately possess in the future.

Other New Testament Passages Pertaining to the Inauguration of the Land Promises

Bruce Waltke has helpfully observed that because the NT rarely uses the term "land," very closely related terms must be studied that refer to significant parts of Israel's real estate in the land—terms such as "Jerusalem," "Zion," "temple," and "throne of David."[30] I have discussed the first three of these with respect to their final fulfillment in the new heaven and new earth. I have already argued that the temple prophecies began to be fulfilled in Jesus and the church (see chap. 19). The same is true with the end-time Jerusalem. Paul says that "the Jerusalem above," the true latter-day Jerusalem, is "our mother" (Gal. 4:26). Likewise, Heb. 12:22 says believers "have come to Mount Zion and to the city of the living God, the heavenly Jerusalem." In some way, Christians have reached this destination, even while still journeying as exiles on the earth (Heb. 11:13). How can this be so? It is because Christ has already become true Israel and thus also the "new Jerusalem," and all who identify with him likewise become part of the new Jerusalem. Revelation 3:12 says that Christ now possesses a "new name" that is equated with "the name of the city of My God, the new Jerusalem."

That Christ has begun to fulfill and be the beginning of the prophesied end-time Israel and new Jerusalem is evident in that the reference to a "new name" in Rev. 2:17; 3:12 is an allusion to Isaiah's repeated prophecy that in the eschaton God's people will have a "new name" (62:2; 65:15). In particular, Isa. 62:2 is about Israel's new standing in the future (cf. *kaleō* ["to call"] + *to onoma sou to kainon* ["new name"] in this text, as well as in 56:5).[31] The saints

---

30. Bruce K. Waltke, *An Old Testament Theology: An Exegetical, Canonical, and Thematic Approach* (Grand Rapids: Zondervan, 2007), 559.

31. Cf. perhaps Isa. 56:5, which probably also is evoked in Rev. 3:12 together with 62:2; 65:15, especially in view of the Jewish attitude toward gentile Christians in Philadelphia and the emphasis on permanent residence in the eternal temple mentioned at the beginning of Rev. 3:12: "Let not the foreigner who has joined himself to the LORD say, 'The LORD will surely separate me from His people.' . . . To [those who] hold fast My covenant, to them I will give in My house and within My walls a memorial, and a name better than that of sons and daughters; I will give them an everlasting name which will not be cut off" (Isa. 56:3–5). For "memorial," the LXX has the gentile being given "a named place." Thus, Rev. 3:12, in light of its OT background, is

of Israel are, by metonymy, referred to as "Zion" and "Jerusalem" (62:1), which "will be called by a new name" (not different, personal new names). There, the "new name" designates Israel's future kingly status (62:3) and restoration to Yahweh's covenantal presence (62:4a; cf. the same significance for "name" in 56:4–8; 65:15–19), and it especially emphasizes end-time Jerusalem's new marital relationship with Yahweh: he will "delight in her," and Jerusalem's land will be called "married" (cf. 62:4b–5, which also refers to Israel as a "bride" and God as the "bridegroom"). And just as Yahweh will come into an intimate covenant relationship with "Jerusalem," so will her "sons marry" her (62:5b). This probably explains why Christians in Rev. 2:17 also receive a "new name": they are identified with Christ, who first began to fulfill Isaiah's prophecy of the true end-time renewed Jerusalem (= the "new name"). Indeed, Rev. 3:12 says, for the same reason, that written upon believers who "overcome" will be "the name of My God, and the name of the city of My God, the new Jerusalem . . . and My new name."

With respect to the expansion of the true Jerusalem and its implications for the expansion of the temple, we read in the conversation between Jesus and the Samaritan woman in John 4:19–24,

> The woman said to Him, ". . . Our fathers worshiped in this mountain, and you people say that in Jerusalem is the place where men ought to worship." Jesus said to her, "Woman, believe me, an hour is coming when neither in this mountain nor in Jerusalem will you worship the Father. You worship what you do not know; we worship what we know, for salvation is from the Jews. But an hour is coming, and now is, when the true worshipers will worship the Father in Spirit and truth; for such people the Father seeks to be his worshipers. God is [the] Spirit, and those who worship him must worship in Spirit and truth."

Now, true worshipers do not worship in any one particular place—Jerusalem—but "must worship in Spirit and truth." The place of true worship has been universalized to any place where the Spirit resides in true worshipers. "Spirit" is to be capitalized in this phrase because it likely refers to the end-time Spirit who was prophesied to come, on which Jesus has just elaborated in 4:10–18 through the image of "living water." Jesus later explicitly identifies this "living water" with the giving of the Spirit (7:37–39).[32] "Truth" in 4:24 probably includes the notion that in Jesus the truth of eschatological realities that have begun have come to possess a greater realization than their OT equivalents.[33] Jerusalem and the temple, which in the OT pointed to the whole renewed earth,

---

another example of Jerusalem, Zion, and the temple being overlapping realities, combining all three significant places of the land into one reality.

32. Here too "living water" is identified with having its source in the prophesied end-time temple (on which, see Beale, *Temple*, 197–200).

33. E.g., Jesus is "true bread [or 'manna'] out of heaven" (John 6:32) and the "true vine" (John 15:1), of which Israel was only a faint foreshadowing (Ps. 80:8–16; Isa. 5:2; Jer. 2:21; Ezek.

have finally begun to reach their universal design. This design will be finally completed in the whole new creation depicted in Rev. 21:1–22:5.

And why has this universalization now begun? It is because Christ's first coming has inaugurated the new creation, which for him individually was climaxed with his resurrection, which established the true temple (John 2:19–22). As a consequence of his resurrection, he gave his life-giving Spirit to empower his people on earth to begin to partake of the new creation (e.g., John 20:19–23; Acts 2:29–36). These invisible, spiritual, new-creational realities will be completed in the physical and visible land of the entire earth. But recall that the beginning of the new creation in Christ himself is physical, in that he was resurrected with the body that he will have forever in the new creation. Also recall that for believers their new-creational resurrection begins by being raised from spiritual death to new-creational life (John 5:24–29). This spiritual phase of their resurrection, which will be followed by physical resurrection at the last day, is still a beginning literal fulfillment, since the OT resurrection prophecies (e.g., Dan. 12:2) predicted a literal resurrection of the whole person, both spiritually and physically.

Similarly, that 1 Pet. 2:4–7 depicts Christ and his people as part of the temple is also an inauguration of the land promises, especially since this is an inauguration of the prophecy in Isa. 28:16 that the temple "cornerstone" would be laid in "Zion."[34] It is not coincidental that Judaism believed that the temple and Jerusalem were the center point of the earth; and now Jesus and his people have begun to take that position as the bridgehead of the new temple, new Jerusalem, and new creation.[35]

Finally, comment is needed on the prophesied "throne of David." David's old throne was located as a specific part of Israel's geography, but the NT prophecies of the reestablishment of David's throne in the eschaton have begun in Christ through his resurrection and ascension. Acts 2:29–36 is one of the NT passages expressing this notion most clearly. Peter says,

> Brethren, I may confidently say to you regarding the patriarch David that he both died and was buried, and his tomb is with us to this day. And so, because he was a prophet and knew that God had sworn to him with an oath to seat one of his descendants on his throne, he looked ahead and spoke of the resurrection of the Christ, that He was neither abandoned to Hades, nor did His flesh suffer decay. This Jesus God raised up again, to which we are all witnesses. Therefore having been exalted to the right hand of God, and having received from the

---

17:6–10; Hos. 10:1); with respect to the latter, Jesus fulfills the latter-day prophecies about Israel being made a fruitful vine forever (e.g., Hos. 14:7; Mic. 4:4; cf. Isa. 27:2–6).

34. Note that, in addition to the temple identification in 1 Pet. 2, the "cornerstone" in Isa. 28:16 is part of a prophesied temple. This is evident in that 28:16 is an intertextual development of 8:13–16, which refers to God as a "sanctuary" who is to be trusted ("feared"), and who is pictured as a "stone."

35. For Jewish references in support of this, see Beale, *Temple*, 333–34.

Father the promise of the Holy Spirit, He has poured forth this which you both see and hear. For it was not David who ascended into heaven, but he himself says:

> "The Lord said to my Lord,
> 'Sit at My right hand,
> until I make Your enemies a footstool for Your feet.'"

Therefore let all the house of Israel know for certain that God has made Him both Lord and Christ—this Jesus whom you crucified.

In an earlier chapter (chap. 17) I discussed the descent of the Spirit at Pentecost as the commencement of the descending eschatological temple. In light of Acts 2:29–36, the resurrected and ascended Jesus is the inaugurated fulfillment of the promised Davidic Messiah, whose resurrection itself is the beginning construction of the latter-day temple (e.g., John 2:19–22). He is also the king of the heavenly temple and has caused it to descend through his Spirit. Hence, Jesus is both sitting on the prophesied Davidic throne, which is the locus of the temple in heaven, and is extending that temple on earth. Thus, the locations of the temple and the Davidic throne, which were crucial pieces of Israel's land, have begun fulfillment in Jesus and his Spirit. In this way we can see that the land promises have begun fulfillment in Jesus's physical resurrection, not only as the beginning hillock of the new-creational landmass to come but also as the geographical location of the temple and the place where David's throne is.[36]

Conclusion to the Biblical Theology of the Land Promises

Bruce Waltke has argued that "the New Testament redefines Land in three ways: first, *spiritually*, as a reference to Christ's person; second, *transcendentally*, as a reference to heavenly Jerusalem; and third, *eschatologically*, as a reference to the new Jerusalem after Christ's second coming."[37] Generally, the "Land in the Old Testament is a type of the Christian life in Christ."[38] This definition could sound a bit too close to allegorization or undue spiritualization, even though Waltke contends that Christ has the authority to redefine the OT divine authorial intent in this manner. I would elaborate on Waltke's comment in this way: that the land was a type of the new creation in that its true design was for Israel (as a corporate Adam) to be faithful and expand the land's borders to encompass the whole earth. Since Israel failed in this, its old land still pointed to this unfulfilled universal consummated expansion into a new creation at some point in the future.

But from another perspective, there is a literal sense in which Christ's resurrection and the church's identification with Christ's resurrection have begun

36. Waltke, *Old Testament Theology*, 559, 571, drew my attention to the connection of the land promises to Jesus as beginning to fulfill the promises of a coming Davidic king on a throne.
37. Ibid., 560.
38. Ibid.

to fulfill the universal land promises of the OT. It is true that the NT does not mention formally that Christ or the church have begun to fulfill Israel's land promises. Nevertheless, the NT does affirm that Christ has begun to fulfill the end-time prophecies of the expected "Israel," "Jerusalem," "Zion," "temple," and "throne of David," all of which were to be significant pieces of real estate in the coming new land of Israel. In that these prophecies pertained to essential parts of Israel's future landscape, Christ's beginning fulfillment of them in some way is an initial realization of part of the land promises.

But in what particular way has Christ begun to fulfill these land prophecies? On the one hand, he has started to fulfill these promises in a physical manner through his own physical resurrection. But, on the other hand, these prophecies continued to be fulfilled through his present unseen reign in heaven and through his unseen rule over the church through the Spirit on earth. But even though these promises began fulfillment in Christ in an unseen or spiritual manner, such spiritual realities were seen from the OT prophetic vantage point to be inextricably linked to or part of the geographical or physical form of these prophecies. For example, the Messiah's spiritual presence in reigning on the throne of David was prophesied to be part of the physical reality of that reign when it was to be fulfilled. Or, another example, Christ's tabernacling spiritual presence was to be part of the physical temple of the cosmos when it was to come to realization. Thus, from the OT vantage point, the fulfillment of these various aspects of the land promises was to include both spiritual and physical features that were to be inextricably linked and were to happen together, all at once. Another way to say this is that an essential part of the fulfillment of the physical land promises included a spiritual dimension. If the Messiah's spiritual (and not merely physical) presence was not interwoven with, for example, the territorial realm of his Davidic rule, then there would be no such rule. A geographical and physical kingdom without the spiritual presence of a king is hollow and, ultimately, no kingdom, and the same is true of the other prophecies associated with land.[39] But spiritual and material parts of these various associated land promises have not happened all at once. The unseen or spiritual form of these prophecies has begun in Christ, and they will be completed in physical form when he returns a final time.[40]

---

39. One might respond by saying that a ruler without a physical kingdom is also hollow and, ultimately, no king. However, the NT makes clear that although Christ's reign is unseen, his inaugurated rule is exercised over the realm of the entire earth (Rev. 1:5; 2:26–27) through his church, which is empowered to begin to rule by his Spirit even on the old earth (Rev. 1:6; 5:10) (on which, see G. K. Beale, *The Book of Revelation: A Commentary on the Greek Text*, NIGTC [Grand Rapids: Eerdmans, 1999], 192–96, 360–64). The book of Acts can be rightly summarized as Christ's rule through his church on earth, empowered by his Spirit (e.g., Acts 1:8).

40. Although, as I have argued throughout this book, Christ did begin to fulfill the OT resurrection prophecies by rising physically from the dead. Nevertheless, his physically resurrected person is presently in an unseen dimension, where he is still fulfilling the prophecies of the "new

Consequently, since the spiritual and physical aspects of these promises about significant features of Israel's future real estate were to be intertwined with one another and, from the OT vantage point, were to occur simultaneously, and Christ has begun to fulfill these prophecies in an unseen spiritual way, we can say that those real estate prophecies have truly begun partial fulfillment in Christ. Thus, when one dimension begins fulfillment, it is to be seen as an initial "literal" fulfillment, even though the actual material land form of the fulfillment has not yet begun.

But what about the Messiah's people who were to accompany him in these fulfillments? Generally, since saints are identified with Christ, they are identified with his beginning fulfillments of these land promises. Since the OT prophesied that both the spirit and the body were to be literally resurrected, the beginning spiritual resurrection in this age is seen to be the beginning literal, though not complete, fulfillment of these resurrection prophecies.

Thus, a person's identification with Christ and spiritual resurrection in Christ in this age is a beginning unseen though literal fulfillment of the resurrection prophecies, which will be consummated at the very end of time in physical resurrection, which all eyes will see. In commencing to fulfill literally the resurrection prophecies in their identification with Christ's resurrection, believers begin to fulfill the universal land promises in a similar unseen, spiritual manner that Christ does. Accordingly, in the saints' identification with Christ's resurrection, they also come to be identified in an unseen manner with him as the new temple, new Jerusalem, new Zion, new Israel, and as kings ruling with the Davidic king, all of which we have noted are significant pieces of Israelite eschatological real estate. These realities that are true of Christ are attributed to those whom he represents.

There is, however, a significant difference between Christ and the saints in beginning to fulfill these promises: Christ has been resurrected physically, but the saints only spiritually. Although Christ's present rule is unseen in heaven, he is reigning there in a physically resurrected body. Christ is fulfilling the associated land prophecies both physically in his resurrected body and spiritually in the unseen heavenly dimension. For example, as ruling resurrected king, he is exercising his Davidic kingship from heaven by his Spirit through his people on earth. Accordingly, Christ has entered into a more escalated inaugurated fulfillment of the resurrection prophecy and of the land prophecies than have believers.[41]

In order to go into more detail and clarification of how all this is so, the reader needs to return to the discussions earlier in this chapter about how Christ and his followers can be inaugurated literal though unseen fulfillments

---

Jerusalem," end-time "Zion," the "temple," and so on, and his followers on earth participate in these inaugurated fulfillments through the Spirit sent from this unseen heavenly dimension.

41. Likewise, he is expanding the temple of the church on earth through his Spirit.

of the temple, new creation, new Jerusalem, and new Israel. For example, since Jesus sums up true Israel in his one person, all those who identify with him and are represented by him are deemed to be, in a positional or legal sense, literally true Israel, though one cannot see this reality with physical eyes. Their identification with him as messianic king in this respect is with his resurrection as a new creation, and their identification with the new temple, new Jerusalem, and new Israel is a subordinate aspect of the new creation. However, one could argue that since, as we saw earlier in the chapter, the OT viewed the coming new temple, new Jerusalem, and new Israel's land to be a universal cosmic expansion of the old ones, these realities overlap with the new cosmic creation. Thus, Israel's land promises and their fulfillment, which has been the primary subject of this chapter, overlap in their identity with the new cosmic creation. Consequently, again, we see the central role of the new-creational kingdom,[42] which we have repeatedly seen in earlier chapters is a crucial part of the redemptive-historical storyline.

Hence, in all these ways, Christ and the church come to be identified with the beginning fulfillment of the promises relating to Israel's end-time landscape and, thus, the land promises.

Excursus The Issue of Analogy or Fulfillment

Is the NT merely making a comparison, or is it depicting the actual, literal inaugurated fulfillment of the prophecies about the universal expansion of Israel's land? I would respond to this question with a presupposition that is supported by much exegesis of how other OT prophetic passages are used in NT texts elsewhere: should not those with a high view of Scripture begin with the assumption that the NT interprets the OT contextually and with hermeneutical integrity? Accordingly, if an OT passage quoted in the NT is a prophecy in its original context, would not a NT author also see it as a prophecy, and would he not see it as beginning fulfillment if he identifies the prophecy with some reality in his own present time? And, even if there is no fulfillment formula, would not the passage still be seen as fulfillment? Possibly, a NT writer could use the OT analogically, but the weight of the prophetic context of the OT passage tilts toward a notion of fulfillment, if there is no clear evidence to the contrary in the NT context.[43] If this is a correct hermeneutical approach, then the prophecies discussed in this chapter about Israel's land being widened to include the whole earth have an already–not yet fulfillment in the NT.[44]

---

42. Recall that in this chapter the throne of the Davidic kingdom was also to be a central piece of real estate in the eschatological new creation.

43. Or, if context makes it clear, a NT author could be affirming that an OT prophecy has not been fulfilled yet but assuredly will be in the future.

44. This would include the typologically prophetic passages also discussed.

THE DISTINGUISHING MARKS OF THE CHURCH AS STORYLINE FACETS OF THE END-TIME INAUGURATED NEW CREATION

23

The Church's New-Creational Transformation of Israel's Distinguishing Marks

The Sunday Sabbath Observance of the Church as an "Already and Not Yet" New-Creational End-Time Reality

My contention throughout this book is that major NT notions are best understood when viewed consistently through the lens of the new-creational, eschatological kingdom inaugurated by Christ, which I have proposed as the core of the NT storyline. I now address how this lens affects one's understanding of some of the main features that distinguish the faithful church from the world, especially in its gathered meetings. This aspect of God's faithful people is another aspect of my proposed storyline. In particular, five of these distinguishing marks of the faithful church will be addressed in this chapter and the next: the meeting of local churches once a week (Sunday), the sacrament of baptism, the sacrament of the Lord's Supper, the church office of elder, and the NT canon. These ecclesiastical marks are transformations of some of the main identifying tags of Israel.

The first distinguishing mark of the church has to do with its day of worship. Why has worship on the last day of the week in the OT now changed to the first day of the week for the new-covenant community? The reason usually offered by theologians is that Christ's resurrection occurred on the first day of the week, and so the church celebrates its existence in its identification with the resurrected Christ by meeting on the day of the week on which Christ's resurrection existence began.

This issue of the Sabbath has been, and continues to be, vigorously debated. For example, there is much disagreement about the following: (1) whether Gen. 2:3 expresses a creation mandate for humanity to rest on the seventh day; (2) whether Israel's Sabbath commandment is still applicable to the church; (3) whether the "rest" in Heb. 3–4 has been inaugurated or is still in the future. Therefore, I again ask for the reader's patience, since these are difficult issues, and the twists and turns of the following argumentation require careful attention.

Sabbath Rest in Genesis 2:2–3?

Before we can probe further into why the once-a-week worship has been changed from Saturday to Sunday,[1] I must address the OT concept of a day of rest. As I just noted, there is much debate about whether Sunday is the continuation of Israel's Sabbath, or even the continuation of the Sabbath as a creational ordinance, or both. I will argue primarily that the Sabbath continues as a creational ordinance, though transformed.

The notion of a Sabbath rest begins implicitly in the OT even before the formal institution of Israel's Sabbath observance in Exod. 20:8–11. We saw earlier in the discussion of the image of God[2] that Adam's commission in Gen. 1:28 as the image of God (Gen. 1:26–27) clearly involved reflecting God's activity narrated in Gen. 1 in at least two ways: (1) just as God subdued and ruled over the chaos at the inception of creation, so Adam was to subdue and rule over the earth; (2) just as God created and filled the earth, so was Adam to "be fruitful and multiply and fill the earth." But there was one more activity described of God at the very end of his work of creation in Gen. 2:2: "He rested on the seventh day from all His work which He had done." Although Adam is not explicitly said to imitate God in resting on the seventh day of each week, many have discerned in Gen. 2:3 a creational mandate for humanity to rest on the seventh day of each week: "Then God blessed the seventh day and set it apart, because in it He rested from all His work which God had created and made." However, it is possible that God "blessed the seventh day and set it apart" in order to celebrate his own resting, and it has nothing to do with humans resting.

---

1. I acknowledge, of course, that not everyone in the Christian church adheres to such a change, so that the change itself is the subject of debate (e.g., note the Seventh-day Adventist position).

2. See chap. 2 under the heading "Adam's Commission in the First Creation and the Passing On of the Commission to Other Adam-Like Figures," and chap. 13 under the heading "The Creation of Humanity in the Image of God and Humanity's Fall."

Nevertheless, it seems more likely that Gen. 2:3 entails a mandate for Adam and humanity to celebrate every seventh day God's climactic resting from his creative work. Several considerations point to this. First, would not Adam, created in the image of God, be expected to reflect God's goal of resting at the end of the creative process, since clearly he is to reflect the first two creative activities (noted above) leading to that goal? A negative answer to this question seems to demand a greater burden of proof. That what is said about the "seventh day" in Gen. 2:2–3 would include Adam and Eve within its purview seems to follow from the recognition that the account of what God actually created in Gen. 1 reaches its climax with the creation of humanity on the sixth day.[3] Then Gen. 2:1–2 continues by saying that God had "completed" his "work which He had done" in creating by the end of the sixth day. The open-ended nature of the statement that "God blessed the seventh day and set it apart" seems to point to more inclusivity than less, and thus to include humanity as the crown of creation. It would border on hermeneutical narrowness not at least to include Adam within the sphere of application of Gen. 2:3.

In this respect, Meredith Kline has said, "The imitation-of-God principle was to find embodiment in the overall pattern of the history of man's kingdom labor in that this history" was stamped with and composed of seven-day cycles in which Adam was to imitate the pattern of God's activities during the creation week.[4] Through each weekly cycle humanity was to "advance through six days of work to the seventh day of completion," the latter of which pointed typologically to the eternal end-time rest without "morning and evening," into which God had already entered at the completion of his creating activity.[5] Thus, human activity "was to correspond to the course of God's creational working as a movement from work begun to work consummated."[6] "Humanity is reminded in this way that life is not an aimless existence, that a goal lies beyond"[7] this earthly, temporal history of weeks in an eternal Sabbath of eschatological rest.[8] Such an eschatological goal in Gen. 2:2–3 is only

---

3. So W. Stott, "σάββατον," *NIDNTT* 3:406. Brevard Childs suggests something similar: "The entire creation story of ch. 1 focuses on the sanctification of the seventh day, the last part of which only has been used in Exodus [20:11]" (*The Book of Exodus*, OTL [Louisville: Westminster, 1976], 416).

4. Meredith G. Kline, *Kingdom Prologue: Genesis Foundations for a Covenantal Worldview* (Overland Park, KS: Two Age Press, 2000), 78. So also, holding virtually the same position, Gerhard F. Hasel, "Sabbath," *ABD* 5:851; Gordon J. Wenham, *Genesis 1–15*, WBC 1 (Waco: Word, 1987), 36; Walter Brueggemann, *Genesis*, IBC (Atlanta: John Knox, 1982), 36; Bruce K. Waltke, *An Old Testament Theology: An Exegetical, Canonical, and Thematic Approach* (Grand Rapids: Zondervan, 2007), 67.

5. Kline, *Kingdom Prologue*, 78.

6. Ibid.

7. Geerhardus Vos, *Biblical Theology: Old and New Testaments* (Grand Rapids: Eerdmans, 1948), 140.

8. Ibid. See also Kenneth A. Mathews, *Genesis 1–11:26*, NAC 1A (Nashville: Broadman & Holman, 1996), 181; Bruce K. Waltke, *Genesis* (Grand Rapids: Zondervan, 2001), 68, both seeing

implicit, but we will see that later Scripture unpacks these Genesis verses in exactly this eschatological manner.

A second observation suggesting that Gen. 2:3 includes a mandate to humans is that the Hebrew word for "bless" is normally restricted to living beings in the OT [9] and typically does not apply to something being blessed or sanctified only for God's sake. Accordingly, Gen. 2:3 appears to be directed to humanity as a creational ordinance to regard the seventh day of each week to be "blessed and set apart" by God. This is suggested further by the fact that the only uses of the verb for "bless" *in Gen. 1–2 outside of 2:3* refer to God blessing nonhuman animate creation (1:22) or humans (1:28). It is not until Gen. 14:20 that the verb is applied to God ("blessed be God Most High"). Outside of Gen. 2:3, the object of what is "blessed" is never indefinite. Job 42:12 is the only place in the OT where days are "blessed" and the blessing is for humans ("And the LORD blessed the latter days of Job more than his beginning").

With respect to the term "sanctify" or "set apart," in the vast majority of the numerous uses of the Hebrew word (*qādaš*),[10] it is God, people, or religious things (the ark, clothing, etc.) that are the clear objects said to be "set apart." Verbal uses can refer to God being "set apart"[11] or to humans being "set apart," especially for some cultic purpose. In particular, the use of the Piel stem of the Hebrew word *qādaš* found in Gen. 2:3, which is used the most throughout the OT,[12] almost always refers to setting apart humans or things for human cultic use. However, the only days said to be "set apart" or "holy" in the OT are Sabbaths and various festival days. In every case, the day is clearly "set apart" for humans to observe. This is the case with the "Sabbath" day observance[13] and other festival days.[14] Nevertheless, it is sometimes made

---

the lack of mention of "morning" and "evening" concerning the seventh day in Gen. 2:2–3 to have the same eschatological significance; so likewise Brueggemann, *Genesis*, 36. Others seeing a notion of end-time rest signaled in Gen. 2:2–3 include Martin Luther, *Lectures on Genesis*, LW 1 (Saint Louis: Corcordia, 1958), 80; C. F. Keil and F. Delitzsch, *The Pentateuch*, vol. 1 of *Biblical Commentary on the Old Testament* (repr., Grand Rapids: Eerdmans, 1971), 69–70.

9. Wenham, *Genesis 1–15*, 36. Although in the Pentateuch the vast majority of uses of the word "bless" (*bārak*) apply to humans being blessed, there are times in which God is said to be "blessed" (e.g., Gen. 9:26; 14:20; 24:27, 48; Exod. 18:10; Deut. 8:10). But never in the Pentateuch is some part of the creation "blessed" for the sake of God, though there are times when God blesses not people themselves but things for the sake of people (e.g., Gen. 27:27; 49:25; Exod. 23:25; Deut. 7:13; 26:15; 28:4–5, 12; 33:11, 13). Even when God blesses people, he is causing various aspects of their immediate environment to prosper or their offspring to increase.

10. Here are included both verb and noun forms.

11. E.g., about twenty-five of the forty-five uses of the Hiphil verb stem refer to God being "set apart."

12. This particular verb stem occurs about 75x in the OT.

13. So Deut. 5:12; Jer. 17:22, 24; Ezek. 20:20; 44:24 ("sabbaths"); Neh. 13:22 (all in the Piel stem); Isa. 58:13b (adjective); Exod. 16:23; 31:14, 15; 35:2; Isa. 58:13a (all in the noun form).

14. The fiftieth year of Jubilee (Lev. 25:12), "new moons and fixed festivals" (Ezra 3:5, in the Pual stem), "a holy day" (Neh. 10:31 [10:32 MT], as a noun), a "festival" day (Isa. 30:29,

explicit that these holy days are "holy to the LORD" and yet also clear that the people were to keep these days "holy." For example, Exod. 31:14 says that the Sabbath is "holy to you [Israel]," and 31:15 says that it is "holy to the LORD." Likewise Neh. 8:9–10 says that a special festival day is "holy to the LORD," yet verse 11 states it merely as "the day is holy," and it is clear from verses 10, 12 that the people were also to observe it as "holy." All the above references to Sabbaths and festival days, most of which have human observance primarily in view, include both humans and God, who were to consider the days holy. Thus, outside of Gen. 2:3, all other sacred days include humans and, at least implicitly, God, in their purview. Accordingly, Claus Westermann asserts that one should have an "exegetical instinct" that not only is the seventh day solemn to God, but also the day "must in some way or other signify something related to people," because of the "fact that the verb 'to sanctify' expresses a cultic idea [elsewhere in the OT] and cannot be referred to a day destined [only] for God himself."[15]

It is likely that this pattern of referring to both humans and God in such sanctified holy days holds true for Gen. 2:3 as well, since these other uses of "sanctify a day" are the only other ones analogous to that in Gen. 2:3. Especially interesting is Neh. 8:11, which I noted above merely refers to a festival indefinitely as "the day is holy," which in context includes humans and God in its perspective (see Neh. 8:10–12). Even the vast majority of the uses of the Piel verb stem used in Gen. 2:3, which have in view setting apart humans or cultic things for human use, also have in ultimate view that the cult is to serve and worship God (and sometimes this twofold notion is explicit [e.g., Exod. 28:3, 41; 29:1, 44; 30:30; 40:13; Ezek. 20:12, 20]). The indefinite statement in Gen. 2:3 seems likewise to have the same dual perspective as the examples above.

Thus, the immediate context of Gen. 2:3 and the pattern of uses of "sanctify a day" elsewhere in the OT point to the seventh day being "blessed" and "set apart" for humans to observe and celebrate.[16] According to Isa. 45:18, the earth

---

in the Hithpael stem; Neh. 8:9, 10, 11, in adjective forms). In addition, on Sabbaths and other festival days, there was to be a "holy convocation" (Lev. 23:3, 7, 36; Num. 28:18, 25–26; 29:1, 7, 12, all using the noun form). Such days are even called "holy convocations" (using the noun form in Lev. 23:2, 4, 8, 21, 24, 27).

15. Claus Westermann, *Genesis 1–11*, trans. John J. Scullion (London: SPCK, 1984), 170.

16. The following commentators are among those who hold that Gen. 2:3 includes the notion of a day "blessed and set apart" for humans: John Calvin, *Genesis* (Edinburgh: Banner of Truth, 1965), 105–7; Luther, *Lectures on Genesis*, 79–81; Keil and Delitzsch, *Pentateuch*, 69–70; Umberto Cassuto, *From Adam to Noah: A Commentary on Genesis I–VI*, vol. 1 of *A Commentary on the Book of Genesis*, trans. Israel Abrams (Jerusalem: Magnes Press, 1961), 64, 68; Walther Eichrodt, *Theology of the Old Testament*, trans. J. A. Baker, 2 vols., OTL (Philadelphia: Westminster, 1961–67), 1:133; Gerhard von Rad, *Genesis*, OTL (Philadelphia: Westminster, 1972), 62–63 (although von Rad does not think Gen. 2:3 is an explicit human mandate to rest, he concludes by saying that "it is tangibly 'existent' protologically as it is expected eschatologically in Hebrews" [p. 63]); idem, *Old Testament Theology*, trans. D. M. G. Stalker, 2 vols, OTL (New York: Harper, 1962–65), 1:148. More recent commentators who acknowledge a creation

was created for humans to inhabit: "For thus says the LORD, who created the heavens (He is the God who formed the earth and made it, He established it and did not create it a waste place, but formed it to be inhabited). . . ." Could such a human-focused purpose for the created earth suggest further that the six-day work of God followed by a seventh day divinely "blessed" and "set apart" would regulate human existence on the earth? Did God create only the material space in which humans were to live, or did he not also create the temporal sphere that would regulate their existence? I think that the overall evidence of this chapter so far points to a positive answer to these questions. Genesis 1:14, reporting part of the fourth day of creation, is further evidence that God created a temporal structure within which humans were to live: "Then God said, 'Let there be lights in the expanse of the heavens to separate the day from the night, and let them be for signs and for seasons and for days and years.'" The phrase "and for seasons" (*ûlĕmô'ădîm*) is better translated "and for festivals" or "and for festivals and [cultic] seasons."[17] Since we have seen that the notion of "sanctify" elsewhere in the OT often is related to setting apart people, things, and certain days as holy for cultic purposes, it is natural to see that God's sanctifying of the seventh day in Gen. 2:3 is one of those festival days included in Gen. 1:14, which is part of the temporal divisions within which Gen. 1:14 says humans are to live.

Accordingly, the observance of every seventh day was to recall God's seventh day of resting, and this observance of every seventh day apparently was to remind humanity of a final, eternal Sabbath rest without "morning or evening" that would no longer need to be repeated. That is, the ultimate goal of humanity was to enter into the kind of consummative rest into which God himself had entered (Gen. 2:2). God is included within the purview of Gen. 2:3 in that the day is dedicated to him, so that it is "blessed" and "set apart" to recall his climactic rest. This day of rest appears not to have ceased but

---

mandate in Gen. 2:3 include Brueggemann, *Genesis*, 35–36; Westermann, *Genesis 1–11*, 169–72; Nahum M. Sarna, *Genesis*, JPSTC (Philadelphia: Jewish Publication Society, 1989), 15; Victor P. Hamilton, *The Book of Genesis: Chapters 1–17*, NICOT (Grand Rapids: Eerdmans, 1990), 143; Mathews, *Genesis 1–11:26*, 180; John E. Hartley, *Genesis*, NIBC (Peabody, MA: Hendrickson, 2000), 50–51; Waltke, *Genesis*, 67, 73; John H. Walton, *Genesis*, NIVAC (Grand Rapids: Zondervan, 2001), 157–61; Wenham, *Genesis 1–15*, 36.

17. In support of this translation, see David J. Rudolph, "Festivals in Genesis," *TynBul* 54, no. 2 (2003): 23–40. Rudolph observes that the vast majority of the uses of *mô'ēd* in the OT refer to a cultic context, and, especially, the plural form of *mô'ēd* always indicates cultic "festivals" in all eight of its only other occurrences in the Pentateuch. Twenty-two of twenty-six plural forms in the OT signify cultic "festivals." In addition, the very same lexical form *lĕmô'ădîm* in Gen. 1:14 refers to religious "festivals" in all its other five OT uses (though Ps. 104:19 is one of the uses, referring back to Gen. 1:14). Interestingly, the plural form of the word in Lev. 23:2 includes reference to the Sabbath in Lev. 23:3, and the singular in Num. 28:2 includes reference to the Sabbath in Num. 28:9–10. Rudolph also observes that several English translations render this plural word in Gen. 1:14 as "festivals" or, more expansively, "festivals and seasons" (e.g., GNB, NJB, NEB, REB), as do the standard Hebrew lexicons and theological dictionaries.

rather to be continuing on into the course of primeval history (since it is not like the other creation days, having no morning or evening, and, as we will see, Heb. 3–4 sees that God's rest continues on throughout time and can be shared in).

The Institution of the Sabbath in Israel

This analysis of Gen. 2:3 is supported additionally by the Sabbath commandment later given to Israel. First, this commandment is the only one of the Ten Commandments that begins with "remember" (Exod. 20:8). It is possible that this expression is projecting ahead to a time when Israel in the future is to "remember" to observe the Sabbath "as the LORD your God commanded you" in the past at Sinai (Deut. 5:12). However, if, as I have contended, the Sabbath was a creational ordinance first given to Adam, then it makes much sense that "remember the sabbath day to keep it holy" is a reference back to Gen. 2:3.[18] That Israel's Sabbath commandment has reference back to Gen. 2:3 receives some corroboration from the basis for keeping the Sabbath (Exod. 20:8–10), which is "in six days the LORD made the heavens and the earth, the sea and all that is in them, and rested on the seventh day" (20:11a). This then becomes the basis also for the following statement: "therefore the LORD blessed the sabbath day and made it holy" (20:11b), a clear reference back to Gen. 2:3.[19] In the immediate context of 20:8–10, when God "blessed the sabbath day and made it holy" (20:11b), the intent was that Israel, not primarily God, would "remember the sabbath and keep it holy" (20:8).

Therefore, if it is granted that Exod. 20:8–10 is interpretatively unpacking the thicker description of "blessed" and "sanctified" in Gen. 2:3,[20] then God's setting apart the Sabbath day in Gen. 2:3 probably does not refer primarily to his own celebrating of the day by resting. This is especially the case because in Gen. 2:3 and Exod. 20:11 God's resting on the seventh day is distinguished from his setting apart the seventh day; the distinction is highlighted in both passages by the resting being the basis for the sanctifying of the day.[21] And the day is clearly "set apart" for Israel to observe, not for God to observe by resting (so also Exod. 31:13–15; 35:2; Lev. 23:3). Nevertheless, the day is a way

18. This was a view sometimes held by Puritan interpreters. More recently, see Childs, *Exodus*, 416. Childs also says that the Sabbath for Israel mentioned in Exod. 16:22–30 presupposes the existence of the Sabbath before the law given at Sinai (p. 290).

19. Hasel ("Sabbath," *ABD* 5:851) adduces other common language between Gen. 2:2–3 and Exod. 20:9–11: "seventh day," "make," and "work." These two passages are the only places where the two Hebrew verbs "bless" and "sanctify" occur in close combination.

20. Which would mean that the Exodus passage is not a mere application of Gen. 2:3 or an alien or noncontextual interpretation.

21. Kline, *Kingdom Prologue*, 79.

to honor God, so that God is likely to be viewed implicitly as continuing to observe the seventh day as special as well.

In this light, Exod. 20:11 shows Gen. 2:3 to have application to Israel and that Israel was to imitate God's six days of creative work by working for six days and imitating his rest on the seventh day by ceasing from work on the last day of every week. That Israel was to imitate God's resting is another element that connects the Exod. 20 commandment back to Gen. 2:2–3, where, I contended, Adam was made in God's image to reflect God's subduing, ruling, increasing and multiplying, and also resting.[22] Those who do not see Gen. 2:3 as a mandate to Adam would conclude that the fourth commandment is a new application of Gen. 2:3 and not an interpretation of it that further clarifies its anthropological intention. In view, however, of the overall thrust of the argument so far about Gen. 2:3 in this section, it is quite natural to see the fourth commandment as clarifying Gen. 2:3 as a creation mandate to humanity. A biblical-theological notion that I have tried to establish in earlier parts of this book is that Israel was a corporate Adam.[23] If so, it is much more natural that a creational mandate to rest given to Adam should be carried over and applied also to the corporate Adam, Israel.

New Testament Testimony to the Sabbath

NT evidence may point further to my conclusion about Gen. 2:3. In Mark 2:27, in response to the Pharisees' accusation that his disciples had broken the Sabbath by picking grain from the fields, Jesus says, "The Sabbath was made for man, and not man for the Sabbath." This appears to be a generic reference to all humanity's role in keeping the Sabbath and not merely to the fourth commandment given to Israel. This is pointed to further in the directly following verse, where Jesus refers to himself as "the Son of Man" (equivalent to "the son of Adam") instead of "the son of David," which he could well have employed, since Jesus has just adduced David as an example of justly breaking the Sabbath.[24] Jesus is the faithful last Adam, ruling over creation in the way the first Adam should have and faithfully celebrating the Sabbath as the first Adam should have.

Is Hebrews 3–4 a Reference to a Present or a Future Eschatological Rest?

Hebrews 3:7–4:11 is another NT passage that contributes to an understanding of the relevance of the Sabbath for the church:

22. So Vos, *Biblical Theology*, 139–40.

23. See, e.g., chap. 2 under the subheadings "The Differences between the Commission to Adam and What Was Passed On to His Descendants" and "Conclusion," and chap. 19 under the heading "Israel's Tabernacle in the Wilderness and Later Temple Were a Reestablishment of the Garden of Eden's Sanctuary."

24. Following Kline, *Kingdom Prologue*, 79–80.

Therefore, just as the Holy Spirit says,

> "Today if you hear His voice,
> Do not harden your hearts as when they provoked Me,
> As in the day of trial in the wilderness,
> Where your fathers tried Me by testing Me,
> And saw My works for forty years.
> Therefore I was angry with this generation,
> And said, 'They always go astray in their heart,
> And they did not know My ways';
> As I swore in My wrath,
> 'They shall not enter My rest.'"

Take care, brethren, that there not be in any one of you an evil, unbelieving heart that falls away from the living God. But encourage one another day after day, as long as it is still called "Today," so that none of you will be hardened by the deceitfulness of sin. For we have become partakers of Christ, if we hold fast the beginning of our assurance firm until the end, while it is said,

> "Today if you hear His voice,
> Do not harden your hearts, as when they provoked Me."

For who provoked Him when they had heard? Indeed, did not all those who came out of Egypt led by Moses? And with whom was He angry for forty years? Was it not with those who sinned, whose bodies fell in the wilderness? And to whom did He swear that they would not enter His rest, but to those who were disobedient? So we see that they were not able to enter because of unbelief. Therefore, let us fear if, while a promise remains of entering His rest, any one of you may seem to have come short of it. For indeed we have had good news preached to us, just as they also; but the word they heard did not profit them, because it was not united by faith in those who heard. For we who have believed enter that rest, just as He has said,

> "As I swore in My wrath,
> They shall not enter My rest,"

although His works were finished from the foundation of the world.

For He has said somewhere concerning the seventh day: "And God rested on the seventh day from all His works"; and again in this passage, "They shall not enter My rest." Therefore, since it remains for some to enter it, and those who formerly had good news preached to them failed to enter because of disobedience, He again fixes a certain day, "Today," saying through David after so long a time just as has been said before,

> "Today if you hear His voice,
> Do not harden your hearts."

For if Joshua had given them rest, He would not have spoken of another day after that. So there remains a Sabbath rest for the people of God. For the one who has entered His rest has himself also rested from his works, as God did from His. Therefore let us be diligent to enter that rest, so that no one will fall, through following the same example of disobedience.

This section of Hebrews needs some analysis before conclusions about its bearing on the Sabbath question can be addressed. This is a difficult passage, and so I ask for the reader's patience in following my discussion.

The segment of 3:7–19 explains that the exhortation to persevere in "hope firm until the end" (3:6) is an exhortation continued from the OT itself. The giving of this exhortation to the readers is the reason that the similar encouragement to persevere was given to the Israelites, both in their wilderness wandering and later during the generation of the psalmist (who wrote Ps. 95, which is quoted repeatedly in Heb. 3–4 [3:8–11, 13, 15; 4:3, 7]). In other words, the command to Israel to continue in its faith and its failure to do so pointed forward to the Christian age, when a positive response would come, first in Christ (3:6a) and then in his true people. First-generation Israel in the wilderness did not "enter God's rest" because it was unbelieving (3:8–10, 15–19). Psalm 95 addresses later generations of Israelites, saying that the time was ripe ("Today") for them to believe and enter into God's rest in contrast to their unfaithful forefathers (3:7–8; 4:7–8). But neither were they faithful, nor did they enter God's rest (cf. 4:6). The rest that Israel was to achieve was to be in the promised land (with Jerusalem and the temple as focal points of this rest),[25] but although the second generation and subsequent generations entered that land, they were not faithful in the land and thus did not enjoy the "rest" that was to occur there (e.g., Heb. 4:8: "For if Joshua had given them [the second generation] rest, He [God] would not have spoken of another day after that").

So the promise of God's people entering into his rest remained unfulfilled until the time of the writer of Hebrews, who repeats the exhortation of the psalmist. The time is still "Today" for God's people to heed the exhortation, since the rest has not been obtained. It is noteworthy that persevering "until the end" to "become partakers of Christ" (3:14) is parallel with "entering His rest" (4:1), so that being identified with Christ at the end of the age is inextricably linked to "entering His rest." The close parallelism suggests that Christ himself has achieved final end-time rest, and those who are identified with him at the end will share in that final rest.

25. On which, see G. K. Beale, *The Temple and the Church's Mission: A Biblical Theology of the Dwelling Place of God*, NSBT 17 (Downers Grove, IL: InterVarsity, 2004), 60–63; Andrew T. Lincoln, "Sabbath, Rest, and Eschatology in the New Testament," in *From Sabbath to Lord's Day: A Biblical, Historical, and Theological Investigation*, ed. D. A. Carson (Grand Rapids: Zondervan, 1982), 207–10.

An interpretative debate has raged about the timing of this rest in this section of Hebrews. Some view the "rest" as completed, so that the believer has achieved final, complete rest in Christ, instead of a rest yet to be obtained. A second view is that the "rest" in this passage is inaugurated for believers but is not final and complete, which is a more viable and possible view than the preceding one. All the complex details of this debate cannot be entered into here,[26] but the present approach, which represents a third view, understands all references to the "rest" in this segment of Hebrews to be something not yet obtained. However, as we will see, there are other passages in the NT outside of Hebrews that do affirm a notion that the rest has been inaugurated for Christians and not yet consummated. My purpose here is to show that Heb. 3–4 envisions only a future consummated form of this rest.

There are two verses in the Hebrews context, however, that on the surface appear to refer to a beginning realization of the "rest" for Christians:

Heb. 4:3 "For we who have believed enter that rest."

Heb. 4:10 "For the one who has entered His rest has himself also rested from his works, as God did from His."

Hebrews 4:10 seems at first glance to indicate that the "rest" has begun to be experienced in the past. Nevertheless, it is more likely that this is an expression of the so-called prophetic perfect, whereby a biblical author sees the future as being so certain to occur that he speaks of it using a past tense, as though it had already happened.[27] That 4:10 is also future is apparent in that "rested from his [the believer's] works" refers not to becoming a Christian in the present age and ceasing from the ungodly works of an unbeliever but rather to resting from the performance of "good works" throughout the Christian life, on analogy with the good works of creation from which God ceased on the seventh day. Thus, this is a resting that comes after one's life has ended and at the end of the age.

26. See Lincoln, "Sabbath," 197–220. Lincoln sees the "rest," esp. in Heb. 4:3, 10, to be inaugurated in the experience of believers. This means for him that the weekly observance of a Sabbath day has been abolished because the Sabbath day pointed forward to such rest, and it has now been fulfilled. See also Richard B. Gaffin Jr., "A Sabbath Rest Still Awaits the People of God," in *Pressing Toward the Mark: Essays Commemorating Fifty Years of the Orthodox Presbyterian Church*, ed. Charles G. Dennison and Richard C. Gamble (Philadelphia: Committee for the Historian of the Orthodox Presbyterian Church, 1986), 33–51. Gaffin sees the "rest" as completely future, with the implication that the Sabbath ordinance continues until its sign-pointing significance is fulfilled at Christ's final coming.

27. In 4:10 the verb "he has rested" (*katepausen*) is an aorist, which designates past time in this context, and the preceding phrase, "the one who has entered" (*eiselthōn*) likewise in context is best taken to indicate past time. However, both are used with a perfective perfect sense, as just explained.

This leaves Heb. 4:3 as the only remaining possible reference in Hebrews to be a present rest. The reference in 4:10 is likely the key to understanding the present tense of "enter that rest" in 4:3. It apparently is a so-called futuristic present.[28] What brings 4:3 even closer to 4:10 is that the directly following context of 4:3 also implicitly portrays Christians to be resting from works that are analogous to God's good works of creation from which he rested on the seventh day (so 4:3b–5). And 4:9 concludes on the basis of the preceding discussion in 4:1–8, "So there <u>remains</u> a Sabbath rest for the people of God." An exclusively future orientation of 4:3 also is pointed to by the surrounding context of 3:7–4:11, where everything else in this passage is about a future-oriented "rest." Christians are pictured throughout as still wandering in the wilderness of the world, but wandering with the aim of finally and truly achieving the final eschatological "rest" in the true promised land of the coming completed new creation.

It has been necessary to summarize Heb. 3:7–4:11 in order to see what light it may shed on the biblical theology of the Sabbath. Hebrews 4:3–6 is particularly relevant for this consideration:

For we who have believed enter that rest, just as He has said,

"As I swore in my wrath,
They shall not enter My rest,"

although His works were finished from the foundation of the world.

For He has said somewhere concerning the seventh day: "And God rested on the seventh day from all His works"; and again in this passage, "They shall not enter My rest." Therefore, since it remains for some to enter it, and those who formerly had good news preached to them failed to enter because of disobedience. . . .

To reiterate a most important point: Heb. 4:3b–5 says that the "rest" that Israel did not obtain and that "remains for some to enter" is the "rest" first achieved by God when "He rested on the seventh day from all His works" (4:4), a quotation from Gen. 2:2, anticipated by allusion to the same passage

---

28. For a listing of commentators who prefer the interpretation that 4:3 refers to entering into the rest in the present and others who affirm that the present tense has an exclusive future sense, see Paul Ellingworth, *The Epistle to the Hebrews: A Commentary on the Greek Text*, NIGTC (Grand Rapids: Eerdmans, 1993), 246; Craig R. Koester, *Hebrews*, AB 36 (New York: Doubleday, 2001), 270–71, 278. Ellingworth and Koester prefer the latter view, as does Luke Timothy Johnson, *Hebrews*, NTL (Louisville: Westminster John Knox, 2006), 124–26. However, the "rest" of 4:3 is seen to include the present by William L. Lane, *Hebrews 1–8*, WBC 47A (Dallas: Word, 1991), 99. Koester (*Hebrews*, 272–73, 279–80) and Johnson (*Hebrews*, 130) also see the "rest" of 4:10 to be a future reference, while Lane (*Hebrews 1–8*, 101–2), views it as including the believers' present experience. For an example of a commentator who is unclear about precisely when the "rest" for God's people begins, see the comments on 4:10 by F. F. Bruce, *The Epistle to the Hebrews*, NICNT (Grand Rapids: Eerdmans, 1990), 110.

in 4:3 ("although His works were finished from the foundation of the world"). If Israel had been faithful, it would have entered into the rest that God began to experience on the seventh day of creation. But Israel was not faithful, so God said, "They shall not enter My rest" (4:5), but still "it remains for some to enter it" (4:6).

In addition, I want to reiterate that 4:9–11 is likewise significant in making reference to God's rest in Gen. 2:2 and the Christian's rest:

> So there remains a Sabbath rest for the people of God. For the one who has entered His rest has himself also rested from his works, as God did from His. Therefore let us be diligent to enter that rest, so that no one will fall, through following the same example of disobedience.

The "Sabbath rest" that "remains" for the believer (v. 9) is a resting "from his [good] works" in the same way "as God did from his," which is another reference to Gen. 2:2, first quoted in full in 4:4. It is this same "rest" that Christians are to "be diligent to enter" at the end of the age (4:11). The rest for believers is not merely analogous to that of God's rest at creation; it is the rest that God himself experienced and still enjoys and into which believers finally and fully enter at the eschaton.[29] The sameness of the rest is highlighted by the repeated mention that the future rest for God's people is called "My [God's] rest" (3:11; 4:3, 5; likewise 4:10), which began to be experienced by God on the seventh creation day.

Hebrews 3–4 and Its Relation to the Question of a Creational Sabbath Mandate in Genesis 2:3

Although the Heb. 3–4 passage does not provide any direct evidence that Gen. 2:3 was a creational mandate for humanity to rest on every seventh day, it does shed light on it as an end-time mandate for humans. The text of Heb. 3–4 provides clear indication that God's "rest" after his six days of creating was to be imitated by humanity. That is, God has designed that his people finish their good works in this life and enter that same rest at the end of history that he experienced, when he had finished his good creative works. In other words, God's resting in Gen. 2:2 is to be imitated by his people at the eschatological consummation. This is not some new purpose for humanity instituted only at the beginning of Israel's history; most likely it is the purpose inherent and implicit in Gen. 2:2. Adam was designed to fulfill this purpose of eschatological resting as a divine image-bearer.

Thus, Heb. 3–4 provides good evidence for one of the points that I argued earlier in the introductory OT discussion of this chapter: God's resting in Gen. 2:2–3 pointed forward to the eschatological resting of his people. But

29. On which, see Gaffin, "Sabbath Rest," 30.

does the Hebrews text shed any light on my contention that Gen. 2:3 was a creational mandate for humanity to commemorate God's rest every seventh day throughout the course of history? Certainly, there is no direct reference to this. However, if Gen. 2:2 implicitly points forward to the latter-day human goal of resting in imitation of God, then the step to Gen. 2:3 being a reference for humanity to rest every seventh day is not such a long one. Even if 2:3 is not a mandate for humanity to rest every seventh day, at the least the end-time goal of resting for humans included in Gen. 2:2 is also included in 2:3b, which repeats the wording of 2:2 concerning God resting. Furthermore, Heb. 4:9 does refer to "a Sabbath [*sabbatismos*] rest" that still "remains" for God's people. What is striking about this is that God's "rest" in Gen. 2:3 (which Heb. 4:9–10 directly links with God's rest in Gen. 2:2) is not referred to elsewhere in the OT except in Exod. 20:11; 31:17, where it is seen to be the basis for Israel resting on the "sabbath" (*sabbaton*).[30] Thus, the only linking between God's rest in Gen. 2:2–3 and a noun form of "sabbath" in all of the OT is in these two pentateuchal texts, where "sabbath" refers to every seventh day that Israel was to rest.[31] In this way, Israel's Sabbath observance may come into the purview of Heb. 4.

Conclusion to the Significance of Hebrews 3–4 for the Sabbath Concept

To sum up, Heb. 4 has defined "rest" for Christians to be (1) eschatological; (2) entirely future; (3) "Sabbath rest"; (4) based on God's rest at creation. From this, certain things may be inferred about the weekly observance of the Sabbath day. First, in light of the first two items, there is included in the weekly Sabbath observance, especially of Israel, a sign or pointer to an ultimate end-time rest. If this is not the case, the only alternative is that the writer of Hebrews creatively coined the term "sabbath-resting" for end-time rest and, indeed, by himself linked that rest with Gen. 2:2–3. This is possible, but it is more probable that he was influenced by the OT's (Exod. 20:11; 31:17) own reuse of Gen. 2:2–3 to provide a basis for Israel's weekly Sabbath rest. If so, it would seem that to some degree Israel's weekly Sabbath rest came into the writer's peripheral vision in Heb. 4:9–10, when he referred to "sabbath-resting" in direct connection to God's rest of Gen. 2:2.

---

30. Note the use of *sabbaton* in Exod. 20:8, 10 and 31:13–16, which is used synonymously with "seventh day." Furthermore, the vast majority of uses of "sabbath" (*sabbaton*) in the OT refer to the seventh day, when Israel was to rest.

31. The word *sabbatismos*, found in Heb. 4:9, does not occur in the LXX or elsewhere in the NT; however, it does appear in extrabiblical Greek to refer to Israel's Sabbath (Plutarch, *Superst.* 3 [*Mor.* 166A]); Justin, *Dial.* 23.3; Epiphanius, *Pan.* 30.22; *Mart. Pet. Paul* 1; *Apos. Con.* 2.36.2 (following here Lincoln, "Sabbath," 213). Likewise the verbal form, *sabbatizō*, used five times in the OT, also refers to Israel's Sabbath (Exod. 16:30; Lev. 23:32) and to the seventh year, when the land was to rest (Lev. 26:34–35; 2 Chron. 36:21).

Another inference from the particular conclusion that the "rest" is entirely future is that the creational ordinance of a weekly Sabbath and Israel's weekly Sabbath have not ceased during the church age. If the eschatological reality of final Sabbath rest has not consummately come, then it is unlikely that the typological sign pointing to that ultimate rest has ceased. That is, if the weekly Sabbath included the function of pointing forward to consummate rest, and that rest has not yet come, then that weekly Sabbath should continue.

That the weekly Sabbath is a creation mandate for humanity is a final possible inference that may be drawn from the conclusion that the "rest" of Heb. 3–4 is based on God's rest at creation. We have observed that the author of Hebrews sees in Gen. 2:2 not only a description of God's rest on the seventh day of creation but also the eschatological goal and mandate that humanity enter and enjoy God's rest[32] (which supports my contention earlier in the chapter that implicit in Gen. 2:2 is that humanity is to imitate God's rest at the end of the age). The author of Hebrews undoubtedly would have seen the same end-time goal and mandate in the repeated mention of God's resting in Gen. 2:3. This is very close to finding a creation mandate in Gen. 2:2–3. To say that God's rest in Gen. 2:2–3 was to be viewed as an eschatological goal and eschatological mandate for Adam, as I have said, is only one step away from seeing in these verses a creational mandate that Adam was to observe every seventh day as a pointer to this end-time goal and end-time mandate. But it is still a step away. However, in light of the cumulative argumentation earlier in this section about Gen. 2:3 being a creational mandate, we may view the evidence of Hebrews to be compatible with this conclusion.[33]

Conclusion to the Sunday Sabbath Observance of the Church as a New-Creational, End-Time Reality

The upshot of this difficult chapter so far is that the observance of a Sabbath at the end of each week is an end-time sign. This weekly Sabbath sign is grounded in God's creation rest and is still to be observed by the church until Christ's final coming, at which time the weekly observance will cease. Some

32. Hippolytus views Gen. 2:3 and the weekly Sabbath to have ultimate reference to the end of time, when "the Sabbath may come, the rest, the holy day 'on which God rested from all His works.' For the [weekly] Sabbath is the type and emblem of the future kingdom of the saints, when they 'shall reign with Christ'" (*Comm. Dan.* frg. 2.4). Likewise, *Barn.* 15:3–5, 9 interprets God's finishing of the six-day creation referred to in Gen. 2:2–3 to have ultimate reference to the time when "the Lord will bring everything to an end" (15:4), and the seventh day of rest in Gen. 2 refers to "when his Son comes . . . [and] will destroy the time of the lawless one and will judge the ungodly" and create a new cosmos, "and then he will truly rest on the seventh day [i.e., for eternity]" (15:5).
33. The preceding analysis of Heb. 3–4 is shaped by Gaffin, "Sabbath Rest," though I have supplemented his understanding here and there.

contend, however, that the Sabbath ordinance was unique to Israel and is no longer relevant for the church as a weekly ordinance. The main reason for this argument is that Christ has come and achieved the rest pointed to by Israel's Sabbath, and those trusting in Christ also fulfill completely the Sabbath rest in him. Andrew Lincoln has argued this in the most depth in his exposition of Heb. 3:7–4:11. His main argument, already noted above, is that Heb. 4:3 and 4:10 respectively refer to believers presently entering the rest and as already having begun to enter it. Thus, believers identify fully with Christ's rest, which has been achieved fully at his resurrection and ascension. For Lincoln, this means that the weekly Sabbath observance of Israel is no longer in force, since all to which it pointed has been fulfilled in Christ and believers, the latter achieving salvation rest in Christ.

I have also tried to show in some detail that Heb. 4:3, 10 are best understood as referring not to an inaugurated rest whereby believers experience full rest through Christ's attainment of it, but rather to a consummated one still to come at the very end of the age. The context of everything else in Heb. 3:7–4:11 supports a notion of an entirely future rest for Christians. If this is so, then there is no strong reason to object to the notion that a weekly Sabbath continues for God's people in the present age. But even if Heb. 3–4 were understood to be affirming an already–not yet end-time Sabbath rest, this would not mean that a weekly Sabbath would not continue, since the end-time rest has *not been consummated*.

Other NT texts point to the likelihood that even for believers, inaugurated rest in Christ has begun but is not completed.[34] Christ, as the last Adam, has himself fully entered into the eschatological Sabbath rest through his resurrection, which has been pointed to by both Gen. 2:3 and Israel's Sabbath ordinance. Those who have believed in Christ are represented by Christ's full Sabbath resurrection rest and thus are identified positionally with that rest, and in this positional sense they have begun to share in that rest. They have also begun existentially to enjoy that rest by virtue of their real inaugurated resurrection life, which also stems from Christ's resurrection life, which has been communicated to them through the life-giving Spirit. But their rest is still incomplete because their resurrection existence has begun only spiritually and has not been consummated bodily. Their final personal accomplishment

---

34. This appears to be expressed in Matt. 11:28–29, where Jesus says, "Come to Me, all you who are weary and heavy-laden, and I will give you rest. Take My yoke upon you, and learn from Me, for I am gentle and humble in heart, and you will find rest for your souls." Such rest may also be implicit in Heb. 3:14, where to "become partakers of Christ" by persevering "until the end" is parallel with believers partaking of rest by persevering until the very end (Heb. 4:1, 6, 11). Thus, partaking of Christ and of the rest are parallel in this context, and it may indicate that at the end of the age believers will partake of the rest that Christ achieved at the end of his life. But even if these passages did not express a notion of inaugurated rest, the biblical-theological deduction of such rest is still a plausible inference.

of rest will occur at the end of the age, when they experience bodily resurrection. Accordingly, the weekly sign of rest still continues for believers living on earth until all that it points to is completely fulfilled at the very end of the age in their bodily resurrection. Therefore, those who contend that a weekly Sabbath is annulled because believers have begun to experience salvific rest in Christ appear not to be consistent in their already–not yet eschatology. To say that a special recognition of one day in seven as a continuation of the Sabbath has been annulled seems to express an overrealized eschatology.[35] Such a Sabbath observance is tied into an already–not yet framework, so that the weekly sign will not pass away until the complete fulfillment to which the sign points takes place. And as I will elaborate more on below, it is not the Israelite Sabbath ordinance per se that continues for the church but rather the creation ordinance, which also was partly expressed as a basis for Israel's Sabbath observance. This is an important qualification about how we see Israel's Sabbath law carried over into the NT.

It is significant to recall that Hebrews expresses a whole-Bible canonical view of end-time Sabbath rest that entails that God's rest was to be imitated by his people at some future point. This has been seen through appeal to Gen. 2:2–3 and, implicitly, its use in Exod. 20:8–11, and through affirming that the wilderness generation, Joshua's generation, and later Israelite generations could have entered into this final divine rest, and that the church will actually enter that rest at some future point.

But even if one agrees with this argument so far about the relevance of the Sabbath and its eschatological significance, unsolved problems remain. First, does not the NT clearly say that Israel's Sabbath law is no longer valid for the church? Second, if the Sabbath law is valid, does not the church have an obligation to keep it in the very same way as Israel and incur the same penalties for disobedience, which involved capital punishment for disobedient Israelites? Third, if Sabbath observance continues, why does the church not observe it on Saturday instead of Sunday, the first day of the week?

Does the New Testament Definitively Abolish the Sabbath Ordinance?

The first objection concerns the contention that several Pauline texts affirm that Israel's Sabbath is no longer applicable:[36]

35. A typical representative of such a position is Lincoln, "Sabbath," 214–16.
36. E.g., Lincoln ("Sabbath," 214) argues that the Jewish Sabbath does not carry over into the church age, since Hebrews clearly views the OT law and the old covenant and its institutions to have been completely annulled by Christ and his work. Lincoln never discusses, however, the relevance for the new covenant of the Genesis creation mandate for humanity to observe the seventh day in commemoration of God's rest because he does not see that Gen. 2:3 expresses such a mandate. A major omission in this respect is that Lincoln merely assumes that Gen. 2:3 is not a creational mandate to humanity—he offers no arguments against this view. An additional omission that is striking, however, is that although Lincoln acknowledges that Gen. 2:3

> **Rom. 14:5–6** "One person regards one day above another, another regards every day alike. Each person must be fully convinced in his own mind. He who observes the day, observes it for the Lord, and he who eats, does so for the Lord, for he gives thanks to God; and he who eats not, for the Lord he does not eat, and gives thanks to God."
>
> **Gal. 4:9–10** "But now that you have come to know God, or rather to be known by God, how is it that you turn back again to the weak and worthless elemental things, to which you desire to be enslaved all over again? You observe days and months and seasons and years."
>
> **Col. 2:16–17** "Therefore no one is to act as your judge in regard to food or drink or in respect to a festival or a new moon or Sabbaths—things which are a mere shadow of what is to come; but the substance belongs to Christ."

Each of these texts is best understood through viewing the "sabbath day" to be the Sabbath as it was particularly observed in Israel, since most commentators agree that all three texts involve false teachings that entailed a return to Israel's old laws in disregard of how Christ's coming has changed those laws. Furthermore, that this is the case is indicated in that what is being nullified is not just the Sabbath according to the specific ways in which Israel was to observe it, but rather the whole Sabbatical system of not only Sabbath "days" but also of Sabbath "months and seasons and years" (Gal. 4:10) and a Sabbath "festival or a new moon" (Col. 2:16). This would include the observance of the Sabbatical Year (every seventh year the ground was to rest) and the Jubilee Year (after seven weeks of years, there was to be restoration of property that had been lost). Accordingly, the nullification of the Sabbath day of rest was part of a nullification of all of Israel's laws dealing with Sabbatical patterns and other laws such as dietary laws (Col. 2:16).[37] Therefore, the plural "Sab-

---

points to an eternal Sabbath rest for humanity (pp. 198–99), he is unconvinced that the lack of consummation of such rest in the church age means that the sign of the Sabbath day must continue on, especially on Sunday (p. 216). The reason for this is due in great part to his denial that there is a creation mandate in Gen. 2:3 for a Sabbath rest day, and that there is no NT evidence for such a mandate (p. 216). However, throughout and below, I have tried to provide a biblical theological rationale for such a mandate being valid for NT believers. It must be remembered that even non-Sabbatarians cannot provide an explicit exegetical rationale for why the church changed the worship day for the people of God from Saturday to Sunday, though I believe that their biblical-theological rationale (Christ's resurrection) is viable.

37. The Hellenistic Jewish false "philosophy" (Col. 2:8) focuses on keeping regulations about "food or drink . . . a festival or a new moon or Sabbaths" (2:16), which concern "decrees such as 'Do not handle, do not taste, do not touch'" (2:20b–21). That this language is Jewish and not pagan is apparent also from the *Let. Arist.* 142: God "hedged us [Jews] round on all sides by rules of purity, affecting alike what we eat, or drink, or touch, or hear, or see." Likewise, the combination of "feast," "sabbath," and "new moon" occurs repeatedly in the LXX to refer to the festivals that were specifically a part of the system of Israel's law, which every Israelite was

baths" (*sabbatōn*) in Col. 2:16 probably includes not only the Sabbath at the end of each week but also the whole system of Sabbath days held at various times. It needs to be recalled that the nullification of these laws came about because Christ has fulfilled them typologically.

Would not the point of these passages be that the church no longer is obliged to observe the Sabbath day? Yes and no. Yes, in the sense that Israel's institutions were typological pointers to Christ, so that they were "a shadow of what is to come," which was Christ as the "substance" of these shadows (Col. 2:17). In general, the reason that the external rites (dietary laws, circumcision, Sabbaths, etc.) of the law are no longer necessary is that their redemptive-historical purpose was to function as a "shadow of what is to come" in Christ (Col. 2:17). In one way or another, Paul understood that the various external expressions of the OT law pointed to the advent of the Messiah, who now has come, so that the purpose of the typological function of the various Israelite institutions is now finished. Christ has completely fulfilled these things.

But we must also answer no. It is true that the Sabbath day as Israel was commanded to observe it, and as a part of the whole system of the nation's calendrical Sabbath observances and festivals, has ceased because what it pointed to (Christ) has come. Yet if, as I have argued, Israel's Sabbath ordinance is based partly on the creational mandate of Gen. 2:2–3, then part of this ordinance has not ceased. Its eschatological goal pointed not only to Christ's final resurrection rest and believers' inaugurated salvific rest in Christ, but also to the final and complete rest of God's people in the new heaven and earth,[38] a goal that I have contended is embedded in Gen. 2:2–3 itself. Christ himself has completely fulfilled what part of the Israelite Sabbath pointed to, which is the rest of the messianic king, who would represent true Israel finally at rest. This view of the ceasing of the Israelite Sabbath because it is fulfilled in Christ is analogous to other unique Israelite laws finding typological fulfillment in Christ—for example, circumcision as key to incorporation into the Israelite covenant community (Christians have now been circumcised from the old world in Christ

---

to obey (1 Chron. 23:31; 2 Chron. 2:4; 31:3; Neh. 10:34 [10:33 ET]; Isa. 1:13–14; Ezek. 45:17; Hos. 2:13 [2:11 ET]; 1 Esd. 5:52; Jdt. 8:6; 1 Macc. 10:34).

38. Judaism believed that the weekly Sabbath pointed to the eternal rest of the new creation (note *L.A.E.* [*Vita*] 51:1–2: "Man of God, do not prolong mourning your dead more than six days, because the seventh day is a sign of the resurrection, the rest of the coming age, and on the seventh day the Lord rested from all his works"; see also *m. Tamid* 7.4; *b. Roš Haš.* 31a; *b. Ber.* 57b; *Mek. Exod.* Shabbata 2.38–41; *Midr. Ps.* 92; *Pirqe R. El.* 19; *'Abot R. Nat.* 1; *Gen. Rab.* 44.17; *S. Eli. Rab.* 2). Other texts possibly assume that the end-time rest may have been pointed to by the weekly Sabbath (4 Ezra 8:52; 2 Bar. 73–74). In *Apoc. Mos.* 43:3 Seth is told that "on the seventh day" he should "rest and rejoice on it, because on that very day, God rejoices (yes) and we angels (too) with the righteous soul, who has passed away from the earth." There were also variants of viewing world history and its consummation on the model of God's seven-day creation week (the preceding Jewish material follows the discussion by Lincoln, "Sabbath," 199–200).

by being cut off in death),[39] the dietary laws by which Israelites maintained ritual cleanness (Christians now are clean in Christ's blood),[40] and the temple (fulfilled in Christ as the new temple).[41] In fact, Israel's entire law, which was the epitome of divine wisdom in the old age, pointed to and was fulfilled in Christ, the greater revelation of divine wisdom in the new age.[42]

With respect specifically to the temple typology, the Sabbath was inextricably linked to temple worship and thus was part of temple typology fulfilled in Christ's construction of the new temple, reigning on the throne and resting in that temple as Israel's end-time Messiah.[43] But that aspect of the Israelite Sabbath that continued the creational mandate continues on into the church age because it pointed not only to the Messiah's rest as representative of Israel but also to the final rest of his people, which did not consummately occur at Christ's first coming. Thus, the creational mandate and its goal that predates Israel's Sabbath and was partially expressed through the nation's Sabbath continues on after Israel's institutions find their completion in and are abolished in Christ. In this regard, John Calvin affirms,

> Therefore when we hear that the Sabbath was abrogated by the coming of Christ, we must distinguish between what belongs to the perpetual government of human life, and what properly belongs to ancient figures [i.e., what was

39. Colossians 2:11–13.

40. Colossians 2:16–17.

41. Colossians 1:19 (on which see G. K. Beale, "Colossians," in *Commentary on the New Testament Use of the Old Testament*, ed. G. K. Beale and D. A. Carson [Grand Rapids: Baker Academic, 2007], 855–57).

42. Colossians 2:3; cf. Col. 1:15–20 (on which, see ibid., 851–55).

43. In this regard, it is particularly relevant that the phraseology combining "Sabbath," "new moon," and "feast" found in Col. 2:16 appears elsewhere in the OT often as part of the description of temple liturgy and worship; as noted generally above, see again 1 Chron. 23:31; 2 Chron. 2:4; 8:13; 31:3; Neh. 10:33; 13:22; Ezek. 45:17; 1 Esd. 5:52 (with a view to temple worship); the other occurrences in Isa. 1:13–14; Hos. 2:11; Jdt. 8:6; 1 Macc. 10:34 probably presuppose a liturgical context in the temple. Likewise, Lev. 26:2 reflects the inextricable link between Sabbath worship in the context of the temple: "You shall keep My sabbaths and reverence My sanctuary; I am the Lord." Other references to the Sabbath also relate it to the context of temple worship (e.g., Lev. 24:8; Num. 28:9–10; 1 Chron. 9:32). Jon Laansma has made the same observation, adding texts such as Lev. 23:3; Ezek. 46:4–5 (*"I Will Give You Rest". The "Rest" Motif in the New Testament with Special Reference to Matthew 11 and Hebrews 3–4*, WUNT 2/98 [Tübingen: Mohr Siebeck, 1997], 68). For Israel's temple and its laws as a key to understanding the relation of Israel's other laws to the NT, see chap. 26 below. Similarly, the "food" and "drink" in Col. 2:16 likely have as part of the background food and drink offerings that were to take place in the temple, though the same Greek words found in Colossians (*brōsis* and *posis*) do not occur in these OT references (e.g., for "food" offerings, see Lev. 3:11, 16, and seven other times only in Leviticus; "drink" offerings are also given in the same context of the temple [e.g., Exod. 25:29, and often throughout the Pentateuch]). Indeed, the combination of "meat" and "drink" offerings occurs often in the Pentateuch (in the LXX see "whole burnt offering" [*holokautōsis*] and "drink offerings" [*spondē*] [e.g., 13x in Numbers, mainly in chaps. 28–29]). "Grain offerings" are often found in this combination.

unique to Israel], the use of which was abolished when the truth was fulfilled [when Christ came].[44]

That part of Israel's Sabbath observance was based on a creational mandate and part on the nation's unique observance is clear from the two versions of the Sabbath law, in Exod. 20:8–11 and Deut. 5:12–15. The first gives God's rest after creation as the basis of Israel's Sabbath, and the second appeals to God's deliverance of the nation from Egypt as the basis, when God delivered them from laborious bondage to the rest that came with freedom. The Sabbath commemoration of the exodus redemption also pointed forward to the greater end-time exodus redemption through Christ, which has been fulfilled in his death and resurrection as the Passover Lamb (e.g., John 19:34–37; 1 Cor. 5:7–8). Thus, there are various ways that the Sabbath pointed to and was fulfilled in Christ, but that aspect of Israel's Sabbath that was based on and reflected the creational mandate of Gen. 2 continues on into the church age. "Creation and redemption are both motives for its [Israel's Sabbath] observance, the one for all men [including Israel], the other especially for Israel."[45] Geerhardus Vos sums up well the relationship of the creational mandate to Israel's Sabbath and to the church's Sabbath:

> The Sabbath . . . has passed through the various phases of development of redemption, remaining the same in essence but modified as to its form, as the new state of affairs at each point [epoch] might require.[46]

> From all this [the various laws related to Israel's Sabbath and typological sabbatical celebrations] we have been released by the work of Christ, but not from the Sabbath as instituted at Creation.[47]

Thus, the unique nationalistic aspects of Israel's laws that explicitly distinguish them from the gentiles, including the way the Sabbath was practiced and on what day it was observed, do not continue.[48] For example, the regulation that Israelites could do no work at all on the Sabbath, under threat of capital punishment (Exod. 35:2; Num. 15:32–36), does not continue into the practice of the Sabbath in the new age.[49] In contrast, the form of Sabbath celebration

44. Calvin, *Genesis*, 106–7.
45. Stott, "σάββατον," *NIDNTT* 3:406.
46. Vos, *Biblical Theology*, 139.
47. Ibid., 143.
48. All the calendrical holy days that Israel celebrated find fulfillment in Christ, including the unique ways that Israel celebrated her Sabbath. The fuller reasons that the unique nationalistic elements of Israel's law are not carried over into the new-covenant age must await further elaboration below (see chap. 26).
49. In this respect, notice the strict requirements about doing no work on the Sabbath day in Exod. 16:23–26; 34:21; 35:3.

in this age on the first day of the week is the meeting of the church in worship. This weekly worship gathering commemorates Christ's inauguration of rest and points to the eschatological rest of saints gathered in worship of God and Christ through his word, songs of praise, prayer, and fellowship at the very end of the age. Accordingly, saints in this age gather on the Sabbath to worship Christ and God by means of his word, praise, song, prayer, and fellowship, which foreshadow the greater worship in the new cosmos. This maintains the creational pattern of a one day among seven that is "blessed" and "set apart" from the others (Gen. 2:2–3).

Should the Church Keep the Sabbath in the Very Same Way as Israel Did?

Of course, if one were to argue persuasively that the creational mandate included the ceasing from all work on the Sabbath, as in Israel, then this would continue into the new age. However, this is difficult to contend. To argue in this manner is problematic because all of Israel's specific Sabbath laws would be hard to carry over. For example, should a Christian be put to death for breaking the Sabbath, since this was the penalty for Israelites who did so? Even the strictest Sabbatarians, who believe that the Christian Sabbath is modeled on Israel's, would not believe that death is a fitting punishment for those who fail to keep the Sabbath. My brief response to this must go back again to discussion of Gen. 1. God's rest on the seventh creation day was not inactivity but only a ceasing of his creative work. Once he had brought creation into being, he continued to exercise his sovereign maintaining of it.[50] Furthermore, in support of this last point, it has been argued by others persuasively that God's creation was a temple-building process, at the end of which God sat and rested on his throne as king of his inaugurated cosmic temple. This is analogous with several descriptions later in the OT that say that after Israel defeated its enemies through divine strength, the temple was built in Jerusalem so that God would "rest" there as sovereign king (e.g., 1 Chron. 28:2; 2 Chron. 6:41; Ps. 132:7–8, 13–14; Isa. 66:1; Jdt. 9:8; *Tg. Onq.* Exod. 25:8; cf. the similar implications of Exod. 15:17–18). Since Israel's temple was a small model of the entire creation, it is appropriate to compare God's resting in Israel's temple, after Israel's enemies have been overcome, with his resting on the seventh day, after his subduing and ruling over the unformed chaos of creation.

Thus, the resting is best understood as the enjoyment of a position of sovereign rule in a cosmic temple, after the quelling of chaotic forces. One

---

50. Could John 5:16–17 reflect some aspect of this notion when Jesus responds to those accusing him of breaking the Sabbath by healing a man who was unable to walk? Jesus responded by saying, "My Father is working until now, and I Myself am working," putting himself on a par with God (see Stott, "σάββατον," *NIDNTT* 3:409). Judaism rightly understood that after finishing his works of creation, God continued to be active in sustaining his creative work, in giving life, and in executing temporal judgments (see Lincoln, "Sabbath," 203).

may compare God's rest at the helm of his holy of holies headquarters in the temple to a US president beginning to reside in the White House. First comes the work of campaigning, and after being elected, the president does not go to live in the White House in order to sit in an easy chair and relax and do nothing. Rather, the new president begins to live in the White House to "settle down" (i.e., rest from the campaigning work) and begin doing the work of the presidency, being chief executive over the country. God, of course, was not campaigning for election in the first six days of creation, but he was setting up his cosmic temple to be his "holy headquarters," from which, after creating, he would run the world.[51]

God has "blessed the seventh day and set it apart" so that his people would commemorate his assumption of kingship and beginning rule over the cosmic temple, which he had created. Before the Mosaic era, at the least, God's people would commemorate God's seventh day of beginning rule probably through some kind of worshipful acts. Since the coming of Christ, there is commemoration not only of God's kingship rest after creation but also of Christ's achievement of rest as messianic king at the right hand of God. This also occurs through worshipful acts at the assembling of saints on Sunday. As noted earlier, the activities of the once-a-week gathering should be modeled after and point to the kingly rest of eschatologically gathered saints in worship of God and Christ through his word, songs of praise, prayer, and fellowship at the very end of the age.[52] After such gathered worship, on Sunday saints can do "work," though in conscious imitation of God's and Christ's management of creation, which is a conscious "work" to be done on other days of the week, since it should be remembered that believers have begun to enter into Christ's own rest. Nevertheless, it must be recalled that believers are still involved in building God's temple on earth. In the midst of their temple-building activities of "good works" throughout the week,[53] every seventh day they need to punctuate that activity by this special commemoration of the completion of God's and Christ's temple-building

51. This illustration comes from John H. Walton, *The Lost World of Genesis One: Ancient Cosmology and the Origins Debate* (Downers Grove, IL: IVP Academic, 2009), 73. Walton (p. 76) also gives the example of buying a new computer and taking time to set it up (getting the equipment placed rightly, connecting the wires, installing the software, etc.). After doing the setting-up work, one stops that work in order to begin the new work of actually using the computer. God did the same thing in setting up the cosmos, after which he began to reign over and manage it. For Walton's elaboration of the kind of "active rest" that God enjoyed on the seventh day of creation, see pp. 72–77.

52. The model for such end-time liturgical activities is provided by passages throughout Revelation that show the heavenly saints gathered around God or the Lamb and his word, praying, singing, and praising (e.g., 5:9–14; 11:15–17; 14:1–5; 15:2–4; 19:1–7).

53. Hebrews 4:10 says that at the end of the age, the person who has completely "entered His [God's] rest" has "also rested from his [good] works, as God did [rest] from His [good works of creating]." Thus, until the final resurrection, saints imitate God's creative good works by doing good works of their own.

activities and consequent position of kingship. Thus, the "bottom line" duty of the day of Sabbath "rest" for the church is the commemoration of God's and Christ's creative work and rest in worshipful assembly.

It remained for Adam and his progeny to complete this temple, after ruling over opposition (i.e., the serpent), and to enter into the temple rest into which God had already entered. There is not space here to repeat my extended argument that Gen. 1 is to be seen as a cosmic temple built by God in which he rested as sovereign king, after he had overcome the chaotic forces. For the same reason, I cannot elaborate further here on Adam's temple-building purpose in relation to his kingship.[54]

The Relationship between the Church's Inaugurated Sabbath Rest in Christ and the Once-a-Week Sabbath Observance

It is important at this juncture to reiterate and underscore that Christ has completely fulfilled for himself the eschatological rest of the last Adam pointed to in Gen. 2:2–3, after having built his end-time temple by his resurrection (e.g., John 2:18–22). And, by doing so, Christ has inaugurated Sabbath rest now for all who trust in him, are identified with his resurrection, and thus are represented by him in his position of rest. The inaugurated spiritual rest that saints have obtained presently in identification with Christ's resurrection rest is one that continues every day of the week and not merely on Sunday. They have not yet, however, obtained the complete end-time rest in their bodily resurrected persons, since the continued expansion of Christ's temple through them by means of the Spirit is not yet completed. There is, therefore, still a one-day special observance on Sunday for the church, the purpose of which is to look forward to the consummation of end-time rest in the new heaven and earth. This Sunday observance is a continuation of the creational Sabbath ordinance of Gen. 2:3, whose purpose also was to look forward to consummate eschatological spiritual and physical rest.

This perspective on the Sabbath is a biblical-theological conclusion, since there is no NT text that says that Christ achieved latter-day rest at his resurrection and that this rest represents others who identify with him.[55] However, some texts explicitly affirm that believers will consummately achieve that rest at the very end of time (Heb. 4:1, 3, 6, 9–10).[56]

---

54. On both these points, see Beale, *Temple*, 81–93, where also supporting bibliography is cited. In addition, for Gen. 1 as a temple-building project by God, see Walton, *Lost World*, 72–92, 102–7 (see also Walton's more detailed monograph on the same subject, *Genesis One as Ancient Cosmology* (Winona Lake, IN: Eisenbrauns, forthcoming).

55. Although, as noted above, this seems to be suggested by Matt. 11:28–29 and implicit in Heb. 3:14; 4:1, 6, 11.

56. Cf. Rev. 14:13: "And I heard a voice from heaven, saying, 'Write, "Blessed are the dead who die in the Lord from now on!"' 'Yes,' says the Spirit, 'so that they may rest from their labors, for their deeds follow with them.'"

Has the Sabbath Worship Day Changed from Saturday to Sunday?

One final problem with holding to the ongoing validity of the Sabbath for the church is to explain why it has been changed to the first day of the week from the last day of the week. There is no exegetical evidence supporting such a change, just as there is no explicit evidence supporting the notion that Christ's resurrection has consummated rest for him and inaugurated it for believers. But change there was. Even those who do not hold to a weekly Sabbath rest but do hold that Sunday is the normative time for the church's weekly worship have no explicit exegetical or theological evidence for why the weekly worship of God's people has been changed from the last day of the week to the first day. There is only occasional description in the NT that weekly church worship was on Sunday (Acts 20:7; 1 Cor. 16:2), and even this is implicit. Most non-Sabbatarians affirm the validity of worship on the first day of the week because that was when Christ rose from the dead.[57] Accordingly, the church met from earliest times on the first day of the week to commemorate Christ's resurrection. Non-Sabbatarians even acknowledge that although the church did not carry over the Jewish Sabbath, it did continue to hold to the Israelite "division of time based on the Old Testament sabbath," which is evident from the fact that the early church speaks of the "first day of the [seven-day] week," which is the day after Israel's Sabbath day.[58] In this respect, Lincoln strikingly says,

> Thus despite the radical discontinuity involved in the church's beginning to assemble on the first day to commemorate their fellowship with the risen Lord, there is also a definite continuity with the Old Testament people of God in that this was done on a weekly and not a monthly or yearly basis. In this the early church acknowledged the sabbatical sequence of time.[59]

This is a surprising concession by a non-Sabbatarian. If the early church carried over the "sabbatical sequence of time," why would not this broad calendrical continuity include a one-in-seven special day of commemoration and worship that is also part of this continuity? In fact, the early church did have such a one-in-seven worship day. Lincoln's argument posits too much discontinuity. My overall discussion in this chapter so far points to Sunday as the Sabbath day, not just the weekly scheme, being carried over from the OT, especially as a continuation of the one-in-seven creation mandate that the seventh day be "blessed" and "set apart."

While non-Sabbatarians believe that the day of congregational worship has changed from Saturday to Sunday because of the earth-shattering event of Christ's resurrection, Sabbatarians also hold that the Sabbath day observance

---

57. Note the Gospel texts that repeat that Christ was raised on "the first day of the week" (Matt. 28:1; Mark 16:2, 9; Luke 24:1; John 20:1, 19).

58. Lincoln, "Sabbath," 200–201.

59. Ibid., 201.

was changed for the same reason. Both perspectives affirm that Christ's resurrection was the beginning of the new creation and the consummation of Christ's "rest" as king; both also hold that Christ's resurrection was the inauguration of believers' rest in positional identification with Christ's resurrection and their beginning personal experience of that resurrection existence. The continuation of a weekly day of rest not only commemorates this past rest but also points forward to Christ's final coming, when believers themselves will be resurrected bodily and completely enter the same rest that Christ has already fully entered. Sabbatarians, however, continue to label this commemorative day to be the "Sabbath," since the sign to which the weekly Sabbath points has not yet been finally and completely fulfilled. This is not a simple carry-over of Israel's Sabbath ordinance; it is a continuation of the expression of the creation ordinance (partially expressed in Israel's Sabbath), which mandated that humanity rest on the seventh day. This seventh day of the creational mandate has been changed to the first day because of the aforementioned significance of Christ's Sabbath-fulfilling resurrection and inaugurating Sabbath rest for his people. This transferred Sabbath on Sunday is likely to be identified with "the Lord's day" (*kyriakē hēmera*) found in Rev. 1:10 (as identified in the *Didache* [14:1],[60] by Ignatius [Ign. *Magn.* 9:1], and by subsequent patristic writers).[61]

Lincoln's final conclusion to his article, which contends for a non-Sabbatarian view, fits just as well, if not better, into a Sabbatarian perspective. With respect to the Heidelberg Catechism's view that the ongoing relevance of Israel's fourth commandment lies in saints doing good works by the Spirit and beginning to experience in this life "the eternal sabbath," he says,

> Such a theology suggests that as Christian believers meet together on the Lord's Day, they will commemorate the true Sabbath rest Christ has brought through his death and resurrection, and under the Word of God and through mutual exhortation, they will be encouraged to continue in this rest so that their participation in its eschatological fullness will be assured.[62]

When the Lord's Day is also seen as the continuation of the Sabbath, the redemptive-historical nature of this commemoration of "the true Sabbath rest" is expressed even more clearly and with appreciation of its roots all the way back in Gen. 2:2–3. But there is a transformation of the Sabbath as it continues into the new age. First, the seventh-day commemoration in Gen. 2:3 and Israel's Sabbath ordinance is transferred to the first day of the week because of Christ's resurrection. Second, Israel's way of observing the Sabbath, with

---

60. Although it is not explicitly specified there that it is the first day of the week or Sunday.
61. Following Stott, "σάββατον," *NIDNTT* 3:411–12. Stott (pp. 412–15) provides extensive bibliography on Sabbath issues in both Testaments; see also the briefer bibliography in Wenham, *Genesis 1–15*, 34.
62. Lincoln, "Sabbath," 216–17.

all its detailed requirements, falls away, and there is a return to the creational mandate. The observance of this mandate is a day of commemoration of God's creative rest, a celebration that Christ has entered that rest, that believers have begun to enter such rest, and a pointing forward to believers completely entering that rest. In addition, Christ's coming fulfills Israel's unique Sabbath commandment, since he is Israel's Messiah, accomplishing Israel's end-time exodus and representing true Israel and the end-time temple. Christ fulfills all of Israel's types, including that to which Israel's Sabbath pointed.

Conclusion

I have argued throughout this book that significant NT ideas have been facets of Christ's death and resurrection as an end-time new creation and kingdom. We have seen this to be the case again with the notion of the Sabbath. God's work in building the first creation as his temple was concluded with his rest on the seventh day, which we have seen was a sign of his kingship. His rest pointed to the final rest of humanity, after it was to finish its good work of serving God on earth. This was first fulfilled by Christ, the son of Adam, who, after completing his work of building the temple and of redemption in his ministry, death, and resurrection, rested at God's right hand as a king in resurrected glory. Christ's ongoing resurrected status is a new-creational condition, as we have seen. All believers are identified with his ongoing resurrected, new-creational rest. But this rest is not consummated for them individually until they receive resurrection bodies and become consummately part of the new creation. Until then, Christians still observe the Sabbath as a sign pointing to their final resurrection rest. The Sabbath has shifted from Saturday to Sunday because that is the day on which Christ rose and obtained his kingly new-creational rest.[63]

---

63. See John M. Frame, *The Doctrine of the Christian Life* (Phillipsburg, NJ: P&R, 2008), 513–74, for a thorough theological discussion of the Sabbath in the OT and in the NT, which is generally consistent with the overall approach in this chapter, though differing to some degree over the precise activities suitable for NT Sabbath observance.

24

The Church's New-Creational Transformation of Israel's Distinguishing Marks

Baptism, the Lord's Supper, the Church Office, and New Testament Canon

I n this chapter we continue to see that important elements of ecclesiology are aspects of the eschatological new-creational storyline.[1] These elements also show how the church as the faithful people of God—another important aspect of the storyline—is distinguished from the world.

The Church's Sacraments of Baptism and the Lord's Supper as Markers of New-Creational, End-Time Realities

Baptism and the Lord's Supper, which N. T. Wright would refer to as the "symbols" associated with the biblical "story,"[2] are also charged with notions of new creation.

---

1. The following sections of this chapter on baptism, the Lord's Supper, and the office of elder are a revision of G. K. Beale, "The Eschatological Conception of New Testament Theology," in *"The Reader Must Understand": Eschatology in Bible and Theology*, ed. K. E. Brower and M. W. Elliott (Leicester: Apollos, 1997), 39–44.

2. N. T. Wright, *The New Testament and the People of God* (Minneapolis: Fortress, 1992), 447–48.

Baptism

Baptism connotes the believer's identification with Christ's death and resurrection:[3] the old self or "old man" (positioned in Adam) was crucified with Christ, and Christians have risen with him in "newness of life" (e.g., Rom. 6:3–11). In addition, two other significant NT discussions of baptism compare it respectively with Noah's salvation through water (1 Pet. 3:20–21) and Israel's exodus through water (1 Cor. 10:1–2), both of which have been discussed above as major parts of the overall OT storyline of re-creation.[4] Also important in this regard is the description of salvation in Titus 3:5 through baptismal and new-creational imagery: "He saved us . . . by the washing of regeneration [*palingenesia*] and <u>renewing</u> by the Holy Spirit."[5]

The possible relationship of baptism to circumcision needs to be addressed.

BAPTISM AND CIRCUMCISION IN COLOSSIANS 2:11–13

The only passage in the NT that brings the two ideas together is Col. 2:11–13. What is the relationship between the two in this passage? A brief analysis of Col. 2:9–13 must be conducted to try to answer this question. The connection of baptism to circumcision in this passage had been greatly debated, since the link is not explicit. As with the difficult question and discussion of the Sabbath in the preceding chapter, I again plead for the reader's forbearance in following the dense exegetical and biblical-theological connections in this thorny passage.

The Context of Colossians 2:9–13

For in Him all the fullness of Deity dwells in bodily form, and in Him you have been made complete, and He is the head over all rule and authority; and in Him you were also circumcised with a circumcision made without hands, in the removal of the body of the flesh by the circumcision of Christ; having been buried

---

3. For the foundation of baptism being in Christ's death and resurrection, see Oscar Cullmann, *Baptism in the New Testament*, trans. J. K. S. Reid, SBT 1 (Chicago: Allenson, 1950), 9–22.

4. For a fuller discussion of the relationship of these two OT events as a background through which to understand baptism, see chap. 2 under the heading "The Repeated Cosmic Judgment and New Creation Episodes of the Old Testament"; Meredith G. Kline, *By Oath Consigned: A Reinterpretation of the Covenant Signs of Circumcision and Baptism* (Grand Rapids: Eerdmans, 1968), 63–83. Against this OT backdrop, baptism can be seen as "a sign of the eschatological ordeal" (ibid., 79). Subsequently, in support of Kline, Wright has observed that exodus typology and Christ's death and resurrection are associated with baptism, and that baptism was "the mode of entry into the eschatological people . . . *because* it had to do with Jesus, who had himself brought Israel's history to its appointed destiny, and who as Messiah summed up Israel in himself" (*New Testament and the People of God*, 447).

5. Not coincidentally the term *palingenesia* is used by Philo (*Mos.* 2.65) to refer to the renewal of the earth after the flood, and by Josephus (*Ant.* 11.66) to the return of Israel from captivity. Likewise, Wis. 19:6 describes the exodus event as the time when "the whole creation was again formed in its own kind anew" (see also 19:18).

with Him in baptism, in which you were also raised up with Him through faith in the working of God, who raised Him from the dead. When you were dead in your transgressions and the uncircumcision of your flesh, He made you alive together with Him, having forgiven us all our transgressions.

Paul has told the readers that they are to focus on Christ as the one "in whom are hidden all the treasures of wisdom and knowledge," so that they will not be "deluded by persuasive argument" otherwise (2:3–4). They are to continue to trust Christ, as they had done in the beginning, and become increasingly established in their faith so that "no one takes you captive through philosophy and empty deception, according to the tradition of men, according to the elements of the world and not according to Christ" (2:6–8). The word "philosophy" (*philosophia*) and the phrases "empty deception," "the tradition of men," and "the elements of the world" must be understood in light of the following context in chapter 2. In particular, in view is a wrong understanding of the meaning and application of OT law for the new age. This appears to be part of erroneous Jewish doctrines that focused on the law instead of Christ as the epitome of divine revelation.[6]

Verse 10 changes the focus to Christ, who has begun to fulfill all to which God's dwelling in the OT pointed: he is the end-time temple.[7] "In Christ" believers are eschatologically "completed" in that they share in the fulfillment of the OT that Christ has brought about. For example, they are part of the new temple in Christ (v. 10a, and see v. 9 above), and they share in Christ's messianic kingdom reign, which he has commenced (v. 10).

Verses 11–13 introduce another OT institution that is a type that finds its fulfillment in Christ and believers. The reference to "circumcision made without hands" (2:11) implies a contrast with "circumcision made with hands," which Paul refers to in Eph. 2:11 ("circumcision in the flesh made by hands"). The word "handmade" (*cheiropoiētos*) always refers to idols in the LXX and is without exception a negative reference, with overtones of idolatry, in the NT.[8] Thus, the implied reference to "circumcision made with hands" in Col. 2 further enforces the notion that it is idolatrous to continue to trust in the OT "shadows" once their fulfillment has come.[9]

---

6. See N. T. Wright, *The Epistles of Paul to the Colossians and to Philemon*, TNTC (Grand Rapids: Eerdmans, 1986), 23–30.

7. For exegetical argumentation supporting this conclusion, see G. K. Beale, "Colossians," in *Commentary on the New Testament Use of the Old Testament*, ed. G. K. Beale and D. A. Carson (Grand Rapids: Baker Academic, 2007), 855–57. See also chap. 16 under the subheading "Colossians 1."

8. On which, see further G. K. Beale, *The Temple and the Church's Mission: A Biblical Theology of the Dwelling Place of God*, NSBT 17 (Downers Grove, IL: InterVarsity, 2004), 224–25.

9. This identification with idolatry is developed further in Col. 2:18, 22–23, on which, see Beale, "Colossians," 860–62.

The Typological Function of the Old Testament Laws and Institutions

The clearest reason for the fading away of OT types and institutions in the church age comes in Col. 2:17, which, together with 2:9–15, serves as the basis for refuting the false idolatrous teaching in Colossae. I will not repeat everything said in the preceding chapter about Col. 2:16–17, so my comments here can be more focused on circumcision.

The external rites (dietary laws, special cultic feast days, Sabbaths, circumcision, etc.) of the law are no longer necessary in that their redemptive-historical purpose was to function as a "shadow of things about to come, that is, the [substantial] body of Christ" (Col. 2:17 [my translation]), which has come. In one way or another, Paul understood that the various external expressions of the OT law pointed to the coming Messiah, who has now arrived. Therefore, the law's preparatory adumbrating function has come to an end because the messianic "substance" to which it pointed has arrived. The idea here is very similar to that in Matt. 5:17: Jesus "fulfilled" the "Law" and "the Prophets" by fulfilling in his actions and words the OT's direct verbal prophecies, foreshadowing events (e.g., the Passover lamb) and institutions (e.g., sacrifices and temple), the ultimate meaning of the law, and the true and enduring authority of the OT.[10]

Hebrews 8:5 and 10:1 likewise speak respectively of the tabernacle and the sacrifices as a "shadow" pointing forward to the true end-time temple and of Christ's once-for-all sacrifice. Colossians 2:17 and the Hebrews texts are classic expressions of the NT's typological view of the OT. Especially emphasized in this context of Colossians are dietary laws (2:16, 21–22), which were designed to make a person clean for participation in worship at the tabernacle or temple.[11] Accordingly, Paul apparently sees that these specific laws foreshadowed the time when believers would be made clean by Christ's redemptive work in order to qualify them for worship in the true temple, founded upon Christ and consisting of Christians.[12]

The Typological Function of Old Testament Circumcision

The first explicit expression of this "shadow to substance" notion in Colossians is in 2:11–13, which anticipates 2:17. In verses 11–13 Paul appears to view the external rite of circumcision to be a pointer to the greater redemptive reality of Christ and his followers being "circumcised" or "cut off" from the

---

10. For the full argument, see D. A. Carson, *Matthew 1–12*, EBC (Grand Rapids: Zondervan, 1995), 140–45.

11. For this view of the original design of the dietary laws, e.g., see K. Kohler, "Dietary Laws," in vol. 4 of *The Jewish Encyclopedia: A Descriptive Record of the History, Religion, Literature, and Customs of the Jewish People from the Earliest Times to the Present Day*, ed. I. Singer (New York: Funk & Wagnalls, 1903), 596; see similarly H. Rabinowitz, "Dietary Laws," *EncJud* 6:120–40.

12. See on 1:19 in Beale, "Colossians."

old, sinful world and set apart to a new one. Accordingly, Paul speaks in 2:11 of believers' redemption consisting of being "circumcised with a circumcision made without hands," which has occurred by means of the "circumcision of Christ" (i.e., his death).[13] "Uncircumcision [*akrobystia*] of your flesh [*sarx*]" (v. 13a) represented sinful unbelief from which one needed to be "circumcised." This phrase, "uncircumcision of your flesh," is likely an analogical allusion to Gen. 17:10–27 LXX, where "the flesh [*sarx*] of your/his uncircumcision [*akrobystia*]" appears four times (see also Gen. 34:24 LXX; Lev. 12:3; Jdt. 14:10). There the point of the narrative is that those who are in covenantal relationship with God should express that relationship through being "circumcised in the flesh of his uncircumcison." This was a symbol expressing that a true Israelite was one whose heart had been cut apart from unbelief and sin (Deut. 10:16; Jer. 4:4b; 9:26; Ezek. 44:7, 9),[14] and who was set apart to God (Jer. 4:4a [see further Gen. 17 below]). Similarly, Paul compares this physical circumcision to the spiritual reality of the new-covenant relationship with Christ. When believers are identified by faith with Christ's death, they are "cut off" from the old world and subsequently raised and set apart to new life (the point of 2:12–13).[15] Paul's reference to the "removal of the body of the flesh" is likely also part of the allusion to Gen. 17, where too "flesh" is part of the description of the symbolic sinful condition directly preceding circumcision.

But Paul seems to be making more than an analogy here. His likely acquaintance with another OT background outside of Genesis suggests that he viewed circumcision in the flesh to be pointing to a coming spiritual circumcision to be performed by the Messiah on behalf of eschatological Israel. Paul seems to be developing the forward-looking, end-time meaning of circumcision that had been expressed already in Deuteronomy. It is said that the majority

13. The "circumcision of Christ" could be an objective genitive (Christ as the object of the circumcision) or a subjective genitive ("circumcision by Christ"). The former may be indicated by the fact that Christ's death is referred to twice in the directly following v. 12. It is difficult to choose, but I prefer the latter because the ruling idea of v. 11a and vv. 12–14 is what has happened to the Colossians (in line with Martin Salter, "Does Baptism Replace Circumcision? An Examination of the Relationship between Circumcision and Baptism in Colossians 2:11–12," *Themelios* 35 [2010]: 24–25, discussing both options).

14. So also Josh. 5:8–9, where the circumcision of the second generation of Israel is said to symbolize God having "rolled away the reproach of Egypt from you." There are various interpretations of the symbolism here, but I think that the best identification is that the circumcison is a reference to a contrast with the Israelite generation who came from Egypt and were unfaithful and disobedient in the wilderness and died there because of their unbelief (Josh. 5:4–7) (see Richard S. Hess, *Joshua*, TOTC [Downers Grove, IL: InterVarsity, 1996], 119–22). The second generation's circumcision represented a "cutting off" from its identification with such an unbelieving condition.

15. Alternatively, if "the circumcision of Christ" is an objective genitive, the idea would be that when believers are identified by faith with Christ's death, which "cut him off" from the old world and led to his resurrection, they are likewise "cut off" from the old world and subsequently raised (the point of 2:12–13).

of Israelites need to "circumcise" their spiritual "heart," though they are physically circumcised (Deut. 10:16 [cf. Jer. 4:4; 9:25–26]). This command to "circumcise the heart" includes both a reference to cutting oneself off from an old manner of life (i.e., in Deut. 10:16 from a "stiff" heart," ultimately equivalent to spiritual death) and being separated to a new condition of life. This is expressed even more explicitly in Jer. 4:4a: "Circumcise yourselves to the LORD [for life] and remove the foreskins of your heart [the old, sinful heart of death]." Circumcision here in verse 4a signifies being set apart to God and not set apart from a negative condition as expressed in 4:4b. However, at the time of the latter-day restoration of Israel, Deuteronomy prophesies that it will not be human Israelites but rather God who "will circumcise your heart and the heart of your seed to love the LORD . . . so that you may live" (Deut. 30:6).[16] This future circumcision appears to focus more on a setting apart to love God than a setting apart from the sinful world, though these are two sides of the same coin. In this respect, Deut. 30:6 is similar to Jer. 4:4a: the future circumcision will be a setting apart to a new sphere where one can love God and have life. Genesis 17 itself indicates that circumcision is a setting apart to a positive sphere of blessing (esp. vv. 5–16), since there it "is the sign of the covenant" (vv. 10–11), which is "everlasting" (vv. 7, 13, 19). The covenant of which circumcision is a sign is God's pledge that "I will multiply you exceedingly" (v. 2 [likewise vv. 4–7]).

Paul himself elsewhere also expresses the notion that circumcision represents a setting apart to a positive reality: Abraham "received the sign of circumcision, a seal of the righteousness of the faith which he had while uncircumcised" (Rom. 4:11). Although this does not use the word "life," the idea that circumcision signified "righteousness" is very close to the sphere of life, since Abraham's righteousness is linked in the context to new life (4:17–25).[17] Similarly, Paul sees that fleshly outer circumcision should signify positively inner circumcision that is "of the heart, by the Spirit, not by the letter" (Rom. 2:25–29). Again, this is very close to symbolizing life, since elsewhere Paul contrasts "letter" and "Spirit" in contexts of new life (Rom. 7:6; esp. 2 Cor. 3:6: "not of the letter but of the Spirit; for the letter kills, but the Spirit gives life").[18]

Thus, it is apparent from several OT and NT passages that physical circumcision was not merely to be a symbol for being cut off from the sphere of cursing but also was to be an outer symbol of a positive inner spiritual reality of life or blessing for Israelite saints. In addition, likely against the background of the positive symbolism of physical circumcision, Deut. 30:6 implies that physical circumcision was a pointer to the eschatological time when spiritual

---

16. For the explicit latter-day time of this promise, see Deut. 4:27–31; 31:29; cf. possibly 32:29; Lev. 26:41.

17. Paul at points in Romans sees the sphere of resurrection life to be overlapping with the sphere in which saints do "righteousness" (e.g., 6:13).

18. Although, the dative occurs in Rom. 2:29 and the genitive in 2 Cor. 3:6.

circumcision would occur on a grander scale and would result in the life of the age to come. So, in line with this, in Col. 2:11–13 Paul views the circumcision of Christ (implicitly) and of believers to be a setting apart not only from death but also to resurrection life. After Christ's death and resurrection, the practice of the physical rite of circumcision is no longer required, since the end-time reality to which it pointed had come and its proleptic purpose had been accomplished. My purpose in pointing out the dual significance of circumcision up to this point is to prepare to see circumcision as closely parallel to baptism, which also signifies separation from the old world and being set apart to life (i.e., in Christ).

The Relationship between Circumcision and Baptism

Commentators have noticed the close connection of "circumcision" and "baptism" in Col. 2:11–13. At the least, the two are analogous: just as "circumcision" of the believer is equated with "the circumcision of Christ" (i.e., the cutting off of believers from their identity with the old world and their old, sinful self) (v. 11),[19] so too "baptism" signifies "having been buried with him" (referring to believers' identification with Christ's death), though it also represents Christians being "raised up with him" (v. 12).[20] If, as I have argued, the Deuteronomy background is in view, then the spiritual circumcision does not merely refer to identification with Christ's death but also includes resurrection life, since the spiritual circumcision text of Deut. 30:6 says that end-time Israelites would be circumcised to be set apart to such life. This inclusion of "life" within the notion of "circumcision made without hands" in verse 11 is pointed to further by verse 13: "When you were dead in your transgressions and the uncircumcision of your flesh, He made you alive together with Him." Being "made alive together with Him" suggests the process of coming out from under "the uncircumcision of the flesh," which conceptually is equivalent to the earlier reference in 2:11 to being spiritually circumcised. However, it should be kept in mind that such spiritual circumcision, in the light of Paul's use of Deut. 30:6 and Gen. 17, includes reference not only to death but also to spiritual life.

Thus, both spiritual circumcision and baptism in Col. 2:11–13 refer to identification with Christ's death and resurrection, though it is true that in verse 12 Paul attaches explicitly this dual death/life notion only to baptism. Accordingly, OT physical circumcision as a type has been fulfilled in eschatological spiritual circumcision and is no longer relevant for entrance into

19. Or, alternatively, "the cutting off of Christ" from his place in the old world, in line with the following phrase, "the circumcision of Christ," possibly being an objective genitive.

20. The dative clause *en hō* in v. 12 likely refers to the directly preceding dative "in baptism" (*tō baptismō*), so that it is baptism "in which you were also raised," though it is possible that its antecedent is the more distant "with him" (*autō*), in which case the dative phrase in question would be rendered "in whom you were also raised." But even if the focus were only on being "raised in Christ," it would likely still be that, as with the death, so also the resurrection in Christ is implied in the context of baptism.

the new-covenant community. Instead, spiritual "circumcision made without hands" and "baptism" are ongoing realities designating entrance into the covenant community.[21] If spiritual circumcision in Christ is the fulfillment of the type of physical circumcision, and since spiritual circumcision is virtually equated here with spiritual baptism, it seems plausible that such baptism is also seen as the fulfillment of the physical type of circumcision. One more deduction can be made: if behind spiritual baptism lies the physical rite of baptism (as most commentators hold), then the equation of physical circumcision can be seen to have its typological fulfillment also in the physical rite of baptism.

The inextricable link or overlapping reality between spiritual "circumcision" and spiritual "baptism" is evident in vv. 11–12a:

> And you were circumcised
> > also
> > in him
> > by means of a circumcision made without hands
> > by means of the removal of the body of flesh
> > by means of the circumcision of Christ
> > by means of having been buried with him in
> > > baptism.

The main verb in this sentence is "you were circumcised" (*perietmēthēte*), and this verb is modified by six following Greek adverbial clauses. The first and second modifier ("also" and "in him") merely explain that verses 11–12 are giving another way, in addition to verses 9–10, that believers are identified with Christ: they "were circumcised also in him." The following four clauses of verses 11–12a explain something about the concept that believers "were circumcised" in Christ. All four adverbial clauses define the means by which the believers were circumcised.[22] That is, they were circumcised (1) by means of a spiritual circumcision ("without hands," i.e., by God or Christ), (2) by "removal of the body of flesh" (taking away people from their old identification with the sinful world), and (3) by being made to identify with Christ's own death, which is referred to both as "the circumcision of Christ" and (4) as being "buried with him in baptism."

Or, just as plausibly, these four adverbial clauses could indicate the manner of how saints "were circumcised":

21. "Baptism" here is probably a reference to spiritual identification with Christ, though as we will see below, the physical rite of baptism likely lies in the background.

22. The phrase "by [or in] the removal of the body of flesh" could modify the preceding "circumcision made without hands," indicating the means or manner of that preceding phrase; alternatively, the phrase "by [or in] the circumcision of Christ" could specifically modify and indicate the means or manner of the preceding phrase, "by the removal of the body of flesh." These alternatives do not affect my overall argument in this section, which will focus below on the relationship of the adverbial participle "having been buried" to the main verb, "were circumcised."

> And you were circumcised
>> also
>> in him
>> in the manner of a circumcision made without
>> hands
>> in the manner of the removal of the body of flesh
>> in the manner of the circumcision of Christ
>> in the manner of having been buried with him in
>> baptism.

Accordingly, each adverbial clause would describe in what manner the action of the verbal circumcision occurred. It is hard to know whether means or manner is best, though they are very close in meaning. Whichever is the case, the phrases would be qualifying the action of the verb "circumcise," so that they would be seen not as a separate concept from the circumcising action but rather as overlapping with it.

What, if any, is the ruling idea between the verb "were circumcised" at the beginning of verse 11 and these following last four modifying clauses? It is likely that "you were circumcised" is the dominant or logical main point. The four last clauses support the verbal notion of "were circumcised" by indicating the means or manner by which this verbal action was carried out. Each supporting phrase is piled one upon another, the first three pertaining to spiritual circumcision and the last to spiritual baptism. Therefore, since the three adverbial phrases following the "in whom also" (*en hō kai*) clause are explained to be the means or manner by which they "were circumcised,"[23] it is probable that the directly following phrase, "buried with him in baptism," is also the means or manner by which they "were circumcised."[24] Furthermore, since the first three adverbial clauses of

23. Each of these three clauses consist of Greek datives, the last two of which are preceded by the preposition *en*, which, in addition to means or manner, could indicate time, apposition, or location. But these three options are unlikely, as is evident from attempting interpretatively to translate them (e.g., note respectively these three options with regard to the second of the three phrases "in the putting off of the body of the flesh": "when you put off" or "which is the putting off" or "in the sphere of putting off"). However, a dative of means ("by means of [or 'with'] the putting off") or manner ("by way of putting off") is natural and smooth not only for the last two *en* + dative clauses but also for the first stand-alone dative clause (which could have the same options of understanding as the *en* + dative clauses just noted above) (for why a temporal or appositional or locative use respectively is syntagmatically unlikely for this first dative clause, see Daniel B. Wallace, *Greek Grammar beyond the Basics* [Grand Rapids: Zondervan, 1996], 152–57). What further supports means or manner as the best option is that the first and third dative phrases are cognate datives (and the second is virtually synonymous), the force of which is "*to emphasize the action of the verb*" (ibid., 168–69) with respect to either the manner by which the verb is carried out or the means (though Wallace stresses manner).

24. The phrase "having been buried" is a rendering of the adverbial aorist passive participle (*syntaphentes*), which indicates not an action that precedes the main verb ("were circumcised") but rather a generally contemporaneous action (which occurs typically when an aorist adverbial participle modifies an aorist indicative verb [on which, see ibid., 624–25]). However, along with this general

verse 11 appear to be lexical equivalents conceptually ("circumcision . . . removal . . . circumcision") to the initial "were circumcised," then, in line with these three preceding clauses, "buried in baptism" likely designates the same thing as the spiritual notion of "were circumcised" in verse 11a. Syntactically, if "having been buried" is a qualification of the verb "were circumcised," then it is an aspect of that verbal action and essentially equivalent to it. Or, alternatively, "buried in baptism" could perhaps be seen to be a subordinate logical notion included within the larger concept of spiritual circumcision, since it is the "means" to achieving or the manner of such circumcision.[25] *Thus, spiritual baptism is likely equivalent to spiritual circumcision in this passage or, at the least, is considered to be an integral though subordinate part of such circumcision.[26] In the latter case, one could conclude that baptism and circumcision are not precisely equivalent. There is, however, enough overlap between the two (both representing death and resurrection) that they can still be considered roughly equivalent.[27]*

It is important to reiterate a conclusion that I reached at the beginning of this section: if spiritual circumcision in this passage is the fulfillment to which physical circumcision pointed, then spiritual baptism, the conceptual

---

contemporaneous time element, the participle likely also more specifically indicates the means or manner by which the action of the main verb is carried out. (Wallace says that "even if a participle is labeled as temporal, this does not necessarily mean such is its only force. Often a secondary notion is present, such as means or cause" [ibid., 624n30], though I would say that sometimes also the temporal element could be secondary.) Context is one of the main clues in determining how an adverbial participle functions, and since the participle here is structurally parallel to the preceding adverbial phrases that indicate the means or manner of the main verb, so likewise probably does the participle function. If a participle of means is in mind, then the participle would define how the action of the main verb is carried out (ibid., 629). It is possible that this is a participle of purpose, but this would be exceedingly rare in the aorist (ibid., 636). Other logical uses of the participle are also not as likely here as means or manner. Salter ("Does Baptism Replace Circumcision?," 25–28) too narrowly categorizes the participle as only temporally contemporaneous. For more in-depth analysis of the thorny issue of the adverbial phrases in Col. 2:11–12, see G. K. Beale, *Colossians and Philemon*, BECNT (Grand Rapids: Baker Academic, forthcoming), where also more exegetical analysis of and interaction with secondary literature on vv. 11–13 in general may be found, especially with respect to the relation of circumcision to baptism and my view of the equivalence of the two.

25. The same is true of the first three adverbial phrases, though they are also more obviously conceptual equivalents to "were circumcised."

26. Salter ("Does Baptism Replace Circumcision?," 26–28) concludes that circumcision is subordinate to and a part of baptism on the basis that in vv. 11–13 baptism includes both death and resurrection, whereas circumcision connotes only death. However, my position on the equivalence or overlapping (i.e., subordinating) aspect of baptism to circumcision is based not only on the syntactical structure of all four adverbial clauses but also on the background of OT circumcision as connoting both separation from a sinful condition and a setting apart to a condition of life (which has been discussed above [Gen. 17; Deut. 10:16; Josh. 5:8–9; Jer. 4:4; 9:26; Ezek. 44:7, 9], including Paul's specific allusions to the OT, which associate spiritual circumcision with life [Gen. 17; 30], though it is likely that he also would have held to that aspect of circumcision signifying being set apart from the sphere of cursing or sin [as in, e.g., Deut. 10:16a; Jer. 4:4b]).

27. Contra Salter ("Does Baptism Replace Circumcision?"), who denies such an equivalence.

equivalent to spiritual circumcision in this passage, should also be seen as the typological fulfillment of OT circumcision. This is still a step removed from saying that the physical rite of baptism for entrance into the covenant community is the equivalent of the physical rite of circumcision, since spiritual baptism is the focus in this passage. However, if, as is likely, physical baptism stands in the background behind spiritual baptism here, then even the liturgy of baptism is secondarily seen to function equivalently to the OT physical rite of circumcision, since the latter probably stands behind spiritual circumcision in this passage. Consequently, both physical and spiritual circumcision are likely identified respectively with physical and spiritual baptism in this passage.[28] Moreover, the obvious fact that circumcision and baptism are, sociologically speaking, entrance markers respectively into the OT community of the people of God and that of the NT means that one would naturally expect that baptism is the NT equivalent to OT circumcision.

Circumcision (physical and spiritual) and its equivalent in baptism (physical and spiritual) represent another example of the transformation of one of Israel's most explicit distinguishing marks.

CIRCUMCISION AND BAPTISM AS DUAL-OATH SIGNS

What also more broadly brings OT circumcision together with NT baptism in the Colossians passage (and in the NT generally) is not only that each was the main sign for entrance into its covenant community but also that both expressed dual-oath signs that signified blessing and cursing. Meredith Kline has developed this notion in most depth.[29] Circumcision represented, on the

---

28. Salter (ibid., 15–29), who concludes that even though circumcision is to be considered conceptually a subordinate part of baptism (against my view that they are equivalent or virtually so), wants to be "cautious" in applying this to the church for all times and places because the Colossians passage is "polemical," being "concerned primarily with addressing false teaching, not with providing the church with a theology of baptism" (pp. 28–29). In fact, he sees this polemical aspect as a partial basis for judging the "circumcision = baptism" view to be illegitimate in terms of applicability to the contemporary church. His approach suffers from a failure to appreciate that the false teaching in Colossae is part of the latter-day tribulation that extends throughout the church age. Consequently, Paul's solution to the problem also extends throughout the church age (on which, see the following section below on the office of elder in relation to the eschatological tribulation of deception).

29. Kline, *By Oath Consigned*, of which only a brief sketch can be given here, though some aspects may veer in a minor way from Kline. His view in *By Oath Consigned* is summarized in his later book *Kingdom Prologue: Genesis Foundations for a Covenantal Worldview* (Overland Park, KS: Two Age Press, 2000), 312–18, 361–65. This part of the chapter is based on the assumption that Kline points us in the right direction about both circumcision and baptism having dual-oath signs of cursing and blessing. Readers are encouraged to consult Kline for his more thorough argument. See Duane A. Garrett, "Meredith Kline on Suzerainty, Circumcision, and Baptism," in *Believer's Baptism: Sign of the New Covenant in Christ*, ed. Thomas R. Schreiner and Shawn D. Wright. NAC Studies in Bible and Theology (Nashville: B&H Publishing, 2006), 257–84, who has written a blistering critique of Kline and has made plausible points, while nevertheless, in my opinion, still not striking at the heart of Kline's position. For example, even

one hand, the "cutting off of the flesh" to designate that the sinful flesh around the heart was cut off, signifying the regeneration of the heart and the setting apart of a person to the Lord. On the other hand, circumcision also represented being "cut off" from the Lord. If an Israelite child came to faith, the sign of blessing was applied. If, however, a child grew up in unbelief, the sign of cursing was applied. Baptism also is associated with a dual-oath sign. As we have seen in Col. 2:12, baptism signified being identified both with Christ's curse of death and with his resurrection to life. The descent into the water represented the former, and the ascent from the water symbolized the latter.[30]

My discussion in the preceding section has focused only on the twofold positive aspect of circumcision that signifies being set apart from a cursed condition and being set apart to a blessed condition. This is the twofold nature of what the sign positively should have meant for the believing Israelite. But what about the Israelite who was circumcised and did not believe? I think that Kline is on a promising track to propose that the unbelieving Israelite's circumcision signifies that the person is not cut off from the curse but rather remains under the curse: the implication is that the person is cut off from the living God. Kline's conclusion is a plausible biblical-theological deduction made on the basis that covenants have dual-oath signs of cursing and blessing. Applied to baptism, for the true believer the sign represents being separated from the old world by identification with Christ's death and being set apart to the new world through his resurrection. It is this positive twofold meaning of circumcision (cut off from the old, set apart to new life) that is uppermost in mind in Col. 2 and precisely parallels baptism there.

But what about professing but false Christians, pseudobelievers, who fail to persevere despite having been baptized? As members of the visible covenant community, they are outwardly identified in the liturgy with Christ's death and resurrection. For such people, however, the inward spiritual significance of these outward signs is not realized in them. These people do not overcome the curse of death through the resurrection of Christ, since they do not possess the reality symbolized by the signs of Christ's vicarious death and of resurrection in the liturgical act of their baptism. However, one could say that they are partly spiritually identified only with the baptismal curse sign of death but not at all spiritually with the sign of resurrection, so that they remain in the

---

if it were the case that Kline were wrong in highlighting judgment over blessing in circumcision and baptism, it does not nullify the notion that judgment is still included to some degree together with blessing. Unfortunately, limits of space prevent the further interaction with Garrett's criticisms that they deserve.

30. Note also Rom. 6:3–6, where having "been baptized into [Christ's] death" (v. 3) is equated with having "been buried with Him through baptism unto death" (v. 4) and with "our old man was crucified with Him" (v. 6). Thus, the water liturgy of apparent immersion standing behind this language refers to identification with the curse through which Christ went, though union with Christ is more the focus than any apparent mode of baptism.

condition of spiritual death. Thus, they remain in their sins and condemned state because they also do not possess the full reality of the baptismal curse sign symbolizing Christ's substitutionary death on their behalf.[31] Therefore, they spiritually experience death, which is the inward reality of the external curse sign of their baptism.

This dual-oath sign is supported by the fact that the NT sometimes understands baptism against the background of major redemptive-historical events that expressed blessing and cursing. In 1 Cor. 10:1–2 Paul says that "our fathers were all under the cloud and all passed through the [Red] sea; and all were baptized into Moses in the cloud and through the sea." Here Israel's baptism is a way of speaking of their identification with Moses in God's redemption from Egypt. The "sea" connotes ideas of blessing on those redeemed through the waters and of cursing on the Egyptians judged in the same waters.

A similar background is conjured up in Matt. 3:11–17, where the "baptism" of Jesus in the Jordan River is narrated. John baptizes Jesus in the water of the Jordan River, along with other Israelites (Matt. 3:5–6, 13–17). Why is it apparently so important that Jesus be baptized with water in a river, along with other Jews, at the inception of his ministry? I argued in an earlier chapter that there is an OT backdrop against which to view this incident.[32] Just as Israel was led by Moses and had to go through the Red Sea at the exodus, and just as second-generation Israel had to do the same thing at the Jordan River under Joshua's leadership, as a replayed second exodus, so again, now that Israel's restoration is imminent through Jesus, true Israelites must identify with the water and the Jordan and their prophetic leader in order to begin to experience true restoration.[33] In this respect, we saw that this incident shows that Jesus is beginning to fulfill the prophecies of Israel's restoration as a second exodus through water (Isa. 11:15; 43:2, 16–17; 44:27–28; 50:2; 51:9–11), especially through "rivers" (Isa. 11:15; 42:15; 43:2; 44:27; 50:2). Thus, the blessing/cursing sign of the Red Sea likely carries over to Jesus's baptism by John (where the Spirit descended on Jesus), which is confirmed in Matt. 3:11,[34] where John's

31. In 1 Cor. 15 Paul tells readers that if Christ has not been raised, then "your faith is in vain" (v. 14) and "you are still in your sins" (v. 17), which he says is not the case for true Christians. However, for pseudobelievers it is the case because their baptism identifies them ultimately only with the curse of death that Christ suffered vicariously for true believers but not for them, so that they remain under that curse.

32. See chap. 13 under the subheading "Jesus as Israel and God's Son Elsewhere in Matthew: The Baptism of Jesus, His Wilderness Testing, and Other Aspects of His Earthly Ministry."

33. Intriguingly, second-generation Israel is also circumcised in direct connection with passing through the divided waters of the Jordan (Josh. 5:1–9).

34. Interestingly, 1QS III:4–9 refers to entering the Qumran community through baptism, which is referred to as "cleansing waters" and "seas or rivers," at which time the Spirit will "cleanse" the one being baptized. It appears that the best background against which to see Qumran baptism is that of Israel's exodus through the Red Sea and again later through the Jordan under Joshua. It would appear that Qumran understood such baptism to include reference to

baptism is said to point to a greater baptism: Christ himself "will baptize you with the Holy Spirit and fire." This likely refers to the Spirit of blessing and the fire of judgment, which is described further in twofold manner in v. 12b: "And He will gather his wheat into the barn, but He will burn up the chaff with unquenchable fire."[35]

I mentioned earlier the circumcision of second-generation Israel in Josh. 5:2–9, which represented that God "rolled away the reproach of Egypt" (v. 9). I contended that this indicated that the second generation was separated from the sinful condition of the wilderness generation, which was identified with Egypt.[36] This circumcision of the second generation in Josh. 5:2–9 is likely a narrative interpretation of what it meant when they went through the divided waters of the Jordan in 5:1. That is, crossing the Jordan was another exodus, and, like the first exodus, it separated Israel from a prior realm of sin and death (i.e., if it had remained in that realm). The circumcision episode in Josh. 5 interprets the Jordan crossing very similarly. I raise this subject here to highlight that the Jordan crossing as an exodus event is identified with the meaning of circumcision, though it underscores only the positive meaning of circumcision. Such a background brings the meaning of the covenant sign of circumcision closer together with the meaning of the exodus as a background for Jesus's baptism.

Likewise, 1 Pet. 3:20–21 refers to Noah and his family being "brought safely through water" in the ark, and "corresponding to that, [is] baptism." Like the Red Sea, the waters of the great flood were a sign of blessing for those in the ark but a sign of judgment for those outside the ark, who perished in the water. In 1 Cor. 10 and 1 Pet. 3 baptism is associated only as a sign of blessing, though the idea of judgment stands in the background of the OT allusions.[37]

How could what I have discussed so far in this section relate to the issue of whether infants should be baptized? This issue certainly cannot be resolved in my conclusion here, but I will make some suggestions that I believe are relevant to the debate. First, since both circumcision and the Red Sea deliverance, as well as the second generation's passage through the Jordan, included

---

a new exodus, especially in the light of comparing Isa. 37:25 (referring to the "rivers" of the first exodus) with Isa. 11:15–16; 41:18; 43:2, 19–20; 44:27; 50:2, which all refer to the "river" or "rivers" of a second exodus (though Qumran does not explicitly refer to these Isaiah texts in discussing the water imagery).

35. Although we saw earlier that the coming of the Spirit in fire in Acts 2 is itself a sign of both blessing and judgment (see chap. 18 under the heading "The Link between the Story of the Church and That of the Spirit: The Spirit's Descent at Pentecost as the Eschatological Temple to Transform People into the Temple").

36. This is further indicated by Judg. 2:10, where the second generation is distinguished from the following generation by the fact that the latter "did not know the LORD, nor yet the work which He had done for Israel," which was like the first generation.

37. For fuller explanation of the significance of these OT backgrounds for these two NT passages with respect to baptism as a dual-oath sign, see Kline, *By Oath Consigned*, 65–73.

infants as participants, it seems natural that infants be included in the new-covenant sign of baptism, since both circumcision and the exodus deliverance through water are two of the main OT backgrounds through which the NT understands baptism. Second, since the NT typically represents a widening of people groups who share in the eschatological blessings (women and gentiles are now included), it would be unusual in the case of a covenantal entry sign to have a narrowing from the old to the new, whereby a major people group (infants) is now excluded. Third, there is the fact that infants underwent the sign of circumcision. If, as I have tried to show throughout this chapter so far, baptism is the redemptive-historical and typological equivalent to circumcision, then it seems natural that the NT equivalent to circumcision, which is baptism, also be applied to infants. It needs also to be remembered that even with "adult baptism" or "believer's baptism," baptism does not necessarily connote only salvation, but as a covenantal sign it conveys notions of both blessing and cursing. It is only a person's life of perseverance that determines which aspect of the water sign is realized in the baptized person.

The issue of the connection of circumcision to baptism, especially with respect to infants, is complicated by the debate about whether the church is to be defined only as the regenerate or whether it is considered to be a community in which it is acknowledged that, as in the OT, the new-covenant community is a mixed community of true believers and professing believers who actually are pseudo-Christians. Also, the issue is complicated by how much correspondence there is between the type of circumcision and the antitype of baptism, which is a difficult issue. There is space here only to indicate in what direction I think that the evidence of the OT and the NT points on this issue, not to present a full discussion of this debate.

The Lord's Supper

Like baptism, the Lord's Supper (or Eucharist) evokes new-creational imagery. It was part of the weekly worship service in which Christians remembered Christ's resurrection on the first day of the week, which, as we saw above, set in motion the end-time Sabbath rest intended for Adam in the first creation.[38]

38. Justin Martyr (*Dial.* 138) says that the eight people preserved through water in the ark "were a symbol of the eighth day [Sunday, the first day of the week], wherein Christ appeared when he rose from the dead. . . . For Christ, being the first-born of every creature, became chief of another race regenerated by himself through water and faith"; accordingly, the church fathers viewed Sunday as "the eighth day going beyond the present 'week' into the future age," so that it is natural that believers could be understood to be already tasting "the life of the new creation in the bread and wine of the eucharist" (Geoffrey Wainwright, *Eucharist and Eschatology* [repr., New York: Oxford University Press, 1981], 77, likewise observing Justin's remark). "The earliest reason given for celebrating Sunday is that it is the day of the resurrection (*Barn.*, 15.9)," and, according to Justin (*1 Apol.* 67), Christians also believed that they were commemorating

Christ's Last Supper and the eucharistic meal of the early church were overtly linked to Israel's Passover and thus to the exodus.[39] Perhaps not coincidentally, Jewish tradition associated the Passover with the original creation and the coming future destruction and renovation of the cosmos, when the Messiah would come[40] and God's kingdom would be established.[41] Such an association makes it natural that each of the Synoptic accounts of the Last Supper includes a saying by Jesus with respect to the cup: "I will not drink of this fruit of the vine from now on until that day when I drink it <u>new</u> with you in my Father's kingdom" (Matt. 26:29) (cf. Mark 14:25; Luke 22:18 ["until the kingdom of God comes"]). This could be a figurative reference echoing the promised fruitfulness of the coming new creation, which would be formally inaugurated by

---

both the first creation, which was on the first day of the creation week, and the resurrection of Christ, who rose on the first day of the week (Peter G. Cobb, "The History of the Christian Year," in *The Study of Liturgy*, ed. Cheslyn Jones et al., rev. ed. [New York: Oxford University Press, 1992], 457).

39. See Joachim Jeremias, *The Eucharistic Words of Jesus*, trans. Norman Perrin (New York: Scribner, 1966), 15–88. Jeremias sees a Passover background eliciting a context of *Heilsgeschichte* and of "promise and fulfillment" for Jesus's Last Supper (see p. 88). In 1 Cor. 5:6–8 Paul refers to Christ as the Passover sacrifice and speaks of celebrating "the feast, not with old leaven" but with "new," which Jeremias believes echoes Jesus's own words at the Last Supper, "This is My body which is given for you" (Luke 22:19), and which he sees as an eschatological interpretation of the loaves used in the Passover (pp. 59–60). See also Gordon D. Fee, *First Epistle to the Corinthians*, NICNT (Grand Rapids: Eerdmans, 1987), 218. Fee sees a possible allusion to the Lord's Supper in 1 Cor. 5:8 and cites others making this suggestion. Likewise, John 19:31–36 portrays the Roman soldiers not breaking Jesus's bones at his crucifixion to be the fulfillment of not breaking the bones of the Passover lamb in Egypt and subsequently, an event pointing to Christ as the key means to redemption in the new age.

40. Interestingly, the "Four Nights" midrashic hymn in various versions of the Targum is inserted into Exod. 12, which gives instructions for the Passover meal; this insertion explains what events have taken place or will occur in the future on the same night in which Passover takes place. These events are none other than some of the key constituent elements of the biblical-theological storyline mentioned above in chaps. 3, 4, 6 (and following chapters). In the Targum these events are the major stepping-stones from the beginning of biblical history to its end: (1) the creation of the world in Gen. 1; (2) God's covenantal dealing with Abraham, which is described figuratively with cosmic conflagration imagery; (3) the exodus Passover; (4) when the earth reaches its appointed time to be dissolved, at which time the Messiah will come to redeem Israel (so *Tg. Neof.* Exod. 12; likewise *Tg. Ps.-J.* Exod. 12; cf. the various translations in Martin McNamara and Robert Hayward, *Targum Neofiti 1: Exodus*, and Michael Maher, *Targum Pseudo-Jonathan: Exodus*, ArBib 2 [Collegeville, MN: Liturgical Press, 1994]; J. W. Etheridge, *The Targums of Onkelos and Jonathan ben Uzziel on the Pentateuch, with the Fragments of the Jerusalem Targum from the Chaldee* [New York: KTAV, 1968], 479–81; Martin McNamara, *The New Testament and the Palestinian Targum to the Pentateuch*, AnBib 27 [Rome: Pontifical Biblical Institute, 1966], 210–11). For other eschatological hopes, including new creation, associated with Passover, see Jeremias, *Eucharistic Words*, 58–59, 206–7.

41. See McNamara, *New Testament*, 210. McNamara discusses manuscript Paris 110 of *Tg. Ps.-J.*, which inserts the "Four Nights" segment at Exod. 15:18, which says, "The Lord shall reign forever and ever."

the resurrection.[42] This is further indicated by the reference that the drinking will take place at the time when "the kingdom comes," a further installment of the inaugurated end-time kingdom. This saying of Jesus apparently began to be fulfilled during his resurrection appearances to his disciples.[43]

Israel's Passover meal was inextricably bound to the event of the Passover and reminded Israel of its exodus redemption, which pointed to the new creation. The equivalent NT meal, the Lord's Supper, is the antitypical correspondence, fulfilling the type of Israel's meal. Very closely connected to this Passover meal typology is Christ as the Passover lamb, who fulfills that to which Israel's Passover lamb pointed.[44] It appears that 1 Cor. 5:6–8 supports both the Passover meal and the Passover lamb typology[45] (note the underlined clauses):

> Your boasting is not good. Do you not know that a little leaven leavens the whole lump of dough? Clean out the old leaven so that you may be a new lump, just as you are in fact unleavened. <u>For Christ our Passover also has been sacrificed.</u> <u>Therefore let us celebrate the feast,</u> not with old leaven, nor with the leaven of malice and wickedness, but with the unleavened bread of sincerity and truth.

However, 1 Cor. 11:20–34 affirms that when partaking at the Lord's table, saints must judge themselves in order to partake worthily or else they will be judged by God in the present. Whichever is the case (and the latter is the focus), true believers receive a form of their eschatological judgment now at the Lord's Supper so that they "may not be condemned along with the world" at the last judgment (1 Cor. 11:32).[46] Hence, the Lord's Supper contains in itself a beginning form of the last judgment, which will be consummated at the end of time. Consequently, as Geoffrey Wainwright concludes, the Lord's Supper is "a projection, from the future . . . of the coming of the Lord . . . who comes to judge and re-create. . . . It includes a present moment of judgment

42. The OT and Judaism expected abundant fruitfulness in the coming creation, including specifically fruitful "vineyards" producing "new wine" (e.g., Isa. 62:8–9; 65:17–22; Hos. 14:7–8; Zech. 9:17; 10:7).

43. According to Acts 10:41, the apostles "ate and drank with Him after He rose from the dead" (so A. J. B. Higgins, *The Lord's Supper in the New Testament*, SBT 6 [Chicago: Allenson, 1956], 62).

44. See Peter Stuhlmacher, *Biblische Theologie des Neuen Testaments*, vol. 1 (Göttingen: Vandenhoeck & Ruprecht, 1992), 130–43, who discusses Jesus's Last Supper as a reenactment of the Passover meal, which recalled Israel's redemption from Egyptian bondage, but which now indicates the end-time release of Israel from bondage by Jesus's death.

45. John 19:36 also indicates that Jesus is the typological fulfillment of what the Passover lamb pointed to.

46. The precise eschatological nature of this judgment for the believer cannot be elaborated on here, although it includes, at least, the penal judgment of the body through sickness or death. Even though such judgment of the believer is called "discipline" (1 Cor. 11:32), Paul must think of it as part of the coming final judgment, where the unbeliever's body, along with the soul, will suffer an eternal, second death.

and renewal which is the projection of the cataclysm[47] that will inaugurate the universal and incontestable reign of God."[48]

The Church Office of Elder as an Eschatological Necessity because of the End-Time Tribulation of Deception and of the New Creation

The origin of the creation of the office of elder is likely related, at least in part, to the inaugurated latter-day tribulation. I discussed in an earlier chapter how the expected eschatological tribulation had begun in the early church but was not consummated. It is important to rehearse that discussion briefly here in order to see how it could form a background against which the church position of elder can be seen as arising.

The Inauguration of Eschatological Tribulation in the Covenant Community

The OT predicts that a final tribulation will precede the dawning of the new cosmos. For example, Dan. 12:1–3 prophesies a time of great distress before the climactic resurrection of the righteous and the wicked. I noted earlier that Daniel refers to the coming trial as one in which there will be deception within the covenant community and persecution of noncompromisers. In addition, other OT and NT texts affirm that the final tribulation will be one in which there will be a breakdown of various parts of the natural order of the cosmos, which will be culminated by complete destruction of the heavens and earth.[49] Against this background, one can see how the final tribulation is but an inextricable prelude to the eventual destruction and re-creation of the cosmos. Actual phenomena of cosmic dissolution are not the typical characteristic of the inaugurated phase of the tribulation; rather, false teaching and deception are among the predominant expressions of this initial stage. Nevertheless, we have seen above that literal physical phenomena of cosmic breakup were expressed at Christ's death: "darkness fell upon all the land" (Matt. 27:45) and "the earth shook; and the rocks were split, and the tombs were opened" (Matt. 27:51–52a). Such literal expressions of initial destruction will again occur at

47. In this respect, *Did.* 10:6, part of the conclusion to the instructions on the Eucharist begun at 9:1, says, "May grace [= Christ] come, and may this world pass away."

48. Wainwright, *Eucharist and Eschatology*, 151 (on this judgment theme, see also pp. 80–83). For more thorough elaboration on the "already–not yet, end-time, new-creational" nature of the Eucharist argued for in the present discussion, see ibid., esp. 37–41, 68–70, 77, 80–83, 106, 147–54.

49. For NT examples, see Mark 13:8; Luke 21:11, 23–26 ("earthquakes" and "famines," which are "the beginning of birth pangs," which are inaugurated before the very end of the age). For some OT and especially scattered early Jewish texts that depict similar convulsions of nature, see Dale C. Allison Jr., *The End of the Ages Has Come: An Early Interpretation of the Passion and Resurrection of Jesus* (Philadelphia: Fortress, 1985), 5–25.

the very end of history when the body of Christ, the church throughout the world, will experience climactic, universal persecution like Christ before them (see Rev. 11:3–13; 20:7–10). The apparent OT prophetic perspective about the coming tribulation was that (1) deception and persecution would occur at the same general period as (2) the convulsions of nature. The NT, however, understands these to occur in stages in which the first feature predominates throughout the age, but then the two converge at the very end.[50]

Throughout the Synoptic Gospels, Paul's writings, 1 Peter, and Revelation, false teaching, deception, and Christian suffering as a result of persecution[51] compose an essential feature of the inaugurated end-time tribulation. When saints refuse to compromise with false teaching, they often must face persecution (cf. Dan. 11:30–35; Rev. 2:8–17). Every manner of suffering is part of the scheme of the overlap of a fallen world that is passing away in the midst of an inaugurated new world.[52] It is important to note that even the saints' persecution must be seen against the background of their resistance to compromising with false teaching, whether from within or outside the covenant community (the latter, e.g., when Roman authorities would threaten Christians with death lest they compromise and worship idols, esp. the emperor).

Elders and Eschatological Tribulation

The origin of ecclesiology, particularly with respect to the hierarchical structure of the church, is to be viewed, at least in part, within this context of the latter-day tribulation of false teaching.[53] On the one hand, "elders" or "bishops" are needed in order to maintain the doctrinal purity of the covenant community, which is always either being influenced by or threatened from the infiltration of fifth-columnist movements. Titus 1:5–16 gives this as the formal reason for the establishment of elders throughout the churches of Crete, and the same rationale is apparent in 1–2 Timothy (cf. 1 Tim. 1:3–7, 19–20; 4:1–7 with 3:1–15; 5:11–17; 6:20–21; cf. 2 Tim. 2:14–18, 23–26; 3:1–13).

---

50. On which, see chap. 7.

51. Accordingly, in the Synoptic Gospels suffering is related to following the Son of Man, whose own suffering is rooted in the prophecy of Dan. 7 (also chaps. 8; 11 12), where the Son of Man, representing true Israel, must be confronted with the deception and suffer hardship for not compromising (among the closest equivalents in the Synoptics, cf. Matt. 8:18–22; Mark 8:31; 14:21, 53–65); Paul also links the church's sufferings as the "body" of Christ with its identification with "Christ's afflictions" (Col. 1:24), as do Hebrews (cf. 9:26 with 12:1–7), James (cf. 1:2–4 with 5:1–11), 1 Peter (cf. 1:5–6, 20 with 2:19–23; 3:14–5:10), and Revelation (cf. 1:5–6 with 1:9, and 5:6 with 6:9).

52. Cf. Rom. 8:18–23 with 8:35–39, where in the former text suffering of believers, and of all creation, is viewed as a result of being part of a new creation emerging from the old corrupted creation, which is portrayed by the image of suffering birth pangs.

53. In this respect, note the overt references in 1 Tim. 4:1–3; 2 Tim. 3:1 (cf. 3:2–9) to the inaugurated end-time trial of deception within the church community.

On the other hand, such an ecclesiastical authority structure ensured the Christian community that it was continuing in the truth and life of the kingdom, which would enable it to be strong in accomplishing its mission of witness to the world, which is also a significant theme in the Pastoral Epistles.[54] This positive element of mission is part of the larger positive role of the church in its responsibility of carrying out the original Adamic commission to subdue the ends of the earth and Israel's similar commission to be priests for and a light of witness to the world.[55] Of course, Acts highlights this eschatological light-bearing mission of the new creation more than any other NT book.[56] In fact, the mention of deacons in Acts 6 and elders in Acts 20 is, at least in part, to indicate their role in speeding on the spread of the kingdom, and in the latter case also to encourage elders to guard against false teaching.

This notion that the interadvent age is one during which the eschatological tribulation and the new creation continue throughout and not just at particular moments has some interesting implications. For example, one scholar has argued that the prohibitions in 1 Tim. 2:11–15 against women teaching authoritatively in the church at Ephesus were a response to women who had become influenced by the rampant false teaching there. However, it is often argued that since this situation of false teaching was a local and unique problem and was the occasion causing Paul to issue the prohibition, then his prohibition does not apply to other churches in places and times throughout the age where false teaching is absent.[57] But, if false teaching is a part of the inaugurated end-time tribulation that continues throughout the whole epoch before Christ's final parousia, then Paul's prohibitions are a response not just to a local situation but rather to that situation as it is an expression of the broader end-time trial. Since the inaugurated latter-day trial means that the churches will be either affected or, at least, threatened by false teaching and deception, Paul's prohibitions are always valid. Therefore, Paul's prohibitions are a part of eschatological ethics pertinent to the entire church age, during

---

54. Indeed, Royce Gordon Gruenler ("The Mission-Lifestyle Setting of 1 Tim 2:8–15," *JETS* 41 [1998]: 215–38) has contended that mission is the dominant theme and concern of the Pastoral Epistles, especially highlighting the significance of 1 Tim. 1:10–16; 2:1–4, among other passages.

55. See Frank Hawkins, "Orders and Ordination in the New Testament," in Jones et al., eds., *Study of Liturgy*, 344–45, which has helped crystallize my own thoughts on these negative and positive factors leading to the establishment of church offices in the NT.

56. E.g., Acts 1:6–8; 2:17–3:26; 13:47; 26:16–18. For the relationship of the eschatology of Acts to the notion of resurrection and new creation, see G. K. Beale, "Eschatology," *DLNTD* 330–45.

57. See, e.g., Gordon D. Fee, "Issues in Evangelical Hermeneutics, Part III: The Great Watershed—Intentionality and Particularity/Eternality: 1 Tim. 2:8–15 as a Test Case," *Crux* 26 (1990): 31–37. Fee shows that 1 Timothy is shot through with reference to false teaching, which is an occasion that must control the interpretation of the epistle. Unfortunately, Fee assumes that such false teaching is evidence of a unique, local situation to which Paul's prohibitions against women teaching in 1 Tim. 2:11–12 is partly a response. Accordingly, for Fee, this prohibition cannot be universalized for all times and places, since it is an ad hoc response to such a local and limited occasion.

which the end-time tribulation of false teaching is either actually affecting churches or threatens to corrupt them.

For the same reason, the office of elder is not a response to occasional or temporarily unique conditions[58] but rather owes its existence to the ongoing, uninterrupted eschatological tribulation of false teaching and deception. In addition, we saw that the office was also created to protect the church's doctrine so that it will remain healthy as it conducts its mission to the world to expand the invisible boundaries of the new creation. Such an office is needed until the time when the new creation is consummated.

In general, it appears that the office of elder in the church is the continuation of the position of elder in Israel. Whereas elders in Israel had both civil and religious authority, elders in the new covenant have full religious authority over the sphere of the new Israel, the church. Several observations point to this equivalence. Besides the use of the same word, "elders" (*presbyteroi*), the book of Acts repeatedly juxtaposes the phrase "rulers and elders" of Israel (4:5, 8) or "chief priests and elders" (4:23; 23:14; 25:15), or "elders and scribes" (6:12) with "apostles and elders" of the church (15:2, 4, 6, 22, 23; 16:4). Just as the Jewish "rulers and elders and scribes were gathered together in Jerusalem" to judge the validity of the emerging Christian movement (4:5–23), so too in "Jerusalem . . . the apostles and the elders came together to look into this matter" about the Jewish-Christian teaching that new gentile converts had to keep the law of Moses (15:1–6). The function of the Jewish elders in Acts 4 and the Christian elders in Acts 15 appears virtually identical. Both are in an official position in their respective covenant communities to adjudicate whether a new theological teaching is valid.

Acts 15 may have light shed on it by the earlier discussion that the position of elder was created, at least partly, to help protect the church's theological health in the midst of an inaugurated end-time tribulation of deceptive teaching. Accordingly, it seems not to be coincidental that directly before the Acts 15 account of the council at Jerusalem, Paul and Barnabas exhorted the believers "to continue in the faith" by saying, "Through many tribulations we must enter into the kingdom of God" (14:22). And the very next verse asserts, "And when they had appointed elders for them in every church, having prayed with fasting, they commended them to the Lord in whom they had believed" (14:23). This is significant because it is the first reference to appointing elders outside Jerusalem, and it leads directly into the dispute needing judgment by the Jerusalem elders in Acts 15. This dispute was none other than a false teaching that, if allowed to continue, would destroy the emerging Christian movement. So the connection of the elders in Acts 14 to "tribulations" and false

---

58. Against the argument by Gordon D. Fee, "Reflections on Church Order in the Pastoral Epistles, with Further Reflection on the Hermeneutics of Ad Hoc Documents," *JETS* 28 (1985): 141–51.

teaching is reflective of their eschatological role to guide the church theologically through the end-time theological threats. Likewise, this inextricable link
of false teaching with elders is developed in Acts 20:27–32, where Paul says,

> For I did not shrink from declaring to you the whole counsel of God. Be on guard
> for yourselves and for all the flock, among which the Holy Spirit has made you
> overseers, to shepherd the church of God which He purchased with His own
> blood. I know that after my departure savage wolves will come in among you,
> not sparing the flock; and from among your own selves men will arise, speak-
> ing perverse things, to draw away the disciples after them. Therefore be on the
> alert, remembering that night and day for a period of three years I did not cease
> to admonish each one with tears. And now I commend you to God and to the
> word of His grace, which is able to build you up and to give you the inheritance
> among all those who are sanctified.

In laying the foundation for the church in Ephesus, Paul explained to the readers "the whole counsel of God" (v. 27 [cf. v. 20]). A part of this counsel was
to remind them that "the Holy Spirit has made you overseers to shepherd the
church of God," especially to "be on guard for yourselves and for all the flock"
(v. 28). They are to "guard" against false teachers who arise "from among your
own selves" (vv. 29–30). This guarding is to be done by being faithful to God's
"word" (the gospel and the Scriptures testifying to that gospel [vv. 31–32]).
While it is true that the imminent false teaching was to be a local problem, it
is also implicit that the function of the overseers to guard the Ephesian church
from error is a function also for elders in every church, since the reference to
the Ephesian church is generalized by "the church of God which he purchased
with his own blood" (v. 28).[59] Such a description is likely intended to go beyond
merely the local situation of the Ephesian church, which is supported further
by my observation above about why Paul and Barnabas "appointed elders for
. . . every church" in Acts 14:23.

Thus, once again we find a major NT notion, the office of elder, to be an
important feature of inaugurated eschatology. The origin of this office is best
understood in the light of the beginning end-time tribulation, as well as of the
new creation (though the former has been the focus here).

The New Testament Canon as an Eschatologically Generated
Foundation of the Church

The canon of the NT as a latter-day reality is not on a par with the Sabbath,
baptism, the Lord's Supper, and the office of elder, which are ecclesiological

---

59. This universal scope is pointed to further by the conclusion in v. 32 that if the elders
are faithful to Paul's admonition, then they will receive "the inheritance among all those who
are sanctified."

markers of the end-time church. Rather, the argument here is that the NT canon is to be seen as an eschatological foundation for the church, which is inextricably linked to Jesus as the beginning of the new creation and the messianic kingdom. This is close to being a marker or sign of the church because the NT Scriptures are to be an integral part of the meeting of the church.[60] Nevertheless, it is not on the same level as the other markers discussed in this chapter.

The Evidence of Luke-Acts[61]

Some allusions to OT prophecies refer to the latter days as a time in which God will promulgate a new "law" and "word," which the NT understands to take both oral and written form. For example, Jesus relates his ministry to OT prophecy in Luke 24:44–47:

> Now He said to them, "<u>These are my words</u> which I spoke to you while I was still with you, that all things which are written about Me in the Law of Moses and the Prophets and the Psalms must be fulfilled." Then He opened their minds to understand the Scriptures, and He said to them, "Thus it is written, that the Christ would suffer and rise again from the dead the third day, and that repentance for forgiveness of sins would be proclaimed in His name to <u>all the nations</u>, beginning from Jerusalem."

It is not only Christ's death and resurrection (= new creation) that is said to have been prophesied, but also "that repentance for forgiveness of sins would be proclaimed in his name to all the nations, beginning from Jerusalem." A redemptive proclamation of "the word of the Lord" to "all the nations" arising from Jerusalem in the end-time (after the beginning resurrection of the dead) is likely an allusion to Isa. 2:2–3:

> Now it will come about that in the last days
> The mountain of the house of the LORD
> Will be established as the chief of the mountains,
> And will be raised above the hills;
> And all the nations will stream to it.
> And many peoples will come and say,
> "Come, let us go up to the mountain of the LORD,
> To the house of the God of Jacob;
> That He may teach us concerning His ways

---

60. On which, see, e.g., Col. 4:16; 1 Thess. 5:27; Rev. 1:3; cf. 2 Thess. 3:14; 1 Tim. 5:17; 2 Tim. 2:15.

61. This section is based on a thumbnail sketch of Charles E. Hill, "God's Speech in These Last Days: The New Testament Canon as an Eschatological Phenomenon," in *Resurrection and Eschatology: Theology in Service of the Church; Essays in Honor of Richard B. Gaffin Jr.*, ed. Lane G. Tipton and Jeffrey G. Waddington (Phillipsburg, NJ: P&R, 2008), 203–54, esp. 209–11.

And that we may walk in His paths."
For the law will go forth from Zion
And the word of the LORD from Jerusalem.

The allusion is strengthened by the fact that Luke 24:49 ("I am sending forth the promise of my Father upon you, but you are to stay in the city until you are clothed with power from on high") is part of an allusion to Isa. 32:15 ("until the Spirit is poured out upon us from on high"), which itself is developed further in Acts 1:8, which likewise we have seen alludes to Isa. 32:15; 49:6.[62] The proclamation of the eschatological word in Isa. 2:3 is developed later in Isaiah: "O Jerusalem, bearer of good news" (40:9); "For a law will go forth from Me, and I will set My justice for a light to the peoples" (51:4) (see also 45:22–24; 55:10–11).

The repeated phrase "the word of God" (or "of the Lord") over twenty times in Acts likely has its roots in Isaiah, especially 2:2–3 and its development later in Isa. 40–55. Particularly noteworthy is Acts' portrayal of the "word" journeying in creating a community based on the word, which is highlighted at significant literary transitions in Acts (e.g., 6:7; 12:24; 19:20). These phrases refer to the prophetic written word of the OT in its beginning preached form of fulfillment in Christ. Thus, it is an oral word based on the written prophetic word (e.g., note Acts 8:26–36, where Isa. 53:7–8 is read by the Ethiopian eunuch and then interpreted through Philip's explanation that it had been fulfilled in Christ; see also Acts 17:11; 18:24–28). Despite opposition, the word makes its way and accomplishes its goal of creating the church community, which, in contrast to the Jewish establishment, is identified as the true heir of Isaiah's new-exodus promises.[63]

In that Jesus is addressing the apostles in Luke 24 and Acts 1:8, he is saying that the end-time mission of the "word" of God begins with the apostles, so that Isa. 2:2–3 is foundational for their mission. In addition to being a foundation,

> by natural extension the prophecy [in Isa. 2:2–3] of a new law, a new word of the Lord going forth out of Jerusalem, is part of the old covenant foundation for a new "canon" of Scripture, wherein the new word-revelation is preserved and from which it will be continually propagated.[64]

Certainly this new "law" and divine "word" announced by the apostles is both oral and written, the latter of which becomes the church's canon. According to Isaiah, the proclamation of the eschatological word would come through

62. On which, see chap. 17 under the subheading "The Eschatological Role of the Spirit in Acts."
63. For the most part, this paragraph is a very brief summary of David W. Pao, *Acts and the Isaianic New Exodus*, WUNT 2/130 (Tübingen: Mohr Siebeck, 2000), chap. 5.
64. Hill, "God's Speech," 211.

the messianic Servant, and the NT affirms this to have begun fulfillment in Jesus (note Isa. 52:7 and 61:1–2, which are respectively alluded to and quoted in Acts 10:36 and Luke 4:16–22). But the NT alludes to some of these same Isaianic texts and applies them to the apostles, since they are seen to be continuing the proclamation that Jesus began to deliver (see Acts 10:43 in relation to 10:36). In this respect, Paul changes the singular of Isa. 52:7 ("How lovely on the mountains are the feet of him who brings good news"), which he likely understood to have originally referred to the Servant, to a plural in Rom. 10:15 ("How beautiful are the feet of those who bring good news"). Thus, the mission of Jesus the Isaianic Servant is to be carried on by the apostles.[65]

Similarly, other commissions to the Servant in Isaiah are taken and applied to Paul (see Isa. 49:6 in Acts 13:46–47, and Isa. 42:6–7 in Acts 26:17–18). Acts 26:17–18 and 26:23 are particularly striking because the latter applies Isa. 42:6 and 49:6 to Jesus, and the former applies Isa. 42:6 to Paul.[66] Consequently, for Isaiah, the eschaton would see the streaming of the nations to the house of the Lord, the going forth of the word of the Lord from Jerusalem, and the pouring out of the Spirit from on high; Luke-Acts shows this to be beginning fulfillment in Jesus, the apostles, and the formation of the early church. We have also seen how Isa. 40–66 is riddled with prophecies of new creation, so that the notion of new creation is likely to be included in the above Isaianic background.

Thus, Paul and the apostles carry on the end-time witness begun by Jesus, so that they are "commissioned witnesses to bear authoritatively the word of the Messiah to the nations," which includes not only their oral testimony but also their written testimony that authoritatively preserves their word, which we now have in the collection of documents known as the NT canon.[67]

The Evidence of Hebrews

Hebrews 1:1–2 is another significant text in this regard:

> God, after He spoke long ago to the fathers in the prophets in many portions and in many ways, in these last days has spoken to us in His Son, whom He appointed heir of all things, through whom also He made the world.

If the revelation of the OT prophets not only was oral but also took written form in a canonical collection, it seems that the greater eschatological revelation

---

65. Note that in Eph. 2:17 Paul refers to Isa. 57:19 ("Peace, peace to him who is far and to him who is near") together with allusion to Isa. 52:7 ("him who brings good news of peace") to speak of Jesus as the one who fulfilled Isaiah's prophecy: "He came and proclaimed good news of peace to you who were far away, and peace to those who were near."

66. Note that Luke 2:30–32 also alludes to Isa. 42:6–7, 16; 49:6 and applies them to Jesus's ministry. For comparisons of these texts, including those of Acts 13; 26, see chap. 8 under the subheading "The Damascus Road Christophany as a Resurrection Appearance."

67. Hill, "God's Speech," 217–18.

through the "Son" likewise would not only be oral but also take the form of an authoritative written collection. It is probably no accident that here the greater revelation is inextricably linked, as I have already discussed, with the cosmic land promises, the new creation, and messianic kingship,[68] which are vital elements of my proposed NT storyline.

And it is clear that the apostles considered their written word as an indispensible part of their authoritative eschatological commission to carry on Christ's witness (for some of the substantial evidence for this, see the excursus below on "The Written Form of the Apostles' Eschatological Testimony").

The Evidence of the Book of Revelation

One more example of the eschatological basis for the writing of a NT book as divine Scripture is the book of Revelation.

In Rev. 1:19 Christ commissions John to write by saying, "Therefore, write the things which you have seen, and the things which are, and the things which will take place after these things." This passage is open to various translations, though the one that appears to be most viable in interpretative paraphrase is this: "Therefore, write the things which you have seen [the apocalyptic vision of the book], and what they mean, and what things must come to pass in the already–not yet latter days."[69] Accordingly, John's vision is "apocalyptic" (visions revealed from heaven); it is symbolic or figurative, needing interpretation; and it is about eschatology. Thus, verse 19 is a statement of the threefold genre of the entire book.

Revelation 1:19–20 is the conclusion of the Rev. 1 vision. The third part of the formula in verse 19, "what things are about to take place after these things" (*ha mellei genesthai meta tauta*),[70] reflects the wording of verse 1, "what things must take place quickly" (*ha dei genesthai en tachei*), and is drawn from Dan. 2:28–29a, 45–47, "what things must take place in the latter days" (*ha dei genesthai ep' eschatōn tōn hēmerōn*).[71] Since the Dan. 2 references treat "after these things" (*meta tauta*) as synonymous with "in the latter days" (*ep' eschatōn tōn hēmerōn*) (on which, see n. 72 and table 24.1), John may also be using "after these things" (*meta tauta*) as an eschatological reference, particularly to the general period of the latter days that had commenced, was presently ongoing, and would continue in the future until the consummation.

---

68. On which, see chap. 22 under the subheading "'Already and Not Yet' References to the Land Promises."

69. For the various translation possibilities of Rev. 1:19 and an explanation of the above paraphrase, see G. K. Beale, *The Book of Revelation: A Commentary on the Greek Text*, NIGTC (Grand Rapids: Eerdmans, 1999), 152–70.

70. Although *mellei* replaces Daniel's *dei* in most manuscripts of v. 19, *dei* is present in some: א* (C) *pc* (*dei mellein*), 2050 latt (*dei*). Cf. Josephus, *Ant.* 10.210.

71. The wording most resembles Dan. 2:45 TH: "what things must take place after these things" (*ha dei genesthai meta tauta*). On which, see further Beale, *Revelation*, 152–55.

This would not be an exclusively future reference, but would be consistent with the inaugurated end-time outlook of the immediate context throughout Rev. 1 and the NT generally.[72] A comparison of the Daniel and Revelation texts may help to highlight the equivalence of the "latter days" of Dan. 2:28 with the "after this" of Dan. 2:29, 45 and Rev. 1:19c (see table 24.1).

Table 24.1

Daniel 2:28–29, 45

LXX	Theodotion	Revelation 1:19
Dan. 2:28: *ha dei genesthai ep' eschatōn tōn hēmerōn* ("what must take place in the latter days")	Dan. 2:28: *ha dei genesthai ep' eschatōn tōn hēmerōn* ("what must take place in the latter days")	*ha mellei genesthai meta tauta* ("what is about to [what must] take place after these things")
Dan. 2:29: *hosa dei genesthai ep' eschatōn tōn hēmerōn* ("what must take place in the latter days")	Dan. 2:29: *ti dei genesthai meta tauta* ("what must take place after these things")	
Dan. 2:45: *ta esomena ep' eschatōn tōn hēmerōn* ("the things which will be in the latter days")	Dan. 2:45: *ha dei genesthai meta tauta* ("what must take place after these things")	

Evidence for this all-important assertion that the last clause of Rev. 1:19 is an expression about the "latter days" is found in that the MT "after this" (*'aḥărê dĕnâ*) of Dan. 2:29 is in synonymous parallelism with "in the latter days" of Dan. 2:28, which strongly implies that the former phrase has eschatological import.[73] The Greek translations confirm the synonymous nature of these phrases by using them to translate the MT. Theodotion uses "after these things" (*meta tauta*) for Dan. 2:29, 45, while in the very same verses the LXX version reads "in the latter days" (*ep' eschatōn tōn hēmerōn*), making more explicit the latter-day sense implicit in the "after this" (*'aḥărê dĕnâ*) of the Aramaic text.[74] Thus, in Dan. 2 "after these things" (*meta tauta*) is an eschatological expression that is synonymous with, but not as explicit as, "in the latter days" (*ep' eschatōn tōn hēmerōn*).

Likewise in Revelation, "after these things" (*meta tauta*) may be a packed eschatological expression in 1:19 (as well as in 4:1b: "Come up here, and I will show you what things must take place after these things"). That is, with reference to 1:19 (and 4:1), "after these things" (*meta tauta*) likely does not function as a simple literary or general temporal transition marker to the next

72. On which, with respect to Revelation, see the remainder of this section.

73. See C. F. Keil, *Biblical Commentary on the Book of Daniel*, trans. M. G. Easton, K&D (repr., Grand Rapids: Eerdmans, 1971), 111–12.

74. Note also that Acts 2:17 renders the "after this" (*'aḥărê-kēn*) of Joel 2:28 (= 3:1 LXX: *meta tauta*) with "in the latter days" (*en tais eschatais hēmerais*).

vision but rather is a specific allusion describing the end times, the eschato-logical "after this" of which Daniel spoke.[75] Thus, Christ's commission for John to "write" the book of Revelation from 1:11 is reiterated and expanded on in 1:19 by explaining that John is to "write" about the latter days, which have been inaugurated.

The "therefore" at the beginning of 1:19 explains the basis for John writing about the eschatological vision that he has seen. Verses 12–18 give that basis. John is commissioned to write the churches because the initial vision that he receives demonstrates that the saints' confidence ("do not be afraid" [v. 17b]) is grounded in Christ's installment as cosmic latter-day judge, end-time priest, and eschatological ruler of the church as a result of his victory over death through resurrection. For example, Jesus portrays himself as beginning to fulfill the prophecy from Dan. 7:13–14 that a "Son of Man" would rule for-ever over a worldwide kingdom. This expands on Rev. 1:5, where Jesus calls himself "ruler of the kings of the earth." Jesus's description of his resurrec-tion in 1:17–18 is also an elaboration of 1:5, where Jesus refers to himself as "the firstborn of the dead." Thus, Jesus's resurrection has commenced the end-time resurrection of the saints. The "sharp two-edged sword" proceed-ing from Jesus's mouth in 1:16 is based on the prophecies of Isa. 11:4 and 49:2, which depict him as an eschatological judge who has begun to fulfill this judicial messianic expectation.[76]

Therefore, the basis for John to "write" the entire book of Revelation about the already–not yet latter days is that those days have been inaugurated by Jesus himself as the king, Son of Man, and resurrected new creation, and he will bring those latter days to consummation. In addition, John is writing about the fulfillment of the "latter days" spoken of by Daniel,[77] which we

75. The semantic equivalence of "after these things" (*meta tauta*) with a "latter days" escha-tological idea has significance for previous views of Rev. 1:19. Some futurists have proposed that 1:19 serves as a chronological outline of the book, so that "what will take place after these things" at the end of the verse is taken to be an exclusively future reference for the very end of history. However, as argued above, if "after these things" (*meta tauta*) refers to the eschatological age, which John sees as already being inaugurated, then 1:19 cannot express such a tidy chronological formula. Accordingly, the third clause in 1:19 would have reference to the eschatological period that includes inauguration in the past, present, and future.

76. For more in-depth elaboration of this paragraph, see Beale, *Revelation*, 211–13.

77. Another piece of evidence in favor of the assertion that Dan. 2:29a, 45 stand behind Rev. 1:19b may be confirmed not just from textual similarities between the verses themselves but also by the similarities of their respective contexts. In this respect, Rev. 1:20 is important: "As for the mystery of the seven stars which you saw in My right hand, and the seven golden lampstands: the seven stars are the angels of the seven churches, and the seven lampstands are the seven churches." The word "mystery" (*mystērion*) most probably comes from Dan. 2:29, 47. Both references in Daniel and Revelation have nearly identical contexts. In Dan. 2 God is twice praised as the consummate revealer of mysteries (*mystēria*), and the references occur at the beginning and the end of Daniel's divinely inspired interpretation of Nebuchadnezzar's dream. Similarly, in Rev. 1 the divine Son of Man figure begins the interpretation of John's initial vision

have seen is primarily about the establishment of the kingdom and the temple of the new creation. All these are themes bound up with the new-creational kingdom, which is a fundamental aspect of the NT storyline that I have been developing throughout this book.

Since John's commission to write is based on Dan. 2:28–29, 45, not only in Rev. 1:19 (the introduction to chaps. 2–3) but also in 1:1 (the introduction to the book), 4:1 (the introduction to the visionary section in 4:2–22:5), and 22:6 (the formal beginning of the conclusion of the book), John should be seen as commissioned to write God's word about the latter days, just as was Daniel, except that John is explaining how Daniel's latter days have been commenced and will be consummated. Likewise, John is commissioned with the same prophetic commission given to Ezekiel (see 1:10; 4:2a; 17:3a; 21:10a), who also was greatly concerned with eschatology (e.g., see Ezek. 40–48, to which John alludes repeatedly in Rev. 21:9–22:5).[78] This, then, is another example of a NT written document being generated by the reality of a dawning eschatology.

Conclusion

Just as Israel had its book from God, so does the new Israel, the church, have its book, which is an already–not yet eschatological unpacking of the meaning of Israel's book. Both are ultimately one book, with each redemptive-historical installment throughout the OT into the NT progressively interpreting the earlier. But since the Bible is one book written ultimately by one divine author, the NT interprets the OT, and vice versa. The choice to put the NT message into writing, in addition to the oral message, must have been motivated partly by its nature as God's word, by its role as part of the foundation for the church, and by the desire to preserve it for the duration of the end-time period, since the apostles were aware that this period might last beyond their own lifetime.[79] In that the OT background for the church's eschatological book is derived partly from Isa. 2:1–3 and Isa. 40–55, eschatological new creation may also hover in the background, since these sections in Isaiah have to do with prophecies of new creation.

---

by revealing (and being the revealer of) the lampstand "mystery" (*mystērion*). Furthermore, John's vision describes a "mystery" containing (1) the inaugurated fulfillment of the office of the Danielic "Son of Man" (cf. Dan. 7:13) as messianic king, the beginning fulfillment of which is participated in (2) ironically by the suffering and sinful church and (3) guardian angels of the churches (cf. also vv. 6, 9).

78. On Rev. 21:9–22:5, see Beale, *Revelation*.

79. On which, see Hill, "God's Speech," 232–33.

Excursus The Written Form of the Apostles' Eschatological Testimony

Paul provides the best examples. In 1 Thess. 2:13 he says that when the Thessalonians "received from us the word of God's message, you accepted it not as the word of men, but for what it really is, the word of God, which also performs its work in you who believe." In 2 Thess. 3:1 he prays "that the word of the Lord may run and be glorified, just as it did also with you." It is evident that Paul's authoritative oral message is also expressed in authoritative written form: "So, he who rejects this [the instructions in Paul's letter] is not rejecting man but the God who gives His Holy Spirit to you" (1 Thess. 4:8); "I adjure you by the Lord to have this letter read to all the brethren" (1 Thess. 5:27); "So then, brethren, stand firm and hold to the traditions which you were taught, whether by word of mouth or by letter from us" (2 Thess. 2:15); "If anyone does not obey our instruction in this letter, take special note of that person and do not associate with him, so that he will be put to shame" (2 Thess. 3:14).

The Corinthian correspondence expresses the same notion: "If anyone thinks he is a prophet or spiritual, let him recognize that the things which I write to you are the Lord's commandment. But if anyone does not recognize this, he is not recognized" (1 Cor. 14:37–38); "It is in the sight of God that we have been speaking in Christ" (2 Cor. 12:19); "Since you are seeking proof of the Christ who speaks in me . . ." (2 Cor. 13:3); "For this reason I am writing these things while absent, so that when present I need not use severity in accordance with the authority which the Lord gave me for building up and not for tearing down" (2 Cor. 13:10). These statements highlight Paul's ironic statement in 2 Cor. 11:17: "What I am saying, I am not saying according to [or "on the basis of"] the Lord, but as in foolishness" (of course, Paul's ironic point is that indeed he is "speaking according to the Lord" in this letter).

In Eph. 3 Paul says that the prophetic "mystery" of OT prophecy was "revealed" to him, and he did not just speak his explanation of this mystery finding fulfillment in Christ but "wrote" about it in his letter, and when the addressees "read" it, they "can understand" his "insight into the mystery of Christ" (vv. 3–4). In this respect, Paul ranks himself with the "holy apostles and prophets" to whom the mystery has been "revealed . . . by the Spirit" (v. 5), and, in his case, part of his apostolic testimony about the mystery is put in authoritative letter form.

Peter too, in 2 Pet. 3:15–16, puts Paul's writings on an authoritative par with OT Scripture:

> And regard the patience of our Lord as salvation; just as also our beloved brother Paul, according to the wisdom given him, wrote to you, as also in all his letters, speaking in them of these things, in which are some things hard to understand, which the untaught and unstable distort, as they do also the rest of the [OT] Scriptures, to their own destruction.

There is even fragmentary evidence of a collection of Gospels during Paul's time that were equal in authority to the OT. In 1 Tim. 5:18 Paul says, "For the Scripture says, 'You shall not muzzle the ox while he is threshing' [Deut. 25:4], and 'The laborer is worthy of his wages' [Matt. 10:10; Luke 10:7]."

The book of Revelation is one of the clearest examples of a NT book that considers itself to be the word of God in written form. Thirteen times John is commanded to "write" (e.g., 1:11, 19; the beginning of each of the letters). What he writes in the letters of chapters 2–3 is both the word of Christ and the words of the Spirit (e.g., 2:1, 7, which is a pattern repeated in each letter). At various points throughout the book what he is commanded to "write" is also viewed as the words of the Spirit (14:13) or of God (19:9; 21:5). So authoritative is the written form of Revelation that not even its written words are to be altered, under threat of curse, as is made clear in 22:18–19:

> I testify to everyone who hears the words of the prophecy of this book: if anyone adds to them, God will add to him the plagues which are written in this book; and if anyone takes away from the words of the book of this prophecy, God will take away his part from the tree of life and from the holy city, which are written in this book.[80]

Consequently, the book of Revelation in its written form is referred to as "the words of the prophecy of this book," which must be kept (22:7 [likewise 22:9]) and adhered to (22:18–19). The conclusion forms a nice inclusio with the introduction to the book: "Blessed is he who reads and those who hear the words of the prophecy, and heed the things which are written in it; for the time is near" (1:3). The clear implication here is that the authoritative nature of the book demands that it be read and reread in Christian communities and be given "heed" (i.e., obeyed, because it is God's word).

This elaboration of the written authoritative witness of the apostles shows that their eschatological testimony was not only oral but also written.

---

80. The context for these verses involves distortion of the book of Revelation with false teaching, partly against the background of Deut. 4:2, where Moses issues virtually the same warning to false teachers distorting his written witness to the law (see Beale, *Revelation*, 1150–54).

PART 9

THE STORY OF CHRISTIAN LIVING AS INAUGURATED END-TIME NEW-CREATIONAL LIFE

25

Christian Living as the Beginning of Transformed New-Creational Life

The End-Time Indicative-Imperative Pattern and Ongoing Return from Exile

The preceding chapters, especially chapters 20–21, focused on God bringing his new-covenant people, end-time Israel, into existence as an eschatological new creation in fulfillment of OT prophecy. Chapters 23–24 focused on the new creation and kingdom as distinguishing marks of this new, faithful covenant community, all of which compose crucial parts of my formulated storyline. This chapter will concentrate more on how this newly created covenant community of faith is to act and why it is to do so. We can call this new living "ongoing Christian living" or "new-creational life" or "sanctification" (as systematic theology has traditionally termed it). I use "sanctification" to refer to ongoing Christian life that is set apart from the old creation and set apart to the eschatological new creation. Thus, inherent to the continuation of Christian living is resurrection life that has transported a person from the old, fallen world into the new creation. And when people begin to become part of the new creation, eschatological righteousness sets in to their lives, a righteousness that was promised to be part and parcel of the new heaven and new earth.[1] When this happens, they become a living part of the redemptive-

---

1. On which, see 2 Pet. 3:13, which is probably formulated on the basis of alluding to a combination of Isa. 61:21; 65:17 (so also Isa. 66:22a).

historical storyline, in which they are not only a part of the new creation but are also involved in the expansion of it in their own lives.

This section and the next will address the vexed problem of how the indicative relates to the imperative in various parts of the NT, especially in Paul's writings. That is, how does being in Christ relate to how one behaves as a Christian? Are Christians defined primarily by what they do, or by what they are, or by both?

A series of passages in the NT Epistles address this issue. We will observe that in passage after passage, what a person is in the resurrected Christ is the basis for how that person should behave. Many passages describe this basis in various ways: sometimes merely "in Christ" or "redeemed" or "saved" or "reconciled" or "justified" or "washed" or "sanctified" or "being a new creation" or "resurrected" or "born again," and so on. This section will focus on people who are described specifically as being part of the end-time new creation as resurrected beings, and then, on that basis, they are addressed with commands. All these descriptions are really facets of a general new-creational condition, which all believers share, a point that this book has tried to make from different angles.

The thesis of this segment is that only people who are part of the new creation and kingdom have the ability to obey the commands. It was in the light of such texts as we are about to study that Augustine formulated his famous prayer, "Grant what Thou dost command and command what Thou wilt" (*Conf.* 10.29). I have already addressed this issue in passing,[2] but now I will place direct focus on it. The point in this section is not to interpret these passages thoroughly but rather to concentrate on how a person's standing in Christ is the basis for being able to fulfill God's commands. The following texts are but a sampling from among many.

Paul

Romans 6

In Rom. 6:4–11 Paul says,

Therefore we have been buried with Him through baptism into death, so that as Christ was raised from the dead through the glory of the Father, so we too might walk in newness of life. For if we have become united with Him in the likeness of His death, certainly we shall also be in the likeness of His resurrection, knowing this, that our old man was crucified with Him, in order that our body of sin might be done away with, so that we would no longer be slaves to sin; for he who has died is freed from sin. Now if we have died with Christ, we believe that we shall also live with Him, knowing that Christ, having been raised from

2. See, e.g., chap. 10 under the subheading "What Difference Does It Make for Christian Living That the Latter-Day New Creation Has Begun?"

the dead, is never to die again; death no longer is master over Him. For the death that He died, He died to sin once for all; but the life that He lives, He lives to God. Even so consider yourselves to be dead to sin, but alive to God in Christ Jesus.

Believers have been identified with Christ's death and his resurrection (vv. 4–5, 8–11), so that they have begun to experience resurrection existence, which will continue on into the eternal age to come (the inaugurated aspect is most clear in vv. 4b, 11b). As we have seen in earlier chapters, this resurrection is the beginning of new creation, and Paul even uses a near synonym of new creation in verse 4b ("newness of life" [*kainotēs zōēs*]).[3] It is important also to see with what Christians are not identified: their "old man was crucified with [Christ]" (v. 6). Many translations render this as "our old self was crucified with him" (e.g., NRSV, NIV, NAB, TNIV), but the literal and better translation of *palaios anthrōpos* here is "old man" (KJV, NET).[4] This rendering fits nicely in this context because Paul has just finished discussing the first or old "Adam" (5:14), whom he also refers to as "man" (*anthrōpos* [5:19]) in contrast to Christ, who also is referred to as a "man" (*anthrōpos* [5:15]) and of whom the first Adam was a type (5:14b). To translate *palaios anthrōpos* as "old self" and not "old man" is to obscure this identification with the old Adam and the new Adam, Christ. Against the background of Rom. 5, the point in Rom. 6 is that believers were formerly part of the old world and identified with the old Adam ("man"), who represented that world in his sin and condemnation. Now, believers' part in the old world has been removed because they are identified with the new man, Christ. Since he has died to the old world and been raised as a new man, his followers too have died and have been raised with him and are new people.

This identification with Christ's resurrection as a new creation is crucial for understanding how saints can be obedient to God. Their new-creational existence, on which Paul elaborates in Rom. 6:4–11, is the basis for them having the ability not to sin but to serve God in 6:12–14:

> Therefore do not let sin reign in your mortal body so that you obey its lusts, and do not go on presenting the members of your body to sin as instruments of unrighteousness; but present yourselves to God as those alive from the dead, and your members as instruments of righteousness to God. For sin shall not be master over you, for you are not under law but under grace.

The "therefore" refers back to verses 2–11 and the climax and main point in verse 11, which asserts that believers are "dead to sin, but alive to God in

---

3. As we saw in an earlier chapter, the Spirit is the agent of resurrection life, and accordingly in Rom. 7:6 Paul says, "We serve in newness by means of the Spirit [*en kainotēti pneumatos*] and not in oldness of the letter," which further develops Rom. 6:4b.

4. The NASB and ESV have "old self" but acknowledge "old man" as a marginal alternative. The NEB well interpretatively paraphrases with "the man we once were."

Christ Jesus." On that basis, repeated in verse 13b ("as those alive from the dead"), Paul's readers can be confident of their ability to "not let sin reign" in them and not to do "unrighteousness" but instead to be "instruments of righteousness." Their resurrection existence in Christ gives them the ability to "walk in newness of life" (v. 4b). This conclusion has already been briefly anticipated not only in verse 4b but also in verses 6b–7.

As we have seen, Ezek. 36–37 is part of the background for understanding resurrection as the power that breaks the hold of sin and death in Rom. 6–8. In Ezek. 36:25–29 God says,

> Then I will sprinkle clean water on you, and you will be clean; I will cleanse you from all your filthiness and from all your idols. Moreover, I will give you a new heart and put a new spirit within you; and I will remove the heart of stone from your flesh and give you a heart of flesh. I will put My Spirit within you and cause you to walk in My statutes, and you will be careful to observe My ordinances. You will live in the land that I gave to your forefathers; so you will be My people, and I will be your God. Moreover, I will save you from all your uncleanness.

And in Ezek. 37:12–14 God tells Ezekiel,

> Therefore prophesy and say to them, "Thus says the Lord GOD, 'Behold, I will open your graves and cause you to come up out of your graves, My people; and I will bring you into the land of Israel. Then you will know that I am the LORD, when I have opened your graves and caused you to come up out of your graves, My people. I will put My Spirit within you and you will come to life, and I will place you on your own land. Then you will know that I, the LORD, have spoken and done it,' declares the LORD."

Notice that in 36:26 God's "Spirit" will give "a new heart" and "a new spirit," which is defined as resurrection life in 37:12–14. This new resurrection life is the basis for God's end-time people to obey God: I "will . . . cause you to walk in My statutes, and you will be careful to observe My ordinances" (36:27). Romans 6–8 sees this beginning fulfillment in Christians.[5]

Ephesians

Ephesians 4:20–32 also exhibits the pattern of the necessity of being a new creature as a foundation for being able to obey God's new-creational commands:

> But you did not learn Christ in this way, if indeed you have heard Him and have been taught in Him, just as truth is in Jesus, that, in reference to your former

---

5. For an elaboration of the validity of the Ezekiel background and its significance for Paul's understanding of resurrection by the Spirit in Rom. 6–8, see chap. 9 under the heading "Resurrection in Romans."

manner of life, you lay aside the old man, which is being corrupted in accordance with the lusts of deceit, and that you be renewed in the spirit of your mind, and put on the new man, which in the likeness of God has been created in righteousness and holiness of the truth. Therefore, laying aside falsehood, speak truth each one of you with his neighbor, for we are members of one another. Be angry, and yet do not sin; do not let the sun go down on your anger, and do not give the devil an opportunity. He who steals must steal no longer; but rather he must labor, performing with his own hands what is good, so that he will have something to share with one who has need. Let no unwholesome word proceed from your mouth, but only such a word as is good for edification according to the need of the moment, so that it will give grace to those who hear. Do not grieve the Holy Spirit of God, by whom you were sealed for the day of redemption. Let all bitterness and wrath and anger and clamor and slander be put away from you, along with all malice. Be kind to one another, tender-hearted, forgiving each other, just as God in Christ also has forgiven you.

Paul reminds his readers what they learned when they first came to faith (vv. 20–21). At that time they were instructed to "lay aside the old man . . . and be renewed in the spirit of your mind, and put on the new man, which in the likeness of God has been created in righteousness and holiness of the truth" (vv. 22–24). Therefore, it is in the past that the "old man" has been laid aside, "the spirit" has been renewed, and the "new man" has been put on. Paul is assuming that the people whom he addresses are "renewed" and are a "new man."[6] It is important to recognize that "lay aside . . . be renewed . . . put on" are not present commands for those who have already become Christians, as is sometimes thought by commentators to be the case. The phrases "lay aside . . . be renewed . . . put on" are descriptions of what Christians were taught to do when they first trusted in Christ. Thus, Paul is addressing Christians who in the past have "laid aside the old man" and "been renewed in the spirit" and "put on the new man." Furthermore, the three Greek verbs in question are not imperatives but infinitives, giving the content of what saints "were taught" (v. 21) at the time of their conversion. These verbs should be seen as having had a past imperatival sense in that they were part of the gospel presentation and exhortation to these believers at the past time of the inception of their faith.

That the verbs refer to what has happened in the past is apparent also from verse 22, where it says that the "old man" refers to "your former manner of life," and it was "being corrupted in accordance with the lusts of deceit." The latter phrase about corruption refers not to believers' present existence but rather to their "former manner of life" as nonbelievers. Furthermore, they are those whose "new man" has "been created" in God's image, another pointer that they have come to be identified with Christ, "the ultimate new man," the

6. Although he leaves room for the possibility that some may not have been so transformed in the past: "if indeed you have heard Him and been taught in Him" (v. 21).

last Adam. That this is so will become even clearer when we examine Col. 3 below in this section.

Some translations of verses 22, 24 have "the old self" and "the new self," but this neutralizes the redemptive-historical allusions and background. The Greek phrases are better rendered as "the old man" (*ton palaion anthrōpon*) and "the new man" (*ton kainon anthrōpon*); this translation is the most formally equivalent, and it suits admirably the contrast of the former old epoch with the new eschatological epoch.[7] Thus, the expressions here are the same as in Rom. 6. As in that passage, these are redemptive-historical references to two ages represented by two all-determinative persons, the first Adam and Jesus, who is the new man or last Adam.

The wording of verses 22, 24 recalls and develops Eph. 2:15, where it says that Christ "abolished the law of commandments in decrees in order that in himself he should create the two [Jew and gentile] into one new man, thus establishing peace." Accordingly, the "one new man" in Eph. 2:15 is composed of Christian Jews and gentiles, but they are "one new man" because Christ created the two "in himself." Jew and gentile were two groups, separate from each other, but after their creation in Christ they are "one new man" because Christ himself is "the one new man." Christ as the "new man" has been anticipated in Eph. 1:22, where the allusion to the ideal end-time Adam is applied to the resurrected Christ's rule and saints are then identified with this position of Adamic rule (Eph. 2:5–6).[8] In addition, Eph. 5:29–32 portrays Christ as the Adam of the new creation, whose wife, believers in the church, "are members of His body" (v. 30, with v. 31 citing Gen. 2:24 in support). This further supports the notion that Eph. 2:15 speaks of a corporate Adam, the individual Christ, who represents believers, who are part of his body. Although the first, historical Adam is not explicitly mentioned in Ephesians, the reference to the "old man" in Eph. 4:22 not only alludes to believers' "former" ungodly existence (e.g., Eph. 2:1–3, 11–12) but also secondarily echoes the "old man" by whom they were represented (the first Adam).

Paul moves from the new-creational condition of his readers in verses 22–24 to the series of commands in verses 25–32 by the transitional word "therefore" (*dio*). This word indicates that what has preceded is the foundation for what follows. Accordingly, on the basis that the believers are a "new man," thus breaking the determinative power of sin from the old world, they are given commands. The "indicative" of the new creation must precede the "imperative" to act as a new creation. Without the power of the new creation, there is no ability to obey God and please him.

7. The KJV and NET have "old/new man." The NAB, NRSV, and TNIV have "old/new self," and the RSV and NEB have "old/new nature," which likewise is less preferable to the "man" rendering. The NASB and ESV have "old/new self" but in a footnote give the alternative "old/new man."

8. For substantiation and discussion of this allusion, see chap. 5.

In fact, the phrase "therefore, laying aside [*apothemenoi*] falsehood" in verse 25 is a continuation of the earlier "laying aside [*apothesthai*] of the old man" in verse 22. The point is that once the "old man" has been laid aside, the sins that characterized the "old man" also begin to be laid aside. As one grows as an inaugurated new-creational being, one increasingly sheds the sinful lifestyle traits that characterized the former existence of the "old man."

Colossians: The Old Man and the New Man in Colossians 3

Colossians 3:1–12 is very similar to Eph. 4:20–32:

> Therefore if you have been raised up with Christ, keep seeking the things above, where Christ is, seated at the right hand of God. Set your mind on the things above, not on the things that are on earth. For you have died and your life is hidden with Christ in God. When Christ, who is our life, is revealed, then you also will be revealed with Him in glory. Therefore consider the members of your earthly body as dead to immorality, impurity, passion, evil desire, and greed, which amounts to idolatry. For it is because of these things that the wrath of God will come upon the sons of disobedience, and in them you also once walked, when you were living in them. But now you also, put them all aside: anger, wrath, malice, slander, and abusive speech from your mouth. Do not lie to one another, since you laid aside the old man with its evil practices, and have put on the new man who is being renewed to a true knowledge according to the image of the One who created him—a renewal in which there is no distinction between Greek and Jew, circumcised and uncircumcised, barbarian, Scythian, slave and freeman, but Christ is all, and in all. So, as those who have been chosen of God, holy and beloved, put on a heart of compassion, kindness, humility, gentleness and patience.

On the basis ("therefore," *oun* [v. 5]) of believers' identification with Christ's death and resurrection (vv. 1–4), Paul exhorts them to live like resurrected new creatures and not like those who belong to the old world (3:5–4:6). After explaining the sample listing of sins that they are not to commit, the basis for being able to refrain from these sins is given again in verses 9–10. In particular, Paul tells them to "not lie to one another." Almost identically to Eph. 4:22–25, Col. 3:9–10 says that true believers are not to "lie" because they have "laid aside the old man" and have "put on the new [man]" (not "old self" and "new self," as in some translations).[9]

Thus, the basis for not living sinfully is stated in verses 1–4 to be believers' resurrected status, and that basis is given again in verses 9–10 as being a new-creational status. Although the "new man" is not perfected, saints are

9. For the reasons supporting the translation of *ton palaion anthrōpon* and *ton kainon* [*anthrōpon*] in Col. 3:9–10 as "the old man" and "the new man" (versus "the old self" and "the new self"), see the discussion earlier in this chapter of Eph. 4:22–24.

growing in their new-creational existence: the "new man" is "<u>being renewed</u> . . . according to the image of the One who created him" (v. 10b). Accordingly, the "image" in which they are being renewed is Christ's image, especially in light of the link back to 1:15 (portraying Christ as "the image of the invisible God"), and "the One who created" them in this image is God. As in Eph. 2:15, Christ again is identified with the "new man" in which believing "Greek and Jew" (and other people groups) exist (Col. 3:11: "a renewal in which . . . Christ is all, and in all"). Even the reference in 3:10 to being "renewed to a true knowledge [*epignōsis*]" may echo the Genesis context, where "knowledge" was at the heart of the fall (cf. Gen. 2:17: "From the tree of the knowledge of good and evil you shall not eat").[10]

In light of the two allusions above to the divine "image" and "knowledge" in Col. 3:10 from Gen. 1–3, the imagery of removing old clothing and donning new clothing in Col. 3:9–10 may be alluding to Gen. 3. Genesis 3:7 says that Adam and Eve, directly after their sin, tried to cover their sinful nakedness by their own autonomous efforts: "They sewed fig leaves together and made themselves loin coverings." However, in an apparent expression of their beginning restoration to God after the fall (esp. in light of 3:20), Gen. 3:21 says, "The LORD God made garments of skin for Adam and his wife, and clothed [*endyō*] them." The clear implication is that their first suit of clothes was taken off and replaced by divinely made clothing, indicating that the humanly made clothing was associated with their alienated condition and sinful shame (Gen. 3:7–11) and was an insufficient covering for those who have begun to be reconciled to God.[11]

Likewise Col. 3:9–10 refers to believers who have "removed the clothes" (*apekdyomai*) of "the old [sinful] man" and "put on the clothes" (*endyō*) of "the new man," which indicates their inaugurated new creation relationship with God.[12] The imagery is not precisely "laying aside" and "putting on," the usual rendering of the English translations; it is sartorial language. They have removed the clothing that is the first Adam (the "old man"), in which neither Adam nor they could come into God's presence, and have clothed themselves with the last Adam (the "new man"), in whom they have been "renewed."[13]

---

10. On which, see James D. G. Dunn, *The Epistles to the Colossians and to Philemon: A Commentary on the Greek Text*, NIGTC (Grand Rapids: Eerdmans, 1996), 221–22.

11. That Adam's and Eve's "loin coverings" were not proper attire to wear in God's holy presence is clear from the fact that "they hid themselves from the presence of the LORD God" and still considered themselves "naked" (Gen. 3:8–10); this view of the clothing in Gen. 3:8 is also taken by *Sib. Or.* 1:47–49.

12. The NRSV and NLT use apparel metaphors: "you have stripped off . . . and have clothed yourselves" (cf. similarly NJB, NET); see Eph. 4:22–24 for closely parallel wording; similarly *Barn.* 6:11–12, which also quotes Gen. 1:26, 28.

13. So likewise John Calvin, *Commentaries on the Epistles of Paul the Apostle to the Philippians, Colossians, and Thessalonians* (repr., Grand Rapids: Baker, 1999), 211; E. K. Simpson and F. F. Bruce, *Commentary on the Epistles to the Ephesians and the Colossians*, NICNT

By donning their new clothing they have begun to return to God and will do so consummately in the future.[14] Paul seems to be using the Gen. 3 "clothing" language analogically: the new clothes with which Adam himself was clothed to indicate his restored relationship with God are analogical to and proleptic of Christians being clothed with the new clothes of the last Adam.

Hence, one is in the position either of the old, fallen, first Adam, the corporate "embodiment of unregenerate humanity" or of the new, resurrected, last Adam, the corporate "embodiment of the new humanity."[15]

The participles often translated as "putting off" (apekdysamenoi) and "putting on" (endysamenoi) in Col. 3:9–10 are likely not commands and are understood better as a description of the reality of what has happened in the past: "since you have put off the old man . . . and since you have put on the new man";[16] in the light of the intended clothing imagery of these words, an even better rendering is "since you have stripped off the old man . . . and since you have clothed yourselves with the new man." On this basis, Paul is exhorting them to stop being identified with the traits of the former life in the first Adam and to be characterized by those of the new life in the last Adam. Again, as in Ephesians, the reason Paul commands his readers to lay aside sinful traits is that they have already and decisively laid aside their old, unregenerate man and put on the new, re-created man, which gives them the power to obey the commands.[17] Therefore, on the basis that the readers are a "new man," Paul again issues commands to them (vv. 12–17).

Titus

Titus 3:5–8 says,

> He saved us, not on the basis of deeds which we have done in righteousness, but according to His mercy, by the washing of regeneration and renewing by

---

(Grand Rapids: Eerdmans, 1957), 84; Peter T. O'Brien, *Colossians, Philemon*, WBC 44 (Waco: Word, 1982), 190–91. These commentators see a contrast here between the figures of the first Adam and the last Adam.

14. So likewise Ralph P. Martin, *Colossians and Philemon*, NCB (repr., London: Oliphants, 1974), 107; N. T. Wright, *The Epistles of Paul to the Colossians and to Philemon*, TNTC (Grand Rapids: Eerdmans, 1986), 138. Both also see a contrast between identification with the old Adam and the new Adam.

15. O'Brien, *Colossians, Philemon*, 190–91. The latter side of the identification is made clear by Rom. 6:5–11; 13:14; Gal. 3:27.

16. These two aorist participles are likely adverbial of cause (modifying the verb "do not lie") and could be translated "because you have put off . . . and because you have put on."

17. For a fuller exegetical analysis of the OT background in Gen. 1–3 of "disrobing [oneself of] the old man" and "donning the new man," see chap. 14 under the subheading "The Image of the Last Adam in Colossians 1:15–18; 3:9–10"; G. K. Beale, "Colossians," in *Commentary on the New Testament Use of the Old Testament*, ed. G. K. Beale and D. A. Carson (Grand Rapids: Baker Academic, 2007), 866–68.

the Holy Spirit, whom He poured out upon us richly through Jesus Christ our Savior, so that being justified by His grace we would be made heirs according to the hope of eternal life. This is a trustworthy statement; and concerning these things I want you to speak confidently, so that those who have believed God may be careful to engage in good deeds. These things are good and profitable for men.

Although the language of the "old man" versus the "new man" is not employed here, terms that convey the same notion of new creation are used: "regeneration and renewing by the Holy Spirit" (v. 5b),[18] which, together with "justification" (v. 7a), are the basis for being "saved" (v. 5a) and being "made heirs according to the hope of eternal life" (v. 7b). All this is set in contrast to the old, sinful lifestyle (v. 3). On the basis of this condition of new creation and justification, which will lead to eternal life, Paul exhorts his readers "to engage in good deeds" (v. 8), some of which are elaborated on in verses 9–14. Again, in light of the analysis of Pauline texts so far in this section, it is not accidental that Paul posits that new creation is the basis for the expectation that Christians will do "good deeds."

The Implications of the "Old Man" and the "New Man" in Paul's Thought

Before proceeding to more relevant texts elsewhere in the NT, it is important to reflect on the theological and anthropological implications of the above analysis. I have concluded that in Rom. 6, Eph. 4, and Col. 3 believers are part of a beginning new creation. This means that their part in the old creation has been "laid aside," and they, though not a perfected new creation, are growing in their new-creational existence. Because they still physically live in the old, material world, and their new-creational being is not completed, sin still dogs them. However, slowly but surely they are increasingly progressing in their new-creational existence. This means that they are in the process of shaking the sinful shadow of the "old man" that lingers over them, even though the old man is gone. In a real sense, true believers are still part of the old creation in that they still possess physical bodies, which are being corrupted and will one day die, unless the Lord returns beforehand. Nevertheless, the unseen part of a person, that person's soul or "spirit" (as Eph. 4:23 terms it), or "inner man is being renewed day by day" (2 Cor. 4:16). To perceive the reality of this increasingly renewed "inner man," one must "look not at the things which are seen, but at the things which are not seen; for the things which are seen are temporal, but the things which are not seen are eternal" (2 Cor. 4:18).

---

18. See also Gal. 4:29, which refers to Ishmael, "who was born according to the flesh," and Isaac, "who was born according to the Spirit." Similarly, see the language of "born again" versus "born of the flesh" in John 3:5–8.

Therefore, "we walk by faith and not by sight" (2 Cor. 5:7) in believing that our resurrection and new-creational existence are true and growing.

It is crucial to clarify here that Paul is not saying that both an "old man" and a "new man" exist together in a person, so that there is a battle between the two inside each Christian. Those who hold such a view conceive that sometimes the "old man" wins the battle, and sometimes the "new man" wins. Some would go so far as to say that the "old man" can dominate a Christian most of the time, so that the "new man" barely ever shows himself. Some believe that Rom. 7:15–25 supports such a dual picture:

> For what I am doing, I do not understand; for I am not practicing what I would like to do, but I am doing the very thing I hate. But if I do the very thing I do not want to do, I agree with the Law, confessing that the Law is good. So now, no longer am I the one doing it, but sin which dwells in me. For I know that nothing good dwells in me, that is, in my flesh; for the willing is present in me, but the doing of the good is not. For the good that I want, I do not do, but I practice the very evil that I do not want. But if I am doing the very thing I do not want, I am no longer the one doing it, but sin which dwells in me. I find then the principle that evil is present in me, the one who wants to do good. For I joyfully concur with the law of God in the inner man, but I see a different law in the members of my body, waging war against the law of my mind and making me a prisoner of the law of sin which is in my members. Wretched man that I am! Who will set me free from the body of this death? Thanks be to God through Jesus Christ our Lord! So then, on the one hand I myself with my mind am serving the law of God, but on the other, with my flesh the law of sin.

It is debated whether this section of Rom. 7 refers to a conflict within the believer or within the unbeliever. I see it as more likely that here Paul is speaking not of turmoil within his ongoing Christian life but rather of the conflict that characterized his life before he came to faith. In this regard, the "I" in this section could represent Paul before his conversion, or unbelieving Adam, or unbelieving Israel at Sinai, or unbelieving humanity or the unbelieving Jewish people.[19] It is likely that Paul is viewing himself as a personal representative of the conflict that the majority of unbelieving Israel had gone through up to the coming of Christ, though the ultimate focus is on Israel's unbelieving response to the law at Sinai, with which Paul identifies himself and all unbelieving Israelites.[20] Secondarily, Paul is also identifying himself with Adam's experience, which Israel later reflected.[21] Paul will say that this

19. Douglas J. Moo, "Israel and Paul in Romans 7:7–12," *NTS* 32 (1986): 122. However, Moo sees an initial focus on Paul's experience as a non-Christian.

20. Moo (ibid.) argues for this view, though he concentrates on showing how Rom. 7:7–12 is best understood in this manner.

21. So Dennis E. Johnson, "The Function of Romans 7:13–25 in Paul's Argument for the Law's Impotence and the Spirit's Power, and Its Bearing on the Identity of the Schizophrenic 'I,'"

conflict has ceased for those Israelites who, like Paul, now believe in Christ (in this respect, see Rom. 7:24–8:3).

I cannot present a more in-depth examination of this passage here, but the following observations point to this section of Romans as a portrayal of an unbeliever,[22] especially of Paul representing unbelieving Israel before the coming of Christ. The following expressions in Rom. 7, which are used by Paul of himself (attributed to the "I" in Rom. 7), point strongly to this conclusion because elsewhere in his epistles they characteristically refer to unbelievers: (1) "I am of flesh" (7:14);[23] (2) "sold under sin" (7:14);[24] (3) "who will deliver me from the body of this death" (7:24);[25] (4) "I know that nothing good dwells in me, that is in my flesh" (7:18 [contrast this with 8:9]);[26] (5) "wretched [talaipōros] man that I am" (7:24).[27] Although some view the "I" of Rom. 7 to be a "struggling Christian," the description is not of someone who has the ability both to do

---

in *Resurrection and Eschatology: Theology in Service of the Church; Essays in Honor of Richard B. Gaffin Jr.*, ed. Lane G. Tipton and Jeffrey C. Waddington (Phillipsburg, NJ: P&R, 2008), 30–34. That Israel's conflict could reflect that of Adam's predicament is understandable given Israel's identification as a corporate Adam who inherited Adam's Gen. 1:28 commission but also, like Adam, did not obey it (I have argued this throughout this book; e.g., see chap. 2 under the subheadings "The Differences between the Commission to Adam and What Was Passed On to His Descendants" and "Conclusion," and chap. 15 under the subheading "The Expectations for Adam's Obedience and the Application of These Expectations to Other Adam-Like Figures and Finally to Christ").

22. I am grateful to my former colleague T. David Gordon for an unpublished paper from the late 1980s that summarizes some of the scholars representing this view (e.g., Kümmel, Käsemann, Ridderbos, Ladd, Achtemeier) and has shaped the present discussion of Rom. 7. Most recently, an in-depth argument has been presented by Dennis Johnson ("Function of Romans 7:13–25," 3–59), who independently expanded in much detail the main outline of Gordon's analysis, including a good representative bibliography of scholars representing both positions on Rom. 7.

23. In particular, Paul uses "flesh" (*sarx*) in Rom. 8:3–13 to designate unbelieving humanity, which is typical of his uses elsewhere. On the contrast between "flesh" and "Spirit" in Paul highlighting how humanity is either in the old world or in the inbreaking new creation, see Gordon D. Fee, *God's Empowering Presence: The Holy Spirit in the Letters of Paul* (Peabody, MA: Hendrickson, 1994), 816–22.

24. The wording and idea of "selling" or "redeeming" are used by Paul elsewhere as metaphors of commerce or slavery to indicate the notion of Christ "buying" or "redeeming" unbelievers, who are in spiritual debt or bondage. These are not metaphors to describe the lives of those who are already Christians (1 Cor. 6:20; 7:23; Gal. 3:13; 4:4–5); likewise, this imagery in Rom. 6 refers either to unbelievers enslaved to sin or to believers enslaved to righteousness (Rom. 6:6, 12, 14, 16–20, 22).

25. Nowhere else in Paul's writings do believers cry out wondering who will free them from the death of the body, since Christians, whose bodies will die, have the confident hope that in Christ their bodies will be raised from the dead at the end.

26. Whereas Paul says in 7:18 that "nothing good dwells in me," in 8:9 he says that "the Spirit of God dwells in you [the believer]," which is a good thing that dwells in the believer. Paul completes Rom. 8:9 by concluding that "if anyone does not have the Spirit of Christ, he does not belong to Him."

27. Note also the cognate word *talaipōria* ("miserable") in Rom. 3:16; James 5:1, which describe the condition of unbelievers.

good and to sin but rather of someone who can only wish to do good but in reality cannot (7:15–23). Accordingly, 7:7–25 is an exposition of those in the nonsalvific state of "the flesh" introduced in 7:5, and 8:1–39 is an exposition of the condition of those who are true Christians introduced in 7:6. This is apparent in that there is a repetition of ideas and terms from 7:5 in 7:7–25 and an absence of concepts and terms from 7:6 in 7:7–25.[28]

If Rom. 7 is describing a conflict not within the Christian but rather within an unbelieving Israelite, what is the nature of that conflict? Paul has already said that unbelieving Jews know God's truth but do not do it. Even though they often break God's law (Rom. 2:21–27), they "know [God's] will," "approve the things that are essential," are "a light to those who are in darkness," and possess "in the Law the embodiment of knowledge and truth" (Rom. 2:17–20). Although they had "a zeal for God," they "did not subject themselves to the righteousness of God [in the law]" (Rom. 10:2–3). It is likely that Paul's conflicted "I" in Rom. 7 reflects a representative personalization of this unbelieving condition of the Jew.[29]

If this line of argumentation is on the right track, which I think it is, Rom. 7 should not be seen as supporting the idea that Christians have within themselves a conflict between an "old man" and a "new man." Thus, this passage is not a major obstacle to the anthropological picture that Christians are only a new, inaugurated end-time "man."

Conclusion to Christian Living in Paul

The upshot of my discussion of Rom. 6, Eph. 4, and Col. 3 is that when persons have identified with Christ, their position in the old, sinful creation has been destroyed, and they have begun to be part of a new creation (see also Gal. 6:14–15). If Paul's addressees were both an "old man" and a "new man" at the same time, there would be redemptive-historical and psychological schizophrenia. The true believer is someone who is no longer an unbelieving "old man" but instead is a believing "new man." Since the "new man" is not perfected, sin

28. Johnson, "Function of Romans 7:13–25," 28–29.
29. See ibid., 51–53. Johnson, after citing some of the above Romans passages, adduces striking references from ancient pagan writers who testify to the notion that pagans had a sense of what is right but violate that sense in their actions. Some of these are closely parallel to Paul's language in Rom. 7:15—e.g., "Every sin involves a contradiction. For since he who is in sin does not wish to sin but to be right, it is clear that . . . he is not doing what he wishes and what he does not wish he does" (Epictetus [AD 55–135]). Note likewise that unbelieving gentiles "do instinctively the things of the Law," with "their thoughts alternately accusing or else defending them" (Rom. 2:14–15). This conflict within unbelieving gentiles may be echoed insofar as Adam stands behind Paul's focus on Israel's sinful condition (I am aware of the disagreement among commentators about whether Rom. 2:14–15 refers to gentile Christians or to unbelieving gentiles, though my own view accords most with the latter perspective (as represented by, e.g., Douglas J. Moo, *The Epistle to the Romans*, NICNT [Grand Rapids: Eerdmans, 1996], 148–57; Thomas R. Schreiner, *Romans*, BECNT [Grand Rapids: Baker Academic, 1998], 119–26).

still indwells believers as a result of the powers of evil, the world's influence, the deleterious effects of living with a fallen body, and the inner imperfected being of believers themselves. But the important point is that the major battle is over because believers have experienced a decisive death in Christ and a decisive victory through being identified with his resurrection. It is true that sin remains, but the power of the new is dominant, and slowly (perhaps) but surely it will dominate over the sinful impulses, though perfection will never be reached until the final resurrection of the body at the end of the age.

C. S. Lewis pictures this theological reality in his *Voyage of the Dawn Treader*. The character Eustace was a very spoiled boy who had become so enamored with a dragon's treasure that he became the dragon itself. Lewis's point is that Eustace's transformation into a dragon represented his dragon-like heart. In a subsequent scene, Lewis depicts Aslan, the messianic lion, leading Eustace up to a mountain, at the top of which is a garden (echoing the garden of Eden) and a big pool of water with marble steps leading down into it (reflecting a baptismal scene). Aslan tells Eustace to undress himself by shedding his dragon skin and go into the water. Eustace realizes that he has no clothes, except for his dragon skin. So he begins to scratch off a layer like a snake sloughs off its old skin. But after doing so, he still looks like a dragon, with dragon skin. So he scratches off the next layer, but he still appears as a dragon; so he scratches off yet a third layer of scales, but he cannot change the fact that he is still a dragon. No matter how hard he tries, Eustace has no ability to change his dragon-like nature.

Finally, Aslan tells Eustace to lay down, and he will remove his dragon skin once for all:

> The very first tear he made was so deep that I thought it had gone right into my heart. And when he began pulling the skin off, it hurt worse than anything I've ever felt. . . .
>
> Well, he peeled the beastly stuff right off—just as I thought I'd done . . . — and there it was lying on the grass: only ever so much thicker, and darker, and more knobbly looking than the others had been. . . . Then he caught hold of me and . . . threw me into the water. . . . After that . . . I'd turned into a boy again.
>
> After a bit the lion took me out and dressed me.[30]

Afterward, Eustace rejoins his friends, and he apologizes for his bad, spoiled behavior: "I'm afraid I've been pretty beastly."[31] With regard to Eustace's subsequent behavior, Lewis concludes,

> It would be nice, fairly nearly true, to say that "from that time forth Eustace was a different boy." To be strictly accurate, he began to be a different boy. He

---

30. C. S. Lewis, *The Voyage of the Dawn Treader* (New York: Harper Trophy, 1994), 115–16.
31. Ibid., 117.

had relapses. There were still many days when he could be very tiresome. But most of those I shall not notice. The cure had begun.[32]

Lewis's description is clearly his attempt to represent the biblical portrayal of the reality that people, on the basis of their own innate ability, cannot do anything to take out their old, fallen, sinful heart and create a new heart for themselves. Only God can bring people back to Eden and create them anew in the last Adam, and when he does, the bent of one's desires and behavior begins to change and to reflect the image of the God who has re-created them into a new creation. Immediate perfection does not come about, but a progressive growth in doing those things that please God does occur. That is, people who have been made into a new creation continue to develop as a new creation until, at the end of the age, that development reaches full maturity in the final resurrection of the body and the spirit.

Consequently, while there are ups and downs in the Christian life, Christians can be confident that they will progressively conquer the remaining sin in their lives, though in this age that victory will never be complete. Believers as already–not yet new creations may be compared to an incomplete puzzle. We all have had the experience of putting a puzzle together and reaching a stage where we have assembled much of the central part of the puzzle and some of the outer parts. Nevertheless, there are still some significant pieces that we have not yet been able to put into place to complete the full picture. God has constructed believers into new creations at the core of their inner, unseen beings, but that core is not perfected, nor are their bodies, until the final resurrection, when all the parts of the believer will be pieced together by God in Christ (cf. Phil. 1:6; 1 John 3:2).

It is this theological and anthropological outlook about the "new man" that Paul and other NT writers use as the rhetorical basis to exhort and encourage believers on to godliness. Again and again, the indicative new creation (or resurrected status in Christ) is given as the foundation for believers being able to perform God's commands. The point is this: Because Christians have the power to obey and please God, they should be motivated to do so when God's commands are issued to them. Sometimes this basis for obedience is supplemented with the additional basis that since God has planned that his newly created eschatological people will be faithful, they should have even more motivation to please him, since he will give them the ability to fulfill his plan (e.g., Eph. 2:10: "For we are his creation, having been created in Christ Jesus for good works, which God prepared beforehand that we should walk in them").[33] At other times, this basis is seen as God actually active "to will

32. Ibid., 119–20.
33. So likewise 1 Thess. 3:12–13 in relation to 4:1; 5:15 in relation to 5:23–24, where a series of commands comes first, then the basis for fulfilling them; 2 Thess. 2:13–14 in relation to 2:15; 2:16–17 in relation to 3:1–2; 3:3 in relation to 3:4.

and to work" in a Christian to bring about that Christian's obedience. In Phil. 2:12–13 Paul says,

> So then, my beloved, just as you have always obeyed, not as in my presence only, but now much more in my absence, work out your salvation with fear and trembling; because it is God who is at work in you, both to will and to work for His good pleasure.

Here Paul tells his readers to continue to obey in working out their salvation, and then he explains that the basis for how they are able to do this is God "willing and working" in them (which is likely a development of Phil. 1:6, 29). Here the order is reversed: the commands come first, then the basis for doing the commands is given.

Some might respond, "Since I have the power, I don't need to be motivated to obey, since God's power will work through me regardless of whether I am motivated to obey. I can just sit back and do nothing, and God will nevertheless work through me." On the contrary, those who are not motivated to obey God's commands are those who have no power to do so and are "dead in [their] trespasses and sins" (Eph. 2:1), are captive to the powers of evil (Eph. 2:2), and "by [their fallen] nature" do sin (Eph. 2:3).

Instead, true saints should be psychologically motivated to fulfill God's precepts because they know that God has given them the power to do so. Commands by themselves do not imply that people have the innate strength to obey (contrary to what Pelagius and later Erasmus contended); commands only set a standard of what is expected. Rather, the reason Paul so often mixes the commands with believers' standing in Christ is to show that the basis for fulfilling the commands is in Christ's and God's power, which provides the motivation to obey.[34]

This kind of motivation is comparable to my neighbor's desire to remove snow from his driveway. He has a powerful snowblower in his garage, and after a few inches of snow have fallen, he hops right out of his house, starts up his snowblower, and quickly cleans off his driveway. I, however, own only a rusty shovel. When it snows a few inches, I have no desire to go out to shovel. After it keeps on snowing and I still do not go out to clear it off, my wife gives me a polite command implied by way of a question: "When are you going to shovel the driveway?" But I have no desire to respond positively to her command. I continue to let the snow build up until after the snow has finished falling, and then I go out rather reluctantly to shovel. I have no motivation to clear away the snow because I do not have the power to do it effectively. My neighbor has all the desire in the world because he has the power to remove

---

34. On which, see Martin Luther, *The Bondage of the Will: A New Translation of De servo arbitrio (1525), Martin Luther's Reply to Erasmus of Rotterdam*, trans. J. I. Packer and O. R. Johnston (Westwood, NJ: Revell, 1957).

the snow effectively. When one has the power to do something, the motivation for doing it follows.

I often travel by airplane to various destinations. However, I would have no desire to get to those destinations if I had to walk or ride a bicycle, since it would take a ridiculous amount of time and effort to do so. But because I can board an airplane and fly to my destinations, I am motivated to travel. When you have the power to do something, there wells up a desire to do it.

It is the same with the commands of Scripture, which are addressed to believers. The authentic Christian, who is a true new creation, has the moral power to please God and is therefore typically motivated to fulfill God's commands when those commands are heard. Christians should want to please God because he is their Father, who has created them as adopted sons and daughters. This is why Paul and other NT writers repeatedly assert their readers' participation in eschatological realities in the midst of exhorting them to be obedient to God.[35]

Other New Testament Texts Relating to the Relationship between the Indicative and the Imperative

James

Other NT writers testify to believers' participation in the new creation as a basis for their ability to fulfill God's commands. James 1:18–22 is another classic example:

> In the exercise of His will He brought [generated] us forth by the word of truth, so that we would be a kind of first fruits among His creatures. Know this, my beloved brethren. But everyone must be quick to hear, slow to speak and slow to anger; for the anger of man does not achieve the righteousness of God. Therefore, putting aside all filthiness and all that remains of wickedness, in humility receive the word implanted, which is able to save your souls. But prove yourselves doers of the word, and not merely hearers who delude themselves.

Here the imperative in verse 19, "know [iste] this," appears to be James's way to draw attention to his preceding statement that God brought them into being according to his will (and not their autonomous will). He then issues the commands to hear and speak with a wise demeanor and to be "slow to

---

35. See Herman Ridderbos, *Paul: An Outline of His Theology* (Grand Rapids: Eerdmans, 1975), 253–58, whose discussion on the indicative in relation to the imperative is along the same lines as in this chapter so far. Also see Peter Stuhlmacher, *Biblische Theologie des Neuen Testaments*, vol. 1 (Göttingen: Vandenhoeck & Ruprecht, 1992), 374, who says, e.g., that "in Paul the indicative of justification provides the grounds of the imperative" of walking according to the Spirit.

851

anger." In verse 21 James returns to part of his regenerative picture: on the basis ("therefore," *dio*) that they have been given new birth (v. 18), they are to "put aside all filthiness and excessiveness of evil[36] and receive the word implanted." That is, just as the word of God was the agency by which they were initially regenerated (v. 18), so they must continue to rely on that same word, since it will continue to be the agent that will maintain their newly created condition (v. 21b). At the same time, their new creation is also the basis for their ability to "put aside" the ways of their old life (v. 21a). And as they continue in this condition of new creation, it will be the basis for them to be "doers of the word,[37] and not merely hearers" (v. 22). Hence, again we see the repeated pattern of new creation followed by the issuing of commands (v. 18 → v. 19, and v. 21 → v. 22), since the newly created state is the basis for keeping the commands.[38] That new creation is in mind is further evident in that the "born again" believers are "a kind of first fruits among his creation [or 'creatures']"—that is, the beginning renewal of the whole creation that will eventually be completely renewed. The idea is much like that of Rom. 8:18–23, where Christians who have begun to experience resurrection life through the Spirit (see 8:11–15) are called "the first fruits of the Spirit" and await their physical resurrection, at which time the whole creation will be renewed.

1 Peter

Similar to James is 1 Pet. 1:22–2:3:

> Since you have in obedience to the truth purified your souls for an unhypocritical love of the brethren, fervently love one another from the heart, for you have been born again not of seed which is perishable but imperishable, that is, through the living and enduring word of God.
> For,

---

36. The adverbial participle "putting aside" (*apothemenoi*), which modifies the aorist imperative "receive," likely explains that the "putting aside" of sin is a process that occurs at the same time as the ongoing reception of the "implanted word." In this regard, the participle may be adverbial of time or, more likely, a participle of attendant circumstance, which "communicates an action that, in some sense, is coordinate with the finite verb" and "in effect, 'piggy-backs' on the mood of the main verb" (Daniel B. Wallace, *Greek Grammar beyond the Basics* [Grand Rapids: Zondervan, 1996], 640 [see also pp. 641–46]); thus the participle takes on an imperatival sense here.

37. The "word" throughout this passage is likely the word of God in the OT, as is apparent from the reference to "the law" (1:25), and "the royal law" that is part of "Scripture" (2:8); so also 2:11; 4:5–6.

38. See likewise Douglas J. Moo, *The Letter of James*, PNTC (Grand Rapids: Eerdmans, 2000), 85–88, and Luke Timothy Johnson, *The Letter of James*, AB 37A (New York: Doubleday, 1995), 197–205. Both commentators generally agree that being "born again" in v. 18 is foundational for accepting and doing the word in vv. 21–22; both also take the participle "putting aside" to have an imperatival sense.

"All flesh is like grass,
and all its glory like the flower of grass.
The grass withers,
and the flower falls off,
but the word of the Lord endures forever."

And this is the word which was preached to you. Therefore, putting aside all malice and all deceit and hypocrisy and envy and all slander, like newborn babies, long for the pure milk of the word, so that by it you may grow in respect to salvation, if you have tasted the kindness of the Lord.

First, the readers are said to have expressed "obedience to the truth" (1:22). What truth? It is the truth just spoken of in 1:18–21: they have been "redeemed . . . with precious blood, as of a lamb unblemished and spotless, the blood of Christ" (vv. 18–19), who came to do his work of redemption "in these last times" (v. 20); through Christ they have become "believers in God, who raised Him from the dead and gave him glory," which has also boosted their "faith and hope in God" (v. 21).

In "obedience" to this eschatological "truth," Peter's readers have "purified their souls." The verb "purify" (*hagnizō*) occurs in the LXX, the Gospels, and Acts to indicate a religious ceremony by which people set themselves apart or consecrate themselves to God for various purposes of serving him.[39] The moral or spiritual nature of the consecration here is apparent in that it was done "by means of obedience to the truth," and is evident also from the fact that the only other two uses of the verb "purify" in epistolary literature likewise refer to acts whereby Christians set themselves apart spiritually and morally (James 4:8; 1 John 3:3). A ceremonial aspect may still stand behind this action of setting apart, since Peter later says that "baptism" is "not the removal of dirt from the flesh, but an appeal to God for a good conscience" (3:21).[40]

One of the purposes of this purification is to enable "an unhypocritical love of the brethren," which is commanded at the end of 1:22: "fervently love one another from the heart." But does this purifying action by believers through their "obedience to the truth" occur by their own innate, independent ability? According to 1:1–2, the work of the Spirit in setting apart believers is the cause leading to their obedience: Christians are "chosen on the basis of the foreknowledge of God the Father, by means of the sanctifying work of the Spirit, for the purpose of [their] obedience [*hypakoē*][41] and to be sprinkled with the blood of Jesus Christ." This likely refers to the initial conversion of the readers. Thus, in light also of the reference to regeneration in 1:23 (developing the same word and idea from 1:3, referring to the cause of conversion),

39. So Karen Jobes, *1 Peter*, BECNT (Grand Rapids: Baker Academic, 2005), 123, citing in support the examples of usage in Exod. 19:10; Num. 6:3; Josh. 3:5, and other passages.
40. See ibid., 123–24, which I have followed in this discussion of the word "purify."
41. This is the same Greek word for "obedience" as in 1:22.

Christians' "obedience" in 1:22 probably focuses on initial conversion life[42] but may include secondarily postconversion obedience.[43]

As in 1:2, verse 22 is immediately followed by an assertion of God's inner renovating basis for the ability to obey and to love: "for you have been born again not of seed which is perishable but imperishable" (v. 23a). This divine begetting is a further development of 1:3, where it is said that "according to His great mercy [God] has caused us to be born again," a rebirth that is likely carried out by the Spirit (in 1:2). The instrumentation of the begetting in 1:23 is "through the living and enduring word of God."[44] This "word of God" as the agent of new birth is immediately identified in verses 24–25a with Scripture (Isa. 40:6–8), the main point being that this word is not perishable but instead "endures forever." At the end of verse 25 Peter adds a brief comment that "this" Scripture, as representative of the OT Scriptures, was "the word which was preached as good news to you."[45] Although neither James 1 nor 1 Peter explains precisely how God's word is the agent for causing people to be born again, it is likely that God's Spirit uses the word to cause this rebirth.[46] And since this "word" is imperishable and eternal, the love that is based on regeneration through this word will grow and last forever.[47]

Then directly in the next verse (2:1), on the basis of their newly created nature ("therefore," *oun* [2:1a]), Christians are said to be those "putting aside" various sins characteristic of the old, sinful lifestyle. And as they are "putting aside"[48] the old lifestyle (2:1a) because they have been "born again" (1:23), they are to act like "newborn babies" and "long for the pure milk of the word, so that by it [they] may grow with respect to salvation" (2:2). This is virtually identical to what we just saw in James 1:21: "receive the word implanted, which is able to save your souls." Peter likewise affirms that just as the word of God was the means

42. So Thomas R. Schreiner, *1, 2 Peter, Jude*, NAC 37 (Nashville: Broadman, 2003), 92–93.
43. So Wayne Grudem, *The First Epistle of Peter*, TNTC (Leicester: Inter-Varsity, 1988), 86–90.
44. In this respect, the adverbial participle "having been born again" (*anagegennēmenoi*), which modifies the main verb "love" in the preceding verse, designates the cause or basis of that love.
45. Most in focus may be the segment of Scripture in Isa. 40–54, which found beginning fulfillment in Christ, though Peter quotes and alludes throughout 1 Peter not only from this segment (see 2:22–25) but also, e.g., from earlier parts of Isaiah (2:6, 8; 3:14–15), from the Pentateuch (1:16; 2:9), Hosea (2:10), Psalms (2:7; 3:10–12), and Proverbs (3:13; 4:18).
46. This appears to be part of the point of 1 Thess. 1:5–6: "For our gospel did not come to you in word only, but also in power and in the Holy Spirit and with full conviction; just as you know what kind of men we proved to be among you for your sake. You also became imitators of us and of the Lord, having received the word in much tribulation with the joy of the Holy Spirit." See also Acts 16:14 and perhaps Eph. 6:17; Titus 3:5.
47. On which, see Grudem, *First Epistle of Peter*, 90–93.
48. The participle "putting aside" (*apothemenoi*) may be adverbial of time or in relation to the main verb that it modifies, "long for," but it is better taken as a participle of attendant circumstance (which also takes on the imperatival mood of the main imperative verb that it modifies), just as I took it in James 1:21 above (so also Jobes, *1 Peter*, 135; Grudem, *First Epistle of Peter*, 93).

through which the readers were initially born again (1:23), so they must continue to be spiritually nourished on that same word, as "newborn babies," since it will continue to be the means by which they will be able to sustain and grow in their newly created condition.[49] Peter acknowledges that it should not be assumed that all confessing believers have really experienced this inner transformation (2:3).

The pattern observed throughout this section is seen here repeatedly again: a command (to love [1:22b]) is grounded in a new inner spiritual transformation, which is referred to as "having been born again" (1:23), which is also the foundation for believers "putting aside" their old, ungodly lifestyle (2:1) and "longing for the pure milk of the word" in order to "grow in respect to salvation."[50]

1 John

The last passage to be discussed on new creation as a basis for obedience to God's commands is 1 John 5:1–4:

> Whoever believes that Jesus is the Christ is born of God, and whoever loves the Father loves the child born of Him. By this we know that we love the children of God, when we love God and observe His commandments. For this is the love of God, that we keep His commandments; and His commandments are not burdensome. For whatever is born of God overcomes the world; and this is the victory that has overcome the world—our faith.

Verse 1 affirms that "whoever believes that Jesus is the Christ" is someone who already "has been born of God." The present born-again condition results from a begetting action in the past that also precedes and thus is likely foundational to the believing.[51] The born-again state seems also to be the basis for loving God and others (vv. 1b–2a) and "doing God's commandments" (vv. 2b–3a).[52] John says that God's "commandments are not burdensome" (v. 3b) apparently because of the regenerative power that those who have been born again possess.

49. The Greek phrase *to logikon adolon gala* can be translated "the pure milk of the word" or "the pure spiritual milk." Either way, it is a packed expression including reference to the preached or oral word (1:25b), the scriptural word (1:23–25a), and the Spirit and Christ, who nourish through that word (on which, see Jobes, *1 Peter*, 130–41). For the likelihood that the phrase includes reference to Scripture, see Grudem, *First Epistle of Peter*, 95–96. That the phrase is a development of the preached and inscripturated "word of God" from 2:23–25 is likely not only because of the nearness of the context but also because of the similar wording of *logos* in 1:23 with *logikos* of 2:2 (see further Schreiner, *1, 2 Peter, Jude*, 100–101).

50. Schreiner (*1, 2 Peter, Jude*, 90) observes the same indicative-imperative pattern.

51. "Has been born" (*gegennētai*) is a perfect passive verb, which typically highlights the present or resulting condition produced by a past action and likely stands in the background, esp. in light of v. 4. Therefore, the one characterized in the present as a "believing one" (*pisteuōn*, a present substantival participle) possesses an ongoing born-again condition as a result of a begetting action in the past.

52. There is no formal logical linking word between v. 1a and vv. 1b–3a, but it is likely that some logical connection exists, and a causal connection seems viable.

Likewise, "everyone who has been born again from God" has been given the ability to "overcome the world" (v. 4a). Therefore, since "the victory that has overcome the world" is defined as "our faith" (v. 4b), this means that being "born again from God" is also the ground from which faith arises.[53]

Conclusion

As in Paul's writings, so also in the General Epistles, one must be made into a new creation in order to be able to obey God's commands.

The Ongoing Return from Exile as a Basis for Christian Living

We have just seen how the inaugurated new creation is a basis for being able to fulfill God's commands. In earlier chapters we observed that salvation can be portrayed as the church beginning not only to be a new creation but also initially fulfilling the prophecies of Israel's return from exile, though this restoration was seen to be the other side of the coin of new creation and thus integrally linked to it.[54] The majority of NT studies on this topic, especially Pauline scholarship, have focused on the notion that the restoration has begun in Christ and in the church.[55] But there has been little, if any, attempt to view the ongoing postconversion life of Christians as a life of those who are still coming out of exile. This is an important perspective because if the restoration promises have not been completed, then there is some sense in which believers are still in the process of coming out of exile.

This focus on still being in exile needs much more study and deserves more development than can be given here.[56] However, I will examine a few relevant texts from this viewpoint.

"The Way" in the Book of Acts

The significance of the citation from Isa. 40:3–5 in Luke 3:3–6 appears at the commencement of Jesus's public ministry:

53. For an analysis of 1 John 5:1–4 in agreement with this one, especially with respect to spiritual rebirth being the basis for belief, love, and keeping the commandments, see Robert W. Yarbrough, *1–3 John*, BECNT (Grand Rapids: Baker Academic, 2008), 268–75. F. F. Bruce (*The Epistles of John*, NICNT [Grand Rapids: Eerdmans, 1970], 117) agrees that "the new life imparted to the family of God" gives them a desire and power to obey him as well as power to overcome the world. Colin Kruse (*The Letters of John*, PNTC [Grand Rapids: Eerdmans, 2000], 172) is explicit only about the command for believers to love not being burdensome "because they have been born by God."

54. E.g., see chaps. 16, 20, 21.

55. E.g., see chap. 20, excursus 2, under the heading "The Inauguration of Israel's Restoration Prophecies in the Gospel of Mark."

56. This is a fruitful area for further research that I have not carried out. Here I give only my initial ideas on the subject.

And [John] came into all the district around the Jordan, preaching a baptism of repentance for the forgiveness of sins; as it is written in the book of the words of Isaiah the prophet,

> "The voice of one crying in the wilderness,
> Make ready the way of the Lord,
> make His paths straight.
> Every ravine will be filled,
> and every mountain and hill will be brought low;
> the crooked will become straight,
> and the rough roads smooth;
> and all flesh will see the salvation of God."

David Pao has rightly argued that this quotation provides the key interpretative framework within which the remainder of Luke-Acts is to be understood. The Isaiah quotation is the beginning of an extended section in Isaiah that prophesies the coming of a new exodus whereby Israel will be delivered from bondage in Babylon.[57] The various motifs found in the prologue (Isa. 40:1–11) to Isa. 41–55 are developed extensively throughout the following chapters of Isaiah and in Acts. The best expression of this new-exodus paradigm is the "way" terminology (derived primarily from Isa. 40:3) in Acts as a name for the nascent Christian movement, polemically identifying the church as God's true people in the midst of his rejection of Israel. Notice the repeated reference to the Christian movement as "the Way" in Acts, which most of the time occurs in contexts of persecution or opposition:

Acts 9:2 "And [Paul] asked for letters from him [the high priest] to the synagogues at Damascus, so that if he found any belonging to the Way, both men and women, he might bring them bound to Jerusalem."

Acts 19:9 "But when some were becoming hardened and disobedient, speaking evil of the Way before the people, [Paul] withdrew from them and took away the disciples, reasoning daily in the school of Tyrannus."

Acts 19:23 "About that time there occurred no small disturbance concerning the Way."

Acts 22:4 "I [Paul] persecuted this Way to the death, binding and putting both men and women into prisons."

Acts 24:14 "But this I [Paul] admit to you, that according to the Way which they call a sect I do serve the God of our fathers, believing everything that is in accordance with the Law and that is written in the Prophets."

---

57. See David W. Pao, *Acts and the Isaianic New Exodus*, WUNT 2/130 (Tübingen: Mohr Siebeck, 2000), chap. 2. For a summary and evaluation of Pao's book, see chap. 20 under the heading "The Inauguration of Israel's Restoration Prophecies in the Gospel of Mark"; also G. K. Beale, review of *Acts and the Isaianic New Exodus*, by David W. Pao, *TJ* 25 (2004): 93–101.

Acts 24:22 "But Felix, having a more exact knowledge about the Way, put them off, saying, 'When Lysias the commander comes down, I will decide your case.'"[58]

This name for the Christian movement, "the Way," thus designates that the Christians were the true end-time Israel beginning to fulfill the prophecies of Israel's return from exile. They were on "the Way" out of exile to returning to God. The name "the Way" indicates that one could begin to participate in this restoration journey by believing in Christ and joining others who already believed and were walking on "the Way," progressing in their new-exodus journey. Consequently, "the Way" described both those first joining it and those who had belonged to it for some time, so that the name included reference to a manner of ongoing Christian living as part of a restoration journey.

Paul's Exhortation to the Church to Continue to Come Out of Exile

I have already presented substantial and even repeated discussion of 2 Cor. 5:14–7:1, arguing that Paul understands his concept of reconciliation in light of the commencing fulfillment of the prophecies of new creation and of Israel's restoration from exile. We saw that this segment of 2 Corinthians is chock-full of quotations and allusions to promises of Israel's restoration.[59] The chain of OT references in 2 Cor. 6:16–18 deserves to be revisited here because they are excellent examples of "return from exile" prophecies being inaugurated in the church, and they are a conclusion to this section dominated by the background of restoration from exile:

> Or what agreement has the temple of God with idols? For we are the temple of the living God; just as God said,
>
> > "I will dwell in them and walk among them;
> > And I will be their God, and they shall be My people.
> > Therefore, come out from their midst and be separate," says the Lord.
> > "And do not touch what is unclean;
> > And I will welcome you.
> > And I will be a father to you,

---

58. In addition, see perhaps also Acts 18:25–26: "This man had been instructed in the way of the Lord; and being fervent in spirit, he was speaking and teaching accurately the things concerning Jesus, being acquainted only with the baptism of John; and he began to speak out boldly in the synagogue. But when Priscilla and Aquila heard him, they took him aside and explained to him the way of God more accurately." In this respect, note "the way of the Lord" in Luke 3:4, citing Isa. 40:3. See also Acts 16:17.

59. The list of these OT references will not be restated here, since they were listed and discussed in chap. 16 (under the subheading "'Reconciliation' in 2 Corinthians 5:14–21") and chap. 21 (under the subheading "2 Corinthians"). The only allusion in the list that may not be linked to return from exile is Ps. 118:17–18, though there is a notion of the victory and restoration of one (probably a king of Israel) who has been oppressed by the nations.

And you shall be sons and daughters to Me,"
Says the Lord Almighty.

On the basis that believers "are the temple of the living God" (v. 16a), in fulfillment of the restoration prophecies of the temple (v. 16b), the readers are commanded, "Come out from their midst and be separate, . . . and do not touch what is unclean" (v. 17). This is a quotation of Isa. 52:11: "Depart, depart, go out from there, touch nothing unclean; go out of the midst of her, purify yourselves, you who carry the vessels of the LORD." This was a command for Israel to go out of Babylonian captivity when the time for restoration was ripe (a development of Isa. 52:2: "Shake yourself from the dust, rise up, O captive Jerusalem; loose yourself from the chains around your neck"). In particular, the command in Isa. 52:11 is to the priests who are to "carry the vessels of the LORD," which were to be restored to the temple that would be rebuilt at the time of the restoration.

Isaiah's command for Israel to get out of Babylon appeared to begin to be fulfilled when the remnant of the tribes of Judah and Benjamin returned after seventy years of bondage (significantly, the majority did not heed the prophetic dictate). But even these returning Israelites proved to be unfaithful, and their restoration was ultimately a physical one and not a true irreversible eschatological fulfillment[60] until the coming of Jesus. Thus, Israel had physically returned from exile but remained in spiritual captivity. Jesus announces the decisive restoration, which is spiritual and which the church continued to announce after his ascension. But after people first believe and commence coming out of exile, joining the movement of "the Way," they continue to walk on the restoration road, as we saw in the preceding section.

Therefore, Paul understands Isa. 52:11 to have continued relevance as a command for the true Israel, the church. In line with Isa. 52:11, he thus conceives of the Corinthian church as a group of priests participating in the restoration and rebuilding of the temple. But on the one hand, Paul is addressing professing Christians who are acting like unbelievers because they are rejecting his apostleship and are aligning themselves with the "false apostles," who "disguise themselves as apostles of Christ" but actually are servants of Satan (2 Cor. 11:13–15). It is quite likely that Paul is addressing a mixed "professing" audience, since some who claim to be genuine saints have become such ardent adherents of the unbelieving and satanic false apostles that they are revealing themselves actually not to be authentic Christians. Paul is exhorting these pseudo-Christians to be restored for the first time.

On the other hand, some whom Paul is addressing with the same commands in 2 Cor. 6:17 are true believers and need to be shocked into the reality of their

60. As I contended earlier in, e.g., chap. 13 under the subheading "The Problem of the Timing of the Fulfillment of the Restoration Promises to Israel."

genuine faith and stop acting like unbelievers (e.g., "What has a believer in common with an unbeliever?" [2 Cor. 6:15b]). They are entertaining the teaching of the false apostles, who contend that Paul is not a true prophetic spokesman of God. Paul is commanding such people to continue their restoration journey back to God, a journey that for them has truly already begun in the past. Accordingly, Paul's imperatives for this group are intended to motivate these true though confused Christians to continue in their restoration pilgrimage, which had begun when they first believed in the past. Their behavior is to comport with those who really are on the restoration road.

The commands in 2 Cor. 6:17 function to spur them on further in their restoration. They are to "come out from the midst of and be separate" from the party of the false teachers, "whose end shall be according to their deeds" (2 Cor. 11:15). That Paul is clearly addressing a significant group whom he considers to be true saints is further evident from 2 Cor. 7:1: "Therefore, having these promises, beloved, let us cleanse ourselves from all defilement of flesh and spirit, perfecting holiness in the fear of God." On the basis of the fulfillment of the restoration "promises" among the Corinthian Christians described in 6:16–18, Paul issues them another command. Those who have begun to be restored as priests in the end-time temple, and thus are part of the temple itself, must "cleanse [themselves] from all defilement of flesh and spirit." That is, they must "not touch what is unclean" (6:17). To have dalliance with the false teachers will contaminate their entire being ("flesh and spirit"). As priests, they must increasingly "cleanse" themselves, "perfecting holiness in the fear of God" (7:1). The combined mention of "cleanse," "perfecting," and "holiness" employs OT priestly language.[61] The readers are to continue to consecrate themselves as priests to God in continuing to serve him in the restored temple and in walking on in their journey of being restored to God.[62]

Therefore, Paul sees a need to encourage those who have begun to come out of exile to continue to do so. A constant coming out of exile and leaving

61. In chap. 21 we saw that, in light of the LXX, the verb *teleioō* and its noun forms in Hebrews, usually translated as "to perfect" and "perfect," have the connotation of "to complete" or "completion" (though not including the precise verbal form *epiteleō* of 2 Cor. 7:1) and are close in meaning to "consecrate" or "set apart" (i.e., "sanctify," which is a typical rendering of the Greek verb *hagiazō* and some of its noun forms). The addition of "cleanse" (*katharizō*) to "perfecting" and "holiness" in 7:1 increases the likelihood of the link to priestly language and imagery. The word *katharizō* is used often for things or people (including priests being cleansed to be qualified for acceptable worship in connection to the temple: about 25x in the Pentateuch, 6x in Ezra-Nehemiah [5 with respect to priestly cleansing], and 7x in the Apocrypha [6 of which refer to the sanctuary]). The combination of the verbs *katharizō* and *hagiazō* occurs only 5x in the LXX, 4 of which refer to "purifying" the temple "altar" that then "makes it holy" (Exod. 29:36, 37; Lev. 8:15; 16:19), and one that refers to priestly purification that qualifies them to "make holy the sabbath day" (Neh. 13:22).

62. For more in-depth analysis of the OT theme of restoration from exile in 2 Cor. 5:14–7:1, see G. K. Beale, "The Old Testament Background of Reconciliation in 2 Corinthians 5–7 and Its Bearing on the Literary Problem of 2 Corinthians 4:14–7:1," *NTS* 35 (1989): 550–81.

behind of old baggage forms a lens through which the apostle understands the ongoing nature of the Christian life, or sanctification.

John's Exhortation to the Church to Continue to Come Out of Exile

Just as Israel had been in captivity to Babylon in the OT, the book of Revelation refers to "Babylon" as the ungodly religious and economic system that dominates the world, including its political institutions (e.g., 17:18). The church lives in exile in this world dominated by this universal Babylon. This global Babylonian system exercises control of the nations by seducing them to live according to its sinful ways: "For all the nations have drunk of the wine of the passion of her immorality, and the kings of the earth have committed acts of immorality with her, and the merchants of the earth have become rich by the wealth of her sensuality" (18:3 [cf. 14:8]). Here, the abhorrent behavior of the nations and kings refers figuratively to their acceptance of Babylon's religious and idolatrous demands. The nations' and kings' cooperation with Babylon ensures their material security (cf. 13:16–17).[63] Wherever the church exists on earth, it still is living in a region that is under the influence of "Babylon" (cf. Rev. 17:1, 15; 18:4). Believing Israelites such as Daniel and his three friends had to live "in Babylon," but they were not to be "of Babylon," and they were faithful in this respect. Through John, an angel commands first-century churches in like manner not to allow themselves to be conformed to the worldly standards of Babylon. In Rev. 18:4–8 John reports,

> I heard another voice from heaven, saying, "Come out of her [Babylon], my people, so that you will not participate in her sins and receive of her plagues; for her sins have piled up as high as heaven, and God has remembered her iniquities. Pay her back even as she has paid, and give back to her double according to her deeds; in the cup which she has mixed, mix twice as much for her. To the degree that she glorified herself and lived sensuously, to the same degree give her torment and mourning; for she says in her heart, 'I sit as a queen and I am not a widow, and will never see mourning.' For this reason in one day her plagues will come, pestilence and mourning and famine, and she will be burned up with fire; for the Lord God who judges her is strong."

The point of this passage is that God's people are to separate from and cease to cooperate with the Babylonian system lest they too suffer its judgment. The mention of Babylon's coming judgment in 18:1–3 and 18:5–8 is the basis in

63. An economic interpretation is confirmed by allusion to Isa. 23:17b, which views Tyre as a major power in seafaring commerce at the time of Isaiah: Tyre is said to "play the harlot with all the kingdoms of the earth"; Isa. 23:17b is also alluded to with the same economic sense in Rev. 17:2a: "with whom the kings of the earth fornicated." For further analysis of Rev. 18:3, see G. K. Beale, *The Book of Revelation: A Commentary on the Greek Text*, NIGTC (Grand Rapids: Eerdmans, 1999), 895–97.

verse 4 for commanding wavering believers not to participate in the compromising idolatrous system and for encouraging uncompromising believers to maintain their faithful course. The revelation of Babylon's sin and punishment should cause true believers to continue not to be seduced by her and not to cooperate with her sinful ways.

The demand to separate from Babylon's ways is modeled after repeated exhortations by Isaiah and Jeremiah, especially Jer. 51:45: "Come forth from her midst, My people" (see also Isa. 48:20; 52:11; Jer. 50:8; 51:6). These prophets exhorted Israel to separate from the idolatry of Babylon by leaving it and returning to Israel at the appropriate time of restoration. As here in Jer. 51 and the other OT parallels, the coming judgment that Babylon must suffer forms the basis for the prophets' exhortation to God's people to separate (see above all Jer. 51:35–45).[64]

The charge is to disassociate from Babylon before the judgment occurs, though the judgment itself will accomplish the full freedom of true saints from the world. The goal of separating is not only to "not participate in her sins" but also to escape the coming judgment (not "receive of her plagues"), as also in Jer. 51.[65] Whereas the dictate to disassociate in Jeremiah involved both physical and spiritual/moral escape, that of Rev. 18:4 involves only the latter.[66]

As we saw in the case of Isa. 52:11 in 2 Cor. 6:17, Jeremiah's virtually identical command for Israel to get out of Babylon seemed to begin fulfillment when part of Israel returned from Babylonian exile. However, its eschatological fulfillment did not become decisive and irreversible until Christ came. Jesus announced the decisive inaugurated restoration, which is spiritual and which the church continued to proclaim after his ascent to heaven. Yet even after people first believe and start coming out of exile, joining the movement of "the Way," they continue to walk on the restoration road in further separation from captivity and its idolatrous influence. The consummation of their restoration will be when they are raised from the dead[67] and thus are completely separated from Babylonian exile, both physically and spiritually.

---

64. The judgment that gives rise to the mandate from Jer. 51 is portrayed with comparable pictures of desolation as in Rev. 18:2: "[Babylon] has become a dwelling place of demons and a prison of every unclean spirit, and a prison of every unclean and hateful bird." Jeremiah 51:37 reads, "Babylon will become . . . a haunt of jackals, an object of horror . . . without inhabitants."

65. Cf. Rev. 18:4b, "so that you will not . . . receive of her plagues," with Jer. 51:45b, "each of you save yourselves from the fierce anger of the LORD."

66. The imperative of Rev. 18:4 also strongly echoes that in Isa. 52:11: "Go out from the midst of her." The inclusion of this echo is evident from the immediately preceding phrase in the Isaiah text, "do not touch the unclean [akathartos]," which refers to the idols of Babylon. The exhortation in Rev. 18:4 directly follows the threefold reference to Babylon as "unclean" (akathartos), which is also associated with idolatry (see 18:2). This background is significant because, as we have seen above, Paul too refers to Isa. 52:11 in appealing to believers to continue to come out of exile. For additional OT background for Rev. 18:4, see Beale, Revelation, 897–99.

67. See Rev. 20:12–15, which refers to the resurrection of both the righteous and the unrighteous (on which see Beale, Revelation, 1032–38).

Summary

Although the NT focuses on the commencement of restoration in Christ, there is some development of an ongoing aspect of continuing to come out of a partial exile to which Christians are still subjected. Believers are still sinful, so that not all "the old things" that characterized their past captivity "have passed away" (this is implicit in light of 2 Cor. 5:17). Consequently, believers need encouragement to continue to walk as godly saints on the road that will end in full restoration to God and Christ in the new heaven and earth. The passages in Paul's writings and Revelation have focused mainly on the need for Christians to continue to progress in their restoration to God because they have been entertaining sin in a way that they should not have.

There are at least two other senses in which Christians are still partly in exile. First, the church lives physically as a pilgrim in the world as a place of exile (Rev. 18:4) and awaits its final homecoming in the eternal land and city (Heb. 11:13–16; Rev. 21:1–22:5). Second, in connection to the first point, Christians possess physical bodies that are a part of the old world in which they were in spiritual exile. Although they have decisively made a break with their spiritual bondage, such a break has not been made with their bodies. Their bodies will be destroyed at death or at the end of time and will be re-created in resurrection, when the church will be finally and fully restored to God. Conceptually, this is part of the point of the final vision of Rev. 21:1–22:5. Last, this need for coming out of exile may be referred to theologically as a need to continue in "sanctification" and in the "perseverance of the saints."

Conclusion: The Purpose of the Commands in the New Testament

Most of the following points derive from the discussion in this chapter of the implications of new creation.

(1) The commands must be seen within the context of the "indicative in relation to the imperative." That is, the Christian's condition of being a new creation (or having begun to return from exile) in Christ is repeatedly given as the basis for obeying the commands. This new eschatological condition gives believers the power to obey the imperatives. Thus, commands are given to those who have the power to obey them.

(2) Commands and warnings are God's means to unlock the power of regenerate people so that they may live a righteous life. Without the commands, regenerate people have nothing to which they may positively respond. It is likely that God continually confronts his people with commands in Scripture in order to unlock their regenerate ability for obedience and to cause their growth as new-creational people.

(3) Commands are given to enable newly created people to learn how to live in a new creation and to grow as new children of God in his family. A

corollary of this is that the commands protect God's people from the sins that were characteristic of the lifestyle of the "old man."

(4) The preceding study implies that commands convict regenerate people who are not living up to God's standard to begin to do so, if they really are regenerate (see, e.g., the implications of Eph. 4:30 in connection to the discussion above of 4:20–32; likewise see 1 Pet. 2:1–3).

(5) Commands convict unregenerate people who confess faith and live in the covenant community but do not characteristically keep the commands. Such conviction can lead such people to realize that they are actually unbelieving and to trust in the gospel (see, e.g., the conditional statements in 2 Cor. 13:5; Eph. 4:21; 1 Pet. 2:3).

Truly regenerate people are also convicted when they are not obedient because of the eschatological Spirit within them. We have seen that God's Spirit was to be an end-time gift, and that one of its main eschatological functions is to raise the dead, both spiritually in the present and physically at the very end. The former has been inaugurated, and the latter is yet to be consummated. Once the Spirit has regenerated a person, the Spirit continues to indwell that person, causing growth in new resurrection life until the goal of complete resurrection is reached. This goal is also final ethical perfection. The Spirit's initial work of setting apart a person from the old, sinful creation to the new (2 Thess. 2:13) will be completed at the end of time (1 Thess. 5:23–24 [though God, not the Spirit, is the subject here]; 1 Pet. 1:2–5).[68]

Therefore, when Christians think or do unholy things, there should be immediate conflict and dissonance with the indwelling Holy Spirit, who is in the eschatological process of causing the believer to reach the goal of final righteousness in the eternal new creation. The depth of this dissonance is better understood when it is remembered what the latter-day Spirit in the believer is repeatedly called or associated with. The Spirit is repeatedly referred to as the "*Holy* Spirit,"[69] and the "Spirit" is inextricably linked to, characterized by, or leads to things such as "truth" (John 14:17; 15:26; 16:13), "love" (Rom. 5:5; 15:30; Gal. 5:22), "righteousness" (Rom. 14:17 [cf. 8:4, 13]; Gal. 5:5), "purity" (2 Cor. 6:6), "peace" (Rom. 8:6; 14:17; Gal. 5:22), and "goodness" (Gal. 5:22). It was likewise prophesied in the OT that in the eschaton the Spirit would come to produce new-creational ethical "fruits,"[70] such as "righteousness" and "peace" (Isa. 32:15–17 [cf. 42:1]), and "cause [God's people] to walk in My statutes, and . . . be careful to observe My ordinances" (Ezek.

68. The Spirit's inaugurated "sanctifying" work in 1 Pet. 1:2 is likely, to some degree, linked to the "inheritance which is imperishable and undefiled and will not fade away" (v. 4) and to the "salvation ready to be revealed in the last time" (v. 5).

69. So 93x in the Bible, 90 of which occur in the NT, esp. in the Gospels, Acts, and Paul's writings.

70. On which, see G. K. Beale, "The Old Testament Background of Paul's Reference to the 'Fruit of the Spirit' in Gal. 5:22," *BBR* 15 (2005): 1–38.

36:27).[71] When Christians "grieve the Holy Spirit of God, by whom they were sealed for the day of redemption" and for attaining the goal of righteousness (Eph. 5:30), they too should be grieved. That which is unholy is not meant to dwell with that which is holy, so that there should be a high-level of conflict within Spirit-filled believers when sin occurs. We may call this "eschatological discord," which inevitably will result in conviction of sin and repentance for the genuine saint.[72]

This is a good example of the practicality of inaugurated eschatology for Christian living.

(6) The commands show God's standard of accountability, which he expects of both regenerate and unregenerate people. The imperatives by themselves do not imply that people have the innate ability to fulfill the commands. Rather, the commands by themselves reveal only what God expects people to do.[73] Of course, I have argued earlier in this chapter and summarized in the first of these six points that the wider context of the commands shows that true believers have the regenerate ability to fulfill the commands.

Excursus The Implications for "Assurance" in Relation to Ongoing Christian Living as Transformed New-Creational Life

One of the consistent conclusions throughout this section is that those who have begun to be a part of the new creation will inevitably progress and grow in this new-creational life, which means that they will grow in godly living. This is not an option. It is not something that may or may not happen. All the passages studied above (and many others) assert that true believers will necessarily and increasingly be characterized by obedience. This may happen slowly, but it will come about surely, as Eph. 2:10 asserts: "For we are His [new] creation, created in Christ Jesus for good works, which God prepared beforehand so that we would walk in them."

We saw in an earlier chapter on already–not yet justification[74] that those who have been justified by faith in Christ still need the badge of good works at the time of the final resurrection and judgment in order to gain entrance to the

71. Note also Ezek. 36:25b: "I will cleanse you from all your filthiness and idols," which is attributed to the Spirit in vv. 26–27.
72. I am thankful to Allen Mawhinney, who many years ago first brought to my attention this eschatological role of the Spirit.
73. In line with Luther's *Bondage of the Will*, who argued against Erasmus's contention that the commands assumed that people have a significant degree of independent volition to fulfill them.
74. See chap. 15 under the subheading "The Final Resurrection and Good Works in Connection to the Justification/Vindication of the Saints" and the heading "The Saints' Final Eschatological Justification/Vindication through Public Demonstration of Their Good Works." Also see chap.

new heaven and earth. This conclusion is at odds with a popular notion that the only thing needed for salvation is belief, and that good works may or may not follow such belief.[75] Accordingly, this popular viewpoint tends to construe the idea that believers must be characterized by good works as "salvation by works," whereby people earn their salvation by doing more good deeds than sinful ones.

In response, in that earlier chapter I explained that the ultimate basis of our justification comes by faith in Christ's work, and that good works are necessary evidence that vindicates us on the last day as having truly been justified. Thus, the necessity of works for final salvation does not have to include the idea of earning salvation by doing good deeds. The evidence of the present chapter similarly highlights that for someone to be considered a true part of the beginning new creation, that person needs to reflect a change from an ungodly lifestyle to a godly one, making progress in righteous living over the course of subsequent life.

But this anthropological portrayal raises a question: if works are a necessary badge for Christians, how many good works does one need in order to be assured of salvation? Of course, Scripture gives no formula to answer this question. However, Paul does give a broad "black and white" answer. For example, in 1 Cor. 6:9–11, Paul says,

> Do you not know that the unrighteous will not inherit the kingdom of God? Do not be deceived; neither fornicators, nor idolaters, nor adulterers, nor effeminate, nor homosexuals, nor thieves, nor the covetous, nor drunkards, nor revilers, nor swindlers, will inherit the kingdom of God. Such were some of you; but you were washed, but you were sanctified, but you were justified in the name of the Lord Jesus Christ and in the Spirit of our God.

After coming to faith, people should not remain in the sinful lifestyle that characterized their pre-Christian life. For example, an adulterer or a homosexual or a drunkard or a swindler, once having become a Christian, should decisively stop living in those kinds of sins. Such people do not become perfect, but they do repent from committing the sins to which they were in bondage. They still sin, but the power of their former sinful bondage has been broken. Because their former, fallen heart has been removed and a spiritual heart has been put in, they now increasingly desire to please God by obeying him instead of pleasing themselves. But they do not perfectly obey God, since there are still unruly desires and sins to which they succumb. Nevertheless, perhaps slowly but surely they increasingly desire to make progress in actually doing those things that are pleasing to God.

---

16 under the heading "The Concept of Reconciliation as the Inaugurated Fulfillment of New Creation and of Israel's Restoration from Exile Prophecies Elsewhere in the New Testament."

75. On which, see Zane C. Hodges, *The Gospel under Siege: A Study on Faith and Works* (Dallas: Redención Viva, 1981). Hodges has been one of the main scholarly proponents of this position.

There is a sense in which the more Christians grow and become closer to the holy God, the more aware they become that they are still unholy sinners. A Puritan once said, "What I once was, I now am not, and what I now am, I will not be." That is, true Christians no longer are dominated by their old, sinful nature, since they are a new creation. Yet, whatever progress believers have made up to the present, they must continue to advance in godliness in the future, so that, as they grow in faith, what they were as Christians in the past they will not be in the future.

So the question presses itself: since Christians do not reach perfection and they sin to varying degrees and in varying ways, and even the most righteous saints become increasingly aware of how sinful they are, how can they be assured that they have a true saving relationship with God? There is no simple answer to this, but there is what may be understood as a cumulative answer that comes from different angles of consideration. We may view the believer's assurance from three angles, with each angle contributing to an aspect of assurance.

Each point of the triangle represents a truth about how a Christian receives assurance.

Trust in God's Promise of Salvation through Christ

First, God promises throughout the NT that those who place their faith in Christ and his redemptive work will receive an inner assurance that they have truly benefited from Christ's work (the top of the triangle). This truth can be found at various places in the NT, 1 John 5:9–15 being a classic example:

> If we receive the testimony of men, the testimony of God is greater; for the testimony of God is this, that He has testified concerning His Son. The one who believes in the Son of God has the testimony in himself; the one who does not believe God has made Him a liar, because he has not believed in the testimony that God has given concerning His Son. And the testimony is this, that God has given us eternal life, and this life is in His Son. He who has the Son has the life; he who does not have the Son of God does not have the life. These things I have written to you who believe in the name of the Son of God, so that you may know that you have eternal life. This is the confidence which we have before Him, that, if we ask anything according to His will, He hears us. And if we know

that He hears us in whatever we ask, we know that we have the requests which we have asked from Him.

God "has testified" that "eternal life" comes through belief in "His Son," and those "who believe" in the Son "have the testimony in" themselves (vv. 9–12). This "testimony" is none other than the internal witness of the Spirit (see, e.g., 1 John 2:20, 27).[76] We can be assured that God's testimony is true that we have life in the Son, since otherwise God would be a liar (which cannot be [v. 10]). The gospel message about the Son is elaborated throughout 1 John and is "written" so that those who "believe in the name of the Son of God . . . may know that [they] have eternal life" (v. 13). Such genuine believers have "confidence" that God hears the prayers of those who pray "according to His will" and will grant "the requests which we have asked from Him" (vv. 14–15). In the context, one such implied request is that if they have asked for life in the Son, then on the basis of God's promise to give such life, they can be assured that he has given them this life. Thus, further assurance of genuine faith comes from this confidence that Christians have about the way God responds to prayer.

In sum, in this passage from 1 John assurance of true faith comes from (1) the internal witness of the Spirit; (2) the reliability of God's word that he will give life in the Son to those who believe; (3) the confidence that God hears and answers the faithful prayers of those who ask for salvation in the Son. In fact, the purpose of the entire epistle of 1 John is to give this assurance (v. 13).

Good Works

The role of "good works" is a second angle from which to view the nature of assurance (the bottom left part of the triangle). As we have seen, one who has truly been resurrected (Eph. 2:4–6) and thus becomes a part of the new creation will inevitably and increasingly be characterized by good works (Eph. 2:10) instead of behaving like "dead people" in bondage to "trespasses and sins" (Eph. 2:1–3). Likewise, 2 Pet. 1:3–4 explains that Christians possess God's "divine power" and reflect God's image (the "divine nature"), and on this basis they are to grow in the fruits of godliness (vv. 5–8). Then, on the grounds that believers are expected to have such spiritual traits, the following conclusion is reached in verses 10–11:

> Therefore, brethren, be all the more diligent to make sure about His calling and choosing of you; for as long as you practice these things, you will never stumble; for in this way the entrance into the eternal kingdom of our Lord and Savior Jesus Christ will be abundantly supplied to you.

76. E.g., see Kruse, *Letters of John*, 102–4, 108; Yarbrough, *1–3 John*, 148–53, 165–68, though he affirms that the "Holy One" in v. 2 may be God, Christ, or the Spirit, or a combination of all three.

How can believers "make <u>sure</u> about [God's] calling and choosing" (v. 10a)?[77] Verse 10b explains the basis for such assurance: "as long as [believers] practice these things" (the godly fruits of vv. 5–8), they can be assured that they "will never stumble," which adds to the basis of the assurance in verse 10a. Verse 11 reiterates verse 10: "in this [same] way" of practicing these godly fruits, they can be sure that "entrance into the eternal kingdom . . . will be abundantly supplied" to them. Thus, assurance of one's "calling and choosing" and final "entrance into the eternal kingdom" increases with growth in doing godly things.

Accordingly, believers' assurance of truly being part of the new creation comes as they look back at their former life and see the changes that have come about since they became Christian. Those who may have grown up from an early age as a Christian may not have such radical differences between their past and present. Nevertheless, they should not be characterized by the kinds of sins that Paul lists in 1 Cor. 6:9–10.[78] Such people also gain a degree of assurance from this recognition. All Christians, to one degree or another, ought to be able to look back and see that they have progressed in godliness during the course of their Christian lives (recalling also that as such growth occurs, ironically so does increasing awareness of remaining sin). This observation ought to bolster Christians' confidence that they are genuine.

Given time, if confessing believers have not changed the ungodly lifestyles of their former unbelieving lives, then such people should not be given assurance that they have truly believed. Perhaps they are true Christians, but they should not have affirmation that they are. Accordingly, the confidence that such persons claim to have from the top part of the triangle is contradicted by the bottom left of the triangle and poses such dissonance that the profession of belief should be questioned. Possibly, such a lack of assurance might shock them either into the reality of their faith, so that they change, or shock them into truly believing for the first time.

Conviction by the Spirit

The presence of the conviction of sin within professing Christians is a third angle from which to understand assurance. As we saw earlier (under the heading "Conclusion: The Purpose of the Commands in the New Testament" above), people who are part of the new creation should be convicted of their sin because of the eschatological Spirit within them. When Christians think or do unholy things, there should be immediate conflict and dissonance with the indwelling Holy Spirit, who is in the process of causing the believer to reach the goal of complete end-time righteousness. Those who are accordingly convicted about their sin will express repentance and change their sinful ways. Those

---

77. Here the Greek word rendered as "sure" is *bebaios*, which can also carry the notions of "certain, steadfast, firmly grounded, firm," and in three of its other seven uses in the NT it refers to Christians being "sure" of their hope (2 Cor. 1:7; Heb. 6:19) and having "firm assurance" (Heb. 3:14). Thus, *bebaios* is virtually synonymous with "assurance."

78. On which, see the discussion earlier in this excursus.

who have no conviction about indwelling sin should have no conviction that they are genuine saints.

Therefore, faithful, growing Christians should receive multiple assurances from these three angles, which have a cumulative force, enhancing the overall sense of confidence about the reality of their Christian existence. What if a Christian is inconsistent in progressing in good works, and an area of life is not under submission to the Lord of the new creation? Such a person should be under great conviction about this sin, and if so, it is a good sign that the Spirit is really in the person, bringing about conviction. Such a person should not doubt knowing God, unless as time goes on the conviction over sin does not issue into repentance, a turning away from the sin being committed.

However, no confidence should exist in those who profess to believe in Jesus but who reflect no discernible change for the good in their lifestyles and who have no conviction about changing their sinful ways.

Generally, the closer people get to God as faith grows, the more such people will desire to please God by what they do, and the more they will be convicted by the remaining sin in them. As a result, they will have even greater assurance as they progress in their Christian lives.[79]

79. Obviously, much more could be said about the notion of assurance. For an excellent and well-balanced article that summarizes many of the important and debated issues, see D. A. Carson, "Reflections on Christian Assurance," *WTJ* 54 (1992), 1–29.

26

Christian Living as the Beginning of Transformed New-Creational Life

The Role of the Law and Marriage

This chapter will show how the OT law and institution of marriage relate to Christian living and faithfulness as a facet of the inbreaking new creation, which are key threads of the redemptive-historical storyline developed throughout this book.

The Relationship between Christian Living and Obedience to the Law in the Inaugurated New Creation

Christians have long debated about what parts of the OT law, if any, carry over into the NT. Many in the past have categorized the law into three parts: ceremonial, civil, and moral. Although this has no exegetical basis, it is a broadly helpful way to conceive of the law. Many scholars disagree with such a tripartite classification of the law and see it as being overly simplistic. The attempt to fit the law into these three categories is indeed a complex issue, and it needs more nuanced argumentation than I can give here. For example, certainly the entire law is moral, but there do appear to be sections of the law that highlight the nationalistic (civil) and ceremonial (temple) functions of some laws, whereas other laws appear to be more purely moral without such functions. Thus, I still think that the threefold classification is a generally helpful way to think of the law.

There have been three major views among Christians about how the OT law relates to the NT. The following description of each position is a general summary, since there are permutations of viewpoints within each, and the intent here is merely to state the most basic elements of each view. So, at the risk of oversimplification, I will attempt briefly to summarize each vantage point.

One perspective is known as theonomy, which contends that the entire law is carried over into the NT. This view sees the ceremonial laws (of priesthood, sacrifices, etc.) to find their typological fulfillment in Christ, but the so-called civil and moral laws carry over and apply to the church. Some forms of theonomy also propose that Christians should work toward inculcating these parts of the law into the government of the countries in which they live.[1]

A second view is represented by the Westminster Confession (Article XIX, "Of the Law of God"), which contends that only the purely moral part of the law, represented by the Ten Commandments, carries over to the church because the ceremonial laws were typologically fulfilled in Christ, and Israel's civil laws ceased when the commonwealth of Israel ceased in AD 70.[2]

A third view is that of classic dispensationalism, which holds that no part of the law is carried over into the church age.[3]

In my view, the most persuasive position is the second one, where only what we may call the purely moral part of the law is seen to be applicable to the church. The most obvious argument in support of this view is that the majority of the Ten Commandments are carried over, quoted, and applied to saints living in the church age. Jesus sums up the Ten Commandments, or the whole moral law, as "love of God and neighbor." For example, note Matt. 22:36–40:

> "Teacher, which is the great commandment in the Law?" And [Jesus] said to him, "'You shall love the Lord your God with all your heart, and with all your soul, and with all your mind.' This is the great and foremost commandment. The second is like it, 'You shall love your neighbor as yourself.' On these two commandments depend the whole Law and the Prophets."

Jesus's first commandment appears to be a summary of the first part of the Ten Commandments, which regulates divine-human relations, and his second

---

1. For a classic view of this form of theonomy, see Greg L. Bahnsen, *Theonomy in Christian Ethics* (Nutley, NJ: Craig Press, 1979).

2. Although the Westminster Confession (Article XIX.4) goes on to say that NT believers are not obliged to keep the civil laws "further than the general equity thereof may require." This phrase has been debated and will not be elaborated on here.

3. See, e.g., Charles C. Ryrie, *Dispensationalism Today* (Chicago: Moody, 1967). Like the other two views, dispensationalism affirms that the ceremonial laws were fulfilled typologically in Christ.

one a summary of how humans are to relate to one another.[4] What makes it likely that these two statements summarize the Ten Commandments is that when Paul says that "he who loves his neighbor has fulfilled the law" (Rom. 13:8), he explains that what he has in mind are the moral laws of the last section of the Ten Commandments, citing four of the six in that section: "You shall not commit adultery, you shall not murder, you shall not steal, you shall not covet" (Rom. 13:9). He cites a fifth in Eph. 6:2: "Honor your father and mother." In responding to the rich young man about which commandments are important to keep, Jesus cites the same ones as Paul, though he adds "You shall not bear false witness" and omits "You shall not covet" (Matt. 19:16–22). Thus, together, Jesus and Paul cite all six of the Ten Commandments that pertain to loving one's neighbor.

While it is true that the first four of the Ten Commandments are not quoted in the NT, it is likely that they are summarized in Jesus's statement that "the great and foremost commandment" in the OT is "You shall love the Lord your God with all your heart, and with all your soul, and with all your mind" (Matt. 22:37–38). We have also seen in an earlier chapter that the Sabbath commandment (Exod. 20:8–11) is part of a creational ordinance that continues to be applicable to the church age.

Thus, at the least, we may say that those moral laws not related to the so-called civil and cultic functions carry over into the church age. But why does this part of Israel's law carry over while the ceremonial and civil parts do not apply? The answer to why the ceremonial laws do not apply is the same for each of the three above viewpoints: they are typologically fulfilled in Christ. For example, he is the true and final end-time priest and sacrifice, so that a priesthood that offers sacrifices is no longer needed. But why do only the moral laws that have no civil function continue into the NT epoch and not also the laws that focus on civil functions? In answering this question, I believe that the lens of the inaugurated new creation in Christ is helpful.

The Bearing of the Inaugurated New Creation in Christ on the Relevance of the Old Testament Law

The law, especially in Paul's thinking, is a prime example of an important biblical concept that not only relates to the new age but also can best be understood in the light of the beginning destruction of the old creation and the emergence of the renovated creation. In this respect, the notion of the law is bound up with the idea of reconciliation (as discussed earlier in chap. 16). The best place to see this is Eph. 2:13–18. Verses 14–15 are the crucial verses, where it is said that Christ made Jew and gentile one when he "broke down the dividing wall of the barrier, by abolishing in His flesh the enmity, which is

4. Paul says that "the whole law is fulfilled" in the statement "You shall love your neighbor as yourself" (Gal. 5:14); likewise Rom. 13:8–10.

the Law of commandments contained in decrees [or 'ordinances'']." This likely refers to Christ nullifying not the whole law but only part of it, as I believe the remainder of Ephesians bears out, since Paul repeatedly quotes and alludes to OT moral law and not cultic or civil laws. Christ has abolished that part of the law which divided Jew from gentile so that they could become one. Gentiles no longer need to adopt the signs and customs of national Israel's laws to become true Israelites. For example, they need to be circumcised not in the flesh but rather in the heart by Christ's death, which was their true circumcision, since it cut them off from the old world and set them apart to the new (see Col. 2:10–14; Gal. 6:14–15). Gentiles do not need to make pilgrimage to Israel's temple to approach God; they merely need to make pilgrimage to Jesus, the true temple, of which the Ephesian Christians were a part (see Eph. 2:20–22). This is the significance of defining the "mystery" in Eph. 3:6 as gentiles being "fellow heirs and fellow members of the body, and fellow partakers of the promise."

The parallel passage to Eph. 2:13–18 in Col. 2 defines the "decrees" (*dogma*) of Eph. 2:15 that Christ abolished as the external nationalistic expressions of the law: food, drink festivals, new moons, or Sabbaths (see Col. 2:15–17, 20–21). Colossians 2:20–22 even refers to these "decrees" with the verbal form of *dogma*: "[Why] do you submit yourself to decrees [*dogmatizō*], such as 'Do not handle, do not taste, do not touch!' (which all refer to things destined to perish with use)—in accordance with the commandments and teachings of men." Note that Col. 2:20 says that they died *apo tōn stoicheiōn tou kosmou* ("to the elements of this world"). There is much debate about the meaning of *stoicheia* in Paul's writings (plural of *stoicheion*, which Paul uses only in Gal. 4:3, 9; Col. 2:8, 20). Many see it referring to demonic powers, which is possible. The most usual meaning of *stoicheia* in the Greek world, however, is the four basic elements of the cosmos: air, fire, water, and earth.[5] How could this basic meaning have relevance for Colossians 2?[6] The old, fallen cosmic order was based on cosmic "elements." These elements included moral or spiritual "elements of division among humanity," ultimately held in place by the devil and his evil forces.

However, now that Christ has come and has launched a new cosmos, the old cosmos has begun to be destroyed. The only element or fundamental building

---

5. As illustrated in, e.g., 2 Pet. 3:10, 12, though here the "elements" of the cosmos are destroyed by means of fire.

6. For a listing of the possible interpretative identifications of *stoicheia* as demonic powers, the four elements of the universe, and supernatural powers in some way connected to the four elements, among other possible views, see C. E. Arnold, "Returning to the Domain of the Powers: STOICHEIA as Evil Spirits in Galatians 4:3, 9," *NovT* 38 (1996): 55–76, including extensive bibliography. In particular, the phrase the "elements of the world" (*stoicheia tou kosmou*) in the Hellenistic Greek of the time referred, as far as I can tell, exclusively to the four elements that were viewed to have composed the world (on which, see Dietrich Rusam, "Neue Belege zu den στοιχεῖα τοῦ κόσμου (Gal 4,3.9; Kol 2,8.20)," *ZNW* 83 (1992): 119–25.

block of the new creation is Christ. And since there is only one Christ, of whom the new creation consists and upon whom it is built, there can be only one newly created people subsisting in that renovated creation. In what sense can it be said that the old world has already begun to be destroyed? The elements of divisiveness that sustained the sinful structure of the old world have been decisively decimated by Christ, and he himself has replaced them as the only foundational pillar of the new world. This is what Paul has in mind in Gal. 6:14–16, where he says that through the cross of Christ "the world has been crucified to me, and I to the world. For neither is circumcision anything, nor uncircumcision, but a new creation. And those who <u>will walk by the elements</u> (*stoichēsousin*)[7] of this rule, peace and mercy be upon them, even upon the Israel of God." That is, those who conduct their lives on the foundational "elements" of Christ, who is the inaugurated new creation, are partakers of the new creation, and they will experience the peace and unity promised to occur in the new heaven and earth.

We could picture Christ as a hermeneutical filter through which the law must pass in order to get to the new creation. Those parts of the law that are nationalistic in nature do not pass through the filter.[8] Those parts of the law that are more moral and less ethnic in nature are able to pass through the filter. This appears to be the significance of 1 Cor. 7:19: "Circumcision is nothing, and uncircumcision is nothing, but <u>what matters is</u> the keeping of the commandments of God." This is parallel with Gal. 5:6 and 6:15, both of which begin with the same negative statement about circumcision and then add a positive contrastive clause, respectively, "faith working through love" and "a new creation." The "commandments" to be kept in Christ, in the "new creation," are summed up in the statement "love your neighbor" (cf. Gal. 5:6 with 5:14) and are in contrast to what distinguishes people ethnically, which must, therefore, exclude those parts of the law that distinguish Israelites as a unique racial group.[9]

This renewed order in Gal. 6 and Eph. 2, as well as Col. 2, in which Jews and gentiles become unified and at peace, is a reflection of Isa. 11 and 66,

7. This is my interpretative paraphrase of this Greek verb, since it may well be a positive contrast to the negative reference to "the <u>elements</u> [*stoicheia*] of the world" in Gal. 4:3, where the phrase refers to the law's negative function to be part of the fallen and corrupted cosmos in line with the cosmological meaning of the word in relation to the law that I have discussed above in Colossians.

8. These nationalistically oriented laws stop in Christ because they become typologically fulfilled in him. That is, since these laws function to regulate civil relationships in the land, they cease such a function when Christ comes because he is the beginning fulfillment of the land promises (on this, see chap. 22). In the same way, the laws regulating temple worship are typologically fulfilled in Christ because he is the fulfillment of all to which the temple pointed.

9. The parallelism between 1 Cor. 7:19; Gal. 5:6; 6:15 has been pointed out by Daniel P. Fuller, *The Unity of the Bible: Unfolding God's Plan for Humanity* (Grand Rapids: Zondervan, 1992), 348–49.

where likewise there are prophecies that Jews and gentiles will be unified and at peace with one another in the coming new cosmos.[10] For example, in Isa. 11:6–9 there is prophetic description of antagonistic animals from the old creation that will be at peace with one another in the coming new creation (e.g., Isa. 11:6: "The wolf will dwell with the lamb, and the leopard will lie down with the young goat, and the calf and the young lion and the fatling together"). The harmonious relation between the animals in Isa. 11 and 66 is a reflection of the peaceful parading of animals before Adam in Gen. 2:19–20[11] and of the peaceful pilgrimage of the animals into the ark in Noah's presence, which prepared for the second new creation at the conclusion of the flood. The verses directly following the Isa. 11 passage indicate that such unity among these formerly antagonistic animals points to the end-time fellowship that will occur between Jew and gentile, the crown of creation. Isaiah 11:10–12 says,

> Then in that day
> The nations will resort to the root of Jesse,
> Who will stand as a signal for the peoples;
> And His resting place will be glorious.
> Then it will happen on that day that the Lord
> Will again recover the second time with His hand
> The remnant of His people, who will remain,
> From Assyria, Egypt, Pathros, Cush, Elam, Shinar, Hamath,
> And from the islands of the sea.
> And He will lift up a standard for the nations
> And assemble the banished ones of Israel,
> And will gather the dispersed of Judah
> From the four corners of the earth.

The same pattern more broadly occurs in Isa. 65–66, where Isa. 11:6–9 is summarized in one verse (Isa. 65:25), and then Isa. 66:18–23 explains that a believing remnant of ethnic Israel will join with gentiles who are considered to be true Israelites (see, e.g., Isa. 66:20).[12] There should be no divisions of people groups in the new creation, just as there was to be no such division in the first creation. The nationalistic divisions in the old world inspired antagonism because they inspired nationalistic pride. For example, it is clear that the many laws that distinguished Israel as a people from gentiles became a source

10. The reference to "new creation" in Gal. 6:15 alludes more directly to Isa. 65:17; 66:22 (on which, see chap. 10 under the heading "Paul's Conception of Death and Resurrection as the Beginning End-Time New Creation: Galatians 5:22–25; 6:15–17").

11. The reference in Isa. 11:6, 8 to a child living in peace with the animals may also echo Adam's peaceful relationship with the animals in the first paradise.

12. For a more extended analysis of Isa. 66:18–22, see chap. 20 under the heading "The Old Testament Notion of Gentiles Becoming Latter-Day True Israel as Background for the New Testament Presupposition That the Church Is True Israel."

of irritation and antagonism among gentiles (dietary laws, Sabbath laws, etc.).[13] These distinctive laws sometimes led to ridicule and persecution, such as happened in the Babylonian exile. Likewise, the same dietary laws caused antagonism and persecution in the time of Antiochus Epiphanes (e.g., 4 Macc. 5:1–38) and ridicule during the Roman domination (e.g., Philo, *Legat.*, 362). In addition, these nationalistic distinctions became objects of idolatrous trust under the influence of demonic forces, which provoked further antagonism. Thus, these divisive laws separating people groups had to be nullified, with only the moral laws left remaining as suitable for the new creation.

It could be simpler to think about OT nationalistic laws being laid aside because in Christ God's covenant people now are constituted not as a nationalistic entity but rather as a transnational church. But the reason for the new-covenant community being transformed into a transnational entity is that it has been transformed to become part of a new creation, which entails not just ethnic Jewish believers living in a localized part of the Middle East but also gentiles who live throughout the whole created cosmos.

Thus, the various racial differences of the redeemed in the final form of the new creation will still be apparent, but their former nationalistic identifications and the concomitant idolatrous nationalistic customs must fall by the wayside and be swallowed up in the identification of all in Christ, the bridgehead and only distinguishing mark of the new creation.[14] The lack of antagonism among animals and the lack of division among humanity is likely a recapitulation of the original paradisal conditions of Eden, which is suggested by the reference to "new heavens and new earth" in Isa. 65:17; 66:22.[15] That is, the coming cosmos is called "new" because it is not only a return to, but also an escalation of, the conditions of the original first world before the incursion of sin and its effects. For example, unlike the prefall world, the new cosmos is incorruptible, so that it is an irreversible renovation of not only the fallen world but even the prefall world.

13. Note, e.g., the problems that Daniel had in refusing to eat unclean foods in Babylon (see Dan. 1). Although it is probably true that Daniel abstained from the Babylonian foods because they were tainted by idolatrous purposes, the reason that Israel's food laws were originally given was likewise to prevent Israel from being tainted by unclean foods associated with Canaan's idolatrous practices.

14. Racial distinctions between people will not be erased in the consummate new creation, but redeemed humanity's identification as true Adam/Israel transcends all former nationalistic distinctions. The precedent for this in the OT was the conversion of Egyptians and Canaanites to the faith of Israel, in which such foreigners became so incorporated into Israel that they were considered now to be Israelites and no longer Egyptians and Canaanites. Although their Egyptian or Canaanite racial distinctions continued, they shook off their idolatrous customs, and their greater identification was with Israel.

15. Furthermore, the duration of those who live in the new cosmos are described in Isa. 65:22 LXX this way: "As the days of the tree of life [i.e., in Eden] shall be the days of my people" (cf. the MT: "As the lifetime of a tree, so will be the days of My people").

Therefore, because of the OT prophecy of new creation that has begun fulfillment in Christ, there can no longer be any nationalistic distinctions between Jew and gentile; the only distinguishing element is Christ, in whom the two are now unified. Therefore, those nationalistic signs entailed in the law that distinguished Jew from gentile are no longer valid. This is why Paul quotes only from the moral law, or when he quotes other facets of the OT law (such as the civil), he uses it in a typological or nontheocratic manner in employing it within the covenant community of the church (e.g., see his use of Deuteronomy in 1 Cor. 5:13). Ephesians and Col. 2 have focused on the so-called ceremonial parts of the law, which were nationalistic identification markers for Israelites and therefore have passed away because Christ is now the only identification marker for the true people of God.

Therefore, according to this criterion of the obsolescence of Israel's laws as identification tags distinguishing Jews from gentiles, it seems likely that the civil or judicial laws have been unable to pass through the new-creational filter of Christ and thus unable to enter the beginning sphere of the new creation. Now that Christ's kingdom has begun to be extended over the whole creation and not only over Israel's land, the laws that were peculiar to the regulation of life in that land are no longer necessary. And since there is no longer a theocratic land of Israel, the laws regulating life in that land are likewise no longer needed.

Consequently, understanding how Christ has instituted the new creation gives insight into understanding which parts of the OT law relate to the new age and which parts do not.[16] Nevertheless, more needs to be said about the basis for why Israel's civil laws do not carry over into the new age.

Paul's Negative and Positive Views of the Law in Light of the Eschatological New Creation

There are numerous references to the law in Paul's writings, especially in Romans. The focus here is on the use of the law in Romans because this will be sufficient to make the point of this section. As elsewhere in Paul's writings, in Romans some references to the law are negative and some are positive. For example, Rom. 3:19–20 says negatively,

> Now we know that whatever the Law says, it speaks to those who are under the Law, so that every mouth may be closed and all the world may become

16. Again, I realize that the cogency of the preceding section depends to some extent on the validity of ceremonial, civil, and moral distinctions in the law and on the assumption that what is "moral" as distinct from "civil" and "ceremonial" can be identified. At the least, Paul seems to make a twofold distinction between those laws that are nationalistic identification markers (civil and ceremonial) and those that are more essentially moral and do not separate Jew from gentile in the new age.

accountable to God; because by the works of the Law no flesh will be justified in His sight; for through the Law comes the knowledge of sin.

However, Rom. 8:4 is one of several texts in Romans that speak favorably about the law: God sent his Son "so that the requirement of the Law might be fulfilled in us, who do not walk according to the flesh but according to the Spirit." Table 26.1 compares these alternating negative and positive views within Romans.

Table 26.1

The Present Age in Romans	The Age to Come in Romans
works/flesh	faith/spirit
disobedience of the law	obedience of the law
2:17–25	2:12–16; 26–29
3:19–20	3:21–4:25
5:12–14	5:15–21
7:7–13	7:1–6; 8:4
9:31–33; 10:1–3, 5	9:30; 10:4, 6–13
13:12b–13	13:8–12a; 14

Some scholars have concluded that Paul contradicts himself, and that no solution can explain how these apparently opposing viewpoints are compatible in Paul's mind.[17] However, once one places these kinds of statements within the context of the already–not yet age of the eschatological new creation, Paul's contrasting assertions about the law make excellent sense. Recall that the new-creational age has broken into the lives of believers through the eschatological work of Christ and the Spirit, thus making them part of the last Adam, Jesus. Yet, unbelievers do not participate in the realities of the new age and are still living in the old age, dominated by their solidarity with the old, fallen Adam.

Consequently, as we have seen already, those who have been resurrected and created by the Spirit to be a beginning new creation have the power of the Spirit to give them new desires and the moral power to begin to fulfill the law. In contrast, unbelievers do not possess the eschatological Spirit and are not part of the new creation, and therefore they have no desire or ability to obey the law. Paul's contrasting view of the law is an excellent example of how the inaugurated eschatological new creation clarifies what one might otherwise consider as inconsistencies in Paul's thought.[18]

17. See, e.g., Heikki Räisänen, *Paul and the Law*, 2nd ed., WUNT 29 (Tübingen: Mohr Siebeck, 1987), 83.

18. This section is based on C. Marvin Pate, *The End of the Age Has Come: The Theology of Paul* (Grand Rapids: Zondervan, 1995), 143, though he does not discuss the notion of the implications of the new creation.

Marriage as a Transformed New-Creational Institution in Ephesians 5

In an earlier chapter I attempted to show that Eph. 1:19b–23 portrays Christ as having begun to fulfill the prophetic hopes of an end-time Adam:[19]

> These are in accordance with the working of the strength of His might which He worked in Christ, when He raised Him from the dead and seated Him at His right hand in the heavenly places, far above all rule and authority and power and dominion, and every name that is named, not only in this age but also in the one to come. And He put all things in subjection under His feet, and gave Him as head over all things to the church, which is His body, the fullness of Him who fills all in all.

Christ's exalted rule in verses 20–21 is expressed by way of reference to Ps. 8:6: "You have put all things under his feet." In this connection, the concluding phrase in verse 23, "Him who fills all in all," likely reflects "fill the earth" in Gen. 1:28, which was part of the original commission to Adam. Paul views Christ himself as having decisively fulfilled the Adamic commission of Ps. 8; this probably indicates Paul's belief, against the background of the Ps. 8 context, that Christ himself, individually and flawlessly, ruled, subdued, multiplied spiritual progeny (though this element is missing in Ps. 8), and filled the earth with God's glory, as fully as one human could in one lifetime.[20]

After instructing husbands to love their wives as Christ loved the church (Eph. 5:25–27), in verses 28–33 Paul appeals to husbands specifically to love their wives as they love themselves:

> So husbands ought also to love their own wives as their own bodies. He who loves his own wife loves himself; for no one ever hated his own flesh, but nourishes and cherishes it, just as Christ also does the church, because we are members of His body. For this reason a man shall leave his father and mother and shall be joined to his wife, and the two shall become one flesh. This mystery is great; but I am speaking with reference to Christ and the church. Nevertheless, each individual among you also is to love his own wife even as himself, and the wife must see to it that she respects her husband.

In verse 31 Paul quotes from Gen. 2:24, which is part of the conclusion of the Adam and Eve narrative. The introductory phrase, "For this reason," of Gen. 2:24 indicates that the verse in Genesis is based on the preceding section. Probably strands from the entire section of Gen. 2:15–23 are in

---

19. See chap. 15 under the subheading "The Expectations for Adam's Obedience and the Application of These Expectations to Other Adam-Like Figures and Finally to Christ."

20. Three times elsewhere Christ is viewed as having achieved the position of the Adamic kingship of Ps. 8:6: "You have put all things under his feet" (see 1 Cor. 15:25–27; Heb. 2:6–9; more briefly, Phil. 3:21).

mind as forming this basis,[21] which means that the directly preceding verse, Gen. 2:23, provides part of the basis. Accordingly, the fact that the woman was part of Adam's body is part of the basis for saying that "a man shall leave his father and his mother, and be joined to his wife; and they shall become one flesh." That is, since Adam and Eve were one, all subsequent marriages should accomplish the same unity. Such subsequent marriages should take the unity of Adam and Eve as their model and strive for that same kind of unity.[22]

The statement in Gen. 2:24 is directed to all those who desire to be married. It is a prefall statement, which means that although it still had application to the postfall marital state, the prefall creation was the ideal context and environment in which this "leaving and cleaving" was to take place.

Paul's teaching in Eph. 5:28–33 reflects this one-flesh union of husband and wife in Gen. 2:24 as the basis for husbands loving their wives (see Eph. 5:31, where Gen. 2:24 is quoted). The Ephesians text goes further than the Genesis passage by saying that the reason why husbands are to maintain unity with their wives is that this is what Christ does with the church (cf. Eph. 5:29–30). Thus, believers "are members of [Christ's] body" (v. 30). Then Eph. 5:31 quotes Gen. 2:24 in support of Eph. 5:30. But how does Gen. 2:24 support the notion in Eph. 5:30 that we "are members of [Christ's] body"? Ephesians 5:32 is the answer: Gen. 2:24 is called a "mystery," and the Genesis passage is said to have "reference to Christ and the church." This answer is not obvious and so needs some explanation.

First, Paul says in Eph. 5:32 that Gen. 2:24 is not primarily about the relationship of husbands to their wives but rather that of Christ to the church. And this relationship described by Gen. 2:24 is a "mystery" (*mystērion*) that is "great." Why is the Gen. 2 statement a mystery? Paul is saying that what appeared to be a pattern describing only the human institution of marriage is now, in view of Christ's coming and the formation of his church, a description not solely applicable to the marriage of a man and a woman. The pattern wherein a man leaves his family and becomes one with a wife contains within it a reflection of a grander marriage: Christ leaving his heavenly home and Father and becoming one with the church. Until the end of history, Christians are to view their own marriages in this manner: husbands should sacrifice for

---

21. Likewise, this seems to be suggested by, e.g., Gordon Wenham, who says that v. 24 "is not a continuation of the man's remarks in v. 23, but a comment of the narrator, applying the principles of the first marriage to every marriage" (*Genesis 1–15*, WBC 1 [Waco: Word, 1987], 70). Likewise, Gordon Hugenberger says that v. 24 is "a climactic summary for the whole of Gen. 2:18–24" (*Marriage as a Covenant: Biblical Law and Ethics as Developed from Malachi*, VTSup 52 [Leiden: Brill, 1994], 152). In this respect, part of the woman's role in context likely was to be a "helper suitable" (Gen. 2:18) to aid Adam in cultivating and guarding the garden (Gen. 2:15) and in remembering and obeying God's command (Gen. 2:16–17).

22. See Hugenberger, *Marriage as a Covenant*, 151–56. He concludes that Gen. 2:24 "offers a normative paradigm marriage."

their wives in order to reflect what Christ has done, and wives should respect (or trust in) their husbands in order to reflect what the church has done (and should do) with respect to Christ.

Such an understanding would not have been obvious to the OT writer or reader of Gen. 2:24, but now, retrospectively, on the other side of Christ's cross and resurrection and by the revelation of the Spirit (cf. Eph. 3:5), it can be seen how such a meaning could organically grow out of the Genesis text. Christ is the ultimate, eschatological "man" (ideal Adam), and the church is the ultimate, eschatological bride (e.g., 2 Cor. 11:2–3; Rev. 19:7–9; 21:2, 9–27). The identification of Christ as an end-time Adam figure may be pointed to also by Eph. 5:23–24, where wives are to "be subject" (*hypotassō*) to their husbands because the latter are the "head" (*kephalē*), just as the church is "subject" to Christ because he is the "head." This combination of the Greek words "be subject" and "head" occurs elsewhere in Paul's letters only in Eph. 1:22, where the verb "be subject" is part of an allusion to Ps. 8:6 (8:7 LXX), which, as we just noted above, was applied to Christ as the one who had begun to fulfill the expectations of the eschatological Adam.

The vast majority of uses of "mystery" (*mystērion*) in the NT are associated with beginning eschatological fulfillment of OT prophecy,[23] as we saw earlier in discussion of Matt. 13:10–11[24] and 2 Thess. 2:3–7[25] (see also Rom. 11:25; Eph. 3:3, 9).[26] If "mystery" carries a prophetic sense in connection to Gen. 2:24, then the Genesis passage would be seen as a typological prophecy, much as I argued in the case of Hos. 11:1 in Matt. 2:15,[27] whereby a historical pattern (in this case, repeated marriages) from OT history foreshadows or adumbrates some redemptive event in the NT age.[28]

How could the use of *mystērion* in Eph. 5:32 be related to that in Eph. 3? Both concern unity of diverse people groups: Jews and gentiles in Eph. 3, and married men and women in Eph. 5. Paul is concerned to say not only that Christ has inaugurated the new-creational unity of fragmented humanity in

23. See G. K. Beale, *John's Use of the Old Testament in Revelation*, JSNTSup 166 (Sheffield: Sheffield Academic Press, 1998), 215–72.

24. See chap. 13, in the excursus, under the heading "The Inaugurated, Unexpected, and Transformed Nature of the End Time Kingdom."

25. See chap. 7 under the subheading "2 Thessalonians 2 and the Great Tribulation."

26. See chap. 20 under the heading "The Presuppositional Basis for the Church Being True Israel."

27. See chap. 13 under the subheading "Jesus as Latter-Day Israel and Son in Matthew 2."

28. See Markus Bockmuehl, *Revelation and Mystery in Ancient Judaism and Pauline Christianity*, WUNT 2/36 (Tübingen: Mohr Siebeck, 1990), 204. Bockmuehl views Eph. 5:32 as inspired exegesis of Gen. 2:24, drawing out a deeper meaning that is prophetically typological in nature (and he cites others generally following this view). Skeptical about a typological sense are Andreas J. Köstenberger, "The Mystery of Christ and the Church: Head and Body, 'One Flesh,'" *TJ* 12 (1991): 94; Thorsten Moritz, *A Profound Mystery: The Use of the Old Testament in Ephesians*, NovTSup 85 (Leiden: Brill, 1996), 142–46.

general (Jew and gentile), but also that he has begun to put back together the broken relationships within the family in particular.[29] We saw in the preceding section on the law that there could be no divisions of people groups in the new creation, just as there were to be no such divisions in the first creation. Similarly, there was not to be any division between Adam and Eve or between all subsequent husbands and wives living in the prefall paradise. The effect of the fall into sin caused such a separation between Adam and Eve (Gen. 3) and in subsequent marriages. With respect to the "mystery" of Jewish and gentile unity in relation to Christ and with regard to husband and wife unity in relation to Christ, Paul sees that the way Christ has fulfilled OT expectations and historical patterns is somewhat unexpected and mysterious from an OT perspective, yet nevertheless developing some organic strands of continuity.[30]

It is quite fitting for Paul to appeal to a prefall creation text about unity in marriage as a prototype for the unity of Christ and the church in the new creation. Accordingly, husbands and wives now should be motivated to maintain the unity that Adam and Eve first experienced (Gen. 2:23) in the original creation and the unity that all humans were designed to experience before the fall (Gen. 2:24). This unity is to be maintained not only because this is the original purpose of marriage according to Gen. 2:24, but also because husbands and wives have the model of Christ and the church to follow as the paradigm for marriage relationships for those living in the new creation, to which Gen. 2.24 ultimately pointed.[31] Just as there were to be no divisions between husband and wife in the original pristine creation, so such unity in the new creation must be preserved.[32]

This is a very practical notion for Christian husbands and wives to remember. It is true that marriage is for the purposes of fulfillment in love (physically, spiritually, and emotionally), for propagation, and for sanctification. When problems arise in the marriage relationship, husbands and wives need to remember that there is an ultimate redemptive-historical purpose for marriage that transcends their own human relationship. As husbands unconditionally love their wives and as wives respond to this love in a faithful manner, they are actors on a redemptive-historical stage performing a play before the onlooking audience of the world. As husbands and wives perform their roles on this stage in the way God has designed, their roles are an object lesson to

29. An insight I have subsequently also found in Köstenberger, "Mystery," 94.

30. For the elements of continuity, in this respect, see G. K. Beale and Benjamin L. Gladd, *Hidden But Now Revealed: A Biblical Theology of Divine Mystery* (Downers Grove, IL: InterVarsity, forthcoming).

31. Moritz (*Profound Mystery*, 146n124) comes close to saying this, which is not consistent with his reticence about a typological view of Gen. 2:24.

32. The last part of this section on the "mystery" of marriage is based on Beale, *John's Use of the Old Testament*, 246–47.

the watching world[33] that Christ has left his Father to love and become one with his bride, and that those who respond in faith can become part of this corporate bride. In doing so, people will leave the sphere of the old world and enter into the new. Christian mates are part of the new creation, and the ethic regulating their marriage is a recapitulation of the original design of marriage in Eden, which pointed to Christ and the church. When conflict enters the marriage relationship and division begins to occur, both partners need to remember that they have covenanted with each other before God to love each other, to remain loyal to that covenant, to continue to become one and, hence, to maintain the peace of the new creation of which they are a part.[34] In contrast to the divisions and conflicts that remain elsewhere in the old creation, husbands and wives are to reflect the peaceful unity that was to have been characteristic of Adam and Eve in Eden before sin (and that would have been characteristic of all marriages in imitation of Adam and Eve's marriage if sin had not occurred). This peaceful unity that was to be true of the first marriage in history is to be characteristic of all those living in the inaugurated phase of the new creation in Christ.

Consequently, at the heart of Christian marriage is a new-creational ethic that has the ultimate purpose of pointing to the relationship of Christ, the last Adam, to the church, the new Eve, in the new creation.

33. This watching world likely includes "the rulers and authorities in the heavenly places" to whom the "wisdom" of the "mystery" of Jew and gentile unity was proclaimed "through the church" (Eph. 3:9–10). These "rulers and authorities" are likely evil (in light of Eph. 6:10–12). The purpose of this proclamation in Eph. 3 was to remind these authorities that their attempts to divide believers have been decisively nullified by Christ's work, as made evident through actions tending toward unity in the church. Likewise, when husbands and wives overcome divisions among themselves, their actions make the same proclamation to the powers of evil and to the world in general.

34. For the notion that marriage in Gen. 2 is a "covenant," see Hugenberger, *Marriage as a Covenant*.

PART 10

CONCLUSION

27

The Relationship of Inaugurated and Consummated Eschatological Realities to the Parallel Realities Experienced by Old Testament Saints

This part of the conclusion has three aims. First, we will look back to see how each of the "already–not yet, end-time, new-creational kingdom" realities discussed in this book correlate with their equivalents in the OT. That is, how do these NT notions relate to the people of the OT epoch? For example, how do the trials of Israel relate to the trials described in the NT, which are considered to be part of the latter-day tribulation? How do the inaugurated NT realities represent a transformation of the OT realities?

A second aim is to discuss the continuity and discontinuity in the inaugurated eschatological stage of prophetic fulfillment.

A third aim is then to look forward and to relate each of the inaugurated ideas to the consummation. How does the commencement of each latter-day reality find its completion at the very end of history?

This chapter will serve to pull together and summarize the various thematic strands throughout the book, especially with respect to the various facets of inaugurated eschatology discussed throughout in relation to the NT storyline repeated in this book. Here I will not repeat all the various ways that the following themes in this chapter are related to the biblical-theological storyline developed throughout the book, except for some summarizing comments (see under the heading "The New Creation and Kingdom" below). A few topics that received less discussion earlier will be highlighted to show how they relate to the biblical-theological storyline noted throughout the book. Some theological ideas that others have seen to be significant have not been addressed in the book nor will they be in this conclusion, since I have not seen them as integral to the biblical-theological storyline. I will make no attempt in this chapter to substantiate most of the points made about the OT and inaugurated eschatology in the NT, since I have done that throughout the book.[1]

Broadly speaking, the OT epoch was a time of prophetic expectation, and the NT age is the beginning fulfillment of that expectation. The very end of the age is the final, complete fulfillment of what had been inaugurated earlier. Each of the inaugurated aspects corresponds to some degree to facets of life lived under the old covenant. Yet the pressing question remains of how the church, the covenant community living in a new age, experiences certain realities differently from how its OT counterpart experienced similar realities. Then we will see how the corresponding consummated realities relate to the inaugurated ones.

NT realities are qualitatively different from their closest OT counterparts in that they are the beginning fulfillment of end-time prophecies. That is, the OT anticipates, and the NT begins to fulfill. But how does the fact that these end-time realities are part of such latter-day fulfillment make them qualitatively different from their OT complements? We will see that many of the inaugurated realities of the new-covenant age are eschatological transformations of old-covenant realities. Another important question is this: how do the inaugurated prophetic realities reach their completion at the very end of the age? To try to explain briefly the similarities and differences between the old age and the new is the task of the remainder of this chapter.[2]

The Latter Days[3]

The Old Testament Reality

The OT prophesies that various events will happen in the latter days, most of which do not find fulfillment within the OT itself. Among OT latter-day prophecies to be fulfilled in the future end-time period are the coming of the Messiah or Davidic king, the kingdom, the restoration of Israel, the new creation, resurrection, the Spirit, the new covenant, the defeat of the enemy of God's people, the final tribulation, and the end-time temple. There are also

---

1. Readers who want more substantiation of points made in this chapter usually will find it in earlier chapters of the book, where there is more elaboration on the same points, much of which I attempt to signpost below. This chapter, however, will also further develop some of the topics discussed earlier.

2. The comparisons and contrasts for the most part will be made between Israel and the church, not the pre-Israelite covenant community.

3. For further elaboration of this section, see chaps. 3–5.

many other OT passages that concern eschatology but do not use the precise terminology of "end-time" language.

Some prophecies appeared to begin fulfillment in the OT age. However, these seeming fulfillments were faint and hollow because they did not reach an eschatologically irreversible condition. Real irreversible fulfillment was still awaited in the future. Israel's restoration,[4] temple, and participation in new creation are good examples of this. Such hollow fulfillments nevertheless represent an ostensible incipient inaugurated eschatology within the OT era itself. I will elaborate further on the nature of this evident but ultimately unreal incipient inauguration in the discussion below concerning the restoration, temple, and new creation.

The Corresponding Inaugurated End-Time Reality

The NT repeatedly uses precisely the same phrase "latter days" as found in the OT prophecies, though other synonymous expressions are also employed. Many of these uses are likely echoes of the OT expression, while others seem to be specific allusions to some of the specific OT texts that employ the expression "latter days." The eschatological idea of the wording is generally identical to that of the OT, except for one difference: in the NT the latter days predicted by the OT are seen as beginning fulfillment with Christ's first coming. All that the OT prophesied would come to pass in the end times has started to be fulfilled in Jesus and the early church and continues until the final coming of Christ. In particular, this indicates that the following OT end-time expectations have been set in motion by Christ's earthly ministry, death, resurrection, and the formation of the Christian church: the great tribulation, God's domination of the gentiles, the defeat of Israel's enemies and deliverance from its oppressors, Israel's restoration, Israel's resurrection, the new covenant, the promised Spirit, the new creation, the new temple, a messianic king, and the establishment of God's kingdom.

The Corresponding Consummated End-Time Reality

The latter-day period that began with Christ and the earliest church and continues throughout the age will be completed at the final coming of Christ and the final judgment, when the old cosmos is destroyed and the new cosmos is created. The inaugurated eschatological realities noted in the preceding paragraph will also be consummated at this time, on which the following discussion will also elaborate.

---

4. E.g., Deut. 4:30 and 31:29 predict that Israel's end-time restoration will presumably begin at the time of the return of the remnant from Babylon. In such cases, the NT would see that what supposedly began realization did not bring about irreversible conditions, and that such permanent conditions of restoration truly become inaugurated at Christ's first coming and finally are consummated at his second coming.

The New Creation and Kingdom

Here there will be more focus on new creation, and a later section will address the specific notion of the kingdom more pointedly.

The Old Testament Reality

We saw in chapter 2 that there were cyclical episodes of what appeared to be a beginning stage of new creation that did not carry through to completion.[5] We saw this with the Noahic flood narrative, the exodus narrative, Israel's second exodus through the Jordan River, and the return from Babylon, which Isa. 40–66 repeatedly referred to as a new exodus and a new creation. These partial repeated fulfillments nevertheless represent what seem to be an incipient inaugurated eschatological new creation within the OT era itself. We observed that essential to the OT storyline was the kingdom of a new creation and the obligation of God's people to extend it throughout the world. The pattern of judgment in the form of (1) cosmic chaos followed by (2) new creation, (3) commission of kingship for divine glory, (4) sinful fall, and (5) exile composes the major events of OT redemptive history. This pattern is first observed in Gen. 1–3 and then in other episodes that have the same five narratival elements; these later episodes are thus recapitulations of the primeval creation narrative.

On the basis of observing this repeated pattern, I drew the conclusion that the OT storyline is best summarized as follows: *The Old Testament is the story of God, who progressively reestablishes his new-creational kingdom out of chaos over a sinful people by his word and Spirit through promise, covenant, and redemption, resulting in worldwide commission to the faithful to advance this kingdom and judgment (defeat or exile) for the unfaithful, unto his glory.* The movement back to the establishment of the kingdom of the new creation is paramount, being achieved by means of God's word and Spirit working through promise, covenant, and judgment. The goal of all this is God's end-time glory. However, although it appeared at points that this kingdom and new creation were being reestablished, the substantial fulfillment never came to fruition.

The Resurrection of Christ and His People as the Corresponding Inaugurated End-Time Reality of New Creation

The repeated restarts of a movement back toward the new-creational kingdom were never irreversibly realized in the OT era. What seemed to be fulfilled faded and wilted like flowers without water. Christ's first coming as the kingly last Adam is another new-creational start-up, but unlike the others, this one did not stop because of sin. This book has especially endeavored to demonstrate

---

5. See especially table 2.2 under the heading "The Repeated Cosmic Judgment and New Creation Episodes of the Old Testament."

that Christ's death and especially resurrection were a further escalation of the new-creational rule begun in his ministry, and then the church's identification by the Spirit with his resurrection also caused it to become part of this new creation kingship as coruler. In this respect, building on the OT storyline, I have posited the following storyline for the NT, with resurrection as new-creational kingship and its expansion being the major stepping-stone to final divine end-time glory: *Jesus's life, trials, death for sinners, and especially resurrection by the Spirit have launched the fulfillment of the eschatological already–not yet new-creational reign, bestowed by grace through faith and resulting in worldwide commission to the faithful to advance this new-creational reign and resulting in judgment for the unbelieving, unto the triune God's glory.* In fact, in this light, as argued earlier, it is apparent that the general notion of eschatology is better defined more specifically as movement toward a new-creational kingdom for God's ultimate glory.

That the establishment and expansion of Jesus's new-creational kingdom is the key means toward accomplishing God's glory is apparent from my earlier contention that Gen. 1–3 and the last vision of Revelation (21:1–22:5) form an inclusio for the entire Bible (see chap. 2 under the heading "The Repeated Cosmic Judgment and New Creation Episodes of the Old Testament"). Genesis 1–3 highlights Adam as a king who was to spread the new-creational kingdom for God's glory, and the main thrust of Rev. 21 shows how what Adam should have done is finally brought to pass. Other important theological aspects are included in the beginning and the end of this scriptural inclusio, but the movement toward a new-creational kingdom for divine glory forms the major contours of it, as I have argued throughout this book.

The inaugurated form of the kingdom in the Gospels is a beginning fulfillment of the OT kingdom prophecies, but it occurs in unexpected forms and ways: invisible rather than visible; small rather than big; over an extended period of time rather than quickly; in victory over and judgment of spiritual enemies rather than physical ones.

The Corresponding Consummated End-Time Reality

The new creation that began with Christ's earthly ministry and escalated with his resurrection, accompanied by the sending of his Spirit working in the church, will be consummated at the end of time. The manifestation of this consummation will be the resurrection of the bodies of saints and the renewal of heaven and earth. The re-creation of the cosmos is prophesied in 2 Pet. 3:13; Rev. 21:1–22:5. The latter passage especially depicts an escalated recapitulation of the garden of Eden as the final temple and new Jerusalem, within which Christ will reign with his resurrected people. The inclusio of a priest-king reigning over a first unspoiled creation and a priest-king reigning over a final new creation is one of the clearest indications that the movement toward this new-creational kingdom is the major stepping-stone in the scriptural storyline toward bringing about God's final, everlasting glory. At the very end, God's kingdom will appear visibly over the entire new creation, after there has been final judgment of the enemy and reward for the faithful subjects of the kingdom.

Conclusion to New Creation in Relation to the Topics Remaining to Be Discussed

The other eschatological realities prophesied by the OT and beginning fulfillment in the NT should be seen to be either subordinate to and/or integrated within this more overriding framework of movement toward the new-creational kingdom for divine glory. In fact, each of these ideas is so inextricably linked to this concept that they should be seen as essential facets of it.

In the remainder of this chapter I will discuss other eschatological realities, some of which are more explicit in the NT, though having roots in the OT. All the major eschatological notions dealt with so far in the book will receive some kind of summary in the rest of this chapter. The end-time concepts that remain to be discussed are new exodus, salvation and justification, reconciliation, regeneration, image of God (including Adamic sonship), the church's salvation and restoration as true Israel, sanctification (i.e., ongoing Christian living), Sabbath, baptism, the Lord's Supper, the church office of elder, the canon of Scripture, the law, and marriage. These concepts will be connected to the core of the biblical storyline—new-creational rule and its expansion—as I have contended throughout[6] and as I will continue to argue that they are best understood as subordinate aspects of that new-creational reality. As indicated in the introduction of this chapter, other ideas not emphasized earlier in the book will receive more attention in order to see how they relate to the storyline (e.g., judgment). I have not presented much discussion of the grand goal of the storyline—the glory of God—but I will address this in the next chapter, which concludes the book.

It certainly is conceivable that many of these notions cited in the preceding paragraph are so overlapping with the concept of the new-creational kingdom that they are merely ultimately synonymous with it. In such a case, all these ideas could be pictured as one diamond with multiple facets. Nevertheless, I believe that the overall evidence points to Christ's kingdom of the new creation to be the diamond itself, with the other ideas being facets of it. And all this needs to be understood in the context of my proposed NT storyline, in which the new-creational rule and the mandate to extend it is the main stepping-stone or thread leading to God's glory. Regardless of whether agreement can

---

6. E.g., in chap. 6, I argued explicitly for the predominance of the new-creational kingship over these concepts.

be reached on this point, my hope is that readers can see that all these realities are interconnected and are inherently eschatological.[7]

In the remainder of this chapter my purpose is to bring more clearly into view the NT inaugurated aspect of each of the aforementioned notions in relation to the corresponding OT reality and the consummated end-time reality, as I have begun to do with "eschatology" and "new creation" so far.

A King and Kingdom

The Old Testament Reality

God began to rule through his vice-regent, Adam, until Adam's fall. This kingship was picked up more formally later in Israel's kings and kingdom, which were the channel through which God ruled the nation. But throughout this period the majority of Israel's kings failed in fulfilling their commission. Even the few faithful kings still fell short of the ideal. Also, throughout this period hopes were expressed for an eschatological king who would come and fulfill the kingly commission in the way God had designed it.

Thus, Israelite kingship was imperfect compared to the prophesied messianic kingship, which would completely fulfill the divine design for kingship. The Israelite kings were typological anticipations of the ideal messianic king to come. Likewise, Israel's kingdom ebbed and flowed with judgment and blessing depending on the faithfulness of its kings, who corporately headed up the nation's kingdom. Most of the time this judgment took the form of varying degrees of foreign oppression, until climactically the northern and southern kingdoms were decisively defeated respectively by Assyria and then Babylon and went into exile in those places.

The Corresponding Inaugurated End-Time Reality

Whereas in the OT age Israel's kingship and kingdom were characterized by unfaithfulness, in the new era Jesus is the perfectly faithful end-time king who represents and blesses those who compose his invisible kingdom. Also, the OT period was one in which there were repeated prophecies of an ideal messianic leader to come, and the Gospels portray Jesus as the inaugurated fulfillment of those prophecies. Thus, the OT age is one of direct prophecy of an eschatological leader and typological anticipation for such a leader, while the NT age is an epoch of fulfillment and realization of these anticipations.

Christ inaugurated his kingship and kingdom at his first coming when he began to rule over the powers of evil and over the hearts of people, whom he called to participate in his kingdom. This stage of the kingdom represented a

7. For more in-depth methodological discussion of the nature of a biblical-theological storyline in relation to "centers" and the preference for the storyline as stated above, see chap. 6.

mysterious or transformed period of fulfillment, since there was only a spiritual rule and not a physical and fully visible rule of Christ, nor was there a final and complete defeat and judgment of the enemy. At his resurrection and ascension his kingship was escalated to the point where he was "seated on David's throne" in heaven. From there, Jesus expresses his sovereignty on earth through the Spirit, who works through his body on earth (as noted throughout Acts). He will "reign" from over earth "until He [God] has put all His enemies under His feet" (1 Cor. 15:25, alluding to Ps. 110:1). Thus, at the time of his resurrection and ascension Christ was "ruler of the kings of the earth" (Rev. 1:5). But even after the ascension Christ's rule through the Spirit in the realm of the church was unseen by unbelieving eyes, though it was perceived by believers through faith in the unseen but true spiritual power of the present kingdom.

The Corresponding Consummated End-Time Reality

Christ will return at the end of time and "judge the world" (Acts 17:31) and then destroy it and create a new cosmos. At that time, Christ ("the Lamb") will reign together with the Father, and the saints "will reign" with them "forever and ever" (Rev. 21:22; 22:3–5) in the new heavens and earth. Although there is still some opposition to Christ's inaugurated, unseen, and spiritual rule in the old world, in the new world there will be absolutely no resistance to this reign; not even death can affect the king and his coregents, since death will be abolished (1 Cor. 15:25–29; Rev. 21:4; 22:3). Christ will rule over every nook and cranny of the new cosmos. This rule will be both spiritual and physical in that Christ will be physically present on the new earth and functioning as king.

Israel's Return from Exile

The Old Testament Reality

What is striking, as we have noted, is that some of the OT predictions about the end times evidently began fulfillment within the OT epoch itself. The promise of Israel's return from exile is a good example of this phenomenon. For example, Deut. 4:27–29 foretells that when Israel becomes idolatrous and evil,

> The LORD will scatter you among the peoples, and you will be left few in number among the nations where the LORD drives you. There you will serve gods, the work of man's hands, wood and stone, which neither see nor hear nor eat nor smell. But from there you will seek the LORD your God, and you will find Him if you search for Him with all your heart and all your soul. When you are in distress and all these things have come upon you, in the latter days you will return to the LORD your God and listen to His voice.

This eschatological prophecy seemed to begin fulfillment in Israel's climactic idol worship and sin that directly led to exile and then, seventy years later, the restoration that began with only a fraction of the tribes of Judah and Benjamin returning to the land. However, only a very small remnant among those returning also "returned" in faith to God. The majority of the returnees were not faithful to God. Directly after the return, the leaders of the restoration even describe the Israelites condition in the land still to be a captivity: "for we are slaves" who are "in our bondage" (Ezra 9:9; so also Neh. 9:36). Although Israel had physically returned to the land, it was still in both physical and spiritual bondage. Its physical captivity was clear from the fact that it continued to be under foreign domination, first by the Persians, then the Greeks, and finally the Romans. The temple of the restoration began to be built, but it became evident that this was not the glorious temple that was expected in the restoration period (see Ezra 3:12; Hag. 2:3), especially by the time Jesus renounced the temple and predicted its destruction in AD 70.

The motor of Israel's latter-day restoration started with the physical return from Babylonian exile,[8] but then it sputtered during the so-called Second Temple period, and the fulfillments associated with the prophecies of restoration did not come to pass and thus awaited their realization for a later time. Thus, the motor started, but then it stalled or, worse, it seized up and broke down.

The Corresponding Inaugurated End-Time Reality

As I have repeatedly observed, the OT prophecies of various events to happen in the latter days decisively began to be fulfilled with the coming of Christ and the establishment of the church. One such prophecy that Jesus and the church begin to fulfill is that of the long-awaited end-time restoration of Israel.

The fulfillment of Israel's end-time restoration that allegedly faintly started but then sputtered and died out within the old epoch is started up in a clear manner by Jesus, who represents true Israel both in his life and in his restoration from death through resurrection. The return from exile began through Christ's ministry, redemptive death, resurrection, and the coming of the Spirit, who works through the church. The application of Israel's restoration prophecies to the church indicates that the church is beginning to fulfill true eschatological Israel's expected restoration to God through its identification with Jesus, the true Israel. Christ's restorative work was primarily a spiritual restoration of one's soul back into a salvific relationship with God. And, as we have also seen, the ongoing character of the Christian life is a continuation of a pilgrimage of returning from exile spiritually. All these things are still part of an inaugurated restoration from exile. Interestingly, therefore, the eschatological pattern of restoration begins within the OT period itself and blossoms in the NT, so

8. Recall that Jeremiah predicted that the restoration would begin after Israel's "seventy years" of captivity (cf. Jer. 25:11–12 with 29:10). The prophecy was fulfilled in part in the physical return of the remnant of Israel, but the true physical and spiritual promises of that prophecy remained unfulfilled, as just explained.

that Israel's physical return from Babylon comes to be seen as a typological foreshadowing of the true return launched in Jesus.

The Corresponding Consummated End-Time Reality

As with the kingdom, the inaugurated fulfillment of the restoration was spiritual and would not be fully realized in physical and spiritual form until the creation of the new cosmos. At the very end of the age the restoration of Israel, the physical typological pattern of which began in the OT and reached an antitypical escalation in its inauguration in Jesus and the church, will reach its final fulfillment. After the destruction of the old cosmos there will be the final resurrection of saints' physical bodies, which will inhabit an eternal, new physical creation. Although believers have begun to be restored to God spiritually in this age, their bodies are still part of the old world and thus are part of an old, decaying world that is estranged from God. Their final resurrection, which launches them into the new cosmos, is the end of the pilgrimage and is the final, complete return from exile. This is not only a complete physical restoration but also a complete spiritual restoration, since the former spiritual restoration was only inaugurated. This means that believers will be transformed into perfect physical and spiritual beings. This will be a transformation according to the pattern prophesied in Phil. 3:20–21:

> For our citizenship is in heaven, from which also we eagerly wait for a Savior, the Lord Jesus Christ; who will transform the body of our humble state into conformity with the body of His glory, by the exertion of the power that He has even to subject all things to Himself.

It is also important to recall that Jesus's own resurrection and ascension were his own individual consummate restoration from the exile of death in summing up and representing Israel. The king went ahead of his people in being completely restored, and they will follow as eschatologically true Israelites at the end of the age in their own resurrection bodies. In this respect, 1 Cor. 15:22–23 shows that Christ first experienced the consummation of resurrection existence, which will be followed by the resurrection of his people at the very end, which will be their final restoration to their God. Thus, Jesus's announcement of the true latter-day spiritual return from exile is consummated later with a physical return in a new cosmos.

God's Deliverance as a Second Exodus in Relation to the Restoration from Exile

The Old Testament Reality

Israel's exodus deliverance from Egypt was recapitulated on a small scale when the second generation of Israel went through the Jordan River, whose waters were parted by Joshua. Just as the first generation had to go through water to get to the promised land (though they failed because of sin), so the second generation had to follow the same path to the land of inheritance.

We have seen that Isaiah prophesied that Israel would be restored to the land from Babylonian captivity, and that this deliverance would be patterned after that of Israel's earlier exodus from Egypt. Accordingly, this "second"[9] exodus is one of the ways that Isa. 40–66 portrayed Israel's restoration. Consequently, everything I said earlier about the latter-day restoration of Israel being inaugurated but being delayed and finally stopping is true of the prophecy of Israel's second exodus from Babylon. That is, because this restoration did come to the fruition of true fulfillment, its faint beginning of release from Babylon nevertheless became a foreshadowing pattern. Subsequently, Isaiah's prophecy of Israel's end-time exodus resumed again in a true eschatological sense with the coming of Jesus.

The Corresponding Inaugurated End-Time Reality

We saw that both the Gospel of Mark and Acts use the notion of a second exodus as one of the main ways to explain respectively the coming of Jesus and the ongoing phenomenon of the growth of the church.[10] Other NT books likewise appeal in significant ways to this background (esp. Luke). Jesus is depicted as leading God's people in a spiritual exodus from spiritual bondage. This exodus is one of the ways that the NT portrays eschatological Israel's restoration from exile, which I discussed just above. Jesus begins to show his sovereignty in defeating the spiritual powers of evil and releasing people from captivity to those powers. His death and resurrection were escalated stages of continuing that exodus and winning victory over the evil powers, thus releasing his people from bondage to those powers and to death. In executing this exodus, Jesus is both an eschatological Moses figure[11] and the Passover Lamb.[12] But although this latter-day exodus was irreversibly begun, it has not yet been completed for God's people.

The Corresponding Consummated End-Time Reality

This eschatological exodus that began only spiritually and in an unseen manner will be consummated finally at the end of history when God's people will themselves finish defeating opposition and leave this old world and enter

9. Or perhaps I should say "third" exodus in light of the second generation of Israel crossing through the divided waters of the Jordan on dry land.

10. See chap. 20 under the heading "Conclusion."

11. See Dale C. Allison Jr., *The New Moses: A Matthean Typology* (Minneapolis: Fortress, 1993).

12. See, e.g., John 19:36; 1 Cor. 5:7. Also recall my earlier discussion of the institution of the Lord's Supper by Christ in the upper room as corresponding to the Passover meal.

into the new, physical, eternal world. This future and last stage of the end-time exodus is portrayed in Rev. 15:2–4:[13]

> And I saw something like a sea of glass mixed with fire, and those who had been victorious over the beast and his image and the number of his name, standing on the sea of glass, holding harps of God. And they sang the song of Moses, the bond-servant of God, and the song of the Lamb, saying,
>
> > "Great and marvelous are Your works,
> > O Lord God, the Almighty;
> > Righteous and true are Your ways,
> > King of the nations!
> > Who will not fear, O Lord, and glorify Your name?
> > For You alone are holy;
> > For all the nations will come and worship before You,
> > For Your righteous acts have been revealed."

The entrance into the eternal new world is pictured in Rev. 21:1–5, where several allusions to Isaiah's prophecies of new creation are made,[14] which in Isaiah are inextricably linked to hope of a new exodus and restoration from exile.[15]

Reconciliation as a Return from Exile

The Old Testament Reality

True saints throughout the OT time also participated in "reconciliation" in the same way that we will soon see that they were "justified" in anticipation of Christ's justifying work on the cross and at the resurrection. We have also seen that Israel's eschatological restoration prophecies outwardly seemed to have been inaugurated after the seventy years of captivity in Babylon. Nevertheless, the majority of those returning were not faithful, so Israel continued in spiritual and theological exile. Even though they had returned to their land, they were still in spiritual captivity and physical captivity (to those foreign powers that ruled over them). Thus, they did not become restored or reconciled to God's very presence in the way the prophets such as Isaiah, Jeremiah, and

13. For the rich exodus background of these verses, see G. K. Beale, *The Book of Revelation: A Commentary on the Greek Text*, NIGTC (Grand Rapids: Eerdmans, 1999), 789–800.
14. Note, e.g., Isa. 65:17; 66:22 (in Rev. 21:1); 43:18; 65:17 (in Rev. 21:4); 43:19 (in Rev. 21:5). For various possible allusions or echoes to Israel's exodus in Rev. 21:1–4, especially with respect to the background of the phrase "and there is no longer any sea" (21:1b), see ibid., 1043–51. In this respect, sometimes the exodus was described as the removal of waters.
15. For this inextricable link in some of the Isaiah passages, see G. K. Beale, "The Old Testament Background of Reconciliation in 2 Corinthians 5–7 and Its Bearing on the Literary Problem of 2 Corinthians 4:14–7:1," *NTS* 35 (1989): 555–57.

Ezekiel had prophesied. Accordingly, this initial physical restoration became a typological pattern foreshadowing a future true restoration and reconciliation.

The Corresponding Inaugurated End-Time Reality

In an earlier chapter we saw that reconciliation to God through Christ is partly to be understood as the church participating in Israel's prophesied restoration from exile (chap. 16). The complete reality of this return was from spiritual death and alienation from God and restoration into God's salvific presence. This takes place when one believes in and identifies with Christ, the true Israel, who was restored to the presence of the Father by resurrection from the bondage of death. Accordingly, Israel's restoration that had begun superficially in a physical but not spiritual manner at the time of the return from Babylon reached a greater escalated typological fulfillment with the coming of Christ and the church. However, as noted just above, the restoration that Christ launched can be seen only with the eyes of faith and remains veiled to unbelievers.

The Corresponding Consummated End-Time Reality

We saw earlier in this chapter that at the final return from exile believers would be delivered from the old bodies that they possessed during their earthly exile in the old world. They would then be restored to God's full end-time presence by physical resurrection, in which they would enter the new, eternal world. The same is true with reconciliation. Believers begin to be spiritually reconciled to God through belief in Christ's death and resurrection, and then at the end of the age they are fully reconciled to God's intimate presence, both spiritually and physically.

Salvation and Justification[16]

The Old Testament Reality

Believers in the OT experienced genuine salvation. David and Abraham are representative examples of OT saints whom Paul says were "justified by faith" (Rom. 4:1–8, 22–23; Gal. 3:6–9; cf. James 2:23).

The Corresponding Inaugurated End-Time Reality

It is clear that both OT and NT believers experienced spiritual salvation from sin. The difference is that in the older epoch this experiential salvation was an anticipation of the salvation to be achieved in space-time, latter-day

16. For a much fuller discussion of justification, see chap. 15.

history in Christ. The inauguration of this salvation in the NT reveals that "the Christian idea of salvation is essentially an eschatological conception."[17] Romans 3:24–26, to be elaborated upon further below, is classic evidence of this, which pertains specifically to the doctrine of justification in connection to old-covenant and new-covenant believers; note especially verse 25: "God displayed [Christ] publicly as a propitiation in His blood through faith. This was to demonstrate His righteousness, because in the forbearance of God He passed over the sins previously committed." Other NT passages point in this same direction:

> **Heb. 11:13** "All these [OT saints] died in faith, without receiving the promises, but having seen them and having welcomed them from a distance, and having confessed that they were strangers and exiles on the earth."
>
> **Heb. 11:39–40** "And all these [OT saints], having gained approval through their faith, did not receive what was promised, because God had provided something better for us, so that apart from us they would not be made complete."

In a similar vein, Rev. 12:7–13 concerns the salvific status of believers in relation to Satan in the pre-Christian time and how this changed with the coming of Christ:

> And there was war in heaven, Michael and his angels waging war with the dragon. The dragon and his angels waged war, and they were not strong enough, and there was no longer a place found for them in heaven. And the great dragon was thrown down, the serpent of old who is called the devil and Satan, who deceives the whole world; he was thrown down to the earth, and his angels were thrown down with him. Then I heard a loud voice in heaven, saying, "Now the salvation, and the power, and the kingdom of our God and the authority of His Christ have come, for the accuser of our brethren has been thrown down, he who accuses them before our God day and night. And they overcame him because of the blood of the Lamb and because of the word of their testimony, and they did not love their life even when faced with death. For this reason, rejoice, O heavens and you who dwell in them. Woe to the earth and the sea, because the devil has come down to you, having great wrath, knowing that he has only a short time."

Verses 7–12 describe actions that are the heavenly counterpart of earthly events recorded in verses 1–6 that radically telescope Christ's life and resurrection (vv. 2–5), followed by the church's flight from persecution (v. 6; see also vv. 13–17). The point of these verses is that Christ's death and resurrection result in

---

17. See George R. Beasley-Murray, "The Eschatology of the Fourth Gospel," *EvQ* 18 (1946): 102. This article gives a brief overview of already–not yet eschatology in John's Gospel.

Christ's and the saints' victory over the satanic accuser and in the inaugurated end-time messianic kingdom. It likely is Christ's resurrection that unleashes the effect of Michael's victory in heaven and defeat of the satanic powers. The remainder of Rev. 12 and of the entire book reveals that Christ's death and resurrection have resulted in significantly curtailing the devil's role of deception and nullifying his role of slanderer. This curtailment and nullification is what is meant by the depiction of Michael and his angels throwing the devil and his angels out of heaven. The "place" that the devil lost was his hitherto privileged heavenly place of accusation, formerly granted him by God as a privilege (see further v. 10b).

The meaning of Christ's ascension and the devil's expulsion from heaven (vv. 3–9) is explained in verse 10 to be the long-awaited inauguration of the prophesied messianic kingdom (e.g., Ps. 2; Dan. 2 [see 12:5, 7]): "The salvation, and the power, and the kingdom of our God, and the authority of His Christ have come." It is repeated in the second part of verse 10 that the devil "had been cast out" from heaven. But now the devil is called "the accuser of our brethren . . . who accuses them before our God day and night." His accusations have been ceaseless. On the basis of this description and the description of Satan in Job 1:6–11; 2:1–6; Zech. 3:1–2, it can be concluded that the devil was permitted access to heaven by God in order to accuse his people of sin. Various OT texts portray Satan accusing saints of unfaithfulness, with the implication that they did not deserve God's salvation and gracious blessings.[18]

In light of Rev. 12:11, the accusations in verse 10 appear to be directed against the apparent illegitimacy of the saints' participation in salvation. The devil's accusation is based on the correct presupposition that the penalty of sin necessitates a judgment of spiritual death and not salvific reward. The charges are aimed against all OT saints who do not receive the deserved punishment at the time of their death but instead are given entrance into God's glorious presence in the invisible heavenly realm. Until the death of Christ, it could appear that the devil's accusations were valid, since God ushered all deceased OT believers into his saving presence without exacting the due penalty of their sin. Satan was allowed to lodge these complaints because there was a degree of truth in the accusations. However, the devil's case was unjust even before the death of Christ because the sins about which he was making accusations and for which he wanted to punish people were significantly instigated by his deceptions. This is why he is called both "deceiver" and "accuser" in verses 9–10. Therefore, OT saints were protected from the damning danger of these accusations.[19]

The death and resurrection of Christ have banished the devil from this privileged accusatorial position formerly granted him by God. The reason

18. See Zech. 3:1–5, 9; cf. *Num. Rab.* 18.21.
19. See *1 En.* 40:7 with 40:9–41:2.

901

for this is that Christ's death was the penalty that God exacted for the sins of all those who were saved by faith. Romans 3:25 says that saints under the old covenant were not judged for their sins, "because in the forbearance of God He passed over the sins previously committed," but finally in Christ God punished those sins at the cross (Rom. 3:19–28). Such people were allowed to enter into God's presence in heaven at death as "justified" people, despite the fact of their sin and even though their sin had not been punished. God was delaying the eschatological punishment finally to exact it in Christ's death. In this sense, we may say that true OT believers were justified in anticipation of the future judgment of their transgressions through Christ's redemptive death. Scripture explicitly says that OT saints were "justified" in this manner (see Rom. 4:1–3, 6; Gal. 3:6–9). In this regard, OT saints were ultimately protected from Satan's accusations because of the coming death of Christ on their behalf, which would finally nullify these accusations.

The sinless Christ vicariously took on himself the wrath that threatened the saints so that they might be delivered from the final wrath to come and be "declared righteous" or "justified." Consequently, no one can "bring a charge against God's elect," not even "angels," "principalities," or "powers" (Rom. 8:33–34, 38), because of the saving effects of Jesus's death and resurrection (Rom. 8:32, 34).[20] Christ's resurrection was also seen to be crucial for justification because believers could be identified with acceptable righteousness before God only by virtue of their identification with the *risen* last Adam, who had been perfectly obedient and continued to maintain that status of perfect obedience. He was raised as the completely righteous last Adam, who was in the glorious image of God. Thus, Christ's death and resurrection mark a significant redemptive-historical change for the relationship of believers in the old covenant to Satan's accusations against their salvific status in comparison to those living under the new covenant. The principle of being justified by faith runs throughout both Testaments.

Believers have begun to be "saved" from bondage to Satan and from final judgment through Christ's death and resurrection. Christ has come and suffered the end-time penalty of that sin, so the price has finally been paid. Nevertheless, it is clear that Satan is still active in blinding unbelievers (Acts 26:18; 2 Cor. 4:3–4) and attempting to influence God's people to sin or trying to harm them (2 Cor. 11:14; 12:7; Rev. 2:9–10).

The Corresponding Consummated End-Time Reality

At the time of the final judgment of humanity, Satan will be judged as well, so that he will never again exercise any kind of harmful influence on the church (e.g., Rev. 20:10). Accordingly, Satan's initial defeat occurred

20. This discussion of Rev. 12:7–12 is derived from a longer analysis in Beale, *Revelation*, 650–60.

at Christ's victorious death and resurrection, and his complete defeat will happen at the very end when Christ comes to consummate his kingdom in final victory over the forces of evil. The saints' inaugurated salvation is also from spiritual death, over which Satan rules (Eph. 2:1–5), and this salvation is completed at the end when believers are freed also from physical death by resurrection.

Just as inaugurated latter-day eschatological salvation is to be understood through the lens of justification, so likewise there is a consummative phase of justification (e.g., 1 Thess. 1:10: "Jesus, who delivers us from the wrath to come"). Believers are declared definitively "justified" or "vindicated" in this age through faith in Christ's death and resurrection. I found it necessary earlier in this book to use the somewhat awkward wording "justified/vindicated" in order to express clearly the vindicatory element in justification. Christians are vindicated because Christ's vicarious death on their behalf removes the penalty of their sin, so that they are declared "not guilty" of judgment for their sin. In addition, believers are declared righteous because Christ achieved representative righteousness for them in his resurrected person, as the perfect image of the last Adam, and *was vindicated from injustice (showing that he had been righteous all along), a vindication with which the saints are also representatively identified.* Accordingly, they are vindicated from God's just condemnatory verdict upon them.

Despite the definitive nature of a person's justification by faith in the present age, there is a consummative aspect to believers' justification, which will occur at the final coming of Christ. In the earlier chapter on justification I suggested that there are three aspects of future "justification" or "vindication":

1. public demonstration of justification/vindication through the final, bodily resurrection;
2. justification/vindication of the saints through public announcement before all the world;
3. public demonstration to the entire cosmos of believers' justification/vindication through their good works.

First, Christians are "justified/vindicated" before all eyes by bodily resurrection. It is true that Christians have been declared absolutely not guilty from the complete spiritual and physical penalty of sin, but they have not yet been delivered from the physical death penalty of sin that has been pronounced upon them, the corrupting effects of which they endure in the present age. The resurrection of the body is the ultimate overturning of this death penalty, the verdict from which they had already been declared as having been vindicated. This removal of the execution of the judgment of physical death is the last phase of the two-part already–not yet effects of justification: (1) resurrection of the "inner man" followed by (2) resurrection of the "outer man."[21] Richard Gaffin refers to this double justification as "justified by faith" and "yet to be justified by sight."[22] Since the complete overturning of the death penalty still lies in the future, there is a sense in which the full justification/vindication from that penalty is also still yet to be implemented, though this implementation is ultimately an effect of the earlier pronouncement of justification by faith from the full penalty of sin. At the very end, their bodily resurrection also vindicates them from the unjust verdict pronounced upon them during their earthly sojourn.

Second, God publicly announces at the time of the final judgment to all in the cosmos that his people are justified/vindicated and thus are exempt from that last great judgment. Although saints have been declared righteous before God and the covenant community in this age, the world has judged them to be in the wrong, with respect to both their belief in Christ and their loyalty to living according to the values of God's word. The world's judgment has expressed itself in the execution of saints, imprisonment, social and economic ostracism, and other forms of contempt. In the final end-time courtroom God's people will be acknowledged before all to have been in the right all along, and their justifying belief and righteous actions will be vindicated and the world's verdict of "guilty" will be finally and forever overturned.

Third, how can one be said to be definitively "justified/vindicated" by Christ's death and resurrection and yet also to be "justified by works"? I have argued that justification by deeds does occur at the time of the believer's final resurrection. At the climax of the church age Christians' good works (which are imperfect) justify/vindicate that they have already been justified by Christ. This final form of justification is not on the same level as the prior justification by faith in Jesus, though it is integrally connected to it. Good works are the badge that vindicates the saints by providing declarative proof that they have been actually justified by Christ in the past. The good works not only demonstrate the past, genuine, justified status of a person but likely also reveal the world's unjust verdict in rejecting such works as a witness to Christ. It should also be recalled that already-justified Christians will appear before the "judgment seat" *in their resurrection bodies*. They will not be judged on whether their deeds have been perfect but rather on whether they have borne the fruit of good works in keeping with and as a result of their resurrection existence and character that comes through union with the resurrected Christ. And, of course, this resurrection existence is none other than new-creational existence. Consequently, the vindication that saints receive through their resurrected bodies is a vindication through being a part of the new creation.

21. Here I am following Richard B. Gaffin Jr., *By Faith, Not by Sight: Paul and the Order of Salvation* (Waynesboro, GA: Paternoster, 2006), 86.
22. Ibid., 88.

The Role of Christ's Death in the New-Creational Kingdom Part of the New Testament Storyline

Throughout this book much discussion has been devoted to Christ's resurrection as the beginning of the new-creational kingdom, which, I have concluded, is the major means by which the goal of the storyline is achieved: the glory of God. Some readers might well contend that I have unduly underemphasized the death of Christ. Certainly, I showed Christ's death to be crucial in the accomplishing of justification (chap. 15) and reconciliation (chap. 16), though in both cases I tried also to show the important role of resurrection in these redemptive ideas. Christ's death, however, has not been discussed in as prominent a way as has resurrection in the other chapters of the book.

It is true that Christ's resurrection represents a farther redemptive-historical progression in the achievement of eschatological salvation than does his death. In this respect, the resurrection achieves a more full-blown inauguration of the new creation or of redemption than occurred in his ministry or death. Nevertheless, I want to underscore that Jesus's death is conspicuously crucial, not only in the achievement of justification, reconciliation, and redemption but also in combination with his resurrection in launching the new creation.

I have argued that Gal. 6:14–16, one of the four most prominent "new creation" passages in the NT, formally states that Christ's death itself was vital in launching the end-time new creation. No doubt, the resurrection is implied in this passage, but Christ's death is explicit. Paul's point is that his identification with the death of Christ is the actual inception of his separation from the old, corruptible, and sinful world, and it is the precise commencement of the old world's separation from him (v. 14). Paul's separation from the old cosmos leads him to being set apart to another world, which in verse 15 he calls a "new creation." Galatians 1:4 is close to the point of 6:14–15: Christ "who gave Himself for our sins, that He might deliver us out of this present evil world." Apparently, in this connection, Irenaeus, *Haer.* 5.23.2 says, "The Lord, therefore, recapitulating in Himself this day [the day of the first Adam's death], underwent His sufferings upon the day preceding the Sabbath, that is, the sixth day of the creation, on which day man was created; thus granting him a second creation by means of His passion, which is that [creation] out of death." (I am indebted to my student Daeil Chun for the Irenaeus reference.)

Directly before Jesus's physical resurrection, he appears to have been transported to "paradise" (Luke 23:43). Could it be that, while Jesus's body lay dead in the tomb for three days, nevertheless his spirit was living in the new creational sphere of "paradise"? And, if this were the case, would believers' historical and positional identification only with Christ's death also entail some sense in which they too were considered to be in the very inception of the new creation? To answer these questions in the affirmative would require more exegetical evidence than the above Lukan passage. So we must leave that to others to ponder and research further.

Likewise, 2 Cor. 5:14–17 views Christ's death (vv. 14–15) and then his resurrection (v. 15) as leading to "new creation" (v. 17). On the one hand, this gives the redemptive-historical order and progression, resurrection being a greater climax of redemption and new creation. On the other hand, resurrection and new creation without Christ's death would be hollow and meaningless.

In addition, Eph. 2:14–16 highlights Christ's death repeatedly as the means to bring about the "one new man" of Jew and gentile, which results in "peace" and "reconciliation." This reference to "one new man" continues to develop the theme of resurrection as new creation from Eph. 1:20–23; 2:2–7, 10.

But there are other ways that Christ's death is connected to new creation. This is natural, since we saw earlier (chap. 13) that many of the most crucial aspects of Jesus's ministry are portrayed in the Synoptic Gospels as episodes of the inbreaking new creation. In this respect, Christ's healings were seen to be the beginning reversal of the physical effects of Adam's fall and a foreshadowing of full healing in Christ's and believers' physical resurrection, in which all the effects of the curse are abolished. For example, Matthew says that Jesus's ministry of healing (8:13–16) was a beginning fulfillment of Isa. 53:4 ("He Himself took our infirmities and carried away our diseases" [8:17]). So also 1 Pet. 2:24 asserts through allusion to Isa. 53:5 that Christ "bore our sins in His body on the cross, that we might die to sin and live to righteousness; for by His wounds you were healed." Significantly, again in 1 Pet. 2:24 Christ's death is inextricably linked to the notion that believers "live to righteousness," which identifies them with resurrection life. Certainly it would be strange if Christ's death were not seen as a climactic event leading to the emerging new creation in him, especially since, as we just observed, his death is inextricably linked to his resurrection. In fact, Christ's obedience to death should be seen as the cause resulting in the effect of the Father raising him from the dead. Thus, Christ's death effects the dawn of the new creation.

There is another way that Jesus's death in justifying believers is linked to new creation. Recall that "justify" actually means "declare/vindicate to be righteous." In this respect, at least one other NT text understands that full righteousness comes only in the new creation. In 2 Pet. 3:13 Peter says:

> But according to His promise we are looking for new heavens and a new earth, in which righteousness dwells.

Peter is likely combining Isa. 60:21 ("Then all your people will be righteous; they will possess the land forever") with Isa. 65:17 ("I [will] create new heavens and a new earth" [likewise Isa. 66:22]). Peter is predicting again, using the words of Isaiah, that God's people will be fully righteous in the final end-time state of the new creation. In this light, Christ's substitutionary death, which declares people righteous, must be considered theologically essential to the inauguration of the saints into the initial stage of the new creation. They will be consummately declared and actually made righteous when the new creation itself finally comes in its fullness.

On the one hand, the NT mentions Christ's death formally much more than it does the expression "new creation," which occurs rarely. On the other hand, mention of Christ's and believers' resurrection life, which we have seen is new creation, occurs more than does mention of Christ's death and believers' connection with that death, although word-usage statistics alone do not always indicate how important or unimportant a biblical concept is.[23] The reason that resurrection life is mentioned more in the NT may be that it is the goal toward which death worked, and it represents a further historical progression in the accomplishment of redemption.

It is relatively rare for Paul to link formally Christ's death or the death of believers with the idea of new creation (though, as we have seen, it does occur in 2 Cor. 5:14–17; Gal. 6:14–15; Eph. 2:13–15). Nevertheless, it is likely that most of the time when there is mention of Christ's death, included implicitly to some degree is the notion of a beginning separation from the old world, which Gal. 6:14–15 (cf. Gal. 1:4) and 2 Cor. 5:14–17 formally view as an absolutely necessary element leading to the inception of new creation. To prove this would take an extensive essay, which the present project does not allow, since the explicit exegetical evidence for this is scarce. My point here is that Christ's death and believers' connection with it is vitally linked to the notion of new creation. Christ's death paves the way toward new creation, which has some parallel with expectation of the Messiah in Judaism.[24]

We have observed repeatedly that new creation and kingdom are two sides of one coin. Accordingly, it should not be surprising that Jesus's death itself is viewed as establishing his rule. And this is precisely what Heb. 2:14–15 indicates in direct connection to identifying Christ as an eschatological Adam (2:6–9). Hebrews 2:14–15 reads,

> Therefore, since the children share in flesh and blood, He Himself likewise also partook of the same, that through death He might render powerless him who had the power of death, that is, the devil, and might free those who through fear of death were subject to slavery all their lives.

Even before Christ's resurrection, his death itself was the means by which he was able to "render powerless" the devil's power and free those who had been held in slavery to that power. Christ's power is likely linked in some way to the authority of his Adamic office. Thus, his death is a victory over Satan,

---

23. By a very approximate count, words referring to Christ and/or believers' resurrection life appear in about 150 verses of the NT, and words referring to death appear in about 95 verses (based on searching words in the semantic domains for "life" and "death" in Johannes P. Louw and Eugene A. Nida, eds., *Greek-English Lexicon of the New Testament: Based on Semantic Domains*, 2nd ed., 2 vols. [New York: United Bible Societies, 1989]). This count is rough because, e.g., words for "life" can be used negatively for Christ's or the saints' death, together with other complicating factors, such as when verb, noun, or adjective forms for words for "life" appear in the same verse, making any exact count difficult. Also, the concept of resurrection life or death may be expressed without using any of its main synonyms.

24. On which, see *4 Ezra* 7:28–32, where "the Messiah" comes to earth for an extended time and then dies together with all other humans, at which time "the world shall be turned back to primeval silence for seven days, as it was at the first beginnings" (v. 30) (translation in James H. Charlesworth, *The Old Testament Pseudepigrapha*, 2 vols. [New York: Doubleday, 1983–85], 1:537). Although the "age" to come is said to occur after this, the author nevertheless identifies the Messiah's death even with the very beginning of the first creation in Gen. 1.

perhaps understood as divesting the devil's kingdom of his captive subjects.[25] Colossians 2:14–15 strikes almost the same note:

> . . . having canceled out the certificate of debt consisting of decrees against us, which was hostile to us; and He has taken it out of the way, having nailed it to the cross. When He had disarmed the rulers and authorities, He made a public display of them, having triumphed over them through it [the cross].

Verse 14 says that the sins deserving punishment were "taken out of the way" at "the cross." This means that those for whom Christ died were in a noncondemnatory state at the time immediately after Christ died for them, even before his resurrection. This state is a crucial element necessary for the believer to be transferred into the beginning of the new world. Verse 15 proceeds to affirm that the evil powers (likely spiritual powers) were made powerless at the cross, through which Christ "triumphed over them."[26]

Similarly, John's Gospel directly links God's glory to Jesus judging "the ruler of this world" through his death and even before his resurrection, thus expressing Christ's victory at the cross (John 12:28–34).

Throughout this section, we have been focusing on Christ's death in terms of "active justification" (what was accomplished by Christ for the believer at the time of his death) in contrast but vitally linked to passive justification (when believers personally receive by faith what Christ has actively accomplished by his death on the cross). The two notions are sometimes blurred in Paul's writings.

The Spirit's Gifting Role

The Old Testament Reality

The Spirit of God was active in both Israel and the church. In the old epoch the Spirit empowered prophets, priests, and kings to perform their tasks, and such empowerment could be taken away (cf. Ps. 51:11). This was a gifting function whereby the Spirit imparted ability for people to carry out the commissions of these three roles. These roles often were performed in connection with the temple, especially in the case of priests and kings, as well as sometimes in the case of prophets (e.g., Isa. 6; Ezek. 1–2).

---

25. This is in line with a Christus Victor idea (on which, see Gustaf Aulén, *Christus Victor* [New York: Macmillan, 1969]), according to which Christ's death at the cross was a triumph over the devil and the powers of evil and liberated people held captive by them in sin.

26. The NASB margin notes the translation "having triumphed over them through it" (i.e., the cross) at the end of v. 15. The Greek phrase at the end of that verse, *en autō*, seems to have its antecedent in "the cross" ("through it") at the end of v. 14, though it may refer to "God" ("through him"), in which case it could still refer to God's work through Christ at the cross, though it possibly could refer to God's work through the resurrection. Here I do not have space to elaborate further on this problem.

The Corresponding Inaugurated End-Time Reality

The Spirit gifted Christ to perform the three roles of prophet, priest, and king. At his ascension Christ sent forth the Spirit on all his people to gift them to be prophets, priests, and kings when they identify with Christ by faith. To be more precise, the Spirit enabled the church to assume the revelatory position that had been carried out by prophets, priests, and kings in the OT. However, this revelatory position was even greater than any OT person could achieve because the climactic revelation of Christ was greater than any revelation in the former age of prophetic anticipation.[27] In addition to elevating people to this new and escalated revelatory position of prophet, priest, and king in Christ, the Spirit also distributes a number of individual gifts to different people. All have some gifts, but not all have the same gifts (see Rom. 12:6–8; 1 Cor. 12–13; Eph. 4:7–13; 1 Pet. 4:9–11). All these gifts, to one degree or another, are ways that believers function as a body and in their position of being prophets, priests, and kings.[28]

Accordingly, the Spirit was selective in gifting people in the OT, but there was a democratization of the Spirit among God's people in the new age. There are at least two reasons for this democratization. First, whereas in the OT the Spirit gifted only prophets, priests, and kings, in the new age all of Christ's people are gifted by the Spirit because they are "in" Jesus, the ultimate prophet, priest, and king. Second, whereas in the OT the Spirit often gifted prophets, priests, and kings in some connection to the temple, in the new age all of Christ's people employ their gifts in service in the temple because they are all "in" Jesus, the true temple.[29]

The Corresponding Consummated End-Time Reality

At the consummation the Spirit will complete his work of placing all of God's people in the revelatory position of prophets, priests, and kings, a work that began at Pentecost and that continued throughout the church age. The Spirit will complete this threefold work by resurrecting them from the dead and placing them in the new heaven and earth.

Christians are presently priests (1 Pet. 2:5; Rev. 1:6; 5:10) and dwell in the holy place of the unseen temple (Rev. 1:12, 20; 2:1, 5; 11:1–4). However, when they receive resurrection bodies, they will be in the position of the high priest, dwelling in the holy of holies in the new creation and in God's glorious intimate and special revelatory presence (Rev. 22:4–5).

27. See an elaboration of this in the discussion of Matt. 11:11–13 (chap. 13, in the excursus, under the heading "Other Examples of the Unexpected and Transformed Presence of the Inaugurated Eschatological Kingdom"), where believers are viewed as being in a greater revelatory position than even John the Baptist.

28. This is especially evident in the gifting functions in 1 Cor. 12–14; Eph. 4:7–13.

29. See the discussion in chap. 18 on the Spirit's role in creating the church as the temple in Acts 2.

God's people have begun to be prophets, though their prophetic knowledge is not eschatologically complete, and they do not have a full understanding of how OT prophecy will be finally fulfilled (cf. 1 Cor. 13:12). Final fulfillment will flesh out details previously unknown, and the Spirit will enable the saints to be in the full revelatory presence of God, and then they will understand the final phase of fulfillment.

And while believers have begun to reign with Christ as kings in the midst of opposition (Rev. 1:6, 9; 2:26–27; 5:10), their kingship will reach its final form in the new heaven and earth, where they will rule together with Christ without any elements of opposition (Rev. 22:1, 5).

The Resurrection as Regeneration or New Creation by the Spirit[30]

The Old Testament Reality

In addition to the gifting function of the Spirit, a related issue that arises is the role of the Spirit in new creation and spiritual renewal. My discussion earlier in this book of the Spirit's role in giving new life concerned the OT prophecies that the Spirit would resurrect people in the eschatological age (see Ezek. 36–37). Although the OT looks forward to the Spirit's work of eschatological resurrection, is it not true that OT saints went through the process of unbelief to belief, and thus went from an unbelieving unspiritual condition to a new spiritual condition? Certainly this was the case, but this new spiritual condition is never called "resurrection" or "new creation" in the OT era, as it later is in the NT. Israelites are commanded, "Circumcise your heart, and stiffen your neck no longer" (Deut. 10:16), and are told, "Make yourselves a new heart and new spirit! For why will you die, O house of Israel?" (Ezek. 18:31). However, the majority of the nation never obeyed this command, though we must presume that the faithful remnant did. This is very close to new-creational language, especially since the contexts of Deuteronomy (e.g., Deut. 30:6) and Ezekiel (e.g., Ezek. 36:26; 37:1–14) use the same language in prophecies that will be fulfilled in Israel in the latter days. Strikingly, Gal. 4:29 affirms that OT believers were indeed "born according to the Spirit": "But as at that time he [Ishmael] who was born according to the flesh persecuted him [Isaac] who was born according to the Spirit, so it is now also." The Galatians text shows a remarkable continuity between the Spirit's regenerating work in OT believers and what we find to be the case later in NT believers.

The Corresponding Inaugurated End-Time Reality

The OT looks forward to the Spirit's work of eschatological resurrection of body and spirit, and in the church age this prophecy begins fulfillment.

---

30. For further elaboration of this section, see chaps. 9 and 17.

The Spirit's role in giving new life that was prophesied in the OT began to be fulfilled in the ascended Jesus, who sent forth the Spirit to gift and regenerate those who became added to the church (e.g., Acts 2:30–33; 1 Cor. 15:45).[31] The NT provides abundant evidence that the Spirit began to create new-creational life in believers. The inaugurated phase of the eschatological resurrection life was spiritual. This was an unexpected form of fulfillment, since the body was not raised along with the spirit, but physical resurrection would follow at the end of the age. This was a staggered fulfillment that was a temporal transformation of the OT prophecy that apparently predicted that the raising of soul and body would occur at the same time. Another unexpected and transformed fulfillment of the resurrection prophecy was that the Messiah would experience physical resurrection apart from those whom he represented, and that they would experience such resurrection only after a certain interim period (cf. 1 Cor. 15:4 with 15:20–23).

But we have seen that the Spirit regenerated people in the OT just as in the NT. This presents a problem. The NT describes the regeneration of people as a part of being a new eschatological creation through identification with Christ's resurrection, which was the inception of the new creation. The eschatological resurrection and new creation began only with the coming of Christ and did not exist in the OT epoch. So how could Israelites be "born according to the Spirit" in the pre-Christian period?

The most plausible answer seems to be that such saints were spiritually renewed on the basis of the future coming of the new creation and resurrection. In a similar manner, as we saw earlier in this section, Rom. 3:25 says that OT believers were not punished for their sins "because in the forbearance of God He passed over the sins previously committed," but finally in Christ he punished those sins at the cross (Rom. 3:19–28). Such people were allowed to enter into God's presence in heaven at death despite their sinfulness because God was delaying the punishment of their sin until the coming of Christ.

The Corresponding Consummated End-Time Reality

At the end of the age the Spirit will physically resurrect all God's people, thus making them part of the new creation, and will cause them to inhabit the new creation forever.[32] Accordingly, their beginning new creation of the heart (or inner "man" or spirit) is itself completed, since it was only formerly inaugurated. Likewise, what also began spiritually in this age will be completed by physical resurrection of the body in the age to come.

---

31. On this, see Richard B. Gaffin Jr., "The Last Adam, the Life-Giving Spirit," in *The Forgotten Christ: Exploring the Majesty and Mystery of God Incarnate*, ed. Stephen Clark (Nottingham, UK: Apollos, 2007), 191–231.

32. On which, see the full implications of Isa. 44:3–5; Ezek. 37:1–14; see also 1 Cor. 15:45 in comparison with 15:35–58.

The Temple and the Church's Mission[33]

The Old Testament Reality

God has dwelled with his people from the very beginning in various forms of temple dwellings. Eden was the first sanctuary, where Adam was to expand God's presence throughout the earth but failed. At that time Adam and Eve were cast outside the immediate presence of God in his temple. Temple reestablishment began formally again with Noah and the patriarchs, with the latter building altars in garden settings on mountains in the promised land to replicate that of the primeval temple and to point forward to God's dwelling in the big temple in Jerusalem. Even with the establishment of the large temple in Jerusalem, only the high priest could stand in God's immediate presence once a year on the Day of Atonement. The temple was dominated by sacrifices for the forgiveness of people's sin, which separated them from their God, whose glorious revelatory presence was sequestered in the back room of the temple in the holy of holies.

The Jerusalem temple itself was symbolic of the invisible and visible heavens and the earth. This cosmic symbolism of the temple pointed forward to the eschatological heaven and earth, which would become God's cosmic temple, where his immediate revelatory presence would dwell universally. Other prophecies also looked forward to God's final temple in the new creation (e.g., Ezek. 40–48). The cosmic symbolism of the temple included the notion that some in Israel should have been cognizant that God purposed to extend his tabernacling presence over the whole earth. Accordingly, they should have been aware that they were designed to be agents in this extension of the temple and thus motivated to be a "kingdom of priests" (Exod. 19:6), mediating between the nations and God, moving outward to spread the divine temple presence over the nations. Therefore, the cosmic symbolism of the temple represented Israel's mission to the world. The repeated attempts to build God's temple ended in failure and became typological adumbrations of the true eschatological temple to come in the future.

The Corresponding Inaugurated End-Time Reality

The eschatological temple expected by OT prophets was truly and irreversibly inaugurated in Jesus. His incarnation represented the beginning of God's presence coming out of the holy of holies: "And the Word became flesh, and tabernacled among us, and we beheld His glory, glory as of the only begotten from the Father" (John 1:14). Jesus especially inaugurated the end-time temple through his resurrection (John 2:19–21). In John 2:19–21 Jesus indicates that his resurrection is the rebuilding of the temple because resurrection is the beginning of the cosmic new creation (as I have argued throughout this book), to which Israel's old temple symbolically pointed. At Pentecost Jesus

---

33. For further elaboration of this section, see chap. 19.

sent his Spirit to incorporate the church into his temple (Acts 2). Accordingly, all those who identify with Jesus are identified with his resurrection, and the Spirit builds them into Jesus as the temple. This is why Paul, Peter, and John (in Revelation) refer to the church as the temple of God.

During the interadvent period, as the church evangelizes, those who believe continue to be added to the temple, and thus the temple expands with God's spiritual presence among more and more people in the way it should have in the first place in Eden and in Israel. Therefore, the mission of Adam and Israel to expand the temple of God's presence is taken up by Christ and the church. They finally accomplish the task left undone by both Adam and Israel. Accordingly, to understand the church as the end-time temple of God is to understand that the church's mission is to spread God's presence throughout the earth through the gospel. The temple prophecies were fulfilled in an unexpected and transformed manner. That is, they began fulfillment not in an architectural structure, which some OT prophecies appeared to foresee, but rather through Christ in his earthly ministry and then resurrection and subsequently through the Spirit's residing in God's people.

The Corresponding Consummated End-Time Reality

When Jesus returns the final time as the last Adam, he will successfully complete this temple building and expanding of God's indwelling presence by destroying the old cosmos. At that time the unseen eschatological temple that had begun to be built spiritually during the church age will weather the destruction of the old world and pass through and become part of the visible physical final construction of a new cosmos, all of which will be Christ's and God's temple (Rev. 21:22). In this cosmic temple the divine glory will abide forever and ever, in every nook and cranny of the new creation. This worldwide temple is a fulfillment of the typological function of the OT temple in that it is a transformation of the old temple's symbolism of the cosmos. Various sections of Israel's old temple that symbolized parts of the coming new heavens and earth find their corresponding realization in that new cosmos, when it finally comes. Israel's old temple was but a little model of the coming cosmos that would be expanded and transformed into the entire new creation. In Christ the original mission of the Eden sanctuary is finally fulfilled on behalf of his people, who had begun to spread the temple during the interadvent era.

Christ as the Image of God: The Last Adam, Son of Man, and Son of God

The Old Testament Reality

I have discussed in some detail how the first Adam was to rule, multiply, and fill the earth (see, e.g., the first part of chap. 2). As such, he was to be a

913

faithful son of God, fully reflecting the image of his divine Father. And we saw how he miserably failed. The commission given to him was passed on to Noah and the patriarchs, and they were to act as an Adamic son of God and do what Adam should have done. In this respect, the commission was passed on to Israel as a nation, who were also to act as a corporate son of God or a corporate Adam. They too failed, like Noah and the patriarchs, but beginning with the patriarchs a promise was mixed in with the passing on of the Adamic commission. This promise was that a "seed" would finally bring about the blessing that Adam should have. Accordingly, the OT also prophesied that this promise would come to be fulfilled in eschatological Israel.

The Corresponding Inaugurated End-Time Reality

Christ came to restore the marred image of God in humanity by completely doing what Adam should have done. He accomplished this restoration through his ministry of obedience, healing, teaching, and then climactically through his death and resurrection.[34] In doing so, he was functioning as a truly faithful eschatological Adam, son of man (i.e., of Adam), and son of God. In this respect, Christology is eschatology (or vice versa) because Christ's activities are centered as eschatologically establishing activities (e.g., in his role as the Son of Man and Son of God).[35]

The Corresponding Consummated End-Time Reality

At the end of history Christ will come a final time to consummate all things. In this respect, he will have brought to completion his Adamic rule in this redemptive-historical age (1 Cor. 15:20–28). In particular, he will complete multiplying his progeny by giving them physical resurrection life (1 Cor. 15:20–23), and he will finish the victory and rule that he began to accomplish over the enemy (including death) at his first coming (1 Cor. 15:24–27). He will then again be seen as God's completely faithful Adamic "son" (1 Cor. 15:28).

The Image of God: The Adamic Sonship of Christ in Relation to Believers

The Old Testament Reality

All people throughout history, even before coming into a redemptive relationship with God, are still in the image of God, though that image is distorted (e.g., Gen. 9:6; James 3:9) because of Adam's representative sin. We have seen

---

34. On which, see the first part of chap. 13, where I tried at length to demonstrate this conceptually in the Synoptic Gospels.

35. On which, see Beasley-Murray, "Eschatology of the Fourth Gospel," 101.

that the NT describes Christ as the last Adam, Son of Man (i.e., Adam), and Son of God coming to restore the marred image of God in those who believe in and identify with him.[36] Those who identify with Christ's Adamic sonship also become identified as "adopted sons" of God (e.g., Rom. 8:15, 23). This is an essential part of the commencement of the new creation.

But were not pre-Christian saints also sharers in the redemptive restoration of the image of God?

The Corresponding Inaugurated End-Time Reality

There is no explicit scriptural evidence that speaks to the issue of whether OT saints were in the beginning stage of the restored image of God. However, there are OT allusions in the NT that appear to address this to some degree.

My analysis of Col. 3 in the chapter on the image of God (chap. 14 under the subheading "The Image of the Last Adam in Colossians 1:15–18; 3:9–10") argued that the point in Col. 3:9–10 is that believers have left their identification with the old world and Adam and have begun to be identified with Christ's resurrection: they "have stripped off the clothes of the old man" and "have donned the clothes of the new man," the resurrected Christ, the eschatological Adam. They are those who have begun to be identified with the new creation in Christ. Here the tone is on new creation in the divine image.

The references to clothing in the Colossians passage may be an allusion to Gen. 3. Genesis 3:7 says that directly after their sin, Adam and Eve tried ineffectively to cover their sinful nakedness by their own autonomous efforts: "they sewed fig leaves together and made themselves loin coverings." However, in an apparent expression of their beginning restoration to God after the fall (esp. in light of 3:20), Gen. 3:21 says, "The Lord God made garments of skin for Adam and his wife, and clothed [LXX: endyō] them." The clear implication is that their first suit of clothes was removed and replaced by divinely made clothing, indicating that the humanly made clothing was associated with their alienated condition and sinful shame (Gen. 3:7–11) and was an insufficient covering for those being reconciled to God. The new set of clothes given to Adam and Eve in Gen. 3:21 likely possessed some degree of glory or pointed to a greater inheritance of the final glorious clothing of immortality, ideas that seem to lie behind the image of clothing in Col. 3:10.

I concluded this earlier discussion by saying that Paul seems to be using the Gen. 3 "clothing" language analogically and, we may add, perhaps typologically: believers are seen to have discarded the clothes of the old, fallen Adam and have been clothed with the attire of the last Adam, with which Adam himself was proleptically clothed to indicate his restored relationship with God and renewed status in the divine image.

---

36. See the first part of chap. 13. Much of what I discussed about Christology is contained in that chapter.

The most that can be said is that saints of the old covenant, following the pattern of the first Adam, began to experience an actual renovation in the image of God, but this renovation was an anticipation of the renovation that Christ, the last Adam, would accomplish in his new-covenant people. There is also a connection between God's people being in the image of God and also being part of God's new temple. If Christ is the temple of God and Christians are a part of this temple and live in the context of this temple, then it is appropriate that they, like Adam in the Eden sanctuary and Christ as the last Adam in the end-time sanctuary, are created in the renewed image of God to be set up as God's images in his new temple.

The Corresponding Consummated End-Time Reality

When Christ returns a final time and raises his people from the dead, they will be raised in the full end-time image of the last Adam (1 Cor. 15:45–54), since they are identified with his image in the interim period and will be fully conformed to him at the end (Phil. 3:21; 1 John 3:2). They began to reflect Christ's glorious image during the church age (2 Cor. 3:18) and will do so completely, both spiritually and physically, at the final day (2 Thess. 1:10, 12).

The Covenant

At points throughout this book I have discussed the covenant (e.g., chap. 21 under the subheading "Hebrews"), though I have not addressed it as a major topic. The discussion here is a limited attempt to relate more formally so-called covenant theology to the overall argument of this book. How does covenant relate to the pre-Christian believers and to those living in the Christian age?

The Old Testament Reality

At the beginning of chapter 2, I addressed the subject of God's commission to Adam in Gen. 1–3 to be God's vice-regent and high priest. The focus was on the notion of ruling over and subduing creation, which first came to expression in whether Adam would carry out God's command in Gen. 2:16–17. Genesis 3 reveals that this also entailed whether Adam would faithfully guard the garden sanctuary from threats to its peaceful existence. I labored to show that there were several indications of escalated eschatological blessings that Adam would enjoy if he faithfully obeyed and carried out his commission. Among such heightened blessings were:

1. no more threats from evil;
2. eternal and incorruptible physical and spiritual life;

3. an unending and absolute kingship;
4. unending physical and spiritual rest;
5. living in the context of an incorruptible creation;
6. he, his progeny, and the cosmos in their consummated state reflecting more greatly the glory of God.

These blessings were contingent on Adam's successful obedience to the Gen. 2:16–17 command, especially as it was to find expression initially in his encounter with the predatory serpent. This was to be the climactic test of his fealty to God. Upon such an act of fidelity, he would have received the escalated blessings, which also would have been passed on to his progeny, who would have been born as children of life, not of death. This implies that Adam was a representative figure for his progeny, an implication that Paul draws out explicitly in Rom. 5:12–21.

My attempted contribution to support the traditional argument that there was a "covenant of works" in Eden is the adducing of these elevated blessings or conditions. One can speak of the prefall conditions as an original creation and of the yet-to-come escalated creation conditions as a consummate, eschatologically enhanced stage of final blessedness. The period leading up to the reception of these escalated conditions would be the time when it would be decided whether Adam would obey or disobey (traditionally referred to as the period of "probation" or "testing"). These heightened conditions are a telltale indication that Adam was in a covenant relationship with God, obedience to which would bring great reward. Thus, if Adam faithfully obeyed, he would receive greater eternal blessings, but if he disobeyed, he would receive the curse of death. The discernment of escalated blessings on the condition of faithful obedience is an indication that Adam was never intended to continue unendingly in the prefall conditions in which he lived prior to his sin. Rather, there was to be a climactic blessing or judgment in response to his obedience or disobedience. Although the word "covenant" is not used in Gen. 1–3 to describe the relationship between God and Adam, I argued that the concept of a covenant is there.

In chapter 2, I also traced a pattern throughout the OT in which Adam's covenantal commission was passed on through such representative redemptive-historical figures as Noah, Abraham, Isaac, Jacob, and Israel and its kings. None could perfectly fulfill the Adamic commission passed on to them. At the same time, I also observed that mixed with the repeated passing of the commission, beginning with Abraham, was the promise that a "seed" would carry out the Adamic commission. Even in the OT this "seed" was identified with an eschatological king (see Gen. 22:17–18 and its use in Ps. 72:17, which in the context of a psalm is about the ideal end-time Israelite king).[37]

37. See likewise, e.g., Ps. 8.

The Corresponding Inaugurated End-Time Reality

The NT identifies Jesus as this eschatological king (Heb. 2:5–16) and "seed" of Abraham (Gal. 3:16) who has carried out the task of Adam.[38] Jesus has fully carried out the Adamic commission (i.e., the covenant of works), and he represents his spiritual progeny in this, so that they are also identified with him in this obedience, though they did not personally participate in it.[39]

In this respect, the Mosaic covenant was primarily a republication of the Adamic covenant, although, like the Abrahamic, it was intermingled with promises of salvation through a coming messianic leader who would do what Adam had failed to do. The mandates of this "old covenant" would not be obeyed, and the "new covenant" would be a republication of the Adamic one, but with the primary view of the Messiah carrying out the Adamic covenant on behalf of his people. This task of the Messiah would include his own death for their violations of that covenant and his resurrection for their identification with his glorious Adamic image.[40]

In this light, the concept of the covenant is a crucial strand of the biblical-theological storyline, being inextricably linked to whether Adam would inherit escalated blessings of ruling over a new creation. The first Adam failed to obtain those blessings, but the last Adam was faithful and inherited those eschatological blessings and represented his people in doing so, in order that they would inherit along with him.

The Corresponding Consummated End-Time Reality

We saw in an earlier chapter on Gen. 2–3, which I rehearsed just above, that there would be a sixfold bestowal of escalated blessings for Adam's covenantal obedience. In reality, these were promised eschatological blessings that the first Adam forfeited and the last Adam inherited. However, the last Adam, who perfectly carried out what the first Adam should have, received all these escalated and consummated blessings at his resurrection and ascension, and

---

38. For discussion in this respect of Eph. 1:22, see chap. 15 under the subheading "The Expectations for Adam's Obedience and the Application of These Expectations to Other Adam-Like Figures and Finally to Christ."

39. Some theologians refer to this as a "covenant of grace" whereby Christ, as the last Adam, agreed to be under the "covenant of works" in order to execute what the first Adam failed to do. Christ did this on behalf of those whom he represented, on condition that they believe in him, and so they are identified with his carrying out of the Adamic covenant (see Louis Berkhof, *Systematic Theology* [Grand Rapids: Eerdmans, 1976], 214, 270–71).

40. The references to "old" and "new" covenants primarily in mind here are those in Jer. 31:31–34; 32:40; 33:20–21; Ezek. 37:26; and the references to "covenant" in Heb. 7–12. Although I discussed these texts in earlier chapters, much more discussion is needed to establish the point, which the limits of the present project do not allow. For a biblical theology of the covenant throughout Scripture, see Scott W. Hahn, *Kinship by Covenant: A Canonical Approach to the Fulfillment of God's Saving Promises*, AYBRL (New Haven: Yale University Press, 2009).

in doing so he represented his people so that they are identified with obtaining these blessings. Thus, for all intents and purposes, the consummation has come personally for Christ in his resurrection and ascent to heaven. In this sense, we can say that the consummate "end" has already come for Christ as an individual. Christians are identified vicariously with Christ their representative in obtaining these blessings, but they do not experience the consummate form of the blessings existentially (e.g., resurrection of the body and perfection of spirit).

That Christ has fully inherited these blessings and that the consummate "end" has already come for him, however, requires some qualification. It is true that Christ has entered the unseen dimension of the new creation in his newly created resurrection body, but this sphere of the heavenly new creation has not yet been consummated physically. It will be so consummated when the old cosmos is destroyed and this heavenly dimension of the new creation becomes the only real dimension: "I saw the new Jerusalem, coming down out of heaven from God" (Rev. 21:2).[41]

Recall that during the interadvent epoch Christ's followers are identified with these consummate blessings through the representation of Christ and have begun to participate in an inaugurated stage of the blessings. At the Messiah's final advent, his people will existentially and personally experience the consummation of the blessings that Christ has already inherited:

1. they will reign as kings with Christ,
2. with a resurrected spirit and body that are incorruptible,
3. which is in a new, incorruptible cosmos;
4. there will be no satanic opposition to their rule;
5. they will perfectly reflect God's glory in their new existence and
6. find complete, never-ending rest.

At this time also, Christ's own reign will reach an even greater consummation because he will reign *in the environment of a final, consummated cosmos.*

At this time, the new covenant will be consummated. The consummate covenantal blessings that Christ already personally inherited by his faithful

---

41. When God destroys the old cosmos, he will re-create the new one from the elements of the old destroyed world, an analogy with the resurrection body, which will be the raising and the renewal of the old body. Thus, there is some kind of continuity between the old creation and old body and the new creation and new body. How does God's creation of the new cosmos out of the destroyed elements of the old cosmos relate to the portrayal of the new creation and new Jerusalem descending from heaven to earth? One possible view is that the unseen dimension that Rev. 21:2 portrays as descending from heaven is somehow combined with God's creating, and the two are combined to form the "new creation." This is pointed to by the juxtaposition of allusions to prophecies of new creation from Isa. 65:17 and 66:22 in Rev. 21:1 (so also allusions to new creation from Isa. 43:18–19 in Rev. 21:4–5), where the focus is on God's creating activity and the picture of the new Jerusalem's descent in 21:2.

obedience, which represented his people, are consummated among his people personally in the final form of the new cosmos.

Distinguishing Marks of the Covenant Community

We saw earlier (esp. chaps. 23–24)[42] that there are several distinguishing marks of God's genuine covenant community.

Jesus as the Ultimate Identifying Mark of the Church as True Israel[43]

THE OLD TESTAMENT REALITY

One became a part of true Israel in the OT epoch either by being born into the community and then responding positively to God's revelation or by coming from outside the community to the land of Israel and joining the Israelite community by believing in God's revelation and identifying with the distinguishing marks of that community (receiving circumcision, obeying the dietary laws, worshiping at the temple, etc.).

The OT prophesied that in the latter days gentiles would make pilgrimage to Israel, become a part of Israel, and not merely be redeemed people who maintain the name "gentiles." Yet these OT prophecies did not envision that the gentile identity of these converts to Israel would be completely erased, although they would come to be identified with Israel and Israel's God. Such eschatologically converted gentiles would become identified with Israel as had gentiles in the past, like Rahab, Ruth, and Uriah, except that they would not have to take on the distinguishing nationalistic identification tags of ethnic Israel, as gentile converts had done formerly. Their gentile identity would not be eradicated, but they would still come to have a greater identity as true Israelites.[44]

THE CORRESPONDING INAUGURATED END-TIME REALITY

The one difference, however, between converted gentiles of the past and those in the future eschaton, which is revealed more clearly in the NT (e.g., Eph. 2:12, 19; 3:4–6), is that the latter did not have to move to geographical Israel. Old Testament prophets appeared to predict that in the end-time, converted gentiles would make a pilgrimage to Israel. But the NT reveals that such gentiles do not have to move to the Middle East, be circumcised, worship at the temple, obey dietary laws, observe holy days, and follow the other laws distinguishing national Israel from the nations. Rather, in the end-time period

---

42. Although chaps. 20–22 also fall generally into this category.

43. This subsection is a brief summary of chaps. 20–21.

44. For elaboration on this, see chap. 20 under the heading "The Old Testament Notion of Gentiles Becoming Latter-Day True Israel as Background for the New Testament Presupposition That the Church Is True Israel."

it had been revealed that gentiles who identify with Jesus, the true Israel, would become part of true Israel and the temple in Christ and would be circumcised by his death and made clean in him. Jesus as the true Adam/Israel is the only ultimate identification tag that transcends gentile identification marks or the old nationalistic Israelite identifying marks of the law.

This NT revelation is called a "mystery" in Eph. 3:6. The mystery is that "the Gentiles are fellow heirs and fellow members of the body, and fellow partakers of the promise in Christ Jesus through the gospel" (cf. the context of Eph. 3:3–6). The core of this mystery is twofold: (1) the Messiah reconstituted true end-time Israel; (2) in the end-time period gentiles now identify with Jesus, the true Israel, and do not have to make a pilgrimage to geographical Israel and identify with the nationalistic identification tags of the old theocratic nation. Rather, gentiles now become true Israelites by moving to Jesus.

These two inaugurated end-time truths were not as clear from the OT prophetic vantage point "as it has now been revealed to His holy apostles and prophets in the Spirit" (Eph. 3:5). Ephesians 3:4 terms this lack of clarity a "mystery." Here again we find a transformation of prophetic expectations that goes beyond yet grows out of the OT prophetic perspective, since the Messiah was considered to be one who would represent Israel as its end-time king (Dan. 7:13–27; Isa. 49:3–6; 53), just as kings throughout Israel's history represented the nation. This messianic representative element was at least part of the seed that was developed into the more fully flowered truth of the "mystery" of Eph. 3:3–6.

THE CORRESPONDING CONSUMMATED END-TIME REALITY

At the final coming of Christ and the very end of the age, all of eschatological Israel, both believing ethnic Jews and gentiles, will have been restored to God through Jesus, the true Israel. They will experience ultimate physical resurrection of body and soul and will enter and dwell in the promised land and the new Jerusalem, which is none other than the entire completed new creation. In doing so, these new-covenant saints will join with old-covenant saints, who also will be resurrected in Christ. This conclusion is not to be construed as a narrow, parochial perspective, since it should be recalled that Israel was to be a corporate Adam. Thus, end-time Israel will also be an end-time Adam, identified with Jesus as their representative true Israel and last Adam.

The Promised Land of Israel as an Identifying Mark of True Israel[45]

THE OLD TESTAMENT REALITY

When the people of Israel were to be restored from exile, they were to return to the land, where they would build a massive temple and come into intimate

---

45. This section is a very brief summary of chap. 22.

fellowship with God, as well as experience other concomitant promises (summarized above in chap. 19). At the time of the return to the promised land, that land would expand and envelop the whole world in the new creation, so that the whole earth would become coequivalent to Israel's land. We have seen that this promise was not fulfilled in the OT era.

THE CORRESPONDING INAUGURATED END-TIME REALITY

Some commentators believe that Israel's return to the land will not occur in any way until after the final coming of Christ, the Messiah. Others believe that it will never be fulfilled in any literal sense. My argument in this book is that the promise did indeed begin to come to realization in Christ and the church. But how could this be said to have begun in any literal manner, since a physical return of the nation to the actual geographical land did not happen at the first coming of Christ? And the NT does not explicitly mention that Jesus or the church has begun to fulfill Israel's land promises. Additionally, recall that when the fulfillment was to come, Israel's land was to expand and cover the entire new world, which certainly did not happen in Christ or through the work of the church in the present age.

However, in that the resurrection of Jesus, as the true eschatological Israel, is the beginning of the new creation, he is to be seen as the very inception of the land promise.[46] The identification of the church with Christ's resurrection also identifies the church as participating with him as the beginning fulfillment of the same land promise.[47] Furthermore, the NT does affirm that Christ has begun to fulfill the latter-day prophecies of the restoration of "Israel," "Zion," "temple," and "throne of David." Each of these prophetic realities was to be an important parcel of real estate in the coming new land of Israel. In that these prophecies pertained to essential parts of Israel's future landscape, Christ's beginning fulfillment of them in some way is an initial realization of part of the land promises.

These promises were fulfilled in both a physical (Christ's resurrection and physical reign in heaven) and a spiritual manner (his unseen rule from heaven exercised through the Spirit in the church on earth).[48] Consequently, there is a real sense in which the land promise begins to be literally fulfilled in Christ and the believers, who are identified with his resurrection and who rule with him in his temple.

46. See the discussion of Heb. 1:2 in chap. 22 under the subheading "'Already and Not Yet' References to the Land Promise."
47. We saw that several texts indicate this, among which are Rom. 8:18–23; Eph. 1:13–14; Col. 1:12–14 (on which, see chap. 22 under the subheading "'Already and Not Yet' References to the Land Promises").
48. Recall that along with a physical dimension, there was always a spiritual dimension in the "literal" fulfillment of all OT prophecies pertaining to God's Spirit and presence being a crucial component.

The Corresponding Consummated End-Time Reality

The land promises that began fulfillment in Jesus and the church will be consummated in the new creation, where the temple and the land overlap and are viewed as covering the total territory of the new creation. At this time, all the prophecies about Israel, the land, David's throne, the temple, and the kingdom, which overlap and began fulfillment in Christ and the church, will be brought to completion.[49]

Sabbath Observance

The Old Testament Reality and the Corresponding Inaugurated End-Time Reality

The weekly observance of a Sabbath was an eschatological sign based on God's creation rest and was designed to be observed from the beginning of human existence and throughout the OT era.[50] This Sabbath ordinance is still to be observed by the church until Christ's final coming, at which point the weekly observance will cease. Consequently, this weekly ordinance is binding for all forms of the covenant community throughout history.

Some contend, however, that the Sabbath ordinance was unique to Israel, was not an ordinance before Israel's existence, and is no longer an obligation for the church. My response was that Israel's Sabbath rest was based partly on the Sabbath as a creational ordinance in Gen. 2:2–3 and partly on it as a remembrance of the exodus. I contended that the Sabbath day as Israel was to observe it uniquely in all its detailed requirements, and as a part of the whole system of the nation's calendrical Sabbath observances and festivals, has ceased because that to which it pointed (Christ) has come. Thus, all the detailed ways that Israel was to keep the Sabbath are related to Israel's unique laws as a nation and commemorated that nation's deliverance, but when Christ came he fulfilled that to which the first exodus pointed. Therefore, only the

---

49. My analysis of the land promises here and in chap. 22 is generally in line with the argument of Gary M. Burge, *Jesus and the Land: The New Testament Challenge to "Holy Land" Theology* (Grand Rapids: Baker Academic, 2010), esp. 125–31. Burge contends that "the New Testament relocates the properties of the Holy Land and discovers them in Christ himself" (p. 129) and in his body, the church, throughout the interadvent age. Burge, however, sees the land promises to be fulfilled in the inaugurated interadvent age; he does not see any physical consummation of the land promises in the new creation, nor does he see the inaugurated phase of fulfillment in Christ and the church to be the beginning of the fulfillment of the new-creational land promises. Neither does he see the OT roots for the univeralization of the land promises. See also the earlier book by Walter Brueggemann, *The Land: Place as Gift, Promise, and Challenge in Biblical Faith* (Philadelphia: Fortress, 1977), 167–96. Brueggemann generally follows W. D. Davies, *The Gospel and the Land: Early Christianity and Jewish Territorial Doctrine* (Berkeley: University of California Press, 1974), in holding that Jesus is the central focus of the land promises. Although Bruggemann thinks that Davies has overly spiritualized the land, his explanation of his own position is ambiguous.

50. See the discussion in chap. 23 under the heading "Sabbath Rest in Genesis 2:2–3?"

Sabbath as a creational ordinance carries over into the NT age, an ordinance that, I argued, existed before the creation of Israel as a nation. Not just the detailed Sabbath laws but Israel's entire law, which was the epitome of divine wisdom in the old age and distinguished the nation as unique in relation to other nations, pointed to and was fulfilled in Christ, the greater revelation of divine wisdom in the new age. But the Sabbath as a creational ordinance, which preceded Israel's unique way of observing the Sabbath, and which was part of the reason that Israel kept the Sabbath, continues on as relevant for the church.

This Sabbath now is observed not on Saturday but rather on Sunday, the first day of the week, since that is the day that Christ, as the glorified last Adam, rose from the dead, inaugurated the new creation, and began to enjoy Sabbath rest. Believers in Christ begin to enjoy that rest by virtue of their identification with his resurrection and commemorate the consummation of that rest at the end of the age by setting apart Sunday as a day of worship and fellowship, which fulfills the church's obligation to keep the Sabbath. Thus, for the church, the observance of the Sabbath day looks back to God's rest after his creative work and looks forward to the consummation of rest that has begun to be enjoyed in Christ, to which also God's initial rest in Gen. 2 looked forward.

THE CORRESPONDING CONSUMMATED END-TIME REALITY

Christ began to enjoy complete Sabbath rest when he ascended to God's right hand at the heavenly throne, where he reigns in his bodily resurrected form. Believers are identified with Christ's complete rest through his representation of them, but they begin to enter that rest personally and spiritually only during the church age. When they are resurrected physically at the end of time, they too will experience full Sabbath rest in their completely resurrected body and spirit. That the Messiah could experience full Sabbath rest at his resurrection and ascent, and that his people would experience it only partially during an interadvent age and consummately afterward, was apparently unforeseen in the OT expectation. Again, this represents a transformed, temporal, already–not yet fulfillment.

Ritualistic Signs of Entrance into the Covenant Community: Circumcision and Baptism[51]

THE OLD TESTAMENT REALITY AND THE CORRESPONDING INAUGURATED END-TIME REALITY

Throughout most of redemptive history God's covenant community has had signs symbolizing the entry of a person into the community. Circumcision and

51. For further elaboration of this section, see chap. 24 under the subheading "Baptism."

baptism are two of the signs that designated, respectively, entry into Israel's and the church's covenant community.

Two important backgrounds against which the NT understands baptism are the deliverance of Noah and his family through the waters of the flood and Israel's deliverance through the waters of the Red Sea. I discussed that both backgrounds are associated with ideas of new creation, especially two episodes that we observed in chapter 2 that were part of recapitulations of creation in Gen. 1. These backgrounds served to enhance the new-creational notion of baptism, which symbolizes identification with Christ's death (submerged in the water) and identification with his resurrection (coming up from the water), which is the beginning of new creation.

I also argued that circumcision is another OT backdrop against which baptism is to be understood. Physical circumcision in the OT symbolized the reality of spiritual circumcision of the heart and thus spiritual life. This symbol expressed that a true Israelite was one whose heart had been cut apart from unbelief and sin and was regenerated (cf. Deut. 10:16; Jer. 4:4). Included in this symbolism in Deuteronomy was that physical circumcision of Israel also pointed to the end time, when God would "circumcise the heart," which would result in "life" (Deut. 30:6). This eschatological life is very close to the notion of end-time resurrection life. In fact, I argued that they are one and the same.

Circumcision and baptism were the main signs for entrance, respectively, into the old-covenant and the new-covenant communities, and both expressed dual-oath signs that signified blessing and cursing. I argued from Col. 2, based on allusions to Gen. 17:10–27 and Deut. 30:6, that circumcision not only was analogous to baptism but also was a typological pointer to eschatological spiritual circumcision (which is actually prophesied in Deut. 30), which is equated with baptism. Baptism in this Col. 2 passage connotes identification with Christ, but also the rite of water baptism likely stands in the background. Accordingly, OT circumcision finds its typological transformation in the antitype of baptism because of the death and resurrection of Christ. Accordingly, spiritual circumcision is virtually identical to spiritual baptism. Since water baptism likely stands behind the reference to spiritual baptism in Col. 2, so likewise probably does physical circumcision stand behind spiritual circumcision in the same passage. Thus, in this passage both physical and spiritual circumcision are identified with physical and spiritual baptism.

I also concluded that the application even to infants of the covenantal entry sign continues into the NT age, which is pointed to by the two backgrounds of circumcision and the exodus deliverance, which also included infants. This is also supported by the broad flow of redemptive history whereby the NT end-time blessings encompass broader people groups than in the OT. In this light, to think that a major people group—infants—is excluded from entry into the new-covenant community seems to go against the grain of the otherwise wider span of the NT's inclusiveness of blessing. It is important to recall that even the baptism on condition of profession is a covenantal sign proleptically connoting both blessing and judgment,[52] and that it is a person's perseverance that becomes decisive for whether the blessing or the curse is applied. Thus, infants are considered not definitively "saved" by baptism, but rather to be entering into the sphere where blessings or curses can come upon them depending on their response to the revelation of the covenant church community in which they grow up.

The Corresponding Consummated End-Time Reality

We saw that the new-creational background of baptism in the Noahic flood and Israel's exodus through the Red Sea lends to NT baptism a heightened sense of inaugurated new creation through Christ's death and resurrection, of which the rite of baptism was emblematic. Likewise, I discussed that in the OT circumcision of the flesh symbolized "circumcision of the heart," which would lead and point to end-time life. Further, circumcision was seen to be both analogous to and, in Col. 2, even equated with baptism. Accordingly, both circumcision and baptism concern the life of the new creation, the former being typological of such life, and the latter fulfilling the type and symbolically expressing the confession of entrance into the new creation by those baptized. This symbolic indication of the actual beginning of new creation in the one being baptized is completed at the end of time in that person's resurrection, which is the person's final state of new creation.

In addition, both circumcision and baptism convey a dual covenantal notion of curse and blessing. Those who persevere in faith receive the blessing, while those who do not persevere receive the curse. With respect to baptism, those who endure in their faith are finally resurrected in the flesh because they have been identified with Christ's substitutionary death on their behalf and with his resurrection. Such people also receive the blessing of resurrection life, to which circumcision pointed and baptism is the antitype (i.e., they will be set apart from the old world to the Lord in new-creational life). Those baptized but not persevering in faith, and thus proving to be pseudosaints of the covenant community, will suffer the curse part of the sign of baptism: they will be identified only with the death aspect that it represents. Since they are not identified with Christ's death for them, they must suffer this eternal curse of death themselves. That aspect of circumcision that symbolizes being cut off from the Lord will also find complete latter-day typological fulfillment in those who do not remain faithful to the end.

52. Recall here that part of the background for baptism lies in the waters of the Noahic flood and of the Red Sea at the exodus, both of which involved judgment and redemption.

A Communal Meal[53]

THE OLD TESTAMENT REALITY AND THE CORRESPONDING INAUGURATED END-TIME REALITY

Israel and the church had in common a communal meal as part of their worship. Israelites celebrated the Passover meal to commemorate the nation's exodus deliverance, and Christians celebrate the Lord's Supper to commemorate Christ's redemptive death and to remember that he is coming again to consummate the salvation that he inaugurated. Christ's Last Supper and the eucharistic meal of the early church were explicitly linked to Israel's Passover and hence the exodus. Israel's Passover meal, because it was so closely linked to the exodus event of the Passover, reminded Israel of its exodus redemption and pointed to the new creation. The equivalent NT meal (the Lord's Supper) to Passover is the antitypical correspondence, fulfilling the type of Israel's meal. Likewise, inextricably linked to this typology of the Passover meal, Christ as the final Passover lamb fulfills that to which Israel's Passover lamb pointed (see John 19:36; 1 Cor. 5:6–8). Just as Christ's death is the transformed fulfillment of that to which the Passover lamb pointed, so likewise is the Lord's Supper the transformed equivalent to the old-covenant Passover meal. We have seen that Judaism associated the Passover with the first creation and the coming end of that creation, as well as the renovation of creation, when the Messiah would come and establish the divine kingdom. This tradition reflects the biblical notion that the exodus itself, of which Passover was a part, was a recapitulation of creation and thus portrayed as an episode of new creation.[54] Therefore, the modeling of the Lord's Supper on the Passover meal likely entails some degree of a continued notion of eschatological new creation.

THE CORRESPONDING CONSUMMATED END-TIME REALITY

In my earlier discussion of the Eucharist, the Passover meal was shown to be its OT typological counterpart. We saw that the Passover had overtones that pointed to a coming new creation. Likewise, Christ's institution of the Lord's Supper at Passover carried with it end-time connotations. With regard to the cup, Jesus said, "I will not drink of this fruit of the vine from now on until that day when I drink it <u>new</u> with you in my Father's kingdom" (Matt. 26:29) (cf. Mark 14:25; Luke 22:18 ["until the kingdom of God comes"]). In addition, every time the church celebrated the Lord's Supper, it "proclaimed the Lord's death until he comes" (1 Cor. 11:26). Thus, even the backward glance at this meal to Christ's death entailed a secondary notion of a reminder

53. For further elaboration of this section, see chap. 24 under the subheading "The Lord's Supper."

54. On which, see chap. 2 under the heading "The Repeated Cosmic Judgment and New Creation Episodes of the Old Testament."

that he was coming again and that the inaugurated form of the Lord's Supper would cease at that time.

The Eucharist carries eschatological notions of new creation, kingdom, and Christ's coming, which were inaugurated during his earthly ministry and ascension. The inauguration of the new creation and kingdom, as I have argued throughout the book, will be perfected at the eschaton, when Christ returns for the final time. At that time, since the Lord's Supper has multiple inaugurated eschatological connotations, it is likely that there will be the second and full course of the eschatological meal that Christ inaugurated. This will be the last installment of the eschatological banquet prophesied in Isa. 25:6: "The Lord of hosts will prepare a lavish banquet for all peoples on this mountain; a banquet of aged wine, choice pieces with marrow, and refined, aged wine."[55] This last banquet will occur at the time that God "will swallow up death for all time" and "will wipe tears away from all faces" (Isa. 25:8), which Revelation sees to take place in the final form of the new heaven and earth (Rev. 21:4; so also 7:17).[56]

The Lord's Supper also has an already–not yet notion of judgment in 1 Cor. 11:27–32:

> Therefore whoever eats the bread or drinks the cup of the Lord in an unworthy manner, shall be guilty of the body and the blood of the Lord. But a man must examine himself, and in so doing he is to eat of the bread and drink of the cup. For he who eats and drinks, eats and drinks judgment to himself if he does not judge the body rightly. For this reason many among you are weak and sick, and a number sleep. But if we judged ourselves rightly, we would not be judged. But when we are judged, we are disciplined by the Lord so that we will not be condemned along with the world.

Those who partake of the Lord's Supper "in an unworthy manner shall be guilty of the body and the blood of the Lord" (v. 27). Verse 29 explains that to partake unworthily is to "not judge the body rightly"; instead, believers are to "examine" (v. 28) themselves to see if they have "judged [themselves] rightly" (v. 31). "Many . . . are weak and sick, and a number sleep" (v. 30), who have "not judged the body rightly" (v. 29b).[57] Since they have not "judged [themselves] rightly," they "are judged" in the present, so that they "will not be condemned along with the world" in the future eschaton (vv. 31–32). Thus,

55. This seems to be the same banquet spoken of in Luke 13:28–29: "In that place there will be weeping and gnashing of teeth when you see Abraham and Isaac and Jacob and all the prophets in the kingdom of God, but yourselves being thrown out. And they will come from east and west and from north and south, and will recline at the table in the kingdom of God."
56. On which, see Beale, *Revelation*, 1049–50.
57. "Judging the body" likely refers to examining one's relationship with the rest of the "body" of the church. For elaboration of 1 Cor. 11:27–32, see Gordon D. Fee, *First Epistle to the Corinthians*, NICNT (Grand Rapids: Eerdmans, 1987), 558–67, which I have followed here.

the Corinthians were beginning to undergo divine judgment, which was to be viewed as "discipline" (v. 32), not final punishment, since those suffering were genuine believers. This judgment, however, which begins within the covenant community in the suffering of believers, will be consummated by the judgment and condemnation of those outside the community in the world at the last judgment.[58]

The "Elder" Leaders of the Covenant Community[59]

The Old Testament Reality and the Corresponding Inaugurated End-Time Reality

I contended that the office of elder in the church, the new Israel, is to some degree the continuation of the position of elder in Israel. The elders in the new covenant have only full religious authority over the sphere of the new Israel, the church, whereas the Israelite elders had civil authority and, it appears at times, some religious authority in the theocracy.[60]

The redemptive-historical basis and circumstance that led to the establishment of elders in the new-covenantal community was the inaugurated end-time tribulation, especially as that tribulation manifested itself in the form of false teaching and apostasy. This false teaching and apostasy that were taking place were a beginning fulfillment of OT prophecies of the coming end-time trial that would be more intense than any other that Israel had experienced (see, e.g., Dan. 7–12).[61] The new community needed leaders to guard the faith of the fledgling church in order to keep it doctrinally healthy and in order that it might be able to expand and spread robustly. Such robust expansion would result in the beginning fulfillment of the original Adamic commission (also passed on to Israel) to subdue the earth and be a light-bearing agent, spreading the realm of the unseen dimensions of the new creation.

---

58. This is parallel with the "judgment to begin with the household of God" that will be consummated in the final judgment at the very end "for those who do not obey the gospel of God" (1 Pet. 4:17). This is also consistent with 1 Cor. 6:1–6, where Paul says that "saints will judge the world" at the very end of time (v. 2), which means that the Corinthian Christians should begin that eschatological role by judging lawsuits among themselves.

59. For further elaboration of this section, see chap. 24 under the heading "The Church Office of Elder as an Eschatological Necessity Because of the End-Time Tribulation of Deception and of the New Creation."

60. On which, see, e.g., where the elders are inextricably linked with the priests in performing certain roles (Exod. 24:1, 9; Lev. 4:15; 9:1; Num. 16:25; Deut. 31:9; 2 Chron. 5:4; Ezek. 7:26), they are empowered by "the Spirit" to "prophesy" (Num. 11:24–25), they confirm the validity of earlier prophecies (Jer. 26:17–23), and they have some capacity of a teaching role (Deut. 32:7). By the time of the first century AD, Israel's elders more explicitly shared authority in religious affairs together with the chief priests (on which, see J. B. Taylor, "Elders," in vol. 1 of *The Illustrated Bible Dictionary*, ed. J. D. Douglas [Leicester, UK: Inter-Varsity, 1980], 434–35).

61. See the discussion in chap. 24 on this subject of why the church's latter-day tribulation of false teaching and apostasy is worse than anything that had occurred previously in Israel's history.

The Corresponding Consummated End-Time Reality

In the new heaven and earth there will be no need for a group of "elders" to guard the faith of the community, since there will be no false teaching or apostasy there: "nothing unclean, and no one who practices abomination and lying, shall ever come into" the new, eternal cosmos (Rev. 21:27; cf. 21:8; 22:15). Also, every member of the consummated covenant community will be in the position of the high priest of Israel, the highest cultic authority in Israel. In fact, every saint will be even higher than the former high priests: "they shall see His face, and His name shall be on their foreheads" (Rev. 22:4). Whereas Israel's high priests could enter the holy of holies once a year but could not gaze directly on the Shekinah glory of God, all believers in the final form of the new earth (which is the expanded form of the holy of holies)[62] will not only be in God's immediate presence forever and continually but also will gaze directly upon his face.[63]

The Biblical Canon of the Covenant Community

The Old Testament Reality and the Corresponding Inaugurated End-Time Reality

The OT community had a growing collection of Scriptures that was completed in about 400 BC. These Scriptures were God's authoritative word, which guided saints in their beliefs and ethical actions.

Just as Israel has its book of Scriptures from God, so does the church, whose book is an already–not yet eschatological unpacking of the meaning of Israel's book, which continues to be Scripture for the church. Both books are ultimately one, with each redemptive-historical installment throughout the OT into the NT progressively interpreting the earlier. But, since the Bible is one book written ultimately by one divine author, the NT interprets the OT, and vice versa. I argued that part of the motivation for putting the NT oral message into writing was its nature as God's word, its role as part of the foundation for the church, and the desire to preserve it for the duration of the end-time period, since the apostles were aware that this period might last beyond their own lifetimes.[64] Because the OT background for the church's eschatological book is derived partly from Isa. 2:1–3 and Isa. 40–55, notions of eschatological new creation may also hover in the background, since these sections in Isaiah involve prophecies of new creation.

---

62. On this point, see chap. 19.

63. For the notion that all saints stand in the position of an escalated high priest in the new cosmos, see Beale, *Revelation*, 1113–14.

64. On which, see Charles E. Hill, "God's Speech in These Last Days: The New Testament Canon as an Eschatological Phenomenon," in *Resurrection and Eschatology: Theology in Service of the Church; Essays in Honor of Richard B. Gaffin Jr.*, ed. Lane G. Tipton and Jeffrey G. Waddington (Phillipsburg, NJ: P&R, 2008), 232–33.

Accordingly, the church's task of fulfilling the Adamic commission to fill the earth with God's presence includes filling it with the light of God's truth, which is encased in both Testaments. In this respect, the Scriptures are absolutely necessary in carrying out the Adamic commission that was reiterated by Christ in Matt. 28:18–20 (note esp. the last verse):

> And Jesus came up and spoke to them, saying, "All authority has been given to Me in heaven and on earth. Go therefore and <u>make disciples of all the nations</u>, baptizing them in the name of the Father and the Son and the Holy Spirit, <u>teaching them to observe all that I commanded you; and lo, I am with you always, even to the end of the age</u>."

The Scriptures are a necessary basis on which the church is able to "make disciples" of new believers, since people become disciples partly (and crucially) by the church "teaching them to observe all that [Christ] commanded" them. "All that Christ commanded" was first preserved orally and then preserved in writing in the Gospels, part of the NT Scriptures. These Scriptures reveal God's truth that is necessary and sufficient for salvation, sanctification, and honoring God.

THE CORRESPONDING CONSUMMATED END-TIME REALITY

At the end of the church's earthly sojourn, its faithful carrying out of the Adamic commission, reaffirmed by the last Adam, will be instrumental in fulfilling the OT prophecy that "the earth will be full of the knowledge of the LORD as the waters cover the sea" (Isa. 11:9 [cf., almost identically, Hab. 2:14]). This spread of knowledge will be completed by Christ himself at his final return. As full of revelation as the Scriptures are for the church's healthy life, believers still do not have the fuller revelation that will be given at the end. Peter acknowledges even that in Paul's writings there "are some things hard to understand" (2 Pet. 3:16). Paul himself likewise says in 1 Cor. 13:9–13 that during the interadvent age the church has sure and sufficient knowledge for its well-being, but it is still "partial" knowledge that will be completed at the time Christ returns and raises up believers as full "mature" resurrected beings:

> For we know in part and we prophesy in part; but when the perfect [eschatologically complete] comes, the partial will be done away. When I was a child, I used to speak like a child, think like a child, reason like a child; when I became a man, I did away with childish things. For now we see in a mirror dimly, but then face to face; now I know in part, but then I will know fully just as I also have been fully known. But now faith, hope, love, abide these three; but the greatest of these is love.

This is a classic statement of an already–not yet knowledge of God's truth. Paul would have understood that this truth was contained in the OT, and the revelation in the NT community was developing this truth, which was in the process of being inscripturated. When the completion of this age comes, then the church's knowledge will no longer be partial. When we become grown up and a mature "man" (i.e., fully mature humans in resurrected bodies), we "will know fully" God's revelation.[65] At that time, we will be "face-to-face" with God,[66] who will reveal to us what we have not hitherto known.

Conclusion

The distinguishing marks of the Sabbath, baptism in relation to circumcision, the Eucharist, eldership, and the biblical canon are understood differently by various Christian scholars and denominations. These issues are debated because Scripture is not as clear about these as it is about other notions more central to understanding the gospel. Even the topic of whether Jesus is the ultimate representative of the church as true Israel is debated. Nevertheless, my analysis above is an attempt to understand these issues through a biblical-theological approach, realizing that not everyone will agree with the conclusions reached here. Much more could also be said about these subjects, especially baptism (e.g., its modes) and the Lord's Supper.[67] I have tried to discuss these subjects from the perspective of inaugurated eschatology, especially as this pertains to the beginning of the new-creational kingdom, in order to see what light this perspective might shed on the subject. The topic of the biblical canon I leave for another time and place because it has unique problems that I cannot adequately address here.[68]

The Ongoing Nature of the Genuine Believer's Life (Sanctification) in Connection with New Creation

The Old Testament Reality and the Corresponding Inaugurated End-Time Reality

What is the nature of the saints' spiritual growth or experience in the old age and the new age? Systematic theology has termed the nature of the believer's

---

65. Of course, Paul does not think that Christians will be omniscient like God at the end of time, but only that they will know a fuller measure of revelatory truth than they had formerly known.

66. The language of "face-to-face" and "knowing fully" is strikingly similar to "see [God's] face" in Rev. 22:4, which describes all saints being in the new cosmos and in the immediate presence of God, who will "illumine them" (Rev. 22:5).

67. E.g., the debate about transubstantiation and consubstantiation, as well as various Protestant perspectives such as spiritual presence and memorialism.

68. However, for an example of an outline of my own approach, see Herman Ridderbos, *Redemptive History and the New Testament Scriptures*, trans. H. de Jongste, rev. Richard B. Gaffin Jr. (Phillipsburg, NJ: P&R, 1988).

ongoing life "sanctification," a term that I am sufficiently happy to employ. The saints' lives are those that have been "set apart" from the old world and sin and to the service of God. Just as those living in the old epoch experienced a form of genuine beginning salvation that anticipated the experience of salvation in the new epoch, so it is with sanctification, especially since ongoing spiritual growth is the continuation of an initial salvation experience. I contended that sanctification in the NT conveys the idea of a believer who continues increasingly to be set apart from the old creation to the new creation, and who bears fruits in keeping with being a part of the new creation. The same concept of a renewed spiritual being can be found in Psalms, for example. David cries out in Ps. 51:2, 7–10,

> Wash me thoroughly from my iniquity
> And cleanse me from my sin. . . .
> Purify me with hyssop, and I shall be clean;
> Wash me, and I shall be whiter than snow. . . .
> Hide Your face from my sins
> And blot out all my iniquities.
> Create in me a clean heart, O God,
> and renew a steadfast spirit within me.

The whole of the lengthy Ps. 119 refers to various facets of the psalmist's spiritual condition that could hardly be described in more escalated spiritual terms of a NT believer:

> 119:28 "My soul weeps because of grief;
>   Strengthen me according to Your word."
> 119:32 "I shall run the way of Your commandments,
>   For You will enlarge my heart."
> 119:36 "Incline my heart to Your testimonies
>   And not to dishonest gain."
> 119:40 "Behold, I long for Your precepts;
>   Revive me through Your righteousness."
> 119:92 "If Your law had not been my delight,
>   Then I would have perished in my affliction."
> 119:93 "I will never forget Your precepts,
>   For by them You have revived me."
> 119:97 "O how I love Your law!
>   It is my meditation all the day."
> 119:98 "Your commandments make me wiser than my enemies,
>   For they are ever mine."
> 119:99 "I have more insight than all my teachers,
>   For Your testimonies are my meditation."
> 119:143 "Trouble and anguish have come upon me,
>   Yet Your commandments are my delight."

On the one hand, the ongoing experience of the psalmist and others of his time is not linked to a growth in redemptive-historical terms of new creation and of no longer being an "old man" but rather being a "new man" in the Messiah, the last Adam. Nevertheless, all other descriptions of such experience are virtually identical to the Christian saint. It is one's restored relationship with God through his grace that provides the "indicative" reality, which empowers believers to obey God's commands. In Ps. 119 the psalmist can pray, "Give me understanding, that I may learn Your commandments" (v. 73); "Their heart is covered in fat, but I delight in Your law" (v. 70); "Open my eyes, that I may behold wonderful things from Your law" (v. 18). The psalmist's opponents within his own community could not pray this way because they did not have such a renewed relationship with God through which his grace flowed.

This suggests that the experience of the true Israelite was proleptic of that of the Christian's renewed relationship with God through Christ.

The Corresponding Consummated End-Time Reality

The process of God's people being set apart from the old world and to the new creation will reach its completion at the final resurrection, when all saints will be fully set apart to the new creation, both spiritually and physically. Their new-creational fruit of righteousness that they began to bear in the old world[69] will come to full ripeness in the new cosmos and undergo an eternal harvest then because of an unending bearing of perfect spiritual fruit.

In this respect, for example, Ps. 1:3 compares the saint to "a tree firmly planted by streams of water, which yields its fruit in its season, and its leaf does not wither; and in whatever he does, he prospers." This is a description of the ongoing life of the vibrant OT saint (as found also in Jer. 17:7–8). Ezekiel 47:12 alludes to the Ps. 1 description and applies it to the fertile arboreal conditions of the climactic new creation:

> By the river on its bank, on one side and on the other, will grow all kinds of trees for food. Their leaves will not wither and their fruit will not fail. They will bear every month because their water flows from the sanctuary, and their fruit will be for food and their leaves for healing.[70]

Ezekiel 47:1–12 is a depiction intended to be a recapitulation of the garden of Eden, which Ps. 1:3 itself may well echo. In light of the Ezekiel allusion to the psalm, may we conclude that what the psalmist was experiencing was a foretaste of the fertile conditions of the coming new creation? That the Ps. 1:3 believer is experiencing in proleptic manner conditions of the coming

69. On which, see G. K. Beale, "The Old Testament Background of Paul's Reference to the 'Fruit of the Spirit' in Gal. 5:22," *BBR* 15 (2005): 1–38.

70. The underlining represents unique wording or unique conceptual parallels to Ps. 1:3.

new creation is also pointed to by Rev. 22:1–2, which alludes to Ezek. 47:12. Revelation 22:1–2 reads,

> Then he showed me a river of the water of life, clear as crystal, coming from the throne of God and of the Lamb, in the middle of its street. On either side of the river was the tree of life, bearing twelve kinds of fruit, yielding its fruit every month; and the leaves of the tree were for the healing of the nations.

Both Ezek. 47 and Rev. 22:1–2 picture a recapitulation of the original garden of Eden, though in an even more escalated fertile form. Accordingly, Rev. 21:3 says that "there will no longer be any curse" in this final form of Eden, unlike what came to be in the first Eden. Believers receive eternal life from "the tree of life," to which all the redeemed have access and from which Adam was cut off. Although neither Ezek. 47 nor Rev. 22 says that believers themselves are like trees that bear fruit, but rather that they are "healed" by the fruit,[71] the notion conveyed is that they will receive eternal health, not only physically in a renewed body but also spiritually. Their robust, unending spiritual health is suggestive of the notion that they will everlastingly bear spiritual fruit themselves, since it is metaphorically implied that they ingest the "leaves" and receive medicinal healing of body and soul and thus abundant life.[72]

This implication of ingestion of the leaves and close identification with the tree's fruit-bearing property in Rev. 22:2 is explicitly expressed in Rev. 2:7: "To him who overcomes I will grant to eat of the tree of life which is in the Paradise of God."[73] Revelation 22:19 identifies the confessing believer even more closely with "the tree of life" itself: "And if anyone takes away from the words of the book of this prophecy, God will take away his part from the tree of life

---

71. Ezekiel 47:12 mentions only that the trees' "leaves [were] for healing," which in context should not be limited to animals but especially appears to be for humans in light of Gen. 2:22, to which it alludes, and of Rev. 22:1–2, which alludes to Ezek. 47:12 (both the Genesis and Revelation texts apply the tree or its leaves to the benefit of humans).

72. Early Judaism identified saints with the trees of Eden. See, e.g., *Pss. Sol.* 14:3–4 (which alludes to Ps. 1:3); 1QHᵃ XIV:14–19; *2 En.* 8–10; for elaboration on these references, see Beale, *Revelation*, 235–36, 1108, and for fuller discussion of the OT allusions in Rev. 22:1–3, see ibid., 1103–13.

73. The promise of "eating of the tree of life" probably represents an inaugurated reality that will be consummated in the final paradise, since the church of Ephesus has clearly been identified with the temple "lampstand" (Rev. 1:20; 2:1, 5), which in Israel's temple was a recollection of the tree of life, since the lampstand was styled to look like an almond tree (see further Beale, *Revelation*, 235–36). In this respect, could the seven lamps on the lampstand be related to the hymnist's affirmation in 1QHᵃ XV:24: "I will shine with a seven-fold light in the Eden which Thou hast made for Thy glory" (on which, see A. Dupont-Sommer, *The Essene Writings from Qumran*, trans. G. Vermes [Oxford: Blackwell, 1961], 224)? Also, in *Barn.* 11:10–11 the image of eating from the trees of the new creation (so Ezek. 47:1–12; cf. Rev. 22:2) is used to describe the present experience of baptism; *Odes Sol.* 11:16–24 refers to those who are presently identified with the blessing of the trees of paradise (so likewise 20:7).

and from the holy city, which are written in this book." This could merely refer to "the part from the tree of life" from which the persevering believer metaphorically eats, as in Rev. 2:7 and implied in 22:2. However, the language of not inheriting a "part from the tree of life" together with not inheriting "a part from the holy city" points to a closer identification with the tree than merely eating from it, in which the pseudobeliever will not participate but the genuine saint will. This, together with the close connection to access to "the water of life" in 22:17, as in Ps. 1:3 and Ezek. 47:12, points further to the saints' identification with the tree itself.

The Law in Both Testaments in Connection to the Believer's Life

The Old Testament Reality and the Corresponding Inaugurated End-Time Reality[74]

How do God's people in both covenantal periods relate to the law? One conclusion from my earlier discussion of the law in relation to Christian living was that unbelievers do not have the desire or the ability to obey God's law and only stand condemned by it. Those in Christ, in the new creation, have both the desire and the ability to fulfill the law. The same appears to be the case in life under the old covenant, as is evident from the verses from Ps. 119 quoted above that speak of the psalmist's great delight in the law. In contrast to the ungodly (Ps. 119:50–53), the psalmist does not merely delight in the law but actually observes it as a trait of his life (e.g., Ps. 119:22: "Take away reproach and contempt from me, for I keep Your testimonies"; Ps. 119:44: "I will keep Your law continually"). Such statements by the psalmist here and in the preceding section are mere tips of the iceberg of Ps. 119, the entire Psalter, and the OT in general.

We also saw in the chapter on the law that the so-called moral, civil, and ceremonial aspects of the law were to be kept by Israelites, but that with the coming of Christ the civil and ceremonial (i.e., the nationalistically distinguishing laws) are fulfilled in him as the new creation, while the moral laws continue to have the same binding power on Christians. The ceremonial and civil laws function as typological pointers to Christ in the new age (e.g., the laws about the annual Day of Atonement sacrifice are fulfilled once and for all in Christ as the final eschatological sacrifice and, at the same time, as the ultimate and final definitive priest).

The Corresponding Consummated End-Time Reality

At the end of the age the purpose of the OT law will be completed. On the one hand, unbelievers throughout the ages have stood under the law's condemnation

---

74. For further elaboration of this section, see chap. 26 under the heading "The Relationship between Christian Living and Obedience to the Law in the Inaugurated New Creation."

for breaking the law.[75] Their punishment began during their life of separation from God,[76] and after death this separation was intensified with some degree of added suffering. This inaugurated judgment will be consummated on the last day (John 12:48).[77] Thus, God has "fixed a day in which He will judge the world in righteousness" (Acts 17:31) on the basis of his law.[78] The unbelieving dead will finally be "judged from the things which were written in the books, according to their deeds"[79] and "thrown into the lake of fire"[80] (Rev. 20:11–15). Those who do not believe that Christ has taken their punishment for breaking the law will have to suffer that final curse themselves.[81]

On the other hand, the positive prophetic purpose of the law will reach its full goal at Christ's final coming. This is likely the point of Matt. 5:18: "For truly I say to you, until heaven and earth pass away, not the smallest letter or stroke shall pass from the Law until all is accomplished." This "simply means the entire divine purpose in Scripture must take place; not one jot or tittle will fail of its fulfillment."[82] With specific respect to the law more narrowly understood as precepts to obey, Jesus has fulfilled the law perfectly at his first coming, his Spirit inspires his people to begin to fulfill the law during the interadvent age, and they will be resurrected and perfected in observing the law in the new heaven and earth.

But what part of the law will they obey in the new cosmos? We saw that in Christ's first coming he fulfilled the typological parts of the ceremonial and civil law (the final priest, temple, sacrifice, etc.). Likewise, we saw that only the nonnationalistic parts of Israel's law carry over from the old age to the new. In essence, this means that the purely moral parts of the law carry over (though it needs to be remembered that the more nationalistic expressions of the law did have a moral dimension). The reason why there can be no nationalistic

75. Note Rom. 4:15: "For the Law brings about wrath."

76. Cf. John 3:18, 36; Rom. 1:18–32; Gal. 3:10; James 2:10.

77. Here the judgment on "the last day" is based on breaking Christ's "commandment," which is the full end-time interpretation of the law (cf. Matt. 5:17).

78. Cf. Rom. 3:19: "Now we know that whatever the Law says, it speaks to those who are under the Law, so that every mouth may be closed and all the world may become accountable to God."

79. The phrases "the books were opened" and "the things written in the books" (Rev. 20:12) are based on Dan. 7:10b, where the end-time enemy is judged by his unrighteous deeds found in "the opened books" at the last judgment; the repeated expression that people will be judged "according to their deeds" (Rev. 20:12–13) is based on the repeated OT phrase whereby God renders "according to deeds" (LXX of Pss. 27:4 [28:4 MT]; 61:13 [62:12 MT]; Prov. 24:12; Jer. 27:29 [50:29 MT]; cf. Jer. 17:10 ["according to ways"]). The significance of the OT background is that the unrighteous deeds by which people will be judged would have been seen as actions in violation of the law.

80. Revelation 21:8 sees that those who break major parts of the OT law ("unbelievers and abominable and murderers and immoral persons and sorcerers and idolaters and all liars") will be placed "in the lake that burns with fire and brimstone, which is the second death."

81. See Gal. 3:10–14.

82. D. A. Carson, *Matthew 1–12*, EBC (Grand Rapids: Zondervan, 1995), 146.

laws to be obeyed in the church during the interadvent era is that the church in Christ is the beginning of the new creation, and the OT prophesied that there would be no nationalistic distinctions of ethnicity in the new age (Isa. 11:6–12). We saw Christ as a new-creational filter through which the so-called nationalistic tags of the law (or so-called civil and ceremonial aspects of the law) could not pass through to the other side into the beginning form of the new creation. Only the nonnationalistic or purely moral laws could pass through the christocentric filter and could remain valid for God's new-covenant people to obey. This was how the law was eschatologically transformed for Christians from what it was during the epoch of Israel.

But will God's people still be bound to obey the moral law in the eternal state? There is no clear statement in Scripture about this, but these commandments will likely continue, and God's people will do them perfectly from the heart forever.[83] Although there is no direct assertion in Scripture that Adam had God's law written on his heart, I think that it was likely, and that he would have continued to obey the law in perpetuity had he been faithful. If this is a reasonable presupposition, then it is viable to think that the same would be true of all of God's people in the everlasting new world.

Continued Return from Exile and Ongoing Exodus as a Picture of the Ongoing Life of Believers

The Old Testament Reality and the Corresponding Inaugurated End-Time Reality[84]

We noted earlier that the inception of a person's salvation can be viewed as the beginning fulfillment of returning from the exile of Satan and bondage to sin into the presence of God. But this return continues for the true saint because it will not be complete until there is complete return to God in the resurrection body in the new heaven and earth. Saints do not get rid of all their spiritual baggage when they come to know Christ, but they do keep shedding it as they proceed on the restoration highway to the final destination of the new cosmos. This is another angle from which to understand the ongoing life of believers, which Paul and other NT writers sometimes refer to as "sanctification." And since the return from exile is portrayed also as a second exodus, the church's pilgrimage throughout the interadvent epoch can also be viewed as an ongoing coming out of Babylon, and not only as the inception of deliverance from sin and bondage to Satan. This picture also involves that of a continual divesting oneself of the sinful baggage that remains from the

83. Of course, laws about fathers and mothers and husbands and wives will not be relevant because there will be no marriage or bearing of children in the eternal state.
84. For further elaboration of this section, see chap. 25 under the heading "The Ongoing Return from Exile as a Basis for Christian Living."

former life of exile and unbelief. This ongoing, long duration of returning from exile was not foreseen in the OT, so that its fulfillment is temporally transformed into a long, drawn-out, already–not yet period. The nature of the continuing restoration is also transformed in that the OT expectation was to be both spiritual and physical return, but in the inaugurated era it is only a spiritual return, which cannot be seen by unbelieving eyes.

Israelites who were restored to a saving relationship with God in anticipation of the climactic restoration in Christ also continued along a proleptic restoration pathway in the remainder of their walk with God.

The Corresponding Consummated End-Time Reality

At the time of the final resurrection of the body on "the last day" (e.g., John 6:39–40, 44, 54), the saints' pilgrimage on earth in continuing exodus from bondage to "spiritual" Egypt and Babylon (cf. Rev. 11:8; 18:4) will finally end, both spiritually and physically. Since God's people are not yet fully perfected as new creations both spiritually and physically, they are still in partial exile, though continuing to make progress on the restoration highway to the country of their final destination (e.g., Heb. 11:13–16). When they experience the final resurrection and are placed in the full new creation, they will have completely arrived home to the eternal promised land of the new heaven and earth, where the new Jerusalem and temple will be.[85] Their long and arduous journey out of exile finally will be over, and they will experience eternal rest.

Marriage in the New Age[86]

The Old Testament Reality and the Corresponding Inaugurated End-Time Reality

Although not all people are called to marriage (see 1 Cor. 7), it is an institution established at the beginning of creation and continuing until the very end of the age. Our focus passage in discussing marriage was Eph. 5, where Paul quotes Gen. 2:24. This description was to be characteristic of all marriages in the old epoch, even after sin had entered into the world: a man left the authority of his household and cleaved to a wife, and together they established a new family unit (they became "one"). Paul employs this Genesis text in Eph. 5:31 in order to appeal to the prefall creation reality of marriage as a typological pattern that he sees pointing to the unity of Christ as the husband and the church as his bride in the beginning of the new creation. Paul wants husbands

---

85. Indeed, as we saw in chaps. 19 and 22, these two locations are coequal with the promised land of the new creation.

86. For further elaboration of this section, see chap. 26 under the heading "Marriage as a Transformed New-Creational Institution in Ephesians 5."

and wives in the inaugurated new creation to maintain the unity that humans were designed to experience before the fall, which was to be modeled on the initial unity that Adam and Eve shared before their sin (Gen. 2:23). This unity is important because not only is it the initial purpose of marriage according to Gen. 2:24, but also it is a redemptive-historical parable before the onlooking world of the relationship of Christ to the church, especially during the church age. Through the acting out of this marital parable, husbands and wives can teach the world about how Christ loves his people and how his people are to respond to that love and thus become one with him.

Ephesians 5:32 says that Gen. 2:24 is not primarily about the relationship of husbands to their wives but rather about the relationship of Christ to the church, and that this relationship is a "mystery" that is "great." Paul is saying that what appeared to be a pattern describing only the human institution of marriage now describes, in view of Christ's coming and the formation of his church, much more. The pattern of a man leaving his family and becoming one with a wife found in Gen. 2:24 contains within it a mirror image of a greater marriage: the Messiah leaving his heavenly home and Father and becoming united with the church. Until the climax of the age, believers are to view their marriages in this way: wives should faithfully "respect" (Eph. 5:33) their husbands in order to reflect what the church has done (and should do) in regard to Christ, and husbands should give of themselves for their wives in order to reflect what Christ has done (Eph. 5:25).

This conception of marriage would not have been evident to the OT writer or reader of Gen. 2:24. Now, however, on the other side of Christ's cross and resurrection and by the revelation of the Spirit (cf. Eph. 3:5), it can be understood how such a meaning could organically grow out of the Genesis text. Christ is the ultimate, eschatological "man" (ideal Adam), and the church is the ultimate, eschatological bride (e.g., 2 Cor. 11:2–3; Rev. 19:7–9; 21:2, 9–27). It is in this way that the understanding of the OT institution of marriage has become eschatologically transformed in the light of Christ's coming and his relationship to the church.

Therefore, marriage for the present age is a new-creational ethic, which is based on and is a recapitulation of the original ethical mandate about marriage in the original creation and points to the relationship of Christ and the church.

The Corresponding Consummated End-Time Reality

Once the church age ends, so too does the need for human marriage end, since its redemptive-historical purpose is no longer required. The ultimate design of marriage, as presaged by Gen. 2:24, was to point people to the relationship of Christ to the church. This design will no longer be required when all whom God has ordained have come into his covenantal family. Then the resurrection of the bride, the church, will come about, and all will enjoy the consummated marriage relationship to Christ, to which former human marriages pointed. It is likely for this reason that Christ says that "in the [final] resurrection they neither marry nor are given in marriage, but are like angels in heaven" (Matt. 22:30).

Deception, Trials, Persecution, and Cosmic Breakup as Tribulation

The Old Testament Reality

The OT saints did not experience the great tribulation that the church began to experience, but they lived in an age of expectation of that eschatological trial.

Nevertheless, Israelite saints experienced deception by false prophets, apostasy, persecution from within the covenant community and by foreign nations, and exile, which was intense. Daniel 7–12 prophesied an even more intense tribulation and persecution to come in the latter days (e.g., note the incomparable "day of tribulation" in Dan. 12:1 OG).

God's people also suffered trials from the interruption of the normal patterns of the way the cosmos operated: the cataclysm of the Noahic flood is a classic example, as are the various cosmic anomalies of the Egyptian plagues, which were seen as calamities greater than and incomparable to any other up to that point in history (Exod. 9:18, 24; 10:6; 11:6). There were severe trials of horrible inhumanity, described as God doing to Israel what "I have not done, and the like of which I will never do again" (Ezek. 5:9). The oppression and exile of Israel were prophesied to be "the time of Jacob's distress," a "day" so "great" that there had been "none like it" (Jer. 30:7). Also included here should be the times when God's theophanic presence expressed itself in judgment through severe cloud, rain, thunder, and hail in a manner similar to that of the exodus plagues. The coming distress that Joel announces will come upon Israel as "a day of darkness and gloom, a day of clouds and thick darkness. . . . There has never been anything like it, nor will there be again after it, to the years of many generations" (Joel 2:2). These OT realities of incomparable tribulation have parallels with that in the age of fulfillment.

At the least, these experiences of Israel were adumbrations of a greater tribulation to come. We saw in chapter 2 (under the heading "The Repeated Cosmic Judgment and New Creation Episodes of the Old Testament") that these trials were part of a recapitulating pattern of cosmic chaos. Strikingly, some of these tribulations were described as so severe that they had never happened before and would not happen again. Likely, the language is figurative to some degree, but it shows that the OT era had its share of trials that were comparable to what would come in the eschatological age. Daniel 12:1 prophesies "a time of distress such as never occurred since there was a nation until that time."

The phrase is an allusion to Jer. 30:7[87] and possibly Ezek. 5:9, though the quite similar phrases from Exod. 9–11 about the incomparable Egyptian plagues may be echoed. The distress mentioned in Dan. 12:1 is primarily that introduced by an end-time opponent that expresses itself in deception within the covenant community and persecution of the "many" who do not compromise. The "incomparable tribulation" formula also occurs in description of the persecution of Israel by the Greek army (early second century BC). For example, 1 Macc. 9:27 says, "So there was great distress in Israel, such as had not been since the time that prophets ceased to appear among them."[88] This was a tribulation in which Israel suffered severe military defeat, "the lawless" dominated in Israel, and there was famine. This likely was understood at the time as a beginning fulfillment of the Dan. 12:1 prophecy of the "time of distress," though there was no significant deliverance of Israel, which Dan. 12:1–2 had also prophesied. Accordingly, this event itself became a foreshadowing of the later end-time fulfillment of Dan. 12:1–2. The Dan. 12:1 prophecy of tribulation focused on coming deception and persecution but likely also included some notion of cosmic breakup, since resurrection of the wicked and righteous is mentioned in Dan. 12:2, which presupposes the end of the natural world in some significant manner. Such inclusion of a breakup in the cosmos in Dan. 12:1 is reflected also by its allusion to earlier OT passages describing significant interruptions of the regular order of nature, which indicate trials for refinement of the faithful and judgment for the hardened.

But what makes the church's tribulation "great" in a way that Israel's was not?

The Corresponding Inaugurated End-Time Reality

In chapter 7 (under the subheading "The Son of Man and the Great Tribulation") I discussed the OT prophecies of end-time tribulation (esp. Dan. 7–12), which were inaugurated in the trials experienced by Jesus and in the church.

First, the church's trial is a fulfillment of OT prophecy that was never fulfilled in the OT, making the tribulation greater because what was prophesied had never taken place on such an intense scale. But this point must be fleshed out by the following two points.

Second, the church's tribulation is greater than that of Israel's because it is part of the end-time "great tribulation" that Christ, representing true Israel, began to suffer, which was climaxed by his death. As we have seen, Jesus's trials and death as tribulation compose a very significant element of the NT storyline. The church as corporate true Israel participates in this tribulation throughout the interadvent age and thus follows in the footsteps of its Lord.

---

87. Note the common language of "the time of distress" and incomparability.
88. This is likely a reference to a trial ultimately caused by the Greek invaders. So also see *As. Mos.* 8:1, which likely refers to the Greek king Antiochus Epiphanes.

For example, note Rev. 1:9: "I, John, your brother and fellow partaker in the tribulation and kingdom and perseverance which are in Jesus, was on the island called Patmos because of the word of God and the testimony of Jesus." It was through tribulation that Christ persevered and ironically began to establish his kingdom, and his people share in the same three realities at the same time (note again, in Rev. 1:9, that they are those who share in these three realities, which are "in Jesus").[89]

In Col. 1:24 Paul portrays this same notion: "Now I rejoice in my sufferings for your sake, and in my flesh I do my share on behalf of His body, which is the church, in filling up what is lacking in the Messiah's tribulations." Some commentators rightly understand "the tribulations of the Messiah" to reflect the background of the expected sufferings of the Messiah prophesied in Dan. 7 and 9, as well as in Isa. 53. Here Paul is not saying that he could add to Christ's atoning suffering, but rather that he does his part in participating in and "filling up what is lacking" in these messianic tribulations, the things that the Messiah's people are prophesied to suffer in following after Jesus. Paul shares in the corporate "body" of Christ in the decreed end-time tribulations that have been patterned after Christ's. Therefore, the tribulation was more intense than in the OT because it was being experienced not merely by any human or any believer but by Jesus, the divine messianic man. The greatness of Jesus necessitates the "greatness" of the "tribulation" and thus a trial that had never happened before.

Third, the OT also prophesied an end-time opponent of the saints and of the messianic leader (again see Dan. 7–12) who would deceive people in the covenant community. The letter of 1 John refers to this figure as "the antichrist," who has come in "spirit" (4:1–6) and begun to work through "many antichrists," who have come at "the last hour" (2:18; see also 4:1–6). Their main work is that of deception about the truth (e.g., 2:21–26) in fulfillment of the Daniel prophecy. The actual presence of the spirit of the antichrist in the covenant community for the first time makes the deception of the latter-day tribulation more intense than that of the deception in the Israelite community of faith.[90]

The fact that the great tribulation could begin without the actual physical presence of the antichrist but with the presence of his deceptive false prophets shows that the prophecy was fulfilled unexpectedly. This is expressed vividly in 2 Thess. 2:3–4, where Paul predicts that the prophesied "man of lawlessness" has not yet come, but his prophesied false prophetic helpers have come. This was a beginning but not complete fulfillment of Dan. 11:30–32, 37. That

89. For a fuller explanation of Rev. 1:9, see chap. 7 under the subheading "The Idea of the Great Tribulation in the Book of Revelation."

90. For further analysis of the Dan. 8–12 background of the "last hour" in 1 John 2:18, see chap. 7 under the subheadings "1 John and the Great Tribulation" and "The Relation of 1 John 2–3 and 2 Thessalonians 2."

the end-time opponent's false prophets could be present without their leader also being present was a "mystery" for Paul: "the mystery of lawlessness is already at work" (2 Thess. 2:7). This unexpected fulfillment was a temporal transformation of the prophecy, since it no doubt appeared from Daniel's perspective that all this would happen at the same time.[91]

But as we saw that there were incomparable trials of cosmic disruption in the OT era, so also are there in the NT latter-day epoch. The "incomparable tribulation" formula from the OT is alluded to in Matt. 24:21 (// Mark 13:19), which itself prophesies of the future: "For then there will be a great tribulation, such as has not occurred since the beginning of the world until now, nor ever will." Most commentators acknowledge that this wording is from Dan. 12:1. The surrounding context of Matt. 24:21 defines this as tribulation by deception (esp. through "false Christs and false prophets") and apostasy, but it also is linked to catastrophic disruptions of the cosmos. There is much debate about when Matthew's prophecy began to be fulfilled. Some see its fulfillment in the defeat of Jerusalem in AD 70, others see it as happening only at the very end of history directly preceding Christ's final coming, and still others see it occurring at AD 70, as just noted but also that this event of fulfillment becomes typological of the very end. I prefer the first view, though the third may be included and is not mutually exclusive of it.[92]

Likewise, the coming of the Spirit in Acts 2 is described in terms of cosmic destruction (Acts 2:2–4, 19–20), as I have discussed elsewhere.[93] The description there is not primarily about the future but partly about the Spirit's coming in inaugurated judgment of the old world,[94] a judgment that will be completed at the very end.

91. For fuller study of the nature of the tribulation in 2 Thess. 2:1–7, see chap. 7 under the subheading "2 Thessalonians 2 and the Great Tribulation."

92. For the "incomparable tribulation" formula applied to the AD 70 famine and crime that took place in Jerusalem during its siege, see Josephus, *J.W.* 5.442.

93. See further G. K. Beale, "The Descent of the Eschatological Temple in the Form of the Spirit at Pentecost: Part I," *TynBul* 56, no. 1 (2005): 97–99.

94. The quotation of the latter part of the Joel 2 prophecy in Acts 2:19–20 is important here: "And I will grant wonders in the sky above and signs on the earth below, blood, and fire, and vapor of smoke. The sun will be turned into darkness and the moon into blood, before the great and glorious day of the Lord shall come." Some see this as not yet fulfilled at Pentecost, since these signs did not appear to happen "literally" in the physical world. However, Peter gives no indication of nonfulfillment of this part of Joel; he says that everything occurring at Pentecost is the fulfillment of "what was spoken of through the prophet Joel" (Acts 2:16). Hence, in some way, even this language of cosmic dissolution from Joel 2 is beginning fulfillment, part of which can be seen with the eyes (Acts 2:2–4; cf. also the cosmic sign of darkness at the time of Christ's death [Matt. 27:45]), though part of the fulfillment probably is in an unseen spiritual dimension (e.g., the judgment language is seen partly to indicate the judgment of Israel [again, see Beale, "Eschatological Temple: Part I," 97–99], though, of course, the first part of Joel's quotation indicates or includes blessing). For further discussion of this language of cosmic conflagration in the OT, see under the heading "Judgment" following below.

The Corresponding Consummated End-Time Reality

At the end of the church age there will be a more severe intensity of the "great tribulation." Christ underwent an inaugurated tribulation during his life, experiencing selective trials and attempted deception, which was consummated by a lethal attack by Satan at the cross. Likewise, Christ's body, the church, will experience the beginning of eschatological trials. Not every sector of the church will experience these trials, but those not affected directly will still be threatened by them. Then this partial tribulation will be consummated at the very end of time by an attempt to exterminate completely the covenant community throughout the earth. Thus, the commencement of the latter-day tribulation in the church will be consummated at the very conclusion of history by becoming more intense, severe, and universal than any other prior trial for God's people. These trials will include primarily deception and persecution. But just as Christ's resurrection overcame the trial of death, so will the church be resurrected before it can be decisively annihilated (Rev. 20:7–15).[95]

But it is not merely the trials of deception and apostasy that will reach a zenith at the end of history. The partial cosmic trials of the disruption of part of nature's regular course likewise will reach a crescendo at that time.[96]

The complete, definitive, end-time cosmic breakup of the earth and judgment of the entire world system is elaborated upon in Rev. 16:19–21:

> The great city was split into three parts, and the cities of the nations fell. Babylon the great was remembered before God, to give her the cup of the wine of His fierce wrath. And every island fled away, and the mountains were not found. And huge hailstones, about one hundred pounds each, came down from heaven upon men; and men blasphemed God because of the plague of the hail, because its plague was extremely severe.

As part of the introduction to this depiction, the formula of incomparable tribulation is found one last time in canonical literature in Rev. 16:18 to describe this final breakup: "And there were flashes of lightning and sounds and peals of thunder; and there was a great earthquake, such as there had not been since man came to be upon the earth, so great an earthquake was it, and so mighty."

95. On which, see Beale, *Revelation*, 1021–38.
96. Not only does Dan. 12:1 predict the zenith of the final "tribulation," but also parts of early Judaism foresee the same climax to history. The Qumran *War Scroll* prophesies that there will be a final battle between the forces of "darkness" and those of "light," and that this struggle "will be a time of distress for the people redeemed by God, and among all their afflictions there will have been nothing to equal it from its beginning until its end in final redemption" (1QM I:1–12). On this, see further G. K. Beale, *The Use of Daniel in Jewish Apocalyptic Literature and in the Revelation of St. John* (Lanham, MD: University Press of America, 1984), 59–60.

The lightning, thunder, and earthquake of Rev. 16:18 are images that depict the last judgment. This imagery is based in large part on Exod. 19:16–18, which describes the Sinai theophany. Elsewhere the OT and Judaism also allude to the same Exodus imagery to depict the last judgment, which is likewise the case in Rev. 4:5; 8:5; 11:19.[97] The phrase "there was a great earthquake" occurs in Rev. 6:12 as part of a scene of the last judgment. The reference to Exodus in Rev. 16:18 is in keeping with the preceding Exodus allusions, which have served as the pattern for the first six bowls in Rev. 16.

Therefore, these features of cosmic destruction are now applied typologically to the final judgment at the end of world history. The escalated nature of the application is expressed in Rev. 16:18 by the phrase "such as there had not been since man came to be upon the earth, so great an earthquake was it, and so mighty." And it is beyond chance that this wording is taken from Dan. 12:1: "at that time . . . such tribulation as has not come about since a nation has come about on the earth until that time" (cf. TH). Daniel describes the "tribulation" at the end of history, when God's "people will be rescued" and undergo a resurrection to life, but the wicked will be raised for "disgrace and everlasting contempt" (Dan. 12:1–2). The connection to Dan. 12 points further to Rev. 16:18 being a description of the end of the "great tribulation," which reaches its climactic point in the last judgment and the end of the present cosmos.

Furthermore, the appropriateness of the Daniel allusion is apparent in that Daniel's wording itself is a typological application of Exod. 9:18, 24. For example, Exod. 9:18 LXX says, "at this hour . . . a very great hail, such as has not occurred in Egypt from the day which it was founded until this day" (a similar formula occurs as a description of two other plagues in Exod. 10:6, 14; 11:6). The Exodus woe of hail also is in mind, since Rev. 16:21 concludes with a "very great plague" of hail.[98]

Judgment

The topic of judgment has already been addressed directly above through discussion of that aspect of the tribulation that entails the disruption of parts of the regular order of the cosmos (both partially in the OT and NT ages and climactically at the close of the age). In addition, judgment was addressed above in analyzing justification, as a summary of the earlier discussion of justification in the book. Thus, this discussion on final judgment will be more limited.

97. For discussion of the background of virtually the same introductory phrase of Rev. 16:8 in Rev. 8:5, see Beale, *Revelation*, 457–60.
98. On the notion that Rev. 16:18 in its immediate context of vv. 17–21 refers to the final breakup and judgment of the earth, see ibid., 841–46.

The Old Testament Reality

The OT frequently describes God's judgment on both the enemies of his people and on his people themselves when they persist in sin and deserve judgment. A number of OT passages describe the judgment of a particular nation within history using language usually reserved for the destruction of the cosmos.[99] A classic instance of this is Isa. 13:10–13 (introduced in 13:1 as "the oracle concerning Babylon"), which describes the coming judgment of Babylon:

> For the stars of heaven and their constellations
> Will not flash forth their light;
> The sun will be dark when it rises
> And the moon will not shed its light.
> Thus I will punish the world for its evil
> And the wicked for their iniquity;
> I will also put an end to the arrogance of the proud
> And abase the haughtiness of the ruthless.
> I will make mortal man scarcer than pure gold
> And mankind than the gold of Ophir.
> Therefore I will make the heavens tremble,
> And the earth will be shaken from its place
> At the fury of the LORD of hosts.
> In the day of his burning anger.

Here the language about the end of the world is applied not to the literal end of the world but rather to the destruction of Babylon by Persia. Such language describes the defeat not only of Babylon (Isa. 13:10–13) but also of Edom (Isa. 34:4), Egypt (Ezek. 32:6–8), enemy nations of Israel (Hab. 3:6–13), and Israel itself (Joel 2:10, 30–31; cf. *Sib. Or.* 3:75–90). There are other examples in the OT of figurative "cosmic disruption" language.[100] Interestingly, *Midr. Ps.* 104.25 says, "Wherever the term 'earthquake' occurs in Scripture it denotes the chaos between [the fall of] one kingdom and [the rise of] another." There are also passages where the same language might be understood literally of the actual destruction of the entire world (Ps. 102:25–26; Isa. 24:1–6, 19–23; 51:6; 64:1;[101] Ezek. 38:19–20; Hag. 2:6–7).[102]

99. E.g., Isa. 13:10–13; 24:1–6, 19–23; 34:4; Ezek. 32:6–8; Joel 2:10; 2:30–31; 3:15–16; Hab. 3:6–11; possibly also Ps. 68:7–8; Jer. 4:23–28; Amos 8:8–9.

100. E.g., 2 Sam. 22:8–16 // Ps. 18:7–15 (figuratively referring to David's victory over his enemies); Eccles. 12:1–5 (referring to human death); Isa. 2:19–21; 5:25, 30; Jer. 4:23–28; Ezek. 30:3–4, 18; Amos 8:7–10; Mic. 1:4–6.

101. Although this may refer to a future local theophany modeled on that at Sinai, inaugurating a new eschatological age, just as the Sinai revelation inaugurated a new age.

102. In addition, this literal language can describe the past local theophanic events at Mount Sinai (Exod. 19:18; Deut. 4:11; Pss. 68:7–8; 77:18).

Typically, this kind of language is used figuratively to refer to the historical end of a sinful nation's existence through divine judgment and the emerging dominance of a victorious kingdom. God executes the judgment by employing one nation to defeat another in war. Although the tone of judgment is dominant, sometimes there is a positive aspect resulting in the deliverance or refinement of a faithful remnant (esp. when Israel is the object of the judgment). Such figurative language occurred because prophets had a literal conception of the end of history, and they applied this metaphorically to the ends of various epochs or kingdoms during the OT era. If this explanation for the use of this language describing local judgments throughout history is correct, then we may say that the prophets saw such judgments being like what would happen at the end of time in the "literal" breakup of the world by God's judicial hand. In this respect, such limited judgments likely were also seen to some degree to point forward to the final, universal discomfiture of the cosmos. For example, when Isaiah describes Babylon's judgment by Persia through "end of the world" language, he is likely including the notion that this local judgment is a small example of what the macrocosmic destruction will look like.[103]

In addition to the "cosmic conflagration" language that refers to the universal destruction of the earth, there are straightforward references to God's final, universal judgment (e.g., Ps. 96:13: "The LORD . . . is coming to judge the earth. He will judge the world in righteousness and the peoples in His faithfulness").[104] References to an *everlasting* judgment, however, are far and few between in the OT, though they do occur.[105]

The Corresponding Inaugurated End-Time Reality

We have seen that the NT portrays the final judgment as beginning, and that it begins with Christ's crucifixion, where he suffers the final judgment as a substitute on behalf of his people for whom he died. In this sense, the final judgment has been pushed back from the very end of history to the cross of Christ in the first century.[106]

---

103. See G. B. Caird, *The Language and Imagery of the Bible* (Philadelphia: Westminster, 1980), 256–60. Caird has sparked my thinking about the application of eschatological language to various events in the OT. He contends that since biblical writers believed in a literal beginning and ending to history, they used the language of the end metaphorically to apply to events in the midst of history. I agree with Caird, but I think that the description of these events with eschatological language also suggests that such events are so much like the literal end that they point to that end and are proleptic of it (which Caird hints at [see p. 256]).

104. So also, e.g., 1 Sam. 2:10; Pss. 82:8; 98:9.

105. See Daniel I. Block, "The Old Testament on Hell," in *Hell under Fire*, ed. Christopher W. Morgan and Robert A. Peterson (Grand Rapids: Zondervan, 2004), 43–65. Block discusses Dan. 12:1–3 in this respect and sees Isa. 66:24 as pointing in the same direction.

106. I elaborated on this earlier in this chapter under the heading "Salvation and Justification."

There is another sense in which the final judgment has begun. Those who reject Jesus in this age are said to be those on whom "the wrath of God abides" (John 3:36), and they are considered to "have been judged already" (John 3:18), so certain is the coming judgment that hangs over them. This beginning form of judgment is not merely a present declaration of one's certain-to-come judgment; such people also exist in a condition of spiritual "death," which is a beginning phase of the punishment to come (cf. John 5:24 with 5:29). Romans 1:18 is another example of the beginning of the last judgment on the unbeliever: "For the wrath of God is revealed from heaven against all ungodliness and unrighteousness of men." This eschatological wrath manifests itself during the present age in God's "giving over" of such intractably unrepentant people to further sin and recalcitrance (Rom. 1:24–32).

The Corresponding Consummated End-Time Reality

The NT continues to predict the coming, final, universal judgment[107] in continuity with some passages of the OT (see the previous section). This judgment will be immediately preceded by the resurrection of the righteous and the ungodly, the latter being raised for judgment (esp. John 5:28–29). This final judgment of all unbelieving humans throughout world history will be directly preceded by the full destruction of the present heavens and earth (2 Pet. 3:7–12), which itself is directly preceded by the defeat and destruction of the last generation of ungodly people living on the earth (2 Pet. 3:7b). The inaugurated judgment of death as separation from God begun in the preconsummation era will be consummated by the completion of this death penalty. In this respect, 2 Thess. 1:7b–9 affirms,

> The Lord Jesus will be revealed from heaven with His mighty angels in flaming fire, dealing out retribution to those who do not know God and to those who do not obey the gospel of our Lord Jesus. These will pay the penalty of eternal destruction, away from the presence of the Lord and from the glory of His power.

Throughout the book of Revelation there are repeated references to the final judgment. Some of these portray the beginning of the final judgment by describing God's judgment of the last generation of unbelievers on the earth together with the beginning destruction of the earth itself (6:12–17; 11:13–18; 16:16–21).[108] Sometimes there is focus on the defeat of the last generation of enemies on the old earth, which is then described together with the execution

---

107. E.g., Matt. 25:31–46; Acts 17:31; Rom. 2:5–6, 8, 12; Heb. 9:27; 10:27.

108. Sometimes the focus is only on the defeat and judgment of the last generation of opponents to God's people without mention of a cosmic breakup (Rev. 14:14–20; 18:1–24).

of their final judgment in "the lake of fire" (19:17–21; 20:8–10).[109] There is also focus on the declaration and execution of eternal judgment in "the lake of fire" of all the impious who have ever lived (20:11–15).[110] The execution of the final judgment takes place directly after the final defeat of earthly foes and destruction of the cosmos. This judgment will involve not only all the unrighteous outside of Christ, but also Satan (20:10)[111] and his demonic forces.[112]

Other Theological Concepts Not Covered in This Book

Some themes that form parts of my proposed NT biblical-theological storyline and were discussed earlier have not been addressed as distinct topics in this book. Recall this storyline once more: *Jesus's life, trials, death for sinners, and especially resurrection by the Spirit have launched the fulfillment of the eschatological already–not yet new-creational reign, bestowed by grace through faith and resulting in worldwide commission to the faithful to advance this new-creational reign and resulting in judgment for the unbelieving, unto the triune God's glory.*

A theology of God,[113] the subject of the OT storyline, has not been formally developed in this book. Nevertheless, we have seen God to be the main actor throughout in sovereignly accomplishing the acts of the OT storyline. However, in the NT Jesus joins God as the subject in the storyline (though I have not formally stated God as part of the subject) and yet is the faithful Son who achieves his Father's will. Of course, God is active throughout the NT story. Furthermore, God is the formal goal of that storyline. It is the goal of God's glory that will form the main subject of the next and final chapter.

I also have not devoted chapters specifically to the subjects of "grace" and "faith," both of which are important components of the NT storyline. I wish there were space in this project to develop these concepts! If my proposed storyline is correct, it is divine grace that enables one to see and have faith

109. Although only the false prophet and the beast are cast into this lake in the former passage, and only Satan in the latter passage.

110. On which, see also Rev. 21:8; perhaps 20:10 can be added here. Limitations of space do not allow discussion here of whether this is a judgment that results in eternal annihilation or is one that entails a never-ending conscious punishment on the ungodly. For further discussion of this issue in support of the latter position, though interacting with the so-called annihilationist view, see Morgan and Peterson, eds., *Hell under Fire* (Grand Rapids: Zondervan, 2004).

111. On the texts from Revelation in this paragraph that have been adduced in support of the notion of climactic end-time judgment, see Beale, *Revelation*, in loc.

112. Cf. 2 Pet. 2:4; Jude 6, which are almost identical, the latter reading, "And angels who did not keep their own domain, but abandoned their proper abode, He has kept in eternal bonds under darkness for the judgment of the great day." These two texts also indicate that the judgment of these evil beings began in the OT age, continued into the NT age, and will continue until the climactic judgment at the end of history.

113. E.g., a study of each of God's attributes.

in the new-creational and kingdom-building work of Christ in his death and resurrection.

Although I have discussed the idea of "fulfillment" (another element of the storyline) throughout this project, the very next section of this chapter will formally address that subject. Other topics also deserve analysis, for which there has not been space. Among these are election, prayer, fellowship of the saints, and various consummative eschatological topics (e.g., millennial issues and the nature of final punishment as either eternal suffering or annihilation).[114] One might get the impression that the subject of ethics is not covered, but that is addressed in my two chapters on Christian living (chaps. 25–26), though perhaps not in the detail that some might like.

These omissions merely highlight the fact that it is virtually impossible to write an "exhaustive" biblical theology of the NT! Nevertheless, I have tried to focus in this book on what I consider to be the main thrusts of such a theology, as it relates to our proposed NT storyline.

Conclusion: Inaugurated Fulfillment as Unexpected and as Organic Transformation of Old Testament Prophecy

This chapter has been an attempt to relate the inaugurated end-time realities of the NT discussed throughout this book to both the corresponding past OT and future consummated realities, which have not received much attention prior to this chapter.

Throughout this discussion I have reflected on how inaugurated new-covenant realities represent a transformation of the corresponding OT realities. Numerous fulfillments of OT prophecy begin realization in a way that was unforeseen, though all continuity is not broken between the prophecy and the fulfillment. For example, there is almost always a temporal transformation. What appeared to be foreseen in the OT to occur as one fulfillment all at once, at the very end of history happens unexpectedly in two stages or in a staggered manner: an inaugurated and a consummated fulfillment. Sometimes the transformation goes beyond temporal unexpectedness. That is, the reality or nature of what begins to be fulfilled appears to be different from what was predicted. There are times when the two-stage temporal unexpectedness necessitates that the fulfilled reality appears to be different from the original prophecy. Accordingly, since the beginning fulfillment is not completely what was predicted, and as long as the consummated stage is not reached,

114. Other theological topics could be added to the list: creation, providence, predestination and the nature of the human will, perseverance, eschatological imminence, the Trinity, and the relation of the humanity to the deity of Christ, as well as Jesus as Messiah and Son of David. The issues of divorce and slavery, among others, could likewise be included here. The list goes on, though some of these topics belong more properly in a systematic theology.

the inception of fulfillment may be only part of the reality prophesied. For instance, there may be a prophecy of a physical reality that begins fulfillment only in a spiritual or unseen manner.

One of the clearest examples of this is the beginning fulfillment of the resurrection prophecy: it begins literal fulfillment spiritually and in an unseen manner, but it is consummated in a physically, visible manner. But as the consummated stage remains yet to come, from the OT perspective, the inaugurated fulfillment is not what appeared to be literally prophesied. However, from the vantage point of the consummation, one can see how the inaugurated stage was a literal beginning of the final, consummated fulfillment.

Some of the inaugurated fulfillments are even more radically unexpected than others and are more thoroughgoing transformations of the way they were prophesied. Good examples of this are Christ and the church as true Israel, and Christ and the church as the eschatological temple. Other examples of far-reaching transformation of OT prophecy are typological fulfillments of the OT in the NT (e.g., Christ as the Passover Lamb; the Passover meal as a type of the Lord's Supper; marriage). In this respect, a narrated OT event or pattern of events becomes truly transformed and is seen as a prophecy of an event in the NT.

Another example of the kinds of transformed OT fulfillments that one encounters are those where the word "mystery" occurs in direct connection, though such transformations are indicated often without the use of "mystery." "Mystery" (*mystērion*) occurs twenty-eight times in the NT. A feature noticeable in a number of the occurrences is that the word is directly linked to OT quotations or allusions. In these cases, at least, "mystery" appears in order to indicate two things: (1) OT prophecy is beginning fulfillment, and (2) this fulfillment is unexpected from the former OT vantage point. With respect to this last point, it is apparent that the various NT authors are interpreting OT texts in light of the Christ event and under the guidance of the Spirit, which results in new interpretative perspectives. I will not examine all these references, since that has been done elsewhere,[115] but it is sufficient to reflect on uses of "mystery" that have been discussed at points throughout this book.

We have seen representative examples of such uses of "mystery" with the way the NT understands the inauguration of the latter-day tribulation (2 Thess.

---

115. See, e.g., G. K. Beale, *John's Use of the Old Testament in Revelation*, JSNTSup 166 (Sheffield: Sheffield Academic Press, 1998), 215–72; Benjamin L. Gladd, *Revealing the* Mysterion: *The Use of* Mystery *in Daniel and Second Temple Judaism with Its Bearing on First Corinthians*, BZNW 160 (Berlin: de Gruyter, 2008), and see relevant bibliography therein. On the concept of "mystery" in Paul's thought, see D. A. Carson, "Mystery and Fulfillment: Toward a More Comprehensive Paradigm of Paul's Understanding of the Old and the New," in *The Paradoxes of Paul*, vol. 2 of *Justification and Variegated Nomism*, ed. D. A. Carson, Peter T. O'Brien, and Mark A. Seifrid (Grand Rapids: Baker Academic, 2004), 393–436. See also Beale and Gladd, *Hidden But Now Revealed*.

2:3–7), the kingdom (Matt. 13:10–52), the church as true Israel (Eph. 3:2–6), and marriage as a new-creational ethic (Eph. 5:28–33). The first passage about tribulation represents unexpected fulfillment in that it occurs in two stages. The inaugurated stage includes the beginning coming of the "man of lawlessness" (or of the "antichrist" in the parallel of 1 John 2:18, 22), even though that "man" has not yet come in the flesh, as will happen at the very end of history. Thus, the prophesied end-time opponent of Dan. 8 and 11 who will attempt to deceive God's people has begun fulfillment but has done so through his prophesied false teachers who have already come in the flesh. Yet even here there is transformation beyond that of temporal unexpectedness or two-stage fulfillment. There is a real, personal spiritual sense in which the evil opponent is on the scene in the present. In 1 John 4:3 the writer says that "the spirit of the antichrist" is present, "of whom you have heard that he is coming, and now he is already in the world."[116] That the end-time adversary can be *spiritually present apart from his bodily presence* is a transformed understanding of how the Daniel prophecy would have been understood to be fulfilled. There, the prophecy was about a personal, incarnate, end-time fiend who was to appear very visibly and deceive and persecute God's people.

We also saw the initial form of the fulfillment of the kingdom prophecies in Matt. 13 to be a "mystery" (see Matt. 13:11). This is both because the fulfillment was occurring in two stages and because there was a transformation in the way the prophecies were beginning to come about in comparison to how they had been predicted in the OT. The kingdom was expected to come quite visibly and immediately to cover the entire world, and the wicked were to be judged and the righteous rewarded. Jesus explains that the "mysteries of the kingdom" are that the kingdom has come but it grows invisibly like leaven, that it begins as a tiny reality ("like a mustard seed"), and that the wicked and the righteous will continue to live together in this initial form of the kingdom before judgment and reward come.

Although the kingdom fulfillment begins in a transformed manner from the way it was expected, it is still understood to be a fulfillment of the OT. That is, there is a transformed element that appears to represent discontinuity, but there is still continuity. This is what the conclusion of the kingdom parables in Matt. 13 affirms: "Every scribe who has become a disciple of the kingdom of heaven is like a head of a household, who brings forth out of his treasure things new and old" (v. 52). The point is that teachers of the kingdom "must manage God's household with the resources of Jesus's new definitive teachings about the eschatological inauguration of God's reign, which fulfills the old Scriptures of Israel."[117] The new is not a completely "new" addition to the

116. Here the Greek word for "whom," *ho*, is neuter, but the spirit is to be understood as personal, just as references to God's Spirit are grammatically neuter even though the Spirit is a person, not a thing.

117. David L. Turner, *Matthew*, BECNT (Grand Rapids: Baker Academic, 2008), 355.

OT revelation but rather is part of the revelation of the old itself. The focus of the revelation, however, is the new that has begun fulfillment and renewed and transformed the old.[118] Thus, "the Old Testament promises of Messiah and kingdom, as well as Old Testament law and piety, have found their fulfillment in Jesus's person," which has caused the "transformation."[119] This has been anticipated in Matt. 5:17, where Jesus says, "Do not think that I came to abolish the Law or the Prophets; I did not come to abolish but fulfill." It is the lens of the person of Jesus through which the prophecies have been understood and transformed: Jesus fulfills the whole OT in that he fulfills direct predictions; events typologically point to him; he gives the full, intended meaning of the OT; and he perfectly "fulfills" the law's demands by perfect obedience.[120] This results in unanticipated ways that the OT is fulfilled. Sometimes there is straightforward fulfillment, but just as often there is unforeseen fulfillment. A classic example of the latter is the use of Hos. 11:1 in Matt. 2:15, which I discussed earlier in the book.[121]

Other examples of NT uses of "mystery" are in Eph. 3 (the church as true eschatological Israel) and Eph. 5 (marriage). Both represent new, fuller understandings of the OT passages that are either directly prophetic (prophecies of end-time Israel) or typologically forward-looking (Gen. 2:24).

Therefore, the focus of these uses of "mystery" is on the kind of fulfillment that often is different from what one would have expected in the pre-Christian era as a reader of the OT prophecies. These references to "mystery" are the tip of the hermeneutical iceberg, where in many other places of the NT the same kind of transformed fulfillment occurs but without the use of "mystery." The NT's christological and eschatological presuppositions,[122] based on the revelation of Christ's acts in history and the historical response to those acts, are the justification of such readings. Indeed, Christ and the NT writers would see such apparently unexpected fulfillments not as a twisting of the OT Scripture or a reading into Scripture of foreign meanings but rather as organic, transformed outgrowths of it. In this respect, William Sanford LaSor has said,

> In one sense, it [the *sensus plenior*, the fuller meaning] lies outside and beyond the historical situation of the prophet, and therefore it cannot be derived by grammatico-historical exegesis. But in another sense, it is part of the history of redemption, and therefore it can be controlled by the study of Scripture taken in its entirety.

118. D. A. Carson, *Matthew 13–28*, EBC (Grand Rapids: Zondervan, 1995), 333.
119. Ibid.
120. See ibid., 141–45.
121. See chap. 13 under the subheading "Jesus as Latter-Day Israel and Son in Matthew 2."
122. On which, see G. K. Beale, "Did Jesus and His Followers Preach the Right Doctrine from the Wrong Texts? An Examination of the Presuppositions of the Apostles' Exegetical Method," *Themelios* 14 (1989): 89–96.

> Perhaps an illustration will make [this] clear. . . . An ordinary seed contains in itself everything that will develop in the plant or tree to which it is organically related: every branch, every leaf, every flower. Yet no amount of examination by available scientific methods will disclose to us what is in that seed. However, once the seed has developed to its fullness, we can see how the seed has been fulfilled . . . [and] we have sufficient revelation in the Scriptures to keep our interpretations of *sensus plenior* from becoming totally subjective.[123]

I think it better to speak of "transformed organic development" than *sensus plenior* because the latter term has been understood and misunderstood in different ways. Geerhardus Vos has also likened what appears to be later transformed fulfillments to the organic development of a tree. As an apple seed develops into a small stalk and then into an apple tree with branches and leaves, and as the tree buds and the flower opens from it, so does biblical revelation develop.[124] And one does "not say that in the qualitative sense the seed is less perfect than the tree."[125] A blooming apple tree does not look like the seed from which it came, but the two are still organically related and are to be identified as the same organism. Jesus as the Passover Lamb is a good example of this. John says that when the soldiers did not break Jesus's legs at his crucifixion (John 19:33), this was the fulfillment of the historical description of not breaking the bones of the Passover lamb in Exod. 12:46 (John 19:36).[126] It is likely that John would not have insisted that both the original readers and the writer of Exodus would have apprehended that this historical narration about the Passover lamb was a prophetic pointer to the death of the Messiah. Nevertheless, John believes that such a prophetic notion lay unseen there in seed form in the text of Exodus, waiting to be revealed at a later time.[127]

Would Moses have been surprised by how John has understood the Passover lamb? Perhaps. But presumably he would have understood how John came up with such a typological view, since Moses himself likely had an understanding that some aspects of the very events in the lives of the patriarchs and of Israel had a foreshadowing character, pointing to later events. For example, would not Moses have perceived that Abraham's entering into Egypt due to a famine, the pharaoh suffering plagues, and Abraham's coming out of Egypt (Gen. 12:10–20) had such parallels with Israel's later coming out of Egypt that the former was designed to point to the latter? In fact, in some cases of typology, which scholars have seen to be unique interpretations only from a New Testament retrospective viewpoint, there is evidence in the OT text itself

123. William Sanford LaSor, "Prophecy, Inspiration, and *Sensus Plenior*," *TynBul* 29 (1978): 55–56.

124. Geerhardus Vos, *Biblical Theology: Old and New Testaments* (Grand Rapids: Eerdmans, 1948), 7, 17.

125. Ibid., 7.

126. See also Num. 9:12; Ps. 34:20.

127. See Carson, "Mystery and Fulfillment," 427.

that the OT writer had some degree of knowledge that the history he was narrating was pointing forward. In such cases, the NT writer is building on the already incipient typological view of the OT text itself and developing it further in the light of progressive revelation of the Christ event. We have tried to show just such a phenomenon with the use of Hos. 11:1 in Matt. 2:15 (on which, see chap. 13 under the subheading "Jesus as Latter-Day Israel and Son in Matthew"). And there are other cases where the same phenomenon likely can be seen (e.g., see Isa. 7:14 in Matt. 1:21–23; Isa. 22:22 in Rev. 3:7), and ongoing research will likely reveal more such instances.

This kind of approach to understanding earlier biblical texts may suitably be termed "canonical" interpretation (versus "grammatical-historical" interpretation), whereby later revelatory parts of the biblical canon unpack, interpret, unfold, and develop earlier, "thicker" parts. If the assumption that God ultimately has authored the canon is true, then later parts of Scripture unpack the "thick description" of earlier parts. If a later OT or NT text is truly unpacking the idea of an earlier text, then the meaning developed by the later text was originally included in the "thick meaning" of the earlier text, whose "seed" had now organically developed, so that both the earlier and the later form of the tree are still to be identified as the same organism.

Thus, unanticipated interpretations of OT passages in the NT may go beyond the original intention of the OT human author. Nevertheless, the original sense of the OT text remains in view even as the NT writer creatively develops that original meaning beyond what may appear to be the "surface meaning" of that earlier passage. Part of what may be developed is the wider divine meaning of the earlier passage, of which the human author was unaware, but which was not in contradiction to the original human meaning. James Dunn puts it this way with respect to Paul:

> In every case Paul understood the newness as a fresh and final unfolding of ancient promise. . . . Without that ancient promise the new would have been so strange and foreign that it would not have been recognized or preached by Paul as gospel. . . . In short, we may say that it was the continuity in the discontinuity, the apocalyptic climax of the salvation-history which constituted the heart of his gospel.[128]

Consequently, my use of "transformation" in speaking of transformed meanings of OT passages in the NT is to be understood as an organic unfolding and transformation, in light of the organic metaphor of biblical revelation, and is

128. James D. G. Dunn, "How New Was Paul's Gospel? The Problem of Continuity and Discontinuity," in *Gospel in Paul: Studies on Corinthians, Galatians and Romans for Richard N. Longenecker*, ed. L. Ann Jervis and Peter Richardson, JSNTSup 108 (Sheffield: Sheffield Academic Press, 1994), 367. However, for qualification of how Dunn understands the above wording in the wider context of his article, see Carson, "Mystery and Fulfillment," 434.

not to be thought to convey the notion of a complete discontinuity. However, the very fact, for example, that some passages say that the fulfillment of an OT passage is a revealed "mystery," hitherto hidden, indicates some measure of significant discontinuity and newness of understanding.[129] In this connection, is it not understandable that fulfillment typically fleshes out details that may not have been precisely foreseen by the OT prophet?

We turn now to the grand goal of the redemptive-historical issues that have been the subject of this book.

129. See Carson, "Mystery and Fulfillment," 415. Carson's article lays out well the continuities and discontinuities between the OT revelation and that of the NT, especially with respect to the conceptual notion of "mystery" as it relates to the tension.

28

The Purpose
of the Redemptive-Historical Story
and Implications for Christian Living
in the "Already and Not Yet"
Eschatological Age of the New Creation

W hat is the ultimate purpose of both the inaugurated and the consummated facets of redemptive history? The initial part of this chapter will attempt to answer this question. Then I will offer a further and final reflection on the practical implications of the transforming power of the new creation for Christian living and preaching.

The Purpose of the Already–Not Yet New Creation:
The Glory and Adoration of God

The purpose of this section is to summarize the works of others who have contended that the glory of God is the grand goal of the entirety of redemptive history. The bulk of the argument of this book is that the new-creational kingdom, in its multifaceted aspects, is the major stepping-stone to this great goal. The glory of God is the climax of the NT storyline, building on that of the OT, that I have proposed throughout this book: *Jesus's life, trials, death for sinners, and especially resurrection by the Spirit have launched the fulfillment of the eschatological already–not yet new-creational reign, bestowed by grace through faith and resulting in worldwide commission to the faithful to advance this new-creational reign and resulting in judgment for the unbelieving, <u>unto the triune God's glory</u>.*

God's desire and purpose throughout history is to glorify himself.[1] This is first suggested in Gen. 1:28, where the purpose of God's creation of humanity in his image is that humanity would reflect that image. This means that humanity would reflect God's glorious attributes and "fill the earth" with image-bearers who reflect the divine glory. We have seen that texts such as Ps. 8 interpret Gen. 1:28 as affirming that the creation of humanity in God's image was so that God's "name" would be "majestic" in "all the earth" (Ps. 8:1, 9). Therefore, the grand goal of creating such image-bearers was that all the earth would be full of the glory of the Lord (so likewise Isa. 11:9; Hab. 2:14).

Indeed, all the significant redemptive-historical events of the biblical record are said to be for this grand goal of God's glory. At Babel human beings wanted to "make a name" for themselves instead of making God's name glorious, with the result that they were judged by being scattered throughout the earth (Gen. 11:1–8).[2] Although it is not made explicit in the OT, Abraham's life was one in which he was "giving glory to God" (Rom. 4:20–21).

Israel's exodus from Egypt was also to accomplish God's glory: "I will be glorified through Pharaoh" (Exod. 14:4, 18 [cf. 9:16]). The very preservation of sinful Israel in the wilderness after its escape from Egypt was for the divine glory: "I acted for the sake of my name" (Ezek. 20:22). When God gave Israel the law at Mount Sinai, "the glory of the LORD" was revealed there (Exod. 24:16–17). Sinai itself was a mountain sanctuary that pointed to the tabernacle that would soon be erected in order that God might dwell in Israel's midst in the wilderness. The broader purpose of Israel's exodus—the giving of the law and Israel's subsequent preservation—was that God would establish his glory in Israel's midst in his tabernacle (Exod. 40:34–35):[3]

> Then the cloud covered the tent of meeting, and the glory of the LORD filled the tabernacle. Moses was not able to enter the tent of meeting because the cloud had settled on it, and the glory of the LORD filled the tabernacle.

The purpose of the conquest of Canaan and Israel's settlement there was that Israel would eventually establish David's kingdom and build a temple so that God's glorious "name" and presence would be manifested there (2 Sam. 7:5–30; see also 1 Kings 8:1–21).[4] When Solomon dedicated this temple, it was filled with "the glory of the LORD," which was none other than God making mani-

---

1. The remainder of this section is based to a significant extent on John Piper, *Desiring God: Meditations of a Christian Hedonist* (Portland, OR: Multnomah, 1986), 227–38.

2. As we will see directly below, God's name represents his glorious attributes, so that the two are virtually synonymous.

3. See also Lev. 9:23; Num. 16:19, 42; 20:6.

4. See also Deut. 12:5, 11, 21; 14:23–24; 16:2, 4, 6, 11; 26:2; cf. Exod. 15:13, 17–18. Even the beginning of Israel's sinful monarchy was linked in some way to God's "great name" (1 Sam. 12:19–23).

fest that this was the place where he had chosen to dwell (1 Kings 8:10–12).[5] Later, Solomon interpreted this sacred space of God's glorious dwelling to be the "house" that is "called by your Name" and was "built for your Name" (1 Kings 8:41–45). Thus, God's glorious presence and name in the temple are virtually the same, which is a natural equation, since it is common in the OT that the name of a person represented that person's essential character, and this notion is particularly applicable to God's name.[6]

God says that the exile and promised restoration were for "the sake of My name," and "For My own sake . . . my glory I will not give to another" (Isa. 48:9–11). Part of the restoration was the rebuilding of Jerusalem and the temple, which, again, was to glorify God: "Rebuild the temple that I may be . . . glorified" (Hag. 1:8).[7]

Jesus's entire life and ministry were for God's glory: "I glorified You on earth" (John 17:4 [cf. 7:18]). And God glorified Jesus, thus indicating Jesus's own deity (John 8:54; 11:4; 12:23; 13:31; 17:5, 10, 24). In particular, Jesus's death glorified God (John 12:28–34). And at Jesus's final coming and judgment of unbelievers, he will "be glorified in His saints" (2 Thess. 1:9–10).

We saw earlier in the book that all the major biblical events mentioned directly above that were designed to achieve God's glory were moving toward an eschatological climax of God's dwelling in a temple in a new creation.[8] This movement, however, stopped because of the sin of God's people. Then an initial start-up of another such apparent eschatological movement would begin, but again it would cease because of sin.

These cycles repeated themselves until the coming of Christ. He inaugurated a new latter-day creation through his earthly ministry, death, resurrection, and sending of the Spirit. This movement toward a final new-creational reign would not cease this time; it will not be reversed but will continue to build throughout the interadvent age until Christ comes a final time to judge and create the final form of the new heaven and earth, all to God's eschatological glory. This is the main point of the vision of Rev. 4–5, which recounts the already–not yet victory of God and Christ, which is to

---

5. Note also 1 Kings 8:13–18. In addition, note "the glory of the LORD" as a reference to his glorious presence in the first temple (Ezek. 3:12; 10:4, 18; 11:23).

6. E.g., Isa. 48:9–11 equates God's "name" and "glory": "For the sake of My name I delay My wrath. . . . For My own sake, for My own sake, I will act. . . . My glory I will not give to another." Divine glory and God's name are in synonymous parallelism in Pss. 72:19; 102:15; 148:13; Isa. 42:8; 43:7; 59:19. Similarly, these two are inextricably linked in the phrase "the glory of [God's] name" (probably to be understood appositionally: "the glory which is My name") in Pss. 66:2; 79:9; 96:8.

7. See also Zech. 1:16–2:5; Hag. 2:7–9; cf. 2 Chron. 36:23; Mal. 2:2.

8. This included even the building of small tabernacles by the patriarchs (on which, see chap. 19).

accomplish their glory.[9] "To Him be the glory and the dominion forever and ever. Amen" (Rev. 1:6b).

Since God's glory is the grand end-time goal of the redemptive-historical storyline,[10] we may conclude that the goal of God in everything is to glorify himself and enjoy that glory forever. Since this is God's goal, so should it be ours. Thus, the chief end of humanity is to glorify God by enjoying him forever.[11] If this is so, all people must ask themselves these questions: "In all that I think, say, and do, do I glorify God or myself?"[12] and, "Do I enjoy myself and the creation more than I enjoy God?" Thus, biblical theology, as I understand it, presents to us the imperative not only to extend his kingdom of the new creation but also to love and worship God for his glory!

The Transforming Power of the New Creation for Christian Living and Preaching

Here I will address one of the main practical and pastoral implications of this book: if the end-time new creation has truly begun, how should this affect the way Christians live?[13] Recall that for the Christian, to be a new creation is to begin to experience spiritual resurrection from the dead, which will be consummated in physical resurrection at the very end of time. This stage of spiritual resurrection is the beginning fulfillment of the OT prophecy of the resurrection of God's people, whereby both the spirit and the body were to be resurrected. Therefore, though being only a spiritual resurrection, it is not a metaphorical or figurative resurrection but rather a literal beginning resurrection from the dead.

We have seen, for example, that throughout his epistles Paul views true believers as those who have begun to experience actual eschatological resurrection existence. Paul's affirmation of this is absolutely critical, since the many commands and exhortations that he gives assume that true saints can obey

9. The endings of Rev. 4 and 5 recount that God's sovereignty in history is to accomplish the glory of God and Christ respectively. See more specifically, G. K. Beale, *The Book of Revelation: A Commentary on the Greek Text*, NIGTC (Grand Rapids: Eerdmans, 1999), 311–69. There I see the main point of both visions being that "God and Christ are *glorified* because Christ's resurrection demonstrates that they are sovereign over creation to judge and to redeem" (pp. 145–46).

10. On which, see also Rom. 11:36, "For from him and through him and to him are all things. To him be the glory forever. Amen."

11. Taken from the answer to Question 1 of the Westminster Larger Catechism, which actually reads, "Man's chief and highest end is to glorify God and fully to enjoy him forever." Piper (*Desiring God*, 13–14) likely rightly interprets "and . . . to enjoy" of the Catechism as "by enjoying." Likewise, see Matt. 5:14; 1 Pet. 4:11.

12. This question should be reflected upon in light of 1 Cor. 10:31: "Whether, then, you eat or drink or whatever you do, do all to the glory of God."

13. On which, see, e.g., chap. 10 under the subheading "What Difference Does It Make for Christian Living That the Latter-Day New Creation Has Begun?" and chap. 25.

them because they have the resurrection power to do so. This is why Paul and other writers emphasize the readers' participation in eschatological realities in the midst of exhorting them to obedience to God. Those who merely profess to be saints, but are not truly regenerate, have no persevering desire to do God's will because they do not have the power of the new creation to obey. Genuine eschatological saints have both the desire and the ability to obey and please God. I have given a number of examples illustrating how having the power to do something gives one the desire to do it.

This notion is important for all Christians to know, but those who teach and preach in the church should especially have an awareness of the inaugurated end-time new creation. Such awareness should color all that they exposit from God's word. It is especially important that pastors make clear to their congregations the eschatological resurrection power that they possess, since awareness of this power enables believers to realize that they have the ability to carry out God's commands. On this basis, God's "commandments are not burdensome" (1 John 5:3). And, as we have seen, it is God's life-giving Spirit who empowers his people to carry out his commands, which otherwise, indeed, would be too burdensome to obey.

This already–not yet end-time framework for knowing who we are and what God consequently expects from us cannot be communicated effectively in just a few sermons or Sunday school lessons; it must be woven into the warp and woof of a pastor's teaching and expository preaching over the years. Only then can such a notion be absorbed effectively by God's grace. Augustine's well-known prayerful dictum adequately sums this up: "Grant what Thou dost command and command what Thou wilt" (*Conf.* 10.29).

Consequently, the NT's interpretation of the OT has been "written for our instruction" because "upon us the ends of the ages have come," giving us the ability "to stand and endure and not fall into sin" (1 Cor. 10:11–13).[14]

A book on practical theology and preaching could be written on this topic, but I must leave that task to others because of the length that this book has already reached.

The upshot of this book ultimately is this: To God be the glory.

---

14. This is a highly interpretative paraphrase of 1 Cor. 10:11–13.

Bibliography

Abbott, T. K. *A Critical and Exegetical Commentary on the Epistles to the Ephesians and to the Colossians.* ICC. New York: Charles Scribner's Sons, 1905.

Achtemeier, Paul J. *1 Peter.* Hermeneia. Minneapolis: Fortress, 1996.

Aletti, Jean-Noël. *Saint Paul, Épître aux Colossiens: Introduction, traduction et commentaire.* EBib 20. Paris: Gabalda, 1993.

Alexander, Joseph A. *Commentary on the Prophecies of Isaiah.* 2 vols. 1847. Reprint, Grand Rapids: Zondervan, 1970.

Alexander, T. Desmond. *From Eden to the New Jerusalem: An Introduction to Biblical Theology.* Grand Rapids: Kregel, 2008.

Alkier, Stefan. *Die Realität der Auferweckung in, nach und mit den Schriften des Neun Testaments.* Neuetestamentliche Entwürf zur Theologie 12. Tübingen: Narr Francke Attempto Verlag GmbH & Co., 2009.

Allison, Dale C., Jr. *The End of the Ages Has Come: An Early Interpretation of the Passion and Resurrection of Jesus.* Philadelphia: Fortress, 1985.

———. "Eschatology." *DJG* 206–9.

———. *The New Moses: A Matthean Typology.* Minneapolis: Fortress, 1993.

Anderson, A. A. *The Book of Psalms.* 2 vols. NCB. Grand Rapids: Eerdmans, 1972.

Ansberry, Christopher B. "Be Wise, My Son, and Make My Heart Glad: An Exploration of the Courtly Nature of Proverbs." PhD diss., Wheaton College Graduate School, 2009.

Arnold, C. E. "Returning to the Domain of the Powers: STOICHEIA as Evil Spirits in Galatians 4:3, 9." *NovT* 38 (1996): 55–76.

Attridge, Harold W. *The Epistle to the Hebrews.* Hermeneia. Philadelphia: Fortress, 1989.

Aune, David E. "Apocalypticism." *DPL* 25–35.

———. "Early Christian Eschatology." *ABD* 2:594–609.

Averbeck, Richard E. "The Cylinders of Gudea (2.155)." Pages 418–33 in *Monumental Inscriptions from the Biblical World.* Vol. 2 of *The Context of Scripture: Archival Documents from the Biblical World.* Edited by William. W. Hallo and K. Lawson Younger Jr. Leiden: Brill, 2000.

Bahnsen, Greg L. *Theonomy in Christian Ethics.* Nutley, NJ: Craig Press, 1979.

Bailey, Daniel P. "Jesus as the Mercy Seat: The Semantics and Theology of Paul's Use of *Hilasterion* in Romans 3:25." *TynBul* 51, no. 1 (2000): 155–58.

———. Review of *Der Tod Jesu als Heiligtumsweihe,* by Wolfgang Kraus. *JTS* 45 (1994): 247–52.

Baldwin, Joyce G. *Daniel.* TOTC. Leicester: InterVarsity, 1978.

Bandstra, A. J. "History and Eschatology in the Apocalypse." *CTJ* 5 (1970): 180–83.

Barclay, John M. G. *Colossians and Philemon: A Commentary*. NTG. Sheffield: Sheffield Academic Press, 1997.

———. *Obeying the Truth: A Study of Paul's Ethics in Galatians*. SNTW. Edinburgh: T&T Clark, 1988.

Barker, Margaret. "Isaiah." Pages 489–542 in *Eerdmans Commentary on the Bible*. Edited by James D. G. Dunn and John W. Rogerson. Grand Rapids: Eerdmans, 2003.

Barnett, Paul. *The Second Epistle to the Corinthians*. NICNT. Grand Rapids: Eerdmans, 1997.

Barr, James. *The Concept of Biblical Theology: An Old Testament Perspective*. Minneapolis: Fortress, 1999.

Barrett, C. K. "The Background of Mark 10:45." Pages 1–18 in *New Testament Essays: Studies in Memory of Thomas Walter Manson, 1893–1958*. Edited by A. J. B. Higgins. Manchester, UK: Manchester University Press, 1959.

———. "The Eschatology of the Epistle to the Hebrews." Pages 363–93 in *The Background of the New Testament and Its Eschatology: Studies in Honour of C. H. Dodd*. Edited by W. D. Davies and D. Daube. Cambridge: Cambridge University Press, 1956.

Bartholomew, Craig G., and Michael W. Goheen, eds. *The Drama of Scripture: Finding Our Place in the Biblical Story*. Grand Rapids: Baker Academic, 2004.

Bartholomew, Craig G., and Michael W. Goheen. "Story and Biblical Theology." Pages 144–71 in *Out of Egypt: Biblical Theology and Biblical Interpretation*. Edited by Craig G. Bartholomew, Mary Healy, Karl Möller, and Robin Parry. Hermeneutics Series 5. Grand Rapids, Zondervan: 2004.

Bartholomew, Craig G., Mary Healy, Karl Möller, and Robin Parry, eds. *Out of Egypt: Biblical Theology and Biblical Interpretation*. Hermeneutics Series 5. Grand Rapids: Zondervan, 2004.

Bass, Derek Drummond. "Hosea's Use of Scripture: An Analysis of His Hermeneutics. PhD diss., Southern Baptist Theological Seminary, 2008.

Bauckham, Richard. *The Climax of Prophecy: Studies on the Book of Revelation*. Edinburgh: T&T Clark, 1993.

———, ed. *The Gospels for All Christians: Rethinking the Gospel Audiences*. Grand Rapids: Eerdmans, 1998.

———. "The Great Tribulation in the Shepherd of Hermas." *JTS* 25 (1974): 27–40.

———. "James and the Jerusalem Church." Pages 415–80 in *The Book of Acts in Its Palestinian Setting*. Edited by Richard Bauckham. Vol. 4 of *The Book of Acts in Its First Century Setting*. Edited by Bruce W. Winter. Grand Rapids: Eerdmans, 1995.

———. *Jesus and the God of Israel: God Crucified and Other Studies on the New Testament's Christology of Divine Identity*. Grand Rapids: Eerdmans, 2008.

———. "Jesus and the Wild Animals (Mark 1:13): A Christological Image for an Ecological Age." Pages 3–21 in *Jesus of Nazareth: Lord and Christ; Essays on the Historical Jesus and New Testament Christology*. Edited by Joel B. Green and Max Turner. Grand Rapids: Eerdmans, 1994.

Baugh, S. M. "Covenant, Priesthood, and People in Hebrews." Online: http://baugh.wscal.edu/PDF/NT701/NT701_Hebrews_CPP.pdf.

Bayer, Hans F. "Christ-Centered Eschatology in Acts 3:17–26." Pages 236–50 in *Jesus of Nazareth: Lord and Christ; Essays on the Historical Jesus and New Testament Christology*. Edited by Joel B. Green and Max Turner. Grand Rapids: Eerdmans, 1994.

Baylis, Albert H. *From Creation to the Cross: Understanding the First Half of the Bible*. Grand Rapids: Zondervan, 1996.

Beale, G. K. *1–2 Thessalonians*. IVPNTC. Downers Grove, IL: InterVarsity, 2003.

———. *The Book of Revelation: A Commentary on the Greek Text*. NIGTC. Grand Rapids: Eerdmans, 1999.

———. "Colossians." Pages 841–70 in *Commentary on the New Testament Use of the Old Testament*. Edited by G. K. Beale and D. A. Carson. Grand Rapids: Baker Academic, 2007.

———. *Colossians and Philemon*. BECNT. Grand Rapids: Baker Academic, forthcoming.

———. "The Descent of the Eschatological Temple in the Form of the Spirit at Pentecost: Part I." *TynBul* 56, no. 1 (2005): 73–102.

———. "The Descent of the Eschatological Temple in the Form of the Spirit at Pentecost: Part II." *TynBul* 56, no. 2 (2005): 63–90.

———. "Did Jesus and His Followers Preach the Right Doctrine from the Wrong Texts? An Examination of the Presuppositions of the Apostles' Exegetical Method." *Themelios* 14 (1989): 89–96.

———. "Eden, the Temple, and the Church's Mission in the New Creation." *JETS* 48 (2005): 5–31.

———. "The Eschatological Conception of New Testament Theology." Pages 11–52 in *"The Reader Must Understand": Eschatology in the Bible and Theology*. Edited by K. E. Brower and M. W. Elliott. Leicester: Apollos, 1997.

———. "Eschatology." *DLNTD* 330–45.

———. "The Final Vision of the Apocalypse and Its Implications for a Biblical Theology of the Temple." Pages 191–209 in *Heaven on Earth: The Temple in Biblical Theology*. Edited by Simon J. Gathercole and T. Desmond Alexander. Carlisle, UK: Paternoster, 2004.

———. "Isaiah VI 9–13: A Retributive Taunt against Idolatry." *VT* 41 (1991): 257–78.

———. *John's Use of the Old Testament in Revelation*. JSNTSup 166. Sheffield: Sheffield Academic Press, 1998.

———. "The Old Testament Background of Paul's Reference to the 'Fruit of the Spirit' in Galatians 5:22." *BBR* 15 (2005): 1–38.

———. "The Old Testament Background of Reconciliation in 2 Corinthians 5–7 and Its Bearing on the Literary Problem of 2 Corinthians 4:14–7:1." *NTS* 35 (1989): 550–81.

———. "The Old Testament Background of Rev 3.14." *NTS* 42 (1996): 133–52.

———. "The Old Testament Background of the 'Last Hour' in 1 John 2:18." *Biblica* 92 (2011): 231–54.

———. "Peace and Mercy upon the Israel of God: The Old Testament Background of Galatians 6,16b." *Bib* 80 (1999): 204–23.

———. Review of *Acts and the Isaianic New Exodus*, by David W. Pao. *TJ* 25 (2004): 93–101.

———. "Review of D. A. Carson, P. T. O'Brien, and M. A. Seifrid, eds. *Justification and Variegated Nomism*, vol. 2: *The Paradoxes of Paul*. Grand Rapids: Baker Academic, 2004." *Trinity Journal* 29 NS (2008): 146–49.

———. Review of *The End of the Beginning*, by William J. Dumbrell. *Themelios* 15 (1990): 69–70.

———, ed. *The Right Doctrine from the Wrong Texts? Essays on the Use of the Old Testament in the New*. Grand Rapids: Baker Academic, 1994.

———. *The Temple and the Church's Mission: A Biblical Theology of the Dwelling Place of God*. NSBT 17. Downers Grove, IL: InterVarsity, 2004.

———. *The Use of Daniel in Jewish Apocalyptic Literature and in the Revelation of St. John*. Lanham, MD: University Press of America, 1984.

———. *We Become What We Worship: A Biblical Theology of Idolatry*. Downers Grove: IVP Academic, 2008.

Beale, G. K., and Benjamin L. Gladd, *Hidden But Now Revealed: A Biblical Theology of Divine Mystery*. Downers Grove, IL: InterVarsity, forthcoming.

Beasley-Murray, George R. "The Eschatology of the Fourth Gospel." *EvQ* 18 (1946): 97–108.

———. *John*. WBC 36. Waco: Word, 1987.

Beetham, Christopher A. *Echoes of Scripture in the Letter of Paul to the Colossians*. BIS 96. Leiden: Brill, 2008.

Beisner, E. Calvin, ed. *The Auburn Avenue Theology, Pros and Cons: Debating the Federal Vision*. Ft. Lauderdale, FL: Knox Theological Seminary Press, 2004.

Bell, Richard H. *No One Seeks for God: An Exegetical and Theological Study of Romans 1.18–3.20*. WUNT 106. Tübingen: Mohr Siebeck, 1998.

Belleville, Linda. "'Born of Water and Spirit': John 3:5." *TJ* 1 (1980): 125–41.

Berges, Ulrich. *Das Buch Jesaja: Komposition und Endgestalt*. HBS 16. Freiburg: Herder, 1998.

Berkhof, Louis. *Systematic Theology*. Grand Rapids: Eerdmans, 1976.

Best, Ernest. *The First and Second Epistles to the Thessalonians*. Peabody, MA: Hendrickson, 1972.

Betz, Hans Dieter. *Galatians*. Hermeneia. Philadelphia: Fortress, 1979.

Betz, Otto. "Der Katechon." *NTS* 9 (1963): 276–91.

———. "The Eschatological Interpretation of the Sinai-Tradition in Qumran and in the New Testament." *RevQ* 6 (1967): 89–107.

Bird, Michael F. "Incorporated Righteousness: A Response to Recent Evangelical Discussion concerning the Imputation of Christ's Righteousness in Justification." *JETS* 47 (2004): 253–75.

———. "Justification as Forensic Declaration and Covenant Membership: A *Via Media* between Reformed and Revisionist Readings of Paul." *TynBul* 57, no. 1 (2006): 109–30.

Bitner, Bradley J. "The Biblical Theology of Geerhardus Vos." MA thesis, Gordon-Conwell Theological Seminary, 2000.

Black, Jeremy. "Ashur (god)." Page 36 in *Dictionary of the Ancient Near East*. Edited by Piotr Bienkowski and Alan Millard. Philadelphia: University of Pennsylvania Press, 2000.

Blaising, Craig A., and Darrell L. Bock. *Progressive Dispensationalism*. Grand Rapids: Baker Academic, 1993.

Blenkinsopp, Joseph. *Ezekiel*. IBC. Louisville: John Knox, 1990.

———. *Isaiah 56–66*. AB 19B. New York: Doubleday, 2003.

Bloch-Smith, Elizabeth. "'Who Is the King of Glory?' Solomon's Temple and Its Symbolism." Pages 18–31 in *Scripture and Other Artifacts: Essays on the Bible and Archaeology in Honor of Philip J. King*. Edited by Michael D. Coogan, J. Cheryl Exum, and Lawrence E. Stager. Louisville: Westminster John Knox, 1994.

Blocher, Henri. *In the Beginning: The Opening Chapters of Genesis*. Translated by David G. Preston. Downers Grove, IL: InterVarsity, 1984.

Block, Daniel I. *The Book of Ezekiel: Chapters 25–48*. NICOT. Grand Rapids: Eerdmans, 1998.

———. "The Old Testament on Hell." Pages 43–65 in *Hell Under Fire*. Edited by

Christopher W. Morgan and Robert A. Peterson. Grand Rapids: Zondervan, 2004.

Blomberg, Craig L. "Matthew." Pages 1–109 in *Commentary on the New Testament Use of the Old Testament*. Edited by G. K. Beale and D. A. Carson. Grand Rapids: Baker Academic, 2007.

———. "The Unity and Diversity of Scripture." *NDBT* 64–72.

Bock, Darrell L. *Luke 9:51–24:53*. BECNT. Grand Rapids: Baker Academic, 1996.

Bockmuehl, Markus. *Revelation and Mystery in Ancient Judaism and Pauline Christianity*. WUNT 2/36. Tübingen: Mohr Siebeck, 1990.

Booij, Thijs. "Some Observations on Psalm LXXXVII." *VT* 37 (1987): 16–25.

Borgen, Peder. "Moses, Jesus, and the Roman Emperor: Observations in Philo's Writings and the Revelation of John." *NovT* 38 (1996): 145–59.

Box, G. H. *The Book of Isaiah*. London: Pitman, 1908.

Branham, Joan R. "Vicarious Sacrality: Temple Space in Ancient Synagogues." Pages 319–45 in vol. 2 of *Ancient Synagogues: Historical Analysis and Archaeological Discovery*. Edited by Dan Urman and Paul V. M. Flesher. StPB 47. Leiden: Brill, 1995.

Bratsiotis, N. P. "בָּשָׂר." *TDOT* 2:313–32.

Brendsel, Daniel J. "Centers, Plots, Themes, and Biblical Theology." Paper presented at the Doctoral Seminar on Theological Interpretation of Scripture, Wheaton College, December 18, 2008.

———. "Plots, Themes, and Responsibilities: The Search for a Center of Biblical Theology Reexamined." *Themelios* 35, no. 3 (2010): 400–412.

Brenton, Lancelot C. L. *The Septuagint with Apocrypha: Greek and English*. 1851. Repr., Peabody, MA: Hendrickson, 1986.

Briggs, Charles A. *A Critical and Exegetical Commentary on the Book of Psalms*. 2 vols. ICC. Edinburgh: T&T Clark, 1986–87.

Brown, Colin. "Resurrection." *NIDNTT* 3:259–309.

Brown, J. K. "Creation's Renewal in the Gospel of John." *CBQ* 72 (2010): 275–90.

Brown, Raymond E. *The Epistles of John*. AB 30. Garden City, NY: Doubleday, 1982.

Broyles, Craig C. *Psalms*. NIBC. Peabody, MA: Hendrickson, 1999.

Bruce, F. F. *1 and 2 Corinthians*. NCB. Greenwood, SC: Attic Press, 1971.

———. *1 & 2 Thessalonians*. WBC 45. Waco: Word, 1982.

———. *The Book of Acts*. NICNT. Grand Rapids: Eerdmans, 1954.

———. *The Epistle of Paul to the Galatians: A Commentary on the Greek Text*. NIGTC. Grand Rapids: Eerdmans, 1982.

———. *The Epistle of Paul to the Romans*. TNTC. Grand Rapids: Eerdmans, 1963.

———. *The Epistle to the Hebrews*. NICNT. Grand Rapids: Eerdmans, 1990.

———. *The Epistles of John*. NICNT. Grand Rapids: Eerdmans, 1970.

———. *The Epistles to the Colossians, to Philemon, and to the Ephesians*. NICNT. Grand Rapids: Eerdmans, 1984.

———. "Eschatology in Acts." Pages 51–63 in *Eschatology and the New Testament: Essays in Honor of George Raymond Beasley-Murray*. Edited by W. Hulitt Gloer. Peabody, MA: Hendrickson, 1988.

Brueggemann, Walter. *Genesis*. IBC. Atlanta: John Knox, 1982.

———. *The Land: Place as Gift, Promise, and Challenge in Biblical Faith*. Philadelphia: Fortress, 1977.

Buchanan, G. W. "Eschatology and the 'End of Days.'" *JNES* 20 (1961): 188–93.

Bullock, C. Hassell. *Encountering the Book of Psalms: A Literary and Theological Introduction*. Grand Rapids: Baker Academic, 2001.

Bultmann, Rudolf. *Theology of the New Testament*. Translated by Kendrick Grobel. 2 vols. London: SCM, 1952–55.

Burge, Gary M. *Jesus and the Land: The New Testament Challenge to "Holy Land" Theology*. Grand Rapids: Baker Academic, 2010.

Burney, C. F. "Christ as the APXH of Creation (Prov. viii 22, Col. i 15–18; Rev. iii 14)." *JTS* 27 (1926): 160–77.

Buttmann, Alexander. *A Grammar of the New Testament Greek*. Andover, MA: W. F. Draper, 1873.

Buzzard, Anthony. "Acts 1:6 and the Eclipse of the Biblical Kingdom." *EvQ* 66 (1994): 197–215.

Byrne, Brendan. *Romans*. SP 6. Collegeville, MN: Liturgical Press, 1996.

Cadbury, Henry J. "Acts and Eschatology." Pages 300–321 in *The Background of the New Testament and Its Eschatology: Studies in Honour of C. H. Dodd*. Edited by W. D. Davies and D. Daube. Cambridge: Cambridge University Press, 1956.

Caird, G. B. *The Language and Imagery of the Bible*. Philadelphia: Westminster, 1980.

———. *Paul's Letters from Prison*. NClarB. Oxford: Oxford University Press, 1976.

Caird, G. B., and L. D. Hurst. *New Testament Theology*. Oxford: Clarendon, 1994.

Callender, Dexter E., Jr. *Adam in Myth and History: Ancient Israelite Perspectives on the Primal Human*. HSS 48. Winona Lake, IN: Eisenbrauns, 2000.

Calvin, John. *Commentaries on the Epistle of Paul the Apostle to the Hebrews*. Reprint, Grand Rapids: Baker Academic, 1984.

———. *Commentaries on the Epistles of Paul the Apostle to the Galatians, Ephesians, Philippians, Colossians, and 1 and 2 Thessalonians, 1 and 2 Timothy, Titus, Philemon*. Reprint, Grand Rapids: Baker Academic, 1984.

———. *Commentaries on the Epistles of Paul the Apostle to the Philippians, Colossians, and Thessalonians*. Reprint, Grand Rapids: Baker Academic, 1999.

———. *Genesis*. Edinburgh: Banner of Truth, 1965.

Carlston, Charles E. "Eschatology and Repentance in the Epistle to the Hebrews." *JBL* 78 (1959): 296–302.

Carnegie, David R. "Worthy Is the Lamb: The Hymns in Revelation." Pages 243–56 in *Christ the Lord: Studies in Christology Presented to Donald Guthrie*. Edited by Harold H. Rowdon. Downers Grove, IL: InterVarsity, 1982.

Carroll, John T. *Response to the End of History: Eschatology and Situation in Luke-Acts*. SBLDS 92. Atlanta: Scholars Press, 1988.

Carroll R., M. Daniel. "Blessing the Nations: Toward a Biblical Theology of Mission from Genesis." *BBR* 10 (2000): 17–34.

Carson, D. A. "1–3 John." Pages 1063–67 in *Commentary on the New Testament Use of the Old Testament*. Edited by G. K. Beale and D. A. Carson. Grand Rapids: Baker Academic, 2007.

———. "Current Issues in Biblical Theology: A New Testament Perspective." *BBR* 5 (1995): 17–41.

———. *The Gagging of God: Christianity Confronts Pluralism*. Grand Rapids: Zondervan, 1996.

———. *The Gospel according to John*. PNTC. Grand Rapids: Eerdmans, 1991.

———. "The *homoios* Word-Group as Introduction to Some Matthean Parables." *NTS* 31 (1985): 277–82.

———. "Locating Udo Schnelle's *Theology of the New Testament* in the Contemporary Discussion." *JETS* 53 (2010): 133–41.

———. *Matthew 1–12*. EBC. Grand Rapids: Zondervan, 1995.

———. *Matthew 13–28*. EBC. Grand Rapids: Zondervan, 1995.

———. "Mystery and Fulfillment: Toward a More Comprehensive Paradigm of Paul's Understanding of the Old and the New." Pages 393–436 in *The Paradoxes of Paul*. Vol. 2 of *Justification and Variegated Nomism*. Edited by D. A. Carson, Peter T. O'Brien, and Mark A. Seifrid. Grand Rapids: Baker Academic, 2004.

———. "New Testament Theology." *DLNTD* 796–814.

———. "Reflections on Christian Assurance." *WTJ* 54 (1992): 1–29.

———. "The Vindication of Imputation: On Fields of Discourse and Semantic Fields." Pages 46–78 in *Justification: What's at Stake in the Current Debates*. Edited by Mark A. Husbands and Daniel J. Treier. Downers Grove, IL: InterVarsity, 2004.

Carson, D. A., and Douglas J. Moo. *An Introduction to the New Testament*. 2nd ed. Grand Rapids: Zondervan, 2005.

Carson, D. A., P. T. O'Brien, and M. A. Seifrid, eds. *The Complexities of Second Temple Judaism*. Vol. 1 of *Justification and Variegated Nomism*. Grand Rapids: Baker Academic, 2004.

Carson, Herbert M. *The Epistles of Paul to the Colossians and Philemon*. 2nd ed. TNTC. Grand Rapids: Eerdmans, 1966.

Cassuto, Umberto. *From Adam to Noah: A Commentary on Genesis I–VI*. Vol. 1 of *A Commentary on the Book of Genesis*. Translated by Israel Abrams. Jerusalem: Magnes Press, 1961.

Cazelles, Henri. "Sacral Kingship." *ABD* 5:863–66.

Charles, R. H. *The Apocrypha and Pseudepigrapha of the Old Testament*. 2 vols. Oxford: Clarendon, 1913.

Charlesworth, James H. *The Old Testament Pseudepigrapha*. 2 vols. New York: Doubleday, 1983–85.

Cheyne, T. K. *The Prophecies of Isaiah*. 6th ed. 2 vols. London: Kegan Paul, Trench, Trübner, 1898.

Childs, Brevard S. *Biblical Theology of the Old and New Testaments: Theological Reflection on the Christian Bible*. Minneapolis: Fortress, 1993.

———. *The Book of Exodus*. OTL. Louisville: Westminster, 1976.

Chilton, Bruce D. "Galatians 6:15: A Call to Freedom before God." *ExpTim* 89 (1978): 311–13.

Clements, R. E. *God and Temple*. Philadelphia: Fortress, 1965.

Clifford, Richard J. *Creation Accounts in the Ancient Near East and in the Bible*. CBQMS 26. Washington: Catholic Biblical Association of America, 1994.

———. "Isaiah 40–66." Pages 571–96 in *Harper's Bible Commentary*. Edited by James L. Mays. San Francisco: Harper & Row, 1988.

Clines, David J. A., ed. *The Dictionary of Classical Hebrew*. Vol. 6. Sheffield: Sheffield Phoenix Press, 2007.

Clowney, Edmund P. "The Final Temple." *WTJ* 35 (1972): 156–89.

Cobb, Peter G. "The History of the Christian Year." Pages 455–72 in *The Study of Liturgy*. Edited by Cheslyn Jones et al. Rev. ed. New York: Oxford University Press, 1992.

Cohen, Jeremy. *"Be Fertile and Increase, Fill the Earth and Master It": The Ancient and Medieval Career of a Biblical Text*. Ithaca, NY: Cornell University Press, 1989.

Cohn, Norman. *Cosmos, Chaos, and the World to Come: The Ancient Roots of Apocalyptic Faith.* New Haven: Yale University Press, 1993.

Collins, C. John. "Galatians 3:16: What Kind of Exegete Was Paul?" *TynBul* 54, no. 1 (2003): 75–86.

Craigie, Peter C. *Deuteronomy.* NICOT. Grand Rapids: Eerdmans, 1976.

Cranfield, C. E. B. *A Critical and Exegetical Commentary on the Epistle to the Romans.* 2 vols. ICC. Edinburgh: T&T Clark, 1975.

Croatto, J. Severino. "The 'Nations' in the Salvific Oracles of Isaiah." *VT* 55 (2005): 143–61.

Cullmann, Oscar. *Baptism in the New Testament.* Translated by J. K. S. Reid. SBT 1. Chicago: Allenson, 1950.

———. *Christ and Time: The Primitive Christian Conception of Time and History.* Translated by Floyd V. Filson. Philadelphia: Westminster, 1950.

Currid, John D. *A Study Commentary on Exodus.* 2 vols. Auburn, MA: Evangelical Press, 2000–2001.

Curtis, Byron G. "Hosea 6:7 and the Covenant-Breaking like/at Adam." Pages 170–209 in *The Law Is Not of Faith: Essays on Works and Grace in the Mosaic Covenant.* Edited by Bryan D. Estelle, J. V. Fesko, and David VanDrunen. Phillipsburg, NJ: P&R, 2009.

Curtis, Edward M. "Image of God (OT)." *ABD* 3:389–91.

Dahood, Mitchell. *Psalms.* 3 vols. AB 16, 17, 17A. Garden City, NY: Doubleday, 1964.

Davids, Peter H. *The Epistle of James: A Commentary on the Greek Text.* NIGTC. Grand Rapids: Eerdmans, 1982.

———. *The First Epistle of Peter.* NICNT. Grand Rapids: Eerdmans, 1990.

Davidson, Richard M. *Flame of Yahweh: Sexuality in the Old Testament.* Peabody, MA: Hendrickson, 2007.

———. *Typology in Scripture: A Study in Hermenuetical τύπος Structures.* AUSDDS 2. Berrien Springs, MI: Andrews University Press, 1981.

Davidson, Robert. *The Vitality of Worship: A Commentary on the Book of Psalms.* Grand Rapids: Eerdmans, 1998.

Davies, John A. "Solomon as a New Adam in 1 Kings." *WTJ* 73 (2011): 39–57.

Davies, W. D. *The Gospel and the Land: Early Christianity and Jewish Territorial Doctrine.* Berkeley: University of California Press, 1974.

Davies, W. D., and Dale C. Allison Jr. *A Critical and Exegetical Commentary on the Gospel according to Saint Matthew.* 3 vols. ICC. Edinburgh: T&T Clark, 1988–97.

De Graaf, S. G. *Promise and Deliverance.* Translated by H. Evan Runner and Elisabeth Wichers Runner. 4 vols. St. Catherines, ON: Paideia, 1977–81.

Delitzsch, Franz. *Biblical Commentary on the Prophecies of Isaiah.* Translated by James Martin. 2 vols. K&D. Grand Rapids: Eerdmans, 1949.

Delling, G. "στοιχέω, κ.τ.λ." *TDNT* 7:666–69.

Dempster, Stephen G. *Dominion and Dynasty: A Biblical Theology of the Hebrew Bible.* NSBT 15. Downers Grove, IL: InterVarsity, 2003.

Dibelius, Martin, and Heinrich Greeven. *A Commentary on the Epistle of James.* Translated by Michael A. Williams. Hermeneia. Philadelphia: Fortress, 1975.

Dillard, Raymond B. "Intrabiblical Exegesis and the Effusion of the Spirit in Joel." Pages 87–93 in *Creator, Redeemer, Consummator: A Festschrift for Meredith G. Kline.* Edited by Howard Griffith and John R. Muether. Greenville, SC: Reformed Academic Press, 2000.

Dodd, C. H. *According to the Scriptures: The Sub-Structure of New Testament Theology.* London: Nisbet, 1952.

Douglas, Mary. *Leviticus as Literature.* Oxford: Oxford University Press, 1999.

Dowd, Sharon E. Review of *Isaiah's New Exodus in Mark*, by Rikki E. Watts. *JBL* 119 (2000): 140–41.

Driver, S. R. *A Critical and Exegetical Commentary on Deuteronomy.* ICC. 1895. Repr., Edinburgh: T&T Clark, 1996.

Dubis, Mark. "The Land in Biblical Perspective." Paper presented at the Annual Meeting of the Evangelical Theological Society, Valley Forge, PA, November 17, 2005.

———. *Messianic Woes in First Peter: Suffering and Eschatology in 1 Peter 4:12–19.* SBL 33. New York: Peter Lang, 2002.

Duguid, Ian W. *Ezekiel*. NIVAC. Grand Rapids: Zondervan, 1999.

Dumbrell, William J. *Covenant and Creation: A Theology of the Old Testament Covenants*. Nashville: Thomas Nelson, 1984.

———. *The End of the Beginning: Revelation 21–22 and the Old Testament*. Homebush West, NSW: Lancer, 1985.

———. *The Faith of Israel: A Theological Survey of the Old Testament*. 2nd ed. Grand Rapids: Baker Academic, 2002.

———. "Genesis 2:1–17: A Foreshadowing of the New Creation." Pages 53–65 in *Biblical Theology: Retrospect and Prospect*. Edited by Scott J. Hafemann. Downers Grove, IL: InterVarsity, 2002.

———. *The Search for Order: Biblical Eschatology in Focus*. Grand Rapids: Baker Academic, 1994.

Dunn, James D. G. "The Danielic Son of Man in the New Testament." Pages 528–49 in vol. 2 of *The Book of Daniel: Composition and Reception*. Edited by John J. Collins and Peter W. Flint. Leiden: Brill, 2001.

———. *The Epistle to the Galatians*. BNTC. Peabody, MA: Hendrickson, 1993.

———. *The Epistles to the Colossians and to Philemon: A Commentary on the Greek Text*. NIGTC. Grand Rapids: Eerdmans, 1996.

———. "How New Was Paul's Gospel? The Problem of Continuity and Discontinuity." Pages 367–88 in *Gospel in Paul: Studies on Corinthians, Galatians and Romans for Richard N. Longenecker*. Edited by L. Ann Jervis and Peter Richardson. JSNTSup 108. Sheffield: Sheffield Academic Press, 1994.

———. *Romans 1–8*. WBC 38A. Dallas: Word, 1991.

———. "Spirit, New Testament." *NIDNTT* 3:693–707.

Dupont, Jacques. "ΛΑΟΣ ΈΞ ἘΘΝΩΝ." *NTS* 3 (1956): 47–50.

Dupont-Sommer, A. *The Essene Writings from Qumran*. Translated by G. Vermes. Oxford: Blackwell, 1961.

Eberhart, Christian A. "Atonement. I. Old Testament/Hebrew Bible." Pages 23–31 in vol. 3 of *Encyclopedia of the Bible and Its Reception*.

Edited by Hans-Josef Klauck et al. Berlin: de Gruyter, 2010.

Eichrodt, Walther. *Theology of the Old Testament*. Translated by J. A. Baker. 2 vols. OTL. Philadelphia: Westminster, 1961–67.

Eliade, Mircea. *The Myth of the Eternal Return*. Translated by Willard R. Trask. London: Routledge & Kegan Paul, 1955.

Ellingworth, Paul. *The Epistle to the Hebrews: A Commentary on the Greek Text*. NIGTC. Grand Rapids: Eerdmans, 1993.

Elliott, John H. *1 Peter*. AB 37B. New York: Doubleday, 2000.

Elliott, Neil. *The Rhetoric of Romans: Argumentative Constraint and Strategy, and Paul's Dialogue with Judaism*. JSNTSup 45. Sheffield: JSOT Press, 1990.

Ellis, E. Earle. "II Corinthians V.1–10 in Pauline Eschatology." *NTS* 6 (1960): 211–24.

———. "Present and Future Eschatology in Luke." *NTS* 12 (1965): 27–41.

Emerton, J. A. "The Problem of Psalm 87." *VT* 50 (2001): 183–99.

Enns, Peter. *Exodus*. NIVAC. Grand Rapids: Zondervan, 2000.

———. *Inspiration and Incarnation: Evangelicals and the Problem of the Old Testament*. Grand Rapids: Baker Academic, 2005.

Etheridge, J. W. *The Targums of Onkelos and Jonathan ben Uzziel on the Pentateuch, with the Fragments of the Jerusalem Targum from the Chaldee*. New York: KTAV, 1968.

Evans, Craig A. *Mark 8:27–16:20*. WBC 34B. Dallas: Word, 2001.

———. "The Prophetic Setting of the Pentecost Sermon." *ZNW* 74 (1983): 148–50.

Fee, Gordon D. *The First Epistle to the Corinthians*. NICNT. Grand Rapids: Eerdmans, 1987.

———. *God's Empowering Presence: The Holy Spirit in the Letters of Paul*. Peabody, MA: Hendrickson, 1994.

———. "Issues in Evangelical Hermeneutics, Part III: The Great Watershed—Intentionality and Particularity/Eternality: 1 Timothy 2:8–15 as a Test Case." *Crux* 26 (1990): 31–37.

———. *Pauline Christology: An Exegetical-Theological Study*. Peabody, MA: Hendrickson, 2007.

———. "Reflections on Church Order in the Pastoral Epistles, with Further Reflection on the Hermeneutics of Ad Hoc Documents." *JETS* 28 (1985): 141–51.

Feinberg, Charles L. "Jeremiah." Pages 357–694 in vol. 6 of *The Expositor's Bible Commentary*. Edited by Frank E. Gaebelein. Grand Rapids: Zondervan, 1986.

———. "The Rebuilding of the Temple." Pages 91–112 in *Prophecy in the Making*. Edited by Carl F. H. Henry. Carol Stream, IL: Creation House, 1971.

Fekkes, Jan. *Isaiah and Prophetic Traditions in the Book of Revelation: Visionary Antecedents and Their Development*. JSNTSup 93. Sheffield: Sheffield Academic Press, 1994.

Findeis, Hans-Jürgen. *Versöhnung, Apostolat, Kirche: Eine exegetisch-theologische und rezeptionsgeschichtliche Studie zu den Versöhnungsaussagen des Neuen Testaments (2 Kor, Rom, Kol, Eph)*. FB. Würzburg: Echter, 1983.

Fiorenza, Elisabeth Schüssler. "Redemption as Liberation: Apoc 1:5f. and 5:9f." *CBQ* 36 (1974): 220–32.

Fishbane, Michael. *Text and Texture: Close Readings of Selected Biblical Texts*. New York: Schocken, 1979.

Fitzmyer, Joseph. A. *The Gospel according to Luke (X–XXIV)*. AB 28A. Garden City, NY: Doubleday, 1985.

Foulkes, Francis F. *The Acts of God: A Study of the Basis of Typology in the Old Testament*. London: Tyndale, 1958.

Frame, James E. *A Critical and Exegetical Commentary on the Epistles of St. Paul to the Thessalonians*. ICC. New York: Scribner, 1912.

Frame, John M. *The Doctrine of the Christian Life*. Phillipsburg, NJ: P&R, 2008.

France, R. T. *The Gospel of Mark: A Commentary on the Greek Text*. NIGTC. Grand Rapids: Eerdmans, 2002.

———. *Jesus and the Old Testament: His Application of Old Testament Passages to Himself and His Mission*. Downers Grove, IL: InterVarsity, 1971.

———. "Old Testament Prophecy and the Future of Israel: A Study of the Teaching of Jesus." *TynBul* 26 (1975): 53–78.

Francis, Fred O. "Eschatology and History in Luke-Acts." *JAAR* 37 (1969): 49–63.

Franklin, Eric. "The Ascension and the Eschatology of Luke-Acts." *SJT* 23 (1970): 191–200.

Fuller, Daniel P. *The Unity of the Bible: Unfolding God's Plan for Humanity*. Grand Rapids: Zondervan, 1992.

Fung, Ronald Y. K. *The Epistle to the Galatians*. NICNT. Grand Rapids: Eerdmans, 1988.

Furnish, Victor Paul. *II Corinthians*. AB 32A. New York: Doubleday, 1984.

Furter, Daniel. *Les Épîtres de Paul aux Colossiens et à Philémon*. CEB. Vaux-sur-Seine: Edifac, 1987.

Gaffin, Richard B., Jr. *By Faith, Not by Sight: Paul and the Order of Salvation*. Waynesboro, GA: Paternoster, 2006.

———. *The Centrality of the Resurrection: A Study in Paul's Soteriology*. Grand Rapids: Baker Academic, 1978.

———. "The Last Adam, the Life-Giving Spirit." Pages 191–231 in *The Forgotten Christ: Exploring the Majesty and Mystery of God Incarnate*. Edited by Stephen Clark. Nottingham, UK: Apollos, 2007.

———. "A Sabbath Rest Still Awaits the People of God." Pages 33–51 in *Pressing toward the Mark: Essays Commemorating Fifty Years of the Orthodox Presbyterian Church*. Edited by Charles G. Dennison and Richard C. Gamble. Philadelphia: Committee for the Historian of the Orthodox Presbyterian Church, 1986.

Gage, Warren Austin. *The Gospel of Genesis: Studies in Protology and Eschatology*. Winona Lake, IN: Carpenter Books, 1984.

Garcia, Mark A. "Imputation and the Christology of Union with Christ: Calvin, Osiander, and the Contemporary Quest for a Reformed Model." *WTJ* 68 (2006): 219–51.

Gardner, Anne E. "The Nature of the New Heavens and New Earth in Isaiah 66:22." *ABR* 50 (2002): 10–67.

Garland, David E. *1 Corinthians*. BECNT. Grand Rapids: Baker Academic, 2003.

Garrett, Duane. *Hosea, Joel*. NAC 19A. Nashville: Broadman & Holman, 1997.

———. "Meredith Kline on Suzerainty, Circumcision, and Baptism." Pages 257–84 in *Believer's*

Baptism: Sign of the Covenant in Christ. Edited by Thomas R. Schreiner and Shawn D. Wright. NAC Studies in Bible Theology. Nashville: B&H Publishing, 2006.

———. "The Ways of God: Reenactment and Reversal in Hosea." Inaugural address for the installation of Duane Garrett as professor of Old Testament at Gordon-Conwell Theological Seminary, South Hamilton, MA, fall 1996.

Gaventa, Beverly R. "The Eschatology of Luke-Acts Revisited." *Encounter* 43 (1982): 27–42.

George, Timothy. *Galatians.* NAC 30. Nashville: B&H, 1994.

Gese, Hartmut. "Tradition and Biblical Theology." Pages 301–26 in *Tradition and Theology in the Old Testament.* Edited by Douglas A. Knight. Philadelphia: Fortress, 1977.

Gesenius, W. *Hebrew Grammar.* Edited and enlarged by E. Kautzsch. Translated by A. E. Cowley. Oxford: Clarendon, 1970.

Gignilliat, Mark. *Paul and Isaiah's Servants: Paul's Theological Reading of Isaiah 40–66 in 2 Corinthians 5.14–6.10.* LNTS 330. London: T&T Clark, 2007.

Giles, Kevin. "Present-Future Eschatology in the Book of Acts (I)." *RTR* 40 (1981): 65–71.

———. "Present-Future Eschatology in the Book of Acts (II)." *RTR* 41 (1982): 11–18.

Gill, John. *A Body of Doctrinal Divinity.* London: M. & S. Higham, 1839.

Gilmour, S. MacLean. "The Revelation to John." Pages 945–70 in *The Interpreter's One-Volume Commentary on the Bible.* Edited by Charles M. Laymon. Nashville: Abingdon, 1971.

Ginzberg, Louis. *The Legends of the Jews.* Translated by Henrietta Szold. 7 vols. Philadelphia: Jewish Publication Society, 1909–38.

Gladd, Benjamin L. *Revealing the Mysterion: The Use of Mystery in Daniel and Second Temple Judaism with Its Bearing on First Corinthians.* BZNW 160. Berlin: de Gruyter, 2008.

Glazov, Gregory Yuri. *The Bridling of the Tongue and the Opening of the Mouth in Biblical Prophecy.* JSOTSup 311. Sheffield: Sheffield Academic Press, 2001.

Glickman, S. Craig. *Knowing Christ.* Chicago: Moody, 1980.

Gnilka, Joachim. *Der Kolosserbrief.* HTKNT. Freiburg: Herder, 1980.

Goldingay, John E. *Daniel.* WBC 30. Dallas: Word, 1989.

———. *Psalms.* 2 vols. BCOTWP. Grand Rapids: Baker Academic, 2006.

Goldsworthy, Graeme. *According to Plan: The Unfolding Revelation of God in the Bible.* Leicester: Inter-Varsity, 1991.

Goodwin, Mark J. "Hosea and 'the Son of the Living God' in Matthew 16:16b." *CBQ* 67 (2005): 265–83.

Goppelt, Leonhard. *A Commentary on 1 Peter.* Translated by John E. Alsup. Edited by Ferdinand Hahn. Grand Rapids: Eerdmans, 1993.

———. *Theology of the New Testament.* Translated by John E. Alsup. Edited by Jürgen Roloff. 2 vols. Grand Rapids: Eerdmans, 1981–82.

———. "τύπος κτλ." *TDNT* 8:246–59.

———. *Typos: The Typological Interpretation of the Old Testament in the New.* Translated by Donald H. Madvig. Grand Rapids: Eerdmans, 1982.

Gordon, T. David. "The Problem at Galatia." *Int* 41 (1987): 32–43.

Goulder, M. D. *Type and History in Acts.* London: SPCK, 1964.

Gowan, Donald E. *Eschatology in the Old Testament.* Philadelphia: Fortress, 1986.

Grayson, A. Kirk. *Assyrian Rulers of the Third and Second Millennia BC (1114–859 BC).* RIMA 2. Toronto: University of Toronto Press, 1991.

Grimm, Werner. *Weil Ich dich liebe: Die Verkündigung Jesu und Deuterojesaja.* ANTJ 1. Bern: Herbert Lang, 1976.

Grudem, Wayne. *The First Epistle of Peter.* TNTC 17. Leicester: Inter-Varsity, 1988.

———. *Systematic Theology.* Grand Rapids: Zondervan, 1994.

Gruenler, Royce Gordon. "The Mission-Lifestyle Setting of 1 Timothy 2:8–15." *JETS* 41 (1998): 215–38.

Gundry, Robert H. "The Non-imputation of Christ's Righteousness." Pages 17–45 in *Justification: What's at Stake in the Current Debates.* Edited by Mark A. Husbands and Daniel J. Treier. Downers Grove, IL: InterVarsity, 2004.

———. "On Oden's Answer." *Books and Culture* 7, no. 2 (2001): 14–15, 39.

———. "Why I Didn't Endorse 'The Gospel of Jesus Christ: An Evangelical Celebration' . . . Even Though I Wasn't Asked To." *Books and Culture* 7, no. 1 (2001): 6–9.

Gunkel, Hermann. *Schöpfung und Chaos in Urzeit und Endzeit: Eine religionsgeschichtliche Untersuchung über Gen 1 und Ap Joh 12.* Göttingen: Vandenhoeck & Ruprecht, 1895.

Guthrie, Donald. *Galatians.* NCB. Camden, NJ: Thomas Nelson, 1969.

———. *New Testament Theology.* Downers Grove, IL: InterVarsity, 1981.

Hafemann, Scott J. *2 Corinthians.* NIVAC. Grand Rapids: Zondervan, 2000.

———. *Paul, Moses, and the History of Israel: The Letter/Spirit Contrast and the Argument from Scripture in 2 Corinthians 3.* WUNT 81. Tübingen: Mohr Siebeck, 1995.

———. "'The Righteousness of God': An Introduction to the Theological and Historical Foundation of Peter Stuhlmacher's Biblical Theology of the New Testament." Pages xv–xli in *How to Do Biblical Theology,* by Peter Stuhlmacher. PTMS 38. Allison Park, PA: Pickwick, 1995.

———. "'Self-Commendation' and Apostolic Legitimacy in 2 Corinthians: A Pauline Dialectic?" *NTS* 36 (1990): 66–88.

———. *Suffering and Ministry in the Spirit: Paul's Defense of His Ministry in II Corinthians 2:14–3:3.* Grand Rapids: Eerdmans, 1990.

Hagner, Donald A. *Hebrews.* NIBC. Peabody, MA: Hendrickson, 1990.

Hahn, F. C. "Siehe, jetzt ist der Tag des Heils." *EvT* 33 (1973): 244–53.

Hahn, Scott W. *Kinship by Covenant: A Canonical Approach to the Fulfillment of God's Saving Promises.* AYBRL. New Haven: Yale University Press, 2009.

Hailey, Homer. *A Commentary on Isaiah, with Emphasis on the Messianic Hope.* Grand Rapids: Baker Academic, 1985.

Hamilton, James. "The Glory of God in Salvation through Judgment: The Center of Biblical Theology?" *TynBul* 57, no. 1 (2006): 57–84.

———. *God's Glory in Salvation through Judgment: A Biblical Theology.* Wheaton: Crossway, 2010.

Hamilton, Neill Q. *The Holy Spirit and Eschatology in Paul.* SJTOP 6. Edinburgh: Oliver & Boyd, 1957.

Hamilton, Victor P. *The Book of Genesis: Chapters 1–17.* NICOT. Grand Rapids: Eerdmans, 1990.

———. *The Book of Genesis: Chapters 18–50.* NICOT. Grand Rapids: Eerdmans, 1995.

Hansen, G. Walter. *Galatians.* IVPNTC. Downers Grove, IL: InterVarsity, 1994.

Harris, Murray J. *The Second Epistle to the Corinthians: A Commentary on the Greek Text.* NIGTC. Grand Rapids: Eerdmans, 2005.

Hartley, John E. *Genesis.* NIBC. Peabody, MA: Hendrickson, 2000.

Hartman, Lars. *Prophecy Interpreted: The Formation of Some Jewish Apocalyptic Texts and of the Eschatological Discourse Mark 13 par.* ConBNT 1. Lund: Gleerup, 1966.

Harvey, A. E. "The Use of Mystery Language in the Bible." *JTS* 31 (1980): 320–36.

Hasel, Gerhard F. *New Testament Theology: Basic Issues in the Current Debate.* Grand Rapids: Eerdmans, 1978.

———. *Old Testament Theology: Basic Issues in the Current Debate.* Grand Rapids: Eerdmans, 1972.

———. "Sabbath." *ABD* 5:850–56.

Hatch, Edwin, and Henry A. Redpath. *A Concordance to the Septuagint and the Other Greek Versions of the Old Testament.* Graz: Akademische Druck- & Verlagsanstalt, 1954.

Hatina, Thomas R. "Exile." Pages 348–51 in *Dictionary of New Testament Background.* Edited by Craig A. Evans and Stanley E. Porter. Downers Grove, IL: InterVarsity, 2000.

Hawkins, Frank. "Orders and Ordination in the New Testament." Pages 339–47 in *The Study of Liturgy.* Edited by Cheslyn Jones et al. Rev. ed. New York: Oxford University Press, 1992.

Hay, David M. *Colossians.* ANTC. Nashville: Abingdon, 2000.

———. *Glory at the Right Hand: Psalm 110 in Early Christianity*. SBLMS 18. Nashville: Abingdon, 1973.

Hays, Richard B. "Can Narrative Criticism Recover the Theological Unity of Scripture?" *JTI* 2 (2008): 193–211.

———. *The Conversion of the Imagination: Paul as Interpreter of Israel's Scripture*. Grand Rapids: Eerdmans, 2005.

———. *Echoes of Scripture in the Letters of Paul*. New Haven: Yale University Press, 1989.

———. *First Corinthians*. IBC. Louisville: John Knox, 1997.

———. *The Moral Vision of the New Testament: Community, Cross, New Creation; A Contemporary Introduction to New Testament Ethics*. San Francisco: HarperSanFrancisco, 1996.

Hemer, Colin J. *The Letters to the Seven Churches of Asia in Their Local Setting*. JSNTSup 11. Sheffield: JSOT Press, 1986.

Hendriksen, William. *Exposition of I and II Thessalonians*. Grand Rapids: Baker Academic, 1979.

———. *Exposition of Ephesians*. Grand Rapids: Baker Academic, 1967.

Heppe, Heinrich. *Reformed Dogmatics Set Out and Illustrated from the Sources*. Translated by G. T. Thompson. Revised and edited by Ernst Bizer. London: Allen & Unwin, 1950.

Hess, Richard S. *Joshua*. TOTC. Downers Grove, IL: InterVarsity, 1996.

Hiebert, D. E. "Peter's Thanksgiving for Our Salvation." *SM* 29 (1980): 85–103.

Higgins, A. J. B. *The Lord's Supper in the New Testament*. SBT 6. Chicago: Allenson, 1956.

Hildebrandt, Wilf. *An Old Testament Theology of the Spirit of God*. Peabody, MA: Hendrickson, 1995.

Hill, Charles E. "God's Speech in These Last Days: The New Testament Canon as an Eschatological Phenomenon." Pages 203–54 in *Resurrection and Eschatology: Theology in Service of the Church; Essays in Honor of Richard B. Gaffin Jr.* Edited by Lane G. Tipton and Jeffrey C. Waddington. Phillipsburg, NJ: P&R, 2008.

Hill, David. "The Spirit and the Church's Witness: Observations on Acts 1:6–8." *IBS* 6 (1984): 16–26.

Hirsch, E. D. *Validity in Interpretation*. New Haven: Yale University Press, 1967.

Hodges, Zane C. *The Gospel under Siege: A Study on Faith and Works*. Dallas: Redención Viva, 1981.

Hoekema, Anthony A. *The Bible and the Future*. Grand Rapids: Eerdmans, 1979.

Höffken, Peter. *Das Buch Jesaja: Kapitel 40–66*. NSKAT 18/2. Stuttgart: Katholisches Bibelwerk, 1998.

Hofius, Otfried. "Erwägungen zur Gestalt und Herkunft des paulinischen Versöhnungsgedankens." *ZTK* 77 (1980): 186–99.

Holtz, Traugott. *Die Christologie der Apokalypse des Johannes*. TUGAL 85. Berlin: Akademie-Verlag, 1971.

Hooker, Morna D. *From Adam to Christ: Essays on Paul*. Cambridge: Cambridge University Press, 1990.

Horton, Michael S. *Covenant and Eschatology: The Divine Drama*. Louisville: Westminster John Knox, 2002.

Hoskier, H. C. *Concerning the Text of the Apocalypse*. 2 vols. London: Bernard Quaritch, 1929.

Hossfeld, Frank-Lothar, and Erich Zenger. *Psalms 2: A Commentary on Ps 51–100*. Translated by Linda M. Maloney. Edited by Klaus Baltzer. Hermeneia. Minneapolis: Fortress, 2005.

Hubbard, Moyer V. *New Creation in Paul's Letters and Thought*. SNTMS 119. Cambridge: Cambridge University Press, 2002.

Hübner, Hans. *An Philemon, an die Kolosser, an die Epheser*. HNT 12. Tübingen: Mohr Siebeck, 1997.

———. *Biblische Theologie des Neuen Testaments*. 3 vols. Göttingen: Vandenhoeck & Ruprecht, 1990–95.

———. *Vetus Testamentum in Novo*. Göttingen: Vandenhoeck & Ruprecht, 1997.

Huey, F. B., Jr. *Jeremiah, Lamentations*. NAC 16. Nashville: Broadman, 1993.

Hugedé, Norbert. *Commentaire de L'Épître aux Colossiens*. Geneva: Labor et Fides, 1968.

Hugenberger, Gordon P. *Marriage as a Covenant: Biblical Law and Ethics as Developed from Malachi.* VTSup 52. Leiden: Brill, 1994.

———. "A Neglected Symbolism for the Clothing of Adam and Eve (Genesis 3:21)." Paper presented at the annual meeting of the Tyndale Fellowship, Cambridge, July 1996.

Hughes, Philip E. *Paul's Second Epistle to the Corinthians.* NICNT. Grand Rapids: Eerdmans, 1967.

Hurley, James B. *Man and Woman in Biblical Perspective.* Grand Rapids: Zondervan, 1981.

Hurst, L. D. "Eschatology and 'Platonism' in the Epistle to the Hebrews." *SBLSP* 23 (1984): 41–74.

Hutter, Manfred. "Adam als Gärtner und König (Gen 2:8, 15)." *BZ* 30 (1986): 258–62.

Iwry, Samuel. "*Maṣṣēbāh and Bāmāh* in 1Q Isaiah[a] 6 13." *JBL* 76 (1957): 225–32.

Jackson, T. Ryan. *New Creation in Paul's Letters: A Study of the Historical and Social Setting of a Pauline Concept.* WUNT 2/272. Tübingen: Mohr Siebeck, 2010.

Jenson, Robert W. *Ezekiel.* BTCB. Grand Rapids: Baker Academic, 2009.

Jeremias, Joachim. *The Eucharistic Words of Jesus.* Translated by Norman Perrin. New York: Scribner, 1966.

Jewett, Robert. *Romans.* Hermeneia. Minneapolis: Fortress, 2007.

Jobes, Karen H. *1 Peter.* BECNT. Grand Rapids: Baker Academic, 2005.

———. "Jerusalem, Our Mother: Metalepsis and Intertextuality in Galatians 4.21–31." *WTJ* 55 (1993): 299–320.

Johnson, Aubrey R. *The One and the Many in the Israelite Conception of God.* Cardiff: University of Wales Press, 1960.

Johnson, Dennis E. "The Function of Romans 7:13–25 in Paul's Argument for the Law's Impotence and the Spirit's Power, and Its Bearing on the Identity of the Schizophrenic 'I.'" Pages 3–59 in *Resurrection and Eschatology: Theology in Service of the Church; Essays in Honor of Richard B. Gaffin Jr.* Edited by Lane G. Tipton and Jeffrey C. Waddington. Phillipsburg, NJ: P&R, 2008.

Johnson, Luke Timothy. *The Gospel of Luke.* SP 3. Collegeville, MN: Liturgical Press, 1991.

———. *Hebrews.* NTL. Louisville: Westminster John Knox, 2006.

———. *The Letter of James.* AB 37A. New York: Doubleday, 1995.

Johnson, S. Lewis. "Paul and the 'Israel of God': An Exegetical and Eschatological Case Study." Pages 181–96 in *Essays in Honor of J. Dwight Pentecost.* Edited by Stanley D. Toussaint and Charles H. Dyer. Chicago: Moody, 1986.

Joüon, Paul. *A Grammar of Biblical Hebrew.* Translated and revised by T. Muraoka. 2 vols. SubBi 14. Rome: Editrice Pontificio Istituto Biblio, 1991–93.

Kaiser, Otto. *Isaiah 1–12.* Translated by John Bowden. 2nd ed. OTL. Philadelphia: Westminster, 1983.

Kaiser, Walter C. *The Uses of the Old Testament in the New.* Chicago: Moody, 1985.

Käsemann, Ernst. *Commentary on Romans.* Translated and edited by Geoffrey W. Bromiley. Grand Rapids: Eerdmans, 1980.

Katanacho, Yohanna I. "Investigating the Purposeful Placement of Psalm 86." PhD diss., Trinity International University, 2006.

Keel, Othmar. *The Symbolism of the Biblical World: Ancient Near Eastern Iconography and the Book of Psalms.* Translated by Timothy J. Hallett. New York: Crossroad, 1985.

Keesmaat, Sylvia C. "Exodus and the Intertextual Transformation of Tradition in Romans 8:14–30." *JSNT* 54 (1994): 29–56.

———. *Paul and His Story: (Re)Interpreting the Exodus Tradition.* JSNTSup 181. Sheffield: Sheffield Academic Press, 1999.

Keil, C. F. *Biblical Commentary on the Book of Daniel.* Translated by M. G. Easton. K&D. Reprint, Grand Rapids: Eerdmans, 1971.

———. *Prophecies of Ezekiel.* Translated by James Martin. Vol. 2. K&D. Reprint, Grand Rapids: Eerdmans, 1970.

———. *The Prophecies of Jeremiah.* Translated by David Patrick and James Kennedy. 2 vols. K&D. Reprint, Grand Rapids: Eerdmans, 1968.

Keil, C. F., and F. Delitzsch. *The Pentateuch.* Vol. 1 of *Biblical Commentary on the Old*

Testament. Reprint, Grand Rapids: Eerdmans, 1971.

Kellermann, D. "גּוּר." *TDOT* 2:439–49.

Kelly, J. N. D. *The Epistles of Peter and Jude*. BNTC. Peabody, MA: Hendrickson, 1969.

Kennedy, Joel. *The Recapitulation of Israel*. WUNT 2/257. Tübingen: Mohr Siebeck, 2008.

Kidner, Derek. *Genesis*. TOTC. Downers Grove, IL: InterVarsity, 1967.

———. "Isaiah." Pages 629–70 in *New Bible Commentary: 21st Century Edition*. Edited by D. A. Carson et al. Downers Grove, IL: InterVarsity, 1994.

Kim, Jung Hoon. *The Significance of Clothing Imagery in the Pauline Corpus*. JSNTSup 268. London: T&T Clark, 2004.

Kim, Seyoon. *The Origin of Paul's Gospel*. Grand Rapids: Eerdmans, 1982.

———. "Paul's Common Paranesis (1 Thess. 4–5; Phil. 2–4; and Rom. 12–13): The Correspondence between Romans 1:18–32 and 12:1–2, and the Unity of Romans 12–13." *TynBul* 62 (2011): 109–39.

———. *"The 'Son of Man'" as the Son of God*. WUNT 30. Tübingen: Mohr Siebeck, 1983.

Kirk, J. R. Daniel. *Unlocking Romans: Resurrection and the Justification of God*. Grand Rapids: Eerdmans, 2008.

Kissane, Edward J. *The Book of Isaiah*. 2 vols. Dublin: Browne & Nolan, 1943.

Kline, Meredith G. *By Oath Consigned: A Reinterpretation of the Covenant Signs of Circumcision and Baptism*. Grand Rapids: Eerdmans, 1968.

———. *Images of the Spirit*. Grand Rapids: Baker Academic, 1980.

———. *Kingdom Prologue: Genesis Foundations for a Covenantal Worldview*. Overland Park, KS: Two Age Press, 2000.

———. *The Structure of Biblical Authority*. Grand Rapids: Eerdmans, 1972.

Koester, Craig R. *Hebrews*. AB 36. New York: Doubleday, 2001.

Kohler, K. "Dietary Laws." Pages 596–600 in vol. 4 of *The Jewish Encyclopedia: A Descriptive Record of the History, Religion, Literature, and Customs of the Jewish People from the Earliest Times to the Present Day*. Edited by I. Singer. New York: Funk & Wagnalls, 1903.

Koole, Jan L. *Isaiah III/3: Chapters 56–66*. Translated by Antony P. Runia. HCOT. Leuven: Peeters, 2001.

Köstenberger, Andreas J. *John*. BECNT. Grand Rapids: Baker Academic, 2004.

———. "The Mystery of Christ and the Church: Head and Body, 'One Flesh.'" *TJ* 12 (1991): 79–94.

Kraft, Heinrich. *Die Offenbarung des Johannes*. HNT 16A. Tübingen: Mohr Siebeck, 1974.

Kraus, Hans-Joachim. *Psalms 60–150*. Translated by Hilton C. Oswald. CC. Minneapolis: Fortress, 1993.

Kraus, Wolfgang. *Der Tod Jesu als Heiligtumsweihe: Eine Untersuchung zum Umfeld der Sühnevorstellung in Römer 3,25–26a*. WMANT 66. Neukirchen-Vluyn: Neukirchener Verlag, 1991.

Kreitzer, Larry J. "Eschatology." *DPL* 253–69.

———. "Parousia." *DLNTD* 856–75.

Kruse, Colin G. *The Letters of John*. PNTC. Grand Rapids: Eerdmans, 2000.

Kuhn, K. "προσήλυτος." *TDNT* 6:727–44.

Kümmel, Werner Georg. *The Theology of the New Testament according to Its Major Witnesses*. Translated by John E. Steely. Nashville: Abingdon, 1973.

Kurz, W. S. "Acts 3:19–26 as a Test of the Role of Eschatology in Lukan Christology." *SBLSP* 11 (1977): 309–23.

Kutsko, John F. *Between Heaven and Earth: Divine Presence and Absence in the Book of Ezekiel*. BJS 7. Winona Lake, IN: Eisenbrauns, 2000.

Laansma, Jon. *"I Will Give You Rest": The "Rest" Motif in the New Testament with Special Reference to Matthew 11 and Hebrews 3–4*. WUNT 2/98. Tübingen: Mohr Siebeck, 1997.

Lacocque, André. *The Book of Daniel*. Translated by David Pellauer. London: SPCK, 1979.

Ladd, George Eldon. *A Commentary on the Revelation of John*. Grand Rapids: Eerdmans, 1972.

———. *The Presence of the Future: The Eschatology of Biblical Realism*. Grand Rapids: Eerdmans, 1974.

———. *A Theology of the New Testament*. Grand Rapids: Eerdmans, 1974.

———. *A Theology of the New Testament*. Rev. ed. Grand Rapids: Eerdmans, 1993.

Landy, Francis. *Paradoxes of Paradise: Identity and Difference in the Song of Songs*. BLS 7. Sheffield: Almond, 1983.

———. "The Song of Songs." Pages 305–19 in *The Literary Guide to the Bible*. Edited by Robert Alter and Frank Kermode. London: Collins, 1987.

Lane, William L. *Hebrews 1–8*. WBC 47A. Dallas: Word, 1991.

LaRondelle, Hans K. *The Israel of God in Prophecy: Principles of Prophetic Interpretation*. AUMSR 13. Berrien Springs, MI: Andrews University Press, 1983.

LaSor, William Sanford. "Prophecy, Inspiration, and *Sensus Plenior*." *TynBul* 29 (1978): 49–60.

Lee, Archie. "Gen. 1 and the Plagues Tradition in Ps. 105." *VT* 40 (1990): 257–63.

Lemcio, Eugene E. "The Unifying Kerygma of the New Testament." *JSNT* 33 (1988): 3–17.

———. "The Unifying Kerygma of the New Testament (II)." *JSNT* 38 (1990): 3–11.

Leupold, H. C. *Exposition of Genesis*. 2 vols. Grand Rapids: Baker Academic, 1942.

Levenson, Jon D. *Creation and the Persistence of Evil: The Jewish Drama of Divine Omnipotence*. San Francisco: Harper & Row, 1988.

———. *Sinai and Zion: An Entry into the Jewish Bible*. San Francisco: Harper & Row, 1987.

———. *Theology of the Program of Restoration of Ezekiel 40–48*. HSM 10. Cambridge, MA: Scholars Press, 1976.

Levine, Baruch A. *Leviticus*. JPSTC. Philadelphia: Jewish Publication Society, 1989.

Levison, John R. "The Spirit and the Temple in Paul's Letters to the Corinthians." Pages 189–215 in *Paul and His Theology*. Edited by Stanley E. Porter. PS 3. Leiden: Brill, 2006.

Lewis, C. S. *The Voyage of the Dawn Treader*. New York: Harper Trophy, 1994.

Lewis, Theodore J. "Beelzebul." *ABD* 1:638–40.

Lightfoot, J. B. *Saint Paul's Epistles to the Colossians and to Philemon*. Rev. ed. CCL. Grand Rapids: Zondervan, 1961.

Limburg, James. *Psalms*. WestBC. Louisville: Westminster John Knox, 2000.

Lincoln, Andrew T. "Colossians." *NIB* 11:551–669

———. *Ephesians*. WBC 42. Dallas: Word, 1990.

———. *Paradise Now and Not Yet: Studies in the Role of the Heavenly Dimension in Paul's Thought with Special Reference to His Eschatology*. SNTSMS 43. Cambridge: Cambridge University Press, 1981.

———. "Sabbath, Rest, and Eschatology in the New Testament." Pages 197–220 in *From Sabbath to Lord's Day: A Biblical, Historical, and Theological Investigation*. Edited by D. A. Carson. Grand Rapids: Zondervan, 1982.

Logan, Samuel T. "The Doctrine of Justification in the Theology of Jonathan Edwards." *WTJ* 46 (1984): 26–52.

Lohfink, Gerhard. *Paulus vor Damaskus: Arbeitsweisen der neueren Bibelwissenschaft dargestellt an den Texten Apg 9:1–19, 22:3–21, 26:9–18*. SBS 4. Stuttgart: Katholisches Bibelwerk, 1966.

Lohmeyer, Ernst. *Die Offenbarung des Johannes*. 3rd ed. HNT 16. Tübingen: Mohr Siebeck, 1970.

Lohse, Eduard. *A Commentary on the Epistles to the Colossians and to Philemon*. Translated by William R. Poehlmann and Robert J. Karris. Edited by Helmut Koester. Hermeneia. Philadelphia: Fortress, 1975.

Longenecker, Richard N. *Galatians*. WBC 41. Nashville: Thomas Nelson, 1990.

Longman, Tremper, III. *Immanuel in Our Place: Seeing Christ in Israel's Worship*. Phillipsburg, NJ: P&R, 2001.

Louw, Johannes P., and Eugene A. Nida, eds. *Greek-English Lexicon of the New Testament: Based on Semantic Domains*. 2nd ed. 2 vols. New York: United Bible Societies, 1989.

Lundbom, Jack R. *Jeremiah 21–36*. AB 21B. New York: Doubleday, 2004.

Lust, Johan, Erik Eynikel, and Katrin Hauspie. *Greek-English Lexicon of the Septuagint*. 2 vols. Stuttgart: Deutsche Bibelgesellschaft, 1996.

Luther, Martin. *The Bondage of the Will: A New Translation of De servo arbitrio (1525), Martin Luther's Reply to Erasmus of Rotterdam*.

Translated by J. I. Packer and O. R. Johnston. Westwood, NJ: Revell, 1957.

———. *Lectures on Genesis*. LW 1. Saint Louis: Concordia, 1958.

MacDonald, Margaret. *Colossians and Ephesians*. SP 17. Collegeville, MN: Liturgical Press, 2000.

Mackie, Scott D. *Eschatology and Exhortation in the Epistle to the Hebrews*. WUNT 2/223. Tübingen: Mohr Siebeck, 2007.

MacRae, George W. "Heavenly Temple and Eschatology in the Letter to the Hebrews." *Semeia* 12 (1978): 179–99.

Maher, Michael. *Targum Pseudo-Jonathan: Exodus*. ArBib 2. Collegeville, MN: Liturgical Press, 1994.

Maier, Christl M. "Psalm 87 as a Reappraisal of the Zion Tradition and Its Reception in Galatians 4:26." *CBQ* 69 (2007): 473–86.

Manson, William. "Eschatology in the New Testament." Pages 1–16 in *Eschatology: Four Papers Read to the Society for the Study of Theology*. SJTOP 2. Edinburgh: Oliver & Boyd, 1953.

Marcus, Joel. Review of *Isaiah's New Exodus in Mark*, by Rikki E. Watts. *JTS* 50 (1999): 222–25.

Marcus, Ralph, trans. *Philo, Supplement II: Questions and Answers on Exodus*. LCL. London: Heinemann, 1953.

Marshall, I. Howard. *1 and 2 Thessalonians*. NCB. Grand Rapids: Eerdmans, 1983.

———. "Acts." Pages 513–606 in *Commentary on the New Testament Use of the Old Testament*. Edited by G. K. Beale and D. A. Carson. Grand Rapids: Baker Academic, 2007.

———. *The Epistles of John*. NICNT. Grand Rapids: Eerdmans, 1978.

———. *New Testament Theology: Many Witnesses, One Gospel*. Downers Grove, IL: InterVarsity, 2004.

———. "Slippery Words I: Eschatology." *ExpTim* 89 (1978): 264–69.

Martin, Ralph P. *2 Corinthians*. WBC 40. Waco: Word, 1986.

———. *Colossians and Philemon*. NCB. Reprint, London: Oliphants, 1978.

———. *James*. WBC 48. Waco: Word, 1988.

———. *Reconciliation: A Study of Paul's Theology*. Atlanta: John Knox, 1981.

Martínez, Florentino García. *The Dead Sea Scrolls Translated: The Qumran Texts in English*. Translated by Wilfred G. E. Watson. 2nd ed. Grand Rapids: Eerdmans, 1996.

Martínez, Florentino García, and Eibert J. C. Tigchelaar. *The Dead Sea Scrolls Study Edition*. 2 vols. Grand Rapids: Eerdmans, 2000.

Matera, Frank J. "The Culmination of Paul's Argument to the Galatians: Gal. 5:1–6:17." *JSNT* 32 (1988): 79–91.

———. *Galatians*. SP 9. Collegeville, MN: Liturgical Press, 1992.

———. *New Testament Theology: Exploring Diversity and Unity*. Louisville: Westminster John Knox, 2007.

Mathewson, David. *A New Heaven and a New Earth: The Meaning and Function of the Old Testament in Revelation 21.1–22.5*. JSNTSup 238. Sheffield: Sheffield Academic Press, 2006.

Mathison, Keith A. *From Age to Age: The Unfolding of Biblical Eschatology*. Phillipsburg, NJ: P&R, 2009.

Matthews, Kenneth A. *Genesis 1–11:26*. NAC 1A. Nashville: Broadman & Holman, 1996.

Mattill, Andrew J., Jr. *Luke and the Last Things: A Perspective for the Understanding of Lukan Thought*. Dillsboro, NC: Western North Carolina Press, 1979.

Mauro, Philip. *The Patmos Visions: A Study of the Apocalypse*. Boston: Hamilton, 1925.

Mayes, A. D. H. *Deuteronomy*. NCB. Grand Rapids: Eerdmans, 1979.

Mays, James Luther. *Psalms*. IBC. Louisville: John Knox, 1994.

McCartney, Dan G. "*Ecce Homo*: The Coming of the Kingdom as the Restoration of Human Viceregency." *WTJ* 56 (1994): 1–21.

McConville, J. G. *Deuteronomy*. AOTC 5. Leicester: Apollos, 2002.

McKenzie, John L. *Second Isaiah*. AB 20. Garden City, NY: Doubleday, 1968.

McNamara, Martin. *The New Testament and the Palestinian Targum to the Pentateuch*. AnBib 27. Rome: Pontifical Biblical Institute, 1966.

McNamara, Martin, and Robert Hayward. *Targum Neofiti 1: Exodus*. ArBib 2. Collegeville, MN: Liturgical Press, 1994.

McRay, J. "Charismata in Second-Century Eschatology." Pages 151–68 in *The Last Things: Essays Presented by His Students to Dr. W. B. West Jr. upon the Occasion of His Sixty-Fifth Birthday*. Edited by Jack P. Lewis. Austin: Sweet, 1972.

Meadors, Edward. P. *Idolatry and the Hardening of the Heart: A Study in Biblical Theology*. New York: T&T Clark, 2006.

Mell, Ulrich. *Neue Schöpfung: Eine traditionsgeschichtliche und exegetische Studie zu einem soteriologischen Grundsatz paulinischer Theologie*. BZNW 56. Berlin: de Gruyter, 1989.

Merkle, Ben L. "Romans 11 and the Future of Ethnic Israel." *JETS* 43 (2000): 709–21.

Metzger, Bruce M. *A Textual Commentary on the Greek New Testament*. London: United Bible Societies, 1971.

Michaels, J. Ramsey. *1 Peter*. WBC 49. Nashville: Nelson, 1988.

———. "Eschatology in 1 Peter III.17." *NTS* 13 (1967): 394–401.

Middleton, J. Richard. *The Liberating Image: The Imago Dei in Genesis 1*. Grand Rapids: Brazos, 2005.

Mihalios, Stefanos. *The Danielic Eschatological Hour in the Johannine Literature*. LNTS 346. New York: T&T Clark, 2011.

Miller, Patrick D. "Creation and Covenant." Pages 155–68 in *Biblical Theology: Problems and Perspectives*. Edited by Steven J. Kraftchick, Charles D. Myers Jr., and Ben C. Ollenburger. Nashville: Abingdon, 1995.

Minear, Paul S. *I Saw a New Earth: An Introduction to the Visions of the Apocalypse*. Washington, DC: Corpus, 1969.

Miscall, Peter D. *Isaiah*. Readings. Sheffield: JSOT Press, 1993.

Mitchell, Alan C. *Hebrews*. SP 13. Collegeville, MN: Liturgical Press, 2007.

Moessner, David P. *Lord of the Banquet: The Literary and Theological Significance of the Lukan Travel Narrative*. Minneapolis: Fortress, 1989.

Montefiore, Hugh. *A Commentary on the Epistle to the Hebrews*. BNTC. London: A&C Black, 1964.

Montgomery, J. A. "The Education of the Seer of the Apocalypse." *JBL* 45 (1926): 70–80.

Moo, Douglas J. "Creation and New Creation." *BBR* 20 (2010): 39–60.

———. *The Epistle to the Romans*. NICNT. Grand Rapids: Eerdmans, 1996.

———. "Israel and Paul in Romans 7:7–12." *NTS* 32 (1986): 122–35.

———. "Israel and the Law in Romans 5–11: Interaction with the New Perspective." Pages 185–216 in *The Paradoxes of Paul*. Vol. 2 of *Justification and Variegated Nomism*. Edited by D. A. Carson, Peter T. O'Brien, and Mark A. Seifrid. Grand Rapids: Baker Academic, 2004.

———. *The Letter of James*. TNTC. Grand Rapids: Eerdmans, 1985.

———. *The Letter of James*. PNTC. Grand Rapids: Eerdmans, 2000.

———. *Romans 1–8*. WEC. Chicago: Moody, 1991.

Morales, Rodrigo J. *The Spirit and the Restoration of Israel*. WUNT 2/282. Tübingen: Mohr Siebeck, 1992.

Morgan, Christopher W., and Robert A. Peterson, eds. *Hell under Fire*. Grand Rapids: Zondervan, 2004.

Moritz, Thorsten. *A Profound Mystery: The Use of the Old Testament in Ephesians*. NovTSup 85. Leiden: Brill, 1996.

Morris, Leon. *The Apostolic Preaching of the Cross*. Grand Rapids: Eerdmans, 1955.

———. *New Testament Theology*. Grand Rapids: Zondervan, 1986.

Moule, C. F. D. *The Epistles of Paul to the Colossians and to Philemon*. CGTC. Cambridge: Cambridge University Press, 1957.

Muilenburg, James. "The Book of Isaiah: Chapters 40–55." Pages 422–773 in vol. 5 of *The Interpreter's Bible*. Edited by George A. Buttrick. New York: Abingdon, 1956.

Murphy, Frederick J. "Retelling the Bible: Idolatry in Pseudo-Philo." *JBL* 107 (1988): 275–87.

Murray, John. *The Epistle to the Romans*. 2 vols. NICNT. Grand Rapids: Eerdmans, 1965.

Neudecker, N. "'Das ganze Volk die Stimmen . . .': Haggadische Auslegung und Pfingstbericht." *Bib* 78 (1997): 329–49.

Niehaus, Jeffrey J. *God at Sinai: Covenant and Theophany in the Bible and Ancient Near East.* Grand Rapids: Zondervan, 1995.

———. "In the Wind of the Storm: Another Look at Genesis III 8." *VT* 46 (1994): 263–67.

Nielsen, Anders E. "The Purpose of the Lucan Writings with Particular Reference to Eschatology." Pages 76–93 in *Luke-Acts: Scandinavian Perspectives.* Edited by Petri Luomanen. PFES 54. Helsinki: Finnish Exegetical Society; Göttingen: Vandenhoeck & Ruprecht, 1991.

Nolland, John. *Luke 18:35–24:53.* WBC 35C. Dallas: Word, 1993.

O'Brien, Peter T. *Colossians, Philemon.* WBC 44. Waco: Word, 1982.

———. *Introductory Thanksgivings in the Letters of Paul.* NovTSup 49. Leiden: Brill, 1977.

———. "Justification in Paul and Some Crucial Issues of the Last Two Decades." Pages 69–95 in *Right with God: Justification in the Bible and the World.* Edited by D. A. Carson. Grand Rapids: Baker Academic, 1992.

———. *The Letter to the Ephesians.* PNTC. Grand Rapids: Eerdmans, 1999.

———. "Was Paul a Covenantal Nomist?" Pages 249–96 in *The Paradoxes of Paul.* Vol. 2 of *Justification and Variegated Nomism.* Edited by D. A. Carson, Peter T. O'Brien, and Mark A. Seifrid. Grand Rapids: Baker Academic, 2004.

Oden, Thomas C. "A Calm Answer to a Critique of 'The Gospel of Jesus Christ: An Evangelical Celebration.'" *Books and Culture* 7, no. 2 (2001): 1–12, 39.

Olyan, Saul M. *A Thousand Thousands Served Him: Exegesis and the Naming of Angels in Ancient Judaism.* TSAJ 36. Tübingen: Mohr Siebeck, 1993.

Ortlund, Dane. "Justified by Faith, Judged according to Works: Another Look at a Pauline Paradox." *JETS* 52 (2009): 323–39.

Osborne, Grant R. *Revelation.* BECNT. Grand Rapids: Baker Academic, 2002.

Overduin, Nick. Review of *Isaiah's New Exodus in Mark*, by Rikki E. Watts. *CTJ* 37 (2002): 131–33.

Owen, John. *Justification by Faith.* Grand Rapids: Sovereign Grace Publishers, 1971.

Pagolu, Augustine. *The Religion of the Patriarchs.* JSOTSup 277. Sheffield: Sheffield Academic Press, 1998.

Pamment, Margaret. "The Kingdom of Heaven according to the First Gospel." *NTS* 27 (1981): 211–32.

Pao, David W. *Acts and the Isaianic New Exodus.* WUNT 2/130. Tübingen: Mohr Siebeck, 2000.

Patai, Raphael. *Man and Temple in Ancient Jewish Myth and Ritual.* 2nd ed. New York: KTAV, 1967.

Pate, C. Marvin. *The End of the Age Has Come: The Theology of Paul.* Grand Rapids: Zondervan, 1995.

———. *The Glory of Adam and the Afflictions of the Righteous: Pauline Suffering in Context.* Lewiston, NY: Mellen Biblical Press, 1993.

Pate, C. Marvin, et al. *The Story of Israel: A Biblical Theology.* Downers Grove, IL: InterVarsity, 2004.

Patzia, Arthur. *Colossians, Philemon, Ephesians.* GNC. San Francisco: Harper & Row, 1984.

Pennington, Jonathan T. "Heaven, Earth, and a New Genesis: Theological Cosmology in Matthew." Pages 28–44 in *Cosmology and New Testament Theology.* Edited by Jonathan T. Pennington and Sean M. McDonough. LNTS 355. London: T&T Clark, 2008.

Perowne, J. J. Stewart. *The Book of Psalms.* 2 vols. Andover, MA: W. F. Draper, 1876.

Peterson, David. "Atonement in the Old Testament." Pages 5–15 in *Where Wrath and Mercy Meet: Proclaiming the Atonement Today.* Edited by David Peterson. Carlisle, UK: Paternoster, 2001.

Pietersma, Albert, and Benjamin G. Wright, eds. *A New English Translation of the Septuagint.* New York: Oxford University Press, 2007.

Piper, John. *Counted Righteous in Christ: Should We Abandon the Imputation of Christ's Righteousness?* Wheaton: Crossway, 2002.

———. *Desiring God: Meditations of a Christian Hedonist.* Portland, OR: Multnomah, 1986.

———. *The Future of Justification: A Response to N. T. Wright.* Wheaton: Crossway, 2007.

———. "The Image of God: An Approach from Biblical and Systematic Theology." *StudBT* 1 (1971): 15–32.

Pitre, Brant. *Jesus, the Tribulation, and the End of the Exile: Restoration Eschatology and the Origin of the Atonement.* WUNT 2/204. Tübingen: Mohr Siebeck; Grand Rapids: Baker Academic, 2005.

Pokorný, Petr. *Colossians: A Commentary.* Translated by Siegfried S. Schatzmann. Peabody, MA: Hendrickson, 1991.

Porteous, Norman W. *Daniel.* OTL. Philadelphia: Westminster, 1965.

Porter, Joshua R. "The Legal Aspects of the Concept of 'Corporate Personality' in the Old Testament." *VT* 15 (1965): 361–80.

Porter, Stanley E. "Is There a Center to Paul's Theology? An Introduction to the Study of Paul and His Theology." Pages 1–19 in *Paul and His Theology.* Edited by Stanley E. Porter. PS 3. Leiden: Brill, 2006.

———. "Peace." *NDBT* 682–83.

———. "Peace, Reconciliation." *DPL* 695–99.

———. "Two Myths: Corporate Personality and Language/Mentality Determinism." *SJT* 43 (1990): 289–307.

Pritchard, J. B. *Ancient Near Eastern Texts Relating to the Old Testament.* Princeton: Princeton University Press, 1969.

Propp, William H. C. *Exodus 19–40.* AB 2A. New York: Doubleday, 2006.

Provan, Charles D. *The Church Is Israel Now: The Transfer of Conditional Privilege.* Vallecito, CA: Ross House, 1987.

Rabinowitz, H. "Dietary Laws." *EncJud* 6:120–40.

Räisänen, Heikki. *Paul and the Law.* WUNT 29. Tübingen: Mohr Siebeck, 1987.

Ray, Charles A., Jr. "The Identity of the 'Israel of God.'" *TTE* 50 (1994): 105–14.

Ridderbos, Herman. *The Coming of the Kingdom.* Translated by H. de Jongste. Edited by Raymond O. Zorn. Philadelphia: P&R, 1962.

———. *The Gospel according to John: A Theological Commentary.* Translated by John Vriend. Grand Rapids: Eerdmans, 1997.

———. *Paul: An Outline of His Theology.* Grand Rapids: Eerdmans, 1975.

———. *Redemptive History and the New Testament Scriptures.* Translated by H. de Jongste. Revised by Richard B. Gaffin Jr. Phillipsburg, NJ: P&R, 1988.

Rissi, Mathias. *The Future of the World: An Exegetical Study of Revelation 19.11–22.15.* SBT 2/23. London: SCM, 1972.

Rist, Martin. "The Revelation of St. John the Divine (Introduction and Exegesis)." Pages 347–613 in vol. 12 of *The Interpreter's Bible.* Edited by George A. Buttrick. New York: Abingdon, 1957.

Robertson, A. T. *Paul and the Intellectuals: The Epistle to the Colossians.* Revised and edited by W. C. Strickland. Nashville: Broadman, 1959.

Robertson, O. Palmer. "Is There a Distinctive Future for Ethnic Israel in Romans 11?" Pages 209–27 in *Perspectives on Evangelical Theology: Papers from the Thirtieth Annual Meeting of the Evangelical Theological Society.* Edited by Kenneth S. Kantzer and Stanley N. Gundry. Grand Rapids: Baker Academic, 1979.

Robinson, H. Wheeler. *Corporate Personality in Ancient Israel.* Philadelphia: Fortress, 1980.

Robinson, William C. "Eschatology of the Epistle to the Hebrews: A Study in the Christian Doctrine of Hope." *Encounter* 22 (1961): 37–51.

Rofé, Alexander. "Isaiah 66:1–4: Judean Sects in the Persian Period as Viewed by Trito-Isaiah." Pages 205–17 in *Biblical and Related Studies Presented to Samuel Iwry.* Edited by Ann Kort and Scott Morschauser. Winona Lake, IN: Eisenbrauns, 1985.

Rogerson, John W. "The Hebrew Conception of Corporate Personality: A Re-Examination." *JTS* 21 (1970): 1–16.

Rosner, Brian S. "Biblical Theology." *NDBT* 3–11.

Ross, Allen P. *Creation and Blessing: A Guide to the Study and Exposition of the Book of Genesis.* Grand Rapids: Baker Academic, 1988.

Rudolph, David J. "Festivals in Genesis." *TynBul* 54, no. 2 (2003): 23–40.

Rusam, Dietrich. "Neue Belege zu den στοιχεῖα τοῦ κόσμου (Gal 4,3.9; Kol 2,8.20)." *ZNW* 83 (1992): 119–25.

Russell, Ronald. "Eschatology and Ethics in 1 Peter." *EvQ* 47 (1975): 78–84.

Ryrie, Charles C. *Dispensationalism Today.* Chicago: Moody, 1967.

———. "The Mystery in Ephesians 3." *BSac* 123 (1966): 24–31.

Sabourin, L. "The Eschatology of Luke." *BTB* 12 (1982): 73–76.

Sahlin, Harald. "Adam-Christologie im Neuen Testament." *ST* 41 (1986): 11–32.

Sailhamer, John H. "Hosea 11:1 and Matthew 2:15." *WTJ* 63 (2001): 87–96.

Salter, Martin. "Does Baptism Replace Circumcision? An Examination of the Relationship between Circumcision and Baptism in Colossians 2:11–12." *Themelios* 35 (2010): 15–29.

Sanders, E. P. *Paul and Palestinian Judaism.* Philadelphia: Fortress, 1977.

Sarna, Nahum M. *Exodus.* JPSTC. Philadelphia: Jewish Publication Society, 1991.

———. *Genesis.* JPSTC. Philadelphia: Jewish Publication Society, 1989.

Saucy, Robert L. *The Case for Progressive Dispensationalism: The Interface between Dispensational and Non-Dispensational Theology.* Grand Rapids: Zondervan, 1993.

———. "The Church as the Mystery of God." Pages 127–55 in *Dispensationalism, Israel and the Church: The Search for Definition.* Edited by Craig A. Blaising and Darrell L. Bock. Grand Rapids: Zondervan, 1992.

Schlatter, Adolf. *Romans: The Righteousness of God.* Translated by Siegfried S. Schatzmann. Peabody, MA: Hendrickson, 1995.

Schlier, H. "ἀμήν." *TDNT* 1:335–38.

———. "θλίβω, θλῖψις." *TDNT* 3:139–48.

Scholer, David M. "Sins Within and Sins Without: An Interpretation of 1 John 5:16–17." Pages 230–46 in *Current Issues in Biblical and Patristic Interpretation: Studies in Honor of Merrill C. Tenney Presented by His Former Students.* Edited by Gerald F. Hawthorne. Grand Rapids: Eerdmans, 1975.

Schreiner, Thomas R. *1, 2 Peter, Jude.* NAC 37. Nashville: Broadman, 2003.

———. *New Testament Theology: Magnifying God in Christ.* Grand Rapids: Baker Academic, 2008.

———. *Paul, Apostle of God's Glory in Christ: A Pauline Theology.* Downers Grove, IL: InterVarsity, 2001.

———. *Romans.* BECNT. Grand Rapids: Baker Academic, 1998.

Schrenk, G. "δικαιόω." *TDNT* 2:212–14.

Schweizer, Eduard. "πνεῦμα." *TDNT* 6:389–455.

Scobie, Charles H. H. "The Structure of Biblical Theology." *TynBul* 42, no. 2 (1991): 163–94.

———. *The Ways of Our God: An Approach to Biblical Theology.* Grand Rapids: Eerdmans, 2003.

Scott, E. F. *The Epistles of Paul to the Colossians, to Philemon and to the Ephesians.* MNTC. London: Hodder & Stoughton, 1948.

Scott, James M. *Adoption as Sons of God: An Exegetical Investigation into the Background of ΥΙΟΘΕΣΙΑ in the Pauline Corpus.* WUNT 2/48. Tübingen: Mohr Siebeck, 1992.

———. "Luke's Geographical Horizon." Pages 483–544 in *The Book of Acts in Its Graeco-Roman Setting.* Edited by David W. J. Gill and Conrad Gempf. Vol. 2 of *The Book of Acts in Its First Century Setting.* Edited by Bruce W. Winter. Grand Rapids: Eerdmans, 1994.

———. *Paul and the Nations: The Old Testament and Jewish Background of Paul's Mission to the Nations with Special Reference to the Destination of Galatians.* WUNT 84. Tübingen: Mohr Siebeck, 1995.

———. "Restoration of Israel." *DPL* 796–805.

Seebass, H. "אַחֲרִית." *TDOT* 1:207–12.

Seifrid, Mark A. "Romans." Pages 607–94 in *Commentary on the New Testament Use of the Old Testament.* Edited by G. K. Beale and D. A. Carson. Grand Rapids: Baker Academic, 2007.

———. "Unrighteous by Faith: Apostolic Proclamation in Romans 1:18–3:20." Pages 105–45 in *The Paradoxes of Paul.* Vol. 2 of *Justification and Variegated Nomism.* Edited by D. A. Carson, Peter T. O'Brien, and Mark A. Seifrid. Grand Rapids: Baker Academic, 2004.

Selwyn, E. C. "Eschatology in 1 Peter." Pages 394–401 in *The Background of the New Testament and Its Eschatology: Studies in Honour of C. H. Dodd.* Edited by W. D. Davies and D. Daube. Cambridge: Cambridge University Press, 1956.

Shepherd, Norman. *The Call of Grace: How the Covenant Illuminates Salvation and Evangelism*. Phillipsburg, NJ: P&R, 2000.

Shires, Henry M. *The Eschatology of Paul in the Light of Modern Scholarship*. Philadelphia: Westminster Press, 1966.

Silberman, L. H. "Farewell to O AMHN: A Note on Revelation 3:14." *JBL* 82 (1963): 213–15.

Silva, Moisés. *Biblical Words and Their Meaning: An Introduction to Lexical Semantics*. Grand Rapids: Zondervan, 1983.

———. "Eschatological Structures in Galatians." Pages 140–62 in *To Tell the Mystery: Essays on New Testament Eschatology in Honor of Robert H. Gundry*. Edited by Thomas E. Schmidt and Moisés Silva. JSNTSup 100. Sheffield: JSOT Press, 1994.

———. "Galatians." Pages 785–812 in *Commentary on the New Testament Use of the Old Testament*. Edited by G. K. Beale and D. A. Carson. Grand Rapids: Baker Academic, 2007.

———. "Old Testament in Paul." *DPL* 630–42.

———. "Perfection and Eschatology in Hebrews." *WTJ* 39 (1976): 60–71.

———. *Philippians*. BECNT. Grand Rapids: Baker Academic, 1992.

———. "Philippians." Pages 835–39 in *Commentary on the New Testament Use of the Old Testament*. Edited by G. K. Beale and D. A. Carson. Grand Rapids: Baker Academic, 2007.

Sim, David C. *Apocalyptic Eschatology in the Gospel of Matthew*. SNTSMS 88. Cambridge: Cambridge University Press, 1996.

Simpson, E. K., and F. F. Bruce. *Commentary on the Epistles to the Ephesians and the Colossians*. NICNT. Grand Rapids: Eerdmans, 1957.

Skarsaune, Oskar. *In the Shadow of the Temple: Jewish Influences on Early Christianity*. Downers Grove, IL: InterVarsity, 2002.

Sklar, Jay. "Sin and Impurity: Atoned or Purified? Yes!" Pages 1–31 in *Perspectives on Purity and Purification in the Bible*. Edited by Baruch J. Schwartz et al. London: T&T Clark, 2008.

———. *Sin, Impurity, Sacrifice, Atonement: The Priestly Conceptions*. HBM 2. Sheffield: Sheffield Phoenix Press, 2005.

Smalley, Stephen S. *1, 2, 3 John*. WBC 51. Waco: Word, 1984.

Smith, Gary V. "Structure and Purpose in Genesis 1–11." *JETS* 20 (1977): 307–19.

Smith, P. A. *Rhetoric and Redaction in Trito-Isaiah: The Structure, Growth, and Authorship of Isaiah 56–66*. VTSup 62. Leiden: Brill, 1995.

Smith, Robert H. "The Eschatology of Acts and Contemporary Exegesis." *CTM* 29 (1958): 641–63.

———. "History and Eschatology in Luke-Acts." *CTM* 29 (1958): 881–901.

Smyth, Herbert W. *Greek Grammar*. Cambridge, MA: Harvard University Press, 1920.

Snodgrass, Klyne R. "Justification by Grace—to the Doers: An Analysis of the Place of Romans 2 in the Theology of Paul." *NTS* 32 (1986): 72–93.

Stordalen, Terje. *Echoes of Eden: Genesis 2–3 and Symbolism of the Eden Garden in Biblical Hebrew Literature*. CBET 25. Leuven: Peeters, 2000.

Stott, W. "σάββατον." *NIDNTT* 3:405–15.

Strathmann, H. "λαός." *TDNT* 4:29–57.

Strauss, Mark L. *The Davidic Messiah in Luke-Acts: The Promise and Its Fulfillment in Lukan Christology*. JSNTSup 110. Sheffield: Sheffield Academic Press, 1995.

Stuart, Douglas. *Hosea–Jonah*. WBC 31. Waco: Word, 1987.

Stuart, Moses. *A Commentary on the Apocalypse*. 2 vols. Andover, MA: Allen, Morrell & Wardwell, 1845.

Stuhlmacher, Peter. *Biblische Theologie des Neuen Testaments*. 2 vols. Göttingen: Vandenhoeck & Ruprecht, 1992–99.

———. *Das Evangelium von der Versöhnung in Christus*. Stuttgart: Calwer, 1979.

———. "Erwägungen zum ontologischen Charakter der *kaine ktisis* bei Paulus." *EvT* 27 (1967): 1–35.

———. *How to Do Biblical Theology*. PTMS 38. Allison Park, PA: Pickwick, 1995.

———. *Paul's Letter to the Romans: A Commentary*. Translated by Scott J. Hafemann. Louisville: Westminster John Knox, 1994.

———. *Versöhnung, Gesetz und Gerechtigkeit: Aufsätze zur biblische Theologie*. Göttingen: Vandenhoeck & Ruprecht, 1981.

983

Stuhlmueller, Carroll. *Creative Redemption in Deutero-Isaiah*. AnBib 43. Rome: Biblical Institute Press, 1970.

Suh, Robert H. "The Use of Ezekiel 37 in Ephesians 2." *JETS* 50 (2007): 715–33.

Swartley, Willard M. *Israel's Scripture Traditions and the Synoptic Gospels: Story Shaping Story*. Peabody, MA: Hendrickson, 1994.

Sweet, J. P. M. *Revelation*. London: SCM, 1979.

Swete, H. B. *An Introduction to the Old Testament in Greek*. Cambridge: Cambridge University Press, 1902.

Talbert, Charles H. *Romans*. SHBC 24. Macon, GA: Smyth & Helwys, 2002.

Tasker, R. V. G. *The Second Epistle of Paul to the Corinthians*. TNCT. Grand Rapids: Eerdmans, 1958.

Tate, Marvin E. *Psalms 51–100*. WBC 20. Dallas: Word, 1990.

Taylor, J. B. "Elders." Pages 434–35 in vol. 1 of *The Illustrated Bible Dictionary*. Edited by J. D. Douglas. Leicester: Inter-Varsity, 1980.

Terrien, Samuel. *The Psalms: Strophic Structure and Theological Commentary*. ECC. Grand Rapids: Eerdmans, 2003.

Thielman, Frank. *Paul and the Law: A Contextual Approach*. Downers Grove, IL: InterVarsity, 1994.

———. *Theology of the New Testament: A Canonical and Synthetic Approach*. Grand Rapids: Zondervan, 2005.

Thiselton, Anthony C. *The First Epistle to the Corinthians: A Commentary on the Greek Text*. NIGTC. Grand Rapids: Eerdmans, 2000.

Thomas, Robert L. *Revelation 1–7: An Exegetical Commentary*. Chicago: Moody, 1992.

Thompson, Michael B. *Clothed with Christ: The Example and Teaching of Jesus in Romans 12.1–15.13*. JSNTSup 59. Sheffield: Sheffield Academic Press, 1991.

Titrud, Kermit. "The Function of *kai* in the Greek New Testament and an Application to 2 Peter." Pages 240–70 in *Linguistics and New Testament Interpretation: Essays on Discourse Analysis*. Edited by David Alan Black. Nashville: Broadman, 1992.

Toussaint, Stanley D. "The Eschatology of the Warning Passages in the Book of Hebrews." *GTJ* 3 (1982): 67–80.

Towner, Philip. "Response to Prof. Greg Beale's 'The Eschatological Conception of New Testament Theology.'" Paper presented at the Tyndale Fellowship Triennial Conference on Eschatology, Swanick, Darbyshire, July 1997.

Trudinger, L. P. "'O AMHN (Rev. III:14) and the Case for a Semitic Original of the Apocalypse." *NovT* 14 (1972): 277–79.

Turner, David L. *Matthew*. BECNT. Grand Rapids: Baker Academic, 2008.

Turner, Max. *Power from on High: The Spirit in Israel's Restoration and Witness in Luke-Acts*. JPTSup 9. Sheffield: Sheffield Academic Press, 1996.

Turner, Nigel. *Syntax*. Vol. 3 of *A Grammar of New Testament Greek*. Edited by J. H. Moulton. Edinburgh: T&T Clark, 1963.

Turretin, Francis. *Institutes of Elenctic Theology*. Vol. 2. Translated by George Musgrave Giger. Edited by James T. Dennison Jr. Phillipsburg, NJ: P&R, 1994.

Van Der Ploeg, J. P. M. "Eschatology in the Old Testament." Pages 89–99 in *The Witness of Tradition: Papers Read at the Joint British-Dutch Old Testament Conference Held at Woudschoten, 1970*. Edited by A. S. Van Der Woude. OtSt 17. Leiden: Brill, 1972.

VanGemeren, Willem. "Isaiah." Pages 471–514 in *Evangelical Commentary on the Bible*. Edited by Walter A. Elwell. Grand Rapids: Baker Academic, 1989.

Vanhoozer, Kevin J. *Is There a Meaning in This Text? The Bible, the Reader, and the Morality of Literary Knowledge*. Grand Rapids: Zondervan, 1998.

VanLandingham, Chris. *Judgment and Justification in Early Judaism and the Apostle Paul*. Peabody, MA: Hendrickson, 2006.

Von Rad, Gerhard. *Genesis*. OTL. Philadelphia: Westminster, 1972.

———. *Old Testament Theology*. Translated by D. M. G. Stalker. 2 vols. OTL. New York: Harper, 1962–65.

Vos, Geerhardus. *Biblical Theology: Old and New Testaments*. Grand Rapids: Eerdmans, 1948.

———. "The Eschatological Aspect of the Pauline Conception of the Spirit." Pages 91–125 in *Redemptive History and Biblical Interpretation: The Shorter Writings of Geerhardus Vos.* Edited by Richard B. Gaffin Jr. Phillipsburg, NJ: P&R, 1980.

———. *The Eschatology of the Old Testament.* Phillipsburg, NJ: P&R, 2001.

———. "The Idea of Biblical Theology as a Science and a Theological Discipline." Pages 3–24 in *Redemptive History and Biblical Interpretation: The Shorter Writings of Geerhardus Vos.* Edited by Richard B. Gaffin Jr. Phillipsburg, NJ: P&R, 1980.

———. *The Pauline Eschatology.* 1930. Reprint, Grand Rapids: Baker Academic, 1979.

Vriezen, Th. C. "Prophecy and Eschatology." Pages 199–229 in *Congress Volume: Copenhagen, 1953.* VTSup 1. Leiden: Brill, 1953.

Wade, G. W. *The Book of the Prophet Isaiah.* London: Methuen, 1911.

Wagner, J. Ross. *Heralds of the Good News: Isaiah and Paul in Concert in the Letter to the Romans.* NovTSup 101. Leiden: Brill, 2001.

Wainwright, Geoffrey. *Eucharist and Eschatology.* Reprint, New York: Oxford University Press, 1981.

Wall, Robert W. *Colossians and Philemon.* IVPNTC. Downers Grove, IL: InterVarsity, 1993.

Wallace, Daniel B. *Greek Grammar beyond the Basics.* Grand Rapids: Zondervan, 1996.

Waltke, Bruce K. *Genesis.* Grand Rapids: Zondervan, 2001.

———. "Micah." Pages 591–764 in vol. 2 of *The Minor Prophets: An Exegetical and Expository Commentary.* Edited by Thomas Edward McComiskey. Grand Rapids: Baker Academic, 1993.

———. *An Old Testament Theology: An Exegetical, Canonical, and Thematic Approach.* Grand Rapids: Zondervan, 2007.

Waltke, Bruce K., and M. O'Connor. *An Introduction to Biblical Hebrew Syntax.* Winona Lake, IN: Eisenbrauns, 1990.

Walton, John H. *Genesis.* NIVAC. Grand Rapids: Zondervan, 2001.

———. *The Lost World of Genesis One: Ancient Cosmology and the Origins Debate.* Downers Grove, IL: IVP Academic, 2009.

Wanamaker, Charles A. *The Epistles to the Thessalonians: A Commentary on the Greek Text.* NIGTC. Grand Rapids. Eerdmans, 1990.

Warfield, Benjamin B. *Biblical and Theological Studies.* Edited by Samuel G. Craig. Philadelphia: P&R, 1952.

———. *Selected Shorter Writings of Benjamin B. Warfield.* Edited by John E. Meeter. 2 vols. Nutley, NJ: P&R, 1970–73.

Watson, Nigel M. "Justified by Faith: Judged by Works—An Antinomy?" *NTS* 29 (1983): 209–21.

Watts, John D. *Isaiah 34–66.* WBC 25. Waco: Word, 1987.

Watts, Rikki E. *Isaiah's New Exodus in Mark.* Grand Rapids: Baker Academic, 1997.

Webb, Barry. *The Message of Isaiah: On Eagles' Wings.* Bible Speaks Today. Downers Grove, IL: InterVarsity, 1996.

Wedderburn, A. J. M. "Adam in Paul's Letter to the Romans." Pages 413–30 in *Papers on Paul and Other New Testament Authors.* Vol. 3 of *Studia Biblica 1978: Sixth International Congress on Biblical Studies, Oxford, 3–7 April 1978.* Edited by E. A. Livingstone. JSNTSup 3. Sheffield: JSOT Press, 1980.

———. "Traditions and Redaction in Acts 2:1–13." *JSNT* 55 (1994): 27–54.

Weima, Jeffrey A. D. "1–2 Thessalonians." Pages 871–89 in *Commentary on the New Testament Use of the Old Testament.* Edited by G. K. Beale and D. A. Carson. Grand Rapids: Baker Academic, 2007.

———. "Galatians 6:11–18: A Hermeneutical Key to the Galatian Letter." *CTJ* 28 (1993): 90–107.

———. *Neglected Endings: The Significance of the Pauline Letter Closings.* JSNTSup 101. Sheffield: Sheffield Academic Press, 1994.

———. "The Pauline Letter Closings: Analysis and Hermeneutical Significance." *BBR* 5 (1995): 177–98.

Weiser, Artur. *The Psalms: A Commentary.* Translated by Herbert Hartwell. OTL. London: SCM, 1959.

Wenham, David. "Appendix: Unity and Diversity in the New Testament." Pages 684–719 in *A Theology of the New Testament*, by George Eldon Ladd. Rev. ed. Grand Rapids: Eerdmans, 1993.

———. *Paul: Follower of Jesus or Founder of Christianity?* Grand Rapids: Eerdmans, 1995.

Wenham, Gordon J. *Genesis 1–15*. WBC 1. Waco: Word, 1987.

———. *Story as Torah: Reading the Old Testament Ethically*. Edinburgh: T&T Clark, 2000.

Westermann, Claus. *Genesis 1–11*. Translated by John J. Scullion. London: SPCK, 1984.

———. *Isaiah 40–66*. Translated by D. M. G. Stalker. OTL. Philadelphia: Westminster, 1996.

Wevers, John W., ed. *Numeri*. Vol. 3.1 of *Septuaginta*. Göttingen: Vandenhoeck & Ruprecht, 1982.

White, Joel. *Die Erstlingsgabe im Neuen Testament*. TANZ 45. Tübingen: Francke Verlag, 2007.

Whybray, R. N. *Isaiah 40–66*. NCB. Grand Rapids: Eerdmans, 1975.

Wikenhauser, Alfred. "Weltwoche und tausendjähriges Reich." *TQ* 127 (1947): 399–417.

Wilckens, Ulrich. *Theologie des Neuen Testaments*. 5 vols. Neukirchen-Vluyn: Neukirchener Verlag, 2002–5.

Wildberger, Hans. *Isaiah 1–12*. Translated by Thomas H. Trapp. CC. Minneapolis: Fortress, 1991.

Wilder, William N. "Illumination and Investiture: The Royal Significance of the Tree of Wisdom." *WTJ* 68 (2006): 51–70.

Willis, John T. "The Expression *be'acharith hayyamim* in the Old Testament." *ResQ* 22 (1979): 54–71.

Wilson, Robert R. "Creation and New Creation: The Role of Creation Imagery in the Book of Daniel." Pages 190–203 in *God Who Creates: Essays in Honor of W. Sibley Towner*. Edited by William P. Brown and S. Dean McBride Jr. Grand Rapids: Eerdmans, 2000.

Windisch, Hans. *Der zweite Korintherbrief*. 9th ed. KEK 6. Göttingen: Vandenhoeck & Ruprecht, 1970.

Winter, Irene J. "Art *in* Empire: The Royal Image and the Visual Dimensions of Assyrian Ideology." Pages 359–81 in *Assyria 1995: Proceedings of the 10th Anniversary Symposium of the Neo-Assyrian Text Corpus Project, Helsinki, September 7–11, 1995*. Edited by S. Parpola and R. M. Whiting. Helsinki: The Neo-Assyrian Text Corpus Project, 1997.

Wise, Michael O., Martin G. Abegg Jr., and Edward M. Cook. *The Dead Sea Scrolls: A New Translation*. New York: HarperCollins, 2005.

Witherington, Ben. *Letters and Homilies for Jewish Christians: A Socio-Rhetorical Commentary on Hebrews, James and Jude*. Downers Grove, IL: IVP Academic, 2007.

Wolter, Michael. *Der Brief an die Kolosser, der Brief an Philemon*. ÖTK. Gütersloh: Mohn, 1993.

Woods, Clyde. "Eschatological Motifs in the Epistle to the Hebrews." Pages 140–51 in *The Last Things: Essays Presented by His Students to Dr. W. B. West Jr. upon the Occasion of His Sixty-Fifth Birthday*. Edited by Jack P. Lewis. Austin: Sweet, 1972.

Wrede, William. *Paul*. Translated by Edward Lummis. London: Philip Green, 1907.

Wright, G. Ernest. *God Who Acts: Biblical Theology as Recital*. London: SCM, 1964.

Wright, N. T. *The Climax of the Covenant: Christ and the Law in Pauline Theology*. Minneapolis: Fortress, 1992.

———. *The Epistles of Paul to the Colossians and to Philemon*. TNTC. Grand Rapids: Eerdmans, 1986.

———. *Jesus and the Victory of God*. Minneapolis: Fortress, 1996.

———. *The New Testament and the People of God*. Minneapolis: Fortress, 1992.

———. *Paul: In Fresh Perspective*. Minneapolis: Fortress, 2005.

———. *The Resurrection of the Son of God*. Minneapolis: Fortress, 2003.

———. "Romans." *NIB* 10:393–770.

———. *What Saint Paul Really Said: Was Paul of Tarsus the Real Founder of Christianity?* Oxford: Lion Publishing, 1997.

Yarbrough, Robert W. *1–3 John*. BECNT. Grand Rapids: Baker Academic, 2008.

Yarden, Leon. *The Tree of Light: A Study of the Menorah, the Seven-Branched Lampstand*. Ithaca, NY: Cornell University Press, 1971.

Yates, John W. *The Spirit and Creation in Paul*. WUNT 2/251. Tübingen: Mohr Siebeck, 2008.

Yonge, C. D., trans. *The Works of Philo: Complete and Unabridged*. Peabody, MA: Hendrickson, 1993.

Zenger, Erich. "Zion as Mother of the Nations in Psalm 87." Pages 123–60 in *The God of Israel and the Nations: Studies in Isaiah and the Psalms*. Edited by Norbert Lohfink and Erich Zenger. Translated by Everett R. Kalin. Collegeville, MN: Liturgical Press, 2000.

Zerwick, Maximilian. *Biblical Greek: Illustrated by Examples*. Rome: Scripta Pontificii Instituti Biblici, 1963.

Ziegler, Joseph., ed. *Susanna, Daniel, Bel et Draco*. Vol. 14.2 of *Septuaginta*. Göttingen: Vandenhoeck & Ruprecht, 1999.

Zuck, Roy, and Darrell Bock, eds. *A Biblical Theology of the New Testament*. Chicago: Moody, 1994.

Author Index

Brown, Colin, 229n5, 233n16

Brown, Francis, 95, 95n26, 114, 115n80

Brown, J. K., 238

Brown, Raymond E., 152nn52–53, 332n43

Broyles, Craig C., 658n17

Bruce, F. F., 139n21, 200n18, 241n36, 271n41, 313n32, 321n9, 447n33, 450n41, 452n54, 462n80, 491n52, 492n57, 501n79, 531n13, 654n8, 730n53, 740n83, 786n28, 842n13, 856n53

Brueggemann, Walter, 666, 777n4, 778n8, 780n16, 923n49

Buchanan, G. W., 92n18

Bullock, C. Hassell, 75n115, 77n117, 78n119

Bultmann, Rudolf, 19n74, 20n76, 113

Burge, Gary M., 923n49

Burney, C. F., 337, 337n54, 338n60, 339n61

Buttmann, Alexander, 724n40

Buzzard, Anthony, 138n19

Byrne, Brendan, 501n79, 502n81

Cadbury, Henry J., 140n24

Caird, G. B., 7n17, 7n19, 112, 112n73, 113–14, 113nn74–76, 114n77, 178, 178n51, 450n41, 948n103

Callender, Dexter E., Jr., 66nn90–91, 360n7, 618n11, 620n15

Calvin, John, 280, 281n61, 452n54, 666, 710n14, 734n68, 779n16, 794, 795n44, 842n13

Carlston, Charles, 143n36

Carnegie, David R., 348n80, 348n87, 348n89

Carroll, John T., 140n24

Carroll R., M. Daniel, 34n19, 48n55

Carson, D. A., 7n20, 9n32, 10nn35–36, 11n39, 15n60, 25n94, 134n7, 135n12, 164, 164n11, 164n13, 235n26, 237n29, 277n54, 314n36,

334n50, 391n14, 416n77, 426n94, 430, 430n103, 430n106, 470, 470n3, 471n4, 526n135, 570n33, 734n66, 805n10, 870n79, 937n82, 952n115, 954nn118–20, 955n127, 956n128, 957n129

Carson, Herbert M., 452n54

Cassuto, Umberto, 779n16

Cazelles, Henri, 72n106

Charles, R. H., 118n2, 563n12

Charlesworth, James H., 563nn11–13, 564n18, 565n20, 907n24

Cheyne, T. K., 666, 666n34, 667, 668, 668n44

Childs, Brevard S., 8n25, 10, 10n38, 25n94, 666, 777n3, 781n18

Chilton, Bruce D., 310n25

Clements, R. E., 56n74

Clifford, Richard J., 329n37, 666, 668n45

Clowney, Edmund P., 639n45, 642n52

Cobb, Peter G., 817n38

Cohen, Jeremy, 32n13, 32n15, 48n55, 624n23

Cohn, Norman, 58n78

Collins, C. John, 754nn8–9

Cook, Edward M., 403n47, 564n17

Cowles, Henry, 667

Craigie, Peter C., 102n44

Cranfield, C. E. B., 491n52, 502n81, 517n121

Croatto, J. Severino, 666, 668, 668nn45–46, 668n48

Cullmann, Oscar, 17, 17n67, 19, 19n71, 162n4, 803n3

Currid, John D., 368n21

Curtis, Byron G., 43n44

Curtis, Edward M., 31n5, 37n25

Dahood, Mitchell, 658n17

Davids, Peter H., 323n18, 324n24

Davidson, Richard M., 172n38, 617n7

Davidson, Robert, 658n17

Davies, G. J., 666

Davies, John A., 71n103

Davies, W. D., 389n9, 759n16

Delitzsch, Franz, 98n32, 667, 667n39, 778n8, 779n16

Dempster, Stephen G., 29n1, 30, 30n3

Dennefeld, F., 667

Dibelius, Martin, 323n22

Dillard, Raymond B., 603n603, 687n92

Dillmann, A., 667

Dodd, C. H., 4, 4n11, 11, 11n44, 12, 13, 20n76, 699, 699n115

Douglas, Mary, 610n65

Dowd, Sharon E., 695n107

Driver, S. R., 93n18, 95, 95nn26–27, 114, 115n80

Dubis, Mark, 549n49, 550n52, 758n15

Duguid, Ian W., 561

Duhm, B., 667

Dumbrell, William J., 20n76, 21–23, 21nn83–84, 22nn88–90, 29n1, 30n2, 30n4, 32n16, 39n30, 48n55, 48n58, 56nn72–73, 60, 61n81, 74n112, 75nn113–14, 82n128, 82n132, 170n29, 171n35, 174n43, 175n44, 358n2, 533n17, 624n23, 732nn58–59, 732n62, 734n67, 737n74

Dunn, James D. G., 256n14, 313n32, 374n38, 394n22, 397n29, 443n13, 449n39, 451nn47–48, 491n52, 501n79, 502n81, 577n62, 581n81, 583, 583n88, 584, 584n91, 765n29, 842n10, 956, 956n128

Dupont, Jacques, 685

Dupont-Sommer, A., 564n17, 746n90, 935n73

Eberhart, Christian, 488n43

Edwards, Jonathan, 167n18, 506n92, 507

Eichrodt, Walther, 90n10, 779n16

Eliade, Mircea, 629n33

Ellingworth, Paul, 143n33, 320n7, 321n10, 463n83, 465n88, 634n42, 786n28

Scripture Index

Old Testament

Genesis

1 32, 34, 57, 59, 59n79,
60, 79, 83n134, 84,
93n19, 158, 169,
183n66, 229, 278,
326, 329n38, 332,
338, 383, 383n3,
384, 386, 391, 392,
413, 428, 442,
442n10, 445n20,
446, 450, 458, 478,
559, 563n10, 621,
625, 632, 776, 777,
796, 798, 798n54,
817n40, 907n24,
925
1–2 32, 48, 66, 72, 83,
88, 89, 111, 175,
247, 247n44, 277,
277n55, 318, 346,
387, 441, 460, 471,
622, 644, 751, 753,
754, 759
1–3 6, 6n16, 23, 30,
30n2, 33, 36, 37,
39, 42n38, 43, 58,
59, 60, 65, 66, 67,
69n98, 74, 85, 88,
90, 90n10, 93, 95,
115, 116, 167, 176,
177, 178, 183, 223,
228, 257, 257n16,
262, 345n77,
358n3, 374n38,
401, 411n62, 427,
429, 441, 452,
454, 454n61, 459,
462n79, 617, 842,
843n17, 891, 916
1–11 58
1:1 337, 391
1:1–10 383
1:2 37, 82, 84, 93n19,
172, 389, 413,
413n66, 413n69,
444, 559, 565n19,
566
1:2–4 243, 304
1:3 269, 278, 322, 445,
457
1:3–5 323n20
1:4 382n1
1:5 392
1:9 413, 413n69
1:9–10 414n70
1:10 382n1
1:11–12 44n47, 82, 278
1:11–25 383
1:12 382n1
1:14 780, 780n17
1:14–16 323, 629
1:14–18 323n20
1:16–17 450
1:18 382n1
1:20 44n47
1:21 382n1
1:22 778
1:24 44n47
1:25 382n1
1:26 32, 33, 35, 36, 45,
52, 67, 70, 70n101,
111, 358n2, 374n38,
382, 383, 401, 402,
403, 428, 452n53,
463, 842n12
1:26–27 45n51, 378,
382, 393n19, 445,
450n41, 455, 457,
458, 776
1:26–28 30–31, 32,
37, 47, 48n55, 53,
56, 56n74, 63,
66, 70, 78, 83, 84,
85, 247n44, 262,
263n26, 277, 318,
358, 382, 383, 413,
423, 427, 441, 446,
450, 451, 459, 464,
478, 624, 624n23,
625, 652, 670, 752
1:27 75, 358, 444, 445,
463n81
1:27–28 458
1:28 30, 32, 33, 34,
34n19, 35, 37,
42, 45, 46, 47, 48,
48n55, 49, 51, 52,
53, 54, 56, 56n74,
57, 58, 59n79, 64,
65, 67, 70, 70n100,
71, 77, 79, 79n125,
80, 82, 83, 84, 94,
97, 101, 106, 111,
128, 228, 229,
247n44, 262, 278,
345, 345n77, 358,
358n3, 359, 382,
383, 384, 390, 391,
393, 400, 401, 402,
403, 406, 424, 428,
436, 444, 447, 450,
451, 452n53, 455,
463, 477, 478, 479,
564n19, 565n19,
621, 623, 624,
624n23, 625, 626,
631, 644, 753, 757,
762n21, 776, 778,
842n12, 846n21,
880, 959
1:28–29 278
1:29 82, 90n10
1:31 44, 382n1, 621
2 41, 97, 100n38,
228, 329n38, 358,
420n84, 620, 626,
627, 753, 789n32,
795, 881, 884n34,
924
2–3 42, 45, 359, 361n7,
419n81, 618n11,
918

995

40:26 326n28
40:28 326n28
40:28–31 81n128,
  533n15
40:31 326
41–55 701, 857
41:4 128, 342
41:4–10 702
41:8 670n54
41:8–9 415n74
41:14 764
41:17–20 81n128, 82,
  533n15, 533n17
41:18 80n126, 815n34
41:18–20 105, 326n28
41:22–23 105
41:23 105n57
42 242, 568, 684,
  696n110
42–43 741
42:1 82, 242, 415,
  415n72, 415n74,
  416, 495, 562n8,
  567, 689, 689n97,
  696n110, 698, 864
42:1–4 415, 568
42:5–9 81n128, 533n15
42:5–13 348
42:6 241n36, 631, 713,
  715n18, 826
42:6–7 241, 243,
  378n50, 547,
  547n42, 684, 764,
  826, 826n66
42:6–9 533
42:7 423, 713, 764n25,
  765
42:8 960n6
42:9 342, 531
42:12 741
42:15 412, 814
42:16 241, 243, 423,
  547, 547n42, 684,
  697, 698, 764,
  764n25, 765,
  826n66
42:17–20 367n16
42:18–20 698
43 141, 231, 232, 242,
  299, 299n1, 300,
  314, 342, 343,
  378n51, 418, 531,
  533, 534, 537, 576

43:1 378n51, 532,
  685n89, 764
43:1–13 532
43:1–21 532
43:2 412, 415n72, 532,
  814, 815n34
43:3 532
43:3–4 533
43:3–7 532
43:5–21 56
43:6 376n46, 538, 637,
  718
43:6–7 532
43:7 378n51, 532,
  685n89, 960n6
43:8 302, 367n16,
  378n51
43:9 54, 342, 343
43:10 232n10, 241,
  342, 343, 378n51,
  532, 533, 574, 576,
  577n64, 684n87,
  693, 701
43:10–11 532
43:10–12 54, 337, 576
43:10–13 336, 678
43:10–15 576
43:12 342n70, 343,
  574, 576, 577n64,
  693, 701
43:12–13 342
43:13 342
43:14 532, 764
43:14–17 532
43:14–21 532
43:15 532
43:16 633n41
43:16–17 412, 415n72,
  418, 532, 814
43:16–19 342
43:16–21 82, 533n17
43:18 311n25, 532,
  552, 898n14
43:18–19 81, 300,
  339, 342, 376n46,
  418, 530, 531,
  531n13, 532, 533,
  535, 536n24, 538,
  555n58, 576, 718,
  741, 919n41
43:18–20 81
43:18–21 231, 326n28,
  378n51, 689, 741

43:19 231, 309, 341,
  342n69, 536n24,
  552, 722, 898n14
43:19–20 532, 815n34
43:19–21 532
43:20 418, 419, 741
43:21 231, 378n51,
  532, 741
43:22–25 533
43:25 533
44 378
44:1–8 82, 533n16
44:2 378, 415n74, 669,
  670n54
44:2–4 305n7, 306,
  584n91
44:3 82, 236n26, 689
44:3–4 689
44:3–5 415n72, 562,
  576, 911n32
44:6–8 54, 128, 342
44:8 342, 574, 576, 693
44:9–10 378
44:9–17 378
44:9–20 702
44:12 378
44:14 366n14
44:18 367n16, 378
44:19–20 379
44:21 378, 379
44:21–23 81n128,
  533n15
44:22 764
44:23 379, 764
44:24 378, 379, 764
44:24–28 81n128, 82,
  533n15, 533n17
44:24–45:7 82, 533n16
44:25 379
44:26–28 379
44:27 412, 815n34
44:27–28 412, 814
45 39, 446, 523, 632
45:1–8 81n128, 533n15
45:3–4 685n89
45:7–8 533n18
45:8 305n7
45:9–13 81n128
45:14 533
45:18 37, 779
45:18–19 60, 189, 632
45:18–20 81n128,
  533n15
45:18–25 533n18

45:21 342
45:22–24 702, 825
45:22–25 522
45:23 458, 459
45:23–24 522
45:24 522
46:1–13 702
46:10 96, 105
47:6 533
48:1–11 720
48:5–19 63
48:6 531
48:8 342
48:9–11 960, 960n6
48:11 63
48:12–14 128
48:16 342, 495, 562n8,
  689, 689n97
48:18 533
48:20 862
49 242, 416n76, 573,
  656, 661, 661n21,
  671, 684, 693, 713,
  714, 715
49:1–6 293, 416n76,
  684, 684n87
49:1–8 416, 416n76
49:2 344, 829
49:2–6 661
49:3 242, 244, 379,
  416n76, 656, 657,
  684, 693, 706, 712,
  715
49:3–6 416n76, 656,
  731n55, 921
49:4 472n8, 712
49:4–5 712
49:4–6 712
49:5 416n76
49:5–6 684
49:6 139, 241, 241n36,
  242, 243, 379,
  416n76, 574, 631,
  656, 657, 693, 701,
  712, 713, 715, 825,
  826, 826n66
49:7 712
49:8 472n8, 482n19,
  534, 537, 538,
  711, 712, 712n16,
  713, 714, 714n18,
  715n18, 718
49:8–9 533, 712

New Testament

Ancient Sources Index

Apocrypha and Septuagint

Old Testament Pseudepigrapha

Apocalypse of Elijah

1:10 152n53, 203n28
1:13 124n15
2:41 203n28
3:1 152n53
3:5 152n53, 203n28
3:13 152n53
3:18 152n53
4:1–2 203n28
4:2 152n53
4:15 152n53
4:20 152n53
4:20–23 203
4:25–26 120n6, 124n15
4:28 152n53
4:30 152n53
4:31 152n53
5 414n70
5:6 152n53, 453n60
5:9 414n70
5:10 152n53
5:14 414n70
5:32 152n53
5:38 414n70

Apocalypse of Ezekiel

frg. 1,
    introduction 133n5

Apocalypse of Moses

41 244n41
43:3 793n38
43:5 563n12

Apocalypse of Zephaniah

A 601

Assumption of Moses

8:1 942n88

2 Baruch

4:6 246n43
6:5–9 124
10:2–3 120n5
13:2–6 120n6
21:12 246n43
23:5 563n10
25–27 190

25:1–4 125
25:1–27:5 126
27:15b–28:1a 125
28–32 121n8
28:5–7 121n8
29:1–8 121
29:3 125
29:5 121
29:8 121n8, 125
30:1 125
30:1–2 233n17
30:1–3 137
30:1–4 122
30:3–5 120n6
31–32 121
40:3 121
44:12 41
44:12–15 232
48:48–50 122
48:49 246n43
50:1–4 137
52:7 246n43
54:21 120
57:2 233
59:1–12 120n5
59:4 120n5
59:8 120n5
70:2–8 190n4
73–74 793n38
74:1–4 121
74:2–4 41
76:1–5 120n6, 122n10
76:2 120n6
76:5 120n6
78:5–7 119
78:6 120n6
78:7 119
82:2–4 120n6
83:5 120n5
83:6 121n7
83:7 120n6
85:10 121n7

1 Enoch

5:7 756n11
10:2 121n7
14 603, 607n53
14:8–25 600, 610
14:8–15:2 601
16:1 120
27:2 120
37:3 124
40:7 901n19
40:9–41:2 901n19

46:3 246n43
49:2–4 564
49:3 233n20, 306n8
51:1 137
61:5–7 233n20
61:7 306n8, 563n12
61:11 564n18
62:2 564n18
71 603, 607n53
71:1–17 601, 610
71:5 600
71:15–17 122
90:28–36 124n14
91:5–9 190n5
91:6 118n2
91:16 530n9
93:9 118n2
106:13 60
106:17 563n12
108:1 125
108:1–2 122
108:1–3 120n6

2 Enoch

Shorter Recension [A]

1:5 602n41
71:24–25 120n6

Longer Recension [J]

1:5 602n41
8–10 935n72
8:3 619n12
8:5 619n12
18:6–7 121n7
22:8–10 453n60
25–33 158
30:11–12 66n91, 67
31:1 43n46
33:1 11 127
33:11 127
50:2 122
65:6 121n7
65:6–7 120
65:6–11 41
66:6–8 122
71:21–22 454n61

3 Enoch

24:6–7 544
45:3 596n15

4 Ezra

2:33–48 453n60
2:34 126
2:34–35 127
4:26–29 122
4:27 123n13
4:30 120
5:1–19 190
6:13–24 127
6:24 190n4
6:25 127
6:25–28 121
6:27 126
6:58 402, 447n31
7:14 246n43
7:26 246n43
7:26–37 121
7:32 133n5
7:43[113]–45[115] 122, 126
7:75 133n5
7:83 246n43
7:84 120
7:87 120
7:88–101 133n5
7:95 121
7:95–96 232
7:95–97 122
7:96 121
7:97–101 133n5
7:98 553n57
7:113 120
8:50 126
8:51–55 122
8:52 246n43, 793n38
8:63 119
9:2–4 190
9:6 120
10:59 6n20, 120
11:44 120n6
12:9 120n5
12:23–26 126
12:28 126
12:32–34 125
13 432
13:1–3 405
13:6–7 108n62
13:16–20 126
13:18 246n43
13:32 405
13:35–36 108n62
13:37 405
13:46 123
13:52 405

Dead Sea Scrolls

Targumic Texts

Mishnah and Talmud

Other Rabbinic Works

Ecclesiastes Rabbah
1.7.7 233n19
1.4.3 233n19
2.8.1 689n98
3.15 414n70
7.8.1 596n11

Exodus Rabbah
5.9 596n13
19.7 336
20.3 233n19
21.8 413n68
23.11 348n84
28.6 596nn12–13
48.4 565n21

Genesis Rabbah
1.1 337
2.4 565n20
8.1 565n19
8.12 385
11.2 374n38
12.6 385
13.6 590n114
14.5 352n99, 590n114
14.8 565
15.6 619n12
24.7 385
39.11 59n79
44.17 793n38
55.6 319n4
73.4 590n114
95.1 232n11
96 117
96.5 565n21, 590n114
97 565n20
99.5 117

Lamentations Rabbah
2.4.8 689n98
4.9.14 689n98

Leviticus Rabbah
14.9 352n99, 590n114

16.4 596n11
21:12 602n41
27.4 414n70
34.3 385

Mekilta Beshallah
25.27 755

Mekilta de Rabbi Ishmael
Beshallah
3.10–22 414n70

Tractate Shirata
1.1–10 353n104

Mekilta Exodus
20.16 385

Mekilta Exodus Shabbata
2.38–41 793.38

Midrash Exodus
41.7 565m22

Midrash Psalms
2.7 405
2.9 760n20
14.5 565n23
14.6 605, 689n98
18.11 233n19
31.7 117
46.2 232n11
72.3 564n18
73.4 565
87.7 658n16
92 793n38
92.3 596n13
104.25 947
138.2 689n98
145.1 353n104
149.1 353n104

Midrash Song of Songs
1.10.2 596n11

Midrash Tanḥuma
Genesis
1.32 348n84
2.12 233n20, 306n8, 565n21
3.5 48n55, 59n79
5.1 59n79
5.5 59n79
8.23 596n12
9.13 564n18
10.4 689n98
11.9 232n11
12.6 565n21
12.9 117

Exodus
1.22 596n13

Leviticus
7 565n22
10 330n39

Midrash Tanḥuma Yelammedenu
Genesis
2.12 48n55
12.3 233

Exodus
10 565n21
11.3 330n39

Numbers Rabbah
4.8 402
4.20 56n74
11.3 56n74
12.13 629
13.2 633n40
13.12 385
13.20 604n46
15.7 629
15.11 348n84

15.19 604n46
15.25 605
16.24 385
18.21 217, 901n18

Pesiqta de Rab Kahana
12.19 60
15.1 52n63, 402n45
22.5a 565

Pesiqta Rabbati
1.4 233n19
1.6 351–352n99, 565n21
8 602
36.1 233n19

Pirqe Rabbi Eliezer
1 633n41
19 793n38
31 133n5, 232n11
33 351n99
34 133n5, 233n18
35 330n39

Ruth Rabbah
6.4 596n11
7.2 565n20

Seder Eliyahu Rabbah
2 793n38
21 233n19
22 233n19
86 232n11
94 319n4

Song Rabbah
1.1.9 233n20, 306n8, 564, 565n21
2.5 56n74
3.10.4 330n39

Zohar
1.4b 414n70

Apostolic Fathers

Barnabas
1:7 157
4:1 158
4:1–4 152n53
4:1–6 205

4:9 152n53, 158
4:9–11 158
4:11 157
4:12–14 159
5:6 157

5:6–7 157
6:8–19 157
6:11 157
6:11–12 452n53, 842n12

6:13 105, 157, 177, 219, 234, 460
6:14 157
10:11 158n66
11:10–11 935n73

Nag Hammadi

New Testament Apocrypha and Pseudepigrapha

Greek and Latin Works

Other Ancient Sources

Subject Index